THE
TRIPLE REVOLUTION
EMERGING

THE
TRIPLE REVOLUTION
EMERGING

Social Problems in Depth

Robert Perrucci

PURDUE UNIVERSITY

Marc Pilisuk

UNIVERSITY OF CALIFORNIA, BERKELEY

LITTLE, BROWN AND COMPANY · BOSTON

HN
65
.P4
1971

Cover photographs by:

Students, Howard Harrison
Rocket, U.S. Army
Computer, Time-Life photo

Composite development by Ansell

PREFACE

This book was written to achieve a twofold goal: first, to acquaint students with three significant social changes that are shaping the character of life in the twentieth century; and second, to examine various solutions to problems engendered by these changes which will require fundamental shifts in American social institutions.

We have given serious consideration to the point of view that American society is in difficulty, that it is facing demands that question the very viability of our society as we know it. Rather than a society that is essentially healthy while beset by particular problems, we see a society whose very patterns of successful adjustment are causing severe and widening strains in accommodating to new and different circumstances.

In the three years since the first edition, major institutional shifts have occurred. These changes have increased the conflict between divergent trends to the point beyond which violence and social withdrawal become the only predictable outcome. There are clear and coherent issues underlying the changes, issues that reaffirm our original analysis about the basic incompatibility of the military and cybernetic revolutions, on one hand, and the human-rights revolt on the other. Any book of readings is hard put to bring out a coherent underlying framework. We have tried, therefore, in our extended introductions to the chapters, in our own articles, and in some of our selections to make this a more complete and coherent text—an integrated perspective of the meaning of social problems in the United States of the seventies.

Our change from the first edition represents more than a desire to remain topical. The terror of effective voter registration remains in Mississippi even after the civil-rights movement has faded, and one or two quiet summers do not mean that campus confrontation has completely replaced the potential violence of the ghetto. Where we have been obliged to cut descriptions of such historically important events as the Watts riot or the Mississippi voter-registration project, it is not because such events are not still related to the current scene. Rather, our change is in the direction of probing deeper. We are at a point in history where the inner dynamics of modern society have come sufficiently close to the surface to make comprehensible the inadequacy and the outright dangers of time-honored answers to the facts that question both the fitness and the legitimacy of "The Establishment." We are convinced that an appreciation of what is happening to this society requires

v

both a hard head and a soft heart. We cannot see our social system without a grasp of the machinery of strategic thought and decision control, or the seduction of intellectuals by technology and planning, or dehumanization and severely alienating experiences among most Americans (even our largely mythical, silent, satisfied, middle-class majority). The roots of contemporary social problems lie in clandestine but centralized power concentrations, benevolent colonialism, the economics of inequity, the social psychology of trivial work, of participation, of control, and of despair. These concepts and the theories that tie them together are necessary to keep a handle on where we are going. But they are worthless without an appreciation of the anguish that is everywhere about us. In this book we try to do both—push the analysis to its limiting axioms and give a glimpse of the sufferings of our people. We believe we have compiled some of the best social analyses of American problems to be found. But the taste of experience we cannot hope to capture. We hope that when our students do see hunger, police riots, corporate and military arrogance, or the shallow loneliness behind the plastic marketplace culture, they will understand both the conditions that produce them and what must be done to affirm life once again.

We do not intend to be merely prognosticators of gloom; rather we hope that in focusing a social-problems book on future and more basic problems of society, we may be helping to create those conditions from which new and more adaptive institutions will emerge.

Some elements of our approach are not typical of the field of social problems. There is no chapter specifically devoted to crime and delinquency, none on racial prejudice, none on mental illness, alcoholism, or drug addiction. Where these topics are discussed, it is in the context of more basic social trends that are precursors of such symptomatic manifestations of deeper problems.

While the organization of the book is based upon analysis of three converging revolutionary changes, the theory presented is not one clearly associated with a single discipline. We have drawn from the physical sciences and from political science, from depth psychology and urban sociology, from economic theory and strategic analysis—and more. Our sources cover this wide range because the substance of the book is defined by social problems as they are occurring right now—either in the form of human suffering or political controversy. The findings of the National Automation Report, the Moynihan controversy over the Negro family, the controlled-response military doctrine, the urban riots, the plight of the migrant worker, the use of computers in social planning, the lessons of the Vietnam war, the protest movement—all are part of American life.

In our integrating text at the beginning of each chapter, we have tried to apply social science to these problems, rather than defining the problems within the limits of the currently existent concepts of a particular discipline. By so doing we believe that we have assembled a book of readings that will be useful in courses dealing with contemporary American society, as well as in social-problems courses. Ordinarily the sociologist, psychologist, political scientist, historian, or social-welfare specialist teaching courses concerned with contemporary problems will be able to supplement the crystallized problem statements in the selected articles with material from his own disciplinary framework, or with a more orthodox textbook on social theory. What we have tried to present is the basic substance of the problems, and the controversies over their solutions. The problems are delineated against a background that emphasizes their interrelatedness and indicates their future direction.

We would like to express our appreciation to the authors, as well as the publishers, of the readings for allowing us to reprint their works in this book. We also wish to thank Phyllis Pilisuk and Lynn Bozoki for their assistance in the selection of materials, Dena Targ and Joan Flint for their help in the preparation of the manuscript, and Carole Halpin for her careful and extensive work in obtaining the articles selected to appear in this book.

In the revised edition Hillary Turner and Ann DeRosa put in the long and dedicated hours that made possible a major revision in record time. Carol Wych and Suzy Sussman helped with library work and preparation of the final manuscript. We want to make clear that the order of our names on this book does not reflect any distinction in the responsibility or in the work load or in anything. Anyone wishing to take issue with the book will have to take us both on.

May 1971   ROBERT PERRUCCI
                                              MARC PILISUK

CONTENTS

II. Cybernation

THE
TRIPLE REVOLUTION
EMERGING

Introduction

In March 1964 in Washington a meeting of 32 noted social critics produced a policy statement entitled "The Triple Revolution" (1964). The purpose of the statement was to call attention to changes in our society which were so revolutionary in magnitude that the society's current response to them was proving totally inadequate, and to point out that radical new measures were needed. The three revolutions—in warfare, cybernation, and human rights—were seen to reflect the theme of man's being increasingly compelled to play the servant rather than the master role in the technologies he has created. While most of the paper dealt with the cybernetic revolution and with policies appropriate to the resultant large-scale displacement of labor, the authors also presented the idea that the three problem areas were interrelated, and that the points of convergence among them exposed some of the critical foci of balance and stress in American society.

It seemed to us that the authors of the paper had hit upon a compelling theme and one that would be helpful in understanding the mass of seemingly separate and unrelated problems in our society. (An extremely negative press reaction to the proposals of the paper revealed that the analysis had cut into cherished values that were the underpinnings of the social fabric.) We felt this paper provided an excellent starting point from which to define and explore a pattern of illness that gave rise to many diverse symptoms of human distress on the American scene.

Before we can attempt to show the extent to which the umbrella of the triple revolution covers the field of contemporary problems, it is first necessary to give our own definition of a social problem and to explain the nature of the social scientist's concern with the world of problems.

Science and Social Problems. All scientists rely on their value preferences, for these are ultimately their guides to selection of what is worthy of study. The study of social problems has provided social scientists with the particular advantage of permitting them to test the applicability of their knowledge to the resolution of human problems. There are, however, some apparent conflicts between the scholar's motivation to study people and societies and his motivation to study social problems. As an ideal (which is only approximated but, nevertheless, important) the impulse of the social scientist stems from a desire to discover principles governing the operation of social systems. He brings to this task scientific methods involving strict attention to the standards of a value-free approach to his chosen subject matter. For example, when he asserts that certain procedures at meetings are dysfunctional to the achievement of certain outcomes or that certain practices reduce the frequency of deviant actions, he is not passing judgment on whether efficiency in meetings, or deviant actions, should be reduced or encouraged. But as soon as that same "pure" social scientist selects a social problem as the starting point of his inquiry, he is in effect saying, "Certain social conditions are 'bad' and others are 'good.' " His motivation here is to change the "bad," and extend the "good."

These two motives for the study of society have been able to flourish (without creating a major social problem in professional associations of social scientists) because of accommodations between scientific and ameliorative interests. These accommodations include:

1. Assert the reality of the interplay between "pure" theory and applied practical work—theory can be advanced by practical work and much can be accomplished in problem solution by the use of established social theory.

2. Maintain a commitment to the "machinery" of science such that investigations of social problems are carried out according to accepted standards of scientific research.

3. Develop a definition of social problems that will isolate the subject of study without requiring individual social scientists to state their own value preferences.

An examination of many existing definitions of social problems reveals several common properties: Social problems are conditions that (1) affect a large number of people; (2) in ways that negatively affect their own value preferences; and (3) about which they think some action can and should be taken. Most of the elements in this definition can be traced to the early work of Fuller (1938) and Fuller and Myers (1941a; 1941b).

The difficulties involved in maintaining the foregoing view of social problems have become increasingly apparent. First of all, the extreme subjectivism of this approach limits the social analyst to examining those conditions that have been found to be undesirable by consensus. Merton (1966) has raised a similar criticism in his response to Fuller and Myers' definition and has noted how considerations of power and authority enter into the process of defining a condition as a social problem. Becker (1967) has also raised questions about Fuller and Myers' conception of social problems, but he, essentially, supports the view that a defining process by certain persons or groups provides the important starting point for study.

In addition to the above-mentioned limitations there are several other factors that we believe severely limit the usefulness of current social-science perspectives on social problems.

1. Different persons and groups in American society possess varying amounts of social power and prestige. Relative advantage in this connection allows some persons and groups to get items of interest placed on the social agenda (i.e., to define social problems). The differential distribution

of opportunity to place items on the social agenda invalidates the ration of free competition of ideas implicit in current views, and itself represents a social problem.

2. The idea of a collectivity of concerned citizens defining social problems is much like that of participatory democracy of the pluralist society, and the pure competition of the free market. The view seems less well suited in an age of professional social-problem definers, and governmental agencies whose mandate is uncovering and solving social problems. The specialization inherent in the organization of professional problem-solvers serves to fragment definitions of problems in accordance with departmental or bureau interests, and encourages the avoidance of massive attacks on social problems that cut across jurisdictional lines. (In this connection, see the article by Robert Ross in Chapter 4.)

3. The dominant view of citizen as definer of social problems fails to take into account the distinction between "personal problems of milieu" and "public issues of social structure" (Mills, 1959). Definitions made in terms of immediate problems of milieu are most likely to lead to solutions that are ways of *handling* or *combatting* social problems rather than eliminating the social structural conditions responsible for them. Thus, city riots are handled with more portable swimming pools and antiriot legislation; neighborhood youth-gang disturbances are handled with better police protection; unemployment is handled with welfare checks.

4. Related somewhat to point 3 above is the tendency among current social-problems analysts to define in a restrictive and limiting fashion the boundaries of the social system in which problems exist; the most extensive boundaries are usually the nation-state. The growing international involvement of most countries would seem to demand that domestic problems be placed within an international perspective by examining relationships between institutions in the internal system and those in the external system.

5. Current views on social problems may be especially well suited to studying how people respond to social problems *after they have become problems* (in the objective sense that their presence necessarily intrudes on people's consciousness). This may be a part of the reason why social scientists are frequently embarrassed by their failure to anticipate significant national and international events such as the civil-rights movement and frequent foreign entanglements involving shooting wars. We cannot satisfactorily anticipate events if we restrict our study to problems which have already emerged full blown.

The remainder of this introduction will consider the concept of social problems that has guided the editors in this book; the concept is related to the interrelated themes of *the triple revolution.*

Defining social problems. The definition of a social problem reflects the norms and values of the definer. Science helps us little, for in it there are, in a sense, no troubles, pathologies, or evils; there are only conditions and structures which are consequences of other conditions and structures. It is as scientific for a cancerous cell to undergo growth destructive to other parts of the organism as it is scientific for other cells to undergo their more common patterns of growth. The definition of health is a normative concept dependent upon the shared values of longevity, physical capability, and upon the specific preference for normal function as dictated by the theories of medicine about healthy organs.

Our own values and preferences follow from our assumptions about a healthy human being. First, we assume that a healthy individual must be recognized to have intrinsic worth. We believe that his worth is not dependent upon particular achievements but is implicit in the fact of his birth. From this it seems that permitting a child to starve amidst plenty or the loss of a soldier in battle, no less than the assassination of a president, are social problems. This concern with the preservation of life is thrown into the forefront of our attention by the three revolutions occurring in society; particularly by the revolution in the nature of warfare. It is augmented further by a population problem radically different from any that existed previously. During our lives the number of childhood deaths has grown greater than ever before in history and the number is increasing with every year of material progress. Soldiers continue to kill and be killed; deaths of civilians are gradually outweighing those of armies. These are prima-facie evidence of problems. Likewise, the possibility of nuclear war represents a social problem of unprecedented magnitude.

Next in importance to the value of life itself is our belief that an individual's worth entitles him to minimum standards of respect from other people. When police with bullwhips, or insensitive hospital personnel, or unfair voting registrars, or short-tempered parents abuse the dignity of other people, then social problems are present.

A healthy individual must have resources sufficient to meet his most basic physical and psychological needs and leave him free from anxieties over deprivation or resignation to a life of scarcity. The anguish and despair that follow poverty, discrimination, and illness are also social problems.

There are psychologists who claim further that the healthy individual must maintain a measure of freedom in his choices (Rogers, 1951) and a means to actualize his potentialities (Maslow, 1954). We modify these conceptions slightly to conform to the limitations imposed on man as a member of society. People must be free and able to participate in the formation of those policy decisions that will affect their daily existence. An individual left jobless by his company's decision to move or conscripted to serve in an overseas war of which he disapproves is not living in health if his reservations about the policy concerned were not a material part of the policy decision. By this measure apathy is itself a social problem because it represents an absence of power which makes participation impossible and creates resignation and despair.

Last, a healthy society must develop individuals who will contribute to the well-being of other members of the society. In a highly interdependent society, the consequences of one group's actions have widespread repercussions. The scientist who designs methods of chemical and bacteriological warfare, the investor in a new enterprise, the city planner, the ward nurse, and the voting citizen share responsibility for the consequences of their decisions upon the well-being of others. Conscience and existential guilt are needed in human communities. A social problem exists where people do not assume responsibility for the consequences of their own action or inaction.

It should be clear that in our conception conflict, disorder, and value clashes are not by themselves social problems. Disorder could point up an underlying problem, but it could also be indicative of an adaptive attempt to improve upon bad conditions. The emphasis here is *not* upon social harmony but upon the well-being of the individual as we understand the conditions of such well-being. These are our values and the assumptions by which we define what is and what is not a social problem.

In addition to using our own values and assumptions about a healthy person and healthy society, we are also guided in our selection of problems by a notion of central and peripheral problems. When a man considers his own personality, he is prone to think of his achievements, his aspirations, and his ideals as the central and general characteristics of himself. He tends to see his more serious problems as accidents, as specific deficiencies, or as caused by someone else (if indeed he admits to seeing them at all). There is a tendency among social scientists and laymen alike to look upon their own society in much the same way. Its successes and its ideals are the permanent characterization. Its problems, when they are discovered, are accidents, specific casualties, or unfortunate by-products of an otherwise healthy society. The net effect of such social perceptions is to introduce a bias into the analysis of what must be done to meet problems. Perceiving personal problems as superficial and specific permits the individual to carry on his daily activities much as usual without need for a radical and painful reappraisal of himself. Seeing social problems as separate misfortunes or as failures to achieve facile integration into the healthy mainstream of society precludes a search for the underlying pathology beneath such surface eruptions as delinquency, racial violence, bigotry, alienation, conformity, urban slums, and the high-school dropout. But the effects by which we label problems are consequences rather than accidents of the social order. It is our desire to show that these and other problems can be understood as manifestations of larger difficulties which are central and even necessary features of American society as it is currently structured.

The triple revolution. The twentieth century has confronted American society with both unprecedented progress and unprecedented problems. Economic, scientific, and technological advances have brought material abundance, improved health standards, and a phenomenal ability to control nature and turn it to man's uses. Existing alongside all this wealth and mastery over nature are continuing states of international warfare and tension, the debilitation of our physical environment, persistent poverty and despair among millions of Americans, and a growing inability of the many to influence and control the social and political processes that so significantly affect their lives.

Efforts by many public and private groups to deal with these conditions have not yielded results that would encourage optimism. To be sure, in most approaches, war, poverty, and powerlessness are considered either as necessary evils (although not always evil, as wars are fought to preserve our freedoms) or as temporary dislocations which can be remedied. However, under the corrective responses that stem from current approaches, the conditions not only persist but they grow worse. Greater productivity and abundance for some leads to more poverty for the disadvantaged; technological advances that spark economic growth can also be measured in unemployment, worker insecurity, and alienation; and growing sophistication in military weaponry that promised supremacy and reduction of the likelihood of war seems not to have aided in keeping the United States from military involvements in the Middle East, Latin America, Africa, and Southeast Asia.

Conventional attempts to remedy these problems do not seriously question the viability of the American institutions dealing with them. Race relations, delinquency, alienation, and poverty are conceived as problems of specific subgroups which have not yet achieved adequate integration into the larger society or into one of several interest groups providing individuals with a sense of identification and potency. Other current conceptions assume that a problem emerges when interest groups disagree on the existence of, or solution to, some social condition. People experiencing dissatisfaction with existing arrangements, it is argued, can come together and have their views tested in the free marketplace of ideas. When groups are not powerful enough to obtain a public hearing of their complaints, it is argued that larger, more powerful forces (e.g., government, business, unions) do balance each other's interests and power in a way that contributes to the general interest.

These traditional views on the emergence and solution of social problems fail to confront the current distribution of power in American society. Established views on interest-group politics, pluralism, and countervailing power do seem quite appropriate for dealing with problems that are easily absorbed by American institutions; they seem inadequate for dealing with the revolutionary changes that challenge the very nature of these institutions.

A different conception of social problems and of ways of eliminating them is required by the impact of the three revolutions upon the contemporary scene. The solutions to problems may require a basic reexamination and remodeling of our existing values and institutions. It is our belief that the revolutions that have occurred in warfare, in cybernation, and in the mobilization of demands for human rights present the society with pressures that threaten the very bases of its stability. Moreover, these revolutions reflect the increasing difficulty experienced by existing institutions in giving full expression to the simple, yet profound, principles by which American society has chosen to be known: democratic processes and the dignity of man.

The technological-militarism revolution is found in the elaborate nuclear and ballistic-missile technology that is having far-reaching effects on every phase of American life. The psychological impact of nuclear capabilities may lead to "dehumanization" of certain social relationships and of persons in certain social categories. This psychological-defense mechanism is one way of handling anxiety in painful situations. A second consequence is a social-defense mechanism, wherein new forms of social organization are devised to handle the threats posed by international tensions. Among these forms are the shelter-centered society with a regimented populace, and the weakening of such values as individual liberty, democratic values, and a community-based society. At the very time when the most radical of changes are needed to avoid even gross international famine, the highly centralized military and industrial powers have focused upon the technical means for extension of their own control over revolutionary movements abroad and radical protest at home. The final consequence of an existing nuclear technology is its role in maintaining a high level of international tension which permeates many aspects of American life, and gives the military a rationale for its own continuation.

These social and psychological conditions are more than just consequences of nuclear capabilities; they also have the potential for creating greater dependence on military technology to control the fears that the technology itself has created. This process reflects one of the persistent theoretical themes of this book: certain types of technically oriented social patterns become, with time, autonomous and impervious to attempts designed to redirect activities toward new ends.

The cybernation revolution is reflected in the combined efforts of computers and automated machinery largely though not exclusively as they are applied to the processes of production. The result has been increased productive capacity and decreased dependence upon human labor. For some, cybernation brings great material benefits and the promise of release from the degrading and unchallenging aspects of work; others see in cybernation the problems associated with reduced employment, loss of economic security, and the meaning of a life without work.

The secondary effects of cybernation which extend beyond production and employment are those that threaten to reorganize the nature of economic and social life. The emergence of "conglomerates" in American industry and their relationship to governmental power are indicative of patterns of centralization that render a citizen's participation in the affairs of his nation increasingly difficult. Moreover, cybernation technology shapes the patterns of social life through greater planning of social systems and through increased use of the technology to shape and control the behavior and attitudes of citizens by government or other large organizations. The fantastic array of organization and technical measures of control have created a new elite of technicians and experts who make the system run by processes incomprehensible to·most of us and most protective to the powers that employ them. It is important for those left outside the central decision apparatus to see that this emperor, while far from nude, is decked out in garments surprisingly weak at the seams.

The human-rights revolution is found in the growing demand for full economic, political, and social equality by millions of people in the United States and in many other countries around the globe. The demand for equality in all spheres of life reveals that established institutions have adapted to long-standing inequalities. For the black and brown people in our society, for the poorer orientals and white people, and for women generally, demands for equity have been a major focus. The disparities in justice, in welfare, in health care, and in opportunity have been too great. But it has remained for youth to point the finger on their successful elders of American society—to show that success itself in the military, in business, or in the professions can be a degrading, self-deluding, and unconscionable experience. Through its diverse thrusts the movement for human rights is holding a dim hope against the military and cybernetic technologies for the right of an individual to be himself. The revolution in human rights is basic to the transformation of society into a humane environment. It is held in check by a tightening militarization and by technical dominance of the power centers of society as well as by its own fragmentation. But events are confirming the warning of President John F. Kennedy: "Those who make nonviolent revolution impossible make violent revolution inevitable."

The three revolutions are interdependent and mutually reinforcing trends that present us with the progress-problem paradoxes described earlier. The health of a social system must be evaluated relative to the challenges that confront it. The very strengths of American institutions which provide cohesion under moderate challenges may introduce rigidities under conditions that call for a more drastic reorganization of the social order. It is our belief that American society is in serious trouble; that the revolutions wrought by the rapid changes in weaponry, in the utilization of information in cybernetic systems, and in the revolutionary demands of the impoverished around the globe cannot be met by the civilian and military institutions that have so far evolved in our society. Neither does a fair examination of these institutions reveal a capacity for adaptive changes capable of mitigating the emerging problems of centralization in decision-making, of inequitable distribution of opportunities, and of a third world war.

The data presented in this book on cybernetic and militaristic trends describe a civilization in decline—the emergence of a death culture.

To speak of America as an emerging "death culture" is a strong statement, and one that sharply contradicts this country's humanitarian self-concept. Three forms of evidence convince us of the validity of this characterization. First is the nation's apparent commitment to the continued development of weapons of destruction that are designed to terminate life and life-sustaining resources for entire populations. Second is the willingness of the nation to "define away" the needs, desires, and values of large segments of the population, thereby subjecting them to a kind of "social death." The aged, alienated youth, poor, political protestors, hippies, skidders, and other "nonproductive" outsiders have no place in the society and can be ignored, brutalized, and even killed with impunity. Finally, the reactions of those persons who are unhappy with the society turn either to violence or social withdrawal. The despair over their inability to reshape the society increasingly produces such reactions of self or societal destruction.

This is the death culture. It contains no visions of a better life for its citizens. It stimulates no human impulses in its people. It develops no sense of common purpose or challenge that results in a reaffirmation of life.

It is our hope that cyclical processes in history may be responding to the death culture—that power and depersonalization may create their own antithetical trends toward warmth and sharing. If hopes are to be built upon anything beyond blind faith, they must begin with an awareness of how the system operates and where it is moving. The very awareness of system decay is a force in the evolution of society toward a radical restructuring of human institutions in keeping with human dignity. We try also, therefore, to describe some aspects of the forces toward reemergence of human life and growth in society.

REFERENCES AND ADDITIONAL READING

Ad Hoc Committee, "The Triple Revolution," *Liberation* (April 1964), pp. 1–7.

Becker, Howard S. (ed.), *Social Problems: A Modern Approach* (New York: Wiley, 1967).

Dahl, Robert, *Who Governs? Democracy and Power in an American City* (New Haven: Yale Univ. Press, 1961).

Fuller, Richard C., "The Problem of Teaching Social Problems," *American Journal of Sociology,* **44** (November 1938), pp. 415–435.

Fuller, Richard C., and Richard R. Myers, "Some Aspects of a Theory of Social Problems," *American Sociological Review,* **6** (February 1941), pp. 24–32.

Fuller, Richard C., and Richard R. Myers, "The Natural History of a Social Problem," *American Sociological Review,* **6** (June 1941), pp. 320–328.

Maslow, A. H., *Motivation and Personality* (New York: Harper, 1954).

Merton, Robert K., "Social Problems and Sociological Theory," in R. K. Merton and R. A. Nisbet (eds.), *Contemporary Social Problems,* 2nd ed. (New York: Harcourt, Brace, 1966).

Mills, C. Wright, "The Professional Ideology of Social Pathologists," *American Journal of Sociology,* **49** (September 1942), pp. 165–180.

Mills, C. Wright, *The Sociological Imagination* (New York: Oxford Univ. Press, 1959).

Presthus, Robert, *Men at the Top: A Study in Community Power* (New York: Oxford Univ. Press, 1964).

Rogers, Carl R., *Client-Centered Therapy* (Boston: Houghton Mifflin, 1951).

1

TECHNOLOGICAL MILITARISM

Social and Psychological Consequences of Nuclear Capabilities

MECHANISMS OF THE DEATH CULTURE

The Editors

A revolutionary breakthrough has occurred in weapons and in their relation to the men who have created them. We have not merely increased the limits of our destructive capability but have become the first generation easily capable of terminating the complex experiment of human life on this planet. Through the organized efforts of civilized men, all of mankind must live in the shadow of the very real possibility of total destruction. A human or mechanical error, a radar team or a submarine crew acting under stress (imposed perhaps by the fact that no target on the globe is more than fifteen minutes away from a launching device), could cause a war.

How close to an intended gross nuclear attack we have come may never be known since such intentions are usually held in guarded secrecy. Several cases of accidents which have been revealed, however, came close to setting off a nuclear counterattack in response to signals of attack which were later shown to be false. These cases raise a related question of how to determine whether a real attack is in fact an act of aggression or merely an accident. Surely the decision to launch a civilization-destroying counterattack should require time to evaluate whether, and from which source, one has actually been attacked and whether the attack was intended. But unfortunately the speed and finality of missile delivery leaves no time for such evaluations (Livant, 1961).

The expressed purpose of technical capability in nuclear weaponry is to use the threat of annihilation to deter aggression. Society lives under this threat which is now continuous rather than merely sporadic. Threats are a form of stress which lead to certain predictable consequences in the behavior of those threatened. Since threats are psychological messages, some intended to deter war have also the capacity to incite one; such a misjudgment could bring on nuclear war. The threats by rival street gangs to keep off each other's "turf" provide an illustration, on a microscopic scale, of how threats made with intention to deter serve actually to incite. This can happen when threats lack the force of an impartial legal system and must rely instead on the stubbornness or hostility of their tone if they are to be believed. The lack of impartial international jurisdiction and the self-righteousness of military threats are also a part of the international scene.

The possibility of nuclear war does not come only from the reliance on threats of force by major powers. A majority of the world's population lives under conditions of severe deprivation of food, of medical care, of hope to partake in a more constructive shaping of the lives of their children. People who have long been deprived sometimes act out without fear of consequences; a sinister leader of a small power could bring on a major conflagration between large powers.

The ideas and behaviors of modern man have not kept pace with advances in military technology. It appears that people increasingly have to adjust to the realities of military weaponry but that they apparently have lost the capacity for making the technology adjust to them. One adjustment to painful reality is to deny, repress, or merely forget it. With increasing effort and cost, people struggle to achieve inadequate defenses against the weapon systems they have created. Too often the effort goes on automatically, without reflection on the dangers of such pursuits. In this first section we direct attention to the most urgent of social problems, reminding people of nuclear weaponry, and examining the ways in which people are adjusting to its existence.

The Scientists' Committee report describes the effect of a single 20-megaton bomb exploded over a major metropolitan area. It is clear and understated in its account of expected damage. Other reports of probable target areas in the United States suggest that the first bomb would likely be accompanied by another on a second target designed specifically for neighboring military installations, with damage extending well into the region affected by the first blast. The Scientists' Committee report emphasizes blast and incendiary damages. A fuller report of medical effects of thermonuclear attack by the Physicians for Social Responsibility (Ervin et al., 1962) indicates that radiation illness will be a severe disability and a cause of untimely death or genetic damage among the survivors. Moreover, the utter futility of a shelter program is emphasized in the physicians' report by accounts indicating forty years time for decontamination of fertile soil and the dangers inherent in a break in the delicate balance of the ecology that permits the continuation of life.

Nuclear weaponry is but one example of the application of technology to serve military purposes. The technology includes the most sophisticated design for guidance of missiles, the most insidious of airborne chemical and bacteriological agents, and the endless gimmickry of subversion, intrigue, and the covert manipulation of foreign affairs. Could this extensive armory of destruction and force be otherwise when more than half our scientists and engineers are employed in its development?

The creative potential continues to bear fruit. The toxic arsenal already contains stockpiles of tularemia, Q-fever, botulism, and a series of incapacitating psychic and neurologic poisons that produce symptoms of disorientation, paralysis, and severe nausea. The CBW is cheap to produce, easy to launch by small powers as well as major ones, and devastating to man and his environment. The bigger technical options fall into the category of geophysical warfare. They include the triggering of earthquakes through explosives, the creation of tidal waves by loosening material from the continental shelf, and the creation of an ice age through redistribution of the Antarctic ice cap. The planning includes the use of chemical agents to destroy the protective layer of ozone over parts of the earth's surface, thereby allowing it to be burned up by the sun's ultraviolet rays. And again, if chemical and bacteriological incapacitants are not deemed sufficient to immobilize an adversary, it will be possible to increase the natural low-frequency oscillations in the earth's ionosphere cavity—thereby inciting electrical activity in the brain and impairing brain performance in a major segment of the enemy's population. However such innovations may be labeled for public relations, as a deterrent, as humane warfare, or as defensive environmental modification, they will be natural products of the military-oriented society described well in McDonald's article on American militarism.

McDonald points to the largely unquestioned and massive military priorities of American society. The psychic meaning of performing well in such a society has come to be that of accepting the demands of military service, controlling one's shock over massive destruction of civilian populations by one's own nation, accepting a position in a large governmental or industrial organization in which one can do nothing to rechannel the military expenditure to the production of vitally needed health, welfare, recreational, and educational services. Senator J. William Fulbright has called attention to the general debasement of standards—for example, the cost-pinching vulgarity of modern architectural construction—as debasement in every area squeezed by military priorities. Good adjustment has come to mean accepting one's place in a devastating status quo which in turn means a withdrawal of sensitivity to the victims of the system. The psychic mechanisms behind such a withdrawal of human tendencies toward compassion are described in the article on dehumanization in this section.

With the coming of the missile age, a vast controversy emerged regarding the suitability of fallout shelters, or even underground cities, to live out the period of danger following a nuclear attack. In addition to evidence that such a program just would not work, critics reacted unfavorably to the amount of totalitarian discipline required to keep the system in operation, to the value choices involved in deciding who would be admitted and who would not and even who might have to be eaten when other sources of food were consumed, creating a rather bizarre problem of how to serve one's fellow man. Throughout the controversy it was evident that the basis upon which civil defense was founded was the belief that nuclear war is much like a natural disaster. But with this view one accepts a sense of helplessness in averting the dangerous event and rejects one's own responsibility in contributing to the very conditions that make nuclear war more likely (Waskow and Newman, 1962; Melman, 1962).

The shelter issue provides a striking instance of the degree to which persons have come to live with the idea that war in the nuclear age is still a viable institution, that preparation for it and defense against it are inevitable parts of the human condition. The same aura of inevitability is prevalent in much of the debate over military conscription which is summarized in the review by Flacks, Howe, and Lauter in Chapter 2. How men shall be conscripted to meet the military need is up for debate; whether men should automatically and unquestioningly accept the demands of the military appetite is not ordinarily considered.

This section is not asking whether we accept a warlike world as inevitable. Many Americans do accept as inevitable a world of hostility, threats, and weapons and are resigned to the support of a military machine that never delivers the security it promises. But the major question we are asking is: What kind of people, what kind of society have we become, as a result of our defensive accommodations to the danger of total war?

The high level of military preparedness and the consequent threat of destruction are facts of modern life. Considering the utter horror of modern war, it seems remarkable that people go about their daily pursuits with only an occasional concern over such crises as the rise in radioactive fallout in milk, the Berlin blockade, the Cuban missile episode, or Cambodia. This apparent calm in the face of extreme threat is similar to psychological defense mechanisms which sometimes guard the terminal patient against a full realization of the extent of his illness and hence of the proper measures needed to prolong life. The patient gains, by such defense, a false and comforting security which in fact is not appropriate to the real danger. Bernard, Ottenberg, and Redl suggest the manner in which a composite psychological mechanism, dehumanization, may be affecting wide segments of American society with a similar handicap—an inappropriate adaptation to the constant threat of annihilation and the strains of mass technological society. These effects on large numbers of individuals reflect changes in the society as a whole as it also adjusts itself to acceptance of military priorities and military values. These are the effects described in Senator J. William Fulbright's speech, "The Cold War in American Life":

> This . . . is the real meaning of the cold war in American life. It has consumed money and time and talent that could otherwise be used to build schools and homes and hospitals, to remove the blight of ugliness that is spreading over the cities and highways of America, and to overcome the poverty and hopelessness that afflict the lives of one-fifth of the people in an otherwise affluent society. . . .
>
> . . . we must strive . . . to restore the lines of communication between the minority that value excellence and the majority that settle for mediocrity. I do not know how this is to be accomplished, but I think there is a clue in what seems to me to be one

of the major sources of post-war vulgarization of American life: the combination of widespread affluence with the intense anxieties generated by the cold war, resulting both in a fixation on foreign problems and in an almost compulsive search for release from anxiety through trivial and tasteless, but convenient and diverting, channels of popular amusement. (Fulbright, 1964.)

Senator Fulbright's suggestion is that we turn our creative energies away from international power and inward to the people of our cities and country-side. This does not seem to us to be a form of isolationism or a shirking of international responsibility. It is rather a necessary first step in recultivating the human sensitivities dormant in our society that we may become better aware of the purposes for which we live before we are throttled by our own defenses.

REFERENCES AND ADDITIONAL READING

Dentler, Robert A., and Phillips Cutright, *Hostage America: Human Aspects of a Nuclear Attack and a Program of Prevention* (Boston: Beacon, 1963).

Ervin, Frank R., et al., "Human and Ecologic Effects in Massachusetts of an Assumed Thermonuclear Attack on the United States," *New England Journal of Medicine*, **266** (May 31, 1962), pp. 1127–1139.

Frank, Jerome D., "Breaking the Thought Barrier: Psychological Problems of the Nuclear Age," *Psychiatry*, **23** (1960), pp. 245–266.

Frank, Jerome D., *Sanity and Survival: Psychological Aspects of War and Peace* (New York: Random House, 1967).

Fulbright, Senator J. W., "The Cold War in American Life," address to the University of North Carolina, 1964 Symposium, *Arms and the Man: National Security and the Arms of a Free Society* (April 5, 1964); reproduced in R. Perrucci and M. Pilisuk, *The Triple Revolution: Social Problems in Depth* (Boston: Little, Brown, 1968), pp. 35–47.

Gifford, Sanford, "Death and Forever," *The Atlantic* (March 1962), pp. 88–92.

Lapp, Ralph, *The Weapons Culture* (New York: Norton, 1968).

Livant, William P., "Attack Versus Aggression: How Can We Distinguish?," *Committee of Correspondence Newsletter* (October 1961), pp. 20, 22.

McCarthy, Richard D., "Chemical and Biological Warfare Policies and Practices," *Sane Report* (April 21, 1969).

Melman, Seymour (ed.), *No Place to Hide: Fact and Fiction about Fallout Shelters* (New York: Grove, 1962).

Neal, Fred Warner, "Government by Myth," *The Center Magazine*, **2** (November 1969), pp. 2–7.

Physicians for Social Responsibility, "Symposium: The Medical Consequences of Thermonuclear War," *New England Journal of Medicine*, **266** (May 31, 1962), pp. 1126–1155, 1174.

Pilisuk, Marc, *International Conflict and Social Policy* (Englewood Cliffs, N.J.: Prentice-Hall, 1971); see the chapter on "War and the Minds of Men."

Raser, John, "ABM and the MAD Strategy," *Ramparts* (November 1969), p. 36.

Rudin, Stanley A., "The Personal Price of National Glory," *Trans-action* (September-October 1965), pp. 4–9.

Shoup, General David M., "The New American Militarism," *The Atlantic*, **223** (April 1969), pp. 51–56.

Sternglass, Ernest J., "The Death of All Children," *Esquire* (September 1969), pp. 1a–1d.

Stone, Jeremy J., "How the Arms Race Works," *The Progressive* (June 1969), pp. 25–26.

Wald, George, "Therefore Choose Life," speech delivered at ABM/Choice Conference, Washington, D.C.; *Sane Report* (May 2, 1969).

Waskow, Arthur (ed.), *The Debate over Thermonuclear Strategy* (Boston: Heath, 1965).

Waskow, Arthur, and S. L. Newman, *America in Hiding* (New York: Ballantine, 1962).

THE EFFECTS OF A
20-MEGATON BOMB

Scientists' Committee for Radiation Information

This summary will describe in some detail what could happen to the New York metropolitan area and its residents if a single 20-megaton bomb hit Columbus Circle in midtown Manhattan.

While it is not possible to make precise predictions of damage, estimates are possible, based on evidence from test explosions, the atomic drops in Hiroshima and Nagasaki, and various published material. All estimates are derived from unclassified information, with three major sources: *Medical Effects of the Atomic Bomb in Japan; The Effects of Nuclear Weapons;* and *Biological and Environmental Effects of Nuclear War.*[1]

ASSUMPTIONS

Any analysis of effects of nuclear explosion depends on the assumptions made. In this instance:

A 20-megaton bomb is assumed. Bombs of this size are generally believed to exist in substantial numbers. While there is evidence that still larger bombs exist, their effect cannot be estimated here with equal reliability. Nevertheless, one must bear in mind that the results described below could well be exceeded, and perhaps greatly exceeded.

Columbus Circle is assumed as a target or hypocenter. This is a well-known landmark.

Clearly there could be a multibomb attack. Bombs of various sizes might be used. Target points are not entirely predictable. Considering the effect of a single bomb is helpful for illustration. But damage caused by two bombs appropriately spaced and timed can be greater than the sum of their destructive effects taken separately.

The consequences of exploding the bomb at various heights are contrasted. Particularly, destructive features are emphasized by a ground burst, a typical air burst, or a high-altitude burst.

The thermal effects depend strongly on humidity and atmospheric visibility conditions. Assumed here are those conditions that would allow maximal thermal danger. This makes clear the limits of possible destruction and injury; under other condi-

Reprinted by permission of the publishers from New University Thought *(Spring 1962), pp. 24–32.*

[1] *Medical Effects of the Atomic Bomb in Japan*, edited by A. W. Oughterson and S. Warren (New York: McGraw-Hill, 1956); *The Effects of Nuclear Weapons*, edited by S. Glasstone and prepared by the U.S. Department of Defense (Washington: Atomic Energy Commission, 1957); *Biological and Environmental Effects of Nuclear War*, a report of the Special Subcommittee on Radiation of the Joint Committee on Atomic Energy, U.S. Congress (86th Congress, 1st Session) (Washington: U.S. Government Printing Office, June 1959).

tions the thermal effects would be less severe. An attacker planning to assault a number of targets in a brief time might have limited choice of atmospheric conditions.

THE EXPLOSION
AND ITS AFTERMATH

As the bomb explodes, the sky fills with a bluish-white glare. A man standing 60 miles away would see a fireball 30 times brighter than the noonday sun—a fireball hot as the center of the sun.

The fireball rapidly expands until it is 4½ miles wide. As it expands, it begins to rise, scorching an ever-widening area. Meanwhile, if the explosion was a ground *surface burst,* the fireball has sucked up a vast quantity of vaporized earth and debris.

If the bomb were exploded in the *air* on a clear day, the heat would ignite a man's clothing 21 miles away and seriously burn exposed skin at 31 miles. (A contact *surface burst* would cut the distances to 13 and 19 miles.)

The matter sucked up by the fireball in a surface burst starts to condense on reaching upper air layers, 5 to 10 miles up. It spreads out, forming a radioactive, mushroom cloud. The material in this cloud soon begins to descend as fallout.

Meanwhile, an intense pressure wave, or shock, traveling faster than sound, spreads out from the center of the explosion, crushing almost everything in its path until it gradually loses its force.

Following the shock front comes the wind of more than 1000 miles per hour. As it moves outward, the wind diminishes; behind it a vacuum develops. Then the surrounding air rushes in, fanning the fires started by thermal radiation and initial blast damage.

Soon these fires will join and develop into a firestorm that could cover an area many miles across, destroying all that will burn—structures and living things.

The blast itself, from a surface burst, would create a hole 240 feet deep, at its deepest point, and a half mile across. Within a radius of 7.7 miles the destruction would be severe. Up to 15 miles the damage would still be heavy.

The population would face several distinct types of hazards, each of which must be coped with successfully for survival. The effects would vary somewhat, depending on whether the bomb drop were a contact surface burst or an air burst. Both are discussed in the report. In summary, a surface burst produces greater local blast damage, heavy local fallout. An air burst produces little local fallout, more worldwide fallout, greater danger of firestorm, and more widespread blast damage.

Seven types of hazards to be considered are as follows: (1) immediate thermal effects, (2) immediate nuclear radiation, (3) blast effects, (4) firestorm, (5) fallout, (6) economic and social disruption, and (7) long-term effects.

IMMEDIATE
THERMAL EFFECTS

The fireball gives off a tremendous amount of heat, or thermal energy. One can predict the extent of heat damage by noting the number of calories (unit of heat) per square centimeter of surface a given object would receive if exposed to the flash of the bomb. If the explosion occurs within the atmosphere, the energy *required* for igniting a given material is greater the larger the total energy yield of the bomb. For example, for a 20-megaton bomb, about 7 calories per square centimeter (cal/cm²) will ignite shredded newspaper, 13 cal/cm² will ignite deciduous leaves. At 23 cal/cm² most clothing will ignite.

Flash burns are an even more probable danger than the burning of clothing. At Hiroshima and Nagasaki, flash-burn casualties were *the* major problem in medical care, accounting for more than half of all deaths.

On a clear day, a 20-megaton (MT) low air burst would produce these injuries to exposed skin:

Third-degree burns (12 cal/cm²) 27 miles from the explosion

Second-degree burns (10 cal/cm²) 31 miles away

First-degree burns (4 cal/cm²) 45 miles away

For a surface burst these distances would drop by 40 percent because there is less thermal energy to start with, and heat rays near the ground would not travel as far because they are absorbed and scattered by dust, water vapor, and carbon dioxide. Unless medical supplies and facilities were somehow spared, the second- and third-degree burns would probably result in death. Such burns nearly always become infected. And radiation further reduces the chances of recovering from even minor infections.

A high-altitude burst, say 20 miles up, well above most of the atmosphere, would produce even greater fire damage on earth. Atmospheric haze would reduce the range of heat damage. An explosion in clear air under a cloud layer could increase the range.

A person actually seeing the flash of the bomb burst would suffer a burn on the retina, which could lead to blindness. The seriousness of the burn would depend on its size and its location on the retina. For a high burst as opposed to a surface burst, the flash would be seen further away. Only sparse information about retinal burns has been declassified. However, it has been disclosed that "a megaton detonation" 40 miles high produced retinal burns in rabbits 340 miles away.

IMMEDIATE NUCLEAR RADIATION

With a small bomb, say 20 kilotons (KT), immediate nuclear radiation is an important hazard; but with a large bomb, such as 20 megatons, it may be ignored because blast and heat effects of a 20-MT weapon are so great that they would far outweigh the immediate radiation danger. For example, 2.5 miles from ground zero the radiation intensity would be about 300 roentgens, a lethal dose for 3 to 18 percent of those exposed. However, at that distance the 800-mph wind, the flying debris, and the flash heat would alone suffice to kill an exposed person.

BLAST EFFECTS

Blast damage to a building or other structure may result from one or several causes. First, the shock front squeezes everything in its path. A building may collapse because it is being blown over, or because the external pressure is suddenly so great that all four walls collapse inward.

Arriving with the shock front are the drag forces, in the form of a strong wind. Telephone poles and radio towers that may resist the squeezing effect of the shock front are quite vulnerable to being blown over. Within a few seconds, the shock wave and its accompanying winds have passed.

Following the shock front and drag forces, there is a reversal in pressure. Buildings now experience a partial vacuum and winds blowing back toward the center of the explosion. The stress is less, but it can add to damage on an already weakened structure. Also, the ground shock itself can knock a building down as an earthquake does.

A surface burst on Columbus Circle would produce a mammoth hole. It would cover a 20-block area and be deep enough to hide a 20-story building. The hole would extend from 55th to 63rd Streets and from east of Seventh Avenue to west of Columbus Avenue. The subway systems, which are interconnected in the midtown area, would be penetrated.

Any midtown 20-MT hit is likely to penetrate at least one of the subway tunnels. The deepest tunnel is the BMT 60th Street tunnel under the East River, which is down 113 feet. Since all three systems are interconnected in the midtown area, the blast wave would sweep with lethal intensity through a large part of the system. Blast waves in a tunnel maintain their intensity over a longer distance since they cannot spread out.

Within a 7.7-mile radius of Columbus Circle, the blast would produce severe structural damage. At the outer edge of this circle, most unreinforced brick or wood-frame houses would be completely demolished, the result of a peak overpressure of 5 pounds per square inch (psi). Brick apartment buildings would probably still be standing, but need major repairs. However, within a 6.4-mile radius, they too would collapse. An air burst would extend the major damage radius to 10 miles.

Within a 15-mile radius, the damage would be less severe but extensive. At the edge of the circle, a wood-frame house might remain standing but need such major repairs that restoration would not be economical. The peak overpressure at the 15-mile line would be 1.9 psi. This is still enough to tear entrance doors off their hinges, breaking them into pieces, send window glass flying through the house, and dislodge window frames.

Up to 40 miles away, there would be some damage, such as window breakage, in the majority of structures. And under some atmospheric conditions, a New York City explosion could produce shattered windows in Wilmington, Delaware.

The inner circle (7.7-mile radius) of severe blast damage includes, at its outer edges, in Brooklyn, Gowanus Bay, half of Prospect Park, Ebbets Field, and the Bedford-Stuyvesant and Bushwick sections.

In Queens it would include Ridgewood, the western tip of Forest Hills, Corona, and the western edge of the Whitestone section. In the Bronx, Sound View Park, Crotona Park, and New York University. Only the tip of Manhattan above the Cloisters would not be inside this area.

In New Jersey, this zone of mass destruction would include most of Jersey City, Leonia, Ridgefield Park, Teterboro Airport, half of Kearny. The Palisade ridge would probably not provide much protection since blast waves move around such objects.

The 15-mile radius (1.9 psi) from Columbus Circle would include all of New York City, except Far Rockaway and the area beyond Staten Island Airport. In Nassau County, the eastern portion of the circle would be marked by Elmont, Floral Park, Manhasset, and Port Washington. Much of New Rochelle and Yonkers would be within the circle. In New Jersey, these cities would be along the perimeter: Paramus, Paterson, West Orange, and Elizabeth.

It should be noted that not all brick houses would collapse within the inner circle, nor would all brick houses remain standing beyond it. There would be individual variations depending on construction differences and variations in the local behavior of the shock front.

The mass destruction of buildings and other objects would have produced an immense quantity of flying debris. It has been determined that chunks of flying glass and masonry could cause casualties up to 15 miles from ground zero. (A casualty is defined as "an individual sufficiently injured to be unable to care for himself and thus becomes a burden to someone else.") It should be noted that small glass fragments lodging in the eye could produce casualties at distances much greater than those cited.

There would also be a third type of blast effect—displacement, such as picking up a man and smashing him into a wall. This, too, could occur as far away as 15 miles from ground zero. A significant number of head and skeletal injuries would occur, with the extent of the injury depending on the distance traveled prior to impact.

THE FIRESTORM

A prime threat to urban populations after a thermonuclear explosion is the firestorm. Firestorm develops when a mass of fresh air breaks into a large area with a high density of fires and replaces the hot rising air. This mass of fresh air may move with hurricane velocity. The wind causes the fires to merge and encompass the entire area.

The fires can start in two ways. First, thermal radiation would ignite trash, window curtains, dry grass, leaves and, toward the interior of the fire zone, many less-flammable materials. Second, the blast would upset stoves, cause electrical short circuits, break gas lines, and burst underground oil-storage tanks. All of these would become ignition points.

Within the radius of 21 miles from Columbus Circle, it is probably conservative to predict an average of ten ignition points per acre in every part of the city (except for the southern part of Staten Island, which is outside this line and is partly shielded by the terrain). Since New York City covers about 200,000 acres, this would probably result in nearly 2 million fires in the city. The Fire Department could hardly cope with such a staggering number, even if it were prepared. In this case, most of the force would be unable to respond, most equipment would be unusable, water pressure would be inadequate, and many rubble-lined streets would be impassable.

In view of the density of combustible material in many parts of the city, a firestorm is probable. (The contents of a fireproof building are combustible, even if the building is not.)

At Hiroshima, where a far smaller bomb (20 KT) was dropped, a firestorm developed and eventually covered a radius of about 1.2 miles. In Nagasaki, no firestorm developed, apparently because natural winds carried the fire into an area where there was nothing to burn. Still, all buildings in Nagasaki within 1.25 miles of ground zero were destroyed by flames.

There are, however, not enough data to justify quantitative predictions of the firestorm area.

The most complete data on firestorm casualties come from Hamburg, Germany, where a firestorm occurred July 27, 1943, after prenuclear incendiary air raids. Some 60,000 persons were killed, almost as many as in the atomic bomb drop on Hiroshima.

Hamburg police engineers estimated that temperatures in the burning city blocks were as high as 800°C (about 1500°F). Wind velocity exceeded 150 mph. Hundreds of persons were seen leaving shelters as the heat became unbearable. They ran into the streets and slowly collapsed. Days after the raids ended, as home shelters were opened, there was enough heat remaining inside for the influx of oxygen to cause the shelters to burst into flames. Many bodies had been cremated.

Death from intense heat can occur in ways other than burning or disintegration. Heat stroke can occur in a temperature of 140°F. Exterior damage can close off ventilation in a sheltered area.

Also, carbon-monoxide poisoning would

be one of the chief types of injuries expected. In World War II it was a common
cause of death in public air-raid shelters
and improvised home shelters. Carbon-
monoxide casualties are nearly always expected in flaming buildings, where exits
have been blocked by rubble. Under such
conditions, a cellar protected from the blast
could become a tomb. In Hamburg, it is
estimated that 70 percent of all casualties
not caused by mechanical injuries or burns
were brought on by carbon monoxide.

DISRUPTION OF
PHYSICAL FACILITIES

Careful consideration of problems that
arise from wide breakdown of physical facilities and social services in the event of
a nuclear explosion is vitally important to
any discussion of survival. Such consideration, however, leads beyond the competence of the Scientists' Committee for Radiation Information. At best, this segment
of the report can suggest problems of
physical disruption that deserve more systematic study.

In all previous American experience with
large-scale disaster, relief and reconstruction assistance poured in from other communities, state, national, or international
agencies. It seems probable that in the
event of a 20-MT nuclear explosion on
New York City, other major population
centers in the Northeast would be attacked
too. This would limit prospects for outside
help in dealing with consequences of the
attack.

Problems of Transportation Facilities

This problem may be regarded in three
categories: thoroughfares, fuel, and machines. Throughout the area of the 15-mile
radius from ground zero, debris would clog
streets with little hope of early clearance.
No vehicle could be expected to pass. It is

probable that many bridges would not be
serviceable and that tunnel entrances in
Manhattan would be blocked. Rail and
subway lines would most likely suffer com-
mensurately. Transportation equipment remaining after blast and fire would find
extremely limited fuel since local supplies
would be largely consumed in mass fires.
The breakdown of transportation would
immediately hamper or prevent rescue,
evacuation, and emergency assistance measures. Later its impact would be felt in
terms of the absence of such important
products as food, medical supplies, and fuel
—including fuel for central electric gen-
erators.

Problems of Water Supply

It seems probable that many water-stor-
age tanks, some mains, filtering and purification equipment, and pumps would be
destroyed or would become inoperable.
There is, in addition, some risk of radioactive contamination of reservoirs. It is to
be noted, however, that most of the city's
water supply is in covered reservoirs and
that probably 90 percent of the fallout
would be insoluble in water. The main
immediate problems would likely be breakdown of pumping facilities and contamination by germs.

Problems of Food Supply

This question can be examined in two
categories: first, that food which is stored
in the city and, second, that food produced
outside. Food stored under normal conditions would be subject to blast and fire.
Food-processing plants, storage and refrigeration facilities would also be affected by
blast and fire. Metropolitan food supplies
are heavily dependent on transportation.
Sheltered food supplies, if available after
extensive ruin, might provide sustenance
for a limited period. Outside the metropolitan area the extent of damage to stock,

produce, and arable land would depend on fire damage and the quantity of local fallout.

Problems of Housing and Home Fuel Supplies

It is doubtful that many of New York City's approximately 2.5 million dwelling units would provide adequate shelter (in the conventional sense) for survivors, even if mass fires did not consume everything. It is more difficult to predict what would happen in suburbs. Widespread blast damage would extend in a 15-mile radius around Columbus Circle. (The firestorm, a probability within a 15-mile radius, and perhaps beyond, could create further havoc.) Those fortunate enough to have dwelling units remaining, and with a manageable radiation problem, would have a hard time during cold weather. Local supplies of fuel would probably have been destroyed and the breakdown of transportation would curtail further deliveries. Human exposure during winter months is an inevitable source of casualties.

Problems of Medical Facilities

It seems clear that most of the city's hospitals and related facilities would be destroyed or unusable, since virtually all of the city except the southern part of Staten Island lies within the 15-mile radius of heavy damage. The millions of dead and injured would include a sizable proportion of physicians and other trained medical personnel. Those medical centers still able to function would be faced with enormous problems arising from the general destruction, since medical services are heavily dependent on city-wide physical facilities and transportation. Few hospitals, for example, have auxiliary power sources sufficient for more than emergency periods. Destruction of city power plants and limited fuel supplies would therefore limit an important component of hospital services. Insufficient power would affect not only light, x-ray, and other machines, but also refrigeration necessary for important drugs. The failure of transportation of medical supplies and the presumed shortage of water, raising problems of general sanitation, indicate further aggravations of the health situation in even of a 20-MT nuclear explosion.

Problems of Sanitation and Public Health

Sources of epidemic characteristically include: uncollected refuse, sewage, uncontrolled vermin, contaminated water and food supplies, and lack of medical facilities. Collection and disposal of corpses would require large numbers of workers and adequate transportation facilities. Public-health problems created specifically by an extensive radioactive environment have not so far been experienced. Persons suffering from exposure to radiation, however, are particularly susceptible to infection, and a population of weakened and injured survivors, as in all comparable crises, would seem to invite epidemic.

LONG-TERM EFFECTS

The hazards discussed in earlier sections would occur largely within days, weeks, and months after the explosion. There would also be longer-term radiation effects of two types: those that affect the exposed individual (somatic effects) and those that affect his descendants (genetic effects).

These effects are not fully understood by scientists. The knowledge that does exist has been exhaustively studied, but interpretations vary and are not conclusive. The uncertainties of the biology are compounded by uncertainty about radiation doses. While these effects will not be discussed in detail here, certain observations are possible.

Virtually all scientists agree that excess exposure of a population to radiation will have harmful effects on subsequent generations. The disagreements concern the relative incidence of harmful effects. These genetic effects might include miscarriages, stillbirths, neonatal deaths, congenital malformations, reduced mental and physical vigor, feeble-mindedness, and a host of physiological diseases or malfunctions, any one of which might lead to the disablement or death of an individual.

The evidence indicates that it is unlikely that long-term exposure to radiation would result in the genetic extinction of the human species, whatever the other harmful effects might be.

There is particular concern about the effects on fertility of an exposed male generation. Men exposed to a moderately high dose of radiation followed by a continuous low dose over a period of time are likely to exhibit sterility or reduced fertility for years. The gonads are among the most sensitive to radiation of all human organs.

Among other possible somatic effects are: increased incidence of leukemia and other forms of cancer, increased incidence of degenerative diseases, shortening of the life span, development of cataracts, and various adverse effects on growth and normal development, especially in embryos.

DEHUMANIZATION

A COMPOSITE PSYCHOLOGICAL DEFENSE
IN RELATION TO MODERN WAR

Viola W. Bernard, Perry Ottenberg, and Fritz Redl

We conceive of dehumanization as a particular type of psychic defense mechanism and consider its increasing prevalence to be a social consequence of the nuclear age. By this growth it contributes, we believe, to heightening the risks of nuclear extermination.

Dehumanization as a defense against painful or overwhelming emotions entails a decrease in a person's sense of his own individuality and in his perception of the humanness of other people. The misperceiving of others ranges from viewing them *en bloc* as "subhuman" or "bad human" (a long-familiar component of group prejudice) to viewing them as "nonhuman," as though they were inanimate items or "dispensable supplies." As such, their maltreatment or even their destruction may be carried out or acquiesced in with relative freedom from the restraints of conscience or feelings of brotherhood.

Reprinted by permission of the editors and publisher from Milton Schwebel (ed.), Behavioral Science and Human Survival *(Palo Alto: Science and Behavior Books, Inc., 1970).*

In our view, dehumanization is not a wholly new mental mechanism, but rather a composite psychological defense which draws selectively on other well-known defenses, including unconscious denial, repression, depersonalization, isolation of affect, and compartmentalization (the elimination of meaning by disconnecting related mental elements and walling them off from each other). Recourse to dehumanization as a defense against stresses of inner conflict and external threat is especially favored by impersonal aspects of modern social organization, along with such special technological features of nuclear weapons as their unprecedented destructive power and the distance between push button and victim.

We recognize that many adaptive, as well as maladaptive,[1] uses of self-protective dehumanization are requisite in multiple areas of contemporary life. As a maladaptive defense in relation to war, however, the freedom from fear which it achieves by apathy or blindness to implications of the threat of nuclear warfare itself increases the actuality of that threat: the masking of its true urgency inactivates motive power for an all-out effort to devise creative alternatives for resolving international conflict. Dehumanization also facilitates the tolerating of mass destruction through by-passing those psychic inhibitions against the taking of human life that have become part of civilized man. Such inhibitions cannot be called into play when those who are to be destroyed have been divested of their humanness. The magnitudes of annihilation that may be perpetrated with indifference would seem to transcend those carried out in hatred and anger. This was demonstrated by the impersonal, mechanized efficiency of extermination at the Nazi death camps.

The complex psychological phenomenon which we call dehumanization includes two distinct but interrelated series of processes: *self-directed dehumanization* relates to self-image, and denotes the diminution of an individual's sense of his own humanness; *object-directed dehumanization* refers to his perceiving others as lacking in those attributes that are considered to be most human. Despite the differences between these two in their origins and intrapsychic relationships within overall personality development and psychodynamic functioning, both forms of dehumanization, compounded from parts of other defenses, become usable by the individual for emotional self-protection. These two forms of dehumanization are mutually reinforcing: reduction in the fullness of one's feelings for other human beings, whatever the reason for this, impoverishes one's sense of self; any lessening of the humanness of one's self-image limits one's capacity for relating to others.

It seems to us that the extensive increase of dehumanization today is causally linked to aspects of institutional changes in contemporary society and to the transformed nature of modern war. The mushrooming importance in today's world of technology, automation, urbanization, specialization, various forms of bureaucracy, mass media, and the increased influences of nationalistic, totalitarian, and other ideologies have all been widely discussed by many scholars. The net long-term implications of these processes, whether constructive or destructive, are beyond the scope of this paper, and we do not regard ourselves qualified to evaluate them.

---

[1] Adaptive and maladaptive refer to a person's modes of coping with internal and external stress. The distinction hinges on the extent to which such coping is successful with respect to the optimal overall balance of the individual's realistic interests and goals.

We are concerned here, however, with certain of their more immediate effects on people. It would seem that, for a vast portion of the world's population, elements of these broad social changes contribute to feelings of anonymity, impersonality, separation from the decision-making processes, and a fragmented sense of one's integrated social roles, and also to pressure on the individual to constrict his affective range to some machine-like task at hand. Similarly, the average citizen feels powerless indeed with respect to control over fateful decisions about nuclear attack or its aftermath.

The consequent sense of personal unimportance and relative helplessness, socially and politically, on the part of so many people specifically inclines them to adopt dehumanization as a preferred defense against many kinds of painful, unacceptable, and unbearable feelings referable to their experiences, inclinations, and behavior. *Self-directed dehumanization* empties the individual of human emotions and passions. It is paradoxical that one of its major dynamic purposes is protection against feeling the anxieties, frustrations, and conflicts associated with the "cog-in-a-big-machine" self-image into which people feel themselves pushed by socially induced pressures. Thus it tends to fulfill the very threat that it seeks to prevent.

These pervasive reactions predispose one even more to regard other people or groups as less than human, or even nonhuman. We distinguish among several different types and gradations of *object-directed dehumanization*. Thus the failure to recognize in others their full complement of human qualities may be either partial or relatively complete. Partial dehumanization includes the misperceiving of members of "out-groups," *en masse,* as subhuman, bad human, or superhuman; as such, it is related to the psychodynamics of group prejudice. It protects the individual from

the guilt and shame he would otherwise feel from primitive or antisocial attitudes, impulses, and actions that he directs—or allows others to direct—toward those he manages to perceive in these categories: if they are subhumans they have not yet reached full human status on the evolutionary ladder and, therefore, do not merit being treated as human; if they are bad humans, their maltreatment is justified, since their defects in human qualities are their own fault. The latter is especially true if they are seen as having superhuman qualities as well, for it is one of the curious paradoxes of prejudice that both superhuman and debased characteristics are ascribed simultaneously to certain groups in order to justify discrimination or aggression against them. The foreigner, for instance, is seen at once as "wicked, untrustworthy, dirty," and "uncanny, powerful, and cunning." Similarly, according to the canons of race prejudice, contradictory qualities of exceptional prowess and extraordinary defect—ascribed to Orientals, Negroes, Jews, or any other group—together make them a menace toward whom customary restraints on behavior do not obtain. The main conscious emotional concomitants of partial dehumanization, as with prejudice, are hostility and fear.

In its more complete form, however, object-directed dehumanization entails a perception of other people as nonhumans—as statistics, commodities, or interchangeable pieces in a vast "numbers game." Its predominant emotional tone is that of indifference, in contrast to the (sometimes strong) feelings of partial dehumanization, together with a sense of *noninvolvement in the actual or foreseeable vicissitudes* of others. Such apathy has crucial psychosocial implications. Among these—perhaps the most important today—is its bearing on how people tolerate the risks of mass destruction by nuclear war.

Although this communication is primarily concerned with the negative and maladaptive aspects of dehumanization, we recognize that it also serves important adaptive purposes in many life situations. In this respect, it resembles other mental mechanisms of defense. Some of the ingredients of dehumanization are required for the effective mastery of many tasks in contemporary society. Thus, in crises such as natural disasters, accidents, or epidemics in which people are injured, sick, or killed, psychic mechanisms are called into play which divest the victims of their human identities, so that feelings of pity, terror, or revulsion can be overcome. Without such selective and transient dehumanization, these emotional reactions would interfere with the efficient and responsible performance of what has to be done, whether it be first aid, surgery, rescue operation, or burial.

Certain occupations in particular require such selectively dehumanized behavior.[2] Examples of these include law enforcement (police, judges, lawyers, prison officials) ; medicine (physicians, nurses, and ancillary personnel) ; and, of course, national defense (military leaders, strategists, fighting personnel) . Indeed, some degree of adaptive dehumanization seems to be a basic requirement for effective participation in any institutional process. Almost every professional activity has some specific aspect that requires the capacity for appropriate detachment from full emotional responsiveness and the curtailment, at least temporarily, of those everyday human emotional exchanges that are not central to the task at hand, or which might, if present, impede it. The official at the window who stamps the passport may be by nature a warm and friendly man, but in the context of his job the emigrant's hopes or fears lie outside his emotional vision.

Margaret Bourke-White, the noted photographer, was at Buchenwald at the end of World War II as a correspondent. Her account of herself at that time aptly describes the adaptive use of dehumanization, both self-directed and object-directed:

People often ask me how it is possible to photograph such atrocities. . . . I have to work with a veil over my mind. In photographing the murder camps, the protective veil was so tightly drawn that I hardly knew what I had taken until I saw prints of my own photographs. I believe many correspondents worked in the same self-imposed stupor. One has to or it is impossible to stand it. (Bourke-White, 1963.)

The only occasions to date on which nuclear bombs have been used in warfare took place when the "baby bombs" were dropped on the civilian populations of Hiroshima and Nagasaki. Lifton (1963) has reported on reactions among the Hiroshima survivors, as well as his own as investigator. His observations are particularly valuable to us since, as a research psychiatrist, he was especially qualified both to elicit and to evaluate psychodynamic data. According to the survivors whom he interviewed, at first one experienced utter horror at the sudden, strange scene of mass deaths, devastation, dreadful burns, and skin stripped from bodies. They could find no words to convey fully these initial feelings. But then each described how, before long, the horror would almost disappear. One would see terrible sights of human beings in extreme agony and yet feel nothing. The load of feeling from empathic responsiveness had become too much to endure; all one could do was to try to survive.

Lifton reports that during the first few such accounts he felt profoundly shocked, shaken, and emotionally spent. These effects gradually lessened, however, so that he became able to experience the inter-

---

[2] These occupations, therefore, carry the extra risk of their requisite dehumanization becoming maladaptive if it is carried to an extreme or used inappropriately.

views as scientific work rather than as repeated occasions of vicarious agony. For both the survivors and the investigator, the "task" provided a focus of concentration and of circumscribed activity as a means of quelling disturbing emotions.

In these instances, the immediate adaptive value of dehumanization as a defense is obvious. It remains open to question, however, whether a further, somewhat related, finding of Lifton's will in the long run prove to be adaptive or maladaptive. He learned that many people in Japan and elsewhere cannot bear to look at pictures of Hiroshima, and even avoid the museum in which they are displayed. There is avoidance and denial of the whole issue which not infrequently leads to hostility toward the A-bomb victims themselves, or toward anyone who expresses concern for these or future victims. May not *this* kind of defense reaction deflect the determination to seek ways of preventing nuclear war?

We believe that the complex mechanism of dehumanization urgently needs to be recognized and studied because its use as a defense has been stepped up so tremendously in recent times, and because of the grave risks it entails as the price for short-term relief. This paper represents only a preliminary delineation, with main attention to its bearing on the nuclear threat.[3]

Many people, by mobilizing this form of ego defense, manage to avoid or to lessen the emotional significance for themselves of today's kind of war. Only a very widespread and deeply rooted defense could ward off the full import of the new reality with which we live: that warfare has been transformed by modern weaponry into something mankind has never experienced before, and that in all-out nuclear war there can be no "victory" for anyone.

The extraordinary complacency with which people manage to shield themselves against fully realizing the threat of nuclear annihilation cannot be adequately explained, we think, by denial and the other well-studied psychological defense mechanisms. This is what has led us to trace out dehumanization as a composite defense, which draws upon a cluster of familiar defenses, magnifying that fraction of each which is most specifically involved with the humanness of one's self-image and the perception of others. It operates against such painful feelings as fear, inadequacy, compassion, revulsion, guilt, and shame. As with other mental mechanisms of defense, its self-protective distortions of realistic perceptions occur, for the most part, outside of awareness.

The extent to which dehumanization takes place consciously or unconsciously, although of considerable interest to us, is not relevant enough to this discussion to warrant elaboration. This also holds true for questions about why dehumanization as such has not hitherto received more attention and study in clinical psychiatry.[4] At least one possible reason might be mentioned, however. Most defense mechanisms were not studied originally in relation to such issues as war and peace, national destiny or group survival. Instead, they came under scrutiny, during the course of psychotherapy, as part of the idiosyncratic

---

[3] Because of this primary emphasis, we shall refrain from exploring many important facets of dehumanization which seem less directly relevant to the threat of nuclear warfare. Yet, it permeates so many aspects of modern life that, for clarity in describing it, our discussion must ramify, to some extent, beyond its war-connected context. Still we have purposely neglected areas of great interest to us, especially with regard to psychopathology, psychotherapy, and community psychiatry, which we think warrant fuller discussion elsewhere.

[4] No doubt, when the phenomenon is part of a mental disorder, it has been dealt with therapeutically, to some degree, under the names of other defense mechanisms.

pathology of individual patients. This could have obscured the recognition of their roles in widespread collective reactions.

In order to avoid confusion we should also mention that the term "dehumanization," as we are using it, refers to a concept that is different from and not connected in meaning with the words "humane" and "humanitarian." "Inhumane cruelty causes suffering; maladaptive dehumanization, as we point out, may also lead to suffering. Yet even these seemingly similar results are reached by very different routes; to equate them would be a mistake. A surgeon, for example, is treating his patient humanely when, by his dehumanization, he blots out feelings of either sympathy or hostility that might otherwise interfere with his surgical skill during an operation.

No one, of course, could possibly retain his mental health and carry on the business of life if he remained constantly aware of, and emphatically sensitive to, all the misery and injustice that there is in the world. But this very essential of dehumanization, as with other defenses, makes for its greatest danger: that the constructive self-protection it achieves will cross the ever-shifting boundaries of adaptiveness and become destructive, to others as well as to the self. In combination with other social factors already mentioned, the perfection of modern techniques for automated killing on a global scale engenders a marked increase in the incidence of dehumanization. Correspondingly, there is intensified risk that this collective reaction will break through the fragile and elusive dividing line that separates healthy ego-supportive dehumanization from the maladaptive callousness and apathy that prevent people from taking those realistic actions which are within their powers to protect human rights and human lives.

A "vicious cycle" relationship would thus seem to obtain between dehumanization as a subjective phenomenon and its objective consequences. Conscience and empathy, as sources of guilt and compassion, pertain to human beings; they can be evaded if the human element in the victims of aggression is first sufficiently obscured. The agressor is thereby freed from conscience-linked restraints, with injurious objective effects on other individuals, groups, or nations. The victims in turn respond, subjectively, by resorting even more to self-protective dehumanization, as did the Hiroshima survivors whom Lifton interviewed.

One might argue, and with some cogency, that similar conversion of enemies into pins on a military map has been part of war psychology throughout history, so are we not therefore belaboring the obvious? The answer lies in the fundamental changes, both quantitative and qualitative, that nuclear weapons have made in the meaning of war. In fact, the very term "war," with its pre-atomic connotations, has become something of an outmoded misnomer for the nuclear threat which now confronts us. "Modern war"—before Hiroshima—reflected, as a social institution, many of the social and technological developments which we have already noted as conducive to increased dehumanization. But with the possibility of instantaneously wiping out the world's population—or a very large section of it—the extent of dehumanization as well as its significance for human survival have both been abruptly and tremendously accelerated.

In part, this seems to be due to the overtaxing of our capacity really to comprehend the sudden changes in amplitudes that have become so salient. In addition to the changed factors of *distance, time, and magnitude* in modern technology, there is the push-button nature of today's weaponry and the *indirectness* of releasing a rocket barrage upon sites halfway around the world, all of which lie far outside our range of previous experience. When we look out of an airplane window, the earth below becomes a toy, the hills and valleys reduced to abstractions in our mental canvas; but we do not conceive of ourselves as a minute part of some moving speck in the sky—which is how we appear to people on the ground. Yet it is precisely such reciprocal awareness that is required if we are to maintain a balanced view of our actual size and vulnerability. Otherwise, perceptual confusion introduces a mechanistic and impersonal quality into our reactions.

The thinking and feeling of most people have been unable as yet to come to grips with the sheer expansion of numbers and the frightening shrinkage of space which present means of transportation and communication entail. The news of an animal run over by a car, a child stuck in a well, or the preventable death of one individual evokes an outpouring of sympathetic response and upsets the emotional equanimity of many; yet reports of six million Jews killed in Nazi death camps, or of a hundred thousand Japanese killed in Hiroshima and Nagasaki, may cause but moderate uneasiness. Arthur Koestler (1945) has put it poignantly, "Statistics don't bleed; it is the detail which counts. We are unable to embrace the total process with our awareness; we can only focus on little lumps of reality."

It is this unique combination of psychosocial and situational factors that seems particularly to favor the adoption of the composite defense we have called "dehumanization"—and this in turn acts to generate more and more of the same. The new aspects of time, space magnitude, speed, automation, distance, and irreversibility are not yet "hooked up" in the psychology of man's relationships to his fellow man or to the world he inhabits. Most people feel poorly equipped, conceptually, to restructure their accustomed picture of the world all of a sudden, in order to make it fit dimensions so alien to their lifelong learning. Anxiety aroused by this threat to one's orientation adds to the inner stress that seeks relief through the defense.

We are confronted with a *lag in our perceptual and intellectual development* so that the enormity of the new reality, with its potential for both destructive and constructive human consequences, becomes blurred in our thinking and feeling. The less elastic our capacity to comprehend meaningfully new significances, the more we cling to dehumanization, unable to challenge its fallacies through knowledge and reason. Correspondingly, the greater our reliance on dehumanization as a mechanism for coping with life, the less readily can the new facts of our existence be integrated into our full psychic functioning, since so many of its vital components, such as empathy, have been shunted aside, stifled, or obscured.

Together, in the writers' opinion, these differently caused but mutually reinforcing cognitive and emotional deficiencies seriously intensify the nuclear risk; latent psychological barriers against the destruction of millions of people remain unmobilized, and hence ineffective, for those who feel detached from the flesh-and-blood implications of nuclear war. No other mechanism seems to fit so well the requirements of this unprecedented internal and external stress. Dehumanization, with its impairment of our personal involvement, allows us to "play chess with the planets."

Whether it be adaptive or maladaptive, dehumanization brings with it, as we have noted, a temporary feeling of relief, an illusion of problems solved, or at least postponed or evaded. Whatever the ultimate effects of this psychic maneuver on our destiny, however, it would seem to be a wise precaution to try to assess some of its dangerous possibilities.

Several overlapping aspects of maladaptive dehumanization may be outlined briefly, and in oversimplified form, as follows:

1. *Increased emotional distance from other human beings.* Under the impact of this defense, one stops identifying with others or seeing them as essentially similar to oneself in basic human qualities. Relationships to others become stereotyped, rigid, and, above all, unexpressive of mutuality. People in "out-groups" are apt to be reacted to *en bloc;* feelings of concern for them have become anesthetized.

George Orwell (1945) illustrates this aspect of dehumanization in writing of his experience as a patient. His account also serves as an example of the very significant hazard, already mentioned, whereby professionally adaptive uses of this defense (as in medical education and patient care) are in danger of passing that transition point beyond which they become maladaptive and so defeat their original purpose.

Later in the day the tall, solemn, black-bearded doctor made his rounds, with an intern and a troop of students following at his heels, but there were about sixty of us in the ward and it was evident that he had other wards to attend to as well. There were many beds past which he walked day after day, sometimes followed by imploring cries. On the other hand, if you had some disease with which the students wanted to familiarize themselves you get plenty of attention of a kind. I myself, with an exceptionally fine specimen of a bronchial rattle sometimes had as many as a dozen students queuing up to listen to my chest. It was a very queer feeling—queer, I mean, because of their intense interest in learning their job, together with a seeming lack of any perception that the patients were human beings. It is strange to relate, but sometimes as some young student stepped forward to take his turn at manipulating you, he would be actually tremulous with excitement, like a boy who has at last got his hands on some expensive piece of machinery. And then ear after ear ... pressed against your back, relays of fingers solemnly but clumsily tapping, and not from any one of them did you get a word of conversation or a look direct in your face. As a non-paying patient, in the uniform nightshirt, you were primarily a *specimen,* a thing I did not resent but could never quite get used to.

2. *Diminished sense of personal responsibility for the consequences of one's actions.* Ordinarily, for most people, the advocacy of or participation in the wholesale slaughter and maiming of their fellow human beings is checked by opposing feelings of guilt, shame, or horror. Immunity from these feelings may be gained, however, by a self-automatizing detachment from a sense of *personal* responsibility for the outcome of such actions, thereby making them easier to carry out. (A dramatic version of the excuse, "I was only carrying out orders," was offered by Eichmann at his trial.)

One "safe" way of dealing with such painful feelings is to focus only on one's fragmented job and ignore its many ramifications. By blocking out the ultimately destructive purpose of a military bombing action, for instance, one's component task therein may become a source of ego-acceptable gratification, as from any successful fulfillment of duty, mastery of a hard problem, or achievement of a dangerous feat. The B-29 airplane that dropped the atomic bomb on Hiroshima was named Enola Gay, after the mother of one of its crew members. This could represent the psychological defense of displacing human qualities from the population to be bombed to the machine.

One of the crew members is reported to have exclaimed: "If people knew what we were doing we could have sold tickets for $100,000!" and another is said to have commented, "Colonel, that was worth the 25¢ ride on the 'Cyclone' at Coney Island." (*Yank,* 1947.) Such reactions, which may on the surface appear to be shockingly cynical, not only illustrate how cynicism may be used to conceal strong emotions (as seems quite likely in this instance); they also suggest how one may try to use cynicism to bolster one's dehumanization when that defense is not itself strong enough, even with its displacement of responsibility and its focusing on one's fragmented job, to overcome the intensity of one's inner "humanized" emotional protest against carrying out an act of such vast destructiveness.

3. *Increasing involvement with procedural problems to the detriment of human needs.* There is an overconcern with details of procedure, with impersonal deindividualized regulations, and with the formal structure of a practice, all of which result in shrinking the ability or willingness to personalize one's actions in the interests of individual human needs or special differences. This is, of course, the particular danger implicit in the trend toward bureaucracy that accompanies organizational units when they grow larger and larger. The task at hand is then apt to take precedence over the human cost: the individual is seen more as a means to an end than as an end in himself. Society, the Corporation, the Five-Year-Plan—these become overriding goals in themselves, and the dehumanized man is turned into a cost item, tool, or energy factor serving the mass machine.

Even "scientific" studies of human behavior and development, as well as professional practices based on them, sometimes become dehumanized to a maladaptive extent (Kahne, 1959). Such words as "communicate," "adjust," "identify," "relate," "feel," and even "love" can lose their personal meaningfulness when they are used as mere technical devices instead of being applied to specific human beings in specific life situations.[5] In response to the new hugeness of global problems, patterns of speech have emerged that additionally reflect dehumanized thinking. Segmented-fragmented concepts, such as "fallout problem," "shelter problem," "civil defense," "deterrence," "first strike," "preemptive attack," "overkill," and some aspects of game theory, represent a "move-countermove" type of thinking which tends to treat the potential human victim as a statistic, and to screen out the total catastrophic effect of the contemplated actions upon human lives. The content of strategy takes on an importance that is without any relation to its inevitable *results,* the defense of dehumanization having operated to block out recognition of those awesome consequences that, if they could be seen, would make the strategy unacceptable. The defense, when successful, narcotizes deeper feelings so that nuclear war, as "inevitable," may be more dispassionately contemplated and its tactical permutations assayed. In the course of this, however, almost automatic counteractions of anxiety are frequently expressed through such remarks as: "People have always lived on the brink of disaster," "You can't change human nature; there will have to be wars," and "We all have to die some day."

4. *Inability to oppose dominant group attitudes or pressures.* As the individual comes to feel more and more alienated and

---

[5] Within our own discipline this is all too likely to occur when thousands of sick individuals are converted into "cases" in some of our understaffed and oversized mental hospitals. Bureaucratic hospital structure favors impersonal experience. In an enlightening study, Merton J. Kahne (1959) points up how this accentuation of automatic and formalized milieu propensities thwarts the specific therapeutic need of psychiatric patients for opportunities to improve their sense of involvement with people.

On another occasion we hope to enlarge on how and why maladaptive uses of dehumanization on the part of professionals, officials, and the general public hamper our collective effort as a community to instill more sensitivity to individual need into patterns of congregate care, not only in mental hospitals but also in general hospitals, children's institutions, welfare and correctional facilities, etc.

lonely in mass society, he finds it more and more difficult to place himself in opposition to the huge pressures of the "Organization." Fears of losing occupational security or of attacks on one's integrity, loyalty, or family are more than most people can bear. Self-directed dehumanization is resorted to as a defense against such fears and conflicts: by joining the party, organization, or club, and thus feeling himself to be an inconspicuous particle in some large structure, he may find relief from the difficult decisions, uncertainties, and pressures of nonconformity. He may also thereby ward off those feelings of guilt that would arise out of participating in, or failing to protest against, the injustices and cruelties perpetrated by those in power. Thus, during the Nazi regime, many usually kindhearted Germans appear to have silenced their consciences by emphasizing their own insignificance and identifying with the dehumanized values of the dictatorship. This stance permitted the detached, even dutiful, disregard of their fellow citizens, which in turn gave even freer rein to the systematic official conducting of genocide.

5. *Feelings of personal helplessness and estrangement.* The realization of one's relatively impotent position in a large organization engenders anxiety[6] which dehumanization helps to cover over. The internalized perception of the self as small, helpless, and insignificant, coupled with an externalized view of "Society" as huge, powerful, and unopposable, is expressed in such frequently heard comments as: "The government has secret information that we don't have"; or, "They know what's right, who am I to question what they are doing?"; or "What's the use? No one will listen to me. . . . "

The belief that the government or the military is either infallible or impregnable provides a tempting refuge because of its renunciation of one's own critical faculties in the name of those of the powerful and all-knowing leader. Such self-directed dehumanization has a strong appeal to the isolated and alienated citizen as a protective cloak to hide from himself his feelings of weakness, ignorance, and estrangement. This is particularly relevant to the psychological attraction of certain dangerous social movements. The more inwardly frightened, lonely, helpless, and humiliated people become, the greater the susceptibility of many of them to the seductive, prejudiced promises of demagoguery: the award of spurious superiority and privilege achieved by devaluating the full humanness of some other group—racial, religious, ethnic, or political. Furthermore, as an added advantage of the dehumanization "package," self-enhancing acts of discrimination and persecution against such victim groups can be carried out without tormenting or deterrent feelings of guilt, since these are absorbed by the "rightness" of the demagogic leader.

In recent decades and in many countries, including our own, we have seen what human toll can be taken by this psychosocial configuration. It has entered into Hitlerism, Stalinism, U.S.A. "lynch-mobism." If it is extended to the international arena, against a "dehumanized" enemy instead of an oppressed national minority, atomic weapons will now empower it to inflict immeasurably more human destruction and suffering.

The indifference resulting from that form of dehumanization which causes one to view others as inanimate objects enables one, without conscious malice or selfishness, to write off their misery, injustices, and death as something that "just couldn't be helped." As nonhumans, they are not identified with as beings essentially similar to oneself; "their" annihilation by nuclear

---

[6] This has been particularly well described in novels by Kafka and Camus.

warfare is thus not "our" concern, despite the reality that distinctions between "they" and "we" have been rendered all the more meaningless by the mutually suicidal nature of total war.

Although this type of dehumanization is relatively complete, in the sense of perceiving others as not at all human, it may occur in an individual with selective incompleteness under certain special conditions only, while his capacity for other emotional ties is preserved. This may prove socially constructive or destructive, depending on the purposes to which it is put. Thus we have already noted how "pulling a veil" over her mind helped Bourke-White adaptively in her socially positive job of reporting atrocities. But it was compartmentalized dehumanization that also helped many to commit those very atrocities; they were able to exterminate Jews with assembly-line efficiency as the Nazi "final solution" while still retaining access to their genuine feelings of warmth for family members, friends, and associates.

These contradictory emotional qualities, often appearing side by side in the same person, are also evidenced—in the opposite direction—by outstanding deeds of heroic rescue by those who, under different circumstances, might well exhibit dehumanized behavior. Almost daily, the newspapers carry stories of exceptional altruism; individuals or whole communities devote their entire energies to the rescue of a single child, an animal, or perhaps (in wartime), a wounded enemy soldier. What accounts for the difference between this kind of response to the plight of others, and that of dehumanized callousness? How are the adaptive humanized processes released?

One research approach might consist of the detailed description and comparative analysis of sample situations of both kinds of these collective reactions, which have such opposite social effects. A case history of community apathy which could be compared in such a study with instances of group altruism already on record, was recently provided by A. M. Rosenthal (1964), an editor of *The New York Times*. At first glance, perhaps, his account of dehumanization, involving but one individual and in peacetime, may not seem germane to our discussion about nuclear war. But the macrocosm is reflected in the microcosm. We agree with Mr. Rosenthal that the implications of this episode are linked with certain psychological factors that have helped pave the way for such broad social calamities as Fascism abroad and racial crises in this country, both in the North and South. It does not seem too farfetched, therefore, to relate them to the nuclear threat as well.

For more than half an hour, one night in March 1964, thirty-eight respectable, law-abiding citizens in a quiet middle-class neighborhood in New York City watched a killer stalk and stab a young woman in three separate attacks, close to her home. She was no stranger to these onlookers, her neighbors, who knew her as "Kitty." According to Rosenthal, "Twice the sound of their voices and the sudden glow of their bedroom lights interrupted him and frightened him off. Each time he returned, sought her out, and stabbed her again. Not one person telephoned the police during the assault; one witness called after the woman was dead." Later, when these thirty-eight neighbors were asked about their baffling failure to phone for help, even though they were safe in their own homes, "the underlying attitude or explanation seemed to be fear of involvement—any kind of involvement." Their fatal apathy gains in significance precisely because, by ordinary standards, these were decent, moral people—husbands and wives attached to each other and good to their children. This is one of the forms of dehumanization that we have described, in which a reaction of massive indifference—not hostility—leads to grievous cruelty, yet all the while, in another compartment of the self, the same individual's capacity for active caring continues, at least for those within his immediate orbit.

Rosenthal describes his own reaction to this episode as a

peculiar paradoxical feeling that there is in the tale of Catherine Genovese a revelation about the human condition so appalling to contemplate that only good can come from forcing oneself to confront the truth . . . the terrible reality that only under certain situations, and only in response to certain reflexes or certain beliefs, will a man step out of his shell toward his brother. In the back of my mind . . . was the feeling that there was, that there must be some connection between [this story and] the story of the witnesses silent in the face of greater crimes—the degradation of a race, children hungering. . . . It happens from time to time in New York that the life of the city is frozen by an instant of shock. In that instant the people of the city are seized by the paralyzing realization that they are one, that each man is in some way a mirror of every other man. . . . In that instant of shock, the mirror showed quite clearly what was wrong, that the face of mankind was spotted with the disease of apathy—all mankind. But this was too frightening a thought to live with, and soon the beholders began to set boundaries for the illness, to search frantically for causes that were external and to look for the carrier.

As we strive to distinguish more clearly among the complex determinants of adaptive-maladaptive, humanized-dehumanized polarities of behavior, we recognize that stubborn impulses toward individuation are intertwined with the dehumanizing trends on which we have focused. Both humanization and dehumanization are heightened by interpenetrating social and psychological effects of current technological and institutional changes. The progress of the past hundred years has markedly furthered humanization: it has relieved helped to bring about increased leisure and a richer life for a larger part of the world's population. Despite the blurring of permuch of human drudgery and strain, and sonal distinctiveness by excessive bureaucracy, there are now exceptional opportunities, made possible by the same technology that fosters uniformity, for the individual to make rapid contact with, and meaningful contribution to, an almost limitless number of the earth's inhabitants. The same budgets, communication networks, transportation delivery systems, and human organizations that can be used to destroy can also be turned toward the creative fulfillment of great world purposes.

Our situation today favors contradictory attitudes toward how much any individual matters in the scheme of things, both subjectively and from the standpoint of social reality. At one extreme a few individuals in key positions feel—and are generally felt to have—a hugely expanded potential for social impact. Among the vast majority there is, by contrast, an intensified sense of voiceless insignificance in the shaping of events. Objectively, too, there is now among individuals a far greater disparity in their actual power to influence crucial outcomes. More than ever before, the fate of the world depends on the judgment of a handful of heads of state and their advisers, who must make rapid decisions about actions for which there are no precedents. Ideas and events, for better or worse, can have immediate global impact.[7] A push button can set a holocaust in motion; a trans-Atlantic phone call can prevent one.

In spite of humanizing ingredients in modern life, and the fact that men of good will everywhere are striving ceaselessly toward goals of peace, freedom, and hu-

[7] The news of President Kennedy's assassination circled the earth with unparalleled speed, and evoked a profound worldwide emotional response.

man dignity, we nevertheless place primary emphasis, in this paper, on dehumanization because we feel that the dangers inherent in this phenomenon are particularly pervasive, insidious, and relevant to the risk of nuclear war.

From a broad biological perspective, war may be viewed as a form of aggression between members of the same species, *Homo sapiens*. The distinguished naturalist, Lorenz (1963), has pointed out a difference, of great relevance to the relationship between dehumanization and nuclear warfare, in the intraspecies behavior of animals who live in two kinds of groups. In the one, the members live together as a crowd of strangers: there are no expressions of mutual aggression, but neither is there any evidence of mutual ties, of relationships of affection, between individuals in the group. On the other hand, some of the fiercest beasts of prey—animals whose bodily weapons are capable of killing their own kind —live in groups in which intense relationships, both *aggressive and affectionate,* exist. Among such animals, says Lorenz, the greater the intraspecies aggression, the stronger the positive mutual attachments as well. These latter develop, through evolution, out of those occasions, such as breeding, when cooperation among these aggressive animals becomes essential to their survival as a species.

Furthermore—and this is of the utmost importance for survival—the greater the capacity for mutual relationships, the stronger and more reliable are the *innate inhibitions* that prevent them from using the species-specific weapons of predatory aggression, fangs, claws, or whatever, to maim or kill a member of their own species, no matter how strong the hostile urge of one against another. For example, when two wolves fight, according to Lorenz, the potential victor's fangs are powerfully inhibited at what would be the moment of

kill, in response to the other's ritualized signal of immobile exposure to his opponent of his vulnerable jugular.

Man's weapons, by contrast, are not part of his body. They are thus not controllable by reflexes fused into his nervous system; control must depend, instead, on psychological inhibitions (which may also function through social controls of his own devising). These psychic barriers to intraspecies aggression—which can lead to our becoming extinct—are rooted in our affiliative tendencies for cooperation and personal attachment. But these are the very tendencies that, as this paper has stressed, dehumanization can so seriously undermine.

Lorenz speaks of a natural balance within a species—essential to its preservation—between the capacity for killing and inhibition. In that sense, perhaps, man jeopardizes his survival by disturbing, with his invention of nuclear bombs, such a balance as has been maintained throughout his long history of periodic "old-style" wars. Such a dire imbalance would be increased by any shift on the part of the "human animal" toward a society essentially devoid of mutual relationships. For this would vitiate the very tendencies toward emotional involvement and cooperation which are the source of our most reliable inhibitions against "overkilling." Therefore, in terms of the parallels suggested by Lorenz, in order to protect ourselves against the doom of extinction as a species, we must encourage and devise every possible means of safeguarding the "family of man" from becoming an uncaring crowd. Not merely the limiting or halting, but the reversing of maladaptive dehumanization emerges as a key to survival.

What can be done to counteract these dangers? Assuredly, there is no single or ready answer. The development of psychic antidotes of *re*humanization must involve a multiplicity of variables, levels of discourse and sectors of human activity, commensurate in complexity with the factors that make for *de*humanization. Our attempt in this paper to identify this mental mechanism, and to alert others to its significance, its frequency, and its interrelatedness to nuclear risk, represents in itself a preliminary phase of remedial endeavor. For the very process of recognizing a psychosocial problem such as this, by marshaling, reordering, and interpreting diverse sets of facts to find new significances in them, is a form of social action, and one that is especially appropriate to behavioral scientists. Beyond this initial posing of the problem, however, any chance of effectively grappling with it will require the converging efforts of those in many different professions and walks of life.

Rehumanization as a mode of neutralizing the dangerous effects that we have stressed should not be misconstrued as aiming at the reestablishment of prenuclear-age psychology—which would be impossible in any case. We cannot set history back nostalgically to "the good old days" prior to automation and the other changes in contemporary society (nor were the conditions of those earlier days really so "good" for the self-realization of a large portion of the population). On the contrary, the process of rehumanization means to us a way of assimilating and reintegrating, emotionally and intellectually, the profound new meanings that have been brought into our lives by our own advances, so that a much fuller conviction than ever before of our own humanity and interdependence with all mankind becomes intrinsic to our basic frame of reference.

The imperative for speeding up such a universal process of psychological change is rooted in the new and *specific* necessity to ensure survival in the face of the awesome irreversibility of nuclear annihilation. The most essential approaches toward achieving this goal, however, lead us into such *general* and only seemingly unrelated issues as the degree of political freedom and social justice; our patterns of child care and child rearing; and our philosophy of education, as well as the quality of its implementation. For the process of dehumanization, which eventuates in indifference to the suffering implicit in nuclear warfare, has its beginnings in earlier periods and other areas of the individual's life. It is through these areas that influences conducive to rehumanization must be channeled.

We need to learn more, and to make more effective use of what is already known, about how to strengthen people's capacity to tolerate irreducible uncertainty, fear, and frustration without having to take refuge in illusions that cripple their potential for realistic behavior. And we urgently need to find ways of galvanizing our powers of imagination (including ways of weakening the hold of the emotionally based mechanisms that imprison it).

Imagination and foresight are among the highest functions of the human brain, from the evolutionary standpoint, and also among the most valuable. They enable us to select and extrapolate from previously accumulated experience and knowledge, in order to create guidelines for coping with situations never before experienced, whose nature is so far unknown.

Other kinds of learning ordinarily serve us well in the complicated process of establishing behavior patterns for meeting new life situations. We are able to learn by trial and error, for example, from our firsthand experiences and from successively testing the value of alternative approaches as similar situations arise. Also, we learn much by vicariously living through the reported experiences of others.

Through imagination, however, a completely new situation can be projected in the mind in its sensate and vivid entirety, so that the lessons it contains for us can be learned without the necessity of going through it in real life. This form of "future-directed" learning, which creative imagination makes possible, is therefore uniquely advantageous in dealing with the problematic issues of thermonuclear war; it permits us to arrive at more rational decisions for preventing it without having to pay the gruesome price of undergoing its actuality.

The fact is that the "once-and-for-all" character of full-scale nuclear war renders the methods of "learning through experience"—our own or others'—not only indefensible (in terms of the human cost) but also utterly unfeasible. The empirical privilege of "profiting" from an experience of that nature would have been denied to most if not all of humanity by the finality of the experience itself.

Accordingly, it would seem that whatever can quicken and extend our capacity for imagination, in both the empathic and conceptual spheres, is a vital form of "civil defense." It requires, to begin with, all the pedagogic ingenuity that we can muster to overcome the lag in our intellectual development that keeps us from fully comprehending the new dimensions of our existence. Yet, our endeavors to develop new modes of thinking can be canceled out by the constricting and impeding effects of dehumanization. The terrible potential of this subtle mechanism to facilitate the depopulating of the earth lies in its circumventing human restraints against fratricide. We are faced, therefore, with the inescapable necessity of devising ways to increase opportunities for meaningful personal relationships and maximum social participation throughout the entire fabric of our society.

REFERENCES

Bourke-White, M., *Portrait of Myself* (New York: Simon and Schuster, 1963).

Kahne, M. J., "Bureaucratic Structure and Impersonal Experience in Mental Hospitals," *Psychiatry,* **22**:4 (1959), pp. 363–375.

Koestler, A., "On Disbelieving Atrocities," in *The Yogi and the Commissar* (New York: Macmillan, 1945).

Lifton, R., "Psychological Effects of the Atomic Bomb in Hiroshima; the Theme of Death," *Daedalus* (Summer 1963), pp. 462–497.

Lorenz, K., *Das Sogenannte Böse—Zur Naturgeschichte der Aggression* (Vienna: Dr. G. Borotha-Schoeler Verlag, 1963).

Orwell, G., "How the Poor Die," in *Shooting an Elephant* (New York: Harcourt, Brace, 1945).

Rosenthal, A. M., *Thirty-Eight Witnesses* (New York: McGraw-Hill, 1964).

Yank, the Army Weekly (New York: Duell, Sloane and Pearce, 1947), p. 282.

MILITARISM IN AMERICA

Donald McDonald

Is the United States a militarized society? Two quick—and contradictory—answers can be given to this question. The "yes" answer is usually based on a few pieces of evidence; military expenditures and the Vietnam war are the ones most often cited. The "no" answer rests on the fact that a civilian is commander-in-chief of our armed forces and that another civilian, the secretary of defense, exercises direct authority over the administration of these forces. The "yes" proceeds from insufficient evidence; the "no" evades the issue because it assumes that civilians really do control our armed forces and that the mere fact of civilian control—constitutional and/or actual—proves that the control is not leading to a militarization of American society.

Neither of the answers, of course, is satisfactory. I suspect that what must be done is to treat this question as a genuine query. That means we must let our answer develop out of an understanding of the meaning of the key term, "a militarized society," and out of an examination and critical analysis of the contemporary American experience to determine whether our experience fits the definition of such a society.

I

The following seem to be major characteristics of a militarized society:

1. *A militarized society is an authoritarian society.* Free expression is a threat, dissent cannot be tolerated, and disobedience is met with swift repression.

2. *In a militarized society, stability is a cardinal virtue.* Questions of social justice and human rights, when they are not altogether ignored, are viewed with sour suspicion because they cannot be entertained, even abstractly, without at least implying that in certain circumstances stability is not a virtue but a vice.

3. *The militarized society is a fearful society.* The ultimate justification for a militarized society is that it is surrounded by enemies. In such an atmosphere, human trust withers, paranoia becomes a national disease, and it is never possible to have too many weapons.

4. *The militarized society is a self-righteous society.* It regards its motives as the purest, its values as unquestionable, its ideals as unsurpassable. When it wages war or intervenes in the affairs of another people, it is sure it does so only to protect these qualities or enable others to enjoy them.

5. *In a militarized society, the military is not a means to an end, it is the end itself.* Whatever is good for the military is good for society. Military logic is the national philosophy.

6. *A militarized society gives to the military the highest priority in claims on the national resources.* In practice, the military consumes the lion's share of the government's revenues from taxes on the people;

Reprinted by permission from The Center Magazine, **3**:1 *(January 1970), a publication of the Center for the Study of Democratic Institutions, Santa Barbara, Calif.*

a substantial part of what is left over is spent to placate a restless people and to repress those who will not be placated.

7. *A militarized society has an unchallengeable claim on the lives of its young men.* Conscription into military service becomes a natural—and, in time, almost an unnoticed—part of the political and social landscape.

8. *In a militarized society, the military are beyond effective criticism and control.* The institutions that ordinarily exercise such critical control—legislative bodies, courts, press, universities, churches—are silenced, ignored, or drawn into acquiescence.

9. *In a militarized society, deception is accepted as a normal fact of life.* Foreign and domestic espionage, sabotage, subversion, and other paramilitary activities are carefully cultivated within the military; these have the twofold effect of keeping the enemy off balance and one's own citizens ignorant and therefore unable to ask critical questions.

10. *A militarized society perceives most political problems as military problems and the militarized solution is, therefore, the only realistic solution.* The options confronting such a society in a world community are determined and defined by the military. Civilian policymakers who consider other options do so at the risk of being labeled "soft-headed" if not "disloyal."

11. *In a militarized society, the economy is dependent on the military.* The military constitutes the single biggest "industry" and its dissolution would be as catastrophic for the nation as the dismantling of the single industry in a one-industry town.

12. *The militarized society is a sterile society.* Because it turns human and material resources into instruments of death and consequently neglects problems concerned with the quality of life, and because, in the process, it either suppresses or buys off with enormous rewards of money, prestige, and power the possibility of divergent views and voices, the militarized society deprives itself of the life-quickening energies of its artists and its philosophers, its critics and saints, its youth with their idealism, and its elders with their wisdom and experience. The result is sterility, emptiness, barrenness.

13. *The militarized society is a barbaric society.* The barbarian is not necessarily covered with blood, nor does he have to wear a military uniform. In a technologized military society, it is possible for decent people to perform tasks at drawing boards and in laboratories that will ensure the death of hundreds of thousands of people halfway around the world; it is possible for pilots and technicians, pressing buttons and switching on computers, to complete the killing process without seeing the faces of those they are killing. Militarization inevitably makes one indifferent about taking human life. A technologized militarization simply makes it easier and less painful to cultivate that indifference.

II

If the above is an accurate profile of a militarized society, the question is: To what extent is it matched by the contemporary American experience? A review of the evidence is in order.

The Size of the Establishment

The most obvious evidence is the size of the military establishment itself. The Department of Defense has 3.4 million men in the armed forces and 1.3 million civilian workers; its defense contracts give jobs to another 3.8 million industrial workers. Altogether, the DOD furnishes one out of every nine jobs in the United States. The

80-billion-dollar Defense budget accounts for half the total annual expenditures of the national government. If one adds to this the cost of past wars (in veterans' pensions, military hospitals, etc.), the military receive 70 cents from every dollar of taxes levied on the American people. Military weapons projects backed up and awaiting the end of the Vietnam war carry an estimated price tag of 100 billion dollars.

As the largest single activity in the country, the military has contracts with 22,000 prime contractors and 100,000 subcontractors. It subsidizes research in hundreds of universities. Its money flows into 363 of the nation's 435 congressional districts. Some 5300 cities and towns have at least one defense plant or company. Entire towns are wholly dependent on military-industrial activity for their economic life.

Department of Defense Research Activities

As a measure of the extent to which the Department of Defense is involved in foreign policy, the Department spends 7.3 million dollars a year for foreign-area social and behavioral science research, and another 6 million dollars a year for policy-planning studies in foreign politico-military problems. This compares with the 125,000 dollars a year set aside for the State Department's research budget.

The total research budget for the Defense Department in 1968 was 8 billion dollars, of which 1.6 billion was earmarked for basic research (as contrasted with, for example, research in weapons development). This 1.6 billion dollars was about six times the 280 million dollars allocated to the National Science Foundation for basic research in the same period of time.

Under pressure from some congressmen, the Department of Defense is trying to transfer several of its social and behavioral science research projects in foreign-policy problems to other agencies of the government. But Defense officials are opposed to any deep cutback in their own research activity.

The Department of Defense spends several hundred million dollars a year in funding research at American universities. In 1966, the top six were: Massachusetts Institute of Technology, $35,078,000; Stanford, $21,930,000; Michigan, $21,579,000; Columbia, $14,829,000; Illinois, $14,075,000; and the University of California at Los Angeles, $11,492,000.

According to Senator Eugene McCarthy, defense and space programs since 1960 have amounted to 54 percent of total expenditures on research and development in the entire country. Undoubtedly the most controversial Defense-funded research program was Project Camelot, a 1.5-million-dollar annual operation of American University's Special Operations Research Office (now its Center for Research in Social Systems, or CRESS). Through American University, the Department of Defense sought to recruit social scientists from the University of California, MIT, Princeton, and Michigan in order to discover ethnic and other motivational factors concerned with the cause and conduct of small wars. The social scientists' assigned mission was to build a model of a developing society, showing its breakdown possibilities as well as its manipulability. While some American researchers were surveying Chile in 1965, to see whether that country might not serve as a model, word of the project got to the press, some American social scientists started an uproar at finding their colleagues engaged in a project to help the American military manipulate people in small impoverished countries, and the United States canceled Camelot. But CRESS continues, and presumably such research activities are also continuing on

American campuses across the country. When, for example, student and faculty protested the connection between a dozen of the top American universities (MIT, Stanford, California Institute of Technology, Princeton, et al.) and the Institute of Defense Analyses, the universities severed their institutional ties to the IDA, but they kept in touch with the defense organization through individual professors and university officials, who were ostensibly representing only themselves and not their institutions, on IDA's board of trustees. An estimated thirty to forty university professors continue to spend up to a fifth of their time doing IDA work (analysis of defense problems, primarily) for fees of as much as 200 dollars a day, plus expenses.

An indication of the extent to which universities have become dependent on the military for their operating budget was seen in October last year when the president of Stanford University revealed that as a result of some cutbacks in military research Stanford would have a budget deficit of 600,000 dollars this year with no prospect of making it up from other sources.

Despite the Defense Department's insistence on conducting social and behavioral science research, Admiral Hyman Rickover has testified before the Senate Foreign Relations Committee that the Department of Defense

has been able to involve itself in research having only the remotest relevance to the problems encountered by the armed services—matters at no previous time, nor anywhere else in the world, deemed to lie within the province of the defense function—just because it has the money; it has more money than any other public agency.... Already the State Department is, to all intents and purposes, but a junior partner.... Although Congress alone has the constitutional authority to declare war, other branches of the government may confront it with situations that make war inevitable.

Speaking of the entire social-science research program funded by Defense, Rick-

over said: "No harm would have been done to the Republic if none of it had been done."

A Global Military Presence, Open and Otherwise

Admiral Rickover's denial of the relevance of military research in social and psychological areas may have been technically valid a generation ago. Given the military's commitment to both conventional and paramilitary warfare and the military's massive and multifarious activities around the world, however, military logic alone would demand the support of this global presence with researched activity.

The United States now maintains 340 major bases and 1930 minor bases abroad at an annual cost of 5 billion dollars. A million-and-a-half men staff these bases and U.S. fleets; two-thirds of these men are in Asia and the Pacific, the others are in Western Europe and Latin America.

Early in 1968, Senator William Fulbright asked the Department of Defense to make public a study done for it by Douglas Aircraft Corporation at a cost of $89,500. Senator Fulbright had a copy of the report of the study and wanted the American people to share it with him. The report was on how the United States could "maintain world hegemony in the future." It was originally titled "Pax Americana." But when the nature of the report became known, Defense renamed it "Strategic Alignments and Military Objectives." The DOD refused to make its contents public.

American military pursues its tasks overseas in a variety of ways, some of them hidden from the scrutiny of both congressmen and citizens. Senator McCarthy revealed that in 1967, in addition to uniformed men under arms, the United States had 4681 "military agents" scattered throughout the world under our military assistance program. These men, he noted, "are sent without any kind of formal congressional examination" and they "carry on, without publicity and without public awareness in the United States, missions which have strong political overtones."

Although the usual rationale for the American military presence in other countries is that it is in our national interest to be there and that we want to ensure the freedom and the right of other peoples to choose their own form of government, a Senate Foreign Relations subcommittee revealed last June that U.S. armed forces had taken part in at least two major exercises in Spain in the last two years. The purpose of the exercises was to perfect techniques for the quelling of a possible internal insurrection against the Franco government. Several months before this disclosure, the full Senate Foreign Relations Committee warned that the United States, by its very military presence in Spain, had assumed a "quasi-commitment" to defend the Franco regime, possibly even in a civil war. The Committee disclosed that a high-ranking American officer had assured the Spanish government that "the presence of American armed forces in Spain constitutes a more significant security guaranty to Spain than would a written agreement."

Last October, Senator Fulbright revealed that the Department of Defense on its own motion had sent additional jet fighter planes to a base in Spain without informing either the State Department or the Defense Department's Section of International Security Affairs. The increase, he said, meant the stationing of 242 American servicemen and 18 more fighter aircraft in Spain, adding up to a half-million-dollar "blow to our balance of payments." Fulbright said that the lesson of this incident is that "foreign policy has, in all too many instances, become the captive creature of decisions made by planners in the Defense Department."

Another method by which the American military plays a direct role in the affairs of other nations is by engaging in arms sales. According to Jack Raymond, in a *Harvard Business Review* article (May-June 1968), from 1949 to 1962 the U.S. government alone sold 16.1 billion dollars worth of military arms to other countries and gave away about 30.2 billion dollars.

Since 1962, when the current arms-sales program began, Pentagon officials have been as aggressive as private arms merchants, with the result that the United States has sold over 11.1 billion dollars worth of arms. In a speech in Los Angeles in the spring of 1966, the Pentagon official in charge of the sales program proudly estimated that it had yielded one billion dollars in profits for American industry and 1.2 million man-years of employment for companies throughout the country.

Despite the Congress's imposition in 1967 of a limit of 25 million dollars worth of arms sales to Africa and a 50-million-dollar limitation on arms to Latin America, the arms business abroad, Raymond said, remains "very big."

As a result of the Pentagon's arms-sales program, it is not unusual for both sides in international disputes to be waging combat with American weapons: the Turks and the Greeks; the Pakistanis and the Indians; the Israelis and the Arabs. Military expenditures in poor and underdeveloped countries are now said to be rising faster than their gross national product. A study sponsored by the Stockholm International Peace Research Institute revealed last November that the world spent approximately 173 billion dollars for military purposes in 1968. Of this, the United States spent about 80 billion dollars and the Soviet Union 40 billion dollars. The share of the poor countries is small but rising faster than the average: arms spending in developing countries is rising at a rate of 7.5 percent a year compared to the world average of 6 percent. These figures must be put alongside the average annual rate of increase in the world's gross national product, which is 5 percent. The Institute found that world production of nonmilitary goods and services has multiplied about five times in the last fifty years, but that arms spending has multiplied about ten times in that period.

Perhaps the most far-flung, potentially the most lethal, and certainly the most difficult to verify of American military activities in other countries is the work of the secret Central Intelligence Agency. The CIA was established in 1947 by the National Security Act, which placed the armed services under a new Department of Defense and created the National Security Council. Its original assignment was primarily that of gathering, coordinating, evaluating, and disseminating intelligence on behalf of the government, specifically the National Security Council. Today, the CIA employs 15,000 persons, it has an annual budget of a half-billion dollars, and its activities go far beyond intelligence work.

Two years after it was established, the CIA's secrecy was officially sanctioned. By a specific act of Congress, the CIA was allowed to:

1. Disregard laws that required disclosure of the organization, functions, names, official titles, salaries, or numbers of personnel employed by the agency.

2. Expend funds without regard to laws and regulations governing expenditures, and with no other accounting than the director's vouchers.

3. Make contracts and purchases without advertising.

4. Transfer funds to and from other government agencies.

5. Contract for research outside the government.

6. Provide special expense allowances for staff abroad.

7. Admit up to 100 aliens and members of their families a year.

In the twenty-two years of its existence,

more than 150 resolutions have been introduced by congressmen to exercise tighter control over the CIA. Every one of these resolutions has been either defeated or tabled.

The uneasiness of congressmen centers on the suspicion that CIA activities that go beyond intelligence work actually create international situations which then sharply limit the options of American civilian policymakers. Senator Stephen Young has charged that the CIA has, in effect, been making foreign policy. Senator McCarthy echoed this charge and added that, in so doing, the CIA "has assumed the roles of President and Congress." James Reston of *The New York Times* once flatly asserted: "The State Department does not know what the CIA is doing."

Two kinds of evidence indicate the strongly interventionary and paramilitary subversion role played by CIA agents in other countries. The first is found in the book *To Move a Nation,* by Roger Hilsman, an official of the State Department during the Kennedy Administration. Although he asserted that CIA-type operations are justified by the need for national security, Hilsman said that too often the CIA has been "over-used as an instrument of foreign policy." Elaborating, Hilsman referred to CIA actions which included the instigation and carrying through of a coup in Iran against Premier Mohammed Mossadegh, the thousand-man invasion of Cuba, the "covert boost" to Ramon Magsaysay in the Philippines, the unsuccessful effort to create another "Magsaysay" in the person of the unpopular and weak General Phoumi Nosavan in Laos.

According to Hilsman, by the end of the Eisenhower Administration in 1960, secret CIA political action had become a "fad" and United States agents abroad were as "ubiquitously busy" as communist agents. The cumulative effect of several hundred such covert actions, he added, was to tarnish the American image in the world community. "[It] corroded one of our major political assets, the belief in American intentions and integrity."

The second kind of evidence of interventionary (as distinguished from intelligence-gathering) activity by the CIA came in the wake of the disclosures in 1966 that the CIA has operated under cover of American universities, labor unions, book publishers, student organizations, and cultural and religious organizations. Following these stories, American wire services and newspaper correspondents overseas began filing dispatches telling of discontent in foreign capitals, a new wave of anti-American feeling, and allegations of CIA intervention. These reports came from Chile, India, Mexico, Bolivia, West Berlin, Switzerland, France, Spain, British Guiana, and Canada.

Arms Accumulation

One of the most accurate indices of its militarized state of mind is the size of a society's arsenal. According to Jeremy Stone, a member of the Institute for Strategic Studies in London and a Fellow of the Council on Foreign Relations, each of 41 nuclear submarines will soon have the capability of destroying 160 Russian cities. In addition, we have more than 1000 land-based intercontinental ballistic missiles which can take out those same Russian cities six times over. Finally, when, as appears likely, we attach from three to ten thermonuclear warheads to each ICBM, converting them to multiple independently targetable reentry vehicles (MIRVs), we again will have increased by up to tenfold our overkill capacity with regard to the Soviet Union.

Last March, after closed congressional hearings with Army spokesmen concerning the chemical-biological warfare arsenal in this country, Representative Richard D.

McCarthy of New York told newsmen that the United States has enough of one deadly nerve agent—a substance labeled "GB" by the Army—to kill 100 billion people, or to wipe out the present world population of 3.4 billion thirty times over. While Representative McCarthy was expressing alarm over both the existence and transportation by railcar of such deadly agents in the United States, Representative Robert L. F. Sikes of Florida told newsmen he thought the United States was not doing enough in this field. The Russians, said Sikes, have seven to eight times the capability of the United States in chemical-biological warfare. "I think our capability should be expanded," he said.

Last October, Robert M. Smith reported from Washington in *The New York Times* that the Army has produced and stockpiled more than 20,000 poison bullets in the Pine Bluff Arsenal in central Arkansas. The bullets are "reliably reported" to contain botulin—a toxin that produces an acute, highly fatal disease of the nervous system. An Army manual says that "through repeated purification procedures [the toxin] has been obtained in a crystalline form and is one of the most powerful toxins known. Botulism is characterized by vomiting, thirst, general weakness, headache, fever, dizziness, double vision, and dilation of the pupils. Paralysis is the usual cause of death." The *Times* reporter added: "Knowledgeable sources indicate that the poison bullets could logically serve only one purpose: assassination. To kill an enemy leader with a poison bullet, it would be necessary to do no more than nick him."

In the face of mounting disclosures of the extent to which chemical poisons are stockpiled at eight bases from Maryland to Oregon, and against the background of the accidental killing of 6400 sheep in March 1968 in Utah's Skull Valley as a result of an Army nerve gas test at the Dugway

Proving Ground 27 miles away, Secretary of Defense Melvin Laird is reported to have submitted, last October, a secret memorandum to the National Security Council urging that the United States stop producing biological agents for use in warfare. The position of the Joint Chiefs of Staff on the issue was not clear. Also not clear was whether Mr. Laird's recommendation, if approved, would leave intact the overkill capacity of our chemical and biological germ arsenal and whether only biological but not chemical production would be halted. Diseases which can be spread by weapons in Army warehouses now include the plague, anthrax, tularemia, psittacosis, Q-fever, botulism, Rocky Mountain spotted fever, brucellosis, and Venezuelan equine encephalitis. It is estimated that a single ounce of Q-fever rickettsia is enough to infect 28 billion people with its debilitating symptoms. Pneumonic plague is close to 100-percent fatal if treatment is not begun within twenty to twenty-four hours after exposure.

As recently as a month before Secretary Laird's reported recommendation to the National Security Council, Army officials insisted on the need to maintain chemical production on the ground that the best way to dissuade the enemy from using chemical weapons is to have a chemical retaliatory capacity of one's own. Last July, Secretary Laird himself, during a question-and-answer period with student interns in Washington, was quoted as saying that "as much as we deplore this kind of a weapon [chemical and biological], if we want to make sure this weapon is never used, we must have the capability to use it." He noted that the Administration was then conducting a review of the chemical and biological warfare program and said that he did not want to prejudge its results but that he "strongly believed the United States had to continue to develop offensive chemical and biological weapons."

Then, on November 25, 1969, President Nixon announced that he was renouncing the use of all biological warfare weapons, that he would destroy existing stockpiles of such germ weapons, and that he was renouncing "first use" of chemical warfare weapons that could either kill or incapacitate their victims. Excluded from his prohibition were chemical weapons such as defoliant herbicides and riot-control gases.

Although Mr. Nixon's announcement was generally received with favor in both the United States and foreign capitals, enthusiasm was guarded for the following reasons:

1. The huge American chemical-warfare arsenal will remain intact.

2. Renouncing "first use" of lethal and incapacitating chemical agents can be meaningless under wartime conditions; a desperate, or callous, nation can always claim that the other side initiated chemical warfare and, without proving its claim, launch a chemical attack of its own.

3. The United States will continue its research into biological weapons for "defensive" purposes, but in recent years universities and university research professors have justified their Pentagon-sponsored development of germ warfare weapons on precisely this ground—that they were needed in order to develop defensive immunization programs. Indeed, the line between what is offensive research and what is defensive research in this area is extremely difficult to draw. (An anonymous spokesman for the Nixon Administration has said that as much of this biological warfare research would be transferred from the Pentagon to the Department of Health, Education, and Welfare as possible.)

4. Unnamed Army officers told an Associated Press reporter that they "do not regard the present quantities of germ materials as weapons stockpiles, but rather as limited components for biological testing."

If this view prevails, there will be no destruction of germ warfare stockpiles, despite Mr. Nixon's announcement.

5. One of the American riot-control gases, CS-2, is far more than a simple tear gas of earlier years; it is a lung gas causing extreme pain and is used in Vietnam to flush out enemy soldiers so they can be shot.

6. In addition to CS-2 gases and napalm, the United States will continue to use herbicides, as in Vietnam, chemicals that the *The New York Times* has called "triply reprehensible" because they "destroy food supply far into the future, upset the ecology, and threaten future generations with deformity."

Arms Racing and War Gaming

According to columnist James Reston, "the control of military arms is undoubtedly the most important political question in the world today, for the arms race devours the money and influences all other questions of poverty, race, jobs, and housing, both here and abroad." It is estimated that American taxpayers have contributed, since 1946, more than one trillion dollars for national security. The technique of arms racing and war gaming is fairly well known. The military, given the task of defending the nation, research, develop, and produce weapons and weapon systems. They must, they say, immediately assume that since our side can produce and has in fact produced a particular weapon or system, a potential enemy can produce the same weapon. Therefore, we must research, develop, and produce defensive weapons to counter these putative offensive weapons. At that stage, we must further assume that since we have produced a defensive system, the potential enemy can devise a similar defense. Therefore, our next task is to research, develop, and produce a new offensive weapon system which will overwhelm any possible defense devised by the enemy.

With this offense-defense pattern, there is no theoretical limit to the quantity or quality of weapon systems that the military may deem necessary to ensure national security. The only limits are, on the one hand, the imagination of the war gamesmen and war planners and, on the other, the amount of tax money that can be placed at their disposal. The actual development and deployment of weapons by Soviet Russia, for example, is not ultimately a limiting factor in our own weapons program. If the Russians do not have a particular weapon, we must assume that they may soon have it, or certainly that they *should* have it in the future.

These "strategic assumptions" are open-ended and self-justifying. When, for example, American military men claimed in the mid-1960s that the U.S.S.R. was building a thick antiballistic missile system, we proceeded to increase our offensive nuclear striking power by developing multiple warheads for both our submarine and land-based missiles. But when former Defense Secretary Robert McNamara reported in late 1967 that Russia in fact had no significant ABM capability, the Department of Defense did not halt its development of multiple warheads designed to counter the nonexistent Russian ABM threat. Instead, the DOD said: "Nevertheless, knowing what we do about past Soviet predilections for defensive systems, we must, for the time being, plan our forces on the assumption that they will have deployed some sort of an ABM system around their major cities by the early nineteen-seventies."

Mr. McNamara described this arms-racing approach to national security as a "kind of mad momentum" intrinsic to the development of all new nuclear weaponry. "If a weapon system works—and works well—there is strong pressure from many directions to produce and deploy the weapon out of all proportion to the prudent level required." The former Defense Secretary added that if the United States were to deploy a heavy antiballistic missile shield, that would constitute a "strong inducement for the Soviets to vastly increase their own offensive forces. That . . . would make it necessary for us to respond in turn—and so the arms race would rush hopelessly on to no sensible purpose on either side."

Since Mr. McNamara left the Defense Department, Congress has approved a "thin" ABM system. The MIRV system— fitting multiple warheads to our thermo- nuclear missiles—has gone ahead. Once MIRVs are fully deployed the Soviet Union will not know or have any way of knowing whether we have 5000 or 10,000 warheads in our offensive arsenal. We will be similarly ignorant about Russian offen- sive capabilities. It will then be difficult, if not impossible, to have meaningful stra- tegic-arms limitation talks because there will be no way for either side to be sure that the other one is not cheating in any agreement.

Waste, Profits, and Accountability

In an activity of the magnitude of the Department of Defense, it would be sur- prising if there were no waste, no corrup- tion, no profiteering. However, it may be worth looking at some of the evidence in this area as a reflection of a more signifi- cant side of the American military—that which concerns its restraints and the extent to which it can be held in fact accountable under the constitutional prescription of civilian control.

Walter Adams, an economist at Michi- gan State University, in an important article entitled "The Military-Industrial Complex and the New Industrial State" (*The American Economic Review*, May 1968), reported that "a summary of Gen- eral Accounting Office studies covering the period from May 1963 to May 1964 [re-

vealed] ascertainable waste of 500 million dollars in a 5-percent sample of procure- ments." He added that Merton Peck and Frederic Scherer found in their study (*The Weapons Acquisition Process*) that in twelve major weapon-system development programs, actual costs exceeded predicted costs 3.2 times on the average, with a range of actual versus predicted costs of from 70 to 700 percent. Recent prediction errors in the F-111 and Apollo programs, Scherer reported, are of the same order of magni- tude.

The Senate Committee on Government Operations, looking into the matter of the "pyramiding of profits and costs in the missile procurement program," concluded in 1964 that

even the most reputable and ethical contractor is placed in the conflicting position of managing a program where the feasibility, technical and economic decisions which should be made by the customer-government are made by the producer- contractor. . . . The absence of competition, cou- pled with the urgency to get the program under way, removes normal safeguards against large profits and weakens the government's negotiat- ing position.

In 1965, the Comptroller General, an Eisenhower appointee, singled out the fol- lowing characteristics of the military-con- tract system for a House committee looking into the matter:

1. Excessive prices in relation to avail- able pricing information.
2. Acceptance and payment by the gov- ernment for defective equipment.
3. Charges to the government for costs applicable to contractors' commercial work.
4. Contractors' use of government-owned facilities for commercial work for extended periods without payment of rent to the government.
5. Duplicate billings to the government.
6. Unreasonable or excessive costs.
7. Excessive progress payments held by

contractors without payment of interest thereon.

In the five years since the Comptroller General disclosed these practices in defense contracting, there has been little or no change in the system. In 1969, the "cost overrun" on the C-5A transport plane alone was a *cause célèbre,* but not, as it turned out, enough of a *cause célèbre* to reform conventional procurement procedures. The original price for 115 of the Lockheed C-5A's was 3.2 billion dollars. Final cost to the government was 5.2 billion dollars, or 67 percent more. Colonel A. W. Buesking, former director of management systems control in the office of the Assistant Secretary of Defense, has said that control systems essential to prevent excessive costs simply do not exist. According to Senator William Proxmire, "defense spending is out of control. The military-industrial complex now writes its own budgetary ticket."

[Following are] some samples of out-of-control defense procurement practices:

1. Richard A. Stubbing, a defense analyst with the Bureau of the Budget, after a study of the performance of complex weapon systems, concluded: "The low, overall performance of electronics in major weapon systems developed and produced in the last decade should give pause to even the most outspoken advocates of military hardware programs." He found that in 13 missile and aircraft programs produced since 1955 at a cost of 40 billion dollars, more than 60 percent of the electronic components failed to perform acceptably.

2. Defense Department figures in November 1968 disclosed that over the past fifteen years, a total of 8.8 billion dollars has been invested in 67 major military contracts which were subsequently canceled either because the weapons did not meet specifications or the military decided it had no use for them.

3. The cost of the Minuteman-2 missile increased from 3.2 billion dollars to 7 billion dollars.

4. The cost of a rescue submarine increased from 3 million dollars to 80 million dollars (a 2700-percent increase) but only, testified Barry Shillito, Assistant Secretary of Defense, because the submarine had been so improved it was "almost totally different from the one we embarked on."

5. A system to keep track of fuel sent to Vietnam broke down in 1967 and the Air Force was unable to account for 21 million dollars worth of gasoline and oil.

6. The cost of the Short-Range Attack Missile rose from 301 million dollars in January 1968 to 636 million dollars in December 1968.

7. When General Dynamics' plane, the F-111B (the Navy's fighter-bomber version of the TFX) was found to be too heavy to meet the altitude and range requirements of the military, the government reimbured 216.5 million dollars to the company to cover most of its costs, and imposed a small penalty.

8. A. E. Fitzgerald, former deputy for management systems of the Air Force, testified before the Joint Economic Subcommittee on Government Economy that Air Force officials in 1967 had submitted to then Defense Secretary Robert McNamara a cost estimate for the Mark II—the electronic "brain" system of the F-111—that was 229 million dollars below the figure they knew to be correct. They lied, he said, because they feared Mr. McNamara would abandon the system if its true costs were known.

The technique of "buying in" is the proximate explanation for the phenomena of excessive costs, high profits, and low product-reliability in the weapons industry. A defense contractor "buys in" on a prospective new weapon program by grossly underestimating the cost he quotes to the government, by overestimating the performance capability of the weapon, and by promising to deliver the weapon long before he knows it can be done. Ordinarily this would be a sure formula for going bankrupt. But in the defense industry the government and the industrialists have found ways to make sure that does not occur. "The defense industry," according to Richard Kaufman, a member of Senator Proxmire's staff, "is the most heavily subsidized in the nation's history. Thanks to Pentagon procurement policies, large contractors find their defense business to be most lucrative."

The government's subsidization and protection of the defense contractors take a number of forms. As Kaufman puts it: "There are many ways to succeed in the defense business without really trying." For example, 13 billion dollars worth of government-owned property, including land, buildings, and equipment, is in contractors' hands, thereby greatly reducing—in some cases eliminating—the need for any fixed-capital investment by a defense contractor. Working-capital needs are also sharply reduced for the contractor through what is called "progress payments," which have no relation to progress in terms of contract objectives achieved, but correspond only to costs incurred. These two government-subsidized provisions minimize the contractor's investment in the defense business and permit him to use his assets for commercial business or for securing additional defense contracts.

There is also little or no supervision over the way in which contractors use government money and property. Some use it for their own purposes. As an example, Kaufman cited the case of Thiokol Chemical Corporation, Aerojet General (a subsidiary of General Tire & Rubber Company), and Hercules, Inc.:

From 1964 through 1967 they received a total of 22.4 million dollars to be used for work on the Air Force Minuteman missile program. Government accountants found that the three contractors misused more than 18 million dollars of this money, spending it for research unrelated and inapplicable to Minuteman or any other defense program.

When a contractor's costs run higher than he had estimated (and they inevitably do when he has underestimated them in order to get the contract), the Pentagon agrees to pay for the increased costs through the device of "contract-change notices." On a complex weapon system, the changes from original specifications will number in the thousands. Some of these changes are ordered by the Pentagon, some are authorized by the Pentagon at the request of the contractor. Kaufman reports that the opportunities for hiding real or phony cost increases in this system are obvious, "so much so that in defense circles contract-change notices are sometimes referred to as 'contract nourishment.'"

Contract nourishment comes under the more general heading of the "get well" stratagem in defense-contracting circles. No matter how much difficulty a contractor may get into because of his "buying in" promises, he knows that the government will see to it that he "gets well." If his weapon program turns out to be unacceptable to the Pentagon, a contractor stands to lose tremendous sums should the contract be canceled for reason of default. However, if the government cancels his contract for "convenience," the contractor is reimbursed for the costs he has incurred. A classic example of a default overlooked by the government occurred in the case of General Dynamics' F-111B. When it became obvious that the F-111B would simply not come up to performance specifications, Gordon Rule, a civilian procurement official with responsibility for the plane, recommended that General Dynamics' contract be terminated for default. It was Paul

H. Nitze, Deputy Secretary of Defense, under pressure from Assistant Secretary of the Air Force Robert H. Charles and Roger Lewis, chairman of General Dynamics, who made the 216.5-million-dollar reimbursement to the company.

Mr. Rule has testified before a congressional subcommittee that he encountered opposition from both civilian defense officials and the Naval Air Systems Command in 1967 while he was conducting an investigation of inefficiency at the Hartford, Connecticut, plant of the Pratt and Whitney Aircraft Division of the United Aircraft Corporation. He had been sent there when the then Defense Secretary Robert McNamara had learned that Pratt and Whitney's price for F-111 engines had grown from an estimate of $273,910 each to $750,000.

According to Kaufman, profits on defense contracts are higher than those on related nondefense business, they are higher for the defense industry than for manufacturing as a whole, and the differential is increasing. The General Accounting Office found that the average negotiated profit rate had increased 26 percent from the 1959–63 period to late 1966. Admiral Hyman G. Rickover has testified that makers of propulsion turbines are insisting on profits of from 20 to 25 percent, compared with 10 percent a few years ago, and that profits on shipbuilding contracts have doubled in two years.

Kaufman explains that even these profit figures, however, are not a true reflection of actual profits. If figured as a return on investment, rather than as a return on costs, true profits are often phenomenally higher.

An example of the difference was demonstrated in a 1962 tax-court case, *North American Aviation vs. Renegotiation Board*. The contracts provided for 8-percent profits as a percentage of costs; the tax court found that the company had realized profits of 612 percent and 802 percent on its investment in two succeeding years.

The reason for this tremendous return on investment was the Defense Department's policy of furnishing both fixed and working capital to large contractors. "In some cases," Kaufman wrote, "the amount of government-owned property exceeds the contractor's investment, which is sometimes minimal. It is no wonder that contractors prefer to talk about profits as a percentage of costs." A study by Murray Weidenbaum (now Assistant Secretary of the Navy) disclosed that between 1962 and 1965 a sample of large defense contractors earned 17.5 percent net profit (measured as a return on their investment), while companies of comparable size but doing business in the commercial market earned 10.6 percent.

If the proximate causes of excess cost, waste, inefficiency, and profits in the defense industry can be found in the operating arrangements and practices that have been developed by the Pentagon and the industrialists, the deeper causes of why these practices have been allowed to continue must be sought elsewhere.

Senator George McGovern touched on two of these causes in his statement in the Center Occasional Paper, *ABM: Yes or No?*:

Politically, the ability to get support for highly dubious multi-billion-dollar projects such as the ABM rests on two factors: first, exploitation of the national feeling of insecurity that comes anytime we debate a proposal with a defense label attached to it; and second, the perfectly legal and very substantial rewards the military sector can bestow upon communities and states whose congressmen are cooperative.

Thus, after the 2-billion-dollar cost overrun on the C-5A plane had become a matter of common knowledge, the Senate defeated by a vote of 64 to 23 an amendment by Senator Proxmire to the 1970 military authorization bill which called for a reduction of 533 million dollars in further procurement of the C-5A until the General Accounting Office could complete a comprehensive study of its cost—the study was to be finished within 90 days.

Again, after months of hearings disclosing the practices described above, the Senate passed a 20.1-billion-dollar authorization bill for new military procurement last fall; the House passed a 21.3-billion-dollar authorization bill (allowing its members two days to read the 2660 pages of Armed Services Committee hearings on the bill, and 45 seconds speaking time to each representative during the debate of the bill). The final compromise authorization bill came to 20.7 billion dollars. It included, at Representative Mendel Rivers' insistence, 415 million dollars for Navy ships that the Pentagon had not even requested. Senator John Stennis, chairman of the Senate Armed Services Committee, said: "No major weapon has been left out of this bill, and none has been seriously affected."

Just as significantly, the joint conference struck down or seriously impaired every amendment that senators had attached to the authorization bill to curb some of the excesses of the defense industry and the Pentagon and make them more accountable for their actions. The joint conference eliminated one amendment which required that all major Pentagon weapons contracts be subjected to an independent quarterly audit by the General Accounting Office, which is an arm of Congress. The joint conference did retain one amendment providing for the Comptroller General to study defense profits, but the amount of information defense contractors would be required to supply was limited, and the Comptroller General would have to go to the congressional Armed Services Committees (notoriously favorable to the Pentagon) in order to be able to subpoena the contractors' records. Also, a 20-percent cut

in the Defense Department's budget for independent research was reduced to a 7-percent cut.

Senator Proxmire identified two further factors serving to explain the resistance of military-procurement practices to reform. The procurement system, he has said, "permits almost 90 percent of all contracts to be negotiated rather than awarded on a formally advertised competitive basis." This, coupled with the fact that the number of high-ranking retired military officers now working in defense industries has tripled in the last ten years (from 721 in 1959 to 2072 in 1969) represents, the Senator said, a "distinct threat to the public interest. How hard a bargain will officers involved in procurement, planning, or specifications drive with contractors when they are one or two years from retirement and have the example to look at of over two thousand fellow officers doing well on the outside after retirement?"

For a deeper probe of the causes of the present Pentagon and weapons-industry practices, we must turn our attention to their formal relationship.

The Military-Industrial Interlock

The American military and American industry need each other. The military depends on industry to furnish its arsenal. Industry depends on the military for weapons orders to maintain and improve its earnings. It would be surprising if there were an absence of a close, cooperative relationship between the two. The best brief description of this relationship has been provided by Walter Adams. In that relationship, Adams wrote,

government not only permits and facilitates the entrenchment of private power but serves as its fountainhead. It creates and institutionalizes power concentrations which tend to breed on themselves and to defy public control. The scenario of events should be familiar. The "mad momentum" of an international weapons race militates toward large defense expenditures. This generates a demand not only for traditional, commercial shelf items like food, clothing, fuel, and ammunition but also for the development and production of sophisticated weaponry. Lacking a network of government-owned arsenals, such as produced the shot and cannon in the days of American innocence, or having dismantled the arsenals it did have, the government is forced to buy what it no longer can make. It becomes a monopsonistic buyer of products which are not yet designed or for which production experience is lacking. It buys at prices for which there is little precedent and hardly any yardsticks. It deals with contractors, a large percentage of whose business is locked into supplying defense, space, or atomic energy needs. It confronts powerful oligopolists in a market where technical capability rather than price is the controlling variable—in an atmosphere shrouded by multilateral uncertainty and constant warnings about imminent aggression.

In the process, government becomes almost totally dependent on the chosen instruments, i.e. creatures of its own making, for effectuating public policy. Lacking any viable in-house capabilities, competitive yardsticks, or the potential for institutional competition, the government becomes—in the extreme—subservient to the private and special interests whose entrenched power bears the government seal.

This unique buyer-seller relationship, which defies analysis by conventional economic tools, lies at the root of the military-industrial complex and the new power configurations generated by it. The complex is not a conspiracy between the "merchants of death" and a band of lusty generals, but a natural coalition of interest groups with an economic, political, or professional stake in defense and space. It includes the armed services, the industrial contractors who produce for them, the labor unions that represent their workers, the lobbyists who tout their wares in the name of "free enterprise" and "national security," and the legislators who, for reasons of pork or patriotism, vote the sizable funds to underwrite the show. . . . Given the political reality of such a situation and the economic power of the constituencies involved, there is little hope that an interaction of special-interest groups will somehow cancel each other out and that there will emerge some compromise which serves the public interest. [*The American Economic Review*, May 1968]

The example of Lockheed-Georgia illustrates the pervasive economic influence of a defense industry on a city, region, and state. Located at Marietta, Georgia, Lockheed does more than 2 billion dollars of defense business a year. It pays about 200 million dollars a year in wages to 26,000 workers who come from about one-third of the state's 159 counties. According to Jack Raymond in the *Harvard Business Review*, "Lockheed buys everything from soft drinks to metal parts from Georgia suppliers. Last year, the company spent 113 million dollars with about 1730 suppliers, many of them small businesses."

Despite the economic rewards and the national-security argument, which have traditionally kept the military budget on an ever onward and upward course, revelations of waste, excess profits, and plain gouging have become widely known. So many congressmen have become outraged that, for the first time in many years, the future of military spending recently became uncertain. As a result, Secretary of Defense Laird was reported in June of last year to have determined to take a tougher approach toward both defense contractors and the military services.

Mr. Laird and Deputy Secretary David Packard were said to have begun to take steps to slow down the weapons-development cycle so that difficult technical problems could be solved before funds are freed to begin production. It was also reported that they intended to prohibit defense contractors from making unrealistically low bids in order to "buy into" a program and would order the armed forces to tighten up their supervision of contracts and not make costly change-orders once a production contract has been granted. As evidence of the sincerity of Mr. Laird's desire to eliminate gross losses, "knowledgeable sources" in the Pentagon pointed to the cancellation of a multi-million-dollar contract with Lockheed for the Cheyenne helicopter because of costly delays in its development, and the cancellation of several ships authorized by Congress in order to absorb a 600-million- to 700-million-dollar cost overrun on Navy ships already under construction.

It was also pointed out that Mr. Packard had told an Aerospace Industries Association meeting:

You have to eliminate this business of "buying in." Neither the Department of Defense nor the Congress will continue to tolerate large cost overruns which relate to unrealistic pricing at the time of award, or to inadequate management of the job during the contract. In simple terms, you will find it much more difficult for us to consider upward price revisions—and you should plan your affairs accordingly.

However, to judge the sincerity of these *en famille* moves, one should consider the later actions by top Defense officials. The man who played a key role with his testimony disclosing billions of dollars of waste in defense contracting, one A. E. Fitzgerald, was relieved of his job in the Pentagon and was assigned to review construction of a bowling alley in Thailand. Then, in the fall of 1969, when Secretary Laird announced cutbacks in military bases and expenditures, Mr. Fitzgerald was among the first to lose his job.

Last July, Mr. Laird announced the formation of a blue-ribbon panel to make a twelve-month study of the Department of Defense and recommend reforms in its operation. An analysis of the composition of the blue-ribbon panel and its defense-industry connections was made by Senator Proxmire and published in the October 28, 1969, *Congressional Record*. Chairman of the panel is Gilbert W. Fitzhugh, who is also chairman of the board of Metropolitan

Life Insurance Company. Metropolitan Life, the Wisconsin senator noted,

holds $34,000,783 worth of common stock in 24 of the 100 largest companies doing defense business. The Metropolitan also has outstanding loans to 24 of these same defense contractors totaling over 1.3 billion dollars. Of the 15 panel members selected, 8, representing a majority of the panel membership, still hold official positions with 12 different companies which have a combined total of over 815 million dollars in defense contracts.

Although the other panel members are "not plagued by direct personal interests in defense business," Senator Proxmire said, "a number of them lack the needed knowledge of defense procurement practices to counterbalance the long experience in these matters which the eight-man majority brings to the panel."

Senator Proxmire added that he was sorry to report that the panel's top staff man is not an outside critic, but a Pentagon official, J. Fred Buzhardt, a graduate of the U.S. Military Academy, and special assistant to Assistant Secretary of Defense Robert Froehlke. Senator Proxmire concluded,

The inescapable impression one gets ... is that the panel is caught in the embrace of the very individuals it is supposed to evaluate and constructively criticize. ... I have seen all this happen before. The script has become all too familiar. The final report will be carefully noted and highly publicized [for] a few weeks, only to be relegated to the shelf once its publicity value for the Pentagon has been exhausted. ... The panel is at best a sham, at worst an indication of how powerful the Pentagon has actually become, so powerful that it is able to control those who would criticize it.

In the light of what is still a warm and symbiotic relationship between the military and the defense industries, it becomes for both a matter of the highest importance to keep public and congressional opinion favorably oriented toward "national security." The thousands of public-relations men employed by the defense industry are reenforced by the Pentagon's own public-relations manpower. Currently, the Pentagon has 6140 public-relations men around the world. Within Washington itself the Pentagon employs another 339 "legislative liaison" lobbyists with an annual budget of more than 4 million dollars. The next biggest government-worker lobby in Washington is the postal clerk's union, which spent $277,524 in 1967.

The mutuality of interest between Pentagon and industry was underlined last summer with the appearance of a prominently circulated newspaper advertisement to promote the Nixon Administration's antiballistic-missile proposal. An analysis by *The New York Times'* Neil Sheehan of the business connections of the 344 persons who signed the full-page advertisement disclosed that 55 had defense-industry associations. Fourteen of these were directors, officers, or lawyers for companies already doing antiballistic-missile business to the extent of more than one billion dollars in contracts awarded by the Defense Department. Another 20 signers of the advertisement had similar connections with companies among the top 100 defense contractors in the country. The advertisement, which claimed that 84 percent of the American people were in favor of the ABM (a figure publicly disavowed by Opinion Research whose poll, it said, had been misrepresented), made no mention that any of the signers had any defense-business connections.

The widely announced Pentagon cuts in defense spending last fall (e.g., 307 military bases to be "consolidated, reduced, realigned, or closed") were to effect a 3-billion-dollar saving as part of a reported plan to keep total defense spending, after June 30, 1970, to 71 to 73 billion dollars a year and to enable the United States to fight one major war and one minor war

simultaneously, instead of the two major and one minor war doctrine under which the Defense Department had been operating since 1959. However, several aspects of the new "austere" look clouded the picture and served to dampen the enthusiasm of economy advocates. For one thing, Air Force officials said that some of the reductions in missiles, planes, and bases were an acceleration of part of a modernization program announced in 1967; presumably the modernized weapons would be far more costly than the old and the reduction in the arms budget would be temporary, and true only until the new weapons were in production. For another, even though such planes as the B-58 Hustler were being retired, a new fighter-bomber which could cost as much as 9 billion dollars was being recommended. Also, as Senator Proxmire was quick to point out, the Navy, to give the illusion of sharper and more extensive cutbacks, had announced on five different occasions the mothballing of several old ships while virtually ignoring the fact that new ships authorized by Congress would far exceed in cost the savings of those being retired. Finally, Defense Secretary Laird himself, two weeks after the first announcement of a military budget cutback, made what, under the circumstances, seemed a most curious public statement, when on October 31, 1969, he addressed an audience of 800 defense contractors and aerospace industrialists at the Los Angeles Chamber of Commerce aerospace luncheon. According to the *Los Angeles Times* report of the meeting (by its political writer, Richard Bergholz), Mr. Laird

called on the aerospace industry ... to help him convince the American people they should not expect big spending cuts when the Vietnam war ends. ... Laird said many of the defense contractors and aerospace industrialists had supported the Defense Department in its past policies "and I know that we can count on this audience for the same kind of support in the future."

How Foreign Policy Becomes Militarized

American foreign policy becomes militarized in a number of ways. One of the most obvious is that a President of the United States and/or his Secretary of State want to militarize it. They have become convinced that, under certain circumstances and in some areas of the world, it is in the national interest to shoot or subvert first, and talk later. Or they become convinced that it is in the interest of the United States to send troops and planes into neutral countries and from there wage war against elements within those countries deemed dangerous to our interests or to wage war against other nations. These troop deployments are accomplished without the advice and consent of the Senate. The troops are deployed without a formal declaration of war, though they are used in the waging of war and their very use invites reprisal and the enlargement and inflaming of hostilities into a general war. Or a President and his Secretary of State may decide that it is in the interest of the United States to make secret commitments and have private understandings with dozens of nations (as the late Secretary of State John Foster Dulles did), which make the United States liable to an armed defense of those nations without a formal declaration of war.

Foreign policy also becomes militarized when a President is misled by his armed services and the Central Intelligence Agency into thinking that a particular military action (e.g., the 1961 invasion of the Bay of Pigs) is a viable option. President Kennedy said he would never again trust the CIA as he had on that occasion.

Foreign policy becomes militarized when the CIA, in addition to its intelligence work, undertakes operational initiatives (as in the early years of the American intervention in South Vietnam; as in the Dominican Republic in 1965; as in the Congo)

which present *faits accomplis* to Washington and from which Washington can extricate the country only with the greatest difficulty.

Foreign policy becomes militarized when the arms race escalates on both sides in the familiar action-reaction phenomenon—the "mad momentum," as Mr. McNamara described it. The continual piling up of thermonuclear, chemical, and biological weapons, with the consequent "catching up" always present, now on one side, now on the other, makes it increasingly difficult, politically and psychologically, to form a foreign policy in which strategic-arms limitation, and then gradual and progressive disarmament, will be both cornerstone and goal.

Foreign policy becomes militarized when both major American political parties seek partisan advantage in presidential campaigns by accusing the other of permitting a "bomber gap," a "missile gap," or a "security gap" to develop. Even though each of these accusations has been found later to have been false and misleading, the winning party, to make good on its campaign promises, authorizes enormous new increments to the strategic-weapons stockpile and further deepens the militarization of policy.

Foreign policy becomes militarized when, at critical moments, it is the military who seem to offer the crisp, definite, tangible options—while those who argue for negotiation, diplomacy, and respect for the decent opinion of mankind seem to be offering the unattractive, endlessly prolonged, and inconclusive options. Arthur Schlesinger, Jr., recalling the Bay of Pigs crisis, once wrote: "I could not help feeling that the desire to prove to the CIA and the Joint Chiefs that they were not soft-headed idealists but were really tough guys, too, influenced State's representatives at the Cabinet table."

Foreign policy becomes militarized by

the national-security managers, the men who have served as secretaries and assistant secretaries of Defense, State, Air, Army, and Navy; chairmen of the Atomic Energy Commission; directors of the CIA. Richard Barnet, in his book *The Economy of Death,* noted that out of 91 men who have held these offices from 1940 to 1967, 70 have come from the ranks of big business or high finance. The Brookings Institution revealed that 86 percent of the Secretaries of the Army, Navy, and Air Force, from 1933 to 1965, had come from the ranks of either business or the law. The Washington assumption is that there is an inherent correlation between the ability to run a bank, a business, a defense industry, and a law firm, on the one hand, and, on the other, the ability to define the nation's interest and devise a program calculated to enhance it.

It is not easy to determine at what point the President or his Secretary of State, on their own motion, militarize foreign policy, and at what point they are merely responding to a set of conditions and options which are basically militaristic and are presented to them by persons, agencies, and institutions that have no constitutional authority to make foreign policy. Confronted by such options, a President, unless he is extraordinarily well informed, adroit, and agile, cannot go around the options but must work within them.

Authoritarianism, Actual and Potential

According to one view, military conscription, which has been in existence for almost thirty years, cannot be classified as evidence of authoritarianism. The Selective Service law *is* a law, democratically enacted, and like any law, it can be removed by due process. But to young men subject to induction into the armed forces and liable to be sent to fight in the Vietnam war which various senators have described

as "insane," "immoral," "illegal," and "unconstitutional," the military draft and its five-year prison sentence for refusal to serve constitute an unquestioned example of authoritarianism and an unwarranted violation of the human conscience.

In actual practice, as Senator Edward Kennedy has pointed out, government and draft-board officials have used the Selective Service System to punish young men who protest against the Vietnam war and the draft itself by reclassifying them 1-A and accelerating their call-up. Here, says Senator Kennedy, "the fundamental issue is whether the Selective Service System has the right to supplant the courts and substitute an administrative form of punishment."

With respect to freedom of speech and assembly, Americans—judging from the massive turnouts in the moratoriums late last year—do not find it necessary to summon heroic courage to register criticism and dissent on such issues as the Vietnam war. On the other hand, the House Committee on Internal Security (formerly the House Un-American Activities Committee) continues to be funded and it continues to pursue self-styled revolutionaries among the dissenters, such as Thomas Hayden, by holding hearings in the style of the Joseph McCarthy period of the 1950s. Also the Justice Department has instituted a number of "conspiracy" trials against pacifist leaders (e.g., Dr. Benjamin Spock, the Reverend William Sloan Coffin) which, regardless of their legal outcome, may well have the effect of intimidating other citizens and sharply reduce their activity in the peace movement.

Another possible portent of authoritarianism can be found in a report of Army teams which, in the summer of 1968, visited more than one hundred American cities to discuss riot-control plans with local officials. A 180-man Directorate of Civil Disturbance Planning and Operations in the Pentagon maintains "city profile" books containing analyses of population composition, trouble spots, and layouts of police precincts and communications. More than a half-million regular Army servicemen, reservists, and national guardsmen have been given riot training. Former Attorney General Ramsey Clark has said he is opposed to a federal police force and that the American tradition is against it because "there's no telling which way a monolithic military-police organization might go." While the Constitution empowers the federal government to "protect" a state against "domestic violence," the existence of half a million riot-trained troops, a directorate in the Pentagon, and the development of closely coordinated plans between Pentagon and city officials mean that the instruments of quick and massive military suppression are at hand should government officials interpret the constitutional provision in an authoritarian way.

In that connection, statements by Vice-President Spiro Agnew and actions by other members of Mr. Nixon's Administration last fall take on ominous overtones. After Mr. Agnew's widely reported New Orleans speech in which he described peace-protest leaders as an "effete corps of impudent snobs," Mr. Nixon said his Vice-President had "done a great job for this Administration." Later, Mr. Agnew, at a meeting of Republicans in Harrisburg, Pennsylvania, said that peace-protest organizers are "merchants of hate" and "parasites of passion" and asserted that the nation "can afford to separate them from our society with no more regret than we should feel over discarding rotten apples from a barrel." After Mr. Nixon's November 3rd speech on the Vietnam war, Mr. Agnew criticized the three national television networks for, among other things, their analysis and commentary following the speech. Although he affirmed that "every American has a right to disagree with the President of the United

States and to express publicly that disagreement," Mr. Agnew said that

"the President of the United States has a right to communicate directly with the people who elect him, and the people of this country have the right to make up their own minds and form their own opinions about a Presidential address without having a President's words and thoughts characterized through the prejudices of hostile critics before they can even be digested.

Finally, Mr. Nixon's newly appointed chairman of the Federal Communications Commission, Dean Burch, telephoned the heads of the three national television networks two days after Mr. Nixon's Vietnam speech, asking for complete transcripts of the remarks of their reporters and commentators. Jack Gould, television editor of *The New York Times,* said that this procedure

was reported by many radio and TV station owners to be the first time an FCC chairman departed from the protocol usually followed by the regulatory agency in handling complaints. Normally, the broadcasters noted, a complaint is forwarded by mail by Ben F. Waple, secretary of the FCC. The complaint is in written form, and the networks are allotted twenty or more days to reply.

Another potential extension of military authority, if not authoritarianism, lies in the Defense Department's involvement in domestic problems relating to the economy and to the health, education, and welfare of American citizens. Before leaving office, former Secretary of Defense Clark Clifford outlined an extensive Defense program—in being and in prospect—which would place the Defense Department directly into the business of building model housing and hospitals, using defense contracts to stimulate job opportunities in economically depressed areas, and educating hitherto neglected young men. The Nixon Administration kept several parts of this program, notably the involuntary induction of 100,000 poorly educated (and therefore ordinarily noninductible) men each year into the armed forces and educating them under military auspices before returning them to civilian life.

A final indicator of authoritarian style and substance: in 1966, Senator Edward Kennedy demanded that the State Department explain its legal authority for "shadowing" American citizens traveling abroad. A *New York Times* dispatch from Washington (March 23, 1966) said that the Massachusetts senator had sent a "sternly worded letter" to Secretary of State Dean Rusk expressing his dismay on learning that some American travelers are subjected to surveillance by their government because of their political beliefs. " 'I would have assumed that the granting of a passport carried with it for each citizen the privileges given to all citizens and that all passport bearers would have their privacy assured and be able to travel without embarrassment,' the Senator wrote." The *Times* explained that Mr. Kennedy's protest had been prompted by the disclosure that the State Department earlier that month had ordered the American embassies in Paris and Moscow to impose surveillance over the activities of H. Stuart Hughes, a professor of history at Harvard University, because of the Federal Bureau of Investigation's suspicions about his political beliefs. The State Department's order for surveillance was sent to its two embassies on March 8th, but was rescinded March 16th. The earlier message said that Dr. Hughes "reportedly in the past has had strong convictions toward communism." In his letter to Mr. Rusk, Senator Kennedy said:

"While I have had serious disagreements with [Professor Hughes] on matters of policy, I have always considered [him] to be a gentleman of integrity who has expressed his convictions in an honest and forthright fashion.... I feel it is most important to determine who makes the judgment that a traveling citizen is pro-com-munist, whether that judgment is confirmed by the Passport Office when it transmits a request for surveillance, and what further use is made of such a determination and of any information obtained by this investigatory activity among the various government agencies."

The *Times* said that State Department sources would not say how many such surveillance requests it receives, but "it was estimated they might run to hundreds a year."

III

This article began with a question: Is the United States a militarized society? I have listed what I think are dominant characteristics of a militarized society and have critically reviewed what I think is relevant evidence drawn from the contemporary American experience. Each of us must answer the question for himself.

For my part, I think that America has become to a considerable extent a militarized society. In a sense, the real question is whether the march toward a totally militarized America can be stopped and reversed. If it cannot, then we are in principle already a militarized people and it is only a matter of time until the details are all in place and we are militarized in fact. I think there is hope that the march of militarization can be stopped, but with each passing year that possibility dwindles. The combination of forces that have brought us this far down the road to complete militarization—the Pentagon, the weapons industry, military-minded congressmen—shows no sign of weakening. And the circumstances, or context, within which these forces have operated and drawn their strength—the mantling of militarism in "national security," the creation and sustaining of weapons-industry jobs in more than 80 percent of the congressional districts of the nation, the weapons-research orientation of much of university life, the inability of congressmen to make informed technical judgments on complicated weapons and weapons programs—all these show no signs of abatement or reform. Finally, our great social problems—racism, poverty, the decay of our cities, our shameful treatment of the mentally ill and the elderly, the rage of our youth, environmental pollution, the decline and stagnation of our schools, inflation, rising taxes along with spreading public squalor—these pressurized problems may well explode and make an already largely ungovernable society chaotic, thus inviting the domestic military solution: order at the point of the bayonet, an enforced, police-state life if there is to be any life at all.

My hope for a reversal of militarization is narrowly based. The close vote in the Senate on ABM reflected a new high level of senatorial awareness of spurious arguments for new weapons systems and a rebelliousness against traditional congressional rubber-stamping of Pentagon weapons requests. However, the Senate's later behavior on the arms-authorization bill and on the amendments to impose some kind of rational restraint on the Pentagon and the defense industrialists more than canceled out the hopes we had reposed in it.

But the American people have begun to realize that, after spending a trillion dollars for national security since 1945, they have bought insecurity. There is hope, then, that they will demand a breakout from the old, now quite discredited arms-spiral approach to national security.

There is hope, too, in the youth movement which, with the intuitive directness of the young, has gone straight to the point: that militarization is a systemic and structural phenomenon and that it has not made a great deal of difference which man or party occupies the White House because the Vietnam war continues and the prac-

tices and presumptions that led to the Vietnam war continue.

Ten Steps to a Civilized Society

It may be adventitious but it seems appropriate to end this inquiry with some subjective notes about what would, in the author's view, constitute a civilized, as contrasted with a militarized, society. These are the things I think our nation can and should do:

1. Begin the end of the Vietnam war by announcing a unilateral ceasefire and simultaneously asking the United Nations to accept the responsibility, through U.N. inspection teams and police peace-forces, for ensuring that no further bloodshed occurs and for the effective neutralizing of the country. This would be accompanied by a solemn and public pledge to abide by whatever troop-withdrawal timetable the U.N. orders for both North Vietnamese and American forces in South Vietnam.

2. A further pledge by the United States to contribute the major share of the financial support of the U.N. police force and inspection teams in Vietnam, this share to be computed as a percentage of the amount of money the United States has spent in destroying that country and its people since 1964.

3. An order to the CIA to confine its work to intelligence-gathering and intelligence-evaluating and to cease all paramilitary subversive and sabotage activities in all parts of the world.

4. A critical review by appropriate congressional and administration agencies of the practice of all clandestine military activities, and an empowering of the State Department to maintain continuing surveillance over these activities.

5. Announcement by the United States of an immediate freeze on present strategic-arms levels, with a bid to the Soviet Union to do the same, with these two actions

linked to a third: offering diplomatic recognition to Communist China and recommending to the United Nations that China be given a seat on the Security Council.

6. Meaningful strategic-arms limitation talks with all the great powers, leading not only to limitation but also to stage-by-stage deescalation of the strategic-arms stockpile, with appropriate mutual, on-site inspection to prevent the possibility of cheating.

7. Immediate congressional hearings leading to legislation providing for the phasing out of weapons industries and the conversion of these industries, where possible, into domestic-welfare activities. Where conversion is not possible, the hearings must lead to the systematic creation of job opportunities for displaced weapons-industry workers. These opportunities should be sought first in high-priority domestic-problem areas: building of more schools, more mental hospitals, more facilities for the elderly, more parks and leisure-time facilities in the ghettos, more job-training schools for the present unemployables; attacking the problems of air and water pollution; creating national parks in wilderness preserves; revivifying and rebuilding the decaying central cities across the country.

8. An end to military conscription.

9. A pledge to the United Nations of a sizable percentage of our present arms budget (no longer needed as the Vietnam war ends—an annual saving of at least 30 billion dollars—and as we progressively cut back, along with Russia and the other powers, our strategic-arms stockpile). This money would be used by the U.N. for development of Third World countries and for the equipping and staffing of a highly mobile international police force able to put out, or at least isolate, brush-fire disputes in the international community, and prevent them from spreading or being spread by opportunistic nations.

10. Repeal of the Connally Amendment, which allows us to decide which international disputes involving us we will submit to the World Court for adjudication. With this action, we will announce to the world that we recognize not only the existence of world law but the imperative necessity for all nations to abide by it.

The American mythology abounds in legends, some grounded in historical truth, some the product of our wishful thinking. Among the legends is the belief that America has always acted benevolently, unselfishly, nobly in the world community. That legend never was an unqualified truth, but there was truth in it. There has been much less truth in it during the last quarter of a century. I think that most Americans, if they honestly look at the record of these last twenty-five years, feel ashamed. They might even agree with Kilmer Myers, Episcopal Bishop of California, who said that America stands in imminent danger of "losing its soul." These are not easy things to say. And those who say them are too often accused of anti-Americanism.

Dietrich Bonhoeffer, a few years before he was hanged by his Nazi jailors, said that he prayed that Germany would lose the war. He added that this was the most painful thing he had ever done because he loved his country. But he loved it so much he could not bear to think of German atrocities being vindicated by a military victory. Today, we revere Dietrich Bonhoeffer as a hero and a martyr.

I hope this nation will not make martyrs of its heroes. My ten-step approach to a demilitarized and civilized society would vindicate our heroes and redeem the American legend. More importantly, for me at least, is that if it were adopted it would represent a last-minute triumph of hope over experience, of reason over madness.

2

Military Ideology and Influence in Society

THE WARFARE STATE

The Editors

Students of contemporary civilization have different views about the necessity of the extensive military preparedness that characterizes the United States. The proponents of such preparedness, who are frequently found in research institutes for the study of military strategy, argue that war is one of several options that may be required by the national interest. Also the national interest may require using threats of force to deter aggressive nations from taking aggressive actions. Threats in turn require the capability to deliver or they will not be believed. A final or total threat remains unconvincing as a deterrent against relatively minor transgressions and may in fact tempt an adversary to commit minor transgressions short of those that would provoke a full-scale counterattack. Therefore, an entire series of graded threats must be made for lesser offenses than a surprise nuclear attack and these too require preparedness if they are to be credible.

The argument does not end here. Why merely react to provocations from an adversary? Why not have a graded series of offensive actions of one's own, which might range from economic assistance to subversion to counter-guerrilla warfare and to threats of limitless escalation? Activities like these have been studied, planned for, and carried into action in American foreign policy. The mode of thought within which such activity is not only rational but also necessary is expanded in Herman Kahn's book, *On Escalation*, which is carefully summarized in the review by Anatol Rapoport.

Rapoport's review, however, raises the important question of whether the assumptions behind such strategic analyses as these are reasonable. The underlying view that the world is made of self-interested nation-states protecting or extending their national interests in a game which permits various forms of armed conflict among the moves may be quite dangerous. If the strongest nations act as if the world were an arena for competitive national advantages, the belief will likely become a self-fulfilling prophesy.

The dynamics of self-fulfilling prophesy are easily understood. If I say no one likes me, then I will react to signs of friendship with reserve and suspicion; eventually no one will like me. With nations, as with individuals, the expectation of malice serves not only to generate malice, but also to rule out attempts to change hostile motives. Even if the world did look like the interminable conflict world of the strategists, the strategic view may well preclude any opportunity to change the world, to engage in those acts of trust or good will or research into alternatives that will help to build a world more respectful of human values. The Christian admonition to "love thine enemies," while incomprehensible to the strategic view, may also have self-fulfilling properties which have not been explored. Rapoport's analysis of the strategists exposes the utter inhumanity of the assumptions under which they work. His analysis of other strategic works of Herman Kahn and Henry Kissinger is continued in *Strategy and Conscience* (1964). The application of the concepts like dehumanization to the personal style of the defense intellectuals is accomplished with compelling clarity in Robert J. Lifton's *Boundaries: Psychological Man in Revolution* (1970).

The strategists' way of thinking has dominated American foreign policy at least since the start of the cold war. In the writings of scholars there has been a significant convergence between the intellectuals who work directly or indirectly for the Department of Defense and the "realist" school of political-science thought. Both most frequently share the view of men and nations as inherently power-seeking and checked in their aggrandizements only by a calculation of the costs involved. Although the work of Herman Kahn has been influential among military strategists, much of the strategy debate has been window dressing for the actual enactment of strategic policy which necessarily reflects the compromises and the preferences of those responsible for policy making. The actual decision on a particular military action is the outcome not of any particular strategic analysis alone but of the political pressures which the military advisors are able to mount. Serious students of this process should read carefully *The Politics of Escalation* by H. Franz Schurmann, Peter Scott, and Reginald Zelnick (1966); Townsend Hoopes' *The Limits of Intervention* (1969); and Peter Scott's "Air America: Flying the U.S. into Laos" (1970), and "Laos: The Story Nixon Won't Tell" (1970). In general the military use their "intelligence" to create an "urgent" need for an extensive military venture. The administration eventually compromises to competing pressures by acceding to some of the military demands.

It is from just such an amorphous mass of military and industrial pressures (including those of the defense intellectuals who call for a more orderly, "rational" program) that Department of Defense administrators came up with an annual report assuring a portion of the pie to each significant pressure group and packaging the entire program in terms that represent a pragmatic program to achieve military security for this country. The most recent packages contain a rationale for the antiballistic-missile program, which promises a major escalation in the costs of defense, and the MIRV program, which will contribute to the early obsolescence of the ABM. The strategic arguments for and against the ABM received some news coverage during Senate debate on the issue. Not noted in the news were the political and economic pressures on the part of powerful corporations which were consummated by support of ABM. A case study of AT&T and the ABM shows how a giant American corporation was able to delay for years any interference with its profit pyramiding in the missile industry (Goulden and Singer, 1969). In cost-plus contracts, a corporation is assured a fixed percentage of profits over its expenditures. The expenditures are extremely high because the figure includes the cost of work subcontracted from the first corporation to a second one. That cost figure includes the profits already claimed by the second company. Hence the prime contractor receives a double profit for work it has not actually done. The second company's costs (and its fixed-percent profits) are also inflated by subcontracting for that portion of the missile system which it in turn buys from a third company.

By the time the bill comes to the taxpayer, some portions of the contract have been tapped for profits by four separate companies. When the Army, after many years of battle with AT&T, was permitted to buy missile-carrying trailers directly from the firm that produced them, the cost was reduced through competitive bidding to less than half the original. But for the big corporations such a cut in profits does not go without some future compensation. Western Electric, denied its share of profits on Freuhauf trailers, was granted a contract for the dubious ABM system. Other corporations losing out on the competition for defense contracts are receiving huge federal grants for domestic urban programs where subcontracting and purchasing from subsidiaries help to fatten profits before any benefits leak downward to the cities.

Security is a way of feeling—a psychological commodity—and no amount of expenditure on defense will necessarily purchase it. Trusting to the professional military man the judgment of just how much defense is enough is not an entirely satisfactory procedure. The preparedness of one nation provides stimulus for the preparedness of other antagonistic nations, resulting in less security for all nations. The only steady gains from self-reinforcing trends such as an arms race are in those portions of the society most closely associated with military values or with weapon production. The modest antiballistic-missile program currently planned in the United States has already had marked repercussions in Soviet society, strengthening the hard-line and militaristic factions, weakening those who would seek closer accommodation with the United States. The various military establishments of the world hold symbiotic relationships to one another. They cannot survive without competitors, and their growth in power and influence depends on the growth, militancy, and productivity of their enemies.

It must be stressed that policy in a large modern society does not emerge from rational debate, whether by soldiers, scholars, or administration. It emerges rather from the interplay between the large interest groups, public and private, jockeying for the measures most immediately beneficial to their own purposes. Pilisuk and Hayden's article on the military-industrial complex examines the institutions which have an interest in the perpetuation of military preparedness and finds them much more diverse and powerful than the old munitions makers who used to be associated with a primitive desire for the profits of war. The article offers the thesis that, right or wrong, the high level of military preparedness is no accidental policy but rather is a consistent, necessary, and prominent part of the forces that keep the United States functioning in what has been, at least temporarily, a stable course.

The increasing militarization of society might go on indefinitely but for the fact that military production is inherently wasteful and dangerous. The top military officials and the largest defense contractors do consistently well, but for the rest of us the military cow has been giving skimmed milk. At the point of this writing, an army of unemployed scientists and engineers exists, reflecting relatively small cutbacks in certain categories of defense. These professionals should now be considered among the subgroups of American society for whom the system provides no meaningful place. The general problem of persons displaced and alienated from American society is dealt with in Chapter 5.

A substantial body of research exists on the question of economic consequences of disarmament. Most of this research points to a problem which is infinitely more complex than a mere reallocation of the defense dollar into one or another constructive purpose. Some industries suffer a crisis of overspecialization, leaving little margin for convertibility to civilian needs. Similarly, areas like Southern California suffer from overconcentration of governmentally subsidized defense industry. Some economic-offset programs, such as retiring the national debt or drastically reducing taxes, would produce a predictable economic disaster in the country. Reallocation of money into schools, hospitals, or housing requires a high degree of planning based on prediction of population shifts, plans in neighboring areas, the stability of industry in an area, and the economic consequences of related programs. The feeling among several economists is that the United States, on an economic basis, could accommodate to peace, but that the political changes required for such an accommodation are not feasible (Melman, 1965). Inquiry into political changes, or shifts in power, are a relatively taboo topic among behavioral scientists. But the very absence of such inquiry reveals a society geared to retaining a status quo with a high dependence on military machinery and a strategic conception of world affairs.

Absence of active high-level consideration characterizes the recent history of the question of whether a selective-service system should exist in this country. It is around the issue of the draft, however, that heated debate is occurring at lower levels of the policy process. At issue here, as in the proposals for a National Service Corps, is the question, "Who shall decide for the individual his obligations to goals with which he is not necessarily in agreement?" This debate is discussed in the article by Flacks, Howe, and Lauter. The discussion of the draft law and its use to channel the life choice of young men into preferred occupations suggests forms of control over people similar to those discussed later in our section on Decision Control,

Chapter 6. The same basic problem recurs. In an effort to meet conditions imposed by modern technology, our society has found it increasingly necessary to control the choices people are making.

The draft as an issue has brought to a head the vast friction between a military society and its antiwar dissenters. Certainly the draft has been misused to channel people into draft-exempt occupations. There are also cases in which draft reclassifications have been used specifically to stop the organizing work of people who sought to prevent strip mining from driving Appalachian miners from their homes or who worked for getting a black and white coalition political party in Mississippi (SCEF, 1969). It is not only the abuses which include higher fatalities among black and chicano soldiers, or the better abilities of wealthier young men to keep out of service, but also the idea of service to this country in any form that is now being questionned. People once idealistic about alternative nonviolent service to "build instead of burn" now, with increasing frequency, look upon *any* federal service requirement as an infringement upon their personal freedom in service to mindless bureaucracy. Edward Sampson's study, "Two Profiles" (1969), comparing the most dedicated ROTC cadets with a sample of young people under indictment for draft refusal, found the latter to be sensitive, thoughtful, and self-directed people optimistic about their ability to be more than a pawn in influencing social change. By contrast the cadets had a need to show off and thereby reaffirm a waning sense of their own manhood. They saw people as basically evil, thus making wars inevitable and the person unaccountable for the actions he takes while in uniform. Despite heavy sentencing, draft resistance has been increasing at a fantastic rate and the courts are already overloaded with draft cases. While many find a physical deferment, Canada, Vista, or the Peace Corps a compromise, the feeling expressed by one young man is quite prevalent: "I'd like to help other people somehow but not if it means working for the Government. I just don't feel this Government has anything to do with me. They are going to go ahead and do what they want, but I don't want anything to do with them" (Poppy, 1969). Psychiatrist Robert Lifton, in "Vietnam and the Militarized Society" (1969), notes the change from early antiwar protest in which students and faculty were inclined to explore the larger ethical and historical issues behind Vietnam. Now he sees instead a great sense of being betrayed—by a nation, a government official, or by the older generation in general. The feeling is that an outside force has impinged upon young people with the obligation of service to murder or be murdered—and they have been overtaken by the search to pursue their lives without being either consumed or destroyed. Studies show the capacity of the basic training experience to rob people of autonomous identities and convert them into sometimes unconscious carriers of the message that military authority must be legitimate even if the war itself is absurd. The extent of opposition to this acceptance of military authority has grown, however, to a point in which the Army has found it necessary to intimidate its men and close its chapels to prevent the "G.I.'s for Peace" from expressing their ideas.

The depth and spread of opposition to military service raises the charge which no establishment wishes to hear—i.e., that it is illegitimate. Kenneth Boulding (1969) has clarified the relationship between legitimacy and survival. Organizations and societies are held together both by coercion and by concensus as to basic values. Any long-term life for a nation-state requires a good measure of concensus on core values. It is this sense of legitimacy that permits even an unpopular government to collect taxes, pass laws, and fight wars. Institutions, according to Boulding, gain legitimacy with time but sometimes grow rigid and decline. At present the national state has grown to dwarf all other institutions as the holder of ultimate legitimacy. The state demands certain sacrifices and, up to a point, individuals tend to justify these sacrifices by increasing their allegiance to the state. The psychological mechanism of dissonance reduction assists this paralogic of great cost—therefore high value—a model that works well until the returns become dubious. At that time, the individual questions what he gets from the monarchy or the empire or the contemporary national state in return for his investment. Increasingly the answer is very little, particularly very little opportunity for meaningful life and very little security. Industrial technology has made people trivial adjuncts to the production process, and military technology has made the nation incapable of defense against annihilating attack. Unilateral defense by a nation has become an obsolete idea.

The draft, in general, is an evidence for the decline in legitimacy of the nation-state in favor of its coercive powers over its own citizens. Even those who serve without protest see the service as obligation and sacrifice. Beyond a certain point the sacrifices in lives, in regard for the lives of others, in taxes for military preparedness are bringing the very legitimacy of the nation-state into question. Boulding concludes that draft reform is but aspirin for a more far-reaching disease and that "We are very close to the moment when the only way to preserve the legitimacy of the national state will be to abandon most of its power." Neither a change to a lottery, which has occurred, nor an end to the draft and its replacement by a more militaristic professional army can answer the charge of illegitimate power. While young people have negligible political power in this country, they are raising the issue that will cause this society to become either much less militaristic or, if it must retain its militarism, much more totalitarian. The question is how can a society whose direction is toward military bureaucratization command the allegiance of its people.

The thesis of this section is that military modes of thought have contributed to an acceptance of a highly centralized social system in which the disadvantaged who get nondiscriminatory job training in the military; the graduate student on a National Defense and Education Fellowship; the civilian army of scientists, engineers, industrialists, managers, and union workers who live on defense-supported contracts; and the patriots who, cut off from meaningful service, substitute allegiance to nationalistic symbols—all make the domestic costs of a transition to peace quite high. The very successes of the United States as a nation ready for war leave little power in the hands of interest groups who have not yet found success or become dependent on the dominant type of social or economic arrangement associated with military preparedness. The absence of such power is leading young people, poor people, racial minorities, and some professionals to redefine their strengths outside the channels considered legitimate by governmental authority.

REFERENCES AND ADDITIONAL READING

American Friends Service Committee, *The Draft? A Report Prepared for the Peace Education Division of the American Friends Service Committee* (New York: Hill and Wang, 1968).

Barnes, Peter, "All-Volunteer Army?," *The New Republic* (May 9, 1970), pp. 19–23.

Barry, Thomas, "Our Restless Reserves," *Look* (August 12, 1969), pp. 36, 38, 41–43.

Benoit, Emile, and Kenneth E. Boulding (eds.), *Disarmament and the Economy* (New York: Harper and Row, 1963).

Boulding, Kenneth, "The Impact of the Draft on the Legitimacy of the National State," in Sol Tax (ed.), *The Draft: A Handbook of Facts and Alternatives* (Chicago: Univ. of Chicago Press, 1969).

Coser, Lewis A., "The Dysfunctions of Military Secrecy," *Social Problems*, **11** (Summer 1963), pp. 13–22.

Etzioni, Amitai, *The Moon-Doggle: The Domestic and International Implications of the Space Race* (Garden City, N.Y.: Doubleday, 1964).

Flacks, Richard, "Protest or Conform: Some Social Psychological Perspectives on Legitimacy," *Journal of Applied Behavioral Science*, **5** (1969), pp. 127–160.

Ginger, Ann F., *The New Draft Law: A Manual for Lawyers and Counselors* (New York: National Lawyers Guild, 1970).

Goulden, Joseph C., and Marshall Singer, "Dial-a-Bomb: AT&T and the ABM," *Ramparts*, **8**:5 (November 1969), pp. 29–37.

Hoopes, Townsend, *The Limits of Intervention: An Inside Account of How the Johnson Policy of Escalation in Vietnam Was Reversed* (New York: McKay, 1969).

Janowitz, Morris, "American Democracy and Military Service," *Trans-action* (March 1967), pp. 5–11ff.

Kahn, Herman, *On Escalation: Metaphors and Scenarios* (New York: Praeger, 1965).

Kahn, Herman, "The Nature and Feasibility of War Deterrence," in D. Bobrow (ed.), *The Components of Defense Policy* (Chicago: Rand McNally, 1965).

Kissinger, Henry A., "Central Issues of American Foreign Policy," in Kermit Gordon (ed.), *Agenda for a Nation* (Washington: Brookings Institution, 1968), pp. 585–614.

Lapp, Ralph, *The Weapons Culture* (New York: Norton, 1968).

Lifton, Robert J., "Vietnam and the Militarized Society: The Human Cost," address delivered at ABM/Choice Conference, Washington, D. C., May 2, 1969.

Lifton, Robert J., *Boundaries: Psychological Man in Revolution* (New York: Random House, 1970).

Lynn, Conrad J., *How to Stay Out of the Army: A Guide to Your Rights under the Draft Law* (New York: Monthly Review and Grove Press, 1968).

McGovern, Senator George S., et al., "The People versus the Pentagon," *The Progressive* (June 1969), pp. 5–8.

McNamara, Robert S., "Remarks before the Economic Club of New York," address to the Economic Club of New York, Waldorf Astoria Hotel, November 18, 1963. Reproduced in R. Perrucci and M. Pilisuk, *The Triple Revolution: Social Problems in Depth* (Boston: Little, Brown, 1968), pp. 66–76.

Melman, Seymour, *Our Depleted Society* (New York: Holt, 1965).

Poppy, John, "The Draft: Hazardous to Your Health?," *Look* (August 12, 1969), pp. 32–34.

Powell, Elwin, "Paradoxes of the Welfare State," *Trans-action* (March 1964), pp. 3–7.

Rapoport, Anatol, *Strategy and Conscience* (New York: Harper and Row, 1964).

Rechy, John, "The Army Fights an Idea," *The Nation* (January 12, 1970), pp. 8–12.

Sampson, Edward E., "Two Profiles: The Draft Resister and the ROTC Cadet," paper presented at the American Orthopsychiatric Association meeting, Washington D. C., March 1969.

Satin, Mark (ed.), *Manual for Draft-Age Immigrants to Canada* (Toronto: Anansi, 1969).

Schurmann, Herbert Franz, Peter Scott, and Reginald Zelnick, *The Politics of Escalation in Vietnam* (Boston: Beacon, 1966).

Scott, Peter, "Air America: Flying the U. S. into Laos," *Ramparts* (February 1970), pp. 39–54.

Scott, Peter, "Laos: The Story Nixon Won't Tell," *New York Review of Books* (April 9, 1970), pp. 35–41.

Southern Conference Educational Fund (SCEF), *An Enemy of the People: How the Draft Is Used to Stop Movements for Social Change* (Louisville, Ky.: SCEF Press, 1968).

Stern, Sol, "The Defense Intellectuals," *Ramparts*, **5** (February 1967), pp. 31–37.

Stone, I. F., "McNamara and the Militarists," *New York Review of Books* (November 7, 1968).

Tax, Sol, *The Draft: A Handbook of Facts and Alternatives* (Chicago: Univ. of Chicago Press, 1969).

CHICKEN À LA KAHN

Anatol Rapoport

The recent history of warfare is a history of applied science. No other application of science has mobilized human ingenuity on so broad a scale and in such depth. The major wars of our century have been characterized by a shift in scientific focus. Thus World War I has been called with some justification the chemists' war; World War II has been called the physicists' war. Toward its last phases, World War II was also becoming the mathematicians' war. Indeed, the electronic computer was distinctly a by-product of that war.

However, in spite of the shifting focus, it is clear that war is becoming even more a genuine cooperative enterprise among all the fields of science. The crucial role of mathematics in World War III seems definitely assured. In addition, the social sciences will surely be enlisted. Sociology and economics loom in importance as the necessity becomes apparent of preparing for social dislocations of unprecedented magnitude. One envisages also the future role of political science in creating patterns of political control concomitant with social organization required by modern war. Psychology will make its contribution not only with regard to the study of man as a link in the man-machine system but also with regard to the psychic processes of the decision maker. For these psychic processes now constitute an integral part of the new revolutionized strategic science.

It is with some aspects of the new strategic science that *On Escalation* (by Herman Kahn, Frederick A. Praeger, Inc., $6.95) is concerned. Before I undertake the discussion of the book proper, I should like to offer a few conjectures concerning its place in the history of strategic theory.

The art of strategy reached a peak of elegance during the eighteenth century, thanks largely to the genius of Frederick the Great of Prussia. The Napoleonic wars brought in an admixture of vulgarization, thanks to the dilution of professional armies by hordes of conscripts and volunteers. Clausewitz's classical treatise "On War" was a courageous attempt to reestablish austere standards of rationality and professionalism in the theory and practice of war. Clausewitz is justly credited with bringing into focus the cardinal principle of civilized war, namely, that war is a means, never an end in itself. By means of war, one state imposes its will upon another. Such imposition of will, namely the attainment of specific objectives, ought to be, Clausewitz argued, the one and only reason for going to war. Moreover, war ought to be conducted by competent professionals in accordance with sound and rational principles.

It goes without saying that Clausewitz would have been severely disappointed with the conduct of World War I, a war of attrition, in which it should have become immediately clear to all participants (but it didn't) that the costs of the war would far surpass the value of any of the stated objectives. What was worse, World War I

Reprinted by permission of the author and publisher from The Virginia Quarterly Review, **41**:3 *(Summer 1965), pp. 370–389.*

was also almost devoid of strategic elegance. Nor would Clausewitz have approved of World War II for its emphasis on mystical objectives (Blood and Soil; Unconditional Surrender; the Four Freedoms). As for the rash of revolutions, civil wars, resistance movements, and the like which have erupted in our century, Clausewitz would surely have viewed this development as a degradation of a noble art, something like a spectacle of chess players hurling chess pieces at each other.

Since the end of World War II, classical Clausewitzian diplo-military principles have enjoyed a renaissance. I would venture to suggest that no small part in this renaissance was played by the introduction of nuclear weapons. At first, this seems surprising since it was thought for a while that nuclear war would destroy the rational basis of war by making all conceivable objectives prohibitively costly. Moreover, it was next to impossible to conceive of sound strategic principles relevant to the conduct of a war which would last perhaps only a few hours. These apprehensions, however, proved to have been unfounded. A new group of strategists has appeared, recruited largely from the academic rather than the military circles. These progressive thinkers brought fresh ideas to bear upon the art and science of war.

Of these new strategists, one of the most imaginative is Herman Kahn, the author of the volume under review. Mr. Kahn's earlier volume, *On Thermonuclear War,* attracted attention far beyond the defense community. In it he gave full expression to the two main ideas which rescued the art of strategy from oblivion. One idea was that the art of strategy need not be confined to the battlefield but can be extended to the thrusts and parries, threats and counterthreats of mutual intimidation, which usually precede a war. The other idea was a reformulation of objectives for which wars could be fought. Granting that

it is difficult to extend the notion of "victory" to any outcome of a full-scale nuclear exchange, Mr. Kahn insisted that it is still possible for one side or another to "prevail."

Both of these ideas stem from a conceptualization of war as a game of strategy. This conceptualization is already apparent in the military classics, but has come most clearly into focus against the background of recent mathematical developments known as the theory of games. Game theory includes a far-reaching taxonomy of conflict situations classified in accordance with the nature of their strategic structure. Each game is defined by a set of rules, including rules of termination, which define numerical pay-offs to each player associated with each possible outcome of the game. Hence, if we can define the pay-offs associated with various outcomes of a war, say in terms of population and material losses, as well as strategic opportunities with respect to the next war, we can surely decide which side has prevailed in any specific real or hypothetical instance by the simple expedient of keeping score.

It must be stressed that Mr. Kahn does not utilize the technical apparatus of game theory in his formulations. Indeed, his formulations are not of the sort to which formal game theory could be meaningfully applied. It is true, however, that Mr. Kahn's outlook is strongly influenced by the outlook presupposed in game theory. In game theory, it is the strategic structure of a conflict situation which constitutes the exclusive object of analysis. Thus the bulk of game theory rests on a taxonomy of games, which reveals the fundamental distinctions between two-person and N-person games, between zero-sum and nonzero-sum games, between games with solutions in terms of pure strategies and those requiring mixed strategies, etc. Although none of these technical questions are raised in Mr. Kahn's analysis, the spirit of his approach is quite similar. As in game theory, only the strategic structure has been abstracted from each conflict situation. As in game theory, while the magnitude of the pay-offs is relevant, the actual content of the pay-offs is not. For example, it is not legitimate to ask in the context of game theory *why* one outcome of the game is preferred to another, any more than to ask why a yard is longer than an inch. This is also the case with Mr. Kahn's analysis. His analysis always proceeds on the basis of given preference orderings. What determines the preferences and how is entirely beyond the scope of his book.

Next, the specific physical realization of the game is irrelevant to Mr. Kahn's analysis, just as it is in game theory. For example, it is quite irrelevant to the analysis of a game whether the game is played on a board with wooden pieces or on a blackboard with chalk marks or on a battlefield with human bodies or as a nuclear exchange with cities as chips. Nor are the psychological processes of the players relevant except insofar as they have a bearing on strategic choices.

It is in this spirit that Mr. Kahn develops the science of nuclear strategy of which he is said to be an outstanding exponent. The present volume is essentially an exposition of forty-four phases of conflict (among states or power blocs), distinguished mainly by the degree of severity. Mr. Kahn calls these phases the rungs of the escalation ladder.

The simplest model of an escalation ladder has only two rungs. As such it can be formalized as the so-called game of Chicken, with which Mr. Kahn begins his exposition. The designation "Chicken" derives from the game sometimes played by American youngsters on a highway. Two cars rush headlong toward each other. The first driver to swerve from the collision course is "chicken." Thus victory goes to

the bold. Consequently, Mr. Kahn points out, if the driver of one car can convey to the other that he is absolutely determined not to swerve or is drunk or has thrown the steering wheel away, he can prevail, provided the other (1) gets and understands the message; (2) is not equally determined; (3) is not drunk; (4) has not thrown away *his* steering wheel.

On Escalation is essentially an expansion of this idea. The either-or structure of Chicken is here drawn out into a large spectrum, ranging from Rungs 1, 2, and 3 (Precrisis Maneuvering) to Rung 44 (Spasm War). Indeed, refinement of distinctions is one of Mr. Kahn's principal contributions to strategic analysis. His recurring complaint is the crudeness of conceptualization which distinguishes only "peace" and "war" or only "conventional war" and "nuclear war." In contrast, Mr. Kahn's taxonomy of diplo-military conflict is exceedingly rich and refined. Starting with several rungs of increasingly tense internation situations, he does not reach the (sporadic) shooting stage until Rung 8 (Harassing Acts of Violence), and the sustained shooting stage (Large Conventional War) until Rung 12. On the other hand, the nuclear stage is reached already at Rung 15 (Barely Nuclear War), leaving 24–29 rungs of nuclear escalation to reach the serious stages, namely, Slow Motion Countercity War (Rung 39), Countervalue Salvo (40), Augmented Disarming Attack (41), Civilian Devastation Attack (42), Some Other Kinds of Controlled General War (43), and finally the Spasm (the 44th and last rung).

The Spasm, that is, the all-out holocaust, is the layman's conception of nuclear war. It was shared also by John Foster Dulles, who is said by Mr. Kahn to have remarked that if war ever broke out, the State Department would be closed down.

One of Mr. Kahn's contributions to

present-day thinking about war and peace is in dispelling such simplistic notions. The choice, he points out, is not between the total blessing of peace and the total curse of a spasm war. There is a wide choice of positions on the escalation ladder, along which nation-states may wander up and down in the pursuit of their national interests.

The concept of escalation combines brinkmanship with measured response. The former, it will be recalled, was a conception of diplomacy based upon the maximum threat. As long as war and peace were thought of in either-or terms, there seemed to be no choice open to the United States but of threatening the Soviet Union (the then Enemy Number One) with total destruction, if communist subversion should occur anywhere in the world. The measured-response theory (advanced shortly after the Soviet Union developed a nuclear capability of her own) was based on the principle of making the punishment fit the crime, i.e., retaliation was to be tailored to the provocation. The new escalation theory incorporates the best features of both. It has had some precursors. For example, it was proposed at one stage to make massive retaliation depend on a chance outcome. In this way, the threats could be properly graduated. Thus, in response to a minor provocation (say a student riot in Venezuela), the United States could threaten the Soviet Union with massive retaliation with probability .01 (that is, make the implementation of the threat dependent on an outcome of an event whose chance of occurrence was one in a hundred); while to a major provocation (for example, infiltration in South Vietnam) the response might be a threat of massive retaliation with probability .5 (e.g., making the realization dependent on the toss of a coin). Theoretically, this scheme had a great deal to recommend it, for it

made the choice of strategy mathematically tractable. One could rely on a rational opponent to weigh the utilities of the possible outcomes with the respective probabilities and to act so as to maximize his utility. There is no denying, however, that the notion of "probabilistically graduated response" has an academic flavor to it, and it is not surprising that the idea did not elicit enthusiasm in practical men.

Escalation, too, embodies probabilistic ideas, but here probabilities are involved not in deliberate randomization of choices but rather in estimates which the participants make of each other's intentions. The principal feature of the game of Chicken dominates the strategic considerations of the escalation game. He who disbelieves that the opponent is willing to go the limit may thereby be enhancing his own chances of a win. For in that case, he is able to muster "resolve," and the very fact that he does so induces the credibility of *his* willingness to go the limit.

Like many great ideas, this one is simple and not particularly new. Mr. Kahn's contribution is embodied mainly in his systematic and detailed explorations of the techniques available to the participants on each rung of the escalation ladder.

The discussion of the techniques is necessarily brief (this is a survey rather than a handbook), but it is exhaustive in the sense of covering a very large number of contingencies and alternatives. Thus at Rung 2 (Political, Economic, and Diplomatic Gestures) a player may choose among refusing to facilitate negotiations, making overtures to the other side's enemies, arranging for newspaper leaks, etc. At Rung 4 (Hardening of Positions) one starts to "burn the bridges" i.e., to make one's own retreat impossible. At Rung 7 ("Legal" Harassment) "one may harass the opponent's prestige, property, or nationals legally." So it goes to Rung 12

(Large Conventional War), in which fighting has started in earnest but where "quality" weapons (nuclear, bacteriological, chemical) are not yet used. As we have already mentioned, the nuclear stage is reached at Rung 15 (Barely Nuclear War). This is a delicate stage. It may be that the first use of nuclear weapons is unintentional; or it may be "unintentional," i.e., the user has used nuclear weapons deliberately but is conveying the impression that the use was accidental.

"There are at least two reasons for such deceptions," writes Mr. Kahn.

First, the mere fact that a nuclear "accident" has occurred would indicate clearly to the opponent, and to others who could put pressure on him, that the situation was very dangerous. . . . Second, the attacker may feel that it is particularly important to destroy some key enemy installation . . . and find that he can do so only with nuclear weapons. He might destroy this installation and still hope that the opponent would accept it as an accidental and unauthorized use of a weapon. The offending side could offer to punish the guilty individuals, perhaps to provide an indemnification, or to permit a reprisal (but not really a compensating one) by the other side.

Once one has passed the "nuclear threshold," escalation becomes a tricky business. The problem is to keep it under control. Some control seems to be "built in" in the very act of "limited nuclear exchange." In one of the scenarios (a scenario is an imagined course of events, usually involving a crisis or a part of a war. Scenarios are used in training people to think strategically, for example, to foresee the range of options open to the principals at various stages of conflict) Mr. Kahn writes:

The Soviets . . . invade West Germany. They are advancing rapidly. The Americans might then use two or three nuclear weapons to destroy bridges in the Soviet rear . . . the purpose of the destruction is less to degrade logistics than to say, "Having used two or three nuclear weap-

ons, are we not likely to use many more?" . . . [The Soviets] might themselves use two or three nuclear weapons . . . in order to indicate that they have not been frightened by the American use. . . . One can thus easily imagine a cease fire being called immediately after the Soviet retaliation.

On the other hand, the tit-for-tat might not end with one exchange. We read later:

If there should come about more or less continued tit-for-tat exchanges . . . the result would be a war of almost pure resolve. . . . Many strategists believe that reciprocal-reprisal wars of resolve may be a standard tactic of the future, when the balance of terror has become firm and absolute.

By the time Rung 39 is reached, the tit-for-tat exchanges are in the "city trading stage."

This kind of war would be the most extreme and ultimate form of deliberative, selective, and controlled response—but one not necessarily or even likely to be beyond the psychological capabilities of decision makers. . . .

Each of the phases, be it noted, presents its own strategic problems and a plethora of pros and cons for escalating to the next phase. (Deescalation presents its own problems, briefly mentioned toward the end of the book.) Only the last phase (Rung 44—Spasm War) is devoid of strategic significance and hence offers no intellectual challenge. To quote Mr. Kahn once more:

My use of the term "spasm" does not necessarily denote blind overwhelming fury, but might only mean that a response is automatic, unthinking, and uncontrolled—a function of the central nervous system, so to speak, rather than of the brain. [Possibly Mr. Kahn means here the autonomic nervous system; otherwise the end of the sentence makes no sense. The central nervous system includes the brain.]

The exposition of On Escalation is for the most part descriptive. The phase of escalation represented by each rung is illustrated by the diplo-military events characteristic of the phase and by the options of initiative and response open to the participants. Specific recommendations are, for the most part, not definitive, and at times include both pro and con arguments. For example, the important question of "breaching the nuclear threshold" is examined with great thoroughness. In peripheral conflicts, according to Mr. Kahn, a premium is put on the use of blackmail and threats, surprise attacks, anonymous attacks, being willing, politically and morally, to accept a high percentage of casualties, etc. But, he goes on, "these are precisely the desiderata in which the U.S. is most likely to be weak or incompetent." He continues, ". . . by and large the kind of war that the U.S. is most competent to fight . . . is the high explosive [thermonuclear] war." This is clearly an argument for escalation from a phase in which the United States is at a disadvantage to one where it enjoys an advantage.

There are other arguments for breaching the nuclear threshold cited by Mr. Kahn, for example, "a world in which nuclear weapons have been used . . . purposely and effectively to punish an aggressor is a stable world." This is especially true if

. . . one or two dozen nations possess adequate stocks of nuclear weapons, [so that] no single nation or even any reasonable combination is likely to take up aggression. The process of weapon diffusion would enable any one of these nations to strike a painful and even anonymous blow against the aggressors. Such a world would clearly be discouraging for a Hitler. And it is not an improbable international political-strategic order for the future.

Admitting that is is a strong argument for nuclear use, and the consequent proliferation of nuclear weapons, Mr. Kahn nevertheless declares that he is not convinced by it, in any event "in the present climate of opinion in the U.S.—which is bitterly hostile to the proliferation of nu-

clear weapons." For one thing, Mr. Kahn is seriously concerned with the change in the power structure in a world in which twenty or thirty nations possess nuclear weapons—"and not all of them stable democracies." He also sees another argument against the use (and consequently the proliferation) of nuclear weapons which would not, perhaps, occur to many people: namely, the resulting accelerating arms race might act as a "spur to various kinds of ban-the-bomb movements, some wholly irresponsible, thus increasing the pressures of these groups upon democratic governments. Such groups could impair Western morale, leading to diffidence and uncertainty in the pursuit of national objectives."

On the whole, Mr. Kahn recommends prudence in the use of escalation in the pursuit of national interests: ". . . if one wishes to violate thresholds, one must be conscious of the negative effects and act in a manner that minimizes them, as well as exploit the gains that are sought."

Thus, the prescriptions to be found in *On Escalation* are, for the most part, eclectic rather than definitive. On only one point, already mentioned above, Mr. Kahn expresses an emphatic commitment, namely, the necessity of "thinking through" all foreseeable contingencies and of preparing appropriate plans of action. He deplores the attitude which "shuts off thinking" as soon as a scenario reaches an outbreak of a thermonuclear war. He points out that such a war is (1) a distinct possibility and (2) not necessarily an unmitigated disaster. It behooves us, therefore, to extend to the hypothetical situations arising in a nuclear war the same cool, calculating demeanor that has characterized the best in diplo-military tradition. The military profession, Mr. Kahn complains, was almost ready to throw in the sponge with the advent of nuclear weapons. He notes with satisfaction that this loss of heart was only temporary. He rallies the defense community to awaken to the exciting potentialities of a new diplo-military science based on a widened range of coercive capabilities introduced by the nuclear breakthrough. My evaluation of Mr. Kahn's book will be based on the analysis of this plea and on my response to it.

Mr. Kahn supports his plea by an appeal to open-mindedness and to foresight in a rapidly changing world. I take it, then, that the investigations he pursues and encourages are motivated by intellectual curiosity and by patriotism. I assume also that Mr. Kahn is motivated, like any other professional, by pride of craftsmanship. Sophistication is the mental analogue of manual virtuosity. And so I will assume that patriotism, professional pride, and intellectual curiosity are the principal bases of Mr. Kahn's appeal for overcoming inhibitions in exploring the potentialities of escalation and nuclear war.

Let us examine patriotism first. Patriotism is a variant of loyalty, in which the object of allegiance is a nation-state. Nation-states have not always existed and therefore neither has patriotism. Some forms of loyalty, however, are present in all patterns of social life. For example, the basis of the serf's loyalty to the feudal lord was the power of the lord to protect the serf from marauders and from other lords. The henchman's loyalty to the gangster boss has a similar basis. Other forms of loyalty are based on sentimental attachment, for example, family, friendship, and community ties. The nation-state commands loyalty primarily in two ways: first, on the basis of a belief that one's own nation-state can organize life in a better way than other authorities; second, in virtue of complete and unconditional identification with the nation-state. The first type of loyalty is characteristic of "popular" patriotism, for example, the sort widespread in the United States. Most Americans link their loyalty to the United States with the blessings which they believe derive from the "American way of life." The intense patriotism observed in nascent nations, especially during their struggle for independence, also derives from expectations of benefits to be obtained from a national government; and so does the patriotism which emerges as a by-product of a social revolution, for instance, that of the French in the 1790s and of the Russians following 1917. (The distinction between patriotism and nationalism is not relevant to this discussion and is not made here.)

The second type of patriotism amounts to a replacement of one's own identity by that of the state. Psychic transformations of this sort are commonly observed in members of the military castes, the Prussian Junkers being the most commonly cited example. Junker-type patriotism, in contrast to "popular" patriotism, does not depend on current or future blessings expected from the state. It is total, unconditional, and reflex-dominated. We might note here that reflex-dominated patriotism (jingoism) has been often observed in civilian populations as well, particularly during war hysterias. However, these phenomena are usually transient. Following military defeat or an exhaustive war, mass patriotism inspired by war hysteria frequently turns into hatred directed against one's own power elite and military caste. In Russia, this reversal led to a complete liquidation of both the old power elite and of the military caste; in Germany this almost happened, but not quite, so that the military caste lived to see another war. "Antipatriotism" of varying degrees was also observed in England, in France, and even in the United States following World War I. Members of the military castes themselves, however, tend to preserve their original loyalty, sometimes even after the citadel of power to which they had owed allegiance has been destroyed.

In short, popular patriotism conceives the state as a means to an end (real or imagined), while military patriotism conceives the state as an end in itself. In a war, the man motivated by popular patriotism must constantly reassure himself that he is fighting for something of value to himself or to people with whom he identifies or, perhaps, to all people, but at any rate to *people*. Thus in World War II, the American civilian in uniform believed that he was fighting to preserve the patterns of life to which he was accustomed, or else, if he had a broader perspective, to prevent the enslavement of the world by a self-proclaimed elite. The military-caste patriot does not need such reassurances. For him, the preservation of the state and the extension of its power are identical with self-preservation and with the extension of his own power. Thus military patriotism is completely compatible with the Clausewitzian view of international relations, inasmuch as the enhancement of the power of a state vis-à-vis other states is the sole aim of Clausewitzian diplo-military strategy. It is, however, questionable whether popular patriotism is compatible with the Clausewitzian view of international relations. In particular, in the context of a nuclear war, the basis of *American* popular patriotism disappears. For it is absurd to suppose that it is possible to preserve the familiar patterns of American life on any of the upper rungs of Mr. Kahn's ladder. To be convinced, the reader need only read Mr. Kahn's description of city evacuation procedures (Rungs 17, 25, and 30). In a deeper sense, the values underlying American popular patriotism go by the wayside as soon as one accepts the very framework of thought in which Mr. Kahn develops his arguments, namely, the Clausewitzian framework and the values of the military caste. In the United States, popular support for the two world wars could be mobilized only by representing these wars as struggles *against* the Clausewitzian system, i.e., a world system dominated by power politics.

It is interesting to note that Mr. Kahn realizes the irrelevance of popular support in a World War III. He writes:

There would probably not be any drafting, training, war mobilization, bond drives, or voting between the first and the last shots. Such a war most likely would be relatively technical, run by government authorities and technicians, with little or no attention paid to the immediate problems of support from, or the morale of, the civilian population. It would probably be fought relatively coolly, and be guided by considerations of national interest little affected by propaganda or popular emotion.

Clearly, "national interest" is to be understood here in strictly Clausewitzian terms, i.e., independent of whatever might be of interest to the populations involved. World War III, like the wars of the eighteenth century, is envisaged as a war without active participation by the populations. The populations will be affected, of course, but only incidentally, as bystanders, while the professionals do their business.

Thus, if Mr. Kahn's arguments are to be supported by considerations of patriotism, we must keep in mind that only one type of patriotism is relevant in this context, namely that derived from a world view espoused by military castes and by assorted despots from Xerxes to Stalin. This view is fundamentally destructive of the values underlying the entire development of social thought which places man as the center of attention. In particular, the world view shared by Mr. Kahn is destructive of the fundamental values which underlie American political philosophy.

Once one has fathomed the sources of Mr. Kahn's patriotism, one sees also the source of his professional pride. The military caste identifies with the Clausewitzian state; Mr. Kahn identifies with the military caste. Let us not be deceived by the absence of glittering uniforms, duels, cavalry, chandelier-lit balls, and similar trappings which have kept the old European military castes in the public eye. The "defense community," to which Mr. Kahn refers, although socially inconspicuous, is nevertheless a true social organism, and so is the "analytic community" to which Mr. Kahn himself belongs, namely, the conclave of civilians, recruited largely from universities, who serve the "defense community" in the capacity of technical advisors. It is impractical to absorb these specialists into the military profession for various reasons. (For example, the military with its modest rate of professional salaries cannot compete with industry or even with academia in the recruitment of career personnel.) But the absence of military snobbism in the United States has made possible a climate of genuine fraternal solidarity between the military caste and its civilian professional corps. They share a genuine basis of common values, the Clausewitzian world view and the ideals of strategic sophistication and technical excellence.

It is characteristic of professional communities that they elicit loyalties which cut across national and ideological lines. Thus scientists and artists belong to a world community. It is more difficult for the military castes to forge a similar world community since, ostensibly at least, they are sometimes committed to each other's destruction. Nevertheless, a basis for such a community exists in the self-concept of the military professional. It is easy to trace many of Mr. Kahn's strategic arguments to assumptions of such professional solidarity. The "built-in controls" of the escalation process are supposed to be operating on the basis of mutually assumed rationality and mutually perceived common interests of the "players." In fact, the whole philosophy of escalation is based on the supposition that such controls are operating; otherwise, there is no need to distinguish

the forty-four rungs between peace and the Spasm War. Without the "perception of common interests," escalation would be a purely self-catalytic, explosive process.

Now, one might ask, if "perception of common interests" can keep a nuclear war "under control" so as to limit the extent of the damage, why cannot the same "perception of common interests" prevent nuclear war altogether or, for that matter, prevent any war which results in losses to all concerned? These questions are not raised in *On Escalation,* but they were touched upon in Mr. Kahn's earlier books (for example, in connection with his discussion of disarmament). His answers to these questions were in the form of admonitions to stick to "realism." From the point of view of us bystanders, it is difficult to see why it is more realistic to agree to fight a limited nuclear war than to agree not to fight a war at all. From the point of view of the military caste, however, Mr. Kahn's conception of realism makes sense: it is not realistic for any professional community to strive for the abolition of the reason for its own existence.

Let us now examine the last and most clearly stated basis of Mr. Kahn's appeal to explore all the potentialities of nuclear warfare. As we have said, this is an appeal to open-mindedness with allusions to freedom of inquiry unencumbered by fear or sentiment, the time-honored principle of scientific investigation. Mr. Kahn complains that this appeal has met with sharp hostility in some sectors of the intellectual community, and he attributes this hostility to outraged moralistic sensibilities. He has argued (or others have argued for him; cf. Raymond Aron's foreword to Herman Kahn's *Thinking about the Unthinkable*) that a detached attitude toward the genocidal by-products of modern war is no more reprehensible than a physician's detached attitude toward horrendous diseases; that a refusal to discuss the strategy and tactics of nuclear war is analogous to a prudish reluctance to discuss venereal disease, prostitution, drug addiction, and the like. An analogous argument is sometimes drawn between preparedness for natural disasters.

A reply to these arguments can be made along two lines. First, the analogy between nuclear warfare and assorted diseases, earthquakes, floods, etc. is a false one. Diseases and natural disasters are not imposed on populations by decision makers, while wars are. Any dispassionate investigation of war *viewed as an affliction or a disaster* (which is the crux of the analogy) must inquire into the social, psychological, or psychopathological determinants of war. This is not the content of Mr. Kahn's investigations. He teaches how to conduct a war and how to escalate it with a view of imposing the will of one state on another or, if this fails, with a view of inflicting maximum damage on the enemy, while minimizing damage to oneself. Now, since the "defense community" is, in a sense, a world community (as many professional communities are), Mr. Kahn's opposite numbers in other countries will be learning from him and may well improve on his ideas. Thus the results of these investigations can in no way alleviate the curse of war but can only aggravate it, as has been the case throughout the history of progress in military technology and strategy.

Against this conclusion, the defenders of Mr. Kahn's views sometimes advance the "logical consequences" argument. According to this argument, Mr. Kahn does no more than investigate the logical consequences of strategic thinking in the nuclear age. Such an investigation can serve a salubrious purpose, it is argued, for if the implications of strategic thinking are carried to their logical conclusions (as they are by Mr. Kahn), and if the results are revealed to be appalling (as they are), then the decision makers may have sècond thoughts in their conduct of diplo-military

blackmail. If Mr. Kahn's book were truly written with this aim, I would applaud it. However, there is no evidence for this interpretation.

For one thing, the book must have been put together hastily and carelessly. The writing resembles a transcript of a brainstorming session rather than an organized exposition. There are instances of loss of contact with reality, as, for example, in the suggestion that in a "large conventional war" casualties *may* occur. There are lapses of logic, as in a statement to the effect that Khrushchev gave no sign of being *reassured* by the *possibility* that a crisis might not escalate. There are glaring inconsistencies. In discussing evacuation plans (in preparation for nuclear war), Mr. Kahn mentions the "enormous political, social, economic, and psychological problems" which these plans entail (p. 146); while on p. 201 he suggests that civilian support and morale are irrelevant to the conduct of nuclear war. At times, Mr. Kahn's discourse becomes incoherent or nearly so, as in the following passage: "Therefore, in the current situation (for purposes of damage limitation, as distinguished from deterrence only), it may be better—in several ways—to acquire additional capability for rapidly improving the posture rather than to acquire additional capability in being."

Next, the tone of the book gives the impression of being deliberately offensive. Its undercurrent of paranoia and brutality reminds one of certain standardized private-eye stories. The calculated titillation in the deliberate build-up of the war crescendo is modeled after the sex-technique books advertised in pulp magazines. The pages of the book crawl with quotation marks, which turn out to be typographical versions of giggles. Thus Mr. Kahn sees to it that we understand what he means by "unintentional" breaches of the nuclear threshold, "justifiable" attacks, "peaceful" blockades, etc. Quotation marks are used also to frame Mr. Kahn's metaphors, evidently meant to liven up the detached scientific discussion. "The moment of truth" (the final confrontation) is one example.

The author of *On Escalation* is revealed not as a detached analyst, nor even as a cynically bemused observer of human folly, but rather as an enthusiastic choreographer of the dance of death. He relishes the obscene pranks he invents and the cataclysmic phantasies he invokes. Nor does the pornographic implication of his metaphors escape him. He says, for example:

> The term "spasm war" is now almost standard jargon in military and government circles and, to some degree, in journalism as well. I believe the expression originated in briefings I gave some years ago in which some war-plan proposals were referred to as "orgastic spasms of destruction." During one of these briefings, I said to the audience, "You people do not have a war plan. You have a 'war-gasm.'"

Who among us is not convinced that this gem was greeted with guffaws and slapping of thighs, an outburst of jolly fellowship among the initiated? *On Escala-tion*, like Mr. Kahn's earlier books, is essentially a taxonomy of Pandora's zoo, a blueprint for genocide, and a guide for the possessed. It is a recurrent symptom of a repulsive social disease, not unlike the disease to which Germany and Japan succumbed a generation ago. The disease is now incubating in our country. As this is being written (April 1965), the United States is triumphantly climbing the escalation ladder.

Inasmuch as Mr. Kahn's exercises in "thinking about the unthinkable," as he calls them, have been in the public eye since 1960, it does not seem that they have been effective in suggesting second thoughts to the decision makers, as some defenders of Mr. Kahn hoped they would. It is barely possible, however, that Mr. Kahn's books may help ordinary people, thinking ordinary thoughts, to realize that "security through strength" has become a contradiction in terms and that our chances of escaping the unspeakable depend on whether people who think like Mr. Kahn can be removed from positions of influence.

IS THERE A MILITARY-INDUSTRIAL COMPLEX THAT PREVENTS PEACE?

Marc Pilisuk and Tom Hayden

The notion of a military-industrial complex as a potent force or even indeed a ruling elite is not new in American history. From FDR who attacked the "merchants of destruction" and campaigned in 1932 to "take the profits out of war" to a more restrained warning by Eisenhower against the "unwarranted" power of the military-industrial complex, American politics and scholarship have often entertained such a concept. Many scholars, however, have rejected the "power elite" concept implicit in the charge of a military-industrial complex capable of dominating the entire American scene. Implicit in the writings of such pluralist writers as Daniel Bell, Robert Dahl, and Talcott Parsons is the basis for a denial that it is a military-industrial complex that prevents peace. The argument is:

1. It is held that the *scope* of decisions made by any interest group is quite narrow and cannot be said to govern anything so broad as foreign policy.

2. It is held that the "complex" is *not monolithic, not self-conscious,* and *not coordinated,* the presumed attributes of a ruling elite.

3. It is held that the military-industrial complex does not wield power if the term "power" is defined as the ability to realize its will even against the resistance of others and regardless of external conditions.

Since the arguments of the pluralists have been directed largely to the work of C. Wright Mills, it is with Mills that we will begin to analyze the theories which claim there *is* a military-industrial complex blocking peace.

THE THESIS OF ELITE CONTROL

Mills is by far the most formidable exponent of the theory of a power elite. In his view, the period in America since World War II has been dominated by the ascendance of corporation and military elites to positions of institutional power. These "commanding heights" allow them to exercise control over the trends of the business cycle and international relations. The cold war set the conditions that legitimize this ascendance, and the decline and incorporation of significant left-liberal movements, such as the CIO, symbolizes the end of opposition forces. The power elite monopolizes sovereignty, in that political initiative and control stem mainly from the top hierarchical levels of position and influence. Through the communications system the elite facilitates the growth

An earlier version of this essay by Marc Pilisuk and Tom Hayden was published in The Journal of Social Issues, 21:3, pp 67–117, under the title, "Is There a Military-Industrial Complex Which Prevents Peace?: Consensus and Countervailing Power in Pluralistic Systems."

of a politically indifferent mass society below the powerful institutions. This, according to the Mills argument, would explain why an observer finds widespread apathy. Only a small minority believes in actual participation in the larger decisions that affect their existence and only the ritual forms of "popular democracy" are practiced by the vast majority. Mills' argument addresses itself to the terms of the three basic issues we have designated, i.e., scope of decision power, awareness of common interest, and the definition of power exerted.

By *scope*, we are referring to the sphere of society over which an elite is presumed to exercise power. Mills argues that the scope of this elite is general, embracing all the decisions which in any way could be called vital (slump and boom, peace and war, etc.). He does not argue that *each* decision is directly determined, but rather that the political alternatives from which the "deciders" choose are shaped and limited by the elite through its possession of all the large-scale institutions. By this kind of argument, Mills avoids the need to demonstrate how his elite is at work during each decision. He speaks instead in terms of institutions and resources. But the problem is that his basic evidence is of a rather negative kind. No major decisions have been made for twenty years contrary to the policies of anticommunism and corporate or military aggrandizement; *therefore* a power elite must be prevailing. Mills might have improved his claims about the scope of elite decisions by analyzing a series of actual decisions in terms of the premises that were *not* debated. This could point to the mechanisms (implicit or explicit) that led to the exclusion of these premises from debate. By this and other means he might have found more satisfying evidence of the common, though perhaps tacit, presuppositions of seemingly disparate institutions. He then might have developed a framework analyzing "scope" on different levels. The scope of the Joint Chiefs of Staff, for instance, could be seen as limited, while at the same time the Joint Chiefs could be placed in a larger elite context having larger scope. Whether this could be shown awaits research of this kind. Until it is done, however, Mills' theory of scope remains open to attack, but, conversely, is not subject to refutation.

Mills' theory also eludes the traditional requirements for inferring monolithic structure, i.e., consciousness of elite status, and coordination. The modern tradition of viewing elites in this way began with Mosca's *The Ruling Class* in a period when family units and inheritance systems were the basic means of conferring power. Mills departs from this influential tradition precisely because of his emphasis on institutions as the basic elements. If the military, political, and economic institutional orders involve a high coincidence of interest, then the groups composing the institutional orders need not be monolithic, conscious, and coordinated, yet still they can exercise elite power.[1] This means specifically that a military-industrial complex could exist as an expression of a certain fixed ideology (reflecting common institutional needs), yet be "composed" of an endless shuffle of specific groups. For instance, our tables show 82 companies have dropped out of the list of 100 top defense contractors and only 36 "durables" remained on the list from 1940 to 1960. In terms of industry, the percentage of contracts going to the automotive industry dropped from 25 percent in World War II to 4 percent in the missile age. At the same time, the aircraft companies went from 34 to 54 percent of all contracts, and the electronics industry from 9 to 28 percent (Peck and Scherer, 1962). Mills' most central argu-

---

[1] See James H. Meisel, *The Myth of the Ruling Class*, for the best available discussion of the innovation in theorizing about elites.

ment is that this ebb and flow is not necessarily evidence for the pluralists. His stress is on the unities which underlie the procession of competition and change. The decision to change the technology of warfare was one that enabled one group to "overcome" another in an overall system to which both are fundamentally committed. Moreover, the decision issued from the laboratories and planning boards of the defense establishment and only superficially involved any role for public opinion. The case studies of weapons development by Peck and Scherer, in which politics is described as a marginal ritual, would certainly buttress Mills' point of view.

Making this institution analysis enables Mills to make interesting comments on his human actors. The integration of institutions means that hundreds of individuals become familiar with several roles: general, politician, lobbyist, defense contractor. These men are the power elite, but they need not know it. They conspire, but conspiracy is not absolutely essential to their maintenance. They mix together easily, but can remain in power even if they are mostly anonymous to each other. They make decisions, big and small, sometimes with the knowledge of others and sometimes not, which ultimately control all the significant action and resources of society.

Where this approach tends to fall short is in its unclarity about how discontinuities arise. Is the military-industrial complex a feature of American society which can disappear and still leave the general social structure intact? Horst Brand (1962) has suggested a tension between financial companies and the defense industries because of the relatively few investment markets created by defense. Others have challenged the traditional view that defense spending stimulates high demand and employment. Their claim is that the concentration of contracts in a few states, the monopolization of defense and space industry by the largest

75 or 100 corporations, the low multiplier effect of the new weapons, the declining numbers of blue-collar workers required, and other factors, make the defense economy more of a drag than a stimulant (Melman et al., 1963; Etzioni, 1964). Certainly the rising unemployment of 1970 in the midst of expansion of the ABM system and extension of the Vietnam war to Laos and Cambodia show the flaws of relying upon defense spending for an economic stimulant. Mills died before these trends became the subject of debate, but he might have pioneered in discussion of them if his analytic categories had differentiated more finely between various industries and interest groups in his power elite. His emphasis was almost entirely on the "need" for a "permanent war economy" just when that need was being questioned even among his elite.

This failure, however, does not necessarily undermine the rest of Mills' analysis. His institutional analysis is still the best means of identifying a complex without calling it monolithic, conscious, and coordinated. Had he differentiated more exactly, he might have been able to describe various degrees of commitments to an arms race, a rightist ideology constricting the arena of meaningful debate, and other characteristics of a complex. This task remains to be done, and will be discussed at a later point.

Where Mills' theory is most awkward is in his assertions that the elite can, and does, make its decisions against the will of others and regardless of external conditions. This way of looking at power is inherited by Mills, and much of modern sociology, directly from Max Weber. What is attributed to the elite is a rather fantastic quality: literal omnipotence. Conversely, any group that is *not* able to realize its will even against the resistance of others is only "influential" but not an elite. Mills attempts to defend this viewpoint but, in essence, modifies it. He says he is describing a tendency, not a finalized state of affairs. This is a helpful device in explaining cracks in the monolith —for instance, the inability of the elite to establish a full corporate state against the will of small businessmen. However, it does not change the ultimate argument—that the power elite cannot become more than a tendency, cannot realize its actual self, unless it takes on the quality of omnipotence.

When power is defined as this kind of dominance, it is easily open to critical dispute. The conception of power depicts a vital and complex social system as essentially static, as having within it a set of stable governing components, with precharted interests which infiltrate and control every outpost of decision-authority. Thereby, internal accommodation is made necessary and significant change, aside from growth, becomes impossible. This conception goes beyond the idea of social or economic determinism. In fact, it defines a "closed social system." A "closed system" may be a dramatic image, but it is a forced one as well. Its defender sees events such as the rise of the labor movement essentially as a means of rationalizing modern capitalism. But true or false as this may be, did not the labor movement also constitute a "collective will" which the elite could not resist? An accommodation was reached, probably more on the side of capital than labor, but the very term "accommodation" implies the existence of more than one independent will. On a world scale, this becomes even more obvious. Certainly the rise of communism has not been through the will of capitalists, and Mills would be the first to agree. Nor does the elite fully control technological development; surely the process of invention has some independent, even if minor, place in the process of social change.

Mills' definition of power as dominance ironically serves the pluralist argument, rather than countering it. When power is defined so extremely, it becomes rather easy to claim that such power is curbed in the contemporary United States. The pluralists can say that Mills has conjured up a bogeyman to explain his own failure to realize his will. This is indeed what has been done in review after review of Mills' writings. A leading pluralist thinker, Edward Shils, says that Mills was too much influenced by Trotsky and Kafka:

Power, although concentrated, is not so concentrated, so powerful, or so permeative as Professor Mills seems to believe.... There have been years in Western history, e.g., in Germany during the last years of the Weimar Republic and under the Nazis when reality approximated this picture more closely.... But as a picture of Western societies, and not just as an ideal type of extreme possibilities which might be realized if so much else that is vital were lacking, it will not do. (Shils, 1961.)

But is Mills' definition the only suitable one here? If it is, then the pluralists have won the debate. But if there is a way to designate an irresponsible elite without giving it omnipotence, then the debate may be recast at least.

This fundamental question is not answered in the other major books that affirm the existence of a military-industrial complex. Cook's *The Warfare State* and Perlo's *Militarism and Industry* and several more recent works are good examples of this literature which is theoretically inferior to Mills' perplexing account.

Cook's volume has been pilloried severely by deniers of the military-industrial complex. At least it has the merit of creating discussion by being one of the few dissenting books distributed widely on a commercial basis. It suffers, however, from many of the same unclarities typical of the deniers. Its title assumes a "warfare state" while its evidence, although rich, is only a compilation of incidents, pronouncements, and trends, lacking any framework for weighing and measuring. From his writing several hypotheses can be extracted about the "face of the Warfare State," all of them suggestive but none of them conclusive:

1. The Department of Defense owns more property than any other organization in the world.[2]

2. Between 60 and 70 percent of the national budget is consistently allocated to defense or defense-related expenditures.

3. The military and big business join in an inevitable meeting of minds over billions of dollars in contracts the one has to order and the other to fulfill.

4. The 100 top corporations monopolize three-fourths of the contracts, 85 percent of them being awarded without competition.

5. As much as one-third of all production and service indirectly depends on defense.

6. Business and other conservative groups, even though outside of the Defense establishment, benefit from the warfare emphasis because it keeps subordinate the welfare state that is anathema to them. (Pages 20–24, 162–202.)

There is no doubt about Cook's data holding up for the years since his book was written. The federal budget of $154.9 billion for the fiscal year 1971 assigns 64.8 cents of every tax dollar to the cost of past and present wars and war preparation. The Vietnam war costs are concealed in the 48.4 cents per dollar for current military expenditures. Veterans benefits and national debt interest are also sizable items. The Nixon administration claims 41 percent of its budget to be on human resources. The figure, however, includes trust funds like Social Security (for which the government is merely a caretaker), veterans benefits, and even the Selective Service System in this category. The actual human resources figure is 17 percent,

indicating that welfare is still being crushed by warfare (Senator M. Hatfield, address, Feb. 10, 1970, Corvallis, Oregon).

Cook's work, much more than Mills', is open to the counterargument that no monolithic semiconspiratorial elite exists. Even his definitions of vested interests are crude and presumed. Moreover, he suffers far more than Mills from a failure to differentiate between groups. For instance, there is nothing in his book (written in 1962) that would explain the economic drag of defense spending, which Cook preceptively observed in a *Nation* article, "The Coming Politics of Disarmament," in 1963. One year he wrote that big business was being fattened off war contracts, but the next year the "prolonged arms race has started, at last, to commit a form of economic hara-kiri." "Hara-kiri" does not happen spontaneously; it is a culmination of long-developing abnormalities. That Cook could not diagnose them before they became common in congressional testimony illustrates the lack of refinement in his 1962 analysis. Cook's failure lies in visualizing a monolith, which obscures the strains that promote new trends and configurations.

It is in this attention to strains that Perlo's book is useful. He draws interesting connections between the largest industrial corporations and the defense economy, finding that defense accounts for 12 percent of the profits of the 25 largest firms. He adds the factor of foreign investment as one which creates a further propensity in favor of a large defense system, and he calculates that military, business, and foreign investments combined total 40 percent of the aggregate profits among the top 25. He draws deeper connections between companies and the major financial groups controlling their assets.

This kind of analysis begins to reveal im-

---

[2] Swomley (1964) accounts for Department of Defense holdings equivalent in size to eight states of the U.S.A. Kenneth Boulding, including personnel as well as property criteria, calls the Department of Defense the world's third largest socialist state. (Personal discussion, 1963.)

portant disunities within the business community. For instance, it can be seen that the Rockefellers are increasing their direct military investments while maintaining their largest foreign holdings in extremely volatile Middle Eastern and Latin American companies. The Morgans are involved in domestic industries of a rather easy-to-convert type, and their main foreign holdings are in the "safer" European countries, although they too have "unsafe" mining interests in Latin America and Africa. The First National City Bank, while having large holdings in Latin American sugar and fruit, has a more technical relation to its associated firms than the stock-owner relation. The Mellons have sizable oil holdings on Kuwait, but on the whole are less involved in defense than the other groups. The DuPonts, traditionally the major munitions makers, are "diversified" into the booming aerospace and plutonium industries, but their overseas holdings are heavily in Europe. Certain other groups with financial holdings, such as Young and Eaton interests in Cleveland, have almost no profit stake in defense or foreign investments. On the other hand, some of the new wealth in Los Angeles is deeply committed to the aerospace industry.

Perlo makes several differentiations of this sort, including the use of foreign-policy statements by leading industrial groups. But he does not have a way to predict under what conditions a given company would actively support economic shifts away from the arms race. These and other gaps, however, are not nearly as grave as his lack of analysis of other components of the military-industrial complex.[3] There is no attempt to include politicians, military groups, and other forces in a "map" of the military-industrial complex which Perlo believes ex-

ists. This may be partly because of the book's intent, which is to document profiteering by arms contractors, but, for whatever reason, the book is not theoretically edifying about the question we are posing. Nor does it refute the pluralist case. In fact, it contains just the kind of evidence that pluralist arguments currently employ to demonstrate the absence of a monolith.

The newer literature, since 1965, shows a somewhat more penetrating glimpse into the extent of the merger of the military and the defense industry. Lapp, *The Weapons Culture*; Weidenbaum, "Arms and the American Economy"; Galbraith, *The New Industrial State*; and Knoll and McFadden, *American Militarism 1970*, all show the heavy involvement of the Department of Defense with the corporate giants. The two recent and most striking works which provide the most concrete detail on the operation of this military-industrial network are Seymour Melman's *Pentagon Capitalism* (1970) and Richard Barnet's *The Economy of Death* (1969). Both are well written and a must for any serious student of contemporary policy. *Pentagon Capitalism* describes the result of the defense-industrial merger as a giant enterprise controlled by the civilian defense establishment, or "state-management." Through the elaboration of government controls over the firms that carry out defense contracts, the Defense Department's role has changed from that of customer to that of administrator over a far-flung empire of defense production. The Pentagon is able to divert capital and scientific and technical manpower to its own purposes, drawing resources away from productive activity to, what Melman calls, economically "parasitic" activity. He holds that the prime goal of the "state-management" *is to enlarge its decision power.* Thus wars, once begun, tend to ex-

[3] In an earlier book, *The Empire of High Finance* (1957), Perlo documented the close relations of the major financial groups and the political executive. He did not, however, carry this analysis to congressmen and senators, nor did he offer sufficient comparative evidence to demonstrate a long-term pattern.

pand; "security gaps" are invented, causing weapons systems to grow in size and sophistication; and international arms sales increase.

Barnet (*The Economy of Death*) sees the military-industrial complex as more decentralized, like a machine with several separate parts that run together smoothly. Each institution within the complex acts for its own purposes, and all contribute to justifying and maintaining the irrational and dangerous growth of military capability. Barnet documents the interchangeability of personnel between industry and the military. A major strength of Barnet's work lies in his willingness to be specific, to name the key names from among those in his study of 400 top decision makers who come from a handful of law firms and executive suites "in shouting distance of one another in fifteen city blocks in New York, Washington, Detroit, Chicago, and Boston." Many of the names are commonly known (although the extent of their financial-world connections is not)—Charles Wilson, Neil McElroy, Robert Anderson, George Humphrey, Douglas Dillon, John McCone, Adolph Berle, Averell Harriman, William C. Foster, John McCloy, Robert McNamara, Roswell Gilpatric, James Douglas, William Rogers, and Nelson Rockefeller. Men such as these are systematically recruited into the top Cabinet posts and become "national security managers." Their common backgrounds, even membership in the same elite social clubs, assures a measure of homogeneity around their task of defining who or what threatens this nation and what should be done about it. Their views on the national interest reflect their own success in judicious management of risk in the business world. Barnet's assumption about the homogeneity of their club is supported by Dumhoff's "Who Made American Foreign Policy, 1945–1963?" It is clear that a man like William Rogers with the right business background but no particular

knowledge or background in foreign affairs can be made Secretary of State while a civil-rights leader, Martin Luther King, was admonished by official spokesmen for expressing a position against the Vietnam war.

Barnet believes it is the ongoing mechanisms of the system that keep it rutted in old paths. The evils are not incidental, he says, but built into the system. Military solutions to international problems seem more reliable, "tougher," than diplomatic solutions, and they are backed up by millions of dollars worth of "scientific research"; so military solutions are preferred even by civilian defense officials. The military, the civilian defense establishment, and defense contractors constantly work together to develop new weapons systems to meet defense "needs"; so they feed one another's ideologies, and costlier, more elaborate weapons result. It is difficult and expensive for military contractors to convert to peacetime production, so they have done virtually no planning for conversion and many have abandoned all interest in such planning. Perhaps most important for Barnet, those in power see America's chief purpose as consolidating and extending American power around the world; hence military technology is an indispensable tool. Whether this collection of civilian managers is really in control or whether they are merely serving more powerful military bureaucracy is the point at issue, and Barnet leans toward the view of the ascendance of relatively smooth-working military hierarchy. Dumhoff, using very similar evidence, places the aristocratic economic elite at the top of the pinnacle.

Melman, in particular, presents a strong case to suggest that militarism in the United States is no longer an example of civilian corporate interests dictating a military role to produce hardware for profit from the governmental consumer and to defend the outposts of capitalism. Instead, he sees the system as one led by the military managers for their own interests in power, a state socialism whose defense officials dictate the terms of policy, and of profits, to their subsidiary corporations. Melman supports his case by the observation that not only the personnel but the actual procedural ways of operation demonstrate that the Defense Department and the corporations which serve it have interpenetrated one another's operations—to such an extent that there is for all practical purposes really only one organization. The horrible example that comes to mind is the rise of Hitler, first backed and promoted by industrialists who later lost their measure of control over an uncontrollable military machine. Melman's thesis differs from both the pluralist doctrine which sees various groups competing for power and the Marxist doctrine which sees the greed of the capitalists as the prime mover. In Melman's convincing analysis the military is fast becoming the King.

Melman's analysis may yet prove true. For the present, however, corporate capitalism has fared too well to alleviate all suspicions of the hidden hand. The nature of the new interlocking industrial conglomerates like Lytton, Textron, or General Dynamics is that they and the main financial houses of the United States provide an inner core whose interests are permanently protected even as individual corporations prosper or falter. For such centers of elite power, which Barnet shows to be the main source of top Defense Department and other foreign-policy-appointed officials, the terms of the military merger have been highly beneficial. The benefits must be seen not only in profits but in the retention of the entire profit-making system against the demands of a hungry and impatient world. Melman speaks of the drive of the new technocratic military bureaucracy to increase its power and control but de-emphasizes what interests this power is pro-

tecting. Barnet specifies the community of interest and outlooks among the corporate decision managers who are recruited into the inner circles of foreign policy but does not state explicitly what beliefs lie at the core of the practices that are promoted.

Both Barnet and Melman believe that American militarism is a function of institutions directly involved with defense. It can be argued, on the other hand, that a description of something called a military-industrial complex should include all of the power centers of American society. Directorates of the major defense contractors are not separable from those of industries geared primarily to the production of consumer goods. Neither are the consumer industries independent of military and diplomatic actions which protect international marketing advantages. Barnet himself notes that it is not merely the faction of the labor movement directly employed in defense industries, but organized labor in general which is a political supporter of military-industrial power. The universities are heavily involved in defense interests as is the complex of oils, highways, and automotives. Even in education the armed services Project 100,000 has inducted a large number of former draft rejects for resocialization and basic educational development (followed by two years of applied study abroad in Vietnam for the successful graduates) (Little, 1968; Pilisuk, 1968).

Barnet and Melman deal incompletely with the relationship of the sector they regard as the military-industrial complex to the rest of society. Both realize the tremendous power of the military, the civilian defense officials, and the defense industry combined. They are aware that the defense establishment has a powerful hold on public opinion through fear of enemy attack and through control over a large sector of the work force. Yet they seem to hope this power can be curbed by a loud enough public outcry. In the last analysis they too believe that the defense establishment has merely been allowed to get out of hand, and that now the exercise of some countervailing power may bring sanity back into American policy and make peace possible.

REVISING THE CRITERIA FOR INFERRING POWER

After finding fault with so many books and divergent viewpoints, the most obvious conclusion is that current social theory is deficient in its explanation of power. We concur with one of Mills' severest critics, Daniel Bell, who at least agrees with Mills that most current analysis concentrates on the "intermediate sectors," e.g., parties, interest groups, formal structures, without attempting to view the underlying system of "renewable power independent of any momentary group of actors" (Bell, 1964). However, we have indicated that the only formidable analysis of the underlying system of renewable power, that of Mills, has profound shortcomings because of its definition of power. Therefore, before we can offer an answer of our own to the question, "Is there a military-industrial complex that blocks peace?," it is imperative to return to the question of power itself in American society.

We have agreed essentially with the pluralist claim that ruling-group models do not "fit" the American structure. We have classified Mills' model as that of a ruling group because of his Weberian definition of power, but we have noted also that Mills successfully went beyond two traps common to elite theories, *viz.*, that the elite is total in the scope of its decisions, and that the elite is a coordinated monolith.

But we perhaps have not stressed sufficiently that the alternative case for pluralism is inadequate in its claim to describe the historical dynamics of American society. The point of our dissent from pluralism is over the doctrine of "countervailing power." This is the modern version of Adam Smith's economics and of the Madisonian or Federalism theory of checks and balances, adapted to the new circumstances of large-scale organizations. Its evidence is composed of self-serving incidents and a faith in semimystical resources. For instance, in the sphere of political economy, it is argued that oligopoly contains automatic checking mechanisms against undue corporate growth, and that additionally, the factors of "public opinion" and "corporate conscience" are built-in limiting forces.[4] We believe that evidence in the field, however, suggests that oligopoly is a means of stabilizing an industrial sphere either through tacit agreements to follow price leadership or rigged agreements in the case of custom-made goods; that "public opinion" tends much more to be manipulated and apathetic than independently critical; that "corporate conscience" is less suitable as a description than Reagan's terms, "corporate arrogance."

To take the more immediate example of the military sphere, the pluralist claim is that the military is subordinate to broader, civilian interests. The first problem with the statement is the ambiguity of "civilian." Is it clear that military men are more "militaristic" than civilian men? To say so would be to deny the increasing trend of "white-collar militarism." The top strategists in the Department of Defense, the Central Intelligence Agency, and the key advisory positions often are Ph.D.'s. In

---

[4] For this argument, see A. A. Berle, *The Twentieth Century Capitalist Revolution*; and J. K. Galbraith, *American Capitalism*. For sound criticisms, but without sound alternatives, see Mills' and Perlo's books. Also see Michael Reagan, *The Managed Economy* (1963); and Bernard Nossiter, *The Mythmakers* (1964), for other refutations of the countervailing power thesis.

fact, "civilians" including McGeorge Bundy, Robert Kennedy, James Rostow, and Robert McNamara are mainly responsible for the development of the only remaining "heroic" form of combat: counterinsurgency operations in the jungles of the underdeveloped countries. If "militarism"[5] has permeated this deeply into the "civilian" sphere, then the distinction between the terms becomes largely nominal.

The intrusion of civilian professors into the military arena has been most apparent in more than 300 universities and nonprofit research institutions which supply personnel to and rely upon contracts from the Department of Defense. About half of these centers were created to do specialized strategic research. One of these, the RAND Corporation, was set up by Douglas Aviation and the Air Force to give "prestige-type support for favored Air Force proposals" (Friedman, 1963). When RAND strategy experts Wohlstetter and Dinerstein discovered a mythical "missile gap" and an equally unreal preemptive war strategy in Soviet post-Sputnik policy, they paved the way for the greatest military escalation of the cold-war era, the missile race.

The civilian strategists have frequently retained an exasperating measure of autonomy from the services that support them. Such conflicts reached a peak when both the Skybolt and the RS 70 projects met their demise under the "cost effectiveness" program designed by Harvard economist Charles Hitch (then with RAND, later Defense Department comptroller, now President of the University of California). That the civilian and military planners of military policy sometimes differ does not detract from the argument. What must be stressed is that the apparent flourishing of such civilian agencies as RAND (it earned over 20 million dollars in 1962 with all the earnings going into expansion and spawned the nonprofit Systems Development Corporation with annual earnings exceeding 50 million dollars) is no reflection of countervailing power. The doctrine of controlled response under which the RS 70 fell was one which served the general aspirations of each of the separate services; of the Polaris and Minuteman stabile deterrent factions, of the brush-fire or limited-war proponents, guerrilla war and paramilitary operations advocates, and of the counterforce adherents. It is a doctrine of versatility intended to leave the widest range of military options for retaliation and escalation in U.S. hands. It can hardly be claimed as victory against military thought. The fighting may have been intense but the area of consensus between military and civilian factions was great.

CONSENSUS

All that countervailing power refers to is the relationship between groups who fundamentally accept "the American system" but who compete for advantages within it. The corporate executive wants higher profits, the laborer a higher wage. The President wants the final word on military strategies, the Chairman of the Joint Chiefs does not trust him with it, Boeing wants the contract, but General Dynamics is closer at the time to the Navy Secretary and the President, and so on. What is prevented by countervailing forces is the dominance of society by a group or clique or a party. But this process suggests a profoundly important point; that *the constant pattern in American society is the rise and fall of temporarily irresponsible groups.*

---

[5] We are defining the term as "primary reliance on coercive means, particularly violence or the threat of violence, to deal with social problems."

By *temporary* we mean that, outside of the largest industrial conglomerates,[6] the groups which wield significant power to influence policy decisions are not guaranteed stability. By *irresponsible* we mean that there are many activities within their scope which are essentially unaccountable in the democratic process. These groups are too uneven to be described with the shorthand term "class." Their personnel have many different characteristics (compare IBM executives and the Southern Dixiecrats) and their needs as groups are different enough to cause endless fights as, for example, small versus big business. No one group or coalition of several groups can tyrannize the rest as is demonstrated, for example, in the changing status of the major financial groups, such as the Bank of America which grew rapidly, built on the financial needs of the previously neglected small consumer.

It is clear, however, that these groups exist within consensus relationships of a more general and durable kind than their conflict relationships. This is true, first of all, of their social characteristics. In an earlier version of this essay we compiled tables using data from an exhaustive study of American elites contained in Warner et al., *The American Federal Executive* (1963) and from Suzanne Keller's compilation of military, economic, political, and diplomatic elite survey materials in *Beyond the Ruling Class* (1963). The relevant continuities represented in this data suggest an educated elite with an emphasis upon Protestant and business-oriented origins. Moreover, the data suggest inbreeding with business orientation in backgrounds likely to have been at least maintained, if not augmented, through marriage. Domhoff, in

Who Rules America?, has shown that elites generally attend the same exclusive prep schools and universities, and belong to the same exclusive gentlemen's clubs. The consistencies suggest orientations not unlike those found in examination of editorial content of major business newspapers and weeklies and in more directly sampled assessments of elite opinions.[7]

The second evidence of consensus relationships, besides attitude and background data indicating a pro-business sympathy, would come from an examination of the *practice* of decision making. By analysis of such actual behavior we can understand which consensus attitudes are reflected in decision making. Here, in retrospect, it is possible to discover the values and assumptions which are defended recurrently. This is at least a rough means of finding the boundaries of consensus relations. Often these boundaries are invisible because of the very infrequency with which they are tested. What are visible most of the time are the parameters of conflict relationships among different groups. These conflict relationships constitute the ingredients of experience which give individuals or groups their uniqueness and varieties, while the consensus relations constitute the common underpinnings of behavior. The tendency in social science has been to study decision making in order to study group differences; we need to study decision making also to understand group commonalities.

Were such studies done, our hypothesis would be that certain "core beliefs" are continuously unquestioned. One of these, undoubtedly, would be that efficacy is preferable to principle in foreign affairs. In practice, this means that violence is preferable to nonviolence as a means of de-

[6] The term refers to industrial organizations like Textron and Ling-Temco-Vought which have holdings in every major sector of American industry.

[7] For some interesting work bearing upon the attitudes of business and military elites, see Angell, 1964; Bauer et al., 1963; Eells and Walton, 1961; and Singer, 1964.

fense. A second is that private property is preferable to collective property. A third assumption is that the particular form of constitutional government which is practiced within the United States is preferable to any other system of government. We refer to the preferred mode as limited parliamentary democracy, a system in which institutionalized forms of direct representation are carefully retained but with fundamental limitations placed upon the prerogatives of governing. Specifically included among the areas of limitation are many matters encroaching upon corporation property and state hegemony. While adherence to this form of government is conceivably the strongest of the domestic "core values," at least among business elites, it is probably the least strongly held of the three on the international scene. American relations with, and assistance for, authoritarian and semifeudal regimes occurs exactly in those areas where the recipient regime is evaluated primarily upon the two former assumptions and given rather extensive leeway on the latter one.

The implications of these "core beliefs" for the social system are immense, for they justify the maintenance of our largest institutional structures: the military, the corporate economy, and a system of partisan politics which protects the concept of limited democracy. These institutions, in turn, may be seen as current agencies of the more basic social structure. The "renewable basis of power" in America at the present time underlies those institutional orders linked in consensus relationships: military defense of private property and parliamentary democracy. These institutional orders are not permanently secure, by definition. Their maintenance involves a continuous coping with new conditions, such as technological innovation, and with the inherent instabilities of a social structure that arbitrarily classifies persons by role, status, access to resources, and power.

The myriad groups composing these orders are even less secure because of their weak ability to command "coping resources," e.g., the service branches are less stable than the institution of the military, particular companies are less stable than the institutions of corporate property, political parties are less stable than the institution of parliamentary government.

In the United States there is no ruling group. Nor is there any easily discernible ruling institutional order, so meshed have the separate sources of elite power become. But there is a social structure which is organized to create and protect power centers with only partial accountability. In this definition of power we are avoiding the Weber-Mills meaning of *omnipotence* and the contrary pluralist definition of power as consistently *diffuse*. We are describing the current system as one of overall "minimal accountability" and "minimal consent." We mean that the role of democratic review, based on genuine popular consent, is made marginal and reactive. Elite groups are minimally accountable to publics and have a substantial, though by no means maximum, freedom to shape popular attitudes. The reverse of our system would be one in which democratic participation would be the orienting demand around which the social structure is organized.

Some will counter this case by saying that we are measuring "reality" against an "ideal," a technique which permits the conclusion that the social structure is undemocratic according to its distance from our utopian values. This is a convenient apology for the present system, of course. We think it possible, at least in theory, to develop measures of the undemocratic in democratic conditions, and place given social structures along a continuum. These measures, in rough form, might include such variables as economic security, education, legal guarantees, access to information, and participatory control over systems of economy, government, and jurisprudence.

The reasons for concern with democratic process in an article questioning the power of a purported military-industrial complex are twofold. First, just as scientific method both legitimizes and promotes change in the world of knowledge, democratic method legitimizes and promotes change in the world of social institutions. Every society, regardless of how democratic, protects its core institutions in a web of widely shared values. But if the core institutions should be dictated by the requisites of military preparedness, then restrictions on the democratic process, i.e., restrictions in either mass-opinion exchange (as by voluntary or imposed news management) or in decision-making bodies (as by selection of participants in a manner guaranteeing exclusion of certain positions), then such restrictions would be critical obstacles to peace.

Second, certain elements of democratic process are inimical to features of military-oriented society, and the absence of these elements offers one type of evidence for a military-industrial complex even in the absence of a ruling elite. Secretary of Defense Robert McNamara made the point amply clear in his testimony in 1961 before the Senate Armed Services Committee:

Why should we tell Russia that the Zeus development may not be satisfactory? What we ought to be saying is that we have the most perfect anti-ICBM system that the human mind will ever devise. Instead the public domain is already full of statements that the Zeus may not be satisfactory, that it has deficiencies. I think it is absurd to release that level of information. (*Military Procurement Authorization Fiscal Year 1962*.)

Under subsequent questioning McNamara attempted to clarify his statement that he only wished to delude Russian, not American, citizens about U.S. might. Just how this might be done was not explained.

A long-established tradition exists for "executive privilege" which permits the President to refuse to release information when, in his opinion, it would be damaging to the national interest. Under modern conditions responsibility for handling information of a strategic nature is shared among military, industrial, and executive agencies. The discretion regarding when to withhold what information must also be shared. Moreover, the existence of a perpetual danger makes the justification, "in this time of national crisis," suitable to every occasion in which secrecy must be justified. McNamara's statement cited above referred not to a crisis in Cuba or Vietnam but rather to the perpetual state of cold-war crisis. And since the decision about what is to be released and when is subject to just such management, the media become dependent upon the agencies for timely leaks and major stories. This not only adds an aura of omniscience to the agencies, but gives these same agencies the power to reward "good" journalists and punish the critical ones.

The issues in the question of news management involve more than the elements of control available to the President, the State Department, the Department of Defense, the Central Intelligence Agency, the Atomic Energy Commission, or any of the major prime contractors of defense contracts. Outright control of news flow is probably less pervasive than voluntary acquiescence to the objectives of these prominent institutions of our society. Nobody has to tell the wire services when to release a story on the bearded dictator of our hemisphere or the purported brutality of Ho Chi Minh. A frequent model, the personified devil image of an enemy, has become a press tradition. In addition to a sizable quantity of radio and television programming and spot time purchased directly by the Pentagon, an amount of service, valued to $6 million by *Variety*, is donated annually by the networks and by public-relations agencies for various military shows (Swomley, 1959). Again, the pluralistic shell of an independent press or broadcasting media is left hollow by the absence of a countervailing social force of any significant power.

Several shared premises, unquestioned by any potent locus of institutionalized power, were described as:

1. Efficacy is preferable to principle in foreign affairs (thus military means are chosen over nonviolent means).
2. Private property is preferable to public property.
3. Limited parliamentary democracy is preferable to any other system of government.

At issue is the question of whether an America protecting such assumptions can exist in a world of enduring peace. Three pre-conditions of enduring peace must be held up against these premises.

The first is that enduring peace will first require or will soon generate disarmament. Offset programs for the reallocation of the defense dollar require a degree of coordinated planning for the change inconsistent with the working assumption that "private property is preferable to public property" in a corporate economy.

If one pools available projections regarding the offset programs, especially regional and local offset programs, necessary to maintain economic well-being in the face of disarmament in this country, the programs will highlight two important features. One is the lag time in industrial conversion. The second is the need for coordination in the timing and spacing of programs. One cannot reinvest in new home building in an area which has just been deserted by its major industry and left a ghost town. The short-term and long-term offset values of new hospitals and educational facilities will differ in the building and the utilization stages, and regional offset programs have demonstrable

interregional effects (Reiner, 1964). Plans requiring worker mobility on a large scale will require a central bank for storing job information and a smooth system for its dissemination. Such coordination will require a degree of centralization of controls beyond the realm which our assumption regarding primacy of private property would permit. Gross intransigence has already been seen even on the contingency planning for nondefense work by single firms like Sperry Rand which have already been severely hurt by project cutbacks. And the prospect of contingency planning will not be warmly welcomed in the newer aeroframe industry (which is only 60 percent convertible to needs of a peace-time society) (McDonagh and Zimmerman, 1964). Private planning by an individual firm for its own future does occur, but without coordinated plans, the time forecast for market conditions remains smaller than the lag time for major retooling. A lag time of from six to ten years would not be atypical before plans by a somewhat overspecialized defense contractor could result in retooling for production in a peacetime market. In the meantime, technological innovations, governmental fiscal or regulatory policies, shifts in consumer preferences, or the decisions by other firms to enter that same market could well make the market vanish. Moreover, the example of defense firms which have attempted even the smaller step toward diversification presents a picture which has not been entirely promising (Fearon and Hook, 1964). Indeed, one of several reasons for the failures in this endeavor has been that marketing skills necessary to compete in a private-enterprise economy have been lost by those industrial giants who have been managing with a sales force of one or two retired generals to deal with the firm's only customer. Even if the path of successful conversion by some firms were to serve as the model for all individual attempts, the collective result would be poor. To avoid a financially disastrous glutting of limited markets, some coordinated planning will be needed.

The intransigence regarding public or collaborative planning occurs against a backdrop of a soon-to-be increasing army of unemployed youth and aged, as well as regional armies of unemployed victims of automation. Whether one thinks of work in traditional job-market terms or as anything worthwhile that a person can do with his life, work (and some means of livelihood) will have to be found for these people. There is much work to be done in community services, education, public health, and recreation, but this is people work, not product work. The lack of a countervailing force prevents the major reallocation of human and economic resources from the sector defined as preferable by the most potent institutions of society. One point must be stressed. We are not saying that limited planning to cushion the impact of arms reduction is impossible. Indeed, it is going on and with the apparent blessing of the Department of Defense (Barber, 1963). We are saying that the type of accommodation needed by a cutback of $9 billion in R & D and $16 billion in military procurement requires a type of preparation not consistent with the unchallenged assumptions.

Even the existence of facilities for coordinated planning does not, to be sure, guarantee the success of such planning. Bureaucratic institutions, designed as they may be for coordination and control, do set up internal resistance to the very coordination they seek to achieve. The mechanisms for handling these bureaucratic intransigencies usually rely upon such techniques as bringing participants into the process of formulating the decisions which will affect their own behavior. We can conceive of no system of coordinated conversion planning which could function without full and motivated cooperation from the major corporations, the larger unions, and representatives of smaller business and industry. Unfortunately, it is just as difficult to conceive of a system which would assure this necessary level of participation and cooperation. This same argument cuts deeper still when we speak of the millions of separate individuals in the "other America" whose lives would be increasingly "administered" with the type of centralized planning needed to offset a defense economy. The job assignment which requires moving, the vocational retraining program, the development of housing projects to meet minimal standards, educational enrichment programs, all of the programs which are conceived by middle-class white America for racially mixed low-income groups, face the same difficulty in execution of plans. Without direct participation in the formulation of the programs, the target populations are less likely to participate in the programs and more likely to continue feelings of alienation from the social system which looks upon them as an unfortunate problem rather than as contributing members. Considering the need for active participation in real decisions, every step of coordinated planning carries with it the responsibility for an equal step in the direction of participatory democracy. This means that the voice of the unemployed urban worker may have to be heard, not only on city council meetings which discuss policy on the control of rats in his dwelling, but also on decisions about where a particular major corporation will be relocated and where the major resource allocations of the country will be invested. That such decision participation would run counter to the consensus on the items of limited parliamentary democracy and private property is exactly the point we wish to make.

Just as the theoretical offset plans can be traced to the sources of power with which they conflict, so too can the theoretical plans for international governing and peace-keeping operations be shown to conflict with the unquestioned beliefs. U.S. consent to international jurisdiction in the settlement of claims deriving from the nationalization of American overseas holdings or the removal of U.S. military installations is almost inconceivable. Moreover, the mode of American relations to less-developed countries is so much a part of the operations of those American institutions which base their existence upon interminable conflict with communism that the contingency in which the U.S. might have to face the question of international jurisdiction in these areas seems unreal. Offers to mediate, for example, with Cuba by Mexico, are bluntly rejected. Acceptance of such offers would have called into question not one but all three of the assumptions in the core system. International jurisdictional authority could institutionalize a means to call the beliefs into question. It is for this reason (but perhaps most directly because of our preference for forceful means) that American preoccupation in those negotiations regarding the extension of international control, which have taken place, deal almost exclusively with controls in the area of weaponry and police operations and not at all in the areas of political or social justice.[8]

The acceptance of complete international authority even in the area of weaponry poses certain inconsistencies with the preferred "core beliefs." Nonviolent settlement of Asian-African area conflicts would be slow and ineffective in protecting American interests. The elimination, however, of military preparedness, both for projected crises and for their potential escalation, requires a faith in alternate means of resolution. The phasing of the American plan

for general and complete disarmament is one which says in effect: prove that the alternatives are as efficient as our arms in protection of our interests and then we disarm. In the short term, however, the effectiveness of force always looks greater.

The state of world peace contains certain conditions imposed by the fact that people now compare themselves with persons who have more of the benefits of industrialization than they themselves. Such comparative reference groups serve to increase the demand for rapid change. While modern communications heighten the pressures imposed by such comparisons, the actual disparities revealed in comparison speak for violence. Population growth rates, often as high as 3 percent, promise population doubling within a single generation in countries least able to provide for their members. The absolute number of illiterates as well as the absolute number of persons starving is greater now than ever before in history. Foreign aid barely offsets the disparity between declining prices paid for the prime commodities exported by underdeveloped countries and rising prices paid for the finished products imported into these countries (Horowitz, 1962). All schemes for tight centralized planning employed by these countries to accrue and disperse scarce capital by rational means are blocked by the unchallenged assumptions on private property and limited parliamentary democracy. A restatement of the principle came in the report of General Lucius Clay's committee on foreign aid. The report stated that the U.S. should not assist foreign governments "in projects establishing government-owned industrial and commercial enterprises which compete with existing private endeavors." When Congressman Broomfield's amendment on foreign aid resulted in cancellation of a

---

[8] An objective account of the major negotiations related to disarmament which have taken place may be found in Frye (1963).

U.S. promise to India to build a steel mill in Bokaro, Broomfield stated the case succinctly: "The main issue is private enterprise vs. state socialism" (*The Atlantic,* September 1964, p. 6). Moreover, preference for forceful solutions assures that the capital now invested in preparedness will not be allocated in a gross way to the needs of underdeveloped countries. Instead, the manifest crises periodically erupting in violence justify further the need for reliance upon military preparedness.

We agree fully with an analysis by Lowi (1964) distinguishing types of decisions for which elite-like forces seem to appear and hold control (redistributive) and other types in which pluralist powers battle for their respective interests (distributive). In the latter type the pie is large and the fights are over who gets how much. Factional strife within and among military-industrial and political forces in our country are largely of this nature. In redistributive decisions, the factions coalesce, for the pie itself is threatened. We have been arguing that the transition to peace is a process of redistributive decision.

Is there, then, a military-industrial complex that prevents peace? The answer is inextricably embedded into the mainstream of American institutions and mores. Our concept is not that American society contains a ruling military-industrial complex. Our concept is more nearly that American society *is* a military-industrial complex. It can accommodate a wide range of factional interests from those concerned with the production or utilization of a particular weapon to those enraptured with the mystique of optimal global strategies. It can accommodate those with rabid desires to advance toward the brink and into limitless intensification of the arms race. It can even accommodate those who wish either to prevent war or to limit the destructiveness of war through the gradual achievement of arms control and disarmament agreements. What it cannot accommodate is the type of radical departures needed to produce enduring peace.

REFERENCES

Angell, Robert C., "A Study of Social Values: Content Analysis of Elite Media," *Journal of Conflict Resolution,* **8**:4 (1964), pp. 329–385.

Bank Holding Companies: Scope of Operations and Stock Ownership, Committee on Banking and Currency (Washington: U.S. Government Printing Office, 1963).

Barber, Arthur, "Some Industrial Aspects of Arms Control," *Journal of Conflict Resolution,* **7**:3 (1963), pp. 491–495.

Barnet, Richard, *The Economy of Death* (New York: Atheneum, 1969).

Bauer, Raymond A., I. Pool, and L. Dexter, *American Business and Public Policy* (Alberton, N.Y., 1963).

Bell, Daniel, *The End of Ideology* (Glencoe, Ill.: Free Press, 1959).

Benoit, Emile, and K. E. Boulding (eds.), *Disarmament and Economy* (New York: Harper, 1963).

Berle, Adolf A., *The Twentieth Century Capitalist Revolution* (New York: Harcourt, 1954).

Bluestone, Irving, "Problems of the Worker in Industrial Conversion," *Journal of Conflict Resolution,* **7**:3 (1963), pp. 495–502.

Brand, Horst, "Disarmament and American Capitalism," *Dissent* (Summer 1962), pp. 236–251.

Burdick, Eugene, and H. Wheeler, *Fail-safe* (New York: McGraw-Hill, 1962).

Burton, John, *Peace Theory* (New York: Knopf, 1962).

Cartwright, Dorwin, "Power: A Neglected Variable in Social Psychology," in D. Cartwright (ed.), *Studies in Social Power* (Ann Arbor: Research Center for Group Dynamics, 1959).

Catton, Bruce, *The War Lords of Washington* (New York: Harcourt, 1948).

Coffin, Tristran, *The Passion of the Hawks* (New York: Macmillan, 1964).

Cohen, Bernard C., *The Press and Foreign Policy* (Princeton: Princeton Univ. Press, 1963).

Convertibility of Space and Defense Resources to Civilian Needs, 88th Congress, 2nd Session, Vol. 2, Subcommittee on Employment and Manpower (Washington: U. S. Government Printing Office, 1964).

Cook, Fred J., "The Coming Politics of Disarmament," *The Nation* (February 6, 1963).

Cook, Fred J., *The Warfare State* (New York: Macmillan, 1962).

Dahl, Robert A., *A Modern Political Analysis* (New York: Prentice-Hall, 1963).

Dahl, Robert A. *Who Governs?* (New Haven: Yale Univ. Press, 1961).

Dillon, W., *Little Brother is Watching* (Boston: Houghton Mifflin, 1962).

Domhoff, G. William, "Who Made American Foreign Policy, 1945–1963?," in David Horowitz (ed.), *Corporations and the Cold War* (New York: Monthly Review Press, 1969), pp. 25–69.

Economic Impacts of Disarmament, U.S. Arms Control and Disarmament Agency, Economic Series 1 (Washington: U.S. Government Printing Office, 1962).

Eells, Richard, and C. Walton, *Conceptual Foundations of Business* (Homewood, Ill.: Irwin, 1961).

Etzioni, Amitai, *The Hard Way to Peace* (New York: Collier, 1962).

Etzioni, Amitai, *The Moon-doggle* (Garden City, N.Y.: Doubleday, 1964).

Fearon, H. E., and R. C. Hook, Jr., "The Shift from Military to Industrial Markets," *Business Topics* (Winter 1964), pp. 43–52.

Feingold, Eugene, and Thomas Hayden, "What Happened to Democracy?," *New University Thought*, **1** (Summer 1964), pp. 39–48.

Fisher, Roger (ed.), *International Conflict and Behavioral Science* (New York: Basic Books, 1964).

Fishman, Leslie, "A Note on Disarmament and Effective Demand," *Journal of Political Economy*, **70**:2 (1962), pp. 183–186.

Foreign Assistance Act of 1964 (Parts VI and VII), Committee on Foreign Affairs, Hearings, 88th Congress, 2nd Session (Washington: U.S. Government Printing Office, 1964).

Friedman, S., "The RAND Corporation and Our Policy Makers," *Atlantic Monthly*, (September 1963), pp. 61–68.

Frye, William R., "Characteristics of Recent Arms-Control Proposals and Agreements," in D. G. Brennan (ed.), *Arms Control, Disarmament, and National Security* (New York: Braziller, 1963).

Galbraith, J. K., *American Capitalism* (Boston: Houghton Mifflin, 1956).

Galbraith, J. K., "Poverty among Nations," *Atlantic Monthly* (October 1962), pp. 47–53.

Galbraith, J. K., *The New Industrial State* (New York: Signet, 1967).

Galbraith, J. K., *How to Control the Military* (Garden City, N.Y.: Doubleday, 1969).

Gans, Herbert J., "Some Proposals for Government Policy in an Automating Society," *The Correspondent*, **30** (January-February 1964), pp. 74–82.

Government Information Plans and Policies (Parts I–V), Hearings before a Subcommittee on Government Operations, 88th Congress, 1st Session (Washington: U.S. Government Printing Office, 1963).

Green, Philip, "Alternative to Overkill: Dream and Reality," *Bulletin of the Atomic Scientists* (November 1963), pp. 23–26.

Hayakawa, S. I., "Formula for Peace: Listening," *N.Y. Times Magazine* (July 31, 1961).

Heilbroner, Robert, "How the Pentagon Rules Us," *New York Review of Books*, **15**:2 (1970), pp. 5–6, 8.

Horowitz, David, *World Economic Disparities: The Haves and the Havenots* (Santa Barbara: Center for Study of Democratic Institutions, 1962).

Horowitz, I. L., *The War Game: Studies of the New Civilian Militarists* (New York: Ballantine, 1963).

Humphrey, Hubert H., "The Economic Impact of Arms-Control Agreements," *Congressional Record* (October 5, 1962), pp. 2139–2194.

Impact of Military Supply and Service Activities on the Economy, Report to the Joint Economic Committee, 88th Congress, 2nd Session (Washington: U.S. Government Printing Office, 1963).

Isard, Walter, and E. W. Schooler, "An Economic Analysis of Local and Regional Impacts of Reduction of Military Expenditures," *Papers, Vol. 1, 1964 Peace Research Society International*, Chicago Conference, 1963.

Janowitz, Morris, "Military Elites and the Study of War," *Journal of Conflict Resolution*, **1**:1 (1957), pp. 9-18.

Janowitz, Morris, *The Professional Soldier* (Glencoe, Ill.: Free Press, 1960).

Keller, Suzanne, *Beyond the Ruling Class* (New York: Random House, 1963).

Knebel, Fletcher, and C. Bailey, *Seven Days in May* (New York: Harper, 1962).

Knoll, Erwin, and Judith McFadden (eds.), *American Militarism 1970* (New York: Viking, 1969).

Knorr, Klaus, "Warfare and Peacefare States and the Acts of Transition," *Journal of Conflict Resolution*, **7**:4 (1963), pp. 754–762.

Lapp, Ralph E., *Kill and Overkill* (New York: Basic Books, 1962).

Lapp, Ralph E., *The Weapons Culture* (New York: Norton, 1968).

Larson, Arthur, *The International Rule of Law*, a report to the Committee on Research for Peace, Program of Research No. 3, Institute for International Order, 1961.

Lasswell, Harold, *Politics: Who Gets What, When & How* (New York: Meridian, 1958).

Lipset, Seymour M., *Political Man* (Garden City, N.Y.: Doubleday, 1959).

Little, Roger W., "Basic Education and Youth Socialization in the Armed Forces," *American Journal of Orthopsychiatry*, **38**:5 (1968), pp. 869–876.

Long Island Sunday Press (February 23, 1964).

Lowi, Theodore J., "American Business, Public Policy, Case Studies, and Political Theory," *World Politics* (July 1964), pp. 676–715.

Lumer, Hyman, *War Economy and Crisis* (New York: International Publishers, 1954).

Lynd, Robert S., and Helen Merrill, *Middletown* (New York: Harcourt, 1959).

McDonagh, James J., and Steven M. Zimmerman, "A Program for Civilian Diversifications of the Airplane Industry," in *Convertibility of Space and Defense Resources to Civilian Needs*, Subcommittee on Employment and Manpower, U.S. Senate, 88th Congress (Washington: U.S. Government Printing Office, 1964).

McNamara Robert S., "Remarks of the Secretary of Defense before the Economic Club of New York," Department of Defense Office of Public Affairs, Washington, November 18, 1963.

Mannheim, Karl, *Freedom, Power and Democratic Planning* (London: Routledge and Kegan Paul, 1956).

Meisel, James H., *The Fall of the Republic* (Ann Arbor: Univ. of Michigan Press, 1962).

Meisel, James H., *The Myth of the Ruling Class* (Ann Arbor: Univ. of Michigan Press, 1958).

Melman, Seymour (ed.), *A Strategy for American Security* (New York: Lee Offset Inc., 1963).

Melman, Seymour, *The Peace Race* (New York: Braziller, 1962).

Melman, Seymour, *Pentagon Capitalism* (New York: McGraw-Hill, 1970).

Merbaum R., "RAND: Technocrats and Power," *New University Thought* (December-January, 1963-64), pp. 45–57.

Michael, Donald, *Cybernation: the Silent Conquest* (Santa Barbara: Center for the Study of Democratic Institutions, 1962).

Milbrath, L. W., *The Washington Lobbyists* (Chicago: Rand McNally, 1963).

Military Posture and Authorizing Appropriations for Aircraft, Missiles, and Naval Vessels, Hearings No. 36, 88th Congress, 2nd Session (Washington: U.S. Government Printing Office, 1964).

Military Procurement Authorization Fiscal Year 1962, Hearings before the Committee on Armed Services, U.S. Senate, 87th Congress, 1st Session (Washington: U. S. Government Printing Office, 1961).

Mills, C. Wright, *The Causes of World War III* (New York: Simon & Schuster, 1958).

Mills, C. Wright, *The Power Elite* (New York: Oxford Univ. Press, 1959).

Minnis, Jack, "The Care and Feeding of Power Structures," *New University Thought*, **5**:1 (Summer 1964), pp. 73–79.

Mollenhoff, Clark R., *The Pentagon: Politics, Profits, and Plunder* (New York: Putnam, 1967).

Nossiter, Bernard, *The Mythmakers: An Essay on Power and Wealth* (Boston: Houghton Mifflin, 1964).

Osgood, Charles E., *An Alternative to War or Surrender* (Urbana: Univ. of Illinois Press, 1962).

Parsons, Talcott, *Structure and Process in Modern Societies* (Glencoe, Ill.: Free Press, 1959).

Parsons, Talcott, *The Social System* (Glencoe, Ill.: Free Press, 1951).

Paul, J., and J. Laulicht, "Leaders' and Voters' Attitudes on Defense and Disarmament, *In Your Opinion*, Vol. 1, Canadian Peace Research Institute, Clarkson, Ontario, 1963.

Peck, M. J., and F. M. Scherer, *The Weapons Acquisition Process* (Boston: Harvard Univ. Press, 1962).

Perlo, Victor, *Militarism and Industry* (New York: International Publishers, 1963).

Piel, Gerard, *Consumers of Abundance* (Santa Barbara: Center for the Study of Democratic Institutions, 1961).

Pilisuk, Marc, "Dominance of the Military," *Science* (January 18, 1963), pp. 247–248.

Pilisuk, Marc, "The Poor and the War on Poverty," *The Correspondent* (Summer 1965).

Pilisuk, Marc, "A Reply to Roger Little: Basic Education and Youth Socialization Anywhere Else," *American Journal of Orthopsychiatry*, **38**:5 (1968), pp. 877–881.

Progressive, The, "The Power of the Pentagon," **33**:6 (June 1969).

Pyramiding of Profits and Costs in the Missile Procurement Program (Parts 1, 2 and 3), Hearings, Committee on Government Operations, U.S. Senate, 87th Congress, 2nd Session (Washington: U.S. Government Printing Office, 1962).

Pyramiding of Profits and Costs in the Missile Procurement Program, Report No. 970, 88th Congress, 2nd Session (Washington: U.S. Government Printing Office, 1964).

Rapoport, Anatol, *Fights, Games, and Debates* (Ann Arbor: Univ. of Michigan Press, 1960).

Rapoport, Anatol, *Strategy and Conscience* (New York: Harper, 1964).

Raymond, Jack, *Power at the Pentagon* (New York: Harper, 1964).

Reagan, Michael, *The Managed Economy* (New York: Oxford, 1963).

Reiner, Thomas, "Spatial Criteria to Offset Military Cutbacks," paper presented at the University of Chicago Peace Research Conference, November 18, 1964.

"Report on the World Today," *The Atlantic* (September 1964), pp. 4–8.

Rogow, Arnold A., *James Forrestal* (New York: Macmillan, 1963).

Satellite Communications, 1964 (Part 1), Hearings, Committee on Government Operations, 88th Congress, 2nd Session (Washington: U.S. Government Printing Office, 1964).

Scherer, Frederick, *The Weapons Acquisition Process: Economic Incentives* (Cambridge, Mass.: Harvard Business School, 1964).

Shils, Edward, "Professor Mills on the Calling of Sociology," *World Politics*, **13**:4 (1961).

Singer, J. David, "A Study of Foreign Policy Attitudes," *Journal of Conflict Resolution*, **8**:4 (1964), pp. 424–485.

Singer, J. David, *Deterrence, Arms Control and Disarmament* (Columbus: Ohio State Univ. Press, 1962).

Singer, J. David (ed.), "Weapons Management in World Politics," *Journal of Conflict Resolution*, **7**:3; and *Journal of Arms Control*, **1**:4.

Stachey, John, *On the Prevention of War* (New York: St. Martin's Press, 1963).

Strauss, Lewis L., *Men and Decisions* (Garden City, N.Y.: Doubleday, 1962).

Sutton, Jefferson, *The Missile Lords* (New York: Dell, 1963).

Swomley, J. M., Jr., "The Growing Power of the Military," *The Progressive* (January 1959).

Swomley, J. M., Jr., *The Military Establishment* (Boston: Beacon, 1964).

Toward Full Employment: Proposals for a Comprehensive Employment and Man-power Policy in the U.S., a report of the Committee on Labor and Public Welfare, United States Senate (Washington: U.S. Government Printing Office, 1964).

Toward World Peace: A Summary of U.S. Disarmament Efforts Past and Present, U.S. Arms Control and Disarmament Agency Publication 10 (Washington: U.S. Government Printing Office, 1964).

Warner, William Floyd, and J. D. Abegglen, *Big Business Leaders in America* (New York: Harper, 1955).

Warner, William Lloyd, P. P. Van Riper, N. H. Martin, and O. F. Collins, *The American Federal Executive* (New Haven: Yale Univ. Press, 1963).

Watson-Watt, Sir Robert, *Man's Means to His End* (London: Heinemann, 1962).

Weidenbaum, Murray L., "Arms and the American Economy: A Domestic Emergence Hypothesis," *American Economic Review* (1968).

Westin, Alan, "Anti-Communism and the Corporations," *Commentary* (December 1963), pp. 479–487.

Wise, David, and Thomas Ross, *The Invisible Government* (New York: Random House, 1964).

Wright, Quincy, William Evans, and Morton Deutsch (eds.), *Preventing World War III: Some Proposals* (New York: Simon and Schuster, 1962).

ON THE DRAFT

Richard Flacks, Florence Howe, and Paul Lauter

At no time in its history has the draft been opposed, evaded, defied, studied, and pronounced upon with such energy and persistence as it is today. We now have the report of a presidential commission proposing extensive reforms, another report by a congressional commission endorsing most of the present system, and a book presenting the case for replacing the draft altogether by a voluntary army. Yet none of these proposals really deals with the reason why the draft is now a hot political issue: the war in Vietnam.

This war, more than most wars in American history, remains unpopular even with many who do not oppose it. Yet the Administration has been able to wage the war without serious political challenge, in part because of the power to conscript. Many young Americans, still raised to value personal liberty and democratic consent, feel forced by the draft to contribute to a war which they oppose and which is certainly not of their making or liking. Among men of draft age particularly, there is a mood of anger, resistance, and cynicism, and a rapid decline

Reprinted by permission from The New York Review of Books *(April 6, 1967), pp. 3–5; copyright © 1967 by The New York Review.*

of the draft's legitimacy. And for many left or liberal "doves," opposition to the war and opposition to the draft have become synonymous.

But for a much larger group, including Republicans and even some hawks, the war has served only to make visible the draft's inequities. Even now with over 400,000 American troops in Vietnam, the military needs—indeed, can use—only a minority of those eligible for the draft. Thus some men are conscripted for combat, while the majority remain free. Among men who are qualified—as the Marshall Commission points out—those who are white, middle class, and college-educated are likely to escape the mud and death in Southeast Asia, while those who are black, poor, and "unsuitable" for college die on battlefields at a rate double that of their proportion in the population. The economic and social biases of the draft seemed intolerable during cold war; to diverse groups, for various reasons, they are a disgrace during hot war.

Speaking with a traditional American outrage about bumbling and inequality, Bruce K. Chapman documents in *The Wrong Man in Uniform*[1] current complaints about the Selective Service System. Many abuses arise in the name of local autonomy. The bureaucratic jungle described by Chapman consists of over four thousand local draft boards which decide the fate of millions according to obscure criteria. Chapman finds great variation, from state to state, in the proportion of men who are classified as 1-F or who are, for a variety of reasons, deferred from serving. In one state, married men are vulnerable; elsewhere they are not. Peace Corps volunteers are deferred in New York, but drafted in Kansas. Illinois gives special consideration to mortuary trainees, but not Alabama. The system as a whole creaks with age, inbreeding, and inefficiency. Draft

board members, the Marshall Commission documents, are all male, mostly veterans and white-collar workers, and virtually all white —only 1.3 percent are Negro. Twenty-two percent of board members are over seventy years old; the average age is fifty-eight. Although Congress intended that Selective Service be controlled by civilians, its top officials are heavily military in orientation and training.

Recently, the system has begun to stumble over its own manipulations. A year ago, General Hershey claimed that the 1-A pool would be exhausted shortly, and that, therefore, some students would have to lose their deferments. Draft boards began demanding reports on class standings, and hundreds of thousands of students rushed to take the Selective Service qualification test. Some were reclassified; thousands enlisted; thousands more engaged in antidraft and "antiranking" sit-ins. But no manpower crisis did appear; by June 1966, it was clear that Selective Service had simply overestimated its needs by more than a third! According to Chapman, last Spring's crisis was the result of the temporary loss—in the bureaucratic "pipelines"—of 500,000 men classified 1-A. Whether this is so or not, the entire sequence of events dramatized the draft's power to touch even the university sanctuary. General Hershey may have meant to relieve political pressure by publicizing the potential vulnerability of students. But the effect was to provoke students into opposition to the draft—despite the fact that they have been among its chief beneficiaries.

A reader of Chapman's book concludes, correctly, that the present Selective Service System creates a great many absurd inequities because of decentralization as well as the deferment system itself; that it creates enormous uncertainty and unnecessary anxiety for millions; and that it is, moreover, inefficient from the military point of view,

[1] Trident, 143 pp.

since it fails to recruit men with a stable commitment to service.

What Chapman and similar critics miss is that the Selective Service System is *designed* this way—its "flaws" are not accidental, but viewed by its administrators as necessary to its effective operation. For, over the years, General Hershey has evolved the idea that Selective Service functions not primarily for the "delivery of manpower for induction .... It is in dealing with the other millions of registrants that the System is heavily occupied, developing more effective human beings in the national interest."[2] Occupational and student deferments, therefore, are tools to deal with the "ever-increasing problem of how to control the service of individuals who are not in the armed services." In short, young men unfortunately desire to determine their own careers; such unreliable and unpredictable impulses can and must be disciplined and "channeled." Selective Service describes the process:

Educators, scientists, engineers, and their professional organizations ... have been convincing the American public that for the mentally qualified man there is a special order of patriotism other than service in uniform—that for the man having the capacity, dedicated service as a civilian in such fields as engineering, the sciences, and teaching constitutes the ultimate in their expression of patriotism. A large segment of the American public has been convinced that this is true. . . .

It is in this atmosphere that the young man registers at age 18 and pressure begins to force his choice. . . .

The psychological effect of this circumstantial climate depends upon the individual, his sense of good sportsmanship, his love of country and

its way of life. He can obtain a sense of well-being and satisfaction that he is doing as a civilian what will help his country most. . . .

In the less patriotic and more selfish individual it engenders a sense of fear, uncertainty and dissatisfaction which motivates him, nevertheless, in the same direction. He complains of the uncertainty which he must endure; he would like to be able to do as he pleases; he would appreciate a certain future with no prospect of military service or civilian contribution, but he complies with the needs of the national health, safety, or interest—or is denied deferment.

Throughout his career as a student, the pressure—the threat of loss of deferment—continues. It continues with equal intensity after graduation. His local board requires periodic reports to find out what he is up to. He is impelled to pursue his skill rather than embark upon some less important enterprise and is encouraged to apply his skill in essential activity in the national interest. The loss of deferred status is the consequence for the individual who acquired the skill and either does not use it or uses it in a non-essential activity.

The psychology of granting wide choice under pressure to take action is the *American or indirect way of achieving what is done by direction in foreign countries where choice is not permitted.* [Italics added.]

There it is—the lives of American men could not be better described. Are you in a state of perpetual worry about military service? Do you feel yourself pushed into a way of life against which your deeper impulses rebel? Would you rather be a poet than a graduate student in English, an organizer in the ghetto than a law student? Would you like to lumberjack or bum around Europe or "tune in and drop out" or just be free this year? Your anxieties and frustrations are not accidental; U.S. gov-

---

[2] These and the following quotations are taken from the *Selective Service Orientation Kit* memo on "Channeling" (April 1965); available from Chief, Public Information, Selective Service System, 1724 F Street, Washington, D.C. We are indebted to Jean Carper and Peter Henig for drawing our attention to these statements. More detailed analysis of "channeling" may be found in P. Henig, "On the Manpower Channelers," *New Left Notes* (January 20, 1967); and in a forthcoming book on the draft by Jean Casper (*Bitter Greetings*, Grossman).

ernment policy, as interpreted by General Hershey, creates them. And if you happen to rub your eyes and ask, "Tell me, again, what exactly are our objections to totalitarian collectivism?" the answer is really very simple: the American way is the indirect way.

Several years ago, some Republican congressmen began to sense the political potential in the inequitable, inefficient, and undemocratic Selective Service System, and to demand its abolition and replacement by a volunteer army. Similar proposals were urged by a few Democrats like Gaylord Nelson of Wisconsin. Barry Goldwater suggested, during the election campaign of 1964, that a volunteer army was feasible. In response to these early stirrings, President Johnson ordered a study conducted by the Department of Defense. Never fully published, the Pentagon study argued essentially in defense of the present system and against a volunteer force, primarily because of the huge sums needed to hire an army of sufficient size.

But these arguments have not silenced an increasingly articulate and cohesive Republican campaign against conscription and for a volunteer army. Chapman, a leader in the "Progressive Republican" Ripon Society, has provided ammunition for several representatives such as Thomas Curtis and Donald Rumsfeld, as Congress has moved toward a major debate on the draft this session. On this issue, liberal Republicans find common ground with Goldwater conservatives. Professor Milton Friedman, Goldwater's economic advisor, judges that the price of a volunteer army would be substantially lower than Pentagon estimates; and he is supported by the economist Walter Oi, who prepared part of the Defense De-

partment's study. Friedman argues further that men in the armed forces support much of the real cost of the draft by a hidden "direct tax" on their labor, which they are forced to contribute at a price far below its true worth. The pay of an army private, Chapman asserts, is little more than that of a Rumanian peasant on a collective farm. Housing, especially for men with families, ranges from deplorable to insipid; post amenities are primitive; social life, rigid and sterile. Give men freedom to choose, pay them a decent wage (say, $5000 as a minimum), improve their working conditions, offer fringe benefits—in short, apply the techniques of effective business practice—and you will produce an efficient, stable military work force at a socially acceptable cost, and remove a major source of compulsion from the lives of young men.

In response to this developing Republican position, to widespread criticism of the stand-pat Pentagon report, and to growing student protest, President Johnson appointed the "blue-ribbon" Commission[3] headed by Burke Marshall to conduct still another study. The result is a recommendation which would essentially abolish General Hershey's channeling system. So many young men turn eighteen every year (1,800,000 now and over 2 million by 1970), that student and occupational deferments are no longer needed to ensure adequate supplies of manpower in "essential" occupations. To deal with the problem of how to select the minority of available men needed for the military, the Marshall Commission proposes what amounts to a lottery. Their system of random selection is designed to make everybody feel a lot better: it will strike only a fraction of the young, even during a war as large as the present one; it will reduce the

---

[3] *In Pursuit of Equity: Who Serves When Not All Serve?*, report of the President's National Advisory Commission on Selective Service, Burke Marshall, Chairman (Washington: U.S. Government Printing Office), 219 pp.

political problems of current inequities by drawing, with equal arbitrariness, from all races, areas, economic levels. At the same time, complaints about "uncertainty" can be eliminated by drafting younger men first who, in the view of the military, are more malleable anyway.

The Commission proposes to centralize the selection system, replacing idiosyncratic local draft boards with computers that will apply uniform national standards to all registrants. In addition, the Commission recommends the creation of several hundred regional appeals boards, its members to be representative of "all elements of the public," including women, and to serve for no longer than five-year terms. The Commission wants to see local boards function mainly to help registrants appeal their draft status (presumably those with hardship cases, or those wanting to avoid the draft by becoming career officers); it wants to make sure that the claims of conscientious objectors are handled expeditiously (in part, probably, because the present system can be used to stall the draft for up to two years); it wants to make sure that the public understands the working of a new, improved system. In short, the Marshall report would modernize Selective Service by making it more uniform and equitable, more impersonal in its selection, and more inclusive of a wide spectrum of society in its operation. It is a clean, almost surgical effort to eliminate the most laughable and disgusting particularities of the draft as we know it. Besides, it has the distinct virtue that most of its central proposals can be implemented by presidential fiat and without awkward congressional debate.

But the Marshall Commission report implies no departure from the present goals and priorities of American society. It does not suggest how a country which devotes its public resources largely to war can deal with the fundamental problems of social inequality. Instead, it implies that military institutions can be used to patch over the effects of racism; thus, it wants the military to make special efforts to recruit and "rehabilitate" poor youths who are ordinarily rejected because they do not meet induction standards. All eighteen-year-old men would undergo physical, mental, and moral tests. "This universal testing," the Commission comments, "would meet social as well as military needs." In other words, draft registration can be used as a framework for a program of regimented social rehabilitation.

The Marshall Commission would seem to reduce government interference in the lives of young men by abolishing the privileged treatment now given to students and workers in certain occupations. But what will its impact be? The pressure now generated by America's international posture—to coordinate individual lives and careers, to plan "manpower utilization"—seems more irresistible than the Marshall Commission can acknowledge. In the long run, it is unlikely that people will tolerate a system in which a fraction of the young make supreme sacrifices because they have lost a game of roulette. Waiting in the wings are proposals for vast programs of "national service," in which youth will be "expected" to serve as police cadets, teachers, job corpsmen, peace corpsmen, and so on—if they are not inducted. The Commission wants to draw sharp distinctions between military service and "national service," and seems to consider the latter politically impossible at present and of dubious constitutionality. But by reducing the vulnerability of many young men to military service, the Marshall proposal will make national service seem more desirable than ever to those who wring their hands at the individualism, the "lack of patriotism," and the "privatism" of young people.

One of the main hand-wringers, Margaret Mead, describes national service at work:

Every individual, including the physically handicapped, the mentally defective, the emotionally

disturbed, the totally illiterate, would be registered, and every one of these, according to their
needs or potentialities, would be assigned to
types of rehabilitation, education, and different
kind of service with different sorts of risks, benefits, and requirements.

Oddly, despite this description, national-
service advocates persist in calling the system "voluntary." To deal with at least two
million new men annually (to say nothing
of women), the system would require an
enormous federal bureaucracy, fantastic expenditures for training and maintenance,
and expansion of service opportunities beyond anything now imaginable. Besides,
service is probably best rendered by those
who freely give it.

Above all, national service—perhaps servi-
tude is a more appropriate term—would
mean an enormous jump in the degree of
control by a central authority over the lives
of Americans. Assignments to the military,
to service, or to rehabilitation would finally
be made not according to individual ability
or interest, but by a centralized manpower
planning commission, according to established definitions of national priorities. In
this light, national service can be seen as
the present draft writ large: "channeling"
no longer applied "indirectly"—the "American way"—but by compulsion. The system
becomes a machine, in which men are considered as a "national resource," to be developed, channeled, enriched, molded, utilized, exploited, and above all, nationalized
—in the public interest, to be sure. This is a
high and totalitarian price to pay for "social-
izing" unruly youth, controlling early marriage, and eliminating the "sense of unfair-
ness" people feel about the draft.

The Marshall proposal is, in fact, the most
suitable design for an America which intends to consolidate and extend its worldwide military power. Sophisticated strategists in the national leadership believe that
continuing commitments to "stop communism" and to contain revolutions wherever
these occur are militarily and technologi-

cally feasible. There is, however, the problem of how the American people will take
to the role of world policeman. How will
we react to fairly continuous war of one sort
or another run by a huge military establishment? One danger, of course, is an outbreak
of irrational and irresponsible mass jingoism, which could push toward a nuclear
confrontation with the "enemy." At the opposite pole, disruptive protest and disaffection might prove embarrassing or worse.
The Marshall plan meshes nicely with the
"Great Society" at home: it requires no
mass mobilization of the populace, and it
enables the draft to affect only a random
fraction of the young. A volunteer army
would accomplish the same results. But the
Marshall Commission rejects a voluntary
system, primarily because it is not sufficiently
"flexible" to meet the possibility of "crises"
which require "the rapid procurement of
larger numbers of men." That is, a voluntary system might inhibit escalation of wars
like the one in Vietnam.

The Marshall Commission is probably
right in thinking that the volunteer alternative is impossible within the context of present American foreign policy. For although
it makes small-scale military operations even
more simple (hardly anyone will worry if a
few thousand hired hands are shipped off),
it does require a somewhat smaller military
force than the Pentagon has grown accustomed to having at its disposal. More important, what if escalation becomes necessary? Congress would then have to consider
reinstituting conscription; public debate
would then ensue; normally secure National
Guardsmen and Reservists might have to be
called, and months might pass before the
new system got men into the field. From the
perspective of the liberal establishment,
which the Marshall Commission perfectly
represents, the volunteer proposal combines
the imperialist flavor of a mercenary army
with the isolationist quest for a mechanism
to restrain strong (irresponsible, interven-
tionist) presidents. The Marshall proposals

are thus the right ones, *if* one conceives that the most important problem is how to maintain a huge military force, capable of a variety of overseas activities, while keeping the American population at peace.

But for those who are opposed to American interventions and are in favor of disarmament and radical social change in countries where the U.S. stands against it, the draft debate as it is crystallizing becomes increasingly frustrating. How can a choice be made between a system based on Russian roulette and a professional army? Both perpetuate the illusion that Pax Americana is possible. The voluntary army, its opponents say, might intensify caste barriers among the young; it could become a black and poor man's army, could increase the insulation of the military from civilian control (though we already have, in effect, a professional army—with access to conscripts). On the other hand, the volunteer army does seem to offer the slim chance of restraining the president by making mobilization more difficult and more a matter for congressional and public debate. It does remove the undemocratic effects of the draft. Furthermore it would free many men now bound to school by the channeling system to pursue their talents in their own way. It would make it possible for them to move off the campus in order to make something of the thousands of opportunities for catalyzing social change in American communities. The voluntary system is better than the Marshall Commission's draft; just as the Marshall proposal is better than continuing the present system. But all of these proposals avoid the real problem, which is the nature of American foreign policy. A debate about how to raise an army cannot help but be sterile, and finally, unreal, if it evades the question of how the army is to be used.

Ignored by all these proposals, the question of fighting a dirty little war agitates young people in America, who increasingly refuse to participate in the Vietnam war.

Thousands avoid the draft by subterfuge or by managing student, law, or divinity deferments. Mohammed Ali's struggles with Selective Service, chronicled on every sports page in the nation, have educated more young men on how to evade the draft than all the antiwar organizations together. Richard Paterack, a former VISTA volunteer, continues his service to Americans in Canada, where he aids hundreds of others who are also fleeing conscription. David Harris, president of Stanford University's student body, said that going to jail "should be considered a normal part of growing up in America." Many are demonstrating the truth of Harris's statement: the "Fort Hood Three," who have refused orders to go to Vietnam; Specialist Fourth Class Harry Muir, grand-nephew of former Navy Secretary Josephus Daniels, who has refused to wear his uniform; David Miller, the first man to be jailed for burning his draft card; David Mitchell, also jailed after American judges, who established the Nuremberg precedent, rejected his defense based on it. And an increasing number of "We Won't Go" groups, some of them organized by Students for a Democratic Society, have declared their intention to resist the draft and are, in defiance of the law, organizing others to do so.

Those resisting the draft express a new mood, a different concept of heroism. It is a mood in some ways projected by John Kennedy shortly after his World War II service. "War will exist," he said, "until that distant day when the conscientious objector enjoys the same reputation and prestige that the warrior does today." The Marshall Commission has dimly perceived something of the force—and threat—of this mood:

The majority felt that a legal recognition of selective pacifism could be disruptive to the morale and effectiveness of the armed forces. A determination of the justness or unjustness of any war could only be made within the context of that war itself. Forcing upon the individual the necessity of making that distinction—which would be the practical effect of taking away the

Government's obligation of making it for him—could put a burden heretofore unknown on the man in uniform and even on the brink of combat, with results that could be disastrous to him, to his unit, and to the entire military tradition.

Exactly. If individuals are free to make up their own minds about whether or not they will participate in a nation's wars, that would indeed undermine the very goals the Commission's report is so carefully designed to serve.

It seems to us, then, that the issue of the draft comes down not simply and narrowly to how we raise an army. Rather, it is whether the nation will give priority to personal freedom and to building social equality, or to maintaining a policy requiring military intervention on a world scale. In trying to raise *this* issue, perhaps the self-exile, the draft-card burner, the conscientious objector, and the war resister expose what the new draft proposals mask.

3

Pax Americana, the American Empire, and the Third World

GLOBALISM

The Editors

This section examines the implications of American military power and the concomitant cold-war ideology on the other areas of the world, particularly those areas that historically have been under colonial domination by the great powers. In the beginnings of British, Spanish, and French colonialism, the ethical issues of exploitation of poor people were not raised. Poor people were considered neither clean nor Christian nor suited to rule themselves. Five centuries of almost invariably exploitative rule of these people and of the territories they occupy have not bettered their lot. Now they represent a majority of the world's population. They live in shoddy sections of cities surrounding foreign-owned industrial firms or, more frequently, as landless servants in their own countries. For years the poor have survived in their separate cultural settings on a set of values more familially and community oriented than our own and less dependent upon the Western criteria of individual success in the marketplace. But certain factors in the lives of the poor have changed.

First, and perhaps most important, the number of poor people has increased so greatly over their food productivity that malnutrition has become a fact of their daily existence and the specter of mass starvation is imminent. There exists a delicate dependency between the continuity of human life and the manner in which man manages and allocates resources. This perspective is clearly seen in Huxley's "The Politics of Ecology." Among the most affluent countries, there exists a pattern of allocation of resources essentially incongruous with the needs for clean air, clean water, and especially for food. The misallocation of resources is so great that the precarious balance which protects the survival of regions and of races is in danger of being upset. One source of misallocation, from the ecological perspective, lies in the cost of warfare. Currently, the world military budget is equivalent to the entire income of the poorer half of the world's population.

In addition to the change in numbers, there is an increasing income gap between the impoverished colored majority and both their white Western neighbors and the self-serving aristocracies of their countries. While the impoverished have grown poorer or remained the same, their aristocratic enclaves have grown wealthier, as has the affluent Western world.

We do not fully understand why poverty exists, whether the basic or prime deficiency is in education or in capital for industrial investment, in agricultural productivity or in control of the size of families, in job-training opportunities or in the individualistic type of motivation to achieve, excel, succeed, and save for the future. It is clear to the economist, however, that the cost of prime commodities, the exports of poorer countries, has been dropping, while the cost of manufactured goods which these countries must import has been going up. This has amounted to a form of subsidization of the rich nations by the poorer ones. Portions of the deficit are compensated for by foreign aid. However, foreign aid has been largely in the form of credits to foreign governments to purchase American-made weapons. At any rate foreign aid has not been of the type or of the scope sufficient to combat international poverty. But whatever the cause or causes of poverty, the modern revolution in communication has made the income gap highly visible and, perhaps not unexpectedly, a majority of the world's population is in a state of incipient or active revolution.

The policy of selling American arms abroad is a relic of the Dulles foreign policy which sought a "containment" of communism through a series of military security treaties with other nations. Whatever the intention, the weapons have not deterred the formation of revolutionary communist movements. One factor in this failure has been the very misallocation of resources away from the needed domestic production. Such allocations permit nations like India and Pakistan to face each other militarily, as in the Kashmir disputes, both using American weapons and both in dire need of economic uplifting. In Jordan, which purchases Lockheed F-184 supersonic fighter bombers at approximately $2 million each, the annual per-capita income is $233. The planes are said to be needed to offset the sale of American arms to Israel.

Apart from whether such major overseas suppliers as General Dynamics, Lockheed, and McDonald Aircraft could survive a change in this policy, it seems rather clear that a number of the newer countries are expending their intellectual, as well as their material, resources on weapon procurement in preference to nation development. In some instances the younger intellectual leaders of the poorer nations resent the weapons priority.

The resentment reflects yet another difference from the period of unquestioning colonialism. The underdeveloped areas have evolved into nations. The newer and more popular leaders have been influenced by the ideologies of the American revolution as well as the teachings of Marxist socialism. They have great nationalistic pride and a resentment against being used as pawns in a power struggle among larger powers. The thrust of the poorer nations to develop an identity independent of the East-West conflict has led to their common designation as "the third world."

Resentment by third-world rulers is not always visible. A large measure of the military and paramilitary assistance goes directly to aristocratic or military elites and provides them with the means to suppress revolutionary movements aimed at land reform, at nationalization of exploitative industries, at modifications in the tax structure, at domestic rule, or at the ruling elites themselves. Conor Cruise O'Brien, a former Irish delegate to the United Nations, criticizes the tacit assumption of American strategic thought, *viz.*, that revolutions are exportable commodities which may be turned on from afar by communist states intent upon aggrandizement through military subversion. What seems to be ignored in this formulation of the problem are the economic and social conditions that make revolutions necessary. Ignored also is the extent of local support of revolutionary movements that is needed for their success. Forgotten entirely is the fact that, in accordance with American founding precepts of popular rule, such support makes revolution legitimate.

In developed countries it is possible to imagine a social revolution without violent revolution. In those parts of the world where the impoverished are a vast majority, any meaningful social change is at the expense of a privileged aristocracy of landowners or of the new merchant sweat-shop owners and political bosses who assure cheap labor to foreign firms. These ruling classes reign behind a wall of parasitic bureaucrats and a paid army which, because it is not always trustworthy, must be augmented by foreign mercenaries. Under such circumstances there tends to be no social change without a political one and no political change without force.

The American response has been to favor social revolution, at least verbally. When verbal exhortation fails, the United States then favors no revolution and American experts decide for the people of another country just when their revolution is not in their own best interests.

... the expert, for example, on what form a revolution in Cuba should take is not Fidel Castro but Arthur M. Schlesinger, Jr., who, among others, discovered it had been betrayed. Mr. Schlesinger, a connoisseur it seems not merely of revolution but of counterrevolution, has told us in *A Thousand Days* that when the Bay of Pigs operation was under way, the unfortunate Cubans who were supposed to be leading the insurrection drew up a manifesto for distribution in Cuba. The manifesto was aimed, not surprisingly, at eliciting the support of people who had lost money in the revolution, and was apparently judged insufficiently Cuban and revolutionary by Mr. Schlesinger and his colleagues in Washington. So they sent it to two Harvard Latin American experts who rewrote it, putting in a lot of nice liberal notions about Negroes and the like, and in this form it was put out in the name of the corrected Cubans. How the improved manifesto sounded in Havana I don't know, but it certainly sounded a lot better at Harvard, and that was the point. In the lapidary words of the celebrated discoverer of Parkinson's Law, "All propaganda begins, and ends, at home." (O'Brien, 1966.)

It is not the Marxist direction of these revolutions that makes them anti-American. Various socialist and communist countries have better relations with some Western capitalistic countries than with each other. What accounts for the high level of anti-American feeling is the American operation of policing other countries on behalf of unpopular ruling elites.

There have been numerous involvements by the United States in response to revolutionary movements. Some like the Dominican and Lebanon cases have involved direct and open landing of American military forces. More frequently, as in Cuba, Guatemala, Indonesia, British Guiana, and probably Nigeria, the involvement has been largely through the clandestine activities of the Central Intelligence Agency and the Defense Intelligence Agency. There techniques have involved the support and training of local police, the secret subsidization of foreign students and labor unions, and even the bombing of foreign cities with disguised planes. Such operations have included the use of "black radio" employing false radio signals to coerce government officials into surrendering by making them believe their supporters had already given up, and the careful screening of international information, not only from our adversaries but from our own press and from our own United Nations ambassador as well (Wise and Ross, 1964). In Greece and in Brazil the combination of American investors, American paramilitary operations, and local aristocracies has produced a rule by torture which shatters the sensibilities of civilized humanity.

In the late 1950s a number of high-prestige commissions in and out of government were coming to similar conclusions. Representing the wealthiest and most powerful elite of American society, the Rockefeller and Gaither Committees and the Council on Foreign Relations were calling for an end to American reliance on the nuclear arms race. They were heralding in a policy directed at the underdeveloped ex-colonial nations. While ballistic-missile nuclear deterrence was to remain the bulwark of a defense against surprise attack, the new thrust of military policy would go into developing all manner of conventional warfare and of developing novel means to fight against wars of national liberation. The task involved a major development of counterinsurgency training, increased research into chemical and bacteriological warfare, the development of pacification programs, psychological warfare, and espionage techniques, and the utilization of special economic and police assistance to command allegiance to governments sympathetic to American military and corporate interests. The process is described in detail in Marc Pilisuk's *International Conflict and Social Policy* (1971). The present chapter will highlight some case illustrations of the practice.

The most extensive involvement by the United States in the intervention in a revolutionary movement has occurred in Vietnam. Martin Nicolaus in "The Professor, the Policeman, and the Peasant" describes the nature of the early involvement. The details of the case highlight both the assumptions and the tactics of the policy. While the costs have been heavier in the Vietnam case, the strategy shows marked similarity to that of the Soviet Union at the time of the Hungarian uprisings in 1956: support an unpopular "puppet regime" to abet one's own military posture, and fulfill "commitments" to the "legal" puppet to protect it from its own population. Hungary and Vietnam are similar also in that neither revolt began as anti-communist or as anti-western. Both were nationalistic in objectives. Both were said to be sparked by alien agitators, who were said to be solely responsible for the unrest. Yet suppression has left a legacy of extreme anti-Soviet feeling among the Hungarian refugees even now after many objectives of the revolt have been conceded. Similarly, anti-Americanism in Vietnam has become very prevalent and will endure beyond the period of fighting. It is through such reactions that force as a technique of international relations comes frequently to beget further force, and the war to end wars becomes mythology.

In a later article in *Viet-Report,* Nicolaus (1966) describes what the involvement in secret, counterinsurgency work has meant to the academic standards of the university and to the participants themselves. However, the consequences for the domestic character of the United States, as the global counterrevolutionary policeman, go beyond the involvement of small numbers of academicians on specific "classified" projects. The early detection of a revolt, which can be defused, controlled, or managed before it gains momentum, requires a far greater mobilization of domestic energies. Project Camelot was a large social-science endeavor aimed at early detection of revolutionary unrest. When its source of funding (the U.S. Army) leaked out, the showdown in the Chilean Senate brought the program to an embarrassing halt (Horowitz, 1965). The basic corruption of the academic purpose for paramilitary objectives has been reiterated at many levels. This is seen again in DuBoff's review of "U.S. Policy: The Third World," one among several influential treatises providing the policy rationale for counterinsurgency. The low regard for life and the arrogant assumption that American interests and ideas are inherently right for other countries (regardless of their own popular attitudes) is particularly striking.

The final selection by Goff and Locker reveals a second "hidden hand" behind counterrevolutionary moves. If the CIA conducts one set of clandestine operations, the corporate business community appears to conduct another. The poverty in the Dominican Republic and its radical change movements reflect the omnipresence of the sugar industry. In other countries it is oil or bauxite, but the model of international corporate cartels dominating poor countries, dealing directly with their governments, and bringing in U.S. marines when their interests are shaky is a factor as basic to American foreign policy as is the bureaucratic expansion of the military and defense contracting. It is in the coalition between corporate interests, ongoing military and paramilitary programs, and the intellectuals and state department officials who rationalize American intervention that we see the basis of attempts to control the directions of an impoverished and struggling world under an enforced "pax Americana."

REFERENCES AND ADDITIONAL READING

Barnet, Richard J., *The Economy of Death* (New York: Atheneum, 1969).

Boulding, Kenneth, "After Civilization, What?," *Bulletin of the Atomic Scientists* (October 1962), pp. 2–6.

Brightman, Carol, "The 'Weed Killers,' " *Viet-Report,* **2** (June-July 1966) , pp. 9–14.

Buckhout, Robert, "The American Presence in Thailand: Seeds of Escalation," unpublished ms.

Domhoff, William, "Who Made American Foreign Policy, 1945–1953," in David Horowitz (ed.), *Corporations and the Cold War* (New York: Monthly Review Press, 1969), pp. 25–69.

Editors of Ramparts, "3 Tales of the CIA," *Ramparts* (April 1967), pp. 15–28.

Fam, K. T., and D. C. Hodges, *Readings in American Imperialism* (Boston: Porter Sargent, 1970).

Galbraith, John Kenneth, "The Poverty of Nations," *Atlantic* (March 1962), pp. 47–54.

Gordon, Kermit (ed.), *Agenda for the Nation* (Washington: Brookings Institution, 1968).

Horowitz, Irving Louis, "The Life and Death of Project Camelot," *Trans-action*, **3** (November 1965), pp. 3–7; reproduced in R. Perrucci and M. Pilisuk (eds.), *The Triple Revolution: Social Problems in Depth* (Boston: Little, Brown, 1968), pp. 35–47.

Jacoby, Neil, "The Multi-National Corporation," *The Center Magazine*, **3** (May 1970), pp. 37–54.

McCarthy, Eugene J., "The U. S.: Supplier of Weapons to the World," *Saturday Review* (July 9, 1966), pp. 13–16.

McDermott, John, "Two Programs for South Vietnam," *Viet-Report*, **2** (February 1966), pp. 3–10.

Melman, Seymour, *Pentagon Capitalism: The Political Economy of War* (New York: McGraw-Hill, 1969).

Nicolaus, Martin, "The Professor, the Policeman, and the Peasant—II," *Viet-Report*, **2** (March–April 1966) , pp. 3–8ff.

O'Brien, Conor Cruise, "The Counterrevolutionary Reflex," *Columbia University Forum*, **9**:2 (Spring 1966); reproduced in R. Perrucci and M. Pilisuk (eds.), *The Triple Revolution: Social Problems in Depth* (Boston: Little, Brown, 1968), pp. 136–141.

Pilisuk, Marc, *International Conflict and Social Policy* (Englewood Cliffs, N.J.: Prentice-Hall, 1971).

Salam, Abdus, "Diseases of the Rich and Diseases of the Poor," *Bulletin of the Atomic Scientists* (April 1963), p. 3ff.

Wald, George, "Corporate Responsibility for War Crimes," *New York Review of Books*, **15** (July 1970), pp. 4–6.

Wise, David, and Thomas B. Ross, *The Invisible Government* (New York: Random House, 1964).

THE POLITICS OF ECOLOGY

Aldous Huxley

In politics, the central and fundamental problem is the problem of power. Who is to exercise power? And by what means, by what authority, with what purpose in view, and under what controls? Yes, under what controls? For, as history has made it abundantly clear, to possess power is *ipso facto* to be tempted to abuse it. In mere self-preservation we must create and maintain institutions that make it difficult for the powerful to be led into those temptations which, succumbed to, transform them into tyrants at home and imperialists abroad.

For this purpose what kind of institutions are effective? And, having created them, how can we guarantee them against obsolescence? Circumstances change and, as they change, the old, the once so admirably effective, devices for controlling power cease to be adequate. What then? Specifically, when advancing science and acceleratingly progressive technology alter man's long-established relationship with the planet on which he lives, revolutionize his societies, and at the same time equip his rulers with new and immensely more powerful instruments of domination, what ought we to do? What *can* we do?

Very briefly let us review the situation in which we now find ourselves and, in the light of present facts, hazard a few guesses about the future.

On the biological level, advancing science and technology have set going a revolutionary process that seems to be destined for the next century at least, perhaps for much longer, to exercise a decisive influence upon the destinies of all human societies and their individual members. In the course of the last fifty years extremely effective methods for lowering the prevailing rates of infant and adult mortality were developed by Western scientists. These methods were very simple and could be applied with the expenditure of very little money by very small numbers of not very highly trained technicians. For these reasons, and because everyone regards life as intrinsically good and death as intrinsically bad, they were in fact applied on a worldwide scale. The results were spectacular. In the past, high birth rates were balanced by high death rates. Thanks to science, death rates have been halved but, except in the most highly industrialized, contraceptive-using countries, birth rates remain as high as ever. An enormous and accelerating increase in human numbers has been the inevitable consequence.

At the beginning of the Christian era, so demographers assure us, our planet supported a human population of about two hundred and fifty millions. When the Pilgrim Fathers stepped ashore, the figure had risen to about five hundred millions. We see, then, that in the relatively recent past it took sixteen hundred years for the human species to double its numbers. Today world population stands at three thousand millions. By the year 2000, unless something appallingly bad or miraculously good should

Reprinted by permission from The Center Magazine, **2**:2 *(March 1969), a publication of the Center for the Study of Democratic Institutions, Santa Barbara, Calif.*

happen in the interval, six thousand million of us will be sitting down to breakfast every morning. In a word, twelve times as many people are destined to double their numbers in one-fortieth of the time.

This is not the whole story. In many areas of the world human numbers are increasing at a rate much higher than the average for the whole species. In India, for example, the rate of increase is now 2.3 percent per annum. By 1990 its four hundred and fifty million inhabitants will have become nine hundred million inhabitants. A comparable rate of increase will raise the population of China to the billion mark by 1980. In Ceylon, in Egypt, in many of the countries of South and Central America, human numbers are increasing at an annual rate of 3 percent. The result will be a doubling of their present populations in approximately twenty-three years.

On the social, political, and economic levels, what is likely to happen in an underdeveloped country whose people double themselves in a single generation, or even less? An underdeveloped society is a society without adequate capital resources (for capital is what is left over after primary needs have been satisfied, and in underdeveloped countries most people never satisfy their primary needs); a society without a sufficient force of trained teachers, administrators, and technicians; a society with few or no industries and few or no developed sources of industrial power; a society, finally, with enormous arrears to be made good in food production, education, road building, housing, and sanitation. A quarter of a century from now, when there will be twice as many of them as there are today, what is the likelihood that the members of such a society will be better fed, housed, clothed, and schooled than at present? And what are the chances in such a society for the maintenance, if they already exist, or the creation, if they do not exist, of democratic institutions?

Not long ago Mr. Eugene Black, the former president of the World Bank, expressed the opinion that it would be extremely difficult, perhaps even impossible, for an underdeveloped country with a very rapid rate of population increase to achieve full industrialization. All its resources, he pointed out, would be absorbed year by year in the task of supplying, or not quite supplying, the primary needs of its new members. Merely to stand still, to maintain its current subhumanly inadequate standard of living, will require hard work and the expenditure of all the nation's available capital. Available capital may be increased by loans and gifts from abroad; but in a world where the industrialized nations are involved in power politics and an increasingly expensive armament race, there will never be enough foreign aid to make much difference. And even if the loans and gifts to underdeveloped countries were to be substantially increased, any resulting gains would be largely nullified by the uncontrolled population explosion.

The situation of these nations with such rapidly increasing populations reminds one of Lewis Carroll's parable in *Through the Looking Glass*, where Alice and the Red Queen start running at full speed and run for a long time until Alice is completely out of breath. When they stop, Alice is amazed to see that they are still at their starting point. In the looking-glass world, if you wish to retain your present position, you must run as fast as you can. If you wish to get ahead, you must run at least twice as fast as you can.

If Mr. Black is correct (and there are plenty of economists and demographers who share his opinion), the outlook for most of the world's newly independent and economically nonviable nations is gloomy indeed. To those that have shall be given. Within the next ten or twenty years, if war can be avoided, poverty will almost have disappeared from the highly industrialized and contraceptive-using societies of the West.

Meanwhile, in the underdeveloped and uncontrolledly breeding societies of Asia, Africa, and Latin America, the condition of the masses (twice as numerous, a generation from now, as they are today) will have become no better and may even be decidedly worse than it is at present. Such a decline is foreshadowed by current statistics of the Food and Agriculture Organization of the United Nations. In some underdeveloped regions of the world, we are told, people are somewhat less adequately fed, clothed, and housed than were their parents and grandparents thirty and forty years ago. And what of elementary education? UNESCO recently provided an answer. Since the end of World War II heroic efforts have been made to teach the whole world how to read. The population explosion has largely stultified these efforts. The absolute number of illiterates is greater now than at any time.

The contraceptive revolution which, thanks to advancing science and technology, has made it possible for the highly developed societies of the West to offset the consequences of death by a planned control of births, has had as yet no effect upon the family life of people in underdeveloped countries. This is not surprising. Death control, as I have already remarked, is easy, cheap, and can be carried out by a small force of technicians. Birth control, on the other hand, is rather expensive, involves the whole adult population, and demands of those who practice it a good deal of forethought and directed willpower. To persuade hundreds of millions of men and women to abandon their tradition-hallowed views of sexual morality, then to distribute and teach them to make use of contraceptive devices or fertility-controlling drugs—this is a huge and difficult task, so huge and so difficult that it seems very unlikely that it can be successfully carried out, within a sufficiently short space of time, in any of the countries where control of the birth rate is most urgently needed.

Extreme poverty, when combined with ignorance, breeds that lack of desire for better things which has been called "wantlessness"—the resigned acceptance of a subhuman lot. But extreme poverty, when it is combined with the knowledge that some societies are affluent, breeds envious desires and the expectation that these desires must of necessity, and very soon, be satisfied. By means of the mass media (those easily exportable products of advancing science and technology) some knowledge of what life is like in affluent societies has been widely disseminated throughout the world's underdeveloped regions. But, alas, the science and technology which have given the industrial West its cars, refrigerators ,and contraceptives have given the people of Asia, Africa, and Latin America only movies and radio broadcasts, which they are too simpleminded to be able to criticize, together with a population explosion, which they are still too poor and too tradition-bound to be able to control by deliberate family planning.

In the context of a 3, or even of a mere 2 percent annual increase in numbers, high expectations are foredoomed to disappointment. From disappointment, through resentful frustration, to widespread social unrest the road is short. Shorter still is the road from social unrest, through chaos, to dictatorship, possibly of the Communist party, more probably of generals and colonels. It would seem, then, that for two-thirds of the human race now suffering from the consequences of uncontrolled breeding in a context of industrial backwardness, poverty, and illiteracy, the prospects for democracy, during the next ten or twenty years, are very poor.

From underdeveloped societies and the probable political consequences of their explosive increase in numbers we now pass to the prospect for democracy in the fully industrialized, contraceptive-using societies of Europe and North America.

It used to be assumed that political freedom was a necessary precondition of scientific research. Ideological dogmatism and dictatorial institutions were supposed to be incompatible with the open-mindedness and the freedom of experimental action, in the absence of which discovery and invention are impossible. Recent history has proved these comforting assumptions to be completely unfounded. It was under Stalin that Russian scientists developed the A-bomb and, a few years later, the H-bomb. And it is under a more-than-Stalinist dictatorship that Chinese scientists are now in process of performing the same feat.

Another disquieting lesson of recent history is that, in a developing society, science and technology can be used exclusively for the enhancement of military power, not at all for the benefit of the masses. Russia has demonstrated, and China is now doing its best to demonstrate, that poverty and primitive conditions of life for the overwhelming majority of the population are perfectly compatible with the wholesale production of the most advanced and sophisticated military hardware. Indeed, it is by deliberately imposing poverty on the masses that the rulers of developing industrial nations are able to create the capital necessary for building an armament industry and maintaining a well-equipped army, with which to play their parts in the suicidal game of international power politics.

We see, then, that democratic institutions and libertarian traditions are not at all necessary to the progress of science and technology, and that such progress does not of itself make for human betterment at home and peace abroad. Only where democratic institutions already exist, only where the masses can vote their rulers out of office and so compel them to pay attention to the popular will, are science and technology used for the benefit of the majority as well as for increasing the power of the State. Most human beings prefer peace to war, and practically all of them would rather be alive than dead. But in every part of the world men and women have been brought up to regard nationalism as axiomatic and war between nations as something cosmically ordained by the Nature of Things. Prisoners of their culture, the masses, even when they are free to vote, are inhibited by the fundamental postulates of the frame of reference within which they do their thinking and their feeling from decreeing an end to the collective paranoia that governs international relations. As for the world's ruling minorities, by the very fact of their power they are chained even more closely to the current system of ideas and the prevailing political customs; for this reason they are even less capable than their subjects of expressing the simple human preference for life and peace.

Some day, let us hope, rulers and ruled will break out of the cultural prison in which they are now confined. Some day.... And may that day come soon! For, thanks to our rapidly advancing science and technology, we have very little time at our disposal. The river of change flows ever faster, and somewhere downstream, perhaps only a few years ahead, we shall come to the rapids, shall hear, louder and ever louder, the roaring of a cataract.

Modern war is a product of advancing science and technology. Conversely, advancing science and technology are products of modern war. It was in order to wage war more effectively that first the United States, then Britain and the USSR, financed the crash programs that resulted so quickly in the harnessing of atomic forces. Again, it was primarily for military purposes that the techniques of automation, which are now in process of revolutionizing industrial production and the whole system of administrative and bureaucratic control, were first developed. "During World War II," writes Mr. John Diebold,

the theory and use of feedback was studied in great detail by a number of scientists both in this country and in Britain. The introduction of rapidly moving aircraft very quickly made traditional gun-laying techniques of anti-aircraft warfare obsolete. As a result, a large part of scientific manpower in this country was directed towards the development of self-regulating devices and systems to control our military equipment. It is out of this work that the technology of automation as we understand it today has developed.

The headlong rapidity with which scientific and technological changes, with all their disturbing consequences in the fields of politics and social relations, are taking place is due in large measure to the fact that, both in the USA and the USSR, research in pure and applied science is lavishly financed by military planners whose first concern is in the development of bigger and better weapons in the shortest possible time. In the frantic effort, on one side of the Iron Curtain, to keep up with the Joneses—on the other, to keep up with the Ivanovs—these military planners spend gigantic sums on research and development. The military revolution advances under forced draft, and as it goes forward it initiates an uninterrupted succession of industrial, social, and political revolutions. It is against this background of chronic upheaval that the members of a species, biologically and historically adapted to a slowly changing environment, must now live out their bewildered lives.

Old-fashioned war was incompatible, while it was being waged, with democracy. Nuclear war, if it is ever waged, will prove in all likelihood to be incompatible with civilization, perhaps with human survival. Meanwhile, what of the preparations for nuclear war? If certain physicists and military planners had their way, democracy,

where it exists, would be replaced by a system of regimentation centered upon the bomb shelter. The entire population would have to be systematically drilled in the ticklish operation of going underground at a moment's notice, systematically exercised in the art of living troglodytically under conditions resembling those in the hold of an eighteenth-century slave ship. The notion fills most of us with horror. But if we fail to break out of the ideological prison of our nationalistic and militaristic culture, we may find ourselves compelled by the military consequences of our science and technology to descend into the steel and concrete dungeons of total and totalitarian civil defense.

In the past, one of the most effective guarantees of liberty was governmental inefficiency. The spirit of tyranny was always willing; but its technical and organizational flesh was weak. Today the flesh is as strong as the spirit. Governmental organization is a fine art, based upon scientific principles and disposing of marvelously efficient equipment. Fifty years ago an armed revolution still had some chance of success. In the context of modern weaponry a popular uprising is foredoomed. Crowds armed with rifles and home-made grenades are no match for tanks. And it is not only to its armament that a modern government owes its overwhelming power. It also possesses the strength of superior knowledge derived from its communication systems, its stores of accumulated data, its batteries of computers, its network of inspection and administration.

Where democratic institutions exist and the masses can vote their rulers out of office, the enormous powers with which science, technology, and the arts of organization have endowed the ruling minority are used with discretion and a decent regard for civil and political liberty. Where the masses can exercise no control over their rulers, these powers are used without compunction to enforce ideological orthodoxy and to strengthen the dictatorial state. The nature of science and technology is such that it is peculiarly easy for a dictatorial government to use them for its own purposes. Well financed, equipped, and organized, an astonishingly small number of scientists and technologists can achieve prodigious results. The crash program that produced the A-bomb and ushered in a new historical era was planned and directed by some four thousand theoreticians, experimenters, and engineers. To parody the words of Winston Churchill, never have so many been so completely at the mercy of so few.

Throughout the nineteenth century the State was relatively feeble, and its interest in, and influence upon, scientific research were negligible. In our day the State is everywhere exceedingly powerful and a lavish patron of basic and *ad hoc* research. In Western Europe and North America the relations between the State and its scientists on the one hand and individual citizens, professional organizations, and industrial, commercial, and educational institutions on the other are fairly satisfactory. Advancing science, the population explosion, the armament race, and the steady increase and centralization of political and economic power are still compatible, in countries that have a libertarian tradition, with democratic forms of government. To maintain this compatibility in a rapidly changing world, bearing less and less resemblance to the world in which these democratic institutions were developed—this, quite obviously, is going to be increasingly difficult.

A rapid and accelerating population increase that will nullify the best efforts of underdeveloped societies to better their lot and will keep two-thirds of the human race in a condition of misery in anarchy or of misery under dictatorship, and the intensive preparations for a new kind of war that, if it breaks out, may bring irretrievable ruin to the one-third of the human race now living prosperously in highly industrialized societies—these are the two main threats to democracy now confronting us. Can these threats be eliminated? Or, if not eliminated, at least reduced?

My own view is that only by shifting our collective attention from the merely political to the basic biological aspects of the human situation can we hope to mitigate and shorten the time of troubles into which, it would seem, we are now moving. We cannot do without politics; but we can no longer afford to indulge in bad, unrealistic politics. To work for the survival of the species as a whole and for the actualization in the greatest possible number of individual men and women of their potentialities for good will, intelligence, and creativity—this, in the world of today, is good, realistic politics. To cultivate the religion of idolatrous nationalism, to subordinate the interests of the species and its individual members to the interests of a single national state and its ruling minority —in the context of the population explosion, missiles, and atomic warheads, this is bad and thoroughly unrealistic politics. Unfortunately, it is to bad and unrealistic politics that our rulers are now committed.

Ecology is the science of the mutual relations of organisms with their environment and with one another. Only when we get it into our collective head that the basic problem confronting twentieth-century man is an ecological problem will our politics improve and become realistic. How does the human race propose to survive and, if possible, improve the lot and intrinsic quality of its individual members? Do we propose to live on this planet in symbiotic harmony with our environment? Or, preferring to be wantonly stupid, shall we choose to live like murderous parasites that kill their host and so destroy themselves?

Committing that sin of overweening bumptiousness, which the Greeks called *hubris,* we behave as though we were not members of earth's ecological community, as though we were privileged and, in some sort, supernatural beings and could throw our weight around like gods. But in fact we are, among other things, animals—emergent parts of the natural order. If our politicians were realists, they would think rather less about missiles and the problem of landing a couple of astronauts on the moon, rather more about hunger and moral squalor and the problem of enabling three billion men, women, and children, who will soon be six billions, to lead a tolerably human existence without, in the process, ruining and befouling their planetary environment.

Animals have no souls; therefore, according to the most authoritative Christian theologians, they may be treated as though they were things. The truth, as we are now beginning to realize, is that even things ought not to be treated as *mere* things. They should be treated as though they were parts of a vast living organism. "Do as you would be done by." The Golden Rule applies to our dealings with nature no less than to our dealings with our fellow-men. If we hope to be well treated by nature, we must stop talking about "mere things" and start treating our planet with intelligence and consideration.

Power politics in the context of nationalism raises problems that, except by war, are practically insoluble. The problems of ecology, on the other hand, admit of a rational solution and can be tackled without the arousal of those violent passions always associated with dogmatic ideology and nationalistic idolatry. There may be arguments about the best way of raising wheat in a cold climate or of reforesting a denuded mountain. But such arguments

never lead to organized slaughter. Organized slaughter is the result of arguments about such questions as the following. Which is the best nation? The best religion? The best political theory? The best form of government? Why are other people so stupid and wicked? Why can't they see how good and intelligent *we* are? Why do they resist our beneficent efforts to bring them under our control and make them like ourselves?

To questions of this kind the final answer has always been war. "War," said Clausewitz, "is not merely a political act, but also a political instrument, a continuation of political relationships, a carrying out of the same by other means." This was true enough in the eighteen thirties, when Clausewitz published his famous treatise and it continued to be true until 1945. Now, pretty obviously, nuclear weapons, long-range rockets, nerve gases, bacterial aerosols, and the laser (that highly promising, latest addition to the world's military arsenal) have given the lie to Clausewitz. All-out war with modern weapons is no longer a continuation of previous policy; it is a complete and irreversible break with previous policy.

Power politics, nationalism, and dogmatic ideology are luxuries that the human race can no longer afford. Nor, as a species, can we afford the luxury of ignoring man's ecological situation. By shifting our attention from the now completely irrelevant and anachronistic politics of nationalism and military power to the problems of the human species and the still inchoate politics of human ecology we shall be killing two birds with one stone—reducing the threat of sudden destruction by scientific war and at the same time reducing the threat of more gradual biological disaster.

The beginnings of ecological politics are to be found in the special services of the United Nations Organization. UNESCO, the Food and Agriculture Organization, the

World Health Organization, the various Technical Aid Services—all these are, partially or completely, concerned with the ecological problems of the human species. In a world where political problems are thought of and worked upon within a frame of reference whose coordinates are nationalism and military power, these ecology-oriented organizations are regarded as peripheral. If the problems of humanity could be thought about and acted upon within a frame of reference that has survival for the species, the well-being of in-dividuals, and the actualization of man's desirable potentialities as its coordinates, these peripheral organizations would become central. The subordinate politics of survival, happiness, and personal fulfillment would take the place now occupied by the politics of power, ideology, nationalistic idolatry, and unrelieved misery.

In the process of reaching this kind of politics we shall find, no doubt, that we have done something, in President Wilson's prematurely optimistic words, "to make the world safe for democracy."

THE PROFESSOR, THE POLICEMAN, AND THE PEASANT

Martin Nicolaus

On a day in April 1960 in a small town in South Vietnam, the following event took place: an American professor interviewed the chief of the local police in the latter's headquarters, while (according to the professor's report) "curled up on a mat in the corner was a twenty-year-old peasant in tattered clothes. His feet were in manacles, the left side of his face was swollen and his eye and cheek were bruised." The youth was "suspected of Vietcong membership."[1] He had been interrogated by the secret police chief. The professor, who was doing basic research under contract to the U.S. government and to the Saigon government, noted these facts but asked no further questions about the peasant. Neither the police chief nor the professor indicated that the peasant's presence disturbed them or struck them as strange.

Yet it does seem strange for an American professor to have an amiable interview with a secret police chief in the latter's interrogation center, and even more strange that the interview took place while a young man who had been convicted of no crime lay bruised and manacled in the corner. A closer examination of the event yields even more alien facts: the interrogation room had been paid for, and the police chief's

Reprinted by permission of the author and publisher from Viet-Report, **2** *(February 1966), pp. 16–21.*

[1] Joseph Zasloff, *A Study of Administration in Binh Minh District* (Saigon: MSUG, October 1961, mimeo), p. 25.

equipment, including the manacles that held the peasant, had been supplied by an American university—the same university that paid the professor's salary. The professor, the policeman, and the peasant were here assembled in exactly their intended roles, playing the parts the university had designed for them: the professor researching, the policeman interrogating, the peasant silent, bruised. This indeed seems like an extraordinary episode in the annals of American academia. And the fact that the professor did not think the event was worth special comment—that seems inexplicable, inexcusable, scandalous.

Nevertheless, it happened, and it happened regularly. Not that the professors regularly encountered manacled peasants in their interviews; that was not a typical event. Still, this encounter in April 1960 is like a microcosm of the larger drama that had been unfolding since 1950 and ended only in 1962. The peasant lying manacled in a corner of the room symbolizes, perhaps in an exaggerated way, perhaps not, the predicament of a great many South Vietnamese peasants: they were all being bound, beaten, or manacled in one way or another, although not all of them took it as silently as this one, as the professors well knew. The secret police chief was also playing a typical role—getting information out of peasants was his job. The professor, too, was doing his job: asking some questions, not asking other questions, writing down the responses, and not expressing opinions outside his field of professional competence. And the manacles, together with related equipment, were supplied to the police by the university on a regular schedule; there was nothing extraordinary about it. This one event expresses Michigan State University's Vietnam Project in a nutshell.

Nor, for that matter, is the episode an isolated instance in American intellectual history. Certainly the majority of university projects overseas do not involve such collaboration with the secret police—American or foreign—and they do follow a stricter definition of what is "technical" assistance. But the needs which the Michigan State project was designed to serve exist now, or are growing into existence, in many parts of the world. The conditions that made it possible to use American professors as they were used in Vietnam persist. The Michigan State University Group (MSUG) was not an unrepeatable event. More and more it appears as the prototype, the pilot model of a growing family of overseas "research projects" of which the controversial Project Camelot in Latin America was the latest member, but not the last. The MSU project reflects not only a few individual professors, not just one particular university, not merely an especially dark period of American history—although these things were at work too; its roots go back further and deeper into the "normal," the established and enduring life of American professors, universities, and American foreign policy in general.

A STRANGE BEGINNING

Credit for being the first to piece together and publish the outlines of the MSUG story belongs to *Ramparts* magazine's staff writer and some-time foreign correspondent Robert Scheer. Since the publication of Scheer's booklet, *How the United States Got Involved in Vietnam*,[2] in which Scheer made several allegations that disturbed Michigan State University, new evidence

---

[2] Available from the Center for the Study of Democratic Institutions, Santa Barbara, Calif.

has come to light[3] which makes it possible for the first time to substantiate some of these charges with a solid network of proof. This is how the Vietnam project began:

In Tokyo in July 1950, Ngo Dinh Diem, then one of many exiled Vietnamese politicians, met Wesley Fishel, who had just accepted a position as assistant professor of political science at Michigan State University (then called Michigan State College).[4] The circumstances surrounding the meeting are obscure, but it was hardly accidental. Diem had been a frequent guest at American consulates-general in Asia since 1946, and it was rumored that certain elements of the American government—the CIA most frequently mentioned in this regard—were in fact grooming him for the job of eventually replacing Bao Dai, the playboy emperor of Vietnam.[5] Nor is it likely that Wesley Fishel was simply another young Ph.D. off on a lark in Japan, and just happened to run into Diem in a tearoom. In any case, this meeting proved to be an extraordinarily fortunate coincidence for both men. The two exchanged letters when Fishel returned to the United States, and a bare seven months later their friendship had blossomed to the point where Fishel had Diem made a "consultant" to Michigan State's "Governmental Research Bureau."[6] How a mere assistant professor in his first year at MSU was able to pull such strings for his friend is one of the several little mysteries that surround the MSU project and the person of Wesley Fishel. Only one and a half years after

their initial meeting in Tokyo, Diem and Fishel—both without any overt official standing—were engaging in international diplomacy on behalf of the U.S. government. In 1952, Diem "asked the French to permit Michigan State College to furnish technical aid to the Vietnamese government, the cost of which would be borne by the United States government, but the French refused."[7] After that, Diem moved his base of operations from MSU's East Lansing campus eastward into Cardinal Spellman's territory, and began the series of publicity triumphs (recounted in Scheer's booklet) which catapulted him into power in Saigon in mid-1954. Less than two months later, his friend Wesley Fishel hurried to Saigon as Diem's special advisor and as a member of U.S. Special Ambassador Lawton Collins' personal staff.[8] "Not surprisingly," in the words of Professors Scigliano and Fox, both of whom were high-ranking members of the MSU project, Fishel's discussions with Diem led to a request that Michigan State "undertake to help Vietnam in its current difficulties."[9] A team of four officials from the East Lansing Campus, headed by Arthur Brandstatter, chief of MSU's School of Police Administration, made a whirlwind, two-week tour of Vietnam and returned in early October 1954 with a recommendation that MSU undertake a huge project of technical assistance to the Diem government.[10] During subsequent negotiations between Diem, Fishel, MSU, and the U.S. Foreign Operations Administration (now

[3] Robert Scigliano and Guy H. Fox, *Technical Assistance in Vietnam, The Michigan State University Experience* (Prager Special Studies, 1965).
[4] *Ibid.*, p. 1.
[5] Georges Chaffard, *L'Indochine—dix ans d'independance* (Paris: Calmann-Levy, 1964), pp. 24, 27, 53.
[6] Scigliano and Fox, p. 1.
[7] *Ibid.*
[8] *Ibid.*; also Scheer.
[9] *Ibid.*
[10] Scigliano and Fox, pp. 2, 75.

called, less candidly, Agency for International Development), the size of the project was somewhat reduced, but its scope remained broad. Its purpose was to give the Diem government assistance in strengthening nearly all aspects of its functioning, with particular emphasis on the economy, the civil service, and the police.[11]

However, in early 1955, the Diem government was so near collapse that the MSU project almost died stillborn. The majority of Diem's cabinet deserted him, the army was in near revolt, and the city was under virtual siege by one of the armed sects, the Binh Xuyen. Even Special Ambassador Collins sent a pessimistic note to Eisenhower, suggesting that a new man can be found to replace Diem. However, firm support for Diem came from the CIA's ubiquitous Colonel Lansdale, and (via CIA chief Allen Dulles to his brother, John Foster, to Eisenhower) Collins was overruled, and Diem's future was assured.[12] The persons in Saigon who did the most to keep Diem in power during this crisis, according to the French journalist Georges Chaffard, were certain American military counselors and unnamed "activists" from Michigan State University.[13] Their efforts were successful; Diem rode out the crisis, and in the spring of 1955 the U.S. National Security Council formally endorsed Diem. According to Scheer, who says he got it from Fishel, at this time "no less a personage than Vice-President Nixon called John Hannah, the president of Michigan State, to elicit his support."[14] Hannah, an important figure in the GOP and a former

Assistant Secretary of Defense, was told (according to Scheer quoting Fishel) that it was "in the national interest for his university to become involved."[15] According to Hannah, however, there was no request from Nixon. Hannah claims that the request came from "authority even higher than Nixon's."[16] However that may be, Michigan State's interests, Diem's interests, and the national interest were already thoroughly intertwined before this phone call to Hannah took place.

According to Scheer, the MSU project filled a special need of American foreign policy at this time.

The Geneva Accords had prohibited increases in the strength of either side through the introduction of "all types of arms" or buildups in troop strength. The presence of the International Control Commission . . . offered the prospect of unfavorable publicity to the United States if its Military Assistance and Advisory Group, United States Operations Mission, or CIA agents operated openly. The Michigan group would serve as "cover."[17]

It is true that the Geneva accords (Article 17a) forbade arms increases and it is a fact that the International Control Commission could have created heavily damaging publicity. But whether or not the Michigan group served as "cover" is a question that should be suspended for the moment, waiting until more of the evidence is in.

In May 1955, the Michigan State University Group was officially born with the signing of two contracts, one between MSU and the Diem government, the other between MSU and the U.S. government. The

[11] *Ibid.*, p. 3.
[12] See, for example, David Wise and Thomas B. Ross, *The Invisible Government* (New York: Random House, 1964), pp. 157–158.
[13] Chaffard, pp. 75, 82.
[14] Scheer, quoted in Marvin Gettleman (ed.), *Viet Nam* (New York: Fawcett, 1965), p. 249.
[15] *Ibid.*
[16] Quoted in "Deny MSU Fronted for CIA in Vietnam," *The Detroit News* (November 28, 1965).
[17] Scheer, p. 249.

contracts were for two years, and were re-newed with modifications in 1957 and 1959.[18] The first MSUG advisors under the contract arrived at the end of May 1955.[19] For a project of its size, it was prepared in a remarkably short time. Actually "the team of MSU professors," as one is tempted to call the group, were neither predomi-nantly from MSU nor were most of them professors. It was an academic program neither in numbers nor in purpose, only in publicity. From 1955 to 1962, the term of the project, MSUG had 104 American staff members altogether, who served vari-ous lengths of time. Of these 104, 32 were clerical or administrative personnel. Only 72 were full-fledged MSUG advisors. Of these 72 advisors, 33 were in the police division, 34 in the Public Administration Division, and 5 were short-term consul-tants. Of the 33 police advisors, only 4 came from the MSU campus, the remainder being recruited from law-enforcement and other agencies. Of the 34 nonpolice ad-visors, only 11 were from the MSU campus. Only 25 of all 72 advisors were actually professors, and almost all of these were in the nonpolice division. The only reason to call the group the "MSU professors" is that all five of the Chief Advisors were political-science professors at Michigan State, and Michigan State faculty held all other con-trolling positions in the project. But pro-fessors from Yale, Pittsburgh, UCLA,[20] and other universities also took part. While Michigan State lent its name and its re-spectability to the project and acted as co-ordinating agency, the real direction of the program came from the U.S. government and from the Saigon government. In doing

its utmost to cooperate with these powers, MSU did no more than many other Ameri-can universities would have done, and are doing.

Compared to the cost of a jet fighter-bomber, MSUG was a trivial operation, but compared to the cost of most "research" projects even in the physical sciences, MSUG was a behemoth. The cost of sal-aries, transportation, and overhead for the American staff alone was $5.3 *million,* and the equivalent of an additional $5.1 million in Vietnamese piastres was spent on the staff of about 200 Vietnamese scholars, translators, typists, chauffeurs, and security guards. To this tidy subtotal of $10.4 mil-lion must be added another $15 million more, according to the estimate of Scigli-ano and Fox. This amount approximately represents equipment and material-aid funds controlled and disbursed by MSUG.[21] Nearly all of this amount was spent by the Police Division, but there is no way of knowing by how much the estimate is too low, since certain activities of the Police Division were never formally reported to MSUG's Chief Advisors.[22] But if the esti-mate is anywhere near accuracy, it means that MSUG spent the neat sum of about $25 million, or about two dollars for every man, woman, and child in the country. The entire cost, of course, was borne by the U.S. government.

Wesley Fishel became MSUG Chief Ad-visor in early 1956. Scheer quotes Fishel as having said ". . . I surfaced—to use a CIA term—to become head of the MSUG pro-gram,"[23] but Fishel denies that he ever used such language.[24] In any case, it was not a bad job for a man who had begun aca-

---

[18] *Final Report* (Saigon: MSUG, June 1962, mimeo), p. 1.
[19] *Ibid.,* pp. 61, 62.
[20] Scigliano and Fox, pp. 40–41.
[21] *Ibid.,* p. 4.
[22] *Ibid.,* p. 21.
[23] Scheer, p. 249.
[24] *The Detroit News, loc. cit.*

demic life as an assistant professor only six years before.

All these factors are worth keeping in mind when asking the question whether MSUG acted as "cover" for the CIA.

AN URGENT REQUEST

The first MSUG advisors to arrive in Saigon were police experts, and the first task undertaken by MSUG was a police project, so it seems fair to begin to describe the behemoth here. MSUG was divided into two divisions: Police and Public Administration, with the Chief Advisor responsible for both. As the project became organized the two divisions worked quite separately from one another and the Chief Advisor acted as the only channel of information between them, at least formally; but in the first few months the two groups worked together. Throughout 1955 much of Saigon was in ruins from the pitched street battles; frequent plastic-bomb explosions rocked the residential districts, and some MSUG members happened to be living in a hotel that was raided during a riot, and suffered considerable property damage.[25] In the midst of this atmosphere of crisis and chaos came an "urgent request" from the American Embassy in Saigon that MSUG devote all its energies to strengthening the police and security organizations, particularly the Sureté and the Civil Guard, and to reorganizing the refugee commissariat.[26] Since the first advisors on the scene happened to be a secret-police specialist and a civil-guard specialist, MSUG readily acceded to the request. The first real professors who arrived were assigned to the refugees.

The Vietnamese secret police was nothing more or less than a branch of the French Sureté, a name that means to Vietnamese approximately what Okhrana meant to the Bolsheviks and Gestapo meant to German Jews. When the French abandoned Vietnam in 1954–1955, the Saigon government inherited the organization lock, stock, and barrel, and set about patching its war wounds. The first step was to abolish the dreaded name Sureté and replace it with something more suited to a brave new nation. The MSUG advisors had the answer: the secret police was henceforth called the Vietnamese Bureau of Investigation, or VBI.[27] They then devoted a great part of their energies to increasing the organization's efficiency. Its scattered facilities and records were consolidated and expanded in a former French army camp which was later renovated for the purpose. Here, under MSUG guidance and with MSUG-supplied funds, the VBI built an interrogation center, detention center, laboratory, records and identification center, and communications headquarters.[28] They undertook to modernize the Sureté's fingerprint files by reclassifying them from the French to the American system. After a year of work, they had reclassified 600,000 files in the "criminal and subversive" section, and expected the job to take another two years, which gives an idea of how many people the Sureté had its eyes on—perhaps from 10 to 20 percent of the population; not bad for an antiquated outfit, but not good enough by American standards.[29]

In order to improve on this percentage, the University Group in 1959 took charge of the national identity-card program, designed to furnish every South Vietnamese over 21, for a small fee, with an obligatory, nearly indestructible plastic-laminated ID

---

[25] Final Report, p. 2; Scigliano and Fox, p. 5.
[26] Scigliano and Fox, pp. 6, 66.
[27] Sheer, p. 251; also Final Report, p. 61.
[28] Final Report, p. 48.
[29] Ibid., my projections.

card bearing his photograph and thumb-print. MSUG imported specially designed laminating machines and portable photography studios, and it trained, equipped, and advised the heavily armed identification teams which sought, unsuccessfully, to dogtag every peasant in the country, After a number of identification teams were ambushed, the program was abandoned.[30]

MSUG established a special training school under the jurisdiction of the VBI high command, in which the Americans gave instruction in subjects ranging from jeep driving to the use of different types of tear gas. They wrote or had translated manuals on weapons maintenance, riot control, and related subjects.[31] They gave advice on all aspects of the VBI's operations, including the location of training camps and the so-called detention centers.[32] However, despite the advisors' best efforts, when the project ended in 1962, the VBI (in the words of MSUG's *Final Report*) "still fell far short of the revised setup which had been recommended."[33]

The U.S. Embassy's urgent request for help with the Civil Guard was a matter of special importance, but MSUG was less helpful here. The Civil Guard, an ill-equipped body of about 50,000 men staffed with military officers, quartered in army encampments and under control of the province chiefs, played a key role in Diem's strategy for seizing power in a largely hostile countryside. Regular units of the Civil Guard would sweep through an area to soften it up and to overcome whatever resistance was encountered, and then re-mained, using the old French forts to keep the area pacified. The MSUG advisors wanted to reduce the organization in size and to convert it into a rural police force, to take it out of military control and base it in the villages, somewhat on the model of Franco's *Guardia Civil*. USOM and MAAG, on the other hand, wanted the Guard to be "organized into company, battalion, and regimental groups, and armed with rifles, automatic rifles, and machine guns."[34] As a result of this conflict, which was won by USOM and MAAG in 1959, MSUG's role in the Civil Guard was confined to some training and some supply activities.[35]

MSUG advisors also trained and supplied the municipal police; reorganized traffic patterns in Saigon; gave training in pistol marksmanship to the palace guard and to other "special groups"; and advised the government on counterinsurgency.[36]

But all these training and advisory activities paled in importance compared to what Scigliano and Fox call "the core of the police program," the provision of "material aid."[37] From 1955 to 1959, according to Scigliano and Fox, the University Group was for all practical purposes the sole supplier of weapons, ammunition, vehicles, and equipment to the entire South Vietnamese secret police, municipal police, Civil Guard, and palace guard.[38] Scigliano and Fox state that "the major items, some of which came from local stocks of American material that had been given to the French Expeditionary Corps, were revolvers, riot guns, ammunition, tear gas, jeeps and

---

[30] *Ibid.*, p. 49.

[31] *Ibid.*, p. 45

[32] Scigliano and Fox, p. 6.

[33] *Final Report*, p. 47.

[34] Scigliano and Fox, pp. 17, 23.

[35] *Ibid.*, pp. 17, 19; *Final Report*, p. 48.

[36] *Final Report*, pp. 45–51; on the palace guard, Scigliano and Fox, p. 18.

[37] Scigliano and Fox, p. 15.

[38] *Ibid.*

other vehicles, handcuffs, office equipment, traffic lights, and communications equipment."[39] Even MSUG's *Final Report,* available on request from MSU, admits these facts: "The Division arranged to supply, wherever possible, motor vehicles, small arms weapons, and tear gas. . . . Schedules of distribution of weapons to patrolmen and maintenance of training was also established."[40] But "patrolmen" is a characteristic euphemism. The most substantial portion of these supplies and funds went to the secret police directly; and even more, indirectly, in the name of Michigan State University.[41]

The weapons-supply program was the biggest and most successful part of the entire MSU project. It received the lion's share of the project's cost, and the greatest number of man-hours were devoted to it. Most of all of the Police Division's training programs centered around the weapons and equipment supplied by MSUG; Scigliano and Fox note that the Vietnamese were eager to be instructed in the handling of riot guns but turned a deaf ear to attempts to instruct them in the rules of evidence or the rights of prisoners. Americans refrained from trying to impose their cultural values in these matters on the Vietnamese, although some instructors were "guilty" of the attempt.[42] Even when the training programs had been largely completed in 1958, the Police Division still found it necessary to maintain a staff of more than 20 advisors to handle the distribution schedules.[43] During the peak period of MSUG's operations, mid-1957 to mid-1959, the Police Division staff out-

numbered the Public Administration staff —despite the latter's much wider range of tasks—by a ratio of about 5 to 3, and the Public Administration Division never had as many advisors in it at any time.[44] If one did not know that the program was sponsored by a respectable American university, one could easily come to the conclusion that MSUG was primarily a paramilitary-aid program with a research bureau thinly spread over it, like icing on the cake.

Finally, the accusation that MSUG acted as a cover for the CIA can now be regarded as definitely proven. Although both MSU and Wesley Fishel have denied Robert Scheer's allegations to this effect,[45]—Scheer lacked decisive evidence, after all—recent testimony by three top-ranking MSUG members makes these denials extremely dubious. Ralph Smuckler, MSUG Chief Advisor from April 1958 to December 1959 (immediately after Fishel's tenure), stated in a newspaper interview that "a few" of the Police Division's "borrowed helpers were from the CIA." But, he continued, "these were cloak and dagger operations, and the use of CIA agents was a drop in the bucket compared to the overall project."[46] Smuckler is presently Acting Dean of International Programs at MSU. MSU political-science professors Robert Scigliano (Assistant to Chief Advisor, July 1957 to September 1959—covering most of Fishel's term) and Guy Fox (Chief Advisor, May 1961 to June 1962), both colleagues of Fishel, have this to say in their recently published book: "The nonprofessional advisors in the police program were overwhelmingly from state and municipal law-

---

[39] *Ibid.,* p. 16.
[40] *Final Report,* p. 47.
[41] Scigliano and Fox, pp. 16, 21; *Final Report,* p. 47.
[42] Scigliano and Fox, p. 19.
[43] *Ibid.,* p. 18; *Final Report,* p. 66.
[44] *Final Report,* pp. 65–67.
[45] *The Detroit News, loc. cit.*
[46] *Ibid.*

enforcement agencies, although there was also a group of CIA agents."[47] Further: "Lack of adequate information makes it impossible to assess the work that several persons conducted with a special internal security unit of the *Sureté* between 1955 and 1959. Although attached to MSUG, these persons were members of the CIA and reported only to the American Embassy in Saigon."[48] Scigliano and Fox also complain that MSUG's intimate involvement with police work

blurred for too many persons, including its own staff, its primary mission as an educational institution. The last point applies with even greater force to MSUG's somewhat forced hospitality as an organizational cover for certain intelligence functions of the American government until mid-1959. Not only was the cover quite transparent, but what it did not conceal tended to bring the whole MSU endeavor under suspicion.[49]

What the rather vague phrase "somewhat forced hospitality" refers to is not clear; but what is clear is that MSUG's function as a cover for the CIA unit was written into MSUG's original contract. In mid-1959, after reviewing its progress, the group "refused to provide cover for this unit in the new contract period."[50] At that time the CIA unit moved from MSUG to under the wings of USOM, which also absorbed the weapons-distribution program.[51] As soon as these transfers had been accom-

plished, the Police Division staff dwindled rapidly to the vanishing point; its mission had been successfully accomplished.[52] In the light of these circumstances, MSU's protestations of innocence and ignorance are simply not credible.

It is a fact that article 17 (a) of the Geneva Agreements prohibits the introduction into Vietnam of all types of arms and munitions, and it is another fact that from 1954 to 1957 the United States maintained an official posture of strict respect for the Agreements, even while supporting the Diem government's refusal to honor them by holding the 1956 national reunification elections. During Eisenhower's second term the official line changed to open disregard for the Agreements, and about a year later the International Control Commission began growing increasingly ineffectual because of an irreconcilable split between the Canadian and the Polish delegations, so that the Commission no longer represented a publicity threat. Could these facts be related to the fact that the CIA and USOM-MAAG shed their professorial cloaks and began to distribute daggers openly at about the same time? Then, too, by 1957, the manacled peasant had begun his flight from Diem's repression into the *maquis*[53]; for the peasant, his urban sympathizers, together with the sects and certain ethnic minorities, and for the Diem regime, the gloves were off.

[47] Scigliano and Fox, p. 41.
[48] *Ibid.*, p. 21.
[49] *Ibid.*, p. 60.
[50] *Ibid.*, p. 11.
[51] *Ibid.*
[52] *Final Report*, pp. 65–67.
[53] See Philippe Devillers, "The Struggle for Unification," *China Quarterly* (January-March 1962).

U. S. POLICY

THE THIRD WORLD

Richard B. DuBoff

The following article is a review of the book United States Policy and the Third World, *by Charles Wolf, Jr. (Boston: Little, Brown, 1967), 204 pp., $5.75; paperback, $2.75.*

The slogan, "Grab 'em by the balls—and their hearts and minds will follow," attributed to an American general in South Vietnam, should be the subtitle of *United States Policy and the Third World.* For the focus of Wolf's book, as might be expected in this decade of national liberation movements, is "Insurgency and Counterinsurgency" (Chapter 3) : how to freeze a revolution by terror.

The message comes through loud and clear, and it applies to the native population to be liberated by the established authorities as well as to ourselves here on the homefront. Our problem? Wolf, a senior economist at the RAND Corporation, describes it this way:

Because Americans typically start from the previously described "popular-support" view, we frequently feel uncomfortable collaborating with established governments against insurgent movements. Notwithstanding our awareness of the realities of communist subversion and the techniques of "liberation war," the populist tradition in American history disposes us to identify with the insurgent ethos. The initial role of a Castro evokes more sympathy among Americans than that of a Batista. Castro, struggling in the Sierra Maestra, could be easily seen as a popular, Jacksonian crusader for the common man and against the entrenched interests; Batista fitted equally well the role of the ruthless, exploitative tyrant.

That there was reality as well as appearance in this role casting is not the point. The point is that the emotional reaction of Americans to insurgencies frequently interferes with a realistic assessment of alternatives, and inclines us instead toward a carping righteousness in our relations with the beleaguered government we are ostensibly supporting [pp. 57–58].

With that injunction Wolf concludes his dismissal of the "popular-support" thesis which maintains that guerrilla insurgencies depend upon the backing of the indigenous populations. It turns out that this thesis is nothing more than a "new mythology," a style of thinking "as pervasive as it is untested." The author is highly suspicious of it from the beginning, for he informs us flatly, and without factual documentation, that "the growth of the Viet Cong and of the Pathet Lao probably occurred despite the opposition of a large majority of the people in both Vietnam and Laos."

Wolf realizes he is treading on dangerous ground in contradicting popular-support viewpoints held by a wide range of theoreticians from Mao and Giap to Roger Hilsman and Walter Lippmann. The reason for the audacity, however, is soon evident: he has a new theory of his own.

What an insurgent movement requires for successful and expanding operations is not popular

Reprinted by permission from Viet-Report, **3**:4,5 *(January 1968), pp. 15–18.*

support, in the sense of attitudes of identification and allegiance, but rather a supply of certain inputs (e.g., food, recruits, information) at reasonable cost, interpreting "cost" to include expenditure of coercion as well as of money [pp. 50–51; Wolf's emphasis].

How can these key "inputs" be obtained in the absence of popular support? The answer is never made clear, although several explanations are offered. Resource flows in the countryside may simply be appropriated by the insurgents (but regaining them, Wolf recognizes, won't necessarily increase popular support for the government, either). Economic growth may increase the output of goods and services at such a rate that more become available for everybody, including the insurgents. (But in that case, wouldn't prosperity sap the spirit of the rebels and entice them into the ranks of the budding bourgeoisie? And wouldn't the government's income also rise and thus tend to increase its own capacity for dealing with the uprising? Apparently, not. The carrot always needs the stick.)

These logical obstacles notwithstanding, Wolf's theory rolls on to conclusion. To prevent the "outputs" of the insurgent system from materializing—the "outputs" are sabotage, terror, small attacks, then large-scale attacks (not, be it noted, reform and other nonmilitary goals)—the "inputs" must be seized or destroyed. Recruits, information, shelter, and food must be denied the guerrillas. And we are thrown back in the familiar South Vietnamese setting: repression.

Confiscation of chickens, razing of houses, or destruction of villages have a place in counterinsurgency efforts, but only if they are done for a strong reason: namely, to penalize those who have assisted the insurgents. If the reason for the penalty is not sufficient, explicit, and known to the people, exaction of penalties is likely to harm rather than help the counterinsurgency effort.

Military discipline must be tightened and brought under firm control so that whatever harshness is meted out by government forces is unambiguously recognizable as deliberately imposed because of behavior by the population that contributes to the insurgent movement [p. 66].

Of course the effort is to be buttressed by the full panoply of intellectual hardware one expects from RAND. Some examples: offers of amnesty, pecuniary rewards for weapons turned in, "incentive systems" of direct payments to acquire information about guerrillas and officers ("What is the 'price' of a Viet Cong? What would be the price at which the leaders of . . . the National Front for the Liberation of South Vietnam, such as Nguyen Huu Tho, could be located? It might well be less than the price that Magsaysay paid for locating top Huk leaders in the Philippines.") [1] Other "psywar" tricks include "introducing into the country of origin (for example, North Vietnam) counterfeit money, ration cards, and identity cards," as well as rumors, propaganda, and hints of conspiracy. The last tactic is especially promising, we're told, because "the rigidities of communist control systems may make them more vulnerable to such interference . . . [and to] such a high level of 'noise.'" How well schemes like these work in practice may be judged by the ill-fated plan to have shot-down U.S. flyers buy their way out of North Vietnam by offering their peasant captors bullion gold, "redeemable in any free world currency of their choice" (*New York Times,* July 16, 1967).

---

[1] A price that appears to have been either too low or only a down payment. The Huk movement has once again been growing because, among other reasons, "the peasants identify the United States with the sugar barons and other powerful landlords—and once more look for succor to the Huks, just as though Magsaysay had never lived" (*New Republic,* September 9, 1967); see as well "Huks Regaining Luzon Strength," *New York Times* (April 16, 1967).

THE LESSONS OF
COLD-WAR SCHOLARSHIP

The section of counterinsurgency, together with some distilled treatment of "Defense and Development" (Chapter 7), contains most of what Wolf has to contribute to the politics and economics of the "third world" as a field of study. His essay can be faulted on several grounds aside from the political and moral grounds which I have cited above. Its historical probes are, if anything, more open to criticism, but that's the trademark of our "value free" economists and political scientists. For instance, at least five times we are reminded of "the 1962 aggression by China against India," despite the substantial evidence to the contrary (like the testimony of the then Chairman of the Joint Chiefs of Staff, Gen. Maxwell Taylor; *New York Times,* April 19, 1963). Of more interest to readers of *Viet-Report,* however, is the broader significance of such distortions, and what a book like this stands for.

United States Policy and the Third World reveals three important tendencies in cold-war scholarship: (1) the way in which our social sciences automatically tend to articulate the world view of the American power elite; (2) the shift in U.S. cold-war strategy since the advent of the Kennedy Administration in 1961; (3) the perversion of the intellect in service of our militarized foreign-policy apparatus.

The World View of the Power Elite

The opening pages set forth the basic premises of this particular study in U.S. foreign policy: the relentlessness of the cold war and the need to prevent further "losses," understood primarily in military terms.[2] The recurrent theme is that of a political and economic system which feels itself at bay in a world of hostile change. What does one do in face of this situation? If possible, he braces himself, he makes up his mind to control and direct these changes, or better yet, to block them altogether. He hangs on, regardless of the cost. Can American foreign policy since 1945 be described in any other way and still be understood as a consistent, unified whole?

American involvement in foreign areas [arises] . . . perhaps most fundamentally as an inevitable reflection of the size, activity, and power of the United States . . . and a belief by American policymakers that some foreign political leaders, institutions, systems, and options are congenial to American values, while others are hostile. . . . Attempts can be made to compensate for the military and economic consequences of a particular country's loss, but it is more difficult to find ways to compensate for the effect of a dimly perceived notion of "trend" on the loyalties and confidence of other people and countries [pp. 11, 18].[3]

The military, or paramilitary, value of the third world naturally follows from this reasoning:

---

[2] The similarity with other liberal cold warriors is striking. John McDermott has pointed out the same feature in Roger Hilsman's book, *To Move a Nation,* in his review of it in *New York Review of Books* (September 14, 1967).

[3] Two pages later, Wolf adds: "If we consider, further, various extreme contingencies concerning the progressive erosion of the free world, it might ultimately become extremely difficult to determine where the 'iron curtain' began and where it ended. A progressive reduction in the area of the world in which we could travel freely would significantly curtail our freedom, quite apart from the effect of such insulation on the quality of domestic society in the United States . . . a world of such piecemeal and sequential erosion would be one in which new generations of Americans would face increasing temptations to affiliate with the trend rather than oppose it. An inward-directed and withdrawn America might generate its own domestic opponents with an increasing disposition to overturn it from within." The tone of this observation is disturbing, since it views internal opposition as practically seditious and treasonous, but I also believe that the point is well taken. If somehow prevented

In this sense, the denial of communist control in the third world is probably the primary objective of American foreign policy in these areas.... Economic growth and social advancement are important aspects of these aims. But the denial objective is primary [p. 22].

We have before us, I think, the ultimate tragedy of U.S. foreign policy. It is stated quite clearly and unequivocally. Between continued economic underdevelopment and the possibility of a communist regime coming to power, the United States unhesitatingly chooses the former.[4]

Kennedy and the Cold War

The world power balance has undergone a major readjustment since the arrival of the New Frontiersmen in Washington in January 1961. Things had not been going well for the United States in the last years of the Eisenhower Administration. The Soviet Union had forged ahead in space, achieved nuclear deterrence parity with its own ICBMs, and vaulted over the "containment" barrier at several points, most notably in the Middle East. It had also won a string of propaganda victories over this country, thanks largely to our disarmament negotiators, whose sabotaging of the London and Geneva talks from 1955 through 1960 was too much even for certain charter members of the liberal establishment. The Chinese were making astounding economic progress (which was to end abruptly in 1960), and the neutralist countries, in the spirit of Bandung, were showing signs of traveling further from the West toward the East and Marxian socialism. It is against

this background that JFK's promise to "get the country moving again" has to be viewed. The idea was certainly in the best Western tradition: to revitalize the economic and social fabric of the country for the sake of national efficiency. Then, and only then, could its leaders face external challenges with power and confidence.

A premature, frantic lashing out would have to be avoided; that would make matters worse. Any actions taken to reverse the unfavorable world trends would have to be carefully planned. To this end, the old dreams about destroying Soviet and Chinese power in their heartlands were laid to rest. Instead, the battleground was shifted to the "uncommitted" countries, whose allegiance could tip the balance one way or the other. The architect of the new policy, as is now widely acknowledged, was Walt Whitman Rostow, with a healthy assist from Maxwell Taylor.

For his part, Rostow supplied a highly deterministic theory of history, *The Stages of Economic Growth*, which depicted societies as inevitably passing from backwardness through an economic "take-off" to "high mass consumption" affluence. The nations of the third world would sooner or later follow this path if left to their own devices. They would achieve respectable degrees of economic development and reasonable levels of political democracy *unless* —unless somewhere along the way they contracted a "disease" to which they were especially vulnerable in the stages before "take-off." The "disease" is communism. Marx's social and economic analysis, and its related program, was thus interpreted

from externalizing its problems and interfering in the affairs of other nations, the American power structure would find its energies restricted to the domestic arena. In other words, once forced to turn in upon itself, the United States would have to reappraise its own social system. There would be no more excuse for a garrison economy. It would either have to be dismantled, with accompanying political and economic dislocation, or else formally institutionalized, perhaps in a form of fascism.

[4] For a tantalizing, though characteristically cautious analysis of this policy, see Robert Heilbroner, "Counterrevolutionary America," *Commentary* (April 1967).

as a gratuitous intrusion into the historical process, an intrusion that might thwart the march of economic growth toward a future full of proto-Americas. The strategy, then, would be to stifle nascent "communist" and "romantic revolutionary" influence in the third world. The tactics would be counterinsurgency.

Maxwell Taylor's role was to call attention (in *The Uncertain Trumpet,* in 1959) to the inadequate state of the U.S. armed forces for carrying out this tactical mission. (It was no accident that Gen. Taylor was immediately brought back into the councils of power by Kennedy. Antiguerrilla activity would require an overhaul of the Army and Air Force, which had been left in an atomically musclebound state by Ike's "more bang for a buck" advocates. Brushfire, "limited" wars simply could not be waged by a military relying almost entirely on "massive retaliation" nuclear forces to keep the peace.)

The rest is a matter of record. The Kennedy-Johnson Administration used the Cuban missile crisis triumph and the ensuing "detente" with the USSR as a springboard for launching a counterrevolutionary offensive in the third world. Whenever there was any opening or any supposed threat, American power was poured in, politically, financially, and—increasingly—militarily. The fact is that American strength has become so preponderant that the old balance of power (or balance of terror) is now obsolete. The assumption that the Vietnam intervention would generate serious resistance from the communist nations and effectively isolate the United States from all its allies turns out to be incorrect. As the only superpower, this country has eclipsed the rest of the world in military and economic might.

For the foreseeable future, the only real check on Washington's interventionists may prove to be the boundless faith they have in their own power—what D. W. Brogan has called the "illusion of American omnipotence"—and the resultant tendency to overplay their hand. While the United States undoubtedly is "number one," there are forces which, in the long run, it cannot control. It will not be able to dictate the terms of the next three or four decades of history, though it will probably try. And when it does, the chickens will come home to roost, as they have so often in the years since 1945—as they have in Vietnam.

The Perversion of Intellect

Finally, the Charles Wolfs, the W. W. Rostows, the Arthur Schlesinger, Jrs. stand out as monuments to the "responsibility of the intellectuals," a tale documented by Noam Chomsky, Conor Cruise O'Brien, and Christopher Lasch. The perversion of the intellect in service of raw power: so runs the grim chronicle of the past twenty years. It encompasses not only the recent series of revelations concerning liberals and CIA operatives, but also a more fundamental illness, the transformation of the American social sciences into antihistorical analytical tools. Most of our political scientists, sociologists, economists, and historians project a world model in which the behavioral norms are stability, adjustment, and consent to an elite-monitored *status quo,* rather than self-determination, conflict, revolution, and control over public policy. In their eyes any social discord can be resolved by administrators or technicians. Expertise, not ideology, is what is required. This indeed is the "end of ideology."

Of course what it really represents is the end of history. It is a method which has converted social scientists into agents for containing and suppressing the dominant fact of history: change. Upheaval and revolution become either accidents (presumably capable of being "prevented") or products of irrational and conspiratorial forces. Under more normal circumstances any serious disorders in a socioeconomic system, it is assumed, can be eliminated by palliatives correctly applied within the system itself. That a wholly new society might be the only answer is beyond the conceptual range of such an approach. Thus counterrevolution and intervention are inherent in its very structure.

It should be obvious that through this sort of intellectual debasement American social scientists have "ended" neither ideology nor history. They have instead constructed a new ideology more dogmatic than most others precisely because it is so negative. Rather than developing either social theory or history they have instead been manufacturing policy rationales. It is a short and easily negotiable step from here to outright enlistment in the cold-war cause. The intellectuals then become the grease monkeys of *Pax Americana*.

Wolf's efforts are a case in point. They keep natural company with Arthur Schlesinger, Jr.'s 1961 "White Paper" on Castro's Cuba, *The Revolution Betrayed;* with Professor Walter Heller's proud claim to have recast national economic policymaking (as Chairman of the Council of Economic Advisers under Kennedy) so that economists may act as "angel's advocate [in putting at the President's disposal] . . . the resources needed to achieve great societies at home and grand designs abroad . . . [and by providing] the wherewithal for foreign aid and defense efforts and for financing Vietnam on a both-guns-and-butter basis";[5] and with the American University research scholars'

contribution to "Project Camelot," carried out in South America for a U.S. Army searching for the most efficient means to crush insurgency movements in their infancy. The list is a long and ignoble one, and the blackest chapter is being written in Vietnam by men like Wolf. The full flavor of what they are doing can be captured by reading Mary McCarthy's account of the U.S. "intellectuals" in South Vietnam along with any of the available reports on the effects of the bombings of North Vietnam. It would be a difficult task to decide which one paints a picture of greater intellectual depravity: the "pacification" program in the South or the systematic destruction of all sectors vital to a developing economy like North Vietnam's (railroads, schools, hospitals, administrative centers; in short, the entire "social infrastructure," as Wolf might say).[6]

SOME POINTS FOR RESISTANCE

If the peace movement can learn any lesson from books like *United States Policy and the Third World,* it would seem to be in the realm of tactics, broadly conceived. Let us consider that there are (pardon my Pentagonese) "profitable targets" that can be attacked short of taking on the whole political and economic system of the United States. The latter is still a pretty formidable obstacle; anything possible will take far more time than may be left to us by our militarized liberal leadership. But other targets exist—certain points against

[5] Heller, *New Dimensions of Political Economy* (Cambridge, Mass.: Harvard Univ. Press, 1967), pp. 10–11. Heller goes on to say that successful economic policy will also help "ideologically," since "a vigorous American economy is a showcase of modern capitalism for all the world to see." In violating the ban on ideology, this writer at least wins a laurel for his candor.

[6] Miss McCarthy's article appeared in *New York Review of Books* (May 18, 1967), and is reprinted as the third chapter of her book, *Vietnam.* On the bombings of North Vietnam, see the articles by Carol Brightman in *Viet-Report* (April-May 1967); Carl Oglesby, "Vietnam: This Is Guernica," *The Nation* (June 5, 1967); Dave Dellinger, "Report from the Tribunal" (in two parts), *Liberation* (April 1967; May-June 1967).

which guerrilla-type pressure might be brought to bear. I refer to the institutional props of the cold-war machinery: the draft (the "selective service" system); the by-passing of Congress by the President on foreign-policy questions, usually under the cloak of crisis resolutions or special appropriations; and the assimilation of the university and the intellectual into the garrison state.

This third prop should not be over-looked. It is particularly vulnerable. If the U.S. government were eventually denied a smoothly flowing supply of academicians for its global crusade to maintain the *status quo,* its costs might begin to rise toward unacceptable levels. Something like that might do more to stop American aggression than all the peace marches and *New York Times* signature appeals put together.

THE VIOLENCE OF DOMINATION

U. S. POWER AND THE DOMINICAN REPUBLIC

Fred Goff and Michael Locker

INTRODUCTION

The massive U.S. military intervention in the Dominican Republic during 1965 greatly clarified the political situation throughout Latin America. Just as Vietnam focused U.S. interests in Asia, so the Dominican intervention objectified North American intentions throughout the hemisphere. In both places Washington made it painfully clear how far it is willing to go to maintain control over the third world. The more subtle guises by which the U.S. tried to manipulate events since the days of gunboat diplomacy were stripped away when 20,000 soldiers stormed ashore to crush a nationalist rebellion in Santo Domingo. For most Latin Americans the official reasons offered to justify this action

were patently false. To all but most North Americans it was obvious the Dominicans had their independence stolen in order to benefit U.S. economic, political, and military interests. The violence that flared to the surface in this confrontation is buried inside every other covert and overt mechanism the United States utilizes to control the third world. Domination breeds violence and the potential for organized revolution.

In many respects the Dominican Republic is a small carbon copy of Cuba. An island republic close to our shores, it lives on a sugar-export economy, has a large Negro and Spanish population, and suffers from a history marked by violent, cruel dictatorship and U.S. intervention. American efforts to dominate the country stretch

Reprinted by permission of the publisher from I. L. Horowitz, J. deCastro, and J. Gerassi (eds.), Latin American Radicalism *(New York: Random House, 1969), pp. 249–291 (abridged); copyright © 1969, Random House.*

back to the early 1800s, culminating in the Spanish-American War and the gunboat diplomacy days of Theodore Roosevelt, Taft, and Wilson.[1]

Plagued by long-term economic stagnation, extensive debts to European bankers, and by political chaos, the country was invaded in 1898 by a U.S.-supported secret military expedition led by a wealthy exiled Dominican merchant. The venture failed, but in 1903 and again in 1904 revolts broke out and political leaders, vying for control, sought U.S. protectorate status. Troops landed temporarily to "protect" a sugar estate and lend support to a pro-United States faction; Kuhn, Loeb and Co., a large New York banking house, took over the foreign debts and floated a $20 million bond issue.

In a dozen years from 1904 to 1916, the United States moved from the Roosevelt Corollary to full-scale Marine occupation of the Dominican Republic. First we collected customs, then we forbade insurrection in order to maintain stability, then we held elections with warships in the harbor and sailors or Marines at the polls, then we demanded full control over internal revenues and expenditures as well as over customs, then we demanded the disbanding of the Army and establishment of a Guardia Nacional (Constabulary); then we sent the Marines.[2]

DOMINATION THROUGH OCCUPATION: 1916–1930

U.S. military occupation forces literally ran the country for eight years, ignoring even the fiction of a "Dominican government." In strikingly contemporary language the commanding U.S. admiral announced the occupation:

... for the purpose of supporting the constituted authorities and to put a stop to revolutions and consequential disorders ... It is not the intention of the United States Government to acquire by conquest any territory in the Dominican Republic nor to attack its sovereignty, but our troops will remain until all revolutionary movements have been stamped out and until such reforms as are deemed necessary to insure the future welfare of the country have been initiated and are in effective operation.[3]

In order to stabilize the financial situation, the military government repressed nationalist forces through a program of "disarmament and pacification." In two eastern provinces, Seibo and San Pedro de Macoris, where large American sugar estates were established, Dominicans took to the hills, harassed the plantations, and conducted guerrilla warfare. The Marines, terming them bandits, hunted the insurgents down mercilessly, terrorizing the local population and committing atrocities. By 1920 the repression, combined with the award of disputed land to United States and Dominican *latifundistas,* raised nationalistic passions almost to the point of full-scale rebellion. Alarmed, the plantation operators banded together under the leadership of an American, Edwin Kilbourne, to pacify the area. With a new Marine Commander they organized local squads of native Dominicans familiar with the terrain. A program of peaceful inducements was initiated after limiting the guerrilla forays and the more important leaders were persuaded to surrender. "The Marines un-

[1] Histories of the Dominican Republic in English are few and far between. The most thorough account is by the famous State Department diplomat and one-time American Commissioner to the Dominican Republic (1922–25), Sumner Welles, *Naboth's Vineyard: The Dominican Republic, 1844–1924,* 2 vols. (New York, 1928).
[2] John Bartlow Martin, *Overtaken by Events: The Dominican Crisis from the Fall of Trujillo to Civil War* (New York, 1966), p. 28.
[3] Welles, Vol. 2, p. 777.

questionably sowed the seed of anti-Americanism throughout the Republic," especially in the eastern provinces. To this day "in some towns the anniversary of their departure is celebrated as a holiday."[4]

Most of the social and economic programs established during the occupation collapsed when the troops formally withdrew in 1924. But even before withdrawing, the United States insisted on maintaining control over customs until all foreign debts were paid, forced the adoption of a U.S.-drafted electoral code, and further strengthened the National Police as a substitute for the old politicized army. Trained and officered by American Marines, the police quickly became the most organized and powerful force throughout the island. It was through this structure that Rafael Leonidas Trujillo made his way, assiduously cultivating friendships with the American officers, conspicuously demonstrating cooperation and cordiality. As he climbed the promotional ladder, with the aid of favorable American recommendations, he mastered the one essential role for gaining and sustaining political power in the Republic—an understanding that the base of domestic power is rooted primarily in the United States.

DOMINATION THROUGH DICTATORSHIP: THE ERA OF TRUJILLO

When the National Police was transformed back into the army in 1928, Trujillo assumed the role of chief. Maneuvering carefully behind the scenes he engineered a fake uprising followed by the seizure of cities and the confiscation of weapons on the pretext of preserving order and preventing bloodshed. "One of Trujillo's greatest concerns in this plot was to insure that the government he established would be recognized by the United States."[5] Close contact with the American legation and his influential old Marine Commander, Colonel Cutts, guaranteed Trujillo U.S. support and ultimate success.

Once in power Trujillo proceeded to erect a pervasive and repressive totalitarian regime. The army was his private instrument of coercion and terror; the oversize officer corps benefited materially and enjoyed privileged status.[6] At home and abroad he developed a huge espionage apparatus providing the kind of intelligence needed to predict events and manipulate people. By recruiting their sons Trujillo cleverly forced most of the oligar-

---

[4] Martin, p. 29. On the operations and effects of U.S. occupation, see Arthur J. Burks, *Land of a Checkerboard Family* (New York, 1932); Melvin M. Knight, *The Americans in Santo Domingo* (New York, 1928); Dana G. Munro, *Intervention and Dollar Diplomacy in the Caribbean, 1900–1921* (Princeton, 1964); and Marvin Goldwart, "The Constabulary in the Dominican Republic and Nicaragua" in *Latin American Monographs*, No. 17 (Gainesville, 1962).

[5] Robert D. Crassweller, *Trujillo: The Life and Times of a Caribbean Dictator* (New York, 1966), p. 62. Crassweller's book is a highly authoritative account of the Trujillo period. During World War II the author was an officer in the State Department's Economic Warfare Section. Later he was a partner in a Dominican-Puerto Rican iron-mining venture, then became a member of the legal staff of Pan American World Airways. In 1967 he joined the staff of the Council on Foreign Relations to do a two-year study on U.S. policy in the Caribbean.

A discussion of the Dominican armed forces can be found in Howard J. Wiarda, "The Politics of Civil-Military Relations in the Dominican Republic," *Journal of Inter-American Studies*, **2**:4 (October 1965), pp. 465–484.

[6] "During his long rule, the dictator showered continuous favors upon his uniformed backers, the result being that the Dominican Republic built up the most powerful war machine in

chy into collaboration; blackmail, threats, and economic pressure compelled virtually every man of ability to serve him. Torture and assassination awaited those who resisted. Political opposition was erased or manipulated by cooption, imprisonment, exile, or murder. The Generalissimo personally selected all the national and local appointments, and his own party, manned by an endless string of relatives and cronies, administered a sizable social-welfare program. Every official, high or low, was subjected to constant rotation, public humiliation, or sudden elevation on short notice by orders from "El Jefe."

Beyond this traditional *caudillo* system, Trujillo constructed a fantastic personal economic empire. "At the most, . . . other [*caudillos*] had wanted money for its own sake, or for luxury, display, bribery, or a political purpose. Trujillo, far more than any of them, saw in the entire economic process a source of dominion as potent as the army, as strong as the most rigid political structure."[7] Funds collected from the public and from illicit operations were invested in every conceivable agricultural and industrial enterprise; monopolies usually followed. Import-export taxes and license fees facilitated the harassment and eventual takeover of corporations dealing in foreign trade, the lifeblood of the economy. More-

over, U.S. commodity shortages at the end of World War II raised prices on agricultural exports and propelled the island's elite into relative prosperity. After centralizing banking operations, Trujillo could sell any of his unprofitable businesses to the state for a large profit and make timely reacquisitions. It has been estimated that between 65 and 85 percent of the entire economy eventually ended up in his hands.[8] The monetary fortune accumulated from this empire was not trivial, and the variety of devices it afforded for exercising power was crucial to maintaining the regime.

In the late forties and during the fifties, Trujillo made his move for the most coveted prize in the Dominican economy—the cane-sugar industry. A sharp rise in postwar sugar prices attracted Trujillo's attention, but with the exception of relatively small properties held by the Vicini family the entire industry was owned by foreign capital—mainly United States. Fully aware of the financial and political complications involved in entering this economic sector, he proceeded cautiously. After acquiring a small independent mill in 1948, he pushed forward with the construction of an enormous milling installation, Rio Haina, that was put into production in 1953. In order to supply enough cane, he acquired large tracts of land from Dominicans, Canadians,

the Caribbean, a military establishment far out of proportion to the actual security needs of the tiny nation. It included 17,000 troops; 12,000 policemen; light-, medium-, and heavy-tank battalions; and squadrons of fighters, bombers, destroyers, and frigates. The armed forces simply occupied their own nation." Edwin Lieuwen, *Generals vs. Presidents: Neomilitarism in Latin America* (New York, 1964) , p. 55.

[7] Crassweller, p. 123.

[8] *The Hispanic American Report*, **15** (December 1962) reported: "Official sources revealed that Trujillo's share of the national wealth had amounted to the following: bank deposits, 22%, money in circulation, 25%; sugar production, 63%; cement, 63%; paper, 73%; paint, 86%; cigarettes, 71%; milk, 85%; wheat and flour, 68%; plus the nation's only airline, its leading newspapers, and the three principal radio and television stations. According to the Swiss daily (Basel) *National Zeitung*, the Trujillo family had deposited no less than $200 million in Swiss banks in the name of fictitious companies."

In the same journal, **16** (May 1963), p. 463: ". . . the dictator owned 10% of the productive land and 10% of the cattle industry; 45% of the nation's active manpower was employed directly in Trujillo enterprises; a further 35% was engaged in the Armed Forces and the government-operated banking, hotel, and electricity systems."

Puerto Ricans, and finally Americans with small holdings. The largest single sugar complex on the island, La Romana, a subsidiary of the American-owned South Puerto Rico Sugar Co., was then handed the technical task of building a railroad for the efficient transportation of cane and managing the entire operation on a profit-sharing basis.

These accomplishments pushed Trujillo into the largest economic deal of his reign—acquisition of the prized U.S. West Indies Sugar Company. A product of the Marine occupation and the efforts of antiguerrilla expert Edwin Kilbourne (president and director of the company), West Indies was the largest geographically dispersed sugar complex on the island: four high-volume mills, along with 30,000 head of cattle, considerable pasture land, coconut plantations on Samana Bay, some coffee fincas, and a great deal of underdeveloped land. Unlike La Romana with its powerful South Puerto Rico Corp. connections to Kuhn, Loeb & Co. and Rockefeller interests, West Indies could not elicit enough political influence to bring about U.S. intervention.[9] After some pressure was applied and the word of Trujillo's desire to buy got out, the stockholders negotiated a favorable figure ($35,-830,000) in three cash installments. As for South Puerto Rico, Trujillo realized its technical skills were not replaceable and its powerful connections could be mutually advantageous in raising the island's U.S. sugar quota.

The sugar acquisitions demonstrated that Trujillo still retained his keen understanding of power relationships within the United States as well as the limitations they imposed on his actions. Geographic proximity and the economic strength of the United States forced any Dominican government to depend on close and cordial relations with powerful U.S. citizens. To this end, Trujillo devoted boundless energy and resources in the form of business deals, sex, flattery, campaign contributions, bribes, blackmail, even murder. Joseph E. Davies, the archetype of Trujillo's influential American, was a multimillionaire corporate lawyer (with a major interest in General Foods) turned New Deal diplomat. In 1931, Davies visited the Republic for President Roosevelt and brought back a highly favorable assessment of the new regime, which led, in turn, to a lifesaving moratorium on debt payments and opened up new lines of credit. A long friendship ensued; Davies visited often to serve as financial counsel on business ventures and fiscal policy. Along with Davies, industrialist Herbert May, construction tycoon Felix Benítez Rexach, diplomat-businessman William Pawley, and the molasses dealers A. I. and J. M. Kaplan served as Trujillo's economic liaison with the U.S. financial and business community.[10]

Trujillo never found an equivalent to Davies in the political sphere of the U.S. Establishment, though he managed to significantly influence governmental decisions

[9] Originally West Indies Sugar was part of a company controlled by the National City Bank. But in 1931 the company was taken over by less influential stockholders who counted on the considerable skill and influence of the management—which included Kilbourne—within the Republic.

On the other hand, South Puerto Rico's connections to Kuhn, Loeb & Co. (the powerful New York banking house that held the Dominican government's debt until 1940) existed through stock ownership, loans, and interlocking directors. Ties to Rockefeller interests (including the Chase Manhattan Bank and its predecessors, and Standard Oil Co. of New Jersey) were manifest through interlocking directors and the chief Rockefeller law firm, Dewey, Ballantine, Bushby, Palmer & Wood, which was the company's general counsel.

[10] Herbert May was a link to the Pittsburgh Mellon interests which developed a sizable investment in the 1950s for mining bauxite at Cabo Rojo through the Aluminum Company of America. [Footnote 10 continued on next page.]

and public opinion through a chain of well-paid politicians, lawyers, journalists, and lobbyists. Nobody knows how many millions of dollars were passed directly or indirectly to senators, representatives, executive-department employees, and other powerful Americans in public life who might protect and promote Trujillo.[11] Such dignitaries, critics as well as supporters, were often invited to his private fiefdom, wined and dined, provided with women and then secretly photographed. The "blackmail photographic library was extensive."[12] . . .

After 1955, Trujillo built a congressional power base in the United States centered around his periodic attempts to enlarge the island's share of the extremely lucrative U.S. sugar quota. Since 1934, the United States Government has subsidized the price

of raw sugar to regulate supply and stabilize prices for domestic refiners and industrial consumers. A tonnage quota is assigned by Congress (primarily the House Agriculture Committee) to exporting nations and domestic growers guaranteeing the producer a high price and thus assuring delivery. Cuba had always been a preferred nation in the system, receiving the largest quota (providing approximately one-third of all sugar consumed in the United States) by reason of its position as the world's greatest producer. Since the dollar stakes were high and most of the Cuban ventures constituted very substantial *American* investments, the Cuban lobby exercised considerably more leverage than Trujillo and South Puerto Rico Sugar.[13]

Thus, it was not until the Cuban Revolu-

Benítez, a Puerto Rican who fought Muñoz Marin over the issue of independence, raised capital and equipment for public improvement projects undertaken by his company, the Rexach Construction Co. He was selected by Trujillo to be his political agent in Puerto Rico.

William Pawley was ambassador to Peru (1945–46) and Brazil (1946–48), influential in Washington, and a businessman with diverse holdings in Florida and Cuba. He drafted the Dominican legislation on foreign investments for Trujillo, obtained mineral concessions for U.S. investors, and advised the Generalissimo on numerous occasions (e.g., The Galindez Affair).

The Kaplan brothers bought molasses for export to the U.S. and had extensive political power within the liberal wing of the Democratic Party.

[11] The Head of Trujillo's military intelligence (SIM) wrote: "Trujillo had, for instance, price lists for the purchase of some U.S. Congressmen. An ordinary, run-of-the-mill Representative would cost about $5,000 or less. A few House committee chairmen could be had for about three times that much, depending on the committee. Senators came higher, of course. A chairman of a key committee could run from $50,000 to $75,000." Arturo R. Espaillat, *Trujillo: The Last Caesar* (Chicago, 1963), p. 81.

[12] Martin, p. 35.

[13] This was reflected in the prestige of their lobbyist George W. Ball, a partner in the law firm of Cleary, Gottlieb, Steen and Ball, who represented two Cuban sugar associations before Congress during the 1956 consideration of the Sugar Act. Ball went on to become Under-Secretary of State in the Kennedy and Johnson administrations. Neither Trujillo nor South Puerto Rico ever retained a political figure with as much influence as the Cuban lobby.

The role of prestigious political figures in the sugar-quota lobbying is discussed in Daniel M. Berman and Robert A. Heineman's article "Lobbying by Foreign Government on the Sugar Act Amendments of 1962," *Law and Contemporary Problems* (September 1963), pp. 416–427.

The whole quota system really benefits American-owned producers at home or abroad far more than underdeveloped nations, as has been asserted by its backers. Most of the subsidies, eventually paid for by the American public through higher prices, are collected by U.S. corporations, who then determine their use in terms of profit maximization rather than social needs. Those subsidies which end up with foreign nationals only make the oligarchy richer and more powerful.

tion fundamentally altered power relations inside the United States that the Dominican Republic had a chance to sell its greatly expanded sugar exports at preferential quota prices.[14] As United States-Cuban relations deteriorated and Castro cut back sugar production during 1959–60, Trujillo's lobbying in Congress began to bear fruit. By July 1960, the Cuban quota was canceled and the Dominican Republic received the largest portion of its subsequent redistribution.[15] Cane production soared and the value of sugar exports doubled.

Yet Castro's revolution was obviously a mixed blessing. On June 14, 1959, Dominican exiles launched an invasion from Cuba which, though unsuccessful, shook Trujillo's regime to its roots. Torture, arrests, and assassinations of prominent Dominicans followed, and for the first time in thirty years, opposition on a large scale developed. By January 1960, in an unprecedented event, the Roman Catholic Church finally denounced the Trujillo regime. During this same period huge arms expenditures began to sap the economy's strength. In a fit of desperation, Trujillo lashed out in an assassination attempt on an archenemy, Venezuela's social democratic President Romuló Betancourt. The Organization of American States (OAS) was called into session, Trujillo was denounced, and economic sanctions were imposed. . . .

A plot to overthrow Castro in August 1959, financed by Trujillo, attempted to foster an internal uprising backed by a foreign invasion (from Florida and the Dominican Republic). But the Eisenhower Administration was not yet prepared to back such drastic moves and the CIA hampered the invasion operations. When the Cuban-based conspirators double-crossed Trujillo's agents the plot failed miserably.[16] Without Castro's removal relations continued to deteriorate: "The Department of State increasingly viewed the Dominican tyrant as an embarrassment, an awkward inheritance from an earlier time, now lingering too long and imperiling the future and unwittingly preparing the way for Castroism."[17] Increased U.S. reliance on Dominican sugar imports strengthened the push to stabilize the situation by removing Trujillo. Diplomat-businessman William Pawley, along with his close friend Senator George Smathers (D.-Fla.), visited El Jefe to plead for his abdication in order to facilitate a smooth transition toward democracy. Trujillo refused to comply, military assistance and arm shipments were termi-

---

[14] Before 1960, most Dominican cane was sold to the British dealers Tate & Lyle. Though the raw sugar was sold at low world-market prices, Trujillo's control over labor kept wages so depressed that Dominican sugar producers could still turn a handsome profit.

[15] This was largely due to the efforts of Representative Harold Cooley (D-N.C.), Chairman of the House Agriculture Committee and virtual sugar czar when it came to setting quotas. Cooley, along with his staff, made several expense-paid trips to the island to "visit" El Jefe and was very favorably disposed to the dictator.

[16] This whole episode to overthrow Castro in 1960 is still shrouded in mystery, especially the role of the CIA and the American soldier of fortune William Morgan. A substantial number of Cuban exiles and foreign mercenaries were actually enlisted while Morgan was assigned the task of reactivating the Second Front of Escambray and capturing the city of Trinidad for the invasion landing. After Morgan double-crossed his backers and the invasion fell through, many of the Cuban exiles were recruited by the CIA for the Bay of Pigs landing (April 1961). The United States never supported the plot with much zeal, probably because Washington's policy at this time centered around opposing Castro through isolation rather than direct intervention. For some details see Crassweller, pp. 349–352; and Robert Emmett Johnson, "For a Million Bucks I'll Knock Off Castro," *True* (August 1967), pp. 12–18.

[17] Crassweller, p. 421.

nated, and Ambassador Joseph S. Farland contacted the growing internal underground before the United States vacated his diplomatic post in May 1960. . . .

Kennedy's rise to power gave Trujillo's lobbyists a new chance to alter U.S. policy. State Department consultant and sugar-company executive Adolf A. Berle, Jr., and Under Secretary of State Chester Bowles were reached in an effort to have the special sugar tax lifted. Moreover, a special lobbyist (Igor Cassini) convinced Joseph Kennedy that a revolutionary situation was developing and that it would be helpful to send a special envoy to Ciudad Trujillo to assess matters. The State Department's top troubleshooter, Robert Murphy, paid an informal visit and again sought a liberalization of the regime. It was clear to the Kennedy Administration that support among Latin Americans for anti-Castro activities (including the Bay of Pigs) rested in part on anti-Trujillo moves. Without a power base in the executive branch of the United States Government the Dominican dictator was helpless to determine his own fate.

The failure of the Murphy mission set in motion the final stages of a CIA-supported plot to assassinate Trujillo. Chiefly organized by some of his own military officers, the assassination was successfully carried out on May 31, 1961.[18] As an obstacle to, rather than an instrument for, domination, the Great Benefactor had to be removed.

DOMINATION THROUGH STABILIZATION: 1961–1963

With Trujillo's disposal the Kennedy Administration had to choose between maintaining order through support for the remaining repressive apparatus and hated Trujillo cronies or gambling on democracy and social change by favoring the anti-Trujillo forces. U.S. priorities were clearly spelled out by the President in a Cabinet session soon after Trujillo's death.

There are three possibilities in descending order of preference: decent democratic order, a continuation of the Trujillo regime, or a Castro regime. We ought to aim for the first, but we really can't renounce the second until we are sure that one can avoid the third.[19]

In effect, Washington simultaneously attempted to maintain stability and order while encouraging democratization and minor social change. In classical fashion the New Frontiersmen submerged Dominican interests under North American needs. For six months the United States hesitated to dismantle the old structures now administered by Trujillo's last figurehead president, Joaquin Balaguer, but really in the hands of Trujillo's remaining relatives, military officers, business associates, and gangsters. The island was wracked by bloody repressions and severe unemployment, while the United States encouraged Balaguer to "liberalize" and "democratize" his regime. Conservative and left opposition against Trujilloism without Trujillo sought continued suspension of the U.S. sugar quota to restrain the regime's excesses. Kennedy, realizing this was his most powerful weapon, had to postpone moving against the Trujillistas until the U.S. military, the CIA, and its cooperating organizations could penetrate the country's shattered infrastructure, create a conservative alternative regime, and thereby control events. By the end of 1961 a conspiracy of Dominican generals was combined with a show of U.S. naval power offshore near

[18] Norman Gall, "How Trujillo Died," *The New Republic* (April 13, 1963), pp. 19–20.
[19] Arthur M. Schlesinger, Jr., *A Thousand Days: John F. Kennedy in the White House* (Boston, 1965), p. 769.

Santo Domingo to force the last of the Trujillo family to leave the island.[20]

The first real political organization after Trujillo's assassination sprang up within the oligarchy, petty bourgeois, and professional classes who formed an anti-Trujillo civic-minded association which later became the Union Civica Nacional (UCN) political party. In order to gain a base among the youth and intellectuals, the UCN entered into an unholy alliance with the strongly nationalist 14th of June Movement (IJ4). This alliance, however, was quickly sacrificed in January 1962 for control of the U.S.-backed interim Consejo de Estado (Council of State) government which was charged with maintaining stability and holding elections the following December. The United States demonstrated its strong backing of the council by lifting economic sanctions, resuming diplomatic relations, restoring military assistance, extending $25 million in emergency credit, and authorizing the purchase of additional sugar under the premium quota price.[21]

The ending of sanctions and the reestablishment of a Dominican sugar quota was undoubtedly crucial. The cane-sugar industry is the largest industrial operation on the island and the leading contributor to government income in the form of taxes, foreign exchange, and employment. Privately South Puerto Rico Sugar's La Romana produces one-third of the cane output, while the former Trujillo holdings, taken over by the Consejo, produce a little less than the remaining two-thirds. In 1962 over 90 percent of Dominican cane went to American ports, and under a newly enacted sugar quota act, both South Puerto

Rico Sugar and the interim government retained influential lobbyists to jack up quotas even further.

A fundamental question confronting the Consejo and subsequent governments revolved around the fate of the confiscated Trujillo properties. These represented approximately 65 percent of Dominican industry in fifty-seven different product sectors, 35 percent of the arable land, and 30 percent of the animal husbandry.[22] It was an open secret that the UCN hoped to distribute the holdings to favored private interests if they won the upcoming elections.

During the 1962 electoral campaign the Partido Revolucionario Dominicano (PRD), headed by twenty-five-year exile Juan Bosch, presented a platform advocating distribution of Trujillo land to landless *campesinos*, formation of cooperatives, an increase in agricultural wages, construction of small town communal eating halls, public works, and development of new industry around untapped mineral resources to reduce unemployment. The general object was to diversify agriculture and to create a consumer economy.

Despite repeated setbacks and unforeseen complications the holding of elections was guaranteed by the frantic but thorough manipulations of U.S. ambassador John Bartlow Martin, a man with strong ties to the ADA (Americans for Democratic Action) liberals in the United States. For example, at one crucial juncture, Martin wrote:

Then I called the senior Embassy staff and Williams together, told them what I was doing, and told them we must slow down the Dominican reaction before it got completely out of control.

[20] De Lesseps S. Morrison, *Latin American Mission: An Adventure in Hemisphere Diplomacy* (New York, 1965), Chapters 7–10.
[21] For a description of political maneuvering after November 1961, see Julio César Martínez, "Revolution and Counter Revolution: The Chessboard," *New Politics*, 4:2 (Spring 1965), pp. 47–55.
[22] Dr. Emilio Cordero Michel, "The Dominican Revolution," *Progressive Labor* (December 1965), p. 68.

We must immediately talk to all important Dominicans—explain the situation, urge everyone to await developments, and reaffirm our determination not to abandon the Republic. We divided up the people we could see—Consejeros, political party leaders, government men, sugar men.[23]

DOMINATION THROUGH INFILTRATION: THE BOSCH GOVERNMENT

The defeat at the hands of Bosch's social democratic PRD, which received 60 percent of the December 1962 vote, caught the UCN and its conservative backers by surprise. But Bosch, a self-educated intellectual from humble origins, knew his government would not last long; thirty hours before the polls opened he told a television audience:

I do not wish to be a candidate because I know the PRD will win the elections and if it does, the government . . . will be overthrown in a short time on the pretext that it is Communist.[24]

As a skeptical business community looked on, Bosch negotiated a $150-million line of credit with a Zurich-based consortium to finance his larger development projects, a departure from the usual U.S. sources. Next he canceled an oil-refinery contract, which Esso, Texaco, and Shell had negotiated with Trujillo and the Consejo, because of the large profits which would leave the country.[25]

Despite these initiatives toward financial independence, Bosch found it necessary to seek United States aid. The Kennedy Administration hoped to make the Dominican Republic a "showcase of democracy" as a counterweight to Cuba.[26] Nevertheless, Bosch found U.S. financial backing hard to obtain. Former businessman Newell Williams, AID director for the Republic, commented: "Ever since Bosch has been in, we've been turned down."[27] Later, toward the end of Bosch's first one hundred days in office, Ambassador Martin noted, "We had committed something over $50 million

---

[23] Martin, p. 164. Martin was a free-lance journalist and a key speech writer in the 1952 and 1956 presidential campaigns of Adlai Stevenson. He worked on John F. Kennedy's 1960 campaign staff and was subsequently appointed ambassador to the Dominican Republic, arriving in March 1962.

[24] Juan Bosch, *The Unfinished Experiment: Democracy in the Dominican Republic* (New York, 1965), p. 123. This book was originally published in Spanish in 1964 by the Centro de Estudios y Documentación Sociales (CEDS) under the title *Crisis de la Democracia de América en la República Dominicana* (Mexico, 1964). CEDS was run in Mexico by social democrat Victor Alba and was financed by the CIA through the J. M. Kaplan Fund. The English edition does not give the translator's name and was published by Frederick A. Praeger, Inc., which was recently exposed as having contracted with the CIA for numerous printing jobs.

[25] Drew Pearson on May 21, 1965 elaborates: ". . . Third factor operating against Bosch, when he was kicked out in September 1963, was the Texas Oil Co. Sen. Wayne Morse (D-Ore.), in hearings before the Senate Foreign Relations Committee, developed the fact that Duane D. Luther of Texaco, a former member of the cloak-and-dagger OSS, had contributed $2,500 to Bosch's opponent, Viriato Fiallo, and was reported to have plotted the anti-Bosch revolt . . . When I telephoned Luther to get his side of the story, the overseas operator reported that he would not take the call." Drew Pearson, "The Washington Merry-Go-Round" (May 21, 1965) as reported in Gary J. Mounce and Anne H. Sutherland (eds.), *After Santo Domingo, What? U.S. Intervention in Latin America*, pp. 11–18, an inquiry sponsored by the University Colloquy on Public Relations, University of Texas, May 1966, Austin, Texas.

[26] See Schlesinger, pp. 769–773, the section entitled "The Showcase That Failed."

[27] Martin, p. 389.

to last year's Consejo but not a cent for Bosch."[28]

Several aspects of his administration alarmed native and United States investors. An effort was made to rescind several sugar contracts negotiated by the Consejo. While advantageous for U.S. sugar purchasers, these contracts meant a loss of several million dollars in foreign exchange for the Dominican Republic. Former Ambassador Martin wrote:

The Department [State Department] instructed me to inform the Dominican Government that its failure to honor legitimate contracts with U.S. sugar firms would certainly have most serious repercussions for the Bosch government and might even lead to an invocation of the Hickenlooper amendment which would end AID to the Republic.[29]

Within a week of Bosch's inauguration, *Business Week* attacked him for proposing a "revolutionary constitution" and land reform "which would prohibit operations of U.S.-owned sugar companies."[30] An official of La Romana expressed the fear that Bosch's government might make the Puerto Rican "mistake" of subdividing the cane lands. "To break up the Company's lands would wreck Romana."[31] Concern over constitutional provisions about business operations was a constant theme in discussions between U.S. representatives and all Dominican governments. Much later during the U.S. invasion and occupation of the

Republic in 1965, U.S. negotiators demanded that the "rebels," who were fighting for a reinstatement of the 1963 Constitution, modify several of its articles. They were especially troubled by Article 19, giving workers the right to profit sharing in both agricultural and industrial enterprises; Article 23, prohibiting large landholdings; Article 25, restricting the right of foreigners to acquire Dominican land; Article 28, requiring landholders to sell that portion of their lands above a maximum fixed by law, excess holdings to be distributed to the landless peasantry; and Article 66, prohibiting expulsion of Dominicans from their own country. American negotiators in 1965 proposed an amendment to exempt owners of sugar plantations and cattle ranches, the largest of these being South Puerto Rico Sugar's La Romana.[32] . . .

In short time, inflated anti-communism flourished and began to undermine Bosch's legitimacy. Even civil-libertarian Ambassador Martin kept constant pressure on Bosch with advice like the following:

I recommended Bosch couple any changes with other measures—repeal of the old de-Trujilloization law and enactment of a law providing for the trial of military personnel by military tribunals . . . I recommended that Congress adopt a resolution declaring it the sense of the Congress that communism was incompatible with the Inter-American system . . . and that it enact a Dominican version of the Smith act . . . I recom-

---

[28] *Ibid.*, p. 451. AID money was slow in coming. Bosch eventually received authorization for about $50 million in grants and loans.

[29] *Ibid.*, p. 355.

[30] *Business Week* (March 2, 1963), as quoted by Victor Perlo, *The Marines in Santo Domingo* (New York, 1965), p. 10. (A pamphlet published by New Outlook publishers.)

[31] *Latin America Report*, **5**:4 (1963), p. 13. For a discussion of another controversial piece of Bosch legislation directly affecting La Romana, see Franklin J. Franco, *República Dominicana, Clase, Crisis Y Comandos* (Cuba, 1967), p. 141, on the "Precio Tope de Azucar" Act. Basically it provided for any profits from sales of sugar above a ceiling price to be given to the state.

[32] Dan Kurzman, *The Washington Post* (May 25, 1965), as reported by *I. F. Stone's Weekly* (May 31, 1965).

mended he hold back on agrarian reform if it entailed confiscation laws.[33]

In practical terms, Martin's anti-communism reinforced the irrational charges of Dominican rightists which further undermined Bosch's government. A favorite target of right-wing generals was the Inter-American Center for Social Studies (CIDES). Run by a Rumanian-born naturalized American, Sacha Volman, CIDES received its funds and direction from the American-based Institute of International Labor Research (IILR). The IILR in turn was headed by U.S. social democratic leader Norman Thomas and its secretary-treasurer was Volman. All but a fraction of IILR's budget came from the J. M. Kaplan Fund, which was exposed in 1964 by Congressman Wright Patman as a conduit for Central Intelligence Agency funds. Immediately after the armed forces overthrew Bosch, CIDES was sacked and closed while Volman fled the country. Ironically, the military was, in effect, charging that a CIA operation was riddled with communists and communist sympathizers, though it is now clear CIDES' covert purpose was to assure strong U.S. influence in the PRD and Bosch's government.

Earlier this same Institute of International Labor Research played a crucial role in Dominican politics. At the time of Trujillo's assassination (May 1961), Juan Bosch was teaching at the Costa Rican Institute of Political Education which Sacha Volman set up in 1959 with CIA funds channeled through the J. M. Kaplan Fund and the IILR. Immediately after Trujillo's assassination Volman was the first man Bosch sent to the Republic to survey the political situation and recommend strategy for the PRD. During 1962 he proceeded to organize a 300,000-member peasant league (FENHERCA), which played a key role in providing Bosch's PRD with the critical countryside vote in the election (approximately 70 percent of the Dominicans live in rural areas). But once the votes were in Volman abandoned FENHERCA and one of the PRD's strongest bases of organized support deteriorated.

With Bosch in office, Volman reoriented his energies and resources into organizing CIDES, a planning-research center for the government and a training institute for young political organizers and administrators. CIDES was to provide most of the state planning as well as the crucial technical and professional talent for running the government and the infrastructure of the PRD. The Kaplan Fund contributed $35,000 which was supplemented by grants from several other U.S. foundations and government agencies. A $250,000 grant from the Ford Foundation (administered by Brandeis University and ADA leader John P. Roche) paralleled CIDES' work within the government civil-service administration. Along with other similar programs, the U.S. Government was thus able to penetrate and manipulate the social democrats (PRD) in the Dominican Republic as well as the government they formed.

As it turned out, the involvement of J. M. Kaplan in the IILR and its Dominican offshoots (FENHERCA and CIDES) was not a fortuitous occurrence. This Caribbean sugar and molasses speculator had arranged a monopoly of Dominican molasses sales during the latter years of the Trujillo era. Introduced to Bosch by Norman Thomas, Kaplan became the Dominican president's personal emissary to business and political circles in New York and Washington. In reality, Kaplan's interest in Bosch's government, both in terms of channeling CIA funds to Volman's operations and maintaining a favorable image for Bosch among his

[33] Martin, p. 487.

142   TECHNOLOGICAL MILITARISM

powerful U.S. friends, was directly related to his sugar and molasses operations and associations. One month before Bosch was overthrown Kaplan suddenly decided that his administration was infiltrated with communists and he withdrew his influential support. This vital break signaled the collapse of Bosch's power base in the United States.[34]

But the Kennedy Administration never placed all its bets on infiltrating and controlling the social democratic PRD in order to guarantee U.S. domination. In what amounted to a schizophrenic policy, the Kennedy Administration, while supporting Bosch, simultaneously trained and equipped the antireformist forces that eventually brought down his regime—the armed forces and the police. . . .

The Dominican officers were not used to acting alone, however. Judging from accounts like the following, they were given the go-ahead to overthrow Bosch by their U.S. advisers:

Cass [Bevan Cass] was having problems of conscience about Bosch. As our naval attaché, he was obligated to urge Dominican officers to support Bosch, but he himself had misgivings about Bosch's attitude toward the Castro Communists

. . . and didn't know "how much longer I can go on supporting him like this" . . . he was probably our most influential attaché.[33]

Led by the air-force tank commander, Elias Wessin y Wessin, and Trujillo assassin, Antonio Imbert Barrera, the armed forces deposed Bosch on September 25, 1963.

The cross-purpose policy of backing both the right and the left went even deeper. The AFL-CIO Latin American trade union federation, ORIT, split the PRD-oriented labor movement with the formation of CONATRAL, a pro-U.S., parallel confederation of Dominican unions organized along the antipolitical Sam Gompers line. Aiding in the training of anti-Bosch unionists was the American Institute for Free Labor Development (AIFLD), a bizarre hybrid of AFL-CIO, big business, and U.S. Government interests.[36] Not surprisingly, CONATRAL exhorted the Dominicans one week before the coup, through a one-page newspaper advertisement, to put their faith in the armed forces to defend them against communism. Shortly after the coup most other labor leaders were in jail, hiding, or had sought asylum.[37]

[34] For the background on this subject see: Ruth Shereff, "How the CIA Makes Friends and Influences Countries," *Viet-Report* (January-February 1967); Bosch, pp. 97 and 169–178; Dan Kurzman, "Labor Group Got $1 Million From CIA," *The Washington Post* (February 21, 1967); and Sacha Volman, *Latin American Experiments in Political and Economic Training* (Washington: Brookings Institution, 1964).

[35] Martin, pp. 504–505. According to *Time* staffer Sam Halper, the Dominican armed forces ousted Bosch "as soon as they got a wink from the U.S. Pentagon." See Sam Halper, "The Dominican Upheaval," *The New Leader* (May 10, 1965).

[36] Nine young labor leaders attended the AIFLD school in Washington, D.C.; two were sent to Europe and Israel for special training; and twenty additional leaders attended regional AIFLD schools in Latin America.

The working-class spirit of these training sessions is most difficult to comprehend, given the fact that ALFLD's chairman was J. Peter Grace, President of W. R. Grace and Company and a Director of the First National City Bank. Also on the board are several other leaders of U.S. corporations with heavy investments in Latin America.

For further discussion of the ALFLD see: Sidney Lens, "American Labor Abroad: Lovestone Diplomacy," *The Nation* (July 5, 1965); and George Morris, *CIA and American Labor: Subversion of the AFL-CIO's Foreign Policy* (New York, 1967), Chapter 6.

[37] Dominican labor, including the numerous splits within the movement, is reviewed in T. D. Roberts *et al.*, *Area Handbook for the Dominican Republic* (Washington: U.S. Government Printing Office, 1966), Chapter 21; and Susan Bodenheimer, "The AFL-CIO in Latin America. The Dominican Republic: A Case Study," *Viet-Report* (September-October 1967), pp. 17–19 and 27–28.

Ambassador Martin, never overwhelmingly enthusiastic about Bosch, nevertheless sought the State Department's view on the utilization of American warships for reinstating Bosch. The Department refused to intervene unless a "Communist takeover" was imminent. Bosch's downfall was the final blow to the Kennedy hope for peaceful social reform in Latin America. The extremely weak power base in the United States advocating such a program—certain intellectuals, social democrats, some of Kennedy's advisers, and a section of the CIA—was no match for threatened business interests, generals, and liberals who put anticommunism ahead of social change. It should be remembered that Caribbean policy in the early sixties was dominated by a preoccupation with Cuba and the incipient spread of Fidel Castro's revolution. For businessmen, journalists, and State Department officials, the legitimacy of Bosch's administration rested on its ability to contain, through whatever means necessary, the small Castroite left (primarily the nationalistic 14th of June Movement). As mentioned above, Martin went so far as to strongly recommend the enactment of a Dominican Smith Act. Bosch refused. And for the influential power base in the United States concerned with Cuba, this ruled out large-scale support, and therefore survival.

. . . What could have been his strongest base of support, an organized labor and peasantry, had been infiltrated and manipulated by the United States.

DOMINATION THROUGH MANIPULATION: THE TRIUMVIRATE

Kennedy, seeing the *golpe* as a heavy blow to the *Alianza*, refused to recognize the new regime and suspended aid; but Kennedy was assassinated. In an effort to gain U.S. diplomatic recognition and economic aid, a new government, the so-called Triumvirate, dramatically announced it was threatened by an incipient guerrilla movement aided by Fidel Castro. Actually, some June 14th Movement leaders took to the hills shortly after Bosch's downfall, but the arms they acquired were apparently obtained through a CIA agent (Camilo Todemann) and proved useless. When the guerrillas surrendered, they were mercilessly tortured and executed.[38] The plot produced the desired effect, for one of President Johnson's first foreign-policy shifts was to recognize the regimes in the Dominican Republic and Honduras. On the same day (December 14, 1963), Thomas Mann was appointed Assistant Secretary of State for Inter-American Affairs. The subsequent Dominican government was headed by Donald Reid Cabral, former auto dealer, close friend of U.S. business and member of the oligarchy. Realizing his power rested with the military, Reid turned his back on the officers' contraband and smuggling operations, thereby winning their tacit support.[39]

The Reid government put an end to economic and social development. With the shelving of the 1963 Constitution, the Bosch reform legislation, and the Zurich consortium credit, large numbers of United States businessmen turned again to the Dominican Republic. George Walker (of the Mellons' Koppers Company), a close Reid friend, had made a visit to the Dominican Republic during the Consejo period (Reid was one of the seven Consejo members) on behalf of the Businessmen's Council on International Understanding. Walker "had brought in high-level U.S. industrialists to study the former Trujillo properties and advise the Consejo what to do with them."[40]

---

[33] José Francisco Peña Gómez, "U.S. White Paper on the Dominican Republic," *New America* (December 18, 1965), p. 5; and Martin, pp. 631–632.
[39] For a discussion of the Reid Cabral period, see Martin, pp. 47–55.
[40] *Ibid.*, p. 116.

It was from these operations that Bosch had hoped to partially finance his social reforms. But Walker recommended gradually selling or leasing the properties to private investors.

The Midland Cooperatives of Minneapolis, Minnesota, landed an oil-refinery contract. Falconbridge Nickel Mines, a Canadian-American concern, announced plans to built a $78-million refinery. The Inter-American Development Bank and the AFL-CIO launched a joint housing project. The World Bank gave $1.7 million for a hydroelectric study, replacing the one Bosch intended to finance with European capital.[41]

And there was more. At the same time, plagued by plunging world sugar prices, Reid continued Bosch's austerity program and received International Monetary Fund (IMF) and AID credit and loans as well as a $30-million loan from six U.S. commercial banks.

During the Bosch regime the 18,000 workers at South Puerto Rico's La Romana had won a 30-percent increase in their meager wages. Under Reid, that contract was broken and in February 1965, one much more favorable to the company was negotiated with a parallel or "ghost" union set up by La Romana. Since low wages are crucial for profits in this marginal industry requiring surplus labor, the company greatly benefited from Reid's antilabor policy. Reid had previously declared a state of siege in Santo Domingo to offset a general strike called by the Sindicato Independiente de Choferes. By spring of 1965 the country was $200 million in debt; there were rumors of a Reid campaign to sell the former Trujillo properties, now in the hands of the state, to private investors; the armed forces were carrying on increasingly flagrant and publicly known contraband operations; and Santo Domingo itself was facing a serious water shortage—Reid had discontinued the renovation and expansion of the city's water system initiated by Bosch. One other persistent rumor was that Reid was planning to rig the promised elections to ensure his victory. More than one commentator was led to observe that only U.S. support kept Reid in power.[42]

Meanwhile, in exile, Bosch and leaders of the Revolutionary Social Christian Party (PRSC) agreed on the pact of Rio Piedras, a plan to cooperate in overthrowing Reid and restoring the 1963 Constitution. In a more secret move, Bosch also reached a similar but more tenuous agreement with the ex-Trujillo servant and conservative, Joaquin Balaguer.[43] Both agreements involved utilization of disparate military factions in the projected overthrow of Reid Cabral. Many of the conservative senior officers were riding high on corruption involving import rackets. The younger and lower-echelon officers were easily approachable by the various anti-Reid factions who also feared cancellation or manipulation of the promised elections. These clandestine accords, combined with deteriorating economic and social conditions in the country, especially in Santo Domingo (unemployment was as high as 40 percent), precipitated the coup in April 1965. It is quite possible that in the early hours of the uprising as many as three or more separate military factions were vying for power: one faction supporting Bosch, another Balaguer, and one right-wing faction supporting Wessin y Wessin. And it was at this point, when the military split

---

[41] *Hispanic American Report,* **17** (July 1964), p. 621.
[42] For a discussion of the Reid Cabral regime and its relations with labor, see Franco, pp. 170–177; and Bodenheimer, *Viet-Report* (September-October 1967).
[43] This secret Balaguer-Bosch understanding has been confirmed in several personal interviews. See also Dan Kurzman, "Dominican Constitutionalism," *The New Leader* (July 18, 1966), p. 10.

and broke into internecine combat, that the Dominican crisis made international headlines.

DOMINATION THROUGH INTERVENTION AND OCCUPATION

Within three days the constitutionalist forces routed Wessin y Wessin's troops while the other military factions wavered. Obviously the crucial question was whom the United States would back. There is no doubt that the PRD leadership was counting on rather automatic U.S. support for the return of the legally elected Bosch government. It seems they were convinced of U.S. democratic intentions.[44] At the point when the constitutionalists were in control of Santo Domingo—April 27—the United States could have prevented bloodshed and chaos, furthered the development of social reform, and destroyed the antireformist military forces by supporting exiled Juan Bosch. It was simply a matter of permitting Bosch

to reenter the country to take command of the constitutionalist forces. On several occasions Johnson confidant Abe Fortas and ex-Ambassador Martin visited Bosch in San Juan, Puerto Rico, making it clear that Washington would *not* support his return to Santo Domingo. The FBI and CIA kept him under constant surveillance and thwarted his various overt and covert attempts to return.[45]

Public statements notwithstanding, the Johnson Administration decided on April 24 that it would send in the Marines if the rebels gained the upper hand.[46] A massive buildup of troops and equipment was set in motion. When the United States made it apparent, through Ambassador William Tapley Bennett, Jr., that it was going to back the Wessin forces and that the rebels would have to fight or surrender, the PRD civilian leadership passed to the rebel military commanders, who by this time had armed and organized a sizable proportion of the civilian population within Santo Domingo.

On April 28, when it became clear that

---

[44] During an interview in exile in San Juan, Puerto Rico (August 1965), Juan Bosch described his reappraisal of U.S. democratic intentions to Kal Wagenheim, then editor of the *San Juan Review* and *New York Times* stringer in Puerto Rico. A quote from that interview appeared in *The New Leader* (February 28, 1966), p. 10: "I believe that in the Dominican Republic Latin America has been given a lesson: the lesson is that it is not possible to establish a democracy with the help of the United States, and neither is it possible to establish a democracy against the United States." It seems that the constitutionalist military leaders were also convinced their rebellion would *not* arouse the San Isidro right-wing forces led by General Wessin y Wessin to armed opposition. That is, they expected a relatively peaceful palace coup. See Franco, p. 195.

[45] This information has been confirmed in several personal interviews. See also: Juan Bosch, "A Tale of Two Nations," *The New Leader* (June 21, 1965), pp. 3–7; and Juan Bosch, "An Anti-Communist Manifesto," *New York Review of Books,* 9:7 (October 26, 1967), a review of Régis Debray's *Revolution in the Revolution?,* where Bosch wrote: "When I realized that the Americans would stop at nothing to prevent my return to Santo Domingo, I asked the Congress to elect Colonel Camaño constitutional president . . ."

[46] Reports on the decision to intervene are very contradictory and the real reasons have been withheld by the Johnson Administration. The Senate Foreign Relations Committee hearings on the intervention were never made public—a prerequisite agreed to by Senator Fulbright before Administration officials consented to testify. But Max Frankel was evidently "leaked" some of the hearings' highlights, which he described in "Secret U.S. Report Details Policy in Dominican Crisis," *New York Times* (November 14, 1965). Tad Szulc, *Dominican Diary* (New York, 1965) corroborates this information.

Wessin's forces had been routed, the Marines landed, ostensibly to evacuate Americans, but in reality to bolster the military and lay the groundwork for U.S. occupation. This whole process was portrayed as a response to a rump military junta set up by U.S. military attachés and led by Wessin's ally Colonel Bartolomé Benoit. The Marines quickly solidified the fractionalized military forces; wavering elements realized the rebels were doomed in the face of U.S. firepower. The so-called "neutral" landing force quickly equipped the junta units with badly needed radios, food, weapons, medical supplies, and logistic support. Surrounding Santo Domingo, they succeeded in containing and eventually splitting the rebel forces.[47]...

The effects of the rebels' independence and consequent power were tellingly demonstrated when the United States threatened to destroy the constitutionalists by a full-scale attack, including bombing, on the rebel-held sector of downtown Santo Domingo.[48] This attack was deterred, partly because the rebels threatened to set off explosives in the banks (including Chase Manhattan and First National City), the headquarters and offices of many U.S. businesses operating in the Republic, the electric plant and the telecommunications center, all of which were within the rebel-held sector. The United States backed off and thereby demonstrated some of its true interests.

The stated reasons for American military intervention are still veiled in confusion, primarily because many of the official documents have never been made public and the political figures who formulated and executed the policy are still in power. In President Johnson's first public statement on April 28, 1965, the United States intervened to "... give protection to hundreds of Americans who [were] still in the Dominican Republic and to escort them safely back to this country."[49] The President's statement was based on embassy and press cables which exaggerated the constitutionalist threat to American lives. Dispatches described firing squads holding terrorized American tourists at gunpoint in the Embajador Hotel. Moreover, the heads of assassinated victims were supposedly paraded through the streets of downtown Santo Domingo. In reality, from the outbreak of the rebellion not one American civilian was killed by accident or on purpose by the constitutionalists.[50]

[47] For details see Szulc, *Diary*; Dan Kurzman, *Revolt of the Damned* (New York, 1966); and Theodore Draper, "The Dominican Crisis: A Case Study in American Policy," *Commentary* (December 1965), pp. 33–68.

[48] Max Frankel, *New York Times* (November 14, 1965).

[49] "Statement by President Johnson, April 28, 1965," as reproduced in U.S. Senate, Committee on Foreign Relations, *Background Information Relating to the Dominican Republic* (Washington, 1965), p. 51.

[50] In fact, the only atrocities ever documented during this period were all within the military junta's territory. Murder of civilian prisoners took place between May 22 and June 5, 1965. A report submitted to the OAS by a special team of three Latin American criminologists sent to investigate alleged brutalities reached the following conclusions, according to Drew Pearson: "That there had been mass murders and that most of the population had been too terrorized to testify. The Commission was not able to arrive at the number killed though one prison under General Imbert's supervision, once containing 3,000, now has been reduced to 500. General Imbert was picked by the American Embassy to head the military junta immediately after the landing of American Marines. He has been kept in power only by the Marines and U.S. aid...." Drew Pearson, "A Report of Imbert Atrocities," *Washington Post* (August 13, 1965). See also *Washington Post* (June 10, 1965), and the *New York Times* (June 10, 11, and 23, 1965) as well as the criminologists' report to the OAS.

By April 30, President Johnson, after reiterating the purported threat to American lives, hinted at another justification for intervention:

... there are signs that people trained outside the Dominican Republic are seeking to gain control. Thus the legitimate aspirations of the Dominican people and most of their leaders for progress, democracy, and social justice are threatened and so are the principles of the Inter-American system.[51]

By May 2, however, President Johnson clarified the above:

The evidence that we have on the revolutionary movement indicates that it took a very tragic turn. Many of them trained in Cuba, seeing a chance to increase disorder and gain a foothold, joined the revolution. They took increasing control. What began as a popular democratic revolution that was committed to democracy and social justice moved into the hands of a band of Communist conspirators. ... Our goal, in keeping with the great principles of the inter-American system, is to help prevent another Communist state in this hemisphere.[52]

The charges of communist infiltration and control have been refuted by liberal journalists who were on the scene, liberal senators such as J. William Fulbright, noted resident researcher at Stanford University's Hoover Institute, Theodore Draper, and Juan Bosch himself.[53] While agreeing that communist conspiracies are a real danger to democratic revolutions, they proceed to question the strategic influence of the small and fractionalized Dominican communist parties. Given such criteria one could delegitimize any revolution threatening U.S. interests by uncovering a handful of communists. Undoubtedly communists are present in every third-world conflict today; but, from a radical perspective, there is no reason to assume communists cannot also be bonafide nationalists. The supposition that a Communist Party member will place the interests of an international communist conspiracy above those of a nationalist revolution cannot be substantiated from a historical or practical point of view. It should be noted that the international communist conspiracy within the rebel movement never appealed for Cuban, Soviet, Chinese, or any other communist aid, even while under severe duress.

What, then, were the real motives and circumstances of the U.S. intervention? American liberals and social democrats, including Tad Szulc, Dan Kurzman, J. William Fulbright, and Theodore Draper, all agree that the troops intervened to bolster the flagging junta forces. But they fail to offer any comprehensive explanation of why

[51] "Statement by President Johnson, April 30, 1965," Committee on Foreign Relations, p. 53.
[52] "Statement by President Johnson, May 2, 1965," Committee on Foreign Relations, pp. 56–57. A review of Dominican events supporting the Administration's position on Communist infiltration and control can be found in *Dominican Action—1965: Intervention or Cooperation?*," The Center for Strategic Studies, Georgetown University (Washington, 1966). This pamphlet was partially authored by Eleanor Lansing Dulles, ex-State Department official (1942–62) and sister of the late Secretary of State John Foster Dulles and former CIA director Allen Dulles.
[53] Tad Szulc, *Diary*; Dan Kurzman, *Revolt*; Senator J. W. Fulbright, "The Dominican Republic," speech before the U.S. Senate, September 16, 1965, and *The Arrogance of Power* (New York, 1966), Chapter 4; the following works by Theodore Draper: "The Dominican Crisis; A Case Study in American Policy," *Commentary* (December 1965), pp. 33–68; "The Roots of the Dominican Crisis," *The New Leader* (May 24, 1965); "A Case of Defamation: U.S. Intelligence versus Juan Bosch," *The New Republic*, two parts (February 19 and 26, 1966); and Juan Bosch, "A Tale of Two Nations," *The New Leader* (June 21, 1965), pp. 3–7, and "Communism and Democracy in the Dominican Republic," *War/Peace Report* (July 1965), pp. 3–5.

the United States *opposed* a return to a democratic order under the constitutionalists. In their opinion, faulty information about the rebel forces was supplied and evaluated by incompetent policy makers who were overly preoccupied with Cuba and anti-communism. After meticulously refuting the Administration's "cover stories," Draper awkwardly concludes: "We still do not know what was behind the anti-Bosch campaign."[54] The key to this perplexing question lies in an analysis of why the United States *supported* the right-wing junta forces. Johnson and his advisers knew from past experience they could control the military and thus guarantee U.S. domination; however, the constitutionalists, with their independent, armed civilian cadres, presented a more formidable obstacle to manipulation.

The liberals offered no comprehensive explanation for U.S. intervention because they were hopelessly confused about the priorities and objectives of U.S. policy. They assumed the primary goal was to promote democracy and social welfare, and the intervention, with its support of the right-wing military, became a paradox. But if one assumes the most important U.S. foreign-policy objective is maintaining control and domination over Dominican development, the intervention and occupation becomes quite logical. Johnson and his advisers knew from past experience they could penetrate, manipulate, and control the military, thus guaranteeing U.S. domination and its consequent benefits; the constitutionalists, however, lacked a formal structure to penetrate and were willing to employ illegal and violent means which frustrate manipulation. Given the objective of domination, President Johnson had little choice about which side to support.

The forces determining U.S. priorities and objectives in the Dominican Republic were rooted in powerful American economic interests and domestic political considerations. The U.S. corporations with a direct and indirect stake in the outcome of Dominican events had ready access to U.S. Administration officials, and when the April 1965 rebellion broke out they most likely expressed their deep concern. A considerable number of individuals with financial, legal, and social connections to the East Coast sugar complex were well stationed throughout the upper echelons of the U.S. Government. For example, prominent New Dealer and Johnson confidant Abe Fortas was a twenty-year director of the Sucrest Corporation, the third largest East Coast cane refiner. State Department expert and adviser to several presidents on Latin America (including Kennedy and Johnson) Adolf A. Berle, Jr., was postwar board chairman of Sucrest as well as a large stockholder. OAS Ambassador and special envoy to the Dominican Republic Ellsworth Bunker was past chairman, president, and thirty-eight-year director of the second largest East Coast cane refiner, the National Sugar Refining Co.; roving Ambassador W. Averell Harriman (sent to Latin America by Johnson to explain the Dominican intervention) is a limited partner in the New York banking house of Brown Brothers, Harriman, which owns approximately 5 percent of National Sugar's stock. Molasses magnate J. M. Kaplan is a heavy contributor and influential adviser to many Democratic Party candidates and the ADA. State Department consultant and ex-U.S. Ambassador to the Dominican Republic (1957–1960) and Panama (1960–63) Joseph S. Farland has been a director of South Puerto Rico Sugar Co. since 1964. Former Deputy Secretary of Defense Roswell Gilpatric is the managing executive partner of Cravath, Swaine and Moore, the

[54] Theodore Draper, "A Case of Defamation: The U.S. Intelligence vs. Juan Bosch," *The New Republic* (February 26, 1966), p. 18.

Wall Street legal counsel for National Sugar. Wall Street lawyer Max Rabb, in the firm of Stroock, Stroock and Lavan (legal counsel for Sucrest), was a member of the National Committee for Johnson and Humphrey.[55]

[55] Ex-FDR Under Secretary of the Interior Abe Fortas was described by Washington reporter Ben H. Bagdikian as "the most intimate and omnipresent of the President's friends and advisors." See Ben H. Bagdikian, "The 'Inner Circle' Around Johnson," *The New York Times Magazine* (February 28, 1965); and Charles B. Seib and Alan L. Otten, "Abe, Help!— LBJ," *Esquire* (June 1965).

William D. Rogers, Deputy Assistant Administrator of USAID and Deputy U.S. Coordinator of the Alliance for Progress from 1963 to 1965, is a member of Arnold and Porter, prominent law firm and lobbyist which Fortas was formerly associated with. The law firm is described in the *Esquire* article as "a high-powered operation of about 40 lawyers, most of them former government officials or teachers... [The] business is almost completely oriented to the Federal Government cases involving taxes, anti-trust situations, savings and loan regulation cases, proceedings before the Securities and Exchange Commission, and the like."

Fortas was also a board member and general counsel of the Greatamerica Corporation, a holding company with 80 percent of Braniff Airlines; Greatamerica is controlled by Dallas businessmen Troy V. Post and Clint W. Murchison, Jr.

Adolf Berle, Jr., was honored by the Sucrest stockholders on the occasion of his retirement as chairman of the board in 1964 for "the firm hand of his leadership and the uniquely personal quality of his service, to and on behalf of the corporation..." Mr. Berle is also a partner in the New York law firm of Berle and Berle, which specializes in Latin American affairs for U.S. corporations.

Ellsworth Bunker, whose father was a founder of National Sugar, was described by *New York Post* columnist Joseph P. Lash (January 27, 1957) as a "spokesman for the whole [sugar] industry vis-à-vis the government." Before entering the diplomatic corps in 1950, Bunker had extensive business connections centered around the East Coast cane-sugar complex. His directorships included American Hawaiian Steamship, Central Aguirre Associates, General Baking Co., Guantanamo Sugar Co., and Potrero Sugar Co. He was chairman of the U.S. Cane Sugar Manufacturers Association and during World War II served as chairman of the Cane Sugar Refiners War Committee. He is a long-time trustee of the Atlantic Mutual Insurance Company, which uses as its legal counsel Senator George Smathers' Miami law firm, Smathers and Thompson, and whose board includes J. Peter Grace, president and director of W. R. Grace and Co. and director of the First National City Bank of New York. Bunker and his close friend molasses magnate J. M. Kaplan are both honorary directors of the New School for Social Research of New York. The Honorable Ellsworth Bunker's son John B. Bunker is past president of Great Western Sugar Company and currently president of the second largest U.S. sugar-beet refiner, Holly Sugar Company, a subsidiary of Houston Oil Field Material Company (HOMCO). Bunker's brother, Arthur H. Bunker, is a past partner and long-time director of Lehman Brothers, a large New York investment house. Director of a Lehman Brothers subsidiary, Edwin L. Weisl is a close Johnson adviser and New York County Democratic Committeeman.

W. Averell Harriman's brother, E. Roland Harriman, heads Brown Brothers, Harriman, and sits with Ellsworth Bunker on the board of directors of Atlantic Mutual Life Insurance Company. Another Brown Brothers partner, Knight Woolley, is a board member of Bunker's National Sugar Refining Co.

Roswell Gilpatric's law firm, Cravath, Swaine and Moore, includes among its other clients such giants as Time, Inc., and the General Dynamics Corporation.

Max Rabb was also former Secretary to Dwight D. Eisenhower's Cabinet (1953–1958).

Thomas Mann, Assistant Secretary of State for Inter-American Affairs, also prominent in the decision to intervene, "worked closely with the CIA" in the 1954 Guatemala coup and the Bay of Pigs invasion. See Alex Campbell, "The Mann to Watch," *The New Republic* (June 5, 1965), pp. 13–15. He was described by *Business Week* as a "conservative friend of business," who as ambassador to Mexico had been "excessively concerned with leftist influence."

The whole East Coast sugar industry, which is dominated by National Sugar, Sucrest, and the largest U.S. refiner, American Sugar Co., is directly dependent on sizable Dominican sugar and molasses imports. Any disruption in supply, as happened after the Cuban Revolution, would threaten price stability and earnings in this narrow margin of profit industry. The ability of these as well as many other corporations to either place people directly in the government or have access to important government officials was and is a major factor shaping the priorities and objectives of American foreign policy vis-à-vis the Dominican Republic. Even without direct economic interests it would be difficult, if not impossible, for these gentlemen to resist or escape the assumptions and inclinations inculcated by their economic and social milieu.

The domestic political considerations operating in favor of intervention were even more subtle than the economic forces at work. Any foreign country (especially in the third world) which attempts to become truly independent by freeing itself of American economic, military, and political manipulation and control is easily branded in the U.S. public media as communist. The financial and military interests affected by such a move have direct access to the mass media and other organizations shaping public opinion. This could be used as leverage against those political officials responsible for protecting their interests. No domestic political figure can afford to risk the charge of being soft on "communism" which, for all practical purposes, means losing control over actual or potential (1) investments and trade opportunities returning high profits, (2) markets for goods and services, (3) sources of cheap labor, (4) sources of cheap or strategic raw materials, (5) militarily stra-

tegic bases, and (6) influence and votes in international regional organizations. Particularly after the Cuban Revolution any U.S. President would be vulnerable, and therefore sensitive, to a situation like that confronting President Johnson in April 1965. The decision which had to be made was painfully clear. Rather than risk failure by backing a nationalist government promoting democracy and social reform, Johnson intervened militarily to ensure U.S. control and head off any domestic political threat from U.S. financial and military interests. In short, domestic political interests again took priority over Dominican democracy and independence.

With the U.S. occupation, domination and control in the Dominican Republic became, for all practical purposes, absolute. Military operations involving over 30,000 U.S. troops were coordinated out of the office of General Bruce Palmer and not by the Brazilian Inter-American Peace Force Commander-in-Chief.[56] The Assistant Secretary of State for Economic Affairs, Anthony M. Solomon, went to the Republic to coordinate the work of more than sixty U.S. officials "acting for all practical purposes as the civilian government in the Dominican Republic."[57] The U.S. Special Forces' "Operation Green Chopper" flew units throughout the country to inquire about the political views of the citizens at large, to distribute food, and to promise public works.[58]. . .

To further extend its political control, the United States forced out the military junta headed by Imbert, cutting off U.S. funds which were supplying the government payroll. By September 1965, U.S. negotiators were able to put together a provisional government headed by Hector García Godoy, formerly Bosch's foreign minister and subsequently vice-president of Balaguer's Parti-

[56] Szulc, *Diary*, p. 284.
[57] *Ibid.*, p. 267.
[58] *Ibid.*, pp. 314–315.

do Reformista. The U.S. objective for this administration was to maintain stability and hold elections which would further legitimate a U.S.-backed government. In effect, Washington was creating a pro-U.S. political atmosphere and party within the country. Aiding mightily in this task was an OAS mission headed by Ellsworth Bunker, and U.S. gifts and low-interest loans amounting to over $100 million.[59]

Bosch returned from exile in September 1965, and under strong domestic and foreign pressure, agreed to run in the upcoming elections. Well-known social democratic and liberal Bosch sympathizers Norman Thomas and Victor Reuther argued that only through elections and the subsequent establishment of a stable democratic government would the occupation troops leave the island. Obviously, no meaningful election could be held without the participation of the PRD and their candidate Juan Bosch. Thomas, Reuther, civil-rights leader Bayard Rustin, lawyer and New York Reform Democrat Allard Lowenstein, Sacha Volman, and others organized the Committee on Free Elections in the Dominican Republic. They told Bosch they would send a team of "independent unofficial observers" (eventually seventy) to oversee the elections and, through their presence, help moderate possible fraud and coercion. Unbeknownst to Bosch and all but one or two of the committee observers, Allard Lowenstein held several private talks with U.S. officials in Santo Domingo and on the eve of the elections made a secret agreement with Ambassador Ellsworth Bunker. If Bosch won, Bunker would publicly state U.S. support

for his election. And if Balaguer was the victor, Lowenstein promised to use his considerable influence to encourage a public statement of support.[60]

Though nearly blind and over eighty years old, Thomas made a three-day visit to the Republic at election time to lend his prestige as head of the committee. Upon his return to New York immediately after the election, Thomas, accompanied by Lowenstein, made a press statement that was interpreted as a personal endorsement of the election's freedom and fairness. In the eyes of many liberals who had opposed Johnson's intervention policy, the committee's presence and Thomas' statement legitimized the elections. However, the Dominicans who cooperated with the committee (most of whom were Bosch sympathizers) felt betrayed by the premature statement. The committee and most Americans avoided the key question: How can you hold a free election in a country occupied by foreign troops who invaded to prevent one of the two main candidates from assuming the presidency? Even more convinced than in 1962 that he would be overthrown if elected, Bosch first refused to run. After being persuaded otherwise, however, he conducted a campaign aimed at educating the electorate about problems facing any Dominican government. An atmosphere of fear pervaded the country and he never left his heavily guarded Santo Domingo residence to campaign among the peasantry and pro-urban strongholds.

The candidate favored by the United States, the oligarchy, most of the armed forces, the Church, and the U.S.-backed

[59] On February 18, 1966, the *Christian Science Monitor* reported the U.S. had "pumped more than 100 million dollars since last September in gifts and low interest loans" into the Dominican economy. "The bulk of the money—$77 million—went to pay government salaries and other budget items." According to the *New York Times* (January 23, 1967), between July 1, 1965, and June 30, 1966, the Dominican Republic received the highest per-capita economic aid from the United States of any Latin American country—$32.10 compared to $13.40 for Chile, the closest competitor.

[60] From personal experience, interviews, and observations.

Dominican Labor Confederation, CONA-
TRAL, was Joaquin Balaguer. The ex-
Trujillo servant won handily amidst charges
of fraud, coercion, and political pressure
tactics.[61] The much needed peasant backing
organized in 1962 for the PRD by CIA-
financed Sacha Volman was missing. Apparently, Volman had agreed, in accordance
with U.S. State Department wishes, to remain outside the country during the campaign.[62] It was obvious to most Dominicans
that the United States was backing Balaguer
and that a Bosch victory was unacceptable.
Never close to U.S. social democrats and
ADA liberals—the Kennedy operatives for
controlling the PRD—Johnson literally constructed a new pro-American power base
(Balaguer's party and government) that was
largely dependent on, and subservient to,
United States interests.

DOMINATION THROUGH
STABILIZATION AND
INFILTRATION: BALAGUER'S
FIRST YEAR

Balaguer's election victory in June 1966
vindicated U.S. intervention and occupation in the eyes of the Johnson Administration and its supporters. A new Constitution
was drawn up and most of the U.S. objections to the 1963 document were excluded.
Financial and technical resources were

quickly brought to the assistance of the
new regime. Supplementing generous loans
and grants were nearly five hundred Americans serving in official capacities, creating
a virtual parallel government.[63] An outfit
known as the International Development
Foundation, financed and staffed by the
Central Intelligence Agency, replaced Volman's operations in the training of anti-
communist peasant leaders. The U.S. sugar
quota was substantially raised to bolster
revenues. On top of $3 million in military
assistance, the Pentagon sent sixty bilingual
advisers to train a 3,400-man "elite" army
brigade in riot control and counterinsurgency. In addition, AID was spending $800,-
000 on "public safety" (police training). The
military received upward of 40 percent of
the national budget; approximately 40 percent of the labor force was unemployed.[64]

Satisfied that the situation had been sta-
bilized, United States business flocked to
the Republic to make new investments in
housing construction, land and tourist development, and agribusiness.[65] Strikes were
virtually outlawed for one year, the government austerity program (geared to alleviat-
ing the foreign debt) frozen, and in some
cases it forced reduction of wages. And a
program for selling the state-owned properties was instituted. Meanwhile, left political
parties were thoroughly infiltrated while the
return of many feared ex-Trujillistas into
positions of authority brought about a rise

[61] Norman Gall, *The New Leader* (June 20, 1966).
[62] From a personal conversation with Sacha Volman, May 7, 1966.
[63] Ninety-three percent (93%) of the supporting assistance (i.e., primarily budgetary support)
given by AID for fiscal year 1967 was scheduled to go to five countries listed in the following
order: Vietnam, Korea, Jordan, Dominican Republic, and Laos. U.S. Department of State,
Agency for International Development, *Proposed Economic Assistance Plans for FY 1967*
(Washington: U.S. Government Printing Office, 1967), p. 10.
    The 500 official Americans serving as of January 1967 included almost 100 from the State
Department, 160 from the Agency for International Development, 150 Peace Corpsmen, and
60 military advisers. An undetermined number of CIA agents and unofficial Americans were
also present. Susan Bodenheimer, "The Hidden Invaders: Our Civilian Takeover in the
Dominican Republic," *Liberation* (February 1967), p. 14.
[64] Bodenheimer, *Liberation*, pp. 14–15.
[65] *Housing*: Rockefeller's IBEC (International Basic Economy Corporation) and George A.
Fuller Company Pan-Americana. [*Footnote 65 continued on next page.*]

in political assassinations and terriorism.[66] Periodically the Dominican press carried reports of sporadic guerrilla warfare in the countryside.

CONCLUSION

The U.S. intervention and occupation had several far-reaching consequences. Large segments of Dominican society, especially the urban youth, were further alienated from the traditional political leadership with its links to the United States. Anti-Americanism became even more deep-seated. As one Dominican author observed, the intervention "fully revealed those who were culpable for our underdevelopment."[67] As a result of the struggle, during the late spring and summer of 1965 a whole new power base was created and two opposing camps were strengthened, reinforced, and polarized to the extent that few observers feel there will be a peaceful reconciliation. The people were armed with as many as 20,000 firearms which they still possess; they saw how their commando units could hold off and even defeat the regular army; the right-wing military elements acquired new equipment and supplies while solidifying their ties to the U.S. Armed Forces.

The more international effects of the intervention were a further weakening of the Organization of American States and the United Nations. Professor W. Friedman of the Columbia University Law School described how the United States did not even pretend to be guided by international law: "It [U.S. intervention] departs from the principle that international law does not permit interference on the ground of an objectionable political ideology."[68] The "joint" military action in the Dominican Republic was the first such "cooperative" venture in the history of the hemisphere and set the precedent for the creation of a permanent Inter-American Peace Force.

In the United States the intervention led more liberals to conclude that Vietnam was not simply a mistake, but rather part of a new approach to foreign relations. The official policy of nonintervention in the internal affairs of Latin American nations which had been proclaimed with varying degrees of credibility since December 1933 was officially reversed. A less noted though significant effect was the weakening of the Peace Corps' political independence. Frank Mankiewicz, then director of the Corps' Latin American operations (and later Senator Robert Kennedy's press secretary) made a special trip to Santo Domingo to oppose

---

Land development and tourism: Hilton Hotels, Holiday Inn, and the American-Dominican Investment Company (of Boston) have all invested in hotels, or hotel sites. South Puerto Rico Sugar, recently bought by Gulf and Western Industries (whose head, Charles Blundorn, is a close friend and business associate of Edwin L. Weisl, Johnson adviser and political supporter), plans to turn much of its virgin beachfront land into a Caribbean vacation paradise. South Puerto Rico Sugar owns over 275,000 acres in the Republic, constituting 78.9 percent of the total cultivated land in San Pedro de Macoris province and 59.7 percent in El Seibo.

Agribusiness: Central Aguirre bought up a former United Fruit Company 30,000-acre plantation to develop vegetable production for Puerto Rican and U.S. markets. Aside from sugar, South Puerto Rico Sugar's land supports approximately 30,000 head of cattle; much of its land is undeveloped and suitable for cultivation (now being planned).

[66] For some documentation on the return of Trujillistas see Norman Gall, "The Struggle in Santo Domingo," *The New Leader* (January 2, 1967).

[67] Franco, p. 264.

[68] Letter to the Editor, *New York Times* (May 9, 1965).

the threatened en-masse resignation of a sizable number of volunteers as a protest against U.S. policy.[69]

Juan Bosch once again left the Dominican Republic after the 1966 election, declaring that "there is no democratic exit from the present situation." It became clear that the constant priority of United States foreign policy was the maintenance of control and domination for the unequal benefit of U.S. interests. The mechanisms for achieving this objective varied from brutal suppression to subtle manipulation, with a conscious preference for the latter. Military occupation gives way to U.S.-trained and -financed "national" organizations whose dependency is invisible only to North Americans. Democracy, social progress, and independence are subservient to the primary objective and readily disposable if they jeopardize U.S. authority. What is conspicuously absent from most left-liberal and social democratic interpretations is an analysis of political and economic forces *within* American society. Interests, associations, and structures, rather than intentions and rhetoric, largely determine the motivational forces that shape foreign policy.[70] While the Kennedy and Johnson adminis-

trations employed different mechanisms of domination—political vs. military—their objectives remained the same. Kennedy had strong enough links to the PRD through ADA liberals and social democrats to take a chance with democracy and muted nationalism; he hedged his bets by stepping up military assistance. But Johnson lacked Kennedy's connections and when revolutionary nationalist forces took up arms the ability of the United States to maintain effective control, short of occupation, was undermined.

The fate of peaceful democratic modernization in Peru, Brazil, Ecuador, or the Dominican Republic, pivots on the political, corporate, and military structures of American society. This is what the Cuban revolutionaries profoundly understood and the American people, including liberals from the church, university, and the professions, have never confronted. Those who define Latin American problems primarily in terms of conditions external to the United States and offer assistance based on this assumption will only perpetuate U.S. domination. Without fundamental change in American society, violent confrontation is inevitable.

---

[69] Szulc refers in passing to Mankiewicz's trip in May 1965 to the Dominican Republic: Szulc, *Diary*, p. 224. Other information on this topic was obtained from interviews with several Peace Corps volunteers who were directly involved.

[70] Feeling that business and financial information was most lacking in standard interpretations, we concentrated a great deal of effort on recognized business sources, special libraries, and trade journals. For analysis on corporations we found especially helpful *Moody's Industrials*. Senate and congressional hearings as well as executive department data were utilized (e.g., Securities and Exchange Commission listings of corporation stockholders). Tracing the interests and associations of individuals presents a difficult area of research. Some basic reference sources include: various *Who's Who; Current Biography; Poor's Register of Directors and Executives; Martindale-Hubbell Law Directory*; U.S. Department of State *Biographical Register*; and telephone directories at home and abroad.

Data collected from these sources provide knowledge and leads on the potential interrelationships involved in decision making and the exercise of power. The preliminary background knowledge gained from the above enabled us to frame questions and understand answers in interviews with individuals directly or indirectly related to crucial events. Among these individuals were corporation executives, sugar brokers, journalists, and government functionaries. A summer 1967 visit to the Dominican Republic by one of the authors provided an opportunity to conduct interviews and collect statistical data on economic, social, and military conditions.

11

CYBERNATION

4   Automation, Planning, and Centralization

THE MEANING OF THE CYBERNETIC STATE

The Editors

One of the most visible trends in America during the twentieth century has been the rapidly changing occupational structure. Professional and managerial occupations have grown in significance, along with other lower white-collar occupations. In the blue-collar ranks there has been a growing need for skilled workers and service workers, and a sharp decline in farm occupations and unskilled occupations. Such trends are often viewed as a natural outgrowth of a healthy industrial society, reflecting great advances in technology which would relieve man from burdensome work, thereby freeing him for more creative employment.

The pace of change in the occupational structure was made more rapid by the introduction of systems of production that could be carried out without human intervention. Automation in many production areas had the potential for eliminating tens of thousands of jobs, especially those in large-scale manufacturing industries. The efficiencies of these working machine systems soon spread to those occupations that process paper rather than produce products; the lower white-collar clerical employee as well as the middle management could no longer compete with the speed, accuracy, and dependability of information-processing systems (Ginberg, 1964). A rapid extension of these trends suggests a future with a three-class occupational structure: professionals, technicians, and service workers.

The questions and issues raised by the automation-produced occupational structure fall into two main areas: (1) how to maintain employment; and (2) how to reduce unemployment. Virtually all observers of the impact of automation agree that unemployment is one of the most immediate consequences of automation. There is considerable disagreement, however, concerning the manner in which unemployment due to job dislocation can be remedied. One view—the so-called aggregate-demand view—maintains that displacements due to automation are temporary, and can be reduced by a stimulated economy. The structuralist approach to unemployment from automation views job dislocation as permanent, since the people being displaced have little education and available skill to bring to a new occupation. Those with little skill or education will find it increasingly difficult to find a place in the occupational structure except in the third-class service occupations referred to earlier.

The structuralist view of automation-produced unemployment has also led to such proposals as the guaranteed annual income (Theobold, 1967). Starting with the assumption that the technological capability does exist for a very small proportion of the labor force to produce enough for the entire country, the guaranteed income is necessary for allowing the displaced worker to maintain a decent standard of living.

The full significance of automation is not only that it eliminates some jobs, but also that it eliminates an entire class of jobs, leaving the displaced worker without a place in the occupational structure. This clearly points to the close connection between the processes of automation and the revolution in human rights presented in Part III of this book. For example, many of the ameliorative programs of job retraining, or reducing high-school dropout rates, often result in preparing people for occupations that are being rapidly eliminated. One result of this situation is that programs designed to deal with poverty and unemployment are ineffective because they are unrealistically connected to the economic system.

Perrucci's paper, "Work in the Cybernetic State," contains an examination of the effect of automation and mechanization upon unemployment patterns and alienative work. Available solutions to automation-produced unemployment seem incapable of dealing with the young, nonwhite, urban dweller who has either been rejected from the labor force or is unemployable because of limited education or skills. The additional problems of meaningless work can be further traced to a more general pattern wherein production needs, profit, and efficiency take precedence over man's need for work that provides self-respect and a feeling of usefulness. In facing up to the problems of nonwork and work, it will be necessary to realize that solutions will have to be political rather than technological, for technology only works to achieve the ends of those who use it.

The tendency to solve social ills with technical means, as in the case of automation, is a consequence of trying to reduce certain social ills to manageable dimensions in order that precise solutions might be applied. This results in thinking about automation as "the problem" and "manpower planning and retraining" as the technological solution. What is overlooked, however, is the possibility that the solutions are themselves an intimate part of the problem. Automation is only the visible part of that iceberg called the cybernetic revolution. What is less visible is the emergence of large-scale planned systems in the social, political, and economic realms. An experiment in forecasting the future undertaken by the RAND Corporation (Gordon and Helmer, 1964) suggests that there will be major efforts in the years ahead in (1) the establishment of large-scale systems in developing, controlling, and using our energy and natural resources; (2)

continued development of automated manufacturing industries and the emergence of manufactured food to meet the needs of an expanding world population; (3) development of rapid transportation systems for land, sea, and air; (4) the development of biosocial systems concerned not only with medical advances, housing, community development, and pollution control, but with the coordination of these advances into large-scale social systems such as the design of cities; and (5) the expansion of space programs and military defense systems.

The tendency toward planned and controlled systems has raised questions of whether the operation of a computerized government will render the average citizen ineffective in influencing policy, partly through ignorance, and increasingly through apathy (Michael, 1962). One is tempted to conclude from these arguments that while the strengths of a computerized government are in seeking the "best" solutions to national problems, the technology itself leads to an avoidance of certain problems and questions that are not amenable to the techniques. In such a situation there is the possibility that both the definition of problems and the effective solutions will be made within the constraints of the problem-solving technology. Thus the reliance on cybernetic technology minimizes the average citizen's ability to affect national policy, while at the same time limiting consideration of alternatives in national policy to those that are amenable to the problem-solving tools that are available.

Social critics as diverse as Robert Theobold and Eric Hoffer have voiced the opinion that automation and technology are here to liberate us if only they can be utilized with the appropriate wisdom. This proves, however, to be a big "if" and Donald Michael (1966) has called attention to a number of frequently overlooked social impacts of technological progress. Failure to consider social impacts can result in enslavement rather than liberation. Michael is particularly concerned with the ethical and human consequences of radical scientific innovations in three areas: biological technology, cybernetics, and social engineering.

Biological and pharmacological technology creates the possibility for making a target population seriously ill or hopelessly docile (as with germ warfare.) Biological technology can also be used to enhance food productivity with hybrid grains and green belts. Its potential includes replacing, functionally and practically, organs of the human body which can grasp objects, scan the printed page, pump blood, and pace the beatings of the heart. It can replicate intricate neural functions with electronic apparatus and transplant actual organs: retinas, hearts, kidneys, and skin tissue, from a doner to a receiver. It can control fertility and childbirth and affect the genetic engineering of human and animal populations through sperm banks and other devices.

Through drugs and environmental conditioning, the new technology can affect the level of intelligence, the moods, the temperaments, the experiences, and the dependencies of individuals and of populations. Each advance raises a host of unforeseen ethical questions. Who will decide who is to be victim in the application of biochemical warfare—the president, the local sheriff, or the "population"? Will physicians and biochemists become less concerned with life if lethal applications of biological techniques become common? How will the right to bear children be restricted; by whom, for whom? Will poor black people whose work more often entails physical injury become the natural donors of hearts to rich white people who can pay for them? Will drugs be required for some people—as in the use of tranquilizers for control in mental hospitals and schools—and restricted from others? Shall marijuana and the hallucinogens be legalized, taxed, turned into a source of profits to drug companies, or be made freely available?

Analogous concerns may be raised for social engineering. Technical aids break the veil of privacy in collecting data and computers assist in the storage and retrieval of information. Brainwashing, sensory deprivation, and saturation advertising are sophisticated techniques of persuasion which can change values and identities of people. The very notion of "social engineering"—that is, the ability of social scientists, through the refinement of predictive models to manipulate social behavior—raises the political question, "Who is to decide who is to be manipulated and for what ends?" (Michael, 1966.)

Some of the problems inherent in what cybernation has done to the nature of the world of work have been noted. These include the displacement of the unskilled, the remoteness of the individual from the product of his labor, the new place of leisure. Michael alerts us to some of the unplanned social impacts of cybernetic change in sex roles and in education. Technology has contributed to the ability of individuals to reverse sex roles. With the creation of more and more "service" jobs, men, in the course of their work, perform traditional female roles. At the same time an increased emphasis on technique and rational programming tends to deprecate the role of the mother. Simultaneously, sexual mores change but without the needed development of legal and social services for the homosexual. Increased leisure requires reeducation of the individual both to utilize leisure in a meaningful way and to conceive of his identity not based solely on the work he performs. Yet the educational system continues to shape the aspirations and abilities of people for vocational roles which are often meaningless and frequently nonexistent.

Michael raises five points for consideration in evaluating technological consequences within biotechnology, social engineering, or cybernation:

1. The social impacts of past technology on society have not been attended to adequately and those consequences are still emerging.

2. There has been, and continues to be, a gap between technological development and any planning for its extended social impacts.

3. There will be increased generational conflict, not only because of value clash over technology itself, but because the younger generation has new practical and substantive expertise.

4. The question of how and when the consequences of technology become

designated a social problem or a legitimate area of social concern is poorly understood.

5. The tendency to analogize from historical models of past accommodations to technology is prevalent but most often fallacious. Society has never before had as intricate a set of interconnections among its components.

The burgeoning of technology, of course, brings with it the increased importance of the scientist and the scientist-engineer. "The symbiosis between science and technology has . . . evolved into big science and big technology . . . dependent on big money, which inevitably means big politics" (Michael, 1966). Michael expects that the erosion of the integrity of science will be a major problem. The need to use politics to pay for technology leads to the use of technology to manipulate politics. Finally, what about democracy when the mass of people have only partial information and few, if any of us, have the reasoning ability to evaluate the issues with a full accounting of the potential consequences?

In a world of vast complexity and bigger and bigger institutions, how does the individual respond? The first adaptation Michael describes is "selective involvement" where people pick issues they are concerned with and ignore the rest. Secondly, the individual might attempt to "withdraw" by seeking out a less technologized environment; or finally, individuals can "protest" in an attempt to change the immediate environment. The satisfied drone of Huxley's *Brave New World* and the tyrannized pawn of Orwell's *1984* are also models of accommodation which now make these authors appear uncomfortably prophetic. Yet these are possible adaptations to the new technology.

In the face of such potential, scholars and professionals will have to "face some very uncomfortable questions. . . . What about our research techniques? What must we do—and what must we abandon of what we now take status and comfort in—to get methods that adequately tackle the issue? We must find out what we should really be studying, even if it means breaking down cherished disciplinary barriers and repudiating the importance of the issues we have studied up to now . . ." (Michael, 1966).

Existing assumptions and views of the role of technology in shaping society have been examined in detail by McDermott in his paper, "Technology: The Opiate of the Intellectuals." McDermott's critique is of the Report of Harvard University's Program on Technology and Society. In it he examines the expectations invested in technology by the educated public. The promises go everywhere from ending poverty and providing universal opportunity to increasing human freedom, replacing work by leisure, providing continuous constructive social revolution without violence, ending ideological strife, and even population control and permanent peace. The conference report takes a sanitized middle-of-the-road position on the value of technology. It is seen to produce many wonderful things but also some undesirable conditions like pollution. Basically, the difficulty perceived by the technological elites is that certain parts of society are too rigid to permit a free flow of new innovative technology to handle these problems. Unhampered technical innovation is believed to be a self-correcting social mechanism. Lack of public support or selfish practices by business or other vested interests are seen as impediments to the free corrective hand of technical progress.

These social impediments are also considered fair target for organizational and social technology. Hence the government could make more advanced use of the media to get support for more technological progress to meet social problems.

McDermott's major criticism is of the technical experts' claim that their output is always on behalf of the general good of mankind rather than for their own benefit, or for that of people who are involved in technical practice, or for the managerial persons who financially support the technical innovators, or for the corporate profits which always seem to accrue even after such innovations as low-cost housing, supersonic bombers, and medical instruments. The expert's loyalties are not always so pure. Neither is the power which must be granted if he is to apply his special knowledge. Since technological advance requires specialized knowledge and training, decisions based on the "best" knowledge available require the expert to have increasingly concentrated decision-making power.

The more general argument forwarded by professionals and experts is that they have no ax to grind. They are merely problem solvers trained professionally to work for the public good. The altruistic technocrat is, however, more myth than reality. In actuality he serves certain interests and not others. McDermott illustrates the point with his description of a masterful and complex system for probabilistic bombing in Vietnam. The intricate and expensive system increases the probability of hitting an actual enemy target over the alternative of purely random bombing. The interests served are, of course, not those of the antiwar protestors (but they are not experts and do not have to be considered), nor of the Vietnamese soldiers and farmers in the area (but they are probably the enemy and should not be considered). Hence our altruistic expert does assume the values of certain interests and does negate others. In addition, the new system is so complex and so costly, both in trained personnel and in equipment, that it would be foolhardy to feed poor intelligence data into it. Thus more technical elaboration of the intelligence system is called for, perhaps of the transport system as well. Every aspect of support for this system from the application of social science to its management to the application of physical science to its machinery is pressured to become more efficient, better rationalized, more streamlined, and more responsive to the overriding purpose of the probabilistic bombing program. Thus McDermott illustrates that technology, when we recognize its real forms as opposed to its idealized abstractions,

... refers fundamentally to systems of rationalized control over large groups of men, events, and machines by small groups of technically skilled men operating through organizational hierarchy. (McDermott, p. 29.)

The future potential for systems which have such capacity for control and for monitoring and filtering out all interferences are well illustrated by such extreme cases as the Vietnam bombing program.

Hence the most instructive and accurate example should be of a technology able to suppress the humanity of its rank-and-file and to commit genocide as a by-product of its rationality. (McDermott, p. 29.)

The literature in future planning is now replete with the problem of how future societies will require a greater concentration of decision power in the hands of specially talented and knowledgeable experts. This group will assure greater fulfillment and equality for the rest of us through their informed and dedicated efforts. But what has become or will become of democracy? McDermott points out that the rise of democracy was made possible when literacy and roads for travel first began to make it apparent that the aristocracy did not have the mystical qualities which were attributed to them through remote rumor. There is now a great decline in literacy with regard to the new technical elite. Very few people have any real knowledge of how its scientific innovations or its computer-assisted organizational practices really work. Hence the experts are being invested with mystical powers unobtainable by most of us. With the creation of this magical omnipotent elite, democracy is rapidly declining. What the cult of technical innovators fails to grasp is that real participation in planning and the running of one's own life may prove more essential to the mental functioning of the human being than the benevolence of experts. They fail also to see that they are serving the values of a highly inequitable system and protecting it from the legitimate demands of people who are abused by it.

McDermott is critical of those who view technology as nothing more than "organized knowledge for practical purposes." Such a benign definition of technology emphasizes a flexibility and purity of technology that simply requires wisdom and informed planning to make sure that its positive benefits are maximized while its negative consequences must be planned for and thereby controlled. McDermott prefers to look at technology as an institutional system with an ideology, elites, and supportive links with other social institutions. The ties and shared interests among the federal government, military interests, corporations, foundations, and the university suggest a convergence of ideology among technology's leading beneficiaries that promises even greater impact upon the shape of American society.

Bob Ross's analysis "Is Planning a Revolution?" deals with the problems of estimating the consequences of technology. The social planner's tools fall under the heading of systems analysis, cost-benefit analysis, and planned-program budgeting systems. For Ross, these new techniques form the basis for a new ideology of planning, which tends to ignore the role of political processes in influencing social changes. Moreover, there is also the tendency to apply such planning techniques to projects that suit the technology, with the consequence that many hard-core problems are ignored and those most easily helped (i.e., those that may need it least) are selected for attention. Ross is further concerned with the shift in the center of support for planning to the halls of the private corporation rather than governmental agencies (see Introduction to Chapter 8). The move from welfare statism to corporatism raises questions about whether problems that do not promise profits will ever be considered by the new planners.

Technology, then, can be viewed as one of the constraints in choosing among alternative solutions to national problems. The problem posed in this area is reflected in the efforts of many groups to include certain conditions on the list of national problems or national "needs." Further difficulty stems from the fact that even among the subgroups who are able to get their needs represented on the national agenda, there is considerable disagreement concerning the needs that should have priority. Melman (1966) presents a discussion of America's needs in housing, health services, education, transportation, natural-resource development, water, waste, and pollution. His main point is that the pursuit of these needs is seriously hampered by the priority given to military programs and military expenditures, and that there is in fact a priorities problem that is often unrecognized. Within the framework of the popular "guns and butter" debate, the arguments center about whether or not there is a priorities problem, for if there is no need to choose between guns and butter, special group interests are not being slighted by national policy decisions. This is part of the meaning of a "consensual society," where significant national debate is made unnecessary by the fact that all needs are being satisfied.

Assuming, however, that American society must make choices in allocating its resources, it is of vital importance to learn how those who make decisions on behalf of the people learn about the people's needs. Some observers of the cybernetic revolution such as Michael (1962) (mentioned above) McDermott (1969) (in this chapter) and Boguslaw (1965) (see Chapter 6) envision a future where it will become increasingly difficult for the average citizen to make his voice heard on matters related to his interests. A less pessimistic view recognizes the growing complexity of society which makes direct individual participation in government increasingly difficult, but sees the needs and interests of the average citizen being represented through the federal government. This view is often expressed under the theory of "countervailing power," wherein the citizen copes with "big business" through his "big government" and "big unions."

The three remaining papers in this chapter all deal with the question of how power is distributed in American society. The relevance of the countervailing power thesis requires close inspection at a time when the nation's defense establishment has become one of industry's best customers, awarding defense contracts approaching 40 billion dollars. It is the increasingly close association between government and business that is the focus of Barber's paper entitled "The New Partnership: Big Government and Big Business." The emergence of the so-called "conglomerates" in American industry (as one consequence of cybernation) and their relationship to the seats of governmental power becomes one of the major constraints on the policy alternatives for dealing with the consequences of cybernation. Under such conditions of centralization of economic power, government's ability and willingness to protect the "public interest" is severely restricted.

Centralization in the control over the communications media produces a concentration of power which makes possible even greater centralization. During the 1950s and '60s there was a great accumulation of wealth in the aerospace industry. Through its work on contracts from NASA, the industry produced a technological breakthrough in communication satellites. Its consumer promise was worldwide telephone communication at a cost per call as low as the going rate for local calls. Hughes Aircraft actually had a proposal which could have made the vast intercity connections of telephone wires and cables obsolete. Considering that over 25 billion dollars in public research funds had gone into this development, it might have been time for the public to reap some dividend. In actual fact, public control was never considered and Hughes Aircraft was denied permission for development. Instead, a new agency was created by law to control the territory. COMSAT was to be owned half by communication companies and half by publically issued stock. AT&T holds three seats on the 15-member board, and, more important, 58 percent of the stocks. COMSAT serves to control the development of communication satellites to assure that established commercial interests will be protected. To accomplish this, AT&T employed a national advertising campaign, including, of course, the brochures enclosed with our phone bills. Its leverage in the Senate helped to accomplish the first voted termination of a filibuster since 1927 against 10 liberal senators who opposed the public giveaway.

Joseph Goulden summarized the case as follows:

Once again AT&T retained its position in the marketplace of goods and services by virtue of its preeminence in the marketplace of power. But AT&T is not unique in this respect, and focusing on it does not imply that such unofficial "plural monopolies" as exist in steel or autos or elsewhere throughout the economy are substantially more responsive to or constrained by the public interest. Indeed they can fix prices and determine quality with greater arrogance and impunity than AT&T, since not even the forms of regulation hem them in. An indictment of AT&T does not acquit them any more than the ABM makes hydrogen bombs and germ warfare sane and healthful. Rather, both AT&T and the ABM—and, in a sense, the whole military-industrial complex—are the extreme, limiting cases that can epitomize a larger reality. They are the pure idols of the marketplace of power which operates without any regard for human benefit or need. (Goulden, 1969, p. 37.)

There are, of course, a number of reasons why America's most lucrative business, AT&T, would be interested in how the media presents news about itself. The reasons regard its shady practices in tapping the public till. In return for governmental review of rates, the telephone company is assured a monopoly so that we may all call one another on the same phones. But the Bell System need not have the monopoly which it does over the manufacture of telephone equipment through its subsidiary, Western Electric. Western is itself the twelfth largest corporation in America and the major benefactor of the ABM system. AT&T has a stake in paying Western the highest possible profits since its own rates are based on percentage of its costs. The profits paid by the Bell System to Western add to AT&T's costs. The profits on the added costs go into our telephone bills. There have been attempts to investigate this fraud. In 1939 the FCC's Walker Report stated that Western could cut its prices to Bell by 37 percent and still be assured a return of 6 percent on investment. Nothing happened until 1949 when the Justice Department filed suit to require purchase through competitive bidding. The case was granted indefinite postponement when Dr. M. J. Kelly of Bell Laboratories appealed to the Secretary of Defense that the mere trial of the case would divert the attention of Bell officials from vital military projects. The Defense Secretary at that time, himself a member of an investment firm (Brown Bros. and Harriman) which is a major holder of AT&T stock, found the argument convincing. The court resolution came when the Justice Department moved on a consent decree in which seven of the nine points—none damaging to AT&T were approved. Frederick Kappel, who has since moved from head of Western to head of AT&T, referred to the decree as "window dressing" but urged fellow officials in a hasty memo to "use discretion in passing along. Don't brag about having won victory or getting everything we wanted. . . ."

For the corporate state this type of con game is a natural state of affairs. Attorney General Brownell and his golf crony T. Brooke Price, AT&T's general counsel, who worked out the agreement, do not see themselves as embezzlers of public money. They are merely carrying out the daily duties of protecting their corporate interests which they see as ultimately consistent with the best interests of the United States and of the world. They are victims of their own machinery for public relations and decision control (see Chapter 6). Such men are psychologically and culturally shielded from recognizing the inherent loss in personal integrity associated with the maintenance of great empires of wealth and power.

The evidence presented by Barber shows clearly that the days of private enterprise in the United States are past and that the new industrial state must be understood in other terms. An organization like General Motors is more than a corporation. There are only eleven nations in the world with a larger gross national product than GM. The interchange between GM officials and federal policy is basic to the claim once made by GM President Charles Wilson, while serving as Secretary of Defense, that "What is good for General Motors is good for the U.S." Galbraith (1967) has attempted to define the new system in a way which encompasses corporate bigness. What such new models of contemporary capitalism highlight is how protected the core decision authorities have become from the ultimate consequences of their decisions. Sometimes, however, the consequences are driven home with striking clarity. The explosion of interest in ecology raises an issue that the new industrial state can avoid only with the certainty of extinguishing itself. While ecology has frequently been used as a political refuge to take the heat off public concern over poverty and warfare, the facts of the ecological crisis are still upon us. In addition to the matter of population growth which ensures starvation, industrial combustion is raising the CO_2 content of air to a point that will increase global temperature, which could melt the Arctic ice floes and the Arctic ice cap, thereby raising the ocean level and drowning much of mankind. Existing mineral reserves would be exhausted even if the world population were to remain constant in number but merely uplifted, economically, to the American standard. Chemical poisons abound in our foods, now including DDT found in the milk of nursing mothers. A 1968 UNESCO conference concluded that man has 20 years before air pollution alone begins to make the planet uninhabitable for humans.

While technical solutions are continuously sought and the concept of a super birth-control device or a super prolific green belt of new strands of high-protein vegetation are worthy of effort, it should be clear that the spaceship earth is in trouble in its capacity to support life. The Ehrlichs, who have carefully taken into account technological growth (which Malthus could not foresee), still see the day of reckoning to be quite close. For the underdeveloped world, large-scale starvation is already here as is large-scale mental retardation resulting from malnutrition.

In Western societies there is an immediate need, from an ecological viewpoint, to give away resources to support those who are in desperate need. There is an equally urgent need to preserve our resources from our own appetites, to attend to waste absorption and reuse, and to reduce the transportation and manufacturing components of our gross national product. Here we come face to face with the objectives that the new government-corporate state were created to prevent. Military productivity goes to prevent a takeover of resources by those in need. Centralized industrial-governmental settings exist to assure continuous expansion, obsolescence, and security in the exploitation of resources and in manufacturing. Can the new industrial state reform its objectives for the struggle with nature? Heilbroner states the dim hope that "The capitalist and managerial classes may see the nature and nearness of the ecological crisis, and may recognize that their only salvation (as human beings, let alone privileged humans) . . . [will require them] . . . to accept a smaller share of the national surplus, simply because they recognize that there is no alternative." (Heilbroner, 1970).

One problem with this mildly optimistic hope is that decision elites can easily "manage" the problem by introducing all manner of new programs responsive to political pressures but inadequate to the real need. The cooptive capacities of the political system at the middle levels are extremely great. But the ecological threat requires a drastic change at the highest levels. As yet, the public interest has not been foremost at the centers of power.

Domhoff, in his paper "How the Power Elite Set National Goals," argues that the center of power resides in the owners and managers of large corporations, banks, insurance companies, and finance houses. Their power is exercised through interlocking corporation ties, foundations, university experts, and the priority-setting policy groups often established at the highest levels of government. Domhoff uses the particular case of the President's Commission on National Goals, set up in 1960, to illustrate the potential of elite power centers to shape national policy in accordance with their own interests.

THE TOP 22:

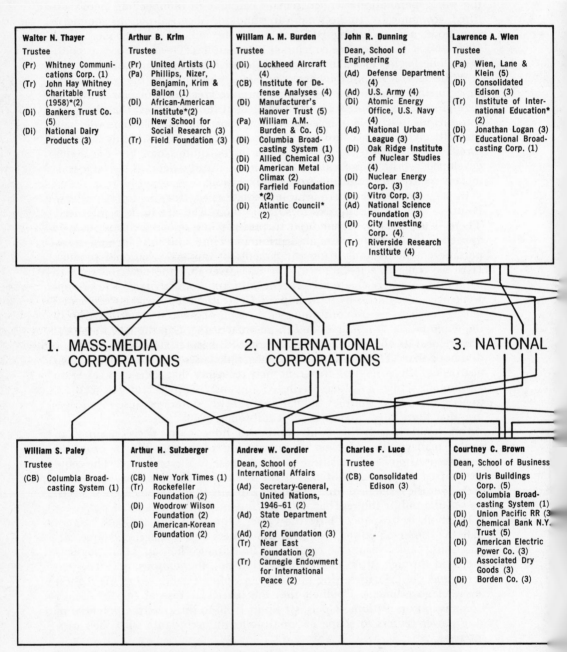

Walter N. Thayer

Trustee

(Pr) Whitney Communi-
       cations Corp. (1)
(Tr) John Hay Whitney
       Charitable Trust
       (1958)*(2)
(Di) Bankers Trust Co.
       (5)
(Di) National Dairy
       Products (3)

Arthur B. Krim

Trustee

(Pr) United Artists (1)
(Pa) Phillips, Nizer,
       Benjamin, Krim &
       Ballon (1)
(Di) African-American
       Institute*(2)
(Di) New School for
       Social Research (3)
(Tr) Field Foundation (3)

William A. M. Burden

Trustee

(Di) Lockheed Aircraft
       (4)
(CB) Institute for De-
       fense Analyses (4)
(Di) Manufacturer's
       Hanover Trust (5)
(Pa) William A.M.
       Burden & Co. (5)
(Di) Columbia Broad-
       casting System (1)
(Di) Allied Chemical (3)
(Di) American Metal
       Climax (2)
(Di) Farfield Foundation
       *(2)
(Di) Atlantic Council*
       (2)

John R. Dunning

Dean, School of
Engineering

(Ad) Defense Department
       (4)
(Ad) U.S. Army (4)
(Di) Atomic Energy
       Office, U.S. Navy
       (4)
(Ad) National Urban
       League (3)
(Di) Oak Ridge Institute
       of Nuclear Studies
       (4)
(Di) Nuclear Energy
       Corp. (3)
(Di) Vitro Corp. (3)
(Ad) National Science
       Foundation (3)
(Di) City Investing
       Corp. (4)
(Tr) Riverside Research
       Institute (4)

Lawrence A. Wien

Trustee

(Pa) Wien, Lane &
       Klein (5)
(Di) Consolidated
       Edison (3)
(Tr) Institute of Inter-
       national Education*
       (2)
(Di) Jonathan Logan (3)
(Tr) Educational Broad-
       casting Corp. (1)

1. MASS-MEDIA CORPORATIONS

2. INTERNATIONAL CORPORATIONS

3. NATIONAL

William S. Paley

Trustee

(CB) Columbia Broad-
       casting System (1)

Arthur H. Sulzberger

Trustee

(CB) New York Times (1)
(Tr) Rockefeller
       Foundation (2)
(Di) Woodrow Wilson
       Foundation (2)
(Di) American-Korean
       Foundation (2)

Andrew W. Cordier

Dean, School of
International Affairs

(Ad) Secretary-General,
       United Nations,
       1946–61 (2)
(Ad) State Department
       (2)
(Ad) Ford Foundation (3)
(Tr) Near East
       Foundation (2)
(Tr) Carnegie Endowment
       for International
       Peace (2)

Charles F. Luce

Trustee

(CB) Consolidated
       Edison (3)

Courtney C. Brown

Dean, School of Business

(Di) Uris Buildings
       Corp. (5)
(Di) Columbia Broad-
       casting System (1)
(Di) Union Pacific RR (3
(Ad) Chemical Bank N.Y.
       Trust (5)
(Di) American Electric
       Power Co. (3)
(Di) Associated Dry
       Goods (3)
(Di) Borden Co. (3)

Source: Adapted from "Who Rules Columbia?" (New York: North American Congress on Latin America, 1968).
Legend: Di, Director; Ad, Advisor; Pr, President; Pa, Partner; CB, Chairman of the Board; Tr, Trustee; Me, Member.

COLUMBIA'S RULING ELITE

Note: The numbers in parentheses after each organization correspond to the numbered groups in the center of the chart. The connecting lines represent primary interests only. Organizations marked with an asterisk (*) secretly received funds from the CIA. Details of the various groups are given on the following page.

1. MASS-MEDIA CORPORATIONS

Eight of the Top 22 are leading figures in major communications firms . . . particularly heavy is CBS' representation (Paley, Burden, Brown) and the prestigious New York Times is represented by their Board Chairman . . .
the Whitney communications empire of television, radio and publishing, owned the now defunct New York World-
Journal-Tribune . . . Krim's law firm is counsel for important communications companies . . . this concentration
of interests is reflected in Columbia's large and expanding School of Journalism which produces skilled labor for
the media industry . . . the School also houses the industry's American Press Institute . . . Columbia avails itself
of these connections to manufacture a favorable public image.

2. INTERNATIONAL CORPORATIONS

Seven Columbia rulers have primary ties to either U.S. corporations or non-profit organizations with an international domain . . . Kirk, McGuire and Kappel are on the boards of oil companies dependent on foreign reserves
for their survival . . . these and other corporations (such as Burden's American Metal Climax with mining interests in Africa) require skilled managers to oversee the corporate fiefdoms carved out by U.S. economic interests
. . . Columbia's School of International Affairs is underwritten by these same corporations and in turn serves as a
finishing school for the managers . . . The School is headed by State Dept. consultant and ex-U.N. administrator
Cordier, who is noted for his role in the execution of the Congolese nationalist Patrice Lumumba . . . the Regional Institutes of the School perform research and intelligence that reinforce anti-nationalist ideology . . . covert financing by the CIA has been uncovered in one institute project on Eastern Europe . . .
     Six of the seven trustees engaged in overseas activity are prominent functionaries in seemingly apolitical or-
ganizations secretly funded by the CIA . . . for instance, Burden was a founder and is a director of the Farfield
Foundation, used by the CIA to pass over $1 million to intellectual projects run by the Congress for Cultural
Freedom . . . Kirk has played a crucial role in the CIA-founded and -funded Asia Foundation, which encouraged
"cultural interaction" through publications, exchange programs and research.

3. NATIONAL CORPORATIONS

Five of the Top 22 have primary relationships with leading national corporations and several of the others have
secondary interests . . . corporations such as Consolidated Edison (represented by Trustees Kirk, Wien and Luce)
gain private advantage through their ties to Columbia . . . the University manipulates land-holdings in and rents
property from Con Ed . . . in addition to direct gain, national corporations benefit from the University's production of highly skilled labor, especially by the professional schools (Law, Business, Engineering and Applied Science) . . . the Watson computer lab is operated by Columbia and IBM (of which Kirk is a Director) . . . Teachers
College and the School of Social Work manufacture the professionals to organize the national and local infrastructure to service corporate needs.

4. THE DEFENSE-RESEARCH NEXUS

The Top 22 include five representatives of the military-industrial complex . . . Burden's Lockheed Aircraft and
Moore's General Dynamics together receive 10% ($3.6 billion) of all U.S. military contracts . . . their existence is
dependent upon production of the aircraft presently used in Vietnam . . . as Chairman of the Board of the Institute for Defense Analyses (IDA), Burden directs $15 million worth of Pentagon-financed war research . . . IDA,
specializing in evaluations of advanced weaponry and counterinsurgency technology, serves as a major idea factory for the Department of Defense . . . sponsored by twelve major universities (including Columbia), IDA is
shielded from attack by its academic facade . . . President Kirk adds to IDA's academic lustre by serving on its
Board of Trustees . . . Columbia officials also provide an academic cover for the Riverside Research Institute
(formerly the Electronics Research Lab of Columbia University), whose secret military work is coordinated by
IDA . . . RRI trustee Dunning, a Defense Dept. consultant and expert on atomic weapons, is a director of three
private corporations dependent on military contracts . . . for example, Dunning's City Investing Corp. is a major
subcontractor of Burden's Lockheed Aircraft and manufactures spray defoliant systems for chemical warfare.

5. REAL ESTATE AND FINANCE

Of the Top 22, at least fifteen have primary interlocking relationships with New York City's major real estate and
finance companies . . . with over 60% of its $245 million endowment in real estate Columbia is one of the largest
property holders in New York City . . . most disturbing is the association of four Columbia rulers (Uris, Massie,
Buttenwieser and Brown) with the real estate and construction empire of Uris Buildings Corporation . . . Uris himself conveniently serves as President Kirk's advisor on University construction and expansion, a position well-
suited for the promotion of his company . . . the proposed "Piers Project" between 125th and 135th streets ad-
jacent to the Hudson River will be constructed by Uris' firm . . . Trustee Hogan, doubling as District Attorney,
can overlook any conflicts of interest . . . Tishman Realty and Construction is represented by Trustee Buttenwieser, and Trustee Wien is famous for his billion dollar speculation in property.
     The lifeblood of real estate is the capital of banks, insurance companies and investment concerns which un-
derwrite mortgages and loans . . . Columbia's real estate men are intimately connected with the largest banking
and insurance firms . . . Dean Brown is an advisor to Chemical Bank New York Trust Co.; Trustee Massie is a
director of Chemical Bank, sits with Kirk on the Board of Greenwich Savings Bank, and is a director of two major
insurance companies; Buttenwieser is a partner in the investment concern of Kuhn, Loeb;—Burden is a director
of Manufacturer's Hanover Trust; Temple is a director of First National City Bank and Atlantic Mutual Insurance
. . . the Rockefeller Brothers, who rent the land under Rockefeller Center from Columbia, have two of their financial concerns (Chase Manhattan Bank and Metropolitan Life Insurance) represented at Columbia by Kappel.

Some believe that enlightened input will enter into national policy from interests outside the centralized power structure via the route of independent university scholarship. The belief tends to be shattered by an examination of just how dependent the "multiversity" is upon the focal points of power. The degree to which the major university is dependent provides but another example of the concentration of power in American society, as detailed in an in-depth case study of the Board of Trustees at Columbia University ("Who Rules Columbia?," 1969). The data of that study, some of it based on private files uncovered during the 1968 occupation of the University's administration building, revealed that Columbia University was contributing, by its land policies, to the continuation of large tracts of ghetto housing and that University expansion needs were met with no regard for the needs of the surrounding community. Moreover, service to military and corporate needs provided a guiding theme underlying the research and training opportunities of Columbia at every level of organization. The extensive interlocking ties between the trustees and the corporate, military, and government agencies are the means by which interests having little to do with education actually shape the programs and policies of one of the country's major universities. The accompanying chart reveals the full extent and nature of these ties. [*See pages 168–170.*]

These interlocking ties provide the source of income for the internal programs of the university that serve the corporate-military-government interests, and they control the decision making that shapes these internal programs. Control of university affairs by nonindigenous persons with nonacademic interests is the central issue behind the often-heard charge that universities have become the provider of experts for the nation's corporate-military interests.

The concentration of power in the hands of a few—and the sense that technology makes the "common" man incompetent to make decisions, anyhow—dramatically increases our sense of helplessness. We watch in impotent fear the progress of what may be the most frightening feature of the cybernetic revolution: its capacity for mindless progress and expansion. Canadian social critic and philosopher George Grant writes:

The supreme example of the autonomy of technique is surely the space programme. If it is possible for man to do something it must be done. Vast resources of brains, money, materials are poured out in the U.S. and U.S.S.R. to keep this fantastic programme proliferating. And it is accepted by the masses in both societies not only as necessary but as man's crowning glory. One leader of the U.S. space programme said that as we cannot change the environment of space, we will have to change man. So we are going to produce beings half flesh, half electronic organs. If it can be done, it must be done and it surely will be done. This is . . . the autonomy of technique. The question whether technique serves human good is no longer asked. It has become an end in itself. (Grant, 1967.)

Similarly, Paul Goodman describes his encounter with General Learning, a subsidiary established by a 40-million-dollar contribution from General Electric and Time, Inc. (which owns a textbook company). Once the new subsidiary was formed, an editor of *Life* was relieved of his duties for five weeks to "prepare a prospectus on the broad educational needs of America and the world, to come up with exciting proposals, so that General Learning might move with purpose in this unaccustomed field." The situation is at the same time bizarre and increasingly common. First, the organization and technology is created. Then they try to dream up a purpose for it. The diffuse expertise in "systems" makes it possible for North American Aviation to contract to reform the penal system of California. Public needs can be manufactured and the only real competence required is "to have a big organization and a sales force, and to be in, to have the prestige and connections . . . to get the subsidy." Without the constraints of Adam Smith's marketplace, the enterprise can expand "like weeds in a well-manured field." But Goodman reminds us that somewhere behind the frenetic collaboration of the electronics giant, the mighty publisher, the National Science Foundation (that made curriculum studies), and the local school board (which wants to be in with the latest fashions) are the real children and classroom teachers—the people engaged in the human function of learning and teaching. They are not involved in the plans which affect them. ". . . the children are quite incidental to the massive intervention of the giant combinations" (Goodman, 1966).

The essence of cybernation is not simply machines, although the displacement of human functions and the remolding of man to meet technical necessities has frightening implications. The heart of cybernation lies in the ability to monitor far-reaching events through continuous and elaborate feedback sources in order that future events may be regulated and controlled from a single nerve center. The monitoring and storage of information and the control of action and events have been made possible by a silent revolution in technology. Hence, technological displacement, the translation of human problems into technical ones, the increased centralization of political power, and the growing interconnectedness among established organizations are all part of the same problem. We are living in the cybernetic state.

REFERENCES AND ADDITIONAL READING

Ayers, E., *What's Good for G. M.* (Aurora, 1970).

Banfield, Edward C., *The Unheavenly City* (Boston: Little, Brown, 1970).

Barber, Richard J., *The American Corporation: Its Power, Its Money, Its Politics* (New York: Dutton, 1970).

Berle, Adolf A., "Second Edition/Corporate Power," *The Center Magazine*, **2** (January 1969), pp. 76–84.

Burke, John G. (ed.), *The New Technology and Human Values* (Belmont, Calif.: Wadsworth, 1967).

Domhoff, G. William, *The Higher Circles: The Governing Classes of America* (New York: Random House, 1970).

Dugger, Ronnie, "Oil and Politics," *The Atlantic*, **224** (September 1968), pp. 66–90.

Ehrlich, Paul, and Anne Ehrlich, *Population, Resources, Environment: Issues in Human Ecology* (San Francisco: Freeman, 1970).

Ellul, Jacques, *The Technological Society* (New York: Knopf, 1964).

Galbraith, John K., *The New Industrial State* (Boston: Houghton Mifflin, 1967).

Gamson, William, *Power and Discontent* (Homewood, Ill.: Dorsey, 1968).

Ginberg, Paul, "Computers: How They're Remaking Companies," *Business Week,* Special Report (February 29, 1964).

Goodman, Paul, "The Empty Society," in *Like a Conquered Province* (New York: Random House, 1966); reproduced in R. Perrucci and M. Pilisuk (eds.), *The Triple Revolution: Social Problems in Depth* (Boston: Little, Brown, 1968), pp. 645–659.

Gordon, T. J., and O. Helmer, *Report on a Long-Range Forecasting Study* (Santa Monica, Calif.: RAND Corp., September 1964).

Goulden, Joseph C., *Monopoly: A Journalistic Study of AT&T* (New York: Putnam, 1968).

Grant, George, "Realism in Political Protest," *Christian Outlook* (November 1967), pp. 3–6; reproduced in R. Perrucci and M. Pilisuk (eds.), *The Triple Revolution: Social Problems in Depth* (Boston: Little, Brown, 1968), pp. 678–683.

Grant, George, *Technology and Empire* (Toronto: Anansi, 1969).

Heilbroner, Robert, "Ecological Armageddon," *New York Review of Books,* **14** (April 23, 1970), pp. 3–4, 6–9.

Kalachek, Edward D., "Automation and Full Employment," *Trans-action* (March 1967), pp. 24–29.

Kohlmeier, Jr., Louis M., *The Regulators* (New York: Harper and Row, 1969).

Lekachman, Robert, "The Automation Report," *Commentary,* **41**:5 (May 1966); reproduced in R. Perrucci and M. Pilisuk (eds.), *The Triple Revolution: Social Problems in Depth* (Boston: Little, Brown, 1968), pp. 178–190.

McDermott, John, "Technology: The Opiate of the Intellectuals," *New York Review of Books* (July 31, 1969).

Melman, Seymour, "American Needs and Limits on Resources: The Priorities Problem," *New University Thought,* Special Issue (1966–67), pp. 3–8; reproduced in R. Perrucci and M. Pilisuk (eds.), *The Triple Revolution: Social Problems in Depth* (Boston: Little, Brown, 1968), pp. 211–217.

Michael, Donald N., "Some Speculations on the Social Impact of Technology," in Morse and Warner (eds.), *Technical Innovations in Society* (New York: Columbia Univ. Press, 1966); reproduced in R. Perrucci and M. Pilisuk (eds.), *The Triple Revolution: Social Problems in Depth* (Boston: Little, Brown, 1968), pp. 191–210.

Michael, Donald N., *Cybernation: The Silent Conquest* (Santa Barbara, Calif.: Center for the Study of Democratic Institutions, 1962).

North American Congress on Latin America Staff, *Who Rules Columbia?* (New York: North American Congress on Latin America, 1968).

Perrucci, Robert, "Engineering: Professional Servant of Power," *American Behavioral Scientist* (1971), forthcoming.

Sennett, Richard, *The Uses of Disorder: Personal Identity and City Life* (New York: Knopf, 1970).

Theobold, Robert, *The Guaranteed Income* (Garden City, N.Y.: Doubleday, 1967).

Weiner, Norbert, "Some Moral and Technical Consequences of Automation," *Science,* **131** (May 1960), pp. 1355–1358.

WORK IN THE
CYBERNETIC STATE

Robert Perrucci

In 1964 a presidential commission was appointed in response to concern over the growing use of computers and automated production systems in factories and offices across the country. A year later the commission released the report of the National Commission on Technology, Automation, and Economic Progress. The report did not agree with those who predicted massive dislocations in the occupational structure and levels of unemployment that would eventually lead to the elimination of most work as we now know it. Instead, the report indicated that automation eliminates jobs, and not work, leaving the central question as one of how to assist displaced workers.

Three major programs were suggested for dealing with automation-produced unemployment and with the level of poverty then facing some 35 million Americans.

1. For workers displaced by automation, the report favored an extensively applied manpower policy for retraining, upgrading, and relocation. Such a program would counter tendencies to accept certain levels of unemployment as "normal" features of the economy.

2. The unemployed who cannot be helped by a retraining program, because of limited skill levels, would have to be helped by the federal government as the employer of last resort. The report estimates that some five million jobs would be created to employ persons who cannot find a place in the economy.

3. The final program is for those Americans who cannot work because they are too young or old, because they must care for their children, or because they are unsuited for work. The report urges the adoption of a negative income tax that would provide supplemental payments to low-income families and guarantee that no family would ever fall below a certain income level.

In the seven years since this commission was formed and its report issued, the unemployment rate has increased sharply. Instead of programs to deal with unemployment we have watched the federal government increase unemployment as part of their program for controlling inflation. Added to the problem of growing unemployment has been an increasing sense of discontent about the very character of work itself and the meaning that work provides to those who carry it out.

Underlying this paper's examination of unemployment and alienative work is a general hypothesis that developments in the technical processes of work and in the way work is organized have reduced *man's* role in the productive processes and have transformed him into a dispensable and replaceable *unit*. The cybernetic state, characterized by a high degree of centralization, coordination, and control, has transformed work into *system inputs* that are necessary to maintain a desired level of efficiency or productivity. The maintenance of employment and satisfactions of work are of secondary concern when compared to the

This paper was written especially for this book.

needs of the industrial system for fewer workers, faster workers, or interchangeable workers.

The remainder of this paper will examine both the character of unemployment in the United States, and the nature and sources of alienative work.

THE DEPERSONALIZED UNEMPLOYED

Patterns of Unemployment

Work is a matter of social definition. The coal miner of West Virginia would perhaps only grudgingly accept the artist at a painting, the writer of a book, or the tennis professional as involved in work. The Peace Corps volunteer or the neighborhood organizer also are not considered as working because their motivations are "different" and their material rewards are only minimal. The common-sense understanding of what constitutes work is that which one does to "earn a living." In American society, work is the activity that provides monetary rewards. It is important to note that such cultural definitions do not consider activities that provide psychic or ideological income as work (a characteristic of American society which we shall discuss later).

Yet if the main feature of work is that it yields pecuniary rewards, it is also clear that there can be important secondary rewards of work which may in fact be more important for individuals and society than the material gain. Work can provide a sense of self-worth that comes with performing a task well and from having that performance valued by others. Whether such a feeling is derived from work depends upon the work itself and the value attached to it. Work can also provide an opportunity for people to come into association with each other; to form associations, to discuss the affairs of their daily lives, and to share their discontent and satisfaction. In short, work can provide a basis for the social fabric of communities, cities, and nation in the opportunities it provides for harmonious social relationships.

Through the experience of work, and the social context of work, people develop a conception of how their society is organized, what the main motivations and personal qualities of their fellow men are like, and what their place in the society means to others. In short, the experiences of work are taken as a microcosm of the larger society; they are carried into domestic life, the community, political life, and every other aspect of the worker's social existence. The worker who is faced with oppressive supervision or isolated, machine-paced work is not very likely to view the world as a place where his feelings are important and where his involvement is welcomed and productive. The worker faced with competitive pressures for wage rates or for jobs quickly finds himself in a hostile world where others are waiting and eager to line their pockets at his expense. The white-collar workers, whose job it is, in an economy of waste, to devise ways to induce people to buy things they don't want, don't need, and which don't work, cannot do such work for long without developing a cynical and misanthropic view of their fellow human beings.

These "secondary" aspects of work receive relatively little consideration in the face of the individualistic-monetary ideology of work that pervades American life. Those who are successful at work are promised high income, which in turn can buy more and better consumer goods, which in turn can provide prestige in the community, which in turn can help to provide offspring with a good education that will provide a good job with a high income. The individualistic-monetary ideology of work sees it as individual activity and initiative which gains for the worker monetary rewards commensurate with his efforts. This conception of work is maintained by an educational system geared toward occupational choice and a lifetime of work, and by a success ideology which extolls the virtues of striving, toil, and ambition as the basis for achieving personal rewards. The persistence and persuasiveness of this success ideology—which can be heard in its finest form at any high-school graduation ceremony—is hard to account for, but that it is widely verbalized cannot be denied. Almost any random sample of Americans will tell you they value success, if not for themselves (for it may be too late), for their children. And social scientists have also vigorously, if inadvertently, supported the success ideology by seeing a desire to "get ahead" in adolescents as more "normal," or in viewing certain occupations as examples of nonsuccess.

The individualistic-monetary view of work becomes more pronounced as the "secondary" motivations for work—intrinsic satisfaction, social relationships, social responsibility—are eliminated by the changing nature of work. There is, of course, nothing wrong with earning money from work. But as the sole motivation and sole reward it is inherently unstable in its ability to maintain a sufficient level of satisfaction and sense of worth.

In order to understand fully the scope and significance of work in American life, it will be useful to examine some of the detailed statistics on the occupational structure and to look behind these statistics to the actual work and the workers they represent.

The occupational structure has changed very dramatically since the turn of the century and with a speed that has forced a major alteration in work within the life span of an individual. In 1900, approximately 17 percent of the labor force was in white-collar occupations, 45 percent in manual and service occupations, and 38 percent in agriculture. Some sixty years later white-collar occupations account for 42 percent of the labor force, manual and service occupations has risen slightly to 48 percent, and agriculture has declined sharply to less than 10 percent of the labor force. The general trend is toward elimination of occupations requiring less skill, training, and education; this is reflected in the changing distribution of workers among the three general occupational categories, and within the categories as well. The greatest growth has been in the occupations requiring higher skill and education. For example, in manual occupations there has been an increase in skilled occupations but a decrease in unskilled; similarly in the white-collar category the greatest growth has been in the professional and technical positions rather than in clerical and sales.

This reshaping of the occupational world has taken place during a period of unprecedented economic growth, providing employment for a record number of Americans. The low rate of unemployment during the latter part of the 1960s (about 3.8 percent) was pointed to with pride by government officials as evidence of the continuing trend of full employment with economic growth.[1] Under the pressure of growing inflation, government measures to "cool off" the economy have increased unemployment to 4.0 percent during the first quarter of 1970 and moved it sharply to 5.1 percent at the present writing (August 1970). Even more important than the overall rate of unemployment, however, is the manner in which that rate is distributed, in

---

[1] This rate is low by American standards, but is still substantially higher than the unemployment rate found in other industrialized societies that are not supposed to be as healthy economically as the U.S.

that it can reach depression-level proportions for certain segments of the population. It is this *form* of unemployment, rather than the rate, which reflects the patterns of growth and change that have taken place in the economy and occupational structure.

Table 1 contains the statistics on the number of persons employed in the major occupational classifications. The table also contains the unemployment rates for each

clearly seen in Table 2. In this table are the employment and unemployment figures and rates for white and nonwhite in the total U.S., in selected poverty neighborhoods, and in other neighborhoods, not classified as below the poverty line. Unemployment is substantially higher for nonwhite Americans and for persons living in "poverty neighborhoods." That the unemployment rate is higher in poverty neighborhoods should not be surprising,

Table 1   EMPLOYMENT AND UNEMPLOYMENT BY OCCUPATION
(1970, FIRST QUARTER)[a]

Occupation	Number Employed (in thousands)	Unemployment Rate (percent)
White collar (total)	37,938	2.4
Professional, technical	11,026	1.9
Managers, proprietors, officials	8,215	1.0
Clerical workers	13,906	3.3
Sales workers	4,791	3.2
Blue collar (total)	28,236	4.9
Craftsmen, foremen	10,264	2.6
Operatives	14,168	5.7
Nonfarm laborers	3,804	7.9
Service workers	9,673	4.7
Farmers, farm laborers	3,153	2.1
Total	79,000	5.1

[a] Source: Adapted from the *Monthly Labor Review*, **93**:5 (May 1970), p. 97.

category of occupation. With a general labor force of about 79 million persons, an overall unemployment rate of 5.1 percent means that there are about 4 million persons who are seeking employment and are without it. Moreover, it can be seen from the table that the rate of unemployment is generally higher for the lower-status occupations. Unemployment of blue-collar workers is twice that of persons in white-collar occupations.

The uneven distribution of employment according to area of residence and color is

since the classification of poverty neighborhoods is so closely tied to employment. What is important, however, is the degree of concentration of the unemployment. We have seen from Table 1 that the high rates of unemployment are concentrated in certain classes of occupation; now we see a further concentration in terms of color and of area of residence.

If we take this concern with the distribution of unemployment one step further we can see the fourth major condition which is related to a concentration of un-

Table 2   EMPLOYMENT STATISTICS BY AREA AND COLOR
(1967 ANNUAL AVERAGES, IN THOUSANDS)[a]

	Total U. S.	Urban Poverty Neighborhoods[b]	Other Urban Neighborhoods[b]
Civilian labor force	77,347	6,664	36,720
Nonwhite	11.2%	41.6%	7.6%
Employed	74,372	6,211	35,464
Nonwhite	10.8%	40.7%	7.4%
Unemployed	2,975	454	1,257
Nonwhite	21.4%	54.6%	13.4%
Unemployment rate	3.8%	6.8%	3.4%
White	3.4%	5.3%	3.2%
Nonwhite	7.4%	8.9%	6.1%

[a] Source: Paul M. Ryscovage and Hazel M. Willary, "Unemployment of the Nation's Urban Poor," *Monthly Labor Review*, **91**:8 (August 1968), pp. 15–21.

[b] Pertains only to civilian noninstitutional population age 16 years and over in Standard Metropolitan Statistical Areas with a population of 250,000 or more. Urban poverty neighborhoods were established "by ranking census tracts in standard metropolitan statistical areas, SMSA's, with populations of 250,000 or more, on the basis of 1960 data in income, education, skills, housing, and proportion of broken families. Those traits falling in the lower quartile were designated as 'poverty areas.' " (P. 21.)

employment. In Table 3 are the unemployment rates by age, sex, and area of residence; it can be noted that unemployment is the highest among the young in urban poverty neighborhoods. Almost one-quarter of the men and women, age 16–19, living in poverty neighborhoods are unemployed. This very high rate of unemployment for 16–19-year-olds is especially high for nonwhites. Using 1968 annual averages we find that the rate of unemployment for nonwhites, age 16–19, is 24.9 percent, while for whites of the same age group 11.0 percent.[2] This depression-level unemployment rate is what is meant by the phrase "poverty amidst affluence."

The concentration of unemployment described in Table 3 is not simply peculiar to poverty neighborhoods. An examination of unemployment patterns in 1967 in twenty of the nation's largest metropolitan areas reveals similar results.[3] The cities studied were Los Angeles-Long Beach, San Francisco-Oakland, Pittsburgh, Newark, Detroit, St. Louis, Buffalo, Cleveland, Baltimore, New York, Philadelphia, Houston, Chicago, Milwaukee, Boston, Paterson-Clifton-Passaic, Cincinnati, Dallas, Washington, D.C., and Minneapolis-St. Paul. There are approximately 26 million workers, or one-third of the nation's labor force, living in these cities; one-third, or one million persons, of the nation's unemployed live in these metropolitan areas. The results of the study are as follows:

1. The 1967 unemployment rate for the 20 largest metropolitan areas combined was 3.9 percent. Rates for individual areas ranged from just

[2] *Monthly Labor Review* (March 1970), p. 4.
[3] Paul O. Flaim, "Jobless Trends in 20 Large Metropolitan Areas," *Monthly Labor Review* (May 1968), pp. 16–28.

Table 3 UNEMPLOYMENT RATES BY AGE, SEX, AND AREA
(1967 ANNUAL AVERAGES, IN PERCENT)[a]

	Total U. S.	Urban Poverty Neighborhoods[b]	Other Urban Neighborhoods[b]
Total	3.8	6.8	3.4
Men	3.1	6.2	2.7
16–19	12.3	23.5	12.8
20–24	4.7	7.5	4.5
25–	2.0	4.3	1.7
25–54	1.9	4.3	1.5
55–	2.5	4.3	2.5
Women	5.2	7.7	4.6
16–19	13.5	23.5	11.8
20–24	7.0	10.1	5.4
25–	3.7	5.3	3.5
25–54	4.1	6.0	3.7
55–	2.5	2.8	2.6

[a] See source note in Table 2.

[b] See note in Table 2.

over 2 percent in Minneapolis-St. Paul and Washington, D.C., to around 5.5 percent in the Los Angeles-Long Beach and San Francisco-Oakland areas.

2. The average unemployment rate was substantially higher for the central cities (4.7 percent) than in the suburban areas (3.3 percent). The suburb-central city difference was substantial for whites (3.1 versus 3.7 percent) but relatively insignificant for nonwhites.

3. Between 1960 and 1967, unemployment rates dropped substantially in most of the 20 SMSA's. But in four areas—Los Angeles-Long Beach, San Francisco-Oakland, St. Louis, and Newark—the 1967 rate was about the same as that in 1960.

4. Nonwhites had higher unemployment rates than whites in all areas surveyed, and for the 20 SMSA's combined the nonwhite rate (7.5 percent) was more than double the white rate (3.3 percent).

5. Unemployment in the 20 SMSA's was particularly high for nonwhite teenagers. Their job-

less rate (33 percent) was three times the rate for white teenagers.

6. Approximately 1 million unemployed workers, 34 percent of the nation's jobless total, lived in the 20 SMSA's. The 270,000 unemployed nonwhites in the 20 areas account for 42 percent of total nonwhite unemployment.

7. Three-fifths of the white labor force in the 20 SMSA's lived outside the central cities. Only one-fifth of the nonwhite labor force lived in the suburbs.

8. One of three nonwhite workers in the nation lived in the central cities of the 20 areas, compared with only 1 out of 8 white workers.[4]

This pattern of unemployment, with its concentration among the young, nonwhite, low-skilled workers, living in the central areas of large cities, is the kind of unemployment that led to the phrase "invisible poor," used by Michael Harrington in 1962 in his book *The Other America*. Per-

[4] *Ibid.*, p. 17.

haps these unemployed men and women were "invisible" because of their concentration in cities, and in certain occupations. But today we can no longer speak of the "invisibility" of the unemployed. Today they are visible and yet they remain unemployed. Unemployment persists in its present form because of its concentration among the "powerless," not the "invisible." They are without the power and influence to bring about those changes in private and public policy that will either result in their employment or in the elimination of the hardships of unemployment.

But to say simply that they are powerless would fail to recognize that there are economic and technological reasons for their condition, as well as political ones. The unemployed persons listed in the foregoing statistics are of two dominant types: the *"rejects"* (a term used by Harrington) and the *young unemployables.* The rejects are those members of the labor force whose occupations are being eliminated by technological advances in mechanization and automation. These are generally occupations classified as "operatives" and "unskilled laborers," and at present they constitute about 18 million workers (see Table 1). But rejects are not drawn solely from blue-collar occupations. The full potential of automation is yet to be realized on tasks that would affect the employment of millions of clerical workers and many persons in middle management positions. The young unemployables, on the other hand, consist of high-school dropouts and graduates who have never been in the labor market. Their level of education is believed to suit them only for those lower-skilled positions that are rapidly being eliminated from the occupational structure. Since the unemployables are young and without family obligations, and often still have the sense of pride and self that is

associated with youth, they do not accept the unprotected and demeaning forms of employment that many rejects wind up accepting—employment in the "economic underworld" of domestic workers, hotel workers, kitchen help, and busboys.

The basic conditions that give rise to this particular form of unemployment, and promise to expand its effects to other occupations, are to be found in the technological processes of work itself. Mechanization and automation are technical innovations of great importance in the economic growth of the United States. They are also responsible for the displacement and exclusion of active and potential workers from the work force. It is nothing new to find the occupational structure modified by technical change; change in the technology of production has always made some skills and occupations obsolete while calling forth new skills and occupations. What is new in the impact of automation on work is the real question of whether those persons who are displaced and excluded from work can ever be reabsorbed in other forms of employment.

Automation and Unemployment

Much of the public discussion surrounding the type of unemployment described above has formed two distinct schools of thought concerning the methods of reducing such unemployment. Each school starts with the view that the immediate impact of automation in industry is unemployment. Exact figures are hard to come by, but there are references to the displacement of some 20,000 workers per week over the last several years when dealing with national statistics;[5] and there are numerous individual incidents of automation-produced worker displacement, such as Ford Motor Company plants where 9 men at 3

[5] Report of the National Commission on Technology, Automation, and Economic Progress.

machines are doing work formerly done by 34 men at 39 machines, or the insurance company that introduced a computer into one of its divisions and reduced personnel from 198 to 85.[6] It should be clear, however, that when we speak of automation as related to unemployment we do not mean mass unemployment of depression-level variety, nor do we envision the complete elimination of work as we know it today. Similarly, when we speak of automation in its *present* form we are not thinking of *totally* automated production systems where workers play little or no part in the productive process. It is not so much that we do not have the technical knowledge to totally automate, but the present costs of such steps are prohibitive. It is important to keep these points in mind, for some social analysts who have argued that automation is not a significant cause of unemployment do so by speaking of "total" automation and "mass" unemployment.[7] These same analysts often consider the 1967 rate of unemployment (3.8 percent) as quite low and perhaps reflecting a condition of "full" employment. Our point in this essay is precisely that we as a nation are becoming prepared to accept this national rate of unemployment as very low and even normal. Still, as the preceding statistics reveal, this low rate of unemployment is distributed in a fashion that is at the heart of some of our major social ills. This rate of unemployment that we have learned to live with is not due to any "natural" laws of economics. This rate is the result of public and private value choices that have shown a preference for "efficiency" and "progress" rather than the basic human needs of people.

One final point should be made in connection with the question of "high" and "low" or "acceptable" and "unacceptable" rates of unemployment. As we have just suggested, a national rate of unemployment that is low (e.g., 3.8 percent) and is often seen as acceptable tells little about the actual conditions of unemployment and the way those conditions may reveal a basic set of difficulties in American life. It is also necessary to see these national rates as related to the costs involved in accepting a certain rate of unemployment. For example, in the early 1960s the rate of unemployment reached a very high level of 7.1 percent. Many students of unemployment problems saw the cause for this high rate as due to automation and mechanization of work, and predicted a continuing rise in the unemployment rate. This did not happen: the rate of unemployment fell to 4.9 percent in 1964 and to 3.8 in 1966. Critics of those who predicted continuing employment, such as Charles Silberman, saw the drop in unemployment as evidence that automation was not responsible for unemployment. Yet he only mentions in passing the reason why unemployment dropped: "In part, of course, the decline in unemployment in 1965 and 1966 was a side effect of the rise in defense spending associated with the war in Vietnam, and unemployment could rise again if defense spending were cut."[8] That the war was responsible for reducing the rate of unemployment is clear, but surely we do not wish to use the existence or continuance of a war as a basic part of labor planning. Employment must be maintained with a peacetime economy, and since the end of World War II we have not had an adequate assessment of whether this is possible

---

[6] John Diebold, *Beyond Automation* (New York: McGraw-Hill, 1964).
[7] See, e.g., Charles E. Silberman, *The Myths of Automation* (New York: Harper and Row, 1966).
[8] *Ibid.*, p. 9.

under our present patterns of resource allocation and utilization in America.

At this point let us turn to the two schools of thought on how to deal with unemployment. The *aggregate-demand* approach views unemployment due to automation as temporary in nature, and as a more or less normal feature of economic systems. This unemployment can be reduced by stimulating the economy through increased federal spending or reduction in private and corporate taxes. The additional buying power and excess money for investment leads to an increased demand for goods with greater demand for workers. The *structuralist* approach views automation-produced unemployment as permanent in nature and insensitive to the influence of a stimulated economy. They see the displaced worker as hampered by his lower skills and education and thus without a place in the labor market. He is suited for employment in those occupations that are already being eliminated and have an excess of men to available positions. Solutions consistent with this view of the problem are programs in job retraining and income maintenance for those who still cannot be reabsorbed into the labor market.

The aggregate-demand view tends to remain philosophically above the battle of the here-and-now problems of unemployment by taking the "long view" of both the past and the future: "all history is a sequence of technical changes and automation is nothing new," or "eventually the economy itself will adapt to the introduction of automation by creating a demand for new goods and services and absorbing workers into other industries." The central deficiencies of this view, however, are first that there is little firm evidence that a stimulated economy will absorb displaced workers; and second, even if the economic

arguments are sound, the assumptions made about men and their motivations are primitive in nature. Even with the stimulated economy of defense spending due to the Vietnam war there is little evidence that the growing economy of the aggregate-demand variety will reduce the hard-core poverty of the young, nonwhite, urban resident. When we look at the rates of unemployment in 1960 and 1967 for the twenty largest metropolitan areas, we find that cities that had the largest increase in employment in this period did not necessarily have a reduction in unemployment.[9] In cities that had the highest increases in employment between 1960 and 1967 (more than 15 percent) —San Francisco-Oakland, Los Angeles-Long Beach, Dallas, Washington, Houston—the first two cities still have the highest unemployment rates of all (5.6 and 5.4 respectively), while the latter three cities are in the low-unemployment range.

The point of all this is that a stimulated economy, especially a defense-stimulated economy, does not necessarily reach those with less education and skill, but rather it increases the need for professionals, technicians, and skilled workers. In fact, it is one reason why the plight of the unemployed is more severe in periods of prosperity and "full" employment. It is not a matter of their relative gains as some have argued, seeing the discontent of the poor as a social-psychological reaction to the fact that their economic gains are not as great as persons in higher positions. It is more a matter of them remaining in the *same* position of unemployment despite the prosperity. It is only with the use of "bloodless" and often meaningless statistics that one can speak of a disparity between relative rates of economic improvement. Yet it would take more than the gifts of a government statistician to interpret an increase in income from $3,500 to $4,000—

[9] Flaim, *op. cit.*, p. 23.

a whopping 20-percent gain—as reflecting any form of improvement in the social and economic life of a family, its aspirations, and the hopes its children can have for the future.

The second difficulty of the aggregate-demand approach to reducing unemployment is that it sees man as motivated mainly by economic rewards and hence a convenient unit in economic analysis. For example, when the plight of displaced coal miners in West Virginia is considered from the point of view of aggregate-demand theory, it is expected that an expanding economy will create new positions for the displaced miners. The only problem is that these new positions may be in South Dakota. There is little or no consideration of the displaced miner's and his family's ties to their community in West Virginia. Geographic mobility is very disruptive to family and community ties that may have developed over a long period of time. Moreover, it is quite clear that many persons who are faced with the choice of continued unemployment or a geographic move will opt for continued unemployment.[10] From the point of view of "economic man" in the aggregate-demand models, such behavior seems irrational. Yet it may be far more rational for an unemployed miner to remain in a community where he is known, has supportive ties, and where he has made some measure of adaptation to his poverty than it would be for him to travel with his family half way across the country for a job which promises little more in the long run than the insecurity he experienced in West Virginia. As a miner, in a time when the technology of mining has become increasingly mechanized, he will be continually faced with the threat of unemployment. No amount of movement to regions of high employment (perhaps temporarily high) will change that fact.

The structuralist approach to automation-produced unemployment has received its fullest expression in the report of the National Commission on Technology, Automation, and Economic Progress.[11] The stress here is upon income-maintenance programs, manpower retraining, and the creation of new jobs in the public sector with the government as the employer. The structuralist position on the nature of unemployment and its intractability even with a stimulated economy clearly seems to be the more valid assessment of the situation. Their solutions, on the other hand, though basically sound, are limited in nature. As with the aggregate-demand approach, the structuralists select their solutions within the framework of assumptions which now dominate our social and economic structure. When dealing with the solution of having the government take the role of employer of last resort, the report indicates that there is a need for approximately 5 million jobs in public-service employment. These positions would be in medical institutions and health services, welfare and home care, national beautification, educational institutions, and similar public institutions which would profit by having more employees to help keep them cleaner, stay open longer, or operate more effectively. These would be positions requiring little skill or education and thus could be filled without the need for retraining. Yet such jobs have the character of "make-work," or similar to that class of jobs that already exist (though not in such large numbers) in the "economic underworld."

---

[10] Robert Perrucci and Kichiro K. Iwamoto, "Work, Family and Community in a Rural Depressed Area," in H. Meissner (ed.), *Poverty in the Affluent Society* (New York: Harper and Row, 1966).
[11] *Op. cit.*

The movement of the "rejects" and young unemployables into these new positions has the character of being more like a transfer of problems than a solution of problems. The depersonalization of nonwork is now a problem of depersonalization of work.

The overriding difficulty with the report's solutions, which has been boldly stated by Robert Lekachman,[12] is that it continually outlines technical solutions to problems without considering the political solutions. The report mentions programs costing 2 billion or 5 billion or 6 billion or 20 billion dollars that would undoubtedly make manpower retraining or income maintenance quite feasible; and they present new and creative programs for developing communities and even whole regions. Yet, as Lekachman points out, we already possess the necessary economic strength and technical knowledge for such solutions. Still they do not exist. And they do not exist because the decision to spend 20 billion dollars on income maintenance or retraining is a political and not a technical decision. In short, the solutions to the problems of unemployment go far beyond the world of work and the economy; they are basically questions of social and political power. The power to force a reexamination of our priorities in terms of whether efficiency and progress must always be more important than a man's job and life.

THE DEPERSONALIZED EMPLOYED

While the problems of unemployment are important, and should continue to grow in numbers and significance for both blue- and white-collar workers, the problem itself has the one "virtue" of being relatively concrete in nature. The character of one's employment status can be determined reasonably well; and the effectiveness of programs to reduce employment are also subject to a high degree of precision. When we turn to the problems of work, however, we find our subject to be more elusive. "Work alienation," "job satisfaction," "degrading work" are characteristics of work that are more diffuse, more subjective, and less subject to precision in measurement. It is for this very reason that the problems of work may be more far-reaching and significant for our society. The significance of the "cybernetic revolution" for work in American society is not only that it provides new "hardware" of production such as mechanization and automation. It is also that this revolution represents a new philosophy of man's place in the world; his relationship to himself, others, and the social institutions of his society. The cybernetic revolution and its underlying philosophy is all the more important to consider because it consists of patterns of social change that have obvious benefits for mankind and are often undertaken with humanistic ends in mind. Cybernation promises an end to the drudgery of work; it promises more and better consumer goods; it promises better systems of education, health care, police protection; and it promises more livable cities. Let us see what else it promises.

Man and the Machine

Recognition of the fact that both man and society are influenced by the conditions of work is neither new nor startling. The ancients, apparently, clearly recognized that certain kinds of work are inconsistent with the development of truly civilized men.[13] But it is mainly among the

---

[12] Robert Lekachman, "The Automation Report," *Commentary*, **41** (May 1966).
[13] Andriano Tilgher, *Work: What It Has Meant to Men Through the Ages* (New York: Harcourt, Brace, 1930).

modern thinkers faced with the harsh realities of industrialization that a concern
with the conditions of work is expressed.
The appearance of the machine age and
new means of production, such as extreme
division of labor, was greeted with concern
about how dehumanizing, monotonous
work would affect the worker's body, mind,
and intelligence. From Adam Smith:

The man whose whole life is spent in performing a few simple operations, of which the effects
are perhaps always the same, or very nearly the
same, has no occasion to exert his understanding
or to exercise his invention in finding out ex-
pedients for removing difficulties which never
occur. He naturally loses, therefore, the habit of
such exertions, and generally becomes as stupid
and ignorant as it is possible for a human creature to become.

To Marx and Engels:

Owing to the extensive use of machinery and to
division of labor, the work of the proletarians
has lost all individual character, and, consequently, all charm for the workman. He becomes
an appendage of the machine, and it is only the
most simple, most monotonous, and most easily
acquired knack, that is required of him.[14]

The early stage of industrialization in
England was accompanied by concern and
criticism in the classical and poetic visions
of Thomas Carlyle and William Blake.
The powerful impact of Blake's poetic and
artistic images provide an intriguing contrast to the "cool," statistical treatment of
the effects of industrialization found in
Engels' *The Condition of the Working-
Class in England in 1844.*[15]

In America, the introduction of machine
technology provided the basis for a core of
literature by such writers as Thoreau, Hawthorne, Emerson, Twain, and Melville that
has since been characterized as the "pastoral tradition." In an excellent book on
the pastoralists in America, Leo Marx provides an absorbing account of America's
response to the machine in the nineteenth
century and of the literary tradition that
emerged as a distinct school of social criticism.[16] The introduction of the machine
in America was greeted with hope, optimism, and naivete by leading industrialists,
educators, and political leaders. The very
tendency to think about the social consequences of new technology was apparently
not an established part of the intellectual
thought of the period. As Leo Marx points
out: "the very notion of 'technology' as an
agent of change scarcely existed."[17] In addition, it was felt that the new technology
was a force for good which could be separated from the evils of the factory system
seen in England in the eighteenth century.
Marx takes the views of Thomas Jefferson,
as a student of the Enlightenment, to symbolize this spirit of hope.

From Jefferson's perspective, the machine is
a token of that liberation of the human spirit to
be realized by the young American Republic;
the factory system, on the other hand, is but
feudal oppression in a slightly modified form.
Once the machine is moved from the dark,
crowded, grimy cities of Europe, he assumes that
it will blend harmoniously into the open countryside of his native land. He envisages it turning millwheels, moving ships up rivers, and all
in all, helping to transform a wilderness into a
society of the middle landscape. At bottom, it is
the intensity of his belief in the land, as a locus
of both economic and moral value, which pre-

---

[14] Quoted in George Friedmann, *Industrial Society* (Glencoe, Ill.: Free Press, 1955), pp.
129–130.
[15] Friedrich Engels, *The Condition of the Working-Class in England in 1844* (London:
Sonnenschein, 1892).
[16] Leo Marx, *The Machine in the Garden: Technology and the Pastoral Ideal in America*
(New York: Oxford Univ. Press, 1964).
[17] *Ibid.*, p. 149.

vents him from seeing what the machine portends for America.[18]

Other leading figures of the period with perhaps greater sensitivity to the fact that the large-scale introduction of machine technology would require public discussion and political decisions, sought to link the image of the machine to the pastoral ideals of the period. Not only would the machine lead to mastery of nature, national wealth, and self-sufficiency, but also the machine is part of nature's plan. Nature is represented in mechanistic images, thereby providing a link between nature and the machine, and creating a kind of natural determinism that is reminiscent of many modern attempts to see technological "advance" as a force which must seek its natural ends.

Of what significance are these remarkable parallels between nineteenth-century critics and advocates of the machine and twentieth-century critics and advocates of automation and mechanization? It is often tempting to draw upon examples from the historical context of work to either justify or criticize the conditions of work as they presently exist. For example, a critic of the contemporary conditions of work would draw upon the work of the preindustrial craftsman or pastoral artisan as a contrasting condition. In this contrast he would judge modern man to be more alienated from his work and less satisfied with his lot in life. On the other hand, the justifier of work in the modern world would select his examples for contrast from the early factory system in Europe. He would then find modern man's work to be "humanized," more sensitive to the general needs of workers, and providing greater satisfaction.

Any such attempts to use history in this fashion are examples of poor social science. If it is argued that the modern worker is comparing his present condition with some historic past, either favorably or unfavorably, then it must be shown how the earlier images of work are embodied in presently existing social and cultural systems. In other words, we cannot make the modern worker "happy" or "alienated" by a contrast that we provide as observers. The problems of work must be sought in the modern conditions of work; what a worker does, what he says about his work, how his work affects his life as a citizen, husband, or father, and how his work is related to other patterns of thought.

A second temptation for those who look at work in a historical context is to respond to the existence of a persistent condition as evidence that the condition itself is somehow a normal state of affairs. For example, when it is found that today's critics of automation are expressing the same concerns as eighteenth-century critics of the machine, it is easy to conclude that "there is nothing new under the sun," that man has always been concerned with work, and, the prophets of doom notwithstanding, the problems of work are "normal" and not really in need of remedy (if it is admitted that a remedy could change things). It seems far more plausible to view such historical similarities as evidence that the conditions of work since the introduction of the machine have followed an orderly and linear progression of making man less and less important in the processes of production. We should be careful not to overstate this point, however, for at the same time that the large majority of workers have been rendered less useful, either through outright displacement or extreme specialization, there have also emerged new work roles that require expanding responsibilities and involvement. This is particularly apparent in scientific, technological, and managerial work roles. A recognition

[18] *Ibid.*, p. 150.

of these new roles, however, cannot be used to deny the conditions of work for most workers.

A frequently used starting point in attempting to determine man's feelings about his work is to look at public-opinion surveys that ask respondents the straightforward question of "How satisfied are you with your work?" and expect the straightforward answers of either "very satisfied," "somewhat satisfied," "somewhat dissatisfied," or "very dissatisfied." When the question of work satisfaction is approached in this fashion, it is found that the large majority of people indicate that they are satisfied with their work.

This is a much too simplified procedure for trying to estimate job satisfaction. The question is too general in nature, while the realities of work are quite varied. Work has to do with material rewards, psychic gratifications and social relationships with co-workers and supervisors. Satisfaction with one aspect of work may not be related to another aspect. The reasons that a man likes his job do not necessarily produce dissatisfaction when they are not present.[19] Moreover, a man who has little alternative with respect to his job may not be too inclined to be overly critical of the work that he is destined to do for his active work life.

It is also known that when people are asked less direct questions about their work and are given an opportunity to choose alternative work roles for themselves, the picture that is derived concerning work satisfaction is quite different. Harold Wilensky has drawn together the results of his own studies and others that have asked workers of different occupational groups whether or not they would choose the same type of work if they could start all over again. While such a question is still very general, it at least has the virtue of not requiring the worker to be directly critical of his present job in a fashion that might be too self-critical as well. Table 4 contains the data on the proportion of workers in each of the listed occupations or occupational categories that would choose not to continue in their present work if given an opportunity. If we take these answers to indicate a degree of dissatisfaction with work, then it is clear that dissatisfaction is somewhat more widespread than indicated by the general and direct questions on satisfaction. It is also clear that regardless of how a question concerning job satisfaction is worded, the level of satisfaction declines for workers in the lower levels of the occupational structure. At the upper professional level some eight or nine out of ten persons indicate they would pursue the same job if given another opportunity to make a career decision. For technical professionals and white-collar workers in general, the level of satisfaction is from seven out of ten engineers to less than one-half of white-collar employees. In the lower ranges of working-class occupations, some six to eight out of ten workers indicate they would not choose the same work again.

If we refer back to Table 1 and think of the number of people working in the different occupational groupings, we get some idea of the magnitude of the problem of job dissatisfaction. The figures represent tens of millions of workers who are sufficiently dissatisfied with their present job that they would change it if given an opportunity. We do not, of course, know anything of the depth of this dissatisfaction. We do not know the extent to which such dissatisfaction represents a serious threat to the stability of American society. To know this would require extensive discussions with workers about the various aspects of

[19] Frank Frielander and Eugene Walton, "Positive and Negative Motivations Toward Work," *Administrative Science Quarterly*, **9** (1964-65), pp. 194–207.

Table 4   WORKERS WHO WOULD NOT CHOOSE SIMILAR TYPE OF WORK IF THEY COULD
START OVER AGAIN[a]

Professional and Lower White-Collar Occupations	Percent	Working-Class Occupations	Percent
Urban university professors[b]	7	Skilled printers	48
Mathematicians	9	Paper workers	48
Physicists	11	Skilled auto workers	59
Biologists	11	Skilled steel workers	59
Chemists	14	Textile workers	69
Firm lawyers[b]	15	Blue-collar workers, age 30–55[b]	76
School superintendents[c]	15		
Lawyers	17	Blue-collar workers, age 21–29[b]	77
Journalists (Washington correspondents)	18		
		Unskilled steel workers	79
Church university professors[b]	23	Unskilled auto workers	84
Solo lawyers[b]	25		
Engineers[d]	27		
Diversico engineers[b]	30		
Unico engineers[b]	30		
White-collar workers, age 21–29[b]	54		
White-collar workers, age 30–55[b]	57		

[a] Adapted from Harold Wilensky, "Work as a Social Problem," in H. Becker (ed.), *Social Problems: A Modern Approach* (New York: Wiley, 1966).
[b] "All probability samples or universes of six professional groups and a cross section of the 'middle mass' (lower-middle class and upper-working class) in the Detroit area, stratified for comparability with respect to age, income, occupational stratum, and other characteristics." (Wilensky, *op. cit.*)
[c] "From a 48 percent sample of all school superintendents in Massachusetts, 1952–1953. Neil Gross et al., *Explorations in Role Analysis, Studies of the School Superintendency Role* (New York: Wiley, 1958)." (Wilensky, *op. cit.*)
[d] From a national sample of engineering graduates employed in industry and government. R. Perrucci et. al., "The Engineer in Industry and Government," *Journal of Engineering Education*, **56** (March 1966), pp. 237–273.
For further details on the samples, see Wilensky, *op. cit.*

their work, about what they find satisfying and what they find degrading. If we are to go beyond merely lamenting the absence of satisfying work to actually changing the conditions of work, this kind of information will be essential.

Yet we will not be put off by the absence of all the information. We sense a widespread discontent in the nation over the nature and rewards of work. We shall try to convey our sense of this discontent by looking at why man works and what he does at work. It is our feeling that the underlying conditions of all work satisfaction and dissatisfaction are connected with the ends that one pursues in working, and the opportunity provided by work to realize certain human needs. The first condition refers to the extent that there is a "grubbing" orientation toward work. A grubbing orientation is concerned primarily with work as a means of expanding income, personal prestige, or power and is a feature of occupations that have already achieved a measure of economic and social stability. It is also a concern for rewards that are decreasingly satisfying because of the instability of the end itself, and, to use the language of economics, because the value of each additional unit of income or power or prestige is not as important as the preceding unit. Let it be clear, however, that a grubbing orientation does not simply mean a concern over income, period; it does not apply to the lower white-collar or blue-collar worker who is interested in increasing his income to reach a standard of living that provides for a family's needs. It is an orientation found in the upper professional ranks, where men are supposed to pursue their careers for altruistic ends; ends which are increasingly relegated to the role of professional rhetoric.

The grubbing orientation is, of course, a feature of the more fundamental pattern of linking work with income. This pattern, which is such an integral part of our society, also affects the job satisfaction of the lower income worker in the sense that he has only one reason for working, and even here he realizes only limited satisfactions. If, on the other hand, his work has some larger social purpose (other than income), and his income for self and family are independent of work, then it is quite possible that he would have a different feeling about the work that he does. In short, what is being suggested in this discussion of the grubbing orientation toward work is that the use of work as a means of attaining external rewards (e.g., income, power, prestige) is closely connected with job discontent for the simple reason that the ends pursued are by their very nature unstable. For the upper professional who has substituted these external goals for the more altruistic ends of his profession, the result will be an increasing ambivalence and self-

doubt concerning the use of his talents. For the white-collar and blue-collar worker who seeks satisfaction through increased income and consumption patterns that are purchased with this income, the result will be an increasing feeling of being trapped in an occupation that he despises and by the consumer behavior that he and his family have come to accept as "needs."

The second dimension of work is concerned with the nature of work itself and its relationship to the attainment of certain human needs. Work can be physically demanding, dirty, and degrading; these conditions are inherent in the tasks required by certain jobs. The conditions of work can also be stifling and repressive concerning the opportunity for a worker to exercise some measure of control over his work, or to exercise his own opinions, judgments, and intellect in the work process itself. Physically demanding or repressive work abuses the dignity of the self in the uses to which the body is put; and it abuses man's special sense of "humanness" that is associated with the exercise of his intellect. When work is found in these conditions, the worker is truly nothing more than a highly inefficient machine. His job persists simply because a technical device that can perform the same work has not been found.

The two dimensions of work—the pursuit of external goals and the satisfaction of basic human needs—must also be seen in their interrelationships and in the particular cultural context in which they exist. It is likely that there will always be work that is physically demanding and dirty, *but whether or not it is degrading depends very much on why the work is being done.* In American society we have increasingly accepted man's value in the marketplace as the measure of his worth, as the measure of how much respect he is entitled to. When hard and dirty work yields both low income and little respect, then that work is degrading. Contrast this, however, with the hard and dirty work of the small farmer in early America, the member of a collective farm in Israel, the medical missionary, a Vista volunteer, and a Peace Corps volunteer. Although the examples deal with work in a rural setting, is it not possible that men would also work toward the collective goals of rebuilding their community or city, or of providing service without a feeling of servility?

Much the same can be said for the freedom to exercise control and intellect in one's work. All work cannot be challenging and exciting for workers. Much work is routine, repetitive, and requiring little skill or ingenuity in its performance. But is it necessary that when a man finds himself in such an occupation he must also be saddled with a self-concept that makes it difficult for him to have any sense of dignity? It is only necessary when a society glorifies white-collar work and a college education to such an extent that it is a national obsession. I cannot help but recall a rather startling conversation with an 18-year-old New York City youth who had only recently graduated from high school. The boy candidly reported that he was not going to college because of a lack of interest, poor high-school grades, and a feeling that he simply could not make it even if he tried. Instead he had taken a job in a gas station and garage with the hope that he could learn how to be an auto mechanic (which in itself is by no means a repetitive, mindless job). What amazed the author so much is that the boy was describing his choice as a personal failure that he was learning to live with. He said he thought that people "didn't think much of a mechanic," and in order to "be somebody" today you had to have a college degree. If this boy is any representative of the noncollege-bound youth today it is clear that our national advertising campaigns aimed at encouraging youth to go to college and making higher education a national resource have been very effective indeed. It is also clear that they may be helping to create a generation of "failures" who feel things are "all over for them" before the age of twenty.

Facing the Crises of Work and Nonwork

The central overriding problem that cybernation poses for the world of work is found in the fact that cybernation represents a new philosophy of progress, of value, and of the relationship between man and his society. It would be a misunderstanding of the cybernetic revolution to view it simply as a new way of handling information, of making decisions, and of coordinating machines. For its danger lies not so much in the fact that it is able to do "old" things faster and cheaper, but in its tendency to define new things, new goals, new standards of worth. In its functioning as a philosophy, cybernation has become identified with national purpose, with maintaining the dominant position of the United States in world affairs, and with the cold-war struggle.[20] Yet its very power as a technique is also responsible for its narrowness and inhumanity as a philosophy. The cybernetic revolution has pro-

---

[20] See, e.g., Diebold, op. cit., "It is significant, I think, that with increasing frequency and forcefulness statements of Soviet political and economic theory refer to automation as the means by which mankind will achieve the highest of estates, no shilly-shallying here, no confusion over whether to move forward. Rather a firm determination to lead tomorrow where our country leads today. . . . It [Soviet Union] is positively embracing automation. Premier Khruschev has stated, 'Automation is good. It is the means we will use to lick you capitalists.' " (P. 10.) "We also need increased productivity if we are to maintain our defense position and yet increase our standard of living." (P. 144.)

duced a great deal of the drudgery of duced great wealth and comfort and re-work; but it is unable to deal with the fact that it cannot use man and the *quality* of man's life as a measure of progress.

Justification of the cybernetic revolution and its continuation is often expressed in the "hard facts" of economics. Industries are faced with the continual problem of maintaining a competitive advantage in national and international markets. The application of automated means of production serves to increase productivity and efficiency, thereby maintaining a steady pressure for "better" and "cheaper" products that will continue to maintain the economic strength of the nation. Workers who are displaced by the new technology or who cannot find a place in it because of low skill level are seen as unfortunate casualties of an otherwise healthy economic system. This tale of justification for the continuation of automated and mechanized production systems is true only within a specific framework of assumptions about costs and efficiency. Certainly, a manufacturing firm can clearly show that they can produce more at less cost per unit of production by reducing the work force by half and introducing automated production systems. But what of the costs to the displaced worker or the unemployable youth? What of the costs in broken lives and broken homes? What of the costs in welfare benefits, delinquency, crime prevention and detention, care for the psychologically disturbed, for all the associated individual and social effects of unemployment. These are real costs, and they are borne by the unfortunate victim of automation and the passive taxpayer who underwrites the casualties of progress.

It is not suggested for one moment that there are no efficiencies or savings associated with reduction in labor force and introduction of automation. But it is being suggested that much of what is done in the name of progress and reduced costs may not be anything of the sort. It is suggested further that if the costs of progress now borne by the average citizen are transferred to the industries that argue for the necessity of automation, it is possible that there might be greater hesitation in trading people for machines.

The most widely used program for dealing with unemployment is found in federally sponsored programs of manpower retraining of displaced workers and teaching basic skills to young unemployables. Such programs have not enjoyed great success in providing employment for those without work. It is difficult to impart new skills in short periods of time, at least if it is to be a skill that provides some semblance of job security. In addition, these programs have often been unrealistically linked to existing job opportunities. It is no easy task to establish accurately the number and type of jobs that are going unfilled, and then train or retrain people quickly enough to fill these jobs. The alternatives are to train people in skill areas that can be quickly learned, and to use city-wide or regional estimates of unfilled jobs. Both alternatives fail to provide secure jobs or jobs that are in fact in areas where the unemployed live.

Although not currently in use, income-maintenance programs such as the guaranteed annual wage or negative income tax are being seriously considered as a means for dealing with unemployment. Once considered quite "radical" and far-reaching, such proposals have become part of the normal rhetoric of congressmen and government officials. Income-maintenance programs have the virtue of providing all families with an income that would provide for a certain standard of living. As such they can be very valuable. Yet it should also be clear that they do nothing in providing a displaced worker with a new job or a young high-school dropout or graduate with meaningful employment. Income maintenance is a *politically radical* step because it intends to spend a great deal of money for a sizable minority of the population with little power to make such demands. But it is being increasingly justified in the jargon of cost-benefit analysis as cheaper than the welfare system, or a small price to pay to keep peace in the cities and minimize the discontent of the poor, the black, and the young.

As usual, when government officials plan to spend a great deal of money, they tend to exaggerate their expected return. Such exaggerations are often necessary to get the program enacted, but unfortunately they come to be believed even by those who should know better. Income-maintenance programs will help to reduce extreme poverty or hunger and protect millions from the fear, insecurity, and want they currently face. But they will do nothing about the problems of being unemployed, of being without a place in society, or of minimizing the discontent of those who feel they are not needed or wanted. It is, moreover, a dangerous matter to render some 10 to 20 million people totally dependent upon the good will and political vagaries of a dominant, affluent majority.

Manpower retraining for the unemployed and unemployables and income-maintenance programs accept the existence of current tendencies in automation and job displacement. They are adaptations to a set of conditions that are felt to be inevitable and even desirable. It would seem, however, that more attention could be given to the ways in which to minimize the unemployment experienced by the young and unskilled. One general suggestion would be to consider programs by which industry could bear a greater share of the costs associated with job displacement. When an industry plans to reduce its labor force for greater efficiency it could be required to bear a part or all of the cost of retraining the displaced worker while providing him with an income comparable to that which he earned prior to displacement. Companies of a certain size and wealth could also be expected to develop job-training programs within their own plants which would provide training and employment for many of the young without work.

Companies that have no interest in providing full income maintenance while retraining takes place, or those that feel they cannot train and employ the young unemployables, would have the option of paying an annual tax that would be used to allow the government to become the employer of last resort. The only problem with the government as employer of last resort is that there might be a tendency to create "make-work" jobs rather than jobs that are community-based and deal with the problems of neighborhoods and cities. Whatever specific procedures are used, however, is less important at this point than the need to open up serious discussion of programs which would serve to maintain full employment among those segments of the population that are currently faced with large-scale unemployment.

Facing up to the problems of meaningless and alienative work is a far more difficult matter than dealing with unemployment. The problems of work are so closely tied to the entire occupational structure and economy that it staggers the imagination to think of proposals for changing the nature of work without trying to return work to its preindustrial form. Moreover, the solutions to problems of work do not all lie in the realm of work, but in the fact that work bears the burden of providing man with all of his essential social relationships and self-concept. In a society where ties to family, clan, community, or religion are still important, a man can approach work with fewer expectations as to the satisfactions he is to realize. Where attachments to other systems of meaning are not present, there we will find work bearing an especially heavy burden.

Yet despite these difficulties there are some plausible levers of change that could have a beneficial effect upon work. They include (1) changing the worker's relationship to his work by experimenting in large-scale job-enlargement programs; (2) increasing worker control over the decision-making aspects of work; (3) separating the relationship between work and income, and minimizing the role of direct income as a reward for work; and (4) tying work to collective goals associated with community needs in health, education, and recreational services.

Job-enlargement programs are nothing new, but they may not have been given a fair chance of being "tested" as a solution to worker alienation. Originally designed to reverse the process of extreme fragmentation of work, enlargement was expected to provide workers with a greater sense of identification with their work by giving them more "complete" tasks. The apparent advantages of extreme fragmentation have made many officials skeptical of trying out plans to reorganize work in a manner quite foreign to their experience.[21]

If dealing with the work process itself presents difficulties which make change in work unrealistic, it is still possible to alter the worker's relationship to his job by increasing his control over it. Some aspects of the work process are controlled by the machine, but others are decided upon by managers, industrial engineers, and labor contracts. Work schedules, pacing, quality standards, productivity, income systems, and the location of the work place are all matters that are decided upon not by the worker himself, but by others who plan, organize, and supervise the work process. Blumberg has argued that a shift in power and decision making to workers will result in an increase in general morale and work satisfaction.[22] However, before such experiments could be considered it would be necessary to think through the relationship between private ownership of industry, managerial control, and worker control. For worker control would have to go beyond mere "participation" in decision making to control over decision making, if it is to be an effective solution to meaningless work.

A third way of making work more meaningful and less alienative is to minimize the role of income as the main reward for work. This, however, is among the most far-reaching changes that would be considered, for it would require extensive changes in how people define their needs concerning a standard of living and how they satisfy these needs. Health needs, retirement programs, and educational costs are some of the present living costs that could be provided for through collective employee and governmental programs that would sharply reduce income levels as a reward for work. This does not necessarily mean a lower standard of living, for it simply shifts the payment for selected family needs from an individual to a collective basis, thereby minimizing the use of work as a device for income enhancement and status gains. Some attention could also be given to questions of income ceilings and income differentials with the objective of providing a more equitable distribution of standard of living by pro-

[21] For indications of the advantages of job enlargement, see E. H. Conant and M. D. Kilbridge, "An Interdisciplinary Analysis of Job Enlargement: Technology, Costs, and Behavior Implications," *Industrial and Labor Relations Review*, **18** (April 1965), pp. 337–395; W. E. Reif and P. P. Schodenbek, "Job Enlargement: Antidote to Apathy," *Management of Personnel Quarterly*, **5** (Spring 1966), pp. 16–23.

[22] Paul Blumberg, *Industrial Democracy* (London: Constable, 1968).

viding for more family needs outside of the sphere of direct income.

Even without the development of new collective and governmental programs to provide for health, housing, education, and retirement needs, it is still possible to consider limiting incomes or equalizing incomes in selected occupations. For example, among professional occupations, academics in the same department or university might consider ways of equalizing incomes; doctors might agree to establish "reasonable" limits on income; congressmen might consider alternatives to obtaining larger salaries (now at $42,000) which still meet established needs and possible income forgone while performing a public service.[23] All such proposals would have the effect of minimizing income inequalities among occupations, and it would make the so-called "service" ethic among professionals and the alleged intrinsic motivation to work more plausible.

A final approach attempts to avoid working with established occupations but to develop new occupations that are undertaken for the purpose of achieving collective goals at the community level rather than pursuing the individual goal of income. The objective here would be to bring work back to the places where people live rather than requiring people to travel long distances to their work, and to radically transform the rewards that people get from work and their motivation for working.

If the problems of work as they are experienced at all levels of the occupational structure are to be dealt with honestly and effectively, it will require serious consideration of new and far-reaching transformations of the way work is organized and rewarded. Perhaps the American labor movement could be revitalized into a genuine progressive force if unions were to undertake an examination of the problems of work facing millions of American workers. Until such efforts are made and new patterns of work developed we will continue to find man replaced by machines, eliminated from secure employment, and subject to work that is increasingly unrewarding in every sense but a monetary one.

---

[23] At least one congressman, Representative Andrew Jacobs of Indiana, has refused to accept the $12,000 pay increase for congressmen and has introduced a bill to repeal the pay raise.

IS PLANNING A REVOLUTION?

Robert Ross

If not too long ago most Americans and their leaders did not realize the enormity of their homefront problems, then the fiery glow of cities by night has enlightened them. Reactions have been characteristically mixed, but nowhere apathetic—an indication that public intervention in domestic crises will be far more deliberate and widespread than it ever was during the years of the Vietnam buildup.

For blacks and major sectors of young people and professionals, the ghetto explosions have triggered a breakthrough to a new political awareness of the necessity for genuine resistance movements. Other Americans have substituted alarm at the problem posed by "riots" in place of concern for the problems which precipitated them in the first place. Like the British in India, lower-middle and working-class white America reasons that it is better that the law be certain than that it be just. And these groups are being joined by articulate liberals whose notions of justice and equality are traditionally dependent upon the preservation of the existing social order.

There are others in Democratic or liberal administrative circles whose only tradition for reform has been the New Deal and the incremental perspective that succeeded it. For them radical changes were expunged as programmatic alternatives when socialism was thought-reformed out of American life. Trapped between what they see as the "crazies" on both sides, most are anxious to do good if that is what "fire insurance" and bipartisan foreign policy require—and it appears that it is. It is the efforts of these groups which are beginning to dominate the agencies of social change within America's racially torn, economically blighted cities, just as they once dominated the attempted reconstruction of a collapsed economy in the thirties. The first task of this paper will be to anticipate and evaluate the impact of their programs on urban America through a study of their defining operational techniques.

THE IDEOLOGY OF PLANNING: WHAT "EFFICIENCY" MEANS

Planning is the more or less efficient and foresightful devising of means to reach specified goals. Aside from military preparations, we have not had much of it in American government. But now wherever one turns a new kind of planning is proposed for solving slum housing, unemployment, consumer exploitation, and the myriad conditions of ghetto oppression.

In the thick undergrowth of the social policy bureaucracies—Departments of Health, Education and Welfare (HEW), Housing and Urban Development (HUD), Labor, Office of Economic Opportunity (OEO), the Ford Foundation, Rockefeller Fund, departments of urban renewal, city planning, and planning firms—lies a series of responses to the urban crises which, in turn, fascinate, repel, and amuse. They all claim to increase the efficiency of social programs but not one challenges the system which creates the crises.

Reprinted by permission from Viet-Report, **3**:*8–9 (Summer 1968), pp. 8–11, 61.*

No one does or should expect reformers to be revolutionaries or expect capitalist politicians to assert socialist principles; but even on their terms, can the various attempts to uplift the blacks, clean up the slums, and re-do the educational system really work? Moreover, at what cost and with what consequences? How efficient *are* the new technocrats?

In recent years systems analysis, cost-benefit analysis (CBA), and planned-program budgeting systems (PPBS) have become the new and revered tools of the technocratic planner. Developed by the high-technology defense complex, today government, business, and municipal leadership look to these tools to locate structural faults and inefficient funding investments in the service bureaucracies.

After a year of listening to government people talk about systems analysis to a group of social-work professors and sociology graduate students, this writer concluded that for all the heat there was little light. For hardware systems, or economic models, in which each component of a process can be quantified and controlled, systems analysis had a particular procedural function. As it moves deeper into social and behavioral problem solving, the variables defy quantification, except arbitrarily. How does one specify a model of a family-maintenance system or labor-market recruitment system? Systems analysis in social problems is merely an attempt to be rational and complete in visualizing what causes and what might change a given phenomenon. But herein lies the rub. The most creative applications of systems analysis still ignore the ordinary political processes for social change—legislation, lobbying, and social movements—and end up being as utopian as any New Left program for decentralization.

Cost-benefit analysis (CBA), a more modest method, can facilitate certain decision-making processes, but it too fails where it counts the most: in its long-range effects on the social life of individuals and groups.

CBA assigns a cost to each element of a program; it then attempts to assign a monetary value to benefits accruing from the program. For example, a study done in a California county on vocational rehabilitation for welfare recipients was "costed out" by including staff time, use of plant, supplies, etc. Two of the several benefits accruing from the project were measured by the savings in welfare payments to ultimately employed recipients and by the taxes the former recipients would pay on earned income. The ratio of monetary cost to monetary benefit was found to be 1:37: a finding which, nevertheless, will neither convince nor have meaning for a cost-conscious Congress when it is asked to fund such a program.

What is not measured in CBA studies is far more important to the creation of a society beneficial to all than those limited instances when ability to compare costs and benefits help to decide the monetary worth of a program investment. Can we measure in monetary or any quantifiable terms how much or how little it hurts a mother to work or to stay at home with her fatherless children? In assessing the cost of compulsory assignment to the ghetto of experienced teachers, can we also measure the extent and effect of black children's resentment to having another white person in authority over them? Repeatedly, these important but immeasurable social and political values are the unmentioned ones in CBA studies.

Within the complex of OEO-HEW, the use of monetary measurement of cost and the search for higher benefit to cost ratio possess systematic biases in the short run which are oppressive in the long run. Specifically, what we should fear from the dominance of CBA is its perpetuation of a permanent underclass. For example, in the rehabilitation project discussed above, the potential participants were screened to ensure the highest possible ratio of benefits. Only the most rehabilitatable were chosen, which ensured fewer dropouts from the program and more employed participants. The efficiency of picking those who least need a service has a contagious logic. You help those who can use help, the argument goes. But the cumulative effect over time and through many such programs is that the search for efficient use of resources will always leave a bottom of the barrel, a "hopeless" section of the population. Once so designated, they remain hopelessly outside the web of service and justice, hopelessly neglected and, in fact, hopelessly unknown. (The last Census missed a substantial number of unemployed inner-city young men.)

The third planning method, PPBS, attempts to use cost-benefit reasoning in the budgeting processes of an administrative agency. This is the system which former Defense Secretary McNamara brought to the Pentagon, and which, by virtue of an Executive Order, will become the standard system in social-policy government agencies. Many students of this process have concluded that PPBS is more than a way of justifying decisions to skeptical publics. By proposing an objective way to measure whether one program or another is more efficient in reaching a goal and by positing the goal and finding the cheapest way to attain it, PPBS is an impressive instrument of power in the hands of central budgeting analysts. In fact, it is *the* centralizing mechanism within agencies and a weapon in the fight for power between agencies. It allows an agent of an administrative leader, by virtue of his claim to a sound basis of judgment, to stop one idea, encourage another, and have final say over many.

That a basis for judgment is needed in social-policy programs is not denied. Social-service workers and the public programs they have for years defended have never developed persuasive empirical justification for any given service program. Even minimum-support programs—Aid to Dependent Children, for example—have not successfully accomplished any of their many aims. This is also true of nongovernment social-policy planners. In comparison to government planning efforts, they have no particular methodology to integrate social and physical policy. They criticize the bricks-and-mortar approach but have not come up with an alternative approach. In the face of the government's Model Cities Program, for example (today's most celebrated catch-all program for the inner city), critics appear mute.

Model Cities contains three objectives: (1) to integrate physical and social planning; (2) to provide for citizen participation; and (3) to accomplish physical renewal without displacing poor people. Reasonable, perhaps laudable goals. Yet there is no reason to believe that Model Cities will accomplish a single one of them.

Take the first. In addition to the traditional contest of power between city planners and social-policy advocates, there seems to be no systematic link between the two types of development. Do the advocates of the physical/social integration also advocate the development of a different kind of economic base for black communities? No, they promise employment of blacks on prospective construction, although no city mayor has yet begun to do battle with the building-trade unions to win even this goal. Occasionally there are sounds about reviving or creating black capitalism for the black community. But is the need really for black grocers, furniture stores, etc.? In an age in which the marginal small businessman is as predatory, or more so, than the big retailing chain, this is an odd benefit to bestow on the exploited black consumer. Or does anyone seriously envision a black IBM rising from the ashes of Watts?

Without a theory of what keeps black people down, of how the whole system works, talk of integrating different types of planning has no content, no concrete meaning.

The second objective, citizen participation, could be important if for no other reason than that it would generate conflict which would be socially educative and a catalyst to organizing in the black community. But participation is not authority. No budgetary power is proposed for the Model Cities Advisory Councils (the name used in Chicago); no actual policy on the use of city resources will be decided by indigenous representatives. At present there is not much hope that *any* decisions at all will be made by "citizens." Fighting in the War on Poverty was also educative: it taught us that the majority of city administrators will struggle, manipulate, dodge, and finally win the battle to keep these power instruments in hands that are friendly and representative of themselves.

Even if honest efforts were made to keep the citizen participation boards in the hands of residents who reflected the diversity of the black communities, and even if "advice" were taken seriously in the absence of power and authority, the idea would still be skewed in the wrong direction. If any community is to decide its fate, it needs a number of things which poor communities often lack; among these is access to technical skills in order to compete with and compel attention from government agencies. Moreover, for citizen participation to be representative and significant, the apparatus which organizes it must be as broad and determined as that which induces response to other major political events. Neither of these is part of

Model Cities plans. For example, to make the technical prerequisites to participation available would entail the release of funds to the citizens' group so it could hire its own planning firm. To legitimize the granting of this money might require obtaining a percentage of the community's signatures on a petition declaring support for the essential ideas of the group soliciting. And for the participation to be intense every plan would have an alternate; groups given monies for planning would each produce at least one, and the choice between plans might be made at the polls, or town meetings, etc. But this entails a true devolution from white to black power, a democratization of planning which is unlikely to be considered by the Daleys, Yortys, or, for that matter, the Stokes of the American cityscape.

There is evidence that Model Cities' third objective represents a sincere effort to avoid massive dislocation. But consider the following situation. A house has an average of 10 six-person families. The 10 families live in 10 units which total, say, 40 rooms. The house will be bought, rehabilitated, and then rented by the local housing authority. Part of the rehabilitation goal is to bring the building up to code standards for overcrowding (average 1.01 persons per room). After rehabilitation perhaps only 8 units will be left; in any case, if the code standards are to be maintained, all those families cannot go back. Therefore, dislocation.

There is no substitute for simply increasing the supply of housing for the poor.

SHAPING A CORPORATE CONSTITUENCY

Most modern politicians recognize the limits of all these techniques and programs. Thus many have turned to private business to meliorate the urban crisis. Senator

Charles Percy started a presidential boom-let for himself with a rather ordinary pro-posal to have government underwrite mortgages for ghetto dwellers of moderate income. The late Robert F. Kennedy raced through Indiana claiming that government can't do everything, that the welfare sys-tem was obsolete, that the greatest un-tapped resource for urban redevelopment was the dynamic of private enterprise. And the Urban Coalition plans to rescue the cities with an alliance comprised of the traditional sources of activist liberalism with the addition of enlightened Corporate Enterprise.

Corporate planners have already taken certain tentative steps. In late 1966 Presi-dent Johnson moved to generate jobs for the hard-core unemployed through the Concentrated Employment Project (CEP). And ever since it became apparent that the basic development and deployment of mis-sile capability had been managed, science-based aerospace and high-technology com-panies have been taking on urban research and development contracts. In San Diego, Ford engineers are designing a long-range transportation plan; in New Jersey, Litton Industries has taken over a Job Corps camp. All over the country hip young men with a smattering of knowledge about com-puterized teaching are working on voca-tional and remedial literacy training.

There are two conditions under which business will welcome or foster both ex-tensions of government subsidies and direct utilization of private enterprise in the realm of social welfare. The first is when domestic crises threaten the foundations of the business system itself, as they did in the dual political and economic crisis of the Great Depression. The second is when business (or the leading sectors of the most advanced industries) believe that cer-tain government policies will lead to secure or attractive profit potentials for them-selves—as with the railroad land grants,

the land grant colleges, the designation of private insurance companies as carriers of medicare insurance, and the federal insur-ance of mortgage loans. Each of these con-ditions obtains today; coupled with the proven incapacity of government welfare programs to meet the needs of the urban poor, they herald a growing investment of corporate planning in the ghettos.

To date, corporate programs have been easy to dismiss as token responses, flashy PR gestures, or simply as irrelevant appli-cations of technology to social conflicts. All this they may be, but the thrust behind them does represent an institutional ide-ology which stands as a far more com-pelling feature of the postwar political landscape than the welfare statism of Dem-ocratic/liberal circles.

After World War II many articulate spokesmen and analysts from within the business community began to extrapolate the accumulated benefits of the Progressive regulatory period and the New Deal-Fair Deal period, while also taking note of the increased scope of corporate enterprise after vigorous government subsidization for capital expansion during and following the War. Radical thinkers claimed to perceive in this discussion the genesis of a new ideological commitment, which they called corporatism. (In the early sixties the founders of Students for a Democratic So-ciety argued that "corporatism"—or cor-porate liberalism—was a distinct ideological formation which represented the gravest threat to those who believed that America needed to *ventilate* not subdue conflict and ideology in the coming years.)

For themselves, the corporate ideologues had mustered an apparently fail-safe social vision. Harmony of interest and the obso-lescence of class keynoted the views of theorists like A. A. Berle and the people William B. White addressed in *Is Anybody Listening?* (an earlier and more pointed version of *The Organization Man*). That social stability could be guaranteed by the unique ability of the professional manager was central to this literature. The ability to coordinate facts, human attributes, and financial possibilities within workable programs, and to motivate people to fulfill them: these were the qualities which brought the manager to the foremost role in the solution of society's problems. Another feature of the work of these laureates was their clarity about the need for collective identity at a time when the intellectual remnants of reform and liberalism were adrift with hocus-pocus theories of alienation and mass society. The corporatists assumed and/or argued that the corporate entity was a fitting and inevitable base to which the roots of identity could be tied. Industrial civilization could be integrated through love, not of Big Brother, but of The Firm. Finally, not without controversy, the image of the corporation with a soul gained ground. Business could and should assume social responsibility for the survival of a civilization which, after all, business had largely engineered.

Much of this was elaborated when the permanent war economy needed to be rationalized, when institutional public relations was coming of age. Fearful memories of the possibilities of depression radicalism lingered to remind business statesmen that they had to have something more than Hobbesian self-interest to legitimize their privileges in the polity. Berle (in the *Twentieth Century Capitalist Revolution*) noted this, and argued that the chief problem of the future would be the legitimation of the sovereign powers now held, but unjustified, by the corporation.

What is so very interesting about the present spate of corporate rhetoric on the "Urban Crisis" is the consistency with which business has sustained—but also crucially modified—these themes.

The important modification is the new perception exemplified by business leadership as well as by political liberals such as Percy and the authors of the Kerner Commission Report, that the welfare system and, more broadly, the welfare state in its American variant is a failure: it holds no promise of completing its task of creating an egalitarian, uniformly affluent society. There is no articulate sector of the polity that maintains confidence in the New Deal bag of tricks. That is the real reason why corporatism is a relevant discussion and why socialism would be if there were a political base for it. There is no longer an articulate constituency which defines its hopes and aspirations as merely more of the same—more unemployment compensation, social security, etc., etc. Confronted with the nature of black destitution in the ghettos, the integrative social mechanisms which brought immigrant groups and dissident labor into the American mainstream have proved to be irrelevant or impotent and, at worst, explicitly repressive.

The technocrats of systems and cost-benefit analyses are beginning to understand this. They seek to harness industry because they have experienced (or anticipate) failure through government welfarism. Their new rhetoric stresses coordination of all efforts, public and private alike. Knowing that the old security planning failed and the new salvage planning is shallow, they look to the efficient corporate managerial planner as a last hope.

But the move from welfare statism to corporatism surely holds no more promise of success. The evidence for this is, literally, the record of our whole civilization. Business can't and won't move into housing or vocational education or preventive medicine unless it can make a good or sure profit. To ensure profit means once again that high-risk sectors—in this case, social reconstruction—must be "baited" with government guarantees (tax incentives, cost-plus contracts, and the like). It means that the most intolerable social ills—more often than not, directly traceable to the anti-social priorities of the profit motive itself —will now be sought *for a price*. It means that over and above immobile or inept municipal governments a far more cynical and politically alien system of power will hold sway. But equally persuasive is the simple fact that modern industry, presently organized, has little or nothing to offer the angry poor.

Consider, for example, the problem of "hard core" unemployment. It is becoming increasingly clear that the location, recruitment, "motivation," training, and hiring of these young men is next to impossible by any means yet in use. There is no reason to believe that private industry will find people the census missed or train people the militants miss. These members of the underclass will become "employable" when the society seems to be theirs, working in their interests, run by their folk.

. . . The difference between a social program and a revolution, as far as poor people are concerned, is the subjective consciousness that in revolution the situation is one which is the people's to define and lead.

Is planning a revolution? One hears the word repeatedly among social-policy planners. No meeting on the inner city or on any aspects of welfare is without the incantation to a revolutionary new scheme of service-delivery, or a revolution in development techniques, or a revolutionary proposal for housing. I don't know what the American Revolution will look like. But another system of coordination, or another invitation to private investment— that it is not.

THE NEW PARTNERSHIP

BIG GOVERNMENT AND BIG BUSINESS

Richard J. Barber

Big business is getting bigger. This year more than a thousand corporations will be consolidated into larger financial enterprises in the greatest merger wave in the country's history. As a result the character of U.S. industry is being radically transformed and the typical corporation of the 1970s is very likely to bear a disturbingly close resemblance to the General Motors Corporation of the mid-1960s. With 735,000 employees, 1.3 million shareholders in more than 80 countries, plants in 24 countries, and a line of products that includes autos, refrigerators, earth-moving equipment, loco-

Reprinted by permission of the author and The New Republic *from* The New Republic *(August 13, 1966), pp. 17–22; copyright 1966, Harrison-Blaine of New Jersey, Inc.*

motives, jet engines, and missile-guidance systems, GM's 1965 net profit (after taxes) of $2.1 billion was greater than the general revenue of 48 states and its sales of $21 billion exceeded the GNP of all except nine foreign nations. Though its proportions are truly massive, GM is by no means exceptional, even now. Many other companies also are sharply increasing their sales (60 U.S. companies reported revenue last year of at least $1 billion), enlarging their profits (82 manufacturers had net earnings of $50 million or more in 1965), and expanding their international commitments (American firms are increasing their overseas investments at a rate of more than $10 million each day). Simply put, the era of the huge, diversified, international company is here.

Just as fundamental changes are taking place in industry, so too are traditional government-business relationships being markedly altered. New economic forces are threatening to outmode the classic American antipathy to bigness. "From this country's beginning," Justice Hugo Black said a few weeks ago in a Supreme Court opinion, "there has been an abiding and widespread fear of the evils which flow from monopoly—that is, the concentration of economic power in the hands of a few." But that attitude, however meritorious, conflicts squarely with what is going on in the economy and with present government policy. In consonance with the prevailing Administration consensus philosophy, the federal government—relinquishing its customary role as a foe of corporate size—is in fact now forging a New Partnership with big business. Naturally this has many troublesome implications, but certainly it means that one no longer can be confident that government will keep the exercise of private economic power within reasonable bounds.

At the moment 200 corporations (out of a total of approximately 200,000) control nearly 60 percent of the country's manufacturing wealth and occupy commanding positions in virtually all principal markets. Just 10 companies, with General Motors at the head of the list reported profits in 1965 equal to the total profits of the next 490 largest firms. Already far larger than modern technology requires, these industrial titans, through internal growth and merger, are certain to increase their relative position even more in the immediate future. Internationally their power will be no less than it is domestically. In the past seven years U.S. firms have more than doubled their overseas investment—it now totals more than $50 billion—with the result that the foreign sales of Standard Oil of New Jersey, Burroughs, Colgate-Palmolive, Mobil, and National Cash Register, among many others, often exceed half their total income. Within a decade a group of 200 American companies plus another 50 to 100 large foreign enterprises will possess most of the world's manufacturing assets and make the great preponderance of sales and profits, having as tight a grip on global industry as our big companies now have at home.

Last year a thousand companies disappeared through merger in the U.S., and in 1966 they will be joined in the graveyard by an estimated 1300. Not only is the absolute number of mergers high by any standard of comparison (fewer than 200 firms a year vanished a decade ago), but a great many large firms are involved. In 1965 Pure Oil (with assets of $750 million), Richfield Oil (assets: $500 million), Consolidation Coal (assets: $465 million), and ABC-Paramount were acquired by, respectively, Union Oil, Atlantic Refining, Continental Oil, and ITT. Between 1948 and 1965 more than 800 companies with assets of at least $10 million each were assimilated into larger empires, mostly those ruled by the 200 biggest manufacturing corporations. At this rate Art Buchwald may well be right in thinking that "the whole country will soon be merged into one large company."

The sheer volume of mergers, important

though it is, must not obscure the most striking fact of all: their changing character. At one time most mergers involved direct competitors or suppliers and their customers. This is no longer true. Today more than 70 percent of all mergers are of the conglomerate variety, bringing together entirely unrelated firms. Horizontal—direct competitor—consolidations currently make up only 12 percent of all mergers, down from more than 30 percent in the early 1950s.

A NEW KIND OF COMPANY

Conglomerate acquisitions have carried many firms into widely diversified product or geographic markets. Borden, usually thought of as a dairy company, is heavily engaged in chemicals. Lipton Tea (a subsidiary of Unilever, the English-Dutch colossus) controls Good Humor. Hershey Chocolate has just entered the macaroni business. R. J. Reynolds, commonly associated with cigarettes, sells poultry, canned soups, catsup, and soft drinks. These and hundreds of other well-established firms have been broadening their product base through the acquisition of going concerns.

An excellent example of the conglomerate is International Telephone & Telegraph. For years engaged in the communications business outside the U.S. (it still is, with 150,000 employees in its foreign manufacturing plants alone), ITT has acquired an odd assortment of enterprises, well described by some of their names: Hayes Furnace Co., Aetna Finance, Great International Life Insurance, Hamilton Management Co. (a $400 million mutual fund), Avis Rent-a-Car, ABC-Paramount (itself diversified, with broadcasting, theatre, phonograph record, and publishing assets), and Airport Parking (with parking facilities at air terminals in 59 of the nation's largest cities).

ITT is only one of an expanding breed of conglomerates. Gulf & Western Industries (from auto-parts manufacture it has broadly expanded into mining and chemicals and soon will acquire Paramount Pictures), Litton Industries (which sells more than a hundred different products, ranging from adding machines to nuclear submarines), Textron, the FMC Corporation, and Olin have similar attributes. A few months ago the U.S. Rubber Company changed its name to Uniroyal, explaining that fewer than half the things it now makes have anything to do with rubber.

Under the pressure of conglomerate mergers many industries are losing their distinctive characteristics. Electronics firms are aggressively moving into the publishing and educational product fields, as signified by RCA's acquisition of Random House (which previously had swallowed Knopf), the sale of D. C. Heath to Raytheon, Xerox's purchase of Wesleyan University Press (rumors now suggest possible merger with Harcourt, Brace), and IBM's absorption of Science Research Associates. From their strong base the computer companies will no doubt continue to diversify, subsuming publishing and educational hardware, and perhaps entertainment and broadcasting (CBS's purchase of the New York Yankees and its interests in Broadway musicals, notably *My Fair Lady*, is suggestive of future trends) in a single amorphous industry— one that does not yield well to traditional tools of economic analysis.

Many factors have helped bring about the conglomerate merger explosion, but one key explanation has been a rising stock market which has permitted mergers to be made on highly advantageous terms. Since most acquisitions take the form of an exchange of stock (usually tax-free), companies whose securities trade in the market at high price-earning ratios have found it particularly easy to purchase lower price-earning companies at relatively small cost. If, for instance, two companies, X and Y, have earnings of $1.00 per share but the X shares sell for $20 and the Y shares for only $10, a merger can easily be arranged that is mutually attractive. Y shareholders might, as one possibility, exchange each of their shares for X shares having a market value of, say, $11 (this gain in value is usually free of tax). With Y's earnings added to their previous profits, X shareholders could also reasonably expect their own holdings to rise in price in view of the market's tendency to capitalize their corporation's earnings at a higher rate. Exactly this kind of swap is involved in Consolidated Food's proposed purchase of United Artists, the nation's most successful film distributor. Under comparable conditions Litton, ITT, and other firms have made many acquisitions on highly advantageous terms in the last few years.

Although the largest corporations have lately been substantially increasing their already tight hold on the country's manufacturing wealth, primarily through conglomerate mergers, the federal government has provided little in the way of an antidote. Antitrust enforcement has served to check mergers between competitors (the merger of Bethlehem and Youngstown Steel was barred, for instance) but no such attention has been given to conglomerate acquisitions. Despite the fact that they are now the most common form of merger (nearly 1000 will be carried out this year) and can seriously lessen competition at the same time they increase concentration, fewer than 1 percent have been formally protested by the federal antitrust enforcement agencies. The green light is on and the race to diversify by acquisition is well underway. The government's unwillingness to challenge conglomerate merger is matched by its refusal to test the legality of established oligopolistic positions. The word is technical but all it refers to are those industries in which a few big companies account for most of the sales. In autos GM, Ford, and Chrysler make 95 percent of the country's new cars; similarly, Alcoa, Reynolds, and Kaiser control about 90 percent of the aluminum market; U.S. Steel, Bethlehem, and Republic produce almost 60 percent of the steel; Anaconda, Kennecott, American Smelting, and Phelps Dodge refine virtually all of the copper. In the same fashion a handful of corporations dominate many other manufacturing industries, with four firms accounting for at least 75 percent of the output of synthetic fibers, soap, salt, flat glass, metal cans, electric bulbs, and computers, to cite only a few specific cases.

Statistics aside, the basic economic significance is that in oligopolistic markets the big sellers come to recognize that it is more profitable not to compete in price. A classic illustration took place in 1956. That year the Ford Motor Company initially announced an average price increase on its 1957 models of 2.9 percent. Two weeks later, however, when GM increased its 1957 model prices by an average 6.1 percent, Ford promptly revised its prices upward to match the GM prices almost dollar for dollar (and Chrysler soon followed suit). Ten years have brought about no change in the situation. Prices for 1966 cars show the same intimate relationship, with dealers' base prices differing by only pennies on comparable Ford, GM, and Chrysler models. This kind of coordinated pricing occurs regularly in the highly concentrated industries. Official government reports reveal the receipt from supposed competitors of hundreds of sealed bids that are identical to the fourth decimal place in the purchase of steel, aluminum, electrical, and other products. The result is the same as if the producers conspired to fix their prices, but while this does occur from time to time, generally it is not necessary. As Chief Justice Warren put it, "an industry which does not have a competitive structure will not have competitive behavior." Yet no steps have been taken to bring about a less concentrated structure.

Quite understandably smaller businessmen feel they are being discriminated against in favor of the giants when it comes to antitrust enforcement. Last May, for instance, the merger of two foodstore chains that together accounted for about 7.5 percent of sales in Los Angeles was held unlawful. Promptly after the decision was handed down, Donald F. Turner, head of the Antitrust Division, announced that he would challenge any merger between competitors having 8 percent or more of any given market. While this may represent sound policy, if it is unaccompanied by action taken against already dominant firms, it means that other companies are forbidden to join forces at the same time that General Motors, U.S. Steel, Goodyear, General Electric, Anaconda, and others of the top 200 are tacitly immunized from antitrust prosecution that would seriously curb or reduce their power.

The government's failure to take steps through antitrust action to block the growth of conglomerate firms and to deconcentrate those industries in which a few companies occupy commanding positions is attributable to a number of factors. First, the myth persists that enterprises become more efficient as they get bigger. To break up General Motors, General Electric, or U.S. Steel thus would run counter to the public interest by destroying their supposed efficiencies of scale. Similarly, while it may not be desirable to let two direct competitors merge, it is thought that there is nothing wrong—quite the contrary—with the formation via merger of a sprawling conglomerate. The entry of Litton or ITT into a new market, so the argument goes, is likely to increase efficiency by bringing in aggressive management, adding capital, and letting in the fresh breezes of modern research. While these arguments are familiar to just about everyone who reads the *Wall Street Journal* or *Fortune*, let alone the *Harvard Business Review*, they are not generally backed up by empirical evidence.

LACK OF ANTITRUST ACTIVITY

Many studies have shown that small and medium-sized firms, specializing in a single product line, are typically more efficient, more innovative (the great bulk of important inventions still are made, not in corporate laboratories, but by individual inventors or small research organizations), and quicker to offer new products and adopt new marketing techniques than their largest rivals. In the steel industry, for example, the two most important technological advances in recent years—the basic oxygen process (it cuts the time needed to make a ton of steel to less than a quarter of that required in an open hearth) and continuous casting—were first used in the United States, not by the steel giants, but by the industry's smaller firms. Nonetheless, many people continue to believe that massive, conglomerate enterprises somehow contribute to greater efficiency. Clearly this attitude, however inaccurate, seriously inhibits antitrust enforcement.

A second reason for the lack of really meaningful antitrust activity is that existing legislation is less than ideally designed to deal with oligopolistic industries and conglomerate mergers. Neither the Sherman Act (passed in 1890) nor the Clayton Act (last amended in 1950), though broad in their coverage, specifically was tailored to cope either with markets in which a small group of firms controls prices or with diversification mergers. As a result, while existing legislation can be used to reach these situations, it makes antitrust enforcement difficult and cumbersome, offering another excuse for the failure to bring the kind of cases that might have made major economic impact.

There is still a third factor and it is probably the most important of all for it places the issue in its political perspective. What is happening is that within the government there is a growing acceptance of business bigness as positively beneficial. Viewed in this light, the disinclination to use antitrust to deal with established dominant positions or to interfere with conglomerate mergers is only one incident of the New Partnership which is being formed by government and big business. This "new interdependence," as *Fortune* calls it, is the product of several forces, economic and political.

GOVERNMENT AS AN ALLY

For one thing, business has prospered immensely under recent Democratic administrations and has come to accept government as a useful ally. Stimulated by a consciously expansionary fiscal policy, the economy has grown rapidly since 1961, sending corporate sales and profits to record heights. Corporate after-tax profits for 1965 totaled $45 billion (up from $27 billion in 1960), equal to a return of 13 percent on net worth—the highest profit rate in history. And based on figures for the first quarter of 1966, corporate profits could go even higher this year. A booming economy, lower tax rates, provisions for larger depreciation allowances, and a generous tax credit have helped show that Democratic government can be great for business.

Billion-dollar expenditures for defense, space, and the Great Society provide additional reason for business' growing appreciation of government. This year defense procurement alone will exceed $23 billion. The cost of putting a man on the moon (and certainly we will not stop there) will be near the $30 billion mark, and most of the money will go to private companies like North American Aviation, Boeing, and McDonnell Aircraft. The Atomic Energy Commission continues to fund large amounts of nuclear research ($1.9 billion in fiscal 1967), much of it done by General Electric and Westinghouse, the world's leading suppliers of nuclear reactors. As well, key AEC installations, such as the Oak Ridge Laboratory, are managed, for a sizable fee, by Union Carbide and other concerns. No one knows for sure how much revenue the government's defense-space-nuclear programs generate for the nation's businesses, but for many industries, government contracts are essential to survival.

How crucial government's support can be is starkly revealed by the aircraft industry. When World War II ended the sales of the big military plane builders abruptly halted. At this point a benevolent defense establishment, in the fashion of the WPA, created enough work to keep them alive. Thus, in 1946, the Air Force—in a then-secret guideline (it was not declassified until 1960)— directed that "contracts [be] parceled out among the old established manufacturers on an equitable basis so that they may be assured enough business to perpetuate their existence." Given this kind of cordial treatment, firms like Boeing, North American, Douglas, and Lockheed were able to survive until they entered the golden days of the 1950s when highly lucrative contracts for aircraft and missiles became commonplace.

Although the large defense-space contractors currently rank among the largest of all manufacturers, they continue to be so closely tied to the government that they still cannot realistically be viewed as private enterprises. Most of the major aircraft corporations—like Lockheed, North American, and Aerojet-General—are engaged in very little nongovernment work. For these companies defense-space sales account for close to 100 percent of their total income. Moreover, they often use government-owned plants and machines in carrying out production contracts. In a fairly typical case a defense firm will be supplied with more than 50 percent of its fixed capital and with as much as 90 percent of its working capital. Actual investment, therefore, is relatively small, with the result that profit rates can be unusually high (in 1965 Boeing's profits came to 21 percent of net worth, and Lockheed 19 percent—more than 50 percent higher than the profit rate for the 500 largest manufacturers.) So intimate is their association with the defense establishment that the big aircraft-missile concerns can most sensibly be viewed as government appendages, with roughly the same status as the Post Office Department. Given this relationship nothing could be more natural than for Air Force and Navy officers to put the supersonic experimental bomber, the XB-70, and other aircraft at the disposal of General Electric as part of the company's ill-fated public relations stunt earlier this year. The XB-70 and one other military aircraft collided in mid-air and crashed with the death of two pilots and the destruction of the $1.2 billion bomber. Answering criticism that the planes should never have been made available to the company, military officials argue that GE—an important defense supplier—is simply a member of the defense family, and in many ways they are right.

Government's essential role in many defense industries is matched by the large part it plays in the nation's research. The federal government today supports nearly 70 percent of all research done in the United States. With annual expenditures of about $16 billion (more than it spent for all purposes during the entire nineteenth century), the government—especially the Defense Department, NASA, AEC, and the National Institutes of Health—subsidizes most of the research done by the universities and the thousands of nonprofit organizations as well as private industry. For all practical purposes American science has been nationalized and government partici-

pation is routinely expected. To cite an instance, when the development of a Mach-3 Supersonic Transport (SST) was proposed, it was considered perfectly normal for the government to offer initially to pay 75 percent of the minimum $1 billion cost—now the government is expected to contribute at least 90 percent.

More is in the government cornucopia, however, than funds for defense and space. The fulfillment of Great Society domestic objectives creates nearly unlimited additional business opportunities. The renewal of our cities ($10 billion a year is a reasonable price tag), urban mass transit (the new rapid transit system in San Francisco will cost $1 billion), improved intercity rail transportation (estimated cost: $15 billion), the alleviation of air and water pollution (the latter alone could call for expenditures of $75 billion over 15 years), better medical care, greater educational opportunities, job training (ITT's Federal Electric subsidiary manages the Kilmer Job Corps Center, for an $11.5 million fee): all of this means billions in sales and profits.

Sensing the economic significance of government defense and domestic programs, big business has now swung its support behind the Democratic Party. In 1964 "Democrats became the party of the 'fat cats'," observes Herbert J. Alexander in his extensive study of campaign spending. Sixty-nine percent of individual contributions received by national Democratic campaign committees was in sums of $500 or more; only 28 percent of individual Republican contributions came in such large amounts.

The key element in the support of Democratic candidates—explaining the large percentage of big contributors—is business. Members of the President's Club, almost all of whom were company executives or their advisers, contributed at least $4 million in aid of President Johnson's campaign. Of the 4000 1964 Club members 532 were in California, home of the biggest defense-space contractors and the state which accounts for about a third of all contract awards. In addition to individual gifts, the Democrats sold 93 full-page advertisements to corporations in their 1964 Official Convention Program, yielding another $1.5 million. Among the takers were several of the biggest defense contractors. If allowance also is made for the sums which came from corporations whose lobbyists bought, with cash, tickets at $25 to $100 per plate luncheons and dinners, business picked up at least three-fourths of the tab for President Johnson's election. And Democratic senators and representatives—and their Republican colleagues—have like cause to be grateful.

In return for its support, big business has received appropriate recognition. Within days after his 1965 inauguration the President held a dinner for a group of business leaders, most of whom were members of the Business Council. The Council, which rose to prominence under President Eisenhower and then fell into disfavor in the early days of the Kennedy Administration (ties were reestablished in September 1961), has once more been extended a cordial greeting at the White House. Its roster is a veritable Who's Who of big business (of its four officers, three are presidents of corporations ranked among the largest 100 manufacturers; the fourth is the head of the country's biggest railroad). With 65 executives comprising its active membership, the Council meets regularly with top government officials in and near Washington.

SCIENCE OF MANAGEMENT

These contacts are strengthened by a steady two-way exchange of personnel. As did its predecessors, the Johnson Administration has drawn heavily on big business and its advisers (the Wall Street and Washington law firms in particular) to fill important policy-making positions at both cabinet and subordinate levels. One example is the Foreign Intelligence Advisory Board, created in 1961 by President Kennedy to monitor the intelligence community. So great is its authority that it is informed in detail about the CIA's plans and methods of operation, precisely the information which will not be given to any senator or congressman who does not sit on the existing oversight subcommittees. Yet, with the present composition of the Board, such details are regularly disclosed to executives at AT&T, the Polaroid Corporation, and Corning Glass. Much other valuable information reaches Robert Kintner, a high White House staff aide and former president of NBC.

The flow of personnel between big business and government is not one-way, of course, and many important executives in private industry can point to earlier public service. Retiring State Department diplomats or AID officials find homes in the companies with extensive international operations. Generals and admirals, by the hundreds, are hired by major contractors anxious to maintain good contacts with the services (Admiral William F. Raborn, former CIA director, is expected to return soon to Aerojet-General). These are well-known instances, but industry has also tapped government for experts in other fields, such as education. Francis Keppel, former U.S. Commissioner of Education, now heads General Learning Corporation, a General Electric-Time, Inc. venture.

In the face of these various indicia of the growing intimacy between government and business—as reflected in procurement contracts, political contributions, and exchanges of key personnel—their old hostility is fast coming to an end. A new breed of corporate executive is on the scene, professionally trained and more oriented to the science of management than to the perpetuation of an ideology which looks upon government as intrinsically evil. The modern company officer accepts government (much like he accepts the labor union) and works actively with it, seeking to take full advantage of the opportunities it offers and striving to influence the policies it adopts. This new attitude toward government comes as a shock to the old conservatives. Barry Goldwater, no doubt reflecting the opinion of many small businessmen, sarcastically views big business leaders as "money manipulators" who are "willing to do almost anything for the dollar."

CHECKING CORPORATE POWER

No assessment of the New Partnership would be complete, however, without an effort to identify some of its larger implications. One thing should be clear: if not restrained, the giant corporations, which, under prevailing circumstances, are likely to tighten even more the control they exert over large segments of the American economy, can act in a manner distinctly contrary to the public interest. Through the manipulation of prices, free from traditional competitive inhibitions, they can levy a monopoly toll on the consumer.

During the last several months big business has been implored on several occasions to exercise restraint in its pricing practices. In each case the White House has met at best only very limited success, demonstrating that the enunciation of guidelines, backed up by no more than jaw-bone diplomacy, is insufficient to ensure that the benefits of increasing productivity are passed along to the consumer. With labor productivity in many industries climbing more rapidly than in the economy generally (meaning that fewer man-hours are required for a given amount of output), prices should be *reduced*, not just held at the existing level. Yet the best the Administration has been able to do—as in copper, aluminum, and molybdenum—is to block further price *increases*. (And in cigarettes, chemi-

cals, and steel it has not even been able to accomplish that much.) A good example is provided by the auto industry. Last fall the car makers increased prices on the 1966 models even though labor productivity was rising so rapidly in the industry that the companies could have cut prices, with full allowances made for higher labor compensation and for the cost of installation of previously optional equipment. With continuing high prices and declining costs it is no wonder that GM and Ford profits rose steeply in 1965. Much the same situation is true of molybdenum. Under government pressure, American Metal Climax, on July 13, rescinded a proposed 5-percent price hike; nevertheless, prices remain high enough to give the corporation an estimated 30-percent return on its molybdenum investment (and an overall profit rate of 17 percent).

Recent price behavior in the major manufacturing industries shows that while the executives of powerful companies like to be regarded as part of the Great Society consensus, generally they give first priority to their own corporate well-being when making decisions about prices and other matters. To curtail the undesirable exercise of their power demands much stronger instruments of control than verbal admonition.

The problem of corporate power could be dealt with at its source by initiating a strong antitrust program that would check further economic concentration (the mere filing of a few cases against conglomerate mergers would alone be insufficient) and weaken the hold of the firms which presently dominate most of our major industries. But can an administration that is wedded to big business undertake this kind of action when it would unquestionably be regarded by industry as a ground for divorce? If it cannot, and there is much evidence to suggest that is the case, the antitrust laws no longer can be regarded as a central instrument of economic policy.

The principal alternative means of checking corporate power is some sort of direct regulation. The possible techniques range from a system that would require companies in concentrated industries to give formal advance notice of price increases and to provide evidence of justification, but that would leave them free to hike their prices if they wished (bills embodying this approach have been introduced in the 89th Congress by Representatives Celler and Reuss) to utility-like regulation that would call for detailed government control of prices. These proposals naturally raise many interesting questions, but any detailed examination would only be academic since the very thought of regulation is anathema to an administration that is anxious to please business. It has steadfastly refused even to acknowledge the possibility that some day it might have to seek explicit statutory authority to back up its wage-price guidelines.

In the process of forming a New Partnership with big business, the harsh fact is that the present Administration has surrendered much of its ability to select the means that will protect the public from concentrated economic power. In effect, through adherence to the consensus philosophy it has become less a partner than a captive of big business. For the foreseeable future, therefore, the American corporate giants will be able to expand their position, at home and abroad, with considerable freedom, and to exert their power much as they wish. Without government protection the best the public can hope for is that big business will be charitable.

HOW THE POWER ELITE
SET NATIONAL GOALS

G. William Domhoff

The subject of this conference has to do with national goals and priorities—what they are, how they are determined, and how they might be changed. It is the latter concern—how they might be changed—that probably inspired this gathering, for national goals are not a topic of explicit concern unless they are being called into question. As we all know, the underlying American goal shared by the majority of the population has been every man for himself doing anything he can to make as much money as he can. However, now that this overriding individualistic materialism has added pollution and youthful revolt to its previous side effects of corruption and social neglect, there is talk of raising the whole problem to the level of a "national debate."

This paper was prepared for a conference on national priorities that was cosponsored by the Stanford Research Institute and the student government of Stanford University. The conference was held January 15–17, 1970, and its proceedings will be edited by Kan Chen of the Stanford Research Institute and published by San Francisco Press.

Topical though comments on how to change American goals may be, I am going to deal with how the present goals are determined. While this may seem rather academic to the practical-minded and action-oriented, I think it provides the necessary basis for more realistic thinking about the problems involved in bringing about change of any significance.

There are those, including some of the participants in this seminar, who think that specific priorities in America are created in the political process via elections, debates in Congress, and discussions in the White House. I also have heard it said that everybody is in on the setting of priorities—consumers, laborers, voters, businessmen, farmers, and so on. I disagree with these views except in the obvious sense that such factors have some part to play. Rather, it is my belief that the national goals are set by those who have been the best at making profits, that is, by the wealthy—who are the winners by the American rules of the game of life.

The wealthy in this country are the owners and managers of the large corporations, banks, insurance companies, and finance houses. Making up perhaps 0.2–0.3 percent of the population, these corporate rich possess about 25 percent of all the privately held wealth in the United States. More importantly, they own perhaps 60–70 percent of all privately held corporate wealth, from whence derives the dividends that underwrite their fabulous life style and the private schools, debutante balls, gentlemen's clubs, summer resorts, and overseas vacations that help to weld the group together as an interacting and intermarrying social class.

I am aware that not all members of this privileged class involve themselves in governing, managing, and goal setting. Some are merely jetsetters, sportsmen, or clothes-horses. However, many do so involve themselves, and these members of the upper class are at the core of a power elite that is the "operating arm" or "leadership group" or "executive committee" that manages the affairs of the corporate rich as a whole. This inner core is filled out and aided in its work by high-level employees in institutions controlled by members of the upper class, which means top-level corporation managers, foundation officials, and university presidents. These latter members of the power elite, I believe, are advanced in terms of their ability to deal with the problems of an economic system that does very nicely by its richest members.

The power elite (which I prefer to think of in the plural rather than the singular because there are some differences of emphasis and style among them) set priorities in two different places, neither of which has been mentioned during this conference. The first is the corporate board room, which is the meeting place of bankers, financiers, corporate lawyers, and businessmen from all over the country. The interlocking and overlapping of these boards almost defies description. Suffice it to say that everybody in this little world is in touch with everybody else through a variety of people and pipelines. As to what priorities are set by this closely knit group—they make investment decisions, decide plant locations, determine the size and shape of the work force, and other such seemingly mundane things that provide the context within which the political process operates. A nice discussion of these matters is by the Republican and quasi-Marxist, Andrew Hacker.[1] If board rooms are as important as Hacker (and certainly others) would suggest, then perhaps it is surprising that they have not been mentioned here.

---

[1] Andrew Hacker, "Power to Do What?," in Irving L. Horowitz (ed.), *The New Sociology* (New York: Oxford Univ. Press, 1964).

Important as corporate board rooms and counting houses are as meeting places for the setting of goals and priorities by the power elite, there is yet a second location for such activity that is perhaps even more important, for it concerns the corporate system as a whole, not just the fortunes of a given company or interest group. This priority-setting process is at its crucial points connected to the government, but it has about as much to do with electoral politics and congressional debates as nothing at all. It is "above politics," "nonpartisan," "bipartisan," "objective," and all other such words that let us know we are in the realm of an issue on which the power elite are going to decide among themselves what is best for the country.

The process to which I am alluding can be conceptualized as having four or five stages, depending on how you want to separate it out, but in reality there is much overlap and feedback between stages, and sometimes several things are going on at once. For simplicity's sake, and as a starting point for discussion, I would diagram the process as follows [see page 213].

The Archimedian point in this little "model" is in the groups I call the consensus-seeking or policy-planning groups of the power elite. It is in these groups that wealthy men from all over the country get together to try to figure out how to react to the general problems facing the corporate system. And I should add, of course, that they have a little bit of help from their friends, the academic experts, particularly the economists, who are well financed via the foundations and enormously flattered by all the attention and acclaim they receive. Some of them even think that experts like themselves run the country.[2]

Among the most important of the or-

ganizations I have in mind are the Council on Foreign Relations, the Committee for Economic Development, and the American Assembly, but there are others, some old, some new, some waning in importance, some just coming into their own. There are many things that could be said about these organizations, but since I have said most of them elsewhere, I want to emphasize only the most germane to the question of goal setting:

1. They bring together big business leaders from all over the country to discuss issues of importance.

2. They retain academic experts housed in corporate and foundation-financed think tanks to serve as consultants to these groups.

3. They receive much of their financial support from power-elite foundations such as Ford, Rockefeller, and Carnegie.

4. Most importantly, members and advisers of these organizations are often called to government service or asked to serve on special "blue-ribbon" commissions or "task forces" concerned with the issues already dealt with in the discussion groups of the policy-planning organizations.

It turns out that this model even applies to the framework within which national goals are being discussed, so I would like to use this opportunity to show how it applies to a specific problem. The story begins in the second half of the 1950s when the concerns were not overpopulation, environmental pollution, and youthful disenchantment but diversifying the military to fight against nationalist uprisings, rebuilding national prestige and morale in the face of Russia's firsts in space, combatting recession and a generally sluggish economy, and bolstering the nation's vigilance against international communism.

---

[2] However, as Arjay Miller pointed out in a discussion after his talk, you can buy 24 economists with the salary of the chairman of General Motors. But I digress.

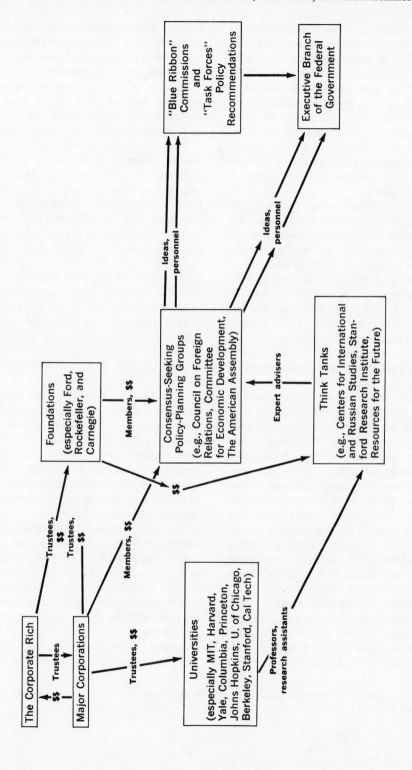

THE POWER-ELITE POLICY-MAKING PROCESS

The anti-communist crusade was especially important, for the Soviets looked like they might be able to make good on their goal of burying the United States economically, the Sino-Soviet split had not developed to a very great extent, and the possibility of wars of liberation not amenable to treatment by A-bombs and H-bombs was making international bankers and businessmen jittery over President Eisenhower's reliance on "massive retaliation" at the expense of conventional forces.

Because I think these concerns could be traced to corporate board rooms and discussions within the aforementioned consensus-seeking groups, I am being slightly arbitrary in starting a detailed account of events with a special panel convened by the Rockefellers in late 1956 under the auspices of one of their foundations, the Rockefeller Brothers Fund. The "panel," which in terms of the process previously diagrammed substitutes for one of the formal consensus-seeking groups, consisted of about 85 people organized into six groups of from 10 to 30 participants. It would be tedious to list the members and their connections, for such information can be summarized by saying that they were predominantly corporate leaders, foundation officials, and leading members of the various policy-planning and discussion organizations, along with several academic advisers and a few labor leaders and journalists. The task of the panels was to take stock of America in such areas as foreign policy, international security, economic policy, and education, and to make recommendations for the future.

Some of the panels also availed themselves of special consultants who, in two or three cases, helped to write the final report. For example, Henry Kissinger, later to be a Kennedy and Nixon adviser on foreign affairs, helped with two of the reports, while a Chase Manhattan Bank official and a Columbia University law professor helped with another.

Four of the panel reports appeared in the first half of 1958. They had two recorded effects in the world of government and politics. First, one of the members of the overall panel guiding the Rockefeller studies, Charles Percy (then president of Bell and Howell, now a senator from Illinois), was named head of a GOP Goals Committee. Second, President Eisenhower announced in his 1959 State of the Union message that he was going to set up a special commission on national goals. According to *The New York Times*, it was Percy who convinced the President to make such a move: "In an interview, White House sources report, Mr. Percy convinced President Eisenhower of the need for a nonpartisan document defining great national goals the country should move toward in the next decade."[3] Important as this explicit connection is between the Rockefeller studies and the national-goals commission, the assertion of a causal relationship does not hang on such a narrow reed as Percy talking to President Eisenhower. There are innumerable connections that could be drawn between the Rockefeller group and several of the most important lawyers, bankers, and businessmen working in the Eisenhower Administration. There is also, as we shall now see, some overlap in personnel between the two groups.

Due to difficulties in picking personnel and in making the plan acceptable for private funding (which Eisenhower insisted upon), the President's Commission on National Goals was not announced until January 1960. The details of the commission's situation are quite interesting. First, it was administered by the American

[3] Russell Baker, "Funds' Wariness Blocks U.S. Study," *The New York Times* (October 29, 1959), p. 19.

Assembly, a discussion organization of big businessmen and their advisers that was set up at Columbia University in 1950 (and which served as a base from which to tout Columbia University President Eisenhower for President of the United States). After accepting its official charge from the President, the American Assembly then received its funding from several private foundations. The foundations read like a Who's Who of the big business world, and, not incidentally, of the Rockefeller panels: the Carnegie Corporation, which had five trustees involved in the Rockefeller panels; the Ford Foundation, which had one trustee involved in the Rockefeller panels; the Rockefeller Foundation, which had two trustees involved in the Rockefeller panels; and the Alfred P. Sloan Foundation, which had two trustees involved in the Rockefeller panels. Four foundations whose trustees were not involved in any of the panels also contributed: the Maurice and Laura Falk Foundation, the Johnson Foundation (Racine), the Richardson Foundation, and the U.S. Steel Foundation.

The commission itself, as of course are all government commissions, was drawn from all walks of life. *The New York Times* tells us that "Included are a jurist, a scientist, a labor leader, four educators, a retired general, two corporation executives, and an editor."[4] Accurate though that statement may be in a narrow sense, I don't think it captures the reality of the matter. True enough, the venerable George Meany of the AFL-CIO was seated at the table, as he so often is on these official blue-ribbon occasions, but the rest of the group has a rather strong power-elite flavor. Seven of the eleven members were in 1960–61 members of one organization alone, the Council on Foreign Relations.

Here is the lineup:

Henry M. Wriston, chairman. At the time Wriston was the president of both the American Assembly and the Council on Foreign Relations. He was formerly president of Brown University.

Frank Pace, Jr., vice chairman. Pace was the chairman of General Dynamics and sat on other corporate boards. (A senior vice president from General Dynamics was on one of the Rockefeller panels.)

Erwin D. Canham, editor of the *Christian Science Monitor,* president of the United States Chamber of Commerce for 1959–60. (The managing editor of the same newspaper was on one of the Rockefeller panels.)

James B. Conant, retired president of Harvard University.

Colgate W. Darden, Jr., retired president of the University of Virginia. He is married to a daughter of Iréneé duPont and sits on the boards of duPont, U.S. Rubber, Life Insurance Company of Virginia, and Newport News Shipbuilding and Dry Dock Company.

Crawford H. Greenewalt, also married to a duPont, and president of E. I. duPont de Nemours & Company. He was also an MIT trustee at the time, which is interesting in light of the fact that a member of the commission yet to be introduced is the chairman of MIT.

Alfred M. Gruenther, retired general, president of the American Red Cross. His brother was on the White House staff during the Eisenhower Administration.

Learned Hand, a retired judge who was 88 years of age and took no part in the writing of the final report.

Clark Kerr, president of the University of California.

James R. Killian, Jr., chairman of MIT,

---

[4] "Goals Group Led by Educator, Long Interested in Government," *The New York Times* (November 28, 1960), p. 24.

a member of the Rockefeller panels, and a director of General Motors and IBM.

George Meany, president of the AFL-CIO.

The commission asked fourteen "distinguished Americans" to write papers on various problems for its consideration. In addition to Wriston and Kerr, who were on the commission itself, the writers include the president of the Carnegie Corporation (who played an important role in the Rockefeller panels), the vice president of the Alfred P. Sloan Foundation, a director of the Twentieth Century Fund (who helped write the sixth and final Rockefeller panel report), the president of IBM, two economists from the Committee for Economic Development, an editor from the Des Moines *Register* and *Tribune* (whose publisher was on the Rockefeller panel), the chairman of the Chase Manhattan Bank (who was also chairman of the Council on Foreign Relations and the Ford Foundation trustees), and five academicians.

The commission also had a staff. It was headed by William P. Bundy, brother of McGeorge, son-in-law of Dean Acheson, and a member of the Council on Foreign Relations. He was "on leave" from the Board of National Estimates of the Central Intelligence Agency, which makes it somewhat academic that the commissioners themselves had "no connection with the government."[5]

I present these details as evidence that the commission is perhaps the inside job

that I believe it to be. In any event, it must have had a meeting of minds rather quickly, for its report was available in book form in early December even though it was not appointed until January. The report, published by Prentice-Hall under the title *Goals for Americans*, was publicized widely as a public service by the Advertising Council, which is yet another outpost of the power elite. And, as the preface duly notes, "The book will also provide a basis for deliberations by regional, state and municipal sessions of the American Assembly as well as by civic groups, classes and discussion meetings." In short, the goals were to be communicated to the underlying population.[6]

The possible impact of the Eisenhower Commission report was undoubtedly muted by the election of John F. Kennedy in 1960, for no Democratic president is going to openly embrace the suggestions of even a "nonpartisan" commission that was set up by an outgoing Republican president. However, it is likely that the effects of the report and the Rockefeller panels could be traced into the special "task forces" that were established by Kennedy in the months before his inauguration, for there is overlap in personnel between the Rockefeller panels and the task forces on foreign and educational policies, while two of those who wrote reports for the Eisenhower Commission also served on task forces. More generally, six Rockefeller panelists served President Kennedy in defense and foreign-policy matters, and two of those who wrote reports for the Eisenhower Commission

---

[5] *Goals for Americans* (Englewood Cliffs, N.J.: Prentice-Hall, 1960), p. xi.

[6] *Goals for Americans* was not the only study on priorities to appear in 1960. A few months earlier the "capstone" report in the Rockefeller series had appeared. Entitled *The Power of the Democratic Ideal*, its writing committee included a Carnegie Corporation vice president and the Twentieth Century Fund director who wrote a paper for the goals commission. Other authors included a Columbia University philosophy professor, a counselor for Radio Free Europe (which is in part supported by the CIA), and the president of the Social Science Research Council (which is a whole story of foundation financing in itself).

had assignments in the Kennedy Administration. From this point the influence of these reports would have to be traced into specific policy decisions, a difficult task which is not our concern here. However, I cannot pass up the opportunity to note that President Kennedy said the following in announcing his task force on "defense frontiers":

The committee will not make another sweeping investigation or study of defense, military policies and resources such as has been so ably and thoroughly done in recent years by various House and Senate Committees, and by such private groups as the Gaither and Rockefeller Committees, the Council on Foreign Relations, the Foreign Policy Association, the Carnegie Corporation, the great universities, and others. Rather it will utilize their spendid work as its primary source for facts, analyses and informed opinion on the narrower field of defense management and administration with which it is called upon to deal.[7]

Returning to the general question of the framework within which goal setting is discussed, the next development concerns the establishment in 1962 of a Center for Priority Analysis by the National Planning Association. This is noteworthy first because the committee "overseeing" the project for the NPA includes one of the fourteen contributors to the commission as well as numerous power-elite types and one or two labor leaders. It is also interesting because the top three officers in the NPA were also members of the Council on Foreign Relations and the Committee for Economic Development (and one of those three served on a Rockefeller panel). However, it is mostly noteworthy because the Center for Priority Analysis explicitly used the framework provided by the Eisenhower Commission report: "For the list of goals to be studied, the report of President Eisenhower's Commission on National Goals was taken as a point of departure."[8] The objective was to put dollars-and-cents figures by each of the goals so decision makers could decide among various alternatives on a more factual basis. A main finding, in addition to "costing out" each goal, was that all the goals could not be pursued at once. In the NPA, which may be of waning importance, we see a nice example of how the power elite provide themselves with the facts and figures necessary to operate their complex corporate system.

The matter does not end here. As problems multiply, the need for rational planning and goal-setting increases. Thus we find retired Ford Motor Company president Arjay Miller calling for a permanent goals institute within the federal government.[9] Thus we hear of Thomas J. Watson of IBM (one of the fourteen contributors to the Eisenhower Commission) calling in early 1970 for a new government agency to be concerned with national goals. And thus we see President Nixon, with whom corporate leaders and foundation officials have conferred so often about so many things, making a first move in this direction with the creation, in July 1969, of a National Goals Research Staff within the

---

[7] *New Frontiers of the Kennedy Administration* (Washington, D.C.: Public Affairs Press, 1961), p. 21; on the importance of task forces see Norman C. Thomas and Harold L. Wolman, "The Presidency and Policy Formation: The Task Force Device," *Public Administration Review* (September-October, 1969).

[8] Leonard Lecht, *Goals, Priorities, and Dollars* (New York: Free Press, 1966), Appendix B, p. 341.

[9] Actually, Miller's contribution to this seminar, with its mentions of the Ford Foundation, The Brookings Institution, the Center for Priority Analysis, the Urban Coalition, and special government committees and agencies, is a nice presentation of the process this paper tries to describe.

White House. In announcing the new group, President Nixon said "the staff would forecast future developments, assess longer-range consequences of present social trends, estimate the range of alternate goals that would be feasible and measure the probable future impact of alternative courses of action to meet anticipated problems."[10] Headed by former Nixon law partner Leonard Garment, the staff includes Raymond Bauer of the Harvard Business School, Anthony Wiener of the Hudson Institute (still another think tank), and experts brought in from such government outposts as HEW and OEO. The staff is concerned with drawing together what has been done on these problems by the government and "private institutions." I take the latter to be the Committee for Economic Development, the National Bureau of Economic Research, Resources for the Future (which has two directors from the goals commission), The Brookings Institution, the National Planning Association, and other power-elite organizations.

Now, the National Goals Research Staff may not grow into anything bigger, but I think it is the straw in the wind that will complete the circuit from corporation to foundation to policy-planning group to blue-ribbon commission to government agency. Speeches at gentlemen's clubs, conferences at elite campuses like Stanford, reports by government groups and commissions, discussions at the American Assembly, a small goals staff in the White House, a friendly editorial about the goals staff in *The New York Times* (July 17, 1969) —soon the word will be out to all nooks and crannies of the big-business community that a new agency is needed, at which time the whole thing can be moved through a stodgy Congress which harbors many resisters who are from the "old school" of thought, worlds apart from the sophisticated circles of internationally minded corporate leaders and their academic advisers.

In closing this discussion of how the power elite set national goals, I want to comment on the question that is so often raised: So what? Does it make any difference? For it goes without saying, at least in business and academic circles, that American leaders act in the interest of all of us when they make their decisions. Sociologist Arnold M. Rose assures us, for instance, that the kind of evidence I have presented "does not prove that the business appointees are running the government for the benefit of business"; to the contrary, his own opinion is that decision makers with business backgrounds promote "their conception of the national interest [in the case of foreign affairs]."[11] Unfortunately, I don't think it is all that straightforward and clear-cut. However much the power elite may try to take us into account (and that is being generous), they have—like all of us—biases, implicit assumptions, and narrowed outlooks based upon their upbringings and their occupations. Psychology and sociology have documented this in detail for the middle and lower levels of Western societies—surely it could not be claimed that it is otherwise among the very affluent, who have a different (and more bountiful) source of income than the rest of us, not to mention a rather unique life style.

Indeed, to even raise the question of "So what?" in the face of the wealth and income distributions—not to mention the

[10] "White House Panel to Study Problems," *The New York Times* (July 13, 1969), p. 51; John Herbers, "U.S. Unit at Work on Social Report," *The New York Times* (December 24, 1969), p. 11.
[11] Arnold M. Rose, *The Power Structure* (New York: Oxford Univ. Press, 1967), pp. 23, 93.

ugly statistics on infant mortality, educational opportunities, health and disease, unemployment, housing, and life span—is to make a cruel joke. The power elite set priorities through the mechanisms I have outlined, and the wealth and well-being statistics suggest that they set them for the benefit of the corporate rich.

5

The Depersonalized
and the Alienated

PEOPLE AS WASTE

The Editors

As the American economy has climbed to unprecedented levels of productivity and national prosperity, it has moved so swiftly that millions of Americans have been left behind. Automated and mechanized industries produce more with fewer people, a trend which has not yet reached a stable equilibrium. Many of the technological changes have displaced those who do not have the necessary skills and education to find jobs that will provide a decent living and some security.

While automation can bring a release from the drudgery of work and an opportunity for more creative uses of human talent, such statements may have little meaning for the condition of life faced by the agricultural poor, the poorly educated, and the unskilled industrial rejects. It is particularly these segments of the population who have felt the effects of technological unemployment.

The urban poor who have been displaced by technological change are the 20 million Americans that Harrington (1963) has called the "rejects." Occupations requiring little skill and education represent the only types of work left for industrial rejects; these are jobs in the "economic underworld" such as domestic workers, hotel employees, kitchen help, and busboys. An added burden of workers in marginal occupations is that they are unprotected by any organization that has their interests in mind; they neither work in large-scale organizations with wage programs, sick leave, and health plans, nor are they in a unionized occupation.

The rural poor live in chronic low-income areas and have high rates of unemployment and underemployment. The far-reaching technological, occupational, and educational changes of the last fifty years have left these areas with a larger supply of human resources than the land and capital resources require to maintain a decent level of productivity. The result has been a marked reduction in farms and farm occupations with large numbers of unemployed who are unsuited for nonfarm occupations even if they should be available in the area.

Most solutions to the problems of the rural poor have not been able to deal with the central issues behind rural poverty, and in many cases solutions have seemed only to exacerbate the problems. Technological-economic solutions have focused upon more intensive and "rational" use of existing resources (i.e., by changing machinery, crops, or land use); however, farms in low-income areas operate with such restricted resources that the usual federal farm programs have little effect upon farm income. Similarly, suggestions to combine smaller farms into larger units with intensive mechanization have the short-run effect of reducing farm occupations. Another solution offered, which is in accord with the aggregate-demand approach to unemployment, has to do with encouraging the rural poor to move into other jobs and other regions. Given the limited education and skills of the rural poor, moving out of farm occupations would mean movement into unskilled nonfarm positions that have their own form of instability and insecurity. The ultimate effect of such job changes might simply be that unemployment is transferred from the rural area to the city, where it may be more difficult to cope with the problems of poverty (Perrucci and Iwamoto, 1966).

The displacement of workers in many industries represents one form of depersonalization. A sense of identification depends on a particular kind of work and the American criterion for status depends upon job level. For these reasons an entire way of life can be disrupted by the loss of occupation. Thus, when one comes into contact with society through a low-status job, or the police, or hospital, or a social-work contact, the experience further reinforces the feelings of worthlessness.

The feeling that one is unwanted or useless can also be part of the very nature of work itself. As was pointed out in the paper by Perrucci in Chapter 4, work can be degrading because it is physically hard and dirty; it can be demeaning because it is repetitive, machine-paced, and mindless; and it can be meaningless because the product is of little social value. In contrast to the oft-repeated view that American workers are middle class, Swados (1957) has suggested that although workers may vote, dream, and consume like the middle class, they still work like workers. He also suggests the possibility that the mindlessness of working-class occupations also seems to be found in white-collar positions, thereby extending the boundaries of depersonalization.

Another form of depersonalization is found in the tendency to ignore the needs and basic human worth of large numbers of persons in certain social categories. The failure to respect their needs is often based upon the fact that they may fail to have the necessary social credentials of worth such as education and a job. The aged represent such a depersonalized social category in our society. Being old, without work and income, in a society that places high value on productive work roles as the key to one's social position, means to be ignored and hidden in nursing homes, mental hospitals, and urban ghettos. Only a society that values men and women independent of what position they hold or how much they earn can learn to care for their old people. The aged in our society have an added problem described by Simone de Beauvoir. If life itself is deprived of meaningful social involvement, then old age must surely leave people with the hollow feeling of having missed out on their one opportunity for a full life (de Beauvoir, 1970).

Depersonalization may also be found in organizations whose official purpose is to serve the needs of clients, but in the day-to-day operations the organization and its members' needs and interests take priority over clients. The article by Morris explores this form of depersonalization as it confronts women in a maternity ward. The intimate and highly personal experience of childbirth is placed within the impersonal hospital setting which transfers mothers and children into objects to be processed, studied, and ignored as human beings. The critical hypothesis offered by Morris is that this impersonal experience, in which the new mother bears and faces her child, affects the mother's response to her child. It is possible that we find here the beginnings of a cycle of pathology that manifests itself in adolescence and adulthood, and is again transmitted across the generations: early rejection, less secure in self-help, less easily helped by existing education and welfare, and more subject to become part of a culture of rejects likely to seek status through gang memberships and narcotics.

The situation described in the Morris essay is most likely to be found among lower-income families and mothers who are on welfare rolls; all of which suggest that medical services in general, and hospital organization in particular, have not adapted their services to the values and life styles of the poor (Strauss, 1967).

Many of society's programs that are originally designed to help people by dealing with their basic needs often wind up being instruments of degradation. Low-income public housing started out as an example of how public monies could be utilized to assist many families without adequate housing. Today many of these technical feats called public housing are nothing more than high-rise slums. They function on par with mental hospitals, prisons, nursing homes, children's homes: they are places to put unwanted persons out of sight and away from the public conscience. A very vivid passage by James Baldwin (1961) attempts to describe the nature of the project dwellers' response to their housing and the reasons for this response.

They began hating it at about the time people began moving out of their condemned houses to make room for this additional proof of how thoroughly the white world despised them. And they had scarcely moved in, naturally, before they began smashing windows, defacing walls, urinating in the elevators, and fornicating in the playgrounds. Liberals, both white and black, were appalled at the spectacle. I was appalled by the liberal innocence—or cynicism, which comes out in practice as much the same thing. Other people were delighted to be able to point to proof positive that nothing could be done to better the lot of the colored people. They were, and are, right in one respect: that nothing can be done as long as they are treated like colored people. (Baldwin, 1961, p. 61.)

The essay by Oscar Lewis, "Even the Saints Cry," reveals how the meaning of a move from a slum to a public-housing project is much more than simply a change of physical surroundings. Living in the slums produces many adaptations which become part of a pattern of living and which do not work in the middle-class project. The issue revealed in this paper is the "gap" that develops between the "planners" and the "planned for." The lack of understanding, the detachment and alienation that comes from not being in on the planning in a responsible way, may be one of the reasons why public housing does not meet the needs of the people involved.

A further problem associated with depresonalization and dehumanization is that persons so responded to tend to internalize the negative definitions of their worth that they are constantly faced with. Alienation, escapism, withdrawal are all attempts to avoid the constantly punishing experience of low self-esteem. The paper by Michael Tabor, "The Plague," takes a hard look at drug addiction and its relationship to racism and capitalism. The drift into drug use is seen as connected with the exploitation and racist dehumanization faced by black people. Tabor also offers the challenging hypothesis that the hard drug traffic could not flourish without capitalist involvement from both legitimate and illegitimate sources, and the cooperation of police to protect the national and international organizations whose business is dope.

The paper by Caudill presents a detailed case of how automated and mechanized coal mining has displaced thousands of workers in eastern Kentucky. In addition to describing the nation's indifference to the needs of these workers, Caudill has also described the inadequacy of government programs to deal with the mass displacement of man by machines. Programs that do exist are mainly concerned with providing food-stamp benefits and welfare checks, while hoping that displaced miners will be absorbed by new industries.

In writing this essay in 1964, Caudill soberly warned of the revolutionary potential of a situation where once prosperous Americans "find themselves slipping inexorably into an economic mire that breeds poverty, despair, (and) dependency. . . ." A *New York Times* news story on March 27, 1967, described the growing militancy in the Appalachian region, which has replaced the apathy that formerly characterized the residents of the region. The article attributed the "rural revolution" to the activities of young workers of the Appalachian Volunteers, and Volunteers in Service to America (VISTA). The views of the workers in some antipoverty programs are similar to those expressed in Chapter 11 by representatives of the Revolution in Expression.

Numerous others in the contemporary society suffer a degree of alienation and depersonalization at the hands of the larger social system. James Spradley's fine study *You Owe Yourself a Drunk* indicates how incarceration, enforced poverty, and the unconcern of bureaucratic agencies force a large number of people into the role of urban tramps or nomads.

Those "successful" in the working class, from which many of the urban nomads come, can hardly be considered healthfully integrated into the larger society. The alienation of working-class life can be traced beyond the realm of the unpleasantness and boredom of their work to the general style of life of millions of low-income white families in America. Although generally employed, and not considered among the poor whites, the lower-middle-class American with his $7500 income is caught between his contempt for the white rich and the black poor. "The Whitetowners" by Binzen gives a clear picture of the needs and problems of the lower-middle-class white, the sources of his alienation, and the targets of his anger. The dilemma of the lower-middle class is that they believe in the "American Dream" which suggests that people willing to work can "make it," while they remain trapped in the historical conditions of a class structure that has always operated against them. This study of "The Whitetowners" describes the origins and shallow lives of that vast portion of society sometimes referred to as the silent majority. Its harsh existence among schools and public services fitted poorly to its needs hinges on the holding of a job, the can of beer, the television, the sports section and comics of the local newspaper, and the flag that covers and justifies every hardship from the dead son in war to their near bankruptcy state. Often living in ethnic tracts of cities, the population is isolated, highly suspect of big government and intellectuals, and bitterly turned against minorities who are seen as invaders of their neighborhoods, competitors for their scarce jobs, and spoilsports for complaining about a fate remarkably like their own. From this group come the "hard hats," the conservative veterans' groups, and the continuous threat of support for the pure repressive society immortalized in history by fascism.

Until recently the youth of Whitetown were permanently trapped. Peter Schrag writes:

Phrases like the "forgotten man" and "the silent majority" are too political to serve as normative descriptions, but there is no doubt that there are forgotten kids who are, indeed, genuine victims: children of factory workers and truck drivers, of shop foremen and salesclerks, kids who live in row houses above steel mills and in ticky-tacky developments at the edge of town, children who will not go to college, who will not become affluent, who will not march the streets, who will do no more, no less, then relive the lives of their parents.

We have all seen them: the kids on the corner with their duck-tail haircuts; the canvas-bag-toting types, lonely and lost, lining up at induction centers; kids in knocked down cars that seem to have no springs in back, whose wedding announcements appear daily in the newspapers of small towns (Mr. Jones works for the New York Central Railroad—no particular job worth mention—Miss Smith is a senior at Washington High) and whose deaths are recorded in the weekly reports from Saigon—name, rank, home town. On the south side of Bethlehem, Pennsylvania, just above the mills, there is an alley called Mechanic Street; once it was the heart of the old immigrant district—the first residence of thousands of Hungarians, Russians, Poles, Mexicans, Germans, Czechs, and Croats. Most of them have now moved on to materially better things, but they regard this as their ancestral home. Think of the children of Mechanic Street; think of places called Liberty High and South Boston High, of Central High and Charlestown High, and of hundreds of others where defeat does not enjoy the ironic distinction of the acknowledged injustice of racial oppression. (Schrag, 1970.)

While the past may have held out only a replay of their parents lives there is now, apparently, a break in the cycle. With jobs scarce and with young men introduced, via Vietnam, to travel and drugs and hip people, there is movement toward a sharing with other American youth, of certain basic anti-Establishment values and life styles. When afforded the opportunity to see how depersonalizing, unfulfilling, and hypocritical the society has been, various segments are breaking their old ties and becoming more estranged and alienated from the myths of the American dream.

Considering the "successful" working-class Whitetowner, a victim of severely constricted and depersonalized patterns of social living, moves the problem of social alienation much closer to the social mainstream. But what of those even more central, more successful, more affluent, middle-class families of the cities and suburbs. Richard Sennett presents a strong case to show that the middle-class family has withdrawn into itself, establishing a complete world of people and experience among four or five persons isolated from neighbors unlike themselves and protected from any dependency upon varied and unpredictable encounters. Outside of the protypical intense middle-class family, metropolitan relations have become ordered and uninteresting.

... the means by which people communicate with each other, work together or exchange services with each other, aided by machines and complex bureaucratic rules—are a cornucopia of tools with which metropolitan man is brutalizing his social relations into ever more simple, ever more controllable, ever less anarchic forms. (Sennett, 1970, p. 29.)

The decline into life without conflict and disorder has led to a fear of diversity and a high degree of passivity with regard to problems which go beyond one's immediate family. Hence the suburbanites' participation in larger social issues, even those related to the nearby urban crisis, tends to be essentially defensive and negative. The middle-class family in America has been isolating itself from the hardships of other people, from the forces of change in society, and from opportunities for creative living. If its members are not depersonalized, they are at least constrained to a self-image with rigid limits—and their children are perhaps the generation most alienated from society that this country has ever known.

It is the paradox of American society that its technological and military expansion and consequent depersonalization has brought us sufficiently close to Huxley's *Brave New World* that the human urge is to recoil and to cry out for survival of the anarchic desire to be free. The alienated of the society are no longer the mentally ill or deviants on the fringe of society. Rather, most of us are living without true communities, alienated from ourselves and from our society.

The relevance of depersonalization for the cybernetic revolution is that it reflects a tendency of the society to act like a coordinated production machine with the social value of "progress" used to justify moving a man out of his job while economic theories tell us that he will be absorbed by the economy somewhere else. It also reflects a tendency to use large numbers of people as unimportant cogs in psychologically meaningless work, to reject them entirely from the production machine and relegate them to a category of problems rather than the category of people.

REFERENCES AND ADDITIONAL READING

Baldwin, James, *Nobody Knows My Name* (New York: Dell, 1961).

Beauvoir, Simone de, "On Aging," *Ramparts*, **9** (September 1970), pp. 19–24.

Bem, S. L., and D. J. Bem, "Case Study of a Nonconscious Ideology: Training the Woman to Know Her Place," in D. J. Bem, *Beliefs, Attitudes, and Human Affairs* (Belmont, Calif.: Wadsworth, 1970).

Benston, Margaret, "The Political Economy of Women's Liberation," *Monthly Review*, **21**:4 (September 1969), pp. 13–27.

Dixon, Marlene, "Why Women's Liberation," *Ramparts* (December 1969), pp. 58–63.

Gans, Herbert, "The Failure of Urban Renewal," *Commentary*, **39**:4 (April 1965), pp. 29–37; reproduced in R. Perrucci and M. Pilisuk (eds.), *The Triple Revolution: Social Problems in Depth* (Boston: Little, Brown, 1968), pp. 264–280.

Harrington, Michael, *The Other America* (Baltimore: Penguin, 1963).

Huxley, Aldous, *Brave New World* (New York: Harper and Row, 1932).

Komarovsky, Mirra, "The Long Arm of the Job," in her *Blue Collar Marriage* (New York: Random House, 1962).

Morgan, Robin (ed.), *Sisterhood Is Powerful* (New York: Random House, 1970).

Perrucci, Robert, "The Neighborhood Bookmaker," in P. Meadows and E. H. Mizruchi (eds.), *Urbanism, Urbanization and Change* (Reading, Mass.: Addison-Wesley, 1969).

Perrucci, Robert, and Kichiro K. Iwamoto, "Work, Family, and Community in a Rural Depressed Area," in H. Meissner (ed.), *Poverty in the Affluent Society* (New York: Harper and Row, 1966).

Schneider, Michael M., "Middle America: Study in Frustration," *The Center Magazine*, **3**:6 (November/December 1970), pp. 2–9.

Schrag, Peter, "Growing Up on Mechanic Street," *Saturday Review* (March 21, 1970), pp. 59–79.

Sennett, Richard, "The Brutality of Modern Families," *Trans-action*, **7**:11 (September 1970), pp. 29–37.

Spradley, James, *You Owe Yourself a Drunk* (Boston: Little, Brown, 1970).

Strauss, Anselm L., "Medical Ghettos," *Trans-action* (May 1967), pp. 7–15.

Swados, Harvey, "The Myth of the Happy Worker," in his *A Radical's America* (Boston: Atlantic-Little, Brown, 1957); reproduced in R. Perrucci and M. Pilisuk (eds.), *The Triple Revolution: Social Problems in Depth* (Boston: Little, Brown, 1968), pp. 234–240.

PSYCHOLOGICAL MISCARRIAGE

AN END TO MOTHER LOVE

Marian Gennaria Morris

Not long ago a mother in the Midwest, while giving her baby its bath, held its head underwater until it drowned. She said that there was something wrong with the child. Its smell was strange and unpleasant; it drooled; it seemed dull and listless. It reminded her of a retarded relative, and the thought of having to spend the rest of her life caring for such a person terrified her. Her husband was out of work, and she was pregnant again. She said she "felt the walls closing in." When, in her confused and ignorant way, she had asked her husband, a neighbor, and a doctor for help, she got promises, preachments, and evasions. So she drowned the baby.

This mother said she had felt "so all alone." But, unfortunately, she had plenty of company. Many thousands of American women do not love or want their babies. Although few actually kill their infants, the crippling effects of early maternal rejection on children can hardly be exaggerated—or glossed over. The number directly involved is large. The social harm, for everybody, is great. An idea of the size of the problem can be gained from the following figures, taken from federal, state, and local sources:

50–70,000 children neglected, battered, exploited annually.

150,000 children in foster homes for these reasons.

Over 300,000 children in foster care altogether.

8 to 10 percent of all school children in one twenty-county study in need of psychiatric examination and some type of treatment for their problems.

But even these figures can hardly begin to describe the violence, deprivation, and dehumanization involved.

Recently we concluded a study of thirty rejecting mothers and their children who can serve as examples. Our findings are supported by a number of other studies of parents and their children who have various physical and psychological disorders. Although the poor are hardest hit by family and emotional problems, it should be noted that the majority of these families were not poverty-stricken. Psychological miscarriage of motherhood attacks all classes and levels.

Twenty-one of the thirty mothers demonstrated clearly from the time of delivery that they could not properly mother or care for their babies—could not even meet their basic needs. Yet no one who had had contact with them—neither doctors, nurses, nor social workers—had apparently been able to help, effectively, any one of them, nor even seemed aware that severe problems existed.

The entire population of mothers was

Reprinted by permission of the author and publisher from Trans-action *(January 1966), pp. 8–13, a publication of the Community Leadership Project (Washington University, St. Louis, Mo.).*

characterized by old troubles and hopelessness, stretching back to the previous generation—and in one-third of the cases, back to the third generation. Half the children were illegitimate, or conceived before marriage. Sixty percent of the families had been in juvenile, criminal, or domestic courts at some earlier time. Two-thirds of the children were either first-borns, or first-borns of their sex—and lack of experience with children increased their mothers' insecurities.

All thirty children needed intensive psychiatric treatment. Only two of the thirty were "well" enough—from homes that were "stable" enough—for out-patient care to even be considered. The remaining twenty-eight were headed for institutions. Their prognoses are grave, their chances doubtful. They will cost us a great deal in the years to come, and their problems will be with us a long time. Some will never walk the streets as free men and women.

Actually, the children were so disturbed that they could not be diagnosed with great accuracy. For instance, it was impossible to tell how intelligent most really were because they were in such emotional turmoil that they could not function properly on tests, and seemed retarded. A fifth of them had been so beaten around the head that it is quite possible their brains were damaged. (One baby had been thrown across the room and allowed to stay where it fell.) Women who feel neglected and less than human in turn neglect their children and treat them as less than human.

FEAR AND REALITY

In our supposedly interdependent society, we are close together in violence, but apathetic to each other's needs. But apathy to their needs constitutes a violence to women facing labor, delivery, and the early and bewildering adjustments of motherhood. And it is in these days and weeks that psychological miscarriage occurs.

During pregnancy, labor, and delivery the basic fears of childhood—mutilation, abandonment, and loss of love—are vividly revived for a woman, and with double force—for herself and the baby. Nor are these fears simply fantasies: mothers *are* frequently cut, torn, and injured, babies *are* born with congenital defects.

The entire pregnancy period, with its lowering of defenses, makes the mother more capable of loving and feeling for her baby. But whether she finds his needs pleasing or threatening depends on what happened to her in the past, and the support she gets in the present.

After delivery, still in physical and emotional stress, under great pressure, she must make the most important, difficult adjustments of all. She must "claim" her baby. That is, she must make it, emotionally, part of herself again; identify it with the qualities and values in herself and her life that she finds good, safe, reassuring, and rewarding. After all the dreams and fears of pregnancy, she now must face and cope with the reality—the baby and his needs. If she miscarries now and rejects the child as something bad that cannot be accepted, then the child cannot grow to be normal. Nor can its society be normal, since the mothers must hand down to each generation the values by which society survives.

In older days, when most women had their babies at home, these adjustments were made in familiar surroundings, with such family support as was available. Now they are made largely in the hospital. What actually happens to mothers in today's hospitals?

Childbirth, once a magnificent shared experience, has increasingly become a technical event. Administrative and physical needs get priority. Emotional needs and personalities tend to get in the way of efficiency. Administrators and medical personnel, like everyone else, respond most readily to those pressures which affect them. Since they are in charge, they pass them down to the patient, whether they help the patient or not.

The mothers of the poor in particular arrive faceless, knowing no one on the ward, with little personal, human contact from before birth until they leave. Increasingly, they arrive already in labor, so that the hospitals cannot turn them away. They also come at this late stage so that they can avoid the constant procession of doctors and the three- and four-hour clinic waits, during which they are called "mother" because their names have been lost in the impersonal clinic protocols. In the wards, they may be referred to simply by their bed numbers.

Birth itself may be subordinated to the schedule: some doctors schedule their deliveries, and induce labor to keep them on time. Even "natural" labor may be slowed down or speeded up by drugs for convenience.

A PUBLIC EVENT

Mothers say that they are allowed little dignity or modesty. Doctors strange to them may, and do, examine them intimately, with little attempt at privacy. They say that without their permission they are often used as live lecture material, giving birth before interested audiences of young interns and students while the obstetrician meticulously describes each step and tissue. How apathetic we have become to the routine dehumanization of mothers is well illustrated by the story of an upper-middle-class woman I know. She was in labor, almost hidden by drapes preparatory to vaginal examination, light flooding her perineum (but not her face). Approached by a nurse and gloved physician she suddenly sat up in her short-tailed hospital gown and said, "I don't know who *you*

are, doctor, but *I* am Mrs. Mullahy." Good for Mrs. Mullahy! She has a strong sense of personal identity, and is determined to preserve it.

Mothers say they are isolated and humiliated. They say that in addition to their own anxieties they must worry about what their doctors think, and be careful to please and propitiate the staff members, who may have power of life and death over them and their babies.

They say that they are kept in stirrups for hours—shackled in what reduces them to something subhuman—yet afraid to complain.

Is it increasingly true, as mothers say, that babies are not presented to them for from four to twelve hours after birth? Social histories show that prompt presentation is necessary for the mental health of the mothers; studies of other mammals indicate that such delay interrupts mothering impulses and may bring on rejection of the young. Is this happening to human mothers and babies? How necessary, medically, is such a delay? Is it worth the price?

Many women become deeply depressed after childbirth. Is this at least partly a reaction to hospital experiences? Is it an early distress signal of psychological miscarriage? There is very little research that attempts to assess early maternal adaptation, and we need such research badly. Are the violent mothers, so brutal to their children, violent at least in part because of our faceless and impersonal birth practices? Clinical studies show that the less sense of identity and personal worth a mother has, the more easily she displaces her aggressions onto others—*any* others. Are we scapegoating our children?

STAKING A CLAIM

To a mother, the birth of her baby is not a technical event. It starts in intimate contact with the father, and has deep roots in her feelings for and relationship with him, whether positive or negative. It reflects her personality, her state of maturity, the experiences of her most intimate anxieties and special hopes, and her associations with the adults who have had most influence on her. She enters the hospital prey to childhood insecurities, and stripped alike of defenses and clothes. Attitudes and cues from the hospital personnel, and from others, strongly affect her self-respect and her feelings about her own and her baby's worth.

It is difficult to observe most normal claiming behavior in a hospital. But some of it can be observed. Most mothers, for example, do find ways to make contact with their babies' bodies—touching and examining them all over delightedly, even to the tiny spaces between fingers and toes —cooing and listening to them, inhaling their odors, nuzzling and kissing them.

Socially, a major way to claim a child is to name it. Names suggest protective good magic; they establish identity and suggest personality; they emphasize masculinity or femininity; they affirm family continuity and the child's place in it.

Nevertheless, it is usually difficult to follow claiming behavior for two reasons. First, because hospital routines and tasks interfere. To the staff, the process of mothers becoming acquainted with infants is seen as merely cute, amusing, or inconvenient. Babies are presented briefly, pinned and blanketed tightly, making intimate fondling—for women who have carried these infants for months—difficult and sometimes even guilt-producing.

The second reason is related to the nature of normal motherhood. The well-adjusted mother is secure within herself, content to confine her communications mostly to her baby, rather than project them outward. As Tolstoy said of marriage, all happy ones tend to be happy in the same way, and relatively quiet. But the unhappy ones are different and dramatic— and it is by observing unhappy mothers that the pathological breakdown of maternal claiming can be most easily traced.

Let us consider two examples.

Tim—Breakdown in Early Infancy

When Tim's mother first felt him move in her, and realized then that all evasion and doubt about her pregnancy was past, she blacked out (she said) and fell down a flight of stairs.

Tim was her second child. Her first pregnancy was difficult and lonely and, she had been told, both she and the baby had almost died during delivery. She suffered from migraine headaches, and was terrified of a second delivery.

For the first four months of Tim's life, she complained that he had virulent diarrhea and an ugly odor, and took him from doctor to doctor. Assured by each one that there was nothing wrong with the child (in the hospital the diarrhea cleared up in one day), she took this to mean that there was something wrong with *her*—so she sought another doctor. She took out thirteen different kinds of cancer insurance on Tim.

During an interview, she told a woman social worker that it was too bad that doctors could not look inside a baby and know he was *all* O.K.

The social worker decided to probe deeper: "You would have a hard time convincing me that you *deliberately* threw yourself down those stairs."

"Who, me? Why I told my mother all along that I would never *willingly* hurt a hair of one of my children's heads."

"But suppose you had, unwillingly. Would you blame someone else for doing it, under the circumstances?"

"No! I was sick and don't even know how it happened."

After that, the demon that had haunted

her was in the open, and recovery began. She had felt that she was both criminal and victim, with the child as the instrument of her punishment. (Only a "good" mother deserves a good baby; a "bad" mother deserves a "bad"—damaged or sick—baby.) The implied criticisms of her mother and doctor had aggravated these feelings. She identified Tim not with the good in her but the "evil"—he was something faulty, something to be shunned.

Under treatment she learned to accept herself and regain her role of mother. She was not really the bad little girl her critical mother and doctor had implied; neither, therefore, was Tim bad—she could accept him. It was no longer dangerous to identify with her. She let Tim see her face; she held him comfortably for the first time; she did not mention his "ugly" smell; she stayed by his bed instead of restlessly patrolling the corridors. She referred to our hospital as the place she had "got him *at*," instead of the hospital, ninety miles away, where he had actually been born.

Jack—Effects on an Older Child

Shortly after Jack was born, his mother asked her obstetrician whether Jack's head was all right. Gently touching the forceps marks, he said, *"These* will clear up." Thinking that she had been told delicately that she had a defective child, she did not talk to Jack for five-and-a-half years—did not believe he could understand speech.

At five-and-a-half, approaching school, he had never spoken. A psychologist, thinking that the child was not essentially retarded, referred the mother to a child-guidance clinic, where the social worker asked whether she had ever found out if the obstetrician had meant the *inside* of Jack's head. For the first time in all the years it occurred to her that there might have been a misunderstanding. Three months later Jack was talking—though many more months of treatment were still necessary

before he could function adequately for his age.

Behind this, of course, was much more than a misunderstanding. Behind it was Jack's mother's feelings of guilt for having caused her own mother's death. Guilt went back many years. During an auto ride long ago, she had an accident in which her mother suffered a mild blow on the head. In the early months of pregnancy with Jack, she had found her mother dead in the tub. The cause was cancer, which had nothing to do with the bump. But deep down she could not believe this, and she developed the fear that Jack's head, too, was damaged—a fitting punishment for a woman who feared she had killed her mother. When her obstetrician seemed to confirm it, she did not question further.

For almost six years Jack was not so much an infant or child as a damaged head. Like her mother he was silent—from "brain injury." It was only under treatment that she accepted the possibility that she might have "misunderstood." . . .

CLUES TO MATERNAL HAZARDS IN MOTHERING

There are several criteria that can be used to assess the adequacy of a mother's behavior during the early weeks of an infant's life. Mother-infant unity can be said to be *satisfactory* when a mother can: find pleasure in her infant and in tasks for and with him; understand his emotional states and comfort him; read his cues for new experience; sense his fatigue points.

For example she can receive his eye contact with pleasure; can promote his new learnings through use of her face, hands, and objects; does not overstimulate him for her own pleasure.

In contrast, there are specific signs that mothers give when they are *not adapting* to their infants, [for example]:

See their infants as ugly or unattractive.

Perceive the odor of their infants as revolting.

Are disgusted by their drooling and sucking sounds. . . .

MOTHERS AS PATIENTS

How can we prevent such psychological miscarriages—and how can we limit their ravages once they have already occurred?

The dynamics of maternal rejection are not completely known—we need far more research, far more detailed and orderly observation of early maternal behavior. Nevertheless, enough is known already about the symptoms for us to be able to work up a reliable profile of the kind of woman who is most likely to suffer damage, and to take steps to make sure that help is offered in time. After all, the ultimate cause of maladaptation is lack of human sympathy, contact, and support, even though the roots may go back for more than one generation. We must, therefore, offer that support. We may not be able completely to heal old, festering wounds, but we can palliate their worst effects, and keep them from infecting new babies.

Mothers in our study identified the periods of greatest danger as just before and after delivery. It is then—and swiftly—that intervention by a psychiatric team should occur. What can be done?

We must have early recognition of trouble. Early signs of maternal maladaptation are evident in the mutual aversion of mother and child. But these signs have to be watched for—they cannot be ignored because of hospital routine that is "more important."

Let the mother have enough time to see and become acquainted with the hospital personnel with whom she will experience birth. Length of hospital stay is geared to technical requirements—five days for middle-class mothers, down (in some places) to twenty-four hours or less for the poor. Therefore, acquaintance should start before birth, at least with the physician, so that when delivery comes the mother will not be faced with a stranger in cap and gown, but a human being she already knows. Nurses and social workers should also be included. (The Hahnemann Medical College and Hospital in Philadelphia already assigns resident physicians to the prenatal clinics to provide this continuity.)

Mothers of young infants suffer from geographical and psychological isolation. Services should work toward reducing both of these isolations. Ideally such services should come from a team, including not only the doctor and nurses, but a sympathetic pediatrician, psychiatric and medical social workers, of both sexes, who could also act as substitute parents. This help should be as available to the middle class as to the poor (middle-class patients are sometimes denied hospital social services).

Help should carry over into home care. *Make sure that each mother has someone to care for her at home.* After their too brief hospital stay, poverty-stricken women, many without husband or family, are often more helpless and lost at home than in the hospital.

Mothers should not be left alone for long periods, whether under sedation or not. Schedules should and must be modified to allow them to have normal family support as long as possible. If they have none, substitutes—volunteers—should be found. Isolated mothers, cut off from support or even contact with their physicians, and treated as objects, much too often displace their loneliness, depression, resentment, bitterness, humiliation, rage, and pain onto their babies.

Get rid of the stirrups—and the practice of using them to hang mothers' legs in the air for hours! Find some other way to hold women on the delivery table until the last moments. Women often spend months recovering from bachaches caused by stirrups.

Present the baby as soon as possible. The most frequent comment from mothers who remain conscious in the delivery room is, "The doctor gave him to me." This is psychologically very sound; when the father-image (doctor) presents the baby with the obvious approval of the mother-image (nurse), latent feelings of guilt about having a baby and about the acceptability of the baby—and of motherhood—are lulled and dispelled. Too often, however, the nurse is cast, or casts herself, in the role of unwilling, stingy, critical giver of the baby —in fact the whole institution lends itself to this. Presentation should precede and not depend on feeding; it should be made gladly and willingly; it should allow time and ease of access for the mother to examine her baby's body.

Doctors, nurses, and aides should understand and come to know pregnancy, labor, delivery, and early growth as a continuing process, rather than in bits and pieces, a series of techniques. They need to understand and see it from the mothers' viewpoint, as well as in terms of bottles, diapers, rooms, instruments, and procedures.

Reassure mothers about their infants. This includes understanding the real meanings of their questions. If a mother continually discounts good reports, rejection may be underway, and psychological miscarriage imminent.

First-born children, and the first-borns of each sex, are the ones most commonly rejected; their mothers need special care—as do the mothers of the poor and those without family, husband, or outside human supports.

None of these proposals are radical— even administratively. Most are quite simple, and could be done directly in the wards and the private rooms. . . .

There is nothing more important in a maternity pavilion, nor in a home, than the experiences with which life begins. We must stop the dehumanization of mothers. We must give all children a chance for life.

EVEN THE SAINTS CRY

Oscar Lewis

You cannot take people out of an old-fashioned slum, where reality has been giving them a grim, distorted education for years, place them in a project, and expect them to exhibit all kinds of gentle, middle-class virtues.—Michael Harrington

This article describes the experiences of a young Puerto Rican mother, Cruz Rios, who moved from La Esmeralda—one of the oldest slums in San Juan only a short distance from the governor's palace—about four miles east to Villa Hermosa, a new government housing project in a middle-class section of Rio Piedras. Cruz' story illustrates the difficult problems of adjustment in her new environment and helps us understand why, in spite of the efforts of well-intentioned governments and the spending of huge sums of money on public housing, the positive effects hoped for by social planners are not always forthcoming.

When I began my study of Cruz in 1963, she was just 17 and living alone on relief with her two children. She lived in a small, dark, one-room apartment for which she paid a rental of eight dollars a month. Her kitchen was a tiny corner alcove equipped with a three-burner kerosene stove and a water faucet jutting out from the wall. She shared a run-down hall toilet with two other families and paid a neighbor $1.50 a month for the privilege of an extension cord which supplied her with electricity.

Cruz, a crippled, mulatto girl with reddish brown kinky hair and a pretty face, was lame since early childhood. She left school after the fifth grade, set up house

with her sweetheart at 14, and gave birth to her first child at 15. Two years later, before the birth of her second child, she separated from her husband, Emilio, who refused to recognize the baby as his own.

Part I gives the reader a glimpse of living conditions in the slum; part II, recorded five months after Cruz had moved, gives her reactions to the housing project. (Names of all places and people in this tape-recorded narrative have been changed to guarantee the anonymity of the narrator.)

I

Here in La Esmeralda, the only thing that disturbs me are the rats. Lice, bedbugs, and rats have always been a problem in my room. When I moved in here a year ago, the first thing I found were little baby rats. "Kill them!" my friend Gloria said. "*Ay Bendito!* I can't do it. Poor little things— they look like children," I said, and I left them there in a hole. The next day they were gone. I didn't kill them, they just disappeared. I cleaned up the house and about a month later they were going back and forth through the room from one hole to another, with me just looking at them.

When Alejandro was living with me, more rats came because there was a hen with eggs under the house. A rat had given birth and had eaten some of the chicks. The owner took the hen and 29 chicks out of there because there were baby rats underneath the hen too. The man threw them out but a week later they came back and were all over the place, even getting into the pan with the baby's milk and eating up whatever I left around.

One Sunday my *mamá* said, "Let's buy a rat trap and see if we can't get rid of some of them." Well, we tried it and that day between us and the next-door neighbor we caught 29 little rats. After a while, more came. Anita used to chase them across the room to see if she could catch them, and the boys who came to the house would say, "Look, a rat."

I would tell them, "Let it be, it's one of the family. They keep me company, now that I'm all by myself. I am raising them for soup."

So I left them alone, but before I knew it, there were great big rats here. One Sunday I said to Catín, who had just eaten a breaded cutlet, "Catín, you'd better go bathe or the rats will eat you up." Then I forgot about it and she lay down. Later I took a bath and went to bed. About midnight, Catín screamed, *"Ay, ay, ay, it bit me!"* The first thing that came to my mind was that it was a snake or a scorpion. "What bit you?" I asked and when I turned on the light, she said, "Look, look!" and I could see a rat running way.

She had been bitten on the arm and I could see the little teeth marks. I squeezed out the blood and smeared urine and bay rum on it.

Then I said, "Catín, you'd better come into my bed with me. God knows whether it was because the crib is dirty or you are dirty." I was wearing only panties, Chuito and Anita were naked, but Catín was wearing a jacket and pants. Well, later that same rat came and bit her again on the other arm. I sprinkled bay rum all over the bed where she was sleeping and rubbed it on her and nothing else happened that night.

The next day I went to the church and told the Sister that the girl had been bitten by a rat. She told me that if Catín didn't start running a fever, to leave her alone, and if she did, to take her to the hospital. Then I said to Catín, "You see? That's what happens when you don't bathe." She took a bath every day after that.

At the end of the year, Anita got a rat bite on the lip. I squeezed it out for her and it dried up and she didn't get a fever or anything. A few days after that, I was sitting in a chair with my arm hanging down when a rat came and *pra!* it tried to take off my finger. It wanted human flesh. I lifted my hand, and the rat ran to a hole and disappeared.

Then I said to myself, "These rats have to be finished off. I can't live like this with so many blessed rats. There are more rats than people." And I bought a trap from the man next door. I fixed the bacon myself and put it in the trap. First I caught a real big rat, then another and another. Three in all that same night. But there were still more left.

The next morning, I heard screams coming from Rosa Maria's room up above. I said, "Rosa, what's wrong?" Her little boy was crying and shaking his hand, with a rat hanging from it. "Kill it," I said, but he answered, "I can't. Its teeth are stuck in my finger." Finally he got it off by dragging it along the floor. Rosa Maria attended him but the next day the child had a fever which kept going up. The doctor said that the boy was getting tetanus and had to go to the hospital.

The people upstairs leave a lot of rotting clothes piled there, and cans of food and rice. If they don't get rid of that filth, the rats won't leave. I asked the landlord to cover the holes because the rats keep coming in and out as if they were in a bus terminal. He said he didn't live here and I should do it myself.

There are lots of cockroaches in my room too. And new fleas have come in, I don't know from where, except probably from the rats themselves. There are also crickets and lizards. These houses are hollow underneath, and below the floor there's a lot of old boards and filth and all kinds of garbage that has accumulated, and at night the animals come crawling up.

I've noticed that it's on Thursday nights that the rats give us the most trouble. Every other Thursday, before the social worker comes, I clean my house from top to bottom so there are no crumbs on the floor for the rats to eat and no dirty dishes for them to clean. I've learned that unless I leave something for them, the rats come closer and closer to us. When the house is clean, we are in more danger of getting bitten.

II

The social worker told me it would be a good idea to get the children out of La Esmeralda because there's so much delinquency there. My moving to the housing project was practically her idea; she insisted and insisted. Finally one day she came to me and said, "Tomorrow you have to move to the *caserio* in Villa Hermosa." I didn't want to upset her because she's been good to me, so I said okay.

You should have seen this place when I moved in. It was bursting with garbage and smelling of shit, pure shit. Imagine, when the social worker opened the door that first day, a breeze happened to blow her way. She stepped back and said, "Wait, I can't go in. This is barbarous." I had to go outside with her. I tell you, the people who lived here before me were dirtier than the

dirtiest pig. When I moved out of my little room in La Esmeralda, I scrubbed it so clean you could have eaten off the floor. Whoever moved in could see that a decent person had lived there. And then I came here and found this pig-sty, and the place looked so big I felt too little and weak to get it clean. So, fool that I am, instead of sending out for a mop and getting right down to work, I just stood in a corner and cried. I locked the door and stayed in all day, weeping. I cried floods.

And this place isn't like La Esmeralda, you know, where there's so much liveliness and noise and something is always going on. Here you never see any movement on the street, not one little domino or card game or anything. The place is dead. People act as if they're angry or in mourning. Either they don't know how to live or they're afraid to. And yet it's full of shameless good-for-nothings. It's true what the proverb says, "May God deliver me from quiet places; I can defend myself in the wild ones."

Everything was so strange to me when I first moved here that I was scared to death. I hated to go out because it's hard to find your way back to this place even if you know the address. The first couple of times I got lost, and I didn't dare ask anybody the way for fear they would fall on me and beat me. If anyone knocked on my door I thought four times before deciding to open it. Then when I did, I took a knife along. But I'm not like that any more. I've made my decision: if someone wants to kill me, let him. I can't live shut in like that. And if anybody interferes with me it will be the worse for them. I have a couple of tricks up my sleeve and can really fuck things up for anybody when I want to.

After a few days, I finally started cleaning up the place. I scrubbed the floors and put everything in order. I even painted the whole apartment, although I had to fight tooth and nail with the man in charge of the buildings in order to get the paint. That old man wanted to get something from me in return, but I wouldn't give it to him. I never have been attracted to old men.

The apartment is a good one. I have a living room, bedroom, kitchen, porch and my own private bathroom. That's something I never had in La Esmeralda. I clean it every morning and when the children use it I go and pull the chain right away.

I never had a kitchen sink in La Esmeralda either, and here I have a brand new one. It's easy to wash the dishes in these double sinks because they're so wide and comfortable. The only trouble is the water, because sometimes it goes off and the electricity, too—three times since I've been here.

I still don't have an ice-box or refrigerator but the stove here is the first electric one I've ever had in my life. I didn't know how to light it the day I move in. I tried everything I could think of, backward and forward. Luckily, the social worker came and she lit it for me, but even so I didn't learn and Nanda had to show me again that afternoon. She has worked for rich people so long that she knows all those things. I really miss my own little kerosene stove, but Nanda wanted it, so what could I do? She's my *mamá* and if she hankered after a star I would climb up to heaven to get it for her if I could.

The main advantage of the electric stove is that when I have a lot of work to do and it gets to be ten or eleven o'clock, I just connect the stove and have lunch ready in no time. In La Esmeralda I had to wait for the kerosene to light up well before I could even start to cook. And this stove doesn't smoke and leave soot all over the place, either. Still, if the power fails again or is cut off because I don't pay my bill, the kids will just have to go hungry. I won't even be able to heat a cup of milk for them. In La Esmeralda, whenever I didn't have a

quarter to buy a full gallon of kerosene, I got ten cents worth. But who's going to sell you five or ten cents worth of electricity?

I haven't seen any rats here, just one tiny little mouse. It doesn't bother me much because it lives down below, in a hole at the bottom of the stairs. There's no lack of company anywhere, I guess—rats in La Esmeralda and lots of little cockroaches here.

This apartment is so big that I don't have to knock myself out keeping it in order. There's plenty of room for my junk. I even have closets here, and lots of shelves. I have so many shelves and so few dishes that I have to put a dish here and a dish there just to keep each shelf from being completely empty. All the counters and things are no use at all to me, because I just cook a bit of oatmeal for the children and let them sit anywhere to eat it since I have no dishes with which to set a table. Half of my plates broke on the way from La Esmeralda. I guess they wanted to stay back there where they weren't so lonely.

Here even my saints cry! They look so sad. They think I am punishing them. This house is so big I had to separate the saints and hang them up in different places just to cover the empty walls. In La Esmeralda I kept them all together to form a little altar, and I lit candles for them. In La Esmeralda they helped me, but here I ask until I'm tired of asking and they don't help me at all. They are punishing me.

In La Esmeralda I never seemed to need as many things as here. I think it is because we all had about the same, so we didn't need any more. But here, when you go to other people's apartment and see all their things. . . . It's not that I'm jealous. God forbid! I don't want anyone to have less than they have. It's only that I would like to have things of my own too.

What does bother me is the way people here come into my apartment and furnish the place with their mouths. They start saying, "Oh, here's where the set of furniture should go; you need a TV set in that corner and this one is just right for a record-player." And so on. I bite my tongue to keep from swearing at them because, damn it, I have good taste too. I know a TV set would look fine in that corner, but if I don't have the money to buy one, how can I put it there? That's what I like about La Esmeralda—if people there could help someone, they did; if not, they kept their mouths shut.

I really would like a TV though, because they don't have public sets here, the way they do in La Esmeralda. I filled in some blanks for that program, Queen for a Day, to see if I can get one as a gift. It was Nanda's idea and she's so lucky that maybe I will get it. If I do, then at least I could spend the holidays looking at TV. And the children might stay home instead of wandering around the neighborhood so much.

The traffic here really scares me. That's the main reason I don't like this place. Cars scud by like clouds in a high wind and, I'm telling you, I'm always afraid a car will hit the children. If something should happen to my little penguins, I'd go mad, I swear I would. My kids are little devils, and when I bring them in through the front door, they slip out again by climbing over the porch railing. Back in La Esmeralda, where our house was so small, they had to play out in the street whenever people came over, but here there is plenty of room to run around indoors.

Maybe I was better off in La Esmeralda. You certainly have to pay for the comforts you have here! Listen, I'm jittery, really nervous, because if you fail to pay the rent even once here, the following month you're thrown out. I hardly ever got behind on my payments in La Esmeralda, but if I did, I knew that they wouldn't put me out on the street. It's true that my rent is only $6.50 a month here while I paid $11.50 in La Esmeralda, but there I didn't have a

water bill and I paid only $1.50 a month for electricity. Here I have already had to pay $3.50 for electricity and if I use more than the minimum they allow in water, I'll have to pay for that too. And I do so much washing!

It's a fact that as long as I lived in La Esmeralda I could always scare up some money, but here I'm always broke. I've gone as much as two days without eating. I don't play the races at El Comandante any more. I can't afford to. And I can't sell *bolita* numbers here because several cops live in this *caserio* and the place is full of detectives. Only the other day I almost sold a number to one of them, but luckily I was warned in time. I don't want to be arrested for anything in the world, not because I'm scared of being in jail but because of the children.

Since I can't sell numbers here, I sell Avon cosmetics. I like the pretty sets of china they give away, and I'm trying to sell a lot so that they'll give me one. But there's hardly any profit in it for me.

In La Esmeralda I could get an old man now and then to give me five dollars for sleeping with him. But here I haven't found anything like that at all. The truth is, if a man comes here and tries to strike up a conversation I usually slam the door in his face. So, well, I have this beautiful, clean apartment, but what good does it do me? Where am I to get money? I can't dig for it.

In La Esmeralda we used to buy things cheap from thieves. They stole from people who lived far away and then they came to La Esmeralda through one of the side entrances to sell. And who the hell is going to go looking for his things down there? Not a chance! You hardly ever saw a rich person in La Esmeralda. We didn't like them, and we scared them off. But so far as I can tell, these dopes around here always steal from the *blanquitos*, the rich people, nearby. Suppose one of them took it into his head to come here to look for the missing stuff? What then?

Since I've moved I'm worse off than I have ever been before, because, before now I realize all the things I lack and, besides, the rich people around here are always wanting everything for themselves. In La Esmeralda you can bum a nickel from anyone. But with these people, the more they have, the more they want. It's everything for themselves. If you ask them for work, they'll find something for you to do fast enough, but when it's time to pay you'd think it hurt them to pull a dollar out of their pocket.

Listen, to get a few beans from some people who live in a house near here I had to help pick and shell them. People here are real hard and stingy. What's worse, they take advantage of you. The other day I ironed all day long for a woman and all I got for it was two dollars and my dinner. I felt like throwing the money in her face but I just calmly took it. I would have been paid six dollars at the very least for a whole day's ironing in La Esmeralda. At another lady's house near here I cooked, washed the dishes, even scrubbed the floor, and for all that she just gave me one of her old dresses, which I can't even wear because it's too big for me.

Right now, I don't have a cent. The lady next door lets me charge the food for breakfast at her husband's *kiosko*. She's become so fond of me, you can't imagine. Her husband won't sell on credit to anybody, but there's nothing impossible for the person who is really interested in helping you out. She trusts me, so she lets me write down what I take and keep the account myself.

I buy most of my food at the Villa Hermosa grocery. It's a long way from here and I have to walk it on foot every time I need something, like rice or tomato sauce. It's a supermarket, so they don't give credit, but everything is cheaper there, much

cheaper. A can of tomato sauce costs 7 cents there and 10 cents in La Esmeralda. Ten pounds of rice costs $1.25 in La Esmeralda and 99 cents here. The small bottles of King Pine that cost 15 cents each in La Esmeralda are two for a quarter here.

Sometimes Public Welfare gives me food, but not always, and I don't like most of the things they give. That long-grained rice doesn't taste like anything. It's like eating hay. The meat they give has fat on top and it comes in a can and it's real dark. They say it's corned beef but I don't know. The same goes for that powdered milk. Who could drink the stuff? In La Esmeralda I saved it until I was really hard up and then I sold it to anybody who was willing to shell out a quarter for it to feed it to their animals or something. But I don't dare do that here because it's federal government food, and it's against the law to sell it. I could get into trouble that way in a place like this, where I don't know anybody. I might try to sell that stuff to a detective without realizing who he was and I'd land in jail.

I haven't been to La Esmeralda often since I moved here, because I can't afford it. Every trip costs 40 cents, 20 cents each way. I want to pay off all my debts in La Esmeralda so that I can hold my head high and proud when I go there. I want people to think I've bettered myself because one can't be screwed all one's life. Even now when I visit, still owing money as I do, I put on my best clothes and always try to carry a little cash. I do this so Minerva, Emilio's aunt, won't get the idea I'm starving or anything like that. She really suffers when she sees me in La Esmeralda, and I do all that just to bother her. I dress up the kids real nice and take them to call on everybody except her.

When I first moved out of La Esmeralda, nobody knew that I was leaving, in the first place because it made me sad and in the second place because that old Minerva had gone around telling everybody she hoped I'd clear out. She even said it to my face. I'd yell back at her, "What right do you have to say that? Did you buy La Esmeralda or something?"

Another reason why I hardly ever go to La Esmeralda is because Emilio spies on me. He has come after me in the *caserio* just the way he did in La Esmeralda, though not as often. He likes to use the shower in my new apartment when he comes. When I start home after visiting La Esmeralda, he gets into his car and drives along behind me, offering to give me a lift. But, listen, I wouldn't get into that car even if I had to walk all the way from San Juan to Villa Hermosa. I put a curse on that car, such a tremendous curse that I'm just waiting to see it strike. I did it one day when Anita had asthma and I had no money to take her to the hospital. I happened to glance out of the window and I saw Emilio stretched out in his car, relaxed as could be, as if he deserved nothing but the best. I let go and yelled with all the breath in my chest, "I hope to God someday you'll wear that car as a hat. I hope it turns to dust with you all fucked up inside it." Now I can't ride in the car, because I'm afraid the curse will come true some time when both of us are in it.

You can't imagine how lonely I feel here. I have friends, but they're sort of artificial, pasted-on friends. I couldn't confide in them at all. For example, I got pregnant a little while ago, and I had to have an abortion. I nearly went crazy thinking about it. Having a baby is nothing, it's the burden you have to take on afterwards, especially with a cowardly husband like mine who takes the easiest way out, denying that the child is his. So there I was, pregnant and, you know, I was ashamed. I was already out of La Esmeralda, see? Well, I know that my womb is weak, so I took two doses of Epsom salts with quinine and out came the kid. You can't imagine

how unpleasant that is. In La Esmeralda you can tell everybody about it, and that sort of eases your heart. But here I didn't tell anybody. These girls I know here are *señoritas*, mere children, and something like that . . . *ay bendito!*

But, to tell you the truth, I don't know what they call a *señorita* here in Villa Hermosa. The way it is in La Esmeralda, a girl and boy fall in love. For a few months they control themselves. Then they can't any more, and the boy does what he has to do to the girl. The hole is bigger than the full moon and that's that. They tell everybody and become husband and wife in the eyes of all the world. There's no trying to hide it. But here you see girls, who by rights should already have had a couple of kids, trying to keep from being found out. They'll go to a hotel with their sweethearts and let them stick their pricks into every hole in their body except the right one. And then they're so brazen as to come out of that hotel claiming they're still *señoritas*. It's plain shameless.

There are some policemen here who make love like this to some girls I know. Well, the policeman who did it to my friend Mimi came and told me that if I loaned him my bed for a little while he would give me three pesos. As that money wouldn't be bad at all and as he wasn't going to do it to me, I rented him the bed and grabbed the three pesos. Let them go screw! They locked themselves in the bedroom for a little while and then they went away. It was none of my business. If they didn't do it here, they would go do it somewhere else. And she didn't lose her virginity or anything here. So my hands are clean.

Sometimes I want to go back to La Esmeralda to live and other times I don't. It's not that I miss my family so much. On the contrary, relatives can be very bothersome. But you do need them in case you get sick because then you can dump the children on them. Sometimes I cry for loneliness here. Sometimes I'm bored to death. There's more neighborliness in La Esmeralda. I was used to having good friends stop by my house all the time. I haven't seen much of this neighborhood because I never go out. There's a Catholic church nearby but I've never been there. And I haven't been to the movies once since I've been living here. In La Esmeralda I used to go now and then. And in La Esmeralda, when nothing else was going on, you could at least hear the sea.

In La Esmeralda nobody ever made fun of my lameness. On the contrary, it was an advantage because everyone went out of his

way to help me: "Let me help the lame girl. Let me buy *bolita* numbers from Lame Crucita, because cripples bring luck." But it isn't like that here, where people just laugh. That's why I'd like to live in La Esmeralda again or have Nanda move in here with me.

The social worker told me that I could go to the hospital and have an operation to fix my back. But who could I leave my little baby crows with? And suppose what they do is take my guts out in order to make me look right? Still, now that I live in a place like Villa Hermosa, I would like to have an operation to make me straight.

THE PLAGUE

CAPITALISM + DOPE = GENOCIDE

Michael Tabor

Michael "Cetewayo" Tabor is one of the Panther 21. He is 23 years old and he is charged, along with the other New York Panthers on trial before Judge John (Mudface) Murtagh, with conspiring to murder policemen, blow up the Botanical Gardens, dynamite department stores and railway lines. The biggest frame-up in the history of New York.

For five years, from age 13 to age 18, while living in Harlem where he was born, Tabor was addicted to heroin, the Plague. At 13 he was "desperate and depressed"

and began shooting up. He became a member of the "Cloud Nine Society" to escape the "ugly realities of ghetto life."

In this essay, which was written in prison, he raps about heroin, about what it is like to be hooked. He describes the world as the addict himself sees it. But, more important, he describes the Plague from the perspective of a revolutionary. He links the problem of drug addiction to capitalist exploitation, racial oppression, the Mafia, cops in the colony, escapism and self-destruction by Black people. And he raps about the solution—Revolution—about the fundamental changes necessary to wipe the Plague from the cities of Babylon.

Malcolm X's Autobiography *changed Tabor. It gave him "a new outlook on life." He became a member of the Black Panther Party, founded in Oakland, California, in 1966 by Bobby G. Seale and Huey P. Newton, and kicked two bad habits—heroin and acquiescence before the white oppressor. He worked on the Panther Breakfast Program to feed hungry Black children and on the Liberation School to teach illiterate Black children to read and write. He was Defense Captain for the Bronx Chapter of the Party.*

On April 2, 1969, he was arrested, held in $50,000 bail, and placed in jail. He had been arrested and imprisoned before, for he had ripped off furs and jewels from the Mother Country to pay for heroin. He told the District Attorney, pig Phillips, "I have been in a penal institution for 23 years. All of AmeriKKKa is a State prison." Phillips asked him if he was scared when a cop with a shotgun arrested him. "No," he said. "I had a gun drawn on me when I was six years old. I've developed an immunity to it. It's standard for police to point guns at Black people."

For Michael Cetewayo Tabor, becoming a Panther meant self-defense against police attacks. It means becoming "a socially productive human being." And, as Fred Hampton said shortly before he was murdered in Chicago, being a Panther means "getting high off the People." For Tabor, there is nothing higher than revolution.

All Power to the People!

Jomo Raskin

I. THE PROBLEM

Recently in the Black colony of Harlem a 12-year-old Black boy was murdered by an overdose of heroin. Less than two weeks later a 15-year-old Black girl met the same tragic fate. During the year 1969 in New York City alone there were over 900 deaths resulting from drug addiction. Of these, 210 were youths ranging in age from 12 to 19. Of the over 900 dead, the overwhelming majority were Black and Puerto Rican. It is estimated that there are at least 25,000 youths addicted to narcotics in New York City—and that is a conservative estimate.

Drug addiction in the colonized ghettos of AmeriKKKa has constituted a major problem for over 15 years. Its use is so widespread that it can—without fear of exaggeration—be termed a Plague. It has reached epidemic proportions, and it is still growing. But it has only been within the last few years that the racist U.S. government has considered drug addiction "a matter of grave concern." It is interesting to note that this growing concern on the part of the government is proportionate to the spread of the Plague into the inner sanctums of the white middle- and upper-class communities. As long as the Plague was confined to the ghetto, the government did not see fit to deem it a problem. But as soon as college professors, demagogic politicians, money-crazed finance capitalists and industrialists discovered that their own sons and daughters had fallen victim to the Plague, a virtual "state of national emergency" was declared. This is significant, for it provides us with a clue to the understanding of the Plague as it relates to Black people.

From the Federal Bureau of Narcotics, to the clergy, to members of the medical profession, so-called educators, psychologists, right on down to the chemically enslaved addicts on the street corner, the hopes for effectively curbing the spread of the Plague are dishearteningly dim. Despite the stiffer jail sentences being meted out to those whom the law defines as drug profiteers—a euphemism for illegal capitalists—there are more dope dealers now than ever before. Despite the ever-increasing number of preventive and rehabilitative programs, the Plague proliferates; it threatens to devour an entire generation of youth.

The basic reason why the Plague cannot be stopped by the drug prevention and rehabilitation programs is that these programs, with their archaic, bourgeois, Freudian approach and their unrealistic therapeutic communities, do not deal with the causes of the problem. These programs deliberately negate or at best deal flippantly with the socioeconomic origin of drug addiction. These programs sanctimoniously deny the fact that capitalist exploitation and racial oppression are the main contributing factors to drug addiction in regard to Black people. These programs were never intended to cure Black addicts. They can't even cure the white addicts they were designed for.

This fascist government defines the cause of addiction as the importation of the Plague into the country by smugglers. They themselves even admit that stopping the entry of the Plague is impossible. For every kilo (2.2 lbs) of heroin they confiscate, at least 25 kilos gets past customs agents. The government is well aware of the fact that even if they were able to stop the importation of heroin, dope dealers and addicts would simply find another drug to take its place. The government is totally incapable of addressing itself to the true causes of drug addiction, for to do so would necessitate effecting a radical transformation of this society. The social consciousness of this society, the values, mores, and traditions, would have to be altered. And this would be impossible without totally changing the way in which the means of producing social wealth is owned and distributed. Only a Revolution can eliminate the Plague.

Drug addiction is a monstrous symptom of the malignancy which is ravaging the social fabric of this capitalist system. Drug addiction is a social phenomenon that grows organically from the social system. Every social phenomenon that emanates from a social system that is predicated upon and driven by bitter class antagonisms that result from class exploitation must be seen from a class point of view.

II. ESCAPISM AND SELF-DESTRUCTION

In regard to Black people, our problems are compounded and take on appalling dimensions as a result of the racist dehumanization that we are subjected to. To understand the Plague as it relates to Black people, we must analyze the effects of capitalist economic exploitation and racist dehumanization.

The heinous and sadistic program of annihilating the humanity of Black people that was initiated over 400 years ago by money-mad slave masters and that has continued unabated until this very day is deliberate and systematic. It is done for the purpose of justifying and facilitating our exploitation. Since the reality of our objective existence seemed to confirm the racist doctrines of white superiority and its antithesis, black inferiority, and since we lacked an understanding of our condition, we internalized the racist propaganda of our oppressors. We began to believe that we were inherently inferior to whites. These feelings of inferiority gave birth to a sense of self-hatred which finds expression in self-destructive behavior patterns. The wretchedness of our plight, our sense of powerlessness and despair, created within our minds a predisposition toward the use of any substance which produces euphoric illusions. We are inclined to use anything that enables us to suffer peacefully. We have developed an escapist complex. This escapist complex is self-destructive.

The depraved capitalist-racist oppressor

exploits these psychological and emotional deficiencies for all they are worth. The oppressor encourages our participation in any activity that is self-destructive. Our self-destructive behavior patterns and our escapist tendencies constitute a source of profits for the capitalists. They also, by weakening, dividing, and destroying us, reinforce the strength of the oppressor and enable him to perpetuate his domination over us.

Fratricidal street-gang fighting is a direct manifestation of a self-destructive behavior pattern. It is also a form of escapism by which Black youths vent their rage, frustrations, and despair on each other rather than deal with the true enemy. Pathological religionism or the fanatical indulgence in religion is essentially escapist because it encourages the victim to concentrate his attention, energy, and hope for salvation and freedom upon a dubious, mystical force. It discourages confronting the actual causes of our misery and deprivation. It encourages the focusing of attention upon pie in the sky, rather than the securing of more lamb chops right here on planet earth. It also serves as a source of profits for those religious charlatans, preachers, and ministers who exploit it.

Alcoholism is both self-destructive and escapist. It is also a source of tremendous profits for the capitalists. The amazingly high number of bars and liquor stores in the Black communities testify to this tragic fact. The capitalist liquor industry would prosper just on the business it does in the Black ghetto alone.

III. THE HEROIN ADDICT

The most escapist and self-destructive activity for us and one of the most profitable for the capitalist, and therefore the most encouraged by him, is drug addiction, specifically heroin addiction.

About 1889 a German chemist discovered diacetylmorphine, heroin. It was hailed as the perfect drug for curing morphine addicts. But soon it became apparent that it was more addictive than morphine. By the 1920s there were addicts who were injecting heroin directly into their veins. Heroin production in the United States was discontinued and the drug was no longer used as an antidote for morphine addiction and as a pain killer.

Heroin addiction, the Plague, the scourge of the Black colonies of Babylon. The Plague, whose spiritual, moral, psychological, physical, and social destructive powers greatly exceed that of any disease hitherto known to humanity. The Plague, opium from Turkey, shipped to Marseilles, converted into morphine base, then processed into heroin, smuggled into AmeriKKKa, cut, diluted, then placed into the Black ghetto. The Plague, poisonous, lethal, white powdery substance, sold by depraved, money-crazed beasts to Black youths who are desperately seeking a kick, a high, a means, anything that will help to make them oblivious to the squalor, to the abject poverty, disease, and degradation that engulfs them in their daily existence.

Initially the Plague does just that. Under its sinister influence, the oppressive, nauseous, ghetto prison is transformed into a virtual Black Valhalla. One becomes impervious to the rancid stench of urine-soaked tenement dungeons, unaffected by the piercing cries of anguish of Black folks driven to the brink of insanity by a sadistic social system. Unaffected by the deafening wail of pig police-car sirens as they tear through the streets of the Black Hell en route to answer a 1013 call from some other pig police who is in a state of well-deserved distress. Unaffected by the trash cans whose decayed, disease-carrying garbage has overflowed to fill the ghetto streets.

Yes, under its ecstatic influence one is

made oblivious to ugly realities. But there is a trick, a cruel monstrous trick, a deadly flim-flam awaiting its naive, youthful victim, for, as the illusionary beauty of the heroin-induced high begins to vanish, correspondingly, the temporary immunity from reality attained under its chemical trance vanishes. The reality that the pathetic victim sought so desperately to escape once again descends upon and re-engulfs him. The rancid stench of urine-soaked tenement dungeons begins to assail his nostrils. Those Black cries of anguish seem to blend with the wailing sirens of pig police cars. He hears them now very loud, and very clear—in stereophonic sound. And that garbage that flows over into the streets from uncollected trash cans is felt underfoot.

The young victim is not long in discovering that only by taking another dosage will he be able to attain sanctuary from his hideous reality. Each shot of the Plague that he injects into his blood system brings him that much closer to the grave. Soon he is strung-out, hooked. He is physiologically and psychologically dependent on the Plague. Both his body and mind have become addicted to heroin. He has now become a full-time, charter member of the Cloud 9 Society. His physical body begins to take on a decimated appearance. A shameless disregard is displayed toward his clothes. That his shirt is filthy and his shoes are soleless, leaving him to walk virtually on his naked feet, does not matter. That his unwashed body now emits a most foul odor disturbs him but little. That his nonaddicted friends now shun him and look upon him with contempt matters not, for the feelings are mutual. They no longer have anything in common. Everything ceases to matter, everything except heroin, the Plague.

As he continues, his body begins to build up an immunity to the drug. Now, in order to attain his euphoric high he must increase his dosage. This means that he must obtain more money. So enslaved has he now become that he will do anything for a bag, for a "shot." To lie, to steal, to cheat, to rob is nothing to him. Whatever he must do for a "shot" he will do, he *must* do, for he is a slave to the Plague.

The vicious cycle grinds into motion. He violates what the ruling class defines as being the law in order to secure money to feed his sickness. Inevitably he gets flagged-off, busted. He goes to jail, and after he has served out his sentence he is released. The first thing he wants is a shot. The cycle continues. And he plunges deeper and deeper into the abysmal pit of degradation. And there, always there and ever willing, for a price of course, to meet the addict's demand for dope is the cop-man, the dealer, purveyor of poison, distributor of death, merciless, murdering scum of the planet, vile capitalists, salesmen of death on the installment plan, the dope pusher, the Plague-man.

IV. CAPITALISM AND CRIME

Dope selling is beyond a doubt one of the most profitable capitalist undertakings. The profits from it soar into billions. Internationally and domestically the trade and distribution of heroin is ultimately controlled by the Cosa Nostra, the Mafia.

Much of the profit amassed from the drug business is used to finance so-called legitimate businesses. These legitimate businesses that are controlled by the Mafia are also used to facilitate their drug-smuggling activities. Given the fact that organized crime is a business and an ever-expanding one at that, it is constantly seeking new areas of investment to increase profits. Hence, more and more illegal profits are being channeled into legitimate businesses. Partnerships between the Mafia and "reputable businessmen" are the order of the day. There is a direct relationship between legitimate and illegitimate capitalists.

Over the years a number of politicians and foreign ambassadors and wealthy businessmen have been arrested in this country for drug activities. Others, because of their wealth and influence, were able to avoid arrest. In the fall of 1969 it was discovered that a group of prominent New York financiers was financing an international drug-smuggling operation. No indictments were handed down. Shortly after that a group of wealthy South American businessmen were arrested in a plush New York City hotel with over $10 million worth of drugs.

Given the predatory and voracious nature of the capitalist, it should come as no surprise that so-called legitimate businessmen are deeply involved in the drug trade. Capitalists are motivated by an insatiable lust for profits. They will do anything for money. The activities of organized crime and the "legitimate capitalists" are so inextricably tied up, so thoroughly interwoven, that from our vantage point any distinction made between them is purely academic.

The legitimization of the Mafia, their increased emphasis upon investing in and establishing corporations, has been accelerated by the stiffer prison sentences that are being meted out to drug profiteers. In New York this has resulted in the gradual withdrawal of the Mafia from their position of actual leadership of the New York drug trade. The New York drug trade is now dominated by Cuban exiles, many of whom were military officers and police agents in the prerevolutionary, repressive Batista regime. They equal the Mafia in ruthlessness and greed.

These new local dope kingpins have established a broad network of international smuggling operations. They utilize the traditional trade routes and create new ones, as indicated by the increased number of Narcotics Bureau seizures of dope coming from South America.

The concept of Black Power has influenced the thinking of every segment of the Black community. It has come to mean Black control of the institutions and activities that are centered in the Black community. Black teachers demand Black community control of the ghetto schools. Black businessmen and merchants advocate the expulsion of white businessmen from the ghetto so that they can maximize their profits. Black numbers-game operators are demanding total control of the ghetto numbers operations. And Black dope dealers are demanding community control of heroin. It is a tragedy that in New York the greatest gains made in the realm of Black community control have been made by Black racketeers, numbers-game bankers and dope dealers, by the Black illegal capitalists. Prior to 1967 it was a rarity to find a Black dope dealer who handled more than 3 kilos (1 kilo = 2.2 lbs) of heroin at any given time. Independent Black importers were unheard of. Now there is an entire class of Blacks who are big-time drug wholesalers and distributors who handle 5 kilos and upward. There is also a number of Blacks who have become importers, using Mafia-supplied lists of European connections.

The extent and instant rate of profits reaped from the dope industry could arouse the envy of U.S. Steel, General Motors, and Standard Oil. From the highest level to the lowest, the profits are enormous. If the individual is sufficiently ambitious, cunning, ruthless, and vicious, he may graduate from the status of street peddler to big-time wholesaler and distributor in a short span of time.

V. PIG POLICE

The Plague could never flourish in the Black colonies if it were not for the active support of the occupation forces, the police. That narcotics arrests have increased in no way mitigates the fact that the police give dope peddlers immunity from arrest in exchange for money payoffs.

It is also the practice of pig police, especially narcotics agents, to seize a quantity of drugs from one dealer, arrest him, but only turn in a portion of the confiscated drugs for evidence. The rest is given to another dealer who sells it and gives a percentage of the profits to the narcotics agents. The pig police also utilize informers who are dealers. In return for information, they receive immunity from arrest. The police cannot solve the problem, for they are a part of the problem.

When you consider that a kilo of heroin purchased by an importer for $6,000, when cut and bagged and distributed will bring back a profit of $300,000 in a week's time, it becomes easier to understand that even if the death penalty were imposed on drug profiteers, it would not deter the trade.

The lying, devious puppets of the bourgeois ruling class, the demagogic politicians of the Capitol Hill, have now passed a law which gives narcotics agents the right to crash into a person's home without knocking, on the pretext of looking for narcotics and "other evidence." This law was ostensibly passed to prevent dope dealers from destroying the dope and "other evidence." Now, anyone who thinks that this law will be confined to just suspected drug dealers is laboring under a tragic and possibly suicidal delusion. To assume that only suspected drug dealers will be affected by this law is to negate the reality of present-day AmeriKKKa. To allow yourself to think for one moment that this law only applies to suspected drug dealers is to deny that the laws being passed, the policies being implemented, and the methods and tactics of the police have become blatantly and shamelessly fascist.

It should come as no surprise when the homes of revolutionaries and other progressive and true freedom-loving people are invaded by the police on the pretext of searching for drugs and "other evidence." A number of revolutionaries have already been imprisoned on framed-up narcotics charges. Lee Otis was given 30 years and Martin Sostre was sentenced to 41 years on trumped-up narcotics charges. Rest assured this policy will be intensified. It would do us well to consider what kicking in a person's door in search of drugs and "other evidence" actually means. What is "other evidence"? The bourgeois, fascist law makers have not specified what constitutes "other evidence." The No-Knock Law is an integral part of the fascist trip that this country has embarked upon.

A characteristic feature of class and racial oppression is the ruling-class policy of brainwashing the oppressed into accepting their oppression. Initially, this program is carried out by viciously implanting fear into the minds and sowing the seeds of inferiority in the souls of the oppressed. But as the objective conditions and the balance of forces become more favorable for the oppressed and more adverse to the oppressor, it becomes necessary for the oppressor to modify his program and adopt more subtle and devious methods to maintain his rule. The oppressor attempts to throw the oppressed psychologically off-balance by combining a policy of vicious repression with spectacular gestures of good-will and service.

Given the fact that Black people have abandoned the nonfunctional and ineffective tactics of the "Civil Rights" era and have now resolved to attain their long overdue liberation by any means necessary, it has become necessary for the oppressor to deploy more occupation forces into the Black colony. The oppressor, particularly in New York, realizes that this cannot be done overtly without intensifying the revolutionary fervor of the Black people in the colony. Therefore, a pretext is needed for placing more pigs in the ghetto.

And what is the pretext? It goes like this: Responsible negro community leaders have informed us, and their reports concur with police findings, that the negro community is ravaged by crime, muggings, burglaries, murders, and mayhem. The streets are unsafe, business establishments are infested by armed robbers, commerce cannot function. City Hall agrees with negro residents that the main cause for this horrible situation is the dope addicts who prey on innocent people. Yes, the dope addicts are to blame for the ever-increasing crime rate. And City Hall will answer the desperate cry of negro residents for greater protection —send in more police!

That victims of the Plague are responsible for most of the crimes in the Black ghettos is a fact. That Black drug addicts perpetrate most of their robberies, burglaries, and thefts in the Black community against Black people cannot be denied. But before, out of desperation, we jump up and scream for more police protection, we better remember who put the Plague in Harlem, Bedford Stuyvesant, and the other Black communities. We better remember who ultimately profits from the drug addiction of Black people. We better remember that the police are alien hostile troops sent into the Black colonies by the ruling class, not to protect the lives of Black people, but rather to protect the economic interests and the private property of the capitalists and to make certain that Black people don't get out of place. Rockefeller and Lindsay give less than a damn about the lives of Black people. And if we don't know by now how the police feel about us, then we are *really* in bad shape.

Before, when the home of a Black person was burglarized by a drug addict, or a sister had her purse snatched, the police took all night to respond to the call, or didn't respond at all. The burglar or purse-snatcher was hardly ever caught. In most instances, when someone was arrested, it was the wrong person. But when an exploiting capitalist business establishment in that very same ghetto, especially a white one, gets ripped-off, there are immediately 15 siren-wailing police cars on the set, and three dozen pigs are running up and down the street, waving guns in everybody's face. And you can lay 5 to 1 odds that somebody is going to jail for it. Whether or not the arrested person perpetrated the act is irrelevant from the pigs' standpoint. The racist pig police use Blacks as an outlet for their sadistic impulses, inadequacies, and frustrations. Now that more police have been sent in, the situation has gone from bad to worse.

VI. REVOLUTION

The racist pig police, the demagogic politicians, and the avaricious big businessmen who control the politicians are delighted that Black youths have fallen victim to the Plague. They are delighted for two reasons: one, it is economically profitable, and two, they realize that as long as they can keep our Black youths standing on the street corners "nodding" from a "shot" of heroin, they won't have to worry about us waging an effective struggle for liberation. As long as our young Black brothers and sisters are chasing the bag, as long as they are trying to cop a fix, the rule of our oppressors is secure and our hopes for freedom are dead. It is the youth who make the revolution and it is the youth who carry it out. Without our young, we will never be able to forge a revolutionary force.

We are the only ones capable of eradicating the Plague from our communities. It will not be an easy task. It will require tremendous effort. It will have to be a revolutionary program, a People's program.

The Black Panther Party is presently in the process of formulating a program to combat the Plague. It will be controlled totally by the people. We, the people, must stamp out the Plague, and we will. Dope is a form of genocide in which the victim pays to be killed.

Seize the Time!
Intensify the Struggle!
Destroy the Plague!
All Power to the People!

THE PERMANENT POOR
THE LESSON OF EASTERN KENTUCKY

Harry M. Caudill

The Cumberland Plateau of Kentucky is one of the great natural-resource regions of the American continent. Industrialists bought up its great wealth three-quarters of a century ago and soon after 1900 commenced the large-scale extraction of its timber and minerals. When the development of the eastern Kentucky coalfields began, mining was largely a manual pursuit. Mining machines were displacing mules and ponies, and electricity was making it possible to do an increasing number of tasks with electric power rather than muscle power. Nevertheless, some of the undercutting of coal, much of the drilling, and practically all of the loading into cars were done by armies of grit-blackened miners. Industrial wages enticed thousands of mountaineers to turn from the plow and hoe to the pick and shovel. Hordes of Negroes were induced away from the cotton rows of Georgia, the Carolinas, Tennessee, Mississippi, and Alabama and forsook plantation life for the mines. Shiploads of Europeans were brought to the southern coalfield. The extraction of the region's mineral wealth was undertaken in the atmosphere of a tremendous industrial boom.

The Depression destroyed the coalfield's prosperity, but the Second World War revived it, and for a few years the boom returned and the miner was again a useful and honored citizen. The coal industry depended upon his skill and courage, and steel production, electric-power generation, and other basic industries were dependent upon coal. The collapse of the war and of the postwar boom is now history, and we have an opportunity to reflect upon the social, political, and economic consequences that result when a modernized industry is able to cast aside three-quarters of its workmen within the span of a decade.

Reprinted by permission of the author and publisher from The Atlantic Monthly *(June 1964), pp. 49–53; copyright © 1964, by The Atlantic Monthly Co. (Boston, Mass.).*

In the postwar years technologists were able to design and manufacture machines of remarkable power and efficiency. Their genius was nowhere better demonstrated than in the coal industry. Devices were developed for boring directly back into the face of the coal seam, and chewing out immense quantities of the mineral, thus eliminating the need to undercut or blast the seam. Simultaneously, the conveyor belt displaced the tracks, mining locomotives, and strings of cars in many mines. Roof bolting made its appearance. This method of supporting the roof eliminated the need for wooden props and proved most effective. A single mechanical loading machine could load more coal than two dozen hardworking shovelers.

Machines were costly, but investment capital was plentiful. The mine operators borrowed from the banks and mechanized and automated the mines and tipples to a remarkable degree. Big, amply financed operations bought up their small competitors. Many inefficient and nearly worked-out pits suspended operations altogether. Thus in a few years the fragmented and archaic coal industry became surprisingly modern and technologically advanced. The operators were delighted. Corporations that were bankrupt only a few years before now basked in a sustained new prosperity. For example, Consolidation Coal Company, which had been in receivership, paid off all its obligations and acquired a controlling interest in Chrysler Corporation.

While a new optimism pervaded the officer of the automated and mechanized companies, disaster befell thousands of the men who had depended for so long upon the old industry. By the thousands they found the scrip offices and payroll windows closed in their faces. Mining companies for which they and their fathers had worked, in some instances for two generations, simply vanished altogether. Some three-fourths of eastern Kentucky's miners found

themselves without work. They had become the victims of a materialistic social order which venerates efficiency and wealth above all other things and largely disregards social and human consequences. When they were no longer needed, their employers dropped them as a coal miner might have thrown away the scrip coins of a bankrupt company.

The legions of industrial outcasts were left with three choices. They could leave the area and find work elsewhere if employment of any kind could be found. Many thousands followed this course, and the population of the mining counties subsided dramatically. A third of the people fled from the shadow of starvation.

They could remain within the region and attempt to live by mining coal from the thin seams not monopolized by the big and highly efficient operations. These men could operate small "doghole" mines with little equipment and trifling capital, pitting their arms and backs against the tireless machines of their big competitors. They were goaded to desperation by the fact that in a camp house or a creek shanty a wife and five to ten children depended upon them for clothes and bread. They had been educated for the mines at a time when little formal education was required for that calling. Thus, in the contest with the big coal corporations they could contribute little except their muscles and their will. Thousands entered these small mines, often "gang-working" as partners and sharing the meager profits at paydays.

In the third situation was the miner who for one reason or another could not or would not leave the area, and found that however hard he toiled in the small mines his income was too meager to provide for the needs of his household. He and his family became charges of the government. Federal and state agencies came to his relief with a wide variety of cash and commodity doles. He was confined to a kind of dull, bleak, reservation existence reminiscent of that imposed by military fiat on the reservation Indians of the Western plains.

Living by welfare, without work and without purpose save existence, these numerous mountaineers settled down to while away the years and await developments.

The men who left the region for the great cities of the North and Middle West did not always find smooth sailing. The rapid process of industrial modernization which had first, and so dramatically, waved its wand across the eastern Kentucky coalfield had penetrated into the immense industrial complexes of the nation's cities. Assembly lines which had traditionally required hundreds of swarming workmen were reorganized, and wonderfully efficient machines were introduced into the automobile and other great manufacturing industries. In many instances, these machines were guided by sensitive electronic masters which, with belts of punched plastic and electric current, could impose unerring and immediate obedience.

In some respects, to be sure, eastern Kentucky is unique. Its people were dependent for fifty years on but a single industry, and, remarkably, they were an industrial people living in a rural rather than an urban setting. The coal industry, like extractive industries generally, invested little of its profits back in the region and allowed its communities to maintain schools of only the most rudimentary sort. It created an environment which left its workmen almost totally dependent upon their employers for bread and leadership, then provided only a small measure of the former and practically none of the latter. Nevertheless, the collapse of coal as a mass hirer of men left in the Kentucky mountains a splendid case study of the social and political implications arising from the displacement of men by machines.

Government at all levels was wholly unprepared for the dramatic developments that ensued. To be sure, these developments were a logical outgrowth of the continuing industrial revolution, which, once set in motion, appears to be destined to carry us inevitably toward a day when a few people and many machines will do the work for a leisurely population of consumers. But between the first spinning jenny and the distant utopia lie many pitfalls, some of which yawn before us today.

In short, government in our democratic society proved practically bankrupt of ideas when confronted with this new challenge. Hoping against hope that expansion in other industries would eventually absorb the displaced miners, government agencies waited. When the stranded miner had exhausted his unemployment insurance benefits and his savings, when he had come to the ragged edge of starvation and was cloaked in bewilderment and frustration, government came to his rescue with the dole. It arranged to give him a bag of cheese, rice, cornmeal, beef, butter, and dried milk solids at intervals, and in most instances to send him a small check. Having thus contrived to keep the miner and his family alive, the government lost interest in him. Appropriations were made from time to time for his sustenance, but little thought was given to his spirit, his character, his manhood. He was left to dry-rot in the vast paleface reservation created for his perpetuation in his native hills.

And, inevitably, he fell prey to the politicians who dispense the bread and money by which he lives. Coal mining and thirty years of subservience to the scrip window had already done much to impair the mountaineer's ability to adapt well to rapidly changing circumstances. He had dwelt too long as a kind of industrial serf in company-owned houses, on company-owned streets, in company-owned towns. For too long the company had buffered

him from the swift-flowing social and economic tides swirling in the world outside
his narrow valleys. When his employers
cast him aside, he still possessed only a
single valuable remnant of his birthright—
the ballot. He was essential to the politicians because he could vote, so he was
placed in a sort of suspended animation in
which he came fully to life only at election
time. He became increasingly dependent
upon the political machines that ran his
counties. He accepted the food doles and
the welfare checks and ratified the arrangement by voting for the men and women
who thus sustained him. The politicians
expanded their operations into other fields
where public funds could make the difference between life and death. In all too
many counties they captured the school
systems, thereby acquiring large new sums
to be dispensed as patronage. The positions
of schoolteacher, bus driver, lunchroom director, truant officer, and a multitude of
others were treated as so many plums to be
dispensed to the acquiescent, the obedient,
and the meek. The union of school politics
and welfare politics resulted in a formidable prodigy indeed. Its power was quickly
recognized at Frankfort and Washington.
New political pacts were made, and a wide
range of state jobs were placed at the disposal of the local overlords. Thus their
power became virtually complete.

Today in many eastern Kentucky counties political machines of remarkable efficiency are to be found. Their effectiveness
surpasses Tammany Hall at its best. In a
typical county the school board and state
agencies control the biggest payrolls. The
politicians who run them can also reach
and influence the many small merchants,
automobile dealers, and service-station operators with whom they do business. Thus
they are masters of the majority of those
who still work for a living.

The state and federal governments act as
tax-collecting enterprises, which funnel vast
sums into the hands of merciless and
amoral local political dynasties. The county
machines dispense the funds so as to perpetuate themselves and their allies at
Frankfort and Washington. Increasingly,
these omniscient organizations manage to
gather into their hands funds and gifts
from private charities, including even the
American Red Cross. Taxpayers in fifty
states, oblivious to what their dollars buy,
pay little heed to this ominous course of
events.

These developments raise a disquieting
question which Americans have never confronted before:

How fares the American concept of government of the people, by the people, and
for the people when a clear majority become permanently dependent upon and
subservient to their elected leaders?

Indeed, can democratic government survive at all in such a setting?

The situation in eastern Kentucky is new
to the American scene, but much of the
pattern is as old as Rome.

In ancient Italy the social order was remarkably healthy so long as the populace
consisted, in the main, of freeholding farmers and self-employed artisans and artificers.
The scene darkened when Roman armies
conquered distant territories and sent home
multitudes of captives. The rich bought up
the small plots of farmers and cultivated
the resultant plantations with the labor of
slaves. Other slaves were set to work in
mass manufactories. Because of their great
numbers, their carefully planned organization, and their specialization, they were
able to produce far more cheaply than
their self-employed, free competitors. The
corporations that ran these huge enterprises provided grain, leather goods, cloth,
and weapons for the empire. The free men
and women flocked to the towns and cities
to cluster in slums. To keep them orderly
the government fed them, clothed them,

and entertained them with games. An astoundingly complex system of doles and subsidies was perfected to sustain the idled millions of Roman citizens. In idleness the Roman decayed. He became bitter, vengeful, irresponsible, and bloodthirsty. The mutterings of Roman mobs came to speak more loudly than the voice of Caesar. Rome withered within, long before alien armies crashed through her walls.

These ancient events cast shadows of portent for us today. The machine is a far more profitable servant than any slave. It is untiring, wears out slowly, and requires no food or medication. Technological progress is inexorable and moves toward perfection. What will be the final consequences of it all for the American ideals of equality, liberty, and justice?

We are in the throes of a rapidly quickening new technological revolution. Fifty years ago 700,000 American coal miners were able to mine less coal than 140,000 dig today. Experts tell us that coal production may double by 1980 without any increase in the number of miners. Automobile production increases year by year, but the number of workmen declines. In every field of manufacturing, sensitive, accurate, unfailing steel monsters crowd men and women from workbench and turning lathe, from well and mine. On the land the number of farmers decreases as farms are consolidated into giant tracts. Tractors and mechanical cotton pickers and threshers have rendered the farm laborer as obsolete as the coal miner of 1945.

New turns of the technological wheel are in sight. In twenty years nuclear power may render all fossil fuels obsolete, valued only for their chemical derivatives. If this occurs, new legions of workmen will follow the coal miner into abrupt obsolescence.

On the material side, this revolution undoubtedly represents only progress. It brings us more and more goods for less and less work, thus bringing to fruition one of mankind's ancient dreams.

But what of man's social, spiritual, and political aspects? Is it possible we are moving rapidly forward on the one hand and going backward to barbarism on the other?

What is to become of the jobless miner who takes his family to a Chicago housing development, there to press in upon a one-time automobile assembler from Detroit and a discarded tool and die maker from Pittsburgh? What results when these men and their wives and children are joined by a Negro from Mississippi whose job as a cotton picker was taken over by a machine, or by a white hill-farmer from Tennessee whose ninety acres could not produce corn in competition with the splendidly mechanized farms of Iowa? Are the mushrooming housing developments of the great cities to become the habitations of millions of permanently idled people, supported by a welfare program as ruinous as the one devised by the Caesars? Are whole segments of American citizenry to be consigned to lifetimes of vexatious idleness, resentment, and bitterness? Are these centers to become vast new slums out of which will issue the ominous rumblings of titanic new mobs?

And what torrents of new bitterness will be added to the nation's bloodstream when computers send multitudes of white-collar workers into abrupt idleness in the mortgaged houses of suburbia?

In my opinion these questions pose the foremost issue of our time.

It strikes me that our scientists may develop the explosive power to send a few Americans to Mars while, simultaneously, our society prepares a vastly greater explosive power among disillusioned millions of Americans who remain behind on our own battered planet.

The industrialists who run the eastern Kentucky coalfield laid careful plans for the creation and use of mining machines but cast aside their mining men as lightheartedly as one might discard a banana peel. Most of the victims of this callous treatment accepted their fate resignedly. Some did not, however, and in the winter of 1962–1963 the hills in four eastern Kentucky counties resounded with gunfire and nocturnal explosions. For several months a situation bordering on anarchy prevailed across a wide region. Tipples and mines were blasted. Automobiles, power lines, and mining machines were destroyed. Such acts were committed by desperate men seeking to strike at a social and economic order which had rejected them.

Today the challenge of eastern Kentucky is a great national challenge. If we can triumph over it, the solutions we find will offer hope to the entire nation. Increasingly, the agony of eastern Kentucky is but a part of the misery that afflicts great cities, mill towns, and mining regions everywhere. The pain grows out of the evil paradox of mass idleness in the midst of booming production.

Liberty, like a chain, is no stronger than its weakest part. If the freedom and well-being of a part of the people are lost, the freedom and well-being of all are mortally imperiled. If the nation writes off our southern highlands as unworthy of rescue and rehabilitation, then the nation as a whole is unworthy of survival. As an optimist and a liberal I believe that the nation will rise to the challenge of the depressed and backward Appalachian region, and that in so doing, it will find many of the answers that democracy requires for survival throughout the nation.

A population equivalent to the present population of New York State is being added to the nation every four or five years. Technology eliminates some 40,000 jobs each week. These facts tell us that we must successfully master new frontiers of social justice, and do so in a hurry, or become another nation of regimented serfs.

A social and political crisis of the first magnitude will confront America before the end of another decade. Substitutes for such presently accepted goals as full employment will have to be found. Fresh definitions of the concepts of work, leisure, abundance, and scarcity are imperatively needed. Economic theories adequate to an infant industrial revolution are wholly unsatisfactory when applied to a full-fledged scientific revolution such as that which now engulfs us. The complexity and interdependence of the scientific-industrial nation call for national planning and action. Government must and will intervene more and more in the nation's industrial life. The destiny toward which we move is a national economy under the law. A radical change in public attitude toward law and government is necessary if the general welfare is to be achieved without the total sacrifice of individual liberty. Having bargained for the benefits of technology on all fronts, law is our only means of assuring that it serves the common good.

In 1963 the American economy brought unprecedented prosperity to some 80 percent of the people. Simultaneously, a segment of the population as numerous as the inhabitants of Poland consisted of paupers, and 5.5 percent of the nation's breadwinners were without jobs. Clearly a new tack must be taken soon unless America the Beautiful is to become a crazy quilt of bustle and sloth, brilliance and ignorance, magnificence and squalor.

For more than a dozen years the prevailing political ideology has implemented a *de facto* return to the Articles of Confederation. This doctrine holds that action at the state or local level is admirable while any direct effort by Washington to deal with social or economic malaise is un-American and dangerous. The result is a growing paralysis of the national government as an instrumentality of the public will. This reasoning has brought tremendous outpouring of federal grants-in-aid to states and communities, under circumstances which entail much waste and, often, minimal benefits.

In eastern Kentucky, and in many other depressed areas, the state government will not act effectively to combat poverty and economic decline because it is allied to or controlled by the interests that produced the problems. Thus, state officials talk piously about reform but strenuously oppose any real effort to attack the status quo. They respond to the political machines nurtured by welfare grants and founded on impoverished and dependent citizens. It is not too much to expect that, as matters now stand, federal funds trickling through state treasuries will finance the rebuilding of new political machines in practically every state—machines more odious than those once bossed by Crump, Pendergast, and Hague.

Common sense and past experience argue strongly for a system of federally administered public works. Only in America are able-bodied men permitted to loaf in idleness amid a profusion of unperformed tasks. Should not the thousands of jobless Kentucky coal miners be set to work reforesting the wasted hills, building decent consolidated schoolhouses and roads, and providing decent housing in lieu of the dreadful shacks that now dot every creek and hollow? And why not a modernized version of TVA—a Southern Mountain Authority—to develop the immense hydro- and thermal-power potential of the Appalachian South for the benefit of the entire nation, and to stop the hideous waste of the land now being wrought by the strip- and auger-mining industries? What of the possibility of an educational Peace Corps to break the old cycle of poor schools, poor job preparation, poor pay, and poor people?

Unless the nation can profit from the terrible lesson eastern Kentucky so poignantly teaches, new multitudes of once prosperous Americans may find themselves slipping inexorably into an economic mire that breeds poverty, despair, dependency, and, eventually, revolution.

THE WHITETOWNERS

Peter Binzen

The Whitetowner's row house is fourteen feet wide.

Five rooms on two floors with a postage-stamp yard out back. One of hundreds of small properties in a vast, dreary industrial landscape—clogged streets, drafty factories, fouled air, a noisy elevated line. Hardly a tree. And the few tiny parks are littered with broken bottles.

The Whitetowner was born and raised in this section and his parents still live near by. They don't think of moving out. Neither does he.

The Whitetowner is a steady worker and

a family man. He quit school in tenth grade to get a job. His wife, also a native of the area, dropped out to marry him two months before her graduation. She was a better student than he was. She manages the family finances. Their house and car are paid for.

It is evening. The Whitetowner's wife is in the front room with their three children watching a bang-bang TV show. Her hair is in pink plastic curlers. The television set is a big new color model. The house is neat and better furnished than its plain gray exterior would lead one to expect. On the wall behind the TV is a proud affirmation in needle point: A MAN'S HOME IS HIS CASTLE. On the kitchen wall is the prayerful GOD BLESS OUR HOME. In both rooms are religious ornaments and bouquets of plastic flowers.

The Whitetowner sits in the kitchen answering the questions of an outsider who is trying to find out what makes Whitetown tick. The questions bear on things that concern the Whitetowner deeply. Despite his lack of formal education, he expresses himself forcefully. Asked if he favors Bible reading in public schools, he says Yes and adds, "The Bible is the beginning of knowledge. A *must* for all!" He supports physical punishment of pupils but explains, "I also believe fairness should be shown and two sides of a story told."

He doubts that his children will go to college. He doesn't really want them to. "It would be a waste of money," he says, "with all this riot nonsense." He thinks the United States would be improved "if people with *guts* were in high places." He complains that his city's schools are too lax on discipline, too political, and too lenient toward student demonstrations.

Proudly, he describes his community:

Whitetown people are, and have been as long as I can remember, people who like to pay their own way. To be sure, there are a lot of "renters" moving in, but they aren't the result of White-

town. They come from God knows where. Whitetown may look run-down to an outsider, but the politicians are to blame for its condition. Compared to other sections, it is a decent place to raise children and to live. If outsiders would stop condemning Whitetown and her people, her future would become brighter. We have a minority that drink too much, but ninety percent are social drinkers.

Asked to comment on Whitetown's reputation as a "provincial, backward section with strong prejudices," the Whitetowner swings both fists:

Who gave it the reputation you stated? And, anyway, just what is wrong with being provincial, backward (if that means opposing someone else's ideas), and having strong prejudices? Rich people have children that commit suicide, drive like maniacs, and are unruly. Rich people live on high parties and are social climbers, the mental hospitals are full of them. Why aren't the Negroes living in the suburbs? The suburbs are full of Whitetown people that are loaded down with high mortgages.

We are honest hard-working people with children we love dearly. If the Negro moves into Whitetown it will only be to push this issue of integration—and the people here are sick of having it shoved down our throats. We are sick of reading in the paper where looters, arsonists, and murderers are allowed to do whatever they damn well please. We don't want them, they would ruin our community and our property values would drop.

And, then, in a parting shot, the Whitetowner asks:

Why the sudden interest in our community? Could it be to help these poor lazy slobs get rent-free houses? Whitetown *does* have a future. When you *eggheads* run out of surveys to take and the dust begins to settle, we will be able to enjoy the life we have always known and feel contented with.

I don't know this Whitetowner's age or even his occupation. He might be a truck driver or a policeman, a turret-lathe operator or a white-collar office worker. All I know for sure is that he is white, he makes between five and ten thousand dollars a year, he owns his house, and he speaks his mind. (The comments are his; I've changed the name of his community.) I'm also certain that he speaks for a vast army of white American workingmen in Boston's Charlestown, New York's Belmont, and Philadelphia's Kensington; in Chicago's Southwest Side, Cleveland's West Side, and San Francisco's Eureka Valley. Law and order is their watchword and, for many, George Wallace was their candidate for President in 1968.

Not long ago this white workingman was almost a folk hero in our national life. He was the honest, respectable, law-abiding citizen, the backbone of the community. More than likely, he was the son or grandson of immigrants, and the melting pot was his kettle. Whether of Irish, Italian, German, Polish, Russian, or Ukrainian extraction, he was a hundred per cent American and proud of it. From Belleau Wood to Anzio and the Chosin Reservoir he fought for his country. He supported his church (usually Roman Catholic), backed his local political leaders (usually Democrats), and provided the votes for most of the progressive domestic and internationalist legislation enacted in Congress.

All this has now changed. Today the white workingman always seems to be *against* things. He's *against* open housing, *against* school bussing, *against* hippies, Yippies, and draft dodgers. He's *against* letting Negroes into unions, and China into the United Nations. He's even *against* his own church when it gets embroiled in civil-rights causes.

In the drama of a nation striving for interracial justice, for true equality in education, housing, and employment, Whitetowners often emerge as deep-dyed racists. While some are silent protesters, others have made spectacles of themselves. In recent years Whitetowners have rioted half a dozen times. Their strong feelings are potentially as explosive as the force that detonated Watts, Hough, Detroit, and Newark.

Who are these people? What are their origins? What makes them act as they do? Robert C. Wood, former Undersecretary of the United States Department of Housing and Urban Development, describes[1] the Whitetowner as the "working American—the average white ethnic male . . . the ordinary employee in factory and office, blue collar and white," who lives in the "gray area" fringe of central cities and constitutes the majority of the nation's work force.

The *New York Times* labels him the "$8,000-a-year shoe clerk." During the 1968 Presidential election campaign, Richard M. Nixon called him "the forgotten American" and George C. Wallace identified him as "the little man." The American Jewish Committee speaks of him as "the reacting American," writer Elizabeth Hardwick considers him "the cheerless American," *Newsweek* magazine describes him as "the troubled American," and social scientist David Riesman rates him "the man in the middle." More recently he's been identified as part of that amorphous mass known as the "silent majority."

By whatever name, the people we are talking about are drawn mainly from the ethnic groups that differ from the basic white Protestant Anglo-Saxon settlers in religion, language, and culture. Many of these "ethnics" are among the thirty-four million foreign-stock Americans—that is, immigrants themselves or having at least one immigrant parent. Most are descendants of Eastern and Southern European peasants. Many others are Irish. Of course, not all white Anglo-Saxon Protestants have

[1] In a speech at Lincoln, Mass., on Dec. 8, 1967.

made their fortunes and moved to the suburbs. Especially in the South but also in Northern cities sizable numbers of Protestants, often fundamentalist or evangelical, are struggling to keep their heads above water. Conversely, a great many immigrants and immigrants' children have enjoyed success beyond their dreams and wouldn't deign to set foot in Whitetown. More often than not, however, the Whitetowns of America are populated by the ethnics and by first- and second-generation (and often third-generation) immigrants.

Whitetowns come in all ages, shapes, and sizes. Chicago's Scottsdale is new. It sprang up after World War II on former prairie in Chicago's extreme southwest corner, ten miles from the Loop. In neat single houses with pink flamingos on front lawns and two cars in many garages live fourteen thousand militant Caucasians, who are, says Scottsdale's school principal "united in their determination to keep their community segregated." Many Scottsdalers are municipal employees required by ordinance to live within the city limits. For them Scottsdale, which extends to the city boundary, is the end of the line. They've run as far as they can. There appears to be no real poverty in Scottsdale, but many men hold two jobs to make ends meet, and average income there was last estimated at just over eight thousand dollars.

Boston's Charlestown is old. Its working-class whites cluster in drab surroundings at the foot of Bunker Hill, which dominates the area. The Boston Navy Yard is near by and many Charlestonians work there. It was in grimy, faded Charlestown that John F. Kennedy began his political career in 1948, and it was to Charlestown that he returned to start every subsequent campaign. Charlestown has poverty and it has Negroes—a few living in public housing. Now it is engaged in a mighty renewal effort, with help from Washington and with the knowledge that along with

new schools, new housing, a beautiful community college, will come meaningful racial integration.

New York's Belmont, in the Fordham section of the Bronx, is a small city of twenty-five thousand people, 95 percent of them first- and second-generation Italians. Theirs is a classic ethnic enclave holding out against pressure from Negroes moving north from Manhattan. Curiously, some of the proudest and bitterest Belmonters are those who have moved to suburban Whitetowns but return regularly to Belmont's markets and its church and desperately want always to be able to do so. Every year brings another three hundred families to Belmont from Italy. Belmont's Our Lady of Mount Carmel Roman Catholic Church is an Italian national parish with six million dollars invested in the neighborhood. As Father Mario Zicarelli says with a smile, "While I take care of all Italians, whatever their color, maybe I have to be interested in my community."

In Cleveland's Near West Side, in Chicago's Uptown, and in sections of Detroit are examples of festering Anglo-Saxon poverty. Here live Appalachian white migrants from the hills of Tennessee, Kentucky, and West Virginia. These are truly forgotten people, just as miscast for city life as the most backward plantation Negroes. And often more miserable because they cannot blame their pigmentation for holding them back. Tough, mean sections of burned-out pride, homesickness, and contention as bitter as that in the hillbilly ballad:

> *Fight like dogs,*
> *If you ain't no kin,*
> *If you kill one another,*
> *It ain't no sin.*

Philadelphia's Kensington is a nineteenth-century mill area, a Dickensian factory town. Here you find working-class whites in their fourteen-foot-wide row houses. Here you also find middle-class workers with boats and summer places at the Jersey shore, still living in Kensington because it is home and they are proud of it. There are many pensioners just scraping by. And elderly widows. And, increasingly, poor white families moving in from mixed sections downtown. To the established homeowners of Kensington these newcoming renters are white trash. The clash between these two groups is almost as bitter and traumatic as the racial collision.

Poverty, we should note, doesn't draw the color line in America's big cities. The 1960 United States census counted almost twice as many poor white families in metropolitan areas as poor nonwhite families. Poverty was then considered to be three thousand dollars a year for a family of four. By this definition, there were 10.7 million impoverished white families in urban America and 5.6 million impoverished nonwhite families. The 1960 census did not reach all the nonwhites, its figures were not very reliable and they are now out of date. Furthermore, since whites in the general population outnumber nonwhites by about ten to one while white poor outnumber nonwhite poor by less than two to one, the poverty problem is obviously greater among nonwhites. But the message of the 1960 census still holds: In American urban areas, life is desperately difficult for great numbers of whites and blacks alike.[2]

What Whitetowners of different classes, sections, backgrounds, occupations, religions, national origins, and even political parties—for they cut across party lines—share is their alienation from the American "mainstream." This alienation is reflected in distrust of most politicians, in contempt for white rich and black poor, in a bristling defensiveness and a yearning for the recent past when life was simpler and loyalties less complex, when children were reared by the Bible and the beltstrap, when the schools stuck to the three R's, and when patriotism meant "My country right or wrong."

Despite wealth and political success, Vice-President Spiro T. Agnew, whose father was born in Greece, is an authentic Whitetown voice. When, in defending the Nixon Administration's Vietnam policy late in 1969, Agnew attacked war critics as "an effete corps of impudent snobs," he spoke for the truckers, policemen, and factory workers of American Whitetowns. When he mentioned the intellectuals' "disdain to mingle with the masses who work for a living" and said it was time for "the preponderant majority, the responsible citizens of this country," to stop dignifying the acts of "arrogant, reckless elements" within American society, he was telling the Whitetowners what they wanted to hear.

In the 1968 Presidential election, many Whitetowners voted not for Nixon but for George Wallace. They helped the Alabama segregationist pile up nine million votes. Theirs was a protest against what's been going on in this country. "The central problem [in America]," Joseph Kraft, the syndicated columnist, wrote in the summer of 1968, when the Whitetowners' wrath first became evident,

is not the visible problem of disaffected Negroes and young people. The central problem is that

---

[2] The very existence of poor whites sometimes seems to be intentionally obscured. A case in point is the March 1968 Report of the National Advisory Commission on Civil Disorders, the Kerner Report. It used 1960 census data to show that in the Milwaukee Standard Metropolitan Statistical Area the proportion of poor nonwhites was three times that of poor whites. That is, 26.1 percent of the nonwhite families had incomes under three thousand dollars a year compared with only 8.8 percent of the white families. A valid point. The report failed to note, however, that in actual numbers the poverty problem in Milwaukee was largely a poor-white problem: 30,026 poor whites to 4,191 poor nonwhites.

the lower-middle-class whites who comprise the great body of the electorate have lost confidence in the upper-middle-class whites who have been running the country for the past decade.

This dilemma was clearly exemplified at the time in New York City as white school-teachers, policemen, and parents revolted against the leadership of Mayor John V. Lindsay. As the *New York Times* noted, these people felt Lindsay was "too interested in the stylish rich and the striving poor." "Lindsay," said the director of a New York civic organization, "just doesn't seem to understand the life of a mailman or a cop. They feel he is buying racial peace by giving away to Harlem what the middle class needs." Lindsay owed his subsequent reelection in 1969 to the fact that two conservative candidates, Democrat Mario A. Procaccino and Republican John J. Marchi, split the Whitetown vote. He also worked hard in the months before the election to win back the Whitetowners. But the *Times,* in a post-election analysis, found that the city's nonwhite poor and the rich were keys to the Mayor's victory.

Whitetown's problem is basically economic. Twenty years ago, seventy-five hundred dollars sounded like easy street. For a family man today it is not enough for real comfort. The havelittles in Whitetown find themselves just one notch above subsistence. Their tax burden is heavy, their neighborhood services poor, their national image tarnished, and their political influence slight. As they stew and fret about their place on the lower rungs of the economic ladder, they see the black man moving up. They worry about job security and about the value of their houses should Whitetown—God forbid—ever be integrated. And so they react bitterly, viscerally, to Black Power, black militancy, the thrust of Negroes in politics, jobs, housing, and education.

This racial crisis poisons our body politic today and preoccupies our politicians and people. The fact is, however, that Whitetown's basic problem transcends the color line. It is rooted in the past, in the class structure of American life, and in the effect that ethnicity, national origins, and religion have had on the ability or inability of individual white Americans to "make it" in America. Many of the Whitetowners haven't made it because the cards have been stacked against them. For many, alienation, underrepresentation, voicelessness, and violence have been historical conditions of life.

"We shall not understand the contemporary United States," wrote Frederick Jackson Turner in 1893, "without studying immigration historically." This is still true. The United States is, of course, a nation of immigrants. But some classes of immigrants have almost always been on top while others remain on the bottom. Changes occur only gradually over a period of not years but generations.

For a long time we deluded ourselves into thinking that such was not the case. We were persuaded that America was one giant mixing bowl where all men became equal. "Here individuals of all nations are melted into a new race of men," wrote St. John de Crèvecoeur in 1782. And much later, in 1908, Israel Zangwill exulted,

America is God's Crucible, the great Melting Pot where all races of Europe are merging and reforming.... Germans and Frenchmen, Irishmen and Englishmen, Jews and Russians—into the Crucible with you all! God is making the Americans.

In the century and a quarter between Crèvecoeur and Zangwill, more than thirty-five million men, women, and children came to the United States. It was the greatest migration in human history. This incredible uprooting reached into every nook and cranny of Europe. More than four and a half million emigrated from Ireland, over four million from Great Britain, six million from what became Germany, eight million from the old Austrian and Russian empires—Poles and Jews, Hungarians, Bohemians, Slovaks, Ukrainians, Ruthenians; three million from the Balkans and Asia Minor—Greeks and Macedonians, Croations and Albanians, Syrians and Armenians.

There were many exceptions, of course, but millions of these immigrants, Oscar Handlin concluded from an exhaustive examination of their letters, were simple peasants. With a heritage of centuries of life on the land in close-knit villages, they were conservative. Their traditions and religious faiths were deeply implanted. In the Old World, these people "knew their place." They were ignorant of democratic processes and American politics.

Even those who quickly learned how one makes one's way in the United States found formidable obstacles massed against them. More than half of the immigrants up to 1860 were Roman Catholics, and millions of Catholics followed in the period up to 1920. But the United States was largely white Anglo-Saxon Protestant turf. Anti-Romanism was the oldest and most deeply entrenched of American prejudices. Discrimination against non-WASPs was almost as pervasive, though certainly not as brutal or relentless, as the repression of Negroes. It was no accident that of the thirty-three American Presidents from George Washington to Dwight D. Eisenhower, twenty-eight were of British stock and thirty were Protestants. John F. Kennedy, who broke the string in 1960, was distinctly Protestant in his education and style, and his religious faith seemed closely attuned to the liberalism and humanitarianism of the "Protestant Pope," John XXIII. Before he could be elected, Kennedy was virtually forced to promise not to side with his coreligionists (in the parochial-school-aid battle). He simply was not perceived as an Irish Cath-

olic in the same way that, for example, Alfred E. Smith was, in his losing race for the Presidency in 1928.

It was no accident, either, that of the scores of Cabinet officers appointed by Presidents between 1789 and 1933, only four were Catholics. Despite the very heavy emigration from Italy, the first Italian-American was not elected governor of a state until 1936 and the first Italian-American United States Senator was not seated until 1950. (In both cases the state was Rhode Island and the successful politician, John Pastore.)

The WASPs who ran the country in the eighteenth and nineteenth centuries welcomed non-WASP immigrants for two reasons. First, America's growing economic machine needed unskilled manpower to dig canals, lay railroad beds, mine coal and iron, work as domestics, and fill the many low-echelon service jobs in burgeoning cities. Second, it was universally accepted that authentic Anglo-Saxons could be produced whatever the mixture of nationality groups. That is, the WASPs thought the immigrants would quickly shed their ethnic identities, forsake their "foreign" cultures and churches, and become "just like us." And so there would be one vast nation of Americans all reflecting the ways of thinking and doing of the majority group. The melting-pot assimilation concept took hold and the WASPs didn't feel threatened.

For the most part, the immigrants came here and did what they were supposed to do. In 1850, 48 percent of Boston's Irish were manual laborers and 15.3 percent were domestic servants—almost two-thirds thus at the very bottom of the economic pyramid. As late as 1900, a study found that for every hundred dollars earned by a native-born worker, the Italian-born immigrant earned eighty-four dollars, the Hungarian sixty-eight, and other Europeans fifty-four. For good jobs the word continued to go out: "Irish need not apply."

Just as Negroes are blamed for most of the urban crime and social unrest today, so were the immigrants a century ago. They were often ill-fed, ill-housed, illiterate—and rebellious. Handlin found that 57 percent of the convicts in Boston's House of Correction in 1862 were Irish and 75 percent of the 12,914 persons arrested in Boston two years later were Irish.

From 1830 to 1870, the Irish caused riots in nearly every major city. Because so many Irish-Americans named Patrick, or Paddy, were carted off to jail, the vehicles that transported them came to be known as paddy wagons. The name has stuck, even though many of today's riders in police vans in the cities are black.

Needless to say, the natives viewed the immigrants' life style with extreme distaste. They blamed the newcomers for the rise in pauperism, crime, drunkenness, and political corruption. In a burst of invective in 1839, Philip Hone, who had formerly been mayor of New York, charged that his city was "infected by gangs of hardened wretches, born in the haunts of infamy, brought up in taverns . . . [who] patrol the streets, making night hideous." Never one to mince words, Hone identified the Irish as "the most ignorant and consequently the most obstinate white men in the world."

His speech was relatively mild compared to the anti-immigrant tirades of Southerners. In the same year that Hone was accusing the Irish of ruining New York, the Louisiana Native American Association outdid him. "When we see hordes . . . of beings in human form," it cried,

but destitute of any intellectual aspirations—the outcast and offal of society, the pauper, the vagrant and the convict—transported in myriads to our shores, reeking with the accumulated crimes of the whole civilized and savage world and inducted by our laws into equal rights, immunities and privileges with the noble, native

inhabitants of the United States, we can no longer contemplate it with supine indifference.

The press was also guilty of incredible excesses. Fortunately for them, many of the immigrants could not read, for they would have seen themselves often maligned in the newspapers. Roman Catholics were abused on every hand. In 1833 the Second Provincial Council of American Bishops issued a pastoral letter accusing the press of being "unkind and unjust" to Catholics.

"Not only do they assail us and our institution in a style of vituperation and offense, misrepresent our tenets, vilify our practices, repeat the hundred-times' refuted calumnies of the days of angry and bitter contention in other lands," cried the bishops, "but they have even denounced you and us as enemies to the liberties of the Republic."

Still, the onslaught against foreign visitors continued.

"Madam Castellan's concert in Philadelphia on Saturday night was a complete failure," reported a Philadelphia paper in November 1843. "We are glad to perceive that the petty parsimony of these foreign adventurers is met by a corresponding want of patronage." The Boston *American Traveller and Farmer's Advocate* reprinted the Philadelphia story and added:

Madam Ciuti and some fiddler who performed here on Saturday night did not come off much better. It is astonishing how our citizens will continue to be humbugged and taxed by these beggars from other shores. . . . Away with your Castellans and Ciutis and give us a concert from our own brigade band or one of our city musical organizations.

The fact was, of course, that the immigrants did bring grave social problems to the cities. But often they became the scapegoat for every urban woe and shortcoming. Certainly, a breakdown in city government similar to what we are witnessing today occurred when immigration tides ran high.

Already in 1888 James Bryce, in *The American Commonwealth,* was saying that "the government of cities is the one conspicuous failure of the United States." He noted that blame was being heaped on the immigrants and wrote:

Nevertheless the immigrants are not so largely responsible for the faults of American politics as a stranger might be led, by the language of many Americans, to suppose. There is a disposition in the United States to use them, and especially the Irish, much as the cat is used in the kitchen, to account for broken plates and food which disappears. The cities have, no doubt, suffered from the immigrants . . . but New York was not an Eden before the Irish came.

Whatever headaches the immigrants gave urban authorities were more than offset by their contributions to America's economy and to its expanding military strength. During the years of heaviest immigration, from 1890 to 1910, United States coal production tripled and steel output multiplied seven times. The foreign-born, Samuel Lubell wrote in *The Future of American Politics,* accounted for 60 percent of the nation's packing-house workers, 57 percent of the iron- and steelworkers, 61 percent of the miners, and 70 percent of the textile and clothing workers. For their labor, the immigrants received low pay and discriminatory treatment. Nowhere was this more evident than in the one-industry coal and steel towns. The separation of foreign-born laborers and WASP managers in these towns was as complete, says Lubell, as that between serfs and lords on a feudal manor.

In fighting for their country, the ethnic Americans have compiled a record that is unexcelled in the annals of United States military history. With the waging of unpopular wars in Korea and Vietnam, their flag-waving patriotism has gone out of style and their exploits on the battlefield have been largely forgotten. Yet they helped make the United States a world power. Of course, it is often the ethnic Americans who are the most militantly anti-communist, the most chauvinistic, the most willing to support higher and higher arms spending, and most inclined to see the world as dividing between the forces of good (us) and the forces of evil (the other guys). But their fighting spirit is unmistakable.

The Irish especially have felt a compulsion to prove their patriotism in battle. In the Civil War, they formed a major portion of the Union Army, not so much because of their devotion to abolition—their anti-draft riots in 1863 shook New York—but because they lacked the financial means to avoid conscription as so many WASPs avoided it. The famed Irish Brigade distinguished itself in combat in the Civil War just as New York's "Fighting Sixty-ninth" Regiment was to do in World War I.

Throughout the Civil War years, immigrants flocked to America. In the first four months of 1863 alone, 38,720 landed in New York. The *Philadelphia Inquirer* printed these figures and editorialized:

Such a phenomenon as is here presented, of vast numbers of immigrants seeking a country afflicted by Rebellion, can scarcely be paralleled in the world's history. It speaks with telling emphasis of the confidence of the European masses in the future of our country, and of the stability of the Government whose blessings they have come to enjoy.

Of the first hundred thousand United States Army volunteers in 1917, no fewer than forty thousand were said to be Polish-Americans. Although the Poles were only 4 percent of the population, they accounted for 12 percent of the United States war dead in World War I. And, according to Army and Navy records, about 20 percent of the American armed forces on the eve of Pearl Harbor consisted of men of Polish extraction.

It appears that even now disproportionate numbers of Whitetowners are in uniform. A *Philadelphia Bulletin* study in

September 1966 found both induction and enlistment rates in Philadelphia higher among whites than nonwhites. The differences were statistically significant. And most of these white servicemen came from working-class sections where the college-going rate—and draft-deferment rate—is low. What's more, the Whitetowners are proud of their record. Drive through an

Germany, and Scandinavia. Besides the much-maligned Irish, these included many urban Jews and middle-class Protestants who adjusted quickly to American life and were assimilated. But then came the great wave of Italian and Polish peasants, Jews fleeing persecution in Russia, and other "undesirables" from Eastern Europe. The figures tell their story:

IMMIGRATION

Country of Origin	1871–1880	1881–1890	1891–1900	1901–1910	1911–1920
Italy	55,000	300,000	651,000	2,045,000	1,100,000
Russia (including many Poles and Jews)	39,000	213,000	505,000	1,500,000	1,000,000
Austria-Hungary (many Poles and Slavs)	72,000	350,000	600,000	2,150,000	unavailable

ethnic neighborhood in Philadelphia or Chicago or Cleveland or Detroit and you will see entire blocks welcoming servicemen home with flags and bunting. In the old sections of every big city there is this kind of spirit; in the suburbs, where properties are bigger and loyalties less intense, you rarely find it no matter how hard you look.

For the last forty-five years immigration has been negligible, and we have tended to forget how the country—and the Congress—treated the immigrants. What happened in the early years of this century may help to explain, however, what's happening in Whitetown today.

Through most of the nineteenth century immigration was unrestricted. There were no national "quotas" and no limit on the number of people admitted to these shores each year. Until roughly 1890 the immigrants came largely from the British Isles,

Among the "right people," the cultural reaction to this tremendous influx of poor foreigners was harsh. It amounted to a WASP backlash. Concerns grew lest the nation be overrun by Catholics, Jews, and radicals and the purity of the race imperiled. Indeed, Henry Steele Commager sees the 1890s as the watershed separating rural, idealistic, confident America and urban, pragmatic, insecure America. By 1900, one-third of all American farmers were tenants. Ignatius Donnelly's preamble to the 1892 Populist platform had warned:

We meet in the midst of a nation brought to the verge of moral, political and material ruin . . . business prostrated, homes covered with mortgages, labor impoverished, and the land concentrating in the hands of capitalists. The [native-born] urban workmen are denied the right to organize for self-protection. Imported, pauperized labor beats down their wages.

In this climate, the Ku Klux Klan gained

wide support in the North and Middle West. To separate the "old" immigrants from the "new," such Protestant patriotic societies as the Daughters of the American Revolution and the Sons of the American Revolution were organized and flourished. To control the newcomers' drinking habits, the Anti-Saloon League was founded in 1893. Together with the older Women's Christian Temperance Union, it successfully led the fight for a nationwide ban on the sale of alcoholic beverages. And later, in Oregon, an attempt to close all Catholic schools reached the Supreme Court, where it was thwarted in a historic decision.

The migration of Southern Negroes to Northern cities during and after World War I lessened the need for cheap foreign labor. With the nation in no mood to accept more immigrants anyway, Congress in 1921 and 1924 drastically reduced immigration and overhauled the entire system.

Previously, the criterion for admission to this country had been personal merit regardless of nationality. Now the criterion was pegged solely to race and ethnic origin. For the first time a quota system was instituted. And each national group's quota was based on its ethnic representation in the United States back in 1890, before the heaviest tide of Italian and Eastern European immigration.

Congress knew what it was doing. By turning back the calendar, it guaranteed that 79 percent of all future immigrants would come from "safe" countries—Great Britain, Germany, the Netherlands, Scandinavia—plus Ireland. For the unwanted Italians and Poles immigration fell to almost nothing. Asians, being considered unassimilable, were excluded altogether. This blatantly racist policy remained in force, with only minor changes, until October 3, 1965, when President Lyndon B. Johnson signed a more liberal law returning to the criterion of individual merit regardless of nationality. Since then immigration from

Southern and Eastern Europe has markedly increased, thus adding to the number of Whitetowners.

Although the last period of heavy immigration is long past, it is important to note that even today half of the Roman Catholic adults in this country are immigrants themselves or the children of immigrants. "We are," Father Andrew M. Greeley, priest-sociologist at the University of Chicago, has written, "but a generation or two away from the peasant farms of Europe."

Many Catholics in the Whitetowns of America have had difficulty throwing off the shackles of their peasant heritage. "It seems that Catholics creep forward rather than stride forward in American society," wrote John J. Kane in *The American Catholic Sociological Review*, "and the position of American Catholics in the mid-twentieth century is better, but not so much better than it was a century ago.

What all this means is that just as Negroes today find it hard to advance in American society so, historically, did large numbers of immigrants and so do many still.

"Today, whites tend to exaggerate how well and quickly they escaped from poverty," reported President Johnson's National Advisory Commission on Civil Disorders, headed by former Governor Otto Kerner of Illinois.

The fact is, among the southern and eastern immigrants who came to America in the last great wave of immigration, those who came already urbanized were the first to escape from poverty. The others who came to America from rural backgrounds, as Negroes did, are only now, after three generations, in the final stages of escaping from poverty. . . . Because of favorable economic and political conditions, these ethnic groups were able to escape from lower-class status to working-class and lower-middle-class status, but it has taken them three generations.

I have no intention of suggesting that the immigrants' existence was totally bleak or in any way comparable to the oppression visited upon black people. There is simply no comparison, and those who attempt to draw comparisons have not read Negro—or American—history. America wasn't the land of milk and honey for all newcomers, as the history books suggested, but it did offer unparalleled opportunities. Rags-to-riches didn't happen often, but it happened. While countless immigrants found life terribly hard, the achievements of others have been remarkable.

It is true that all kinds of stunts were used to entice immigrants here. Steamship brokers recruited throughout Europe, U.S. railroads vigorously colonized for foreign workers, and some states sent agents abroad scouting for laborers. Yet all who came to America came voluntarily. And the greatest inducement to come was provided by those already here. The expectations of the immigrants crowding into the big cities seventy-five years ago were not as high as are those of the urban migrants—the Negroes—in today's affluence. Expecting less, the immigrants made do with less and were pleased with less. And in their letters home many no doubt embellished their own limited successes.

"A letter to those who feared to take the risk of emigration," wrote Joseph A. Wyrtrwal, in *America's Polish Heritage,*

would put the entire Polish village in a state of tingling excitement. Every word was received like a jewel. The clear, detailed sentences were first read and reread by the simple, credulous people to whom they were originally addressed, then widely circulated among relatives and friends, and often through the whole village.

Coming from autocratic Europe, with its rigid class structure, the immigrants found American society, with all its defects, much more open and democratic. For the "huddled masses yearning to breathe free," this *was* the land of opportunity. Their letters were full of poignant references to their new rights and responsibilities. "Schools here are free for everyone." "Any man may speak what is on his mind without the least fear." "If a man will work, he need never go hungry." "Here it is not asked, What or who was your father, but the question is, What are you?" "Learning flows free . . . I saw before me free schools, free colleges, where I could learn and keep on learning."

What's more—and this is of key importance—the political structure in American cities took the special needs of immigrants into consideration. The immigrants needed jobs, loans, and often food, coal, rent money, help in dealing with police and the city bureaucracy. In those days, there were few places to turn for help. There were no social workers or welfare agencies, no United Fund, no aid-to-dependent children programs, no Social Security, no unemployment compensation.

Into the breach stepped the political machines. Reaching down into the wards and the precincts, the bosses took the immigrants by the hand and, in exchange for votes—lots of votes, often more than one vote per man—they helped them survive in the cities. All blessings flowed not from Washington but from the political clubhouse. At wakes and weddings, confirmations and *bar mitzvahs,* your friendly neighborhood committeeman or precinct captain could be counted on. And if a man needed a pushcart license, the party would see that he got one.

So immigration and machine politics fitted hand in glove. "The classic urban machine and the century of immigration which ended in the 1920's," wrote Elmer E. Cornwell, Jr., in the *Annals of the American Academy of Political and Social Science,* "were intimately intertwined phenomena. . . . The machine would probably not have been possible, and certainly would not have been so prominent a feature of the

American political landscape, without the immigrant."

As the Kerner Commission stated in its 1968 report, the political bosses traded economic advantages for political support: "Ward-level grievance machinery, as well as personal representation, enabled the immigrant to make his voice heard and his power felt."

In other words, the kind of local control over political decision making that minority groups now are seeking in big cities actually existed to a marked degree for the immigrants. If they didn't actually control their own destinies, the men who did were down the street. And starting with Alfred E. Smith's bid for the Presidency in 1928, the immigrants found a national voice within the Democratic Party.

With the decline of immigration, a new urban political structure began to take shape. The style that Richard Hofstadter, in *The Age of Reform*, described as stressing "strong personal loyalties above allegiance to abstract codes of law or morals" was gradually discarded. This was the city boss, immigrant Catholic style. In its place came the middle-class Protestant reformer style of city government, emphasizing honesty, efficiency—and a cold impersonality.

"The introduction of a merit system and a professionalized civil service," said the Kerner Commission, "has made management of the cities more businesslike, but it has also tended to depersonalize and isolate government."

City Hall thus became less susceptible to corruption, but swept out with the scandals were the close ties between the people and the political machines. As City Hall reformers installed computers and began accounting for every paper clip, they lost touch with the "little people" in Whitetown and Blacktown.

The Kerner Commission pointed out the damaging effect of this change on urban Negroes. They suffered, it said, a "pro-found sense of isolation and alienation from the processes and programs of government." The same can be said of the foreign-stock Whitetowners. And, as we have seen, there are more low-income whites than low-income nonwhites in every major American city.

Just as city politics changed to the disadvantage of the ethnic Americans so did national politics. In the administrations of John F. Kennedy and Lyndon B. Johnson, the great Democratic coalition begun by Smith and forged masterfully by Franklin D. Roosevelt in the thirties began to fly apart. Always a totally implausible amalgam—blacks and whites, workers and intellectuals, Northern liberals and Southern segregationists—nobody really knew how it lasted as long as it did. But when the coalition weakened in the 1960s it was the Whitetowners who walked out. They turned to Wallace or Richard M. Nixon. They turned to the right, to "law and order" and conservatism.

To them, it appeared that upper-middle-class whites were shaping policies to benefit poor blacks. There didn't seem to be anything in it for them. And they had a point.

"This—majority—group of Americans . . . has to be asking whether the government is playing favorites, or greasing squeaky wheels, or whatever," observed Daniel P. Moynihan, then director of the Harvard-MIT Joint Center for Urban Studies and now President Nixon's Special Assistant for Urban Affairs, in an article in *The Public Interest* early in 1968. "We have established a Job Corps for the dropout and a Peace Corps for the college graduate, but the plain fellow with a high school diploma, and his parents, have little to show from either the New Frontier or the Great Society."

Taking the same position, columnist Joseph Kraft, in June 1968, argued that low-income whites had been "conned" into support of liberal economic and social welfare policies without really approving of them. What the nation must do, said Kraft, is "re-engage the sympathies of the low-income whites . . . for humane purposes."

Politics is not alone, however, in isolating and alienating the Whitetowners. In this period of sexual permissiveness, God-is-dead theology, student revolts, and war protests, their old-fashioned patriotism, religious fundamentalism, and family togetherness have gone out of style. True, the sex revolution, for example, troubles American parents across the board. But in Whitetown, where the authoritarianism has been more rigid and the attachment to old rules of conduct stronger, the blow has fallen harder.

Whitetown was not ready for the technological revolution, either, having traditionally valued brawn over brains. Its youth have gone to vocational schools and then into the mills and blue-collar jobs. But in today's worldwide competition for what Alfred North Whitehead termed "trained intelligence," working-class skills have lost their importance. Only 6 percent of the "working Americans" described by Robert Wood, formerly of the Department of Housing and Urban Development, continued their education beyond high school, while 43 percent stopped at eighth grade. Income and education being inextricably linked in American economics, few high-school dropouts will ever make it. Many Whitetowners are thus lost in the shuffle.

For all of these reasons, Whitetown—to outsiders, at least—appears to be on the skids. Its housing is deteriorating. It is losing population. It has few responsible spokesmen at the local level and no leadership. In the black ghettos of big cities where renewal and redevelopment have been carried out extensively, if often controversially, there is a vitality, a sense of change, even improvement, that is lacking in Whitetown.

Rarely do you see new houses, new businesses or industries in Whitetown. Often, though, you see new expressways slicing through its heart. In many cities freeways crisscross the old ethnic neighborhoods en route to the expensive housing, fancy shopping centers, and modern industrial parks of shiny suburbia. Not only do these freeways destroy the unity of America's Whitetowns but they also hasten the exodus of Whitetowners, thus undermining what little stability these old ethnic neighborhoods have left. The federal government rarely spends a nickel to help Whitetown, but it has put billions into expressways.

In light of these facts and in historical perspective, it should be no surprise that the working-class white is angry and frustrated, that out of economic fear and a sense of his own powerlessness he sees the Negro as his competitor who wants his job, house, and neighborhood.

"No one listens to us and our problems, no one cares about us or appreciates the contributions we have made to American life," Barbara Mikulski, Baltimore social worker and third-generation Polish-American, complained to an American Jewish Committee conference in Philadelphia late in 1969.

I'd like to tell you why we are troubled. First, we are tired of being politically courted and then legally extorted. Second, we are sick and tired of institutions, both public and private, not being responsive or responsible to the people they were instituted to serve. Third, we feel powerless in our dealings with these monoliths. Fourth, we do not like being blamed for all of the problems of black America. Fifth, and perhaps the key, we anguish at all of the class prejudice that is forced upon us.

The combative and articulate four-foot-eleven-inch Miss Mikulski terms immigrants drawn here for unskilled labor and factory work the "urban niggers of the industrialized society."

Those who remain blue-collar workers are the field hands and we who moved up into white-collar positions are the house niggers with all of the brainwashing that it implies. . . . The only place we feel any sense of identity, community, or control is that little home we prize. But there again we feel threatened by black people. Ethnic Americans do not feel that black people are inferior but regard them as territorial aggressors on their residential and employment turfs.

Many ethnic Americans also believe that black people, far from being beaten down by Whitetowners or anyone else, are now getting all the breaks in this country. They reject the Kerner Commission's charge that the United States is infected with "white racism."

"My family came over here to get away from the Russians," said a Polish-American machinist, drinking coffee in his sixty-five-hundred-dollar house in Philadelphia's Whitetown.

This is reality. This is why my mother came here. If my mother, when she was twelve or thirteen years old, was strong enough to get on the boat and make a new life for herself somewhere else, I feel that these people [blacks] should have courage enough to fight for what they want and to get away from this business of, "Why, damn, man, you're screwing me."

And this is the feeling I get. Sometimes they come out and say this. They base their whole argument on this: "We're going to beat you down. We're going to take what you got because you beat us for a hundred years"—and I don't feel that I beat them for a hundred years. I don't feel that I've ever beat them. I didn't come in contact with them until I was twenty-five years old.

Whitetowners are hostile to all outsiders, but for newspapermen and television and radio people they reserve a special animosity. They're convinced that the press, especially the "Eastern internationalist press," unfairly dismisses them all as racists, bigots, and ignoramuses without digging into the real issues to see what makes them react as they do.

There is, I think, some truth to this charge. But the Whitetowners often invite such characterizations by behaving just like bigots, racists, and ignoramuses. For example, I heard a Philadelphia Whitetowner climax a dialogue with a bartender by declaiming proudly, "I'd rather live in a tent than next to a nigger."

In another saloon, this one in Queens, after the tumultuous Democratic Convention in Chicago in August 1968, columnist Jimmy Breslin encountered two Whitetowners whose conversation he felt compelled to share with his readers. I can see why; the two made good copy and they were archetypes of the tough, blunt know-nothings sometimes found in Whitetown. The week before, Chicago's Mayor Richard Daley had converted his city into an armed camp and ordered police to crack down on protestors at the convention. Most of the press and the upper middle class were appalled at Daley's doings. Breslin discovered that the Whitetowners were overjoyed.

"He's a real American," a beer-truck driver was saying to the bartender.
"Yes, he is," the bartender said.
"We could use a mayor like that here in this city, brother could we use him" the beer-truck driver said.
"He makes sense," the bartender said. "This guy Lindsay is a nigger-lover."
"Daley don't care, he takes 'em all on, niggers, hippies, anybody," the beer-truck driver said.

As the election campaign wore on, liberal and New Left writers began to take a new —and less damning—look at the white working class.

After covering the Wallace campaign in New England for New York's Greenwich Village weekly, the *Village Voice*, Paul Cowan reported:

There is a real temptation, in writing about the working-class people who attend the Wallace rallies, to mock their lives and habits or to profess outrage at their new beliefs. . . .

But when you talk to such people you feel a

surge of sympathy, for they are this decade's invisible men. They are not fascists but sad, confused human beings whose lives have turned out to be far worse than they had hoped.

Similarly, reporter and social critic Andrew Kopkind, after a visit to Cleveland's Whitetown for his muckraking weekly, *Mayday,* now called *Hard Times,* found that

while the blacks are baited, the poor programmed, the students beaten, the elites honored, and the New Class celebrated—the white workingmen are ignored. . . .

They are neither quite bad enough for slum-clearance nor quite good enough for segregation. Around them, the atmosphere is thick and heavy —with smoke and dust, boredom and frustration.

Cowan's and, to some extent, Kopkind's observations smacked of condescension. And there's nothing that white working people resent more than being talked down to. Free-lance writer Nicholas Pileggi found this out when, in an article in *New York* magazine, he used the wrong term to describe the clustering of Italian-Americans on Manhattan's Lower East Side. The term was promptly flung back into his teeth: "Ghetto! What ghetto? This ain't no ghetto, this is our home and we got no riots and we got no crime on the streets and we got no Cleveland here."

When John G. McCullough, editor of the *Philadelphia Bulletin's* editorial page, visited South Philadelphia's "Little Italy" following trouble at a predominantly Negro vocational school in the neighborhood, he also got a lecture from one of the residents. "What you have now," the man told the editor, "are a lot of pointed heads and non-degree sociologists making field trips into South Philadelphia to study the natives. They've got everything but butterfly nets. . . . [They think that] we're all just bigots and racists and street fighters."

For a long time, sociologists with or without advanced degrees paid the Whitetowns of America little heed. They failed either

to see the mounting problems that working-class white people faced or to find these problems interesting enough to investigate, or else hesitated to show an interest in them for fear that their peers might think them bigoted or racist themselves.

Now, as I've indicated, these problems are being examined. Robert Wood, in his remarkable but little noticed Lincoln, Mass., speech in 1967, pinpointed the issue:

The future of city-building in America turns less on the indignation of the disprivileged [the urban blacks] or the conscience of the exceptional [well-off suburban whites] than is commonly supposed.

The issue becomes increasingly how to dispose the working American to reorient his life from one of relative isolation and alienation and to find real aspirations in participation in a genuine community.

We neglect the working American at our peril.

Wood also urged an end to name-calling. "To march to the core city, to preach, to scold can only serve to make the working American confront, not encounter, the urban newcomer," he said.

David Danzig, late associate professor of social work at Columbia University's School of Social Work, argued that just because ethnic birds of a feather flock together didn't automatically make them racist hawks. He also opposed rhetorical imprecations.

Few people who live in socially separated ethnic communities, as most Americans do, can be persuaded that because their communities are also racially separated they are morally sick. Having come to accept their own social situation as the natural result of their ethnic affinities, mere exhortation is not likely to convince them—or, for that matter, the public at large—that they are thereby imposing upon others a condition of apartheid.

Put another way, Whitetowners really don't see how they, as comparative newcomers without much power, money, or influence, can be blamed for spreading white racism in America. "They just don't under-stand the concept of collective guilt," said Andrew Valuchek, special assistant on minorities for the Democratic National Committee. "They say, 'We're not in a posi-tion of power. It's unfair to call us collec-tively guilty of discrimination.' "

Possibly the Whitetowners are no more guilty than the rest of white America—but they certainly seem blatantly culpable when they show up on the television news cursing and hooting the "niggers" and encouraging their small children to do the same.

Maybe it takes a Whitetowner to under-stand a Whitetowner. Dennis Clark, writer, urbanologist, and staff member of Temple University's Center for Community Studies, grew up in Philadelphia's Whitetown. A boilermaker's son, he survived "amateur bouts at the Cambria [a neighborhood fight joint, long shut down, that might have been the model for "Stag at Sharkey's"], bad booze in Spud Murphy's, choir practice at the Visitation [Roman Catholic Church] and pursuits by Reading Railroad cops."

Clark thinks many ethnics reflect "the stamp of old tribal grudges" and "the fero-cious prejudices of the Old World."

"They represent failure in the great American sweepstakes and in getting the goodies," he says. "They represent a certain amount of pathology. They represent people set adrift from another culture. They represent insecurity. They represent a lot of free-floating aggression against neighboring groups, whoever the neighbor-ing groups happen to be."

But Clark also says of Whitetown:

The people show the marks of the punishment meted out to the lower echelons of the white working class by industrial society. If their psy-chology is one of self-reliance and pugnacity, cynicism and rude social attitudes, it is because they have themselves been frequently denied, punished and baffled by life.

They know and respect what is closest to them: home and church. Higher education, civic betterment, government, the "organization man" corporate world are all alien. They have strug-gled with the industrial and technical society, not understanding it, and have often lost. They are the stepchildren of the industrial system. For Negroes, the true orphans of the system, they have scant sympathy left over.

Clark was talking about Philadelphia Whitetowners. But much of what he says I think applies to working-class ethnic Americans wherever they are. Many of them are in trouble. It is now widely recog-nized that the "true orphans" of our indus-trial society need all the help that can be marshaled for them. It is time to recognize that the "stepchildren" need help, too.

6 Decision Control

MANIPULATION AND CONTROL

The Editors

The fabric of social life is heavily dependent upon the existence of control techniques and influence processes. Man continually tries to influence or control the behavior of others by manipulating his own behavior and various other resources which he can make available or withhold from others. In fact, social life is only possible to the extent that culture operates as a coercive force influencing members of a society to think and behave in accord with established traditions. As one social scientist has noted, each generation faces the threat that it will be overcome by a wave of barbarians. These barbarians are, of course, the new generation of children—those who as yet are unfamiliar with the patterns of living of the society into which they are born.

Advances in scientific and technological knowledge over the last several decades have increased the current use and future potential of *planned, consciously applied control* techniques on human behavior. We are experiencing, on a scale never thought possible, the application of many techniques and practices, the uses of which have not been fully explored. Centralized data banks bringing together a lifetime of information on every citizen are now in increasing use and have been proposed on a very large scale. Drug therapies and psychological analysis have been widely applied to problems ranging from treating mental illness to selling mouthwash. Highly sensitive and unobtrusive electronic devices for "picking up" and recording sound are now standard equipment available to all.

The existence of this new technology raises serious questions concerning the net balance of consequences (favorable and unfavorable) in their use. Certainly, computerized and centralized record systems developed by the federal government would greatly facilitate the activities of many branches of government in serving the people. Yet such centralized data also increase the totalitarian potential of a society as it slowly encroaches on the private world of every citizen.

There is another sense, however, in which the new technology goes far beyond simply value-based disagreements in the uses and consequences of technology. There is the distinct possibility that centralized and computerized decision-making systems make the issues of value disagreement over uses and consequences an irrelevant one. Many of the new technological advances create problems of removing decision making from the people so that value disagreements do not even occur. This is the real issue behind what is called decision control. The technology itself can become self-perpetuating and self-validating.

This tendency toward the emergence of decision-making systems which are impervious to external validation or control has a well-established home in bureaucracy, whether or not there is an elaborate surveillance technology. This can be seen in the operation of government employment programs which subject prospective employees to testing on such personal matters as sex, politics, associations, and beliefs for the purpose of screening security risks. Once such programs are established they are often found to be used for employees in nonsensitive positions (Ridgeway, 1964).

Similar examples are found in the recent controversy on wiretapping between the Attorney General's office and the Federal Bureau of Investigation (Cipes, 1966). The federal government makes a distinction between the use of electronic devices to overhear a conversation ("bugging") and the interception of a telephone communication (wiretapping). Bugging is not prohibited by federal statute and is used in matters related to national security and high-level organized crime. Wiretapping is prohibited by federal law, but has been used in situations involving intelligence activities and national security. In such cases wiretapping must be carried out with the approval and supervision of the Attorney General. Such approval should be hard to obtain but the evidence shows that even Eleanor Roosevelt and Martin Luther King, Jr., were authorized for wiretapping and the FBI took such authorization as a license, in the case of King, to bug his hotel room and criticize him for his personal behavior (Navasky, 1970).

What many court cases concerning the legality of wiretapping and bugging clearly indicate is the difficulty involved in trying to restrain law-enforcement agencies from full-scale use of the surveillance technology. This is quite understandable, for it is the law-enforcement agent's job to collect information bearing on a certain case whether or not that evidence is admissible in a court of law. Often they may hope that the illegal use of wiretapping may reveal information about a suspect which can then be pursued with legal approval.

Such incidents clearly reflect a situation where the technology itself cannot be adequately restrained. There are also a small but growing number of incidents reported in the press where surveillance technology is used in industry for protection of industrial secrets or the pursuit of a competitor's secrets. The most popularized incident of an attempt by private industry to protect its interests through surveillance techniques is that concerning the author Ralph Nader (*Unsafe at Any Speed*) and General Motors. Nader, who was researching the auto industry for a book on safety standards among auto manufacturers, was faced with an inquiry into his personal and professional life by private investigators in the employ of auto firms. Such investigations can be very effective means of intimidations, as few people can subject their lives to a detailed investigation which would not reveal the elements of an incriminating dossier. Nor should people have to subject themselves to such investigations, which leave the traditional rights to privacy guaranteed only by the discretion of those organizations large and powerful enough to determine whom they wish to have shadowed and for what purposes.

The issue of privacy raises squarely the combined impact of technology and centralization. The techniques for fact finding via bugging, wire taps, personality tests and inventories, record search, microfilming, computerized information storage and retrieval are available. Their use, however, is limited to large governmental agencies like the Internal Revenue Service (which sought help from a Georgia public library in identifying users of certain "militant and subversive material") or private agencies like the tax-exempt American Security Council (which supplies sponsors such as National Airlines, Sears Roebuck, and Quaker Oats with information on over six million Americans including "peaceniks" and "pseudo-intellectuals"). Others like TRW Credit Data have files on 40 million Americans with 50,000 new files added each week.

The Senate Subcommittee on Constitutional Rights has revealed the extent of government file keeping, and has warned of the movement toward a mass surveillance system. The government is currently gathering information on its citizens at the following places: (1) a Secret Service computer containing in its memory the names and dossiers of "activists," "malcontents," and those who would "embarrass" government leaders; (2) a Justice Department data bank containing intelligence on individuals and groups involved in civil "disturbances" like peace rallies and welfare protests; and (3) the Army's Counterintelligence Analysis Division in Alexandria, Virgina, collects data on civilian activity related to civil disturbances, often through the use of agents who are assigned to "penetrate" peace groups and civil-rights organizations. These activities are carried out in addition to the extensive files on criminals maintained by the Federal Bureau of Investigation, and the quite varied information files maintained by the Department of Health, Education and Welfare (Boeth, 1970).

The availability of such data about ordinary citizens to military and investigatory agencies or to corporation credit departments raises the spectre of Big Brother, particularly because the concentration of technological resources in certain hands faces the vision screen in one direction only. The daily private dealings of the military and industrial elites are just not available to the citizen. For this reason it has been suggested that the socially conscious social scientist might do well to refrain from the study of powerless students, mental patients, criminals, and poor people for such sponsors as the giant foundations. He might do well to study instead the behavior of the foundations, corporations, and governmental agencies and to consider the poor and powerless to be his legitimate sponsors. These are the people who could really use a peek at the usually private data (Pilisuk, 1971).

The increased use of control through techniques developed in the behavioral sciences parallels an increase in the ability of large agencies to "manage" the news by withholding information or by exercising sanctions against "uncooperative" reporters or television studios. The process is generally subtle with news going through successive rewrites which filter out much criticism of dominant streams of thought. The process can also be more coercive; for example, an important information officer of the Defense Department threatened reporters who presented news from Vietnam inconsistent with American objectives there. Pulitzer prize-winning reporter Morley Safer reports a meeting of press correspondents in Saigon with the Assistant Secretary of Defense for Public Affairs, Arthur Sylvester.

> "I can't understand how you fellows can write what you do while American boys are dying out here," he began. Then he went on to the effect that American correspondents had a patriotic duty to disseminate only information that made the United States look good.
> A network television correspondent said, "Surely, Arthur, you don't expect the American press to be the handmaidens of government." "That's exactly what I expect," came the reply.
> An agency man raised the problem . . . about the credibility of American officials. Responded the Assistant Secretary of Defense for Public Affairs: "Look, if you think any American official is going to tell you the truth, then you're stupid. Did you hear that—stupid!" (Safer, 1966, pp. 9–10.)

This was followed by a vindictive threat by Sylvester to the effect that he did not even have to talk to reporters since he could deal with them through their editors. Such control over the release of information can be a powerful tool in maintaining popular support or in restricting popular criticism of the activities of government agencies.

Yet perhaps far more significant for the problem of news management or the use of public relations to conceal real conflicts is the growing threat to the free society of informed citizens that is posed by the media barons who are involved in local and regional monopolies of newspapers, radio stations, and television stations; the nationwide control over information exercised by NBC, CBS, and ABC; and the corporate conglomerates that control radio, TV, newspapers, and book-publishing companies. The enormity of the media conglomerates staggers the imagination. Federal Communications Commissioner Nicholas Johnson notes:

> ITT is a sprawling international conglomerate of 433 separate boards of directors that derives about 60 percent of its income from its significant holdings in at least forty foreign countries. It is the ninth largest industrial corporation in the world in size of work force. In addition to its sale of electronic equipment to foreign governments, and operation of foreign countries' telephone systems, roughly half of its domestic income comes from U.S. Government defense and space contracts. But it is also in the business of consumer finance, life insurance, investment funds, small loan companies, car rentals (ITT Avis, Inc.), and book publishing. (Johnson, 1968, p. 44.)

The ITT giant, with its board members including government officials in Britain, France, and Belgium, engineered a successful merger with the ABC network which, in 1966:

... owned 399 theaters in 34 states, 5 VHF television stations (all in the top 10 broadcasting markets), and, of course, one of the 3 major television networks and one of the 4 major radio networks in the world. Its 137 primary television network affiliates could reach 93 percent of the then 50 million television homes in the United States, and its radio affiliates could reach 97 percent of the then 55 million homes with radio receivers. ABC had ... affiliations with stations in 25 other nations, known as the "Worldvision Group." These, together with ABC Films, made the parent corporation perhaps the world's largest distributor of filmed shows for theaters and television stations throughout this country and abroad. ABC was heavily involved in the record production and distribution business, and other subsidiaries published three farm papers. (Johnson, 1968, p. 45.)

The occasion for Nicholas Johnson's inquiry was the merger case before the FCC of ITT and ABC. A minority of the Commission objected to the merger on the grounds that economic interests of ITT might exert an unconscious biasing factor on how ABC presented the news. There was nothing unconscious, however, about the attempts of ITT officials to squelch any reporting of the hearings which placed the merger in an unfavorable light. A radio reporter was pressured with false information about pending legislation to undermine the legitimacy of his station. Such abuses by the media are less likely to come to public light than abuses elsewhere. With media control highly centralized, the ideal of wide dissemination of the greatest range of information becomes increasingly constricted. People in our society have grown passive with regard to the world of outside events. A majority were not shocked even with news of a reported massacre by American soldiers. For most of us, acquaintance with the distant world comes only through the mass media. Failure to break the engineered conglomerate consensus in the media precludes discussion among the electorate of issues that make a difference in the direction in which the country is pointed. These new centers of information control run counter to the belief that a democratic society can remain strong only so long as there is criticism, guidance, and fresh ideas that affect all the constituent groups in society.

The papers in this section describe the capabilities and potentialities for control by government or other large organizations of the behavior and attitudes of the public. Starting first with the specific potentialities for control (as with bugging and wiretapping discussed earlier), the Packard article focuses on the uses of behavioral technology in creating artificial consumption patterns and conditioning buyers to be dissatisfied with last year's models. In the face of this technology, the average consumer finds that his needs are manipulated, his self-estimate is dependent on consumption behavior, and that he suffers from the sense of relative deprivation that is inherent in the patterns of planned obsolescence of products. Manipulation by marketing can sell people as well as products. The campaign that brought President Nixon to office spent 20 million dollars on television advertising. Planned by a marketing firm in much the same way as one would sell toothpaste, an image was created not of the essential characteristics or opinions of Mr. Nixon, but of the elements he seemed to lack in his appeal to voters (McGinnis, 1968). Goldhamer and Westrum describe the way in which political appeals can also be diverted toward specific groups through the use of computerized personal data about the electorate.

There is a growing trend among candidates for political office to use sophisticated techniques to determine what image will best appeal to a given section of the electorate. Most candidates feel that general appeals are not likely to be persuasive in urban areas of great diversity. To many candidates, the task of communicating with this electorate seems very difficult indeed. Campaigning today increasingly focuses on groups that might prove crucial to the candidate's victory. Census data, past election behavior, public opinion research, and a wealth of semi-public personal data (such as credit ratings, credit cards, magazine subscriptions, drivers' licenses, housing, etc.) have been computerized for many electoral districts. By applying this information intelligently, candidates can use a variety of media to make specialized appeals that emphasize those aspects of a candidate's image that each target group is likely to find most attractive and persuasive. (Goldhamer and Westrum, 1970, p. 14.)

An extreme form of behavior control is discussed in a review by Thomas Szasz (1965) of an autobiographical novel, entitled *Ward 7,* written by a Russian writer. In the novel a writer who is highly critical of life in Russia is arrested and committed to a psychiatric hospital after being judged insane. Szasz is concerned with the possible use of psychiatric definitions of illness and psychiatric controls to prevent political controversy, whether it be in the Soviet Union or the United States. These controls, couched in institutional psychiatry, are much more than simply a way to get political dissidents behind bars. Their use is significant because they depoliticize political actions. Militant resistance to racism or militarism becomes transformed into evidence of paranoid thinking and a sick mind. (For an example of this tendency, see Copeland, 1970.) When the bureaucratic mass society (Russian or American style) uses the techniques of institutional psychiatry to "reinterpret" political behavior, citizens become patients. And as Szasz has suggested: "Totalitarian tyranny and popular (non-constitutional) democracy thus rush to meet each other in the Therapeutic State."

Just how great is the potential for use of psychiatry to command conformity in this country? Because every one of us have problems and because unconscious motives play a part in most of our behavior, it is quite easy for the psychiatrist, sometimes unwittingly, to impose his own social values in deciding which behaviors are abnormal. Homosexuals are often considered pathological while cigarette smokers are not. Political dissenters are, of course, prime targets. Robert Coles reports the account of a black civil-rights activist sent by a judge to a mental hospital for observation of his "mental status," for possible delinquent or sociopathic trends, and for possible treatment.

It's quite a setup they've got. We protest our inability to vote, to go into a movie or restaurant everyone else uses, and they call us crazy, and send us away to be looked over by psychiatrists and psychologists and social workers and all the rest of them. The questions I've had put at me since I've been here! Were you a *loner* when you were a boy? Did people consider you *rebellious?* Were you *popular* or *unpopular* as a child? When you were younger did you have trouble *taking orders* from your parents or your teachers? Did your mother *discipline* you firmly, or did she more or less let you do as you please? And on and on they go, one question after another, and none of them very subtle. (Quoted in Coles, 1970.)

The psychiatrist rejected any discussion of what the young man was actually doing and what his objective reasons were. He considered himself to be temperate and the young man to be impulsive—to have a need to disrupt the lives of other people, and to bring harm to himself. Therefore the psychiatrist was recommending treatment instead of jail but it would be "too bad" for the young man if he were "resistant." The smug, self-righteous arrogance in favor of the status quo is an affront not only to the young man but to responsible psychiatry. Coles notes that the game of control by psychiatric invective could cut both ways. One could ask what kind of early childhood and what unconscious conflicts underlie a political leader's willingness to order thousands to fight and kill, what enables a CIA man to lie or a pilot to drop napalm, or anyone to be competitive in a "rat race" or uninterested in the poverty of thousands around them.

Moreover, if students are out to kill their "parent surrogates," what indeed about our desire as grown-ups to squelch the young, subtly and not so subtly degrade them, be rid of them—because they inspire envy in us; because they confront us with all the chances we forsook, all the opportunities we have lost, all the tricks and evasions and compromises and duplicities we have long since *rationalized* or *repressed* or *projected?* (Coles, 1970.)

The entire emphasis on explaining things away psychiatrically is a method of killing dissent for it removes from us the need to ask whose law and whose order are being challenged and for what purposes.

The Szasz warning is against an extreme application of the study of psychological illness and health to the control over people. A more common application exists in the use of human-adjustment techniques in industry. The beneficial use of such methods lies in their ability to help people find some interpersonally rewarding aspects in their work and to increase opportunity for democratic participation in decisions affecting their work. The sinister aspect of these methods is that people can be dissuaded from expressing genuine conflicts of interests, over wages or pensions let us say, through the manipulation of feigned or half-hearted interest in their problems or in the frustrations of their work by a psychiatrically oriented personnel manager. Hence the technical field of human relations is frequently abused as a money-saving or trouble-saving substitute for facing genuine conflicts of interests in large organizations. Like the situation of forced hospitalization of deviants, the abuse of human-relations techniques is particularly frightening because it goes on within a framework in which those with power to control tend to believe that the exercise of their techniques is in the best interests of those controlled. This orientation frequently comes to be shared by those whose behavior is being controlled, hence creating superficial consensus which prevents necessary work on issues of difference. Social systems that preclude expression of conflicting interests are totalitarian, even when the populace is apparently supportive of the contrived consensus.

The two remaining articles deal with the broader context of the new technology, with special emphasis on who is to use this technology and for what ends. The Skinner-Rogers debate is concerned with the frequently unexamined issues in the use of behavioral-science knowledge in controlling human behavior. The capabilities of the scientist's knowledge and the applicability of his own values are of central importance in these essays.

Boguslaw opens up a new dimension of decision control in his examination of the way in which system designers create decision-making organizations which are incapable of revising their implicit values or being redirected by their members. Since these new systems are based on efficiency values rather than humanitarian values, much of the diversity and conflict that characterizes social life is reduced to "manageable" alternative actions where decisions are made by fiat. The emergence of what Boguslaw has called "the new utopians" also suggests a significant shift in power and control away from the public and elected representatives to system specialists.

It is not possible to refer to the problem of decision control in the United States without referring to the workings of the Central Intelligence Agency. This agency has excavated a secret tunnel between East and West Germany, flown reconnaissance planes out of the reach of Soviet antiaircraft, trained the police of innumerable poor countries, assisted in the overthrow of several democratically elected but left-leaning governments, provided false information to an American United Nations ambassador, bombed cities in repainted and disguised planes, and bribed foreign labor movements and foreign students studying in this country. It is the largest member of the nine-agency intelligence community in the United States and its power lies in a secret budget known only to be in the billions of dollars, and not accountable even to Congress.

In 1964 Congressman Wright Patman's investigation into the use of foundations as tax dodges led to a discovery of a vast network of foundations and paper trusts and funds all of which were acting as conduits for CIA funds. The funds were going into the support of one of the most liberal American groups through the 1950s and early '60s, the National Student Association. The domestic NSA program, against the war and draft, in favor of SNCC in the South, proved excellent cover for CIA domination of the NSA international program. The CIA interests were twofold: cultivating an anti-communist youth movement in foreign countries and collecting intelligence on potential leaders of other countries. To NSA the relation was comfortable. It meant jobs, money, offices, travel grants, and draft deferments.

The top officers of NSA, when cleared, were made "witty," that is, privy to knowing NSA's secret support from "the company" (CIA). After fifteen years of secrecy, an independent-minded president of NSA, acting under threat of serious penalty, told another member who leaked the story to *Ramparts* magazine. NSA officers pleaded with the rebellious member to repudiate the story, for its revelation would be disastrous to NSA and its strong liberal programs. The most worrisome of the arguments against reporting the connection was that it would hurt not only NSA but the CIA as well.

Covert Action Division No. Five, after all, was not in the business of assassinating Latin American leftists, it was supporting liberal groups like NSA, groups with international programs in the best tradition of cultural exchanges between countries. NSA might be anti-communist, but certainly no one could ever argue that its anti-communism was more militant or more narrow-minded than that of the average American. Rather, it was less so. Thus the exposure of the NSA-CIA tie would deeply hurt the enlightened, liberal, internationalist wing of the CIA. Conservative congressmen, such as L. Mendell Rivers of the House Armed Services Committee, would cut off Agency funds for these purposes, and the hardliners in CIA's "core" would be proven right in their contentions that the Agency shouldn't give large sums of money to support liberal students, no matter what intelligence it was getting in return.

The twisted sickness of this Orwellian argument should speak for itself. Yet it is extraordinary, and frightening, that it could be so easily made by the talented young liberals at the head of NSA. One would think the idea of "an enlightened wing of the CIA" would be an obvious contradiction in terms. But the idea's acceptance and support by a generation of student leaders indicates how deeply the corruption of means for ends has become ingrained in our society, and how much dishonesty is tolerated in the name of the Cold War. (Stern, 1967.)

Bureaucratic obfuscation, covert manipulation and secrecy are landmarks of the intelligence community and of the cybernetic state in general. Control over others inevitably returns home. This control can remove from basically good people the distinction between honesty and subterfuge. They lose the ability, vital to a democracy, to recognize that time when to be silent is to lie.

REFERENCES AND ADDITIONAL READING

Alexander, Herbert E., and Harold B. Meyers, "The Switch in Campaign Giving," *Fortune* (November 1965), pp. 170, 171, 211–216.

Anonymous, "Deep Therapy on the Assembly Line," *Ammunition*, **7** (April 1949), pp. 47–51.

Ashmore, Harry S., "Electoral Reform," *The Center Magazine*, **2** (January 1969), pp. 2–11.

Boeth, Richard, "The Assault on Privacy, Snoops, Bugs, Wiretaps, Dossiers, Data Banks: Specters of 1984," *Newsweek* (July 7, 1970), pp. 15–20.

Cipes, Robert M., "The Wiretap War," *New Republic* (December 24, 1966), pp. 16–22.

Coles, Robert, "A Fashionable Kind of Slander," *Atlantic*, **226**:5 (November 1970), pp. 53–55.

Copeland, Vincent, *The Crime of Martin Sostre* (New York: McGraw-Hill, 1970).

Ferry, W. H., "Masscomm as Guru," in *Mass Communications*, an Occasional Paper by The Center for the Study of Democratic Institutions (May 1966), pp. 8–19.

Goldhamer, Herbert, and Ronald Westrum, "The Social Effects of Communication Technology," a report prepared for the Russell Sage Foundation and published by the Rand Corporation, R-486-RSF (May 1970).

Johnson, Nicholas, "The Media Barons and the Public Interest," *Atlantic* (June 1968), pp. 43–51.

McGinnis, Joe, *The Selling of the President, 1968* (New York: Trident, 1968).

Michael, Donald N., "Speculation on the Relation of the Computer to Individual Freedom and the Right to Privacy," *George Washington Law Review*, **33** (October 1964), pp. 270–286.

Navasky, Victor S., "The Government and Martin Luther King," *Atlantic*, **226**:5 (November 1970), pp. 43–52.

Pilisuk, Marc, "People's Park, Power and the Calling of the Social Sciences," in Robert Buckhout et al. (eds.), *Toward Social Change* (New York: Harper and Row, 1971).

Ridgeway, James, "The Snoops: Private Lives and Public Service," *New Republic* (December 19, 1964), pp. 13–17.

Safer, Morley, "Television Covers the War," *War Peace Report* (June-July 1966), pp. 9–11.

Schiller, Herbert I., *Mass Communications and American Empire* (New York: Kelley, 1969).

Stern, Sol, "NSA and the CIA," *Ramparts* (March 1967), pp. 29–37; reproduced in R. Perrucci and M. Pilisuk (eds.), *The Triple Revolution: Social Problems in Depth* (Boston: Little, Brown, 1968), pp. 365–384.

Szasz, Thomas S., *Law, Liberty and Psychiatry* (New York: Macmillan, 1966).

Szasz, Thomas S., "Toward the Therapeutic State," *New Republic* (December 11, 1965); reproduced in R. Perrucci and M. Pilisuk (eds.), *The Triple Revolution: Social Problems in Depth* (Boston: Little, Brown, 1968), pp. 325–330.

THE WASTE MAKERS

Vance Packard

The people of the United States are in a sense becoming a nation on a tiger. They must learn to consume more and more or, they are warned, their magnificent economic machine may turn and devour them. They must be induced to step up their individual consumption higher and higher whether they have any pressing need for the goods or not. Their ever-expanding economy demands it.

Where are the Americans drifting under the pressure to make them more wasteful, imprudent, and carefree in their consuming habits? What is the impact of all this pressure toward wastefulness on the nation and on the behavior and character of its people?

In a good-humored forecast of things to come, the senior editor of *Sales Management* asserted on May 6, 1960:

If we Americans are to buy and consume everything that automated manufacture, sock-o-selling and all-out advertising can thrust upon us, each of our mounting millions must have extra ears and eyes and other senses—as well as extra income. Indeed, the only sure way to meet all the demands may be to create a brand new breed of super customers.

Some marketing experts have been announcing that the average citizen will have to step up his buying by nearly 50 percent in the next dozen years, or the economy will sicken. In a mere decade United States citizens will have to improve their level of consumption as much as their forebears had managed to do in the two hundred years from colonial times to 1939.

The challenge of finding significant improvements that can be made in existing products, however, is becoming more difficult each year.

When the Appliance Technical Conference was held in Chicago in 1958, the vice-president of engineering for Whirlpool Corporation made a notably candid statement. He said: "The industry has wrung the last possible ounce of research out of the present appliance products. We can only offer prettier equipment." He urged the industry to start basic research in the properties of clothing and meats in order to come up with radically new products.

All this is not to suggest that genuine technological improvements are not being made—or in prospect of being made—in some products. The pushbutton and long-distance dialing telephone and the jet passenger airplane are improvements that have produced considerable enchantment among consumers. There is the probability that Americans soon will be offered improvements in home products that will produce a degree of enchantment in some circles: refrigerators with no moving parts, ultrasonic dishwashers that reportedly will remove fried egg from plates, remote-control stoves, lighting based on electroluminescent phosphors for ceiling or wall panels.

But how much should we rejoice when General Electric introduces a toaster with nine buttons, which make it possible to obtain a piece of toast in any of nine shades? How much should we rejoice when another company introduces a mechanical martini-stirring spoon, which relieves the person stirring from the labor of twisting his wrist? And what American housewife is dreaming of the day when she can prepare breakfast by simply flicking a bedside switch, which will turn on an electronic recipe maker coded on punch cards?

The recession in the late fifties served as a sharp reminder to many of the developing dilemma posed by the need for ever-greater production. Recessions were nothing new. But this one was the most severe of the three postwar recessions. In many industries, companies found themselves with heavy inventories of goods and began cutting back production. The public was still buying, but not fast enough.

Marketers reacted to the challenge of coping with mounting glut during the recession by shifting to the really hard sell. In Flint, Michigan, sales executives began firing a cannon every time a motorcar was sold. Citizens across the land were admonished by industrialists and government leaders of all stripes to begin buying for their own good. At a press conference, President Eisenhower was asked what the people should do to make the recession recede. Here is the dialogue that followed:

"A.—Buy."

"Q.—Buy what?"

"A.—Anything."

The President was advised that this was possibly an oversimplified response in view of the fact that his own Secretary of the Treasury was then urging people to put their money in government bonds. The President then said the public should buy only what it needs and "wants." An appliance store in Killingsley, Connecticut, immediately responded by putting this sign in its window: "Okay Ike, we're doing our part!"

Thus the challenge was to develop a public that would always have an appetite as voracious as its machines. The emerging philosophy was most fervently and bluntly stated perhaps in two long articles in *The Journal of Retailing* during the mid-fifties. The author was Marketing Consultant Victor Lebow. He made a forthright plea for "forced consumption":

Our enormously productive economy . . . demands that we make consumption our way of life, that we convert the buying and use of goods into rituals, that we seek our spiritual satisfactions, or ego satisfactions, in consumption. . . . We need things consumed, burned up, worn out, replaced, and discarded at an ever increasing rate.

At other points he spoke of the "consumption requirements of our productive capacity" and of the "obligation" of retailers "to push more goods across their counters."

Old-fashioned selling methods based on offering goods to fill an obvious need in a straightforward manner were no longer enough. Even the use of status appeals and sly appeals to the subconscious needs and anxieties of the public—which I have examined in earlier works—would not move goods in the mountainous dimensions desired.

What was needed were strategies that would make Americans in large numbers into voracious, wasteful, compulsive consumers—and strategies that would provide products assuring such wastefulness. Even where wastefulness was not involved strategies were needed that would induce the public to consume at ever-higher levels.

As the marketing experts groped for ways to keep sales soaring in the face of mounting saturation, one of the first thoughts that struck them was that each consumer should be induced to buy more of each product than he had been buying. The way to end glut was to produce gluttons.

The makers of one deodorant introduced a he-she kit for husbands and wives, so that they could get two applicators rather than one in each master bathroom. Men previously had tended to use their wives' applicator rather than buy their own.

Hosiery manufacturers began trying to sell more pairs of stockings to each American woman by introducing colored stockings. Women were told that their stockings should match whatever costume or accessories they would be wearing. This concept of more-sales-through-matching took hold in a number of fields. A spokesman for Revlon, Inc., the cosmetics firm, explained that one of the secrets of the company's fabulous success during the late fifties was that it "taught women to match their nail enamel to their moods and occasions, so that they bought more."

One of the Big Four swim-suit producers, Catalina, began promoting the idea of having one suit for the morning sun, one for the noonday sun, and a third for the evening sun. And another of the Big Four, Rose Marie Reid, began urging that women use one suit for swimming, one for sunning, and one for "psychology."

SAFETY AND STYLE

Makers of eyeglasses set their sights on the goal of selling more spectacles per head. The Optical Wholesalers National Association began promoting the notion that every person wearing glasses needs more than one pair. A spokesman explained: "We want glass wearers to own several pairs now—not only for safety but for style as well."

The concept of color "matching" in order to broaden sales was also used in promoting home accessories. A spokesman for Kleenex tissue announced over a television network that "there's a color for every room in your home." And the Bell System sought to get more telephone extensions in each home by the same there's-a-different-color-for-every-room approach. American Telegraph and Telephone urged,

in fact, that families install a second, entirely new line into the house for extra convenience. A Midwestern telephone company official told me of a study made in motels that showed that telephoning could be increased about 20 percent by the use of phones in a color other than the conventional black. Apparently bright colors promote an impulse to call someone just for the heck of it.

A campaign by the world's largest manufacturer of wedding rings to popularize the "double ring" ceremony greatly increased the sale of gold wedding rings. Several hundred radio commentators and society editors began making special note of the fact if the groom, as well as the bride, wore a nuptial ring.

The makers of a number of products for the home concluded that no home was really a home if it did not have doubles in the products they were promoting. The president of Servel, Inc., announced that the American standard of living now called for "two refrigerators in every home." The chief of the washer division of American Home Laundry Manufacturers Association declared that a well-equipped home should have two washers and two dryers. Meanwhile, the Plumbing Fixture Manufacturers Association began promoting the "privazone" home. In a privazone home, each member of the family has his own private water closet. Radio manufacturers disclosed with pride that they had succeeded in selling an average of three radios to every family in the land.

TWO HOMES FOR
EVERY FAMILY

Perhaps the ultimate of this two-or-more-of-a-kind concept—which began so humbly in the twenties with the political promise of two chickens in every pot—was the promotion of the idea of two homes for every family. Home builders began pressing the idea. Others joined in. Building suppliers, appliance manufacturers, and advertising agencies excitedly grasped the potentialities inherent in spreading the idea that every family needed a town house and a country house, or a work house and play house. The marketing possibilities were spelled out by an official of the plywood association in these terms: "The second home is going to . . . provide tremendous markets for everybody in the building-materials field, for appliance manufacturers, builders, and developers, lending agencies, etc. We in the plywood industry are leading the parade."

Another leader of the two-house parade was the J. Walter Thompson advertising agency, which began pointing out in business journals the inviting potentialities of the two-house family. "With the two-house family," it said, "America has clearly entered a new age of consumption for household equipment." It pointed out that the two-house family is likely to have: three or four bathrooms, two to four television sets, two fully equipped kitchens, four to twelve beds, multiples of furniture, linens, rugs, china, etc.

J. Walter Thompson called for an "aggressive advertising and selling" campaign to overcome the public's "habit lag" in sticking with one car when two cars were obviously needed for modern living. One attempt at aggressive reeducation was conducted by the Chevrolet company. Its announcer on the Dinah Shore program began talking of those deprived citizens who were victims of "one-car captivity." The essence of the message, as television critic John Crosby assimilated it, was that, "You peasants who own only one car . . . are chained to the land like serfs in the Middle Ages."

Another tack that the marketers took was to try to induce Americans to demand more with each product bought. It should be either bigger or more complex, or both, in order to be appropriate for modern living. The goal was to justify a higher price tag. Victor Lebow in his blueprint for "forced consumption" put this imperative of a higher price tag in these words: "The second essential is what we might call 'expensive consumption.'"

The lawn mower offers an excellent illustration of the strategy of upgrading the nation's concept of what is appropriate. A simple-minded, intensely rational person might assume that hand mowers would be increasingly popular today and that power mowers would be almost impossible to sell. After all, lawns are getting smaller all the time. And adult males are feeling more and more the need for physical exercise as they spend more time in sedentary, short-week jobs. They come home from the office beating their chests and growling for exercise. The situation that has developed, however, shows how dangerous it has become to try to anticipate consumer behavior by the application of humorless logic, and ignoring the role marketing strategies may play.

The lawn-mower industry was able to convince American males that it was somehow shameful to be seen pushing a hand mower. And power mowers were promoted as a wonderful new gadget. Power-mowers sales rose seventeenfold in fifteen years! By 1960, more than nine out of every ten lawn mowers sold were powered. Such powered mowers cost three to five times as much as hand mowers. Furthermore, having a mere motor on your mower was not enough in some neighborhoods. You also needed a seat on it. Hundreds of thousands of American males began buying power mowers with seats. These, of course, cost ten times as much as a hand mower.

Another general tack the marketers took was to try to induce people to get rid of the products they already owned. In its broadest form this took the form of encouraging people to throw things away.

In the hair-raising utopia, *Brave New World,* that Mr. Aldous Huxley projected in the 1930s for six centuries hence, babies come in bottles and the zombie-like citizens move about in doped-up bliss. To keep the industrial machines humming, each citizen is "compelled to consume so much a year." To that end, newness as a trait is cherished. And sleep teachers stress love of newness because they have the responsibility of "adapting future demand to future industrial supply." The dictator of the utopia, Mustapha Mond, at one point explains: "We don't want people to be attracted by old things. We want them to like the new ones."

When Huxley wrote his book in 1932, he was visualizing what might come about in the distant future. But within a quarter of a century the people of the United States, without any help from dictators or out-and-out sleep teachers, were exhibiting a throwaway mood that would tickle even Mustapha Mond. Much of this was deliberately encouraged. The voice of the television announcer—in 1960—chanted, "You use it once and throw it away. . . . You use it once and throw it away." This specific chant was used to promote the sale of a deodorant pad.

DISCARD, USE UP, DESTROY, WASTE

Residents of the United States were discarding, using up, destroying, and wasting products at a rate that offered considerable encouragement to those charged with achieving ever-higher levels of consumption for their products. A business writer for *Time* magazine related, as the sixties were about to begin:

The force that gives the U.S. economy its pep is being generated more and more in the teeming aisles of the nation's stores. . . . U.S. consumers no longer hold on to suits, coats, and dresses as if they were heirlooms. . . . Furniture, refrigerators, rugs—all once bought to last for years or life—are now replaced with register-tingling regularity.

The new mood of the disposable era was reflected in the pages of the *Engineering News Record,* which observed: "Nowhere in the world except in the U.S. would a skyscraper office building in sound condition be torn down merely to be replaced by another one."

Dennis Brogan has characterized modern Americans as a people "who go away and leave things." The voluptuous wastefulness of modern Americans could be seen not only in their littered parks but in market surveys. The industrial-design firm, Harley Earl Associates of Detroit, reported: "In most households we found there were two to five rolls of Scotch tape—but no one could locate any of them."

Americans had developed their own democratic version of sleep indoctrination of the young. There were the soft, insistent commercials the youngsters heard during their weekly twenty-odd hours of televsion watching. And there were the breakable plastic toys, which taught them at an early age that everything in this world is replaceable.

All the efforts to keep consumption rising—when taken together—amount to an unprecedented saturation of American life with pleas, hints, and other inducements to buy. The sheer dimensions of the current and contemplated selling efforts are becoming a national problem. Commercialization is becoming so all-pervasive that at times it seems to be getting into the air the public breathes.

"Advertising must mass-produce customers just as factories mass-produce products in a growing economy," stated the publisher of *Printers' Ink.* He suggested that outlays for advertising might reach twenty-five billion dollars by 1965. That meant more than doubling the amount being spent to create want and discontent within a few years.

An official of General Foods reported that a typical American family is exposed to 1518 selling messages in the course of an average day. And this does not include the material stuffed into the nation's mailboxes: a total of sixteen billion pieces a year, or four times the amount found in mailboxes a decade earlier.

Members of this average family, for example, are exposed to 117 television and radio commercials a day. Other studies have shown that on television alone members of an average family are subjected to nearly an hour of commercials a day. This growth of messages beamed at the public over the airways is worth special note because airborne messages are hard to ignore and because the public presumably controls the airways in its own interest.

THE "PRESSURE-COOKER" LIFE

The increase in commercials has complicated the life of television writers, directors, and performers as they have tried to sustain their moods of gaiety, tragedy, or suspense. In the spring of 1959, Peter Lind Hayes gave up his ABC daytime show because of the "pressure-cooker existence" the network proposed to inaugurate by cutting his hour-long show to a half hour. He explained: "When you figure the number of commercials we have to give, it actually takes an hour to do a half-hour show. Can you imagine half a dozen commercial interruptions in thirty minutes? That is what it would amount to." Garry Moore revealed that he left daytime television "because frankly, I couldn't cope with the number of commercials we had to accommodate." And, in 1960, he won a singular battle for his nighttime show by successfully demanding that commercial interruptions of his hour-long show be limited to four rather than the then-prevailing seven interruptions.

The tastefulness of television and radio commercials likewise has shown signs of deterioration as the pressure to sell has mounted. Selling messages for "intimately personal products" such as feminine-hygiene products and hemorrhoid treatments are beamed into many living rooms. At this writing, more than 140 television stations accept commercials for the hemorrhoid treatment Preparation H.

One might speculate also on what it does to a people's sense of values—especially their children's—when discussions of significant events are followed on television by announcers who in often louder and more solemn voices announce a great new discovery for a hair bleach. Or, to consider another kind of juxtaposition, a broadcast appeal to aid hungry children in mid-1960 was followed immediately by a dog-food commercial.

Certain of the magazines, too, showed the impact of commercialism as their publishers sought to create an editorial climate attractive to advertisers. In some cases, articles appeared which, while possibly appealing to readers, were most certainly gratifying to advertisers and potential advertisers. One of the mass women's magazines with a primarily working-class audience carried an article called "What's the Big Attraction?" in early 1960. Its illustration showed an attractive girl surrounded by six handsome men. The article purported to show the secrets of the Feminine Girl who is irresistible with the Water Cooler Set. Before you were eight hundred words into this revealing article, you were aware that she relied upon "hand lotions," "moisture creams," "cleaning fluid," "scarves," "fresh glove supply," "bath salts," "bath oil," "special foot lotion," "creamy depilatory," "silky body lotion," "anti-perspirant," "cologne," "cosmetics," "shampoos," "astringent-saturated cotton balls," "nail enamels," "make-up shades," and "lip-stick."

Advertising messages have begun appearing in places where heretofore they have been banned, usually on grounds of taste or public policy. Entrepreneurs and public officials are proving to be willing to let down the bars in order to gain extra revenue. For the first time in half a century, thousands of buses in New York have been carrying advertising posters on their exteriors. Many railroad terminals are so crowded with billboards and commercial displays that it is difficult for a traveler to find the announcement of departures. A New York television station has begun beaming its programs into more than four hundred supermarkets and into three hundred self-service laundries. In the stores the housewife finds herself exposed to as many as eight television screens and to about twenty commercials in the course of her average shopping trip.

So pervasive have billboards become along many stretches of highway in the United States, that even an outdoor advertising expert publicly lamented that a journey he and his wife took to Florida had been "ruined" because "hundreds" of miles of what would have been beautiful highways had been lined with signboards. Lobbyists for the outdoor advertisers have been charged by a New York state legislator with keeping state legislators in their debt—to forestall restrictive legislation—by giving them free sign space, or space at reduced rates, at election time. An investigator for *The Reader's Digest* concluded that the new 41,000-mile federal highway system would become "a billboard slum" unless state legislators acted to prevent it.

In order to cope with situations that arise when states do outlaw billboards along highways, an enterprising signmaker developed a lightweight sign so gargantuan it can be seen from hundreds of yards away. A still more ingenious entrepreneur has

begun offering admen the chance to plant their messages against clouds and mountaintops. Unexcelled Chemical Corporation has been inviting advertisers to use its giant magic lantern called Skyjector. It is capable of beaming an advertisement one-half mile wide against a cloud five miles away. And the company expects that within a year it will be able to create its own clouds if there are none handy. Columnist Inez Robb commented: "It opens up the prospect of a horizon-to-horizon gray-flannel world with the sky . . . available to nature lovers only in rainy weather."

People who wish to stroll along a few public beaches of Florida's Gold Coast are not able to let their fancies roam too far off the notion of consumption. Every hour or so old biplanes roar along just offshore, hauling hundred-foot-long sky billboards. And on the backs of hundreds of ocean-front benches are tacked small billboards. Advertising men offered to install benches in many downtown areas of Philadelphia—and pay the city in addition $15 a month for each bench if they could merely plaster the backs with ads. The offer was rejected.

Some paperback book publishers have begun accepting paid advertisements in their books. One book on child care has been carrying more than a dozen full-page advertisements scattered through the book.

PRESSURES AND THE PEOPLE

A final price that must be considered in assessing the implications of the current drift of American society under the impact of an economy based on ever-mounting consumption is the change it may be producing in the character of the people involved.

What is the impact on the human spirit of all these pressures to consume?

Business Week made a report on the many subtle and adroit persuasion techniques being developed to encourage Americans to be more zestful consumers and commented: ". . . it looks as though all of our business forces are bent on getting everyone to . . . Borrow. Spend. Buy. Waste."

It is unrealistic to assume that all such pressures are not producing changes at a deeper level than mere consumption habits. For example, a person who finds himself induced to spend beyond his income habitually does not wish to feel guilty about his excesses and welcomes a system of morality that condones such habits. Much of the average American's consumption has been channeled into frivolous or playful or whimsical outlets, which also requires rationalizing. United States residents have been spending more on smoking, drinking, and gambling than they have on education. They have been spending more on admission tickets to pastimes than they have on foreign economic aid. They have been spending more on jewelry and watches than they have on either books or basic research. Further, they spend more for greeting cards than they do for medical research.

In earlier years, economists pondering the controls necessary to keep the seller-buyer relationship in fair balance concluded that ordinary human prudence would protect the buyer from being exploited or overwhelmed. *Caveat emptor,* they intoned.

Letting the buyer beware was thought to be no real problem because the buyer was assumed to hold the whip hand since the money was in his pocket. The consumer was assumed to be sovereign. And marketers and merchandisers still like to flatter the consuming public by referring to it as "king."

Marketers in the mid-twentieth century, however, have been subjecting the consumer to a barrage of selling strategies that has rarely heretofore been matched in variety, intensity, or ingenuity. Millions of consumers are manipulated, razzle-dazzled, indoctrinated, mood-conditioned, and flim-flammed. They are conditioned to be discontented with last year's models, and they are conditioned to accept flimsily built products.

The attitude of all too many marketers was revealed in the January 29, 1960, issue of *Printer's Ink*—"The Weekly Magazine of Advertising and Marketing"—when it earnestly reported efforts being made by marketing researchers to understand how people acquire and retain information and attitudes. It stated: "Perhaps most important of all [the researchers] are edging toward that ultimate question for advertising: How can the consumer, like Pavlov's dog, be taught the habit of buying a specific brand?"

If that truly is the "ultimate question" for advertising, then the industry had better search its soul. And consumers had better take to the barricades.

In the face of all these pressures, the lone consumer of ordinary intelligence and impulsiveness is usually no match for the subtle and massive onslaughts aimed at him. Today, the consumer is far from sovereign. To restore the consumer to any real sovereignty, there needs to be a return on a large scale to pride in prudent buying and informative support for that prudence.

SOME ISSUES CONCERNING THE CONTROL OF HUMAN BEHAVIOR

A SYMPOSIUM

Carl R. Rogers and B. F. Skinner

I—SKINNER

Science is steadily increasing our power to influence, change, mold—in a word, control—human behavior. It has extended our "understanding" (whatever that may be) so that we deal more successfully with people in nonscientific ways, but it has also identified conditions or variables which can be used to predict and control behavior in a new, and increasingly rigorous, technology. The broad disciplines of government and economics offer examples of this, but there is special cogency in those contributions of anthropology, sociology, and psychology which deal with individual behavior. Carl Rogers has listed some of the achievements to date in a recent paper (1956). Those of his examples which show or imply the control of the single organism are primarily due, as we should expect, to psychology. It is the experimental study of behavior which carries us beyond awkward or inaccessible "principles," "factors," and so on, to variables which can be directly manipulated.

It is also, and for more or less the same reasons, the conception of human behavior emerging from an experimental analysis which most directly challenges traditional views. Psychologists themselves often do not seem to be aware of how far they have moved in this direction. But the change is not passing unnoticed by others. Until only recently it was customary to deny the possibility of a rigorous science of human behavior by arguing, either that a lawful science was impossible because man was a free agent, or that merely statistical predictions would always leave room for personal freedom. But those who used to take this line have become most vociferous in expressing their alarm at the way these obstacles are being surmounted.

Now, the control of human behavior has always been unpopular. Any undisguised effort to control usually arouses emotional reactions. We hesitate to admit, even to ourselves, that we are engaged in control, and we may refuse to control, even when this would be helpful, for fear of criticism. Those who have explicitly avowed an interest in control have been roughly treated by history. Machiavelli is the great prototype. As Macaulay said of him, "Out of his surname they coined an epithet for a knave and out of his Christian name a synonym for the devil." There were obvious reasons. The control that Machiavelli analyzed and recommended, like most political control, used techniques that were aversive to the controllee. The threats and punishments of the bully, like those of the government operating on the same plan, are not designed—whatever their success—to endear themselves to those who are controlled.

Reprinted by permission of the author and publisher from Science, **124** *(November 30, 1956), pp. 1057–1066.*

Even when the techniques themselves are not aversive, control is usually exercised for the selfish purposes of the controller and, hence, has indirectly punishing effects upon others.

Man's natural inclination to revolt against selfish control has been exploited to good purpose in what we call the philosophy and literature of democracy. The doctrine of the rights of man has been effective in arousing individuals to concerted action against governmental and religious tyranny. The literature which has had this effect has greatly extended the number of terms in our language which express reactions to the control of men. But the ubiquity and ease of expression of this attitude spells trouble for any science which may give birth to a powerful technology of behavior. Intelligent men and women, dominated by the humanistic philosophy of the past two centuries, cannot view with equanimity what Andrew Hacker has called "the specter of predictable man" (1954). Even the statistical or actuarial prediction of human events, such as the number of fatalities to be expected on a holiday weekend, strikes many people as uncanny and evil, while the prediction and control of individual behavior is regarded as little less than the work of the devil. I am not so much concerned here with the political or economic consequences for psychology, although research following certain channels may well suffer harmful effects. We ourselves, as intelligent men and women, and as exponents of Western thought, share these attitudes. They have already interfered with the free exercise of a scientific analysis, and their influence threatens to assume more serious proportions.

Three broad areas of human behavior supply good examples. The first of these—*personal control*—may be taken to include person-to-person relationships in the family, among friends, in social and work groups, and in counseling and psychotherapy.

Other fields are *education* and *government*. A few examples from each will show how nonscientific preconceptions are affecting our current thinking about human behavior.

Personal Control

People living together in groups come to control one another with a technique which is not inappropriately called "ethical." When an individual behaves in a fashion acceptable to the group, he receives admiration, approval, affection, and many other reinforcements which increase the likelihood that he will continue to behave in that fashion. When his behavior is not acceptable, he is criticized, censured, blamed, or otherwise punished. In the first case the group calls him "good"; in the second, "bad." This practice is so thoroughly ingrained in our culture that we often fail to see that it is a technique of control. Yet we are almost always engaged in such control, even though the reinforcements and punishments are often subtle.

The practice of admiration is an important part of a culture, because behavior which is otherwise inclined to be weak can be set up and maintained with its help. The individual is especially likely to be praised, admired, or loved when he acts for the group in the face of great danger, for example, or sacrifices himself or his possessions, or submits to prolonged hardship, or suffers martyrdom. These actions are not admirable in any absolute sense, but they require admiration if they are to be strong. Similarly, we admire people who behave in original or exceptional ways, not because such behavior is itself admirable, but because we do not know how to encourage original or exceptional behavior in any other way. The group acclaims independent, unaided behavior in part because it is easier to reinforce than to help.

As long as this technique of control is

misunderstood, we cannot judge correctly an environment in which there is less need for heroism, hardship, or independent action. We are likely to argue that such an environment is itself less admirable or produces less admirable people. In the old days, for example, young scholars often lived in undesirable quarters, ate unappetizing or inadequate food, performed unprofitable tasks for a living or to pay for necessary books and materials or publication. Older scholars and other members of the group offered compensating reinforcement in the form of approval and admiration for these sacrifices. When the modern graduate student receives a generous scholarship, enjoys good living conditions, and has his research and publication subsidized, the grounds for evaluation seem to be pulled from under us. Such a student no longer *needs* admiration to carry him over a series of obstacles (no matter how much he may need it for other reasons), and, in missing certain familiar objects of admiration, we are likely to conclude that such *conditions* are less admirable. Obstacles to scholarly work may serve as a useful measure of motivation—and we may go wrong unless some substitute is found—but we can scarcely defend a deliberate harassment of the student for this purpose. The productivity of any set of conditions can be evaluated only when we have freed ourselves of the attitudes which have been generated in us as members of an ethical group.

A similar difficulty arises from our use of punishment in the form of censure or blame. The concept of responsibility and the related concept of foreknowledge and choice are used to justify techniques of control using punishment. Was So-and-So aware of the probable consequences of his action, and was the action deliberate? If so, we are justified in punishing him. But what does this mean? It appears to be a question concerning the efficacy of the contingent relations between behavior and punishing consequences. We punish behavior because it is objectionable to us or the group, but in a minor refinement of rather recent origin we have come to withhold punishment when it cannot be expected to have any effect. If the objectionable consequences of an act were accidental and not likely to occur again, there is no point in punishing. We say that the individual was not "aware of the consequences of his action" or that the consequences were not "intentional." If the action could not have been avoided—if the individual "had no choice"—punishment is also withheld, as it is if the individual is incapable of being changed by punishment because he is of "unsound mind." In all these cases—different as they are—the individual is held "not responsible" and goes unpunished.

Just as we say that it is "not fair" to punish a man for something he could not help doing, so we call it "unfair" when one is rewarded beyond his due or for something he could not help doing. In other words, we also object to wasting *reinforcers* where they are not needed or will do no good. We make the same point with the words *just* and *right*. Thus we have no right to punish the irresponsible, and a man has no right to reinforcers he does not earn or deserve. But concepts of choice, responsibility, justice, and so on, provide a most inadequate analysis of efficient reinforcing and punishing contingencies because they carry a heavy semantic cargo of a quite different sort, which obscures any attempt to clarify controlling practices or to improve techniques. In particular, they fail to prepare us for techniques based on other than aversive techniques of control. Most people would object to forcing prisoners to serve as subjects of dangerous medical experiments, but few object when they are induced to serve by the offer of return privileges—even when the reinforcing effect of these privileges has been created by forcible deprivation. In the traditional scheme the right to refuse guarantees the individual against coercion or an unfair bargain. But to what extent *can* a prisoner refuse under such circumstances?

We need not go so far afield to make the point. We can observe our own attitude toward personal freedom in the way we resent any interference with what we want to do. Suppose we want to buy a car of a particular sort. Then we may object, for example, if our wife urges us to buy a less expensive model and to put the difference into a new refrigerator. Or we may resent it if our neighbor questions our need for such a car or our ability to pay for it. We would certainly resent it if it were illegal to buy such a car (remember Prohibition) ; and if we find we cannot actually afford it, we may resent governmental control of the price through tariffs and taxes. We resent it if we discover that we cannot get the car because the manufacturer is holding the model in deliberately short supply in order to push a model we do not want. In all this we assert our democratic right to buy the car of our choice. We are well prepared to do so and to resent any restriction on our freedom.

But why do we not ask *why* it is the car of our choice and resent the forces which made it so? Perhaps our favorite toy as a child was a car, of a very different model, but nevertheless bearing the name of the car we now want. Perhaps our favorite TV program is sponsored by the manufacturer of that car. Perhaps we have seen pictures of many beautiful or prestigeful persons driving it—in pleasant or glamorous places. Perhaps the car has been designed with respect to our motivational patterns: the device on the hood is a phallic symbol; or the horsepower has been stepped up to please our competitive spirit in enabling us to pass other cars swiftly (or, as the advertisements say, "safely") . The concept of

freedom that has emerged as part of the cultural practice of our group makes little or no provision for recognizing or dealing with these kinds of control. Concepts like "responsibility" and "rights" are scarcely applicable. We are prepared to deal with coercive measures, but we have no traditional recourse with respect to other measures which in the long run (and especially with the help of science) may be much more powerful and dangerous.

Education

The techniques of education were once frankly aversive. The teacher was usually older and stronger than his pupils and was able to "make them learn." This meant that they were not actually taught but were surrounded by a threatening world from which they could escape only by learning. Usually they were left to their own resources in discovering how to do so. Claude Coleman has published a grimly amusing reminder of these older practices (1953). He tells of a school teacher who published a careful account of his services during 51 years of teaching, during which he administered: ". . . 911,527 blows with a cane; 124,010 with a rod; 20,989 with a ruler; 136,715 with the hand; 10,295 over the mouth; 7,905 boxes on the ear; [and] 1,115,800 slaps on the head. . . ."

Progressive education was a humanitarian effort to substitute positive reinforcement for such aversive measures, but in the search for useful human values in the classroom it has never fully replaced the variables it abandoned. Viewed as a branch of behavioral technology, education remains relatively inefficient. We supplement it, and rationalize it, by admiring the pupil who learns *for himself*; and we often attribute the learning process, or knowledge itself, to something *inside* the individual. We admire behavior which seems to have inner sources. Thus we admire one who *recites* a poem more than one who simply *reads* it. We admire one who *knows* the answer more than one who *knows where to look it up*. We admire the *writer* rather than the *reader*. We admire the arithmetician who can do a problem in his head rather than with a slide rule or calculating machine, or in "original" ways rather than by a strict application of rules. In general we feel that any aid or "crutch"—except those aids to which we are now thoroughly accustomed—reduces the credit due. In Plato's *Phaedrus,* Thamus, the king, attacks the invention of the alphabet on similar grounds! He is afraid "it will produce forgetfulness in the minds of those who learn to use it, because they will not practice their memories. . . ." In other words, he holds it more admirable to remember than to use a memorandum. He also objects that pupils "will read many things without instruction . . . [and] will therefore seem to know many things when they are for the most part ignorant." In the same vein we are today sometimes contemptuous of book learning, but, as educators, we can scarcely afford to adopt this view without reservation.

By admiring the student for knowledge and blaming him for ignorance, we escape some of the responsibility of teaching him. We resist any analysis of the educational process which threatens the notion of inner wisdom or questions the contention that the fault of ignorance lies with the student. More powerful techniques which bring about the same changes in behavior by manipulating *external* variables are decried as brainwashing or thought control. We are quite unprepared to judge *effective* educational measures. As long as only a few pupils learn much of what is taught, we do not worry about uniformity or regimentation. We do not fear the feeble technique; but we should view with dismay a system under which every student learned everything listed in a syllabus—although such a

condition is far from unthinkable. Similarly, we do not fear a system which is so defective that the student must *work* for an education; but we are loath to give credit for anything learned without effort—although this could well be taken as an ideal result—and we flatly refuse to give credit if the student already knows what a school teaches.

A world in which people are wise and good without trying, without "having to be," without "choosing to be," could conceivably be a far better world for everyone. In such a world we should not have to "give anyone credit"—we should not need to admire anyone—for being wise and good. From our present point of view we cannot believe that such a world would be admirable. We do not even permit ourselves to imagine what it would be like.

Government

Government has always been the special field of aversive control. The state is frequently defined in terms of the power to punish, and jurisprudence leans heavily upon the associated notion of personal responsibility. Yet it is becoming increasingly difficult to reconcile current practice and theory with these earlier views. In criminology, for example, there is a strong tendency to drop the notion of responsibility in favor of some such alternative as capacity or controllability. But no matter how strongly the facts, or even practical expedience, support such a change, it is difficult to make the change in a legal system designed on a different plan. When governments resort to other techniques (for example, positive reinforcement), the concept of responsibility is no longer relevant and the theory of government is no longer applicable.

The conflict is illustrated by two decisions of the Supreme Court in the 1930s which dealt with, and disagreed on, the definition of control or coercion (Freund et al., 1954, p. 233). The Agricultural Adjustment Act proposed that the Secretary of Agriculture make "rental or benefit payments" to those farmers who agreed to reduce production. The government agreed that the Act would be unconstitutional if the farmer had been *compelled* to reduce production but was not, since he was merely *invited* to do so. Justice Roberts expressed the contrary majority view of the court that "The power to confer or withhold unlimited benefits is the power to coerce or destroy." This recognition of positive reinforcement was withdrawn a few years later in another case in which Justice Cardozo (Freund et al., 1954, p. 244) wrote "To hold that motive or temptation is equivalent to coercion is to plunge the law in endless difficulties." We may agree with him, without implying that the proposition is therefore wrong. Sooner or later the law must be prepared to deal with all possible techniques of governmental control.

The uneasiness with which we view government (in the broadest possible sense) when it does not use punishment is shown by the reception of my utopian novel, *Walden Two* (Skinner, 1948b). This was essentially a proposal to apply a behavioral technology to the construction of a workable, effective, and productive pattern of government. It was greeted with wrathful violence. *Life* magazine called it "a travesty on the good life," and "a menace . . . a triumph of mortmain or the dead hand not envisaged since the days of Sparta . . . a slur upon a name, a corruption of an impulse." Joseph Wood Krutch devoted a substantial part of his book, *The Measure of Man* (1954), to attacking my views and those of the protagonist, Frazier, in the same vein, and Morris Viteles has recently criticized the book in a similar manner in *Science* (1955). Perhaps the reaction is best expressed in a quotation from *The Quest*

for Utopia by Negley and Patrick (1952):

Halfway through this contemporary utopia, the reader may feel sure, as we did, that this is a beautifully ironic satire on what has been called "behavioral engineering." The longer one stays in this better world of the psychologist, however, the plainer it becomes that the inspiration is not satiric, but messianic. This is indeed the behaviorally engineered society, and while it was to be expected that sooner or later the principle of psychological conditioning would be made the basis of a serious construction of utopia—Brown anticipated it in *Limanora*—yet not even the effective satire of Huxley is adequate preparation for the shocking horror of the idea when positively presented. Of all the dictatorships espoused by utopists, this is the most profound, and incipient dictators might well find in this utopia a guidebook of political practice.

One would scarcely guess that the authors are talking about a world in which there is food, clothing, and shelter for all, where everyone chooses his own work and works on the average only 4 hours a day, where music and the arts flourish, where personal relationships develop under the most favorable circumstances, where education prepares every child for the social and intellectual life which lies before him, where—in short—people are truly happy, secure, productive, creative, and forward-looking. What is wrong with it? Only one thing: someone "planned it that way." If these critics had come upon a society in some remote corner of the world which boasted similar advantages, they would undoubtedly have hailed it as providing a pattern we all might well follow—provided that it was clearly the result of a natural process of cultural evolution. Any evidence that intelligence had been used in arriving at this version of the good life would, in their eyes, be a serious flaw. No matter if the planner of *Walden Two* diverts none of the proceeds of the community to his own use, no matter if he has no current control or is, indeed, unknown to most of the other members of the community (he planned that, too), somewhere back of it all he occupies the position of prime mover. And this, to the child of the democratic tradition, spoils it all.

The dangers inherent in the control of human behavior are very real. The possibility of the misuse of scientific knowledge must always be faced. We cannot escape by denying the power of a science of behavior or arresting its development. It is no help to cling to familiar philosophies of human behavior simply because they are more reassuring. As I have pointed out elsewhere (Skinner, 1955), the new techniques emerging from a science of behavior must be subject to the explicit countercontrol which has already been applied to earlier and cruder forms. Brute force and deception, for example, are now fairly generally suppressed by ethical practices and by explicit governmental and religious agencies. A similar countercontrol of scientific knowledge in the interests of the group is a feasible and promising possibility. Although we cannot say how devious the course of its evolution may be, a cultural pattern of control and countercontrol will presumably emerge which will be most widely supported because it is most widely reinforcing.

If we cannot foresee all the details of this (as we obviously cannot), it is important to remember that this is true of the critics of science as well. The dire consequences of new techniques of control, the hidden menace in original cultural designs —these need some proof. It is only another example of my present point that the need for proof is so often overlooked. Man has got himself into some pretty fixes, and it is easy to believe that he will do so again. But there is a more optimistic possibility. The slow growth of the method of science, now for the first time being applied to human affairs, *may* mean a new and exciting phase of human life to which historical analogies will not apply and in which earlier political slogans will not be appropriate. If we are to use the knowledge that a science of behavior is now making available with any hope of success, we must look at human nature as it is brought into focus through the methods of science rather than as it has been presented to us in a series of historical accidents.

If the advent of a powerful science of behavior causes trouble, it will not be because science itself is inimical to human welfare but because older conceptions have not yielded easily or gracefully. We expect resistance to new techniques of control from those who have heavy investments in the old, but we have no reason to help them preserve a series of principles that are not ends in themselves but rather outmoded means to an end. What is needed is a new conception of human behavior which is compatible with the implications of a scientific analysis. All men control and are controlled. The question of government in the broadest possible sense is not how freedom is to be preserved but what kinds of control are to be used and to what ends. Control must be analyzed and considered in its proper proportions. No one, I am sure, wishes to develop new master-slave relationships or bend the will of the people to despotic rulers in new ways. These are patterns of control appropriate to a world without science. They may well be the first to go when the experimental analysis of behavior comes into its own in the design of cultural practices.

II—ROGERS

There are, I believe, a number of matters in connection with this important topic on which the authors of this article, and probably a large majority of psychologists, are in agreement. These matters then are not issues as far as we are concerned, and I should like to mention them briefly in order to put them to one side.

Points of Agreement

I am sure we agree that men—as individuals and as societies—have always endeavored to understand, predict, influence, and control human behavior—their own behavior and that of others.

I believe we agree that the behavioral sciences are making and will continue to make increasingly rapid progress in the understanding of behavior, and that as a consequence the capacity to predict and to control behavior is developing with equal rapidity.

I believe we agree that to deny these advances, or to claim that man's behavior cannot be a field of science, is unrealistic. Even though this is not an issue for us, we should recognize that many intelligent men still hold strongly to the view that the actions of men are free in some sense such that scientific knowledge of man's behavior is impossible. Thus Reinhold Niebuhr, the noted theologian, heaps scorn on the concept of psychology as a science of man's behavior and even says, "In any event, no scientific investigation of past behavior can become the basis of predictions of future behavior." (1955, p. 47.) So, while this is not an issue for psychologists, we should at least notice in passing that it is an issue for many people.

I believe we are in agreement that the tremendous potential power of a science which permits the prediction and control of behavior may be misused, and that the possibility of such misuse constitutes a serious threat.

Consequently Skinner and I are in agreement that the whole question of the scientific control of human behavior is a matter with which psychologists and the general public should concern themselves. As Robert Oppenheimer told the American Psychological Association last year (1956a) the problems that psychologists will pose for society by their growing ability to control behavior will be much more grave than the problems posed by the ability of physicists to control the reactions of matter. I am not sure whether psychologists generally recognize this. My impression is that by and large they hold a laissez-faire attitude. Obviously Skinner and I do not hold this laissez-faire view, or we would not have written this article.

Points of Issue

With these several points of basic and important agreement, are there then any issues that remain on which there are differences? I believe there are. They can be stated very briefly: Who will be controlled? Who will exercise control? What type of control will be exercised? Most important of all, toward what end or what purpose, or in the pursuit of what value, will control be exercised?

It is on questions of this sort that there exist ambiguities, misunderstandings, and probably deep differences. These differences exist among psychologists, among members of the general public in this country, and among various world cultures. Without any hope of achieving a final resolution of these questions, we can, I believe, put these issues in clearer form.

Some Meanings

To avoid ambiguity and faulty communication, I would like to clarify the meanings of some of the terms we are using.

Behavioral science is a term that might be defined from several angles but in the context of this discussion it refers primarily to knowledge that the existence of certain describable conditions in the human being and/or in his environment is followed by certain describable consequences in his actions.

Prediction means the prior identification of behaviors which then occur. Because it is important in some things I wish to say later, I would point out that one may predict a highly specific behavior, such as an eye blink, or one may predict a class of behaviors. One might correctly predict "avoidant behavior," for example, without being able to specify whether the individual will run away or simply close his eyes.

The word *control* is a very slippery one, which can be used with any one of several meanings. I would like to specify three that seem most important for our present purposes. *Control* may mean: (1) The setting of conditions by *B* for *A, A* having no voice in the matter, such that certain predictable behaviors then occur in *A*. I refer to this as external control. (2) The setting of conditions by *B* for *A, A* giving some degree of consent to these conditions, such that certain predictable behaviors then occur in *A*. I refer to this as the influence of *B* on *A*. (3) The setting of conditions by *A* such that certain predictable behaviors then occur in himself. I refer to this as internal control. It will be noted that Skinner lumps together the first two meanings, external control and influence, under the concept of control. I find this confusing.

Usual Concept of Control of Human Behavior

With the underbrush thus cleared away (I hope), let us review very briefly the various elements that are involved in the usual concept of the control of human behavior as mediated by the behavioral sciences. I am drawing here on the previous writings of Skinner, on his present statements, on the writings of others who have considered in either friendly or antagonistic fashion the meanings that would be involved in such control. I have not excluded the science fiction writers, as reported re-

cently by Vandenberg (1956), since they often show an awareness of the issues involved, even though the methods described are as yet fictional. These then are the elements that seem common to these different concepts of the application of science to human behavior.

1. There must first be some sort of decision about goals. Usually desirable goals are assumed, but sometimes, as in George Orwell's book *1984,* the goal that is selected is an aggrandizement of individual power with which most of us would disagree. In a recent paper Skinner suggests that one possible set of goals to be assigned to the behavioral technology is this: "Let men be happy, informed, skillful, well-behaved and productive." (1955–1956.) In the first draft of his part of this article, which he was kind enough to show me, he did not mention such definite goals as these, but desired "improved" educational practices, "wiser" use of knowledge in government, and the like. In the final version of his article he avoids even these value-laden terms, and his implicit goal is the very general one that scientific control of behavior is desirable, because it would perhaps bring "a far better world for everyone."

Thus the first step in thinking about the control of human behavior is the choice of goals, whether specific or general. It is necessary to come to terms in some way with the issue, "For what purpose?"

2. A second element is that, whether the end selected is highly specific or is a very general one such as wanting "a better world," we proceed by the methods of science to discover the means to these ends. We continue through further experimentation and investigation to discover more effective means. The method of science is self-correcting in thus arriving at increasingly effective ways of achieving the purpose we have in mind.

3. The third aspect of such control is

that as the conditions or methods are discovered by which to reach the goal, some person or some group establishes these conditions and uses these methods, having in one way or another obtained the power to do so.

4. The fourth element is the exposure of individuals to the prescribed conditions, and this leads, with a high degree of probability, to behavior which is in line with the goals desired. Individuals are now happy, if that has been the goal, or well-behaved, or submissive, or whatever it has been decided to make them.

5. The fifth element is that if the process I have described is put in motion then there is a continuing social organization which will continue to produce the types of behavior that have been valued.

Some Flaws

Are there any flaws in this way of viewing the control of human behavior? I believe there are. In fact the only element in this description with which I find myself in agreement is the second. It seems to me quite incontrovertibly true that the scientific method is an excellent way to discover the means by which to achieve our goals. Beyond that, I feel many sharp differences, which I will try to spell out.

I believe that in Skinner's presentation here and in his previous writings, there is a serious underestimation of the problem of power. To hope that the power which is being made available by the behavioral sciences will be exercised by the scientists, or by a benevolent group, seems to me a hope little supported by either recent or distant history. It seems far more likely that behavioral scientists, holding their present attitudes, will be in the position of the German rocket scientists specializing in guided missiles. First they worked devotedly for Hitler to destroy the U.S.S.R. and the United States. Now, depending on

who captured them, they work devotedly for the U.S.S.R. in the interest of destroying the United States, or devotedly for the United States in the interest of destroying the U.S.S.R. If behavioral scientists are concerned solely with advancing their science, it seems most probable that they will serve the purposes of whatever individual or group has the power.

But the major flaw I see in this review of what is involved in the scientific control of human behavior is the denial, misunderstanding, or gross underestimation of the place of ends, goals, or values in their relationship to science. This error (as it seems to me) has so many implications that I would like to devote some space to it.

Ends and Values in Relation to Science

In sharp contradiction to some views that have been advanced, I would like to propose a two-pronged thesis: (1) In any scientific endeavor—whether "pure" or applied science—there is a prior subjective choice of the purpose or value which that scientific work is perceived as serving. (2) This subjective value choice which brings that scientific endeavor into being must always lie outside of that endeavor and can never become a part of the science involved in that endeavor.

Let me illustrate the first point from Skinner himself. It is clear that in his earlier writing (1955–1956) it is recognized that a prior value choice is necessary, and it is specified as the goal that men are to become happy, well-behaved, productive, and so on. I am pleased that Skinner has retreated from the goals he then chose, because to me they seem to be stultifying values. I can only feel that he was choosing these goals for others, not for himself. I would hate to see Skinner become "well-behaved," as that term would be defined for him by behavioral scientists. His recent article in the *American Psychologist* (1956) shows that he certainly does not want to be "productive" as that value is defined by most psychologists. And the most awful fate I can imagine for him would be to have him constantly "happy." It is the fact that he is very unhappy about many things which makes me prize him.

In the first draft of his part of this article, he also included such prior value choices, saying for example, "We must decide how we are to use the knowledge which a science of human behavior is now making available." Now he has dropped all mention of such choices, and if I understand him correctly, he believes that science can proceed without them. He has suggested this view in another recent paper, stating that

We must continue to experiment in cultural design . . . testing the consequences as we go. Eventually the practices which make for the greatest biological and psychological strength of the group will presumably survive. (Skinner, 1955, p. 549.)

I would point out, however, that to choose to experiment is a value choice. Even to move in the direction of perfectly random experimentation is a value choice. To test the consequences of an experiment is possible only if we have first made a subjective choice of a criterion value. And implicit in his statement is a valuing of biological and psychological strength. So even when trying to avoid such choice, it seems inescapable that a prior subjective value choice is necessary for any scientific endeavor, or for any application of scientific knowledge.

I wish to make clear that I am not saying that values cannot be included as a subject of science. It is not true that science deals only with certain classes of "facts" and that these classes do not include values. It is a bit more complex than that, as a simple illustration or two may make clear.

If I value knowledge of the "three R's" as a goal of education, the methods of science can give me increasingly accurate information on how this goal may be achieved. If I value problem-solving ability as a goal of education, the scientific method can give me the same kind of help.

Now, if I wish to determine whether problem-solving ability is "better" than knowledge of the three R's, then scientific method can also study those two values but *only*—and this is very important—in terms of some other value which I have subjectively chosen. I may value college success. Then I can determine whether problem-solving ability or knowledge of the three R's is most closely associated with that value. I may value personal integration or vocational success or responsible citizenship. I can determine whether problem-solving ability or knowledge of the three R's is most closely associated with one of these values. But the value or purpose that gives meaning to a particular scientific endeavor must always lie outside of that endeavor.

Although our concern in this symposium is largely with applied science, what I have been saying seems equally true of so-called "pure" science. In pure science the usual prior subjective value choice is the discovery of truth. But this is a subjective choice, and science can never say whether it is the best choice, save in the light of some other value. Geneticists in the U.S.S.R., for example, had to make a subjective choice of whether it was better to pursue truth or to discover facts which upheld a governmental dogma. Which choice is "better"? We could make a scientific investigation of those alternatives but only in the light of some other subjectively chosen value. If, for example, we value the survival of a culture, then we could begin to investigate with the methods of science the question of whether pursuit of truth or support of governmental dogma is most closely associated with cultural survival.

My point then is that any endeavor in science, pure or applied, is carried on in the pursuit of a purpose or value that is subjectively chosen by persons. It is important that this choice be made explicit, since the particular value which is being sought can never be tested or evaluated, confirmed or denied, by the scientific endeavor to which it gives birth. The initial purpose or value always and necessarily lies outside the scope of the scientific effort which it sets in motion.

Among other things this means that if we choose some particular goal or series of goals for human beings and then set out on a large scale to control human behavior to the end of achieving those goals, we are locked in the rigidity of our initial choice, because such a scientific endeavor can never transcend itself to select new goals. Only subjective human persons can do that. Thus if we chose as our goal the state of happiness for human beings (a goal deservedly ridiculed by Aldous Huxley in *Brave New World*), and if we involved all of society in a successful scientific program by which people became happy, we would be locked in a colossal rigidity in which no one would be free to question this goal, because our scientific operations could not transcend themselves to question their guiding purposes. And without laboring this point, I would remark that colossal rigidity, whether in dinosaurs, or dictatorships, has a very poor record of evolutionary survival.

If, however, a part of our scheme is to set free some "planners" who do not have to be happy, who are not controlled, and who are therefore free to choose other values, this has several meanings. It means that the purpose we have chosen as our goal is not a sufficient and a satisfying one for human beings but must be supplemented. It also means that if it is necessary to set up an elite group which is free, then this shows all too clearly that the great majority are only the slaves—no matter by what high-sounding name we call them—of those who select the goals.

Perhaps, however, the thought is that a continuing scientific endeavor will evolve its own goals; that the initial findings will alter the directions, and subsequent findings will alter them still further, and that science somehow develops its own purpose. Although he does not clearly say so, this appears to be the pattern Skinner has in mind. It is surely a reasonable description, but it overlooks one element in this continuing development, which is that subjective personal choice enters in at every point at which the direction changes. The findings of a science, the results of an experiment, do not and never can tell us what next scientific purpose to pursue. Even in the purest of science, the scientist must decide what the findings mean and must subjectively choose what next step will be most profitable in the pursuit of his purpose. And if we are speaking of the application of scientific knowledge, then it is distressingly clear that the increasing scientific knowledge of the structure of the atom carries with it no necessary choice as to the purpose to which this knowledge will be put. This is a subjective personal choice which must be made by many individuals.

Thus I return to the proposition with which I began this section of my remarks—and which I now repeat in different words. Science has its meaning as the objective pursuit of a purpose which has been subjectively chosen by a person or persons. This purpose or value can never be investigated by the particular scientific experiment or investigation to which it has given birth and meaning. Consequently, any discussion of the control of human beings by the behavioral sciences must first and most deeply concern itself with the subjectively chosen purposes which such an application of science is intended to implement.

Is the Situation Hopeless?

The thoughtful reader may recognize that, although my remarks up to this point have introduced some modifications in the conception of the processes by which human behavior will be controlled, these remarks may have made such control seem, if anything, even more inevitable. We might sum it up this way: Behavioral science is clearly moving forward; the increasing power for control which it gives will be held by someone or some group; such an individual or group will surely choose the values or goals to be achieved; and most of us will then be increasingly controlled by means so subtle that we will not even be aware of them as controls. Thus, whether a council of wise psychologists (if this is not a contradiction in terms), or a Stalin, or a Big Brother has the power, and whether the goal is happiness, or productivity, or resolution of the Oedipus complex, or submission, or love of Big Brother, we will inevitably find ourselves moving toward the chosen goal and probably thinking that we ourselves desire it. Thus, if this line of reasoning is correct, it appears that some form of *Walden Two* or of *1984* (and at a deep philosophic level they seem indistinguishable) is coming. The fact that it would surely arrive piecemeal, rather than all at once, does not greatly change the fundamental issues. In any event, as Skinner has indicated in his writings, we would then look back upon the concepts of human freedom, the capacity for choice, the responsibility for choice, and the worth of the human individual as historical curiosities which once existed by cultural accident as values in a prescientific civilization.

I believe that any person observant of

trends must regard something like the foregoing sequence as a real possibility. It is not simply a fantasy. Something of that sort may even be the most likely future. But is it an inevitable future? I want to devote the remainder of my remarks to an alternative possibility.

Alternative Set of Values

Suppose we start with a set of ends, values, purposes, quite different from the type of goals we have been considering. Suppose we do this quite openly, setting them forth as a possible value choice to be accepted or rejected. Suppose we select a set of values that focuses on fluid elements of process rather than static attributes. We might then value: man as a process of becoming, as a process of achieving worth and dignity through the development of his potentialities; the individual human being as a self-actualizing process, moving on to more challenging and enriching experiences; the process by which the individual creatively adapts to an ever-new and changing world; the process by which knowledge transcends itself, as, for example, the theory of relativity transcended Newtonian physics, itself to be transcended in some future day by a new perception.

If we select values such as these we turn to our science and technology of behavior with a very different set of questions. We will want to know such things as these: Can science aid in the discovery of new modes of richly rewarding living? more meaningful and satisfying modes of interpersonal relationships? Can science inform us on how the human race can become a more intelligent participant in its own evolution—its physical, psychological, and social evolution? Can science inform us on ways of releasing the creative capacity of individuals, which seems so necessary if we are to survive in this fantastically expanding atomic age? Oppenheimer has pointed out (1956b) that knowledge, which used to double in millennia or centuries, now doubles in a generation or a decade. It appears that we must discover the utmost in release of creativity if we are to be able to adapt effectively. In short, can science discover the methods by which man can most readily become a continually developing and self-transcending process, in his behavior, his thinking, his knowledge? Can science predict and release an essentially "unpredictable" freedom?

It is one of the virtues of science as a method that it is as able to advance and implement goals and purposes of this sort as it is to serve static values, such as states of being well-informed, happy, obedient. Indeed we have some evidence of this.

Small Example

I will perhaps be forgiven if I document some of the possibilities along this line by turning to psychotherapy, the field I know best.

Psychotherapy, as Meerloo (1955) and others have pointed out, can be one of the most subtle tools for the control of A by B. The therapist can subtly mold individuals in imitation of himself. He can cause an individual to become a submissive and conforming being. When certain therapeutic principles are used in extreme fashion, we call it brainwashing, an instance of the disintegration of the personality and a reformulation of the person along lines desired by the controlling individual. So the principles of therapy can be used as an effective means of external control of human personality and behavior. Can psychotherapy be anything else?

Here I find the developments going on in client-centered psychotherapy (Rogers, 1951) an exciting hint of what a behavioral science can do in achieving the kinds of values I have stated. Quite aside from being a somewhat new orientation in psychotherapy, this development has important implications regarding the relation of a behavioral science to the control of human behavior. Let me describe our experience as it relates to the issues of this discussion.

In client-centered therapy, we are deeply engaged in the prediction and influencing of behavior, or even the control of behavior. As therapists we institute certain attitudinal conditions, and the client has relatively little voice in the establishment of these conditions. We predict that if these conditions are instituted, certain behavioral consequences will ensue in the client. Up to this point this is largely external control, no different from what Skinner has described, and no different from what I have discussed in the preceding sections of this article. But here the similarity ceases.

The conditions we have chosen to establish predict such behavioral consequences as these: that the client will become self-directing, less rigid, more open to the evidence of his senses, better organized and integrated, more similar to the ideal which he has chosen for himself. In other words, we have established by external control conditions which we predict will be followed by internal control by the individual, in pursuit of internally chosen goals. We have set the conditions which predict various classes of behaviors—self-directing behaviors, sensitivity to realities within and without, flexible adaptiveness—which are by their very nature unpredictable in their specifics. Our recent research (Rogers and Dymond, 1954) indicates that our predictions are to a significant degree corroborated, and our commitment to the scientific method causes us to believe that more effective means of achieving these goals may be realized.

Research exists in other fields—industry, education, group dynamics—which seems to support our own findings. I believe it may be conservatively stated that scientific progress has been made in identifying those conditions in an interpersonal relationship which, if they exist in *B*, are followed in *A* by greater maturity in behavior, less dependence on others, an increase in expressiveness as a person, an increase in variability, flexibility, and effectiveness of adaptation, an increase in self-responsibility and self-direction. And, quite in contrast to the concern expressed by some, we do not find that the creatively adaptive behavior which results from such self-directed variability of expression is a "happy accident" which occurs in "chaos." Rather, the individual who is open to his experience, and self-directing, is harmonious not chaotic, ingenious rather than random, as he orders his responses imaginatively toward the achievement of his own purposes. His creative actions are no more a "happy accident" than was Einstein's development of the theory of relativity.

Thus we find ourselves in fundamental agreement with John Dewey's statement: "Science has made its way by releasing, not by suppressing, the elements of variation, of invention and innovation, of novel creation in individuals." (Ratner, 1939, p. 359.) Progress in personal life and in group living is, we believe, made in the same way.

Possible Concept of the Control of Human Behavior

It is quite clear that the point of view I am expressing is in sharp contrast to the usual conception of the relationship of the behavioral sciences to the control of human behavior. In order to make this contrast even more blunt, I will state this possibility in paragraphs parallel to those used before.

1. It is possible for us to choose to value man as a self-actualizing process of becoming; to value creativity, and the process by which knowledge becomes self-transcending.
2. We can proceed, by the methods of science, to discover the conditions which necessarily precede these processes and, through continuing experimentation, to discover better means of achieving these purposes.

3. It is possible for individuals or groups to set these conditions, with a minimum of power or control. According to present knowledge, the only authority necessary is the authority to establish certain qualities of interpersonal relationship.

4. Exposed to these conditions, present knowledge suggests that individuals become more self-responsible, make progress in self-actualization, become more flexible, and become more creatively adaptive.

5. Thus such an initial choice would inaugurate the beginnings of a social system or subsystem in which values, knowledge, adaptive skills, and even the concept of science would be continually changing and self-transcending. The emphasis would be upon man as a process of becoming.

I believe it is clear that such a view as I have been describing does not lead to any definable utopia. It would be impossible to predict its final outcome. It involves a step-by-step development, based on a continuing subjective choice of purposes, which are implemented by the behavioral sciences. It is the direction of the "open society," as that term has been defined by Popper (1945), where individuals carry responsibility for personal decisions. It is at the opposite pole from his concept of the closed society, of which *Walden Two* would be an example.

I trust it is also evident that the whole emphasis is on process, not on end-states of being. I am suggesting that it is by choosing to value certain qualitative elements of the process of becoming that we can find a pathway toward the open society.

The Choice

It is my hope that we have helped to clarify the range of choice which will lie before us and our children in regard to the behavioral sciences. We can choose to use our growing knowledge to enslave people in ways never dreamed of before, depersonalizing them, controlling them by means so carefully selected that they will perhaps never be aware of their loss of personhood. We can choose to utilize our scientific knowledge to make men happy, well-behaved, and productive, as Skinner earlier suggested. Or we can ensure that each person learns all the syllabus which we select and set before him, as Skinner now suggests. Or at the other end of the spectrum or choice we can choose to use the behavioral sciences in ways which will free, not control; which will bring about constructive variability, not conformity; which will develop creativity, not contentment; which will facilitate each person in his self-directed process of becoming; which will aid individuals, groups, and even the concept of science to become self-transcending in freshly adaptive ways of meeting life and its problems. The choice is up to us, and, the human race being what it is, we are likely to stumble about, making at times some nearly disastrous value choices and at other times highly constructive ones.

I am aware that to some, this setting forth of a choice is unrealistic, because a choice of values is regarded as not possible. Skinner has stated:

Man's vaunted creative powers ... his capacity to choose and our right to hold him responsible for his choice—none of these is conspicuous in this new self-portrait (provided by science). Man, we once believed, was free to express himself in art, music, and literature, to inquire into nature, to seek salvation in his own way. He could initiate action and make spontaneous and capricious changes of course.... But science insists that action is initiated by forces impinging upon the individual, and that caprice is only another name for behavior for which we have not yet found a cause. (1955–1956, pp. 52–53.)

I can understand this point of view, but I believe that it avoids looking at the great paradox of behavioral science. Behavior, when it is examined scientifically, is surely best understood as determined by prior causation. This is one great fact of science. But responsible personal choice, which is the most essential element in being a person, which is the core experience in psychotherapy, which exists prior to any scientific endeavor, is an equally prominent fact in our lives. To deny the experience of responsible choice is, to me, as restricted a view as to deny the possibility of a behavioral science. That these two important elements of our experience appear to be in contradiction has perhaps the same significance as the contradiction between the wave theory and the corpuscular theory of light, both of which can be shown to be true, even though incompatible. We cannot profitably deny our subjective life, any more than we can deny the objective description of that life.

In conclusion then, it is my contention that science cannot come into being without a personal choice of the values we wish to achieve. And these values we choose to implement will forever lie outside of the science which implements them; the goals we select, the purposes we wish to follow, must always be outside of the science which achieves them. To me this has the encouraging meaning that the human person, with his capacity of subjective choice, can and will always exist, separate from and prior to any of his scientific undertakings. Unless as individuals and groups we choose to relinquish our capacity of subjective choice, we will always remain persons, not simply pawns of a self-created science.

III—SKINNER

I cannot quite agree that the practice of science *requires* a prior decision about goals or a prior choice of values. The metallurgist can study the properties of steel and the engineer can design a bridge without raising the question of whether a bridge is to be built. But such questions are certainly frequently raised and tentatively answered. Rogers wants to call the answers "subjective choices of values." To me, such an expression suggests that we have had to abandon more rigorous scientific practices in order to talk about our own behavior. In the experimental analysis of other organisms I would use other terms, and I shall try to do so here. Any list of values is a list of reinforcers—conditioned or otherwise. We are so constituted that under certain circumstances food, water, sexual contact, and so on, will make any behavior which produces them more likely to occur again. Other things may acquire this power. We do not need to say that an organism chooses to eat rather than to starve. If you answer that it is a very different thing when a man chooses to starve, I am only too happy to agree. If it were not so, we should have cleared up the question of choice long ago. An organism can be reinforced by— can be made to "choose"—almost any given state of affairs.

Rogers is concerned with choices that involve multiple and usually conflicting consequences. I have dealt with some of these elsewhere (Skinner, 1953) in an analysis of self-control. Shall I eat these delicious strawberries today if I will then suffer an annoying rash tomorrow? The decision I am to make used to be assigned to the province of ethics. But we are now studying similar combinations of positive and negative consequences, as well as collateral conditions which affect the result in a laboratory. Even a pigeon can be taught some measure of self-control! And this work helps us to understand the operation of certain formulas —among them value judgments—which folk wisdom, religion, and psychotherapy have advanced in the interests of self-discipline. The observable effect of any statement of value is to alter the relative effectiveness of reinforcers. We may no longer enjoy the strawberries for thinking about the rash. If rashes are made sufficiently shameful, illegal, sinful, maladjusted, or unwise, we may glow with satisfaction as we push the strawberries aside in a grandiose avoidance response which would bring a smile to the lips of Murray Sidman.

People behave in ways which, as we say, conform to ethical, governmental, or religious patterns because they are reinforced for doing so. The resulting behavior may have far-reaching consequences for the survival of the pattern to which it conforms. And whether we like it or not, survival is the ultimate criterion. This is where, it seems to me, science can help—not in choosing a goal, but in enabling us to predict the survival value of cultural practices. Man has too long tried to get the kind of world he wants by glorifying some brand of immediate reinforcement. As science points up more and more of the remoter consequences, he may begin to work to strengthen behavior, not in slavish devotion to a chosen value, but with respect to the ultimate survival of mankind. Do not ask me why I want mankind to survive. I can tell you why only in the sense in which the physiologist can tell you why I want to breathe. Once the relation between a given step and the survival of my group has been pointed out, I will take that step. And it is the business of science to point out just such relations.

The values I have occasionally recommended (and Rogers has not led me to recant) are transitional. Other things being equal, I am betting on the group whose practices make for healthy, happy, secure, productive, and creative people. And I insist that the values recommended by Rogers are transitional, too, for I can ask him the same kind of question. Man as a process of becoming—what? Self-actualization—for what? Inner control is no more a goal than external.

What Rogers seems to me to be proposing both here and elsewhere (Rogers, 1956), is this: Let us use our increasing power of control to create individuals who will not need and perhaps will no longer respond to control. Let us solve the problem of our power by renouncing it. At first blush this seems as implausible as a benevolent despot. Yet power has occasionally been foresworn. A nation has burned its Reichstag, rich men have given away their wealth, beautiful women have become ugly hermits in the desert, and psychotherapists have become nondirective. When this happens, I look to other possible reinforcements for a plausible explanation. A people relinquish democratic power when a tyrant promises them the earth. Rich men give away wealth to escape the accusing finger of their fellow-men. A woman destroys her beauty in the hope of salvation. And a psychotherapist relinquishes control because he can thus help his client more effectively.

The solution that Rogers is suggesting is thus understandable. But is he correctly interpreting the result? What evidence is there that a client ever becomes truly *self*-directing? What evidence is there that he ever makes a truly *inner* choice of ideal or goal? Even though the therapist does not do the choosing, even though he encourages "self-actualization"—he is not out of control as long as he holds himself ready to step in when occasion demands—when, for example, the client chooses the goal of becoming a more accomplished liar or murdering his boss. But supposing the therapist does withdraw completely or is no longer necessary—what about all the other forces acting upon the client? Is the self-chosen goal independent of his early ethical and religious training? of the folk wisdom of his group? of the opinions and attitudes of others who are important to him? Surely not. The therapeutic situation is only a small part of the world of the client. From the therapist's point of view it may appear to be possible to relinquish control. But the control passes not to a "self," but to forces in other parts of the client's world. The solution of the therapist's problem of power cannot be *our* solution, for we must consider *all* the forces acting upon the individual.

The child who must be prodded and nagged is something less than a fully developed human being. We want to see him hurrying to his appointment, not because each step is taken in response to verbal reminders from his mother, but because certain temporal contingencies, in which dawdling has been punished and hurrying reinforced, have worked a change in his behavior. Call this a state of better organization, a greater sensitivity to reality, or what you will. The plain fact is that the child passes from a temporary verbal control exercised by his parents to control by certain inexorable features of the environment. I should suppose that something of the same sort happens in successful psychotherapy. Rogers seems to me to be saying this: Let us put an end, as quickly as possible, to any pattern of master-and-slave, to any direct obedience to command, to the submissive following of suggestions. Let the individual be free to adjust himself to more rewarding features of the world about him. In the end, let his teachers and counselors "wither away," like the Marxist state. I not only agree with this as a useful ideal, I have constructed a fanciful world to demonstate its advantages. It saddens me to hear Rogers say that "at a deep philosophic level" *Walden Two* and George Orwell's *1984* "seem indistinguishable." They could scarcely be more unlike—at any level. The book *1984* is a picture of immediate aversive control for vicious selfish purposes. The founder of *Walden Two,* on the other hand, has built a community in which neither he nor any other person exerts any *current* control. His achievement lay in his original *plan*, and when he boasts of this ("It is enough to satisfy the thirstiest tyrant") we do not fear him but only pity him for his weakness.

Another critic of *Walden Two*, Andrew Hacker (1955), has discussed this point in considering the bearing of mass conditioning upon the liberal notion of autonomous man. In drawing certain parallels between the Grand Inquisition passage in Dostoevsky's *Brothers Karamazov*, Huxley's *Brave New World*, and *Walden Two*, he attempts to set up a distinction to be drawn in any society between conditioners and conditioned. He assumes that "the conditioner can be said to be autonomous in the traditional liberal sense." But then he notes: "Of course the conditioner has been conditioned. But he has not been conditioned by the conscious manipulation of another *person*." But how does this affect the resulting behavior? Can we not soon forget the origins of the "artificial" diamond which is identical with the real thing? Whether it is an "accidental" cultural pattern, such as is said to have produced the founder of *Walden Two*, or the engineered environment which is about to produce his successors, we are dealing with sets of conditions generating human behavior which will ultimately be measured by their contribution to the strength of the group. We look to the future, not the past, for the test of "goodness" or acceptability.

If we are worthy of our democratic heritage we shall, of course, be ready to resist any tyrannical use of science for immediate or selfish purposes. But if we value the achievements and goals of democracy we must not refuse to apply science to the design and construction of cultural patterns, even though we may then find ourselves in some sense in the position of controllers. Fear of control, generalized beyond any warrant, has led to a misinterpretation of valid practices and the blind rejection of intelligent planning for a better way of life. In terms which I trust Rogers will approve, in conquering this fear we shall become more mature and better organized and shall, thus, more fully actualize ourselves as human beings.

REFERENCES

Coleman, C., "The Hickory Stick," Bulletin of the American Association of University Professors, **39** (1953), pp. 457–473.

Freund, P. A., et al., *Constitutional Law: Cases and Other Problems*, Vol. 1 (Boston: Little, Brown, 1954).

Hacker, A., "The Specter of Predictable Man," *Antioch Review*, **14** (1954), pp. 195–207.

Hacker, A., "Dostoevsky's Disciples: Man and Sheep in Political Theory, *Journal of Politics*, **17** (1955), pp. 590–613.

Krutch, J. W., *The Measure of Man* (New York: Bobbs-Merrill, 1954).

Meerloo, J. A. M., "Medication into Submission: Danger of Therapeutic Coercion," *Journal of Nervous and Mental Disorders*, **122** (1955), pp. 353–360.

Negley, G., and J. M. Patrick, *The Quest for Utopia* (New York: Schuman, 1952).

Niebuhr, R., *The Self and the Dramas of History* (New York: Scribner's, 1955).

Oppenheimer, J. R., "Analogy in Science," *American Psychologist*, **11** (1956a), pp. 127–135.

Oppenheimer, J. R., "Science and Our Times," *Roosevelt Univ. Occasional Papers* (1956b), No. 2.

Popper, K. R., *The Open Society and Its Enemies* (London: Routledge & Kegan Paul, 1945).

Ratner, J. (ed.), *Intelligence in the Modern World: John Dewey's Philosophy* (New York: Modern Library, 1939).

Rogers, C. R., "Implications of Recent Advances in Prediction and Control of Behavior," *Teachers College Record*, **57** (1957), pp. 316–322.

Rogers, C. R., and R. Dymond (eds.), *Psychotherapy and Personality Change* (Chicago: Univ. of Chicago Press, 1954).

Skinner, B. F., *Walden Two* (New York: Macmillan, 1948).

Skinner, B. F., *Science and Human Behavior* (New York: Macmillan, 1953).

Skinner, B. F., "The Control of Human Behavior," *Transactions of New York Academy of Science*, **17** (1955), pp. 547–551.

Skinner, B. F., "Freedom and the Control of Men," *American Scholar*, **25** (Winter 1955–1956), special issue, pp. 47–65.

Skinner, B. F., "A Case History in Scientific Method," *American Psychologist*, **11** (1956), pp. 221–233.

Vandenberg, S. G., "Great Expectations or the Future of Psychology (as seen in science fiction)," *American Psychologist*, **11** (1956), pp. 339–342.

Viteles, M. S., "The New Utopia," *Science*, **122** (1955), pp. 1167–1171.

THE POWER OF SYSTEMS AND SYSTEMS OF POWER

Robert Boguslaw

One of the more popular pastimes developed in the wake of a rapidly burgeoning high-speed computer technology has been the game of "let's play you think computers are bad and I think they are good." In one reported encounter, the protagonists were Norbert Wiener (the father of cybernetics) and Arthur L. Samuel (one of IBM's bright sons). Wiener stated as his thesis that "machines can and do transcend some of the limitations of their designers, and that in doing so they may be both effective and dangerous."[1] Samuel, invoking the familiar argument that "most, if not all, of man's inventions are instrumentalities which may be employed by both saints and sinners,"[2] concluded that "the modern digital computer is a modality whose value is overwhelmingly on the side of the good."[3]

History does not record a score for this particular contest, but one is tempted to question whether the game was played in the right ballpark. The Wiener thesis seems to proceed from a perspective that sees the computer as something like a bow-and-arrow contraption possessing more or less indeterminate, boomeranglike performance characteristics. Samuel seems to see his product essentially as a better mousetrap (and who wants to be on the side of the rats)?

There is, of course, at least one additional perspective from which we may contemplate the computer. This is the perspective that helps us to see it as an integral part of a larger, more encompassing social structure. Computers are not found in nature. They have to be built. And they must take their places within a framework of existing social systems. A decision to place them within a framework redefines existing system arrangements in significant ways. Indeed, as computer complexes assume functions previously performed by bureaucratic hierarchies or disparate units or unorganized work groups, they almost invariably lead to the redesign of existing systems. Specifically, this means changes in information organization (with the aid of computers or other physical equipment), formalized work procedures (that is, customs, computer programs, organizational directives, and so forth), and people.

The process of engaging in this redesign inevitably raises issues about how various system "functions" are to be accomplished. Without becoming embroiled in the intricacies of several hoary controversies among anthropologists and sociologists about the precise meaning of function and the usefulness of "functional analysis" we may note a formulation that defines function as the contribution an activity within a system makes to the whole.[4] This definition points up the importance of "specifying precisely both the part and the whole to which a functional statement refers. A practice which is functional within one social region need not be functional in one which is more (or less) inclusive."[5]

The credo of an engineer designing systems composed exclusively of physical or "hardware" components includes the assumption that all functions performed by the components will be *manifest* (that is, "intended and recognized" by the designer).[6] *Latent* functions (those that are neither intended nor recognized) are hopefully omitted. The same credo is held by designers of classical utopias.

The difficulties that arise when computerized systems are designed *without* deviating from this credo have become legend among sophisticates. Suppose, for example, you wish to "automate" the communication functions carried on within a large system.

[1] Norbert Wiener, "Some Moral and Technical Consequences of Automation," in Morris Philipson (ed.), *Automation Implications for the Future* (New York: Random House, 1962), p. 163.
[2] Arthur L. Samuel, "Some Moral and Technical Consequences of Automation—A Refutation," *ibid.*, p. 179.
[3] *Ibid.*
[4] Harold Fallding, "Functional Analysis in Sociology," *American Sociological Review*, **28**:1 (February 1963).
[5] *Ibid.*, p. 6.
[6] Robert K. Merton, "Manifest and Latent Functions," in *Social Theory and Social Structure*, rev. ed. (New York: Free Press of Glencoe, 1957), p. 51.

A preliminary step must consist of a detailed specification of the various classes of information currently being communicated. To obtain such a specification, one might examine messages transmitted in the past, and perhaps codify the information normally transmitted over telephone or telegraph lines, and so on. In the process of conducting such an examination, it is all too easy for the neophyte to overlook classes of information characteristically transmitted, let us say, during coffee breaks. Ignoring the latent communicative function of the coffee break can result in a highly complex computerized system that has no way of dealing with some of its most crucial categories of system information.

As Robert K. Merton expressed it many years ago, "any attempt to eliminate an existing social structure without providing adequate alternative structures for fulfilling the functions previously fulfilled by the abolished organization is doomed to failure."[7]

Now one of the most pervasive characteristics of all social structures is the fact of social differentiation. This, in itself, does not seem very startling. We are accustomed to the notion that some people are old and some young, some female, some male, and so forth. Social differentiation becomes a matter for controversy only after it is used as a basis for social stratification: the distribution of unequal rewards among the various participants in a social system.

Many years ago, two sociologists (Kingsley Davis and Wilbert E. Moore) tried to explain these differences essentially on the basis that

if the more important, highly skilled, and physically and psychologically demanding positions in a complex division of labor are to be adequately filled both from the standpoint of numbers and of minimally efficient performance, *then* there must be *some* unequal rewards favoring these positions over others.[8]

It seems clear that the particular scale of unequal rewards existing in a society tends to be self-perpetuating. People become accustomed to the allocation of certain differences in reward and tend to resist drastic changes.[9] A president of an industrial firm makes more money than a charwoman—this is considered appropriate and fair; and anyone who suggested a reversal in the reward system for our society would encounter serious resistance, not only from presidents, but from most "reasonable" people—including charwomen.

In designing a computerized system on the site of a previously existing "manual" social structure, one inevitably must deal with the effects the new system will have on previously existing roles and their incumbents. When the role incumbents are unskilled or semiskilled workers whose more or less routinized jobs are assumed by the computerized installation, this takes the form of concern with "technological displacement" and consideration of the consequences of "automation." The dialogue may proceed along lines of "these displaced workers must be trained for new skills—like computer programming; however, some people are untrainable and they constitute the core of the social problem accompanying automation. This is something like what happened when the automobile replaced the horse and buggy—new jobs will emerge for which people can be trained—the blacksmiths will simply have to face reality, and so forth."

---

[7] *Ibid.*, p. 81.

[8] Cf. Dennis H. Wrong, "The Functional Theory of Stratification: Some Neglected Considerations," *American Sociological Review*, **24**:6 (December 1959), p. 774.

[9] *Ibid.*

In terms of social stratification, the human, low-skilled workers are simply eliminated. They are not just placed at the bottom of the status and economic-reward ladder; they are removed from it.

But this removal inevitably has direct consequences for those who remain. The middle-level bureaucrat whose value consisted primarily of the uncodified information in his desk, file, or head now finds that he has been asked to furnish all relevant information to a central repository. Much of the prior basis of his unequal reward has been removed. The second- or third-level executive whose value consisted of an ability to analyze large quantities of data and come up with significant policy recommendations now finds his data analysis can be done more effectively according to predetermined analytical schemes. The highly skilled and psychologically demanding positions become those relating to operations of the computer and the formulation of computer programs.

All this, of course, shakes the foundations of existing stratification realities. Former "key decision makers" begin to feel, and indeed are regarded, as anachronistic hangers-on. Experienced computer experts have many techniques for dealing with this problem. One approach is to point out that the locus of decision making still rests with the former executive or manager. This, of course, is not really true. Disbelievers see the light when they ask for a given set of figures or ask that a pet procedure be implemented.

The answer, all too frequently, becomes "but the program can't handle it." Or, "We can't do that just yet, but in about six months, after these immediate problems are ironed out, I'm sure we can get that for you." Or, "This set of figures will cover about 98 percent of all the cases you could possibly be interested in; it just wouldn't be economical to try to get 100 percent of all the cases," and so on.

To an executive accustomed to getting his own way from human employees, even if they have to work overtime or develop ulcers in the process, this may all sound like an unpardonable affront to managerial prerogatives. He is thus inexorably driven to the next step in the process—the "I want a computer course" step. The feeling seems to be: "If I could only learn a little about computer programming, I could keep those snotty kids from being in a position to tell me how to run my business."

But, unfortunately, computer courses for executives seldom provide enduring solutions. At best, the executive learns to deal with his frustrations by accepting the frame of reference of the computer expert and adjusting his sights accordingly. The exercise of power, which formerly was mediated through conventions of law, custom, "what the union will stand still for," or "principles of human relations"—now must be mediated through the current state of computer technology.

To proceed in this fashion (that is, through technology-screened power) is to adopt an orientation that is essentially formalist in nature (although the work of Newell, Simon, and Shaw in the area of heuristic programming provides the promise of creative alternatives). The specification of future and current system states within this orientation characteristically requires an insistence upon a uniformity of perspective, a standardization of language, and a consensus of values that is characteristic of highly authoritarian social structures. Nonconforming perspectives, language, and values can be and, indeed, must be excluded as system elements.

All this is a familiar pattern in classical utopias. Although the inhabitants of utopian societies were frequently prepared to deal with external threats, internal dissension was almost invariably taboo. The tradition of specifying functions within computer-based systems enhances the points of structural correspondence of these systems and classical utopias. In this connection, Ralf Dahrendorf's summary of the structural features of utopian societies provides some useful insights. He points out that: (1) Utopias do not grow out of familiar reality or follow realistic patterns of development. (2) Utopias characteristically have universal consensus on values and institutional arrangements; that is, they are highly uniform throughout. (3) Utopias are characterized by an absence of internal conflict; that is, they are characterized by social harmony, which helps to account for their stability. (4) All processes within utopian societies follow recurrent patterns and occur as part of the design of the whole. (5) Utopias are characteristically isolated in time and space from other parts of the world.[10]

The simple fact of the matter seems to be that classically designed computer-based systems, like classical utopias, resolve problems of conflict, consensus, and reality by simple fiat. But these old problems do not thereby simply fade away. Environments change. Internal conditions change. Systems and utopias alike must be ready and able to change if they are to survive. But crucial types of change originate *within* systems—out of the contradictions and conflicts existing between two or more opposing sets of values, ideologies, roles, institutions, or groups.[11]

To insist that social structures must always be shaped and controlled from "topside," is to reinforce maladaptive tendencies in systems and to help to ensure their ultimate collapse. A façade of value homogeneity cannot resolve the internal stresses, conflicts, and dilemmas that arise in any system designed to cope effectively with the fact of change.

POWER AND BUREAUCRACY

The problem of understanding what it is that makes human societies "stick together" or cohere has been studied by philosophers and social theorists for thousands of years. In general, two different kinds of explanation are offered. The first of these emphasizes the role of *consensus*—the existence of a general agreement on values within the society. The second explanation emphasizes the role of *coercion*—the use of force and constraint to hold a society together.[12]

One of the interesting limitations of traditional utopias is the relative lack of detailed concern they reflect about the composition of the glue used to hold things together.

In the *consensus* formula for social glue, people with common values voluntarily associate to help ensure more effective cooperation. In the *coercion* formula, positions within the system are defined to ensure effective application of force and constraints.[13] To understand the operation of any system, it is crucial to understand the distribution of authority and power within it. Differences in system design may, in the last analysis, involve little more than different allocations of power and authority throughout the system. Indeed, alternate arguments about the merits of different

[10] Cf. Ralf Dahrendorf, "Out of Utopia: Toward a Reorientation of Sociological Analysis," *American Journal of Sociology*, **64**:2 (September 1958), pp. 116–117.
[11] Cf. Pierre L. Van Den Berghe, "Dialectic and Functionalism: Toward a Theoretical Synthesis," *American Sociological Review*, **28**:5 (October 1963), p. 699.
[12] Ralf Dahrendorf, *Class and Class Conflict in Industrial Society* (Stanford, Calif.: Stanford Univ. Press, 1959), pp. 157–159.
[13] Cf. *ibid.*, p. 169.

system design formats may well involve little beyond implicit rationalizations for alternate modes of power distribution.

Each of these formulas is based upon a set of assumptions about the nature of society or social systems. The consensus formula assumes that society is a relatively stable and well-integrated structure of elements, each of which has a well-defined function. Throughout the system itself, there exists a consensus of values among its various members. The coercion formula assumes that every society is at every point subject to both processes of change and social conflict. It further assumes that every element in a society contributes to the system's disintegration and change. And finally, the coercion formula assumes that every society is based on the coercion of some of its members by others. . . .[14]

The point to be stressed here, however, is the importance of specifying the exact nature of the particular glue to be used in a specific system design. Perhaps the easiest error to make is the one that assumes that a consensus glue exists, when in point of fact the design either requires, or has surreptitiously imposed, a coercion formula.

To clarify this somewhat, it may be helpful to note how power, in the sociological sense, is differentiated from force on the one hand and authority on the other.

Force, in this context, refers to the reduction, limitation, closure, or total elimination of alternatives to the social action of one person or group by another person or group. For example, "Your money or your life," symbolizes a situation in which the alternatives have been reduced to two. Hanging a convicted criminal exemplifies

the total elimination of alternatives. Dismissal or demotion of personnel in an organization illustrates the closure of alternatives. An army may successively place limitations upon the social action of its enemy until only two alternatives remain —to surrender or die.[15]

Power refers to the ability to apply force, rather than to its actual application. It is the "predisposition or prior capacity which makes the application of force possible."[16]

Authority refers to institutionalized power. In an idealized organization, power and authority become equivalent to each other. The right to use force is attached to certain statuses within the organization. "It is . . . authority in virtue of which persons in an association exercise command or control over other persons in the same association."[17] Examples of the use of authority include: the bishop who transfers a priest from his parish, the commanding officer who assigns a subordinate to a post of duty, a baseball team manager who changes a pitcher in the middle of an inning, and a factory superintendent who requires that an employee complete a task by a given time.[18]

"Your money or your life," constitutes what in the computer trade would be called a binary choice. If the alternatives available were extended to include, let us say, "the twenty-dollar bill you now have in your pocket," "room and board at your home for two days," "a serviceable overcoat," "the three bottles of scotch you have in your closet," or "a friendly chat over a good meal," then the intensity of the force being applied might be seen as somewhat diminished. This is simply another way of noting that the exercise of force is related

---

[14] Cf. *ibid.*, pp. 161–162.
[15] Cf. Robert Bierstedt, "An Analysis of Social Power," *American Sociological Review*, **15**:6 (December 1950), p. 733.
[16] *Ibid.*
[17] *Ibid.*, 734.
[18] *Ibid.*

to the range of action alternatives made available. The person with the ability to specify the alternatives—in this case, the person with the gun—is the one who possesses power.

And so it is that a designer of systems, who has the de facto prerogative to specify the range of phenomena that his system will distinguish, clearly is in possession of enormous degrees of power (depending, of course, upon the nature of the system being designed). It is by no means necessary that this power be formalized through the allocation of specific authority to wield nightsticks or guns.

The strength of high-speed computers lies precisely in their capacity to process binary choice data rapidly. But to process these data, the world of reality must at some point in time be reduced to binary form. This occurs initially through operational specifications handed to a computer programmer. These specifications serve as the basis for more detailed reductions to binary choices. The range of possibilities is ultimately set by the circuitry of the computer, which places finite limits on alternatives for data storage and processing. The structure of the language used to communicate with the computer places additional restrictions on the range of alternatives. The programmer himself, through the specific sets of data he uses in his solution to a programming problem and the specific techniques he uses for his solution, places a final set of restrictions on action alternatives available within a computer-based system.

It is in this sense that computer programmers, the designers of computer equipment, and the developers of computer languages possess power. To the extent that

decisions made by each of these participants in the design process serve to reduce, limit, or totally eliminate action alternatives, they are applying force and wielding power in the precise sociological meaning of these terms. . . .

As computer-based systems become increasingly more significant in shaping the realistic terms of existence in contemporary society, it becomes increasingly more relevant to inquire about the implications contained for expression of individual values. The process of obtaining representation for individual values is one of the specific notions contained in popular conceptions of democracy. However, the central idea of democracy has been penetratingly described as "one particular way in which the authority to govern is acquired and held."[19] Thus,

A man may be said to hold authority democratically when he has been freely chosen to hold such authority by those who must live under it, when they have had, and will have, the alternative of choosing somebody else, and when he is accountable to them for the way in which he exercises this authority.[20]

It is, of course, clear that there are limits on the democratic principle and that legal and institutional safeguards must exist to protect values other than those of democracy itself. It is equally clear that at best the democratic principle can be only approximated. No one in our society seriously suggests that every person must be absolutely equal to every other person in power and influence.[21] But,

the working touchstone of a "democratic" system of authority is simply the degree to which it gives individuals legitimate instruments for reaching those who make the decisions that affect them, and for bringing influence to bear upon

[19] Charles Frankel, "Bureaucracy and Democracy in the New Europe," *Daedalus* (Proceedings of the American Academy of Arts and Sciences), **93**:1 (Winter 1964), p. 476.
[20] *Ibid.*
[21] Cf. *ibid.*, pp. 476–477.

them. A system is more or less "democratic" depending on the number, availability, and effectiveness of these instruments, and on the proportion of the population entitled and able to use them.[22]

Now, whether the "masses" are denied legitimate access to decision makers by reason of despotism, bureaucratic deviousness, or simple technical obfuscation, the resultant erosion of democratic process can be much the same. To the extent that decisions made by equipment manufacturers, computer programmers, or system designers are enshrouded in the mystery of "technical" detail, the persons most affected by these decisions (including customers, publics, and employees) will be denied the opportunity to participate or react to the decision made. The spectrum of values represented in the new decision-making order can and is being increasingly more circumscribed by fiat disguised as technological necessity. The paramount issues to be raised in connection with the design of our new computerized utopias are not technological—they are issues of values and the power through which these values become translated into action.

[22] *Ibid.*, p. 477.

III

HUMAN RIGHTS

7

Racism, Poverty, and Inequality

IMPOVERISHMENT AND RACIAL DOMINATION

The Editors

Estimates of the number of poor in the United States range from a low of 20 million to a high of 40 million persons. The great variation in these estimates is due almost entirely to the definitions used to classify an individual or family above or below the poverty line. This reflects the relative nature of poverty (or luxury for that matter) and illustrates an important point: persons are classified as poor in relation to other persons and to a standard of living that is currently accepted as statistically normal. Failure to understand this basic fact often leads to efforts to show how America's "poor" earn more than the vast majority of persons in the rest of the world, or that the "poor" have television sets, cars, and other "luxuries." Such comparisons do not make use of some basic understandings concerning the *social* definitions of poverty.

In 1963 the Department of Health, Education and Welfare found that there were some 34½ million persons in the United States with incomes below a minimum budget; the budget is based on a minimum level of living for families and persons living alone (Miller, 1966). About 5 million of the poor lived alone, and 30 million, one-half of these being children, lived in families. Many of those families below the poverty line are not there because of unemployment. About one-half of the families are headed by males who had full-time employment at some point throughout the year. This indicates that many of the poverty families are working families with poor incomes and with little chance to improve their incomes because of limited skills and education.

In the three years that have passed since the first edition of this book, the number of families *defined* as poor (i.e., with income below the official poverty line) has decreased. This decrease is probably due to the effect of the poverty program in getting money and programs into low-income areas. Despite these gains, however, the rapidly rising cost of living in the last

319

decade has virtually wiped out any of the apparent gains reflected in the declining number of poor families. In 1959, poverty was defined as income for a family of four below $3100, while the Bureau of Labor estimated that $7000 was needed for a "modest but adequate" living. In 1969, the poverty level for a family of four was $3335, and the "modest but adequate" living increased to $9200 (Reissmann, 1969). In short, the gap between the poverty level and what is needed for an adequate living has increased quite sharply.

A substantial number of the poor are the older persons in our society. There are approximately 8 million Americans over 65 with incomes below the poverty line, with about 1.5 million of these who live alone on an income of less than $500 a year. The plight of the aged poor is described in the following account of a man on a pension.

Mr. MacIntosh depended on hard-boiled eggs because his hotel room has no refrigerator and he can't afford to eat out. He is trying to live on his $50-a-month Social Security check. Room rent is $38.50 a month, which provides a room with clean linen every two weeks and clean towels every day. The remainder goes for food and chewing tobacco. Every week friends on the same floor buy him two dozen eggs, seven small cans of V-8 juice, two cans of Spam, a carton of dry cereal (because the box says, "Minimum daily requirement of vitamins") and his tobacco. He boils his eggs at once and eats them morning and evening. He stretches a can of Spam for three days or so. It has cost him violent nausea to discover that hard-boiled eggs and opened Spam need refrigeration in warm weather. (Bagdikian, 1966.)

The effects of poverty are also revealed in the facts of hunger and malnutrition facing millions of Americans. The extent of hunger might still be secret but for the takeover of an abandoned Air Force base in Mississippi in 1955 by 35 Negroes whose leaflets said, "We are here because we are hungry and cold and we have no jobs or land." They were promptly evicted but a furor of federal food-stamp programs, replacing direct surplus-food distribution centers, were claiming success in eliminating hunger in Mississippi. Further investigation, however, showed the new food-stamp programs to be working to the detriment of people too poor to purchase the stamps. The wheels of the Department of Agriculture and the Congress grind slowly. Direct payments to assist people in purchase of food stamps was tried after some delays. Even with this, a team of doctors investigating the health of Mississippi children in 1967 made a report which stated:

In child after child we saw: evidence of vitamin and mineral deficiencies; serious untreated skin infestation and ulcerations; eye and ear diseases, also unattended bone diseases secondary to poor food intake; the prevalence of bacterial and parasitic disease as well as severe anemia, with resulting loss of energy and ability to live a normally active life; diseases of the heart and lungs—requiring surgery—which have gone undiagnosed and untreated; epileptic and other neurological disorders; severe kidney ailments, that in other children would warrant immediate hospitalization; and finally, in boys and girls in every county we visited, obvious evidence of severe malnutrition with injury to the body's tissues—its muscles, bones, and skin as well as an associated psychological state of fatigue, listlessness, and exhaustion.

We saw children afflicted with chronic diarrhea, chronic sores, chronic leg and arm (untreated) injuries and deformities. We saw homes without running water and live with germ-bearing mosquitoes and flies everywhere around. We saw homes with children who are lucky to eat one meal a day—and that one inadequate so far as vitamins, minerals, or protein is concerned. We saw children who don't get to drink milk, don't get to eat fruit, green vegetables, or meat. They live on starches—grits, bread, Kool Aid. Their parents may be declared ineligible for commodities, ineligible for the food stamp program, even though they have literally nothing. We saw children fed communally—that is, by neighbors who give scraps of food to children whose own parents have nothing to give them. (Quoted in Citizens' Board of Inquiry into Hunger and Malnutrition in the U.S., 1968, in this chapter.)

How the federal government operates in the face of such destitute conditions teaches us an important lesson about the workings of American government at all levels. At the county level, local control over food-assistance programs left local governments to request, pay for, and run the programs, thus putting those areas least responsive to their own poor in a position to deny those poor federally offered food. Control by local government is not the same as local democratic control by a community of program participants, and the latter rarely exists in this country.

The politics of the national failure to respond during the Johnson Administration are described in Elizabeth Drew's account of "Going Hungry in America." She summarizes:

Yet so little was accomplished not because of mechanical or industrial failures, but because of what can happen to men in policy-making positions in Washington. When they stay in a difficult job too long, they can be overwhelmed by the complexity of it all, and they become overly defensive. Man's pride, particularly the pride of a man who can tell himself he has done some good, can overtake his intellectual honesty. Thus, not Southern politicians, not Orville Freeman, not Lyndon Johnson could face the fact when it was pointed out that many people were hungry, that they weren't wearing clothes. In this they reflected a national trait: it has been easier to stir sustained national concern over hunger in Bihar or Biafra than places at home for which we are more directly responsible. The problems are looked at in terms of the workings of Washington, not in terms of the problems. Decent men could sit and discuss statistical reliability and administrative neatness and the importance of good precedents while people went hungry. (Drew, 1968, p. 61.)

An even more callous administrative response is found in President Nixon's Administration as revealed by Nick Kotz's recent book so aptly titled *Let Them Eat Promises.* The contrast between bureaucratic political process and the reality of human need cannot be exaggerated. This gap is a measure of governmental failure. In the wealthiest nation in history there are babies who die in infancy because they cannot get milk; there are anemic children, and those with stunted growth stemming from protein deficiency; there are scurvy and rickets through lack of milk and citrus juice; there are the hookworms, roundworms, and other parasitic infections; and there are the thousands who go to school without breakfast and have no money for lunch. The shocking facts of starving children, adults, and old people are contained in *Hunger USA,* a report on the more than 14 million Americans without enough food to maintain health.

The impact of poverty upon the poor has been well documented. The sense of despair, alienation, and hopelessness combine to produce limited aspirations and a sense of powerlessness among the young. It is in the *adaptations* to poverty that these conditions are maintained and transmitted intergenerationally. Poverty does breed poverty! Other adaptations to poverty which have become part of the life style of the poor are often responded to as if they were the causes of the problems of the poor. Claude Brown (1965), in his personal account of growing up in Harlem, illustrates how the role of the "hustler" is simply one of many deviant occupations providing the outward symbols of success that are available to ghetto youth. Similarly, Gertrude Samuels' (1959) description of New York youth gangs reveals how gangs function to provide that sense of security and personal worth that their members cannot obtain in socially acceptable ways.

Yet we must be careful not to place too great an emphasis on the psychological impact of poverty which leads to self-defeating personal and cultural patterns. For to do so would turn our attention away from the more basic causes of poverty which are to be found in existing social institutions in American society. Moreover, an overemphasis on the pathological aspects of poverty leads us to neglect the stable patterns of social organization that are to be found in ghettos and low-income areas. In seeking out such existing strengths we may come to understand that there are many viable patterns of social life in American society in addition to the dominant middle-class patterns. In other words, the poor should not have to be required to be totally transformed in order to enjoy a decent standard of living and equal access to the rights guaranteed to all citizens.

Many of the issues raised here have been brought into very sharp focus within the context of the civil-rights movement. Black men have been given legal equality as many of the unequal-treatment laws have been declared unconstitutional and new legislation has provided guarantees of equality in education and voting. Yet while there have been great strides toward legal equality, the Negro has been denied the economic and political power necessary for social equality. It is hardly likely that Negroes derive any great satisfaction from knowing that racist explanations for his inferiority have been replaced by economic and political ones.

The papers in this section deal with many of these questions. The emphasis, however, is clearly upon the facts of inequality and injustice that are associated with poverty. The articles will attempt to present the scope of the problem as it is found in the North as well as the South. They will also illustrate the nature of the disagreements concerning the causes of poverty, its consequences, and the programs needed to help eradicate it.

The South has been the traditional setting in which the Negroes' quest for equality has taken place. The civil-rights movement as an organizational weapon had its greatest impact with the early boycotts and sit-ins. The nationally televised accounts of beating, police dogs, gas, and cattle prods as the Southern communities' response to the awakened Negro were sufficient to raise a national clamor for much of the civil-rights legislation currently in effect. The experience of the early years of the civil-rights movement has been vividly described by Peter Weiss (1964) in his account of a voter-registration project in Mississippi. He reveals the difficulties in voter registration of poor Negroes and whites after years of subordination and intimidation have left them apathetic or fearful, with little knowledge of their rights as citizens. It took great courage for civil-rights workers to enter Mississippi where the authorities were themselves lawless. Weiss recounts an incident in which a highway patrolman stopped a car with five SNCC workers inside, enroute to a meeting. The patrolman said, "You goddamn niggers want to change our way of life"; (hardly a traffic problem). Four of the occupants were delivered handcuffed to the sheriff at the Lowndes County Jail. The fifth, seventeen-year-old James Black, was taken to a spot a mile away by the patrolman. His affidavit dated June 8, 1964, reads:

> He told me to get out of the car; I refused to get out. So he pulled me out. He started hitting me with his fists, and after about twenty blows he got out his blackjack and hit me one time with it and knocked me down. Then he told me to get back in the car. While he was beating me, he asked if any white folks had ever treated me bad; I told him yes, and he hit me again. He asked me again had any white folks in Mississippi treated me bad, and I told him no. At that point he helped me back into the car.
>
> Then he took me to the county jail (Lowndes) where I was questioned by the sheriff. The sheriff asked for my driver's license and to take everything out of my pockets. . . . I had a friend's I.D. card in my pocket and he asked me if my friend was a Negro or a nigger. I told him a Negro. The same highway patrolman was there, and took out his blackjack and again asked if my friend was a Negro or a nigger. He started to hit me with the blackjack, and I told him my friend was a nigger.

The white Northerner's support of the civil-rights movement *in the South* was often accompanied by a smug complacency that the North was civilized and aware of human decency and the law of the land. The response of the white Northerners to the civil-rights movement was seen in Cicero, Illinois, and Milwaukee, Wisconsin, as Negroes sought to move into white working-class neighborhoods; it was seen in the support received by George Wallace in Democratic primaries in Wisconsin and Indiana; it was seen in the repeal of an open-housing law by the voters of California. As the civil-rights movement attempted to deal with problems in the North, the moral superiority of the white Northerner over the white Southerner vanished. The comforting belief that racist America was only found in the South was shattered.

The response of the middle-class white Northerner to the growing consciousness and militancy of the Negro can only be understood in terms of the more general problem of poverty, inequality, and insecurity in American society. Poverty has to do with the inability of persons to achieve a level of income needed to live according to prevailing standards of living. As indicated earlier, the gap between the official poverty line and what is needed for a modest but adequate living has been increasing rather than shrinking. In contrast to poverty, inequality refers to the distribution of wealth or income among the general population. It is concerned with the relative share of total economic output that goes to different segments of the population. Thus, in 1960, the upper 20 percent of the population received 45 percent of total income, while the lower 20 percent received 5 percent of total income (Miller, 1964).

Unsure of his own economic and social status, the lower-middle class American feels his own chances for middle-class status restricted by technological change and a tightening opportunity structure. One consequence of this is that the working-class white becomes both envious and resentful of the attention being given to the Negro at a time when no one seems concerned with his own plight. The combination of economic insecurity, resentment toward upper-middle-class whites, and envy over the growing consciousness of Negroes is revealed in the following statement by a mother from a working-class family that is barely able to make ends meet.

"They may be poorer than a lot of white people, but not by very much. Anyway, what they don't get in money they more than gain in popularity these days. The papers have suddenly decided that the Negro is teacher's pet. Whatever he does good is wonderful, and we should clap. But if he does anything bad, it's our fault. I can't read the papers anymore when they talk about the race thing. I'm sick of their editorials. All of a sudden they start giving us a lecture every day on how bad we are. They never used to care about anything, the Negro or anything else. Now they're so worried. And the same goes with the Church. I'm as devout a Catholic as you'll find around. My brother is a priest, and I do more than go to Church once a week. But I just can't take what some of our priests are saying these days. They're talking as if we did something wrong for being white. I don't understand it at all. Priests never used to talk about the Negro when I was a child. Now they talk to my kids about them all the time. I thought the Church is supposed to stand for religion, and eternal things. They shouldn't get themselves into every little fight that comes along. The same goes with the schools. I went to school here in Boston, and nobody was talking about Negroes and busing us around. The Negroes were there in Roxbury and we were here.

"Everybody can't live with you, can they? Everybody likes his own. But now even the school people tell us we have to have our kids with this kind and that kind of person, or else they will be hurt, or something. Now how am I supposed to believe everything all these people say? They weren't talking that way a few years ago. The governor wasn't either. Nor the mayor. They're all just like cattle stampeding to sound like one another. The same with those people out in the suburbs. Suddenly they're interested in the Negro. They worked and worked to get away from him, of course, and get away from us, too. That's why they moved so far, instead of staying here, where they can do something, if they mean so well. But no. They moved and now they're all ready to come back—but only to drive a few Negro kids out for a Sunday picnic. Who has to live with all this, and pay for it in taxes and everything? Whose kids are pushed around? And who gets called 'prejudiced' and all the other sneery words? I've had enough of it. It's hypocrisy, right down the line. And we're the ones who get it; the final buck gets passed to us." (Quoted in Coles, 1966, p. 56.)

A detailed account of the facts of poverty and inequality is presented by Parker in the article "The Myth of Middle America." Parker examines the contemporary versions of the Horatio Alger myth that have dominated America's beliefs about its progress and prosperity: we are the middle-class society, wallowing in the abundance of a technological miracle and distributing our material benefits to all regardless of status, class, or ethnic origin. Contrary to the myths, however, there are the tens of millions of Americans who, although above the official poverty line, are nonetheless "deprived." The myth of America as the middle-class affluent society is shattered in the face of its 30 million poor, its 70 million deprived, its inadequate health and welfare system, and its literacy and infant-mortality rates.

As the rich in America keep getting richer, even the liberal solutions of a guaranteed annual wage or negative income tax will not deal with the stubborn facts of poverty, deprivation, and inequality. Such solutions will only serve to institutionalize poverty and detract from the large-scale changes necessary for a more just distribution of the benefits of our economy. The particular relation between poverty and inequality in wealthy Western societies was captured in Paul Jacobs' study of business techniques designed to remove any money from the hands of the poor before it can be used for their betterment. His conclusion reflects the strain of being kept poor amidst apparent wealth.

All of us are born into a state of anxiety, and many, or even most, of us must cope, throughout our lives, with deep-rooted feelings of personal inadequacy. For the poor, these feelings are continuously reinforced by the economic circumstances in which they live and by their relationships with the rest of society. In an egalitarian society where everyone is living in poverty, being poor generates neither much anxiety nor strong feelings of inadequacy. But in a society such as ours, which measures achievement primarily by financial and material standards, to be poor is to be scorned by others, and even worse, by one's own self. It is for this reason that in America the taste and smell of poverty are so sour. (Jacobs, 1966, p. 27.)

Much of the difficulty in dealing with poverty among various subgroups in American society resides in the inability of existing social institutions to adapt to the patterns of life in the disadvantaged groups. Residents of urban ghettos are limited in their contacts with legal and welfare institutions to the policeman and social worker who come into their area but are not from their area. There is often little opportunity for the ghetto resident to make legal and welfare services more adaptable to his needs. The low-status client without power has great difficulty in influencing the professionals who come into the ghetto to serve him. Migratory poor have even less power. The article by Truman Moore deals with the plight of the 2 million migrants who move about the country harvesting crops. For not only are the migrants without the power needed to influence state and federal agencies, but they are also transients who do not remain in an area long enough to be eligible to use existing services or to make agencies feel obligated to provide such services.

Moore indicates the failure of existing agencies at the state and national levels in providing minimum-wage protection, decent housing, health services, and schooling for children. The economic interests of the corporate farms that employ migrants are clearly of greater importance to those who make legislation than are the interests of the migrant. The vulnerability of an unprotected, economically disadvantaged group is probably found in more extreme form among migrants than among urban poor who at least have the *potential* for group power through their more stable residence patterns.

The question raised earlier in this introduction—regarding whether one chooses to emphasize the barriers to full equality that reside within the disadvantaged group, or to emphasize the barriers that exist in the institutional structure which fails to adapt to the needs of the poor—remains as one of the persistent issues surrounding the causes of, and solutions to, poverty. The issue became a matter of public debate in 1965, with the appearance of a Department of Labor report entitled *The Negro Family: The Case for National Action,* written by Daniel P. Moynihan with the assistance of Paul Barton and Ellen Broderich. The essential argument of the Moynihan report was that the government efforts to lift the legal barriers in the area of discrimination would not lead to full equality for the Negro. Moynihan reasoned that the history of slavery and subordination had such a marked impact upon the Negro social structure (particularly the family) that many Negroes would be unable to take advantage of the new opportunities that were made available to them. As stated in the report: "at the heart of the deterioration of the fabric of Negro society is the deterioration of the Negro family." Moynihan used this argument to urge the establishment of a national family policy designed to enhance "the stability and resources of the Negro American family."

Controversy in government circles, the civil-rights movement, the press, and among academic social scientists followed this report. Many of the reactions to the report have been collected in a single volume by Rainwater and Yancey (1967). The controversy over the objectives of the report is less pronounced than the disagreement over its emphasis on the pathology of the ghetto and the breakdown of the Negro family. Such emphases can often serve to turn attention away from the defective features of American society that have failed to provide full equality for the Negro. There is no doubt that black Americans bear some scars from a brutal history inflicted upon them. But the Moynihan report ignored three vital points. First, that female dominance of households in Ireland, Poland, and in Western society generally, has always followed (rather than caused) economic destitution (Carper, 1968). Second, who resides with whom, supports whom, marries whom, or has children with whom is none of the government's business. Diverse cultural life styles remain the right of the individual and the community. Third, Black people no less than women or other disadvantaged minority groups are not currently being victimized by the damage that was done to their ancestors 150 years earlier (about which nothing can be done). They are being damaged by the current racism and current inequitable distribution of wealth and power in American society (about which something must be done).

Despite the fact that the large majority of poor Americans are white, poverty is a condition that has come to be identified with black Americans, Mexican-Americans, and American Indians. It is this identification that is partly responsible for the way Americans continue to ignore the existence of the poor. The nonwhite poor can be ignored more easily when there are also justifying beliefs of the sort that sees nonwhite people as less worthy, less motivated, more immoral, or any other stereotype that goes into the construction of racist beliefs.

The three remaining papers in this chapter all have to do with racism, "a principle of social domination by which a group seen as inferior or different in terms of alleged biological characteristics is exploited, controlled, and oppressed socially and psychically by a superordinate group." The paper by Blauner, "Internal Colonialism and Ghetto Revolt," offers a fresh interpretation of urban disorders, cultural nationalism, and the movement for control over the ghettos by black residents. He suggests that the relationship between blacks and whites in the United States must be seen within the framework of a colonialism model and the struggle of the colonized to throw off the economic, psychological, and legal chains of the white oppressors. Thus the so-called urban riots that were officially interpreted as the work of "riff-raff" criminal elements are seen by Blauner as the early stage of a mass rebellion against a colonial status.

The consciousness and militancy of black Americans has only recently begun to influence other minorities who have for years been ignored and subjected to institutionalized racism without fighting back. The conditions faced by Mexican-Americans of the Southwest is the subject of Salazar's "Stranger in One's Land." In school, the Mexican-American is forced to deny his language and culture, following the pattern of the experience of a "conquered population." In the face of such experiences in school and at work, Mexican-Americans have been moving away from the goal of assimilation into Anglo society and are resisting attempts to become American at the expense of their language, culture, or color.

The experience of any colonized people is only partly in response to the situations they face in the present. Of equal importance is their sense of who they are historically, their origins, past leaders, and their struggles and victories. Colonizers treat the histories of the colonized in a very cavalier fashion, writing them to suit their own historical self-concept rather than to represent faithfully the experiences of the colonized peoples. Only an American history could treat Columbus as the "man who discovered America." An American Indian would surely wonder how you can discover a country that is already occupied and settled. The nature and extent of distortion in the writing of American history on the place of Indians is revealed in the paper by Josephy, "Indians in History." The American Indian population continues to be among the most exploited of all groups in the United States. The tenacity of their various cultures and their ability to resist forced assimilation highlight a deficiency in the shallow, changeable culture of modern society. Only our own cultural arrogance stands in the way of a view of American Indians as a group having something vital to teach the rest of us about cultural identity and group living. As with other minorities we have, instead, insisted upon assimilation as the price for mere subsistence.

REFERENCES AND ADDITIONAL READING

Bagdikian, Ben H., "Ed MacIntosh: Man on a Pension," in H. P. Miller (ed.), *Poverty, American Style* (Belmont, Calif.: Wadsworth, 1966).

Brown, Claude, *Manchild in the Promised Land* (New York: Macmillan, 1965).

Carper, Laura, "The Negro Family and the Moynihan Report," *Dissent* (March-April 1966), pp. 133–140; reproduced in R. Perrucci and M. Pilisuk (eds.), *The Triple Revolution: Social Problems in Depth* (Boston: Little, Brown, 1968), pp. 461–468.

Casavantes, Edward, "Pride and Prejudice: A Mexican American Dilemma," *Civil Rights Digest*, **3** (Winter 1970), pp. 22–27.

Cloward, Richard A., and Frances F. Pivan, "Birth of a Movement," *Nation* (May 8, 1967).

Coles, Robert, "The White Northerner: Pride and Prejudice," *Atlantic* (June 1966), pp. 53–57; reproduced in R. Perrucci and M. Pilisuk (eds.), *The Triple Revolution: Social Problems in Depth* (Boston: Little, Brown, 1968), pp. 398–406.

Coser, Lewis A., "The Sociology of Poverty," *Social Problems*, **13** (1965), pp. 140–145.

Drew, Elizabeth, "Going Hungry in America," *Atlantic* (December 1968), pp. 53–61.

Elman, Richard M., *The Poorhouse State: The American Way of Life on Public Assistance* (New York: Pantheon, 1966).

Ferman, Louis A., Joyce L. Kornbluh, and Alan Haber (eds.), *Poverty in America* (Ann Arbor: Univ. of Michigan Press, 1965).

Harrington, Michael, *The Other America* (Baltimore: Penguin, 1962).

Hayden, Tom, "Colonialism and Liberation in America," *Viet-Report* (Summer 1968), pp. 32–39.

Jacobs, Paul, "Keeping the Poor Poor," *New Politics*, **5** (1966), pp. 3–16, 19–20, 25–27.

Kopkind, Andrew, "Of, by, and for the Poor," *New Republic* (June 19, 1965), pp. 15–19; reproduced in R. Perrucci and M. Pilisuk (eds.), *The Triple Revolution: Social Problems in Depth* (Boston: Little, Brown, 1968), pp. 515–523.

Kotz, Nick, *Let Them Eat Promises: The Politics of Hunger in America* (Englewood Cliffs, N.J.: Prentice-Hall, 1969).

Miller, Herman P., "Facts about Poverty, Revised," in H. P. Miller (ed.), *Poverty, American Style* (Belmont, Calif.: Wadsworth, 1966).

Miller, Herman P., *Rich Man, Poor Man* (New York: Crowell, 1964).

Miller, S. M., "Poverty and Inequality in America: Implications for the Social Services," *Child Welfare*, **42**:9 (November 1963), pp. 442–445; reproduced in R. Perrucci and M. Pilisuk (eds.), *The Triple Revolution: Social Problems in Depth* (Boston: Little, Brown, 1968), pp. 488–493.

Miller, S. M., and Pamela Roby, *The Future of Inequality* (New York: Basic Books, 1970).

Montez, Philip, "Will the Real Mexican American Please Stand Up," *Civil Rights Digest*, **3** (Winter 1970), pp. 28–31.

Moynihan, Daniel P., "The President and the Negro: The Moment Lost," *Commentary* (February 1967), pp. 3–17; reproduced in R. Perrucci and M. Pilisuk (eds.), *The Triple Revolution: Social Problems in Depth* (Boston: Little, Brown, 1968), pp. 431–460.

Negro Family, The: The Case for National Action (Moynihan Report) (Washington D.C.: U.S. Government Printing Office, March 1965).

Newsweek, "Tio Taco Is Dead" (June 29, 1970), pp. 22–28.

Rainwater, Lee, and William L. Yancey, *The Moynihan Report and the Politics of Controversy* (Cambridge, Mass.: M. I. T. Press, 1967).

Reissman, Leonard, *Urban Affairs Quarterly* (March 1969).

Rustin, Bayard, "The 'Watts Manifesto' and the McCone Report," *Commentary* (March 1966), pp. 29–35; reproduced in R. Perrucci and M. Pilisuk (eds.), *The Triple Revolution: Social Problems in Depth* (Boston: Little, Brown, 1968), pp. 469–481.

Samuels, Gertrude, "Why 'The Assassins' Can't Be 'Punks,'" *New York Times Magazine* (August 16, 1959), p. 13ff.

Sutherland, Elizabeth (ed.), *Letters from Mississippi* (New York: McGraw-Hill, 1965).

U.S. Commission on Civil Rights, *The Mexican American* (Washington, D.C.: U.S. Government Printing Office, 1968).

Weiss, Peter "Nightmare in Mississippi," *The Progressive* (September 1964), pp. 19–22; reproduced in R. Perrucci and M. Pilisuk (eds.), *The Triple Revolution: Social Problems in Depth* (Boston: Little, Brown, 1968), pp. 391–397.

HUNGER USA

Citizens' Board of Inquiry
into Hunger and Malnutrition in the U.S.

THE MISSISSIPPI STORY:
A CASE HISTORY IN
BUREAUCRATIC NONRESPONSE

Much of the concern and interest in hunger and malnutrition in the United States is directly attributable to the publicity brought to bear on the conditions of the poor in Mississippi as a result of a Senate Subcommittee investigation and a report by a team of doctors sent by the Field Foundation.

In fact, Mississippi and hunger have become synonymous in the public mind.

The story begins, however, not with the flurry of publicity in the summer of 1967. It goes back to the winter of 1965–66 when 35 Negroes invaded the abandoned Greenville, Mississippi, Air Force base and distributed leaflets saying "We are here because we are hungry and cold and we have no jobs or land." They were promptly evicted by federal troops specially flown in. But that event triggered the creation of a special Federal Interdepartmental Committee on Nutrition and a great show of activities by several federal agencies. The accomplishments of that effort were said by Sargent Shriver to be as follows:

As a result of the Administration's persistent effort over 18 months, there is more antipoverty money, more food, more education, more jobs, more housing, more justice being brought to the citizens of Mississippi than to nearly any other state. These achievements could not have been made without coordinated and unified direction in Washington. For example, about one-fifth of all people in Mississippi are being fed today by Federal programs. [OEO for a period of several months assisted local Mississippi counties to underwrite the administrative costs of the direct food distribution program which is alleged to reach 400,000 in Mississippi.]

Secretary Freeman in early 1967 reported to Senator Joseph Clark that

there are 470,000 persons receiving food stamps and total distribution in Mississippi—nearly 10 percent of the national total. Every county in the state has one of the two distribution programs. Fifty-nine counties receive direct distribution. Twenty-three participate in food stamps. The Mississippi distribution is the largest in the nation. New York is second with 440,000 participants.

A series of revelations destroyed the impression which these claims were calculated to convey.

In February 1967, in Jackson, Mississippi, the Mississippi Advisory Committee to the U.S. Commission on Civil Rights held a hearing and received widespread complaints that the food-stamp program was actually working to the detriment of the poor, that no one had the money to buy the stamps, and that people felt they had been better off under the commodity-distribution program.

On April 21, 1967, the Civil Rights Commission issued a memorandum (earlier drafts of which had been in circulation for some time) setting forth the emergency conditions and analyzing the reason for the drop of participation in food programs as a result of the switch over from commodity distribution to food stamps.

In the eight Mississippi counties that changed from commodity distribution to food stamps, there was a total decrease in participation one year after the change of almost 36,000 recipients.

In Jones County, for example, participation dropped from more than 9940 in October 1964, under the commodities, to 4700 in October 1966, under food stamps—a decrease of more than 5000 participants.

In Harrison County, participation dropped from almost 9600 under commodities in March 1965 to less than 2200 in March 1966, under food stamps—a decrease of more than 7000.

In Coahoma County, the decrease was almost 6700 from March 1965 under commodities to March 1966 under food stamps, and the decrease was more than 3500 in Forrest County from October 1965 to October 1966.

The Commission stated, based in part upon the hearing in Jackson:

1. Negroes were almost unanimously of the opinion that they do not want the food-stamp program, and essentially their reason was that they did not think that they could afford it.

2. Individuals with irregular or little income or receiving only the substandard welfare payments made by Mississippi could not budget the amount of money necessary to buy stamps at the time when needed.

3. The certification procedures which are administered by the local officials are far more strictly enforced for the food-stamp program than was the rule under the direct-distribution program.

4. The value of bonus coupons decreases as income increases and therefore individuals most able to participate were least likely to feel it worth their while to tie up a substantial part of their cash.

5. The program was administered through the State Department of Welfare which is operated

in violation of Title VI of the Civil Rights Act of 1964 and is in violation of any standard of good management.

The Commission set forth a variety of alternative recommendations: reduction of minimum charge for food stamps; simultaneous operation of the food-stamp and commodity-distribution programs; and selective expansion of the food-stamp program.

On April 26, 1967, the Senate Subcommittee on Manpower, Employment, and Poverty held a hearing in Jackson, Mississippi, and conducted field trips. Returning with a sense of shock, the Subcommittee demanded immediate action from the President, stating that:

There is clear evidence of acute malnutrition and hunger among families in the Mississippi Delta. Many families subsist without discernible income and cannot afford to meet the minimum purchase requirements for food stamps.

This Subcommittee recommended (1) distribution of food stamps without cost to persons with no cash income; (2) lowering of coupon-purchase requirements to reflect more realistic standards; (3) investigation of incidents where recipients of food stamps were required to pay more than required by departmental regulations; (4) declaration of an emergency situation so that federally owned foods could be distributed through both public and private agencies; and (5) action by other appropriate federal departments including the Office of Economic Opportunity (to utilize its emergency family-loan authority to subsidize the purchase of food or food stamps) and the Department of Health, Education and Welfare (to extend supplementary welfare assistance on a demonstration basis seeking private matching funds).

On the same day, April 26, Secretary Freeman responded with an acknowledgement of the truth of the findings of the Senate Subcommittee. Investigations by members of his own staff found:

1. Evidence of malnutrition and unmet hunger.

2. Families without jobs and with no discernible income who have difficulty making the minimum food-stamp purchase.

3. Need in some instances for better certification of participants.

4. Some participants who believe they are being asked to pay more of their income for food stamps than they can afford.

In that letter he stated that the Department was considering reducing the minimum requirement from $2 a person to $.50 a person and stated:

We are tightening our procedure to assure that in counties shifting from direct distribution to food stamps there is no period of waiting while recertification for food stamps takes place.

On April 29, 1967, the Office of Economic Opportunity acknowledged the crisis caused by poverty in Mississippi but stated that there were crises caused by poverty in many parts of the country—in Watts, Harlem, Rochester, Syracuse, along the Rio Grande, on Indian reservations, in Alaska, and in Appalachia, to mention only a few.

The release acknowledged that the present crisis had been described over eighteen months ago to Congress and placed the blame on Congress for refusing to grant the fiscal requests of the Administration. It further stated that all the recommendations of the Senate Subcommittee had been complied with except those allegedly proscribed by law, namely: the free distribution of food stamps and the declaration under existing circumstances of an emergency condition so as to run both programs simultaneously.

On May 3, 1967, the Office of Economic Opportunity announced the institution of small cash-loan programs to loan money to the poor to buy food stamps. Four Mississippi counties were included in this program: Bolivar, Leflore, Quitman, Coahoma.

Then on May 27–30, 1967, a team of doctors was dispatched by the Field Foundation to examine the health conditions of children in Mississippi. The now famous report which they submitted upon returning included the following observations:

In child after child we saw: evidence of vitamin and mineral deficiencies; serious untreated skin infestation and ulcerations; eye and ear diseases, also unattended bone diseases secondary to poor food intake; the prevalence of bacterial and parasitic disease, as well as severe anemia, with resulting loss of energy and ability to live a normally active life; diseases of the heart and the lungs—requiring surgery—which have gone undiagnosed and untreated; epileptic and other neurological disorders; severe kidney ailments, that in other children would warrant immediate hospitalization; and finally, in boys and girls in every county we visited, obvious evidence of severe malnutrition with injury to the body's tissues—its muscles, bones, and skin as well as an associated psychological state of fatigue, listlessness, and exhaustion.

We saw children afflicted with chronic diarrhea, chronic sores, chronic leg and arm (untreated) injuries and deformities. We saw homes without running water and live with germ-bearing mosquitoes and flies everywhere around. We saw homes with children who are lucky to eat one meal a day—and that one inadequate so far as vitamins, minerals, or protein is concerned. We saw children who don't get to drink milk, don't get to eat fruit, green vegetables, or meat. They live on starches—grits, bread, Kool Aid. Their parents may be declared ineligible for commodities, ineligible for the food-stamp program, even though they have literally nothing. We saw children fed communally—that is, by neighbors who give scraps of food to children whose own parents have nothing to give them.

On July 12, 1967, Secretary Freeman announced that he had followed through on some of the recommendations laid out in his memoranda of April 26 and June 9. His proposed action placed heavy emphasis upon the need for education and outreach in order to promote increased use of the food-stamp program. His proposed actions were to cope with "four principal weaknesses" which the Department's review of domestic programs discloses:

1. Failure of state and local government to use the programs.

2. Weak administration by local government either by intent, ineptness, or inadequate resources.

3. Failure of the poor to participate because of lack of information, understanding, or, in the case of food stamps, money.

4. Inadequate administrative, informational, and educational support by the federal government.

This analysis and subsequent statements by the Secretary leaned heavily upon a report on USDA food programs conducted in two Mississippi Delta counties. It emphasized that despite the difficulties posed by fluctuating seasonal income in establishing equitable payment schedules and despite transportation difficulties, seven out of ten eligible rural families participated in the food-stamp program. Freeman contrasted that with the far lower rate of participation in the food-stamp program in urban areas elsewhere in the United States and pointed out that in addition participation in the commodity-distribution program also reached approximately 70 percent of the eligible families. Both in his summary of the report and in his transmittal of it to the Senate, the Secretary omitted to include another important finding: that all families studied—those participating in the food-stamp program, those participating in the food-distribution program, and those participating in neither program—were found to have diets of approximately equal nutritional value. The report contains a detailed analysis of the nutritional adequacy of participants and nonparticipants:

1. The food-stamp participants used somewhat more dry beans and peas and nuts, more flour, cereal, and bakery products, more potatoes and more sugars and sweets than the nonparticipants. The nonparticipants had more eggs, more citrus fruit and tomatoes, and somewhat more dark-green and deep-yellow vegetables.

The higher caloried, more filling foods of the participants furnished about 2700 calories per person per day; those of the nonparticipants

about 2400. The diet of the participants was somewhat higher in all but two nutrients. The assortment of foods used by the nonparticipants gave them somewhat more vitamin A value and ascorbic acid. Both groups had similar amounts of protein in their diets.

2. The resulting dietary levels of the participants and nonparticipants were fairly similar. Their diets were about equal in calories and protein. But the participants had diets containing somewhat more calcium, iron, thiamine, and riboflavin, whereas the nonparticipants had diets containing more ascorbic acid and vitamin A value. . . .

Compared with households in the country with incomes under $2000 surveyed in the spring of 1955, the food-stamp participants in Washington County had diets that were lower in all respects. They contained only about 80 percent as many calories, only about 60 to 70 percent as much calcium, riboflavin, and ascorbic acid, and roughly 90 percent of the other nutrients. The diets of the food-donation participants in Sunflower County appeared even worse in comparison with the 1955 diets.

All reports received from mid-summer through December 1967 indicate no substantial change, possibly even a worsening, in the conditions of the poor in Mississippi. Thus, on August 7, 1967, the Child Development Group of Mississippi issued the following report:

Yet, out of 118 families who were studied, the medical teams found that 47 percent never served milk, 53 percent did not serve eggs regularly, and 36 percent served meat only once or twice a week. Only 18 percent of the families had fruit or fruit juices for the children, and only 12 percent had fish.

In a second study the medical department took blood tests of children enrolled in centers in Kemper, Madison, Rankin, and Washington counties. These tests showed that 62.1 percent of the children in these centers were anemic, and that 13.5 percent of this number were severely anemic. The test results from Washington County, where half the children live in towns, are even more critical with 80 percent being anemic and 20.2 percent being severely anemic.

Thus, conditions correspond basically to those reported by the Delta Health Center run by Tufts Medical School in Mississippi.

The December 26, 1967, issue of *Look Magazine* provides one of the latest bulletins yet received from the Mississippi hunger front:

Meanwhile, the Teresa Pilgrims—who are neither statistics nor "causes"—continue to exist on rice, grits, collards, tree bark, laundry starch, clay, and almost anything else chewable. Meanwhile their bodies suffer steady depletion of tissues, slow disintegration, and the progressive, piecemeal abbreviation of life. In time, they become physical and psychological cripples. But still, there is some taste of hope.

And most recently, in February, a television report on hunger in Mississippi, filmed in part on Senator James Eastland's plantation, was produced by the Public Broadcasting Laboratory. This report provided a disturbing glimpse into the lives of people whose plight we have discussed:

No food, no meat, no milk—and the children go to bed hungry. Sometimes they cry.

DOCUMENTING THE EXTENT OF HUNGER AND MALNUTRITION IN THE UNITED STATES

We have found concrete evidence of chronic hunger and malnutrition in every part of the United States where we have held hearings or conducted field trips.

These conditions are *not* confined to Mississippi.

Moreover, on the basis of studies, statements of professionals and lay observers, and newspaper accounts, collected from sources throughout the country, we are convinced that chronic hunger and malnutrition are not confined to those places we visited personally but are national in scope and distribution.

In the course of our research we made an extensive attempt to collect all available medical and nutritional studies evaluating the nutritional status of the poor and found that without exception, those studies reveal a prevalence of chronic hunger and malnutrition hitherto unimagined.

This prevalence is shocking. A thousand people who must go without food for days each month would be shocking in a wealthy nation. We believe that, in America, the number reaches well into the millions. And we believe that the situation is worsening.

Our first impressions of these severe conditions came not from professionals, not from medical journals, but from the people whose lives are virtually consumed in seeking the food they lack the money to buy.

The Litany

Hunger has its own special litany, intoned to us in these words:

There are days without any food four or five at
*   a time the parents go hungry and the child*
*   may live on powdered milk for a week at*
*   a time when we just "make do" and mix*
*   whatever we have with water and the end*
*   of the month when food stamps run out,*
*   commodities run out, the Headstart Doctor*
*   refers to this as a time of "discomfort"; to*
*   a school teacher from South Carolina it*
*   means taking teenagers home suffering from*
*   hunger pains*
or times when we have a little something
*   because you get food from "the white lady"*
*   you work for or you eat what you can while*
*   you have it because you want to know what*
*   a full belly feels like*
or you buy the cheapest meat you can, neck
*   bones and that kind of stuff and have it a*
*   couple of times a month.*
And always there are the days without milk for
the children
*   No fresh milk?*
*   No sir*
*   No milk for the children?*
*   No sir*
*   Do they get milk? The small ones?*
*   No*
*   No milk at all?*

No
Ain't no one of them has milk every day.
They lucky to have it twice a month.
And there are days without meat or vegetables
or fruit. And days with only one meal or two—
or three and they aren't really meals.
And the children go to bed hungry.
　　Sometimes they cry.
　　Sometimes they ask me for something
　　I am not able to buy milk or food or nothing
But when they do eat, they eat the same food,
day in and day out black-eyed peas, grits, flour,
maybe fatback, sometimes potatoes, beans, and
where we visited homes and looked in the
kitchen, the shelves were empty— and the
refrigerator if there was one, was empty,
And the sick do without medicine
　　the tuberculous mother who gets meat once
　　a month the pregnant mother who lives on
　　tortillas the wife with diabetes and the
　　grandfather with bronchitis—who do
　　without medicine to save money for food
　　and who do without food because there
　　isn't enough money
And never enough money to buy food
　　$25 per week plus $10 every two weeks from
　　son's part-time job to feed twelve children,
　　ages 3 to 21 $25 every two weeks planting
　　cotton, to feed ten children from ten
　　months to seven years
　　Eight children living on commodities while
　　the father looks for work; three times
　　rejected by welfare
　　$84 in stamps to feed parents and nine
　　children for a month
　　$112 a month retirement benefits for food
　　for his wife and grandson for medicine for
　　bronchitis, and his wife's diabetes . . .

Wherever we went, we heard the voices of the poor, speaking not in medical terms, not with precise analysis of foods consumed in grams or ounces—but telling us of constant, chronic, unremitting hunger.

After a point, the voices merge into a characterization of a pervasive condition. In Alabama, we were told of a survey just completed of over 1800 Negro heads of households representing families totaling over 10,000 persons. The story that survey told follows the litany:

babies whose mothers are unable to nurse them
　　receiving no milk at all but fed instead
　　with water drawn directly from wells and
　　creeks.
children showing the listlessness characteristic of
　　malnutrition, who let flies climb around
　　their eyes and mouths, who show little
　　interest in playing with each other, who
　　just sit idly when not working, who sleep
　　a great deal in school.
adults suffering from cycles of dizziness and
　　"fallinout," who find upon visiting the
　　doctor that they need to discontinue starchy
　　and fatty food—pork products, especially
　　fatback and cornbread, biscuits, beans, and
　　grits—their basic diet.
women who have become bloated from poor diet.

And the story did not vary when we turned north to Boston—where Dr. Wheeler stated:

Inevitably, I compared what I saw there with my experiences in Mississippi and Appalachia and I left Boston with the strongly held opinion that the problems there are only different in degree from what we have seen elsewhere.

I think we saw enough to conclude tentatively that in the northeastern United States also there is a great group of disadvantaged people living just at or below a minimum level of subsistence and that their children are malnourished, hungry, ill-clothed, and are being deprived of the opportunity of ever becoming healthy, well-adjusted, and productive citizens.

This is, in brief, the story of hunger in the United States that this report will explore. Having heard this testimony and much more, we turned to the medical profession and medical and nutritional journals to learn just how seriously hunger in the United States affected the health of the poor. The unequivocal and uncontradicted thrust of testimony by doctors and the studies we received reemphasized the problems of hunger and malnutrition in objective medical terms.

We were struck by the high incidence of anemia, growth retardation, protein deficiencies, and other signs of malnutrition among the poverty population.

Repeatedly, we found high proportions of poor infants and children—Negro, Mexican-American, and white, urban and rural —suffering from anemia. And we have learned that, among the young, anemia can have serious and lasting medical and even emotional effects.

A young resident physician at Boston City Hospital reported to us the signs of malnutrition which he and his fellow doctors see regularly among poor children. He commented that it was a generally accepted fact among the doctors in the hospital that hemoglobin levels in children from poor districts were significantly lower than in children coming to suburban hospitals from higher economic groups. He also mentioned that in his experience the major cause of death in the first year of life is pneumonia, no longer an important killer except in the weak, malnourished, and chronically ill. . . .

In San Antonio, Texas, the Board heard testimony from doctors at Green Charity Hospital that severe cases of anemia were commonplace, that children one year old frequently weighed less than their birth weights and three-, four-, and five-year-olds weighed around 20 pounds.

In Washington, D.C., Dr. Margaret Gutelius, interviewed by a member of the Board, summarized a study conducted in Washington in 1967 of 460 Negro children from low-income families. Fifteen percent of the children were supported by public assistance. Iron-deficiency anemia was found in 28.9 percent of the total number and reached a peak of 65.0 percent in children from 12 to 17 months of age. . . .

In Cincinnati, Boston, Chicago, St. Louis, Columbus, Ohio, and Augusta, Georgia, reports collected by the Board of hospital admissions of children (poor and nonpoor) 6 to 36 months old revealed an average of 20 percent suffering from nutritional anemia. Presumably in the poverty population, the percentage would be higher. This is in fact borne out by studies of Headstart and other preschool children.

These studies have been summarized by L. J. Filer, pediatrician at the University of Iowa School of Medicine:

In Chicago (1967), 31.6 percent of the children examined were suffering from anemia (hemoglobin levels below 11 gms/100 ml).

In New York City (1963), 41.3 percent of one year olds from low-income families had hemoglobin levels below 10 gms/100 ml. Among children below three years, 27.3 percent had abnormally low hemoglobin levels.

In Pittsburgh, 16.4 percent of all children studied between 6 and 36 months and 19.0 percent of nonwhite children had hemoglobin levels below that considered normal.

In Baltimore (1965), the mean hemoglobin concentration of children from low-income backgrounds was found to be lower than that of rural Pakistani infants.

In addition the Board learned that:

In Mississippi, 62.1 percent of 847 Headstart children in four Mississippi counties have hemoglobin levels well below that considered normal.

In Alabama, "80% of the (709) children tested had hemoglobin values of 9.4 grams or less. An expected normal would be 11.0 to 13.0 grams."

The board found both in hearings and studies that pregnant women in poverty suffered from nutritional deficiencies and were constantly anemic. . . .

The board found evidence of retarded growth (abnormally low heights and weights) attributable to malnutrition in both urban and rural poverty areas.

Dr. David Steinman provided the Board with studies showing that six-year-olds from Appalachia were one to two inches shorter than national (Boston-Iowa) norms. This observation was confirmed in conversations with the Assistant Medical Director of Job Corps, Dr. Macht, who informed members of the staff that doctors at the Job Corps centers reported that the youngsters from Appalachia aged 16–21 who entered the centers tended to be generally below normal in height. The crippling effect that growth retardation can have on lives of the poor is discussed below. (We have learned that if poor nutrition goes unchecked in early childhood and growth is consequently retarded, the effects may include irreversible brain damage.)

Dr. Doane Fisher's recent testimony in eastern Kentucky substantiated these findings:

Our hospital admits 30–50 children per month ... mostly very low income; ... our nutritional problems are borderline but they are real ... example: we surveyed 109 preschoolers for our rural day-care centers ... criteria ... family income less than $1000; 30 percent fell below the third percentile for height; now by definition only 3 percent should have ... fallen below. This means that a third of our children were significantly statistically below the size they should be which is pretty good evidence that something was wrong nutritionally earlier in life....

The Board during its field trip to Boston received a report of a comprehensive biochemical dietary study of low-income children conducted by the faculty of the Harvard School of Public Health. The study established that in the Roxbury District (one of Boston's poorest) teenagers—both white and Negro—ranked in the lowest percentiles for height and weight.

A 1967 Baltimore study characterized median height for 842 low-income preschool children so far below the national (Boston-Iowa) standard as to be closer to norms for underdeveloped countries.

When asked about the dimensions of the food problem in the San Antonio area, Vera Burke reported to the Board that she has seen infants one year old weighing as little as seven pounds and others who actually weigh less than they did at birth....

We have identified severe protein deficiency resulting in the most severe protein diseases—kwashiorkor and marasmus. Protein deficiency in early childhood may cause permanent brain damage.

Dr. James Carter personally identified cases of two severe protein-deficiency diseases—kwashiorkor and marasmus—generally thought to exist only in underdeveloped countries. On a field trip to Hualapi and Navajo Indian reservations in Arizona, Dr. Carter heard reports that three or four cases of kwashiorkor per year have been recorded at the United States Health Service Hospital in Tuba City, Arizona. We were informed that such cases were increasing in frequency....

The board found evidence of a high incidence of parasitic diseases associated with malnutrition on its visits to South Carolina, Florida, Mississippi, Alabama, and Indian reservations.

The "Report of a World Health Organization Expert Committee," 1967, states that:

Studies have not been carried out to determine whether malnutrition affects the susceptibility of the human host to infection with hookworm or is related to the number of adult worms in the gut. On the other hand, there is clear evidence that the development of hookworm disease after infection takes place is influenced by the state of the host's iron reserves, and probably also by depletion of the exchangeable albumin pool.

Some observations indicate that in infected subjects prolonged or periodic starvation may cause increased migration of the worms from the gut to aberrant sites. This may explain the greater frequency of complications requiring surgery and other complications in some regions.

In January 1968, a study of 80 preschool children from two communities in Beaufort County, South Carolina, was conducted.

The results of this study are essentially the same as those of an earlier study described to the Board by Dr. Gatch:

An extremely high rate of parasitic infection was the only outstanding problem. Of the 55 fecal specimens, 30 (54.5%) showed a high incidence of ascaris (round worm) and trichuris (whip worm) infection. Though this rate is not as high as that for the same age group in the prior study, it is still a serious problem. The children tested were primarily infected with round worms. . . .

The seriousness of worm infection is not always realized. . . . The eggs are taken into the body through the mouth. They go into the intestines where they hatch and the larvae (baby worms) enter the circulatory system as if they were food. Eventually the larvae reach the lungs where they mature. While these worms are developing in the lungs there is a danger of pneumonia. As the developing worms grow they cause irritation and are usually coughed up and are then swallowed to return to the intestines. There they grow and thrive on the food which would otherwise be used by the body. Intestinal parasitic infestations, therefore, can be associated with nutritional deficiencies, loss of weight, listlessness, and even bowel obstruction. If left to thrive in a person's body, worms can cause death.

At the Birmingham, Alabama, hearing, Dr. H. F. Drake of Huntsville, Madison County, responded to the question: "Are parasites a big problem for these people?" Dr. Drake:

Much larger than is generally recognized. Very definitely so . . . there was a time in my practice when I disregarded it and said, "oh, there are no worms here," until a four-year-old vomited a double-handful on my examining table one day. Since that time, I have checked for them. But there are parasites here, very definitely . . . I don't see in my area much hookworm disease. I see primarily ascaris infestation, pinworms, and from time to time amoebic dysentery. . . .

Studies that have dealt with the nutritional status of the aged indicate that there may be serious nutritional problems among this population group.

The survey conducted by USDA in Rochester, New York, in 1965, of 283 households composed of individuals 65 years of age or older, revealed that 50 percent of the diets being consumed failed to provide adequate levels of one or more protective nutrients, especially calcium and vitamin C.

Interviews in New York City with nutritionists provide the following composite picture of the nutritional problems of the aged:

The major health problems of the aging include diabetes, arteriosclerosis, heart disease, and hypertension. Diet may be related. But both the health and nutritional status of the aging must be viewed as the sum total of long years of living on the marginal limits of nutritional adequacy.

The elderly were characterized by one nutritionist as living on a "tea and toast" diet and by a doctor as subsisting primarily on "mushy foods and soups."

One of those interviewed, Mrs. Marcella Katz, has personally taken nutritional histories of the aging and noted that the protein intake of the aging is very low. They often do not drink milk. Their meat usually consists of chicken backs and wings.

Some of the nutritional problems of the aging are directly attributable to lack of money. One nutritionist observed that "Older persons living on fixed or limited income find that the one area which can be cut is food." It was reported that some chew gum in lieu of eating because they cannot afford food. The aging are unwilling to use their scant savings for everyday needs such as food. . . .

Restaurants, by and large, try to avoid a clientele of older people who take a long time eating and spend little money.

Eating alone tends to become something to get done and over with. And many older people live in single rooms without cooking facilities. (This tends to be understated in surveys which consider a hot plate or a kitchen in the building to be a "cooking facility" for the residents.) . . .

Roughly one-third of the poor are aged. And they would appear to have a unique set of nutritional problems and nutritional needs. Because they are relatively immobile, have to live on limited and fixed incomes, are lonely, are afraid of the neighborhoods they live in, and because they live and eat alone, obtaining, selecting, preparing, and eating food becomes a chore of overwhelming proportions and with none of the compensating social values that meals and eating traditionally have in the family or communal context. . . .

We are not the only ones, or even the first ones, who have "discovered" hunger and malnutrition in America: others—Senate committees, the Director of the Poverty Program, investigators from the Department of Agriculture, newspaper reporters—have described similar findings.

The report that first opened our eyes to hunger in America told of intolerable conditions in Mississippi.

From New Orleans the Board received a report from Revius Ortique, past President of the National Bar Association, that a reporter from a local TV station had recently uncovered the fact that 1000 persons living in tar-paper shacks surrounding the city dump relied upon the food they scavenged there for survival. This situation came to light when the city decided to institute a charge for dumping garbage at the city dump. The resultant decrease in use of the dump caused severe hardship and an outcry from the families who depended upon the steady flow of garbage in order to survive.

In Des Moines, Iowa, Mark Arnold, a reporter for the *National Observer,* found cases of hunger, sickness, and deprivation that seem inconceivable, especially in a state in the heart of the nation's bread basket and in the state on which national standards of satisfactory nutrition and physical development are based. His stories tell of people digging in the dump for food, sick people unable to afford the diet required to control their illness, and infants dying for lack of milk.

He reported these interviews:

Mrs. Fay L., a thin, 68-year-old widow, who lives alone on $45 a month: "I know I should be eating more meat to get the protein with my heart trouble and all, and most of the time I get a little hamburger almost everyday. Doctor says I should be drinking fruit juices too, but I figure I can get some vitamin C from lemonade, it's a lot cheaper. . . . When you keep busy you don't mind being hungry so much. I don't hardly notice when mealtime goes by if I'm playing the piano or reading my Bible."

Mrs. Florence M., 26 with two small children, whose husband is unable to find work: "We mooch same's other folks, I guess. One thing we always got is milk 'cuz my ma keeps a goat. We don't always eat the same things all the time either. One day I'll fix macaroni for lunch, the next day spaghetti, or potatoes so we get a little variety too. . . . I had a steak once, about three months ago. A boy friend of my husband's was servin' it and invited us over. Imagine that, me going 26 years without tastin' steak. I took one little bitty bite and said, 'Boy, it sure was worth waitin' for.'"

Early in April, two officials from the Department of Agriculture, Howard Davis and William Seabron, traveled to Mississippi to view at first hand the reported conditions of hunger. Their findings were summarized in a report to Secretary Freeman:

There are clear evidences of malnutrition and unmet hunger.

A typical hardship case is that of Mr. and Mrs. Leroy Brown, 514 North Beauchamp, Greenville, Mississippi. They have eight children. Mr. Brown is a cement finisher helper and has intermittent employment. He had gone to work the morning prior to our arrival only to find that a subcontractor had slapped a lien on the job and it had closed down. He was unemployed. We asked him about participating in the food-stamp program and he indicated that he could never save enough money to do this. His children had no shoes and few clothes. He has rent of $20 a month, water $3, and he uses butane gas which costs him $1 a week. He claims he has no winter work and gets behind in all his bills during this period. The children go to school usually with no breakfast and get no lunch at school. They get only one meal a day and this usually is something like beans and white potatoes. Every once in a while they have chicken wings or necks.

Mrs. Annie White, 300 Ethel Street, Cleveland, Mississippi, has six children. She signed up for the food-stamp program but was unable to participate because of no income. We asked what she had had for breakfast and she said rice and biscuits. We asked where she got the food and she said it was left over from March commodities. She had tried to get on welfare but without success. We saw a young baby in her house whose stomach and navel was extended, possibly from malnutrition or hunger.

There are families existing on no discernible income....

Sargent Shriver referred to the results of an NIMH study where social workers listened to the poor and heard:

There was no food in the house and I didn't want them to go to school hungry and then come home hungry too. I felt that if I kept them at home with me, at least when they cried and asked for a piece of bread, I would be with them and put my arms around them. . . .

The testimony of the poor told us there was hunger. Doctors, nutritionists, school teachers, government officials, and many others told us there was hunger and malnutrition. Professional journals, newspaper articles, and various other reports confirmed what we heard. There are hunger and malnutrition in America. They are widespread and are becoming worse.

But why, it may still be asked, should this be a matter either for national con-cern or for priority treatment, given the large number of competing demands on this nation? What happens to infants who are malnourished? If malnutrition at every age is dangerous, is chronic hunger by itself a cause for concern? A number of doctors and psychologists have provided us with the answers to these and other related questions. The answers need no embellishment. The facts, we feel, speak for themselves.

The Effects of Hunger and Malnutrition

In the latest *Rockefeller Foundation Quarterly,* George Harrar writes:

We have long known that severe food shortages and famines can have immediate injurious effects on human beings. We have all seen pictures of children with bloated bellies and emaciated bodies. Their physical constitutions are so weakened by hunger that they are highly vulnerable to all manners of other illnesses. It is also common knowledge that certain dietary deficiencies can later cause severe skeletal damage such as occurs in rickets. Contemporary research, however, has indicated that malnutrition may also have long-range and more insidious effects on children and may even damage internal organs such as the liver.

...There is accumulating evidence to show that an inadequate and unbalanced diet, occurring at a highly crucial and prolonged period in the development of an infant or young child, may affect its mental capacities to a degree where its ability to learn is seriously impaired. The visible effects of malnutrition may be corrected and may disappear, and the child may seem to be restored to full health and vigor. But the effects on mental development may not be readily apparent and often may be perceived only when the child manifests difficulty in competing with normal children.

The damage caused by malnutrition begins even before birth and can affect future generations.

Dr. Frederick Solomon summarized this relationship:

It is well known that low-income women have greatly increased chances of producing premature infants and/or having "complicated" pregnancies and deliveries. It is also known that such offspring will then have greatly increased risk of brain damage or (in the case of prematures) slow development and special needs. As far as I can tell from the medical literature, the causes of prematurity and other complications of pregnancy . . . include: (1) small bone size in the expectant mother (probably due to poor nutrition and illness in her childhood); (2) poor nutrition and infectious disease during the pregnancy . . . .

An article in a recent issue of the *Journal of Pediatrics* reported that women whose small stature is attributable to malnutrition are prone to give birth prematurely, and the substantially higher incidence of birth defects among premature babies indicates that the effects of malnutrition thus may extend beyond a single generation.

There is increasing evidence that lack of protein in the diet of youngsters can cause severe and irreversible brain damage.

Dr. Joseph Brenner briefly summarized the evidence in testimony to the Senate Subcommittee on Employment, Manpower and Poverty:

> . . . Increasing evidence has come from different countries, especially from Mexico and South Africa, to suggest that infants, who both before and after birth were deprived of the kinds of food which are necessary for normal bodily growth, suffer not only visible damage to their bodies but also damage to the central nervous system, to the brain.
>
> Now one of the tragedies of this finding, if, indeed, it proves to be substantiated, is that while the damage to the bodily tissues from early malnutrition can be repaired in the main by subsequent better nutrition and medical care, no matter how well you feed children who are sadly deprived of food during the prenatal and immediate postnatal period, if they have suffered brain damage the likelihood is that this cannot be remedied. . . .
>
> It is a common observation that the children

of the 30 million poverty-stricken people in the United States may get enough food through welfare programs. But do they get enough proteins? Mostly they eat starchy foods—potatoes, grits, cornpone, breads, beans, and so forth. If the family has meat, cheese, nuts, or fish, it goes mostly to adults. So children suffer brain damage that is never overcome, irrespective of the amounts of protein consumed later.

These children, being deprived of normal brain development, do not do well in school. They do not have the intelligence, the initiative, or the motivation that stems from normal brain capacity. The many other deficiencies caused by poverty, the emotional and social damages of broken homes, and the lack of normal living conditions all reinforce the outcome of this early nutritional imbalance, so that these children become adults who perpetuate the same conditions for their children. . . .

Malnutrition causes lowering of resistance to infection and consequently is a prime cause of infant mortality after weaning and a significant contributory cause of parasitic infection, worms, viruses, and bacterial diseases. . . .

Other direct effects of malnutrition include listlessness and apathy, shortened life expectancy, disabilities resulting from inadequate growth, and diseases such as blindness, rickets, scurvy, and pellagra that result from deficiencies of a particular nutrient.

Yet, those consequences which result from classical instances of malnutrition represent only the tip of the iceberg. Each extreme case is indicative of a far greater number of borderline cases. Each case identified and documented is indicative of many undocumented and unreported.

But we wish to emphasize that hunger and a general condition of insufficient nourishment take a toll far greater and at least as significant as any of the classical forms of malnutrition which result from the deficiency of a particular nutrient. . . .

The cost of this chronic hunger and

undernutrition takes many forms: educational, psychological and social.

Hunger for food overrides hunger for knowledge.

A child comes to school with no breakfast—except perhaps a cup of coffee. He has no lunch and no money for a school lunch. He may carry some candy to nibble on to appease his appetite. Teachers and principals have repeatedly told the Board the obstacle which hunger places in their way—in the form of listlessness, fights over food, inattentiveness, acute hunger pangs, withdrawal, a sense of failure.

The ultimate costs are to be found in patterns of social unrest, distrust, alienation, withdrawal, and frustration.

Dr. Robert Coles provides this description of what it means to a child to be hungry more or less regularly. The children, he notes:

become tired, petulant, suspicious, and finally apathetic.

One will talk with them and play with them and observe their behavior and ask them to draw or paint pictures. From all that one can learn the aches and sores of the body become for a child of four or five more than a concrete physical fact of life, bring in the child's mind a reflection of his worth, and judgment upon him and his family of the outside world by which he not only feels but judges himself.

They ask themselves and others what they have done to be kept from the food they want or what they have done to deserve the pain they seem to feel.

In my experience with families in the Delta, their kind of life can produce a chronic state of mind, a form of withdrawn, sullen behavior. I have seen some of the families I know in the South go North and carry with them that state of mind and I am now working with them in Boston. They have more food, more welfare money, and in the public hospitals of the northern city certain medical services.

But as one tape-records their expressed feelings and attitudes month after month, one sees how persistently sickness and hunger in children live on into adults who doubt any offer, mistrust any goodness or favorable turn of events as temporary and ultimately unreliable.

I fear that we have among us now in this country hundreds of thousands of people who have literally grown up to be and learned to be tired, fearful, anxious, suspicious, and, in some basic and tragic sense, simply unbelieving.

All one has to do is ask some of these children in Appalachia who have gone north to Chicago and Detroit to draw pictures and see the way they will sometimes put food in the pictures or draw pictures of trees which they then explain are ailing with branches in some way falling. All one has to do is ask them what they want, to confirm the desires for food and for some kind of medical care for the illnesses that plague them.

The hunger we have seen contributes directly to the schisms which threaten our society today.

In a land of affluence and agricultural plenty, it cannot help but aggravate a sense of injustice, of grievance, of frustration and revolt.

This takes many forms. They range from school absenteeism and food stealing in schools to the massive problems of urban unrest and violence where chronic hunger, combined with other grievances, lowers the frustration level, intensifies one's sense of distrust and outrage at the society as a whole and increases tensions to the breaking point. . . .

We recognize that no definitive estimate can now be made regarding the number of people suffering from hunger and malnutrition in the United States.

On July 12, 1967, Dr. William Stewart, Surgeon General of the United States, stated:

"We do not know the extent of malnutrition anywhere in the United States."

Senator Clark asked: "Are you able to say whether, in your estimate, there is a lot of it, or, on the other hand, not much?"

Dr. Stewart: "Among the population . . . there is a fair amount of it. I cannot say what the extent is because we just don't know. . . . We have been trying to get ourselves to do this kind of work in the United States. We can do it all over the world but not in the United States."

It is hoped that under the new Partnership for Health legislation, such data will soon be available. It is significant that Drs. Arnold Schaefer and Ogden Johnson, the experts responsible for conducting such studies for the Public Health Service abroad, have been designated to take charge of this assignment. The legislation calls for an initial report within a few months—by summer, 1968.

Nonetheless, it is possible to assert, with a high degree of probability, that we face a problem which, conservatively estimated, affects 10 million Americans and in all likelihood a substantially higher number.

We base this conclusion upon the following reasoning: the incidence of malnutrition correlates directly with income levels; the percentage of the poor affected by hunger and malnutrition ranges conservatively between one-third and one-half. The federal government estimates that there are approximately 29 million Americans considered to be below the poverty line.

Correlation: all available evidence indicates that the incidence of malnutrition correlates directly with income levels.

1. This correlation emerges from our hearings and field trips, from professional observations, personal interviews, and newspaper accounts summarized above.

2. This correlation is corroborated by the many medical and dietary intake studies summarized above.

3. This correlation is directly substantiated by both the 1955 and 1965 nationwide Household Consumption Studies conducted by the Department of Agriculture.

The 1955 study states:

Among city families, dietary adequacy, as measured by the percentage of household diets meeting allowances in all of eight nutrients, was closely related to income. At each successively higher income level a greater percentage of diets met allowances, a relationship that existed among both northern and southern families. There was a tendency for those of the higher income levels whose diets did not meet the recommended dietary allowances to fail in a single nutrient only. At the lower income levels a somewhat larger percentage of the households failed in four or more nutrients.

The correlation between income and dietary adequacy is reaffirmed in the recently released dietary analysis of the 1965 nationwide consumption study conducted by the Department of Agriculture. The report states:

At each successively higher level of income, a greater percentage of households had diets that met (recommended dietary) allowances.

Moreover, the nutritional status of Americans has actually deteriorated since 1955 and 1965: "About 20 percent of the diets in 1965 were poor, . . . and about 15 percent in 1955."

4. This correlation (between low income and malnutrition) is further substantiated by the impact of low income upon postneonatal mortality—a nutritionally related phenomenon. Postneonatal mortality rates state the incidence of infant mortality *from one month to one year*.

After the period of weaning, nutrition becomes a chief factor in a child's life. Poor nutrition lowers a child's resistance and increases his susceptibility to disease. Since malnutrition may manifest itself as weakened resistance to disease, the autopsy may conclude that the infant died of pneumonia or flu or some other disease, but the evidence reviewed indicates that malnutrition may make the difference between life and death when infection does occur.

Dr. Joseph Brenner, testifying before the Senate Subcommittee on Employment, Manpower and Poverty on July 11, 1967, called attention to the toll being taken of the infant poor during their first year:

During the first few months of his life an infant has a slowly diminishing immunity to disease that has been acquired from the mother before birth. By the time of his weaning he must start replacing his immune substances by those that his body produces. For that he needs adequate body tissues and adequate nutrition to build them. This is vital between the time of weaning when a few months old and about two years of age.

The correlation between malnutrition and poverty is reflected in postneonatal mortality rates. During the first month of life—the neonatal stage—poverty infants die at only a slightly higher rate than infants from higher income groups.

From the second to the twelfth month, a startling disparity occurs between different income groups. The rate of death for the infant from an affluent family drops to approximately one-third the neonatal (first month) rate. The death rate for the poor infant may drop—but nowhere as radically; and in the poorest counties, the postneonatal rate will actually rise appreciably above the neonatal rate. As a result, the odds that the poor infant will die during the second to twelfth month is approxi- mately three times that of the nonpoor infant. In the poorest counties, the disparity shoots up to five to ten times the national average of postneonatal mortality.

Although nutrition is not the exclusive factor causing death, it is the primary factor *added* as a cause of death during the postneonatal stage. This marked divergence between rich and poor reflects the importance of nutrition which, after weaning, can only be supplied by prepared foods.

Thus, for instance, in Wolfe County, Kentucky, the second poorest county in the United States, a county with a 100 percent white population, the neonatal rate for infants is 16.3 per 1000 births—actually below the national average for white infants, 17.3 per 1000. However, the postneonatal rate in Wolfe County is 13.2 per 1000— higher than twice the national average for white infants, 5.9 per 1000.

The pattern is unbroken from state to state:

1. In virtually every state the highest postneonatal mortality rates occur in counties with higher percentages of poor families. . . .

2. In virtually every state, the postneonatal rate in the poorest county dramatically exceeds the postneonatal rate for the wealthiest county. . . .

THE MYTH OF MIDDLE AMERICA

Richard Parker

It was a tenet of both liberal and conservative dogmas following World War II that, economically, life in America was getting better all the time. Aside from the political flurry of McCarthyism in the early 1950s, the economy was everyone's favorite topic of discussion. After economists had predicted a major postwar recession, the American economy fooled them and began what seemed like a skyrocket burst. Between 1945 and 1965, the gross national product quadrupled, and disposable personal income increased two-and-a-half-fold. Postulating a "trickle-down" theory of income distribution, economists assumed that it was only a question of time before poverty was eliminated in America.

Suckled on the Horatio Alger myth and teethed on depression and war, the American public was glad to hear the news. Madison Avenue blared the New Affluence across front pages, and invited all of us to join the feast of consumption. The new symbol of America was the suburb, the grassy, tree-shaded Eden of responsible Americans. There a family was safe and happy with its two cars, two children, dog, and barbeque pit. Social science and the academy in general took over the affluence myth virtually *in toto,* declaring the end of scarcity, and with it the end of ideology, and the dawn of a new technocratic age where abundance, rather than scarcity, would be our bane. A Gallup poll would most likely have found wide acceptance of David Lilienthal's views that "one finds the physical benefits of our society distributed widely, to almost everyone, with scant regard to status, class, or origin of the individual."

But the myth of the New Affluence was a cruel distortion of reality. Composed of half-truths, it closed our eyes, cut us off from a recognition of America, and blocked off political and social alternatives. Today, poverty in the midst of prosperity seems almost characteristic of mature capitalism. Moreover, deprivation also seems characteristic and, together with poverty, describes the living conditions of nearly half the American people. What once appeared to be a New Affluence, I contend, is in fact an expansion of the economy which has disproportionately benefited the upper and upper-middle classes, while it has left the poor and the deprived to gather what crumbs fall from the table.

Marx contended in *Das Kapital* and elsewhere that poverty was a normal condition of capitalism even in the best of times. He argued that even if workers' actual wages rose, the differential between their wages and the income of the rich would continue to increase. The issue was settled to the satisfaction of most American economists by the performance of their own economy after World War II. A number of them had their faith in capitalism shaken by the Depression, but the postwar boom quickly allayed most of their doubts. The original Marxian criticism that wages might rise but differentials between classes grow larger was lost sight of in the general euphoria of the 1950s.

Reprinted by permission from The Center Magazine, **3**:2 *(March 1970), a publication of the Center for the Study of Democratic Institutions, Santa Barbara, Calif.*

The euphoria, moreover, was not limited to the traditional, or laissez-faire, economists. Liberal interventionists and Keynesians alike joined with conservatives to announce the death of poverty in mature capitalism. John Kenneth Galbraith, for example, claimed that by the late fifties American poverty was limited to "the insular poor" and "the case poor." The former were the inhabitants of areas like Appalachia and the rural South, where shifting employment patterns were causing "painful, but temporary hardship." The "case poor" were the alcoholics, invalids, and elderly who could not, or would not, get ahead. Keynes himself (like Marx) had, of course, foreseen no such amelioration, even in Keynesian capitalism. As Paul Mattick notes in his book *Marx and Keynes,*

Keynesian interventions in the economy necessarily adjust production and consumption in favor of investments. Such adjustments cannot end the paradox of poverty in the midst of plenty, and are not designed to do so.

The problem of economists was to explain *why* poverty was disappearing at such a rapid rate. Census statistics indicated that families with incomes below $3000 had declined from 28 to 14 percent between 1947 and 1966. But why? Obviously prosperity in general, and unionization in particular, had improved the lot of the workingman. But raw data, as well as a few highly sophisticated studies, indicated not only that the economic pie was getting bigger but that a significant reallocation was taking place. It appeared that, for some poorly understood reasons, a real change was taking place in the economy. Arthur Burns, then an Eisenhower adviser, rejoiced: "The transformation in the distribution of our national income . . . may already be counted as one of the great social revolutions of history." Paul Samuelson spoke for the liberals when he said, "The American income pyramid is becoming less unequal." Though still lacking an explanation, the economists' statistical foundations seemed eminently solid. Simon Kuznets' massive study, *Shares of Upper Income Groups in Income and Savings,* indicated a major decline in the percentage of personal income controlled by the upper strata of the society, a decline that "would continue." The late Selma Goldsmith and her associates showed that the share of personal income received by the top 5 percent declined from 30 percent in 1929 to 26.5 percent in 1936–37, and to 20.7 percent by 1944. Similarly, she showed that the share of the top 20 percent declined from 54.4 to 51.7 to 45.8 percent in the same periods. At the other end of the spectrum, the bottom 20 percent began to show some, if sizably smaller, gains.

Using these data, plus rawer data collected by the Bureau of the Census and other government agencies, economists postulated a theory for income distribution. According to the theory, income was slowly but irreversibly "trickling down" the income scale from the rich to the poor, to result finally in Samuelson's "flattened pyramid." It was presumed to be only a question of time before the last vestiges of poverty would disappear entirely; by the late fifties, Galbraith declared calmly, poverty in America was no longer "a massive affliction but more nearly an afterthought."

As a consequence, the study of income distribution as an economic discipline rapidly declined throughout the fifties. The university, like the nation at large, mesmerized by the new Affluent Society, was content to rest its discussions of poverty on clichés and rudimentary data. In economics, the new interest was in "value-free" econometrics; in the popular consciousness, it was in *The Organization Man* and *The Man in the Gray Flannel Suit.* Affluence was the presumed condition of almost all, and discussion centered on suburbia, martinis, and psychoanalysis. Maladies were the result of too much rather than too little.

The "rediscovery" of poverty in America, then, came as a rude awakening to most. Michael Harrington's *The Other America,* which got widespread attention in the early sixties, provided graphic portrayals of the personal impact as well as the extent of poverty. It inspired a major reexamination of the country's goals. Harrington's estimation that one-quarter of the American people lived in poverty shattered not only national pride but also the sublime self-confidence of the economics establishment. To them, his words were heresy.

Discomfiture was not limited to economists. It spread through the social sciences. Two sociologists, S. M. Miller and Martin Rein, looking back on their colleagues' embarrassing mistakes, described the general theory that had governed sociological thinking in the fifties:

The expansion of production and productivity resulted in a much greater economic pie. The graduated income tax, expanded welfare services, and education were more equitably distributing this larger pie. Continued increase in aggregate economic wealth would invariably filter down, more or less equitably, to all income groupings. Marginal economic groups, it was assumed, would in time "gracefully succumb" to continued economic growth and that small residual groups not covered by expanded welfare and social security programs would be handily cared for by the public dole.

But even after Harrington pricked the popular balloon, air leaked out with surprising slowness. Those running the federal government's War on Poverty (and many social scientists) agreed to define as poor only those families with annual incomes below $3000. This swift bit of statistical legerdemain immediately shrank Harrington's one-quarter to a less frightening one-fifth. The effect was not only to minimize the poverty in America but to ignore the basic contradictions in the myth of prosperity.

A reevaluation of postwar prosperity leads to major second thoughts about "trickle-down" theories of income distribution. As early as 1957, Robert Lampman, of the University of Michigan, noted that initial gains by the poor to increase their share of the wealth had not only stopped but were reversing. By the early sixties, the rich were again increasing their control of the lion's share of personal income.

The premature optimism of economists like Burns lay in statistics that took no official notice of their unusual circumstances. During the war and shortly thereafter, the income of laborers and service workers increased almost twice as fast as that of professionals and managerial workers. But this was due chiefly to war-related factors that would be unlikely in a peacetime economy, such as full employment mixed with a shortage of nonskilled labor. By the late fifties, the lower categories no longer showed high-rate gains: laborers' and service workers' income increased only 48 percent while managerial income increased 75 percent. Joseph Pechman concluded in 1969 that "the distribution of income in the 1950s period may not have been very different from what it was in the early 1920s."

These gross figures, some would argue, are misleading because of shifts in the labor market. Thus the small gains for laborers might be offset by the diminishing number of common laborers, or the high incidence of poverty among farmers offset by decreasing numbers of farmers. But Herman Miller, an economist with the Census Bureau, disagreed. Writing in a Bureau monograph, *Income Distribution in the United States,* he concluded that shifts in job distribution did not substantially affect patterns of income distribution.

Of course it could still be argued that the overall stability of income distribution for the urban population masks important changes which have taken place for various subgroups within the population. But this hypothesis . . . does not appear to be supported by the facts. Income distribution within the urban population has not shifted even when that population is further classified by labor force status of wife, age of head, or size of family.

Miller, however, does underline one important trend: the increasing number of families in which both husband and wife work.

It should be noted that incomes are much more equally distributed among families where the wife is working than where she is not working; the sizable increase in the proportion of families with working wives has therefore tended to decrease income inequality during the past decade.

Moreover, Census projections show that the proportion of women in the labor force will continue to grow over the next two decades.

Yet even the increased family income provided by a second earner was unable to offset the gains by upper and upper-middle classes in control of personal income. Using Census data as well as studies by various economic agencies, Joseph Pechman acknowledged that the rich, but not the poor, had prospered in the postwar era. He pointed out that the simplest Census tables, those most often cited, exclude capital gains and therefore grossly misrepresent income trends in the upper fifth of the economy. For example, [Table 1] shows the standard before-tax income shares of the rich, according to Census data:

Table 1

Year	Top 5% of Families	Top 20% of Families
1952	18%	42%
1957	16	40
1962	16	42
1967	15	41

What this table indicates obviously is confirmation of Burns' "great revolution." But are the figures accurate?

Tax data are needed to push the analysis

further. These data are more useful, because they show the realized capital gains of these families and net income after federal taxes. The salient observation here is that, contrary to another popular myth now also on the wane, the federal income tax is *not* progressive in its effect. Computing total disposable (i.e., after-tax) income, we find the following [Table 2].

Table 2

Year	Tax Units Top 5%	Tax Units Top 15%
1952	16%	30%
1963	17	33
1967	17	34

However, this table itself can only be considered an estimate that falls to the low side. Since World War II, innumerable tax benefits and payment forms have grown up which benefit only the rich. Pechman names tax-exempt interest and depletion allowances as sources of income, then adds:

During World War II, methods of compensation were devised to funnel income to business executives in nontaxable forms. The devices used are well known: deferred compensation and pension plans, stock-option arrangements, and direct payment of personal consumption expenditures through expense accounts.

Having listed these varieties of unreported income, he prefers caution, and concludes, "Little is known about the impact on the distribution of income."

Gabriel Kolko is not so timorous. In *Wealth and Power in America*, Kolko announced that "the impact of the federal income tax on the actual distribution of income has been minimal, if not negligible." Drawing on a number of sources for his data, he deduced that adding the uncomputed income of the upper classes would raise their total disposable income two or three percentage points above Pechman's own figures. (Thus the top 5 percent received about 20 percent of the personal income, and the top 1 percent about 10 percent of that income.) Since 1952, the effective federal tax rate on the upper 1 percent of the population has *dropped* from 33 to 26 percent.

What may be said of the federal tax structure can be repeated *ad nauseam* for state and local tax structures. The impact of property and sales taxes is clearly regressive, and, as one economist put it, this is "disturbing because the state-local tax system is the growing element of the national system." Federal tax revenues have remained fairly constant as a proportion of gross national product, hovering around 20 percent since 1951. State and local taxes, by contrast, have risen from 7.1 percent of the gross national product in 1951 to 11.9 percent in 1968.

Assuming that state-local taxes respond more or less proportionately to the rise in the national product . . . the states and local governments must have increased rates by 68 percent in these seventeen years to push up their tax yields to current levels.

The motivation is obviously not simple greed, but a reflection of increased demand on public services and increasing population concentration in metropolitan areas. Nonetheless, the burden of these social changes falls most heavily on those least able to pay.

The Economic Report of the President, 1969 shows the following [Table 3]:

Table 3

Income Classes	State and Local Taxes (percentage of income)
Under $ 2,000	25%
2,000– 4,000	11
4,000– 6,000	10
6,000– 8,000	9
8,000– 10,000	9
10,000– 15,000	9
15,000 and over	7

Analysis of income alone, in the case of the rich, obviously also misrepresents the actual concentration of economic well-being in the country. Affluence for the rich, unlike income for the middle and lower classes, is rarely limited to wages and salaries. Rents, dividends, interests, all go into the total wealth of the upper class. James D. Smith, of the Office of Economic Opportunity, in analyzing data of persons with gross assets in excess of $60,000, found a highly concentrated wealth structure. This group, representing the top 1.5 percent of the wealth-holders in the country, received the following amounts of income [Table 4]:

Table 4

Type	Billions	Percent of Total (each type)
Wages and salaries	$25.9	10.8%
Dividends	8.0	74.8
Interest	3.1	27.9
Rent	6.4	52.5
Capital gains	57.6	71.4

Furthermore, this table is an understatement of concentration. It excludes $1.7 billion in dividends paid to trust funds and nonprofit foundations; it assumes only average yields on assets, rather than optimum figures to be obtained through the advice of investment counselors; finally, its data are for 1958, and all subsequent information shows increasing pyramiding of the wealth structure.

Gabriel Kolko also contributes significant figures on the concentration of total wealth in the upper brackets which supplement Smith's own research. For example, in 1960 the top 10 percent controlled two-thirds of all liquid assets, while 51 percent of the spending units headed by unskilled or service workers, had no assets. Other, more shocking data suggest that between .2 and .3 of 1 percent of the population control 22 percent of the personal wealth and 60 to 70 percent of all privately held corporate wealth.

What in fact was the condition of the poor through the fifties and into the sixties? First of all, we must have a definition of poverty. The federal government has chosen the income-line method, with all families falling below $3000 (now $3700, because of inflation) defined as poor, and therefore eligible for charitable assistance. Before 1962, little was known about this group; since then, a veritable antipoverty industry has dredged up quantities of information about these people, from their illiteracy rates to their reproduction out of wedlock.

Given all this information, what have we learned? First of all, the income-line method is misleading. It fails to account for assets, temporary impoverishment, and several other factors. Second, and more important, the $3000 has been recognized as ridiculously, if not criminally, low.

How in fact was the government's poverty budget originally arrived at? Politically, several factors interacted; methodologically, the explanation is simple. An annual food budget was prepared, and then that figure was tripled. The budget followed Department of Agriculture guidelines that included the notion that food occupies about one-third of normal expenditures. But simple methodology belied the gross underestimation of need. Oscar Ornati, in *Poverty Amid Affluence,* summarized a typical 1960 "adequate minimum" budget for a family of four:

It provides for simple clothing to protect against the weather and maintain cleanliness. A woman's coat, for instance, must last five years. Leftover food must be retrieved. A cup of flour spilled means no thickening that week; a blown bulb, no light for that month; and a chair broken in anger cannot be replaced for a year.

The meat budget allows for stewing lamb, beef liver or heart, picnic shoulder, fillet of haddock, or perhaps a boned veal roast. No frozen foods are provided for. It allows nothing for an occasional glass of beer, tobacco, or telephone calls. The budget assumes a small rented five-room flat. The family living room might have two chairs. A mattress and spring on legs may serve as a couch, a dropleaf table for eating; two straight chairs may also be there. Linoleum may cover the floor, and there can be a lamp or two. An electric refrigerator and iron are allowed. The family may listen to the radio an hour a day, but television is not included in the budget. There will be money to buy aspirin but none for "miracle" drugs. The husband may get a haircut once a month, and the wife a home permanent once a year. She can use a self-service launderette. There will be no money to buy the children candy or ice cream, or to go to the movies, or to offer a visitor a cup of coffee.

The government's budget is unrealistic on other scores. It fails to take account of the overpricing and shoddy quality of food in poor areas, as documented in books like David Caplovitz' *The Poor Pay More.* It ignores the high cost of other items such as housing and furniture, etc. (usually 10 to 25 percent overpriced, according to one Bureau of the Census economist) that drives up maintenance costs in the other two-thirds of its budget. In farm areas, it still relies heavily on the presumption that the rural families produce much of their own food, although as a percentage of the total food consumed, home-grown items have fallen from 70 to 36 percent in the past twenty years. It makes no allowances for the higher education of the children, unless one presumes they will receive full scholarship aid, which is highly unlikely. Finally, it assumes no major medical expenses in the family, although over half of the poor are not covered by medical insurance.

The actual meals upon which the entire budget is based inspire greater disbelief. The words of the Census that "assuming the homemaker is a good manager and has the time and skill to shop wisely, she may prepare nutritious, palatable meals ... for herself, a husband, and two young children" on a budget of 70 cents per day per person inspired one pundit to comment that "Betty Crocker herself would starve." A statistician for H.E.W. describes how a housewife must spend her money:

For a meal all four of them ate together, she could spend on the average only 95 cents, and to stay within her budget she must allow no more a day than a pound of meat, poultry, or fish altogether, barely enough for one small serving for each family member at one of the three meals. Eggs could fill out her family fare only to a limited degree because the plan allows less than two dozen a week for all uses in cooking and at the table, not even one to a person a day. And any food extras, such as milk at school for the children or the coffee her husband might buy to supplement the lunch he carries to work, have to come out of the same food money or compete with the limited funds available for rent, clothing, medical care, and all other expenses. Studies indicate that, on the average, family members eating a meal away from home spend twice as much as the homemaker would spend for preparing one for them at home. The 25 cents allowed for a meal at home in the economy plan would not buy much even in the way of supplementation.

Despite the obvious subminimal character of this "minimum budget," some optimism has been generated by the War on Poverty and a booming economy, inducing people to believe that the poor are "disappearing." But this optimism needs closer scrutiny. First of all, a $3000 limit is a ridiculously low level separating the poor from the nonpoor. Second, the government has continued to play games with its own figures ever since the War on Poverty began. For example, the cutoff limit of poverty is measured by pretax income figures, although the poverty budget was constructed on an after-tax basis. Third, politics has taken a heavy toll on the poor.

According to the McGovern Committee: "In 1968, government statisticians estimated there were between 22 and 27 million Americans living in poverty." But at the beginning of 1969 "the higher of these two figures was dropped without explanation" and the 22 million used as the official estimate. Finally, government economists have consistently underestimated the effect of taxes and inflation on the poor, or so say a group of nongovernment economists (writing in *Life,* August 15, 1969). Since fixture of the $3000 figure in 1960–61 dollars, inflation and taxes have required a gain of 41 percent in actual income to maintain a real-income equivalent. This would require a present definition of the poverty level at $4240, or $540 more than the government now allows. Such an adjustment would add several million more families to the rolls of the poor.

For the extremely poor, times are now even harder. As the Southern Rural Research Project reported:

The poor and the hungry had their brief moment in the sun: America may lionize its victims, but the vogue of compassion passes quickly on; the hungry have now become somewhat passé. Americans seem to take it for granted that once such alarming conditions are publicly known, the appropriate authorities will automatically step in and clear the matter up.

Dr. Arnold Schaefer, who headed the Public Health Service's National Nutrition Survey, had been among the first to document malnutrition in sample counties in Texas and Louisiana; now the survey has been discontinued, and Dr. Schaefer has passed quietly from the scene. One wonders if the 15 million malnourished have disappeared as quietly.

The Nixon Administration's response to the crisis of poverty remains to be seen, since its proposed revamping of the welfare system has yet to pass Congress. The central feature of minimum income is an advance over existing programs, since it recognizes working as well as nonworking poor; but its own ceilings of aid are so low as to offset the extension in coverage. His proposals to tie Social Security to cost-of-living indices also seem designed to benefit one segment of the poor, but this was rejected in favor of a one-shot 15-percent bonus.

The central fallacy, or perhaps the central design, in the government's designation of the poor is its narrowness. Given the present definition of the poor, we avoid the larger contours of our social reality. Compared with the wealthy or near-wealthy, the gains of the poor have been almost immaterial. In 1946, the bottom 20 percent of all families (the government estimate of the "poor" hovers around 16 percent) received 5 percent of the income; by 1967, the same fifth—now 40 million people—received 5.4 percent. In other words, the intonations of "trickle down" by economists of the fifties now sound hollow indeed.

Crucial to the isolation of the poor is not only the government's action, but the basic American myth. We are people of the *middle* class, bourgeois, home folks, people who still like Norman Rockwell and live decent, unextravagant lives. De Tocqueville did not instigate the myth, but *Democracy in America* certainly strengthened it. His comments on the "tendencies toward the equalization of the conditions of life" set the pattern for all later social scientists and historians who sought to capture the fundamental character of the country. Louis Hartz, as recently as the middle 1950s, still wrote of "irrational Lockeanism" as the controlling factor in American political life, and saw this as a reflection of the dominant "middle class."

The belief in progress has always caused Americans to see their past in an ambivalent light. They have viewed the past romantically, choosing to see our problems as smaller and our victories larger than life.

What is imperialism to some has been Manifest Destiny in America. What for some was genocide directed toward the Indian was only "resettlement" of the natives. Even when we made mistakes, there was seldom an accusation of guile or willfulness on our part. The Spanish-American War was "misguided," but it was fought with the best of intentions.

By this kind of logic, our poor today are still better off than 90 percent of the world, and certainly in a better state than they were fifty years ago. The discomfort that greeted disclosures by the muckrakers and writers of the naturalist school at the turn of the century has been replaced today by a comfortable agreement that "things were bad then, but just look at them now." After all, the middle class has always been America's strength and salvation. If we do have poor, well, either they are lazy and inefficient (the conservative view) or they are victimized minorities—blacks, the old, unwed welfare mothers (the liberal view). In any case, nobody opposes welfare anymore—Nixon is pushing the guaranteed income—and besides, as liberal economist Alan Batchelder has assured us, "the poor will continue to disappear as the economy expands."

The fundamental misdirection of all this is away from analysis of the "middle class" to a blind invocation of the myth itself. As recently as October 1969, *Newsweek*, for example, ran an otherwise perceptive article entitled simplistically: *The Troubled American—A Special Report on the White Majority*. Studded with references to "America's vast white middle-class majority," it intoned the familiar lauds: "America has always been the most middle class of nations, the most generous and the most optimistic." But what in fact the article showed most clearly is that for an enormous proportion of the "middle class," embourgeoisement has been a half-filled dream, a set of unsatisfied hopes. These are the people Leon Keyserling has called not the poor but "the deprived Americans"—"above poverty but short of the minimum requirements for a modestly comfortable level of living." In 1964, Keyserling estimated their number at 77 million men, women, and children.

Keyserling's distinction between a family income of $3500 ("poverty") and $4500 ("deprivation") should be clear to an economist: the "deprived" all work. Unlike the poor, whose ranks are swelled by the elderly, the infirm, and the blacks, the "deprived" cannot be dismissed as victims of "nonmarket forces." The "deprived" are functioning, productive members of our economic system: the manual laborers, the clerks, the launderers, the hospital workers of our society. They may have their own home, but it is heavily mortgaged; they may have a late-model car, but it has been financed at steep rates. Their savings, which form a family's cushion against disaster, are marginal: 40 percent are either in debt or have savings of less than one hundred dollars. Liquid assets show even less room for error: 20 percent of all families own no assets, and 48 percent own less than five hundred dollars' worth. Yet, as Kolko rightly points out:

Liquid assets—such as checking and savings accounts, shares in savings-and-loan associations and credit unions, and government savings bonds—are of decisive importance to low- and even middle-income families exposed to layoffs, unemployment, or medical and other emergencies. Often they represent the entire margin between security and the relief rolls.

The myth of the middle class serves as a permanent leash on the deprived. Lacking the income, they are still expected to provide their families with the amenities that advertising, television, and the academic mythmakers have told them the "middle class" enjoys. Constantly under pressure, they retain all the old American virtues as a desperate bulwark against the encroach-

ment of the "shiftless poor." They, like the poor, bear a heavy burden of the taxation because of regressive tax structures. They aspire to better education for their children, their own home, and more leisure. Yet, in a great many cases, both father and mother must work simply to maintain their present condition.

The disparities within the "middle class" and the number of the "deprived" are brought out most clearly when one examines the data of income growth over the past half-century. The accompanying table shows control of the income shares by population tenths since 1910. Omitting the top tenth as "upper class" and the bottom two-tenths as "poor," analysis of the remaining "middle class" yields striking results [Table 5].

The most interesting observation is that there are two distinct strata in the "middle class," the upper of the two having gained markedly greater control of income. Between 1910 and 1959, the second, third, and fourth deciles increased their percentage of the total income more than one-quarter, while the fifth, sixth, seventh, and eighth deciles were able to advance only from 26.5 percent to 27.9 percent in the same period.

This information sheds light on much of the writing over the past two decades on the Affluent Society. The "middle class," as a homogeneous group, has done well; but closer examination reveals that that success becomes smaller and smaller as one moves down the income scale within that class. The astigmatic concern of the social scientists for suburbia, executive anomy, and the crises of "the abundant society" has proceeded from myths that now seem badly worn—from the myth of the New Affluence, from the myth of "trickle-down" income and wealth redistribution and the omnipotence of Keynes, and from the capstone myth of them all—the myth of the American middle class.

As a matter of fact, the "middle class"

Table 5   PERCENTAGE OF NATIONAL PERSONAL INCOME, BEFORE
TAXES, RECEIVED BY EACH INCOME-TENTH[a]

Year	Highest Tenth	2nd	3rd	4th	5th	6th	7th	8th	9th	Lowest Tenth
1910	33.9	12.3	10.2	8.8	8.0	7.0	6.0	5.5	4.9	3.4
1918	34.5	12.9	9.6	8.7	7.7	7.2	6.9	5.7	4.4	2.4
1921	38.2	12.8	10.5	8.9	7.4	6.5	5.9	4.6	3.2	2.0
1929	39.0	12.3	9.8	9.0	7.9	6.5	5.5	4.6	3.6	1.8
1934	33.6	13.1	11.0	9.4	8.2	7.3	6.2	5.3	3.8	2.1
1937	34.4	14.1	11.7	10.1	8.5	7.2	6.0	4.4	2.6	1.0
1941	34.0	16.0	12.0	10.0	9.0	7.0	5.0	4.0	2.0	1.0
1945	29.0	16.0	13.0	11.0	9.0	7.0	6.0	5.0	3.0	1.0
1946	32.0	15.0	12.0	10.0	9.0	7.0	6.0	5.0	3.0	1.0
1947	33.5	14.8	11.7	9.9	8.5	7.1	5.8	4.4	3.1	1.2
1948	30.9	14.7	11.9	10.1	8.8	7.5	6.3	5.0	3.3	1.4
1949	29.8	15.5	12.5	10.6	9.1	7.7	6.2	4.7	3.1	0.8
1950	28.7	15.4	12.7	10.8	9.3	7.8	6.3	4.9	3.2	0.9
1951	30.9	15.0	12.3	10.6	8.9	7.6	6.3	4.7	2.9	0.8
1952	29.5	15.3	12.4	10.6	9.1	7.7	6.4	4.9	3.1	1.0
1953	31.4	14.8	11.9	10.3	8.9	7.6	6.2	4.7	3.0	1.2
1954	29.3	15.3	12.4	10.7	9.1	7.7	6.4	4.8	3.1	1.2
1955	29.7	15.7	12.7	10.8	9.1	7.7	6.1	4.5	2.7	1.0
1956	30.6	15.3	12.3	10.5	9.0	7.6	6.1	4.5	2.8	1.3
1957	29.4	15.5	12.7	10.8	9.2	7.7	6.1	4.5	2.9	1.3
1958	27.1	16.3	13.2	11.0	9.4	7.8	6.2	4.6	3.1	1.3
1959	28.9	15.8	12.7	10.7	9.2	7.8	6.3	4.6	2.9	1.1

[a] In terms of "recipients" for 1910–37 and "spending units" for 1941–59.
Source: Data for 1910–37 are from National Industrial Conference Board, *Studies in Enterprise and Social Progress* (New York: National Industrial Conference Board, 1939), p. 125. Data for 1941–59 were calculated by the Survey Research Center. Figures for 1941–46 are available in rounded form only.

may have escaped the grasp of more than the poor and the deprived. If by "middle class" one means a decent, modest standard of living, it seems that perhaps 60 to 70 percent of the country have difficulty in reaching it. In 1966, the Bureau of Labor Statistics announced that the average urban family required $9191 per year to live comfortably; yet the median income that same year was $1400 less than that figure.

At this point, it seems wise to stop and make two observations: the first an esti-mation of some present and possibly future realities; the second, an historical speculation.

The first observation is about the "un-mentioned middle class," the professional, technical elite and its immediate support structure. These people are the true bene-ficiaries of the Affluent Society, and are the class which has sought to reshape the American myths in its image. College-edu-cated, employed as lawyers, engineers, ad-vertisers, and real-estate dealers, these people are the upper strata of the middle class that experienced the greatest gains in postwar years. The suburban crises of the fifties were *their* crises, the suburban malaise was drowned in *their* martini glasses. If one were to seek a paradigm for their group, one would find it during the Kennedy era, in the bright young men around the seat of power; but one could also find it in the older and younger men, in corporations and universities. They are those whom Daniel Bell described as the "technocratic elite."

An attack on this group here is not immediately relevant. The Vietnam war has already prompted a number of incisive critiques of them, particularly on the university level. However, critique and solution are not synonymous. It seems likely that the import of young people's radicalism will be diffused and coopted back into electoral party politics, and the thrust of radical restructuring lost, as it was in the New Deal. Already the "beautiful people" seem to be emerging as the new archetype of this social caste—human beings who span Establishment and anti-Establishment factionalism, who work for corporations by day, yet smoke dope by night.

The problem is that their amorality is more difficult to detect because it so often hides behind a veil of rhetorical concern. Unlike the industrial captains of the last century, their contemporary lieutenants feign not indifference but impotence. After all, they *are* concerned, God knows, but they are only vice-presidents or mere managers. They may give occasionally to the political *outré* or talk of "repressive tolerance" at cocktail parties, but those gestures mark the boundaries of their social concern.

One index of that social indifference emerges in an ironic place: Michael Harrington in January had an article in *The Atlantic* entitled "The Betrayal of the Poor." The irony is that *The Atlantic*, for all its enlightenment, is still an organ of that upper-middle class who have not so much resisted, as they have ignored, social change.

The article begins:

For all the rhetoric of recent years about the war on poverty, the poor in America are almost as numerous as ever.... Unless the government makes immensely greater commitments of resources and planning, the country is doomed to a social explosion in the seventies that will make the turbulent sixties seem tranquil by comparison.

The article, like articles on the malnourished, on housing conditions, on the quality of education in the ghetto, will be read and then lost in the comfortable notion that once federal programs are established, everything will be taken care of. Enter the New Deal, Phase II.

The error in this remains the presumption of the liberal upper-middle class since the first decade of this century: that social legislation by the federal government will cure what ails us. Jane Addams suggested it; Ralph Hunter, one of the nation's first social welfare workers, endorsed it; the New Deal itself put the seal of approval on it; and now even Republicans have begun to see merit in the idea. Unfortunately, the theory has never worked.

The critical assumption behind liberal optimism about coalition between the federal government and corporate capitalism has been that things keep getting better all the time. There are more cars, more homes, better schools, etc., than ever before and, in the midst of this prosperity, the distribution of all this largesse has been getting better as well.

Taking the first half of this claim—that the total quantity of goods has increased—there is no dispute. But one *can* make some comparisons between the United States and other industrialized nations. Fifteen nations have higher literacy rates. Ten nations have lower infant mortality rates. To my knowl-

edge, the United States is the only industrialized nation that does not offer comprehensive medical insurance for all its people.
It offers perhaps the worst unemployment
protection and the worst welfare system
among the developed countries. It has 15
million malnourished. It has 30 million
poor. It has 77 million deprived. Few other
nations can claim such tawdry conditions
amid such phenomenal growth.

On the second half of the comfortable
liberal optimism—that distribution has
been getting better and better—there is a
fundamental error in the assumption. Since
World War II, the only significant redistribution of income in the United States
has been between the upper and the upper-
middle classes. Overall, distribution has remained essentially stable not only over the
past twenty years but over the entire
twentieth century.

There are three sources for this statement. The first is the chart on income distribution [see Table 5] that shows the
limits of change. The second is from Joseph
Pechman, a conventionally liberal economist, writing in *The Public Interest*, who
states:

The year 1929 must have been the high point
of inequality during the 1920s, so that distribution of income in the more recent period may
not have been very different from what it was
in the early twenties if account is taken of un-
distributed profits.

The third is a much earlier source. Published in 1904, Robert Hunter's *Poverty* is
probably the first attempt made to estimate
the number of poor in America. Highly
sympathetic to the poor, it uses the data of
state and private welfare agencies (since
federal data were nonexistent). While emphasizing the wretched conditions of the
poor, Hunter limits their number to only
12 percent of the population. Today economic historians agree that Hunter's estimate was off the mark by 6 percent, thus
leaving at the turn of the century a min-

ority poor of 18 percent. Yet 18 percent was
the government's estimate of the poor sixty
years later!

None of these three estimates is perfect
(none ever can be, because crucial data are
lacking); but they can give a newer and perhaps more accurate contour of poverty and
affluence in America. We are, as De Tocqueville said, and as American social scientists have reaffirmed ever since, "a people of
the middle class." But to be middle class is
both a social-psychological and economic
problem. Among those who call themselves
"middle class," perhaps a majority have always lacked the money to be in fact what
they believe they are. Not only are the poor
still with us, but they have been there for
years. Michael Harrington's announcement
that our poor are the "first minority poor
in history" has been misunderstood; the
poor have always been a minority in
America, but a stubborn minority that refuses to decrease and disappear. The rich
in America just keep getting richer. All the
talk of income distribution, of flattening
pyramids, and of peaceful economic revolutions has been nonsense, fabricated in part
out of optimism, in part out of a myopia in
the professional classes who themselves
gained so rapidly after World War II.

At the end of an account such as this, it is
usually expected that the author will offer
remedies, specific reforms such as tax legislation or welfare payments—or at least see
reason for hope on the horizon. I cannot.
First, because "reform" has become the
province of politicans and electoral platforms, and deals with our needs about as
realistically as someone using a Band-Aid
on a compound fracture. Yet, even liberals
accept reformism, as they did when they
quietly applauded the Nixon proposal of
a guaranteed annual income for the poor,
despite the dire (and probably accurate)
warning of Michael Harrington that "a
guaranteed annual income could be a way

to institutionalize poverty at the subsistence level in the United States."

Second, and more important, I do not seek "reform" because, at age twenty-three, I have lost faith in the willingness of America to "reform." I have lived with the poor, eaten their food, slept in their beds, and taught their children, in Alabama, in Vermont, in Watts. I know their bitterness, and I share it. John Kenneth Galbraith ob-served recently that "liberalism has been excessively tender toward the rich." A surprise to liberals, but a fact of life for the poor. Attempts at reform have delivered to the poor nothing but promises. They have watched the War on Poverty beaten into ineffectual irrelevance. They have listened to America's liberal politicians promise food as they stare at empty plates. They know the sham of reform.

SLAVES FOR RENT

THE SHAME OF AMERICAN FARMING

Truman Moore

Each year when the harvest begins, thousands of buses haul thousands of crews to fields across America as millions of migrant workers hit the road. They ride in flatbed trucks or old condemned school buses patched together for just one more season. They go by car: Hudson bombers with engines knocking, laying a smoke screen of oil; prewar Fords packed with bags, bundles, pots and pans, children crying. They go in pickups made into mobile tents —a home for the season. They ride the rods of the "friendly" Southern Pacific.

They come from farms in the Black Belt, from closed mines in the mountains of Kentucky and West Virginia, from wherever men are desperate for work. They come by whatever means they can find. These are the migrants—the gasoline gypsies, the rubber tramps—crossing and recrossing America, scouring the countryside in a land where the season never ends. There's always a harvest somewhere.

From Florida to Oregon the fruit tramp pursues the orchards. From Texas to Michigan the berry migrants work from field to field. Two million men, women, and children invade every state of the Union to pick fruit, to chop cotton, to scrap beans, to top onions, to bunch carrots, to pull corn, to fill their hampers with the richest harvest earth ever yielded to man.

The circus and the college house parties leave Florida after Easter. The first week of April, the major-league clubs wind up their spring training and go home to play ball. The snowbirds start back to the cities of the north with their tans. And the migrants

Reprinted from the Atlantic Monthly; *copyright © 1965 by Truman Moore. Another version of this article appears in* The Slaves We Rent, *by Truman Moore. Reprinted by permission of Random House, Inc.*

form crews and follow the sun. Sometimes a single bus will carry a crew; sometimes they pass in ragged convoys as the migrant battalions rumble out of Florida and up the Eastern seaboard.

The invasion hits South Carolina in May, North Carolina and Virginia by June. By late summer they have passed through Pennsylvania into New Jersey and New York State. Some go into Delaware and Maryland, others to Long Island, and a few on to Maine. By October the upstate crops are in, and the migrant tide flows back to the southern tip of Florida.

The workers find little to do in November. It is after a lean Thanksgiving and a bleak Christmas that hands are needed again in the fields and groves of the winter gardens.

From Texas the pattern is much the same. This is the home base of the largest migrant group. The exodus begins in early spring. Storekeepers close down for the season as the little towns depopulate. Everyone who can bend and stoop starts for the great corporate farms of the North and the West. From the steaming valleys of Arizona and California to the great Pacific Northwest comes a string of harvests. There is no crop in the world that can't be grown on the Pacific coast, and relatively few that aren't. Where once was a vast desert wasteland, there are now the rich irrigated valleys, principally the Imperial and the San Joaquin. In steady sun and several inches of water, crop after crop is produced with factorylike precision.

Into all these fields, through state after state, the migrants cut a footpath across America. But in spite of their mobility, the migrants are shut off in their own world. Migrant America is a network of side roads, of farm towns and labor camps and riverbanks, of fields and packing sheds. The famous cities are not New York, Boston, and San Francisco, but the capitals of the agricultural empire of the big growers:

Homestead and Belle Glade in Florida; Stockton in California; Riverhead on Long Island; and Benton Harbor in Michigan. For the migrants, no roadside motel or tavern offers a neon welcome. The host community sees them not as a potential payroll but as a blight to the community's health and a threat to the relief rolls. Businessmen, dance bands, and tourists making their way across the country find many services and comforts at their disposal. The migrant can hope at most for good weather, a grassy bank, and a filling station that will permit him to use the rest room.

There is always blood on the harvest moon. No one knows how many luckless migrants have died on their way to gather the harvest. Only a few of the more spectacular crashes make their way to America's breakfast table by way of the local newspaper. A few years ago, a half-ton truck left Texas for the sugar-beet fields of Wyoming. In it were fifty-four migrant workers. As the truck neared the outskirts of Agate, Colorado, the driver suddenly hit the brakes. The truck spun around and turned over twice, scattering workers across the highway. There was one death, a baby who died in a Denver hospital shortly after the accident. In October 1963, not three miles from the spot in Fayetteville, North Carolina, where a truckload of migrants died in 1957, a truck carrying twenty-four bean-pickers turned over when a tire blew out, strewing its human cargo like a handful of oats. Fortunately no one was killed.

When the ICC was considering regulation of migrant transportation in 1957, a representative of the "jolly" Green Giant Company complained that restriction of travel between 8 P.M. and 6 A.M. was a hardship on the workers and the employers. "It has been our experience," said the company's man, "that these trucks can complete the trip from Texas to Wisconsin in from fifty to sixty hours with stops only for meals, gasoline, and general stretching."

A vegetable packer said that it was practically impossible to attach seats securely and still use the trucks to haul produce. He did not advance this as an argument against carrying workers in produce trucks, but against using seats. Many crew leaders use trucks because of the extra money they can make hauling the crops from the fields to the processors. Jon Misner, the director of migrant labor at Stokely-Van Camp in Indianapolis, said he knew crew leaders who made $15,000 hauling vegetables—in an eight-week season.

THE CREW LEADER

Little Jim was a good crew leader. His bus, the Bean-picker Special, was a bit rundown, and the tires were slick. But the driver was sober and careful. The camps that Little Jim found for his crew while they were on the road were not always what he had promised them, but he could hardly help that. He couldn't demand that the grower put the crew up in the Holiday Inn.

The crew went hungry before the crop came in, but Little Jim never told them he was going to feed them. If he lent them money to buy food before they got work, he charged them no more than the going rates, just as a bank would. And he had not been greedy about the money he took from their pay. A dime out of every dollar was his take. He stuck to it. And he charged a couple of dollars for each job he got them, and there were no more than three or four a season. While they were on the road, he got them to "help on the gas." When he deducted for social security, he always turned it in, as he was supposed to. If there was a big shopping center near the camp, he'd stop on the way back from the field so that the crew could do their shopping there instead of in the little stores near the camps, which always overcharged.

His wife thought he was stupid to pass up any chance to make money. So he sold moonshine. There was a good profit in that. "I keep a little around because some of them—they won't work without it. If you don't have it for them, they'll go out and get it." He bought from a bootlegger for $1.00 a quart and sold it in the fields at $.50 a shot. A heavy drinker gets thirsty in the field. But Little Jim had to be careful not to give a bad drinker too much. He had one worker named Leroy Small, who was a mean drunk. He pulled out a home-made machete one afternoon and almost took a man's head off. After that Little Jim was more careful.

He was usually on the road with the crew four to five months a year. During that time, he was the crew's official representative. It is the crew leader, not the grower or the corporate farm, who is recognized as the employer. Whether or not a migrant ends the season money ahead or money behind often depends on his crew leader.

There are more than 8000 crew leaders in the migrant streams. They come in all shades of reliability and honesty. Good or bad, the crew leaders perform a service that is invaluable to the grower. A grower in Maryland can make a simple agreement with a crew leader to supply a given number of migrants at a specified date and for a stipulated price. The farmer, theoretically, can rest assured that his labor problems will be taken care of. In practice, however, he can never rest easy until he sees the crew pull into camp. An unscrupulous crew leader can shift his crew to a higher-paying farm at the last minute. The first farmer can easily lose his crop for lack of a harvest crew. Because both the migrants and the farmers depend on the crew leader, he is in a good position to take advantage of both. Hamilton Daniels was like that.

You had to admire Hamp. He was a thorough professional, with imagination and style. He usually honored his obligations to deliver the promised number of workers at the agreed price and time. Sometimes he came a little late though, because he would stop for a few small unscheduled jobs on the way. Born in New Orleans, a diplomat and a shrewd judge of character, Hamp had a quick intelligence far beyond what five years in school had given him. He knew how to get along with the white growers. He just played Uncle Tom.

Sometimes when the grower was around, Hamp would ride herd on the crew just to let the man know he was in charge. But the growers knew that. They depended on Hamp to bring the migrants in on time and get them out when the work was done. Neither Hamp nor the grower would profit by argument. His dealings with the growers were usually cordial; a balance of power existed that neither cared to test.

Hamp could make a flat price for harvesting and then cut the crew's pay as low as they'd stand for. On a flat-fee basis, Hamp's profit was the difference between what the grower paid him and what he paid the crew. Hamp didn't care for this because if the weather was too hot or it rained too much, he might even lose money.

If there was a good crop and a high market, the grower might agree to an hourly rate so the crew would take their time and not damage the crop. But the usual agreement was a piece rate. This fixed the cost for Hamp and the grower. The rates were usually set up on a sliding scale. When the crop was good, the rates were lower, and as the fields thinned out, the rates went up. When the fields thinned out, the crew didn't want to work them because it was hard to make any money. So the grower would pay a bonus at the end of the harvest to all the workers who stayed on the job. But it really wasn't a bonus. He just withheld some of their money until the job was finished.

Whatever arrangement was made, the crew seldom knew the details. If the grower gave his camp rent-free as part of the payment, Hamp might still charge the crew rent. He was careful never to cut into a man's pay directly, except to take out social security, which he never turned in to the government.

His dealings with the migrant crew were complex. For one thing, he lived closely with them. His impression on them was important. If a crew leader looked too prosperous, the crew might think he was crooked. If he looked too poor, they might doubt he was a good crew leader. Hamp managed to look just right. He has a pair of brown pants and a red shirt that were ragged to the point of fascination. He was the raggedest man they'd ever seen. Close examination of this costume would have revealed patches sewn over whole cloth, but the effect was one of arresting poverty. To contrast with this, Hamp drove a Cadillac. His garments attested to his humility and his car to his success.

In picking a crew, Hamp seemed to work with little thought or design. Actually, he was very careful about whom he took on. He wouldn't take boys who looked as if they were trying to save money for college in the fall. They held too tight to their money, and most of them would leave the crew to go back to school before the season was over.

Hamp looked for the quirk, the twist: the reason this man or that woman wanted to work the crops. He preferred workers, either male or female, in the first stages of alcoholism. Some crew leaders wouldn't hire the drinkers, but Hamp knew better. You had to wait until a man was hooked. Then he didn't seem to know or care what you took out of his pay as long as he had enough to eat and drink. He might get mad, but he didn't leave. Of course, a hardened wino was worthless. He couldn't stand the pace. It isn't easy to bend over in the broiling sun all day.

Hamp kept a good supply of white mule and had places along the way where he could get it. There was good money in it.

He also kept little white packets of dope. There was the real money. But sometimes it was hard to get. You really had to push it all the time to make it pay, and it was too bad if the government men caught you with junk.

He kept his hand in the ordinary rackets, too. He got a 15-percent cut from the grocery store near the camp. If the storekeeper refused to pay a kickback, Hamp would take the crew to another store. The crew seldom had cash, so Hamp worked out a credit system with the storekeeper. The crew members were never shown an itemized bill; they just paid what Hamp said they owed. Hamp also had beer and cigarettes in his trailer at double the store prices. For a $.50 bottle of wine, he charged $1.45. None of the crew stocked up on these things because they never had cash. With one thing and another, Hamp cleared about $20,000 in a fair year.

On the West Coast, the crew leader is called a labor contractor. (The term "crew leader" refers to the foreman.) Nick Peronni is a labor contractor in California. He has a fleet of buses and trucks that haul workers in and out of the San Joaquin Valley. He operates out of the "slave market," a big fenced-in lot that serves as a hiring hall, just up the street from the Farm Placement Service in the skid-row section. Before a man can work, he has to get a white card from the placement office. If he changes crews, he can't get another card. Even if the grower cheats him, he can't quit without losing his white card.

Most of the growers that Nick works for prefer to contract workers from elsewhere. Part of Nick's job is to keep too many of the local workers from getting on the crews. Nick does not travel with the crews. He loads the buses out of the slave market each day for short hauls into the valley. He also handles the paper work. No one is sure how much Nick makes, but estimates run high. As he himself puts it, "If this thing blows up tomorrow, I'll go fishing.

It'll be a long time before I get cold and hungry."

These men are representative of crew leaders. For the most part their lives are hard to trace. Some use colorful pseudonyms like Sugar Daddy, Cool Breeze, or Meatball. A few years ago, the *New York Times* reported that only half of the crew leaders coming into New York State gave addresses that could be located. Tax investigators in Oregon found that relatively few crew leaders had ever filed personal income taxes, and almost none had filed social-security returns for the crew, even though all presumably deducted from their migrants' paychecks.

In 1964, Congress passed a crew-leader registration law designed to put dishonest crew leaders out of business. The crews have just started to move now. It remains to be seen what effect the new law will have.

THE TAR-PAPER CURTAIN

Across America there are tens of thousands of migrant camps. They are in the valleys and in the fields, on the edges of cities and towns. Some are half deserted. Some are behind barbed wire and even patrolled by armed guards. Migrant camps are within commuting distance of Times Square, under the vapor trails of Cape Kennedy, and surrounded by missile sites in the Southwest. They have names like Tin Top, Tin Town, Black Cat Row, Cardboard City, Mexico City, The Bottoms, Osceola (for whites), Okeechobee (for blacks), and Griffings Path.

Negroes from the Black Belt are dismayed by camps they find up North. Okies and Arkies who migrate today find camps much like those the Joads found in *The Grapes of Wrath*. You can drive from New York to California and never see a migrant camp. You have to know where to look. To borrow a popular analogy, a tar-paper curtain separates the migrants from the rest of America.

Let us look at a typical migrant camp which we will call Shacktown. Shacktown is owned by a corporate farm, one of whose foremen is in charge of the camp. "But mostly," he says, "we just turn it over to the people to run for themselves." In other words, no one collects garbage or maintains the camp in any way. The camp is built on the grower's sprawling farm. It cannot be reached without trespassing, and several signs along the road remind the visitor of this fact. Even finding it is difficult. Local residents are suspicious of outsiders who are interested in migrant camps. Requests for directions are met with icy stares.

Shacktown was built about fifteen years ago. No repairs to speak of have been made since then. Most of the screen doors are gone. The floors sag. The roofs leak. The Johnsons, a Shacktown family, have a six-month-old baby and five older children. "When it rains," says Mr. Johnson, "it leaks on our bed and all over the room. At night when it rains, we have to stand up with the baby so he don't get wet and catch pneumonia."

All the rooms in Shacktown are the same size, eight foot by sixteen. When the Johnsons moved in, they found they needed much more space. They sawed through the wall, a single thickness of one-by-six-inch pine, and made a door to the next cabin, which was not occupied. The exterior walls are unpainted and uninsulated. They keep out neither wind nor rain, sight nor sound. Cracks between the boards are big enough to put your hand through. There is no privacy, and the Johnsons, like most Shacktown families, have learned to live without it. The windows are simple cutouts with a hatch propped open from the bottom. Some have a piece of clothlike screening tacked on.

The only touch of the twentieth century in the Johnsons' cabin is a drop cord that hangs down from the ceiling. It burns a single light bulb, plays a small worn radio and, when it works, an ancient television set that Mr. Johnson bought for ten dollars, through which they get their only glimpse of urban, affluent America.

Although there are trees nearby, the camp is built on a barren red-clay hill, baked by a blazing summer sun. There are four barrack-type frame buildings, divided into single rooms. Behind the barracks are two privies, both four-seaters. The door to the women's privy is missing, but the rank growth of weeds serves as a screen. There are no lights, and no one uses the toilets after dark. The Johnsons use a slop jar at night. It is kept in the kitchen and used for garbage, too.

There is virtually no hope of keeping out the flies that swarm around the privies. But one county health inspector found an unusual way of getting the growers interested in the problem. The inspector would drop by the grower's house just before lunch and ask to see the migrant camp. When they came to the privy, the inspector would throw a handful of flour over the seats, which invariably swarmed with flies. On the way back to the house, the inspector would manage to get invited to stay for lunch. At the table he would remark, "Well, I'm sure glad you asked us all to lunch." And there crawling around on the fried chicken would be a floured, white-backed privy fly.

During most of the season in Shacktown there will be several full- or part-time whores. The going price is $3.00. Prostitution thrives behind open doors. Venereal diseases are sometimes epidemic. In a crew near Morehead City, North Carolina, one woman infected ten men in the course of three days. Six out of eight crews working in the area had at least one syphilitic.

There are two hasps on the Johnson's door in Shacktown. One is for the family to use. The other is for the grower. If the rent is not paid, the family will find when they return from the field that they have been locked out. Some growers provide cabins free. Some charge according to the number of able-bodied workers. Rents run from as low as $10 a month to as high as $50.

The Johnsons, like most Shacktown families, do their own cooking. But grocery shopping is not easy. There is a small cracker-barrel store near the camp, run by the grower, but the prices are a third higher than in town. "We got a ten-cent raise," says Mr. Johnson, "and everything in the store went up a quarter. He wants us to buy from him or move out. It don't seem right."

Cooking is done on a small, open-flame, unvented kerosene stove which serves as a heater in the cold weather. Fires and explosions are not uncommon. The cabins are not wired for electric heaters; natural gas is not available. Bottled gas requires a deposit and an installation fee. Asked if the tenants didn't suffer from the cold nights, the camp manager replied, "Oh, heat's no problem. You'd be surprised how hot it gets in one of them little cabins with so many people."

For most of the year the cabins are miserably hot. Refrigeration is nonexistent, and perishable foods seldom find their way to the migrant's table. The baby's milk sours quickly, and he is given warm Coke. Good water is always scarce in Shacktown. Between the long buildings there is a single cold-water tap. The faucet leaks, and there is no drainage. A small pond has developed, and the faucet is reached by a foot-bridge made of boards propped on rocks. This is the only water in camp.

Just keeping clean is a struggle. Water must be carried in from the spigot, heated over the kerosene stove, and poured into the washtub. In the evening, the oldest children are sent out with buckets to stand in line for water. Sometimes when the line is too long, the Johnsons buy their water from a water dealer, who sells it by the bucket. "We get some of our water down the road about five miles," says Mrs. Johnson.

Sometimes I get so tired I'd just like to go in and die. We have to boil the water and then take it to the tub to wash the clothes. We have to boil water for washing dishes. The last camp we was in had a shower, but you had to stand in line for it half a day, especially in the summer.

The problem of getting water is widespread in migrant camps. A Mexican national in California said his camp was without water for a week.

The contractor said the pump broke. There was a small rusty pipe that brought enough water for washing the hands and the face, but we could not wash our clothes, and we could not take a bath for a week. The inspector ordered the pump be fixed right away. Now the water from the baths is pumped out of a big hole, and it flows through a ditch between the bunkhouse and the tents. When it makes warm weather it smells very bad. To me it looks like the contractor is not afraid of the inspector.

When several children in a Swansboro, North Carolina, camp became ill, a young minister named Jack Mansfield had the water in the camp tested. It was found to be contaminated. He reported this to the county health office, but they said nothing could be done since the camp had been condemned long ago.

Shacktown is a typical migrant camp, but not all migrants live like the Johnsons. Some find better camps. Many will find no room at all, and unfortunate workers will live, as they say in Arkansas, "under the stars." Three hundred migrants were stranded in Nevada when the harvest was late. "For days they had barely enough food to keep alive," the Associated Press reported.

They camped—men, women, and children—in the open, along ditch banks, without protection

from winter rains and freezing night temperatures. They took their drinking water from
irrigation ditches used by cattle. Many children
were sick. And they had no work.

Migrant workers are often housed with
the livestock. A Mexican worker in California described his camp this way:

We are installed in a barn which was used for
the cows when we moved in. You have to slide
the big door and go in and out the same as the
cows. The cracks between the wall planks are
about eight or ten centimeters wide. This makes
very good ventilation for the cattle, but it allows
the wind to pass over our bunks at night. It is
strong and fresh cow smell. It is necessary to use
much Flit, and the smell of this chemical also
affronts us. The Americans are very inventive.
Perhaps someday they will invent a Flit with
perfume. . . . The only person who comes to see
us is the Father, who hears confessions and says
the Rosary. We are ashamed to have him come
on account of the smell of the cows and the stink
of the Flit.

As bad as conditions are in the camps
where the migrants live, they are worse in
the fields where they work. A Florida
Health Department report noted that at
times crews refused to harvest fields because of the human waste deposited there
by an earlier crew.

Americans are probably the most dirt-
conscious people in the world. We are a
bathroom-oriented society. Chains of restaurants, motels, and hotels across the
country appeal to customers almost solely
on the contention that their establishments
are spotlessly clean. In such a society, it
is not pleasant to imagine that beneath
the cellophane wrapper lies a head of lettuce that has been urinated on. A storm of
controversy erupted when a labor union
showed a movie of field workers urinating
on a row of lettuce. Growers charged that
the picture was posed by union men in
old clothes. Perhaps it was, but it need not
have been faked.

The fields of the modern factory farm

are immense. And there are no bathrooms.
A Catholic priest observed that "most consumers would gag on their salad if they
saw these conditions, the lack of sanitary
conditions, under which these products are
grown and processed."

After a tour of leading farm states, Senator Harrison Williams of New Jersey said:

In the fields . . . sanitation facilities are a rarity.
Unlike other sectors of our commerce, agriculture generally does not provide migrant farm
workers with field-sanitation facilities such as
toilets, hand-washing facilities, and potable
drinking water.

We as consumers have good reason to be uneasy about this situation. Much of our soft food
and other products are picked, and often field
packed, by migratory farm workers. If we object
to filth anywhere, we certainly should object to
it in any part of the process that brings the food
from the fields to our tables.

One grower, a woman, docked the workers an hour's pay if they left the field to
go to the bathroom. The woman stayed
with the crew most of the day. The men
had to relieve themselves in front of her.
They found this humiliating but were unwilling to lose the wage.

Antonio Velez, a field worker in the San
Joaquin Valley, said he was told by the
grower to drive a pickup truck into the
fields which carried two chemical toilets.
The grower told him to drive fast so that
the toilets would slosh around and be dirty,
and no one would want to use them. He
was afraid the workers "would lose too
much time going to the bathroom." The
idea of providing field workers with toilets
and clean water strikes most growers as an
unnecessary refinement. Consumers who
realize that diseases such as amebic dysentery, polio, and infectious hepatitis (to
name only a few) can be transmitted
through human excreta may not be so convinced of the frivolity of field sanitation.

Dysentery is often considered a joke. It
is called by a host of humorous euphe-

misms. The facts about dysentery are not funny. It kills 6000 Americans a year, finding its heaviest toll among children less than two years old, many of whom are the children of migrant workers.

It will be argued that to supply field workers with rest rooms would be prohibitively expensive. In 1955, as a result of newspaper articles and state investigations about the lack of bathrooms and hand-washing facilities, a group of Western lettuce growers started a voluntary program. A novel type of mobile toilet and hand-washing facility was developed and tried out in the lettuce fields and found to be successful. Forty of the units were built and put into the fields in the spring of 1956. None of the other growers picked up the idea; so when the pressure abated, the project was abandoned.

THE CHILDREN OF HARVEST

The man put down his hamper. "It sure looks like rain," he said. The skies were a bright crystal blue, with only a trace of clouds to the east. The crew kept working, but a few looked up and saw the three men coming down the row. One was the grower, who seldom came around. The other was the crew leader. The third man was a stranger. He carried a brown leather case and a clipboard. The men just nodded as they passed.

They went up and down the rows, the first two walking easily. The third man, the stranger, stumbled now and then—a city man used to flat sidewalks. They crossed the red-clay road and went into the south field. A woman looked up as they came past the stacks of empty crates. Before they were close enough to hear, she turned to the busy crew. "Sure looks like rain." Two small pickers dropped their boxes and darted through the vines and ran into the woods. Someone on the next

row passed the word. "Sure looks like rain." Two more children ducked into the vines and ran.

The children hid beyond the road in a small clearing in a clump of scrub oaks. From here they could see the man leave. It was their favorite game. Hiding from the inspector was about the only thing that broke up the long hours in the field. In the camp they played hide and seek this way. When you were "it" you were the inspector. But it was more fun when there was a real inspector.

Luis at twelve was the oldest of the children. He had been to school off and on since he was six, but he was only in the fourth grade. If he ever went back he would be in the fifth grade, because he was older and bigger now. But Luis didn't want to go back. He wanted to run away. He had been around the country a lot. Last year his family went to California and Oregon. One year they went to Arkansas. Once long ago—he was too young to remember when—his father took them to Florida for the winter citrus harvest. Luis was an ageless child. He had a way of taking a deep weary drag on a cigarette, and after a long while letting the smoke curve slowly out of his nostrils. His face was wrinkled, marked with a tiny network of fragile lines at the corners of his eyes and deeper lines across his forehead.

Still a child, he liked to play games. He enjoyed the gaiety at the Christmas feast. But at the end of the working day, he would stand stooped over slightly with his hands stuck flat into his back pockets. From behind he looked like a dwarf, a tiny old man whose bones had dried up and warped with age.

Billy was the youngest of the children. He was not quite five but old enough to do a little work. He didn't earn much, but it was better, his father said, than having him sit around the day-care center costing them $.75 every single day. His mother kept the money he earned in a mason jar. When fall came, he'd get a pair of shoes if there was enough money. He could start school, if there was one nearby, in new shoes.

His brother lay beside him in the clearing. John was ten. In the years that separated Billy and John, a brother and sister had died, unnamed, a day after birth. John kept them alive in his imagination. There were few playmates in the camps and fields that he ever got to know.

"I got two brothers and a sister," he would say. "And they's all in heaven but Billy there."

He called his invisible brother Fred, which is what he wanted to be called instead of John. Faith was the name he gave his sister. He saw her as soft and gentle, wearing a dress with white frills, like a china doll. He played over in his mind a single drama with endless variations. Faith was hurt or being picked up by some bully. He would come to her side to help or defend her. Then he and Faith and Fred would sit beneath a tree, and they would praise him for his bravery, and he would say it was nothing. They would have something cold to drink and maybe some candy to eat. He retreated more and more into this pleasant world. His mother had noticed his blank gaze many times and had heard him say "Faith." She thought he was going to be called to the ministry to be a gospel preacher or a faith healer.

Robert was almost as old as Luis. He had been on the season for two years. His father came from the sawmill one day and said, "They don't need me any more. They hired a machine." His father had tried to make a joke of it, but late at night Robert could hear his mother crying. He knew it wasn't a joke about the machine being hired. They sold their house and packed everything into the car. Robert left school, and now they lived in one camp after another. Sometimes they slept in the car.

The man with the clipboard left. The children came out of the bushes, picked up their boxes. They bent over in silence and began to pluck at the vines. These are the children of harvest. "The kids that don't count" they are sometimes called. "The here-today-gone-tomorrow kids."

Inspectors from the Department of Labor find children working illegally on 60 percent of the farms they inspect. And no one knows how many hide in the woods when it "looks like rain." No one really knows how many migrant children there are. Estimates run from 10,000 to 600,000. The most frequently used figure is 150,000. One survey in the olive groves of California showed that nearly three-fourths of the workers were children. An Oregon survey showed the importance of the child's labor to the family. There the average migrant worker earned $32 a week during the weeks he worked. But his wife and children together earned $48. In some crops women and children do more than half the harvest work.

The birth of the migrant child will most likely be in a migrant shack or, at best, in the emergency room of a county hospital. His nursery is the field and his toys the things that grow there. A few camps have day-care centers. There are twenty-four such registered centers in the United States, with a total capacity of less than a thousand children.

The migrant child may never develop any idea of home. His family is never in any place long enough, and home to him is wherever he happens to be. He seldom sees a doctor. It is almost certain that he will have pinworms and diarrhea. Other common ailments untreated are contagious skin infections, acute febrile tonsillitis, asthma, iron-deficiency anemia, and disabling physical handicaps. A poor diet condemns the child from the start. A report on a camp in Mathis, Texas, showed that 96 percent of the children had not drunk milk in six months. Their diet consisted mainly of cornmeal and rice. A doctor commenting in the report said there was evidence of ordinary starvation. The migrant child is prone to scurvy, rickets, and kwashiorkor—a severe protein deficiency. Some reports have put the incidence of dental abnormalities at 95 percent, and others said that bad teeth were universal.

Epidemics, like the one in the San Joaquin Valley a few years ago, take a heavy toll. Shigellosis, a form of dysentery, had been rampant in the valley for years. The infant mortality rate was extremely high. Within a short time, twenty-eight babies died of dehydration and malnutrition. The migrant child is also prey to a host of diseases now rare in the nonmigrant world: smallpox, diphtheria, and whooping cough. A medical survey in California showed that two-thirds of the children under three years of age were never immunized against diphtheria, whooping cough, lockjaw, or smallpox. Two-thirds of the children under eighteen had not received polio shots.

There have been many brave attempts to provide migrant workers with medical service, usually on a shoestring budget and through the energy of a few determined people in a community. In the little farming towns around Morehead City, North Carolina, the Reverend Jack Mansfield got together the first mobile medical clinic, a white trailer called the Rocking Horse, equipped with the rudiments of a doctor's office. The Rocking Horse—so named because it tilted back and forth when you walked around in it—was staffed by a group of local doctors who took turns going out to the migrant camps. The welfare department was persuaded to provide a social worker. The National Council of Churches provided a migrant minister.

By the light of a flickering kerosene lantern, the lines of workers waited to see the doctor. Some had unnamed miseries of the head and the chest, aches and pains that move up the back and seize the neck in a vise. Colds, bad teeth, rheumatism, and chronic headaches could only be treated by the same white pills.

It would take a full staff of psychologists to evaluate the psychic condition of the migrant children. But even in the absence of any thoroughgoing study, the symptoms of frustration, bitterness, and disorganization are easy to see. A day-care center was started in the basement of an Arkansas church for migrant children. One of the most successful parts of the center was a workshop run by a young man named Alec Johnson. The shop was set up in a corner room with small windows for ventilation at the top. It was cool and pleasant on the hottest days.

Alec had assembled the usual carpentry tools and some leatherworking tools. By the end of the season, when the migrants pulled out, he had learned several things about migrant children by watching them at play. Joey Smith was a blond, blue-eyed boy from Kentucky. The family had been on the road for almost ten years, which was most of Joey's life. He was two when the coal mine was closed and his father lost his job. When Joey first came to the shop, he was quiet; by the end of the second week, he was racing around the room banging the chairs with a hammer. Alec had to take the hammer away from him, and Joey sulked and refused to do anything.

Alec got Joey interested in making a leather billfold. "I got all the material together," said Alec,

and Joey started with a flurry of energy. But within an hour, he had put it aside and was toying with some pieces of lumber. I started him back on the billfold. Joey hit it a few whacks with the mallet and then looked around for something else to do. Joey wanted the billfold and had been excited about making it. But he didn't seem to be able to stay with it and finish. There were many of the kids who were like this. It seemed to be a characteristic. They start out with great enthusiasm, but as soon as they hit a snag, they toss whatever it is aside and go to something else. They haven't had any experience in building anything or in solving problems. They have no confidence in themselves.

Teachers, doctors, and ministers have the most contact with the migrant children. They are, understandably, not optimistic about the future.

Children have worked on farms since the first farmer had a son, and it has always been considered part of the rural way of life. But there is a difference between the farmer's boy doing his chores and the migrant child topping onions and digging potatoes. The two are blurred together in the minds of people outside agriculture. The blurring gets help from such spokesmen as North Carolina's Congressman Cooley, who enunciated the Blue Sky Doctrine: "There are no sweat shops on the farms of America," he said. "On the farms of our nation, children labor with their parents out under the blue skies."

Under the blue skies of Idaho, a twelve-year-old girl got her ponytail caught in a potato-digging machine. It ripped off her scalp, ears, eyelids, and cheeks. She died shortly afterward in a hospital. On a farm in California, a ten-year-old girl came back from the fields exhausted from a day's work. She fell asleep on a pile of burlap bags as she waited for her parents. As other workers returned from the fields, they tossed the empty bags on the stack, and the little girl was soon covered up. A two-ton truck backed across the pile and drove off. They did not find her body until the next day.

If children were mangled in steel mills, there would be a storm of public protest. But death and injury on the mechanized farms seem to pass unnoticed. Under the blue sky of the farm factory is no place for little children. Agriculture is one of the three most hazardous industries. In California alone, more than five hundred

agricultural workers under the age of eighteen are seriously injured every year.

The migrants who follow the harvest are the only people in America who are desperate enough for this work to take it. Their children will be another generation of wanderers, lost to themselves and to the nation.

FACTORIES IN THE FIELD

The family farm used to be the citadel of virtue in the American rural tradition. Life was made hard by the vagaries of the weather and complicated only by the bureaucrats in Washington, who always meddled with farming. In 1900, when the population of the United States was under 76 million, 40 percent of the people lived on the farm. Today, only 8 percent live on farms, and more leave every year.

Today, the important farms, as units of production, are more like factories. Great cultivators and harvesting machines lumber through endless fields. Gangs of workers bring in the harvest. One cannot ride past these giant farms after the harvest is over and the crew has left without an eerie feeling of being in a land without people. A verse from Isaiah rides the wind: "Woe to those who join house to house, who add field to field, until there is no more room, and you are made to dwell alone in the midst of the land."

The importance of making the distinction between the big farm and the little farm—between the homestead and the factory in the field—is essential to the story of migrant labor. To begin with, the family farmer and the migrant worker are in the same sinking boat. The family farm, while providing an income and a place to live, no longer contributes significantly to America's food production.

If the earth suddenly swallowed up a million and a half small family farms in

America—nearly half the total number—food production would drop by only 5 percent. Half of our food is produced by only 9 percent of the farms. These highly mechanized, capitalized, and integrated companies use most of the seasonal labor. Only a relatively few big growers (5 percent of the total number) use more than $2000 worth of labor a year. The real giants—the top 3 percent—hire more than a third of all farm labor.

It is through the fields of the farm factories that the migrant stream flows. And these are the growers that have brought foreign farm workers to America each year. The growth of corporation farming and its effect on the traditional family farm have been watched with concern for many years. In 1923 a North Carolina land commission issued a still-urgent report:

It is quite conceivable that under capitalistic or corporation farming, greater gains might be secured than under a system of small individual holdings.

It is quite inconceivable, however, that the . . . farmer would be as good or as efficient a citizen, that he would get as much contentment and happiness for himself and his family out of his home, or that he could develop as satisfactory a community for himself and neighbors as he could and would if he owned the house in which he lives and the farm he cultivates. The problem, then, is that of life on the farm, the development of rural communities and the building of rural civilization with which, after all, we are most concerned. . . . The late Governor Bicket said: "the small farm owned by the man who tills it is the best plant-bed in the world in which to grow a patriot. . . ." Every consideration of progress and safety urges us to employ all wise and just measures to get our lands into the hands of many and forestall that most destructive of all monopolies—the monopoly of the soil.

The policy of the federal government has always more or less agreed with this. Nearly every administration has declared itself in favor of preserving the family farm. It is ironic that each, in turn, has brought it closer to extinction.

In 1963 the government spent $4.7 billion on surplus commodities. Most of the money went to prosperous commercial farms, with only pennies trickling down to the hard-pressed family farms. The government-support price is often more than the production costs of the big commercial farms. This means they can produce without worrying about the market since "Uncle Sucker"—as some of the farmers say—will buy what they can't sell elsewhere.

In 1961 two corporate cotton farms received government subsidies of $2 million each; thirteen great farms each received $649,753 on the average; and 332 farms received $113,657 each. By contrast, 70 percent of the cotton farms were given an average of $60.

The government has subsidized the big operators in a more important way. Until this year the commercial farms have been allowed to draw on the pools of cheap labor from other countries, principally Mexico. The presence of hundreds of thousands of foreign workers has naturally disrupted the domestic labor market, resulting in low wages and poor working conditions. The family farmer, who hires little outside help, has to value his and his family's labor at no more than the commercial farmer pays for gang labor.

The exodus from the farm is proceeding at the rate of about 800,000 people a year, although cities and towns have as little immediate need for surplus rural populations as the nation does for surplus farm production. It has been seriously proposed many times that overproduction is caused by a surplus of farmers and that we should let the natural laws of competition weed out the less successful. This way, the problem of surplus production and surplus farmers would solve itself at no expense to the taxpayers. But, as we have already seen, most of the food is produced by a relatively few big farms. And, of course, when the small farmer finally gives up and goes to the city, his land is taken over eventually by another farmer and remains in production.

As a unit, the larger family farm is not without merit. According to a 1962 government report,

Family farms [in this case those using 1.5 man-years of hired labor] are more efficient than large corporate-type farms. . . . When the management of a farm is taken away from those who supply the labor, there is a loss of incentive, diligence, skill, and prudent judgment which are necessary to maintain efficiency.

The report said that the advantages of the corporate farm lay primarily in superior financing and control of the market.

No farmer, of course, whether big or small, can dominate the market. But the vertically integrated farm is its own market. The perishable harvest from the field goes to the farm's own processing and canning plants and is sold canned or frozen under less urgent conditions. (In 1962, however, the government bought up $1.3 million worth of California canned apricots.) The small farmer selling perishable produce is completely at the mercy of the market or, specifically, the buyer.

Today the position of the buyer is stronger than it has ever been. In 1958, supermarket buying agencies handled 60 percent of the food dollar. At the present time, it is said that chain buyers account for 90 percent of the food dollar.

There are about 3.7 million farms in the United States. What seems to be happening is this: the 312,000 first-class farms are big and getting bigger; the 1,755,000 middle-class farms are struggling, and to survive they need a more equitable marketing structure, some government aid, and an orderly farm labor force; the third-class farms, of which there are 1,641,000, are marked for certain death if agriculture con-tinues for much longer on its present path.

The farm of the classic rural tradition, the family farm, required little outside labor. A hired man or two were enough on the bigger farm for most of the year. And at planting or harvest, neighboring farm families joined together and did the work, going from farm to farm.

THE EXPLOITATION OF LABOR

The history of migrant labor is sketchy, but its dominant themes are quite clear. The rise of the corporate farm and the growth of the migrant labor force were twin developments. It is arguable which came first. Some say the industrialized farm developed because growers saw a chance to utilize a growing pool of unemployed labor. Others say that the development of the giant farm created a demand for gangs of itinerant labor, and the migrants came to fill the need. Whichever way it happened, the result has been that the corporate farm is, and always has been, dependent on cheap, migrant labor.

The migrant force of today still bears the marks of our history. Since early America was largely rural, farm interests dominated the government. While manufacturers adjusted to the industrial revolution early, agriculture was able to win exemption from most of the social legislation passed since the turn of the century. Agriculture has grown from a society, or way of life, into a complex food industry without coming to terms with its labor force. Had the automobile industry been able to import cheap labor from under-developed countries, it is unlikely that the automobile union would have made much headway.

The commercial farm has never adjusted to the realities of modern labor conditions or wages. Furthermore, the modern commercial farmer holds on to the idea that he somehow has a God-given right to un-limited cheap labor. Never has he had to enter the labor market and make serious efforts to attract farm labor. If anything characterizes the history of the seasonal farm worker, it is this—fate, through fam-ine or depression, war or revolution, has time and again delivered to the commercial grower an ample supply of cheap and doc-ile labor.

The migrant drama caught the nation's attention in the thirties. Great dust storms swept the plains and dimmed the sun as far away as the East Coast. Long lines of tenant families, the gasoline gypsies, crossed the desert into California looking for work. The dust-bowl refugees were only one set of characters in the migrant epic that be-gan long before the Joads of *The Grapes of Wrath*.

By 1934 the Anglo population in the labor camps reached 50 percent. As the bit-ter years of dust storms and depression set in, Okies and Arkies continued to stream into California in caravans of jalopies. It was ironic that after so many years of coolies and peons, American workers took over in a time of widespread unemploy-ment. Hence wages and working condi-tions, bad as they were, got worse. For every job that was open, there was a hungry carload of migrants. Men fought in the field over a row of beans. For the first time Western growers admitted there was a labor surplus. The Farm Security Ad-ministration reported that by 1938, 221,000 dust bowlers had entered California.

THE BRACEROS

With the coming of World War II, ship-yards and aircraft industries drained off the surplus labor left by the Draft Board. Food demands climbed to wartime levels. Another source of cheap labor had to be found. The government was induced to

sanction the wetbacks. And in 1944 the United States spent nearly $24 million to supply the growers with 62,170 braceros—Mexican farm laborers.

As the war progressed, prisoners of war were turned over to growers, along with convicts, Japanese-Americans, impounded in concentration camps, were released to the custody of the big growers. Armed guards patrolled the fields. When the war ended, the P.O.W.'s went back to Italy and Germany, and the convicts went back to their cells.

The wetbacks remained, and their ques-tionable legal position became more and more evident. Border patrols, on orders from Washington, looked the other way during the harvest season, and the wet-backs streamed in. The federal government not only condoned wetback traffic during the harvest season but actually encouraged it. The President's commission studying the problems of migratory labor discovered this incredible situation:

... wetbacks (who were apprehended) were given identification slips in the United States by the Immigration and Naturalization Service which entitled them, within a few minutes, to step back across the border and become contract workers. There was no other way to obtain the indis-pensable slip of paper except to be found il-legally in the United States. Thus violators of law were rewarded by receiving legal contracts while the same opportunities were denied law-abiding citizens of Mexico. The United States, having engaged in a program giving preference in contracting to those who had broken the law, had encouraged violation of the immigration laws. *Our government thus has become a contrib-utor to the growth of an illegal traffic which it has the responsibility to prevent.* [Italics mine.]

In 1950 when the "police action" began in Korea, President Truman appointed a commission to study the problems of mi-grant labor. The pressure was building up for more cheap labor to meet the antici-pated new demands for food. The McCarran-Walter Act (Public Law 414) had just been passed over the President's veto. This was a new Immigration and Naturalization Act, which permitted the temporary importation of foreign labor under contract for periods up to three years.

Following completion of the report of the President's commission, the 82nd Congress, on July 12, 1951, passed Public Law 78. The commission had recommended a few months earlier that "no special measures be adopted to increase the number of alien contract workers beyond the number admitted in 1950." In that year 192,000 legal braceros (literally, arm-men) came in under contract to work in the fields of the Southwest. Illegal wetback traffic began to decline, but by the end of the decade the number of braceros had risen far above the wartime emergency levels of either World War II or the Korean War. In 1959 there were 437,000 Mexican nationals scattered across the United States from Texas to Michigan.

Over the years growers have shown a decided preference for the foreign farm workers. The reasons are many. The foreigner many times does not speak English. He is uninformed about his rights and in a poor position to defend them if they are violated. He is willing to work for less and under poorer conditions. Imported farm workers are always single males. Housing and transportation are simpler. And when the farmer has done with them, they can be shipped back where they came from. And if any of them make trouble, they can be shipped home a little early.

Shortage of workers amid mass unemployment; foreign workers in record numbers while American workers can't find jobs—these are long-standing contradictions in farm labor. Growers say they can't find workers. Workers say they can't find jobs. Part of the answer lies in the definition of the terms. A shortage of labor exists for many growers when they don't have more than twice the number of workers they can get by with. Extra hands keep the wages down and the union out. The workers' idea of the proper labor supply is when he can choose between jobs and take the one that pays the most.

The theory of the laws that enable growers to import labor was that both worker and grower could be served. In practice these laws crushed the worker and gave the grower an almost limitless supply of cheap labor. Obviously, when a worker refuses a job at $.35 an hour (the prevailing wage for field workers in Arkansas, for example), he only makes it possible for the grower to get Mexicans. Until very recently, Arkansas was the third-largest user of braceros, employing about 40,000 annually.

An interesting example of the law in action was the shifting wages in the Imperial Valley. For many years domestic workers in the winter lettuce harvest were paid a piece rate of a penny a head for harvesting lettuce. This amounted to an hourly wage of from $1.25 to $2.00, good money for harvesting.

As growers began to use more braceros, the piece rate was finally dropped and the wage level in the valley fell. For several years prior to 1961, it was frozen at about $.70 an hour. When President Kennedy signed the extension of Public Law 78 in 1961 (for two years), he instructed the Secretary of Labor to see to it that the program had no adverse effect on domestic labor. As a result, Imperial Valley growers who sought to use braceros were instructed to reinstate the old piece rate of a penny a head. (It can be noted in passing that if harvest wages were doubled, the labor cost would be only $.02 a head.)

In anticipation of this change, growers had increased the hourly wage from $.70 to $1.00. But as soon as the Labor Department called for the old piece rate, 200 growers flew to Washington to protest. The Department backed down and agreed that the growers could pay either $1.00 an hour *or the piece rate of $.24 a carton. The choice was to be left to the worker.* That the growers were satisfied with the new arrangement indicated that they didn't intend the workers, most of whom were braceros, to have much say in the matter after all. And the nature of the choice—between $1.00 an hour or $2.00 an hour—indicated that the Department of Labor was either naïve or cynical.

The mystery was cleared up when an accountant employed by an El Centro lettuce company announced that she had falsified the payroll records. What she had done, on the orders of the company owners, was to pad the hours reported by the labor crews. This lowered, on paper, the hourly wage. Thus the Labor Department was unaware of what the piece rate earnings actually were. Apparently the wage surveyors had asked the growers what they were paying. But no one bothered to ask the workers what they were earning. If it had been discovered that the piece rate was equal to $2.00 an hour, then the bracero wage of $1.00 would have had to be doubled. It would have been clear that the use of the Mexicans had definitely had an adverse effect on other wages in the valley.

The low wages in agriculture may seem to be of little importance to the rest of society. But "agriculture as a whole," according to the California Democratic Council,

still remains our largest single industry. Depressed farm purchasing power contributes directly and significantly to fewer sales, fewer jobs, lower business profits, and a lower general level of national output and income than what the U.S. economy should be producing.

MEASURED IN PENNIES

The marketing of agriculture products needs a thorough investigation. In many cases neither the grower nor the worker is getting a fair shake. Tomatoes grown in McAllen, Texas, and sold in Denver, for instance, produced a net income to the grower of $68.85 per acre. But the consumers paid $9,660 for this acre of tomatoes. Only a small fraction of retail food prices reflects farm crop prices. And a much smaller fraction represents harvesting wages.

There is room here for fair profits to growers and honest wages to workers. What the harvesters need is the dignity of work done under conditions meant for farm workers, not farm animals. The issues that are fought over are cabin space, hot water, and piece rates, but the real issues are basic human rights and fair play. The migrant doesn't want charity or handouts. He wants a chance, a start, to build his strength and manage his own life.

The wages paid harvest labor constitute a tiny fraction of the retail cost of food. In many cases, an increase in wages as much as 100 percent would barely affect the retail price. The price to consumers of eliminating migrant poverty is measured in pennies.

Legislation designed to help migrant labor is urgently needed. In 1964 a number of bills were enacted which will help states improve migrant education, expand the restrictions on child labor, provide some new day-care centers for children, and help farmers provide field sanitation. Congress could, if it would, establish a minimum wage for migratory workers, improve the methods of recruiting, training, transporting, and distributing farm workers, and extend the National Labor Relations Act to cover agriculture.

The ingrained poverty and underemployment that exist among the seasonal farm workers will be difficult to eliminate. Our agricultural system has made harvest work shameful. It has made the welfare check often more honorable than harvest work. It has made pride and satisfaction impossible. No man goes into a field to harvest crops if there is any other choice open to him. The new laws passed in 1964 do not constitute a complete solution. But they would make a start.

NOTHING BUT DESPAIR

The Brent family is typical of many thousands of migrant families. They were forced off their land in Georgia. They blundered into the migrant stream when the owner combined it with five other "mule and nigger" farms. One afternoon a placard appeared in the window of the filling station-grocery store near their home. It offered "employment opportunities" in the harvest in Homestead, Florida. The family was desperate for work. They loaded their household goods into their 1940 Dodge and started for Homestead.

After a long, hot, and dusty trip, they stopped in Belle Glade, north of Homestead, where the harvest was under way. Once there, they found plenty of work, and the whole family went to the fields. In a month it was all over. They never got to Homestead. Work was finished there, too. They realized, too late, that they would have to go where the crops were. They sold their car and joined a crew headed for Pennsylvania. They had become migrants.

Crew leaders and roving bus drivers make recruiting drives into the South, and many workers enter the migrant stream this way. The promise of "a hundred dollars a week and live in a ho-tel" sounds good. A favorite target of the recruiters is the debt-ridden tenant family. Cash earnings and a place to live are heady inducements.

Some families enter the stream to search for a better place to live. One member will go on the season to look around up north

or out west. Still, many of them wind up in the rural slums that lie at the fringes of the suburbs across the land. There are, for example, many Negroes from North Carolina living in Riverhead, Long Island. They came with migrant crews first and later brought their families.

Settling is a slow and difficult process. A Long Island woman explained it this way:

A man comes alone with a crew and picks a place to settle down. Next season, he may come back with another of the men in the family. If they decide it's OK, he'll come next year with his wife. At the end of the season, they stay in Riverhead. No one wants to hire a migrant because they're supposed to be wild and unstable; no one will rent him a house for fear he'll tear it up. So the first place the family lives is a real chicken house. If he finds a job, he can move his family out of the ex-migrant slum into a regular slum. After that, he's got it made. A lot of them don't, and they get stranded. Sometimes the husband has to leave so the wife can get welfare.

The valleys of California and Arizona and the suburbs of the Middle West are filled with the cabin slums of Mexican-Americans, Negroes, and poor whites trying to settle down. After a few years a migrant who cannot escape the stream is broken by it. The poverty, anxiety, homelessness, and isolation wear away his spirit. It is this apathy that is often called acceptance and makes people say, "They like things that way."

"We're always goin' someplace," said a sandy-haired Oklahoma migrant, "but we never git noplace." In a tired, flat voice, an old woman in a Michigan field put it only a little differently: "I been ever' place, and I got no place."

A migrant minister in a Belle Glade camp asked a woman in his camp church if she was going on the season again. "I don't know. Ever' year I go up broke, and I come back broke. I don't know why I go even."

A migrant in Arkansas sat on the steps of his one-room cabin. For an hour he had talked about where he had been, and the things he had done to keep his family alive. Suddenly it seemed as if the memory of the years crushed him.

I get sick of the world sometimes and ever'body in it. I don't know what's goin' to happen. Used to make a livin' pickin' cotton. Then they started bringin' in them Mexicans by the truckload. Now they're gettin' them machines every day.

Few urban Americans have any awareness of this vast impoverished army that tramps through their country to bring the crops in from the fields. It cannot be seen except as a broken-down car or bus here, a truck there, a ragged crew working somewhere off in a field.

But the harvest cycle yields its own fruits: ignorance, poverty, death, and despair. Until we see the connection between migrancy—the corpses piled up on the roadway, the children left to the darkness of ignorance and illiteracy, the despairing, destitute families groping for a way to live—and the bountiful supply of fruits and vegetables on every corner fruit stand or in every supermarket, no changes will come. Without this understanding, no war on poverty can hope to win more than a few skirmishes.

INTERNAL COLONIALISM AND GHETTO REVOLT[1]

Robert Blauner

It is becoming almost fashionable to analyze American racial conflict today in terms of the colonial analogy. I shall argue in this paper that the utility of this perspective depends upon a distinction between colonization as a process and colonialism as a social, economic, and political system. It is the experience of colonization that Afro-Americans share with many of the nonwhite people of the world. But this

Reprinted by permission from Social Problems, **16**:*4 (Spring 1969), pp. 393–408, a publication of the Society for the Study of Social Issues.*

[1] This is a revised version of a paper delivered at the University of California Centennial Program, "Studies in Violence," Los Angeles, June 1, 1968. For criticisms and ideas that have improved an earlier draft, I am indebted to Robert Wood, Lincoln Bergman, and Gary Marx. As a good colonialist I have probably restated (read: stolen) more ideas from the writings of Kenneth Clark, Stokely Carmichael, Frantz Fanon and especially such contributors to the Black Panther Party (Oakland) newspaper as Huey Newton, Bobby Seale, Eldridge Cleaver, and Kathleen Cleaver than I have appropriately credited or generated myself. In self-defense I should state that I began working somewhat independently on a colonial analysis of American race relations in the fall of 1965; see my "Whitewash over Watts: The Failure of the McCone Report," *Trans-action,* **3** (March-April, 1966), pp. 3–9, 54.

subjugation has taken place in a societal context that differs in important respects from the situation of "classical colonialism." In the body of this essay I shall look at some major developments in Black protest—the urban riots, cultural nationalism, and the movement for ghetto control—as collective responses to colonized status. Viewing our domestic situation as a special form of colonization outside a context of a colonial system will help explain some of the dilemmas and ambiguities within these movements.

The present crisis in American life has brought about changes in social perspectives and the questioning of long-accepted frameworks. Intellectuals and social scientists have been forced by the pressure of events to look at old definitions of the character of our society, the role of racism, and the workings of basic institutions. The depth and volatility of contemporary racial conflict challenge sociologists in particular to question the adequacy of theoretical models by which we have explained American race relations in the past.

For a long time the distinctiveness of the Negro situation among the ethnic minorities was placed in terms of color, and the systematic discrimination that follows from our deep-seated racial prejudices. This was sometimes called the caste theory, and while provocative, it missed essential and dynamic features of American race relations. In the past ten years there has been a tendency to view Afro-Americans as another ethnic group not basically different in experience from previous ethnics and whose "immigration" condition in the North would in time follow their upward course. The inadequacy of this model is now clear—even the Kerner Report devotes

a chapter to criticizing this analogy. A more recent (though hardly new) approach views the essence of racial subordination in economic class terms: Black people as an underclass are to a degree specially exploited and to a degree economically dispensable in an automating society. Important as are economic factors, the power of race and racism in America cannot be sufficiently explained through class analysis. Into this theory vacuum steps the model of internal colonialism. Problematic and imprecise as it is, it gives hope of becoming a framework that can integrate the insights of caste and racism, ethnicity, culture, and economic exploitation into an overall conceptual scheme. At the same time, the danger of the colonial model is the imposition of an artificial analogy which might keep us from facing up to the fact (to quote Harold Cruse) that "the American black and white social phenomenon is a uniquely new world thing."[2]

During the late 1950s, identification with African nations and other colonial or formerly colonized peoples grew in importance among Black militants.[3] As a result the U.S. was increasingly seen as a colonial power and the concept of domestic colonialism was introduced into the political analysis and rhetoric of militant nationalists. During the same period Black social theorists began developing this frame of reference for explaining American realities. As early as 1962, Cruse characterized race relations in this country as "domestic colonialism."[4] Three years later in *Dark Ghetto,* Kenneth Clark demonstrated how the political, economic, and social structure of Harlem was essentially that of a colony.[5] Finally in 1967, a full-blown elaboration of "internal colonialism" provided

[2] Harold Cruse, *Rebellion or Revolution* (New York: 1968), p. 214.
[3] Nationalism, including an orientation toward Africa, is no new development. It has been a constant tendency within Afro-American politics. See Cruse, *ibid.,* especially Chaps. 5–7.
[4] This was six years before the publication of *The Crisis of the Negro Intellectual* (New York: Morrow, 1968), which brought Cruse into prominence. Thus the 1962 article was not widely read until its reprinting in Cruse's essays, *Rebellion or Revolution, op. cit.*

the theoretical framework for Carmichael and Hamilton's widely read *Black Power*.[6] The following year the colonial analogy gained currency and new "respectability" when Senator McCarthy habitually referred to Black Americans as a colonized people during his campaign. While the rhetoric of internal colonialism was catching on, other social scientists began to raise questions about its appropriateness as a scheme of analysis.

The colonial analysis has been rejected as obscurantist and misleading by scholars who point to the significant differences in history and social-political conditions between our domestic patterns and what took place in Africa and India. Colonialism traditionally refers to the establishment of domination over a geographically external political unit, most often inhabited by people of a different race and culture, where this domination is political and economic, and the colony exists subordinated to and dependent upon the mother country. Typically the colonizers exploit the land, the raw materials, the labor, and other resources of the colonized nation; in addition a formal recognition is given to the difference in power, autonomy, and political status, and various agencies are set up to maintain this subordination. Seemingly the analogy must be stretched beyond usefulness if the American version is to be forced into this model. For here we are talking about group relations within a society; the mother country/colony separation in geography is absent. Though whites certainly colonized the territory of the original Americans, internal colonization of Afro-Americans did not involve the settlement of whites in any land that was unequivocally Black. And unlike the colonial situation, there has been no formal recognition of differing power since slavery

was abolished outside the South. Classic colonialism involved the control and exploitation of the majority of a nation by a minority of outsiders. Whereas in America the people who are oppressed were themselves originally outsiders and are a numerical minority.

This conventional critique of "internal colonialism" is useful in pointing to the differences between our domestic patterns and the overseas situation. But in its bold attack it tends to lose sight of common experiences that have been historically shared by the most subjugated racial minorities in America and nonwhite peoples in some other parts of the world. For understanding the most dramatic recent developments on the race scene, this common core element—which I shall call colonization—may be more important than the undeniable divergences between the two contexts.

The common features ultimately relate to the fact that the classical colonialism of the imperialist era and American racism developed out of the same historical situation and reflected a common world economic and power stratification. The slave trade for the most part preceded the imperialist partition and economic exploitation of Africa, and in fact may have been a necessary prerequisite for colonial conquest—since it helped deplete and pacify Africa, undermining the resistance to direct occupation. Slavery contributed one of the basic raw materials for the textile industry which provided much of the capital for the West's industrial development and need for economic expansionism. The essential condition for both American slavery and European colonialism was the power domination and the technological superiority of the Western world in its relation to peoples of non-Western and nonwhite origins. This objective supremacy in tech-

[5] Kenneth Clark, *Dark Ghetto* (New York: Harper and Row, 1965). Clark's analysis first appeared a year earlier in *Youth in the Ghetto* (New York: Haryou, 1964).
[6] Stokely Carmichael and Charles Hamilton, *Black Power* (New York: Random, 1967).

nology and military power buttressed the West's sense of cultural superiority, laying the basis for racist ideologies that were elaborated to justify control and exploitation of nonwhite people. Thus because classical colonialism and America's internal version developed out of a similar balance of technological, cultural, and power relations, a common *process* of social oppression characterized the racial patterns in the two contexts—despite the variation in political and social structure.

There appear to be four basic components of the colonization complex. The first refers to how the racial group enters into the dominant society (whether colonial power or not). Colonization begins with a forced, involuntary entry. Second, there is an impact on the culture and social organization of the colonized people which is more than just a result of such "natural" processes as contact and acculturation. The colonizing power carries out a policy which constrains, transforms, or destroys indigenous values, orientations, and ways of life. Third, colonization involves a relationship by which members of the colonized group tend to be administered by representatives of the dominant power. There is an experience of being managed and manipulated by outsiders in terms of ethnic status.

A final fundament of colonization is racism. Racism is a principle of social domination by which a group seen as inferior or different in terms of alleged biological characteristics is exploited, controlled, and oppressed socially and psychically by a superordinate group. Except for the marginal case of Japanese imperialism, the major examples of colonialism have involved the subjugation of nonwhite Asian, African, and Latin American peoples by white European powers. Thus racism has generally accompanied colonialism. Race prejudice can exist without colonization—the experience of Asian-American minorities is a case in point—but racism as a system of domination is part of the complex of colonization.

The concept of colonization stresses the enormous fatefulness of the historical factor, namely the manner in which a minority group becomes a part of the dominant society.[7] The crucial difference between the colonized Americans and the ethnic immigrant minorities is that the latter have always been able to operate fairly competitively within that relatively open section of the social and economic order because these groups came voluntarily in search of a better life, because their movements in society were not administratively controlled, and because they transformed their culture at their own pace—giving up ethnic values and institutions when it was seen as a desirable exchange for improvements in social position.

In present-day America, a major device of Black colonization is the powerless ghetto. As Kenneth Clark describes the situation:

Ghettoes are the consequence of the imposition of external power and the institutionalization of powerlessness. In this respect, they are in fact social, political, educational, and above all—economic colonies. Those confined within the ghetto walls are subject peoples. They are victims of the greed, cruelty, insensitivity, guilt, and fear of their masters. . . .

The community can best be described in terms of the analogy of a powerless colony. Its political leadership is divided, and all but one or two of its political leaders are shortsighted and dependent upon the larger political power structure. Its social agencies are financially precarious and dependent upon sources of support outside the community. Its churches are isolated

[7] As Eldridge Cleaver reminds us, "Black people are a stolen people held in a colonial status on stolen land, and any analysis which does not acknowledge the colonial status of black people cannot hope to deal with the real problem." "The Land Question," *Ramparts,* **6** (May 1968), p. 51.

or dependent. Its economy is dominated by small businesses which are largely owned by absentee owners, and its tenements and other real property are also owned by absentee landlords.

Under a system of centralization, Harlem's schools are controlled by forces outside of the community. Programs and policies are supervised and determined by individuals who do not live in the community . . . .[8]

Of course many ethnic groups in America have lived in ghettos. What make the Black ghettos an expression of colonized status are three special features. First, the ethnic ghettos arose more from voluntary choice, both in the sense of the choice to immigrate to America and the decision to live among one's fellow ethnics. Second, the immigrant ghettos tended to be a one- and two-generation phenomenon; they were actually way-stations in the process of acculturation and assimilation. When they continue to persist as in the case of San Francisco's Chinatown, it is because they are big business for the ethnics themselves and there is a new stream of immigrants. The Black ghetto on the other hand has been a more permanent phenomenon, although some individuals do escape it. But most relevant is the third point. European ethnic groups like the Poles, Italians, and Jews generally only experienced a brief period, often less than a generation, during which their residential buildings, commercial stores, and other enterprises were owned by outsiders. The Chinese and Japanese faced handicaps of color prejudice that were almost as strong as the Blacks faced, but very soon gained control of their internal communities, because their traditional ethnic culture and social organization had not been destroyed by slavery and internal colonization. But Afro-Americans are distinct in the extent to which their segregated communities have remained controlled economically, politically, and administratively from the outside. One indicator of this difference is the estimate that the "income of Chinese-Americans from Chinese-owned businesses is in proportion to their numbers 45 times as great as the income of Negroes from Negro-owned businesses."[9] But what is true of business is also true for the other social institutions that operate within the ghetto. The educators, policemen, social workers, politicians, and others who administer the affairs of ghetto residents are typically whites who live outside the Black community. Thus the ghetto plays a strategic role as the focus for the administration by outsiders which is also essential to the structure of overseas colonialism.[10]

[8] *Youth in the Ghetto, op. cit.*, pp. 10–11, 79–80.
[9] N. Glazer and D. P. Moynihan, *Beyond the Melting Pot* (Cambridge, Mass.: M.I.T., 1963), p. 37.
[10] "When we speak of Negro social disabilities under capitalism, . . . we refer to the fact that he does not own anything—*even what is ownable in his own community*. Thus to fight for black liberation *is to fight for his right to own*. The Negro is politically compromised today because he owns nothing. He has little voice in the affairs of state because he owns nothing. The fundamental reason why the Negro bourgeois-democratic revolution has been aborted is because American capitalism has prevented the development of a black class of capitalist owners of institutions and economic tools. To take one crucial example, Negro radicals today are severely hampered in their tasks of educating the black masses on political issues because Negroes do not own any of the necessary means of propaganda and communication. The Negro owns no printing presses, he has no stake in the networks of the means of communication. Inside his own communities he does not own the house he lives in, the property he lives on, nor the wholesale and retail sources from which he buys his commodities. He does not own the edifices in which he enjoys culture and entertainment or in which he socializes. In capitalist society, an individual or group that does not own anything is powerless." H. Cruse, "Behind the Black Power Slogan," in Cruse, *Rebellion or Revolution, op. cit.*, pp. 238–239.

The colonial status of the Negro community goes beyond the issue of ownership and decision making within Black neighborhoods. The Afro-American population in most cities has very little influence on the power structure and institutions of the larger metropolis, despite the fact that in numerical terms, Blacks tend to be the most sizable of the various interest groups. A recent analysis of policy making in Chicago estimates that

Negroes really hold less than 1 percent of the effective power in the Chicago metropolitan area. [Negroes are 20 percent of Cook County's population.] Realistically the power structure of Chicago is hardly less white than that of Mississippi.[11]

Colonization outside of a traditional colonial structure has its own special conditions. The group culture and social structure of the colonized in America is less developed; it is also less autonomous. In addition, the colonized are a numerical minority, and furthermore they are ghettoized more totally and are more dispersed than people under classic colonialism. Though these realities affect the magnitude and direction of response, it is my basic thesis that the most important expressions of protest in the Black community during the recent years reflect the colonized status of Afro-America. Riots, programs of separation, politics of community control, the Black revolutionary movements, and cultural nationalism each represent a different strategy of attack on domestic colonialism in America. Let us now examine some of these movements.

RIOT OR REVOLT?

The so-called riots are being increasingly recognized as a preliminary if primitive form of mass rebellion against a colonial status. There is still a tendency to absorb their meaning within the conventional scope of assimilation-integration politics: some commentators stress the material motives involved in looting as a sign that the rioters want to join America's middle-class affluence just like everyone else. That motives are mixed and often unconscious, that Black people want good furniture and television sets like whites is beside the point. The guiding impulse in most major outbreaks has not been integration with American society, but an attempt to stake out a sphere of control by moving against that society and destroying the symbols of its oppression.

In my critique of the McCone report I observed that the rioters were asserting a claim to territoriality, an unorganized and rather inchoate attempt to gain control over their community or "turf."[12] In succeeding disorders also the thrust of the action has been the attempt to clear out an alien presence, white men and officials, rather than a drive to kill whites as in a conventional race riot. The main attacks have been directed at the property of white businessmen and at the police who operate in the Black community "like an army of occupation" protecting the interests of outside exploiters and maintaining the domination over the ghetto by the central metropolitan power structure.[13] The Kern-

---

[11] Harold M. Baron, "Black Powerlessness in Chicago," *Trans-action*, **6** (November 1968), pp. 27–33.

[12] Blauner, "Whitewash over Watts," *op. cit.*

[13] "The police function to support and enforce the interests of the dominant political, social, and economic interests of the town" is a statement made by a former police scholar and official, according to A. Neiderhoffer, *Behind the Shield* (New York: Doubleday, 1967), as cited by Gary T. Marx, "Civil Disorder and the Agents of Control," *Journal of Social Issues*, forthcoming.

er report misleads when it attempts to explain riots in terms of integration:

What the rioters appear to be seeking was fuller participation in the social order and the material benefits enjoyed by the majority of American citizens. Rather than rejecting the American system, they were anxious to obtain a place for themselves in it.[14]

More accurately, the revolts pointed to alienation from this system on the part of many poor and also not-so-poor Blacks. The sacredness of private property, that unconsciously accepted bulwark of our social arrangements, was rejected; people who looted apparently without guilt generally remarked that they were taking things that "really belonged" to them anyway.[15] Obviously the society's bases of legitimacy and authority have been attacked. Law and order has long been viewed as the white man's law and order by Afro-Americans; but now this perspective characteristic of a colonized people is out in the open. And the Kerner report's own data question how well ghetto rebels are buying the system: in Newark only 33 percent of self-reported rioters said they thought this country was worth fighting for in the event of a major war; in the Detroit sample the figure was 55 percent.[16]

One of the most significant consequences of the process of colonization is a weakening of the colonized's individual and collective will to resist his oppression. It has been easier to contain and control Black ghettos because communal bonds and group solidarity have been weakened through divisions among leadership, failures of organization, and a general dis-

spiritment that accompanies social oppression. The riots are a signal that the will to resist has broken the mold of accommodation. In some cities as in Watts they also represented nascent movements toward community identity. In several riot-torn ghettos the outbursts have stimulated new organizations and movements. If it is true that the riot phenomenon of 1964–68 has passed its peak, its historical import may be more for the "internal" organizing momentum generated than for any profound "external" response of the larger society facing up to underlying causes.

Despite the appeal of Frantz Fanon to young Black revolutionaries, America is not Algeria. It is difficult to foresee how riots in our cities can play a role equivalent to rioting in the colonial situation as an integral phase in a movement for national liberation. In 1968 some militant groups (for example, the Black Panther Party in Oakland) had concluded that ghetto riots were self-defeating of the lives and interests of Black people in the present balance of organization and gunpower, though they had served a role to stimulate both Black consciousness and white awareness of the depths of racial crisis. Such militants have been influential in "cooling" their communities during periods of high riot potential. Theoretically oriented Black radicals see riots as spontaneous mass behavior which must be replaced by a revolutionary organization and consciousness. But despite the differences in objective conditions, the violence of the 1960s seems to serve the same psychic function, assertions of dignity and manhood for young Blacks in urban

---

[14] Report of the National Advisory Commission on Civil Disorders (New York: Bantam, March 1968), p. 7.

[15] This kind of attitude has a long history among American Negroes. During slavery, Blacks used the same rationalization to justify stealing from their masters. Appropriating things from the master was viewed as "*taking* part of his property for the benefit of another part; whereas *stealing* referred to appropriating something from another slave, an offense that was not condoned." Kenneth Stampp, *The Peculiar Institution* (Vintage, 1956), p. 127.

[16] Report of the National Advisory Commission on Civil Disorders, *op. cit.*, p. 178.

ghettos, as it did for the colonized of North Africa described by Fanon and Memmi.[17]

CULTURAL NATIONALISM

Cultural conflict is generic to the colonial relation because colonization involves the domination of Western technological values over the more communal cultures of non-Western peoples. Colonialism played havoc with the national integrity of the peoples it brought under its sway. Of course, all traditional cultures are threatened by industrialism, the city, and modernization in communication, transportation, health, and education. What is special are the political and administrative decisions of colonizers in managing and controlling colonized peoples. The boundaries of African colonies, for example, were drawn to suit the political conveniences of the European nations without regard to the social organization and cultures of African tribes and kingdoms. Thus Nigeria as blocked out by the British included the Yorubas and the Ibos, whose civil war today is a residuum of the colonialist's disrespect for the integrity of indigenous cultures.

The most total destruction of culture in the colonization process took place not in traditional colonialism but in America. As Frazier stressed, the integral cultures of the diverse African peoples who furnished the slave trade were destroyed because slaves from different tribes, kingdoms, and linguistic groups were purposely separated to maximize domination and control. Thus language, religion, and national loyalties were lost in North America much more completely than in the Caribbean and Brazil where slavery developed somewhat differently. Thus on this key point America's internal colonization has been more total and extreme than situations of classic colonialism. For the British in India and the European powers in Africa were not able—as outnumbered minorities—to destroy the national and tribal cultures of the colonized. Recall that American slavery lasted 250 years and its racist aftermath another 100. Colonial dependency in the case of British Kenya and French Algeria lasted only 77 and 125 years respectively. In the wake of this more drastic uprooting and destruction of culture and social organization, much more powerful agencies of social, political, and psychological domination developed in the American case.

Colonial control of many peoples inhabiting the colonies was more a goal than a fact, and at Independence there were undoubtedly fairly large numbers of Africans who had never seen a colonial administrator. The gradual process of extension of control from the administrative center on the African coast contrasts sharply with the total uprooting involved in the slave trade and the totalitarian aspects of slavery in the United States. Whether or not Elkins is correct in treating slavery as a total institution, it undoubtedly had a far more radical and pervasive impact on American slaves than did colonialism on the vast majority of Africans.[18]

Yet a similar cultural process unfolds in both contexts of colonialism. To the extent that they are involved in the larger society and economy, the colonized are caught up in a conflict between two cultures. Fanon has described how the assimilation-oriented schools of Martinique taught him to reject his own culture and Blackness in favor of Westernized, French, and white values.[19] Both the colonized

---

[17] Frantz Fanon, *Wretched of the Earth* (New York: Grove, 1963); Albert Memmi, *The Colonizer and the Colonized* (Boston: Beacon, 1967).

[18] Robert Wood, "Colonialism in Africa and America: Some Conceptual Considerations" (December 1967), unpublished paper.

[19] F. Fanon, *Black Skins, White Masks* (New York: Grove, 1967).

elites under traditional colonialism and perhaps the majority of Afro-Americans today experience a parallel split in identity, cultural loyalty, and political orientation.[20]

The colonizers use their culture to socialize the colonized elites (intellectuals, politicians, and middle class) into an identification with the colonial system. Because Western culture has the prestige, the power, and the key to open the limited opportunity that a minority of the colonized may achieve, the first reaction seems to be an acceptance of the dominant values. Call it brainwashing as the Black Muslims put it; call it identifying with the aggressor if you prefer Freudian terminology; call it a natural response to the hope and belief that integration and democratization can really take place if you favor a more commonsense explanation, this initial acceptance in time crumbles on the realities of racism and colonialism. The colonized, seeing that his success within colonialism is at the expense of his group and his own inner identity, moves radically toward a rejection of the Western culture and develops a nationalist outlook that celebrates his people and their traditions. As Memmi describes it:

Assimilation being abandoned, the colonized's liberation must be carried out through a recovery of self and of autonomous dignity. Attempts at imitating the colonizer required self-denial; the colonizer's rejection is the indispensable prelude to self-discovery. That accusing and annihilating image must be shaken off; oppression must be attacked boldly since it is impossible to go around it. After having been rejected for so long by the colonizer, the day has come when it is the colonized who must refuse the colonizer.[21]

Memmi's book, *The Colonizer and the Colonized*, is based on his experience as a Tunisian Jew in a marginal position between the French and the colonized Arab majority. The uncanny parallels between the North African situation he describes and the course of Black-white relations in our society is the best impressionist argument I know for the thesis that we have a colonized group and a colonizing system in America. His discussion of why even the most radical French anticolonialist cannot participate in the struggle of the colonized is directly applicable to the situation of the white liberal and radical vis-à-vis the Black movement. His portrait of the colonized is as good an analysis of the psychology behind Black Power and Black nationalism as anything that has been written in the U.S. Consider, for example:

Considered *en bloc* as *them, they,* or *those,* different from every point of view, homogeneous in a radical heterogeneity, the colonized reacts by rejecting all the colonizers *en bloc.* The distinction between deed and intent has no great significance in the colonial situation. In the eyes of the colonized, all Europeans in the colonies are de facto colonizers, and whether they want to be or not, they are colonizers in some ways. By their privileged economic position, by belonging to the political system of oppression, or by participating in an effectively negative complex toward the colonized, they are colonizers. ... They are supporters or at least unconscious accomplices of that great collective aggression of Europe.[22]

The same passion which made him admire and absorb Europe shall make him assert his differences; since those differences, after all, are within him and correctly constitute his true self.[23]

The important thing now is to rebuild his

---

[20] Harold Cruse has described how these two themes of integration with the larger society and identification with ethnic nationality have struggled within the political and cultural movements of Negro Americans. *The Crisis of the Negro Intellectual, op. cit.*

[21] Memmi, *op. cit.*, p. 128.

[22] *Ibid.*, p. 130.

[23] *Ibid.*, p. 132.

people, whatever be their authentic nature; to reforge their unity, communicate with it, and to feel that they belong.[24]

Cultural revitalization movements play a key role in anticolonial movements. They follow an inner necessity and logic of their own that comes from the consequences of colonialism on groups and personal identities; they are also essential to provide the solidarity which the political or military phase of the anticolonial revolution requires. In the U.S. an Afro-American culture has been developing since slavery out of the ingredients of African world views, the experience of bondage, Southern values and customs, migration and the Northern lower-class ghettos, and most importantly, the political history of the Black population in its struggle against racism.[25] That Afro-Americans are moving toward cultural nationalism in a period when ethnic loyalties tend to be weak (and perhaps on the decline) in this country is another confirmation of the unique colonized position of the Black group. (A similar nationalism seems to be growing among American Indians and Mexican-Americans.)

THE MOVEMENT FOR GHETTO CONTROL

The call for Black Power unites a number of varied movements and tendencies.[26]

Though no clear-cut program has yet emerged, the most important emphasis seems to be the movement for control of the ghetto. Black leaders and organizations are increasingly concerned with owning and controlling those institutions that exist within or impinge upon their community. The colonial model provides a key to the understanding of this movement, and indeed ghetto-control advocates have increasingly invoked the language of colonialism in pressing for local home rule. The framework of anticolonialism explains why the struggle for poor people's or community control of poverty programs has been more central in many cities than the content of these programs and why it has been crucial to exclude whites from leadership positions in Black organizations.

The key institutions that anticolonialists want to take over or control are business, social services, schools, and the police. Though many spokesmen have advocated the exclusion of white landlords and small businessmen from the ghetto, this program has evidently not struck fire with the Black population and little concrete movement toward economic expropriation has yet developed. Welfare recipients have organized in many cities to protect their rights and gain a greater voice in the decisions that affect them, but whole communities have not yet been able to mount direct action against welfare colonialism. Thus schools

---

[24] *Ibid.*, p. 134.

[25] In another essay, I argue against the standard sociological position that denies the existence of an ethnic Afro-American culture and I expand on the above themes. The concept of "Soul" is astonishingly parallel in content to the mystique of "Negritude" in Africa; the Pan-African culture movement has its parallel in the burgeoning Black culture mood in Afro-American communities. See "Black Culture: Myth or Reality" in Peter Rose (ed.), *Americans From Africa* (Atherton, 1969).

[26] Scholars and social commentators, Black and white alike, disagree in interpreting the contemporary Black Power movement. The issues concern whether this is a new development in Black protest or an old tendency revised; whether the movement is radical, revolutionary, reformist, or conservative; and whether this orientation is unique to Afro-Americans or essentially a Black parallel to other ethnic group strategies for collective mobility. For an interesting discussion of Black Power as a modernized version of Booker T. Washington's separatism and economism, see Harold Cruse, *Rebellion or Revolution, op. cit.*, pp. 193–258.

and the police seem now to be the burning issues of ghetto-control politics.

During the past few years there has been a dramatic shift from educational integration as the primary goal to that of community control of the schools. Afro-Americans are demanding their own school boards, with the power to hire and fire principals and teachers and to construct a curriculum which would be relevant to the special needs and culture style of ghetto youth. Especially active in high schools and colleges have been Black students, whose protests have centered on the incorporation of Black Power and Black culture into the educational system. Consider how similar is the spirit behind these developments to the attitude of the colonized North African toward European education:

He will prefer a long period of educational mistakes to the continuance of the colonizer's school organization. He will choose institutional disorder in order to destroy the institutions built by the colonizer as soon as possible. There we will see, indeed, a reactive drive of profound protest. He will no longer owe anything to the colonizer and will have definitely broken with him.[27]

Protest and institutional disorder over the issue of school control came to a head in 1968 in New York City. The procrastination in the Albany state legislature, the several crippling strikes called by the teachers union, and the almost frenzied response of Jewish organizations makes it clear that decolonization of education faces the resistance of powerful vested interests.[28] The situation is too dynamic at present to assess probable future results. However, it can be safely predicted that some form of school decentralization will be institutionalized in New York, and the movement for community control of education will spread to more cities.

This movement reflects some of the problems and ambiguities that stem from the situation of colonization outside an immediate colonial context. The Afro-American community is not parallel in structure to the communities of colonized nations under traditional colonialism. The significant difference here is the lack of fully developed indigenous institutions besides the church. Outside of some areas of the South there is really no Black economy, and most Afro-Americans are inevitably caught up in the larger society's structure of occupations, education, and mass communication. Thus the ethnic nationalist orientation which reflects the reality of colonization exists alongside an integrationist orientation which corresponds to the reality that the institutions of the larger society are much more developed than those of the incipient nation.[29] As would be expected the movement for school control reflects both tendencies. The militant leaders who spearhead such local movements may be primarily motivated by the desire to gain control over the community's institutions—they are anticolonialists first and foremost. Many parents who support them may share this goal also, but the majority are probably more concerned about creating a new education that will enable their children to "make it" in the society and the economy as a whole—they know that the present school system fails

[27] Memmi, *op. cit.*, pp. 137–138.
[28] For the New York school conflict, see Jason Epstein, "The Politics of School Decentralization," *New York Review of Books* (June 6, 1968), pp. 26–32; and "The New York City School Revolt," *ibid.*, **11**:6, pp. 37–41.
[29] This dual split in the politics and psyche of the Black American was poetically described by Du Bois in his *Souls of Black Folk*, and more recently has been insightfully analyzed by Harold Cruse in *The Crisis of the Negro Intellectual, op. cit.* Cruse has also characterized the problem of the Black community as that of underdevelopment.

ghetto children and does not prepare them for participation in American life.

There is a growing recognition that the police are the most crucial institution maintaining the colonized status of Black Americans. And of all establishment institutions, police departments probably include the highest proportion of individual racists. This is no accident since central to the workings of racism (an essential component of colonization) are attacks on the humanity and dignity of the subject group. Through their normal routines the police constrict Afro-Americans to Black neighborhoods by harassing and questioning them when found outside the ghetto; they break up groups of youth congregating on corners or in cars without any provocation; and they continue to use offensive and racist language no matter how many intergroup-understanding seminars have been built into the police academy. They also shoot to kill ghetto residents for alleged crimes such as car thefts and running from police officers.[30]

Police are key agents in the power equation as well as the drama of dehumanization. In the final analysis they do the dirty work for the larger system by restricting the striking back of Black rebels to skirmishes inside the ghetto, thus deflecting energies and attacks from the communities and institutions of the larger power structure. In a historical review, Gary Marx notes that since the French revolution, police and other authorities have killed large numbers of demonstrators and rioters; the rebellious "rabble" rarely destroys human life. The same pattern has been repeated in America's recent revolts.[31] Journalistic accounts appearing in the press recently suggest that police see themselves as defending the interests of white people against a tide of Black insurgence; furthermore the majority of whites appear to view "blue power" in this light. There is probably no other opinion on which the races are as far apart today as they are on the question of attitudes toward the police.

In many cases set off by a confrontation between a policeman and a Black citizen, the ghetto uprisings have dramatized the role of law enforcement and the issue of police brutality. In their aftermath, movements have arisen to contain police activity. One of the first was the Community Alert Patrol in Los Angeles, a method of policing the police in order to keep them honest and constrain their violations of personal dignity. This was the first tactic of the

---

[30] A recent survey of police finds "that in the predominantly Negro areas of several large cities, many of the police perceive the residents as basically hostile, especially the youth and adolescents. A lack of public support—from citizens, from courts, and from laws—is the policeman's major complaint. But some of the public criticism can be traced to the activities in which he engages day by day, and perhaps to the tone in which he enforces the "law" in the Negro neighborhoods. Most frequently he is 'called upon' to intervene in domestic quarrels and break up loitering groups. He stops and frisks two or three times as many people as are carrying dangerous weapons or are actual criminals, and almost half of these don't wish to cooperate with the policeman's efforts." Peter Rossi et al., "Between Black and White—The Faces of American Institutions and the Ghetto," in Supplemental Studies for The National Advisory Commission on Civil Disorders (July 1968), p. 114.

[31] "In the Gordon Riots of 1780 demonstrators destroyed property and freed prisoners, but did not seem to kill anyone, while authorities killed several hundred rioters and hung an additional 25. In the Rebellion Riots of the French Revolution, though several hundred rioters were killed, they killed no one. Up to the end of the Summer of 1967, this pattern had clearly been repeated, as police, not rioters, were responsible for most of the more than 100 deaths that have occurred. Similarly, in a related context, the more than 100 civil-rights murders of recent years have been matched by almost no murders of racist whites." G. Marx, "Civil Disorders and the Agents of Social Control," op. cit.

Black Panther Party which originated in Oakland, perhaps the most significant group to challenge the police role in maintaining the ghetto as a colony. The Panther's later policy of openly carrying guns (a legally protected right) and their intention of defending themselves against police aggression has brought on a series of confrontations with the Oakland police department. All indications are that the authorities intend to destroy the Panthers by shooting, framing up, or legally harassing their leadership—diverting the group's energies away from its primary purpose of self-defense and organization of the Black community to that of legal defense and gaining support in the white community.

There are three major approaches to "police colonialism" that correspond to reformist and revolutionary readings of the situation. The most elementary and also superficial sees colonialism in the fact that ghettos are overwhelmingly patrolled by white rather than by Black officers. The proposal—supported today by many police departments—to increase the number of Blacks on local forces to something like their distribution in the city would then make it possible to reduce the use of white cops in the ghetto. This reform should be supported, for a variety of obvious reasons, but it does not get to the heart of the police role as agents of colonization.

The Kerner report documents the fact that in some cases Black policemen can be as brutal as their white counterparts. The report does not tell us who polices the ghetto, but they have compiled the proportion of Negroes on the forces of the major cities. In some cities the disparity is so striking that white police inevitably dominate ghetto patrols. (In Oakland 31 percent of the population and only 4 percent of the police are Black; in Detroit the figures are 39 percent and 5 percent; and in New Orleans, 41 and 4.) In other cities, however, the proportion of Black cops is approaching the distribution in the city: Philadelphia 29 percent and 20 percent; Chicago 27 percent and 17 percent.[32] These figures also suggest that both the extent and the pattern of colonization may vary from one city to another. It would be useful to study how Black communities differ in degree of control over internal institutions as well as in economic and political power in the metropolitan area.

A second demand which gets more to the issue is that police should live in the communities they patrol. The idea here is that Black cops who live in the ghetto would have to be accountable to the community; if they came on like white cops then "the brothers would take care of business" and make their lives miserable. The third or maximalist position is based on the premise that the police play no positive role in the ghettos. It calls for the withdrawal of metropolitan officers from the Black communities and the substitution of an autonomous indigenous force that would maintain order without oppressing the population. The precise relationship between such an independent police, the city and county law enforcement agencies, a ghetto governing body that would supervise and finance it, and especially the law itself is yet unclear. It is unlikely that we will soon face these problems directly as they have arisen in the case of New York's schools. Of all the programs of decolonization, police autonomy will be most resisted.

---

[32] Report of the National Advisory Commission on Civil Disorders, *op. cit.*, p. 321. That Black officers nevertheless would make a difference is suggested by data from one of the supplemental studies to the Kerner report. They found Negro policemen working in the ghettos considerably more sympathetic to the community and its social problems than their white counterparts. Peter Rossi *et al.*, "Between Black and White—The Faces of American Institutions in the Ghetto," *op. cit.*, Chap. 6.

It gets to the heart of how the state functions to control and contain the Black community through delegating the legitimate use of violence to police authority.

The various "Black Power" programs that are aimed at gaining control of individual ghettos—buying up property and businesses, running the schools through community boards, taking over antipoverty programs and other social agencies, diminishing the arbitrary power of the police—can serve to revitalize the institutions of the ghetto and build up an economic, professional, and political power base. These programs seem limited; we do not know at present if they are enough in themselves to end colonized status.[33] But they are certainly a necessary first step.

THE ROLE OF WHITES

What makes the Kerner report a less-than-radical document is its superficial treatment of racism and its reluctance to confront the colonized relationship between Black people and the larger society. The report emphasizes the attitudes and feelings that make up white racism, rather than the system of privilege and control which is the heart of the matter.[34] With all its discussion of the ghetto and its problems, it never faces the question of the stake that white Americans have in racism and ghettoization.

This is not a simple question, but this paper should not end with the impression that police are the major villains. All white Americans gain some privileges and advantage from the colonization of Black communities.[35] The majority of whites also lose something from this oppression and division in society. Serious research should be directed to the ways in which white individuals and institutions are tied into the ghetto. In closing let me suggest some possible parameters.

1. It is my guess that only a small minority of whites make a direct economic profit from ghetto colonization. This is hopeful in that the ouster of white businessmen may become politically feasible. Much more significant, however, are the private and corporate interests in the land and residential property of the Black community; their holdings and influence on urban decision making must be exposed and combatted.

2. A much larger minority have occupational and professional interests in the present arrangements. The Kerner Commission reports that 1.3 million nonwhite men would have to be upgraded occupationally in order to make the Black job distribution roughly similar to the white. They advocate this without mentioning that 1.3 million specially privileged white workers would lose in the bargain.[36] In addition there are those professionals who carry out what Lee Rainwater has called the "dirty work" of administering the lives of the ghetto poor: the social workers, the school teachers, the urban development

---

[33] Eldridge Cleaver has called this first stage of the anticolonial movement *community* liberation in contrast to a more long-range goal of *national* liberation. E. Cleaver, "Community Imperialism," Black Panther Party newspaper, **2** (May 18, 1968).

[34] For a discussion of this failure to deal with racism, see Gary T. Marx, "Report of the National Commission: The Analysis of Disorder or Disorderly Analysis" (1968), unpublished paper.

[35] Such a statement is easier to assert than to document but I am attempting the latter in a forthcoming book tentatively titled *White Racism, Black Culture*, to be published by Little, Brown, 1970.

[36] Report of the National Advisory Commission on Civil Disorders, *op. cit.*, pp. 253–256.

people, and of course the police.[37] The social problems of the Black community will ultimately be solved only by people and organizations from that community; thus the emphasis within these professions must shift toward training such a cadre of minority personnel. Social scientists who teach and study problems of race and poverty likewise have an obligation to replace themselves by bringing into the graduate schools and college faculties men of color who will become the future experts in these areas. For cultural and intellectual imperialism is as real as welfare colonialism, though it is currently screened behind such unassailable shibboleths as universalism and the objectivity of scientific inquiry.

3. Without downgrading the vested interests of profit and profession, the real nitty-gritty elements of the white stake are political power and bureaucratic security. Whereas few whites have much understanding of the realities of race relations and ghetto life, I think most give tacit or at least subconscious support for the containment and control of the Black population. Whereas most whites have extremely distorted images of Black Power, many—if not most—would still be frightened by actual Black political power. Racial groups and identities are real in American life; white Americans sense they are on top, and they fear possible reprisals or disruptions were power to be more equalized. There seems to be a paranoid fear in the white psyche of Black dominance; the belief that Black autonomy would mean unbridled license is so ingrained that such reasonable outcomes as Black political majorities and independent Black police forces will be bitterly resisted.

On this level the major mass bulwark of colonization is the administrative need for bureaucratic security so that the middle classes can go about their life and business in peace and quiet. The Black militant movement is a threat to the orderly procedures by which bureaucracies and suburbs manage their existence, and I think today there are more people who feel a stake in conventional procedures than there are those who gain directly from racism. For in their fight for institutional control, the colonized will not play by the white rules of the game. These administrative rules have kept them down and out of the system; therefore they have no necessary intention of running institutions in the image of the white middle class.

The liberal, humanist value that violence is the worst sin cannot be defended today if one is committed squarely against racism and for self-determination. For some violence is almost inevitable in the decolonization process; unfortunately racism in America has been so effective that the greatest power Afro-Americans (and perhaps also Mexican-Americans) wield today is the power to disrupt. If we are going to swing with these revolutionary times and at least respond positively to the anticolonial movement, we will have to learn to live with conflict, confrontation, constant change, and what may be real or apparent chaos and disorder.

A positive response from the white majority needs to be in two major directions at the same time. First, community liberation movements should be supported in every way by pulling out white instruments of direct control and exploitation and substituting technical assistance to the community when this is asked for. But it is not enough to relate affirmatively to the nationalist movement for ghetto control without at the same time radically opening doors for full participation in the institu-

---

[37] Lee Rainwater, "The Revolt of the Dirty-Workers," *Trans-action*, **5** (November 1967), pp. 2, 64.

tions of the mainstream. Otherwise the liberal and radical position is little different than the traditional segregationist. Freedom in the special conditions of American colonization means that the colonized must have the choice between participation in the larger society and in their own independent structures.

STRANGER IN ONE'S LAND

Ruben Salazar

The predicament of a people who are historically part of the Southwest yet paradoxically treated as strangers in their own land was the focus of the hearing the U.S. Commission on Civil Rights held in San Antonio, Texas, in December 1968.

For the first time, in a public setting, the Mexican-American community's problems in civil rights were the central topic of a Commission hearing. It was not, however, the first time that Mexican-American needs and aspirations in the field of equal opportunity and civil rights had been considered by the Commission. At previous hearings in Phoenix, Los Angeles, and San Francisco, Mexican-American spokesmen had presented some of the issues and demands of the Spanish-speaking community. State advisory committees in the five Southwestern states of Arizona, California, Colorado, New Mexico, and Texas had addressed themselves to problems concerning the Mexican-American people, and occasionally had issued reports of their findings.

But the San Antonio hearing concentrated for the first time the Commission's full attention and resources. Texas, where

no hearing had been held before by the Commission and with the second largest Spanish surname population, and San Antonio, the Texas city with the largest Mexican-American community, offered a logical site for the week-long hearing of December 9–14.

For nearly six months prior to the hearing, staff members delved into the conditions of life and work among Mexican-Americans, filtering out the issues related to civil rights and laying the groundwork for the hearing. A field representative was assigned to San Antonio for coordination of on-site activities.

Some 1000 persons were interviewed; volumes of data were collected and analyzed; nearly 80 persons in all were requested to speak under subpoena—from barrio residents to state officials, businessmen to farm workers, students to school superintendents. Clergymen, law-enforcement officials, and three families also testified.

The hearing explored major areas of concern to Mexican-Americans and the Commission: employment, education, and

Reprinted by permission from the U.S. Commission on Civil Rights, Clearinghouse, *Pub. 19 (May 1970), pp. ii–iii, 1–9, 23–49.*

the administration of justice. Problems in housing and political representation were also considered. The total picture of economic deprivation, of relegation to the meanest employment, of educational suppression, and of restricted opportunity in almost every phase of life unfolded.

Expressing great empathy with the story that developed was a predominantly Mexican-American audience that daily filled the auditorium at Our Lady of the Lake College where the hearing was conducted.

What follows is an account of the Commission's hearing by Ruben Salazar, a California journalist. Salazar is currently news director for the Spanish-language television station KMEX of Los Angeles. He also writes a column for the Los Angeles Times *on the problems of the Spanish-speaking people of the United States. He has been a foreign correspondent in Vietnam, in the Dominican Republic, and in Mexico City. His views do not necessarily represent those of the Commission. The report is published for the purpose of stimulating public interest and concern in the problems confronting Mexican-Americans.* [Note: Ruben Salazar was killed recently by a tear-gas canister thrown by Los Angeles police.]

INTRODUCTION

The San Antonio hearing of the U.S. Commission on Civil Rights which probed into the social anguish of Mexican-Americans was born in protest and begun in controversy.

As the country's second largest minority, Mexican-Americans had been virtually ignored by public and private reformers. There was vague realization that they had educational, employment, and cultural problems. But it was felt that language was the basic reason for these problems. And, it was concluded, once this accident of birth was repaired, Mexican-Americans would melt into the Caucasian pot, just as Italians, Germans, and Poles had.

Then came the black revolution.

It exploded partly from a condition which had been known all along but was now the basis for a black-white confrontation: the color of one's skin was all too important in America. White was good. Black was bad.

Faced with an identity crisis, many young Mexican-Americans—excited by black militancy—decided that they had been misled by their elders into apathetic confusion. It came as a shock at first: Mexican-Americans felt caught between the white and the black. Though counted as "white" by the Bureau of the Census, Mexican-Americans were never really thought of as such. Though the speaking of foreign languages was considered highly sophisticated, Mexican-Americans were condemned for speaking Spanish.

The ambivalence felt vaguely and in silence for so long seemed to crystallize in the light of the black revolution. A Mexican-American was neither Mexican nor American. He was neither white nor black. What was he then and where was he going? The young, the militant, and the angry wanted to know.

When the Commission met in San Francisco in May 1967, Mexican-Americans walked out protesting there was not a Mexican-American Commissioner to represent them or enough attention accorded their problems.

In October of that year, the U.S. Inter-Agency Committee on Mexican-American Affairs held a hearing in El Paso on the problems of the Spanish-speaking. The hearing, conducted at the same time President Johnson officially returned to Mexico a disputed piece of border land [El Chamizal], ended on a sour note.

Governor John Connally of Texas, accused of allowing the use of Texas Rangers to break strikes by Mexican-American farm workers in the Rio Grande Valley, was roundly booed and hooted by Mexican-Americans in the presence of President Johnson. Because the President was there, the incident was given wide publicity and it marked a rare national exposure of rising Mexican-American militancy.

In other areas of the Southwest, the strike-boycott of California table grapes led by Cesar Chavez was becoming a national and international cause. Reies Lopez Tijerina's land grants struggle in New Mexico and its adversaries introduced violence to the movement. There were the high-school walkouts in East Los Angeles by Mexican-American students, and Rodolfo (Corky) Gonzales, head of the Denver-based Crusade for Justice, was preaching ethnic nationalism. Many Mexican-Americans joined the Poor People's Campaign in Washington, D.C., in the summer of 1968.

For the first time, many Americans became aware of Mexican-American discontent. There was talk now of brown power.

In November 1968, President Johnson named the first Mexican-American to the Commission, Dr. Hector P. Garcia, a physician from Corpus Christi, Texas, and founder of the American G.I. Forum. A Commission hearing which would center on Mexican-American problems was scheduled for December 9–14, in San Antonio.

Protests helped bring it about. Now the controversy would begin.

Some Mexican-American leaders charged that Washington was meddling in something it knew nothing about and so would make things worse instead of better. They felt any problems Mexican-Americans might have should be solved locally, by local leadership. The younger and the more militant Chicano leadership retorted that the problems had intentionally been ignored and that national exposure would bring new, more imaginative solutions. Traditional leadership, they claimed, had failed.

These strong points of view, aired publicly before the Commission met, hint at the diversity of thought and feeling found among the some six to seven million Mexican-Americans, most of whom live in California, Texas, New Mexico, Arizona, and Colorado.

There are many splits in the black movement. But there's something the American Negro knows for sure—he's black. He can easily define his problems as a race which make him part of a cohesive force. This is what has forged the beginning of black power in the United States. As yet, most Mexican-Americans seem not to identify with any one single overriding problem as Americans. Though they know they're somehow different, many still cling to the idea that Mexican-Americans are Caucasian, thus white, thus "one of the boys."

Many prove it: by looking and living like white Americans, by obtaining and keeping good jobs and by intermarrying with Anglos who rarely think of it as a "mixed marriage." To these people, Mexican-Americans are assimilating well into white American society. They felt uncomfortable about the Commission's hearing because in their eyes it would merely tend to continue the polarization of Anglos and Mexican-Americans at a time in which they felt it was disappearing.

To many other Mexican-Americans, especially the young activists, Mexican-Americans have for too long been cheated by tacitly agreeing to be Caucasian in name only. They say they would rather be proud of their Indian blood than uncertain about their Caucasian status. They feel they can achieve greater dignity by identifying with pre-Anglo Mexican-Indian civilizations and even the Conquistadores than by pretending that they can truly relate to the *Mayflower* and early New England Puritanism.

This division of feeling will continue and perhaps widen. The hearing, however, clearly showed that people who are indigenous to the Southwest seem sometimes strangers in their own land and certainly in many ways curiously alienated from their fellow Americans.

AQUÍ NO SE HABLA ESPAÑOL

You know it almost from the beginning: speaking Spanish makes you different. Your mother, father, brothers, sisters, and friends all speak Spanish. But the bus driver, the teacher, the policeman, the store clerk, the man who comes to collect the rent—all the people who are doing important things—do not. Then the day comes when your teacher—who has taught you the importance of many things—tells you that speaking Spanish is wrong. You go home, kiss your mother, and say a few words to her in Spanish. You go to the window and look out and your mother asks you what's the matter?

Nada, mama, you answer, because you don't know what is wrong. . . .

Howard A. Glickstein, then Acting Staff Director of the Commission, asked witness Edgar Lozano, a San Antonio high-school student, whether he has ever been punished for speaking Spanish at school. Yes, in grammar, in junior high, and in senior high schools, he answers.

". . . they took a stick to me," says Edgar. "It really stayed in your mind. Some things, they don't go away as easy as others."

Edgar relates with some bitterness and anger the times he was beaten by teachers for speaking Spanish at school after "getting a lecture about, if you want to be an American, you have got to speak English."

Glickstein tries to ask Edgar another question and the boy, this time more sad than angry, interrupts and says:

"I mean, how would you like for somebody to come up to you and tell you what you speak is a dirty language? You know, what your mother speaks is a dirty language. You know, that is the only thing I ever heard at home.

"A teacher comes up to you and tells you, 'No, no. You know that is a filthy language, nothing but bad words and bad thoughts in that language.'

"I mean, they are telling you that your language is bad. . . . Your mother and father speak a bad language, you speak a bad language. I mean you communicate with dirty words, and nasty ideas.

". . . that really stuck to my mind."

Edgar, like many Mexican-Americans before him, had been scarred with the insults of an Anglo world which rejects everything except carbon copies of what it has decreed to be "American." You start being different and you end up being labeled as un-American. An Anglo-oriented school in a Mexican-American barrio can do things to the teachers, too. Bad communication can sorely twist the always sensitive relation between teacher and pupil.

Under questioning from David Rubin, the Commission's Acting General Counsel, W. Dain Higdon, principal of San Antonio's Hawthorne Junior High School, 65 percent Mexican-American, asserted that he felt there was something in the background or characteristics of the Mexican-Americans which inhibits high achievement.

Mexicans or Mexican-Americans, Higdon told the Commission, have a "philosophical concept" in dealing with life which says *lo que dios quiera,* "what God wishes."

An Anglo, on the other hand, Higdon continued, says "in God we trust," not "this is how it shall be and you are limited."

". . . you have unlimited horizons," Higdon explained to the Commission.

And whenever some situation befalls me [as an Anglo], I say it is my fault. Whenever some situation befalls a Mexican-American, he may say it is his fault, but more generally and from a heritage standpoint he would be inclined to say, *lo que dios quiera.*

Rubin: Would it be fair to say that you feel there are genetic factors involved which account for the differences in achievements, that mixture of genes causes differences in people?

Higdon: Well, when you were in my office, I made that statement to you and I will stick by it. . . .

The Mexican-American child learns early that he is different. Then he learns that speaking Spanish prevents his becoming a good American. It's at this time, perhaps, when he most needs sensitive guidance. Yet, how do some teachers see the role of their profession?

Rubin: Did you state in an interview with me and with another staff member that the obligations of the teacher were first to complete paperwork and secondly to maintain discipline?

Higdon: Yes, sir, I did.

Rubin: And thirdly, to teach?

Higdon: Yes, sir.

What can a school, in which teacher and student speak not only different languages but are also on different emotional wavelengths, do to a Mexican-American child?

This kind of school, Dr. Jack Forbes of Berkeley's Far West Laboratory for Educational Research and Development, told the Commission:

tends to lead to a great deal of alienation, a great deal of hostility, it tends to lead also to a great deal of confusion, where the child comes out of that school really not knowing who he is, not knowing what he should be proud of, not knowing what language he should speak other than English, being in doubt as to whether he should completely accept what Anglo people have been telling him and forget his Mexican identity, or whether he should listen to what his parents and perhaps other people have said and be proud of his Mexican identity.

The word "Mexican" has been and still is in many places in the Southwest a word of contempt. Mexican-Americans refer to themselves as Mexicanos or Chicanos with the ease of those who know and under-

stand each other. But when some Anglos talk about "Mexicans" the word takes on a new meaning, almost the counterpart of "nigger."

The Mexican-Americans' insistence on keeping the Spanish language is but one aspect of cultural differences between Anglos and Mexican-Americans.

Values differ between these two groups for a variety of historical reasons. Mexicans have deep rural roots which have produced a sense of isolation. Spanish Catholicism has given Mexicans an attitude of fatalism and resignation. Family ties are extremely important and time, or clock-watching, is not.

Luis F. Hernandez, assistant professor of education at San Fernando Valley State College in Los Angeles, has described the differences this way:

Mexican-American values can be said to be directed toward tradition, fatalism, resignation, strong family ties, a high regard for authority, paternalism, personal relations, reluctance to change, a greater orientation to the present than to the future and a greater concern for being than doing.

The contrasting Anglo-American values can be said to be directed toward change, achievement, impersonal relations, efficiency, progress, equality, scientific rationalization, democracy, individual action and reaction, and a greater concern for doing than being.

Distortion of or deletion of Mexicans' contribution to the Southwest in history books can inhibit a Mexican-American child from the beginning of his schooling.

State Senator Joe Bernal of Texas told the Commission that the "schools have not given us any reason to be proud" of being Mexican-Americans. People running the schools "have tried to take away our language," the senator continued, and so Mexican-American children very early are made to feel ashamed of the Spanish language and of being Mexican.

The children start building up defenses such as insisting on being called "Latin" or "Hispano" or "Spanish-American" because, said Bernal, "they want no reference made to being Mexican." One of the reasons for this, Bernal told the Commission, is that "it has been inculcated" in the minds of grammar-school children that the Mexican "is no good" by means of, for instance, overly and distortedly emphasizing the Battle of the Alamo and ignoring all contributions made by Mexicans in the Southwest.

To be Spanish, of course, is something else. Spanish has a European connotation and Europe is the motherland.

Carey McWilliams in his *North from Mexico* explains that

the Hispanic heritage of the Southwest has two parts: the Spanish and the Mexican-Indian. Originally one heritage, unified in time, they have long since been polarized. Carefully distinguished from the Mexican, the Spanish heritage is now enshrined throughout the Southwest. It has become the sacred or templar tradition of which the Mexican-Indian inheritance is the secular or profane counterpart . . . .

Dr. Forbes noticed on his arrival in San Antonio for the hearing that things have not changed.

. . . the San Antonio greeter magazine which I picked up in a hotel lobby and which had the statement about the history of San Antonio said nothing about the Mexican heritage of this region, talking only about the glorious Spanish colonial era and things of this nature. . . .

To be Spanish is fine because white is important and Spain is white.

Dr. Forbes reminded the Commission that

first of all, the Mexican-American population is in great part a native population in the Southwest. It is not an immigrant population. Now this nativity in the Southwest stems not only from the pre-1848 period during the so-called Spanish colonial and Mexican periods, but it also stems from the fact that many people who today identify as Mexican-Americans or in some areas as Hispanos, are actually of local Indian descent. . . .

Aurelio Manuel Montemayor, who taught in San Felipe High School at Del Rio, Texas, explained to the Commission how in his view all this is ignored in the school curriculum.

Quoting from a State-approved textbook, Montemayor said the book related how

the first comers to America were mainly Anglo-Saxons but soon came Dutchmen, Swedes, Germans, Frenchmen, Africans, then the great nineteenth-century period of immigration added to our already melting pot. Then later on, it [the textbook] said, the Spaniards came.

"So my students," continued Montemayor, "had no idea where they came from" and wondered whether "they were part of American society." This frustrated Montemayor so much, he said, that he told his students "let's see if we can write our own textbook." He instructed them to write papers on the subject, "Who Am I?"

"They told me in their words," Montemayor said, "that they were inferior to the standards of this country. That no matter how much they tried they could never be blonds and blue-eyed."

San Felipe High School is located in the San Felipe Independent School District of the city of Del Rio which also contains the Del Rio Independent School District. San Felipe High School has about 97 percent Mexican-Americans and the Del Rio High School has about 50 percent Anglos and 49 percent Mexican-Americans. Though the Laughlin Air Force Base is located in the San Felipe Independent School District, the base children are bused to the more affluent and less Mexican-American Del Rio High School.

Some of Montemayor's students, prompted by the teacher's concern with self-identity, decided to work on a project called: "Does San Felipe Have an Inferiority Complex?"

"They studied the schools, they studied the discontent in the San Felipe Community," Montemayor told the Commission.

A boy and a girl interviewed parents at the air base and asked them what they thought of the San Felipe schools and whether they would allow their children to attend there.

The boy and girl told Montemayor that base officials had them escorted to the gate when they discovered what they were doing. But not before a base mother told the young pollsters what she thought of San Felipe.

Montemayor: . . . [a woman told my students] that she wouldn't send her children to [San Felipe] district schools. They had them there for a semester, the neighborhoods were so dirty and all of that, and that the schools were falling down. And, of course, the students were finding this out on their own and, of course, as far as morale, it couldn't have been lower.

Many Mexican-American youths, despite their low morale, continue on their business as best they can even though lamenting, as some of Montemayor's students, that no matter how much they try they will never be blond and blue-eyed.

Others become ultramilitant as did David Sanchez, prime minister of the Brown Berets in Los Angeles, who told a newsman: "There are very few gabachos [Anglos] who don't turn me off. To the Anglo, justice means 'just us.' "

And many others, as did some 1500 Mexican-Americans from throughout the Southwest who last March attended a "Chicano Youth Liberation Conference" in Denver, will adopt, in their anger, frustration, and disillusion, a resolution which condemns the "brutal gringo invasion of our territories." . . .

LA EDUCACIÓN DE MEXICANOS

When the Mexican-American in the Southwest complains about having nightmares instead of the American dream, he's usually told: "Education is the answer, amigo. Get an education and your problems will be solved."

Who can argue with that? At the San Antonio hearing, however, the Commission heard experts in the field of educating bilingual and bicultural children argue with the premise behind this alleged panacea. The premise, of course, is that the Mexican-American child can receive a meaningful education merely by wanting it.

Dr. George I. Sanchez of the University of Texas told the Commission that in his State "persons of Spanish surname . . . 17 years of age or older averaged 4.7 years of school, whereas the Negroes averaged 8.1, and the average of the population averaged 10 plus."

In California, that State's Advisory Committee to the Commission reported that the median school years completed for Mexican-Americans was 8.6, for Negroes, 10.5, and for Anglos, 12.1.

Why is Juanito so far behind?

One of the reasons is that many Mexican-American children enter school speaking little or no English because, generally, only Spanish is spoken at home. About the first thing that Juanito encounters at school is an IQ [intelligence quotient] test—in English. Usually, he makes a bad showing because of his limited knowledge of English. This means that at best he will be considered a "slow learner" and treated accordingly; at worst he will be placed in classes for the mentally retarded. Either way, the child begins his school career with a stigma which will remain for the rest of his life. Though many educators have recommended abolishing IQ tests in the early grades—as has been done by the Los Angeles School District—others have recommended that the tests be made more realistic.

In California, Mexican-American students once labeled mentally retarded showed dramatic increases in their IQ scores after taking Spanish-language tests. The report of the tests, submitted to the California Board of Education in May 1969, said that some children have been victims of a "retarding influence" by being left in the mentally retarded classes for long periods of time. The children who took part in the study were in such classes on the basis of English-language IQ tests. When they were retested in the Spanish language, the children's IQ scores jumped by as much as 28 points.

Unfortunately, such studies, as enlightening as they are, do not change other realities. Reforms, which cost money, must be implemented to change the shabby education which many Mexican-Americans receive. In Texas, although state allotments to school districts are determined by the average daily attendance, also considered are the level of academic attainment and the length of teachers' experience. Consequently, inequities are created between wealthier "Anglo districts" and less affluent Mexican-American districts.

A Commission staff study of nine school districts in the San Antonio area showed that in the Northeast School District [predominantly Anglo] expenditures per pupil from all revenue sources in 1967–68 amounted to $745.07. In the Edgewood School District [predominantly Mexican-American] expenditures per pupil, also from all revenue sources, amounted to $465.54. The staff report showed that 98 percent of the noncollege-degree teachers employed in the nine San Antonio districts are concentrated in the predominantly Mexican-American districts.

An Edgewood district student told the Commission that a teacher admitted to a class that he was not qualified to teach the course and asked the students to bear with him. Another student testified that Mexican-Americans are counseled away from college and into vocational training. A high-school senior said Armed Forces representatives go to the schools before graduation to induce boys to enter the service. Commissioner Hector Garcia wanted to know whether any scientists, doctors, lawyers, or businessmen ever visited the schools to encourage graduating students to enter these fields. No, the boy answered.

Edgewood's financial situation could be improved, for example, by merging with the San Antonio Independent School District. Edgewood has unsuccessfully petitioned for merger several times to equalize Edgewood's property tax base with that of San Antonio's. But political realities are at work to make this impossible. Indeed, districts are often created to avoid integration of Anglo and Mexican-American students. In one case in Texas, the students residing at Laughlin Air Force Base [89 percent Anglo] are bused through the 97 percent Mexican-American San Felipe School District (in which the base is located) to the Del Rio School District [51 percent Anglo].

As a result, federal funds are awarded the Del Rio district for the education of military dependents. For example, in 1966 Del Rio received more than $200,000 in federal impacted aid funds, while San Felipe, whose district boundaries encompass the Air Force installation, received less than $41,000.

In an impassioned plea to the Commission, Homero Sigala, school superintendent at San Felipe, called this situation "unfair" and asked that the Commission advise the President, Congress, and the Air Force "to direct the Commander at Laughlin Air Force Base to send the students residing at Laughlin to the San Felipe schools."

Unfair though it may be, the political reality of the situation is that even though Val Verde County, where San Felipe is located, is about 50 percent Mexican-American, there are no Mexican-Americans on the five-member county school board. In other words, Mexican-Americans have no political muscle to make much of an impression on Washington.

This might be attributed to what Dr. Jack Forbes of Berkeley's Far West Laboratory for Educational Research and Development described to the Commission as the "conquered population" syndrome. The indigenous people of Mexico, who included those in what is now the American Southwest, first experienced the Spanish conquest, followed by a long period of colonialism, Dr. Forbes explained. This was followed by the Anglo-American conquest of the Southwest, at the end of the Mexican-American War.

To understand the significance of this syndrome, Dr. Forbes continued,

one must of course get past the romance and mythology of the supposed westward movement of the pioneers and look at the Anglo-American conquest of the Southwest as we might look at the German march eastward against the Poles or as we might look at the Franco-Norman conquest of England, in other words, in a purely detached and objective manner.

And if we are to do this, continued Dr. Forbes,

we would see the U.S. conquest of the Southwest as a very real case of aggression and imperialism, that it involved not only the military phase of immediate conquest, but the subsequent establishment of a colonial society, a rather complex colonial society because there was not one single colonial office to administer Mexican-American people. Instead, there were many institutions that were created to control and administer Mexican-American people and also to enable the dominant population to acquire almost complete control of the soil and the other forms of wealth, of the social institutions, cultural institutions, and so on.

Now the conquest in the colonial period can be further understood if we think about a community such as the city of Los Angeles in California which has long had a large Mexican-American population but in which no major institution of any kind is controlled even pro-

portionately to numbers by the Spanish-speaking population.

The concept of conquest, the Berkeley historian told the Commission, is very often ignored but "I can't emphasize it too much because we're beginning to learn the process of conquest," particularly the "tremendous effect upon people's behavior."

"For example," Dr. Forbes continued, "a conquered population tends to exhibit certain characteristics such as apathy, apparent indifference, passivity, and a lack of motivation in relation to the goals of the dominant society."

Another dimension of the Mexican-American educational quandary was posed by Dr. Manuel Ramirez, an assistant professor of psychology at Rice University, Houston, who spoke of the conflict of cultures between the Anglo and the Mexican-American.

"My research has identified two different kinds of conflict," he stated.

The first type arises as a result of the fact that [the Mexican-American] is led to believe that he cannot be identified with two cultures at the same time. There is one message that is given by his parents, his relatives, and other Mexican-American students, who tell him that if he rejects Mexican-American culture and identifies with the Anglo culture, he may be considered a traitor to his ethnic group.

Dr. Ramirez went on to say:

The other message comes from teachers, employers, and Anglo friends, who tell him that if he doesn't reject the Mexican-American culture, he will be unable to reap the educational and economic benefits that are in the Anglo culture.

The second type is really a series of conflicts which come about because the Mexican-American student is bringing with him a series of behaviors, perceptions, methods of viewing the world, of doing things . . . and this conflicts with the value system of the Anglo middle class.

Then he concluded:

The big problem that we face as Mexican-Americans is, how can we have our children maintain as many of the Mexican-American values as possible and still be a success in the Anglo world? ... And if we could have people who are sensitive to our culture, people who understand our problems and don't take this as a criticism to some teachers, I think that people like myself and others in Texas and other parts of the Southwest are living testimony that there were some Anglo teachers who work, but there aren't enough of them.

Giving another view, Dr. Sanchez told the Commission that one of the barriers to educational reform in Texas was "the poverty of Mexican-Americans and their lack of effective statewide political organization."

"[Mexican-Americans] have not been heard yet as an effective political force," Dr. Sanchez said. "We number some 2½ million in the State of Texas and that political weight has not been effectively harnessed to bring about reforms."

Nevertheless, testimony at the San Antonio hearing indicated that young activists are beginning to stir in the "conquered" Mexican-American community.

Homer Garcia, a student at San Antonio's Lanier High School, told the Commission how a group of students and parents fought for a change in curriculum in the predominantly Mexican-American school to include such studies as chemistry, physics, algebra, trigonometry, calculus, and computer programming. According to Homer, about 500 parents and 500 students turned out to a meeting in a community hall to hear the student demands for a better education. At another Mexican-American school, Edgewood High, students demanded better-qualified teachers.

Howard A. Glickstein, then Acting Staff Director of the Commission, asked Homer how the turnout of parents to the Lanier High School meeting compared to the number of parents who usually attend PTA meetings.

Homer: Nobody comes to PTA meetings. For one thing, the parents really don't know what a PTA is, because they're held during the daytime when—well, my parents, for instance, can't go to the PTA meeting because they are held during the day for the convenience of the teachers. My dad works during the daytime. My mother has to take care of my brothers. I mean, it is not to their convenience at all. It's a teachers' organization, not a parent-teacher organization.

The concern of students and parents for better education at San Antonio's Mexican-American schools brought about positive results, according to student testimony. Much credit was given to parents who backed the students in their demands for curriculum reforms. Community participation in implementing school reforms is essential, the Commission was told, if the powerlessness and alienation felt by the Mexican-American community is to be corrected. Ignoring the community while planning reforms is not only an insult to parents, the Commission was told, but it also indicates that groups of elite educational reformers seem to think they are the only ones who know what's best for the children.

In at least three instances, Anglo educators in their testimony to the Commission revealed that cultural differences and the involvement of the Mexican-American community were not even considered in preparing studies or proposing school reforms. The director of the Texas Governor's Committee on Public Education admitted that Mexican-American parents were not consulted during a three-year study on improving education in Texas; a member of the Governor's committee related that not one top-notch Mexican-American educator was consulted during this same three-year study; and the state commissioner of education said he was not familiar with studies which indicate that Mexican-Americans experience culture conflict when they enter an Anglo-oriented school system.

If regular education for Mexican-Americans is inadequate and unrealistic, the education of migrant children is a national scandal.

Dr. Joseph Cardenas, director of Migrant Education for the Southwest Educational Development Laboratory and now superintendent of the Edgewood School District, estimated that the dropout rate for migrant children is about 90 percent. But more "startling," said Dr. Cardenas, is the fact that

one-fifth of migrants are school dropouts at the preschool age. That is, one-fifth of all migrant children never enroll in any school in spite of the state's compulsory attendance laws. So by the time they [migrant children] start the first grade, or they are 6 years old, you have already lost 20 percent of your population.

Of the 65,000 migrant students in Texas, less than 14 percent are in the upper six grades, Dr. Cardenas disclosed. The average income of the Texas migrant, he continued, is $1400 a year and a "person with this amount of money will have a lot of difficulty in educating his children adequately."

The only solution, Dr. Cardenas said, is a multistate educational program geared especially for migrant children, to follow them wherever the parents are following the crops. After agreeing that this would cost a great deal of money, Dr. Cardenas asserted that actually the only real solution is to stop migration altogether. This last drew the applause of the audience. But the perennial question loomed:

How can Mexican-Americans in the border states afford to stop migrating as long as armies of cheap labor are allowed to cross the international border?

While this part of the hearing was intended to probe into the educational problems of Mexican-Americans in the Southwest, something just as important emerged from the testimony: the Anglo children (and for that matter, the Negroes) had been cheated also—they had not been permitted to take advantage of the Southwest's cultural and language heritage. This became clear when Harold C. Brantley, superintendent of the United Consolidated School District of Webb County, Texas, explained his district's bilingual program.

It should be noted that the United States' first full-fledged bilingual program in public schools was not initiated in the Southwest, where its need had been apparent for generations, but in Florida—following the Cuban crisis. It was in Florida that Brantley got some ideas for the bilingual program in his school district.

The philosophy behind his approach, Brantley told the Commission, was that

I don't feel like a kid's ability to speak Spanish is a detriment. I think that it is an asset. . . . It is merely our responsibility as educators to turn this asset that these kids bring to us, where it not only becomes an asset to them, but can become an asset to the little blue-eyed, blond-haired Anglo.

Brantley's district is made up of the larger part of the rural area of border Webb County—some 2400 square miles—and does not include the county's largest city, Laredo. The district has 987 students, 47 percent of them Mexican-American and 53 percent Anglo. Without waiting for more research, specialized teachers, bilingual instructional materials, or substantial financial resources, Brantley in 1964 persuaded his staff, Anglo and Mexican-American parents, and the Texas Education Agency to begin a bilingual program in his bicultural district.

Today, in the district's three elementary schools, instruction is 50 percent in Spanish and 50 percent in English in the first through fifth grades.

"I am not a linguist," Brantley explained to the Commission. "My sole service is creating [an] atmosphere where things can happen."

Brantley said his program does not ignore the fact that it is very important for schools to facilitate Mexican-American children "getting into the mainstream of the dominant culture and the dominant language of the country." By the same token, Brantley continued:

We also try to stress to that child who comes from this other culture, speaking this other language [that] we want to provide him with the opportunity to improve upon his knowledge of his culture and his ability to function in his vernacular.

As for the Anglo child, Brantley said, his district tries

to create an atmosphere in the classroom where the children who come to us from the dominant culture, speaking the dominant language . . . recognize that here this little kid [Mexican-American] has got something that he [Anglo] doesn't have, and that he ought to be interested in getting what this little kid can teach him.

Warming up to the subject, Brantley asked the Commission:

Now, can you begin to see what this does for the stature of this little kid that comes from this other culture with this other language? Where he is made to feel like he can do something that somebody can't do, and that he has something that this other little kid wants to learn about?

The Commission understood.

NO HAY TRABAJO

When Mexico lost the Southwest to the United States, the Treaty of Guadalupe-Hidalgo specifically guaranteed the property and political rights of the conquered native population. The treaty, executed on February 2, 1848, also attempted to safeguard the Mexican culture and language.

Throughout the San Antonio hearing, it became clear that Mexican-Americans in the Southwest cling tenaciously to their ancestors' culture and language. But it also became evident that the spirit of the treaty has been violated.

Though Mexican-Americans persist in retaining the Spanish language, they do so at the price of obtaining a second-rate education because bilingualism has been suppressed and has never been accepted as an asset. Though they have kept their culture, they have had to pay for it by being stereotyped as backward or, at best, quaint. Nowhere is this more evident than in the jobs Mexican-Americans have traditionally held in the Southwest and the jobs they hold now. It is almost the rule that only Mexican-Americans who have been willing to sacrifice their culture and language have succeeded in an Anglo society.

Carey McWilliams in *North from Mexico* says that the "basic factor retarding the assimilation of the [Southwest Mexican], at all levels, has been the pattern of his employment."

"With few exceptions," says McWilliams, "only a *particular class* of employers has employed Mexican labor in the Southwest: large-scale industrial enterprises, railroads, smelters, copper mines, sugar-beet refineries" and, of course, agriculture. . . . "Traditionally," continues the author,

Mexicans have been paid less than Anglo-Americans for the same jobs. These invidious distinctions have reenforced the Mexican stereotype and placed a premium on prejudice . . . the pattern of employment . . . dictated the type and location of residence. Segregated residential areas have resulted in segregated schools, segregated schools have reenforced the stereotype and limited opportunities for acculturation.

In setting this merry-go-around in motion, the pattern of employment has been of crucial importance for it has stamped the Mexican as "inferior" and invested the stereotype with an appearance of reality. . . .

It was revealed at the San Antonio hearing that in some industries Mexican-Americans are not even employed as laborers.

Under questioning, Ralph Allen, director of employee relations, El Paso Natural Gas Company, told the Commission that in the company's Permian division no Mexican-Americans are employed as unskilled laborers. Working for the company is considered unusually beneficial because it does not offer the dead-end jobs Mexican-Americans often get. Allen said the company's Permian division laborers must be high-school graduates "because they advance from that on up through."

Commissioner Hector P. Garcia noted that in part of the operating area of the El Paso Natural Gas Company, the percentages of Mexican-Americans by county are the following: Jeff Davis, 56 percent; El Paso, 44 percent; Brewster, 42.6 percent; Presidio, 40.5 percent; and Hudspeth, 29.4 percent.

In the city of El Paso, where the company makes its headquarters and is about 50 percent Mexican-American, Allen testified that out of 1150 employees only 13 percent were Mexican-American.

Commissioner Garcia noted that El Paso was "practically the first settlement north of the Rio Grande that was colonized by Spaniards and Mexican Americans" and that Spanish-speaking people have been in the area for "hundreds of years." "And yet," Garcia said, ". . . you haven't been able to find one single Mexican-American that you could . . . employ as a laborer . . .?"

Working for the telephone company can be advantageous because of good wages and opportunities for advancement. Telephone companies, as well as any other firms having contracts with federal agencies, must comply with Executive Order 11246 which requires affirmative action in seeking out members of minority groups for employment.

Joe Ridgway, employment manager for the San Antonio metropolitan sector of the Southwestern Bell Telephone Company, was questioned about the Executive Order by the Commission's Acting General Counsel David Rubin.

Rubin: You still haven't answered my question as to whether you have ever received a communication which has directed you to take affirmative action to seek out members of minority groups for employment.

Ridgway: Yes, sir, we have and are following an affirmative action program that has been presented to me.

Rubin: When was that done?

Ridgway: In November.

Rubin: Of this year?

Ridgway: Of this year.

In other words, though Executive Order 11246 was issued in 1965, Ridgway testified that a program of affirmative action in employing members of minority groups was not initiated until November of 1968, a month before the Commission hearing.

Ridgway added, however, that the program was meant to "continue" to "pursue the things that we have historically done in this area."

This exchange followed:

Rubin: Prior to speaking with staff members of the Civil Rights Commission, were you aware that less than 15 percent of your employees were members of minority groups?

Ridgway: As I remember, there was some question as to exact percentages, and that 15 percent mentioned was a little on the low side.

Rubin: Were you aware of the percentage of the total number of employees constituted by minority groups at that time?

Ridgway: Yes, I was conscious that there would be a percentage.

Rubin: But you didn't know what the percentage was?

Ridgway: The actual percentage, I did not know what it was and had no way of knowing it at that time.

Rubin: Now, your 1968 [Equal Employment Opportunity—1] form shows that out of 626 craftsmen, only 12, or under 2 percent, have a Spanish surname. How do you account for this in a city that is close to 40 percent Mexican-American?

Ridgway: Though I would like to answer your question, I am at a loss as to how to historically go back. It predates what I am personally acquainted with and could answer to. . . .

Yet, a couple of minutes before, Ridgway had testified that the company's new program for affirmative action in employing members of minorities was merely "to pursue the things that we have historically done in this area." Despite Ridgway's seeming confusion over the historical practice of employment discrimination, it became apparent at the hearing that historically the Mexican-American and other minorities had been victims of discrimination in employment.

It was put quite bluntly when Rubin questioned Robert A. Wallace, Deputy Assistant Secretary of the Treasury.

Rubin: Mr. Wallace, the banking industry has been said to have been traditionally —and I am quoting, "a white man's industry." Would you agree with that characterization?

Wallace: Until about two years ago, I would have to agree with that, yes. . . .

Wallace's reference to "two years ago," coincides with a 1966 Treasury Department ruling that all banks receiving federal deposits are covered by Executive Order 11246, and therefore are required to undertake affirmative policies to recruit minority-group persons.

A Commission staff report, however, showed that though all banks visited reported that they had federal deposits, only two said they had been informed of this requirement by the Treasury Department. And, only one bank reported the establishment of an affirmative program to recruit minorities. The staff report also revealed that in San Antonio, where almost half of the population is Spanish-speaking, only 5.6 percent of all bank officials were Mexican-Americans, and nearly half of them were found in one bank, the Frost National Bank. Seven banks reported that none of their officials were Mexican-American and five others reported that they had only one Mexican-American official.

Of the clerical and office workers, 16.4 percent were Mexican-American and 1.4 percent were Negro. The percentage of Mexican-American office workers ranged from 100 percent in one bank (located in the predominantly Mexican-American area) to less than 1 percent in two banks.

In the schools, a staff report indicated that in the San Antonio Independent School District there were 14 Mexican-American administrators out of a total of 132 administrators. In the Bexar County [where San Antonio is located] Welfare Department, Mexican-Americans held close to 50 percent of all jobs and nearly one-third of the supervisory and administrative positions. But, the report notes, though Mexican-Americans comprised 75 percent of all welfare recipients in Bexar County, only 20 of 91 social workers, or less than 22 percent, were Mexican-Americans.

In nine restaurants surveyed by the Commission staff, less than 15 percent of the customer-contact positions were held by minorities, while minorities held 93 percent of the noncustomer-contact positions. The staff report showed that at the Texas Employment Commission, the State agency responsible for aiding persons in obtaining employment, Mexican-Americans held less

than 7 percent of the nonclerical and custodial positions in the State of Texas.

In emphasizing that the Commission was
not trying to condemn one section of the
country or any one industry, Commissioner
Theodore M. Hesburgh said that in its
eleven-year history, the Commission has
found that

there isn't a single city, north, south, east, or
west, where we have gone to, where it doesn't
appear very difficult for minority groups to have
some kind of adequate representation in all
kinds of businesses and professions and trades.

"As a matter of fact," continued Commissioner Hesburgh,

I could say quite openly, the most difficult task
we have had is with the construction trades
where the minorities find it very difficult to become members of the unions.

The historical pattern of employment for
Mexican-Americans was perhaps best dramatized by the controversy over employment practices at Kelly Air Force Base, one
of San Antonio's major employers. There
is so much argument on the subject, that
between June 1966 and December 1968,
there were six surveys of equal-employment
practices conducted at Kelly.

One of the reports, that of the Texas
State Advisory Committee to the Commission, issued in June 1968, found that at
Kelly Field there "are broad and glaring
inequities in the distribution of supervisory and higher grade positions among
Mexican-Americans and Negroes. . . ."

The Advisory Committee said that
among Mexican-American white-collar employees at Kelly, 68.9 percent were in
grades 1–5, for which the initial per annum salaries in 1966 were $3609 to $5331.

In the higher pay scales, the committee
reported, even though Mexican-Americans
comprise about 44 percent of the total work
force, only 8 percent of them were in the
$9221 per year and up white-collar jobs

and only 5 percent were in the $7000 and
up blue-collar jobs.

The Advisory Committee also asserted
that

there exists at Kelly Air Force Base and in the
San Antonio community, among a significant
number of Mexican-American citizens and leaders, a lack of confidence in the base's management and equal-employment-opportunity program. The Mexican-American community feels
that it does not receive equal treatment and
that Kelly Air Force Base management has failed
to remedy this situation, despite the community's
protestations. This fact takes on greater significance when it is recognized that Kelly Air Force
Base is one of the largest employers of Mexican-
Americans in the Nation.

Dennis Seidman, Air Force Deputy Chief
of Staff Personnel, on the other hand, curiously concluded, after his staff conducted
a study, that there was a "lack of credibility" on the part of the Mexican-American community, but asserted that there did
not seem "to be a significant number of
employees who felt that the employment-
opportunity program was a negative kind
of program." Seidman also told the Commission that he himself was not personally
at Kelly during this particuar study but
drew his conclusions from reports by twelve
personnel management experts who spent
six weeks at Kelly.

Howard A. Glickstein, then Acting Staff
Director of the Commission, reminded
Seidman that the Commission's Texas
State Advisory Committee report showed
that in 1966, Mexican-Americans held 11.6
percent of the starting high-grade jobs at
Kelly. And that in 1967 that figure was
12.3 percent.

"And your report," Glickstein continued,
"I believe shows that in 1968 it was 13.7
percent.

"Now the Mexican-Americans represent
about 30 percent of the [higher category]
employees, and about 44 to 45 percent of

the total work force. Would you consider that a broad and glaring inequity?"

Seidman: I think we have considered that in the report to be an imbalance in the number of people in each of these grades as related to their proportion in the population.

Glickstein: Mr. Seidman, there is one overriding impression that I receive by reading your report, and I wonder if you would care to comment on it. It seems as though the word discrimination, or the word inequity, is just a dirty word that will not be used. Is there any reason why that is so?

Seidman: . . . We put no value either positive or negative on those words. We have no evidence to indicate that there is discrimination. We have no empirical evidence that there has been discrimination and therefore the word discrimination does not appear.

Glickstein wanted to know whether Seidman disputed a report issued by the subcommittee of the equal-opportunity committee at Kelly before the hearing which asserted that "minority group members employed at Kelly during the period 1917 to 1966 did not have equal-employment opportunities."

Seidman: I think the phrase . . . which projected, as it were, a historical discrimination, is just that, a projection. I don't believe there are any—there are any empirical evidence in our report to indicate that there has been discrimination, by organization, by grade, or by individuals.

Glickstein: Do you think it is possible to find out if there has been discrimination? Do you think that is a relevant consideration?

Seidman: I think it is possible. I wouldn't know at the moment how to find out, historically.

Later, Glickstein pointed out that at the rate Mexican-Americans were obtaining higher grade-level jobs at Kelly it would take about seventeen more years to equalize the situation. "And if they were to attain a proportionate number of jobs in proportion to their representation in the entire work force, it will take until about 2000."

Seidman answered that he thought "there are many, many factors that impinge on predicting the rate of movement," and that minorities had made good progress in moving up to the higher levels especially in the past twelve months.

Later, Matt Garcia, a Mexican-American attorney who had handled job-discrimination cases, told the Commission he felt the Air Force survey team, headed by Seidman, had come to San Antonio, "only in an effort to negate the Texas State Advisory Committee's report." Seidman had earlier testified that it was just a "coincidence" that his team made the study just after the Advisory Committee's and just before the Commission met in San Antonio.

Attorney Garcia also charged that Seidman's contention that members of minorities were obtaining more higher paid jobs at Kelly was misleading because Seidman did not mention that more higher-level positions had been created in 1968. It's true, he said, that in 1966 there were 142 Mexican-Americans in the beginning category of the higher-paying jobs but the number had increased to 208 in 1968. Furthermore, he continued, Seidman did not mention the fact that in 1967 there were 1434 such jobs while in 1968 there were 1520.

Maj. Gen. Frank E. Rouse, Commander of Kelly Air Force Base, told the Commission he didn't believe "there was any necessity for Mr. Seidman and his [surveying] team in the first place," but he agreed that there is "an ethnic imbalance" in the number of good jobs Mexican-Americans have at Kelly. However, he agreed with Seidman that this was not caused by "discriminatory acts either in the recent past, or the fairly distant past."

"I must believe what I see, can touch, and prove. And I think the conclusion I come to is that under the merit promotion system, rightly or wrongly, the opinion is that the best people were promoted."

Despite General Rouse's contention that discrimination must be seen and touched to be proven, Mexican-Americans have long noted that racial prejudice against them has been perpetrated in a more subtle way than against blacks but that it has been just as effective.

Prof. Daniel P. Rodriguez of Trinity University in San Antonio, who also conducted an employment-opportunity study at Kelly, explained to the Commission how this subtle discrimination works.

During his investigation, Rodriguez told the Commission, he got the impression that Kelly management "were complying with the requirement of the [equal-employment opportunity] regulation without complying with the spirit of it."

Some of management's remarks, Rodriguez said, "led me to believe that among some of these men, even though they felt there was no prejudice or bias on their part, they were not even aware of it."

Rodriguez: I had one supervisor tell me that when a Mexican-American was promoted you had to be careful to ensure that the Anglo group there was going to accept him as a supervisor. What he left unsaid of course—and I casually pointed it out to him—was that when an Anglo was being promoted that there was never any question about whether he could handle minority-group people working under him.

Glickstein: Did you think that he thought that he was discriminating?

Rodriguez: I am positive that he didn't feel that he was discriminating, or that the statement he made to me was—that there was anything wrong with it. I think he

was a little bit surprised when he realized what he had said.

The historical pattern of Mexican-American employment can be changed abruptly for the better with imagination, know-how, sensitivity, and money. This was the message conveyed to the Commission by Joseph B. Andrasko, director of industrial relations for the aeronautics division of the Ling-Temco-Vought Aerospace Corporation of Dallas, in one of the hearing's most positive presentations.

Andrasko said that in 1965, his company, which builds airplanes, foresaw the need for about 14,000 semiskilled and skilled workers for its expansion program. Dallas, where the company is located, could not be a main source of labor because that city had a less than 2 percent unemployment rate. It was suggested that the Rio Grande Valley, whose unemployment rate is very high as a result of the cheap labor available just across the border, be considered as a source for workers.

"This came as much of a shocker," Andrasko said, "as the Rio Grande Valley is approximately 450 to 500 miles from our plant. . . ."

Nevertheless, the company took the plunge and after 2½ years of negotiations with local, state, and federal agencies, the company reached an agreement to train 750 persons in the Rio Grande Valley in a period of twelve months. Of the 750 persons who entered the training program, 684 finished the course and 622 were still on the payroll at the time of the hearing. The trainees, 97 percent of them Mexican-Americans, who could not have hoped to earn more than $1200 to $1500 a year in the Valley, started making $5000 to $6000 a year after five weeks' training.

It was quite an undertaking, considering the workers had to be uprooted from the Rio Grande Valley to live in a Dallas suburb, where they would have to look for housing and schools for their children. These problems were solved, Andrasko said, by assigning company counselors to help the workers get settled in Dallas.

"The counselors were Mexican-American," Andrasko said, "all of them. And we did it by design."

Federal and state funds provided wages for the trainees while they trained, salaries for instructors, rent for equipment that had to be taken to the Valley, and transportation for the workers from the Valley to Dallas. It cost the state and federal governments about $1200 per trainee.

Was the money well spent?

Andrasko told the Commission that the company made a survey which showed that when the trainee started working full-time it took about eighteen months for the newly trained worker to pay $1200 in taxes.

"As a taxpayer I'd say you're darn right [the money was well spent]," Andrasko said.

The trainees, Andrasko added, turned out to be "conscientious, hard workers and followed instructions." As a matter of fact, he continued, the first two wing panels which they built after training were found to have no defects by the inspectors.

The team of Mexican-Americans who were brought to Dallas from the Valley broke the myth that Mexican-Americans can do only certain types of work, Andrasko said. All they needed was an opportunity to prove themselves.

LA LEY

Justice is the most important word in race relations. Yet too many Mexican-Americans in the Southwest feel with David Sanchez, Los Angeles Brown Beret leader, that "to Anglos justice means 'just us.'"

La Ley, or The Law, as Mexican-Americans call the administration of justice, takes forms that Anglos—and even Negroes—never have to experience. A Mexican-American, though a third-generation American, for instance, may have to prove with documents that he is an American citizen at border crossings while a blue-eyed blond German immigrant, for example, can cross by merely saying "American."

Besides the usual complaints made by racial minorities about police brutality and harassment, Mexican-Americans have an added problem: sometimes they literally cannot communicate with the police. A Commission report told of a young Mexican-American, who, while trying to quell a potentially explosive situation, was arrested because the police officers, who did not understand Spanish, thought that he was trying to incite the crowd to riot.

In another case, the Commission report told of a Mexican-American in Arizona who was held in jail for two months on a charge of sexually molesting his daughter. As it turned out, he had been mistakenly charged with this offense, but he did not voice any objections at the time because he did not understand the proceedings and no interpreter was provided for him. A probation officer, who spoke Spanish, talked to the defendant later and upon learning the facts explained the situation to the local magistrate, who dismissed the case.

One of the many reasons a Mexican-American cannot relate well to *La Ley* is that he doesn't see many of his own in positions of authority serving on agencies which administer justice. The 1960 census indicated that Mexican-Americans represent about 12 percent of the Southwest's population. In 1968, only 7.4 percent of the total uniformed personnel in law-enforcement agencies in the Southwest were Mexican-Americans, according to those agencies answering a Commission questionnaire.

As for policy-making positions, the Commission learned in its survey that only ten law-enforcement agencies are headed by Mexican-Americans and eight of these are in communities of less than 10,000 in population.

(A Commission study of the grand jury system of 22 California counties concluded that discrimination against Mexican-Americans in juror selection is "as severe—sometimes more severe—as discrimination against Negroes in grand juries in the South.")

In East Los Angeles, which is the largest single urban Mexican-American community in the United States, "friction between law enforcement and the Mexican-American community" is on the increase, according to a psychiatric social worker, Armando Morales.

Morales is state chairman of the California Unity Council, Police Community Relations Committee, which is composed of members from five statewide Mexican-American organizations—the Community Service Organization, the League of United Latin American Citizens (LULAC), the Mexican American Educators, the American GI Forum, and the Mexican American Political Association.

One of the reasons for this increasing friction, Morales told the Commission, was that "gradually the Mexican-American community is becoming much more aggressive as to its social demands, its social needs. It is becoming more active. And, at the same time, law enforcement is becoming much more suppressive, hence creating that much more friction between the two." Morales also contended that police aggressive behavior seems to be condoned by high-level government.

Morales charged "indifference and apathy to the justice and needs of the Mexican-American" by the federal government. He said his council investigated 25 cases of alleged police brutality, five of which were submitted for consideration to the FBI.

The FBI referred them to the U.S. Department of Justice, which in turn ignored the matter, according to Morales.

The Reverend John P. Luce, rector of the Epiphany Parish in East Los Angeles, agreed with Morales that communication between Mexican-Americans and the Los Angeles police had broken down and said he feared "we are on a collision course in Los Angeles" along the lines of a "police-barrio confrontation." Rev. Luce charged that the Los Angeles police and sheriff departments "refuse to talk with militant and political leaders with whom they might disagree, with young people, with a whole variety of activist people who want change."

The Anglo clergyman told the Commission that the indictment of 13 Mexican-American leaders in the March 1968 East Los Angeles High School walkouts has led to the strong feeling that "the [Los Angeles] district attorney has singled out the Mexican community because he thought they were weaker than some other communities" but that he "miscalculated on this point, because the Mexican is organizing even that much more."

A Commission staff report said that

one of the most common complaints (throughout the Southwest) was that Anglo juvenile offenders are released to the custody of their parents and no charges are brought, while Mexican-American youths are charged with offenses, held in custody, and sent to a reformatory.

A counselor for the New Mexico State Employment Office told the Commission's Advisory Committee:

. . . I was very shocked when I became involved in working with young [Mexican-American] people . . . and found that charges were made against them, such as stealing cantaloupes out of a farmer's field, curfew violations, being truant from school, and things like this. These would all be on record and they all have quite extensive juvenile records. Among the Anglo people I work with, this just [isn't] done. I don't think the Anglo children are this much better.

The Commission's report further stated that it is felt throughout the Southwest that "the most serious police harassment involves interference with attempts by Mexican-Americans to organize themselves in order to assert their collective power."

To the advocates of brown or Chicano power, the Texas Rangers, or *Los Rinches,* are the symbols of this repression. The Texas Rangers is an elite 136-year-old statewide law-enforcement agency under the Texas Department of Public Safety. At the time of the hearing there were 62 Texas Rangers, none of them Mexican-Americans.

To the Mexican-American, especially the poor, such as the farm worker in the Rio Grande Valley, the Rangers in their Stetson hats, fancy boots, hand-tooled revolvers, and holsters personify everything they fear: tough-talking, rancher-grower types who can run you out of town at the slightest suspicion that the Mexican-Americans want to assert themselves.

"The Rangers are the cowboys and we're the Indians," say Mexican-Americans.

Farm workers, labor organizers, and civil-rights workers testified before the Commission that the Texas Rangers break agriculture worker strikes in the Rio Grande Valley through force and intimidation. The unionization of farm workers is seen as a holy war in Texas where farm hands get no workmen's compensation, no state minimum wage, no unemployment and disability insurance, and where there are no mandatory standards in farm worker housing. (In contrast, California requires by law all of these things.)

Reynaldo de la Cruz, 26, a farm worker and father of six children, who had been arrested six times for union activities, told the Commission he joined the union because of

what every Mexican-American farm worker faces, that they have been cheated too long . . . because I had been cheated too many times. [I joined the union] so that we could fight for our rights and for the rights of other people that don't know how to defend themselves.

Asked what the feeling of Mexican-Americans is toward the Texas Rangers, José M. Martinez, a farm worker, told the Commission:

Many people hate them, many people are afraid, because the majority of the Mexicans are not armed. They [Rangers] are armed. And when the Rangers are coming, then the people are afraid. They are afraid of being hit, or being pushed around. . . . The minute that you hear the Rangers are coming, everybody hides. If you are on strike, if you know the Rangers are coming, then they don't want to strike. This is the feeling of the people in the Valley. They are afraid.

Trying to determine what Mexican-Americans thought of government as an administrator of justice, Howard A. Glickstein, then Acting Staff Director of the Commission, asked farm worker de la Cruz whether in his work as a union organizer he saw the state government and state officials as friends or enemies.

De la Cruz: Well, considering that the Rangers are state officials, I think they are our enemies.

Glickstein: How do you view the federal government? What do you think of the role the federal government has played or hasn't played?

De la Cruz: Well, I am not too sure about the federal government. But if they were really our friends, then something would have been done when the Texas Rangers were messing with the strike.

Earlier, Pete Tijerina, executive director of the Mexican American Legal Defense and Educational Fund, had noted that the U.S. Attorney General had intervened on behalf of Negro cases throughout the South but that "not once, not once, has the Attorney General . . . intervened in any Mexican-American case."

The Reverend Edgar A. Krueger, an ordained minister whom the Texas Council of Churches sent to the Rio Grande Valley as an observer during a long farm workers' strike, told the Commission of his experiences with the Texas Rangers, including his arrest.

He said he went to Mission, Texas, one night, in the lower Rio Grande Valley, where he heard farm workers would be picketing. When he, his wife, and their 18-year-old son arrived at Mission he learned that twelve farm workers had been arrested. He spotted Ranger Captain Alfred Y. Allee and other Rangers in their parked cars in the drive-in bank on the other side of the railroad tracks. The Reverend Krueger said that since it was Friday night, "when people just gather, visit, and watch the cars go by," there were about 200 people on both sides of the tracks. But no one was trying to gather a crowd, no one was talking to the group, or trying to convince anyone to become a union member," the Reverend Krueger said. "No one was trying to stop the train, nor was anyone carrying a picket sign at that particular time. All we wanted to do was to find out where the persons had been taken that were arrested."

When the train arrived, the Texas Rangers with very long flashlights signaled the train to pass, the minister said, and he decided to take a picture with his wife's small camera from a hundred feet away. "About that time Captain Allee walked right straight down the west side of the street toward me," recalled the Reverend Krueger, "and said, as he was walking up, 'Krueger, I am sick and tired of seeing you around.' He grabbed me by the collar and the seat of the pants and lifted me practically to the center of the street."

Mrs. Krueger then took a picture of what was happening, the Reverend Krueger said.

"And then Captain Allee yelled, 'Grab that woman,'" the minister told the Commission. "Another Ranger grabbed my wife, and I didn't see it when it happened, but he grabbed her. But I did see later on that he had her arm twisted behind her back."

Captain Allee then turned the minister over to another Ranger and walked up to a farm worker, Magdaleno Dimas, who was eating a hamburger, the Reverend Krueger said.

"Captain Allee slapped the hamburger out of his hand," the Reverend Krueger continued,

and then with double hands slapped him in the face. . . . And then they took me [and Dimas] to the passing train. Since they were running around so rapidly there in something of a frenzy, I was very fearful when they held Dimas, it seemed like his head was just a few inches from the metal that was sticking out from the passing train and held us there beside the train while it was passing.

After manhandling Dimas some more, the minister, his wife, Dimas, and a friend were thrown into the back seat of a Ranger car and searched, the Reverend Krueger said. Seeing that the pipe of one of the men had bounced off the car doorway, the minister said: "It seemed like a very natural thing sitting on the edge of the seat like that to reach down and pick up his pipe. At that time Ranger Jack Van Cleve, with tremendous force, slapped me in the cheek." The Reverend Krueger, his wife, and friends were arraigned for unlawful assembly. This was a year and a half before the Commission hearing and up to then their case had not come to trial. In charging that the Texas Rangers and sheriff's deputies were "strike breakers," and completely partial to the growers, the Reverend Krueger told the Commission that a sheriff's deputy told him [Krueger] that if he really wanted to help "these people" he should tell them to go back to work.

"And there was an occasion when Captain Allee did say that if the [striking] farm workers wanted jobs he would see that they would get jobs," the Reverend Krueger told the Commission. "And he also said that if they didn't go to work that it would have a depressing effect on the whole Valley, and they would suffer and the whole Valley would suffer if they didn't get the cantaloupes out."

But perhaps the Reverend Krueger's most serious charge was that mass arrests by Rangers and other law-enforcement officers usually followed any success the strikers or union had. "For example," said the minister,

the night when my wife and 114 other persons were arrested. This was on the same day, I believe, that the Texas Advisory Committee to the U.S. Commission on Civil Rights finished their hearing in Starr County, in Rio Grande City, and it seemed that that hearing gave some support to the union's cause, and that same night people were arrested.

Arnulfo Guerra, a Rio Grande Valley attorney, charged that local and state government openly opposed the strike and the farm workers' right to organize and he said that the Rangers in particular

were entirely and completely partial to the growers. And I say this because the people who called them [Rangers] in was the county administration, and the county administration was completely and totally partial to the growers. It was a one-sided affair, and they [Rangers] were excessively partial....

Ranger Captain Allee, a 36-year veteran of the Texas Rangers, appeared before the Commission on the closing day of the San Antonio hearing.

Commission Acting General Counsel Rubin asked him why the Texas Rangers were sent to Starr County during the farm workers' strike.

Captain Allee: To keep peace and order and to protect the lives and property and to assist the sheriff's department.

Rubin: What was occurring at that time to warrant [the Rangers going to Starr County]?

Captain Allee: It is my understanding that it had been going on a good while and the United Farm Workers Organizing Committee was trying to organize the employees there.

Rubin: And that was the reason why... why... the Rangers [were] sent?

Captain Allee: That's right. There had been trouble, there was a railroad trestle had been burned and I had my sergeant down there before then and had one or two Rangers there.... [the Rangers] were sent... to make [an] investigation....

Asked why he had arrested the Reverend Krueger, Captain Alle said

he came up and talked to me, and he got pretty arrogant about it, and he was poking me on the chest with his finger and accused me of putting his men in jail. My people, he called them, my people. And he was loud and abusive.

And I got the Reverend Krueger by the belt and the collar and took him over to the car. On the way over there Mrs. Krueger, she had a camera and she was with him, and about that time I heard someone say, look out, captain. And he said, give me that camera, Mrs. Krueger, and he was Ranger Jack Van Cleve, and he said she attempted to hit me over the head with it.

Rubin wanted to know why the minister was arrested.

Captain Allee: I just got through telling you this, for [being] loud and abusive, and disturbing the peace. Language, of course, one thing and another is why I arrested him.

Rubin: What charge was placed against him?

Captain Allee: I don't know. I didn't file the complaint. I can get that for you and send it to you, if you wish.

Rubin: Did Reverend Krueger resist arrest?

Captain Allee: No, he didn't resist arrest.

Rubin: What did he do? You said that you lifted Reverend Krueger by the seat of his pants?

Captain Allee: No, I didn't lift him by the seat of the pants, I said I got him by the belt.

Rubin: By the belt?

Captain Allee: Yes, sir.

Rubin: Why was it necessary to do that?

Captain Allee: Well, I don't know why it was necessary to do it. . . . I usually grab a fellow by the belt if I am going to take him somewhere. Of course, he didn't especially want to go after I talked to him there a little while.

Later, Rubin wanted to know about the arrest of farm worker Dimas and whether the captain had slapped him.

Captain Allee: I slapped a hamburger out of his hand.

Rubin: Why did you do that?

Captain Allee: Well, he was trying to tell me something, I don't know what it was, and he was spitting that mustard. . . .

Asked what reputation the Texas Rangers have among Mexican-Americans, Captain Allee said:

Among Mexican-Americans I think they have a good reputation. I worked around the Mexican people all my life. I had a big percentage of the people of Starr, Texas, of Mexican-American people send a petition into Austin and I didn't request it, asking the Rangers to stay there because they feared violence and bloodshed. And that petition is on file. . . .

Questioned whether there were workers in the fields during the strike, Captain Allee responded:

Oh, yes, there were workers in the fields, lots of people working in the fields. I couldn't tell you whether they were from Starr County or not. Some of them were and some of them from across the border, the green card workers.

Glickstein: There were a lot of green card workers?

Captain Allee: I don't know how many.

Glickstein: They come across [the border] in the morning and go home at night?

Captain Allee: That's right.

It was as if Captain Allee was reminding Mexican-Americans what they have known for many years: If they rock the boat, they can always be replaced by cheaper Mexicans from across the border.

CONCLUSION

In restrospect, perhaps the most positive result of the hearing was that barrio Mexican-Americans came out of it with a feeling that the government does care about them.

This was no small accomplishment. To Mexicans *el gobierno,* the government, has traditionally been a natural enemy. Until the Revolution of 1910, which at last made Mexico a free country, Mexicans experienced foreign dictatorships—Spanish colonialism and the French-imposed Emperor Maximilian, for example—and domestic dictatorships, Santa Anna and Porfirio Diaz.

It is not surprising therefore that Mexican-Americans have an inherent distrust of government. The older ones remember that during the depression of the 1930s, the government "incited" Mexican resident aliens to leave the United States to what was almost certain worse poverty in Mexico. Many Mexican-Americans over 30 in the border areas can remember unpleasant moments at the hands of the U.S. Immigration and Customs agents at border crossings. They remember learning to live with the fear of deportation posed by *el gobierno* which at any moment might demand proof that they're American citizens and not Mexican nationals.

To many Mexican-Americans, dealings with *el gobierno* have always been unpleasant. The contacts with teachers, employment officials, social workers, police, and other representatives of *el gobierno* have, in many instances, left behind memories of mistreatment and insensitivity.

With the San Antonio hearing there was a breakthrough for Mexican-Americans who have felt neglected, if not persecuted, in the past by their government. They had been studied many times before San Antonio, but at the hearing, for the first time on a national platform, the problems of the Mexican-American were explored not only in the general sense but also in the specific.

The obvious challenges of discrimination in employment, competition of cheap labor from Mexico, inadequate education, police harassment, and cultural conflicts were again aired with a monotonous consistency, but there was a difference. This time the investigators talked face to face with members of the "establishment" involved in the areas indicated above and the Commission dealt in precise names, organizations, and systems accused of insensitivity toward the Mexican-American.

The hearing did not end in a tone of: "Look, we've got problems and something must be done." Instead, it ended saying in effect: "Look, these people and these situations are keeping us back and this has to be done."

Something else very valuable came out of the hearing—an underscoring of the gravity of the problems that are now bubbling to the surface in the Mexican-American community. Only the most insensitive spectator could miss the sense of urgency of the problems of the Mexican-Americans and the realization that delay in reaching solutions could only exacerbate those problems.

Following the hearing, though not necessarily because of it, the State of Texas appropriated money for its first bilingual education program, passed a minimum wage law for farm workers, raised the ceiling on money to be made available for welfare benefits, and enacted legislation to prevent confiscation of property outright for a missing delinquent house payment.

The hearing represented another step in a trend toward understanding of the Mexican-American which started a few years ago. The creation of the Inter-Agency Committee on Mexican American Affairs in June of 1967, by President Lyndon B. Johnson, showed a growing awareness by Washington of the Spanish-speaking population.

Making the Committee a permanent agency under President Nixon further indicated that the national government recognized that the Mexican-American had unique problems that required separate consideration from the seat of power.

The formation of the Southwest Council of La Raza and the Mexican American Legal Defense and Education Fund with the help of Ford Foundation money showed that the private sector was also interested.

But what probably has most warmed the Mexican-American to *el gobierno* is the government's growing concern for the uneducated and rural Mexican-American.

Congress' refusal to extend the bracero program was a significant victory for the Mexican-American farm workers who claimed braceros were taking jobs away from them.

The federal government's funding of the California Rural Legal Assistance through the Office of Economic Opportunity was further proof that Washington cared about Mexican-Americans, who comprise about 67 percent of the state's agricultural workers.

The CRLA was founded on the philosophy that the poor, like the rich, are entitled to good lawyers who take the time to serve their needs.

Mexican-American farm workers who, with their fellow black and Anglo colleagues, are the only major occupational group excluded from unemployment-insurance coverage and other federally conferred benefits such as collective-bargaining legislation, had now someone to represent them in court.

At least technically, the Mexican-American farm worker could now defend himself not only from powerful growers but from the government itself.

As for education, the passing of the Bilingual Education Act of 1967 recognized the absurdity of punishing children for speaking Spanish in the school grounds.

It also showed that the time would come when the knowledge of a second language would become an asset instead of a liability.

A stirring has occurred in the Mexican-American community itself. New groups are emerging, older ones are moving in new directions. There is a sense of mobility, typified by expressions of solidarity and demands for change. Not untypical of the mood was the gathering, several months after the San Antonio hearing, of some 1000 Mexican-Americans in Del Rio, Texas, to protest the termination of a VISTA program.

The hearing can be described as a piece of a mosaic, and it provided the groundwork for an even better understanding by the government of the Mexican-American. The information from the hearing was also extremely valuable in the comprehensive studies on Mexican-American education and the administration of justice in the Southwest undertaken by the Commission.

So stark was the picture of the Mexican-American in the Southwest drawn by the words of the witnesses, so evident was the need for additional resources, that the Commission subsequently approved the conversion of its temporary field office in San Antonio to a permanent installation.

Despite all this, and because change takes time, those attending the hearing could easily come to the conclusion that Mexican-Americans have been victims of fraud.

Much of the testimony showed how Mexican-Americans have been cheated of things most Americans take for granted: their right to their language, their culture, their color.

This was perhaps most poignantly expressed when Commissioner Hector P. Garcia asked Irene Ramirez, a San Antonio high-school girl, whether she wanted to have "nice things."

"Of course," answered Irene, "but from the very beginning we are taught . . . I mean, this is an impossible dream."

"What is impossible, dear?" Garcia asked.

"Going to college and achieving something . . . ," she answered.

This exchange dramatized to those attending the hearing that though lip service has always been paid to the theory that Mexican-Americans "are like any other Americans," in reality they are not.

The hearing showed that the Mexican-American has been made to feel negatively about his Mexican background—to the point where even the word "Mexican" has become a liability.

As a result, Mexican-Americans have tried to assimilate into Anglo society as quietly as possible. Some have succeeded. But, if the testimony is to be believed, the attempt at assimilation has failed for too many.

The feeling among activist Mexican-Americans—who prefer to call themselves Chicanos—is that Spanish-speaking people should resist any attempt to become American at the expense of their language and culture.

Chicanos also emphasize that assimilation for assimilation's sake has been oversold and that it must be learned once and for all that you can't turn a brown child into a white child through patriotic rhetoric.

The hearing may also have helped kill the myth that with time Mexican-Americans will assimilate as have the Irish, Italians, Polish, and other ethnic groups. This argument crumbles with the obvious fact that the United States and Mexico share an 1800-mile open border, and not an ocean as do the United States and Ireland.

The influence of Mexico on the Mexican-American will continue as long as Mexico is there.

The Americanization of the Mexican-American has too often meant that he must shun his background and assume a ridiculous role of being what has been described as a "tanned Anglo."

The hearing may have helped bring home an obvious historical fact: Mexicans are not strangers to this land, especially in the Southwest. They are indigenous to it.

The hearing may have focused a growing feeling among Mexican-Americans. That is, that they understand the importance of becoming Anglicized but that in the process they insist that Anglos become Mexicanized, if the melting-pot theory of America is to have value.

INDIANS IN HISTORY

Alvin M. Josephy, Jr.

It is only eighty years, less than the life span of men and women still alive, since the so-called Battle of Wounded Knee in December 1890. That massacre, in which some three hundred American Indian men, women, and children were slaughtered on the plains of South Dakota by the raking fire of Hotchkiss guns, ended the last desperate struggle for freedom by the Sioux people and brought to a close within our country what most Indians realize—and what historians must inevitably realize—was the military conquest of one race by another, begun in the Caribbean four hundred years before when Columbus landed on San Salvador Island. The historical significance of the long, armed conflict not only is still with us but is at the root of much of the understanding of the American past and present.

From the beginning, American Indians, their cultures, life styles, values, and history, have been closely interwoven with the course of the white man's affairs. Much of our culture and many of our attitudes about ourselves and peoples in the rest of the world reflect the Indian-white contact. Yet the true nature of the Indian's role is almost unknown to the non-Indian.

Almost twenty years ago Bernard DeVoto put his finger on one of the wellsprings of the problem. "Most of American history," he wrote, in an introduction to Joseph Kinsey Howard's *Strange Empire,*

has been written as if history were a function solely of white culture—in spite of the fact that

Reprinted by permission from The Atlantic *(June 1970), pp. 67–72; copyright ©
1970 by The Atlantic Monthly Co., Boston, Mass.*

till well into the nineteenth century the Indians were one of the principal determinants of historical events. . . . Disregarding Parkman's great example, American historians have made shockingly little effort to understand the life, the societies, the cultures, the thinking, and the feelings of Indians, and disastrously little effort to understand how all these affected white men and their societies.

A perceptive study done recently by Virgil J. Vogel, an assistant professor of history at Chicago City College, underscores what DeVoto wrote in 1952, and what is still pertinent today. Vogel examined more than one hundred major works on American history, many of them used as influential sources by other historians, and concluded that, as a body, they obliterated, defamed, disparaged, and disembodied the American Indian, creating and perpetuating false impressions about him and producing "deformed" history by not relating accurately or in proper proportion his role in our past.

The blackout of information about the Indians Vogel found particularly disturbing. As a case in point, he examined the historical treatment of the Trail of Tears, the forced removal of more than 125,000 Indians from the Southwest during the administrations of Andrew Jackson and Martin Van Buren, a cruel and tensely controversial episode that occurred in defiance of the Supreme Court, cost the lives of thousands of Indians, and brought hardships, suffering, and ruin to tens of thousands of others. Debate over the infamous removal policy racked the nation for a decade, pitted the President of the United States in a dramatic confrontation with the Chief Justice of the Supreme Court, increased conflict between North and South, and added to the states rights and nullification embers smoldering in the South prior to the Civil War.

Yet Vogel found few, and then usually little more than passing, references to the entire episode in the histories he examined. Edward Channing's *History of the United States*, W. E. Woodward's *A New American History*, Carl Becker's *The United States, Experiment in Democracy*, Francis Butler Simkins' *The South, Old and New*, and Charles and Mary Beard's *The Making of American Civilization, Basic History of the United States*, and *The Rise of American Civilization* were among the many general histories that either totally ignored mention of the removal policy or failed to tell what happened to the Indians. Even Arthur M. Schlesinger, Jr.'s full-length, Pulitzer Prize-winning treatment of that particular period, *The Age of Jackson*, included not a single word about the Indians' Trail of Tears.

Defamation and disparagement of the Indians, calling attention to their faults and none of their virtues, ignoring or denying their contributions, and condemning them to an inferior, or even subhuman, species in intelligence and adaptability, colored almost every work of history that Vogel encountered. Many historians termed them dirty, lazy, brutish, unproductive, and on a level with wild beasts.

Vogel found the theme of denigration continuing unabashedly even into modern-day works, whose author added patent untruths about the Indians. "The Indians had no bona-fide medicine to speak of," wrote Alden T. Vaughan in *New England Frontier* (in fact, Vogel pointed out, the Indians of North America used about 150 medicines which were later included in the *U.S. Pharmacopeia* and *National Formulary*, and the Indians of Latin America contributed about fifty more). "American civilization . . . owed very little to the aborigines of the New World," commented Richard N. Current and his collaborators, T. Harry Williams and Frank Freidel, in their *American History, A Survey*: " . . . none had any conception of the wheel." (False: the wheel was known in Middle

America and was used on children's toys.)

Research beyond Vogel's work will provide anyone willing to make the effort with abundant examples to add to his list. The storehouse of sectional, state, cultural, intellectual, and specialized histories shows, almost without exception, the same sort of treatment of Indians. Typical of such works is Charles S. Sydnor's *The Development of Southern Sectionalism 1819–1848,* whose stated purpose was to present a "full and impartial study of the South and its part in American history." In the text's 399 pages, there are only four brief references to the political and legal contest between the federal and state governments over the Indians' presence in the South and none at all to the Indian peoples themselves or to what happened to them. The word Cherokee appears three times in the volume, but not in the index, and there are no references to works on Indian affairs in the otherwise ample bibliography. Similarly, Perry Miller's two volumes on the New England mind in the seventeenth century almost entirely ignore the Indians' presence among the Puritans. The work carries as a frontispiece in both volumes an early New England woodcut view of Boston, with a benign-looking Indian, looming prominently in the foreground as if symbolizing the presence and influence of Indians in New England colonial life. In the text the Indian is given short shrift, even though it is a study of the century that saw the great King Philip's War threaten the presence *of the white man* in New England.

Major works such as these, resting on original research that gives them authority, set the tone and attitude for lowlier but more numerous studies. In recent years, they too—elementary, high school, and college textbooks, readers, and teachers' guides —have begun to come under scrutiny. In an article which appeared last fall in *The Indian Historian,* a respected and authoritative journal of Indian history published in San Francisco by Indian scholars, Lowell John Bean, an anthropology professor at California State College, Hayward, tore apart a children's text used in the fourth grade in the California public-school system, analyzing and correcting a multitude of inaccuracies, distortions, untruths, half-truths, omissions, and stereotyped images of California Indians, and concluded,

What distortions of truth are passed on from one reader to another in California's public schools? What distortions of self-image are being acquired by California's Indian children who are exposed to this book ... ? The children and their teachers have every right to expect a book such as this to represent the truth. This type of literature must not go unchallenged.

Among Indians themselves, as might be expected, dissatisfaction with histories and school textbooks is not new. In 1965, Rupert Costo, a California Cahuilla Indian scholar, wrote in *The Indian Historian,* "No matter who he may be, the Indian backs away in disgust and horror from most textbooks used to teach children American history."

As far back as 1928, Indians living in Chicago and grouped in an organization known as the Grand Council Fire of American Indians addressed a Memorial to William Hale Thompson, the Chicago mayor, who was then criticizing school books for being pro-British. "We do not know if school histories are pro-British," the Indians said,

but we do know that they are unjust to the life of our people—the American Indian. . . . History books teach that Indians were murderers—is it murder to fight in self-defense? Indians killed white men because white men took their lands, ruined their hunting grounds, burned their forests, destroyed their buffalo. . . . White men who rise to protect their property are called patriots—Indians who do the same are called murderers. White men call the Indians treacherous—but no mention is made of broken treaties on the part of the white man. . . . White men called Indians thieves—and yet we lived in frail skin lodges and needed no locks or iron bars. White men called Indians savages. What is civilization? Its marks are a noble religion and philosophy, original arts, stirring music, rich story and legend. We had these . . . . Tell your children of the friendly acts of Indians to the white people who first settled here. . . . The Indian has long been hurt by these unfair books. We ask only that our story be told in fairness.

For many years, California Indian scholars working with the editors of *The Indian Historian* have been engaged in a professional program of evaluating and criticizing books used in the California school system and elsewhere. "Our Committee read 15 basic and supplementary textbooks," an interim report said. "Not one was free from error and misrepresentation. At least three should be replaced as quickly as possible. All others need extensive revision."

In recent years, non-Indian agencies, often under pressure from Indian groups, have begun to make their own studies. Their results, as of last year, were noted in a report on the status of Indian education issued in the fall of 1969 by a subcommittee of the U.S. Senate Committee on Labor and Public Welfare.

A report prepared for the subcommittee by the University of Alaska showed that: (1) twenty widely used texts contain no mention of Alaska Natives at all. . . . ; (2) although some textbooks provide some coverage of the Alaskan Eskimo, very few even mention Indians; and (3) many texts at the elementary and secondary level contain serious and often demeaning inaccuracies in their treatment of the Alaskan Native.

"A similar study by the University of Idaho," the subcommittee's report went on,

found Indians continually depicted as inarticulate, backward, unable to adjust to modern Euro-American culture, sly, vicious, barbaric, superstitious, and destined to extinction. Minnesota has for years been using an elementary-school social-studies text which depicts Indians as lazy savages capable of doing little more than hunting, fishing, and harvesting wild rice. California, with its progressive public-school program, found in a study of 43 texts used in fourth, fifth, and eighth grades that hardly any mention at all was made of the American Indian's contribution or of his role in the colonial period, gold-rush era or mission period of California history, and, when mentioned, the reference was usually distorted or misinterpreted.

The states cited, it might be noted, all have large populations of Indian children being taught about their ancestors from these books. At the same time, in New York, the Association on American Indian Affairs, an Indian-interest group supported by contributions principally from non-Indians, analyzed high-school textbooks used throughout the country and found that only one in the 75 examined was adequate in its treatment of Indians.

What is "adequate" in the historic treatment of Indians? One criterion, certainly, is to treat history accurately and whole, giving fair and balanced attention to all the groups of humans who were involved. The idea is not unique, and, indeed, is being given strong voice today by blacks and other minority groups about the telling of their own roles in American and world history. In the case of the Indians, it means giving proper representation to their side of history and to their presence and achievements in the Western Hemisphere before the "discovery" by Columbus; their spiritual beliefs, social and political organizations; their patriotic motives in fighting to save their homelands and existence; their foods, medicines, utensils, articles of clothing, means of transportation, words, ideas of government, liberty, and the individual worth and dignity of man, much of it bequeathed to the white man by the Iroquois, Delaware, and other tribes. It means conveying an understanding that the so-called "savages" were actually in harmony with nature and their environment; that they had perfect levels of social and political organization, completely right for the size of each group; that they possessed rich and sophisticated cultural heritages that included music, dance, arts, crafts, and lore; and that their values encompassed many that we wish today for modern civilization.

It means, moreover, removing blinders about aspects of Indian-white relations that add perspectives to American history as a whole, such as the Indians' original friendship, everywhere, toward whites; the slave-catchers and others who turned them against whites even before the first settlers arrived; the great Indian war for religious freedom in New Mexico in 1680, when the Pueblos drove all Spaniards out of that region; the organization of the League of the Iroquois and its impact on the political thinking of the English colonists; the struggle of Tecumseh in the early nineteenth century to create an Indian state which might eventually have joined the United States; the victory of Little Turtle and his Indian allies over General Arthur St. Clair in 1791 in which some 600 U.S. troops lost their lives, more than twice the number Custer lost at the Little Big Horn; and the federal government's use of Christian churches to run the Indian reservations in the 1870s (a startling example of the joining of church and state in the United States).

"We are the bad guys who burned the wagon trains," said Vine Deloria, Jr., a Standing Rock Sioux Indian in his book *Custer Died for Your Sins,* an eloquent statement of the problems the white man has made for the Indians. That enduring image of the raiding, war-whooping Indian still dominates textbooks, novels, movies, and television programs. But back in 1883, Sarah Winnemucca, a Northern Paiute Indian woman from Nevada who had received education in the white men's schools, told in her book *Life Among the Paiutes* how the Indian families were so afraid of the hostile white men streaming through their land in covered wagons that, though they had to get from one side of the trail to the other, they hid during the day and crossed only at night. A new image?

The telling of history straight and whole —as it was—about the Indians, so that we see them as real societies of fathers of families, mothers afraid for their children, patriots, statesmen, wise men, cowards, lovers, and fools (not all men were braves and not all spokesmen were chiefs), implies acceptance of concepts and points of view that not all historians will recognize or welcome.

Since the days of Jamestown and Plymouth, and the writings of John Smith and William Bradford, the relating of American history by white historians has reflected their own Western-civilization-based point of view, as well might have been expected, but what they wrote has also been self-serving. The frontier Indian, resisting white expansion and domination, *had* to be a skulking savage. To the seeker of his land, he *had* to be an aimless nomad. To the exploiter, he *had* to be irresponsible and drunken. To the civilizer, he *had* to be lazy. Even the romantic, the poet, and the philosopher had to give the Indian a false image: to them he was the noble child of nature. To almost no one could he be real.

Today, the historian who wishes to convey a better sense of the true history of Indians has little reliable historical literature on which to draw. Three and a half centuries of telling American history from the point of view of the intruder, moving from East to West across the continent in the wake of "discoverers," "explorers," "openers of the country," provide scant groundwork for a new approach. The answer, so far, seems to be to tack on, as a sort of preface prior to discussing "The Age of Discovery," an appreciative survey of 25,000 years of Indian history in the Western Hemisphere before the coming of the white man, and then to touch base conscientiously with the Indians as often as appears correct through the main body of the text.

This approach was followed by Samuel Eliot Morison and Henry Steele Commager's *The Growth of the American Republic* with enough success to win praise from Vogel as "perhaps the most nearly flawless college text" from the point of view of its attention to Indians. Still, the work—though indeed a monumental improvement over most other general histories in its treatment of the Indians—is inexact in many archaeological and anthropological details which, were they errors in history, would not be tolerated by the authors, and the principal body of the text contains enough other flaws to make clear the dimensions of the wilderness in which the historian must wander when he genuinely seeks learning on Indian matters.

He must examine colonial, territorial, War Department, Indian Bureau, and other governmental agency archival records, with which he will feel comfortable, but he must also pore through the very valuable historical researches that accompanied Indian claims cases. He must become familiar with the pertinent diaries, logbooks, letters, and other writings of explorers, trappers, traders, missionaries, artists, soldiers, miners, settlers, and government agents, some of them French, some Spanish, some English, many of them obscure, but all of them potential suppliers of new insights, as well as information, about the Indians with whom they came in contact.

He must learn the versions and lore of the tribes themselves, listen to the oral history of those who kept the records from generation to generation, and read the published and unpublished writings of Indians who tell, truer than most historians have been willing to believe, what really happened, at least on the Indian side. Books like *Black Elk Speaks,* a narrative history of the Oglala Sioux told by an Oglala holy man; *Cheyenne Memories,* a Northern Cheyenne history written by a Cheyenne scholar, John Stands In Timber; and *Two Leggings,* the narrative of a nineteenth-century Crow, relate better than any white man's account could, the thinking and feelings of the people of those tribes that made them act and react as they did during the turbulent period of the Plains wars. Written without the benefit of the perspectives of these books, chapters on the history of those wars—and there have been plenty of such works that reflect only the white man's point of view about what the Indians did and why—must inevitably be deficient. Finally, and perhaps most important of all, the historian will have to enter the door of other disciplines, drawing particularly on the great mass of archaeological and ethnological studies that are already available, and becoming, in the process, enough of an ethnohistorian to make the Indians three-dimensional and understandable when he writes about them.

There are now some 750,000 Indians and Eskimos in the United States, and many of their children are attending schools and colleges where they are subjected to the use of insulting books. Their high dropout rates, self-hatred, a suicide rate far in excess of the national average, and their lack of motivation can be traced in great part to the feelings of disgrace and humiliation they suffer from their continual confrontation with stereotype thinking about them.

From the point of view of the American people as a whole, the damage is just as serious. The problems we have created for the Indians continue to defy solution because we do not know their history or their true nature. To our detriment, we do not know what they might be able to teach us about conservation, the rearing of children, psychosomatic medicine, and the attainment of harmonious and ordered lives. And we fail utterly to appreciate how knowledge of our mistakes in our treatment of the Indians might now help us in our relations with other peoples in the world.

Fortunately, a number of correctives to the long centuries of blackouts, distortions, and misinformation are beginning to appear. More and better books, written by Indians and non-Indians, and explaining the historic causes of present-day problems, are beginning to appear. Notable among them are Vine Deloria, Jr.'s, *Custer Died for Your Sins,* Stan Steiner's *The New Indians,* the Citizens Advocate Center's *Our Brother's Keeper,* Jack D. Forbes's *The Indian in America's Past,* and Stewart Levine's and Nancy O. Lurie's *The American Indian Today.* Even the field of fiction has struck newly realistic notes for the Indian with Thomas Berger's *Little Big Man* (now being made into a movie, with Indians playing most of the Indian roles) and the Pulitzer Prize novel for 1969, *House Made of Dawn,* by N. Scott Momaday.

In the mass-communications field, the television industry, with its endless stock portrayals of Indians that never existed, has many sins to live down, including a series that glorified Custer, which pressure by angry Indians two years ago forced the offending network to cancel. But in its journalistic programs filmed on Indian reservations, its discussion panels on Indian affairs, and its documentaries that are beginning to deal with Indian history, television is starting to make amends. One of TV's outstanding ventures is a documentary history of the Cherokee's Trail of Tears, the first of a projected series of four programs on Indians produced by National Educational Television for countrywide

showing. Filmed on the same sites in the South where the history occurred, the film stars Johnny Cash, himself a descendant of Cherokees, playing the role of John Ross, the principal chief of the Cherokee nation during the time of the tribe's forced removal to the West. The drama of the program is matched by the faithfulness with which it recreates the true history of what happened to the Indians.

At the same time, Indians themselves are beginning to research and write their own tribal histories, principally for the use of their people and for the schools on their reservations or in the states in which the reservations are located. Programs for such histories, undertaken by Indian scholars and sometimes aided by non-Indian historians and anthropologists, are under way among the Poncas, Choctaws, Pawnees, Blackfeet, Navajo, Rosebud Sioux, and Quinaults, among other tribes, while in various cities and on Alcatraz Island, which the Indians occupied in dramatic fashion last November, groups of Indians who have lived urbanized existences and come from many different tribes have created Indian cultural centers to teach their own people Indian history, language, and culture.

Demands by Indians and various of their organizations, including the National Congress of American Indians and the National Indian Youth Council, have also stirred many universities into new activities. With a $500,000 annual grant from the Doris Duke Foundation, six of them—the universities of Utah, Arizona, Illinois, New Mexico, Oklahoma, and South Dakota—embarked several years ago on an ambitious Indian oral-history program, sending interviewers with tape recorders onto reservations to record the legends, lore, and histories from the Indians themselves. Transcripts from the tapes already run into thousands of manuscript pages and will provide the raw materials for many history books of the future. In addition, courses in Indian studies and revised courses in American history that include a fuller and fairer treatment of the American Indian are being included in the curriculum of many colleges and universities. Perhaps the most important milestone was reached in March at Princeton University, with the holding of a four-day convocation of American Indian scholars under the auspices of the American Indian Historical Society and funded by a grant from the Ford Foundation. The Indian participants, who came from Canada, Mexico, and South America, and the United States, met with the determination that

the leadership and authority of the American Indian in all fields affecting our history, culture, economic improvement, and social development must be asserted if any progress is to be attained by our people.

In a series of panels, the participants read and discussed papers that ranged in subject from "Philosophy of the American Indian and Relation to the Modern World" to "Modern Psychology and Child Development: The Native American Case." The meeting was all-Indian; whites were limited to a few academic and professional observers.

On the elementary and high-school level, also, new winds are blowing. In Montana, as an example, the histories of the tribes in that state are being added to the curriculum of the public-school system, largely under the guidance of John Woodenleg, a former tribal chairman of the Northern Cheyenne Indians and a descendant of a Cheyenne leader at the Battle of Little Big Horn.

Finally, the last few years have seen a proliferation of Indian newspapers and magazines, written, edited, and published by Indians on reservations and in various cities, and carrying articles on Indian history and lore, as well as news about Indian affairs. Designed primarily to be read by Indians, they have attracted the attention of many whites also, and some of them enjoy large national circulations among non-Indian readers.

"It is up to us to write the final chapter of the American Indian upon this continent," wrote Vine Deloria, Jr. Perhaps that is the way it will happen. But for the present there is plenty of work to do, by Indians and non-Indians laboring together, to set straight the chapters already written.

8

Programs, Power, and the Poor

ORGANIZING FOR CHANGE

The Editors

The previous section dealt with the current form of domestic poverty and the relation of this poverty to racial inequality and injustice. In this section the emphasis will be upon the programs which have emerged to combat poverty and upon those aspects of the new poverty that have not been met by existing programs. The new poverty is clearly related to the cybernetic revolution which is in turn related to the development of technological militarism. The latter encourages the technician, displaces the untrained, and invests federal funds into the area of defense which does not benefit the poor. Also new is the fact that poverty is occurring at a time of general prosperity which is clearly visible to the poor.

By and large, the modern poor are trapped in islands of rural and inner-city poverty. They own neither the land nor the shops nor industries which they sometimes occupy. The employers, shopkeepers, store managers, landlords, lending agencies, as well as the police, social workers, hospital workers, and teachers who work in these pockets of poverty, represent a culture different from and sometimes alien to the ways of life of the poor residents. These outside helpers and entrepreneurs, who live in ways strangely dependent upon the culture of continuous poverty, are carriers of a different set of norms and values. The values of their culture (the dominant middle-class culture) are that individual success in the competitive marketplace is the mark of individual worth. That the dominance of large organizations dependent on long-range planning has made such a criterion for success illusory does not prevent these culture carriers from retaining the view, or from assuming that it has universal applicability to the large number of disadvantaged. The culture carriers themselves have reached a moderate success in the culture. Why can the impoverished not do the same?

The answer given to this question varies with one's ideology. A conservative will say that the poor are deficient in the motivation or directed intelligence requisite for reaching the good life and therefore are themselves to blame. The liberal will transplant the blame for the deficiencies to inadequate opportunities to develop the appropriate motivation and patterns of thought by which an individual is sometimes capable of raising himself from humble origins. Whatever the cause or the source of blame for the deficiencies may be, this process of transformation from impoverished existence is by no means an easy one. The Negro child who, by four years of age, shows his self-image by selecting the white doll as nicer and more attractive, the child whose father has deserted because the experience of not being a good provider became too great a threat to his manhood—these children are impaired before the agencies of society can reach them. Many other situations make mobility difficult for the poor: jobs depend on good education, education depends on access to good schools, good schools depend on access to good neighborhoods, which is curtailed by discrimination and by poverty itself. This is what is meant by the cycle of poverty.

Where the conservative and liberal statements merge is in the shared view that the poor are individuals who for some reason suffer deficiencies in achievement-motivation, stimulation, education, scholastic ability, training, capacity for saving or for delayed gratification, or employment opportunity. Given such a philosophy the poor are seen as a problem because they lack the virtues and assets of the middle class. Programs for the general welfare have generally been geared for those sufficiently imbued with middle-class characteristics to have the desire and know-how to gain from them. There has developed a communication gap between those who are poor and the agencies which are supposed to help them. Such a gap was clearly in evidence when a convention of representatives of the poor hooted down Sargent Shriver, the Director of the Office of Economic Opportunity, an official and spokesman for the nation's antipoverty program.

The problem stems from the fact that the poor do not see themselves as problem cases in need of restitution. Rather they are inclined to see their better-off peers not as superior in virtue or competence but rather as better placed, more powerful, and wealthier to begin with. Lacking such position, power, or wealth in the dominant culture, the poor have been prone to establish subcultural adjustments. This is not to say that life in the ghetto or in the tenant farm is a tolerable experience or that the junkie culture, the gang culture, the revivalist sects, or even the strong familial ties that sometimes develop can compensate for the degradation of poverty. We are trying to say rather that many of the poor see themselves as people rather than as problem cases; they see the adjustment patterns relevant to living in the slum or amidst a band of sharecroppers as meaningful to their real problems. They see the ways of the middle-class world as lacking in any special virtue, hypocritical in its professions of equality, and certainly irrelevant to the immediate problems of life among the deprived.

This country is now engaged in numerous programs to combat poverty and inequality. Whether these programs were motivated by the United States' embarrassment at having a domestic poor while involved in a cold-war struggle for influence over the poorer countries, or by fears of domestic disorder and violence, or by a long overdue concern for human decency, the programs have not been markedly successful either in the objective raising of living standards or in the subjective change of the opinions of the poor. Parker's article, "The Myth of Middle America" (see Chapter 7), documents this standstill as do Harrington (1970) and Marris and Rein (1969).

The most striking controversy over the focusing of poverty programs toward cultural patterns viewed as untenable in American society occurred over the Moynihan report on the Negro family (discussed in the introduction to Chapter 7). The issue dealt with whether the cycle of poverty among ghetto blacks is due basically to a family pattern of maternal dominance and low self-esteem for males or, on the other hand, whether the absence of jobs and of power is most critical. The Moynihan emphasis in favor of heads of families marked a change of focus from the Economic Opportunity Act of 1964 where the target population was almost exclusively youth. But from the beginning, federal programs have tended to treat the culture of poverty as a deficiency system which would somehow disappear if skills and educational levels were upgraded. The approach favors the most capable among the poor and leaves out the aged, the alienated, the disabled, the handicapped, and the migratory workers, all of whom are harder to reach.

The failure is repeated in housing. Federal planners have decided that slum housing represents a blight to the city. Their response has been to declare certain areas targets for the bulldozer, and large contractors and developers were given subsidies to reduce their costs (but not necessarily their prices) for building new structures. The renewed areas help to meet the housing needs of somewhat more affluent tenants. But what of the original tenants? Despite some legislation aimed at assistance in relocation, studies show that the majority of them have been forced out of the area into other slums where they are paying an even greater proportion of their small income for rents (Gans, 1965). Marc Fried's study of tenants forced out of their rundown housing in the West End of Boston showed that they were seriously distressed by the loss of social ties. Thirty-eight percent of the men and 46 percent of the women showed "a fairly severe grief reaction or worse" resulting from their forced moves. For many the state of depression was still evident at the time of a follow-up interview two years later (Fried, 1963).

The issue of housing illustrates clearly that the effect of governmental programs cannot be understood in a piecemeal approach. Neither urban decay nor suburban sprawl are the product of individual and federal decisions about housing alone. Easing of credit on federally guaranteed loans is a subsidization for the white city dweller's flight to the suburbs. Similarly, the earmarking of gasoline taxes for expressways rather than for public transportation helps to move industry from the central city, leaving a soon-to-be-majority of nonwhite poor living in substandard housing in the central cities with an inadequate tax base to support schools and services. Even the heavy federal subsidization of agricultural research has sped the mechanization of agriculture and the consequent flight of poor southerners, black and white, to northern cities (Weissbourd, 1964).

If we give credence to the view that various poor communities have developed coping methods which are in fact responsive to the poverty inflicted upon them, then we are acknowledging one of the more positive aspects of the culture of poverty. It is not only the marginality and despair of the poor, but also a set of adaptive survival mechanisms that are extremely difficult for the middle-class planner or professional to comprehend. The culture of poverty often has a tenacity that makes unsatisfactory those procedures of assistance and services which have been designed elsewhere. One challenge to professionals, then, is to find representatives of the poor who can translate the need into new programs and who can be sufficiently close to the poor to deliver the service (Miller, 1963). The most frequently designated target population for new services are the children since it is often hoped that early intervention, perhaps in the educational system, will help to break the image of failure which an impoverished existence certainly accentuates. One problem in working at poverty through children is that poor children have already suffered deprivation and enter school with a handicap that tends to increase with time. Another problem is that effective school programs require participation and support from the home and other parts of the community. These requirements mean that programs must come closer to the particular perceptions and strivings of the deprived communities. This is difficult to do; the minority poor have learned to distrust "whitey."

Any attempt to make the schools an agency for eradicating poverty and inequality must soon come to grip with the inadequacy of school resources, the irrelevance of much of the school curriculum, and the vested interests of educational professionals. Edgar Friedenberg's article on school withdrawal points a critical finger at the goals and techniques of the educational system. He feels that the shortcomings of the system cut even more deeply than the pressing need for more teachers and classrooms or better pay for teachers. These shortages, which result in routinized, mechanical procedures, can sometimes be overcome by daring experiments which take the child and his own experience as the starting point for all forms of instruction. Books like *The Open Classroom* and *Teaching as a Subversive Activity* are already beginning to capture the imagination of some teachers. These teachers, however, find little support for reasons shown here by Friedenberg and elaborated in Freire's *Pedagogy of the Oppressed*. The school system is not geared to education. It is more a detention center geared to custodial care of poor children and advancement into the business and professional world for the child least in need of help. With few exceptions, the child in poverty faces a system with almost nothing relevant to offer. The failure is dramatically depicted by Janet Sideman in "Death of a Dropout," an account of a bright black teenager, her student, who dropped out of a high school with inadequate facilities (even the textbooks failed to arrive when needed) and with a program based upon unfounded assumptions about black youth.

Perhaps it is useless to investigate who was to blame for putting Clarence Brooker and hundreds of other dropouts on the street. The Negro child's education must be structured, it must be consistent. So he is taught to identify abstractions with visual things on the assumption that abstractions are too much for him to handle. He then becomes dependent on material symbols and equipment, and then in the cruelest inconsistency of all, is provided with schools that have substandard equipment, and little or no material to satisfy this dependency. His private life is full of tension and conflict, so he is given work where tension and conflict are eliminated and he never learns to cope with them.

He faces inequality, therefore he is taught conformity, which is mistaken for equality. He never conceives of a class as a miniature community, where people of different character and ability have to live together. And he never experiences equality, since he must have authority, which by its very definition means that someone is above him.

Well, one May evening Clarence Brooker, who was too smart for his own good and couldn't stick it out, dropped a bag of cookies in front of a policeman and was shot. Did he know why he dropped it? The policeman symbolized authority? But this authority wasn't going to be walked over, he carried a gun to prove it. If he were not a dropout, would Clarence be alive today? Who can say? He got an A on his adverbs. (Sideman, 1967, p. 14.)

Insufficient funds and a lack of follow-through have been much more a part of the welfare programs designed to be part of a war on poverty than they have been to defense-related programs like the space and anti-ballistic-missile programs. These priorities reflect the process of political decision making at the highest levels. The process has its counterpart at state and local levels. The Mississippi legislature recently met in special session to consider a special dispensation for a large industrial firm. This is not particularly striking except that one week before, a group of physicians had released the findings of their study of health needs in Mississippi. The report stated that a sizable number of rural Mississippians were living under conditions where extreme malnutrition was a cause of death and disease, particularly among the young. No special session was called to remedy this circumstance.

Most federal projects which are intended to provide jobs, or special education, or voting rights to the disadvantaged have been administered by local authorities and local leaders of the community. These authorities and these leaders reflect the positions of the prevailing loci of power in their communities. Programs have not been used to make dramatic changes in power or wealth of the poorer community. They have been inclined rather to reinforce existing lines of power by providing a system of rewards, jobs, ballots, surplus food, or welfare checks which can be used as a means of pacification or for the purchase of patronage. Such use is not conducive to acceptance of the agent of welfare into the poor community and makes little inroad into the cycle of poverty previously described. Again, it is clearly evident that certain dedicated professionals and certain leaders among the poor have not accepted a definition of the program which leaves its direction in the hands of existing authorities. It is to the credit of one Head Start program in particular, the Child Development Group of Mississippi (Levin, 1967), that it sought direction and leadership from the poor community and consequently won the support and community involvement needed for educational improvement. Levin indicates how the group was able to take a Head Start Project that was designed to be a social-service program dominated by professionalism and convert it into a community-action program run by local committees of poor people responsible for the organization and administration of the program. The program's gradual success and its ultimate undoing both stemmed from the fact of community control.

Levin suggests that the success of a community-action program depends on the choices made about its organization and purposes. He further indicates that these choices are reflected in five confrontation positions for evaluating the place of the poor in community programs.

Position 1

POVERTY PROGRAM RUN FROM ABOVE WITHOUT THE
DISABILITIES AND VITALITY OF THE POOR

versus

CHAOTIC MOVEMENT WITH DIRECTION DEVELOPING
THROUGH LEARNING

Position 2

THE "COMMUNITY" DEFINED AS A POLITICAL SUBDIVISION
RESULTING IN A SOCIOLOGICAL MONSTROSITY

versus

ORGANIC INTEGRITY OF THE NATURAL COMMUNITY

Position 3

THE CONCEPT OF "QUALIFIED" AS A WAY OF RELEGATING
THE POOR TO MENIAL AND SUBSERVIENT FUNCTIONS

versus

AN APPRECIATION OF THE POTENTIAL FOR "QUALITY"
TEACHING AVAILABLE THROUGH FULL UTILIZATION OF
THE SKILLS OF THE INDIGENOUS POOR

Position 4

INTEGRATION AS A PROCESS REMINISCENT OF THE
INGESTION OF THE LAMB BY THE WOLF

versus

INTEGRATION POSTULATED ON EQUIVALENT ECONOMIC
AND SOCIAL POWER

Position 5

"FEAR AND TREMBLING" OF THE LAW-ABIDING IN THE
PRESENCE OF THE "LAW-ABIDERS"

versus

AN ACCEPTANCE OF "THE MOVEMENT" (WITHIN ITS
REALITY DEFINITION) AS THE ONLY CHANNEL OF
COMMUNICATION WITH THE NEGRO POOR AND THE ONLY
SOURCE OF ACCEPTABLE LEADERSHIP

Despite Levin's apparent success in organizing 84 action-oriented centers in 50 urban and rural poor communities in Mississippi, the strong sense of community involvement proved to be too great a threat to the existing power alignment of the state. Evidence collected of better health care and nutrition as well as learning proved irrelevant to the program's continuation. Social scientists find it hard to accept the fact that their objective evaluation of programs often has little to do with the real world. To recognize the fact would be to admit that social research which fails to examine political realities is worth very little. Levin, the program director, was obliged by OEO to resign and finally the entire program was attacked and forced to curtail its activities.

The Child Development Group of Mississippi achieved its success in assisting children and their parents out of lives of resignation to impoverishment by recognizing the competencies of poor people and by granting them the responsibilities for their own programs. CDGM refused to be like other programs which fought the war on poverty as if the poor were some remote and irresponsible enemy to be managed, bribed, coerced, trained, and fed but never allowed a place to develop a real sense of potency. The project demonstrated the ability of the poor to run their own community programs. This autonomy proved to be its undoing. The problem is one of power conflict between an existing social order favoring a status quo and an ascending order demanding change. It is not particularly a southern problem as the example may suggest, for Mobilization for Youth in New York City ran into similar conflicts with the existing educational and political hierarchies. It appears that community-action programs based on the participation of the poor were an early casualty in the War on Poverty (Moynihan, 1969).

There is an obvious need for enlisting poor people in roles in which they might obtain social mobility while providing service to their own subcultures. The idea behind use of nonprofessionals as school aides or "medics" in free clinics was captured by Riessman in his assessment of the revolutionary potential of employing paraprofessionals in social work (Pearl and Riessman, 1965). The plan came to national fruition as the New Careers Program which promised not only to reform social services and to meet pressing community needs but, most important, to do all this by employing large numbers of poor people in jobs that gave them alternative ladders to skilled or professional careers. There have been a number of interesting cases of protest and disruption in agencies employing new careerists. The failures of the program appear more noticeable than the successes. First, jobs have been scarce and the new careerists are a threat to those who have acquired skilled jobs through more traditional routes of education, training, or seniority. Second, when the poor do show the ability to perform and manage the services and resources of their own communities, the custodians of these services—professionals and administrators—show a great reluctance to move over (Haber, 1971).

What is generally at issue in the various instances of disapproval and unrest is who sets the terms (the conditions, the priorities for the administration of antipoverty programs), and who is to be protected or sacrificed in the rush of the deprived for greater control over the police, housing, welfare, political, or commercial institutions that establish the constraints under which the poor live.

In some instances OEO has successfully created a federally sponsored organization of the poor which has been effective in wresting control from local interests. In Western Kentucky it was to the interest not only of the impoverished Appalachian miner but also of the liberal governor and of the larger corporations seeking to enter the area to drive out the extremely conservative, independent mine operators whose strip-mining techniques have not only defaced the land but also have displaced the people. Such coalition of interests is not the ordinary case nor does it seem destined to last once the strip miners and small landowners are successfully fought in the courts and driven from the area.

The poor obviously need allies. Even the most successful of their indigenous community-based efforts, as in the case of certain rent strikes (Lipsky, 1969) or such radical groups as the Newark Community Union or Chicago's JOIN project (Gitlin, 1971), must find some coalition for a base of power. When the coalition shows signs of wresting political control from established urban political machines, the organizing group will find itself subject to harassment often leading to violence. There is, however, another coalition that is less vulnerable to harassment. It is the welfare corporation and its key feature is the attempt to make measures for fighting poverty lucrative through federal contracts to giant corporations. The same type of federal subsidy has gone to such major conglomerates as Litton Industries for job training. Litton fulfilled its contract by recruiting poor youth from all over the country, housing them in old army barracks at Pleasanton, California, drilling them to the point where they could pass the selective-service literacy test, encouraging them to enlist, and, that failing, notifying their local draft boards of a change of classification. The effect is almost the same as the Army's Project 100,000 which selected "1Y" draft rejects for a second chance to route them out of the ghettos and into successful careers in the military and beyond. The fact that people here are not considered worthy of having a choice about what happens to them is typical of large programs administered from above by corporate or military planners.

The Urban Coalition of corporations, foundations, financial institutions, and government officials was created in 1967 to bring the corporate state behind the task of ghetto reform. On the local level, affiliate coalitions in forty major cities included responsible representatives from the black community. The natural interests of the business community in this field are (1) maintaining and training the labor supply, (2) preventing property destruction, (3) increasing consumption, (4) maintaining stability and, perhaps first in order of importance, making profits on government-subsidized contracts.

The Boston Urban Coalition, dominated by a number of corporate heavyweights including Louis Cabot and the presidents of Eastern Gas and Fuel and John Hancock Insurance, first attempted to help finance and advise black entrepreneurs. One immediate response from the black community was ". . . this alleged $56 million program is a sham. . . ." Undaunted, the Coalition's major committee, the National Alliance of Businessmen, moved into an ineffectual summer job program and the New England Telephone Company took on a remedial education program. For the major utility and electronics corporations which have been buying up the major publishing houses, the field of education is good business since it frequently involves research contracts and purchases of books and apparatus from subsidiaries. A major foray by the Coalition into Boston's housing resulted in (1) a mortgage fund to assist relatively well off black home buyers, (2) the setting up of the Eastern Associates Properties Corporation to assure large income-tax advantages, and (3) the assuring of more gas business to the utilities corporation. Housing in Boston's ghetto, Roxbury, remains a disgrace.

Hamburg and Smith describe how the vice-chairman of Aero-jet General, a major defense contractor, established a subsidiary employing cheap labor in the Watts section of Los Angeles to make tents for use in Vietnam. When overhead costs from its training program (financed by the Commerce Department) were counted, the profit was handsome and the same vice-chairman, elevated to the role of administrator for a federal program of urban subsidization, sent telegrams announcing the success to the nation's 500 largest corporations. In Boston, the AVCO conglomerate (abrasives, picture studies, radio stations, etc.) responded.

Within a month after AVCO received its telegram it had a federal commitment for $1.3 million to set up a printing plant in Roxbury, which it had planned to build anyway. Like Watts Manufacturing, the Roxbury printing plant is operated by a wholly owned subsidiary, Economic Systems Inc. (ESI). ESI has been engaged in other areas of public-private cooperation such as running a Job Corps center and manpower development training. With the below-market wages it pays, AVCO's 1966 earnings of $32 million will not be threatened; the assistant to the general manager Van Henderson predicts normal profits at the end of the second year. Normal profits for AVCO run about 18% of their sales. When someone boldly suggests that the 18% could be better used by the community if ESI did not own the plant, the facade was dropped: "What do you think we are, a charity?" As for the training program, one disgruntled AVCO job trainee described it as "the biggest brainwashing I ever saw."

In Boston, as elsewhere, the "conscience" of the corporate elite—from Louis Cabot to William Zisch to Henry Ford, II—reveals its major concern: new profits and increased power in social planning. (Hamburg and Smith, 1968.)

This picture is remarkably similar to Chicago where the added ingredient of a strict and powerful political machine intercedes to keep federal monies flowing to "enlightened" corporate structures. All that is precluded is the option for people who are targets of these antipoverty programs to run things in their own interests. Control of programs from powerful and removed sources accentuates the passivity and marginality of the culture of poverty. Similarly the closeness of the expert planner to the corporations and his remoteness from indigenous groups of poor people in the Model Cities Program makes the benefits to the target population dubious and the potential of increasing marginality quite high (see Robert Ross, "Is Planning a Revolution?" in Chapter 4).

While laws sanction great inequity in income in this country it is also true that many poor do not get even what should be their due under law. Even the right to vote can be effectively restricted by biased registrars using unfair literacy tests. The article by Carlin on store-front lawyers shows how legal assistance has been used, sometimes quite effectively, to gain certain benefits from agencies or landlords who had heretofore shielded themselves from the claims of the poor. The article shows, however, that such efforts are slow and costly. Moreover, even advocacy must face the issue of local control. Poor people have through history been betrayed by those claiming to serve them and the demand recurs for local control and democratic participation, even at the expense, sometimes, of what the most dedicated professional allies might view as significant social change.

An adequate combination of programs to combat poverty must come to grips not only with characteristics of individuals who accommodate to poverty but with the social system that requires great inequities of wealth and the institutions that perpetuate this inequity. The articles in Chapter 8 do not place great faith on existing federal programs to remedy poverty. Yet at some point the problems of poverty reflect conditions that cannot be solved solely by local action. A genuine guaranteed income assuring every individual security at a level well above the poverty line would eliminate, with one stroke, some of the worst features of poverty. If the program were to contain some work incentive while still assuring an adequate income, the costs would be quite high. Such plans fall into the category of social-dividend programs and they are a highly important goal because they apply to large numbers of people and remove the stigma of welfare as charity. The professional can have an important role in the attack on poverty by modifying services, particularly vital services such as medical care, to meet the needs of the poor and by advocacy. Radical organizers and the poor also have major roles to play in establishing local organizations that generate demands on the system. Without such demand there is little change. Pivan and Cloward describe a plan of indigenous organization which might accrue power and induce change through the disrupting of normal services.*

There is a difference in philosophy and in style between programs geared primarily to service and those geared primarily to social action. A service program either directly or implicitly accepts the criterion of material well being as the measure of success and assumes the poor to be deficient. An action program assumes that the poor community has resources adequate to its own well being, providing that obstacles to organization and advancement can be removed. The service approach asks, "What can we do to keep your family together, to keep you from dropping out of school, or to turn your gang into a constructive club?" The activists ask, "What are the strong points of your way of life, what is wrong with the school system or the job system which prevents it from meeting your needs?" From the activists' position a potential leader of the deprived community who makes it into a high position in the military or in industry, or an actual leader whose demands grow more cautious as he is employed on some federal program, are examples of failure. For the activist the illness is not poverty but rather the larger social system which permitted it to develop even amidst plenty. For the student organizers who have forsaken their own careers to work among tenant farmers or ghetto residents, the program which takes steam out of the protest serves only to amalgamate a few more cases into a social system with extremely low priorities for human needs. The tenor of the activists will be seen in our last chapter on the revolution in expression. What is relevant in this section is the effort to develop programs in which "maximum feasible participation" is not a substitute for complete control by the poor of their own programs. Such programs are radical in their objectives and sometimes in their methods. They are highly relevant to the theme of this book because they make explicit the basic difficulty that an automated and impersonal society, geared to wasteful productivity and to globalism in foreign policy, may not have the human resources to deal with a struggle which demands not only goods but a share in the nation's power and a sense of self-direction and respect.

REFERENCES AND ADDITIONAL READING

Alinsky, Saul D., "The War on Poverty—Political Pornography," *Journal of Social Issues*, **21** (1965), pp. 41–47.

Caplovitz, David, *The Poor Pay More* (New York: Free Press, 1963).

Cloward, Richard A., and Richard M. Elman, "Advocacy in the Ghetto," *Transaction* (December 1966).

Drew, Elizabeth, "Going Hungry in America," *Atlantic* (December 1968), pp. 53–61.

Dumont, Matthew P., "The Changing Face of Professionalism," *Social Policy* (May/June 1970), pp. 26–31.

* For an analysis relating the functions of indigenous social action, professional action, and legislative policy change, see Pilisuk and Pilisuk, *Poor Americans: Dynamics of Change* (Chicago: Aldine, 1971).

Ellis, William W., *White Ethics and Black Power* (Chicago: Aldine, 1969).

Freire, Paulo, *Pedagogy of the Oppressed* (New York: Herder and Herder, 1970).

Fried, Marc, "Grieving for a Lost Home," in Leonard J. Duhl (ed.), *The Urban Condition* (New York: Basic Books, 1963).

Gans, Herbert J., "The Failure of Urban Renewal," *Commentary*, **39** (April 1965), pp. 29–37; reproduced in R. Perrucci and M. Pilisuk (eds.), *The Triple Revolution: Social Problems in Depth* (Boston: Little, Brown, 1968), pp. 264–280.

Gitlin, Todd, "The Community Union: Tapping the Radical Potential of the Poor," in M. Pilisuk and P. Pilisuk (eds.), *Poor Americans: Dynamics of Change* (Chicago: Aldine, 1971).

Goodman, Paul, "The Present Movement in Education," *New York Review of Books* (April 10, 1969), pp. 14–22.

Graham, James, *The Enemies of the Poor* (New York: Random House, 1970).

Haber, Alan, "Issues beyond Consensus," in M. Pilisuk and P. Pilisuk (eds.), *Poor Americans: Dynamics of Change* (Chicago: Aldine, 1971).

Hamberg, Jill, and David Smith, "The Urban Coalition—Boston," *Viet-Report*, **3** (Summer 1968), pp. 51–53.

Harrington, Michael, "The Betrayal of the American Poor," *Atlantic* (January 1970), pp. 71–74.

Hayden, Tom, *Rebellion in Newark: Official Violence and Ghetto Response* (New York: Random House, 1967); see Chapter 4, "The Terror," pp. 45–61.

Illich, Ivan, "Why We Must Abolish Schooling," *New York Review of Books*, **15** (July 1970), pp. 4–6.

Kohl, Herbert, *The Open Classroom* (New York: Random House, 1969).

Kopkind, Andrew, "Of, by, and for the Poor," *New Republic* (June 19, 1965), pp. 15–19; reproduced in R. Perrucci and M. Pilisuk (eds.), *The Triple Revolution: Social Problems in Depth* (Boston: Little, Brown, 1968), pp. 515–523.

Lauter, Paul, and Florence Howe, "How the School System Is Rigged for Failure," *New York Review of Books*, **14** (June 1970), pp. 14–20.

Levin, Tom, "The Child Development Group of Mississippi: A Hot Sector of the Quiet Front in the War on Poverty," *American Journal of Orthopsychiatry*, **37**:1 (January 1967), pp. 139–145.

Lipsky, Michael, "Rent Strikes: Poor Man's Weapon," *Trans-action* (February 1969), pp. 10–15.

Marris, Peter, and Martin Rein, *Dilemmas of Social Reform* (London: Routledge and K. Paul, 1967).

Miller, S. M., "Poverty and Inequality in America: Implications for the Social Services, *Child Welfare*, **52**:9 (November 1963), pp. 442–445; reproduced in R. Perrucci and M. Pilisuk (eds.), *The Triple Revolution: Social Problems in Depth* (Boston: Little, Brown, 1968), pp. 488–493.

Minnis, Jack "The Care and Feeding of Power Structures," *New University Thought*, **4** (1964), pp. 63–70.

Moynihan, Daniel P., *Maximum Feasible Misunderstanding* (New York: Free Press, 1969).

Murphy, Raymond J., and Howard Elinson (eds.), *Problems and Prospects of the Negro Movement* (Belmont, Calif.: Wadsworth, 1966).

Pearl, Arthur, and Frank Riessman, *New Careers for the Poor: The Non-Professional in Human Service* (New York: Free Press, 1965).

Postman, Neil, and Charles Weingartner, *Teaching as a Subversive Activity* (New York: Delacorte, 1969).

Rein, Martin, and S. M. Miller, "Social Action on the Installment Plan, *Transaction* (January-February 1966), pp. 31–38.

Schorr, Alvin L., *Slums and Social Insecurity* (Washington, D.C.: U.S. Department of Health, Education and Welfare, 1963).

Schuchter, Arnold, *White Power/Black Freedom* (Boston: Beacon, 1968); see Chapter 2, "Undoing the Slum Ghetto System," pp. 98–175.

Sideman, Janet, "Death of a Dropout," *New Republic* (June 3, 1967), pp. 11–14.

Walton, Mary, "Rats in the Crib, Roaches in the Food," *Village Voice* (New York), May 11, 1967.

Weissbourd, Bill, *Segregation, Subsidies, and Megalopolis* (Santa Barbara, Calif.: Center for the Study of Democratic Institutions, 1964); reproduced in R. Perrucci and M. Pilisuk (eds.), *The Triple Revolution: Social Problems in Depth* (Boston: Little, Brown, 1968), pp. 281–298.

Wiley, Peter, and Beverly Leman, "Cities in Crisis: The Business of Urban Reform," *Leviathan,* **1** (March 1969), pp. 11–13.

AN IDEOLOGY OF
SCHOOL WITHDRAWAL

Edgar Z. Friedenberg

Compulsory school attendance in the United States has been justified from the beginning as essential to democratic polity. Everyone knows Madison's statement to the effect that popular government without popular education is the prelude to a tragedy, or a farce, or both. We have had both, continuously, ever since. I have just finished Theodore White's *The Making of the President, 1960;* and I think this book is the strongest indictment of American public education I have ever seen, though Mr. White does not discuss the issue directly. Still, the laws are on the books. Within a century, with the Kalamazoo decision (1874), the legal basis had been laid for what Madison thought so necessary.

And, be it noted, for the reasons he gave. So far as I know, public support of education in this country has never been justified on the grounds that education was beneficial to the individual student, except to the extent that this pertained to equality of opportunity. It is logical to argue that the individuals who share the responsibilities of citizenship must learn what they have to do in order to discharge them. I wouldn't say the logic was watertight. In Louisiana, where I was raised, we have never regarded either ignorance or lunacy as a bar to high public office; and this liberalism has permitted us to enjoy unusually creative leadership. But, on the whole, the point is well taken. If public education can be justified on the grounds

that it is essential to citizenship, it can also claim, for that reason, to be good for the future citizens themselves.

School attendance laws, however, are a very distorted reflection of the purpose implicit in Madison's phrase. They are not *licensing* laws. They do not require attendance until a specified minimum level of competence deemed essential to the conduct of adult life has been attained; this would mean a life sentence for some. Nor are they *contractual*: they do not assure the student any outcome or even any minimum standard of educational service or decent treatment in exchange for his obligation to attend. Other laws, to be sure, do set up such standards, but the student has no remedy against their breach. Even if he can establish that the school is substandard and that he personally is mistreated there, he cannot legally withdraw; he can only try to force the school authorities to make improvements which, usually, they would already have made long ago if they possibly could.

From this point of view, compulsory school attendance appears as a gross violation of civil liberty: a bill of attainder against a specific age group that guarantees no compensation in return. The school may, indeed, benefit the child; but it doesn't have to in order to earn the right to retain him. In talking about the youngsters who drop out, therefore, I am not going to start with the assumption that they ought to be retained. My hunch is that a large proportion of the dropouts may be doing what is best for themselves under the atrocious circumstances that exist. But I do want to analyze those circumstances, and see why the schools have so little to offer these youngsters.

In the small Southern Methodist college I attended, we had chapel services twice a week; and after the opening hymn there was a responsive reading. The Dean—it was a poor school and could only afford one—would read a portion of Scripture aloud; and the students, assembled as a congregation, would read the following portion: his in light-faced type, ours in bold. There was one of these that I liked especially well, and I remember fragments of it distinctly—not accurately, but distinctly. It began:

Dean: *Whereof from a young man's fancy shall he wend his way?*
Students: *By taking heed unto the Lord, and the firmament thereof.*

This responsive reading, in the version in which I recall it, is admirably suited to its purpose. The first line reveals real evidence of poetic influence. It ties in with the culture, showing that we share in its heritage, and it alludes to the necessity for progress and achievement; while the second line asserts the necessity of basing these on a sound moral imperative. By saying it over together we experienced a feeling of mutuality and belonging, of being the same kind. Yet we ran no risk of binding ourselves to too literal an interpretation of its mandate, because it doesn't actually make any sense at all.

For the types of students it is designed for, the public high-school and junior high-school curriculum serves, I believe, exactly the same purpose as this responsive reading. Its function is liturgical. This is not as true of elementary school, because the basic skills really work. If you read as you are taught there, you will understand at least the words; if you write, your words will be understood; if you follow the rules of arithmetic, your calculations will check out and your books will balance, though you may never have the remotest conception of mathematics.

High school, however, is another matter. What would happen to the businessman, or just citizen, who attempted to apply what he was taught in high-school civics to the actual power structure of his community or his country? Who learns to love reading, or to find the kind of reading he can love among the classics and the bitty anthologies of the high-school English course? High-school history, by and large, is not even propaganda, because nobody is expected to believe it or to be moved by it; it is received as official myth. We tell youngsters that the Pilgrims came to New England searching for religious freedom not in order to give them an understanding of the actual root values of Colonial New England, but in order to provide them with the relevant cliché about the relation of church and state in America, and to let them know that a good middle-class American thinks of "my religious affiliation" or "the faith of my choice." This keeps the youngsters from getting hung up on religion, like an Italian peasant or rural Southerner. As for high-school science, it has, since Sputnik, increased its work load enormously and often tries to duplicate the content of college science courses. But essentially, it serves not as an introduction to science but to legitimate the American middle-class epistemology; science proves that Truth is an aggregate of general principles induced from empirical data that observers can agree on. The function of science is to protect people from odd-balls by setting up the rules so that subjective feeling is discounted. The scientific method, then, becomes a way of separating ends and means. When we want to win an election, or spy on the Soviet Union, or redevelop a slum, we go about it scientifically—i.e., by defining what we are trying to do as a technical problem. Naturally, we care about the feelings of the people affected; people's emotions are a very important factor. That's why we have psychologists on our team.

It is even truer than the progressives have always maintained that there is no valid distinction between the curriculum and the extracurriculum. What counts is the total experience of the student, and what he learns in both the classroom and the playing field is a posture, a pattern of anxieties and a pattern of responses for dealing with it. There is seldom any pleasure in scholarship or ideas as such; the classroom and the playing field alike are places where you try to make it, and learn the techniques for making it that alienate you least from your peers. The overall rules are the same in both: learn the ropes; don't get hung up; always be friendly, sincere, and creative. And win!

The important thing about this familiar picture is that it is a picture of a totally instrumental institution. Nothing about the institution is meant to be valuable, here and now, for its own sake. I don't mean that high-school students don't have any fun. Of course they do; in the suburbs, at least, the high school is a "fun place." But this sort of fun is a part of the social pattern to be learned; being "fun" helps you to make it as well or better than anything, and it takes a great deal of social skill which American adolescents, notably, do learn.

We have never had much interest in what education means and feels like to the youngsters who are subjected to it; only in what it might help them to make of themselves. Even the Supreme Court, in its decision against segregation, could not rest on the moral obloquy and insult that segregation imposes on Negro children; that was not enough. It had to support its position further by pointing out that a major reason why separate schools could not be equal even if they were identical was that the Negro students couldn't make the same contacts there that white students could in their school, and that this was what people really go to school for.

So it is: the Court has done our motives no discredit, but merely reaffirmed our tradition. The public school gives poor boys a chance to develop their potentialities, both by formal education and by providing an opportunity to mingle with and learn from their social superordinates. The commonwealth is then the richer for the skills they later contribute, which would otherwise have been forever lost. This is exactly the opportunity our dropouts need, and which they ought presumably to welcome. So what has gone wrong?

What has gone wrong is pretty complicated; but basically I think one might locate it in the schools' perennial assumptions about the nature of what they have had to offer the children of the poor. These assumptions were probably never valid; but both the school and the poor once believed them. Now, only the school continues to assert them, though no longer with much conviction.

The schools assumed that in order to get ahead in America the student had to learn not only a body of skills, but also a set of social conventions, increasingly subtle and refined as he climbed up the ladder. In school he was taught techniques for handling things and manners for getting along with people. The teachers were the transmitters of an alien culture—alien to them, too. Social mobility was a process like preparing to get a job as a rice farmer in China or a coffee-grower in Brazil. There was a strange language to be learned—from instructors who didn't speak it too well themselves; a strange body of techniques to be mastered—from teachers who had never practiced them at first hand. It would all have to be learned over again when he got there; but at the time it seemed relevant, and made the student feel that he was well on his way.

Now, there are three important ways in which this situation differs from the condition in the high school today. In the first place, the problem of dropouts did not then exist. Most of the students who drop out today would never have been in high school fifty years ago; the school-leaving age has risen irregularly over the past decades, and a more rigid and self-confident school policy would not have hesitated to keep students in grade school until they reached it, whatever it was, if they did not pass. A good many of these dropped out, and took unskilled jobs, which existed; and that was the last anyone thought of them till election day six or seven years later. They weren't a dropout problem; they were the working class.

But those who didn't drop out, even though they came from a working-class background, did not feel at the time that they were losing their identity. This happened later, after they had made it, in the classical discovery of the loneliness of the long-distance runner. In school you were still you: *striving* didn't separate you from other poor, immigrant boys; it was exactly what poor, immigrant boys were supposed to do. There was no intimation at the time that you were leaving yourself behind. It

wasn't that you were becoming a different person; the old *you* was learning new tricks. Education was instrumental, all right—it has always been that in America—but the instruments were thought to be in the curriculum. The student didn't have to learn to think of *himself* as one.

And finally, nobody doubted what the norms were. It seemed very clear that the people in the next stratum up were the ones who knew what the student had to learn; he had to be able to do what they did. This wouldn't make them accept him willingly; but it would allow him to work his way in even if they didn't.

I don't mean to imply that the school actually delivered the social mobility it promised; sometimes it did, more often it didn't. But this was the way it was supposed to work, and why there was so little controversy over whether compulsory school attendance was good for the individual as well as for the commonwealth. As long as the students who stayed in school believed in education naïvely, it served—much better than religion could have in this heterogeneous country—as the opiate of the people. And opium vendors don't have dropout problems.

Apparently, however—to judge by the present situation—they can: the American poor are getting over their addiction.[1] It takes more and more education every year to invoke the same dream; and reality breaks through too often, leaving them sick, mean, and edgy. The educational establishment,

---

[1] Thus, in her recent study of the schools in Big City, Patricia Sexton reports dropout rates even in *elementary school* of 15.5 per 10,000 children from families earning from $3000–5000 annually, falling to 3 children per 10,000 for families earning $5000–7000. For families making more than $9000, the rate was less than 1 child per 10,000. In high schools, of course, the rate is enormously greater, but follows the same pattern. There is no high school in Big City whose median family income is less than $5000. For schools with median family incomes ranging from $5000–5999, Sexton found a dropout rate of 19.2 percent of the total registration, falling to 7.9 percent for schools whose students had a median family income of $7000–7999, and to 3.6 percent for the school whose students came from families having median incomes above $9000. (*Education and Income* (New York: Viking, 1961), pp. 97 and 202.)

fearful of losing popular support, is naturally much concerned with the possibilities of a *rapprochement*, of which two have already been tried. The simplest of these is an effort to beef up the traditional, but paradoxically faltering, economic appeal of education. Students are reminded over and over that today, more than ever, you need a high-school diploma to get any sort of job and a college degree to get a good one. They are given the statistics on the fabulous return education, as an investment, brings in over a lifetime in increments of annual income. The unemployment data on adolescents and unskilled labor are stressed so that the youngsters will understand how hopeless things will be for them if they drop out of school. If they and their teacher are sophisticated enough, the demographic shift in job type may be explained: how unskilled and blue-collar work has fallen off, while service and white-collar jobs, demanding a higher level of school achievement, have enormously increased in proportion.

All this is true enough; but the implication is false. It does not follow that most of the students now dropping out would have a better chance, even economically, if they stayed in school. As S. M. Miller and Frank Riessman have pointed out in a recent WBAI broadcast, the illusory success of some of these school-retention efforts in leading students to better jobs is based on the fact that they made hardly a dent in the number of school dropouts; if the programs had been successful in reaching the students they would inevitably have failed in delivering the jobs. In our economy, the demonstrable economic value of an education is partly a consequence of its scarcity. The blue-collar–white-collar figures are relative, and one loses sight of how much smaller the white-collar one was to begin with. The absolute increase in white-collar opportunity does not compensate for the absolute loss in blue-collar jobs—a discrepancy which is rapidly increasing in magnitude as automation proceeds. Today's dropouts are, perhaps fortunately, pretty skeptical kids; if they all believed that the school could deliver them to a brighter economic future we would soon have unemployed IBM operators and technicians hanging around the way India and Africa have lawyers.

The other, and more sophisticated, *rapprochement* is represented by the Higher Horizons Program, about which I wish I could bring myself to be less doubtful, for it is a program that seems to me characterized by much intelligence, ingenuity, enthusiasm, and sheer good will. Its appeal, moreover, is not purely economic. I understand it to be an attempt to convey to students that middle-class culture, *in toto,* is not beyond their grasp. It can be theirs, if only they do their work. As the title implies, the Higher Horizons approach seeks to make education appear more worthwhile to the student, and encourages him to remain in school to develop his potentialities, by raising his level of aspiration not just economically but culturally. As the boy lifts himself to gaze beyond the slum there comes into view the Museum of Modern Art.

It is heartening to find the middle class so generously willing to share its resources, and, for once, apparently confident of their value. It is also obvious that if the middle class cannot somehow make public education acceptable to the poor on its terms rather than theirs, middle-class dominance of public education—a long-established fact of American life—is doomed. But if the effort is successful, it will remind me of a story that a very intelligent, very British, very working-class hospital orderly used to tell, in a sensitive effort to ease his middle-class patients' embarrassment at the services he was obliged to perform for them. This story concerned a small pharmaceutical firm that was facing bankruptcy. It had an established reputation as Britain's most reputable manufacturer of suppositories. But respect for craftsmanship, as is well known, was declining; their customers, apparently, were turning to other sources for satisfaction. Things looked black. Then the firm consulted one of Madison Avenue's most resourceful advertising agencies. And the agency, after much brain-storming, came up with a slogan that at once opened vast markets to the company by motivating the very segment of the population which had hitherto most successfully resisted its appeal. The slogan was, very simply, "If you don't like our suppositories, you know what you can do with them!"

The dropouts, by and large, don't like middle-class culture; and they know quite well what we can do with it. Dropping out is one way of telling us, and it is about time we turned our attention to the things about the school that are bugging them. The school is the arena in which these youngsters encounter middle-class life; this is where the dropouts fight the ten-year's ideological war that ends in their defeat and rout. In this warfare the core values of their culture and the values the school represents are at issue, and any one that we start by considering will lead to the others. I think the most fruitful might be the familiar question of deferred gratification, or impulse control, which is the source of so much conflict with the school authorities.

We all know the school's side of the question; and know that lower-class youngsters act out their conflicts. Retention programs try to face up to this by helping the youngsters learn more self-control and giving them some valid experience of being rewarded for it, so that they will discover for themselves that certain very desirable goals exist that can only be achieved by people who plan, save, and give a soft answer to

wrath-provoking circumstances. In this way the kids learn that there may be more desirable rewards than the immediate pleasure of blowing up and shooting your bolt. "Now, Dionysus, let's think about what we're really trying to get done here," friendly Apollo is always urging; and of course he is right. The difficulty lies in getting Dionysus to listen.

Or does it? Let me return for a moment to Mr. White's account of the 1960 election, and the Apollonian behavior it elicited from the Republican candidate.

And this, finally was the only summary one could make of the campaign that Richard M. Nixon had so valiantly waged, under such personal suffering: that there was neither philosophy nor structure to it, no whole picture either of the man or of the future he offered. One could perceive neither in this last climactic proposal nor in his prepared speeches nor in his personal discourses any shape of history, any sense of the stream of time or flow of forces by which America had come to this point in history and might move on. Nixon's skill in politics was enormous, his courage unquestioned, his endurance substantial. But they were the skills, courage, and endurance of the sailor who knows the winds and can brave the storm and recognize the tide. There was missing in him always the direction of the navigator.... Thus, it is impossible to distinguish, from his campaign performance, what Nixon's personal political attitude was to the arrest of Martin Luther King when that hero figure of American Negroes was arrested in the last days of the campaign.... On the afternoon of the sentencing of Martin Luther King to four months of hard labor in Georgia, the Department of Justice—at the suggestion of a wise yet shrewd Republican Deputy Attorney-General—composed a draft statement to support the application for release of the imprisoned Negro minister. Two copies of the draft were sent out immediately for approval—one to the White House, one to Mr. Nixon's traveling headquarters. No one has yet revealed who killed this draft statement that was so critically important in the tense politics of civil rights. Either President Eisenhower or Vice-President Nixon could have acted—yet neither did. However obscure Eisenhower's motivations were, Nixon's are more perplexing, for he was the candidate. He had made the political decision at Chicago to court the Negro vote in the North; only now, apparently, he felt it quite possible that Texas, South Carolina, and Louisiana might all be won to him by the white vote and he did not wish to offend that vote. So he did not act—there was no whole philosophy of politics to instruct him. There could never be any doubt of the Vice-President's pugnacity or innate courage; yet it was a pugnacity and courage committed without a framing strategy to make them effective.

The terms of Mr. White's criticism are interesting as the incident itself. No philosophy of politics? No framing strategy? On the contrary, he was all strategy. What he lacked was heart and a sense of outrage: the capacity to make moral judgments. Yet, Mr. White cannot say this because his whole book, though very sensitive to moral factors in the contest, shares the assumption that a candidate's first duty is to get elected. Nixon lost, and the figures do indeed show that his expediency on this issue may have cost him the election. But to infer from this fact that the worst thing about Mr. Nixon's behavior was that it didn't work is to share his posture.

Earlier on, Mr. White describes the situations in the campaign that found Mr. Nixon at his best.

One had to see Nixon entering a small Iowa village—the streets lined with school children, all waving American flags until it seemed as if the cavalcade were entering a defile lined by fluttering peppermint-striped little banners—then see him stop at a Harvest Festival (in Red Oaks) —where on the festival tables lay the ripened ears of field corn . . . to see him at his best. For in such small towns he found an echo. These people were his natural constituency, his idiom their idiom. . . . He woke in Marietta, Ohio, on Monday, October 25th, to begin his last "peak" effort, and it was clear from his first speech of the day that he was at one with his audience as he had not been since he had passed through

the corn fields of Iowa in the first week of the campaign. A sign outside the courthouse of Marietta, Ohio, read: HIGH SCHOOL DEBATERS GREET WORLD DEBATER—the sign was apropos and of the essence of this last trip as he revived. For he *was* a high-school debater, the boy who had some thirty years before won a Los Angeles *Times* prize for his high-school oration on the Constitution. He was seeking not so much to score home a message as to win the hearts of his little audiences; his style was homestyle and during the next two weeks told much about him.

In Red Oaks and Marietta they don't have much of a dropout problem. Good, solid communities, with woodsheds ample to the needs of youth, they turn out clean-cut boys and girls among whom Mr. Nixon is right at home. It was the urban proletariat, and overwhelmingly the Negroes, who refused to take part in his Harvest Festival, though the corn be ripe and the harvest long overdue.

To carry this illustration further would not make my point clearer; in any case, it is simple enough. I think the youngsters who drop out are probably, in many ways, a more promising moral resource than those who stay in, and I think they are driven out in part by moral revulsion from the middle-class life of the school. They could never, themselves, identify their feelings as moral repugnance because they view morality as being on the side of the enemy and therefore square; they imagine they dislike morality and have never been allowed to realize that they have morals of their own. They don't have a complete moral *system,* because they are not systematic; they are unprincipled in their behavior, because principles are too abstract for them to handle. But in a concrete situation they can be trusted more safely than their middle-class peers who are trying to make it.

Mr. Nixon and his silent superior are symbols, too; and I am not naïve enough to attribute the lower-class response to them solely to the revulsion they arouse in the breast of the noble savage. The opposition was well-organized and well-manipulated. But there are natural affinities and polarities in politics that set limits to what manipulation can achieve, and these, among other things, are reflected in the class structure of American society. Officially, American society is, however, middle class and opportunistic—in the Land of Opportunity these are the values that receive official support and that in fact prevail. It is surely fair enough to take Mr. Eisenhower, and Mr. Nixon at the zenith of his presidential aspirations, as representative of what is most American. But one need not be wholly partisan. President Kennedy has also stated emphatically that we need technical rather than ideological or philosophical approaches to the problems that confront us.[2]

This moral attitude dominates our life. We are caught in it in crisis after crisis: in the U-2 incident, the Cuban invasion, the presence of our observers in Vietnam organizing the forced evacuation of peasants so that their farms can be burned, and helping the government see to it that the Viet Cong guerrillas don't get any antibiotics. Time after time the world finds a nice, friendly American standing in the middle of somebody else's ruins, with no more to say for himself than a rueful "It shoulda worked, but somebody must have goofed!"

I have a name for this boy. I call him Edsel, and I think it is time we withdrew him from production and got out a more responsive and less hazardous model. Even the practical-minded may not have much use for him any more; the locals seem to be getting pretty tired of Edsel and are about ready to get him out of there, with a hammer and sickle if necessary. But if we

are to grow anything better, the dropouts are the kids to start with, for they have come part way on their own, against heavy opposition, already. They are ill-disciplined. They have no basic skills. They are so sore that any place you touch them hurts, and when they are hurt they hurt back. They are extremely parochial, limited in their experience of the world to a few city blocks of desolate slum, and therefore both gullible and suspicious about anything beyond it. They are sometimes homeless, and never have any quiet place to study and think. They are inconveniently aware of their own sexuality and inconveniently skilled at bringing it to the attention of others. They live, their teachers sometimes say, like animals; and as they say it, a ghost sobs, harshly. But if these youngsters are trapped, it is not in their apprehensions of pseudo-events. They are not alienated from themselves. They still have access to their sense-data, and, on their own terms, they are accustomed to fidelity.

These are the qualities that, I believe, we hoped to preserve and continually renew by building an open society in which a sensitive, compulsively masculine boy could become an Ernest Hemingway and a poor but beautiful waif a Marilyn Monroe. But at this juncture, less fatal alternatives to mediocrity are needed. Can a school geared to success and social mobility help formulate them? Its traditions are against it, its staff is against it, its relationship to the community power structure is against it.

To reach the dropouts and give them a reason for staying, the school would have to start by accepting their *raison d'être*. It would have to take lower-class life seriously as a condition and a pattern of experience —not just as a contemptible and humiliating set of circumstances that every decent

[2] In the 1962 Commencement Address at Yale. See William Lee Miller, "Some Academic Questions About a New Yale Man," *Reporter* (July 5, 1962).

boy or girl is anxious to escape from. It would have to accept their language, and their dress, and their values as a point of departure for disciplined exploration, to be understood, not as a trick for luring them into the middle class, but as a way of helping them to explore the meaning of their own lives. This is the way to encourage and nurture potentialities from *whatever* social class. Talent, and genius, when real, are expressions of individual experience and the inner life. But success and higher status are not the first goal to which talent or genius is devoted—though they are sometimes the last.

I do not mean to imply that I accept Sitwell's Fallacy: that the poor are happier in their station in life and should be left to enjoy it. Most lower-class people of whatever age hate lower-class life, I am sure: the noise, and the filth, and the crowding, and the vulnerability to the police and illness; never feeling quite well or quite rested. Worst of all, perhaps, is the constant din of the mass media—including the school—telling them that if they were any good at all they would be middle class like everybody else, and live in loveliness in Larchmont. But the fact that they have reason to hate their life of fear and deprivation does not give us the right to force ours on them as the only acceptable alternative to it. This is something they must work out for themselves, and the school's job is to help them understand most fully the meaning and nature of what they have to work with. Basically, the problem of reaching the dropout is analogous to that faced by the Peace Corps in reaching the peoples of underdeveloped countries. Can we—do we even really wish to—help them deal with their situation on their terms with our resources, while leaving our way of life aside till somebody asks for it?

Frankly, I doubt it. This is not how the teachers I know approach lower-status youngsters. They are afraid of them, for one thing. The principal is afraid of disorder which looks bad in his record and in the records of his teachers, and they each have their careers to think of, too. So they learn early to keep the kids in line; this comes first. Order *is* helpful to learning, but it doesn't come first, it grows out of the common task; and teachers who put it first are not enthusiastic allies in keeping disorderly youngsters in school till a basis for order can be created. Order is not, to be sure, the central issue, but it will serve to symbolize the sharpness of the issue between those whose security depends on the suppression of impulse, and those who depend on its expression.

In the urban public school today, the former predominate, and I don't think they can be easily changed, within the limits of personality and bureaucracy that characterize the school. If they can be, there is no fundamental reason why the kinds of youngsters who now drop out may not be well served. But this is a big *if*, for the public school, as it is, is profoundly expressive of our culture. And the fate of the "dropouts" is just one more expression of their actual status in our democracy.

The answer, then, may be "No; this plant makes only Edsels." But if it is, I see no dropout problem. Let them go, let them go, God bless them. They may pop up again. St. James (or Santiago, as this chiliastic figure is known in Spanish) is not merely more merciful than the school system; he is far more flexible and versatile. He can accommodate a wider range of talent; he has a great Court, as well as an Infirmary, and though no familiar avenue bears his name, he has, like James Madison, been thus honored by the inhabitants of certain cities. The nearest, unfortunately, in Cuba.

STORE-FRONT LAWYERS
IN SAN FRANCISCO

Jerome E. Carlin

A United States district court on April 22, 1968, invalidated California's residency requirements for persons seeking public assistance. Previously, applicants had to be residents of the state for at least one year before they could become eligible for benefits. According to the *San Francisco Chronicle* of April 25:

The Reagan Administration will try to overturn last week's landmark Federal Court decision.... Health and Welfare Director Spencer Williams said the decision would add another 24 million dollars to welfare costs; and add about 6900 families and 12,000 other individuals to the welfare rolls.

On December 28, 1968, the *New York Times* printed the following story datelined San Francisco:

POOR WIN VICTORY IN A HOUSING SUIT
COURT HALTS COAST RENEWAL UNTIL
RESIDENTS BACK PLAN

A Federal Court has halted the funding of a $100 million urban renewal project here with a decision that is expected to affect similar projects across the country and aid the poor in establishing legal rights for themselves. The court order prohibits the Department of Housing and Urban Development from supplying additional funds for the project until an acceptable plan has been approved for relocating uprooted families.... In taking the action to court, the Western Addition community group was [represented] by the San Francisco Neighborhood Legal Assistance Foundation....

On August 12, 1969, the following appeared on the front page of the *Chronicle*:

BAY JUDGE ORDERS BOOST IN WELFARE

More money must be paid in rent allotments to people in the biggest welfare program in San Francisco and Alameda Counties, a Superior Court judge ruled here yesterday. Judge Alvin E. Weinberger further ordered the State Department of Social Welfare to take steps that will produce another increase in rent money across the State in a few months time.

He acted in a law suit brought by the San Francisco Neighborhood Legal Assistance Foundation on behalf of all persons receiving Aid to Families with Dependent Children (AFDC) in the two counties. Foundation lawyers charged that most AFDC clients are getting a monthly rent allotment less than the actual rent they are paying. Under State law, the Department's standards for rent must ensure "safe, healthful housing." And the Department's own regulations require that its rent standards be based on "current actual costs for housing."

Judge Weinberger said the state and counties must live up to their own laws and regulations.
. . .

The total sum required statewide would be $19 million per year.... This would pay the actual rent. How much more would be required, after the Department hearings, to pay for safe, healthful housing is a matter of dispute. But the total increase could reach $50 million.

These have been some of the more newsworthy activities of a new type of professional organization. The San Francisco Neighborhood Legal Assistance Foundation

Reprinted by permission from Trans-action *(April 1970), pp. 64–73; copyright* © *1970 by Trans-action Magazine, Washington University, St. Louis, Mo.*

is a federally financed, community-controlled legal service agency which has been aggressively advocating the rights of the poor since it began operation in October 1966. It is one of about 300 agencies throughout the United States funded by the Office of Economic Opportunity (OEO) to deliver more effective legal services to the nation's poor.

Since the foundation has probably gone farther than almost any of the other legal service agencies in carrying out this mandate and has served as a model for many other programs in the United States, it may be instructive to examine what it set out to accomplish, the extent to which it was able to achieve its objectives, and the problems it encountered. One of the most important issues that emerges from such an inquiry is the apparent incompatibility of the two principal goals of the organization: control by the client community and institutional change.

Having participated in the creation of the foundation, and having served as its head for the first three years of its existence, I will be presenting an insider's view that may well be biased and self-serving. I trust that my training as a sociologist and lawyer will serve to curb any major excesses.

MONEY AND ORGANIZATION

The foundation is a private, nonprofit corporation with a governing board consisting of representatives of the local bar associations, law schools, and the poverty community. The bylaws require that a majority of the board members be selected by the five poverty areas in San Francisco and that the board must also have a majority of attorneys. This is accomplished by having each poverty area select at least one lawyer representative. The board hires the coordinator, who is the chief executive

officer of the foundation, and the directing attorney (chief counsel) for each of the five neighborhood law offices. The coordinator is responsible for carrying out the overall policies of the organization (which are determined by him and the board), for allocating resources among the various offices and departments, and for hiring and supervising administrative and legal staff at the headquarters office (Main Office) of the foundation. Each chief counsel hires and fires his own staff of attorneys, secretaries, law students, and aides.

In the fall of 1969 there were more than 120 paid staff persons working at the foundation including 50 full-time attorneys and about 30 part-time law students. In addition, about 25 law students and 10 social-work students spent varying amounts of time at the foundation for credit under faculty supervision. Numerous private attorneys, on a volunteer basis, interview clients in the evening at a neighborhood office, make court appearances on default divorces, or perform other services.

The staff attorneys are generally young—about a fourth came to the foundation right out of law school (mostly through the OEO-funded Reginald Heber Smith Fellowship and VISTA programs); only about a third had at least four years of practice experience before joining the foundation. Most attended top-ranking law schools; approximately a third graduated from an Ivy League law school (Harvard, Yale, or Columbia). One out of four foundation attorneys is from a minority group; there are nine black lawyers.

The yearly budget of the foundation is over a million dollars, practically all of which comes from OEO in the form of an annual grant channeled through the local poverty agency, the Economic Opportunity Council of San Francisco (EOC). Although the foundation must deal both with OEO and EOC, it is essentially the former, and particularly the Legal Services Division within OEO, that has played the principal role in articulating and enforcing general guidelines for the foundation (and other legal-service agencies) and evaluating performance.

OEO seeks to shape and control programs and promote certain national objectives, not only through the funding process, but also by means of nationwide training programs, research and back-up centers, and fellowship programs that place bright young law school graduates in funded agencies. Many foundation lawyers (particularly those working in the Main Office) maintain close ties with other poverty lawyers throughout the country by taking an active part in these OEO programs as well as in meetings of the National Legal Aid and Defender Association (which has become largely dominated by OEO lawyers) and other newly developed associations of poverty lawyers. In the national poverty law movement, OEO's Legal Services (in alliance with the American Bar Association, if not all or even most state and local bar associations) continues to play a leading role, giving solid support (with only few lapses) to program goals generally more advanced than most funded agencies are willing or able to realize.

Every month over a thousand new clients come into the five neighborhood offices of the foundation. A large majority of the clients are seeing a lawyer for the first time, most are on welfare, and half are in families with an annual income of less than $3000 a year. About 15 percent of the clients are referred out—mainly to private attorneys or the public defender—because they fall above the foundation's income standard or they have a fee-producing or criminal case. The largest number of clients (about 30 percent) want help with a family problem, and half of these are seeking a divorce. The next biggest group are those having problems with administrative agencies: welfare, unemploy-

ment insurance, social security, immigration and naturalization (the bulk of the cases in the Chinatown Office), and the draft. Problems with landlords and merchants (and their collection agents) each constitute about 15 percent of the cases.

A major portion of the family cases, including all divorce matters, are referred to the Domestic Relations Unit, now located at the Main Office, for more expeditious handling. This innovation has been adopted by a great many other programs and has contributed significantly to reducing the overall time and resources that need be devoted to this largely routine service.

The Main Office also houses a legal staff handling a limited number of cases that are selected because they raise major poverty issues in public housing, welfare, urban renewal, and more recently in the consumer area. The cases are referred to the staff from community organizations or neighborhood office lawyers. In time the Main Office attorneys have become specialists in the particular areas in which they work, in contrast with most attorneys in the neighborhood offices who, given the diversity of legal problems they have to deal with and the relatively little time they have to give any particular case, remain essentially general practitioners.

COMMUNITY CONTROL

The foundation was largely the creation of Charles Baumbach, a politically astute young lawyer who put together a coalition of white militant lawyers (primarily Jewish) and minority professionals (mainly black) who held positions in the local poverty power structure. The founders had a common cause in their insistence on neighborhood control of legal services.

For the lawyer-founders, community control was in part a means of negating control by the organized bar which they felt would be opposed to a more aggressive form of advocacy, one that would seek to use the law as an instrument of social change. The lawyers were also committed to altering the conventional power relation between the poor and the agencies that purport to serve them. Community control would create new opportunities for the poor to participate in determining agency policy and decisions, and this principle should also apply to legal service programs for the poor, or so it was felt.

For their part, the neighborhood poverty leaders had just fought and won a battle with the mayor for majority control of the EOC by representatives from the "target" areas, and they wanted control of the legal-services component as well. Their reasons were complex: in part they were simply extending the demand for self-determination; in part they had learned to resent the paternalism and insensitivity of traditional legal aid. But there was also a desire to expand a new power base by gaining control over jobs, services, and other rewards for constituents.

Majority control of the Board of Directors by representatives of the poor was one expression of the neighborhood leaders' insistence on community control. Another was the very considerable autonomy given the neighborhood offices. The local leaders envisioned that each of the poverty areas would in effect have its own law firm. The chief counsel of the neighborhood office was to be selected by the board, rather than the coordinator, and it was assumed that the representatives on the board of a particular neighborhood would have primary say in choosing the attorney to head "their" office. Also, limiting the powers of the coordinator would, it was hoped, minimize racial and ethnic jealousies—given the ethnic mix of San Francisco's poverty areas —and provide a hedge against a bad director.

Community control was the unifying issue for the lawyers and neighborhood leaders who established the foundation. It was also the major issue in the foundation's sometimes bitter struggle with the legal establishment in San Francisco. After a year-long battle, the foundation won a stunning victory when it finally convinced OEO officials to fund it rather than the bar-supported Legal Aid Society of San Francisco. The foundation became the first OEO-funded legal service agency in the United States with majority control by representatives of the poverty community.

INSTITUTIONAL CHANGE

Although the neighborhood leaders expressed no particular views regarding the content of the legal program, the lawyer-founders had some very strong ideas about it. These ideas were derived from an analysis of traditional legal aid and some conceptions about law and social change. The lawyers wanted to create an agency that would not only provide remedial assistance to individual clients (albeit in a more sympathetic and aggressive fashion than legal aid), but would also work toward altering conditions that keep the poor powerless and victims of injustice. This aim was based in part upon a recognition of the impossibility, with limited resources, of handling more than a small fraction of the problems urgently calling for legal assistance, and the necessity, therefore, of a more "wholesale" approach. It rested also on the understanding that, as Jan Howard, Sheldon Messinger, and I wrote in 1966,

the legal problems of the poor . . . characteristically arise from systematic abuses embedded in the operation of various public and private agencies, affecting large numbers of similarly situated individuals. Effective solution of the problems may require the lawyer to direct his attention away from a particular claim or grievance to the broader interests and policies at stake, and away from the individual client to a class of clients, in order to challenge more directly and with greater impact certain structural sources of injustice.

Very generally speaking, we came in time to conceive of our mission in this way: to find leverage points in the system to bring about a redistribution of power and income more favorable to the poor. Two general approaches were developed: strategic advocacy and economic development. Under the first, we sought to enter into the variety of forums where the law is made and administered, to facilitate the development of new rights in areas where the law was vague or clearly biased against the poor, or to enforce existing law favorable to the poor which had remained unimplemented (e.g., enforcement of health and safety provisions of the housing code, prohibitions against fraud and misrepresentation in sale of consumer goods).

To a remarkable extent, it appeared that "the system"—be it welfare, urban renewal, private slum housing, or the garment industry in Chinatown—could not operate successfully without breaking the law: the cost of compliance is generally greater than the operators of the system are willing to pay, especially since those most likely to be hurt have been least likely to complain. Consequently, we hoped that vigorous law enforcement might serve not only to redistribute income, but also to mount sufficient pressure to change the system.

The test for the efficacy of such activity was whether it would result in increasing the income or political bargaining power of a substantial number of poor persons. Litigation (with an emphasis on class suits) and administrative and legislative advocacy were the principal tools. In time, however, we learned that these measures, particularly court cases, by themselves were frequently ineffective unless combined with the mobilization of political support in the middle class as well as poverty communities.

By means of the second general approach we sought to promote entrepreneurial activity among ghetto residents. This came later and remained a subsidiary strategy.

A FOURTH IN THE CITY

Whatever else the foundation may have achieved, it gained a reputation in the community of being a tough advocate for the poor, of being willing to take on any and all opponents—police department, Housing Authority, United States Army, welfare department, used-car dealers, Redevelopment Agency, City Hall, board of education. In a skit presented at the Bar Association of San Francisco Annual Ball (December 1968), the following, written by an attorney member, was sung to the tune of "Glowworm":

We're from Neighborhood Legal Assistance
We encourage draft resistance
Nasty landlords are our nemesis
We keep tenants on the premises
We give deadbeats our protection
To frustrate any debt collection
The laws we use are not on your shelf
'Cause we make them up ourself

We soon recognized the importance of publicity in building a reputation: it has been said that we won more cases at press conferences than in the courts. We published our own newsletter which reached several thousand persons, mostly private attorneys in San Francisco, with reports of our more important and more interesting cases. We also made it a point to get our cases into the press. Some idea of the coverage, and the developing image, may be seen in the following:

In one of the most unusual cases handled by the Foundation in recent weeks, 20-year-old Ted Townsend, who had been held for three months in the Presidio stockade as a suspected deserter, was freed after his Neighborhood Legal Assistance attorney pointed out . . . . (*San Francisco Progress*, August 24, 1967.)

A poverty-program lawyer has filed a complaint with the State Public Utilities Commission, seeking to end Pacific Telephone's $25 deposit requirement for certain new customers. (*Chronicle*, December 16, 1967.)

The Neighborhood Legal Assistance Foundation filed a suit that seeks to prevent San Francisco policemen from carrying guns while off duty. (*Chronicle*, November 9, 1968.)

The San Francisco Neighborhood Legal Assistance Foundation has fired another salvo at the State Department of Social Welfare. (*Examiner*, June 27, 1968.)

The unit [the Main Office legal staff] is illustrative both of the length to which the young attorneys in Legal Assistance will go to attempt to help their clients and of the crusading idealism of the men who operate it. (*Examiner*, October 9, 1968.)

The Neighborhood Legal Assistance Foundation is seeking a breakthrough in labor practices to make unions more responsive to the needs of their members, especially minority-group members with language and cultural problems. (*Argonaut*, October 26, 1968.)

The San Francisco Neighborhood Legal Assistance Foundation has joined the legal fight against Rudolph Ford, the Daley City car dealer. (*Examiner*, January 14, 1969.)

A San Francisco draftee who couldn't get anybody to listen to him finally was heard by a federal judge who ordered the army to discharge the youth. . . . After a year Bibbs got his story to . . . an attorney with the Neighborhood Legal Assistance Foundation who filed a federal court suit and got Bibbs discharged. (*Chronicle*, March 12, 1969.)

A quiet little war has been going on between the San Francisco Neighborhood Legal Assistance Foundation and the state over welfare recipients' rights. . . . (*Chronicle*, March 17, 1969.)

Realtor Walter H. Shornstein was accused yesterday [in a suit filed by the San Francisco Neighborhood Legal Assistance Foundation] of using his position as president of the Recreation and Park Commission to push the destruction of the International Hotel. (*Chronicle*, March 28, 1969.)

ACCOMPLISHMENTS

Our reputation gave us needed leverage in dealing with landlords, merchants, collection agencies, used-car dealers, and public-agency officials. Often a phone call was all that was necessary; people knew that we meant business and would follow through —indeed we enraged many slumlords' attorneys, who accused us (sometimes in letters to their congressmen) of using taxpayers' money to harass them.

In assessing the clout we developed it must be said that we have primarily benefited particular clients for whom we have been able to get a better deal in bargaining with merchants, landlords, welfare officials, and others. Although often gratifying for the lawyer and his client, the benefits are generally remedial and short-lived— very little is basically changed. Housing is a good example. In three years we probably handled at least 4000 individual cases involving some kind of landlord-tenant dispute. We undoubtedly brought some solace and relief to many individual tenants by delaying an eviction or forcing a landlord to make some repairs. Nevertheless, in those same three years the housing situation for poor people in San Francisco has become a great deal worse. The stock of low-income housing has been further reduced through public and private renewal programs. If plans for the latest renewal project in the Yerba Buena District are not changed, there will be approximately 4000 fewer units in the city, which means more doubling up or worse, because there are virtually no vacancies among low-income units. The bulk of the housing available to the poor is substandard (at least 60,000 units have been so labeled officially) and is deteriorating further. The waiting list for public housing went up to 5000, at which point the Housing Authority stopped adding names. Rents have gone up with the decline in the housing stock and increasing taxes—in some areas they have doubled in the past few years. Against this background it might appear as though the foundation had made the process a little more humane without having any effect on the underlying machinery. But that is not quite the case.

There are two areas—redevelopment and welfare—in which we have made at least a small dent in the system, which may well mark the beginning of an even greater impact.

THE DEVELOPMENT FIGHT

In surveying the general housing situation for the poor in San Francisco, it was clear that top priority had to be placed on preventing any further reduction in the stock of low-income housing. The principal offender in San Francisco, as in other parts of the United States, has been the federal urban-renewal program administered through local redevelopment agencies. This program has proceeded on the understanding that there would be no enforcement of those provisions of the Federal Housing Act which require that persons displaced from a project area be relocated into safe, decent, and sanitary housing at rents they can afford. If these provisions were to be enforced, then the renewal program would have to go into the business of building low-income housing—and this it has never been willing or able to do. As a result, the program has produced a drastic net decline in housing for the poor and has substantially worsened slum conditions.

In 1966 redevelopment was on the move again in San Francisco after nearly a two-year lull caused by the voters' approval of the anti-fair housing Proposition 14. The Redevelopment Agency was eager to proceed with its plans to demolish approximately 4500 dwelling units of predominantly low-cost housing in the Western Addition, thereby displacing close to 10,000 persons—mostly poor and black. Failure of the agency to comply with the relocation provisions of the Federal Housing Act would provide, we hoped, the necessary leverage to challenge the project. (Not only was the relocation plan patently deficient—given San Francisco's unbelievably tight low-income housing market and the absence of any provisions for constructing new housing for displacees—but it turned out that the Department of Housing and Urban Development (HUD) had been honoring agency requisitions for financing the project without having first given its approval of the agency's relocation plan— a clear and gross violation of federal law.) The major obstacle that we faced was the fact that the courts had, unfortunately, refused to monitor federal urban-renewal programs on behalf of project residents, on the theory that persons whose homes were being destroyed did not have sufficient stake in the outcome of litigation to give them standing to sue and that such suits involved technical matters too complex for the courts to get into. Even though public officials might be violating the law to the grievous detriment of thousands of poor residents forced out of their homes into even worse circumstances, the courts refused to open their doors to hear these complaints. The principal hurdle, then, was the court itself. Before anything else could be done we had to establish for our clients a most basic right—the right to be heard before a judicial tribunal.

A year and a day after the suit was filed in conjunction with the NAACP Legal Defense Fund—and sixteen months after filing an administrative protest with HUD—the court finally reached a decision on the jurisdictional question: it found that our clients had standing to challenge the legality of the agency's relocation plan and issued a preliminary injunction bringing the renewal project in the Western Addition to a grinding halt. This was clearly a landmark decision; it finally brought the federal renewal program under the scrutiny of judicial review, and for the first time in the United States a renewal project had been stopped in midstream.

The case had been brought on behalf of the Western Addition Community Organization (WACO), a federation of grassroots neighborhood organizations, put together a couple of years earlier by a Student Nonviolent Coordinating Committee organizer to fight the second round of redevelopment in the Western Addition (the first round had been decisively lost—only a handful of families out of the many thousand previously residing in the area ever returned). As a result of the court victory, WACO and the residents of the project area were at last given a voice in the decisions and plans so vitally affecting their lives—both in the sense of having gained entrée into the court and also by establishing a viable bargaining position with the Redevelopment Agency. Although the injunction was later dissolved by the court, the Redevelopment Agency had been significantly shaken—and a new and broader-based coalition emerged in the Western Addition which, under agreement with the agency, became an official participant in the renewal process.

Pressure on the Redevelopment Agency has been kept up as projects begin to move in other areas. The Yerba Buena project, which calls for the destruction of 4000 housing units to make way for a new commercial complex, was also challenged by the foundation in a federal court suit. The clients, who are generally old as well as poor, have literally no place to go. The fight with the Redevelopment Agency, particularly in Yerba Buena, brought the foundation into a head-on confrontation with the San Francisco power structure, and the pressure began to mount, especially from City Hall. Nevertheless, the political alliances that had been forged in support of our clients' interests—including our allies among respectable middle-class groups and civic organizations—held firm. And once again, and far more rapidly than before, a federal court order was issued temporarily halting relocation of residents.

What then have we accomplished? We have at least slowed down the rate of destruction of low-income housing by public and private agencies. (By saving the International Hotel, which houses the remnant of the Filipino community in San Francisco, from demolition by private developers, we were able to extend some of the principles established in the WACO case into the private sector.) We have also helped fashion a legal-political force that the Redevelopment Agency and the city power structure will have to bargain with in determining housing policies for San Francisco. And we have provided hard evidence that in the area of redevelopment the arbitrary exercise of public power by local authorities and the federal government can be checked.

WELFARE RIGHTS

The other area in which the foundation has made some progress in its goal of institutional change is welfare. To begin with, we have enabled many more poor people to obtain public assistance: at least 60,000 people became eligible to receive welfare benefits as a result of our suit that invalidated California's residency requirement. We also prevented the cutoff of close to 2000 needy persons from general assistance as an economy move by the San Francisco Department of Social Services. The foundation, moreover, has won several court decisions which, if and when they are implemented, will substantially increase dollar benefits to recipients. In the *Ivy* case the Superior Court ordered that rent allotments for AFDC recipients in San Francisco and Alameda counties be raised immediately to cover actual rentals (this will add about $19 million when extended statewide) and that a new list of rent allotments be issued reflecting the cost of safe and sanitary housing as required by state law (and this could add at least $30 million more). In the *Nesbit* case (which we brought with the Alameda County Legal Aid Society), the court held that the state Department of Social Welfare was violating recent state and federal regulations which, as an encouragement to seek employment, exempt a certain portion of the earnings of working recipients in calculating their welfare grant. As a result, it was estimated that working recipients were getting approximately $30 a month less than they were entitled to. Enforcement of this decision could increase payments to recipients by about $9 million. In the *Kaiser* case, also brought with the Alameda County Legal Aid Society, the federal court declared unconstitutional a California statute placing a ceiling on the amount of money that could be granted to AFDC recipients, a ceiling that was actually lower than the state's own determination of the minimum required for subsistence.

Insofar as we have sought to increase the amount of money going to welfare recipients, we appear to have been successful in adding somewhere between $50 and $100 million—this includes the $25 to $30 million a year estimated increase in welfare costs resulting from the residency decision. Not bad for a $3 million investment in legal services in San Francisco.

These figures, however, may turn out to be something less than firm. The state still has many options to limit, delay, or in other ways frustrate the carrying out of the courts' decisions. The state Department of Social Welfare can engage us in lengthy appellate proceedings, it can adopt new regulations to reduce the cost of particular decisions, it can simply refuse to comply with court orders (as it is now doing in the rent case), or the legislature may change the state law that was the basis for the court victory.

It became necessary, therefore, for us to attend to these other arenas. This required not only our presence at hearings and meetings of state and county welfare bodies and appearances before legislative committees, but the mobilizing of welfare recipients and others to bring pressure to bear on administrative and legislative decision makers. Formation of an active city-wide welfare-rights organization was achieved in part through a series of welfare-advocates' classes conducted in various neighborhoods by the foundation's welfare specialists.

Pressure from the poverty community has been fairly effective in San Francisco, much less effective in Sacramento. Effectiveness in Sacramento requires not only statewide organization, but support from other than welfare recipients, and it is certainly questionable whether this support will be forthcoming when most middle-class voters feel that more money for welfare inevitably comes out of their pockets. Nevertheless, an important effect of the residency decision is that states like California, with relatively high benefits, will bring pressure on Congress for some kind of national income-maintenance program.

Our aim has been not only to increase dollar benefits, but to enable recipients to gain some control over the welfare system —to render it less arbitrary and oppressive. We have been able to reform procedures within the welfare department to bring them more in line with constitutional, due-process requirements. One of the cases, in which we have challenged the failure of the state to give recipients a hearing before their benefits are cut off, is now before the United States Supreme Court. In a sense, however, everything we've done in the welfare area has been calculated to maintain constant pressure on the system to maximize its responsiveness to the poor. We have in part succeeded. We have shaken up the system and even encouraged many on the inside to make changes they felt they could not make before.

The retiring director of the state Department of Social Welfare acknowledged the impact of our efforts, and those of other poverty lawyers in California, in the statement he gave at his final news conference on November 28, 1969:

Here in California we have been challenged on dozens of issues, all of them coming back to the fact that for the first time, the poor have real and effective advocacy in our courts. This, again, is the significant point transcending all other considerations and consequences. An era of advocacy has begun out of which, I am sure, public assistance is never going to be the same. Not only is this happening through the courts, but also in the meetings and hearings of welfare boards, advisory commissions, and administrators at every government level. The poor have come out of their apathy, and our accountability for what we do and why we do it is theirs to know—as it always has been under the law but never before so vocally sought.

As I indicated earlier, one of the strategies for institutional change was promotion of economic development in the poverty community. The foundation was one of the first legal-service programs to launch a serious undertaking in this area. The initial project, a laundromat in the Mission District financed with the first SBA loan in the West to a business owned and operated by poor persons, was highly successful. This venture led to the establishment of the San Francisco Local Development Corporation (LDC) which was designed to serve as a catalyst in the development of other ghetto-owned enterprises, and eventually perhaps serve as a neighborhood development bank. This approach seemed to us to provide a more direct route to the redistributive goal than litigation. Although the LDC continues to function, and has assisted a number of ghetto residents in financing and managing new businesses, we have actually accomplished a great deal less over the past year or two in the economic area than we have in the courts. The slow pace of the LDC may be accounted for in part by staff problems and the time and energy that was consumed in obtaining initial funding. We also underestimated the difficulties in accumulating the capital and expertise necessary to move beyond the small retail or service business.

DILEMMAS

As we have seen, the foundation was initially conceived as a collection of largely autonomous neighborhood law firms with a central administrative staff to "keep the machinery running" and to provide liaison among the neighborhood offices and between them and the board and various outside agencies. This highly decentralized system was designed to ensure maximum responsiveness to the particular needs of the various poverty communities.

I had become convinced from a brief study I had conducted for OEO in the summer of 1966 that a central research and planning staff was essential to implement the broader, strategic goals of the legal-services program. Notwithstanding the greater dedication and competence of the attorneys in the OEO-funded agencies, I argued in my report that without structural changes that go beyond simply shifting the location of the office (into the neighborhood) there would be little difference in actual impact and operation between OEO legal programs and conventional legal aid. I suggested, therefore, a division of function between a central office and neighborhood offices. Lawyers in the central office would develop strategies for change and take the necessary steps to implement these strategies through test cases, class actions, and the like. I contended that they should also maintain close relations with neighborhood organizations, "for the task of creative advocacy ought to reflect consultation with the slum community as well as feedback from the caseload of the neighborhood offices." The main task of the neighborhood office would be that "of serving a large volume clientele on something like a mass production basis," with some research and other assistance from the specialist attorneys.

Over the years, a strong central legal staff was built up in the Main Office of the foundation. The attorneys became specialists in housing and redevelopment, welfare, and other areas, and they were responsible for the major cases of the foundation. The office was started with two attorneys. In the fall of 1969, there were approximately 15 attorneys (including most of the foundation's allotment of Reginald Heber Smith Fellows) and a total staff of about 25, not including the many law students working in the clinic program. The Main Office legal staff was now larger than any of the neighborhood offices. The Main Office attorneys were the "cosmopolitans" in the foundation: they were much more likely than the neighborhood attorneys to have contacts with other poverty lawyers across the United States—in OEO programs, the Legal Defense Fund —to attend regional and national conferences and training sessions and to keep up with the growing body of legal literature in their field.

From the very beginning, relations between the neighborhood offices and the Main Office were strained. In my report to OEO I had pointed out that one of the problems that might arise in setting up a separate structure for the strategic cases was

the tension between service to a mass clientele and creative advocacy. At any point the decision to allocate limited resources to a central planning staff may seem arbitrary, even heartless. For the decision will necessitate turning away desperate people who are, after all, entitled to the service. But unless this is done, little will be accomplished for the large majority of slum dwellers, and many of those who are served will receive only temporary relief.

Neighborhood attorneys felt that they were carrying the burden of providing legal services to the poverty community with little or no help or relief from their Main Office colleagues. The latter were viewed as an expensive luxury—their case loads immorally small, the pace of their work annoyingly relaxed and the results highly dubious. Was the WACO case really worth all the time and effort that had gone into it, and what about the welfare cases that put a few more dollars in a recipient's pocket, if that? Is it fair to spend such a large share of the foundation's resources on these highly speculative cases when there are clear, tangible results obtained in eviction cases and divorce cases, where people really hurt? These questions bothered many neighborhood attorneys. Their growing resentment of Main Office attorneys was hardly diminished by the incidental benefits they seemed to enjoy—the many trips to conferences and meetings, the publicity in the newspapers, and neighborhood sovereignty.

From the point of view of the Main Office attorneys, neighborhood lawyers were not only essentially engaged in a Band-Aid operation, but even on a remedial basis were frequently unable to give effective representation to their clients, given the unwillingness of the neighborhood offices either to limit caseloads or to accept more efficient, routinized procedures. Furthermore, several chief counsels were viewed as the prime perpetuators of a system in which the client community was often the loser.

Main Office attorneys were also unhappy about what appeared to be the political restrictions on some neighborhood offices. The principal example was the unwillingness of the Western Addition office to represent WACO in its fight with the Redevelopment Agency. This decision, it was felt, was motivated in part by a reluctance to oppose the black Establishment in the Western Addition (including the local EOC leaders) which supported redevelopment in exchange for more jobs for blacks in the agency and sponsorship of projects within the renewal area. Similarly, the Chinatown office was extremely reluctant to take an aggressive position against established interests in Chinatown. Thus it was fully two years before any action at all was taken against the sweatshops. It was no accident that these were the two offices in which the local Establishment had most to do with the selection of the chief counsel.

Tensions were heightened by racial and ethnic differences. The Main Office legal staff has been predominantly white (it is interesting that a black lawyer who joined the staff has had little sympathy for the goals and methods of the office) and largely Jewish. Criticism of the Main Office has undoubtedly been affected by the feeling that it was inappropriate for white lawyers to be deciding what is best for poor blacks.

Although the neighborhood lawyers continued to be critical of the increase in staff at the Main Office and its failure to operate primarily as a back-up resource for them, an uneasy truce emerged between the neighborhood offices and the Main Office. The chief counsels agreed to leave the Main Office alone if it would not interfere in internal operations of the neighborhood offices. The sovereignty of the neighborhood offices was not to be trifled with. This was not a very happy solution. Indeed, it became increasingly difficult to effect even a modest degree of coordination. At stake was raising the quality of service in the neighborhood offices—and at the very least, preventing a deterioration in quality. This meant being able to do something about recruitment of attorneys, training of new attorneys, and increasing office efficiency. Development of a rational recruitment program to take advantage of the foundation's nationwide reputation to attract top legal talent, particularly minority lawyers, simply was not possible with each office refusing to yield on its absolute power to hire and fire staff. A staff training program never really existed—some chief counsels resented the interference, and one refused to permit his attorneys to attend training sessions. Development of standard legal forms and office procedures, sharing of information on cases, research memos and briefs to avoid duplication of effort and to ensure the best thinking or approach to a case—all of these seemed unattainable despite repeated campaigns to bring them about. In response to a grant condition from OEO, the director of litigation (who is in effect the chief counsel for the Main Office legal staff) drew up a minimal plan to ensure that information on more important or unusual cases would be made available to him and to the chief counsels in advance of filing, but leaving final control over the cases in the hands of the chief counsels. For a long period the chief counsels for one reason or another were unwilling to consider the plan on its merits.

We were caught in a bind. Our efforts to assist neighborhood offices in raising the quality of service to clients were generally opposed as undermining the autonomy of the neighborhood offices. As a result, the neighborhood job got tougher—with increasing resentment against the Main Office and a lowering of the quality of service to the clients in the neighborhoods. The offices continued operating essentially as independent law firms. Within the offices there was no real division of labor or specialization. Attorneys handled as best they could whatever cases and matters came their way on their interview days. Case loads were large and becoming more burdensome as the backlog of unfinished cases slowly but surely built up. Work with neighborhood groups was confined mostly to incorporation of essentially paper organizations. Moreover, the staff became less experienced, given the tendency to fill vacant slots with younger attorneys. And there was little effective supervision, since in most offices the chief counsel was playing primarily a political role in the community, having turned over the day-to-day administration of the office to his senior staff attorney or senior secretary. Consequently, in spite of the dedication and ability of most neighborhood attorneys, the quality of the work product in general declined.

The goal of community control had been institutionalized in the autonomous neighborhood offices, while the aim of institutional change was embodied in the Main Office legal staff. It was obvious that the growing antagonism between these two structures in large measure represented a conflict between the two goals. The lawyer-founders had been wrong in assuming that control by the client community was a necessary condition for, let alone compatible with, a program of institutional change. We were unfortunately burdened with some romantic notions of the poor.

THE OLD WAY UP

The neighborhood leaders, particularly those identified with the poverty program, were following an old pattern fashioned by other ethnic groups as they fought their way up the power ladder. These leaders were, by and large, not out to change or seriously challenge the system; they simply wanted to be cut in. They were willing to have an understanding with the older, white Establishment: in exchange for greater control of public programs aimed at helping the poor, and more control over jobs and other rewards for their constituents, they would keep the peace. The WACO suit was, of course, embarrassing: it was not until the Redevelopment Agency by its arrogance alienated its black allies in the Western Addition that the neighborhood leaders were able openly to support WACO's position.

It may well be the case that, with respect to their conception of legal services, the neighborhood leaders at this point are much closer to the conservative Republicans than to the militant white lawyers.

It is always possible, of course, that the neighborhood leaders may become radicalized—and the violent repression of the Panthers may be doing just that. And it is also possible that the young black lawyers coming out of the Reginald Heber Smith program may press for a more radical approach to legal services. Neither group, so far, however, seems to be prepared to move much beyond the issue of community control. The two principal demands of the black Reginald Heber Smith Fellows in a recent confrontation with OEO officials were higher salaries and control of the program.

By the spring of 1969 I was convinced that there would have to be some basic change in the structure of the foundation: although much of our work, particularly in housing and welfare, was beginning to pay off, the tensions within the foundation were becoming critical. The changes that would have to be brought about would necessarily mean limiting, if not doing away with, the autonomy of the neighborhood offices. In my view, this could only be accomplished by a black coordinator dedicated to institutional change, that is, by a militant black lawyer. I tried unsuccessfully for several months to find such a person. Finally, in October, having held the office for three years, and with a sense that we had accomplished in some ways a great deal more than I had ever expected, I resigned as coordinator of the foundation. It was now up to the board to find my successor, and hopefully a solution to our dilemma.

In December of 1969 my successor was chosen. The new coordinator is a black lawyer who had been a staff attorney in one of the neighborhood offices, and more recently held a top administrative post in the EOC. He is an able attorney, with a strong sense of professionalism and a flair for administrative efficiency. Although not unsympathetic to the aims and approach of the Main Office legal staff, he clearly represents the interests and perspective of the neighborhood offices. The tensions within the foundation should be significantly reduced, the divisions healed. I assume that the commitment to institutional change will gradually become weaker and that the Main Office legal staff will be reduced in size and given a different direction—to serve primarily as back-up resource for the neighborhood offices.

In retrospect, this probably represents the only solution that was realistically open to the foundation Reorganization in the image of the Main Office legal staff would have brought the foundation into more direct and intolerable confrontations with the Establishment and would have seriously jeopardized neighborhood support. Perhaps at this point the main objective should be the survival of the foundation as a major institution serving the ghetto under ghetto control.

If the militant white lawyers move on, this should not be interpreted simply as a reaction to a shift in leadership and possible direction of the foundation. Some have become disillusioned with the capacity of the legal system to respond; others may be following new fashions. In one way or another, however, the old coalition will very likely be dissolved. Looking back, I suppose we have each used the other—the black professionals and neighborhood leaders have gained an organization, and we had the chance to put our theories into practice. Still, it's sad the partnership couldn't last.

DISRUPTING CITY SERVICES TO CHANGE NATIONAL PRIORITIES

Frances Pivan and Richard Cloward

We often say that the nation's poor, especially the black poor, are carrying the main burdens of the war in Vietnam. Yet little is being done to make the poor an effective force in shifting national priorities from war to domestic programs. Mass demonstrations such as the Poor People's Campaign, which rely on "moral confrontation," are at best a limited form of pressure, and then only when conditions are ripe for new political accommodations. So far, the Administration has shown itself to be capable of absorbing countless demonstrations staged in the Capitol itself.

The Administration is most vulnerable, we think, in the cities, especially if tactics more politically disruptive than demonstrations are employed. It is in the cities that the national Democratic Party has its base, and it is there that most of the black poor now live. Whatever happens in the cities reverberates on national Democratic leaders. Indeed, the growing demand from a wide variety of groups that the Administration give priority to trouble in the cities is becoming a major encumbrance on war policies. Trouble has been brewing over a number of years as masses of black poor have been forced off the land and into the cities, where they aggravate municipal fiscal problems because of the public services they need, and aggravate the white working class by competing for scarce housing and jobs. Riots have further escalated tensions within urban Democratic constituencies, pushing municipalities nearer bankruptcy and worsening black-white electoral cleavages. Except for the war, massive federal grants-in-aid for welfare, health, housing, education, and employment could be used to ease this divisiveness between groups in the Democratic coalition, but that money now goes to the military establishment. If strategies can be found which substantially worsen tensions in the cities, the Administration might be forced to alter these priorities.

Disruptive strategies to produce this result are available. The cities are peculiarly vulnerable to disruption at this time, for city agencies serve older Democratic constituents at the expense of blacks who are a vast new electoral force in the cities. The key to disrupting services—and to exposing this anachronism—is to mobilize the poor either to withhold payments to a system from which they do not receive fair services because the system defers to other groups, or to mobilize people to claim benefits which have been withheld, again out of deference to other groups. First, we propose massive rent stoppages to bankrupt slum landlords and to force municipal takeover of slum buildings. Second, we will describe current efforts to organize actual and potential welfare recipients to claim hundreds of millions of dollars which are withheld from them, usually illegally. These strategies could force city governments into fiscal crisis, exacerbating already evident political strains in the cities, and escalating pressure on the Administration

Reprinted by permission from Viet-Report, **3** *(Summer 1968), pp. 27–31.*

to bail out its urban political apparatus with massive subsidies for the poor.

DISRUPTING THE SLUM HOUSING SYSTEM

The slum is the underbelly of the real-estate market: tenants who cannot compete for housing elsewhere are preyed on by entrepreneurs who lack the capital or competence to compete for profit elsewhere. More prosperous and stable real-estate investors put their capital in the regular market, where money can be made in less demeaning ways, leaving the slum to be exploited by men who seek to gain on speculative exchanges or who, restrained by rent-control laws from levying large increases, shore up their declining profits by skimping on repairs and services. The result is inflated prices and deteriorated buildings—a situation that can be remedied only by public subsidies and public action.

But there is little political pressure for housing subsidies for the poor—only for affluent groups. And although deteriorated housing is illegal, public agencies make no effort to enforce housing codes, for a crackdown would produce massive dislocation of landlords and tenants. Repairs are extremely expensive, and building income is limited by the poverty of the captive tenant market. Slum landlords often do not have the funds to rehabilitate their buildings—not, at least, without substantial increases in rents. Just a modest step-up in enforcement activity under a new administration in New York City recently resulted in a rapid upsurge in the number of foreclosures, tax delinquencies, and vacate orders. If slumlords were pushed out, government would have to house the minority poor. So the enforcement agencies use their powers gingerly and selectively, usually paying heed only when tenants have the tenacity or the "pull" to compel

enforcement. In other words, slum profits depend on collusion between city agencies and landlords: in return for nonenforcement of the codes, the slumlord takes the blame for the slum and enables the city to evade the political ire of the ghetto.

To disrupt these collusive arrangements, the funds that fuel the slum system must be cut off. Tenants should be told to keep the rent money, and to spend it rather than put it aside for later payment to the landlord.

Some liberal jurisdictions have laws which authorize tenants in buildings with code violations to hold their rents in escrow accounts while they pursue an elaborate set of procedures culminating in a court action. But legalistic rent strikes have been a failure. Low-income tenants cannot secure redress in housing agencies and courts. At worst, the agencies and courts are corrupt instruments of real-estate interests; at best, they are hamstrung by elaborate statutes and regulations written to safeguard private property. Even if this were not so, the sheer volume of tasks involved in pursuing a court case is overwhelming: canvassing buildings for violations; filling out complaint forms; arranging appointments for housing inspectors; checking to make sure that the inspectors file reports and that violations have been recorded; arranging for lawyers; chauffering tenants to trials—not once, but repeatedly as landlords successfully obtain adjournments. In short, everything we know about the failure of past legalistic rent strikes points to the futility of attempts to solve a widespread problem by making use of cumbersome procedures for individual legal redress.

Phase I: Ending Evictions

The great obstacle to mounting a disruptive rent strike is the danger that tenants may be evicted. Fear of eviction will make tenants reluctant to withhold rent in the first place, and evictions later can break the morale of a rent-strike movement, causing its collapse. Thus the first phase of organizing should concentrate on resisting evictions. During this first phase, the momentum for a strike movement can also be built.

During a campaign to "Stop All Evictions!" in a particular neighborhood, resistance squads could be organized and tactics for dealing with marshals and police could be tested without exposing tenants to risk. In the meantime, organizers could talk up the idea of a rent strike. The key problem in this phase is to develop a neighborhood communications system for reporting evictions. One way is to leaflet a neighborhood, asking tenants threatened by eviction to call a central telephone number so that organizers can be dispatched to watch the apartment. Another way is to have organizers hang around on the block, telling people to let them know the moment the marshal appears in the vicinity.

There are several tactics for resisting evictions. For example: organizers can mass both in front of the building and within the threatened apartment to block the marshal. They can sit on the furniture, return the furniture to the apartment as quickly as it is carried out, or neighborhood people could be deployed along the hallways and stairways through which the furniture must pass. To overcome even such simple tactics, a marshal must call for the police, who then must contemplate mass arrests in order to carry out a routine eviction. (So far, when these tactics have been tried, the police have been very reluctant to do the landlord's job.)

If resistance works, many more neighborhood people may be emboldened to join in. And when more people join, organizers can capitalize on the public's fear of riots. City officials are now extremely sensitive to the temper of ghettos and exert themselves to avoid the minor incidents which have often set off conflagrations. Mayors have emergency power to halt evictions by executive order, and under the threat of riot would be likely to do so. Even tough-talking Mayor Daley of Chicago ordered all evictions halted during July and August of last year.

Phase II: Rent Revolt

Aside from reasonable assurances that they will not be evicted, tenants need an incentive to strike. The rent money is such an incentive, but only if the tenant can pocket it or spend it. Tenants who in past rent strikes were called upon to place their rent in escrow derived some satisfaction in just keeping the rent from the landlord, but the satisfaction would be far greater if that money could also be spent on family needs, particularly since rent absorbs so large a percentage of the typical slum family's income—sometimes more than half. At least as important, only the massive denial of rent will bankrupt the slum system; if the money is left to accumulate in escrow accounts, it will eventually be returned to landlords by the courts (or by tenants themselves, frightened by either the reality or the rumor that court cases are being lost).

The spread of rent-strike action must be controlled. If those withholding rent are dispersed over too wide an area, the logistics of resisting evictions may become overwhelming. It is probably preferable for organizers to work intensively on a few blocks at first, concentrating their energies to ensure complete coverage of eviction threats. As the area of strike action expands, organizers will need to make sure that a viable communication system exists, and that there are neighborhood cadres capable of resisting evictions. In addition, reserve forces—perhaps sympathetic student groups—should be available for quick mobilization to protect a particular block if public officials decide to try to break the strike by a dramatic show of force. (If some money is available, leaders of the strike may want to rent several vacant apartments, holding them in reserve in the event that a few evictions do in fact occur.)

Phase III: Dealing with Responses to the Rent Revolt

The response of landlords and municipal housing agencies to a successful rent revolt will vary depending on local conditions. Where landlords have little equity in their buildings, many may simply abandon them. In other situations, landlords may try to wait out the strikers, exerting counter-pressure by turning off utilities and discontinuing services. But there is nothing a landlord can turn off that tenants can't turn back on. And if marshals can be successfully resisted, so can utility men threatening to turn off gas and electricity.

When landlords terminate services or abandon the buildings, tenants may want to take over the task of providing minimum services. If they have the organizational capability to do so, they can then settle down to rent-free living until politicians decide to institute programs for refurbishing housing or subsidizing the construction of new housing.

But if a neighborhood does not or cannot take over the servicing of buildings, the consequences might turn into a political advantage for the strikers. Under such circumstances, dangerous conditions would quickly develop: hazards to health, threats of fire, the spread of disorder and suffering. Political leaders can ill afford to ignore these conditions in dense urban communities, where disease and fire can readily spread beyond the boundaries of the slum and ghetto.

Warm-weather months afford many tactical advantages. Lack of heat, the most serious inconvenience to tenants, is not a problem, and even the fear of eviction loses some of its force: hot pavements are not so fearsome as ice-covered ones. More important, people are much more likely to be on the streets in warm weather, making it easier to assemble crowds at the sites of attempted evictions. And until now, at least, the potential for riots and mass violence has been greatest in the summer, so that official repression of strikes is not so likely then.

Municipal political leaders, it should be stressed, possess the powers to act in emergencies. They can take over buildings, institute emergency repairs, and otherwise divert public funds from programs for other groups to cope with a crisis in the slum and ghetto. The question is: What will it take to force these actions? The answer, we suggest, is nothing short of a major crisis in the slum system.

DISRUPTING THE PUBLIC-WELFARE SYSTEM

The growing national movement of welfare recipients[1] is already revealing the fiscal punch of tactics which upset the long-standing practices by which local welfare

[1] The National Welfare Rights Organization, formed two years ago, is directed by George Wiley, a former associate national director of CORE. Policies are formed by a committee composed exclusively by welfare-recipient representatives from 36 states. Organizing materials may be obtained by writing the national headquarters at 1762 Corcoran Street, N.W., Washington, D.C., as well as lists of the leaders, addresses and telephone numbers of hundreds of welfare groups throughout the country. A national welfare newsletter, available for $10 per year, describes organizing activities in various locales, announces nationwide demonstrations, and summarizes important legislation and administrative rulings regarding public welfare.

systems withhold lawful benefits from the poor. In New York City, for example, organizing drives to claim benefits have forced the welfare rolls up by 50 percent in less than two years and doubled costs (to $1.3 billion). And this has been accomplished by a movement which has no support at all from civil rights or peace groups, and scarcely any funds or organizers of its own.

Americans regard every dollar spent for public relief to the unemployed and the unemployable as a sign that something is wrong. Many in the middle class are convinced that poverty should be dealt with by "rehabilitating" the poor rather than by redistributing income; the working class is preoccupied with taxes and hostile toward those below them; and many black leaders seem embarrassed to fight for "handouts," even for those who should not or cannot work, or for those who cannot get a decent job at a decent wage. It is in deference to these widespread sentiments that administrators of public-welfare agencies design policies and procedures to keep their budgets low, an objective achieved by keeping the poor ignorant of their eligibility, by erecting a tangle of bureaucratic barriers against those who do apply, by arbitrarily and illegally rejecting many applicants, and by refusing to allot the full benefits provided by law to those who do get on the rolls. The result is that only half of those who are eligible actually get on the rolls, and most of these are cheated out of full allowances.

Phase I: Breaking the Secrecy Barrier

Welfare organizing across the nation has usually begun with efforts to inform people of their rights.

1. Organizers obtain the official manual of welfare regulations. Welfare administrators ordinarily will not release this manual, but a sympathetic welfare worker can usually be found who will steal a copy. Otherwise, recipients can hold a sit-in or, since manuals are public documents, initiate litigation to obtain copies.

2. A simplified handbook for the use of clients and organizers is prepared on the basis of the manual.

3. Thousands of copies are distributed in ghetto neighborhoods, through churches, stores, and other outlets.

The handbook is especially useful if it is written to alert organizers and clients to the ways in which the system withholds benefits from people—e.g., giving illegal grounds for rejecting applicants, describing typical forms of underbudgeting, telling people about the availability of special grants for heavy clothing which are ordinarily kept secret. Overcoming the secrecy barrier is a crucial step in organizing: people cannot fight what they do not understand.

Phase II: Developing Cadres of Recipients

The national welfare movement has been built largely by indigenous leaders (usually mothers on the Aid to Dependent Children rolls). Once information gets around regarding the extent to which recipients are being cheated out of various benefits, groups form quickly. In the early stages, these groups usually focus on settling the individual grievances of their members. Since negotiations with welfare officials over the intricacies of individual cases consume enormous amounts of time and energy, groups which continue to concentrate on settling individual grievances do not tend to grow. Other tactics, noted in the next phase, are necessary to produce mass action. But grievance work has had the useful consequence of developing cadres of recipients who are confident of their knowledge about the system and of their ability to stand up to it. These cadres, in turn, have often become the spearhead of efforts to mount mass campaigns against the system.

Phase III: Mass Claims for Benefits

Large-scale campaigns are based on identifying a benefit to which many people are entitled but which few receive. Most welfare regulations, for example, allow grants for special purposes, but people are rarely told about them and generally don't get them. Staging a "mass benefit campaign" is much simpler than adjusting individual grievances and has far greater impact. Once the particular benefit is identified as the focus of the campaign (such as demands for school clothing), a checklist is mimeographed and distributed widely through the ghetto, together with an announcement of a demonstration. When several hundred people assemble to demand a common benefit, welfare departments usually release the grants, particularly in cities with large ghettos, where public officials fear violence. In New York City, for example, campaigns staged by welfare groups around special grants for household items, clothing, and emergencies have released some 50 million dollars in extra allowances over the past year.

One of the most useful tactics learned from these campaigns is to make the waiting rooms in the welfare center the locus of organizing activity. In the big cities these waiting rooms are constantly jammed with people, many of whom will respond to on-the-spot offers of aid in getting on the rolls or in obtaining special allowances. In a number of places organizers are beginning to go into the centers with leaflets about welfare rights, with checklist forms for special grants, and with simplified eligibility forms which people can fill out before being called to the interviewing cubicle for an initial interview. If organizers are barred from waiting rooms by the police, they set up tables on the sidewalks outside to distribute literature and talk with people moving in and out of the centers.

Similar issues could be raised by mobilizing unemployed and underpaid black men who are kept off the rolls despite jurisdictions which allow some to obtain benefits under a "home relief" or "general relief" category, and others whose wages are less than they would receive on welfare to receive supplementary payments.

Some groups are contemplating mass advertising to inform people of their possible eligibility for welfare, or to inform those who are already on the rolls of the special allowances they are probably not receiving. The actions being considered include:

1. Taking ads in newspapers or making spot announcements on radio stations that reach the ghetto.
2. Placing posters in supermarkets and other stores in slum neighborhoods.
3. Enlisting ghetto clergymen to preach on welfare rights.
4. Mass leafletting of neighborhoods.

Advertising techniques should be especially effective in reaching the millions of poverty-stricken people who are still not on the rolls, sometimes for reasons of pride, but more often because of ignorance produced by secrecy about eligibility barriers.

In summary, strategies to bankrupt the cities have a double thrust. First, rising municipal costs mean that the poor are getting money, whether it's the rent money they keep or the higher welfare payments they receive. The promise of money is a powerful incentive in mobilizing mass action; the continued flow of money is a powerful force in sustaining it. Protest and demonstration tactics, by contrast, depend on the much less certain and usually less compelling appeal of ideology or momentary drama.

Second, the more money the poor get, the greater the leverage on the national Administration. Urban political leaders, already on the brink of fiscal disaster because they are squeezed between the services needed by an enlarging ghetto constituency and the indignation of their white taxpaying constituents, are becoming insistent lobbyists for increased federal subsidies. It will not be easy for a national Administration that depends on the cities to ignore these claims, or to ignore the worsening divisions in their urban constituency which these strategies can generate.

9 Dispensing Justice and Dignity

INJUSTICE AND INDIGNITY

The Editors

In January 1965, a project entitled Neighborhood Legal Services (NLS) was started in Washington, D.C., funded by the Office of Economic Opportunity. The NLS provides lawyers to defend poor clients who are facing legal action, and to represent clients in legal actions to protect their own interests. The impact of the NLS was described in the October 3, 1966, issue of the *Washington Post*.

Imagine a Washington where slum tenants can legally refuse to pay rent until landlords bring their housing up to city standards;

Where public housing tenants can go to court and force the National Capital Housing Authority to eliminate rats from their homes;

Where Welfare Department investigators are banned from homes of public-aid recipients unless they are invited inside or have a search warrant;

Where finance companies dealing largely with the poor suddenly find they can no longer collect on questionable high-interest contracts.

Imagine a Washington where the quarter of a million poor people now hailed without lawyers into Landlord and Tenant, Small Claims, Traffic, Drunk, and Juvenile courts each year started showing up with attorneys, demanding full court hearings, and winning 10, 20, even 50 times as many cases as they do now.

In response to the activities of the NLS, lawyers for landlords have complained that the NLS lawyers have frequently requested jury trials to earn more time for their clients in avoiding evictions; lawyers in private practice have filed suit against the NLS charging unfair competition; lawyers representing landlords and finance companies who have been used to winning scores of judgments without trials now find themselves confronted with long court trials; and city judges looking at their clogged court docket complain about the NLS lawyers who "are trying to take every 15-cent case all the way up to the Supreme Court."

The effects of the Neighborhood Legal Services project are most striking when one considers that all this represents is a situation where the poor have an opportunity to enjoy all the legal rights generally available to more prosperous and more knowledgeable citizens. It also dramatically describes how easily social institutions—in this case the legal institutions—become adapted to a condition of established legal inequality for some citizens and at the same time resistant to attempts to restore those rights.

The legal system is one activity of the national state that has the manifest purpose of protecting the rights of its citizens. Another activity that is manifestly designed to serve the needs of citizens of the state is the system of public welfare. Both activities have in common a grounding in philosophical principles that see men as beings of special worth and value, with certain fundamental rights that must be preserved. However, both activities also share the dubious honors of falling very far short of their noble purposes and destroying the ends they seek to achieve.

Constitutional guarantees of equal protection under the law, legal counsel, grand-jury indictment, and trial by jury have been found frequently to be guarantees more for some citizens than for others. The complex machinery of the law concerning bail, parole, appeals, grand-jury hearings, preliminary hearings, and rights to counsel can be overwhelming to the person who has little knowledge of the law or little money to employ the services of legal representatives. The poor do not fare well in obtaining the benefit of many of their legal guarantees. They are more likely not to get preliminary hearings, not to get bail, to be in jail longer awaiting trial, not to get a grand-jury hearing, to have fewer jury trials, and to be found guilty more frequently (Nagel, 1966).

The Blumberg article in this chapter provides a close-up look at the legal process in terms of the relationships among the lawyer, client, and court. The author provides a description of the pretrial process that is far removed from popular conceptions of the adversary system of a lawyer representing his client. Here we have a version of the lawyer-client relationship played as a confidence game, with the lawyer choosing legal strategies that will lead to a speedy conclusion and an assured fee. The client is caught between two bureaucratic structures—the legal profession and the courts—each of which has an interest in preserving the other and in developing an efficient system for processing defendants. Blumberg's argument raises some doubt as to the effectiveness of Supreme Court decisions which have extended guarantees to counsel to all citizens; he questions whether the poor defendant is any better off with a lawyer than he is without one.

Efforts to extend constitutional guarantees to the poor have not been limited to the trial phase of the legal process. There have also been important Supreme Court decisions designed to protect defendants in the earliest phase of the legal process—while they are in the hands of the police. In 1957, the Supreme Court in the Mallory decision ruled that police in the District of Columbia could hold a suspect only for the shortest time possible before bringing him before a judge. In 1963, the Gideon decision provided a blanket rule on the individual defendant's right to a lawyer. The most far-reaching decision in 1964—the Escobedo case—ruled that an accused person in the custody of the police could not be subjected to a station-house interrogation until his request to see his lawyer was granted.

These decisions have thrust the Court into a position of making policy for running police departments. This has occurred as the Court's decisions on specific cases have tended to become extended as a general standard governing all cases. As Packer (1965) has noted in speaking of the new decisions by the Court:

It is one thing to say: This defendant's confession was illegally coerced because he was illiterate, unadvised of his rights, held incommunicado, subjected to threats, beaten, or whatever. It is quite another to say: No person who is arrested may be questioned by the police until he has been advised of his right to remain silent and to have the assistance of a lawyer and until he has had the chance to see a lawyer if he wants to.

According to Packer, the increasing tendency of the Supreme Court to make the second type of ruling results from the failure of police departments and appropriate state and federal legislative bodies to develop a system of internal controls to protect the rights of accused citizens.

The response of law-enforcement agencies to the court decisions has been to point out how police effectiveness in crime control has been hampered. It is probably true that police interrogation has helped to detect many crimes and criminals. It is probably equally true that interrogation leads to abuse of individual rights and tragic errors in dispensing justice. The reason why courts should bend in the direction of the accused rather than the police stems from the absence of any effective civilian control over police activities. The complaints of minority groups concerning police brutality reflect a situation where the police are generally unaccountable for their actions, and certainly unaccountable to powerless minority-group members.

Another reason to be concerned over the abuses of individual rights in a situation of unrestrained interrogation is the growing use by police of sophisticated behavior-control techniques in their investigative procedures. The article by Zimbardo describes police techniques in interrogations and enhances our understanding of a legal situation which seems highly implausible: that an innocent man can confess to a crime he did not commit.

The new threat to our system of justice under law is found in the recent attempts to alter long-standing constitutional protections for citizens under suspicion, facing arrest, or awaiting trial. The constitutionality of current legislation which allows police to break into private homes (after obtaining a court order) if the occupants are suspected narcotics peddlers is still to be tested. Similarly, the idea of "preventive detention" supported by President Nixon and Attorney General Mitchell would give judges the power to jail without trial persons awaiting trial as a way of limiting the number of crimes committed by persons free on bail for previous crimes. Although designed for "hard-core" criminal suspects, it has potential for intimidating political dissidents seeking to change American society.

The present political climate in the United States strongly suggests the beginnings of a wave of official, government-based repression against student political groups, black militants, and left-wing activists in general. The historical conflict between individual liberties and the demands of the state is once again tipping in the direction of the state, much as it did in the "Red Raids" of the 1930s, the concentration camps for Japanese-Americans in the 1940s, the McCarthy purges of teachers, government officials, and intellectuals in the 1950s, and the attempts to exterminate black and white radicals in the 1960s. The use of the political trial as the "legal" means of repression seems to increase in frequency. The Spock-Coffin conspiracy trial, the trial of the Chicago Seven, and the indictments of students and faculty in the Kent State killings are examples of the perversion of the legal process in order to follow the prejudices and passions of the day.

Still the most serious threat to our system of justice may not be in the failure of the legal process to dispense justice in an even-handed manner. More serious is the growing tendency to disregard the constitutional rights of citizens before they even appear to be charged with a crime. The actions of local police, state police, and National Guardsmen when directed against "protesters" seems to be free of any external control that might hold them responsible for their actions. It has become virtually impossible to expect the legal system, in the present political climate, to take action against lawless lawmen. In addition to the failure to bring any indictments against Guardsmen at Kent State, or state police at Jackson State, the most flagrant violation of citizens' rights (without any attempt to indict the responsible law-enforcement officials), is the case of the killings of Mark Clark and Fred Hampton in Chicago on December 4, 1969 (Lewin, 1970). A federal grand jury appointed to investigate the killings of the two Black Panther Party officials and the shooting of seven other Panthers seemed unable to determine whether any individual's civil rights had been violated by the actions of the police. This conclusion of the grand jury seems inconceivable in the face of objective facts from the voluntary testimony of police officers and FBI ballistics tests which indicated that there was no proof of violent resistance by the Panthers when police attempted to enter the apartment with a search warrant. The purpose of a grand jury is only to determine, without prejudicing a case, whether there is evidence of criminal activity sufficient to merit an actual trial. This particular grand jury, however, issued a public statement criticizing the Black Panthers for their refusal to give information to the inquiry (the Panthers did not feel that the court system would give them fair treatment). The decision of the grand jury to throw out the case against the officers, in the face of the evidence and testimony available to them, suggests that political issues seem to be more important than guaranteeing constitutional protections to all citizens.

Prisoners in our society are perhaps the group most blatantly stripped of their constitutional rights, and the persecution of racism in society is given full expression in the jails. A report by the Black Caucus of the California Legislature included some descriptive material revealing conditions that preceded an incident in which a guard at Soledad Prison was found beaten to death. At Soledad, inmates are kept in a six-by-eight strip cell. They sleep on a stiff canvas mat over a cold floor, and are forced to eat in stench and filth of their own body wastes. Prison guards encourage the food servers to contaminate the food of black prisoners with cleansing powder, ground glass, and excreta. Some of the guards from Southern backgrounds have armed white prisoners and encouraged them to throw excreta and garbage at the blacks. On January 13, 1970, eight white men and seven black men were skin searched and sent into a new exercise yard in the maximum security wing. Predictably, a fight began and a tower guard with a "crack shot" reputation fired without warning. Three black inmates were killed while one white prisoner was wounded in the groin by a bullet that ricocheted. A letter from a convict gives the following report:

> I looked at the tower guard and he was aiming the gun toward me and I thought then that he meant to kill me too, so I moved from the wall as he fired and went over to stand over inmate C, all the time looking the guard in the gun tower in the face.
> He aimed the gun at me again and I just froze and waited for him to fire, but he held his fire. After I saw he was not going to fire, I pointed to where inmate C lay, with two other black inmates bending over him, and started to walk toward the door through which we had entered the yard, and then the tower guard pointed the gun at me and shook his head.
> I stopped and begged him for approximately ten minutes to let me take C to the hospital but all he did was shake his head. Then I started forward with tears in my eyes, expecting to be shot down every second. The tower guard told me, "That's far enough." Then another guard gave me permission to bring C off the yard and I was ordered to lay him on the floor in the officers' area and go to my cell, which I refused to do until C was taken to the hospital. (Armstrong, 1970, p. 27.)

Survivors claimed that one wounded man bled to death on the concrete floor. In any case the Monterey Grand Jury, three days after the incident, found the killings were justifiable homicide. Within a half hour of the verdict a white guard was found beaten to death. Among the three men charged with the murder is George Jackson who was serving his tenth year of a "one year to life" sentence for stealing seventy dollars from a gas station. Jackson was a prime target of prison officials. He had spent seven of his ten years in solitary confinement and his letters from Soledad Prison document the unsuccessful efforts of prison officials to transform him into a docile kowtowing Negro. The Soledad defendants were brought into two court hearings chained and without counsel. Their case might never have been known but for a note by one of the defendants that was smuggled out asking his mother to get a lawyer.

The circumstance is repeated throughout the jail system. In the Cummins Prison Farm in Arkansas the bodies of three inmates were excavated from the mule pasture. Two were decapitated and the skull of a third had been crushed to the size of a grapefruit. The incident was, according to a criminologist and one time official of the Arkansas penal system, not unusual.

> The state's prison system had been operated on fear for a century, and most of the traditional methods had been used to instill it: beatings, needles under the fingernails, stompings, the "hide" (a leather strap 5 inches wide and 5 feet long), starvation, and an electric device whose terminals were attached to the genitals of the inmate while a trustee or "warden" gleefully turned the crank. True, the prison

had made a profit during the previous fifty years. The champions of the Arkansas prison system proudly boasted—and still do—that no appropriated funds were required to support the "convicts." But exploitation of inmates was effective only under the spur of threats, and the ultimate threat was murder. There is ample evidence that the illegal executions uncovered that January day were not isolated events. (Murton, 1970, p. 12.)

In 1967 a progressive superintendent hired at the Arkansas Tucker Prison Farm established a new program developed around the strategy of treating the inmate with dignity. The use of prisoners as slave labor for private citizens was ended. An elected inmate council dealt with work assignments and matters of discipline. Even death-row inmates were permitted out to work assignments, church, vocational service in the prison, playing in the prison band, and eating in the dining hall. Prison dances were arranged to maintain the inmates social contacts with girl friends and wives and interracial contacts with prison staff were permitted. Civil functions such as weddings occurred. Such routine abuses as whippings and the rape of female inmates en route between prison and state hospital were eliminated. Modern procedures of livestock management were introduced and the farm work became tolerable. In short, the prison was becoming a correctional institution.

On the verge of success, Governor Winthrop Rockefeller succumbed to the pressures of a conservative prison board. The courts refused to prosecute people who stole supplies in an effort to subvert the new reform and accused the new superintendent of "grave robbing." The superintendent was fired as a poor administrator (by a man who had praised his genius in prison reform) and for knowing nothing about agriculture (ignoring the fact that he had farmed, taught farming, and held a degree in agriculture). Within a short time all the old horror of the prison farm had returned. For a system that dispenses justice poorly, the penal aspect remains the last word in dehumanized treatment of human beings.

Turning to the system of public welfare in the United States, we often find that what is intended as a device to help the less fortunate becomes a way of punishing those whose misfortunes are seen as signs of immorality and fundamental deficiencies in character. There are today in the United States nearly 8,000,000 persons on public-welfare rolls; over one-half of these are children, while another third are the aged and the incapacitated. These figures do not include millions of others who live on substandard incomes but are not eligible for public assistance. The two million migrant workers do not meet residency requirements in most states and are ineligible for benefits.

Welfare issues seem to have gained public attention in recent years, and the attention has paralleled the migration of poor whites and Negroes to urban centers, the increased agitation of civil-rights groups for protection against rising unemployment rates, and the increasing public-welfare budgets.

Many of the issues surrounding public welfare were given national prominence in 1960–1961 in Newburgh, New York, in a series of events that was characterized as *The Battle of Newburgh* (the title of a CBS television report on the subject). Not only did Newburgh spark a national debate over public welfare but it also gave public attention to the manner in which a welfare system can be used to punish and degrade those persons it is designed to assist. In an effort to discourage the alleged inflow of more welfare cases and get rid of its reputation as a welfare resort (according to the city manager who proposed the plan), the city required welfare recipients to pick up their checks at the police department rather than in the mail and proposed a list of thirteen operating procedures governing the welfare programs:

1. All cash payments which can be converted to food, clothing, and rent vouchers and the like without basic harm to the intent of the aid shall be issued in voucher form henceforth.

2. All able-bodied adult males on relief of any kind who are capable of working are to be assigned to the chief of building maintenance for work assignment on a 40-hour week.

3. All recipients physically capable of and available for private employment who are offered a job but refuse it, regardless of the type of employment involved, are to be denied relief.

4. All mothers of illegitimate children are to be advised that should they have any more children out of wedlock, they shall be denied relief.

5. All applicants for relief who have left a job voluntarily, i.e., who have not been fired or laid off, shall be denied relief.

6. The allotment for any one family unit shall not exceed the take-home pay of the lowest-paid city employee with a family of comparable size. Also, no relief shall be granted to any family whose income is in excess of the latter figure.

7. All files of all Aid to Dependent Children cases are to be brought to the office of the corporation counsel for review monthly. All new cases of any kind will be referred to the corporation counsel prior to certification of payment.

8. All applicants for relief who are new to the city must show evidence that their plans in coming to the city involved a concrete offer of employment, similar to that required for foreign immigrants. All such persons shall be limited to two weeks of relief. Those who cannot show evidence shall be limited to one week of relief.

9. Aid to persons except the aged, blind, and disabled shall be limited to three months in any one year—this is a feature similar to the present policies on unemployment benefits.

10. All recipients who are not disabled, blind, or otherwise incapacitated shall report to the Department of Public Welfare monthly for a conference regarding the status of their case.

11. Once the budget for the fiscal year is approved by the Council, it shall not be exceeded by the Welfare Department unless approved by Council by supplemental appropriation.

12. There shall be a monthly expenditure limit on all categories of welfare aid. This monthly expenditure limit shall be established by the Department of Public Welfare at the time of presenting its budget, and shall take into account seasonal variations.

13. Prior to certifying or continuing any more Aid to Dependent Children cases, a determination shall be made as to the home environment. If the home environment is not satisfactory, the children in that home shall be placed in foster care in lieu of welfare aid to the family adults. (May, 1964, pp. 25–26.)

Other proposals that were considered and rejected by the city council included a requirement that applicants for relief be photographed and thumbprinted before eligibility is established and a plan to publish the names, addresses, and amount of assistance received by all welfare recipients in the city newspaper.

While the motives for such measures as were employed in the Newburgh case are, at least in part, to guard against misuse, the effects of such a program are not only degrading to the recipient but they make him a pawn in the hands of agencies on which he depends. Moreover, such policies effectively block the payments to many individuals whose particular pattern of needs just do not fit the requirements laid out.

The welfare system is plagued by two central problems: inadequate cash payments, and paternalistic, degrading regulations governing eligibility for welfare. The articles by Lebeaux and Richan provide documentation of the position that the present social-welfare system not only is an inadequate solution to poverty, but also that the manner in which the welfare system is administered is dehumanizing. Greater dependence on welfare, rather than independence, is fostered by the present system since budgets allotted are not sufficient to provide opportunities for realistic planning, nor are they enough to provide the children of the poor with much hope for themselves. Richan further indicates how the meaning of "welfare colonialism" is revealed in the growing movement by welfare clients to control their own affairs and to exercise choice over which services they do and do not wish to participate in.

The shortcomings of the welfare system give support to those who propose the guaranteed annual income as the best solution to poverty. The guaranteed income could help to reverse the growing tendency toward the development of a centralized state which exercises control over the detailed choices of daily existence among a significant portion of its population. Unfortunately the guaranteed income is not an item on the national agenda. Instead, we are faced with President Nixon's Family Assistance Program which is being sold as a major reform but which really promises more of the same with a few new twists. The FAP would provide a minimum income of $1600 a year to a family of four, and, for the first time, both working families and families with fathers present would be eligible. Thus the FAP presumably would be an incentive to work and would not force male heads out of their homes in order for the family to qualify for welfare benefits. The actual benefits proposed in relation to earned income are as follows:

Earned Income	Benefit	Total Income
$ 0	$1600	$1600
720	1600	2320
1000	1460	2460
1500	1210	2710
2000	960	2960
2500	710	3210
3000	460	3460
3500	210	3710
3920	—	3920

Aside from the inadequacy of the benefit for meeting even the lowest possible living standard, the FAP still locates the strong controls over determining eligibility in the hands of the states, and requires all able-bodied family heads, except mothers of children under six years of age, to make themselves available for jobs as determined by local public-employment offices. Thus the unemployed can be conveniently channeled into the cheap-labor market of domestics, farm labor, or street cleaning with little consideration given to the needs of the individual cases.

The proposed FAP program is hailed as a bold effort that will eliminate 60 percent of the poverty in the nation. It will certainly increase benefits in those states (about eight, mainly in the South) that pay benefits below the $1600 minimum proposed by the FAP. This plan, however, seems to pay more attention to reducing the official levels of poverty than to developing an income floor for all Americans that would allow more than a subsistence level of living.

The Guaranteed Annual Income still remains as one alternative to the current or proposed welfare system. Its importance is not so much in the amount of money that is proposed (since the minimum benefit for the FAP could certainly be modified to have an income floor of $5500 rather than $1600), but in the fact that those Americans who cannot be employed at a decent income in our present economy would be free of the degrading experience of being a "welfare case."

Elsewhere in this book we have referred to the practices of large corporations and large federal agencies assuring the continuation of their federal contracts and tax advantages. Such security is achieved through lobbying and planning activities conducted at public expense. The profits as well as the executive and professional salaries of such organizations are an example of welfare for the well-to-do. It occurs without the media scandals that follow when some poor person is discovered collecting more than his due in unemployment checks. When corporate illegalities are detected the judicial system works very differently from the manner described in this chapter. In our highly interdependent economy we are all recipients of the federal dole. Surely there is a way in which this security can be assured without turning the professional and business world into con men with fingers in the cookie jar and without subjecting the poor to colonial control by the judicial and welfare systems.

REFERENCES AND ADDITIONAL READING

Acosta, Oscar, "The East L.A. 13 vs. the L.A. Superior Court," *El Grito* (Winter 1970), pp. 12–18.

Armstrong, Greg, "Soledad Brother: Two Prison Letters from George Jackson," *New York Review of Books*, **15** (October 8, 1970), pp. 27–36.

Atherton, Charles R., " 'Growing Up Obscene': The By-product of Life on AFDC," *Public Welfare*, **27** (October 1969), pp. 371–375.

Barr, Sherman, "Budgeting and the Poor: A View from the Bottom," *Public Welfare* (October 1965), pp. 246–250; reproduced in R. Perrucci and M. Pilisuk (eds.), *The Triple Revolution: Social Problems in Depth* (Boston: Little, Brown, 1968), pp. 571–577.

Bell, Winifred, "The 'Rights' of the Poor: Welfare Witch-hunts in the District of Columbia," *Social Work*, **13** (January 1968), pp. 60–67.

Cloward, Richard A., and Frances Fox Pivan, "We've Got Rights! The No-Longer Silent Welfare Poor," *New Republic* (August 5, 1967), pp. 23–27.

County Welfare Directors Association of California, "The View of the Administrator: A Critique of the Family Assistance Proposal," *Journal of Public Social Services*, **1** (June 1970), pp. 62–66.

Elias, Steve, "The Legal Perspective," *Journal of Public Social Services*, **1** (June 1970), pp. 4–9.

Jackson, George, *Soledad Brother* (New York: Coward-McCann, 1970).

Jacobs, Glenn, "The Reification of the Notion of Subculture in Public Welfare," *Social Casework*, **49** (1968), pp. 527–536.

Lewin, Nathan, "Justice Cops Out," *New Republic* (June 6, 1970), pp. 14–18.

May, Edgar, *The Wasted Americans* (New York: New American Library, 1964).

Murton, Tom, "One Year of Prison Reform," *The Nation* (January 12, 1970), pp. 12–16.

Nagel, Stuart S., "The Tipped Scales of Justice," *Trans-action* (May-June 1966), pp. 3–9.

Packer Herbert L., "Policing the Police: Nine Men Are Not Enough," *New Republic* (September 4, 1965), pp. 17–21.

Shaffer, Anatole, "The Nixon Welfare Program: The Mythology of Reform," *Journal of Public Social Services*, **1** (June 1970), pp. 45–52.

Skolnick, Jerome A., *Justice Without Trial* (New York: Wiley, 1966).

Skolnick, Jerome A., "Judicial Response in Crisis," in Jerome A. Skolnick, *The Politics of Protest* (New York: Simon and Schuster, 1969), pp. 293–324.

Van Dyke, Jon M., "The Jury as a Political Institution," *The Center Magazine*, **3** (March 1970), pp. 17–26.

Wade, Alan D., "On the Radicalization of the Welfare State," *Journal of Public Social Services*, **1** (March 1970), pp. 7–12.

COVERT CONTINGENCIES IN THE RIGHT TO THE ASSISTANCE OF COUNSEL

Abraham S. Blumberg

A recurring theme in the growing dialogue between sociology and law has been the great need for a joint effort of the two disciplines in illuminating urgent social and legal issues. Having uttered fervent public pronouncements in this vein, the respective practitioners go their separate ways. Academic spokesmen for the legal profession are somewhat critical of sociologists of law because of what they perceive as the sociologist's preoccupation with the application of his methodology to the solution of legal problems. Further, it is felt that ". . . contemporary writing in the sociology of law . . . betrays the existence of painfully unsophisticated notions about the day-to-day operations of courts, legislatures, and law offices."[1] Regardless of the merit of this seemingly harsh criticism, it is evident that scant attention—apart from explorations of the legal profession itself, has been given to the sociological examination and understanding of legal institutions, or their supporting ideological assumptions. Thus, for example, very little sociological effort is expended to ascertain the validity and viability of important court decisions, which may rest on wholly erroneous assumptions in the light of the contextual realities of social structure. A particular decision may rest upon a legally impeccable rationale: at the same time it may be rendered nugatory by contingencies imposed by aspects of social reality of which the lawmakers are themselves unaware.

It is in this context that I wish to examine two recent landmark decisions of the United States Supreme Court, which have been hailed as destined to effect profound changes in the future of criminal law administration and enforcement in America. The first of these, *Gideon* v. *Wainwright*, 372 U.S. 335 (1963), was a historic milestone in that it requires states and localities henceforth to furnish counsel in the case of indigent persons charged with a felony.[2] The Gideon ruling raised

Reprinted by permission of the author and Law and Society Review; *this is a slightly abridged version of the paper presented at the American Sociological Association meetings (Miami, August 30, 1966) and subsequently published in* Law and Society Review, **2** *(1967), pp. 15–39.*

[1] Harry W. Jones, "A View from the Bridge," *Social Problems*, Law and Society Supplement, **13** (Summer 1965), p. 42. See Gilbert Geis, "Sociology, Criminology, and Criminal Law," *Social Problems*, **7**:1 (Summer 1959), pp. 40–47, and N. S. Timasheff, "Growth and Scope of Sociology of Law," in Howard Becker and Alvin Boskoff (eds.), *Modern Sociological Theory in Continuity and Change* (New York: Dryden, 1957), pp. 424–449, for further evaluation of the strained relations between sociology and law.

[2] This decision represented the climax of a line of cases which had begun to chip away at the notion that the VIth Amendment of the Constitution (right to assistance of counsel) applied only to the federal government, and could not be held to run against the states

an interesting question: What is the precise point in time at which a suspect is entitled to counsel?[3] The answer came relatively quickly in *Escobedo* v. *Illinois, 378 U.S. 478* (1964), which has aroused a storm of controversy. Danny Escobedo confessed to the murder of his brother-in-law after the police had refused to permit retained counsel to see him, although his lawyer was present in the station house and requested to confer with his client. In a 5–4 decision, the court asserted where the process of police investigative effort shifts from merely investigatory to that of accusa-tory—"when its focus is on the accused and its purpose is to elicit a confession—our adversary system begins to operate, and, under the circumstances here, the accused must be permitted to consult with his lawyer."

As a consequence Escobedo's confession was rendered inadmissible, triggering a national debate among police, district attorneys, judges, lawyers, and other law-enforcement officials, which continues unabated, as to the value and propriety of confessions in criminal cases.[4] Regardless of the relative merit of the various shades of opinion

through the XIVth Amendment. An exhaustive historical analysis of the XIVth Amendment and the Bill of Rights will be found in Charles Fairman, "Does the Fourteenth Amendment Incorporate the Bill of Rights? The Original Understanding," *Stanford Law Review,* **2** (December 1949), pp. 5–139. Since the Gideon decision, there is already evidence that its effect will ultimately extend to indigent persons charged with misdemeanors—and perhaps ultimately even traffic cases and other minor offenses. For a popular account of this important development in connection with the right to assistance of counsel, see Anthony Lewis, *Gideon's Trumpet* (New York: Random House, 1964). For a scholarly historical analysis of the right to counsel, see William M. Beaney, *The Right to Counsel in American Courts* (Ann Arbor: Univ. of Michigan Press, 1955). For a more recent comprehensive review and discussion of the right to counsel and its development, see note, "Counsel at Interrogation," *Yale Law Journal,* **73** (May 1964), pp. 1000–1057.

With the passage of the Criminal Justice Act of 1964, indigent accused persons in the federal courts will be defended by federally paid legal counsel. For a general discussion of the nature and extent of public and private legal aid in the United States prior to the Gideon case, see Emery A. Brownell, *Legal Aid in the United States* (Rochester, N.Y.: Lawyers Cooperative Publishing Co., 1961); also Robert B. vonMehren et al., *Equal Justice for the Accused* (Garden City, N.Y.: Doubleday, 1959).

[3] In the case of federal defendants the issue is clear. In *Mallory* v. *United States,* 354 U.S. 449 (1957), the Supreme Court unequivocally indicated that a person under federal arrest must be taken "without any unnecessary delay" before a U.S. commissioner where he will receive information as to his rights to remain silent and to assistance of counsel which will be furnished, in the event he is indigent, under the Criminal Justice Act of 1964. For a most interesting and richly documented work in connection with the general area of the Bill of Rights, see Claude R. Sowle, *Police Power and Individual Freedom* (Chicago: Aldine, 1962).

[4] See *New York Times* (November 20, 1965), p. 1, for Justice Nathan R. Sobel's statement to the effect that based on his study of 1000 indictments in Brooklyn, N.Y., from February through April 1965, fewer than 10 percent involved confessions. Sobel's detailed analysis will be found in six articles which appeared in the *New York Law Journal,* beginning November 15, 1965, through November 21, 1965, titled "The Exclusionary Rules in the Law of Confessions: A Legal Perspective—A Practical Perspective." Most law-enforcement officials believe that the majority of convictions in criminal cases are based upon confessions obtained by police. For example, the District Attorney of New York County (a jurisdiction which has the largest volume of cases in the U.S.A.), Frank S. Hogan, reports that confessions are crucial and indicates "if a suspect is entitled to have a lawyer during preliminary questioning . . . any lawyer worth his fee will tell him to keep his mouth shut," *New York Times* (December 2, 1965), p. 1. Concise discussions of the issue are to be found in

as to the role of counsel in criminal cases, the issues generated thereby will be in part resolved as additional cases move toward decision in the Supreme Court in the near future.[5] They are of peripheral interest and not of immediate concern in this paper. However, the Gideon and Escobedo cases pose interesting general questions. In both instances, the Supreme Court reiterates the traditional legal conception of a defense lawyer which is reflective of the ideological perception of a criminal case as being an *adversary, combative* proceeding, in which counsel for the defense assiduously musters all the admittedly limited resources at his command to *defend* the accused.[6] The fundamental question to be asked is does the Supreme Court's conception of the role of counsel in a criminal case square with social reality? That is the focus of my concern, and it shall be the task of this paper to furnish some preliminary evidence toward the illumination of that question. For it would seem that there exist only some ideologically oriented generalizations and commitments, but limited empirical apprehension of the function of defense counsel.

There is by now ample evidence that the overwhelming majority of convictions in criminal cases (usually over 90 percent) are not the product of a combative, trial-by-jury process at all, but instead merely involve the sentencing of the individual after a negotiated, bargained-for plea of guilty has been entered.[7] Although more recently the overzealous role of police and prosecutors in producing pretrial confessions and admissions has achieved a good deal of notoriety, scant attention has been paid to the organizational structure and personnel of the criminal court itself. In-

David Robinson, Jr., "Massiah, Escobedo, and Rationales for the Exclusion of Confessions," *Journal of Criminal Law, Criminology and Police Science*, **56**:4 (December 1965), pp. 412–431; Donald C. Dowling, "Escobedo and Beyond: The Need for a Fourteenth Amendment Code of Criminal Procedure," *Journal of Criminal Law, Criminology and Police Science*, **56**:2 (June 1965), pp. 143–157.

[5] On June 13, 1966, the Supreme Court in a 5–4 decision underscored the principle enunciated in Escobedo in the case of *Miranda* v. *Arizona*—U.S.-police interrogation of any suspect in custody, without his consent, unless a defense attorney is present, is prohibited by the self-incrimination provision of the Fifth Amendment.

[6] Even under optimal circumstances a criminal case is a very much one-sided affair, the parties to the "contest" being decidedly unequal in strength and resources. See Abraham S. Goldstein, "The State and the Accused: Balance of Advantage in Criminal Procedure," *Yale Law Journal*, **69** (June 1960), pp. 1149–1199.

[7] F. James Davis et al., *Society and the Law: New Meanings for an Old Profession* (New York: Free Press of Glencoe, 1962), p. 301; Lester Orfield, *Criminal Procedure from Arrest to Appeal* (New York: New York Univ. Press, 1947), p. 297.

Donald J. Newman, "Pleading Guilty for Considerations: A Study of Bargain Justice," *Journal of Criminal Law, Criminology and Police Science*, **46**:6 (March-April 1954), pp. 780–790. Newman's data covered only one year, 1954, in a midwestern community; however, it is in general confirmed by my own data drawn from a far more populous area, and from what is one of the major criminal courts in the country, for a period of fifteen years from 1950 to 1964 inclusive. The English experience tends also to confirm American data; see Nigel Walker, *Crime and Punishment in Britain: An Analysis of the Penal System* (Edinburgh: Edinburgh Univ. Press, 1965). See also Donald J. Newman, *Conviction: The Determination of Guilt or Innocence Without Trial* (Boston: Little, Brown, 1966) for a comprehensive legalistic study of the guilty plea sponsored by the American Bar Foundation. The criminal court as a social system, an analysis of "bargaining" and its functions in the criminal court's organizational structure, are examined in my forthcoming book, *The Criminal Court: A Sociological Perspective*, to be published by Quadrangle Books, Chicago, Ill.

deed, the extremely high conviction rate produced without the features of an adversary trial in our courts would tend to suggest that the "trial" becomes a perfunctory reiteration and validation of the pretrial interrogation and investigation.[8]

For it is in that institutional setting that the actual role of defense counsel in a criminal case is radically different from the one traditionally depicted.[9] Sociologists and others have focused their attention on the deprivations and social disabilities of such variables as race, ethnicity, and social class as being the source of an accused person's defeat in a criminal court. Largely overlooked is the variable of the court organization itself, which possesses a thrust, purpose, and direction of its own. It is grounded in values, bureaucratic priorities, and administrative instruments which exalt maximum production and the particularistic designs for career enhancement of organizational incumbents, whose occupational and career commitments tend to generate a set of priorities exerting a higher claim than the stated ideological goals of "due process of law," and are often inconsistent with them. . . .

At the outset, one must distinguish between the "lawyer regulars," i.e., those defense lawyers who, by virtue of their continuous appearances in behalf of defendants, tend to represent the bulk of a criminal court's nonindigent case workload, and those lawyers who are not "regulars," who appear almost casually in behalf of an occasional client. Some of the "lawyer regulars" are highly visible as one moves about the major urban centers of the nation, their offices line the back streets of the courthouses, at times sharing space with bondsmen. Their political "visibility" in terms of local clubhouse ties, reaching into the judge's chambers and prosecutor's office, are also deemed essential to successful practitioners. . . .

However, lawyers, whether privately retained or of the legal-aid, public-defender variety, have close and continuing relations with the prosecuting office and the court itself through discreet relations with the judges via their law secretaries or "confidential" assistants. . . .

The client, then, is a secondary figure in the court system as in certain other bureaucratic settings.[10] He becomes a means to other, larger ends of the organization's incumbents. Doubts, contingencies, and pressures he may present, which challenge existing informal arrangements or are disruptive of them, tend to be resolved in favor of the continuance of the organization and its relations as before. There is a greater community of interest among all the principal organizational structures and their incumbents than exists elsewhere in

[8] George Feifer, *Justice in Moscow* (New York: Dell, 1965). The Soviet trial has been termed "an appeal from the pretrial investigation," and Feifer notes that the Soviet "trial" is simply a recapitulation of the data collected by the pretrial investigator. The notions of a trial being a "tabula rasa" and presumptions of innocence are wholly alien to Soviet notions of justice. . . . "The closer the investigation resembles the finished script, the better . . ." (p. 86).

[9] For a concise statement of the constitutional and economic aspects of the right to legal assistance, see Monrad G. Paulsen, *Equal Justice for the Poor Man* (New York: Public Affairs Pamphlets, No. 367, 1964); for a brief traditional description of the legal profession, see Paul A. Freund, "The Legal Profession," *Daedalus* (Fall 1963), pp. 689–700.

[10] There is a real question to be raised as to whether, in certain organizational settings, a complete reversal of the bureaucratic ideal has not occurred. That is, it would seem in some instances the organization appears to exist to serve the needs of its various occupational incumbents, rather than its clients. Amitai Etzioni, *Modern Organizations* (Englewood Cliffs, N.J.: Prentice-Hall, 1964), pp. 94–104.

other settings. The accused's lawyer has
far greater professional, economic, intellectual, and other ties to the various elements
of the court system than he does to his
own client. The court is a closed community. This is more than just the case of the
usual "secrets" of bureaucracy which are
fanatically defended from outside view.
Even all elements of the press are zealously
determined to report only that which will
not offend the board of judges, the prosecutor, probation, legal-aid, or other officials,
in return for privileges and courtesies
granted in the past and to be granted in
the future. Rather than any view of the
matter in terms of some variation of a
"conspiracy" hypothesis, the simple explanation is one of an ongoing system dealing
with delicate, tension- and trauma-produc-
ing law-enforcement and administration,
which requires the almost pathological distrust of "outsiders" bordering on group
paranoia.

The virtually hostile attitude toward
"outsiders" is in large measure engendered
by a defensiveness produced by the inherent deficiencies of assembly-line justice, so
characteristic of our major criminal courts.
Intolerably large case loads of defendants,
which must be disposed of in an organizational context of limited resources and
personnel, potentially subject the participants in the court community to harsh
scrutiny from appellate courts, and other
public and private sources of condemna-
tion. As a consequence, an almost irreconcilable conflict is posed in terms of intense
pressures to process large numbers of cases
on the one hand, and the stringent ideological and legal requirements of "due
process of law" on the other hand. A rather
tenuous resolution of the dilemma has
emerged in the shape of a large variety of
bureaucratically ordained and controlled
"work crimes," short cuts, deviations, and
outright rule violations on the part of
court occupational incumbents ranging

from judges to stenographers in order to
meet production norms. Fearfully anticipating criticism on ethical as well as legal
grounds, all the significant participants in
the court's social structure are bound into
an organized system of complicity. This
consists of a work arrangement in which
the patterned, covert, informal breaches,
and evasions of "due process" are institutionalized, but are, nevertheless, denied to
exist.

These institutionalized evasions will be
found to occur to some degree in all criminal courts. Their nature, scope, and complexity will be largely determined by the
size of the court, and the character of the
community in which it is located, e.g.,
whether it is a large urban institution, or
a relatively small rural county court. In
addition, idiosyncratic local conditions may
contribute to a unique flavor in the character and quality of the criminal law's
administration in a particular community.
However, in most instances a variety of
stratagems are employed—some subtle, some
crude, in effectively disposing of what are
often too large caseloads. A wide variety of
coercive devices are employed against an
accused client, couched in a depersonalized,
instrumental, bureaucratic version of due
process of law, and which are in reality a
perfunctory obeisance to the ideology of
due process. These include some very explicit pressures which are exerted in some
measure by all court personnel, including
judges, to plead guilty and avoid trial. In
many instances the sanction of a potentially
harsh sentence is utilized as the visible
alternative to pleading guilty, in the case
of recalcitrants. Probation and psychiatric
reports are "tailored" to organizational
needs, or are at least responsive to the
court organization's requirements for the
refurbishment of a defendant's social biography, consonant with his new status. A
resourceful judge can, through his subtle
domination of the proceedings, impose his

will on the final outcome of a trial. Stenographers and clerks, in their function as record keepers, are on occasion pressed into service in support of a judicial need to "rewrite" the record of a courtroom event. Bail practices are usually employed for purposes other than simply assuring a defendant's presence on the date of a hearing in connection with his case. Too often, the discretionary power as to bail is part of the arsenal of weapons available to collapse the resistance of an accused person. The foregoing is a most cursory examination of some of the more prominent "short cuts" available to any court organization. There are numerous other procedural strategies constituting due-process deviations, which tend to become the work-style artifacts of a court's personnel. Thus, only court "regulars" who are "bound in" are really accepted, others are treated routinely and in almost a coldly correct manner.

The defense attorneys, therefore, whether of the "legal-aid," public-defender variety, or privately retained, although operating in terms of pressures specific to their respective role and organizational obligations, ultimately are concerned with strategies which tend to lead to a plea. It is the rational, impersonal elements involving economies of time, labor, expense, and a superior commitment of the defense counsel to these rationalistic values of maximum production[11] of court organization that prevail, rather than any particularistic, affective ties an accused may have reasonably

expected to be the character of his relationship with his lawyer. The lawyer "regulars" are frequently former staff members of the prosecutor's office and utilize the charisma, "know-how," and contacts of their former affiliation as part of their stock in trade. But an accused and his kin, as with others outside the court community, are unable to apprehend the nature and dimensions of the close and continuing relations between the lawyer "regular" and his former colleagues in the prosecutor's office. Their continuing colleagueship is based on real professional and organizational needs of a *quid pro quo*, which goes beyond the limits of an accommodation or *modus vivendi* one might ordinarily expect under the circumstances of an otherwise seemingly adversary relationship. Indeed, the adversary features which are manifest are for the most part muted and exist even in their attenuated form largely for external consumption. The principals, lawyer and assistant district attorney, rely upon one another's cooperation for their continued professional existence, and so the bargaining between them tends usually to be "reasonable" rather than fierce.

The real key to the apprehension of the role of defense counsel in a criminal case is to be found in the area of the fixing of the fee to be charged and its collection. The problem of fixing and collecting the fee tends to influence to a significant degree the criminal court process itself, and not just the relationship of the lawyer and

[11] Three relatively recent items reported in the *New York Times* tend to underscore this point as it has manifested itself in one of the major criminal courts. In one instance the Bronx County Bar Association condemned "mass assembly-line justice," which "was rushing defendants into pleas of guilty and into convictions, in violation of their legal rights." *New York Times* (March 10, 1965), p. 51. Another item, appearing somewhat later that year, reports a judge criticizing his own court system (the New York Criminal Court), that "pressure to set statistical records in disposing of cases had hurt the administration of justice." *New York Times* (November 4, 1965), p. 49. A third and most unusual recent public discussion in the press was a statement by a leading New York appellate judge decrying "instant justice" which is employed to reduce court calendar congestion, . . . "converting our courthouses into counting houses . . . , as in most big cities where the volume of business tends to overpower court facilities." *New York Times* (February 5, 1966), p. 58.

his client. In essence, a lawyer-client "confidence game" is played. Almost everyone is familiar with the oft-told tale of "The Emperor's New Clothes." A true confidence game is unlike the case of the emperor's new clothes wherein that monarch's nakedness was a result of inordinate gullibility and credulity. In a genuine confidence game, the perpetrator manipulates the basic dishonesty of his partner, the victim or mark, toward his own (the confidence operator's) ends. The two phenomena must be distinguished—the case of the emperor's clothes and the true confidence game. In the case of the emperor, who was possessed of great personal vanity, cupidity, and naiveté, a fraud was perpetrated by some crafty operators who duped him and his subjects. For truly, up to a point, everyone believed that the reality of the emperor's nakedness was but the most clever, artful, and miraculously wrought gossamer. However, in the confidence game, the victim is not an innocent dupe, for he seeks some undue advantage or some shady, illegitimate goal of his own. Thus, "the victim of a con scheme must have some larceny in his heart."[12]

In many of the so-called "server-served" relationships for a fee, which include not only the practice of law, medicine, or dentistry, but also plumbing, there is not always a visible end product or tangible service involved. Usually, a plumber will be able to demonstrate empirically that he has performed a service by clearing up the stuffed drain, repairing the leaky faucet or pipe—and therefore merits his fee. He has rendered, when summoned, a visible, tangible boon for his client in return for the requested fee. A physician, who has not performed some visible surgery or otherwise engaged in some readily discernible procedure in connection with a patient, may be deemed by the patient to have "done nothing" for him. As a consequence, medical practitioners may simply prescribe or administer by injection a placebo to overcome a patient's potential reluctance or dissatisfaction in paying a requested fee, "for nothing."

In the practice of law there is a special problem in this regard, no matter what the level of the practitioner or his place in the hierarchy of prestige. Much legal work is intangible in its dimensions either because it is simply a few words of advice, some preventive action, a telephone call, negotiation of some kind, a form filled out and filed, a hurried conference with another attorney or an official of a government agency, a letter or opinion written, or a countless variety of seemingly innocuous, and even prosaic procedures and actions. These are the basic activities, apart from any possible court appearance, of almost all lawyers, at all levels of practice. Much of the activity is not in the nature of the exercise of the traditional, precise professional skills of the attorney such as library research and oral argument in connection with appellate briefs, court motions, trial work, drafting of opinions, memoranda, contracts, and other complex documents and agreements. Instead, much legal activity, whether it is at the lowest or highest "white-shoe" law-firm levels, is of the brokerage, agent, sales representative, lobbyist type of activity, in which the lawyer acts for someone else in pursuing the latter's interests and designs, furnishing an intangible service.[13]

---

[12] Robert L. Gasser, "The Confidence Game," *Federal Probation*, **27**:4 (December 1963), p. 47.
[13] C. Wright Mills, *White Collar* (New York: Oxford Univ. Press, 1951), pp. 121–129; Jerome E. Carlin, *op. cit.*, passim.

The large-scale law firm may not speak as openly of their "contacts," their "fixing" abilities, as does the lower-level lawyer. They trade instead upon a facade of thick carpeting, walnut paneling, genteel low pressure, and superficialities of traditional legal professionalism. There are occasions when even the large firm is on the defensive in connection with the fees they charge because the services rendered or results obtained do not appear to merit the fee asked.[14] Therefore, there is a recurrent problem in the legal profession in fixing the amount of fee, and in justifying the basis for the requested fee.

Although the fee at times amounts to what the traffic and the conscience of the lawyer will bear, one further observation must be made with regard to the size of the fee and its collection. The defendant in a criminal case and the material gain he may have acquired during the course of his illicit activities are soon parted. Not infrequently the ill-gotten fruits of the various modes of larceny are sequestered by a defense lawyer in payment of his fee. Inexorably, the amount of the fee is a function of the dollar value of the crime committed, and is frequently set with meticulous precision at a sum which bears an uncanny relationship to that of the net proceeds of the particular offense involved. On occasion, defendants have been known to commit additional offenses while at liberty on bail, in order to secure the requisite funds with which to meet their obligations for payment of legal fees. Defense lawyers condition even the most obtuse clients to recognize that there is a firm interconnection between fee payment and the zealous exercise of professional expertise, secret knowledge, and organizational "connections" in their behalf. Lawyers, therefore, seek to keep their clients in a proper state of tension, and to arouse in them the precise edge of anxiety which is calculated to encourage prompt fee payment. Consequently, the client attitude in the relationship between defense counsel and an accused is in many instances a precarious admixture of hostility, mistrust, dependence, and sycophancy. By keeping his client's anxieties aroused to the proper pitch, and establishing a seemingly causal relationship between a requested fee and the accused's ultimate extrication from his onerous difficulties, the lawyer will have established the necessary preliminary groundwork to assure a minimum of haggling over the fee and its eventual payment.

In varying degrees, as a consequence, all law practice involves a manipulation of the client and a stage management of the lawyer-client relationship so that at least an *appearance* of help and service will be forthcoming. This is accomplished in a variety of ways, often exercised in combination with each other. At the outset, the lawyer-professional employs with suitable variation a measure of sales-puff which may range from an air of unbounding self-confidence, adequacy, and dominion over events, to that of complete arrogance. This will be supplemented by the affectation of a studied, faultless mode of personal attire. In the larger firms, the furnishings and office trappings will serve as the backdrop to help in impression management and client intimidation. In all firms, solo or large scale, an access to secret knowledge, and to the seats of power and influence is inferred, or presumed to a varying degree as the basic vendible commodity of the practitioners.

The lack of visible end product offers a special complication in the course of the professional life of the criminal court law-

[14] Erwin O Smigel, *The Wall Street Lawyer* (New York: Free Press of Glencoe, 1964), p. 309.

yer with respect to his fee and in his relations with his client. The plain fact is
that an accused in a criminal case always
"loses" even when he has been exonerated
by an acquittal, discharge, or dismissal of
his case. The hostility of an accused which
follows as a consequence of his arrest, incarceration, possible loss of job, expense,
and other traumas connected with his case
is directed, by means of displacement,
toward his lawyer. It is in this sense that
it may be said that a criminal lawyer never
really "wins" a case. The really satisfied
client is rare, since in the very nature of
the situation even an accused's vindication
leaves him with some degree of dissatisfaction and hostility. It is this state of affairs
that makes for a lawyer-client relationship
in the criminal court which tends to be a
somewhat exaggerated version of the usual
lawyer-client confidence game.

At the outset, because there are great
risks of nonpayment of the fee due to the
impecuniousness of his clients, and the fact
that a man who is sentenced to jail may
be a singularly unappreciative client, the
criminal lawyer collects his fee *in advance*.
Often, because the lawyer and the accused
both have questionable designs of their
own upon each other, the confidence game
can be played. The criminal lawyer must
serve three major functions, or stated another way, he must solve three problems.
First, he must arrange for his fee; second,
he must prepare and then, if necessary,
"cool out" his client in case of defeat[15] (a
highly likely contingency) ; third, he must
satisfy the court organization that he has
performed adequately in the process of

negotiating the plea, so as to preclude the
possibility of the occurrence of any sort of
embarrassing incident which may serve to
invite "outside" scrutiny.

In assuring the attainment of one of his
primary objectives, his fee, the criminal
lawyer will very often enter into negotiations with various members of the accused's
kin group, including collateral relatives.
In many instances, the accused himself is
unable to pay any sort of fee or anything
more than a token fee. It then becomes
important to involve as many of the accused's kin group as possible in the situation. This is especially so if the attorney
hopes to collect a significant part of a proposed substantial fee. It is not uncommon
for several relatives to contribute toward
the fee. The larger the group, the greater
the possibility that the lawyer will collect
a sizable fee by exacting contributions from
a diverse number of individuals.

A fee for a felony case which ultimately
results in a plea, rather than a trial, may
ordinarily range anywhere from $500 to
$1500. Should the case go to trial, the fee
will be proportionately larger, depending
upon the length of the trial. But the larger
the fee the lawyer wishes to exact, the
more impressive his performance must be,
in terms of his stage-managed image as
being a personage of great influence and
power in the court organization. Court
personnel are keenly aware of the extent
to which a lawyer's stock in trade involves
the precarious stage management of an
image which goes beyond the usual professional flamboyance, and for this reason
alone the lawyer is "bound in" to the au-

[15] Talcott Parsons indicates that the social role and function of the lawyer can be therapeutic, helping his client psychologically in giving him necessary emotional support at
critical times. The lawyer is also said to be acting as an agent of social control in the
counseling of his client and in the influencing of his course of conduct. See Talcott Parsons,
Essays in Sociological Theory (New York: Free Press of Glencoe, 1954), pp. 382 et seq.;
Erving Goffman, "On Cooling the Mark Out: Some Aspects of Adaptation to Failure," in
Arnold M. Rose (ed.), *Human Behavior and Social Processes* (Boston: Houghton Mifflin,
1962), pp. 482–505. Goffman's "cooling out" analysis is especially relevant in the lawyer-
accused client relationship.

thority system of the court's organizational discipline. Therefore, to some extent, court personnel will aid the lawyer in the creation and maintenance of that impression. There is a tacit commitment to the lawyer by the court organization, apart from formal etiquette, to aid him in this. Such augmentation of the lawyer's stage-managed image as this affords is the partial basis for the *quid pro quo* which exists between the lawyer and the court organization. It tends to serve as the continuing basis for the higher loyalty of the lawyer to the organization; his relationship with his client, in contrast, is transient, ephemeral, and often superficial.

The lawyer has often been accused of stirring up unnecessary litigation, especially in the field of negligence. He is said to acquire a vested interest in a cause of action or claim which was initially his client's. The strong incentive of possible fee motivates the lawyer to promote litigation which would otherwise never have developed. The criminal lawyer develops a vested interest of an entirely different nature in his client's case: not to promote the litigation, but to limit its scope and duration. Only in this way can a case be "profitable." Thus, he enlists the aid of relatives not only to assure payment of his fee, but he will also rely on these persons to help him in his agent-mediator role of convincing the accused to plead guilty, and ultimately to help him in "cooling out" the accused if necessary.

It is at this point that an accused-defendant may experience his first sense of "betrayal." While he had perhaps perceived the police and prosecutor to be adversaries, or possibly even a judge could be cast in a somewhat similar role, the accused is wholly unprepared for his counsel's role performance as an agent-mediator. In the same vein, it is even less likely to occur to an accused that members of his own family or kin group may become

agents, albeit at the behest and urging of other agents or mediators, acting on the principle that they are in reality helping an accused negotiate the best possible plea arrangement under the circumstances. Usually, it will be the lawyer who will activate next of kin in this role, his ostensible motive being to arrange for his fee. But soon latent and unstated motives will assert themselves, with entreaties by counsel to the accused's next of kin, to appeal to the accused to "help himself" by pleading. *Gemeinschaft* sentiments are to this extent exploited by a defense lawyer (or even at times by a district attorney) to achieve specific secular ends, that is, of concluding a particular matter with all possible dispatch.

The fee is often collected in stages, each installment usually payable prior to a necessary court appearance required during the course of an accused's career journey. At each stage, in his interviews and communications with the accused or, in addition, with members of his kin group, if they are helping with the fee payment, the lawyer employs an air of professional confidence and "inside-dopesterism" in order to assuage anxieties on all sides. He makes the necessary bland assurances, and in effect manipulates his client, who is usually willing to do and say the things, true or not, which will help his attorney extricate him. Since the dimensions of what he is essentially selling, organizational influence and expertise, are not technically and precisely measurable, the lawyer can make extravagant claims of influence and secret knowledge with impunity. Thus, lawyers frequently claim to have inside knowledge in connection with information in the hands of the DA, police, probation officials, or to have access to these functionaries. Factually, they often do, and need only to exaggerate the nature of their relationships with them to obtain the desired effective impression upon the client.

But as in the genuine confidence game, the victim who has participated is loath to do anything that will upset the lesser plea which his lawyer has "conned" him into accepting.[16]

In effect, in his role as double agent, the criminal lawyer performs an extremely vital and delicate mission for the court organization and the accused. Both principals are anxious to terminate the litigation with a minimum of expense and damage to each other. There is no other personage or role incumbent in the total court structure more strategically located, who by training and in terms of his own requirements is more ideally suited to do so than the lawyer. In recognition of this, judges will cooperate with attorneys in many important ways. For example, they will adjourn the case of an accused in jail awaiting plea or sentence if the attorney requests such action. While explicitly this may be done for some innocuous and seemingly valid reason, the tacit purpose is that pressure is being applied by the attorney for the collection of his fee, which he knows will probably not be forthcoming if the case is concluded. Judges are aware of this tactic on the part of lawyers, who, by requesting an adjournment, keep an accused incarcerated awhile longer as a not-too-subtle method of dunning a client for payment. However, the judges will go along with this, on the ground that important ends are being served. Often, the only end being served is to protect a lawyer's fee.

In still another way will the judge help an accused's lawyer. He will lend the official aura of his office and courtroom so that a lawyer can stage-manage an impression of an "all out" performance for the accused in justification of his fee. The judge and other court personnel will serve as a backdrop for a scene charged with dramatic fire, in which the accused's lawyer makes a stirring appeal in his behalf. With a show of restrained passion, the lawyer will intone the virtues of the accused and recite the social deprivations which have reduced him to his present state. There is a speech which varies somewhat, depending on whether the accused has been convicted after trial or has pleaded guilty. In the main, however, the incongruity, superficiality, and ritualistic character of the total performance is understood by a visibly impassive, almost bored reaction on the part of the judge and other members of the court retinue. Afterward, there is a hearty exchange of pleasantries between the lawyer and district attorney, wholly out of context in terms of the supposed adversary nature of the preceding events.

The fiery passion in defense of his client is gone, and the lawyers for both sides resume their offstage relations, chatting amiably and perhaps including the judge in their restrained banter. No other aspect of

---

[16] The question has never been raised as to whether "bargain justice," "copping a plea," or justice by negotiation is a constitutional process. Although it has become the most central aspect of the process of criminal law administration, it has received virtually no close scrutiny by the appellate courts. As a consequence, it is relatively free of legal control and supervision. But, apart from any questions of the legality of bargaining, in terms of the pressures and devices that are employed which tend to violate due process of law, there remain ethical and practical questions. The system of bargain-counter justice is like the proverbial iceberg, much of its danger is concealed in secret negotiations, and its least alarming feature, the final plea, being the one presented to public view. See Arnold S. Trebach, *The Rationing of Justice* (New Brunswick, N.J.: Rutgers Univ. Press, 1964), pp. 74–94; Dominick R. Vetri, note, "Guilty Plea Bargaining: Compromises by Prosecutors to Secure Guilty Pleas," *University of Pennsylvania Law Review*, **112** (April 1964), pp. 865–895.

their visible conduct so effectively serves to put even a casual observer on notice, that these individuals have claims upon each other. These seemingly innocuous actions are indicative of continuing organizational and informal relations, which, in their intricacy and depth, range far beyond any priorities or claims a particular defendant may have.[17]

Criminal law practice is a unique form of private law practice since it really only appears to be private practice.[18] Actually it is bureaucratic practice, because of the legal practitioner's enmeshment in the authority, discipline, and perspectives of the court organization. Private practice, supposedly, in a professional sense, involves the maintenance of an organized, disciplined body of knowledge and learning; the individual practitioners are imbued with a spirit of autonomy and service, the earning of a livelihood being incidental. In the sense that the lawyer in the criminal court serves as a double agent, serving higher organizational rather than professional ends, he may be deemed to be engaged in bureaucratic rather than private practice. To some extent the lawyer-client

"confidence game," in addition to its other functions, serves to conceal this fact.

The "cop-out" ceremony, in which the court process culminates, is not only invaluable for redefining the accused's perspectives of himself, but also in reiterating publicly in a formally structured ritual the accused person's guilt for the benefit of significant "others" who are observing. The accused not only is made to assert publicly his guilt of a specific crime, but also a complete recital of its details. He is further made to indicate that he is entering his plea of guilty freely, willingly, and voluntarily, and that he is not doing so because of any promises or in consideration of any commitments that may have been made to him by anyone. This last is intended as a blanket statement to shield the participants from any possible charges of "coercion" or undue influence that may have been exerted in violation of due-process requirements. Its function is to preclude any later review by an appellate court on these grounds, and also to obviate any second thoughts an accused may develop in connection with his plea.

However, for the accused, the concep-

---

[17] For a conventional summary statement of some of the inevitable conflicting loyalties encountered in the practice of law, see Elliot E. Cheatham, *Cases and Materials on the Legal Profession*, 2nd ed. (Brooklyn: Foundation Press, 1955), pp. 70–79.

[18] Some lawyers at either end of the continuum of law practice appear to have grave doubts as to whether it is indeed a profession at all: Jerome E. Carlin, *op. cit.*, p. 192; Erwin O. Smigel, *op. cit.*, pp. 304–305. Increasingly, it is perceived as a business with widespread evasion of the Canons of Ethics, duplicity and chicanery being practiced in an effort to get and keep business. The poet Carl Sandburg epitomized this notion in the following vignette: "Have you a criminal lawyer in this burg?" "We think so but we haven't been able to prove it on him." *The People, Yes* (New York: Harcourt, Brace, 1936), p. 154.

Thus, while there is a considerable amount of dishonesty present in law practice involving fee splitting, thefts from clients, influence peddling, fixing, questionable use of favors and gifts to obtain business or influence others, this sort of activity is most often attributed to the "solo," private-practice lawyer. See Arthur Lewis Wood, "Professional Ethics Among Criminal Lawyers," *Social Problems*, 7:1 (Summer 1959), pp. 70–83. However, to some degree, large-scale "downtown" elite firms also engage in these dubious activities. The difference is that the latter firms enjoy a good deal of immunity from these harsh charges because of their institutional and organizational advantages, in terms of near monopoly over more desirable types of practice, as well as exerting great influence in the political, economic, and professional realms of power.

tion of self as a guilty person is in large measure a temporary role adaptation. His career socialization as an accused, if it is successful, eventuates in his acceptance and redefinition of himself as a guilty person.[19] However, the transformation is ephemeral, in that he will, in private, quickly reassert his innocence. Of importance is that he accept his defeat, publicly proclaim it, and find some measure of pacification in it.[20] Almost immediately after his plea, a defendant will generally be interviewed by a representative of the probation division in connection with a presentence report which is to be prepared. The very first question to be asked of him by the probation officer is: "Are you guilty of the crime to which you pleaded?" This is by way of double affirmation of the defendant's guilt. Should the defendant now begin to make bold assertions of his inno-

cence, despite his plea of guilty, he will be asked to withdraw his plea and stand trial on the original charges. Such a threatened possibility is in most instances sufficient to cause an accused to let the plea stand and to request the probation officer to overlook his exclamations of innocence. [Table 1] is a breakdown of the categorized responses of a random sample of male defendants in Metropolitan Court[21] during 1962, 1963, and 1964 in connection with their statements during presentence probation interviews following their plea of guilty.

It would be well to observe at the outset that of the 724 defendants who pleaded guilty before trial, only 43 (5.94 percent) of the total group had confessed prior to their indictment. Thus the ultimate judicial process was predicated upon evidence independent of any confession of the accused.[22]

---

[19] This does not mean that most of those who plead guilty are innocent of any crime. Indeed, in many instances those who have been able to negotiate a lesser plea have done so willingly and even eagerly. The system of justice-by-negotiation, without trial, probably tends to better serve the interests and requirements of guilty persons, who are thereby presented with formal alternatives of "half a loaf," in terms of at worst possibilities of a lesser plea and a concomitant shorter sentence as compensation for their acquiescence and participation. Having observed the prescriptive etiquette in compliance with the defendant role expectancies in this setting, he is rewarded. An innocent person, on the other hand, is confronted with the same set of role prescriptions, structures, and legal alternatives, and in any event, for him this mode of justice is often an ineluctable bind.

[20] "Any communicative network between persons whereby the public identity of an actor is transformed into something looked on as lower in the local scheme of social types will be called a 'status degradation ceremony.'" Harold Garfinkel, "Conditions of Successful Degradation Ceremonies," American Journal of Sociology, 61:5 (March 1956), pp. 420–424. But contrary to the conception of the "cop out" as a "status degradation ceremony," is the fact that it is in reality a charade, during the course of which an accused must project an appropriate and acceptable amount of guilt, penitence, and remorse. Having adequately feigned the role of the "guilty person," his hearers will engage in the fantasy that he is contrite, and thereby merits a lesser plea. It is one of the essential functions of the criminal lawyer that he coach and direct his accused-client in that role performance. Thus, what is actually involved is not a "degradation" process at all, but is instead a highly structured system of exchange cloaked in the rituals of legalism and public professions of guilt and repentance.

[21] The name is of course fictitious. However, the actual court which served as the universe from which the data were drawn is one of the largest criminal courts in the United States, dealing with felonies only. Female defendants in the years 1950 through 1964 constituted 7–10 percent of the totals for each year.

[22] My own data in this connection would appear to support Sobel's conclusion (see footnote 4), and appear to be at variance with the prevalent view, which stresses the importance of confessions in law enforcement and prosecution. All the persons in my sample were

Table 1 DEFENDANT RESPONSES AS TO GUILT OR INNOCENCE AFTER
PLEADING (N-724; 1962–1964)

Nature of Response	Comments	Number of Defendants
Innocent (manipulated)	"The lawyer or judge, police or DA 'conned me' "	86
Innocent (pragmatic)	"Wanted to get it over with" "You can't beat the system" "They have you over a barrel when you have a record"	147
Innocent (advice of counsel)	"Followed my lawyer's advice"	92
Innocent (defiant)	"Framed"—betrayed by "complainant," "police," "squealers," "lawyer," "friends," "wife," "girlfriend"	33
Innocent (adverse social data)	Blames probation officer or psychiatrist for "bad report," in cases where there was prepleading investigation	15
Guilty	"But I should have gotten a better deal" Blames lawyer, DA, police, judge	74
Guilty	Won't say anything further	21
Fatalistic (doesn't press his "innocence," won't admit "guilt")	"I did it for convenience" "My lawyer told me it was only thing I could do" "I did it because it was the best way out"	248
No response		8
Total		724

As the data indicate, only a relatively small number (95) out of the total number of defendants actually will even admit their guilt, following the "cop-out" ceremony. However, even though they have affirmed their guilt, many of these defen-

originally charged with felonies ranging from homicide to forgery, in most instances the original felony charges were reduced to misdemeanors by way of a negotiated lesser plea. The vast range of crime categories which are available facilitates the patterned court process of plea reduction to a lesser offense, which is also usually a socially less opprobrious crime. For an illustration of this feature of the bargaining process in a court utilizing a public defender office, see David Sudnow, "Normal Crimes: Sociological Features of the Penal Code in a Public Defender Office," *Social Problems*, **12** (Winter 1964), pp. 255–276.

dants felt that they should have been able to negotiate a more favorable plea. The largest aggregate of defendants (373) were those who reasserted their "innocence" following their public profession of guilt during the "cop-out" ceremony. These defendants employed differential degrees of fervor, solemnity, and credibility, ranging from really mild, wavering assertions of innocence which were embroidered with a variety of stock explanations and rationalizations, to those of an adamant, "framed" nature. Thus, the "innocent" group for the most part, it must be stressed, were largely concerned with underscoring for their probation interviewer their essential "goodness" and "worthiness," despite their formal plea of guilty. Assertion of his innocence at the post-plea stage resurrects a more respectable and acceptable self-concept for the accused defendant who has pleaded guilty. A recital of the structural exigencies which precipitated his plea of guilt serves to embellish a newly proffered claim of innocence, which many defendants mistakenly feel will stand them in good stead at the time of sentence, or ultimately with probation or parole authorities.

Relatively few (33) maintained their innocence in terms of having been "framed" by some person or agent-mediator, although a larger number (86) indicated that they had been manipulated or "conned" by an agent-mediator to plead guilty, but, as indicated, their assertions of innocence were relatively mild.

A rather substantial group (147) preferred to stress the pragmatic aspects of their plea of guilty. They would only perfunctorily assert their innocence and would in general refer to some adverse aspect of their situation which they believed tended to negatively affect their bargaining leverage, including in some instances a prior criminal record.

One group of defendants (92), while maintaining their innocence, simply employed some variation of a theme of following "the advice of counsel" as a covering response, to explain their guilty plea in the light of their new affirmation of innocence. It was a shorthand method of invoking a catch phrase to preclude any further discussion of an otherwise seemingly inconsistent position.

The largest single group of defendants (248) were basically fatalistic. They would only verbalize weak suggestions of their innocence in rather halting terms, wholly without conviction. By the same token, they would not admit guilt readily and were generally evasive as to guilt or innocence, preferring to stress aspects of their stoic submission in their decision to plead. This sizable group of defendants appeared to perceive the total court process as being caught up in a monstrous organizational apparatus, in which the defendant role expectancies were not clearly defined. Reluctant to offend anyone in authority, fearful that clear-cut statements on their part as to their guilt or innocence will be negatively construed, they adopt a stance of passivity, resignation, and acceptance. Interestingly, they would in most instances invoke their lawyer as being the one who crystallized the available alternatives for them, and who was therefore the critical element in their decision-making process....

Based on data which are admittedly tentative and fragmentary, the furor over confessions, whether of the coerced or voluntary variety, would appear to be not too meaningful. It is suggested that the process of criminal law enforcement has always depended, and will continue to do so in the foreseeable future, on judicial confessions in open court (i.e., pleas of guilty), rather than on confessions wrung from an accused in the back room of a police station. The decision of *Gideon* v. *Wainwright,* requiring states and localities to furnish counsel in the case of indigent persons charged with a felony, has been regarded in legal circles as a most important development in American jurisprudence. No doubt, in time, the various states will make administrative provisions to implement this decision. Although there has been great enthusiasm expressed in connection with the decision, my limited data would appear to suggest that results at the felony level in the future will not be significantly different from those which presently obtain in the respective communities affected by the Gideon decision.

The organizational and structural variables of the criminal court will continue to be present, and perhaps be even further augmented, in addition to any race, class, ethnic, or other socio-demographic variables which are to be found in the respective jurisdictions. Together, these are formidable. The organizational features, which in the pursuit of rationality tend to promote the present system of justice, will not be easily overcome by additional counsel and similar resources,[23] for they may in turn be coopted and become part of the organizational structure, if they are not already.

[23] Some of the resources which have become an integral part of our courts, e.g., psychiatry, social work, and probation, were originally intended as part of an ameliorative, therapeutic effort to individualize offenders. However, there is some evidence that a quite different result obtains than the one originally intended. The ameliorative instruments have been coopted by the court in order to more "efficiently" deal with a court's caseload, often to the legal disadvantage of an accused person. See Francis A. Allen, *The Borderland of Criminal Justice* (Chicago: Univ. of Chicago Press), passim; Thomas S. Szasz, *Law, Liberty and Psychiatry* (New York: Macmillan, 1963); and also Szasz's most recent, *Psychiatric Justice* (New York: Macmillan, 1965); Lewis Diana, "The Rights of Juvenile Delinquents: An Appraisal of Juvenile Court Procedures," *Journal of Criminal Law, Criminology and Police Science*, **47**:5 (January-February 1957), pp. 561–569.

COERCION AND COMPLIANCE
THE PSYCHOLOGY OF POLICE CONFESSIONS

Philip G. Zimbardo

The fascination that the police have for the thief is manifested by the thief's temptation to confess when he is arrested. In the presence of the examining magistrate who questions him, he is seized with giddiness: the magistrate speaks gently to him, perhaps with kindness, explaining what is expected of him; practically nothing: an assent. If only once, just once, he did what was asked of him, if he uttered the "yes" that is requested, harmony of minds would be achieved. He would be told, "That's fine," perhaps he would be congratulated. It would be the end of hatred. The desire to confess is the mad dream of universal love; it is, as Genet himself says, the temptation of the human.—From *St. Genet*, by Sartre (New York: Braziller, 1963)

INTRODUCTION TO THE PROBLEM

The basic issue with which I will concern myself in this paper raises the question of whether the protection of our "great society" by means of quick and efficient law enforcement is more important than the loss of individual freedoms and rights which may result from such "protection." More specifically, how far is it permissible for the police to go in interrogating a suspect or a witness in order to guarantee public safety and the swift execution of justice?

Usually we don't consider that

most defendants have, in effect, two trials. They are first tried by the police. If found guilty by the police, they are held for trial by the courts. If found innocent by the police, they are acquitted then and there. This procedure has no basis in law ... but we know from practical experi-

ence that far more cases are disposed of in this manner than ever reach our courts. (3, pp. 15–16.)

Consequently, the question of police procedures becomes one of the most complex legal issues ever to face the courts.

Critics of the police claim that due process of law and constitutional rights are being abrogated by police techniques and are calling for reforms. On the other hand, law-enforcement agencies point to the rising tide of crime and violence in our society and the need to control it before it engulfs us. They want to pursue what they see as "their job" unhampered by restrictions imposed by the Supreme Court.

In the last national election the Republican vice-presidential candidate ascribed the increase in crime and Northern race riots to the moral atmosphere engendered by "so-called liberals of this Administration, and some of the bleeding hearts who often

Reprinted by permission of the author; this is a slightly abridged version of the paper presented at the American Psychological Association meetings (New York, September 3, 1966).

center more sentiment and concern on the criminal than the victim" (30).

What makes the problem an especially difficult one legally is that the basic questions to be resolved are not inherently legal but psychological in nature, and psychologists have ignored the problem and been ignored by those who would solve it. How can the court formulate criteria to assess "psychological coercion," "voluntariness of a confession," "ability to resist pressure" and similar concepts without reference to psychology? Central in the definition and analysis of these concepts is a knowledge of personality, behavior deviations, performance under stress and deprivation, the effects of social demand characteristics, research on persuasability and attitude change, and many other areas of psychology in which many of the readers of this paper are expert.

One of the few limitations imposed upon the interrogators is self-imposed; interrogation techniques are legally acceptable, they assert, so long as the interrogator believes they would not make an innocent man confess (6). However, the *only* evidence that this indeed is a limitation, that an innocent man would *not* confess, is the "feeling" of the authors of the police interrogation manual, unreliable by any standard of judgment.

We know from our close study of American prisoners of the Korean War in Communist interrogation camps (cf. 13; 22; 23) that many good soldiers gave false confessions, incriminated themselves, and betrayed their fellow soldiers. "Prior to the confessions in the Korean War we usually refused to recognize how easy it was to break the will of individual human beings" (20, p. 201). "It has appeared that they [the Communists] can force men to confess to crimes which have not been committed, and then, apparently, to believe in the truth of their confessions and express sympathy and gratitude toward those who have imprisoned them" (13, p. 116).

What I will contend in this essay is that the techniques employed by our American police are more highly developed, more psychologically sophisticated and more effective than the Chinese Communist "brainwashing" techniques which we have denounced.

It is the primary intention of this paper to convince the psychologists among my readers of the theoretical and practical importance of the phenomena of police-elicited confessions. As psychologists concerned with discovering truths about human behavior and establishing valid generalizations based upon sound evidence, I hope they will become sufficiently concerned to contribute their talents to illuminating with relevant research an area of confusion and error. But more important, I expect that any citizen of this country will react with surprise and disgust at the canker we have allowed to grow within our system of justice by our indifference.

The recent Supreme Court decisions which make it mandatory to warn a suspect of his right to remain silent and of his right to counsel might seem to many of you to vitiate not only my remarks but any serious questioning of the legal issues involved. I will present evidence to show that this ruling has had only the slightest effect on the exceedingly high confession rate police obtain. Secondly, Senator Sam J. Ervine of North Carolina has proposed to overturn the Supreme Court ruling by means of a constitutional amendment. He is against "unfair, illegal or reprehensible pressure" but not for the "removal of all pressure." I will leave it to your judgment to determine whether the techniques the police secretly use qualify for what the senator is against. Finally, and most important for us as Americans, is the fundamental issue of democratic guarantees for the individual regardless of the public's demands to get a loose killer, the insistence by the House Un-American Activities Committee on finding Communists in all protest movements, or the President's demand that we unquestioningly support his foreign policies during this time of national emergency (Vietnam).

My paper will first consider a case familiar to many of you in which a "voluntary" confession of murder was subsequently proven false. Then I will examine at length a selection of specific techniques, tactics, and approaches which the police employ in order to secure confessions. Each of these should be viewed in light of the degree to which it violates what you consider to be a fundamental human right. Following this there will be a brief assessment of the allegation that police enforcement demands "efficiency," which in turn justifies the use of such interrogation tactics. Finally, I would like to suggest some lines of research which psychologists ought to be doing in their labs, in the field, or better yet, with the help of their local police academies.

A FALSE CONFESSION— THE WHITMORE CASE

Can a man be induced to give a confession which virtually sentences him to the electric chair when in fact he is "innocent?" If this extreme statement of the proposition can be shown to be true, then it is likely that under appropriate circumstances men will admit to lesser crimes bearing less severe penalities when they are not guilty. The interrogative tactics and techniques (to be described in the next section of this paper) do, according to the authors of police manuals, "certainly measure up to the fundamental test that not one of them is apt to induce an innocent man to con-

fess" (6, Preface). Since the authors present no evidence except their own personal opinion to support this sweeping generalization, I will leave it to you to judge the validity of the assertion by exposing for you a sampling of the recommended interrogation tactics. However, before doing so, let us consider our initial question of whether a man would falsely confess to murder by examining a recent concrete instance of such confession.

Two years ago a policeman, Patrolman Frank Isola, came to the aid of a woman who was being molested in the Brownsville section of Brooklyn, New York City, but was unable to apprehend the attacker. The woman, Mrs. Elba Borrero, reportedly described her assailant as a Negro, 5 feet 9 inches, 165 pounds, pock-marked face, wearing a raincoat from which she had torn a button.

The next day the patrolman and a detective, Richard Aidala, picked up George Whitmore, Jr., in the vicinity of the crime, since he vaguely fit the description (although 4 inches shorter and 25 pounds lighter, he was a Negro with a button missing from his raincoat). He was asked to go to the police station for questioning, which he agreed to do. The probable cause for taking him into custody was stated in the vaguest possible terms in the affidavit as "a reasonable ground for suspicion supported by circumstances sufficiently strong in themselves."

After viewing him through a peephole, the woman identified him as her attacker, and then the interrogation began in earnest. Within a few hours he had confessed to the attempted rape.

Armed with this confession, Whitmore's coat with the missing button, Brooklyn District Attorney S. A. Lichtman was able to say in his summation to the jury, "We have nailed George Whitmore on the button, so to speak." However, the prosecution had conveniently suppressed a report from the FBI laboratory, stating that the remaining buttons on Whitmore's coat were "different in size, design and construction" from the one torn off the coat of the molester.

But this is the least interesting aspect of this case. Let us return to the East Brooklyn precinct house where Whitmore was being questioned. He was picked up at 8 A.M., had confessed by 10:30, then around noon made a second confession of a knife slaying of a Mrs. Edwards. At this time a detective from the Brooklyn North Homicide Squad, E. J. F. Bulger, had witnessed the confession and in looking over the suspect's belongings, noticed a picture of a white girl. He, along with many other detectives, had been working without success for the previous eight months on the sensational dual killing of Janice Wylie and Emily Hoffert (slain August 28, 1963, on East 88th Street in New York City). The detective identified the girl in the photo as Miss Wylie, and then the interrogation began with renewed intensity.

By 4 A.M. the next morning, after 26 hours of questioning, Whitmore "broke" and confessed, for a third time, to the slaying of the two girls. The press, and undoubtedly the public, were delighted by the announcement of Chief of Detectives (now Chief Inspector) L. J. McKearney, "We've got the right guy, no question about it."

Just to be sure there was no question about it, Manhattan Assistant District Attorney Peter Koste, who took the confession, noted that Whitmore was "composed" and "alert" at the end of the interrogation. In addition, the principal interrogator, Detective Bulger, swore to District Attorney Hogan's aides that he obtained the confession without "feeding" any information to Whitmore.

These statements are remarkable when one considers the nature of the confession, what we have learned of the interrogation procedures used, and subsequent events which proved Whitmore was innocent.

The confession "was quite persuasive and convincing" and went into such great detail that it required *61 typed pages!* It included drawings of the apartment and innumerable minor details that only someone at the scene of the crime could know.

Although Whitmore claimed that the police beat him, they denied the charge, and who would take the word of a rapist-killer to that of our police? In an excellent article (cf. 36), *New York Times* reporter Sidney E. Zion (formerly an Assistant United States Attorney for the State of New Jersey) noted that the police used to advantage a technique to be described in the next section of this paper as "the Mutt and Jeff" approach. Arresting Detective Aidala was the "heavy"—mean, stern, demanding—while Detective Joseph Di Prima (present at all three confessions) was the sweet guy with whom Whitmore was able to develop "rapport." Whitmore is reported to have said that Di Prima was nicer to him than his own father had been!

Two weeks later the police concluded that the photo which had started all the gears going was *not* of Miss Wylie. They then spent the rest of the summer trying to prove that nevertheless it did come from her apartment, where Whitmore must have found it and thus he still had to be guilty.

In October the police were informed by one Nathan Delaney that his friend, Richard Robles, admitted to the murder of the two girls.

Now mildly suspicious of the validity of the confession, the police engaged in some brilliant investigatory work and pinpointed the locale of the photo as the picnic area in the Belleplain State Forest, northwest of Wildwood, New Jersey, and the girl in the photo as Arlene Franco. Whitmore lived in Wildwood and had claimed he found the photo, which the girl admitted she threw away.

Only after two witnesses reported that Whitmore was seen in Wildwood on the eve of the murder, and Robles had confessed to the Wylie-Hoffert murders, was George Whitmore released in January 1965—after eight months in jail.

How could it be that a man confesses—61 pages worth—to murders which he did not commit? Whitmore was quite lucky, for as one assistant district attorney said (31):

If this was what we so-called professionals call a run-of-the-mill murder, Whitmore might well have been slipped into the electric chair and been killed for something he didn't do. Let's face it. We've had executions in the past based on nothing more than a dead body and a confession.

An officer in the Police Department was concerned about the unfavorable publicity and the consequences this case might have on the public's image of the police (to be discussed later). He said, "It's an awful thing, but sooner or later things like this happen. I hate to say this but I'm sure that sometime in history we've sent innocent men to their death by an unjust verdict."

But *why* did Whitmore confess? "Call it what you want, brainwashing, hypnosis, fright. They made him give an untrue confession" is what one assistant district attorney close to the case reported (31). A second assistant district attorney confessed, "I am positive the police prepared the confession for Whitmore. . . . I am also sure that the police were the ones who gave Whitmore all the details of the killings that he recited to our office (31).

Finally, it is also instructive to note the remarks at Robles' trial of Lt. T. J. Cavanaugh, commander of the Manhattan detective squad investigating the Wylie-Hoffert murders. He stated that he always believed that the interrogation was "improper" because the confession was inconsistent with the known facts (34).

But perhaps it is not fair to argue a general point with the evidence from one isolated case which happens to provide an affirmative answer to the question I posed: Do innocent men falsely confess to murder?

Time does not permit me to present much more of the available evidence, but it may be adequate to note that last year in New York State alone there were over 500 appeals made by prisoners to reopen cases which were based on confessions (33). A specific instance of these appeals is the case of a Bronx, New York, factory worker who confessed to the murder of a woman, and after spending a year in jail was found innocent by polygraph data which contradicted his confession. The accused, Santo Sanchez, a 40-year-old Puerto Rican father of six children who speaks little English, went into the 41st Street Precinct in good physical condition, and after his indictment on December 21, 1964, was hospitalized for bruises, etc. on Riker's Island for more than six weeks. Incidentally, the major link to the crime was a photo of the accused which was found in the dead woman's apartment. But since they were relatives this does not seem like such a strange phenomenon (38).

There are many other cases of false arrest and conviction which have been uncovered, but how many have not and will never be? This is an idle conjecture for which we have no answer.

Suppose for a moment that you wanted more information about the nature of the interrogation to which Whitmore was subjected. You'd like to know what were the conditions which could exercise such extreme control over a human being's behavior that he would change his overt behavior, admit to murder, and "voluntarily" sign a written confession of it. There are only two direct sources of information available to you: the accused,

Whitmore, and his accuser, the interrogating detective.

Whitmore says he was beaten, the interrogator says he was not. The police claim the confession was a voluntary, uncoerced document freely given by the suspect; he claims it was forced out of him. "Since no outsider is permitted in the interrogation room, it is not possible to know for a certainty what methods the police use in obtaining confessions" (37). What develops is a swearing contest in which almost everyone prefers to believe the law enforcer.

In this vein it was surprising to read that Chief Justice Joseph Weintraub of the New Jersey Supreme Court called for a study of what goes on in "squad rooms" (40). "So far all we have are opinions and what we read in the press. . . . What we need are the facts. Do judges really know what goes on in squad rooms?"

POLICE INTERROGATION TECHNIQUES

If judges do not know what happens during police interrogations, then how can we as merely interested citizens ever find out? One secondary source of evidence which was pointed out to me a number of years ago by Abraham Goldstein, professor of law at Yale, are the manuals[1] used by the police to train detectives and interrogators. These manuals, written largely by police officers, detectives, or former staff members of police scientific crime-detection laboratories, all include at least a chapter or a whole section on techniques of interrogation. The most recent book, a 1962 revision of an earlier 1953 book written by Fred Inbau and John Reid, is entirely "devoted to a discussion of the psychological tactics and techniques of effective interrogation."

I verified that these manuals are used in training interrogators by calling several police academies and requesting source material that I could use in a college course on interviewing.

Although it is not the purpose of this paper to enumerate all of the many different approaches suggested and used by the police in questioning informants, witnesses, and suspects, it will be necessary to present a sampling of them in order to permit you to evaluate whether or not they are "psychologically coercive," and thereby deprive an individual of his fundamental rights and maybe even of his human dignity.

While there are many ways of organizing this material, I have arbitrarily chosen to classify my sample into the following categories:

1. *Demand characteristics of the interrogation environment*—which includes all attempts to manipulate the *current stimulus* environment in order to create a given set or expectation in the person being questioned.

2. *Perceptual and judgmental distortion* —which includes all attempts to manipulate the suspect's perception of the *past crime* and events associated with it.

3. *Distortion of the social-psychological situation*—which includes all attempts to: (a) manipulate the interpersonal relationship between interrogator and suspect to achieve a desired goal, and (b) capitalize on social variables or social characteristics of the suspect.

4. *Utilization of personality and clinical-psychology phenomena*—which includes all attempts to control the subject's personal motives and needs, to establish a therapeutic relationship, and to tailor tactics to personality traits.

5. *Semantic and verbal distortion*—which

---

[1] All references are to police manuals listed in the references, especially items numbered 2 through 9.

includes all attempts to create a given impression by use of specific verbal formulas or words charged with emotion and affect.

It will be obvious that these are not exclusive or exhaustive categories, but will suffice for our present limited interest which is focused on questions of the "voluntariness" of confessions obtained using these approaches, the degree of coercion and psychological force implied, and also the extent to which they violate what we believe are our basic constitutional and human rights.

Do *you* think they could make a guilty man incriminate himself against his will? Do *you* think they could make a reluctant witness reveal the known identity of a criminal? Do *you* think they could make an innocent man confess falsely?

Demand Characteristics of the Situation

Our image of the "squad room" from old movies as a dingy office with a light shining in the eyes of the suspect while a team of police shout questions and accusations has gone the way of Humphrey Bogart. Modern psychology has entered and alerted the police to the potential significance of every detail in the stimulus situation which they can manipulate and control.

The environment. The interrogation should never take place in an environment familiar to the suspect or with anyone he knows present. "By going to the police station the suspect has made the first act of yielding" (3). The suspect is the "guest" of the police and never should the reverse be true; all psychological support from a familiar environment is thereby destroyed. The room must be quiet, free of all external and internal distractors. It must guarantee privacy for the interrogator and not permit of unplanned interruptions.

It is suggested that since most of the appeals (to be mentioned later) depend upon dissociating the interrogating officer from his law-enforcing police-officer function, the room itself should not resemble a jail or police office. While it is preferable that it should not have windows, if they do exist, then bars on them should be of an ornamental nature. In fact, one author (7) suggests Italian garden gate as a particularly suitable style. The bareness of the room (no pictures, only two chairs, and maybe a desk) should all serve to focus attention on the purpose it is serving. No "tension-relieving" activities or objects (paper clips, etc.) should be allowed the suspect or available (6). There should not even be ash trays present, since they "represent a tacit invitation to smoke"—a distracting tension-reliever (6). No phone should be present because it permits interference with a line of questioning, and represents a symbolic "object of contact with the outside world" (7). Another investigator (8), on the other hand, feels that a fake telephone should be present so that the interrogator can surreptitiously ring it when he feels he needs a break and wants an excuse to leave the room. He also feels that "since the subject should be deprived of every psychological advantage," the atmosphere should suggest the invincibility of the law.

It is also good practice to sit the suspect in an armless, straight-back chair so that he cannot become too comfortable, and so all of his bodily movements are observable.

The interrogator. Since relay questioning is less effective than intensive questioning by a single interrogator, the interrogator should be alone with the suspect and "the full weight of his personality must be brought to bear on the emotional situation" (8). He should sit or stand as close to the suspect as possible, with no furniture intervening. "When a person is close to another one physically, he is closer psychologically" (6).

He should not be dressed in uniform and

no guns or police symbols should be present. The interrogator should wear a conservative suit, avoid loud ties or conspicuous clothing. "A short-sleeved interrogator does not command the respect his position requires" (6). Moreover, he should not offend or distract the suspect by unpleasant breath odors, which should be checked first by a fellow officer, and remedied with mouth wash or "a chlorophyll mint" (6).

The interrogator must at all times be in full control of the interview and possess no distracting mannerisms or lose his composure. With a difficult subject he can immediately establish his authority by small gestures like prohibiting smoking or directing the suspect where to sit, etc. (8). Whenever a witness or other prospective informant refuses to cooperate, the bond of loyalty between him and the offender should be weakened by accusing *him* of the offense, and proceeding to interrogate him as if he were the criminal until he agrees to cooperate. . . .

Thus psychology has generally replaced the physical abuses of the third degree, not only because the courts have made invalid physically coerced confessions, but largely because the third degree is not as effective. "When you break a man by torture, he will always hate you. If you break him by your intelligence, he will always fear and respect you" (3, p. 49). To this end an environment is created which minimizes sensory stimulation for the suspect, maximally exposes the suspect's vulnerability, and provides for complete control and domination by the interrogating officer. . . .

Perceptual and Judgmental Distortion Techniques

Confessions are often obtained by either minimizing the seriousness of the offense and allowing the suspect a "face-saving" out, or by the opposite through misrepresenting and exaggerating the seriousness of the crime.

The first approach can be accomplished through "extenuation"—in which the investigator reports that he doesn't take too seriously a view of the subject's indiscretion, since he's seen thousands of others in the same situation. Or he may "shift the blame" to circumstances, the environment, a subject's weaknesses, any of which might lead anyone to do what the suspect did. A more morally acceptable motive may be suggested for the crime, such as self-defense, an accident, a mistake, heat of passion, etc. In order to "open up" a suspect, it is recommended that good "bait" is blaming anyone who might be associated with the crime other than the suspect, e.g., an accomplice, a fence, a company, loan sharks, or even the victim.

Some provocative examples of the way in which experts use this approach in order to misrepresent the nature of the crime to the suspect in order to get him to talk about it are provided by Inbau and Reid (6):

1. A 50-year-old man accused of having taken "indecent liberties" with a 10-year-old girl was told: "This girl is well developed for her age. She probably learned a lot about sex from the boys in the neighborhood and from the movies and TV; and knowing what she did about it, she may have deliberately tried to excite you to see what you would do" (p. 45).

2. Or, they note that in forcible rape cases, "where circumstances permit, the suggestion might be offered that the rape victim acted like she might be a prostitute . . . that the police knew she had been engaged in acts of prostitution on other occasions" (p. 46).

3. "During the interrogation of a married rape suspect, blame may be cast upon the subject's wife for not providing him with the necessary sexual gratification. 'When

a fellow like you doesn't get it at home, he seeks it elsewhere' " (p. 51).

Once the suspect is in a state of emotional confusion, then "he is unable to think logically and clearly, since his sense of values has been disturbed and his imagination is distorting his perspective. It is possible for the investigator to obtain admissions or even a confession from the suspect by further misrepresenting the picture" (8, p. 105). . . .

Distortion of Social-Psychological Phenomena

Even before the questioning begins, the interrogator is urged to role-play the position of the subject in order to be able to respond to him—"man to man, not as policeman to prisoner" (6, p. 19). The interrogator is cautioned that "it is a mistake . . . to look upon the subject as an animal" (*ibid.*).

Under this category would fall all the appeals which depend upon the interrogator being friendly, kind, sympathetic, understanding, "a Dutch uncle," or an older brother. He is the one who provides social approval and recognition, who accords the suspect status, and is aware of and able to manipulate the suspect because of his social values, feelings of pride and class or group membership.

We are told, "It is a basic human trait to seek and enjoy the approval of other persons" (6, p. 69). Therefore, it is wise to flatter some subjects, for example, by complimenting an accused driver of a getaway car for his maneuvering and "cornering," or compare a juvenile with his movie idol, or a member of a racial group with a respectable, outstanding member of that group. This approach apparently works best with "the uneducated and underprivileged," since they "are more vulnerable to flattery than the educated person

or the person in favorable financial circumstances" (6, p. 72). . . .

To create rapport, the interrogator could pat the suspect on the shoulder, grip his hand, or offer to do a favor for him—get water, talk to his wife, employer, etc. "Gestures of this type produce a very desirable effect. They impart an attitude of understanding and sympathy better than words."

In order to know what "to pit against what," one interrogator suggests that a suspect be asked to name all the people and ideals that are important to the suspect, as well as all those to which he is violently opposed.

For suspects who have pride in their family, an attempt is made to get parents to cooperate. If they refuse, their attention is called to a (faked) circular being prepared for broadcast and distribution throughout the country. It not only describes the fugitive, but lists all of his known relatives' names and addresses as possible leads for apprehending him. Cooperation is quite often obtained in this way, Kidd (3) notes.

It will be remembered that in the case of George Whitmore one of the techniques reportedly used involved the arresting detective instilling fear in him, while the interrogating detective was protective, supportive, and sympathetic. Whitmore responded to this technique which the police call the "Mutt and Jeff" approach by actually believing that Jeff was sincerely concerned about his welfare. While Mutt is typically a big, cruel, relentless investigator, Jeff is a kind-hearted family man, perhaps with a brother in a similar scrape once. Jeff asks Mutt to leave the prisoner alone and get out of the room. He then confides that he, too, detests Mutt's tactics (which unfortunately will get worse), and the suspect's only hope is to cooperate quickly with his friend Jeff by telling the truth and confessing. . . .

These tactics and deceptions appear to support Hugo Munsterberg's classic analysis of untrue confessions (18). He said that there are a number of social motives which make it conceivable from the start that an accused makes of his own accord a confession against himself which is not true. In the face of seemingly overwhelming damaging circumstantial evidence, an individual may prefer to make a false confession in the hope of a recommendation of mercy. The brothers Boorn of Vermont confessed to a killing in order to have the charge changed from homicide to manslaughter, only to have the "corpse" turn up alive. He concludes, "The untrue confessions from hope or fear, through promises and threats, from cunning calculations and passive yielding, thus shade off into others which are given with real conviction under the pressure of emotional excitement or under the spell of overpowering influences" (p. 147).

Let us now consider how the personality and character of the suspect become prime instruments of coercion in the police's arsenal of psychological weapons.

Utilization of Personality and Clinical-Psychology Phenomena

Theodore Reik's brilliant analysis of "the compulsion to confess" (19) focuses attention not only on the obviously mentally ill who flock to police stations to confess after every major crime is publicized, but on all of us who harbor some deep-seated guilt for some real or imagined childhood transgression. Since guilt can be completely relieved only by confession, punishment, and absolution, he would hold that we all have a need to confess which, although varying in intensity, is nevertheless there in every one of us. He compares the criminal suspect with the patient in therapy who he says confesses something

and does not know what he has said in so doing. He notes further that the confession is often not an end in itself, but has the additional meaning of an appeal to one's parents or their substitutes—the police. Because the emotional processes which underlie our motives for a lifetime of petty crimes are largely unconscious, they are reflected in a compulsion to confess—in slips of the tongue, symptoms, self-incriminations, and even in criminal false confessions.

Part of the initial "sizing-up" of the suspect involves an assessment of his personality, his strengths and weaknesses (without the aid of standard psychological measuring instruments). Suspects who appear nervous are left alone to "sweat it" for a long time. For some "apparently guilty" subjects, it may be necessary to reduce their guilt feelings by providing justifications for their behavior in order for them to be able even to talk about their feelings and their crimes.

For subjects who don't appear nervous, it is well to point out supposed psychological and physiological symptoms of guilt which they are manifesting. As any hypnotist will tell you, merely calling attention to and making salient some part of the body or bodily process causes the person to react in accordance with the suggestion. Thus, Inbau and Reid (5, 6) say attention should be directed to the: (a) pulsation of the carotid artery (in the neck), (b) movement of the Adam's apple, (c) dryness of the mouth, (d) any movement of the limbs, and (e) a "peculiar feeling inside" which is due to a troubled conscience.

While practicing one or more of these tactics on the suspect, the interrogator must be constantly alert and able to recognize "moments of indecision, during which his [the suspect's] struggle to avoid the consequences of his criminal act will be partially overcome by, or temporarily deadlocked with, his impulse to confess" (6).

This is the time to "move in" on him. If he is a youngster, the interrogator could play on shame by asking him if or how often he masturbates. This is so embarrassing for most youngsters that they will be eager to change the topic of conversation, and can easily be led into talking about the crime.

On the other hand, with sex offenders of the so-called "intellectual type," it may be helpful to note that the Kinsey reports reveal human beings are not so different from animals in matters of sex. Because female sex victims are usually reluctant to talk about the activities which transpired (and some may even be feeling some guilt at not being more disturbed than they are after having been raped), the interrogator may have them write out details rather than speak them or he may ease the situation for them by asking them to view him as their gynecologist whom they are consulting about "a sex organ problem" (6, p. 36).

It is also well (say Inbau and Reid) for an interrogator to ask the suspect if he ever dreamed about committing the offense in question, since there is an "obvious relationship between dreaming and acting out."

"Fears of novel contrivances" allow the police to capitalize on the public's belief in the validity of lie-detector tests, truth serums, etc. The suspect is told he will have to undergo such tests and they will prove conclusively his guilt. If he refuses, then that too is taken as a sign of his guilt. It is also permissible to falsify the tests to make the subject think the machine singles him out as guilty. While this evidence obviously cannot be used in court, his confession based on it is admissible.

Before turning to the final category in this catalog of interviewing techniques, it would be remiss not to mention the deception which Kidd (3, p. 141) refers to as "fear of the insane asylum." He says that "we find that some mentally affected persons fear the asylum more than they do jail. Threat of confinement in an asylum may secure a ready admission in the hope that they will go to jail." . . .

CONCLUSIONS, EXAMINATION OF ALLEGATIONS, AND RECOMMENDATIONS

It is my professional opinion as a psychologist who has been concerned with the experimental modification of attitudes and behavior, that these techniques represent a highly sophisticated application of psychological principles which for many people are more compelling and coercive than physical torture. These techniques involve confusing the suspect, lying, misrepresenting the situation, perjury, arousing and manipulating his social values and personal needs, as well as capitalizing on repressed motives.

I feel that not only are they likely to make a guilty man incriminate himself *against his will,* but they also can lead to false confessions by the innocent and involuntary testimony by witnesses. It is for the courts to act on this problem as a legal issue, and for the reader to judge for himself whether he wants his police force to be empowered to use such techniques on citizens of this country, which is to say, ultimately, whether he wants his police force to be able to use such techniques on himself or some member of his family. As far as I am concerned, this catalog of interrogation techniques represents a debasement of human nature and stands as a disgraceful slur on the American system of justice.

Obviously, I am on the side of the individual and feel that society's major function is safeguarding *his* rights, *your* rights. Apparently such a position conflicts with the concepts of "efficiency" and "necessity." Fred Inbau and John Reid, the authors of the most recent textbook on criminal interrogation from which I have quoted so freely, declare that they "approve of such psychological tactics and techniques as trickery and deceit that are not only helpful but frequently necessary in order to secure incriminating information . . ." (6, pp. 203–204).

In fairness to the positions of these men, it must be noted that crime is increasing at a phenomenal rate in America and in most countries of the world. Since 1958 serious crimes in the United States have increased by 60 percent, six times the population increase! Statistics like these, as well as the mass murders, the "unmotivated" killing of innocent victims, the rapes and kidnappings (which are exploited for dramatic effect by our communication media) cause the public to be justifiably afraid and to demand quick vengeance. The police respond to public pressures and their concern centers on the immediate goal of convicting a particular suspect. In the course of responding to public fear they are in danger of losing their true function. They forget that they are the *enforcers* of our laws, *not* the makers of them, nor yet the judges of those who may have broken them. . . .

It is claimed by the police that over 80 percent of all criminal cases are solved by confessions, so that these trials are mere formalities. This efficient system of justice in the face of our crime wave may be the major reason for the implicit conspiracy of silence and ignorance about police interrogation tactics by our judges and lawyers. *Why do we demand confessions?* It is also interesting to speculate why such a high premium is placed on confessions in our country. Even in the face of sufficient material evidence, the police insist on a confession. This overzealousness in securing a confession sometimes results in a guilty de-

fendant going free (on a legal technicality) when the material evidence alone would have convicted him. It is my hypothesis that the police need to have the criminal *participate in his own destruction* and that a confession of guilt not only absolves the police of the man's subsequent punishment and maybe death, but also absolves the judge, the prosecuting attorney, the jury, the victim (and his relations). Reik (19) notes that the criminal reveals in his confession his intention to reenter society by declaring himself deserving of punishment. Once done, then the court and police authorities function unconsciously as the "typical representative of the father who condemns and forgives, who judges and comforts." There is a strange similarity between our insistence on confessions from criminal suspects, and our forefathers' insistence upon a declaration of guilt and a renunciation of the devil before a woman suspected of being a witch was burned. "It is rare that a man is acquitted once his confession is admitted in evidence" (37).

The act of confession not only absolves the agents of society of the consequences of their sentence and punishment of the criminal, it does much more. It helps to reestablish (at least in their perception) the bond of human communication between society and one of its transgressors, between the many and the social outcast. Confession "personalizes" the criminal act and makes it an object lesson for all of us who could under other circumstances be judged rather than judging. For the criminal, the act of confession may alleviate not only the guilt of the particular crime, but also that stemming from other crimes which shade off into real or imagined childhood aggressions and sins against society. It is likely that for the nonhabitual criminal, confession leads to "an exhilarating sense of relief that may have the characteristics of a religious conversion" (Hinkle & Wolff, 13, p. 612, in describing the reactions of POWs of the Chinese Communists).

Will all hell break loose if police have to change their tactics? Recently critics have questioned the need for the police to rely on confessions, as well as the allegation that legal restrictions upon law enforcement only result in a weakened police force and a higher crime rate. Justice Nathan Sobel of the New York Supreme Court, after reviewing 1000 Brooklyn indictments from February to April, 1965, concluded that fewer than 10 percent involved confessions! (27). A *New York Times* reporter commented after the recent Supreme Court ruling (41) that "while a number of police departments have been issuing warnings, the method probably has been cursory with the words mumbled. Or, it has likely been done as a tactic to establish a rapport with the suspect." It is estimated that 60 percent of United States criminal defendants cannot afford a lawyer, and an even larger percentage do not even know a lawyer or place any trust in lawyers. For most people of the so-called lower socioeconomic classes, lawyers are not friends when in need, but rather fast-talking shysters who are in it only for the money. Moreover, some interrogation tactics explicitly suggest that a suspect's request for a lawyer is a sign of guilt, and a lawyer is only a "stranger" who will come between the "man-to-man conversation" of the suspect and his "friend in the police station." In addition, maintaining one's right to silence is countered by the police with statements that if the suspect didn't have anything to hide he could talk freely, and his silence is therefore incriminating.

A system of justice based upon secret trial by the police and confession-elicitation has, according to the late Justice Felix Frankfurter, "manifest evils." One evil is "the threat that a police system which has grown to rely too heavily on interrogation will not pursue or learn other crime-detection methods, and the consequent danger that police will feel themselves under pressure to secure confessions" (28). It is not only more efficient to rely on confession-getting than tracking down clues and material evidence, but it is simply easier for the police. The framers of the India Evidence Act back in 1872 recognized this when they eloquently stated that: "It is far pleasanter to sit comfortably in the shade rubbing pepper into a poor devil's eyes than go about in the sun hunting up evidence."

Detroit's Chief Detective Vincent Piersante substantiated Justice Frankfurter's assertion with statistics showing that in the year prior to the ruling advising a suspect of his rights, confessions were deemed "essential" in 21 percent of Detroit's murder cases. In 1965, with warnings to suspects of their rights, the absolute number of confessions *increased,* but they were "essential" in only 9 percent of the murder cases—due to sharper sleuthing which uncovered additional, more solid evidence.

The contention made by many police officials that the Supreme Court rulings would "force them to close down" and abandon the city to the criminals receives little support from two other police sources. In Philadelphia the police began giving carefully worded verbal warnings to suspects last year, and since then 76 percent of all felony suspects voluntarily confessed, 60 percent of all robbery suspects, and 83 percent of all murder suspects did likewise. A week after the most recent Supreme Court ruling, Lt. A. E. Schultheiss of the 14th Detective Squad based at the West 30th Street station of New York City (which makes 1500 arrests a year) said, "By and large they readily admit what they've been doing even after they've been told of their rights." It is only "the hardened criminal who won't talk" and who often has legal counsel available anyway (42).

Therefore, it appears that giving citizens their constitutional rights against self-incrimination and for legal counsel has not crippled or "shackled" police work, and they have not had, nor fear of having to "close down the shop" (43).

It is instructive, in fact, to note evidence to the contrary. In Washington, D.C., Police Chief Robert Murray complained that the Mallory decision "will result in a complete breakdown in law enforcement in the District of Columbia." In comparing crime rates in Washington, D.C., which has supposedly been "handcuffed" by having to follow federal rulings while its neighbors, Virginia and Maryland, operated under more lenient state court statutes, it was found that the overall felony rate increased by only 1 percent in Washington from 1950 to 1960, while it went up 69 percent in comparable Maryland and Virginia suburbs (16).

The techniques the police use alienate them from society. It should be mentioned in passing that one of the most serious consequences of the use of interrogation tactics and approaches like those mentioned in this paper is the debasement of the *police themselves* who have to employ them. When one human being aggresses against another either verbally or physically, deceives and tricks him, and finally "breaks his man" and does so under conditions where the "victim" is helpless to retaliate, then we have the conditions under which cognitive dissonance should be aroused in the aggressor. This state of psychological tension results from behavior which is discrepant with the police officer's ideals of fair play, of the rights of every citizen, of human dignity, and is contrary to any feelings of empathy and social/emotional comparison he may have toward the human being he is interrogating. According to Festinger's theory of cognitive dissonance (12a), the existence of the psychological state of dissonance will motivate

the individual to behave in ways which will reduce its magnitude or intensity. Our interrogating officer can readily reduce his dissonance by modifying several of his cognitions; by derogating the suspect, seeing as necessity all coercive techniques designed to expose criminals, and feeling a moral obligation to persecute and convict those suspected of crimes.

Similar consequences have been observed in recent laboratory studies (summarized by Brock and Pallak, 11a) in which a person choosing to be aggressive toward a "victim" (who ostensibly benefits in some way from such aggression, e.g., his errors are punished), minimizes the seriousness of the pain inflicted, evaluates the victim negatively, and feels obligated to have acted in this way.

The long-range effects of such psychological coping mechanisms leave the typical police officer regarding "the public as his enemy," and feeling "his occupation to be in conflict with the community" (according to Westley, 25, p. 35). He comes to hate the petty criminal, to be suspicious of everyone, and to find a strange kinship with the smart, hardened criminal. Where the law "blocks the path from suspicion to disposition, the law becomes an enemy of its ostensible servants" (Toch, 24, p. 6). Eventually many police officers come to redefine for themselves the concepts of justice, criminals, and even graft. They cease using the "average person" as a source of social comparison, may lose the ability to empathize with him, feel compelled to operate "extralegally" when necessary, in order to harass prostitutes, homosexuals, "beatniks," Negroes, and other minority-group members (as documented recently in the Danny Escobedo affair in Chicago, 28). In so doing, they lose contact with the society they serve, and by feeling above most of its average citizens, alienate themselves from it. Part of this attitude of the police is succinctly summarized by Inbau and Reid: "Of necessity, criminal interrogation must deal with offenders on a somewhat lower moral plane than that upon which ethical, law-abiding citizens are expected to conduct their everyday affairs" (6, p. 208).

Chief Circuit Judge David L. Bazelon, of the United States Court of Appeals, has said, "We must deter not only crime, but also the debasement of the individual" (10a). This imperative should include *both* the suspected criminal and the police officer. . . .

It is clear, then, that because the phenomenon we have been discussing has such broad psychological implications, psychologists who insist on working within the secure confines of their self-defined fields of expertness can nevertheless make a significant contribution with their relevant research to the psychology of police-elicited confessions.

America is at a critical stage in her development (cf. Irving Sarnoff's analysis, 21), with the rights of the individual to protest being challenged all the way from Washington, D.C., to Texas and Sacramento. Responsible citizens and concerned professional psychologists must view the issues raised here in the broadest possible terms.

I prefer to see them in the light of Chief Justice Warren's wisdom:

The methods we employ in the enforcement of our criminal law have aptly been called the measures by which the quality of our civilization may be judged (cited in 16, p. 18).

REFERENCES

Police Manuals

1. "Criminal Investigation," *Department of the Army Field Manual*, FM 19–20 (July 1951).

2. Dienstein, W., *Technics for the Crime Investigator* (Springfield, Ill.: Thomas, 1952).

3. Kidd, W. R., "Police Interrogation," *Police Journal*, New York (1940).

4. Gross, H., *Criminal Investigation*, 3rd ed., adapted by J. C. Adam, edited by N. Kendal (London: Sweet and Maxwell, 1934).

5. Inbau, F. E., and J. E. Reid, *Lie Detection and Criminal Interrogation* (Baltimore: Williams & Wilkins, 1953).

6. Inbau, F. E., and J. E. Reid, *Criminal Interrogation and Confessions* (Baltimore: Williams & Wilkins, 1962).

7. Mulbar, H., *Interrogation* (Springfield, Ill.: Thomas, 1951).

8. O'Hara, C. E., *Fundamentals of Criminal Investigation* (Springfield, Ill.: Thomas, 1956).

9. Söderman, H., and J. J. O'Connell, *Modern Criminal Investigation* (New York: Funk & Wagnall, 1945).

Relevant "Professional" Sources

10. Arens, R., and A. Meadow, "Psycholinguistics and the Confession Dilemma," *Columbia Law Review*, **56** (1956), pp. 19–46.

10a. Bazelon, David L., "Law, Morality, and Individual Rights," unpublished address to Juvenile Court Judges Institute and Juvenile Officers Institute (Minneapolis, August 20, 1963), p. 10.

11. Bem, D., "Inducing Beliefs in False Confessions," *Journal of Personality and Social Psychology*, **3** (1966), pp. 707–710.

11a. Brock, T. C., and M. S. Pallak, "The Consequences of Choosing to Be Aggresive," in P. G. Zimbardo (ed.), *The Cognitive Control of Motivation* (Chicago: Scott, Foresman, in press).

12. Carlton, C. O., R. C. Dillehay, and J. Holey, "The Criminal, the Penalty and the Crime: A Study of Social Perception and Judgment," paper presented at the American Psychological Association (New York, September 1966).

12a. Festinger, L., *A Theory of Cognitive Dissonance* (Stanford, Calif.: Stanford Univ. Press, 1957).

13. Hinkle, L. E., and H. C. Wolff, "Communist Interrogation and Indoctrination of 'Enemies of the State,' " *Archives of Neurology and Psychiatry*, **76** (1956), pp. 115–174.

14. Horowitz, M. W., "The Psychology of Confession," *Journal of Clinical and Experimental Psychopathology,* **18** (1957) , pp. 381–382.

15. Johnson, N., "Sources of Distortion and Deception in Prison Interviewing," *Federal Probation*, **20** (1956), pp. 43–48.

16. Kamisar, Y., "The Police Chief, the College Coach and the Problem of 'Absentee Management' . . . and Other Reflections on the Tactics of 'Police Persecution-Minded Critics of the Courts,' " paper presented at American Psychological Association (September 1963).

18. Munsterberg, H., *On the Witness Stand* (New York: Clark Boardman, 1949).

19. Reik, T., *The Compulsion to Confess* (New York: Farrar, Strauss, 1959).

20. Rogge, O. J., *Why Men Confess* (New York: Nelson, 1959).

21. Sarnoff, I., *Society with Tears* (New York: Citadel, 1966).

22. Schein, E. H., "Reaction Patterns to Severe, Chronic Stress in American Army Prisoners of War of the Chinese," *Journal of Social Issues*, **13** (1957), pp. 21–30.

23. Schein, E. H., W. E. Hill, H. L. Williams, and A. Lubin, "Distinguishing Characteristics of Collaborators and Resisters among American Prisoners of War," *Journal of Abnormal Social Psychology,* **55** (1957) , pp. 197–201.

23a. Skolnick, J. H., *Justice without Trial* (New York: Wiley, 1966) .

24. Toch, H. H., "Psychological Consequences of the Police Role," paper presented at American Psychological Association (September 1963).

25. Westley, W. A., "Violence and the Police," *American Journal of Sociology*, **59** (1953), pp. 34–41.

Relevant "Popular" Sources (Mass Media)

26. *Civil Liberties in New York* (March 1963 issue).

27. Law section, *Time Magazine* (Dec. 3, 1965).

28. Law section, *Time Magazine* (April 29, 1966).

New York Times (arranged in chronological order)

29. "New York Curbs Third Degree," J. Roth (Nov. 7, 1963).

30. "Miller Says 'Distorted' Idea of Goldwater Fades" (Oct. 10, 1964).

31. "Hogan Clears Whitmore in Two East Side Murders" (Jan. 28, 1965) .

32. "Bar Leader Finds High Court Too Lenient in Criminal Cases," Edith E. Asbury (Jan. 30, 1965).

33. "Confession Cases May Rise Sharply," P. Benjamin (Feb. 15, 1965).

34. "Police Doubted Whitmore Story," T. Jones (April 1965).

35. "High Court Scored in Crime Rulings," S. E. Zion (May 14, 1965).

36. "The Suspect Confesses—But Who Believes Him?" S. E. Zion (May 16, 1965).

37. "What about Confessions?" S. E. Zion (July 5, 1965).

38. "Confessed 'Slayer' Cleared after Year," B. Weinraub (Nov. 9, 1965).

39. "Confessions Held Crucial by Hogan," S. V. Roberts (Dec. 1, 1965).

40. "Study of Confessions Asked by Weintraub," R. Sullivan (Dec. 11, 1965).

41. "The Court on Confessions" (June 19, 1966).

42. "Police Find Suspects Willing to Talk," B. Weinraub (June 25, 1966).

43. "No Shackles on the Law," editorial (Aug. 15, 1966).

44. "Detroit Police Plan to Put Confessions on Television Tape" (Jan. 20, 1967).

LIFE ON ADC
BUDGETS OF DESPAIR

Charles Lebeaux

In September 1962 a grave crisis occurred in 6000 needy families with children in Detroit. These families were recipients of Aid to Families with Dependent Children (AFDC), the aid program commonly known as ADC (Aid to Dependent Children) until its title was changed in 1962. In the early 1940s the Detroit welfare departments began supplementing AFDC grants out of general relief funds, because the Michigan state grant in AFDC was in many cases too small for the family to live on, and because it was often *less* than the same family would receive from general relief.[1] But due to Detroit's financial straits, about four years ago the city began

Reprinted by permission of the author and publishers from New University Thought, *3:4 (1963), pp. 26–35.*

[1] AFDC is one of five categorical public-assistance programs set up in the Social Security Act, in which the federal government shares costs with the states. These programs (AFDC, Old Age Assistance, Aid to the Blind, Aid to the Disabled, and Medical Aid to the Aged) are separate financially, and for the most part administratively, from general relief, which is run by the states and localities with no federal involvement. Detroit is in Wayne County where there are three relief offices: the Wayne County Bureau of Social Aid, which administers the categorical aid programs (including AFDC) for the entire county; the Detroit Department of Public Welfare, which handles general relief in Detroit; and the Wayne County Department of Social Welfare, which handles general relief in the rest of the county.

cutting the amount of the supplement. In September 1962 the supplement was out entirely. This last cut affected 6000 of the city's 13,000 AFDC families—many more had been affected by earlier cuts. These many thousands of families are thus living below the minimum standards of health and decency, even as defined by this welfare program itself.

Few people in Michigan know about the plight of these families and even fewer seem to care. The AFDC mothers themselves, many without the clothes or carfare to go out of their homes, have almost no power to influence public policy or opinions. Although in the fall of 1962 members of the Detroit Chapter of the National Association of Social Workers (NASW) organized and supported efforts of some Negro organizations (primarily the Trade Union Leadership Council and the Federation of AFDC Mothers, a group of the mothers themselves), none of their appeals to rescind the cut, either to the mayor or the welfare department, were successful. When these efforts failed, the following survey of the families affected by the cut was made, in order to arouse the moribund consciences of the city and state.[2]

THE PEOPLE ON AFDC

There are now about 7½ million people in the United States getting public assistance under all programs, special and general. Around four million of these are in AFDC families. There are about 33,000 AFDC families in Michigan; about 13,000 of these families, with some 40,000 children, live in Detroit. AFDC is the most controversial of the public-assistance programs, not only because of its size and persistent growth, but because of the social characteristics of the recipients. When the program started in the late 1930s, death of the father was the most common cause for being in need of aid. Today, more than 60 percent of AFDC cases are due to estrangement of parents—divorce, separation, desertion, or unmarried motherhood. The American public regards these as bad or unworthy reasons to be in need, and is less inclined to give help.

Over 40 percent of AFDC families are Negro (compared to about 10 percent of the general population). In northern industrial cities the caseload is largely Negro (about 81 percent in Detroit), and in cities like Detroit, the proportion of illegitimate children is unusually high (although less than one-quarter of all illegitimate children in the country receive AFDC assistance).

The federal law says that to qualify under AFDC a child must be in "need," but the states define that status and determine the actual amount of money that each child and his family receive. The Michigan AFDC law says that they shall

[2] After we were unable to obtain a list of the 6000 from city, county, or state agencies, which made a full random sample impossible, the NASW decided that it had to proceed on its own, and quickly. A list of some hundred-odd names was supplied by the Federation of AFDC Mothers, and a questionnaire was devised by faculty and students of the Wayne State University School of Social Work. Twenty-five members of NASW and twenty-five social-work students volunteered to do the home interviewing, which was accomplished in April 1963. Ninety-three usable interviews were held, and are the basis of this report.

Because we could not obtain the list of 6000 supplement-cut cases, we could not pick a statistically correct sample; but when a population is quite homogeneous with respect to the characteristic under investigation, just a few cases may represent all. So with the poverty aspect of our AFDC families. In fact, my guess is that our group is better off than the typical AFDC family, because women who participate in the Federation of AFDC Mothers also probably will be better managers than the average woman receiving AFDC.

receive enough to permit them to live with "health and decency," at a level below which something suffers—health, church and school attendance, or self-respect. However, most states, including Michigan, interpret a health and decency standard to mean "minimum subsistence."

Dollar costs of a minimum-subsistence budget are determined by home economists and other experts in the Federal Department of Agriculture, the State Department of Social Welfare, and home-economics departments in universities by adding together minimum amounts for food, shelter, utilities, clothing, household supplies, and personal incidentals. For example, on the scale prepared by the Family Budget Council of the Detroit Visiting Nurses Association, $266.21 per month was the minimum income required in January 1960, by a family consisting of a mother age thirty-five, a boy age fourteen, and two girls, nine and four, with rent assumed to be $55 per month. For the identical family, paying identical rent, the Michigan State Department of Social Welfare in January 1961, has $223.05 as the monthly amount required to meet basic needs.

In practice, the welfare worker on the case adds up the amount needed to meet basic needs of the family according to state standards, subtracts any income there may be, and the unmet need should be the amount of the AFDC check. But in most cases in Detroit that is *not what the family gets.* The state sets ceilings on what each family can get, no matter what the budget figures show they need, according to the 1963 formula shown in Table 1.

HOW ARE THEY LIVING?

Without important error, we can think of these families as living on the schedule of state ceiling grants. No income other than the relief grant was reported for seventy-nine families. This means that for 85 per cent of the group, income is fixed by the state ceilings—$120 for a mother and one child, $140 for a mother and two children, and so on. Whenever income plus the ceiling grant exceeds the state subsistence standard for the family, the grant is reduced accordingly.

Court-ordered or voluntary support payments by the absent fathers of families on relief is the weakest of financial reeds. In many cases they are not actually forthcoming, and families dependent on them are

Table 1   THEORETICAL AND ACTUAL GRANTS

Family Size	Budget Requirements[a]	Maximum Grant
Mother and 1 child	$151	$120
Mother and 2 children	191	140
Mother and 3 children	228	160
Mother and 4 children	263	180
Mother and 5 children	300	200
Mother and 6 children	334	220
Mother and 7 children	368	240 (absolute maximum)

[a] Includes food and incidentals allowance of $34 per person, $67 rent, and heat and utilities according to a standardized allowance based on family size.

chronically on the verge of utter destitution. Children over seventeen are excluded from the state-federal AFDC program, and since September 1962 are also eliminated from city welfare support. There are at least six families among our ninety-three with an unemployed child over seventeen living in the home with no provision for his support.

Out of the ceiling grant rent and utilities must get paid, usually first. Table 2 shows the combined cost of rent and utilities to these families in the month of March 1963.

Fifty-two of the families live in city public-housing projects, thirty-seven in private housing. Living in public-housing projects is cheaper—the median rent and utility cost is $56, compared with $86 in private housing, but few public-housing units are large enough for the biggest families, who naturally pay more for bigger private quarters.

What do these reasonable rent and utility costs mean to an AFDC family? Consider a mother with two children. Say that rent and utilities are $70 per month. Out of their $140 grant that leaves $70. But the state welfare department says that three people need $102 a month for food and incidentals. It is clear that for these families "something suffers."

One mother, three days after receipt of her check (and twelve days before the next one would come), had 56¢ left. She had bought food and coal and paid the rent, but held off on the gas and electricity bills because there was no money to pay them. The gas and electricity may be cut off, she says, as they have been twice in the last two years. And what of school supplies, clothing, or carfare?

Sixteen mothers reported they were behind in rent. Half of these owed $50 or less, but one woman was $140 behind because her grant had stopped while the agency checked out a report that "a man was living with her." The lost income was never made up. Twenty-five families were behind in utilities; you need a roof overhead, at least in the winter, but you can exist without heat and light.

A surprising proportion of the mothers considered themselves not badly housed. In the words of the women:

(Private housing): *"It's good because the rent is fair and it's near school, relatives and shopping. But the house is too small and the neighborhood is unfriendly."* (High-rise public-housing project): *"It's cold in winter, causing excess use of electricity. It's too far from the children outside, too small, and the elevators are a problem. But it is burglar and fire proof, and there's a good incinerator."* (Also highrise): *"It's too crowded, noisy, and too high"* (woman has hypertension), *"but it's*

Table 2   COMBINED COST OF RENT AND UTILITIES—MARCH 1963

Dollars	Public Housing	Private Housing	Type of Housing Not Ascertained
40–59	44	3	1
60–79	6	10	1
80–99	2	18	2
100–above	0	5	0
Total	52	36	4

warm, fire-proof, and the Neighborhood Service Organization has good programs for the kids."

HOW DO AFDC FAMILIES EAT?

To get some detail on the quality of economic life on AFDC, we asked the mothers how much food they had on hand (meat, dairy products, and fresh or canned fruit). The information obtained was voluminous and interesting, but difficult to summarize and liable to misinterpretation. Just before check day, food stocks will naturally be low, and just after, there may be two weeks supply of food newly purchased. Averages here would make no sense.

However, the trend of the information gathered indicated that hardly any mother had as much as a half-gallon of milk on hand, and very little meat. Ofter the meat listed was an inexpensive cut like neck bones, or a canned variety. There was a nearly universal report, "No fruit," "No fruit." And something we didn't inquire into was frequently volunteered: "No vegetables either." And in home-economics courses in the schools they teach children about balanced diets!

Asked "Is your family adequately fed?" forty of the mothers answered "yes," six answered "sometimes," and forty-seven answered "no." "Never enough near the time the check is due. Hungry at other times too." "Before transfer to AFDC (from Detroit welfare) we ate well, but now food is inadequate." So the mothers respond who feel their families are inadequately fed. One mother had a doctor-prescribed high-protein diet (and TB too) that she has been unable to follow for two months.

Those that consider their families adequately fed have often given up something else. They say that they are getting behind in the rent, are without adequate clothing, and in one case without a phone, which was necessary because of a brain-damaged child with frequent convulsions. Those who feel they are adequately fed usually go without fruit, and eat little meat and vegetables.

FOOD STAMPS IN THE AFDC PROGRAM

For many years now the federal government has been disposing of some of the surplus foods accumulated under the farm subsidy program by giving it to local relief agencies across the country who distribute it to poor people. In 1962 the food-stamp program, which had been used before World War II, was started in a number of localities including Detroit to test whether it was a better way of distributing surplus foods. As a result, in Detroit surplus commodities are not now given directly to families, but food stamps are distributed by the City Department of Public Welfare to all low-income people who wish to participate. The participant takes his cash to a stamp office and buys stamps which are worth more than the cash paid—for example, you may get $14 worth of stamps for $10. The amount one may purchase depends mostly on the size of the family, but most AFDC families qualify for less than a 50-percent bonus, e.g., for $30 cash, $43 in food stamps.

All AFDC families in Detroit are eligible to buy food stamps. Forty-seven out of our ninety-three families reported buying food stamps; forty-six did not. Most mothers who get the stamps say they are a great help. Those who do not get the stamps gave the following reasons (in order of frequency): not enough cash, restricts purchase selection, timing is off, and can't get to the stamp office.

Twenty-four families found the stamps restricted purchase selection. For example, the stamps don't buy soap, cleaning supplies, or toilet paper. They don't buy coffee or cocoa. These restrictions occur because the program, financed by the U.S. Department of Agriculture with farm subsidy funds, is designed to get rid of surplus food stores, not to help feed poor people. The resulting rules and procedures guard the interests of the farmers, who don't grow coffee or toilet paper, instead of the interests of the stamp users. Even a very careful home manager is penalized by the program's procedures; however, she still gains in dollars by using the stamps.

Not enough cash. This is the most important reason; and it causes all kinds of difficulties even for the families that buy food stamps. What happens is this: A family of mother and three children when receiving its semimonthly AFDC check of $80 is certified to buy $30 worth of food stamps. But the rent of $55 is due and must be paid first; there is not enough left to get the food stamps. Suppose they pay only half the rent now (which many do); but some utility bills are due and a child must have a pair of shoes—again, not enough cash to buy the food stamps. They are not permitted to buy less than the amount they are certified for by the welfare department (this would be against the Department of Agriculture regulations). And they must buy regularly. Every time a family fails to buy the stamps at the appointed time, it is automatically decertified and must go through the application procedure again. If the family is very irregular in buying stamps, it becomes ineligible for the program for a while—a Department of Agriculture penalty to force regular participation. Thus those who most need the added food-buying power of the stamps are least able to get them.

Some find the "timing is off"—that the fixed time for buying stamps comes several days after (or before) the check comes. Meanwhile you have to eat, and there is then insufficient cash to buy stamps when the time comes. This problem is much less severe now than it was when the program was started because local relief officials, after fighting a long battle with Washington, have been able to get the check and stamp-buying dates into approximate coincidence.

WHAT DO THE CHILDREN WEAR?

As a further measure of the level of living on AFDC, information was obtained on the total wardrobe of the oldest school child in each family. As with the food data, the information obtained was voluminous and enlightening, but difficult to summarize and liable to misinterpretation. However, some startling facts emerged regarding what is one of the most critical problems in AFDC life, clothing for school children.

Only about half of the clothing is purchased, a good deal of it was bought before the supplement cut of September 1962, and a good deal of this purchased clothing is used. For the other half of their clothing the children depend on gifts, from relatives and neighbors, and from school teachers. About eight out of ten boys have but one pair of shoes; about half the girls have only one pair of shoes, and half have two pairs. About half the children have no rubbers or boots of any kind, and about three-fourths have no raincoats of any description. There is obviously no room in a state ceiling grant for clothing.

WHAT ELSE DO THEY SPEND MONEY ON?

Although the grants hardly allow for it, the mothers are forced from time to time to spend money on things other than rent, utilities, and food. For the month prior to the interview they reported the following other expenditures—which, of course, are estimates from memory.

Sixty-nine had some expense for transportation, ranging in amount from under a dollar to $45 for a trip South to resettle a burned-out mother. Thirty spent one or two dollars, nineteen more spent three or four dollars. One woman said it cost $20 in carfare to make trips to the clinic for an asthmatic son. Twenty-four families apparently rode not at all.

A good deal of medical expense is reflected in the transportation figure, since the free clinic is their only medical provision. Many find Receiving Hospital care unsatisfactory because of long waits and responsibility for young children; thus we find thirty-one who had expenses for doctors, dentists, or medicines during the month. In twenty-four of these cases the amounts expended were less than $7, but one woman reported $48.68 for doctor and $4.25 for medicine, while another "pays what she can" on a $300 bill for braces for her son's teeth.

Eight families reported insurance-premium payments of from $3 to $15 in the preceding month, and undoubtedly many more neglected to report such expenditures. Only ten families reported any expenditure for recreation, although all were specifically asked about this. Nine reported church expenses, from $1 to $6; nine had school expenses, from $1 to $10; eleven paid telephone bills; one paid $7.50 for house screens; one $2 for a horn mouthpiece for a child; one $3.09 for brooms and a mop; several had bought newspapers; one girl lost $10 from the sale of Girl Scout cookies and the mother had to make it good.

LIFE IN OUR "AFFLUENT SOCIETY"

The significance of these other expenditures is twofold. First, that they should exist at all, since there is usually no allowance at all for them in the grim budgets of these families; and second, even more important, that they should be so few and so small considering that we live in a money economy. What does it mean that families should spend nothing at all for transportation for a whole month in a city like Detroit? That most should spend nothing at all for recreation in families averaging over three children apiece? That with hundreds of school kids represented, only nine families reported expenses for school supplies?

As a refined measure of the economic situation of these families, they were asked the combined value of cash and food stamps on hand, and how many days until the next check came. AFDC checks are now issued twice monthly, rather than once as formerly, to help families spread their income over the entire month, although this interferes with rent payment and purchase of food stamps. The essence of the financial situation of these people is contained in the fact that thirty-one families had between nothing and $4 on hand to last from three to fourteen days. Asked if they ever ran out of money, they all answered yes.

When asked what they did about running out of money, two-thirds said they borrowed, either from relatives and friends or storekeepers, and one-third said they just "stayed run out." "Stay run out" is the theme of their lives—and for those who borrow too, because the loan must be paid back, and each month they sink a little deeper. Besides borrowing and staying run out, some found other ways to cope with the continuing crisis: One "lets the bills go." (Where does this end?) One cashes in bottles and borrows food. One cried in shame: "The lady downstairs gives us food." One said, "If the children get sick, I call the police to take them to Receiving Hospital."

One has been "borrowing" secretly from the funds of a Ladies' Club of which she is treasurer. The club is her one meaningful adult social contact. There is soon to be an election for new club officers and she will be exposed. Her children ask: "Mama, why are you always so sad?" Half crazy with worry, she feels sick; at Receiving Hospital they have referred her to the psychiatrist.

One was in despair because a retarded son who delights in his monthly visit home from the County Training School was coming tomorrow, and there was little food and no money or food stamps in the house. One said bitterly: "A woman could always get $10 if she had to. I prefer not to resort to this."

Consider our affluent society: in an economy generating wealth sufficient to supply every family of four with nearly $10,000 per year income, we reduce a family to cashing in pop bottles to get food, we push a woman to thoughts of prostitution to feed her children, we force an honest woman into theft and then provide her with $25 an hour psychiatric treatment.

IMPACT OF THE
SUPPLEMENTATION CUT

As noted above, only about two-thirds of the ninety-three families received a supplement cut in September 1962. The families that had been cut were asked: Where did it hurt? What did you stop buying?

"No more clothes, fruit, milk. Clothes hurt most because mostly for school boy. Borrowed clothes to go to church." "Got behind in utilities—over $100." "Had to cut out food stamps. Hurt because came at time when children needed school supplies and clothing." "Shoes. Children have hard to fit feet so can't buy cheap shoes. Special treats cut out. We used to go as a family for small treats on holidays, but no more." "School clothing. They are ashamed of their ragged clothing. No spending money in school. This makes my children want to quit." "Boy dropped out of Boy Scouts.*

No shows, no getting away from the house."

No clothing, no school supplies, no gym shoes, no church, no Boy Scouts, no movies, no little treats, no ice-cream cones—nothing like this if you want to keep the roof overhead. But after a while you lose interest even in that, and you quit school, quit church, quit Boy Scouts, begin to steal, or perhaps take money from a boy friend. Every single family which has its supplement cut was seriously hurt by the income reduction—all gave stories like those above.

When the 6000 AFDC cases were cut off supplemental relief in September 1962, it was expected at the welfare department that many would come to the department asking for reinstatement of supplementation. But few showed up. It was then suggested by some public-assistance officials, "Maybe they are not so bad off as we thought. Maybe they don't really need it." As we have seen they are wrong.

But how many went, what happened, and why didn't the rest go? Actually thirty-one of the sixty-five mothers who had received a budget cut *did* go to the city welfare to ask for help. None got it. Why didn't the other thirty-four mothers go? Perhaps they were wiser in anticipating refusal; they decided to save the time, the carfare, and the effort. Of course, in refusing aid the intake workers are simply carrying out departmental policy. So often in the position of having to deny aid to people who in their heart they know need help, the workers tend to develop what one former worker calls "the culture of intake"—methods of denying aid without fully examining the circumstances of the family.

SOCIAL POVERTY

These people are not starving or out on the street. But in our world, lack of buying power, even when it is not so absolute as to lead to starvation or death, leads to a very real social starvation and social death.

Well-off people easily forget that almost all social relationships depend on the ability to spend some money. To go to school costs money—for books, notebooks, pencils, gym shoes, and ice cream with the other kids. Without these the child begins to be an outcast. To go to church costs money—for Sunday clothes, carfare to get there, and a little offering. Without these, one cannot go. To belong to the Boy Scouts costs money—for uniforms, occasional dues, shared costs of a picnic. Without these, no Scouts.

Poverty settles like an impenetrable prison cell over the lives of the very poor, shutting them off from every social contact, killing the spirit, and isolating them from the community of human life.

THE TWO KINDS OF SOCIAL SERVICE IN PUBLIC WELFARE

Willard C. Richan

Last year, as a member of the Cleveland Mayor's Commission on the Crisis in Welfare, I attended a meeting whose subject was the social service (noncash) component of public welfare. We had with us a number of middle-rank and upper-rank administrators from the local welfare department and also some welfare recipients. Everybody was for better services, but it soon became clear that not everybody had the same conception of what social services were.

The senior welfare administrator talked about child protection and family breakdown and rehabilitation. The clients talked about emergency aids of a tangible nature: getting the gas turned back on; providing dental care and clothing. The two conceptions overlapped at points, but the orders of priorities were directly reversed.

Client representatives said quite pointedly that they had more experience at raising children than most caseworkers. As for cleaning house, this was the closest they came to having a professional career. The discussion was amicable, but the impasse remained. It is a basic impasse which overhangs any discussion of social services in public welfare. It is a central focus of the conflict which is erupting in welfare departments across the country. Next to the inadequacy of cash benefits, it is probably *the* major point of conflict today. The bill of goods we sold Congress in 1962 was rehabilitation, by which we meant intervening in clients' lives so as to remold their behavior. But this is not what the clients are looking for when they tear up welfare centers in cities around the country.

The impasse must be understood in its wider implications. It must be seen in relation to the total crisis that grips public

Reprinted by permission of the American Public Welfare Association from Public Welfare, **27** *(October 1969), pp. 307–311.*

welfare in America. For decades, relief programs had the function of maintaining a pool of low-skilled labor at subsistence levels low enough to make low-paying jobs in private industry attractive. This surplus of cheap labor provided an important cushion for the ups and downs of the labor market. Recently public assistance has fulfilled the same function for public and other nonprofit institutions, also providing a buffer against the inroads of organized labor in these fields. It is no accident that the hospital administrators in one community complained about a drive to raise AFDC grants because of the potential impact on recruitment of female help at prevailing wage levels.

But recent technological changes are making cheap, mass labor a thing of the past. Thus, public assistance is losing one of its central functions. As it becomes dysfunctional to goad the poor into competing for jobs in the regular economy, the notion of an automatic benefit system unrelated to work—the guaranteed minimum income—emerges. It is noteworthy that support for this scheme cuts across the full spectrum of ideologies regarding the work ethic. There emerges also "work and training," the euphemism for a system that holds some welfare recipients on a treadmill and syphons others into jobs which cannot attract workers from the regular labor force. The early experience with the Work Incentive Program (WIN) underscores this point. In most jurisdictions, WIN has been very slow in getting off the ground.

There emerges also the drive to provide birth-control services to AFDC recipients. A reduction in the birth rate means one thing in parts of the world where the exploding population is outrunning total national economies and quite another in American ghettos. Incidentally, I am talking neither about the merits of birth-control services in the ghetto nor the motivation of planned-parenthood advocates. Smaller family size may well be a factor in emancipating thousands of black people from the depths. Rather, I am trying to understand why the advocates have suddenly gotten a receptive audience and the opposition has pretty well collapsed. America is always embarrassed by unused surpluses, be they agricultural products or people.

This crisis in public welfare's function in society comes at a time of violent unheaval in our sociopolitical order. There is eruption in the ghetto and countereruption elsewhere. And a major point where these forces collide is public welfare. The conflict makes both a shift in the conception of public welfare more urgent and at the same time constricts its freedom to change.

THE FUNCTIONS OF SOCIAL SERVICES

In public welfare as elsewhere, the social services have a major function in times of crisis. Historically, the social worker has buffered social conflict and averted disruptions of the established order. When the alienated poor threaten the system, the social worker seeks to quell the disturbance. At times he has sought to persuade the poor that their misery stemmed from their own inadequacies and moral turpitude. At other times he has helped them focus their discontent at the level of clean streets and recreation facilities. At other times he has dealt with the unrest by defining it as "sick." I disparage this role as the suppressor of discontent insofar as the poor are unable to extract genuine improvement in their living conditions as the price of keeping the peace. In other words, those early settlement workers and more recently the gang workers and the outreach workers who joined in the political struggle for truly better conditions made the role of pacifier a morally defensible one.

What has been the function of the case-worker in public assistance? One function has been to harass the recipient—enough to make nonrecipient status look attractive but not enough to bring on a revolt in the ranks. Another has been to teach recipients how to make creative use of a totally inadequate budget. The provision of irregular "emergency" benefits has been especially important to the social worker's role. On the one hand, it has taken the edge off the discontent at strategic points. On the other, it has made the recipient self-demeaning and compliant. The social worker has sought to help the recipient understand how her own behavior and that of her children has contributed to her misery.

Yet, at the same time, some social workers have gone to bat for their clients, fought school administrators and hospital administrators and landlords and even their own bosses in behalf of the recipients; even engaged in political action for a more humane welfare system. But this role has been gratuitous.[1] By and large, the welfare recipient has not made demands. Not until now. Now the demanding recipient and the political crosscurrents and the change in the function of welfare are all forcing on the social worker a new definition of his own role and of social services in general.

The term "social services" is a marvel of imprecision. Generally it refers to benefits which are outside of the normal rules of the marketplace. In Europe it includes health care and education; in the United States it ordinarily does not. Social services have come to take on special meaning in public assistance in this country, being restricted to benefits other than cash or direct cash substitutes. A useful distinction has been made between two basically different kinds of social services. On the one hand, there are *social utilities,* provisions which are available to a total population or to clearly defined segments of the population.[2] On the other hand, there are *social interventions,* individualized attempts to control or alter client behavior.[3]

The distinction is less in the content of the service than in the circumstances under which it is made available and the purposes it is intended to fulfill—not what is done to or for a person as much as how he becomes eligible.

Because social utilities are available for a total population or for persons falling within clearly defined categories, eligibility for them is unambiguous. The potential beneficiary comes as a claimant; it is he who decides whether or not he needs the particular provision. Social interventions are class-related provisions. The potential beneficiary does not make the decision as to whether he should receive the service; that decision requires the special expertise of the provider of the service. Furthermore, the ground rules for the decision are not understood by the potential recipient but tend to be wrapped in a professional mystique. Thus, the question of whether a social service is a social utility or a social intervention has crucial importance for the relationship between provider and recipient, the prerogatives of the latter and the locus of major decisions about his status.

[1] This, too, may be changing. The National Association of Social Workers has adopted a policy position which defines advocacy for one's clients as a professional obligation, not just an option.

[2] The term was introduced in the social-work literature by Alfred J. Kahn. See "New Policies and Service Models: The Next Phase," *American Journal of Ortho-psychiatry,* **35**:4 (July 1965), pp. 658ff. See also Willard C. Richan, "The Responsibilities of the Social Work Profession in the Delivery of Social Services," unpublished paper (July 1968).

[3] *Ibid.*

Now it needs to be pointed out that the lines between these two kinds of provisions are not clear. Adoptive applicants take the initiative in deciding whether to seek a child; the subject of rehabilitative efforts in AFDC ordinarily does not decide to seek "rehabilitation." Both, however, are subject to a professional decision as to whether and how the service is to be provided.

THE DIVISION OF FUNCTIONS IN PUBLIC WELFARE

The principle that the same public-assistance caseworker should do everything related to his client's needs died hard. On the surface it makes supreme sense for one person to integrate all help to the recipient. But several things have become clear in recent years. The first is that, given the pressures and expectations of public-assistance programs, the more punitive functions tend to drive out the more humane, in a kind of Gresham's Law of welfare. Both official demands and unofficial pressures have made the policing and investigating activities the central ones. In the early 1960s, we saw training and workload reduction as the solution to this problem. But experience has demonstrated that the trained worker with 60 families tends to act like the untrained worker with 160 if nothing else changes.[4]

Thus, what was controversial in 1962—the separation of the income and social-service functions in public assistance—has suddenly become "in" in the late 1960s. The rapidity with which this particular shibboleth was knocked down is impressive. Consider, for instance, the fact that the Advisory Council on Public Welfare, loaded with forward-looking social workers, made no reference to this rather basic change in its 1966 report.[5]

But this salutary step is only a beginning. We need to go the next step and separate the provision of social utilities from social interventions in public welfare. In 1962, we urged Congress that it could do well (reduce welfare rolls) by doing good (provide social services). In this merging of the negative and the humanitarian aspects of welfare, the humanitarian came out on the short end of the stick. Take, for instance, this quote from a spokesman for the National Association of Social Workers, before the House Ways and Means Committee in 1962:

Financial assistance . . . is essential, but alone, is not enough. Expenditures for assistance unaccompanied by rehabilitative services might actually increase dependency and eventually cost the community. . . . Assurance that aid goes only to those legally eligible for it is best safeguarded by adequate numbers of well-qualified staff to evaluate the needs of recipients and determine their qualifications for receiving help.[6]

It is proposed that, in like manner, the lumping together of social utilities and

---

[4] The evidence is persuasive, although not entirely consistent. See David Wallace, "The Chemung County Evaluation of Casework Service to Dependent Multiproblem Families: Another Problem Outcome," *Social Service Review*, **41**:4 (December 1967), pp. 379–389. See also Edwin J. Thomas and Donna L. McLeod, *In-Service Training and Reduced Workloads* (New York: Russell Sage Foundation, 1960).

[5] *Having the Power, We Have the Duty* (Washington, D.C.: U.S. Government Printing Office, 1966). See also Gordon Hamilton, "Editor's Page," *Social Work*, **7**:1 (January 1962), p. 2; Eveline M. Burns, "What's Wrong with Public Welfare?" *Social Service Review*, **36**:2 (June 1962), pp. 111–122; and Samuel Mencher, "Perspectives on Recent Welfare Legislation, Fore and Aft," *Social Work*, **8**:5 (July 1963), pp. 59–64.

[6] Wayne Vasey, in testimony in behalf of the National Association of Social Workers (February 3, 1962) (mimeographed).

social interventions within the social-service component will lead to a general application of the ground rules governing social interventions. In other words, the recipient will in both cases tend to be subjected to the judgment of the provider, a judgment whose rationale he will not understand. To expect that the social worker will in one instance exercise his diagnostic thinking and fashion individualized treatment plans, then turn around and allow the recipient the full prerogatives implied by the concept of social utilities, is unrealistic. The authority role implicit in social interventions will permeate the whole.

The present crisis in public welfare adds a note of urgency to this question. A major focus of welfare-client antagonism, aside from the inadequacy of the grants, is the business of being subject to the control—hostile or beneficent—of the social worker. This is the real meaning of "welfare colonialism." This is the real meaning of the demand by black militants that the ghetto control its own affairs. It is no accident that a major target of the welfare-rights movement has been to place in the hands of clients and applicants knowledge about their rights. It is also no accident that many welfare workers are particularly threatened when the manual gets into clients' hands. In order to be a claimant and demand my rights. I have to know what they are.

I am saying that as long as social interventions are merged with social utilities in public welfare, clients will remain in colonial status. The only solution is to separate out those areas of service where the ground rules can be stated explicitly and the client is truly free to take or not to take. It goes without saying, of course, that such explicit benefits need not be restricted to persons who also need cash assistance. They can be made available to all who need them.

This separation of functions would make feasible two current proposals for giving more power to the recipients of service. One is the principle of "community control"—in which the recipient of services has power over them.[7] The other is the proposal to use some form of vouchers or certificates which would allow the consumer to shop around among competing agencies.[8] It is in relation to social interventions that the exercise of power by consumers will present the greatest problems; both types of power are resisted strongly by all helping professions. It is much easier to argue that welfare clients should control the dispensation of social utilities or shop around among the providers.

The separation of the social-intervention and social-utility functions in public-welfare social services, then, is an important "next step" in moving toward a more rational welfare system. What I have said about these functions in public assistance also applies to other public social services. The worker charged with providing both types of services will tend toward the social-intervention model as an overall orientation. He will tend to focus first on the client's level of social functioning and last on the merits of the expressed need. He will use clinical criteria in determining the client's need for items such as a new apartment or an extra bed. Such criteria are irrelevant, as he himself would hasten to assert if the same criteria were applied to

[7] See Warren C. Haggstrom, "The Power of the Poor," in Frank Riessman, Jerome Cohen, and Arthur Pearl (eds.), *The Mental Health of the Poor* (New York: Free Press of Glencoe, 1964), pp. 205–223.

[8] The rationale for interagency competition for consumers is discussed in John B. Turner, "In Response to Change: Social Work at the Crossroads," *Social Work*, **13**:3 (July 1968), pp. 12ff. See also Robert Morris, "Strategies for Innovation in the Delivery of Services," paper presented to Second NASW Professional Symposium (San Francisco, May 26, 1968).

his attempts to purchase these items. Thus it is important that different workers deal with these respective classes of service.

There are a number of reasons why the division of functions I am suggesting seems particularly timely right now. In the first place, Washington has laid the groundwork for such a step by disengaging money payments from social services. Any welfare department ought to be able to carry out this change with a minimum of red tape. Secondly, in the current national climate, a liberalized form of cash benefits for "those people" may be hard to sell. Finally, there is the social upheaval in America's cities. No, I am not threatening that, unless welfare starts responding to the clients' order of priorities in social services, then more welfare centers are going to get torn up. Some welfare offices may get torn up regardless of how much the system changes. The real issue is whether social services are going to fulfill an important function— whether, in the process of suppressing discontent, they will be morally defensible.

10 Dissent and Social Control

PROTEST AND SUPPRESSION

The Editors

In an earlier section we dealt with the application of the new technology to the control of human behavior. Electronic wiretapping, computerized data banks, centralized wire service, concentrated ownership of the media, and the sophisticated application of the social and biological sciences provide a giant step toward the regulation of individual behavior. But these new technologies have not created the problem of social control. The coercive control of one group of people by another is a major theme of the human historical record. In this section we direct attention to dissent against the established order and to the institutional legitimation of oppressive controls.

The most abusive methods of control in modern history are identified with slavery and with the practices of the Nazis in Germany. The Nazi case is particularly illuminating because it took place in a "civilized" society like our own in many important respects. The very sadism of the atrocities inflicted by the Nazis helps us to isolate the case as something apart, something which could not conceivably happen here. With ruthless pride the Elite Guard—the Nazi S.S.—contrived and carried out acts of perverse cruelty—drowning people in excrement, whipping people to climb trees while others were forced to shake the trees with those falling kicked to rise and, that failing, shot on the ground. In due time a program of mass liquidation in the gas chamber was added as the *Endloesung* (final solution) to the elimination of six million people. Try as we may the horror is too great to stick in our minds. In an article written in 1948, following his discussions with Germans in the postwar period, Everett Hughes raises two basic questions. How could some people be so far released from the inhibitions of civilized life to perform such obscene actions? Where were the millions of ordinary citizens of this civilized country during this period of cruel mass murder?

Hughes provides a compelling analysis of the mutual interdependence of the relatively small number of human butchers who did the dirty work and the millions of disinterested bystanders who either condoned it as being the legal prerogative of the state or, even more frequently, refused either to be involved or to let themselves become aware of the distress of other people. The good people had only to accept passively the designation of some group of human beings as the outgroup (hence expendable) and then maintain a psychological distance from the actual crimes. The practice in the American media of presenting the weekly "body count" or "kill ratio" in the Vietnam war suggests a similar immunity, in the general public, to the suffering of other people.

The case of Kitty Genovese who was assaulted three separate times while 38 persons turned on their lights to see but neither gave nor sought help, is frequently cited to demonstrate the unwillingness of Americans to get involved. And there are also some, including a small American Nazi Party and the Minutemen armed against a communist plot (exactly as the Nazis in Germany first described their purpose), who can be counted upon, when the time is right, to do the dirty work.

The atmosphere conducive to a circumstance in which one group of people (in the American case those designated as communist or subversive) can become the scapegoats and victims of another has been greatly favored by the rapid growth of the radical right. Many a local community has found members of its school board, or particular teachers, or even particular books in its libraries fall victim to well-disciplined attempts of extremist organizations. Such groups seek to purge their country from what they sincerely believe to be the efforts of a conspiratorial movement. The extremist movement finds many adherents from stable middle-class families who feel alienated from meaningful participation in a mass society. A citizen of certain historical powerful empires might have substituted a nationalistic identification for his own failing sense of importance. Now one finds the substitution of national glory for personal pride made impossible by the revolutionary state of the world, the stalemate in nuclear weapons, and the gradual gain in authority or reputation of international agencies. Since 1955 the organizations of the extreme right have grown by an annual average of 22 percent. The budgets of the thirty largest of these organizations rose from close to 5 million dollars in 1958 to more than 14 million dollars in 1963. The vindictive message reaches its audiences through publications with a combined circulation of over one million and more than 7000 radio broadcasts every week. Social scientists are not completely agreed upon the causes for this rapid expansion, but its growth is a fact.

The effects of a hostile super-patriot group upon the larger community are not always apparent. Certain individuals targeted for suspicion are ruined through techniques which were long associated with the name of Senator Joseph McCarthy. During the fifties, described by many as the McCarthy era, the issue of coercive control was particularly salient. This was the period of ascendance of the cold war.

Sociologists and other observers of the social setting were impressed by the general silence, apathy, and acquiescence of the American public at this time. It was the period of investigation and intimidation when Senator McCarthy and his counterparts discredited their opposition by using innuendo in charges made before the press and by hiring paid informants who produced what was wanted for money or out of fear of being subjected to abusive investigation themselves.

Certain procedures of the McCarthy era are strongly reminiscent of excesses during the Stalin era in the Soviet Union—many of which were substantially more extreme, more brutal, and more direct. There is an important parallel to be drawn here between the conditions for military predominance and the condition for restriction in the rights of expression for individuals. Both military preparedness and witch-hunting are partly products of externally perceived threat. Ideologically sanctioned total warfare, whether hot or cold, helps to push both antagonists to measures which transgress the very values which the society is said to be protecting. It is also clear from the Stalin example that totalitarian excesses may be reflections of left-wing as well as right-wing governments. In fact, as control techniques are improved it seems quite conceivable that a totalitarianism of the center, à la Huxley's *Brave New World,* could overcome the technologically advanced societies.

In America, in the fifties particularly, the effects upon those subjected to these procedures was enormous. One victim, a prominent millionaire named Edward Lamb, was subjected to intensive investigation in which he was faced by witnesses paid to perjure by attorneys for the Federal Communications Commission. It took Lamb, who was an attorney and businessman, three and one-half years of court fighting and $900,000 to clear his name and have the license for his radio and television stations renewed (Lamb, 1963). Hundreds of government workers, college professors, and entertainers were ruined because they lacked such resources. But the major effects were caused by the larger number of silent people who just did not find the time or were a little frightened or didn't think anything good would come of being involved. It is this period of silence, which prevented active critical discussion of the revolutionary forces of technological militarism, cybernation, race, and poverty, that has shaped the present period.

During the late fifties, an important Supreme Court decision was made by a 5–4 vote against a defendant who had refused to answer before the House Committee on Un-American Activities. Justice Black's dissent to the majority ruling provides an interesting documentation of the conditions under which the limits of free criticism are reduced. In his dissent Black shows how a committee of Congress bent upon discrediting one of its critics and harassing an individual long associated with civil rights can, with the Supreme Court apparently approving, permit a contempt citation which effectively limits the First Amendment protection afforded by the Bill of Rights to criticize public officials. Justice Black's dissent (with Warren and Douglas concurring) ends with the following warning. "There are grim reminders all around this world that the distance between individual liberty and firing squads is not always as far as it seems."

The House Committee on Un-American Activities as an agency of the federal government was granted great discretionary power and substantial fiscal support in the conduct of its investigations. So, too, is the authority of state and local government a strong adversary against even the most enterprising of dissenters. The state of Arkansas managed to "lynch" its most independent and critical newspaper through an intricate series of legal and financial maneuvers. The local sheriff and police and some of the more politically motivated court officials have great power to determine what persons and what action shall be impeded, which shall be punished severely, and which shall go unnoticed.

Martin Luther King once took the opportunity of his detention by local authorities in a Birmingham jail to answer some of his clerical colleagues who were critical of the methods he employed of sit-ins, marches, and boycotts. King's eloquent reply expressed the reasons why strong dissent is the lifeblood of social change. His view is that the stimulation of tension was a demonstrated necessity before the segregationist South would even open a dialogue. He points also to the crucial aspect of nonviolent techniques in those instances where the practices do constitute violation of a law. The practitioner of this form of civil disobedience openly violates the unconscionable law and willingly accepts the penalty. Such practice avoids the trap of the German citizens who carried out the Nazis' orders because they were legal.

King's response to the question of whether he has allowed due time for progress is particularly relevant to the functions of dissent. Time itself is neutral, King notes, and progress is not inevitable. Progress comes about through tireless human effort. In the face of gross injustice the silence of good people proves as appalling as the hateful actions of the evil-doers.

Wherever the demand for change occurs there tends to be a reciprocal set of forces put in motion to retain or revert to some earlier state of equilibrium; hence, a major tool in any movement, including the contemporary revolution in human rights, is the right to dissent. A major weapon in the hands of forces resisting this revolution is the power of control.

One of the mainstays of power is the ability of the holders to monopolize the symbols of legitimacy (e.g., royal birth, electoral process, executive or officer's status, etc.). Under such circumstances dissent from a loyal subject, a disenfranchised voter, a lower-echelon clerk, or an enlisted man is severely diminished. Furthermore, power tends to become imbedded in certain patterns of communication and certain fiscal transactions which go on behind the closed doors of the Joint Chiefs of Staff or at the local Business Development Councils. Thus, many significant decisions are made outside the clear view of those who would be most disturbed by the dealings transacted. For this reason, verbal dissent is frequently without a platform for confrontation of the particular part of the social system which it would like to change. Before workers could effectively confront their employers it was necessary for them to go through a harrowing period of organization which resulted in acquisition of their own bureaucratic power structure. From positions of equal power, big labor and big business now do engage in direct negotiations and dialogues.

There are numerous examples of attempts by the existing power to prevent organized action that challenges established power. The British attempt to curtail town meetings that protested taxation without representation, the hiring of the Black Legion by major American corporations to use sniping, poison gas, and the fanning of ethnic hatreds to prevent unionization, and even the objectives of the American Project Camelot (see introduction to Chapter 3) to identify and deter insurgent elements in Latin America are important examples. The modern-day examples of "The Crucible," Arthur Miller's drama of the Salem witch hunt in which those labeled as heretics are effectively smothered, are both numerous and tragic. Most relevant to the modern American struggle for human rights, however, are the methods of direct action employed by the "heretics" comprising the amorphous civil-rights groups to induce change. One case, the Montgomery bus boycott, is of particular importance historically because it marked a turning point in the participation of Southern Negroes in what had, till then, been a very cautious, "respectable" organization of middle-class Negroes and whites. The details of the case described in the article by Reddick are particularly helpful in illuminating the interplay between the persistence of dissent and the measures devised by the powers of the community to resist the challenge. The case is remarkable, in retrospect, when one considers the extremely modest demands of the group to hire Negro drivers in all-Negro routes, and to change the seating customs to do away with segregation only in the middle sections of the buses, but to leave the front and rear reserved for whites and Negroes respectively. That such modest demands could create so great a reaction reveals the depth of conviction of those who would resist change. Sometimes, as in the jailing of King in Montgomery, in the slaying of three Mississippi summer-project workers, or in the use of bull whips and cattle-prodding devices, the intense conviction resulted in such provocative recriminations that the protestors become more unified and more militant.

Humor and music have both been factors in maintaining the morale of the civil-rights movement. Negro comedian Dick Gregory suggested that Negro bus drivers need not interfere with segregated seating patterns on the buses if they could only be provided with a 30-foot-long steering column.

The protestors, of course, are equally prone to errors of judgment which set back their own course. Even the most sophisticated forms of resistance to the protestors, such as the hiring of Negro policemen, the establishment of Job Corps training centers and integrated housing projects, attempts by the mass media to associate parts of the movement with communist leanings—even these attempts have been serving to fan the militancy of the civil-rights movement. As a group, however, they have become increasingly strong as the techniques to control them evolved from the bull whip to the most benevolent tokens of equality. The reasons for this relate back to the very isolation and concealment of American poverty. Segregation itself helped keep the poor congregated in separate communities. This helped to fortify the people against a complete internalization of such dominant American values as the mystique of the do-it-yourself Horatio

Alger legend, or the respect for order even above justice. When the protestors see measures organized from without ostensibly for the benefit of the deprived, they appear suspicious and strangely ungrateful.

When well-intentioned programs are not well received, the following questions emerge. Why can't they overcome their distrust of the political system which has long been unrepresentative of their interests? Why don't they respond to the ads to stay in school, seek out the job-training programs, appear more respectable to earn the tolerance of white neighbors? Increasingly among the dissenters, the mood is militant and alienated. In the slums and on the university campuses there is evidence, among the protestors, of an unwillingness to accept a groove, even an apparently desirable groove in a society which is geared, at best half-heartedly, to the provisions of human needs. For most, the alternatives are either to enter the social ladder at the bottom-most rung and remain dependent upon others for providing such limited opportunities as may exist or to assume responsibility themselves for the future of their own communities. The psychological rewards of the more militant and separatist attempts appear to be greater. Picketing realtors who charge exorbitant rents for inferior housing, destroying stores which charge high interest rates, engaging in a political struggle, demanding effective control of the Head Start program may seem more relevant to the poor person than job training, whether in or out of the military, to become a keypunch operator for an electronics firm whose extensive defense contracts use the same funds which might otherwise go to the support of needed community programs. The issue of protest is more than a matter of material gains. It has become a matter of the search for meaningful activity related to the nature of one's problems. The participation in decisions is less easily achieved in a mass bureaucratic society than the initiation of particular welfare programs. If the objective of participation sought by the greater revolution for human rights is achieved, it will probably be through new and imaginative ways of permitting people to have a say in the operation of their communities. Such at least is the hope of certain social critics who would see in the protest movement a means for aiding not only the protestors or the poor but the society as a whole.

It is difficult to make predictions about the future of protest and control in the revolution in human rights in this country. Eventually the rights movement is likely to develop its own sources of bureaucratized power and to be assimilated as a pluralist power group in American society. Until such time its message seems likely to be more revolutionary than reformist, its demands more embarrassing to the centers of American power, and its potential for violence exacerbated by increases in unemployment and the return of young Negro soldiers to their homes in urban ghettos or rural shanty towns. There is always danger that, with the disenchantment from slow progress, a proneness for demagoguery will develop, leaving the entire race issue even more volatile than the summer rioting of 1965 through 1967 would lead us to anticipate.

While the protest increases its pitch it seems also likely that greater efforts at suppression will be attempted and, not inconceivably, that the entire apparatus of police control designed for assisting counterrevolutionary governments abroad will be tried in this country. Tighter police control, stiffer jail sentences, and more harassment of "black power" sympathizers would not be an unreasonable prediction.

Just how far we have gone already in the machinery of control is becoming obvious. When civil-rights workers armed only with their voter-registration pads were drenched in their own blood by police and local hoods alike, there was a widespread moral revulsion aimed at Mississippi. But now in the North apartments of black leaders have been raided, guns have been fired into crowds of minority people and students, and the court system has been stretched to use bail as illegal preventive detention and to harass protestors with vague charges of conspiracy. Following the police riot at the Chicago Democratic Convention in 1968, it was the protest leaders who were brought to trial. In this trial a black man, Bobby Seale, accused of conspiring with persons whom he had not met prior to the demonstration, was gagged and shackled to his courtroom chair for trying to speak in his own defense after the judge, Julius Hoffman, refused to delay the trial until Seale's attorney had recovered from an illness.*

Selected cases do not tell the story of the more carefully planned and more deadly approach to social control in the ghetto. Beverly Leman's article on "Social Control of the American Ghetto" describes the manner in which the defense intellectuals have brought their tools of pacification home to roost in the form of domestic counterinsurgency. It is an important article which suggests how the technical and military revolutions have begun to use the most horrible means of the totalitarian state to maintain domestic control.

Barring the unwanted, but possible, onset of nuclear war, the military revolution and the cybernetic revolution could probably go on indefinitely, gradually accommodating human beings to the nonhuman technologies. Where the clash and the essential crack in American society seems most likely is in the area in which the military and cybernetic revolutions run counter to the demands being expressed in the human-rights revolution.

Conflict is probably a healthy sign in societies, provided that its toll from violence is low and its capacity to find meaningful and satisfactory compromises for conflicting demands remains high. But the prospects for the accommodation of a highly automated warfare-oriented state to meet the challenges behind the extraordinary forms of dissent in this country do not seem good. If we are in fact entering a period of increased suppression then it will do to bear in mind Hughes' warning about good people whose moderate dehumanization and detachment make possible the dirty work of others.

---

* Read Tom Hayden's *The Trial* and Bobby Seale's *Sieze the Time* for accounts of the details of an amazing trial.

REFERENCES AND ADDITIONAL READING

Black, Hugo L., "From Justice Black's Dissent (with Warren and Douglas concurring) in the Braden Case," *United States Reports Cases Adjudged by the Supreme Court,* **365**, pp. 415–423; reproduced in R. Perrucci and M. Pilisuk (eds.), *The Triple Revolution: Social Problems in Depth* (Boston: Little, Brown, 1968), pp. 608–611.

Chmaj, Betty, "Paranoid Patriotism: The Radical Right and the South," *Atlantic* (November 1962), pp. 91–98.

Gleason, Ralph J., and Paul Krassner, "Obituaries on Lenny Bruce," *Ramparts* (October 1966), pp. 34–38.

Hayden, Tom, *The Trial* (New York: Holt, 1970).

Hughes, Everett C., "Good People and Dirty Work," *Social Problems,* **10:**1 (Summer 1964), pp. 3–11; reproduced in R. Perrucci and M. Pilisuk (eds.), *The Triple Revolution: Social Problems in Depth* (Boston: Little, Brown, 1968), pp. 596–607.

Lamb, Edward, *Trial by Battle: Case History of a Washington Witch Hunt* (Santa Barbara, Calif.: Center for the Study of Democratic Institutions, 1963).

McCormack, Thelma, "Intellectuals and the Mass Media," *American Behavioral Scientists* (December 1965–January 1966).

Marine, Gene, "Nobody Knows My Name," *Ramparts* (June 1967), pp. 11–16.

Reed, Robert, "How to Lynch a Newspaper," *Atlantic* (November 1964), pp. 59–63.

Seale, Bobby, *Sieze the Time* (New York: Random House, 1970).

LETTER FROM BIRMINGHAM JAIL
APRIL 16, 1963

Martin Luther King, Jr.

My Dear Fellow Clergymen:

While confined here in the Birmingham city jail I came across your recent statement calling my present activities "unwise and untimely." Seldom do I pause to answer criticism of my work and ideas. If I sought to answer all the criticisms that cross my desk, my secretaries would have little time for anything other than such correspondence in the course of the day, and I would have no time for constructive work. But since I feel that you are men of genuine good will and that your criticisms are sincerely set forth, I want to try to answer your statement in what I hope will be patient and reasonable terms.

I think I should indicate why I am here in Birmingham, since you have been influenced by the view which argues against "outsiders coming in." I have the honor of serving as president of the Southern Christian Leadership Conference, an organization operating in every southern state, with headquarters in Atlanta, Georgia. We have some 85 affiliate organizations across the south, and one of them is the Alabama Christian Movement for Human Rights. Frequently we share staff, educational, and financial resources with our affiliates. Several months ago, the affiliate here in Birmingham asked us to be on call to engage in a nonviolent direct-action program if such were deemed necessary. We readily consented, and when the hour came we lived up to our promise. So I, along with several members of my staff, am here because I was invited here. I am here because I have organizational ties here.

I

But more basically, I am in Birmingham because injustice exists here. Just as the prophets of the eighth century B.C. left their villages and carried their "thus saith the Lord" far afield and just as the Apostle Paul left his village of Tarsus and carried the gospel of Jesus Christ to the far corners of the Greco-Roman world, so am I compelled to carry the gospel of freedom beyond my own home town. Like Paul, I must constantly respond to the Macedonian call for aid.

Moreover, I am cognizant of the interrelatedness of all communities and states. I cannot sit idly by in Atlanta and not be concerned about what happens in Birmingham. Injustice anywhere is a threat to justice everywhere. We are caught in an inescapable network of mutuality, tied in a single garment of destiny. Whatever affects one directly affects all indirectly. Never again can we afford to live with the narrow, provincial "outside agitator" idea. Anyone who lives inside the United States can never be considered an outsider anywhere within its bounds.

You deplore the demonstrations taking

place in Birmingham. But your statement, I am sorry to say, fails to express a similar concern for the conditions that brought about the demonstrations. I am sure that none of you would want to rest content with the superficial kind of social analysis that deals merely with effects and does not grapple with underlying causes. It is unfortunate that demonstrations are taking place in Birmingham, but it is even more unfortunate that the city's white power structure left the Negro community with no alternative.

II

In any nonviolent campaign there are four basic steps: collection of the facts to determine whether injustices exist, negotiation, self-purification, and direct action. We have gone through all these steps in Birmingham. There can be no gainsaying the fact that racial injustice engulfs this community. Birmingham is probably the most thoroughly segregated city in the United States. Its ugly record of police brutality is widely known. Its unjust treatment of Negroes in the courts is a notorious reality. There have been more unsolved bombings of Negro homes and churches in Birmingham than in any other city in the nation. These are the hard, brutal facts of the case. On the basis of these conditions Negro leaders sought to negotiate with the city fathers. But the latter consistently refused to engage in good-faith negotiation.

Then last September came the opportunity to talk with leaders of Birmingham's economic community. In the course of the negotiations certain promises were made by the merchants—for example, the promise to remove the stores' humiliating racial signs. On the basis of these promises the Rev. Fred Shuttlesworth and the leaders of the Alabama Christian Movement for Human Rights agreed to a moratorium on all demonstrations. As the weeks and months went by we realized that we were the victims of a broken promise. The signs remained.

As in so many past experiences, our hopes had been blasted and our disappointment was keenly felt. We had no alternative except to prepare for direct action, whereby we would present our very bodies as a means of laying our case before the conscience of the local and the national community. Mindful of the difficulties involved, we decided to undertake a process of self-purification. We began a series of workshops on nonviolence, and we repeatedly asked ourselves: "Are you able to accept blows without retaliating?" "Are you able to endure the ordeal of jail?" We decided to schedule our direct action program for the Easter season, realizing that except for Christmas this is the main shopping period of the year. Knowing that a strong economic withdrawal program would be the by-product of direct action, we felt that this would be the best time to bring pressure to bear on the merchants.

But Birmingham's mayoral election was coming up in March, and when we discovered that Commissioner of Public Safety Eugene "Bull" Connor was to be in the run-off, we decided to postpone our demonstrations until the day after the run-off so that they could not be used to cloud the issues. It is evident, then, that we did not move irresponsibly into direct action. Like many others, we wanted to see Mr. Connor defeated, and to this end we endured postponement after postponement. Having aided in this community need, we felt that our direct-action program could be delayed no longer.

III

You may well ask, "Why direct action? Why sit-ins, marches, etc.? Isn't negotiation a better path?" You are quite right in calling for negotiation. Indeed, this is the very purpose of direct action. Nonviolent direct action seeks to foster such a tension that a community which has constantly refused to negotiate is forced to confront the issue. It seeks so to dramatize the issue that it can no longer be ignored. My citing the creation of tension as part of the work of the nonviolent resister may sound rather shocking. But I readily acknowledge that I am not afraid of the word "tension." I have earnestly opposed violent tension, but there is a type of constructive, nonviolent tension which is necessary for growth. Just as Socrates felt that it was necessary to create a tension in the mind so that individuals could shake off the bondage of myths and half-truths and rise to the realm of creative analysis and objective appraisal, so must we see the need for nonviolent gadflies to create the kind of tension in society that will help men rise from the dark depths of prejudice and racism to the majestic heights of understanding and brotherhood.

The purpose of our direct-action program is to create a situation so crisis-packed that it will inevitably open the door to negotiation. I therefore concur with you in your call for negotiation. Too long has our beloved southland been bogged down in a tragic effort to live in monologue rather than dialogue.

One of the basic points in your statement is that the action that I and my associates have taken in Birmingham is untimely. Some have asked, "Why didn't you give the new city administration time to act?" The only answer that I can give to this query is that the new Birmingham administration must be prodded about as much as the outgoing one before it will act. We are sadly mistaken if we feel that the election of Albert Boutwell as mayor will bring the millennium to Birmingham.

While Mr. Boutwell is a much more gentle person than Mr. Connor, they are both segregationists, dedicated to maintenance of the status quo. I have hope that Mr. Boutwell will be reasonable enough to see the futility of massive resistance to desegregation. But he will not see this without pressure from devotees of civil rights. My friends, I must say to you that we have not made a single gain in civil rights without determined legal and nonviolent pressure. Lamentably, it is a historical fact that privileged groups seldom give up their privileges voluntarily. Individuals may see the moral light and voluntarily give up their unjust posture; but, as Reinhold Niebuhr has reminded us, groups tend to be more immoral than individuals.

We know through painful experience that freedom is never voluntarily given by the oppressor; it must be demanded by the oppressed. Frankly, I have yet to engage in a direct-action campaign that was "well timed" in the view of those who have not suffered unduly from the disease of segregation. For years now I have heard the word "Wait!" It rings in the ear of every Negro with piercing familiarity. This "Wait" has almost always meant "Never." As one of our distinguished jurists once said, "Justice too long delayed is justice denied."

IV

We have waited for more than 340 years for our constitutional and God-given rights. The nations of Asia and Africa are moving with jetlike speed toward gaining political independence, but we still creep at horse-and-buggy pace toward gaining a cup of coffee at a lunch counter. Perhaps it is easy for those who have never felt the stinging darts of segregation to say "Wait." But when you have seen vicious mobs lynch your mothers and fathers at will and drown your sisters and brothers at whim; when you have seen hate-filled policemen curse, kick, and even kill your black brothers and sisters with impunity; when you see the vast majority of your 20 million Negro brothers smothering in an air-tight cage of poverty in the midst of an affluent society; when you suddenly find your tongue twisted as you seek to explain to your six-year-old daughter why she can't go to the public amusement park that has just been advertised on television, and see tears welling up when she is told that Funtown is closed to colored children, and see ominous clouds of inferiority beginning to form in her little mental sky, and see her beginning to distort her personality by unconsciously developing a bitterness toward white people; when you have to concoct an answer for a five-year-old son asking, "Daddy, why do white people treat colored people so mean?"; when you take a cross-country drive and find it necessary to sleep night after night in the uncomfortable corners of your automobile because no motel will accept you; when you are humiliated day in and day out by nagging signs reading "white" and "colored"; when your first name becomes "nigger," your middle name becomes "boy" (however old you are) and your last name becomes "John," and your wife and mother are never given the respected title "Mrs."; when you are harried by day and haunted by night by the fact that you are a Negro, never quite knowing what to expect next, and are plagued with inner fears and outer resentments; when you are forever fighting a degenerating sense of "nobodiness"—then you will understand why we find it difficult to wait. There comes a times when the cup of endurance runs over, and men are no longer willing to be plunged into an abyss of injustice where they experience the bleakness of corroding despair. I hope, sirs,

you can understand our legitimate and unavoidable impatience.

V

You express a great deal of anxiety over our willingness to break laws. This is certainly a legitimate concern. Since we so diligently urge people to obey the Supreme Court's decision of 1954 outlawing segregation in the public schools, at first glance it may seem rather paradoxical for us consciously to break laws. One may well ask, "How can you advocate breaking some laws and obeying others?" The answer lies in the fact that there are two types of laws: just and unjust. I agree with St. Augustine that "an unjust law is no law at all."

Now what is the difference between the two? How does one determine whether a law is just or unjust? A just law is a man-made code that squares with the moral law or the law of God. An unjust law is a code that is out of harmony with the moral law. To put it in the terms of St. Thomas Aquinas, an unjust law is a human law that is not rooted in eternal law and natural law. Any law that uplifts human personality is just. Any law that degrades human personality is unjust. All segregation statutes are unjust because segregation distorts the soul and damages the personality. It gives the segregator a false sense of superiority and the segregated a false sense of inferiority. Segregation, to use the terminology of the Jewish philosopher Martin Buber, substitutes an "I-it" relationship for an "I-thou" relationship and ends up relegating persons to the status of things. Hence segregation is not only politically, economically, and sociologically unsound, it is sinful. Paul Tillich has said that sin is separation. Is not segregation an existential expression of man's tragic separation, his awful estrangement, his terrible sinfulness? Thus it is that I can urge men to disobey segregation ordinances, for such ordinances are morally wrong.

Let us consider some of the ways in which a law can be unjust. A law is unjust, for example, if the majority group compels a minority group to obey the statute but does not make it binding on itself. By the same token a law in all probability is just if the majority is itself willing to obey it. Also, a law is unjust if it is inflicted on a minority that, as a result of being denied the right to vote, had no part in enacting or devising the law. Who can say that the legislature of Alabama which set up that state's segregation laws was democratically elected? Throughout Alabama all sorts of devious methods are used to prevent Negroes from becoming registered voters, and there are some counties in which, even though Negroes constitute a majority of the population, not a single Negro is registered. Can any law enacted under such circumstances be considered democratically structured?

Sometimes a law is just on its face and unjust in its application. For instance, I have been arrested on a charge of parading without a permit. Now there is nothing wrong in having an ordinance which requires a permit for a parade. But such an ordinance becomes unjust when it is used to maintain segregation and to deny citizens the First Amendment privilege of peaceful assembly and protest.

I hope you are able to see the distinction I am trying to point out. In no sense do I advocate evading the law, as would the rabid segregationist. That would lead to anarchy. One who breaks an unjust law must do so *openly, lovingly,* and with a willingness to accept the penalty. I submit that an individual who breaks a law that conscience tells him is unjust and who willingly accepts the penalty of imprisonment in order to arouse the conscience of the community over its injustice is in re-

ality expressing the highest respect for law.

Of course, there is nothing new about this kind of civil disobedience. It was evidenced sublimely in the refusal of Shadrach, Meshach, and Abednego to obey the laws of Nebuchadnezzar, on the ground that a higher moral law was at stake. It was practiced superbly by the early Christians who were willing to face hungry lions rather than submit to certain unjust laws of the Roman empire. To a degree, academic freedom is a reality today because Socrates practiced civil disobedience. We should never forget that everything Adolf Hitler did in Germany was "legal" and everything the Hungarian freedom fighters did in Hungary was "illegal." It was "illegal" to aid and comfort a Jew in Hitler's Germany. Even so, I am sure that had I lived in Germany at the time I would have aided and comforted my Jewish brothers. If today I lived in a communist country where certain principles dear to the Christian faith are suppressed, I would openly advocate disobeying that country's antireligious laws.

VI

I must make two honest confessions to you, my Christian and Jewish brothers. First, I must confess that over the past few years I have been gravely disappointed with the white moderate. I have almost reached the regrettable conclusion that the Negro's great stumbling block in his stride toward freedom is not the White Citizen's Counciler or the Ku Klux Klanner but the white moderate who is more devoted to "order" than to justice; who prefers a negative peace which is the absence of tension to a positive peace which is the presence of justice; who constantly says "I agree with you in the goal you seek, but I cannot agree with your methods"; who paternalistically believes he can set the timetable for another man's freedom; who lives by a mythical concept of time and who constantly advises the Negro to wait for a "more convenient season." Shallow understanding from people of good will is more frustrating than absolute misunderstanding from people of ill will. Luke-warm acceptance is much more bewildering than outright rejection.

I had hoped that the white moderate would understand that law and order exist for the purpose of establishing justice and that when they fail in this purpose they block social progress. I had hoped that the white moderate would understand that the present tension in the south is a necessary phase of the transition from an obnoxious negative peace, in which the Negro passively accepted his unjust plight, to a substantive and positive peace, in which all men will respect the dignity and worth of human personality. Actually, we who engage in nonviolent direct action are not the creators of tension. We merely bring to the surface the hidden tension that is already alive. We bring it out in the open where it can be seen and dealt with. Like a boil that can never be cured so long as it is covered up but must be opened with all its pus-flowing ugliness to the natural medicines of air and light, injustice must be exposed, with all the tension its exposure creates, to the light of human conscience and the air of national opinion before it can be cured.

In your statement you assert that our actions, even though peaceful, must be condemned because they precipitate violence. But is this a logical assertion? Isn't this like condemning a robbed man because his possession of money precipitated an act of robbery? Isn't this like condemning Socrates because his unswerving commitment to truth and his philosophical inquiries precipitated the act by the misguided populace in which they made him drink hemlock? Isn't this like condemning Jesus because

his unique God-consciousness and never-ceasing devotion to God's will precipitated the evil act of crucifixion? We must come to see that, as the federal courts have consistently affirmed, it is wrong to urge an individual to cease his efforts to gain his basic constitutional rights because the quest may precipitate violence. Society must protect the robbed and punish the robber.

I had also hoped that the white moderate would reject the myth concerning time in relation to the struggle for freedom. I have just received a letter from a white brother in Texas. He writes: "All Christians know that the colored people will receive equal rights eventually, but it is possible that you are in too great a religious hurry. It has taken Christianity almost 2000 years to accomplish what it has. The teachings of Christ take time to come to earth." Such an attitude stems from a tragic misconception of time, from the strangely irrational notion that there is something in the very flow of time that will inevitably cure all ills. Actually, time itself is neutral; it can be used either destructively or constructively. More and more I feel that the people of ill will have used time much more effectively than have the people of good will. We will have to repent in this generation not merely for the hateful words and actions of the bad people but for the appalling silence of the good people. Human progress never rolls in on wheels of inevitability; it comes through the tireless efforts of men willing to be co-workers with God, and without this hard work time itself becomes an ally of the forces of social stagnation. We must use time creatively, in the knowledge that the time is always ripe to do right. Now is the time to make real the promise of democracy and transform our pending national elegy into a creative psalm of brotherhood. Now is the time to lift our national policy from the quicksand of racial injustice to the solid rock of human dignity.

VII

You speak of our activity in Birmingham as extreme. At first I was rather disappointed that fellow clergymen would see my nonviolent efforts as those of an extremist. I began thinking about the fact that I stand in the middle of two opposing forces in the Negro community. One is a force of complacency made up of Negroes who, as a result of long years of oppression, are so completely drained of self-respect and a sense of "somebodiness" that they have adjusted to segregation, and of a few middle-class Negroes who, because of a degree of academic and economic security and because in some ways they profit by segregation, have unconsciously become insensitive to the problems of the masses. The other force is one of bitterness and hatred, and it comes perilously close to advocating violence. It is expressed in the various black nationalist groups that are springing up across the nation, the largest and best-known being Elijah Muhammad's Muslim movement. Nourished by the Negro's frustration over the continued existence of racial discrimination, this movement is made up of people who have lost faith in America, who have absolutely repudiated Christianity, and who have concluded that the white man is an incorrigible "devil."

I have tried to stand between these two forces, saying that we need emulate neither the "do-nothingism" of the complacent nor the hatred of the black nationalist. For there is the more excellent way of love and nonviolent protest. I am grateful to God that, through the influence of the Negro church, the way of nonviolence became an integral part of our struggle.

If this philosophy had not emerged, by now many streets of the south would, I am convinced, be flowing with blood. And I am further convinced that if our white brothers dismiss as "rabble-rousers" and "outside agitators" those of us who employ nonviolent direct action and if they refuse to support our nonviolent efforts, millions of Negroes will, out of frustration and despair, seek solace and security in black nationalist ideologies—a development that would inevitably lead to a frightening racial nightmare.

VIII

Oppressed people cannot remain oppressed forever. The yearning for freedom eventually manifests itself, and that is what has happened to the American Negro. Something within has reminded him of his birthright of freedom, and something without has reminded him that it can be gained. Consciously or unconsciously, he has been caught up by the *Zeitgeist,* and with his black brothers of Africa and his brown and yellow brothers of Asia, South America, and the Caribbean, the U.S. Negro is moving with a sense of great urgency toward the promised land of racial justice. If one recognizes this vital urge that has engulfed the Negro community, he should readily understand why public demonstrations are taking place. The Negro has many pent-up resentments and latent frustrations, and he must release them. So let him march; let him make prayer pilgrimages to the city hall; let him go on freedom rides—and try to understand why he must do so. If his repressed emotions are not released in nonviolent ways, they will seek expression through violence; this is not a threat but a fact of history. I have not said to my people, "Get rid of your discontent." Rather, I have tried to say that this normal and healthy discontent can be channeled into the creative outlet of nonviolent direct action. And now this approach is being termed extremist.

But though I was initially disappointed as being categorized as an extremist, as I continued to think about the matter I gradually gained a measure of satisfaction from the label. Was not Jesus an extremist for love: "Love your enemies, bless them that curse you, do good to them that hate you, and pray for them which despitefully use you, and persecute you." Was not Amos an extremist for justice: "Let justice roll down like waters and righteousness like an everflowing stream." Was not Paul an extremist for the Christian gospel: "I bear in my body the marks of the Lord Jesus." Was not Martin Luther an extremist: "Here I stand; I can do no other so help me God." And John Bunyan: "I will stay in jail to the end of my days before I make a butchery of my conscience." And Abraham Lincoln: "This nation cannot survive half slave and half free." And Thomas Jefferson: "We hold these truths to be self-evident, that all men are created equal. . . ." So the question is not whether we will be extremists but what kind of extremists we will be. Will we be extremists for hate or for love? Will we be extremists for the preservation of injustice or for the extension of justice? Perhaps the south, the nation, and the world are in dire need of creative extremists.

I had hoped that the white moderate would see this need. Perhaps I was too optimistic; perhaps I expected too much. I suppose I should have realized that few members of the oppressor race can understand the deep groans and passionate yearnings of the oppressed race, and still fewer have the vision to see that injustice must be rooted out by strong, persistent, and determined action. I am thankful, however, that some of our white brothers have grasped the meaning of this social revolution and committed themselves to it. They are still all too few in quantity, but they are big in quality. Some—such as Ralph McGill, Lillian Smith, Harry Golden, and James McBride Dabbs—have written about our struggle in eloquent and prophetic terms. Others have marched with

us down nameless streets of the south. They have languished in filthy, roach-infested jails, suffering the abuse and brutality of policemen who view them as "dirty nigger lovers." Unlike so many of their moderate brothers and sisters, they have recognized the urgency of the moment and sensed the need for powerful "action" antidotes to combat the disease of segregation.

IX

Let me take note of my other major disappointment. Though there are some notable exceptions, I have also been disappointed with the white church and its leadership. I do not say this as one of those negative critics who can always find something wrong with the church. I say this as a minister of the gospel, who loves the church; who was nurtured in its bosom; who has been sustained by its spiritual blessings and who will remain true to it as long as the cord of life shall lengthen.

When I was suddenly catapulted into the leadership of the bus protest in Montgomery, Alabama, a few years ago, I felt we would be supported by the white church. I felt that the white ministers, priests, and rabbis of the south would be among our strongest allies. Instead, some have been outright opponents, refusing to understand the freedom movement and misrepresenting its leaders; all too many others have been more cautious than courageous and have remained silent and secure behind stained-glass windows.

In spite of my shattered dreams I came to Birmingham with the hope that the white religious leadership of this community would see the justice of our cause and with deep moral concern would serve as the channel through which our just grievances could reach the power structure. But again I have been disappointed.

I have heard numerous southern religious leaders admonish their worshipers to comply with a desegregation decision because it is the *law*, but I have longed to hear white ministers declare, "Follow this decree because integration is morally *right* and because the Negro is your brother." In the midst of blatant injustices inflicted upon the Negro I have watched white churchmen stand on the sideline and mouth pious irrelevancies and sanctimonious trivialities. In the midst of a mighty struggle to rid our nation of racial and economic injustice I have heard many ministers say, "Those are social issues with which the gospel has no real concern," and I have watched many churches commit themselves to a completely otherworldly religion which makes a strange, unbiblical distinction between body and soul, between the sacred and the secular.

We are moving toward the close of the 20th century with a religious community largely adjusted to the status quo—a taillight behind other community agencies rather than a headlight leading men to higher levels of justice.

X

I have traveled the length and breadth of Alabama, Mississippi, and all the other southern states. On sweltering summer days and crisp autumn mornings I have looked at the south's beautiful churches with their lofty spires pointing heavenward, and at her impressive religious education buildings. Over and over I have found myself asking: "What kind of people worship here? Who is their God? Where were their voices when the lips of Governor Barnett dripped with words of interposition and nullification? Where were they when Governor Wallace gave a clarion call for defiance and hatred? Where were their voices of support when bruised and weary Negro men and women decided to rise from the

dark dungeons of complacency to the bright hills of creative protest?"

Yes, these questions are still in my mind. In deep disappointment I have wept over the laxity of the church. But be assured that my tears have been tears of love. There can be no deep disappointment where there is not deep love. Yes, I love the church. How could I do otherwise? I am in the rather unique position of being the son, the grandson, and the great-grandson of preachers. Yes, I see the church as the body of Christ. But, oh! How we have blemished and scarred that body through social neglect and through fear of being nonconformists.

There was a time when the church was very powerful—in the time when the early Christians rejoiced at being deemed worthy to suffer for what they believed. In those days the church was not merely a thermometer that recorded the ideas and principles of popular opinion; it was a thermostat that transformed the mores of society. Whenever the early Christians entered a town the power structure immediately sought to convict them for being "disturbers of the peace" and "outside agitators." But the Christians pressed on, in the conviction that they were "a colony of heaven," called to obey God rather than man. Small in number, they were big in commitment. By their effort and example they brought an end to such ancient evils as infanticide and gladiatorial contest.

XI

Things are different now. So often the contemporary church is a weak, ineffectual voice with an uncertain sound. So often it is an archdefender of the status quo. Far from being disturbed by the presence of the church, the power structure of the average community is consoled by the church's silent—and often even vocal—sanction of things as they are.

But the judgment of God is upon the church as never before. If today's church does not recapture the sacrificial spirit of the early church, it will lose its authenticity, forfeit the loyalty of millions, and be dismissed as an irrelevant social club with no meaning for the 20th century. Every day I meet young people whose disappointment with the church has turned into outright disgust.

Perhaps I have once again been too optimistic. Is organized religion too inextricably bound to the status quo to save our nation and the world? Perhaps I must turn my faith to the inner spiritual church, the church within the church, as the true *ecclesia* and the hope of the world. But again I am thankful to God that some noble souls from the ranks of organized religion have broken loose from the paralyzing chains of conformity and joined us as active partners in the struggle for freedom. They have left their secure congregations and walked the streets of Albany, Georgia, with us. They have gone down the highways of the south on torturous rides for freedom. Yes, they have gone to jail with us. Some have been kicked out of their churches, have lost the support of their bishops and fellow ministers. But they have acted in the faith that right defeated is stronger than evil triumphant. Their witness has been the spiritual salt that has preserved the true meaning of the gospel in these troubled times. They have carved a tunnel of hope through the dark mountain of disappointment.

I hope the church as a whole will meet the challenge of this decisive hour. But even if the church does not come to the aid of justice, I have no despair about the future. I have no fear about the outcome of our struggle in Birmingham, even if our motives are at present misunderstood. We will reach the goal of freedom in Birming-

ham and all over the nation, because the goal of America is freedom. Abused and scorned though we may be, our destiny is tied up with America's destiny. Before the pilgrims landed at Plymouth we were here. Before the pen of Jefferson etched across the pages of history the mighty words of the Declaration of Independence, we were here. For more than two centuries our forebears labored in this country without wages; they made cotton king; they built the homes of their masters while suffering gross injustice and shameful humiliation— and yet out of a bottomless vitality they continued to thrive and develop. If the inexpressible cruelties of slavery could not stop us, the opposition we now face will surely fail. We will win our freedom because the sacred heritage of our nation and the eternal will of God are embodied in our echoing demands.

XII

Before closing I feel impelled to mention one other point in your statement that has troubled me profoundly. You warmly commended the Birmingham police force for keeping "order" and "preventing violence." I doubt that you would have so warmly commended the police force if you had seen its angry dogs sinking their teeth into six unarmed, nonviolent Negroes. I doubt that you would so quickly commend the policemen if you were to observe their ugly and inhuman treatment of Negroes here in the city jail; if you were to watch them push and curse old Negro women and young Negro girls; if you were to see them slap and kick old Negro men and young boys; if you were to observe them, as they did on two occasions, refuse to give us food because we wanted to sing our grace together. I cannot join you in your praise of the Birmingham police department.

It is true that the police have exercised discipline in handling the demonstrators. In this sense they have conducted themselves rather "nonviolently" in public. But for what purpose? To preserve the evil system of segregation. Over the past few years I have consistently preached that nonviolence demands that the means we use must be as pure as the ends we seek. I have tried to make clear that it is wrong to use immoral means to attain moral ends. But now I must affirm that it is just as wrong, or perhaps even more so, to use moral means to preserve immoral ends. Perhaps Mr. Connor and his policemen have been rather nonviolent in public, as was Chief Pritchett in Albany, Georgia, but they have used the moral means of nonviolence to maintain the immoral end of racial injustice. As T. S. Eliot has said, there is no greater treason than to do the right deed for the wrong reason.

XIII

I wish you had commended the Negro sit-inners and demonstrators of Birmingham for their sublime courage, their willingness to suffer, and their amazing discipline in the midst of great provocation. One day the south will recognize its real heroes. They will be the James Merediths, with a noble sense of purpose facing jeering and hostile mobs and the agonizing loneliness that characterizes the life of the pioneer. They will be old, oppressed, battered Negro women, symbolized in a 72-year-old woman in Montgomery, Alabama, who rose up with a sense of dignity and with her people decided not to ride segregated buses, and who responded with ungrammatical profundity to one who inquired about her: "My feet is tired, but my soul is rested."

They will be the young high-school and college students, the young ministers of the gospel, and a host of their elders courageously and nonviolently sitting in at lunch counters and willingly going to jail for conscience' sake. One day the south will know that when these disinherited children of God sat down at lunch counters they were in reality standing up for what is best in the American dream and for the most sacred values in our Judeo-Christian heritage, thereby bringing our nation back to those great wells of democracy which were dug deep by the founding fathers in their formulation of the Constitution and the Declaration of Independence.

Never before have I written so long a letter. I can assure you that it would have been much shorter if I had been writing from a comfortable desk, but what else can one do when he is alone for days in a narrow jail cell, other than write long letters, think long thoughts, and pray long prayers?

If I have said anything in this letter that overstates the truth and indicates an unreasonable impatience, I beg you to forgive me. If I have said anything that *under*-states the truth and indicates my having a patience that allows me to settle for anything less than brotherhood, I beg God to forgive me.

I hope this letter finds you strong in the faith. I also hope that circumstances will soon make it possible for me to meet each of you, not as an integrationist or a civil-rights leader but as a fellow clergyman and a Christian brother. Let us all hope that the dark clouds of racial prejudice will soon pass away and the deep fog of misunderstanding will be lifted from our fear-drenched communities and in some not too distant tomorrow the radiant stars of love and brotherhood will shine over our great nation with all their scintillating beauty.

THE BUS BOYCOTT
IN MONTGOMERY

L. D. Reddick

Before last December, a visitor to Montgomery would have noticed Negroes standing up in the city buses, while there were empty seats right before them. Somebody could then explain that according to local practice, these unoccupied seats were reserved for "whites only." No matter how packed a bus might be with Negro passengers, they were prohibited from sitting in the first four seats (which hold about ten persons). Theoretically, the last three back seats (holding about ten persons) were similarly reserved for Negroes. In fact this was not so. Moreover, if white passengers were already occupying all of their reserved seats and additional white passengers boarded the bus, Negro passengers, sitting in the unreserved section immediately behind the whites, might be asked to get up and "move back" by the bus driver. At times this was done courteously; all-too-often it was an undisguised insult.

Race relations in Montgomery have traditionally been "good" in the sense that Negroes have seldom challenged their state of subordination. The structure of the society was more or less set. Opposition seemed futile. Personal difficulties might be adjusted through some prominent Negro, who would speak with an influential white person. This was the established pattern of paternalism; and it did not disturb the status quo.

But for some reason on Thursday afternoon, December 1, 1955, Mrs. Rosa Parks refused to "move back" when she was ordered to do so by the bus driver. She was *not* sitting in the section reserved for whites (as the *New York Times* mistakenly reported) but in the first seat of the unreserved section. At the time every seat in the bus was taken. So the command for her to "move back" meant that she would have to stand while a white male passenger, who had just taken the bus, would sit. And so she was arrested and for a brief moment jailed.

Mrs. Parks was ideally fitted for her role. She is attractive and quiet, a churchgoer who looks like the symbol of Mother's Day. Her trial was set for the following Monday, December 5. Out of nowhere, it seems, written and mimeographed appeals appeared in the Negro community, saying: ". . . This has to be stopped . . . if Negroes did not ride the buses they could not operate . . . every Negro stay off the buses Monday in protest of this arrest and trial. . . ."

Only a fraction of Negro bus riders saw these unsigned appeals but one of the notices did fall into the hands of the local paper, which put it on the front page. Negroes laugh when they tell about this. They say that the newspaper was mostly interested in letting the white folks know what the Negroes were up to. But through this story many Negroes got the news of the Monday plan for the first time. At the Sunday church service, Negro ministers

Reprinted by permission from Dissent *(March 1956).*

hammered home their endorsement of the projected one-day "protest"—as they consistently called the boycott.

Physically, Montgomery is ideally fitted for a bus boycott. It is just 27.9 square miles in area. Its population, 130,000, is about 40 percent Negro. Most residents *could* walk to most places in the city.

The judge who tried Mrs. Parks, had he looked into his crystal ball, would have probably dismissed the case. Instead, he found her guilty, fining her $14. She appealed.

All day long on December 5 Negroes stayed off the buses. They did so with such enthusiasm that there was a general feeling that "we ought to continue this."

The Negro ministers had hastily scheduled a mass meeting for Monday evening. Normally, the church holds about 1500 persons. Hours before meeting time, 7:00 P.M., people began filling up the place. By 7 o'clock every seat had been taken and some three or four thousand standees overflowed into the street. Outdoor loudspeakers were set up.

Nobody expected such a response. The Negro ministers, rising to the occasion, improvised a declaration of principles. Amid the singing of hymns and some first-class oratory—led by Rev. M. L. King, Jr.—the audience unanimously adopted the following declaration as read by Rev. Ralph Abernathy: Negroes were not to resume riding the buses until (1) courteous treatment by bus operators was guaranteed; (2) passengers were seated on a first-come, first-served basis—Negroes seating from the back of the bus toward the front while white seat from the front toward the back; (3) Negro bus operators were employed on predominately Negro routes.

Then without the usual money-raising salesmanship, the crowd—inside and outside of the church—filed in and placed dimes, quarters, and dollars on the collec-tion table. This was altogether spontaneous.

Since the Negro ministers were cagey about revealing who was directing the movement, that seemed to whet the appetite of the reporters. As a matter of fact, at this point every thing was *ad hoc* and tentative. The emergence of King and Abernathy was almost by chance. No leader was calling the shots. As Abernathy said later, it was never "a one-man-show." The indignation and demands for action by the "common people" swept everyone along like a flood.

II

There had been a long history of abuse by the bus operators. Almost everybody could tell of some unfortunate personal experience that he himself had had or seen. Montgomery Negroes were fed up with the bus service in particular and, like Negroes throughout the South, with race relations in general. The outrage of the Emmett Till murder was alive in everybody's mind. The silence and inaction of the federal government, in the face of the daily abuse, beatings, and killings of Negro citizens, was maddening. Negroes have no faith at all in Southern law-making and law-enforcing agencies, for these instruments of "justice" are all in the hands of "the brothers of the hoodlums who attack us."

Negroes themselves wanted to get into action. Here and elsewhere they were willing to fight it out—if the fighting was "fair." But Negroes knew on whose side the police and the lily-white militia would be when they came in to "put down disorder." And after that, there would be the local judges and juries. To remain human, the Negroes could not stand by and do nothing. Under the circumstances, the channel into which the Negroes of Montgomery have poured their energies and resentments is the best answer thus far to the question of what to do. Here is organized struggle and group solidarity. It is legal, nonviolent, and effective.

And so the one-day boycott passed into an indefinite protest that, as of this writing, has run for fourteen weeks.

Both the press and the police expected violence. Early newspaper stories started off in this fashion: "Negro goon squads reportedly have been organized here to intimidate Negroes who ride . . . in violation of a Negro boycott. . . ." This was untrue.

The police were equally sure of the image in their minds. Accordingly, they arrested a college student, saying that he had pulled a Negro woman from a bus as she was attempting to get on it. In court it came out that the two were good friends and that they were merrily crossing the street, arm in arm, near a bus. She had told the cops this before the arrest was made but the police believed that there were goons—there had to be—so they saw what they were looking for: "believing is seeing."

The first reaction of the bus-company officials was one of arrogance. They pretended that the Negroes were demanding that the company violate the law. This was absurd. The law required segregation, but did not specify the manner of seating so long as it was segregated. The bus company summarily rejected the proposal of the Negroes.

The city commission sided with the bus company, condemning the boycott and declaring that "first come, first serve" would be illegal. And so almost everybody—the bus company, the city commissioners, and the white public—expected Negroes to be back on the buses in a few days.

This was only the first of a series of misjudgments on the part of the city fathers. All along they demonstrated that their conception of the Negro was the stereotype of the tired field hand or the witless house servant who could be cajoled or forced to do what the white folks wanted him to do. Even now, after fourteen weeks of "education," the commissioners seem not to comprehend the intelligence, resourcefulness, and resolve of the people with whom they are dealing.

III

The ex-bus riders soon found themselves face to face with a practical problem: since the buses were taboo, how were the Negroes to get about the city? At first, they called upon the taxis for cheap-rate jitney service. The police stopped this by warning the taxis that by law they must charge a minimum fare of 45 cents. Next, private cars began giving "friends" a lift, along the bus routes. The charge was 15 cents for "gasoline expense." The cops stopped this, too, by insisting that drivers had to have a taxi permit and license.

In reply, the Negroes organized a voluntary motor pool. Almost overnight Montgomery saw a network of private cars spread over the city, picking up and depositing passengers, from dawn until early evening. It was a marvel of quick organization. Even the local press had to concede that the pick-up system moved with "military precision." Some transportation problems that the bus company had grappled with for twenty years were, apparently, solved overnight.

The police searched the books for laws that would dry up the motor pool. One old rule forbade more than three persons to sit on the front seat of an automobile. Lights, brakes, even the position of license tags, were checked by the police frequently. Minor regulations that are seldom invoked in this normally easy-going town were resurrected and severely enforced. Negro taxi drivers really caught it!

The Negro community of Montgomery has neither its own radio station (as does Atlanta, Ga.) nor a widely read local newspaper. Communication is by word of mouth and through churches mainly. This is probably why frequent mass meetings have proved a necessity. The pattern was established during the first week of the boycott; mass meetings each Monday and Thursday evening. It has been adhered to ever since.

These twice-a-week get-togethers are the soul of the boycott; the Montgomery Improvement Association is the brains. The meetings are rotated from church to church. The speakers, in turn, represent the various denominations. Thus the ground is cut from under any institutional or sectarian jealousy. Rev. King and Rev. Abernathy make it plain by their words and by their sharing of the speakers' platform that they are not self-appointed "leaders" but only "spokesmen" of the movement. Incidentally, the people have "fallen in love" with King, a boyish-looking Ph.D. They look upon Abernathy, also young and an M.A., as a tower of strength. These two men symbolize the poise, the thoughtfulness, and the ability of the independent ministers. They are the real and obvious leaders of this mass upsurge. The more vulnerable intellectuals stay discreetly in the background. Rufus Lewis, an ex-football coach and presently a civic-minded business man, is the cool-headed chairman of the motor-pool committee.

People come hours ahead of time to get a seat at these mass meetings. A few read papers and books while waiting, but mostly the audiences sing. Hymns such as "Onward Christian Soldiers," "Abide With Me," and "Higher Ground" are moving but the really stirring songs are the lined, camp-meeting tunes of low pitch and long meter. These seem to recapture the long history of the Negro's suffering and struggle.

IV

By 7 P.M., the time the meeting starts, virtually every inch of space is taken, including standing room. Often as many listeners are outside as inside. Many others do not come at all because they know they cannot get near the church. It is curious that meetings were never scheduled in different parts of the city at different hours on the same night or rotated to different parts of the city on different nights—in order to accommodate the crowds. This suggestion was made but the planning committee never got around to it or concluded that "the people prefer to be together," as several persons had said.

The mass-meeting pattern is relatively simple: songs, prayer, latest news and plans, a "pep talk," collection. Often the pastor in whose church the meeting was held would preside or, after preliminary remarks, would turn the meeting over to some official of the Montgomery Improvement Association.

The meetings are serious but thoroughly relaxed. There are quips and jokes—a great deal of genial humor. All classes are present in the audiences but the bulk of the attendants are working-class people. It is here that morale is built and sustained. Unity is expressed in words and in the little kindnesses that the people show to each other. The automobile-owning folk, who never rode the buses, and the maids and day-laborers, who depended upon the buses, have come to know each other. The interdenominational, interclass integration of the Negro community has called forth much comment. Moreover, the mass meetings have given many persons some place to go; something to think about; something to absorb their energies. There is high purpose these days in the Negro community.

Few whites attend these meetings although they are open to all. Aside from a Lutheran minister who has a Negro congregation, no local white preacher has publicly identified himself with the Negro cause. Many, of course, give assurances privately. A few are in "hot water" for real or suspected sympathies with the boycotters.

But the main force that keeps the people and their leaders together is the idea of the movement itself. These people know that they are fighting a big battle and that it is a vital part of a larger war. Messages and money contributions from many parts of the nation as well as from remote parts of the world have confirmed this belief.

At first, the demands of the boycotters were limited—courtesy, fair play, fair employment. These were all within the segregation laws of the city and state. At one point, the Negroes would have called off the boycott for just the "first-come, first-serve" arrangement. That day, of course, has long since passed.

Apparently to impress the Negro community with what it could lose, the bus company abruptly stopped all service to Negro neighborhoods. This was supposed to bring Negroes to their knees, crying for the buses. But nobody was impressed. Instead, doubtful would-be bus riders were pushed into the motor pool. The water, they found, was just "fine." On second thought, the bus company decided to reestablish the discontinued lines. So the buses were put back on the routes in the Negro areas. They continued to roll empty.

For about a month negotiations were on and off. Neither side would yield. The boycott held its own. This meant that 75 percent of the bus-riding public was "out," and it cut some $3000 from each day's revenue. Moreover, fewer whites—probably out of sympathy with the boycott—seem to be riding.

To counteract this economic squeeze, the mayor called on the white public to support the buses. The so-called White Citizens Council solicited contributions for the poor suffering bus company. No figures were ever given out but the general impression is that very few persons were willing to subsidize the National City Lines, an economic giant that is spread out over the cities and towns of the Middle West and South and has its main office in Chicago. A forced subsidy was made possible by raising the bus fare from 10 to 15 cents. At which point, additional whites stayed off the buses.

V

To break the impasse, the city commission pulled a fast one. On Sunday, January 22, the Negro community was astounded to read in the morning paper that a settlement had been reached. The article said: "The above agreement is concurred in by all three members of the City Commission, as well as by representatives of the bus company and the group representing the Negroes of Montgomery." The terms of the "agreement" were: (1) courtesy to all; (2) white reserve section at the front of the bus, Negro reserve section at rear of bus; (3) special, all-Negro buses during the rush hours. "First come, first serve" would obtain for the unreserved, middle section. The city commission stated that it had nothing to do with the question of employment. The declaration of courtesy carried no machinery for assuring its practice. In short, this latest "agreement" was merely a restatement of the *status quo ante bellum*. Nevertheless, it sounded like a settlement and many persons who read the story felt that the boycott was over. Some whites were jubilant. Some Negroes were ill. "Why had the leaders given in?" they asked.

A very careful reading of the article raises the question whether it was just poor reporting or something much worse. For example, the names of the "prominent ministers" were not given. Other omissions were equally strange. If this was a release from the city commission, would any newspaper naively print such an important front-page story without first checking with the known Negro representatives, who had been negotiating with the bus company and city commission for weeks? Obviously, this announcement was a calculated maneuver to get the ex-bus riders back on the buses Sunday morning. Perhaps once the spell of not riding was broken, the boycott would dissolve.

The Negroes foiled this maneuver by a combination of luck and quick action. The story had been sent out Saturday evening by the Associated Press. As it came over the wires into the office of the *Minneapolis Tribune,* the reporter Carl T. Rowan, who had been down to Montgomery to cover the boycott, did what any good reporter would do: he called Rev. M. L. King, Jr., to verify the story.

King was amazed. He knew absolutely nothing about any settlement. Rowan then contacted one of the Montgomery commissioners who confirmed the story but refused to give the names of the Negro ministers involved. Under prodding, the commissioner did reveal the denominations of the ministers. Rowan then called King again. This clue was enough. King and his colleagues by a process of checking soon identified the "three prominent Negro ministers." It turned out that they were neither prominent nor members of the negotiating committee.

It was now late Saturday night. Like minutemen, the ministers of the Montgomery Improvement Association went themselves or sent messages to all of the night clubs and taverns in the Negro community, informing the Saturday night revelers of the attempted hoax. Rev. King himself humorously stated that he got a chance to see the insides of many a night spot! Result: word got around so well that the next day the buses rolled empty as usual. At the Sunday morning services, the ministers excoriated the "fake settlement" and repeated that the "protest" was still on. The commissioners lost face. The Negroes were brought closer together.

By the next day, the "three prominent Negro ministers" had publicly repudiated the commission's press announcement. One of the three stated before an open meeting that he had been "tricked" into the conference on the basis of a telephone invitation, asking that he join in a discussion of group insurance for the city. This man said that neither he nor the other two ministers present agreed to any settlement, declaring that they were unauthorized to speak for the ex-bus riders.

Few persons thought that these three Negro ministers would dare challenge the veracity of the city fathers; but they did. This, everybody was sure, would make front-page news. But the local press reduced the sensational disclosure to a bare statement of denial that was buried near the end of a long story. When the local dailies did not print his statement, one of the ministers purchased space for a three-inch ad saying: "The rumor that is out that I agreed with the commissioners on the proposal that they issued is an untrue statement." These words have never been contradicted.

Things now took a turn for the worse. The mayor and the other commissioners embarked upon a "get tough" policy. With a show of anger the mayor denounced the boycott, declared that the white people did not care if another Negro ever rode the buses again, and called upon white employers to stop taking their Negro employees to and from work. He said that white businessmen informed him that they were discharging Negro workers who were participating in the boycott. All three commissioners let it be known that they had joined the White Citizens Council. Even the timid member of the trio mustered up enough bravado to go on television and join the "get tough with Negroes" act. All this, of course, was the traditional, Confederate, flag-waving appeal to white supremacy.

It was to be a field day. The police would "cut the legs off" the boycott by a campaign of arrests for real and imaginary traffic infractions. Negro drivers, who appeared to be in the motor pool, would be questioned about their employment, the balance due on the purchase of their automobiles, and the firms with which they had their insurance.

VI

For a moment the protest movement seemed to be wavering. Again, Negroes saw that the very instruments of law and order were being used against them. Surely, a man had the right to give someone a ride in his own automobile. Persons who had not received a traffic ticket in years were booked. Some ex-bus riders, while waiting to be picked up, were told that there was a law against hitch-hiking; others were accused of "loud talking," walking on lawns and "congregating in white neighborhoods." The daily press printed next to nothing about the wholesale arrests and harassment.

Under such heavy blows the voluntary pick-up system began to weaken. Some drivers were already tired; others disliked "tangling with the law"; still others feared that they could not stand much more provocation without striking back.

The high point of the "get tough" operation was the arrest of Rev. King himself. But if this move was intended to frighten King, it fell flat. He calmly submitted to arrest and jailing. At first, he was not to be let out on bond. The news spread through the Negro community like wildfire. Negroes began rushing down to the jail in such numbers that King was released without having even to sign his own bond.

Meanwhile, a group of Negro business and professional men asked the city for permission to operate a jitney service. This was turned down on the grounds that sufficient transportation was already available. The mayor said, let them ride the buses now rolling empty through the streets. A strange stand for one who didn't care if another Negro rode a bus again!

But the city did care. It stood to lose part of the $20,000 in taxes it received from the bus company each year. Downtown merchants cared, too, for some of their businesses were off by as much as a third since the boycott had begun. Most of all, the bus company cared—each day it cared more and more. It let it be known that it would agree to any seating arrangement that the city commissioners would approve.

The worse was yet to come. The inflammatory appeals seemed to give the signal to the violent elements. A stick of dynamite was thrown on the porch of Rev. King's home. The job was amateurish; the damage slight; the intent vicious. Within minutes hundreds of Negroes flocked to King's home; also the police. It was at this moment that nonviolent resistance almost faded. Many Negroes wanted to launch a counteroffensive. Rev. King, standing on the front porch of his "bombed" home, pleaded with the angry Negroes: "We are not harmed. Do not get your weapons. Let us not answer hate with hate, violence with violence. But we will continue to stay off the buses." Probably this saved the city from a race riot.

There had been other incidents. Some Negro and white high-school students had clashed; one or more cars of white youths had made commando raids on the nearby Negro college, dashing through the campus with lights out, throwing out bags of water, eggs, rocks, and a tiny flaming cross. One evening the commandos were ambushed and bombarded with bricks. Another commando car was captured by special police. Another clumsy bomb-thrower hit the fence of E. D. Nixon, the president of the local NAACP chapter.

This flurry of violence had no noticeable effect on the boycott. The leaders were careful but nobody seemed to be at all afraid. On the other hand, it helped convince the patient hopefuls that an all-out fight was the only kind that made any sense.

For two months the Negroes had clung to the hope of a settlement on the basis of their limited demands. But failure of negotiations and the crude brutality of the "get tough" policy convinced the most conservative ex-bus riders that an attack had to be made upon bus segregation itself. Accordingly, on February 1 a suit was filed in the local federal courts, asking for the end of bus jim crow on the grounds that it is contrary to the 14th Amendment of the Constitution of the United States. Furthermore, the court was asked to stop the city commissioners from violating the civil rights of Negro motorists and pedestrians.

This was a sobering jolt for the city commissioners. The "get tough" policy evaporated overnight. The city fathers, who had been making speeches at the drop of the hat, lapsed into their usual quietude.

VII

Meanwhile, a fresh effort was made to reopen negotiations. This time a white businessmen's club intervened. Many of them had stores that had been hurt. It is estimated that the boycott had cost Montgomery $1,000,000. The businessmen's club met several times, separately, with the city commission and a committee from the Montgomery Improvement Association. Chicago Negroes had thrown a picket line around the offices of the parent bus company, so it was more willing than ever to come to terms. The city commissioners, however, remained adamant. They seem to feel that they cannot afford to yield. So the best that the businessmen could offer was little more than the old "fake" settlement that had been palmed off on the "three prominent Negro ministers."

Some of the drivers in the motor pool were becoming exhausted. Twelve or thirteen weeks of free, voluntary service, four or five hours per day, is fatiguing. Most of these drivers have jobs and other obligations. Several of the leaders felt that maybe the boycott might as well be called off since in the end the courts would settle the issue. Understandably, people were becoming battle-weary. For over three months, life had been like a military operation for the Negro Improvement Association.

So the leaders, though reluctantly, submitted the proposals of the businessmen to the rank and file at one of the mass meetings. The answer was an almost total rejection. Out of approximately four thousand persons present, *only two* voted in favor of calling off the boycott. The morale of the masses, once again, revived the morale of the leaders.

To date the latest move to break the boycott has been the indictment of the leaders of the Improvement Association. This was based on an old antilabor law of doubtful constitutionality. And again nobody was frightened. Nobody tried to hide. Many inquired of the sheriff's office: "Is my name on that Grand Jury list?" If it was, the caller let it be known that he would come down immediately. Confident, orderly, loyal to each other, the Negroes again manifested their collective will and *esprit de corps*.

As for the future, nobody can be sure. The white people of Montgomery have been amazed by the group discipline of the Negro community and by the intelligence and organization with which the boycott has been maintained. "I didn't think they had it in them," is a frequent comment.

Many whites who would like to see the boycott ended and who feel that the demands of the Negroes are reasonable, are afraid to admit this. They fear that to "give in" on this means that "all" is lost. There are sincere apprehensions that desegregation at any one point will lead to general racial integration—and that means intermarriage! An absurd goblin hovers over every white household. The politicians and white councils exploit these fears. The chief weakness of the movement for desegregation is that so little is done to remove the unfounded alarms of the thousands who in desperation are flocking to the hate organizations.

The fact is that desegregation has been magnified so greatly in the minds of so many Americans, both Negro and white, that they do not realize how ordinary and natural a nonsegregated society is. Nonsegregation already prevails in many areas of Southern life—the supermarkets, for example—with scarcely passing notice. Negroes seem to feel that desegregation will work overnight miracles. Southern whites feel that it will precipitate disaster. They are both wrong. It is neither so glorious nor so dangerous as pictured, even in terms of the values of the opposing groups. A nonsegregated society is merely a crude, basic precondition for creating a social order in which the higher sensibilities can flourish.

We are all indebted to the Negroes of Montgomery. They say that they are confident of ultimate victory. In a sense, they have already won. They have given us a magnificent case study of the circumstances under which the philosophy of Thoreau and Gandhi can triumph. Moreover, the boycott movement has brought something new into the lives of the Negroes of Montgomery. They would be loath to give it up. Whenever the boycott ends, it will be missed.

SOCIAL CONTROL OF
THE AMERICAN GHETTO

Beverly Leman

To "resist" the Vietnam war—or the new Vietnams which threaten throughout the third world—has for thousands of young Americans become a moral imperative. But if this resistance is to take political root inside the United States, it must bring to domestic oppression the same intellectual clarity, moral force, and political courage which it has brought to bear on the American oppression of the people of Vietnam. For there can be no mistaking the present warlike character of official "solutions" to the threat or fact of black rebellion in the American ghetto. In fact, not only have domestic law-enforcement agencies derived much of their empirical data from the Vietnam war, but as we shall see they share the same army of social-scientist planners, think-tank analysts, and weapons developers and manufacturers.

After a short period of local improvisation during the 1964–66 urban disturbances, these agencies have today developed a centralized system of social and paramilitary controls designed alternatively to prevent or repress organized dissident action *wherever* it might occur. For months the budget allocations for law enforcement have exceeded anything previously known in American history. New York City alone has a police force which, in the words of Mayor Lindsay, "is larger than most armies of most countries of the world."

Explicitly military-serving institutions, like the Rand Corporation, have expanded into "urban planning." In New York City,

for example, the Rand headquarters is staffed with 40 social scientists who have divided into teams and moved into key city agencies to study municipal operations. And the largest research budget was awarded the police-department team. Its investigation has so far ranged from how to get an infrared detector that will sense a fire behind a wall to pondering incentives and rewards that will draw more people into police work.

Like Rand, the Institute for Defense Analyses studies police technology—the development and application of new riot-control weaponry. Equally important, IDA has developed systems for more comprehensive intelligence-gathering and more versatile manpower deployment which have made the Institute the prime contributor to the emergence of "law enforcement" as a major political and economic institution.

Private enterprise has responded in kind by expanding its interests to service law-enforcement needs while investing in the slums it has helped to create. Industries, too numerous to name here, have produced Orwellian riot-control equipment, electronic security devices, and more conventional military hardware to stimulate a market which grows more lucrative daily.

Liberal politicians who tacitly approved the waging of the Vietnam war—until they decided we weren't winning after all—now openly defend counterinsurgent actions for America's ghettos. But they are nervous. Having lost much of their Northern black

Reprinted by permission from Viet-Report, **3** *(Summer 1968), pp. 12–19.*

constituency through the failure of promised reforms, they know they will lose the rest when the weapons that stun, sicken, and incapacitate—but do not kill—are substituted in their place.

All of the above forces have joined together to maintain the social order. While some still argue the need for improved social-welfare programs, job-training or "community-development" campaigns, all agree that a key effect of America's "ghetto policy" should be the emasculation of insurgent uprisings. Clearly, this objective has led even the most reformist liberals to sanction armed repression, if need be:

A new set of signs tells us something that is painful, even fateful to have to hear: We must prepare for the onset of terrorism. Indeed it may already have begun. How widespread and how successful remains to be seen, but the probability is so great that ignoring it would be an act of irresponsibility or of cowardice. . . . Liberals must align with conservatives to deal with extremists of right and left. . . . Only such a coalition can create . . . stability. (James Reston quoting MIT urbanist, Daniel Moynihan, *N. Y. Times*, 11/1/67.)

THREE-PRONGED STRATEGY FOR THE GHETTO

Out of this shared concern professional planners have devised short-, mid-, and long-range methods for dealing with the crisis. Sensitive to the pressing material needs of the ghetto but also to the lack of federal funds, they have arranged their plans accordingly. Short-term measures must pacify and contain black rebellions; mid-term measures will appeal to business for job-training and plant investment; long-term solutions entail the consolidation of the public/private partnership to reclamate America's underdeveloped "native quarters."

For the immediate goal, they have turned to the law-enforcement establishment to carry out two distinct but interdependent functions which are also prerequisite to all subsequent plans: (1) to provide enough sufficiently trained and well-equipped men to maintain order; and (2) to help implement a social-control apparatus designed to pacify and prevent disorder. The first function is not new, but its application has expanded. Witness the recent police action at Columbia University. The administrators labeled the students' protests a threat to the social order. They called in the police who became the agents of the university by seeking to make dissenting students conform to accepted patterns; hence the punitive police beatings students received. The second function has required the creation of a new in-ghetto police role, which has undergone notable refinement since the Watts riot in August 1965.

Until Watts urban ghettos had been relatively tranquil with most of the violence taking place during the late 1950s and early 1960s against civil-rights workers in the south. After Watts began a more turbulent period: antiwar demonstrations which escalated with the Vietnam war into confrontation politics, draft protests which moved into draft resistance, and then the 1967 summer rebellions in many core cities across the nation. The profusion of activity saw police action shift back and forth from enforcing order in the ghetto to containing political demonstrations.

Those who allied for stability agreed on the need for instituting new controls if present domestic power relationships were to survive. What had, in Watts, been seen as a nonpolitical "riot" to be quelled by local police was in 1967 viewed as an incipient crack in the social order and a breakdown in institutional sanctions. Thus were new controls instituted through legislation (antiriot laws, extension of the subversive control board, weapons appropriations, etc.) .

In one sense, however, it was already too late for laws to act as punitive deterrents. The black uprisings had indeed focused attention on the oppressive and futile existence of ghetto life; and a growing number of young nonghetto persons already mobilized by their opposition to the war began to move on racism and ghetto impoverishment. The combination of punitive legislation and the patent failure of the "war on poverty" created an atmosphere in which persons became disillusioned *and also freer,* an atmosphere in which ideas for change were deemed unimportant unless backed up by action.

However, the more charged the atmosphere, the more anxious became the search for better control:

Since almost no one wants (at least publicly) ideas to be controlled, the casual power of ideas is rarely asserted. . . . Only a fear of being thought illiberal may prevent us from considering that the probability of a riot is increased by demands for "Black Power," by a constant reiteration that white bigotry and racism are at the root of all problems besetting the Negro, by the reaffirmation of the (untrue) assumption that most Negroes live wretched lives and that matters are going from bad to worse. . . . (James Q. Wilson, Professor of Government, Harvard University, *N.Y. Times Magazine,* 5/19/68.)

Wilson's important perception was that when an alienated people, especially the young, begin to achieve a sense of collective identity *at odds* with the prevailing values of the dominant society, the breakdown of the social order has begun. Ideas are indeed infectious, and for men like Wilson, the natural response is to locate and seal off the wounds. Thus, as the inner city became both vanguard for change and a threat to the stability of the outer city, so it also became the focal point for the application of the new social-control apparatus.

I: Policing the Store

San Francisco, Los Angeles, Baltimore, Atlanta, and New York City were the first major cities to implement experimental storefront precincts, satellite stations, mobile substations, and neighborhood task forces (the latter, cited by the Kerner Commission as the prototype for the nation, was modeled after New York City's experiment). Each of the cities has heavily populated ghettos in which unmet needs pose a constant threat. Police can use the storefront, for example, as a base for surveillance; geographically, it places them in direct contact with the ghetto resident "who supplies information or requires assistance."

Ghetto intelligence is gathered along the lines originally set down by the Army in the early 1960s for the civic-action teams going abroad:

(a) . . . become acquainted with key members of the district; (b) . . . gather data on key personnel of district to include: birth, education, skills, family, character, personality, is he pro-American. Gathering information will be a continuing process, record it and pass it on to second team. . . . (*Army Field Manual,* FM31-32.)

These field and investigative data provide vital inputs to the larger computer-assisted military system of command and control. At the heart of this system is a centralized communications center set up under the direction of a "precinct watch commander." He receives the field intelligence and keeps track of events in each beat and the status of each unit. In any given situation, the commander is prepared to transform a loose collection of individual units into a coordinated force. Assisted by the computer, he then monitors patrol activities, allocates resources for emergency needs, and deploys officers to handle special situations. In essence, the center's role involves the "organization of personnel and facilities to perform the functions of planning, situation intelligence, force status monitoring, decision making and execution." (IDA, *Task Force on Science and Technology*, 1967.)

During an emergency the system has a dual impact. First, it minimizes disruption in the outer city, and second, maximizes control in the inner city. For example, during the 1967 rebellion in the Milwaukee ghetto, Mayor H. Maier imposed a curfew on the entire city which cost millions of dollars in lost business. Although the Mayor proclaimed the curfew a "strategic success," it was obvious that more of the same would not be sound policy. However, with the combination of a communications precinct to monitor the inner city's boundaries and the storefront bases for obtaining field data, the military system of command and control could have easily transformed the curfew into a cage outside of which business could go on as usual. And with such a curfew, the control system would permit mass arrests within the contained area on the minor charge of curfew violation. This was already demonstrated after Dr. Martin Luther King's assassination when the Washington, D.C., curfew yielded more than one half of the 6000 arrests made.

However, when the Harlem community indicated its reaction to the police storefront on 125th Street by burning it down, it indicated to the planners that, as one expert has said, "for their work of prevention, the police will . . . need to become agents of social welfare. To succeed in detection and investigation they will have to become scientists, rather than persons involved in . . . subtle extractions of self-incriminating information" (Joseph D. Lohman, Dean, School of Criminology, University of California, "On Law Enforcement and the Police," 8/67). In short, in addition to their field and investigative functions, the police would now have to establish links with the community in the same way that the civic-action teams abroad are instructed to establish links between the armed forces and the native population.

II: Policing Social Conflicts

In the summer of 1967, New York City Police Commissioner Howard Leary explained this second stage of the experiment. The storefront bases, he said, would become social information centers where "slum dwellers could receive advice on health, housing, and welfare problems." Soon he hoped to begin using "carefully trained civilian volunteers . . . some of whom might work for the police department and others for relevant social agencies." When asked whether these counselors might develop into spies for the department, Mr. Leary replied that "the problem could be avoided if the right control procedures developed"—and did not elaborate. At that time New York City officers began to receive in-service training about social problems in the community. Soon after, the Police Department began training selected officers to serve on "conflict teams," which could be called on to cope with family disputes and to refer ghetto people to available social services.

In Atlanta, police began working in neighborhood centers as counselors to school dropouts. In Los Angeles, they joined in local affairs within their area. "This helps them to know the attitudes of the people in their neighborhood. Negro officers project the police image to their segments of the community. . . . Male and female officers also act as liaisons between [police] and Negro news media" (*American City*, 3/67). In San Francisco, a five-officer team works exclusively with the local anti-poverty program attending monthly meetings where they act as a sounding board for complaints.

In offering these services and favors the storefront began to resemble the now-defunct system of neighborhood political clubs which once served as brokers between white ethnic groups and city hall. This likeness is obviously deliberate. It provides a framework within which the police can expand their function and make deals with community and antipoverty groups as well as with established institutions—schools, welfare agencies, etc.

These links have also enabled the police to organize propaganda campaigns inside the ghetto. Typically these campaigns are focused on elementary and secondary schools. In Los Angeles, police launched a "Policeman Bill" program in which first-graders receive a colorful brochure illustrating the policeman as their friend and offering helpful suggestions to both child and parent. While distributing the pamphlets, police explain their role and entertain the children with demonstrations of patrol-car equipment. In Maryland a course has been initiated in which ninth- and tenth-graders visit with law-enforcement personnel and take field trips. In Michigan, the state police place officers in schools to teach 10- to 17-year-olds about law enforcement and the problems of policing. The New York Police Department conducts annual training sessions for public-school civics teachers.

Most of these program materials originate in the universities. For example, Columbia University is now developing materials for a curriculum concerning crime and criminal justice for an integrated program to be taught from the first through twelfth grades; and the University of Cincinnati is developing criminal-justice materials for junior high-school students.

By the close of 1967, however, neither the social scientists nor the federal government were satisfied that the police-community experiment could really maintain order. The only experiments which seemed effective were those which involved hand-picked men who in the main had not patrolled the beat. For example, in New York City the Neighborhood Task Forces operating out of satellite stations in eighteen "trouble spots" were headed up by ranking members of the Mayor's staff. Often referred to as the "Community Cabinet," they functioned primarily to take the heat off of the police. Each satellite had a governing board whose members did not include rank-and-file police, but precinct commissioners, public-service supervisory staff, school principals, and, "in some instances, street agitators." Nevertheless, even this experiment suffered from a credibility gap. Although in each city the in-ghetto service programs received the solid support of the social-planning agencies, neither they nor the storefront operators could break through the bureaucratic morass of city government to answer such simple community demands as a daily garbage pickup. Moreover, the storefront operators were held accountable for all the undelivered promises made by politicians seeking to enlarge their constituencies.

Beyond this the overriding obstacle to the programs' success was the image of the cop himself. To ghetto residents "The Man in Blue" is anathema whether he patrols the ghetto beat or provides medical referrals. For too long he has tread an almost invisible line between protector and oppressor. Recent newspaper items recount the heated exchanges between police spokesmen and ghetto residents who accuse the police of openly allowing heroin trafficking to brutalize young blacks. There is nothing new about this accusation and any seven-year-old child in Harlem will tell you the same story.

Changing the cop image raises a peculiarly American dilemma. Traditionally,

America's finest have been drawn from the same class which produces criminals, and, unlike other countries, they have a very low ratio of racial tolerance and no special education. To the policeman's way of thinking, good police work consists of protecting property and seeing that the "important" people don't get hurt. He believes he will succeed only if he pleases the people for whom he works—and he does not for one moment believe he works for the ghetto residents. In return for the services he provides to the majority, his image is accepted—that is, as long as he unquestionably implements society's double standards:

Janus-like, we have always turned two faces toward a policeman, we expect him to be human and yet inhuman. . . . We resent him when he enforces a law in our own case yet demand his dismissal when he does not elsewhere. We offer him bribes, yet denounce his corruption. . . . (Ben Whitiker, *The Police*, London, 1964.)

In a recent *Nation* report on the "Off-Duty Cop," Kenneth Gross quotes Dr. Ralph S. Banay, consulting psychiatrist to the New York City Police Department, who argues that "the policeman is apart and must maintain a certain status . . . too much familiarity with the community at large could create problems of contempt for authority." Dr. Banay "insists that it is important to make policemen feel apart and obliged to sustain a greater image of law enforcement." Precisely because this attitude has been successfully inculcated, rank-and-file reaction to the community-relations experiments has been decidedly negative.

Although sporadic courses in social problems have been initiated, there is nothing in their content to contradict rank-and-file beliefs. In fact, as the following illustrations show, they provide classical descriptions of mob violence which only reinforce traditional police thinking. In Paterson,

N.J., training courses break "Civil Disturbances" into the following categories:

Race—uprising . . . usually in conjested area but not restricted to such areas

Catastrophe—results from incidents committed when confusion and panic exist, looting, rape, attack, arson *are causes* [emphasis added]

Economic—promoted by professional agitators, based on unemployment, want, etc.

Un-American—clash between American and un-American groups advising the overthrow of the government

Correction—lynchings and other . . . measures by persons taking the law into their own hands (*American City*, 2/68).

In Kansas City, Mo., recruits are trained to look for the leaders within a threatening group:

The Dominant Leader—who tries to secure action, has knowledge of the conflict, is not a thinker, does not concern himself with details, is cold and aloof and will suppress conflicting ideas

The Persuasive Leader—who maintains a personal following with each member . . ., is seemingly sincere, but reshapes thoughts of people . . . to gain credit for organization's good

The Opportunist Leader—who feeds on the emotions and conflicts already underway (*ibid.*).

The content of these programs is geared to riot control, not riot prevention. It has indicated to both social-scientists planners and the Justice Department that localities do not understand the dimensions of the new in-ghetto service function of the police. When confronted with instituting new training methods, rank and file are reticent ("The policeman is not a social worker"). Their own belief is comparable to those who advocate preventing World War III by bombing China now, and their response to last summer's uprisings was more armament for this summer:

The police are buying everything politicians will let them; politicians are letting them buy everything the voters will allow; the voters are allowing (or demanding) more every day (*The Second Civil War*, by Garry Wills, p. 17).

III: Policing the Police

To balance this frantic mobilization with more effective community relations, the Justice Department and the International Chiefs of Police initiated a series of closed training meetings last winter. More than 400 police chiefs attended along with sociology, criminology, and law professors. Federal officials stressed the fact that police civic action was the most important job for local police in the coming decade. They advised police to caution gun restraint "because this was at least half a tactical necessity. The other side has guns." Sponsoring officials later admitted to the press that they were still unsure whether local police who retain authority until federal force is requested would follow a policy of restraint. However, it was reported that police chiefs were won over to the in-ghetto concept by the federal funds promised for police training, research, and recruitment. They were most impressed by the design of local command and control systems, two-way computer patrol systems, and by Attorney General Ramsey Clark's description of the intelligence computer set up in the basement of the Justice Department.

With the close of these sessions it became apparent that elitism had begun to creep into traditional police strongholds. Rank-and-file thinking was to go unheeded while the IACP and police commissioners across the country prepared to implement a new and permanent special force in the ghetto. Redefined by both academic planners and federal officials, the new training standards were a response to the accumulated dislike and distrust between cop and ghetto resident. The IACP's contribution was to draw up a "Model Act" which required that selection and training standards be administered under state law. More rele-

vant training was also the plea of the President's Crime Commission which reported an "almost universal need for higher selection standards, higher compensation, more training, reexamination of traditional roles, and an infusion of more highly educated people" (First National Conference on Crime Control, Washington, D.C., 1967).

The Crime Commission specifically addressed itself to recruitment incentives. It suggested that the old procedure requiring all police candidates to enter the department at the same level, no matter what their background or education, be replaced with three levels of entry, each requiring special training. First was to be the *Community Service Officer*, "uniformed but unarmed," with two major responsibilities: to "maintain close relations with juveniles in the area and be especially alert to crime-breeding conditions that other city agencies have not dealt with. . . ." He might work "out of a storefront office . . . [and] be a member of a team with a police officer and a police agent." The second was the *Police Officer*, who would perform routine duties, make arrests (relieving the CSO from this duty), and enforce traffic regulations, etc. And the third member of the team, the *Police Agent*, would do whatever jobs were "most complicated, most sensitive, and most demanding. He might be a specialist in police-community relations or juvenile delinquency." Although the Commission recommended that all levels have at least two years of college, it preferred the Police Agent to have a degree in the liberal arts or social sciences.

These suggestions were quickly adopted by New York City's John Jay College of Criminal Justice (autonomous but accredited by CCNY) which offers a BS degree. The College hired a new president, Donald H. Riddle, who said that he had left Rutgers University because of his "concern with urban problems." He emphasized what he believed to be true about the police role in an urban society. "There are two important things police have to be taught: the sources of human behavior, normal and abnormal, and the nature and character of social control. You simply cannot control a citizenry with gun and club. A policeman has to know the limits of coercion as a means of social control and be aware of alternatives to brute force." (Dr. Riddle, an ex-Air Force turret gunner and bombardier, and former efficiency expert, teaches one literature course to senior police in which Frantz Fanon is read.)

In Suffolk County, Mass. (which includes Roxbury), the "unarmed but uniformed" CSO has already become part of the police pacification team. Primarily, his functions lend credibility to the rest of the armed team. Elsewhere, new recruitment and training efforts have been undertaken. Chicago, Minneapolis, and Dallas have lowered their minimum police age. The Department of Labor is financing programs in several cities specifically to train black policemen. In New Orleans, business sponsors college education for police personnel; and the Western Interstate Compact for Higher Education (WICHE) has begun financing a traveling contingent of university instructors to provide in-service training for those living away from the city. The New Detroit Committee, a post-riot coalition headed by Henry Ford II, has hired the Michigan State University Dean of Police Administration (who set up the Vietnam secret police for Diem in the early 60's) to direct a $1 million study of reform in the Detroit Police Department.

There is still another and more fruitful reservoir for recruitment: the Vietnam soldier who returns home at the rate of more than 70,000 per month. (Here the major emphasis is on enlisting black and Puerto Rican soldiers, because government officials fear these men will turn their fighting skills against the local agents of law and order. The same officials also view the young soldier-turned-policeman as one whose professional training can be applied domestically without a civilian interruption.) In November 1967 the Defense Department issued a directive to the Army which ordered the early discharge of those G.I.'s who pledged to enter police work in major cities. Several weeks later a complimentary program, Project Transition, was set up "to ensure jobs for men leaving the military service." Lending Administrative support to these projects, President Johnson in January 1968 earmarked $50 million in his new budget for incentive payments to veterans who agreed to take special public-service jobs such as "manning understrength police forces," and also ordered that Vietnam veterans be hired on a priority basis and without examination for the first five levels of civil service.

In the past, the Justice Department has kept a close watch on all recruitment efforts. But except for the projects under Army direction, the federal government has had little unifying jurisdiction over lags and contradictions between states, and little legal authority to press its preferred programs. This has now been changed by the 1968 Federal Omnibus Crime Bill which implements uniform training standards for those states applying for federal funds. The new law places priority on control of riots and civil disturbances (which pleases localities). It encourages training in community services of officers "whose mission will be to ease tensions in the ghetto"; and it expands training for state and local police officers at federal institutes including the National Academy of the FBI. In addition the Bill established a National Institute of Law Enforcement and Criminal Justice which is authorized to contract with colleges and universities to do research and demonstration projects. (It should be noted that with the exception of the wiretapping ruling and the reversal of certain Supreme Court decisions, the Crime Bill derives its provisions from the recommendations made in the IDA-sponsored *Task Force on Law Enforcement.*)

Knowing the conservatism of the police establishment, Attorney General Ramsey Clark had underplayed his hand until the Bill passed into law. Now the federal government has placed complete authority in the Justice Department and Ramsey Clark intends to run the show his way. True, he cannot control the individual behavior of rank and file, but he can withhold funds where federal standards are not met. And where localities are slow to respond, the Department will exert pressure on district attorneys to expose police corruption, or else send officials into the areas to investigate police incidents attached to civil-rights complaints. Even before the crime bill became law, the Justice Department had made plans to facilitate federal intervention. It had, for example, expanded the functions of its Community Relations Service staff—80 men who will go as teams into a city before or as soon as trouble develops in order "to conciliate between hostile elements in the community."

FEDERAL PACIFICATION

But why this federal concern? And what does it mean for the ghetto? Ramsey Clark is not responsive to the sufferings of ghetto residents, but he is responsible for preventing and containing ghetto uprisings. He had insisted that his order for gun restraint was a tactical measure because "the other side has guns, too." Maybe; but federal forces are hardly intimidated. More likely, gun restraint is a result of the impressive array of urban studies which have concluded that unprofessional (shoot-to-kill) police actions will trigger violent political reactions. Traditional force threatens to increase the ranks of dissenters more than it serves to control them. Moreover,

the new and diversified "nonlethal" weaponry is more relevant to ghetto pacification.

Unlike Vietnam where pacification was a political promise but where little is ever spared the match, the bomb, and the bulldozer, the strategies for ghetto pacification lie hidden between the rhetoric of slum redevelopment and the threat of military repression. If the strategy for the ghetto is gun restraint now, then the trade-off is a permanent pacification team—the ramifications of which are already visible.

As one Harlem resident remarked about the Neighborhood Task Force, "It's not touching the real problems . . . and the danger is that the people who might really move for change feel they're not needed." That is the deliberate premise behind ghetto pacification and why it is prerequisite to any subsequent solutions. In the long run pacification seeks not only to prevent riots but to make self-determination irrelevant.

The storefront concept—presently termed "decentralization"—is one of the key factors in this process. Whether it functions as a little city hall or a mobile police precinct, the storefront is in no way detached from its central power; rather it becomes a satellite through which that power is able to reach directly into a neighborhood and maintain its control. For example, the police storefront concept was a direct response to community groups who wanted to replace local police forces with police who had a stake in their community, whose upward mobility depended on meeting *their* needs and, most important, who would provide a buffer between them and federal armed intervention. This is precisely why ghetto residents will *not* be permitted to select their own police, just as they are not permitted control over their own schools or other vital institutions. It is also why the satellite concept is now central to most slum reclamation programs such as Model Cities.

But while gun restraint is enforced to give the satellite concept a chance to develop, there still remain those voters who demand visible assurances that riots will be crushed. In the conflict, the municipal governments have become the mediators. While treading lightly on ghetto streets to keep tensions from snapping, they are increasing their police manpower. In fact, they have had to cut back on essential services to initiate various patrols for special deployment, such as the elite Tactical Patrol Force in New York City.

Consisting of about 500 men (1000 can be mobilized from various areas), the TPF bases its "crowd-control" mission on one factor—mobility. They travel in buses, belong to no precinct, and stay with their unit no more than three years. (They are ideologues—not the graft-takers.) At the same time there is a 200-man Special Events Squad, created to control parades and "mild" demonstrations.

Naturally, this diversification and expansion of law enforcement is seriously straining city resources, and it is interesting to note how this problem lends credibility to a new plan which would undermine municipal police authority altogether.

.... On the basis of technical and organizational considerations, this country requires a metropolitan-regional police force system which would relate to actual urban population concentration. [Such] a force would have 10 or 12 command centers, corresponding to the major population concentrations in the country. It would leave many police functions to local control, such as ... community policing. It would constitute a distinct law enforcement system under federal jurisdiction with crucial function in dealing with ... control of civil disturbances (Morris Janowitz, *The Social Control of Escalated Riots*, p. 22, University of Chicago Center for Policy Study).

The federal government appears to agree with Professor Janowitz for it has provided the means to implement such a force in its new crime bill. The new law already subsidizes regional plans for police training and research much more generously than it does local ones. Correspondingly, it looks to science and technology to further develop centralized police precinct systems in order to decentralize police functions.

The role of the National Guardsman has also been affected. He now receives standard Army rather than state-developed training courses. This prepares him to coordinate his functions with the Pentagon whose plans go beyond riot control to combatting insurgency. In fact, the prototypes of the "metropolitan-regional" force are the Army units themselves, trained in domestic counterinsurgency.

In one of the on-going clandestine military-in-mufti operations which took place in New York City during July 1967, 116 Army Reserves made an intensive study of the city's major departments. The purpose of their investigation was to learn how to take over a city government if necessary. They met with commissioners of key departments and at one point watched Deputy Mayor Costello coordinate operations during rioting in East Harlem. The men were from the 356th Civil Affairs Area Headquarters in Fort Devens, Mass., which in 1965 had begun training for this program. In 1966, the men attended a course in public administration at New York University which is now given at the City College of New York.

On July 29, 1967, they completed a textbook for use by Army Civil Affairs Units elsewhere in the nation. They had also been asked by Deputy Mayor Costello to submit a confidential critique of the operations they had observed. A few weeks later, Deputy Mayor Costello contracted with a management consulting firm, McKinsey and Company, to construct a "demonstration chart room" in Gracie Mansion. The firm then proposed establishing a "war room" at 51 Chambers Street where researchers would develop subsequent issue charts outlining problem areas. The room will be permanently staffed by eight city employees who, it was suggested to the Mayor, "should resemble Robert McNamara's whiz kids."

While the Justice Department, the Pentagon, and the urban planners are establishing their bases, Congress has provided the legal means to mobilize them. First, there is the array of selective control legislation passed in 1967–68: drug control, crime control, riot control, etc. Each of these bills also facilitates the development of federal data systems which will store a reservoir of personal information. Unlike the name-calling McCarthy years, the computer's harassment will be more subtle. An employer will be more disposed to hiring a college dropout than a computer reject. And obviously its impact will be felt most by those who refuse to limit their dissent to acceptable channels.

In a grim reminder of Vietnam pacification techniques, a recently released HUAC report suggests that authorities can make further use of intelligence. To seal off a violent ghetto, for example, HUAC proposes that identification cards for slum-dwellers be issued by an office for the "Control and Organization of the Inhabitants." "Various detention centers . . . for the temporary imprisonment of warring guerrillas" could then be utilized, and "search and seizure operations" launched during daylight hours (*Los Angeles Times*, 5/6/68).

It would be easy to dismiss HUAC's proposals but for several facts which underscore their immediacy. When *Look* Senior Editor William Hedgepeth made an investigation of six detention centers set up by the federal government in 1952, he discovered that:

Military planners in Washington acknowledge that detention of dissenters on at least a limited basis could conceivably take place should prolonged, simultaneous, and seemingly coordinated urban riots reach . . . nationally disruptive proportions so as to require . . . martial law. . . . [This] would mean full military control of the designated area, suspension of bail, and mass arrests on the basis of suspicion alone (*Look*, 5/28/68).

The Executive Secretary of the Citizens Committee for Constitutional Liberties cites as an operational but limited policy of internment the "picking up of a few hundred people in a demonstration and [the] cordoning off of an area to hold them before arrests are made."

Moreover, the Justice Department has given new life to the McCarren Act and Congress has appended six new provisions. These permit the Subversive Activities Control Board to legally invade the lives of dissenters. Notable among them are: (a) all privileges under the Fifth Amendment have been revoked; SACB itself will grant immunity and witnesses are therefore obligated to appear; and (b) no affirmative legal action can be brought against SACB to halt or interfere with its proceedings.

Federal, state, and local guardians of law and order are concluding that programs developed with a summer mentality are unable to meet accumulated expectations; and that the $18,000-a-year directors hired to lend legitimacy to city programs cannot effectively harness the energies of the young. While the alliance for stability attempts to pacify, the black and the poor continue to learn that living with rats is as oppressive as guns are repressive, and that an inferior education subjugates them in the same way that whips and chains subjugate the slave to the master. And while the professionals plan a 10-block Model City in a 10-mile ghetto, the people have come under another influence. Call it the impulse to survive—it is equally the determination to resist and to establish new power among themselves. And it has placed them in conflict and competition with the remote and formal power-holders who dominate their lives and make ghettos out of their communities.

The Revolution in Expression

THE MOVEMENT AT
THE CROSSROADS

The Editors

In the preceding chapters we have tried to indicate that many of the social ills of contemporary American society could be understood as products of the coming together of three very general trends, each sufficiently different from its antecedents to be considered revolutionary. What will emerge from these sometimes conflicting and sometimes overlapping trends may be radically different from the society we have known until now. It is no longer possible to demark clearly which are the groups carrying the revolutionary trends. Surely student activists have been one such group and radical racial groups, of which the Black Panthers are the striking example, are carriers of the potential for change. Two articles in this chapter are historical and analytical accounts of these major focal points of the movement. Belden Fields' comparative view of student revolt in France and the U.S. indicates first how the effects of protest can be far reaching and what consequences follow from the repressive response to student revolt. It should be noted that despite many similarities there were no students shot during all the years of severe disorder in France. Ronald Steel's account of the Panthers helps to correct the unbalanced press image of a revolutionary political group. The Panther program calls for local control over Black communities by the residents and for socialism. Rhetoric of the Panthers notwithstanding, it seems clear from Steel's description that the reason for repression of the Panthers is their political threat to the system's sacred economic and governing institutions. In the main, neither the Panther program nor the programs of activist students include among their goals the incitement of violence. Rather violence emanates from the fact that the system often cannot allow itself to hear, no less tolerate, the movement's political threat to its basic economic structure or to its educational, legal, and political institutions of control.

Social change is likely to emerge from the clash between the demands of the militants and the repressive capacities of the system. The direction of this change is likely to remain erratic through much of the 1970s. What is already distinct is the form of expression that the modern American protest movement is taking. We have called this departure in the expression of disaffection with contemporary society "the revolution in expression" and have selected the writings of Carl Oglesby, Eldridge Cleaver, Kate Millett, and Tom Hayden to convey the pulse of "the movement," diverse as it may be.*

In our earlier edition we included two criticisms of the new left movement by George Grant and Michael Harrington, respectively. Both were more sophisticated and more accurate than other liberal critics who wrote at the time. The liberal thesis was that the application of technology and informed rationality to political and social problems promised a new and more humanitarian hope for society. The liberal theories which suggested that the Vietnam war was but an unfortunate mistake of earlier policies or that the failure of the war on poverty was but a matter of inadequate planning have been discredited by events. Both Grant and Harrington agreed with more radical critics that the social mainstream produced an overwhelming emptiness and dehumanization at the hands of a self-serving manipulative bureaucracy. Grant's essential argument was that the success of the civil-rights movement in the South in the early sixties came within an operating concensus in which federal marshalls, the media, in short the power of the empire, stood, however slowly or reluctantly, on the same side as the civil-rights workers and martyrs. But that support ends with the turn to real reform which intends to stop the manipulation of humans through schools, universities, job and welfare programs, or with resistance to the draft or other agencies that transform people and feed them into a society in which technique in every form—in space, weapons, city planning, productivity, efficiency, and order—has become the autonomous king. To hope that such a system will break of its own internal contradictions, as Grant accurately notes, is to engage in dangerous delusion.

Similarly, Harrington sees a liberal center somewhat remote from the protestors. The loose majority coalition behind the welfare state is seen to have many components, some more humanitarian and less manipulative than the radicals charge. He asks the activists not to assign the poor the role of isolated hero in a morality play which will assure for them the continuous role of minority and of loser. Harrington calls for new and intensive organization in the ghettos, not as an isolated political force but as a catalyst to the alignment of a new majority political movement. Interestingly,

---

* Certain key items are missing here and interested individuals should note new Puerto Rican and Chicano spokesmen from the Young Lords and the Brown Berets, and such Indian voices as Clyde Warrior and Vine Deloria, Jr. While Abbie Hoffman captures a taste of the mocking political life style of the counterculture in *Revolution for the Hell of It*, other works deal with the serious social, political, and personal significance of the alternative life style, i.e., Theodore Roszak, *The Making of the Counter Culture*, Paul Potter, *A Name for Ourselves*, and Charles Reich, *The Greening of America*. The significance of drug use, particularly marijuana, to the counterculture is seen in Joel Fort's article "Pot: A Rational Approach." A very important source of films about "the movement" is San Francisco Newsreel, 1232 Market Street, San Francisco, Calif., 94102, (415) 621-6196.

this was precisely the objective of the Students for a Democratic Society as documented by its early papers before its widespread growth. The objective was a realignment of electoral politics. It was precisely the objective of new-left organizing groups in Boston, Baltimore, Chicago, and Cleveland who tried to go beyond the brilliant organization techniques of Saul Alinsky and to relate the poverty of their constituents to larger issues of war, racism, and welfare capitalism (Flacks, 1970). And it was the failure or inability to respond on the part of the organized liberal community, the unions, the intellectuals, the older Negro groups, and civil libertarians which had a major effect on splintering the movement.

Grant's analysis calls less for a particular strategy than for a depth of thought, of conviction and love which must not be blinded by slogans into false hopes that the technological straitjacket is weakening or that it has lost appeal to and control over a vast majority of the citizenry. Surely the quest for truth is needed as never before and Grant's view of the body politic was certainly correct in 1967. But is it today? Chapter 5, "The Depersonalized and the Alienated," was expanded from three articles in our earlier edition to five in the current one. Even now we fail to include the expressions of alienation to be found among women in our society, or among the youth counterculture generally, or among the large number of unemployed scientists and engineers during the major recession of 1970. The exiles to Canada or to rural communes are not included nor is the movement for a democratic military or the underground. The list of alienated might also have included the growing drug culture or the conservative group of hard hats and fundamentalists. The point, if not yet clear, should emerge lucidly in the articles of this chapter. The society has alienated a much larger segment of its membership than could heretofore be imagined. The movement to change the U.S. radically is here to stay whether or not a new political alignment can be found.

The article by Carl Oglesby was selected to indicate why some people in the movement for radical change do not assume an existing good will on the part of the liberal-moderate establishment. The selection by Eldridge Cleaver shows the depth of feeling among militant leaders of oppressed people as they respond to domestic colonialism. Kate Millet's article on "Sexual Politics" is representative of some of the good writings emerging from women's liberation as women are discovering the common features of an inferior status which has been cast upon them. The culture presses them toward the image of the unthinking, shallow feminine mystique. They are discriminated against in jobs and in pay, exploited as cheap, available, part-time labor according to the needs of the market, looked upon as sex objects, denied the status and rewards that should accrue from such important tasks as child rearing, and not usually afforded with adequate child care to make available a free choice among alternate roles.

Tom Hayden's article gives some assessment of where the movement is after such landmark events as the Democratic National Convention in 1968, the subsequent Chicago conspiracy trials, and the shooting of students on college campuses. Hayden's analyses of world events have frequently been prophetic and here he points to the need for a rallying point around which the forces of protest may regroup. The movement has many voices. The writings of slain Black leader Malcolm X and the poetry and theatre of LeRoi Jones convey the militancy, the sense of urgency, the desire to shake off oppressive authority and the demand of the group to shape their own lives without accepting terms set by outsiders. Some of the emotional message is delivered by a theatre of protest which has grown through the efforts of such groups as the San Francisco Mime Troupe. In the arts, folk music also remains a traditional medium for expressing feelings about the waste and horror of war and the emptiness of modern life. In the last few years gigantic music festivals have turned on millions of individuals as they express the need for a sense of community, however brief, with others of the counterculture. The hip clothing, the movement toward communes, the evolution of free clinics, all give testimony to the fact that people are seeking a sense of community, however fleeting, with others who, like themselves, are rejecting the values and life styles of the cybernetic state.

The techniques of the movement have been evolving, gradually bypassing the small discriminating barber shop or lunch counter, against which the sit-in or picket line may have been well suited. Marches for peace or civil rights are new occurrences in American society. Also new are the practices of leaving the country in preference to being drafted, individual cases of refusal to be inducted or, after induction, refusal to serve in Vietnam. "Teach-ins" which subjected American foreign policy to the guns of its academic critics, free universities and student protests for a voice in the administration of their universities, rent strikes and consumer boycotts, third-party politicking, tax withholding, programs of assistance to the victims of American firepower, and attempts to close down induction centers all reflect an amorphous groping for techniques for effective involvement.

The content of the expression is also different. Luis Valdez in his "Tale of La Raza" (1966) indicates how, in the aftermath of the organization of the grape-picking braceros in the Delano Grape Strike, the crowd demanded that the platforms be used for poor grape pickers of their own race and regions and not for benevolent officials or outside helpers. Similarly, American Indians have spoken out against governmental failure to understand them or to allow them to preserve their sense of community against the arbitrary legal fictions of towns, cities, and states which are recognized by federal programs (Warrior, 1965).

The content of the new expression goes deeply into the latent feelings of individuals long forced to wear their color or their neighborhoods as a badge of inferiority. The topics of the new literature of protest deal with brutal frankness about amphetamines, addictive narcotics and psychedelic drugs, the problems of sex liberation, the meanings of interracial social and sexual ties to the self-image of the Negro ghetto worker or of the civil-rights reformer.

In all this diverse new literature there is an overwhelming sense of disillusionment with modern American society. In much of it there is a sense of hope for a better way.

The data in this book call for revolution. The essays in this chapter give voice to the forms that resistance is taking against the inhumane and uncaring authority of mindless, busy bureaucrats hanging on to their roles in institutions no longer serving people's needs adequately. Taken collectively, they offer one answer to the question posed by Paul Potter when he addressed the first march on Washington to end the war in Vietnam,

> What kind of system is it that disenfranchises people in the South, leaves millions . . . impoverished and excluded from the main stream and promises of American society, that creates faceless and terrible bureaucracies . . . that consistently puts material values before human values—and still persists in calling itself free and in finding itself fit to police the world? What place is there for ordinary men in that system and how are they to control it, make it bend itself to their wills rather than bending them to its? We must. We must name that system. We must name it, describe it, understand it, and change it.

That American society must change and will change with increasing rapidity is beyond doubt. But the means of change seem to us as critically important as the direction. Charles Reich, in his book, *The Greening of America*, shows a full awareness of the convergence of public and corporate power, the end of pluralistic competition, and the orientation toward people as objects of controlled production and consumption. Reich's case is that as strong as the monster has become, it is still vulnerable to a real revolution and one in which violence plays no part.

The essential vulnerability of the system, Reich contends, lies in its failure to meet real human needs. This argument is supported by Paul Potter's analysis of contemporary protest (Potter, in press). The fight for power is doomed, not only because of the amount of concentrated power amassed against the movement but because the majority of people do not feel that what is missing most from their lives is the ability to control the corporations, the military, or the government. What is missing most is the ability to experience one's own life. The real experience of being treated like a "nigger" (or Yippie) during a demonstration is soon eradicated in the media report of the small number of protestors and ineffectiveness of the demonstration. Even the experiences of love and creative human relationships are lost to the demands of filling the roles of housewife, good student, compulsive consumer, productive worker, harried professional, or manipulative elite. Most people view this deficiency in highly individual terms, blaming themselves or their partner for a relationship gone bad. Yet "success" within the media-dominated, military, technocratic society virtually requires such deficiency in experience.

The possibilities for revolutionary change here lie precisely in the fact, according to Reich, that the existing system depends for its existence not merely upon its unjust and unwarranted concentration of wealth and power but also upon an ideology which tells us to produce, consume, deny our experience, postpone our pleasures, and accept the rules of the game as set for us by the Establishment. The revolution in consciousness, led by the young, rejects all that. Its appeal lies in the demand that real human needs be allowed to develop and be met *with or without a change in power.* Reich's prediction is that even among the affluent elite, perhaps particularly among them, the task of preserving privilege and power may weaken and yield to the desire to experience warmth or community. And with its consumers, workers, soldiers, teachers, and its children resisting the old order and living the new one, there may be no alternative but to yield to the insight of a more caring society.

Whether or not this nonviolent transformation toward a new level of human evolution is really forthcoming, the model of taking individual responsibility to live fully and with dedication to the real tasks of experiencing life and assisting others to greater growth and freedom is an important one. There is, however, another, less optimistic, view that sees the sources of power to be essentially unyielding except through direct pressure. For this latter group, confrontation is often the preferred strategy and direct acts of resistance are used to impede the machinery of the cybernetic state from drafting men, waging war, destroying forests, gouging consumers, or denying jobs and income to needy people. There is a strong case to be made for direct acts of resistance to morally indefensible authority. (See Dr. Martin Luther King's letter in Chapter 10.) Increasingly, acts of violence against the Establishment have followed this originally nonviolent tradition, particularly with the wave of bombings following repressive legal and police action against Panthers and white radicals. In one such bombing of the University of Wisconsin Army Math Center, Robert Fassnacht was accidentally killed. The question raised by this and other bombings goes beyond whether the Establishment can easily reproduce its buildings, banks, draft files, beyond any ability to destroy them—or even whether the action was productive or counterproductive in producing social change. The important question regards the use of any means which (actually or potentially) takes human life.

Many rationales have been offered for such action. Some contend that the more dangerous means will be in the same language which the oppressor uses and understands. Others say that the damage to one or two individuals is in no way comparable to the mass death inflicted through worldwide hunger and war which our society inflicts on others. Fassnacht might even have been killed, like many of his peers, if he were sent to Vietnam. Alan Brick, writing in October 1970 in *Resist,* helps to answer these rationales. He states that one must not confuse such acts as the Wisconsin bombing with other protests like the destruction of draft files with napalm—outside of the building—by the Catonsville 9. The moral authority in the latter case was clear even if the act was illegal. Moreover, Brick continues, while the agents of the Wisconsin bombing "certainly cannot be ranked in *degree* with those of the Establishment, they must be ranked with them in kind."

The tragedies at Kent State and Georgia State (where Guardsmen fired at students) clarify the reasons why the police and military use of guns against students—or against anyone—is power devoid of moral legitimacy.

In a book that takes the value of human life as the starting point for defining social problems, it seems imperative to state a value position on the means used to create a more humane society. Lethal weapons when used on people for political goals are "an inseparable part of the continuum of violence that ends in the mass murder of war and the oppression of Third World people in economic slavery." (Brick, 1970.)

The few bomb throwers on the political left play into the hands of the reactionary mentality which plants undercover provocateurs to subvert protest. The real question, however, is a moral one. Violence to people is wrong. The society we seek follows the biblical teaching,

I have set before you life and death, blessing and curse; therefore choose life that you and your dependents may live. (Deuteronomy, Chapter 30.)

To create a more humane social order is a task befitting the inherent dignity of the individual and worthy of the efforts of an educated person.

REFERENCES AND ADDITIONAL READING

Brick, Alan, "Sabotage: Some Questions about Morality," *Resist*, Newsletter No. 4 (October 4, 1970), pp. 2–4.

Carmichael, Stokely, "Toward Black Liberation," *The Massachusetts Review* (Spring 1966); reproduced in R. Perrucci and M. Pilisuk (eds.), *The Triple Revolution: Social Problems in Depth* (Boston: Little, Brown, 1968), pp. 668–677.

Deloria, Vine, Jr., *Custer Died for Your Sins* (New York: Macmillan, 1969).

"Detroit: Violence on the Urban Frontier," *Trans-action*, Special Supplement (September 1967), pp. 6–32 (articles by Irving L. Horowitz, Roger Montgomery, Tom Parmanter, and Lee Rainwater).

Detwiler, Bruce, "A Time to Be Black," *New Republic* (September 7, 1966), pp. 19–22.

Domhoff, William G., "How to Commit a Revolution," text of a speech given at the Student Strike Rally at the University of California, Santa Cruz (April 28, 1969); reprinted in the *Peninsula Observer*.

Epstein, Jason, "The Trial of Bobby Seale," *New York Review of Books* (December 4, 1969), pp. 35–51.

Flacks, Richard, "Protest or Conform: Some Social Psychological Perspectives on Legitimacy," *Journal of Applied Behavioral Science*, **5** (1969), pp. 127–160.

Flacks, Richard, "The New Left and American Politics: After Ten Years," paper presented at annual meeting of American Political Science Association, Los Angeles (September 1970).

Fort, Joel, *The Pleasure Seekers: The Drug Crisis, Youth and Society* (New York: Bobbs-Merrill, 1969).

Fort, Joel, "Pot: A Rational Approach," *Playboy* (October 1969).

Friedenberg, Edgar Z., "National Self-Abuse," *New York Review of Books*, **14** (1970), pp. 36–38.

Goodman, Mitchell (ed.), *Movement Toward a New America* (New York: Knopf, 1971).

Goodman, Paul, "The Empty Society," from *Like a Conquered Province* (New York: Random House, 1966); reproduced in R. Perrucci and M. Pilisuk (eds.), *The Triple Revolution: Social Problems in Depth* (Boston: Little, Brown, 1968), pp. 645–659.

Grant, George, "Realism in Political Protest," *Christian Outlook* (November 1967), pp. 3–6; reproduced in R. Perrucci and M. Pilisuk (eds.), *The Triple Revolution: Social Problems in Depth* (Boston: Little, Brown, 1968), pp. 678–683.

Gray, Francine, "The Panthers at Yale," *New York Review of Books*, **14** (June 1970), pp. 29–35.

Halpern, Manfred, "A Redefinition of the Revolutionary Situation," in Norman Miller and Roderick Aya (eds.), *Redefinition of Revolution: New Perspectives* (New York: Free Press, 1969).

Hamowy, Ronald, "Left and Right Meet," *New Republic* (March 12, 1966), pp. 14–16.

Harrington, Michael, "The Mystical Militants," *New Republic* (February 19, 1966), pp. 20–22; reproduced in R. Perrucci and M. Pilisuk (eds.), *The Triple Revolution: Social Problems in Depth* (Boston: Little, Brown, 1968), pp. 648–689.

Hoffman, Abbie, *Revolution for the Hell of It* (New York: Dial, 1968).

Howard, John R., "The Making of a Black Muslim," *Trans-action* (December 1966), pp. 15–21.

Jacobs, Paul, and Saul Landau, *The New Radicals* (New York: Vintage, 1966).

Jerome, Judson, *Culture Out of Anarchy: The Reconstruction of American Higher Learning* (New York: Herder and Herder, 1970).

Langer, Elinor, "The Oakland Seven," *Atlantic*, **224** (October 1969), pp. 76–82.

Marcuse, Herbert, "Love Mystified: A Critique of Norman O. Brown," *Commentary* (February 1967), pp. 71–84.

Marine, Gene, ". . . as Outlaws, as Gangsters, as Evildoers," from *The Black Panthers* (New York: New American Library, 1969).

Newfield, Jack, *A Prophetic Minority* (New York: New American Library, 1966).

Oppenheimer, Martin, George Lakey, and Bayard Rustin, *A Manual for Direct Action* (Chicago: Quadrangle, 1967).

Playboy Panel, "The Drug Revolution," *Playboy* (February 1970).

Reich, Charles, *The Greening of America* (New York: Knopf, 1970).

Rexroth, Kenneth, *The Alternative Society* (New York: Herder and Herder, 1970).

Roszak, Theodore, *The Making of a Counter Culture* (Garden City, N.Y.: Doubleday, 1969).

Sale, J. Kirk, "Ted Gold: Education for Violence," *The Nation* (April 13, 1970), pp. 423–429.

Schaar, John H., and Sheldon Wolin, "Where We Are Now," *New York Review of Books*, **14** (May 1970), pp. 3–10.

Seabury, Paul, "Gideon's Army and Moynihan's Pros," *New Republic* (March 19, 1966), pp. 23–25.

Seale, Bobby, *Seize the Time* (New York: Random House, 1970).

Slater, Philip E., *The Pursuit of Loneliness: American Culture at the Breaking Point* (Boston: Beacon, 1970).

Solomon, David (ed.), *The Marihuana Papers* (New York: Bobbs-Merrill, 1966).

Stern, Sol, "America's Black Guerrillas," *Ramparts* (September 1967), pp. 24–27.

Valdez, Luis, "The Tale of La Raza," *Ramparts* (July 1966), pp. 40–43.

Warrior, Clyde, "Poverty, Community and Power," *New University Thought*, **4** (Summer 1965), pp. 5–10.

Waskow, Arthur, "The New Student Movement," *Dissent*, **12** (Autumn 1965), pp. 486–493.

Waskow, Arthur, *Running Riot* (New York: Herder and Herder, 1970).

LETTER FROM OAKLAND

THE PANTHERS

Ronald Steel

I went to Oakland, dead end of the westward course of empire, and home of the Black Panthers, to take a look at a conference of the revolutionary left. Oakland, where the American dream ends at the Pacific, and the nightmare begins, is a familiar kind of industrial city: high-rise office buildings and apartments downtown, plasticene shopping centers on the fringe, and slowly decaying wooden houses in between. West Oakland, facing the Bay and the gleaming hills of San Francisco beyond, is the ghetto where the Black Panthers were born. It is a California-style ghetto, with one-family houses and neglected yards, where poverty wears a more casual face and despair is masked by sunshine.

The Panthers in July summoned their friends—a mixed bag of revolutionaries, radicals, pacifists, and liberals—to assemble in Oakland to form what they called a "united front against fascism." The phrase itself had a defensive ring, reminiscent of the ill-fated popular fronts of the 1930s, and it seemed to indicate that the Panthers were in trouble. White radicals, few of whom were consulted about the agenda, privately expressed doubts about the usefulness of such a conference, and many SDS chapters did not send representatives. As it turned out, they would not have had much of a role to play anyway, since the Panthers were very much running their own show and not accepting criticism from those who came to hear them.

Like so many other gatherings of the radical left, the conference produced little unity but a great deal of dissatisfaction. Most of the sessions were disorganized and, with a few exceptions, the speeches were little more than an interminable series of spot announcements denouncing the evils of rampant fascism. No one seemed interested in discussing whether fascism had indeed arrived in America. This, like so much of the other rhetoric of the revolutionary left, was simply taken for granted.

When the three-day conference finally rambled to an end, the dwindling band of white radicals drifted away in dismay, wondering what kind of bag the Panthers had got themselves into. The more militant radicals from Berkeley feared that the Panthers had turned reformist, while socialists and Trotskyites complained about their dictatorial methods. The "united front," whose creation was the ostensible purpose of the conference, had not been formed and most participants expressed doubts that it ever would be. The general consensus was that the Panthers didn't have a very clear idea of what they were up to. They wanted to enlist allies, and they hoped that some kind of united front would develop. But they had no real plan worked out, and certainly no intention of letting anyone else supply one.

Why did the Panthers call such a conference in the first place? At least in part because they have been under increasing harassment and intimidation by the police

Reprinted by permission from the New York Review of Books, **13:4** *(September 11, 1969), pp. 14–22; copyright © 1969.*

and the FBI. During the past few months more than forty leaders and 100 members have been arrested, and some of them are now facing life imprisonment or the death penalty. The party's founder and chief theorist, twenty-seven-year-old Huey P. Newton, is serving a fourteen-year sentence for allegedly shooting an Oakland policeman. Its most articulate spokesman, Eldridge Cleaver, has chosen to go into exile rather than return to prison on dubious charges of parole violation. Its treasurer, seventeen-year-old Bobby Hutton, was killed by police during last year's Oakland shootout. And its acting chairman, Bobby Seale, is under federal indictment for conspiring to incite a riot at last year's Democratic Convention, although he was not a member of any of the organizations sponsoring the protests, and spent less than a day in Chicago.

The Panthers see a concerted plot by the federal government, with the assistance of local police, to destroy them. Recently Spiro Agnew has described them as a "completely irresponsible, anarchistic group of criminals," and J. Edgar Hoover has called them, among black militants, the "greatest threat to the internal security of the country." This summer the Justice Department set up a special task force to investigate the party in the hope of nailing it on violation of some twenty federal laws, including those making it a crime to cross state lines to foment civil disorder, to interfere with persons participating in programs supported by the federal government, and to damage government buildings. Senator McClellan's Permanent Subcommittee on Investigations has been providing a forum for police officers and their informants to denounce the Panthers, as well as white radical groups. Recently they heard Larry Clayton Powell and his wife Jean tell how the Panthers forced them to rob for the party. The Panthers, however, claim that the Powells were kicked out of the party because they were criminals, and that they are telling the McClellan committee what it wants to hear in order to win clemency.

From the record it is clear that the campaign against the Panthers has been stepped up in recent months. In March Bobby Seale was linked to the Chicago conspiracy case and placed under federal indictment. On April 4 New York District Attorney Frank Hogan announced in banner headlines that his office had smashed a Panther plot to blow up several midtown department stores, a police station, and, inexplicably, the Bronx Botanical Gardens. A grand jury indicted twenty-one Panthers and bail for thirteen of them was set at $100,000 each. No bondsman will touch the case, and the party, of course, is unable to raise such an amount of money. Meanwhile the Panthers remain in jail, some under maximum security, not for having actually committed a crime, but for having *conspired* to do so, an extremely vague charge that rests on circumstantial evidence and the testimony of informers.

On May 22, in a case which police claim was linked to the New York twenty-one, eight New Haven Panthers were arrested and charged with kidnapping and murdering Alex Rackley, a New York Panther. Police claim he was killed because he was an informer, the Panthers charge that the police murdered him themselves in order to justify nationwide raids on chapter offices in a search for his alleged assassins. Whatever really happened to Rackley, federal agents did in fact carry out raids in Washington, D.C., Salt Lake City, Denver, and Chicago in conjunction with the case. Two Denver Panthers are being held on $200,000 bail—not for murder or even conspiracy but on the vague catchall charge of unlawful flight to avoid prosecution.[1]

---

[1] On August 19, shortly after this article was completed, Bobby Seale was arrested in Berkeley by FBI agents in connection with the Rackley case. So far, fourteen other Pan-

In the Chicago raid, which took place on June 4, FBI agents blocked off the street at 5:30 in the morning and confiscated Panther literature, a list of donors, and copies of a petition signed by 15,000 people calling for the release of Illinois party chairman Fred Hampton, who is in prison on a two-to-five-year sentence for allegedly stealing $71 worth of ice-cream bars distributed to ghetto children.

The day after the Chicago raid, police broke into the Panther office in Detroit, photographed documents, and arrested three Panthers, who were later released. On June 7, during racial disturbances, police entered the Panther office in Indianapolis and arrested thirty people. On June 10 a grand jury in Chicago indicted sixteen Panthers on charges of conspiracy, kidnapping, and threatening to murder two people who allegedly refused to return weapons entrusted to them by the Panthers. Bond was set at $100,000 each for six of the sixteen. One of the charges, aggravated kidnapping, carries a maximum death penalty. On June 15 San Diego policemen shot their way into Panther headquarters, where they claimed a sniper had taken refuge.

That same day in Sacramento the Panther office was torn apart by police during a shootout. On July 31, again in Chicago, police raided Panther headquarters during the pre-dawn hours, destroyed office equipment, medical supplies, and food for the children's breakfast program, and arrested three unarmed men for shooting at policemen from the office windows. The Panthers insist they were attacked by the police and tried to defend themselves.

Now that the federal government has joined the local police in operations against the Panthers—Attorney-General Mitchell is trying to get the courts to admit wiretap evidence against the Panthers and other groups ostensibly threatening "national security"—the strengthening of their links with white radical groups is more important than before. This is partly a question of ideology, for the Panthers—popular impressions to the contrary—are not racist. Indeed, they are virtually the only black militant group that actually welcomes white allies. It is also a question of survival, for without support from the white community they fear they will be picked off and destroyed.

Vilified and distorted by the press, which has little understanding of their program, they are generally viewed as an anarchistic band of gun-toting, white-hating thugs. This allows the police and federal officials to abridge their constitutional rights in a way they would not dare to use against whites. Provocation, false arrests, trumped-up charges, illegal detention, barbaric treatment, excessive bail, and even legal murder—this is everyday treatment for the Panthers. They have been defined as threatening to white society, and therefore beyond the normal protection of the law.

Is it likely that members of a white political organization, even the Ku Klux Klan, would be rounded up in the middle of the night, thrown into jails dispersed around the city, kept under maximum security and even solitary confinement, detained in prison for months on exhorbitant bail for a crime that was never committed, and charged with plotting irrational actions, without the liberal press voicing its indignation? Yet this is precisely what has happened to the New York twenty-one. If you let it happen to us, the Panthers are saying to white liberals, it will happen to

thers have been arrested in various states on similar charges. The day before Seale's arrest David Hilliard, the Panther Chief of Staff, was ordered to face trial on charges of attempted murder arising from last year's Oakland shootout. With these arrests, the chief national Panther leaders are in exile, in jail, under or facing indictment, or dead.

anyone who dissents. After the lessons of Chicago and Berkeley, white radicals, at least, are beginning to believe the Panther contention that we're all niggers now.

The Panthers are convinced that those in power are out to get them as much for their socialist ideology and their efforts to organize the black community into an effective political force as for their defensive actions against the police. Heavily into the economics and sociology of Marxism, the Panthers see racism in this country as an integral part of the capitalist system. "Capitalism deprives us all of self-determination," Huey Newton has said. "Only in the context of socialism can men practice the self-determination necessary to provide for their freedom."

The Panthers are absolutely serious when they talk of the need for "socialism"; and this is what distinguishes them from the other black militant and black power groups. They see themselves as "revolutionary nationalists," as opposed to "cultural nationalists," who seek black pride in separatist movements, religious cults, and emulation of ancient African culture. "The revolutionary nationalist," according to Huey Newton, "sees that there is no hope for cultural or individual expression, or even hope that his people can exist as a unique entity in a complex whole as long as the bureaucratic capitalist is in control." On the other hand, "cultural nationalism," explained David Hilliard, "is basically related to the physiological need for a return back to Africa in the culture, and we don't see that that is really relevant to any revolution, because culture never frees anyone. As Fanon says, the only culture is that of the revolution."

The reference to Fanon is instructive, for the Panthers, as can readily be seen from the writings of Huey Newton and Eldridge Cleaver, have been deeply influenced by the black psychiatrist from Martinique who died in the service of the Algerian revolution. *The Wretched of the Earth* is a kind of revolutionary Bible for them, and one with far more emotional impact than the Little Red Books which are so often quoted. Both Newton and Cleaver, freely acknowledging their debt to Fanon, have described black people as forming an oppressed colony within the white mother country, the United States. The colony is kept in line by an occupying army—white policemen who live outside the ghetto—and is exploited by businessmen and politicians.

The exploiters can be black as well as white, for the enemy, they insist, is not so much racism as capitalism, which creates and nourishes it. As would be expected of socialist revolutionaries, the Panthers are opposed to black capitalism, which Huey Newton has described as a "giant stride *away* from liberation..." since "...the rules of black capitalism, and the limits of black capitalism are set by the white power structure." Explaining his opposition, Newton has written:

There can be no real black capitalism because no blacks control the means of production. All blacks can do is have illusions. They can dream of the day when they might share ownership of the means of production. But there is no free enterprise in America. We have monopoly capitalism which is a closed society of white industrialists and their protectors, white politicians in Washington.

According to the Panthers, black power has been absorbed into the establishment, shorn of its horns, and transformed into innocent black capitalism, which even Richard Nixon can praise because it poses no threat to the white power structure.

As an alternative they offer "revolution," to liberate oppressed minorities in the United States and break the stranglehold of capitalism on the economically underdeveloped countries of the third world. Until there is some form of socialist "revolution" in America, they believe, small countries will remain prey to neocolonialism and imperialism. The revolutionary in America, therefore, carries the world upon his shoulders. The black man in America will not be free until the white man is free, and until the white man is free, until America is transformed by a socialist revolution, the underdeveloped countries of the world will remain in economic chains.

Such a comprehensive theory clearly has its inadequacies. Although blacks can be described as forming an internal colony within the United States, they do not supply raw materials, labor, or markets to capitalism in the same way as the colonies did. There is, moreover, no evidence at present that the U.S. is entering a revolutionary crisis that will involve the mass of workers. Nor can the Panthers have much success in breaking away into a separate state. What happens, as has been asked, when there's a border dispute? (It is not fair, however, to charge the Panthers with advocating political separatism. They claim neither to favor it nor to discourage it; they simply demand that a U.N.-supervised plebiscite be held on the issue in the black colony. In any case, this is not an immediate problem, and certainly not a major objective for them.)

The Panthers' Marxist-Leninist language, combined with their Fanonist theories of psychological alienation and third-world solidarity, makes them particularly appealing to middle-class white militants, who share their ideology but lack their discipline. White radicals also lack the black man's nonreducible commitment to black liberation: the fact that he is black. A white radical can cop out any time he wants by cutting his hair and behaving like a square. A black man cannot escape. In fighting

against the system he becomes, by his very act of resistance, a hero to white radicals. As Huey Newton has explained:[2]

Black people in America, in the black colony, are oppressed because we're black and we're exploited. The whites are rebels, many of them from the middle class, and as far as any overt oppression this is not the case. So therefore I call their rejection of the system somewhat of an abstract thing. They're looking for new heroes. . . . In pressing for new heroes the young white revolution found the heroes in the black colony at home and in the colonies throughout the world . . . .

While Newton favors alliances with white radicals, he points out that "there can be no black-white unity until there first is black unity." Only blacks can decide the proper strategy for the black community.

White radicals, divided on tactics and ideology, and split into a plethora of competing, often hostile, groups, have only recently begun to deal with some of the problems of "black liberation." There has always been sympathy for the black struggle, and even participation when it was permitted during the civil-rights movement. But things have changed greatly since Stokely Carmichael kicked the whites out of SNCC and the Panthers moved into the streets with guns. Unable to lead the black movement, white radicals are no longer even sure how they can aid it. Uncertain of their tactics, and confused about their goals, they revert to ready-made formulas, like "revolution," to deal with a multitude of complexities that are too difficut to analyze right now. Some assert that groups like the Panthers are the "vanguard" of the revolution—as though this justified white radicals' inability to work out a coherent theory or strategy.

The Vietnam war no longer serves as the great rallying point for the left that it used

[2] The quotations from Huey Newton are from an interview in *The Movement*, August 1968, republished as a pamphlet, and available from SDS.

to. Radicals have a good deal to protest about, but they seem to focus their energies on largely symbolic issues, such as the People's Park, or on the predictable seizure of university administration buildings. The radical left is hung up on revolution, but doesn't seem to have the vaguest idea of how it should be organized, or how the country would be run if such an event ever took place.

For the time being the left is divided, confused, and hopelessly weak and inept, and there is no more telling sign of the insecurity of those who hold power in America than that they are seriously worried about its activities. The McClellan committee solemnly listens to the "threats to national security" posed by campus agitators, while Congress debates[3] unconstitutional limitations on dissent and hysterical punishments against demonstrators. Not only do conventional politicians fear the Panthers, who at least carry guns and who can be described as a paramilitary organization, but even the scholastic debaters of the Students for a Democratic Society. In spite of all the spies and *agents provocateurs* it planted at the SDS convention in Chicago this past June, the politicians and the police apparently failed to learn that the left is too schismatic and ego-centered to threaten anybody.

Everyone now knows that SDS split in two this year, with the national leadership, through its RYM (Revolutionary Youth Movement) faction, expelling the rival Progressive Labor group for being, of all things, "counterrevolutionary." Among its sins the Maoist-oriented PL, through its Worker-Student Alliance (WSA), opposed the People's Park fight in Berkeley as a liberal-reformist move, branded many student demonstrations as "adventurous, diversionary, and alienating to the working people," accused Ho Chi Minh of selling out to the Washington-Moscow axis, criticized Fidel Castro, and condemned the Panthers for "bourgeois nationalism" in fighting the struggle on racial rather than exclusively class lines.

When the Panthers at the convention accused PL of deviating "from Marxist-Leninist ideology on the national question" and called its members "traitors," the SDS national leadership had the issue it needed to read PL out of the organization (although this violated SDS's own constitution) and established itself as the defender of the black liberation movement.

While PL's position is indeed bizarre on many issues, it is a determined, well-disciplined, ideologically trained organization. In the past it has supported the Panthers, but a break was inevitable, since PL argues that even the revolutionary nationalism of the Panthers is "counterrevolutionary." People are oppressed, PL argues, as workers, not as blacks, browns, or women. Naturally this has won PL the enmity not only of the

[3] The level of congressional discussion is exemplified by the following dialogue, from *The Congressional Record*, between Senators Long (D., La.) and Byrd (D., Va.):

   Long: Has the Senator ever heard of the Students for a Democratic Society?

   Byrd: Yes, I have heard of that group.

   Long: Does he agree with me that they are about the scum of the earth?

   Byrd: I do not know whether I would use the same phraseology the Senator uses.

   Long: They're about the most contemptible people I know of. They're the most over-privileged group in this country. Is the Senator familiar with the fact that the parents of these people have put up the money to pay all their expenses and buy soap for them? But they refuse to take baths. That they have put up the money to buy them razor blades? But they refuse to shave. That they put up the money to buy food for those children? And they spend it on marijuana. They are the most sorry, contemptible, overprivileged people in the world and I say those people are a good element for the Communists to move in on.

Panthers but of militant women opposed to "male chauvinism," as well as Puerto Rican groups like the Young Lords, and Mexican-American (Chicano) militants.

The RYM group tried to summarize its position in a lengthy, not always coherent, document it called Weatherman ("you don't need a weatherman to know which way the wind blows") . Among other things, it took the curious position that "the blacks could do it [the revolution] alone if necessary because of their centralness to the system," and signed off with friendly greetings to such enlightened outposts of proletarian freedom as Albania and North Korea.

In Oakland a few hundred SDS people joined others from some forty organizations to form a gathering of about 3000 people: Trotskyites and women striking for peace, Communist Party veterans and anarchists, factory workers and ministers. And, of course, a contingent of Panthers who, in spite of the interracial theme of the meeting, sat in a roped-off section at the back of the Oakland auditorium.

The conference not only got off to a late start, owing to the Panthers' frisking everyone who entered the auditorium, but a bad one, with an interminable address by Communist Party stalwart, Herbert Aptheker, who cut into the time allotted to the women's panel (thereby producing cries of "male chauvinism"—a serious issue for the Panthers and certain radical groups) , and, even worse, a charge that the Panthers had sold out to the bourgeois, reformist Communist Party. The Trotskyites and PL people were particularly upset by this, but the complaint is unjustified. The CP is useful to the Panthers because it furnishes bail money and teams of hard-working organizers who go out and get names on petitions. While the CP is happy to ride the Panthers' tail, it by no means calls the shots.

The Panthers ran the conference without help from the CP or anyone else. There were no workshops and no discussion from the floor, until the final night when a few questions were permitted. "When you begin to develop a united front you do not start off with a bunch of jive ideological bullshit," Bobby Seale declared to cries of "Right on" from the Panther cheering section and much waving of Little Red Books. But as the Trotskyite ISC observed in one of the leaflets it surreptitiously distributed at the conference, ". . . A left which lacks respect for its own ideas and programs and cannot stand internal debate cannot possibly hope to win the support of the masses." The Panthers, however, weren't interested in internal debate or jive ideological bullshit (although they produced a good deal of their own in the course of three days) , but support for their own programs—or, as they would say, "solidarity."

The major program they are now emphasizing is community control of police, with cities divided into districts, each with its own police force controlled by an elected neighborhood council, and with policemen living in the district they control. "If a policeman's brutalizing somebody in the community and has to come back home and sleep that night," Bobby Seale explained, "we can deal with him in our community." Participants at the conference were urged to get out and work on such petitions for decentralization—whites in white communities, browns in Latin communities, and blacks in the ghettos. For blacks and other minority groups such decentralization makes sense. It would not bring about the millennium, but it could sharply reduce the slaying and beating of ghetto people by trigger-happy, frightened, or racist white cops.

The white revolutionaries, however, were put off by such reformist proposals—particularly the Berkeley contingent, which seemed hung up on violence, with some members talking about guerrilla warfare in the streets. Even the pro-Panther SDS leadership felt that decentralization, however good it might be for the ghettos, was a bad policy for white neighborhoods, where it might lead to the creation of vigilante teams under the guise of police forces. The SDS interim committee voted against endorsement of the petition campaign unless it were limited to black and brown communities.

This didn't go down well with the Panthers. On his return from Algiers, where he attended the Pan-African Arts Festival, Chief of Staff David Hilliard told newsmen that "The Black Panther Party will not be dictated to by people who are obviously bourgeois procrastinators, seeking made-to-order revolution which is abstract, metaphysical, and doesn't exist in the black or white community." He derided the SDS argument that community control would make police forces in white areas worse than they already are, and defined the issue as one of revolutionary solidarity. "We're not going to let SDS worm their way out of their revolutionary duties," he warned. "If they are revolutionary, then this is what we, as the vanguard of the revolution in Babylon, dictate—that they circulate that petition, not in our communities but in their own."

Never very comfortable with SDS, the Panthers feel much more at home with the "brothers off the block," the street people, the lumpenproletariat, to use another phrase they are fond of, than with the guilt-ridden children of the white bourgeoisie. With a few exceptions, such as Huey Newton and Bobby Seale, they have had little formal education beyond high school, and some of the most intelligent do not even have that. "We got our education on the street, in the service, or in jail," the Panthers' soft-spoken minister of education, Ray "Masai" Hewitt, told me. The Panther leaders are self-made intellectuals or, in political scientist Martin Kilson's term, "paraintellectuals."[4]

"We relate to the Young Patriots" (a white, recently radicalized Chicago group that is organizing nationally), David Hilliard stated, "because they're operating on the same class level as the Black Panther Party." They also share a similar rhetoric. Speaking at the conference on the eve of the moon landing, a leader of the Young Patriots named Preacherman, in black beret and shades, gave a moving speech which was, in effect, a tribute to the Panthers' ability to reach traditionally apolitical, racist white groups:

Our struggle is beyond comprehension to me sometimes, and I felt that poor whites was (and maybe we felt wrongly, but we felt it) was forgotten, and that certain places we walked there were certain organizations that nobody saw us until we met the Illinois chapter of the Black Panther Party and they met us. And we said,

[4] Describing such leaders as Malcolm X and Eldridge Cleaver, Kilson has written: "Unlike the established elements in the Negro intelligentsia, the paraintellectuals share a cultural experience similar to that of the black lower classes. They share too the lower classes' brutalizing experience with the coercive arm of white-controlled cities, especially the police power. These common experiences enabled the paraintellectuals to be spokesmen for the Negro masses as they emerged into a militant politicalization through riots. The paraintellectuals came onto the scene as legitimate and *natural* leaders. Moreover, they advance the politicalization of the black urban masses, after a fashion, by formulating descriptions of black-white relations, past and present, and policies for altering these relations that the Negro lower class finds meaningful. Few of the established elements among the black intelligentsia have, until very recently, had such success." (Martin Kilson, "The New Black Intellectuals," *Dissent* (July-August 1969), p. 307).

"Let's put that theory into practice about riddin' ourselves of that racism." You see, otherwise, otherwise to us, freeing political prisoners would be hypocrisy. That's what it'd be. We want to stand by our brothers, dig? And, I don't know. I'd even like to say something to church people. I think one of the brothers last night said, "Jesus Christ was a bad motherfucker." Man, we all don't want to go that route, understand. He laid back and he said, "Put that fuckin' nail right there, man. That's the people's nail. I'm takin' it." But we've gone beyond it . . . .

The Young Patriots started out as a street gang and gradually developed a political consciousness that led them in the direction of the Panthers. A similar attempt at radicalizing organized labor is being made with the creation of the League of Revolutionary Black Workers, a federation of several Detroit-based workers' groups such as the Dodge Revolutionary Union Movement (DRUM) and its equivalents at Ford (FRUM), Chrysler (CRUM), and elsewhere. The all-black League was started, according to John Watson, one of its founders, "because the working class is already divided between the races, and because it is necessary for black workers to be able to act independently of white workers."

White workers have been encouraged to form radical organizations of their own to work out a common strategy with black union revolutionaries, but progress has been slow. Speaking of such a group at the *Detroit News*, Watson observed, ". . . although a number of the white guys who were down there had risen above the levels of racism and understood the exploitative nature of the company and of the system, they had very little experience in organizing to fight oppression and exploitation." As with the Panthers, these black workers consider themselves to be in the "vanguard of the revolutionary movement," and see most whites still on the fringes of the real struggle.

These "revolutionary" union groups were started to protect black workers who felt they were being treated unfairly and even victimized by racist white union leaders. Also, they believed, together with like-minded white workers, that union chiefs were in collusion with the bosses to speed up work schedules and ignore grievances over intolerable working conditions. The radical union groups are, first of all, self-protective associations for people unprotected or abused by the regular, bureaucratized unions. Secondly, they hope to stimulate a political awareness that will lead to a revolutionary situation in America.

For the time being, however, it is clear that the ghettos are potentially the most explosive places in the country. This is where the Panthers are organized (although they are trying to establish closer contacts with the revolutionary union movements, as well as with student groups) and where they draw their main support. Much of their appeal for ghetto youths (shared by many whites) is their image of a powerful black man with a rifle. In his recent book of essays,[5] Eldridge Cleaver describes his own first encounter with the Panthers at a meeting in the Fillmore district ghetto of San Francisco: "I spun round in my seat and saw the most beautiful sight I had ever seen: four black men wearing black berets, powder blue shirts, black leather jackets, black trousers, shiny black shoes—and each with a gun!"

Since then Cleaver has learned that there is more to being a Panther than carrying a gun. But the image of power and violence is still the basic one created by the Pan-

[5] *Eldridge Cleaver* (New York: Random House), 211 pp., $5.95.

thers. When ghetto youths learn that party membership is not like joining a street gang but more like taking religious vows, many of them become disillusioned and turn away from the Panthers. They are put off by the strict discipline,[6] the political indoctrination, the discouragement of racism, and such community service projects as the Panther program to provide free breakfast to ghetto children. The Panthers have had to purge people who turned out to be basically criminals or racists unable to relate to the party's political and intellectual program.

Unlike many of the ghetto youth, who want action, retribution, and loot, young black idealists are drawn to the Panthers' philosophy of social justice and equality through power. Where there have been spontaneous black riots, such as those following the assassination of Martin Luther King, the Panthers have tried to cool it, to discourage violence that could lead only to further repression without any political gains. Unfortunately the political leadership in most cities is too dense to realize that the Panthers are actually a force for stability in the ghettos. An intelligent white ruling class would encourage the Panthers rather than try to destroy them; that it has failed to understand this does indeed argue for its own inherent instability.

Lately the Panthers have been emphasizing programs directly related to the needs of the ghetto community, such as free breakfasts and health clinics. This summer they have also been setting up black "liberation schools," where children between two and sixteen are taught some things about American history, economics, and politics that they never learn in the public schools. Clearly much of this is indoctrination, although the Panthers claim that they are correcting the distorted image that black children receive of themselves and their society.

White middle-class revolutionaries tend to patronize such activities as reformist. But the breakfasts, the schools, and the clinics have won the Panthers support within the ghetto that they never could have gained by guns alone or by Marxist-Leninist analyses of the internal contradictions of capitalism. In Oakland, where the party has existed for nearly three years, it is an important element of the black community, respected even though it is not often fully understood. Just as the police have been forced to respect the power of the Panthers, so the white power elite has had to deal with an organized, politically conscious force within the black community. Throughout much of the Bay area, where the Panthers are particularly well organized, they are an articulate, alert defender of black people's interests. The Panthers are there when the community needs them, and they are there when no one else seems to be listening.

An example that comes to mind, simply

[6] There are twenty-six rules of discipline that all members must follow, of which the first is "no party member can have narcotics or weed in his possession while doing party work." In addition, there are eight "points of attention":
1. Speak politely.
2. Pay fairly for what you buy.
3. Return everything you borrow.
4. Pay for anything you damage.
5. Do not hit or swear at people.
6. Do not damage property or crops of the poor, oppressed masses.
7. Do not take liberties with women.
8. If we ever have to take captives, do not ill-treat them.

because it occurred while I was in San Francisco, concerned a sixteen-year-old boy who was shot in the back by a member of San Francisco's Tactical Squad while he was fleeing the scene of an alleged auto theft. The shooting occurred near his home and was heard by his mother, a practical nurse, who was thrown to the ground by the police when she ran to his side screaming, "Don't shoot my boy again." The wounded boy was thrown into a police truck and nearly an hour elapsed before he actually reached the hospital. It is the sort of thing that happens every day in Hunter's Point and a hundred other black ghettos around America. The only difference is that, miraculously, the bullet was deflected by a rib bone and the boy was not killed, and that the Panthers brought it to the attention of the public by calling a press conference which Bobby Seale, David Hilliard, and Masai, the party's three top leaders, attended.

At the conference were a few representatives of the local press (the television stations were invited but refrained from sending anyone), myself, a few Panthers, their lawyer, Charles Garry, the boy, Jimmie Conner, and his parents. The boy, soft-spoken and composed, spoke of the incident as though it were a normal part of life, and when asked why he ran away, replied, with the tedium of one explaining the obvious, "Why did I run? Because I'm scared of police." With him sat his parents, an attractive, quiet woman in her mid-thirties and a handsome, somewhat stocky, graying man who works in aircraft maintenance. Both very light-skinned, eminently respectable, and both bitter and confused about what had happened to them.

Had they been white, their son would have been reprimanded, or at most taken to court. But they are black and their son was almost killed, as other boys have been killed in Hunter's Point and elsewhere for even lesser crimes—if indeed Jimmie Conner was guilty of a crime. When asked about the incident, Mrs. Conner replied, "Just another Negro gone, that's the way we believe that they think about the kids up here. Too many of our kids are dying for nothing. They see police three blocks away and they start running because they're scared. I'm gonna fight them. If I have to go to jail, OK. If I have to work for the rest of my life, I will. If they shoot me that's fine. I'm gonna fight, this has got to stop." The story so far has included the radicalization of Mrs. Ozella Conner, housewife, mother, nurse, and now friend of the Black Panthers.

How did the Panthers get involved in this incident, although none of the Conners is a member of the party? Because a doctor at the hospital where Jimmie was taken was so shocked at his treatment by the police that he called Charles Garry, who in turn called Bobby Seale. What followed was a press conference, followed by a lawsuit under the 1964 Civil Rights Act, followed by press coverage—which of course could never have occurred had the Panthers not been called in.

The cynical would say that the Panthers have something to gain from this publicity, which indeed they have. But that is to miss the point, which is that by such actions they are establishing themselves, in the eyes of the black community, as the defenders of the black man too humble to interest anyone else. They can sink their roots in the black community and win its allegiance partly because no one else is fulfilling that role. This is one of the things that the Panthers mean by "educating" the people, informing them of their rights and making them activist defenders rather than passive victims. This education is carried on through meetings, discussions, leaflets, and the party newspaper. While their tactics have shifted several times since the formation of the party in October 1966, their objectives remain the ones set out in their ten-point program of black liberation.[7]

Looking at this program and talking to the Panthers, as well as reading their newspaper, *The Black Panther* (which everyone interested enough to read this essay ought to do in order to gain, if nothing else, an idea of the atrocities that are going on under the name of law and order), make one realize that the "revolution" they talk about is not necessarily the cataclysmic upheaval that sends the white middle class into spasms. Rather, it is the achievement of constitutional guarantees and economic justice for black people. These gun-carrying, Mao-quoting revolutionaries want what most middle-class Americans take for granted. As Huey Newton has said, if reformist politicians like the Kennedys and Lindsay could solve the problems of housing, employment, and justice for blacks and other Americans at the bottom of the social heap, there would be no need for a revolution. And, it goes without saying, little support for such groups as the Black Panther Party.

The Panthers have a voice in the black community (although not necessarily so large as many whites imagine) because they offer hope for change to ghetto people whom the civil-rights movement and the poverty program bureaucrats have been unable to touch. They walk proudly through the streets of Oakland in their black leather jackets, and they hold mass rallies for the liberation of Huey Newton in the shadow of the Alameda County Court House where he was sentenced. They speak to the black man's image of himself. They tell him that he is no longer powerless against the forces that oppress him, and that his struggle for freedom is part of a worldwide liberation movement. In this sense they fulfill a real psychological need.

While they have not yet shed white blood, except in self-defense, does this mean that they never will, that their talk of guerrilla warfare is simply rhetoric? It would be rash to say so, for the Panthers have declared that they are ready to kill anyone who stands in the way of "black liberation." And they are convinced that racism in this society is so pervasive and deeply rooted that there can be no freedom for black people until it is extirpated

[7] 1. We want freedom. We want power to determine the destiny of our Black Community.

2. We want full employment for our people.

3. We want an end to the robbery by the CAPITALIST of our Black Community. [N.B. Recently changed to "capitalist" from "white man."]

4. We want decent housing, fit for shelter of human beings.

5. We want education for our people that exposes the true nature of this decadent American society. We want education that teaches us our true history and our role in the present-day society.

6. We want all black men to be exempt from military service.

7. We want an immediate end to POLICE BRUTALITY and MURDER of black people.

8. We want freedom for all black men held in federal, state, county, and city prisons and jails.

9. We want all black people when brought to trial to be tried in court by a jury of their peer group or people from their black communities, as defined by the Constitution of the United States.

10. We want land, bread, housing, education, clothing, justice, and peace. And as our major political objective, a United Nations-supervised plebiscite to be held throughout the black colony in which only black colonial subjects will be allowed to participate, for the purpose of determining the will of black people as to their national destiny. [Followed by an explanatory paragraph taken from the U.S. Constitution: "When in the course of human events...."]

by some form of revolution. Even Gene Marine, who, in his highly informative book, *The Black Panthers,*[8] freely admits his admiration for the Panthers, confesses, "I am frightened by them." Like some of the white revolutionaries who emulate them, the Panthers seem to have over-learned *The Battle of Algiers,* and have tried to apply its lesson to a society where the situation is totally different. The United States today is not Algeria of 1954, nor Cuba of 1958, nor even France of 1968. It is a deeply troubled, but nonetheless largely stable society which is capable of putting down an insurrection ruthlessly and quickly.

Don't the Panthers realize this? They seem to, at the present moment anyway. This is why they are serving free breakfasts to ghetto children; attempting to form alliances with white radicals, liberals, workers, and pacifists; and urging people to sign petitions for the decentralization of the police. They may be going through a temporary stage, but the direction in which they are heading is clearly marked reformism. Right now they seem interested in maximum publicity, which is why they hold meetings and press conferences, and complain about the way the mass media ignores or distorts their actions. Some of their sympathizers fear that the Panthers are pushing themselves too much in the public eye, and that this only aids the enemies who are trying to destroy them. But since the police and politicians are out to get the Panthers in any case, perhaps such an effort to convince the public that they are not really monsters is their only chance for survival.

It is curious, to say the least, that the federal government has decided to come down hard on the Panthers at the very time that they are emphasizing ballots and petitions, community self-help, and political alliances, rather than shootouts. The severe harassment and repression they are now suffering may, if anything, improve the Panthers' appeal among the black bourgeoisie and white liberals. It would be one of the ironies of our irrational political life if John Mitchell and J. Edgar Hoover, together with the so-called "liberal" mayors of cities like San Francisco and Chicago, succeeded in giving the Panthers a new vitality just at the time when the party seemed in difficulty.

Mention of the word "revolution" is enough to send most politicians and police officers into a rage. Like radicals in general, the Panthers naturally talk a good deal about revolution, and use such other catchwords as fascism, imperialism, and the dictatorship of the proletariat. They connect racism with the evils of capitalism, and quote freely from the sacred texts of Marx, Lenin, and Mao. Walk into any Panther office and you are likely to find not only Little Red Books lying about, but the officer of the day with his nose buried in the works of Mao, or one of Lenin's many pamphlets. Slogans, often vague and even meaningless in the context in which they are used, become part of the revolutionary vocabulary. This is true not only of the Panthers, who use such slogans to reach an audience with little formal education, but of young radicals generally. The deliberate inflation and distortion of language is a disease of the left.

The Panthers, however, realize that racism is deeply embedded in the cultural history of Europe and America and is not, as certain Marxists still argue, simply a by-product of class society. As Huey Newton has said, "Until you get rid of racism . . . no matter what kind of economic system you have, black people will still be oppressed." What revolution seems to mean for the

[8] Signet, 1969, 224 pp., $.95 (paper).

Panthers is the transformation of the ghetto and the "liberation" of black people, and of all oppressed people, from lives of poverty, degradation, and despair. The steps by which this will take place are not specified precisely, but they need not be violent ones unless every other road to radical change is closed. Having defined the problem, the Panthers now ask white America what kind of solution it proposes. So far as the Panthers are concerned, the answer has been harassment, repression, and even murder.

The Panthers are not racist, but they refuse to take any instructions from their white sympathizers. Indeed, this may be what makes it possible for them to be antiracist. Commenting on the antiwhite sentiment in SNCC before it became an all-black organization, Huey Newton recently said, "We have never been controlled by whites, and therefore we don't fear the white mother-country radicals." Their willingness to work with allied white radicals is not shared by most black militant groups. When Stokely Carmichael recently left the Panthers, his stormy letter of departure[9] centered on just this issue.

As the Carmichael-Cleaver exchange indicated, the black militants are just as fragmented into feuding factions as are the whites. Their rivalry, however, is a good deal more violent, and the struggle between the Panthers and the "cultural nationalist" U.S. group of Ron Karenga led to the murder of two Panthers in Los Angeles last year. The Panthers are serious about wanting to carry on programs of education, and in spite of the terrible repression they are now facing have an enduring faith in the democratic system of petitions and ballots— far more than do the young white radicals. But like most revolutionaries, they are highly authoritarian and want loyal and unquestioning followers (as Stokely Carmichael rightly pointed out in his letter) rather than critical colleagues.

Unlike the white revolutionaries, however, the Panthers do have some fairly clear ideas of what they want—even though they are uncertain about the best way to get it. Whatever their shortcomings, they did not seem to me self-indulgent, romantic, or part-time players at revolution. They are in this struggle for keeps. Anyone who is a Panther today, or who contemplates join-

[9] In spite of his official title of Prime Minister, Stokely Carmichael was not much more than a figurehead in the party. From his self-chosen exile in Guinea, he sent an open letter to the party, distributed by his wife at Kennedy airport to the press, in which he declared:

"The alliances being formed by the party are alliances which I cannot politically agree with, because the history of Africans living in the U.S. has shown that any premature alliance with white radicals has led to complete subversion of blacks by the whites through their direct or indirect control of the black organization."

He also criticized the "present tactics and methods which the party is using to coerce and force everyone to submit to its authority," and declared that unless the Panthers change their political direction they "will at best become a reformist party and at worst a tool of racist imperialists used against the black masses."

To this denunciation Eldridge Cleaver, Minister of Information in enforced exile, replied in the pages of *Ramparts*:

"That you know nothing about the revolutionary process is clear, that you know less about the United States and its people is clearer, and that you know even less about humanity than you do about the rest is clearest of all.... You should know that suffering is color blind and that the victims of imperialism, racism, colonialism, and neocolonialism come in all colors and that they need unity based on revolutionary principles rather than skin color."

ing the party, knows that there is a good chance that he will be jailed or die a violent death. Panthers have already been murdered by the police, many have been beaten and wounded, and others are almost certain to be killed in the months and years ahead. It takes courage to join the party, to submit to its discipline, and to face the likely prospect of imprisonment or death. But for some there is no other way. As Eldridge Cleaver has written, "A slave who dies of natural causes will not balance two dead flies on the scale of eternity."

The Panthers have come a long way since Huey Newton and Bobby Seale first formed the party three years ago in Oakland. It has spread across the nation and has eclipsed such groups as SNCC and CORE to become the most powerful black militant organization in America. This rapid expansion has created problems—not only increasing police harassment and repression as the Panthers became more influential within the black community, but also the difficulty of maintaining the high standard of membership that its leaders would like. Not all Panthers have the organizing ability of Bobby Seale or the analytical minds of David Hilliard, Eldridge Cleaver, and Huey Newton. Which is to say that the Panthers are not superhuman, as some white radicals would like to believe, any more than they are devils.

Beneath an inflammatory vocabulary of ghetto hyperbole and a good deal of facile Marxist sloganizing, the Panthers seemed to me serious, hard-working, disciplined, and essentially humanistic in their work within the black community and in their vision of a more just society. For the Panthers, weapons are an instrument of self-protection, and ultimately the means to achieve the revolution that, in the absence of a peaceful alternative, will make liberation possible. For some of the white militants I spoke to around Berkeley, however, it seemed that revolution is the means, and

denouncing or shooting up the "fascists" (who seem to include just about everyone who disagrees on tactics or strategy, and many readers of this magazine) is conceived as the end. Since Chicago, and particularly since the brutal suppression by the police during the battle of People's Park, some West Coast militants seem to have become traumatized by violence, convinced there is no other way to carry on radical politics.

But Che's prescription is no more relevant in the tree-lined streets of Berkeley or Cambridge than it was in the mountains of Bolivia. The Panthers are prepared for guerrilla warfare, as a last-ditch stand, because they think they may have no other alternative. There are white revolutionaries, on the West Coast and elsewhere, who, in the impatience of their rage and their inability seriously to change a society whose policies they find oppressive, accept this prescription uncritically, and, in view of the forces marshalled against them on the right, with a half-conscious quest for martyrdom. As its frustration increases, the new left becomes more shrill in its rhetoric and dogmatic in its politics. Instead of focusing on the most blatant inequalities and injustices of American life, it is assaulting the periphery. Instead of trying to educate the people to inequities of the social-economic system and the cost of maintaining an empire, it has successfully alienated the working class—without whose support no radical change, let alone "revolution," is possible.

In its resistance to the draft, the war, and racism, the radical left has aroused parts of the nation. More people now realize there is something seriously wrong with American society but are not certain how to deal with it. Many are frightened and attribute all unrest to a conspiracy of "trouble-makers." Others know that change must come, but would like it to be as unobtrusive as possible. It remains to be seen how many can be reached, whether it be on the plane of morality or self-interest, and

convinced that change need not be personally threatening to them. To do this
radicals must have plausible ideas on how
a transformed society would produce a better existence for the mass of people. It does
little good for the radical left to dismiss
everyone who disagrees as "fascist," for
these are a majority, and if they are treated
as fascists long enough, they may begin behaving in such a way as to make the current
repression seem like libertarianism in comparison.

America is not now a "fascist" country,
nor is it likely seen to become one, although
this is not impossible. Probably it will continue to be an advanced capitalist society
in which cruel inequalities and repression,
unlivable cities, and inhuman conditions of
work continue to exist along with consider-

able liberty to take political action, while
our rulers control an empire of poor nations abroad. It is the duty of the left to
find ways to change this system: to educate
people rather than simply abuse them; to
understand what is happening in the factories and farms and lower-middle-class
neighborhoods and be in touch with the
people in them; to use the universities as
places where the complex problems of replacing repressive capitalism and imperialism with a better system can be studied
seriously; to stop playing Minutemen and
begin acting like radicals. If there is ever
going to be a revolution in this country,
it will have to happen first in people's
heads. What takes place in the streets of a
society like this one has another name. It
is called repression.

THE EFFECTS OF STUDENT ACTIVISM
IN INDUSTRIALIZED COUNTRIES

Some Comparative Reflections on France and the United States

A. Belden Fields

*La jeunesse n'a pas toujours raison. Mais la société qui la frappe a
toujours tort.—François Mitterand[1]*

INTRODUCTION

When I first agreed to present this paper
I was convinced that it would be almost
impossible to talk intelligently about the

effects of student activism without discussing its causes and the nature or characteristics of the activism. I still think that this
is true but, in the interest of time and
space allotments, compromises have to be

*Reprinted by permission of the author and the American Political Science Associa-
tion; an earlier version of this essay was presented as a paper at the Sixty-sixth
Annual Meeting of the American Political Science Association (September 1970);
copyright © 1971, A. Belden Fields.*

[1] Cited in Alain Ayache (ed.), *Les Citations de la Révolution de Mai* (Paris: Jean-Jacques
Pauvert, 1968), p. 32.

made. Still I am very bothered by the unsystematic picking and choosing of variables to explain student activism and by some of the polemics which have issued out of the pens of social scientists with the main intent of proving how evil and dangerous the most active individuals really are. In both France and the United States there is a complex cluster of variables which are mutually reinforcing. While they can be dealt with intellectually in isolation, none of them suffices alone as a total explanation of behavior. Moreover, the nature and situational contexts of activism vary on some very important dimensions. The limitations imposed upon this presentation did not permit me to deal with these questions in the systematic way that I would have liked to.

This is particularly disquieting to me because, as I am sure the reader will detect, I am convinced that the material with which we are dealing involves the most important social and political phenomena facing us today. While this paper is an attempt at accurate social analysis, the writer is not dispassionate about the conclusions and would regard it as a great tragedy if the audience remained dispassionate. Critical, the more the better. But dispassionate, no. The stakes are too high.

In the long run I am optimistic as to the effects of student activism. I find hope in aspects of what I refer to as the "counter-culture" of American youth. In the short term I fear for that youth and for all of us who share its humanitarian concerns. If our political system and leaders are capable of positive responses to those concerns, then they had better offer some demonstrative proof very soon.

I will be discussing two kinds of effects. First, there is the question of effects upon specific policy outputs and/or the personnel responsible for making decisions. While in the United States we must differentiate between university policy and personnel and general governmental policy and personnel, in France basic education policy had been determined by the government in Paris until 1968. This pattern provided one target for positive demands and negative expressions of disapproval on both educational questions and general political issues.

Second, there is the question of more basic systemic change. By more basic systemic change is meant fundamental changes in social relationships which involve redistribution of rights, power, or resources. Basic change can be either immediate (corresponding to the traditional use of the term "revolution") or longer term. My intention here is to suggest succinctly certain characteristics of the situation as indicators of future basic change. The admittedly important question of strategies by which students might become a conscious and coordinated force to affect the tempo and direction of such change is not dealt with in this essay.

EFFECTS ON SYSTEM OUTPUTS AND PERSONNEL

A number of attributes attached to the status of student work against students exercising power in industrialized societies the way some of the more successful categories of people do. Stated a little differently, students are deprived of the kind of resource base which has been translated into power by these groups.

First, there is the short duration of the student status in the life of any given individual. This creates difficulties when students attempt to organize. There are rapid shifts in leaders, constituencies, attitudes, and policies. Not only are decision-makers kept off-guard (this may be an asset) but so are potential or real allies.

Second, students tend to be unfamiliar with the exercise of political skills. Engagement in politics as a student is often the first engagement in politics and there is considerably less time for in-group training than there is among many other categories.

Third, students generally lack financial and material resources that other groups have. Students are often dependent upon parents, the government, universities, or poorly paying part-time or summer jobs for their money. When students do engage in large-scale organization or campaigns that involve high financial costs, they run the risk of losing independence to their benefactors.

Fourth, a good proportion of the student population does not enjoy full civil rights. France, like most industrialized countries, permits only those who have reached their twenty-first year to vote. This situation changed last year in Britain when the voting age was reduced to eighteen. This year eighteen-year-olds were given the right to vote in national elections in the United States and a constitutional amendment which would extend this to all elections is in the ratification process.[2] Thus, while the situation may be remedied in the United States, in both France and the United States students have been able to pose an electoral threat only indirectly through publicity campaigns aimed at the general voting population. They have no voting block of their own to speak of.

Fifth, students lack informal channels of access to decision-makers based upon friendship ties, socioeconomic similarity, or lateral shifts in institutional affiliations—e.g., between government, business, and the military.

Sixth, in industrial societies, students do not hold the same strategic position which some other groups enjoy in terms of being able to have an immediate and direct impact upon the political or economic life of a country. The withholding of services by labor, business, or the military is much more immediately felt than is a student strike.

It is this problem of a weak resource base in comparison with other categories which have exerted power that gives the phrase "student as a nigger" some measure of truth. And just as in the case of other minorities which must contend with a weak resource base, one variable of extreme importance is the degree to which decision-makers are predisposed to act in accordance with student demands despite this weak resource base. A positive attitude toward students can be the result of a favorable image which the decision-makers themselves have of students or the perception on the part of the decision-makers that the students enjoy a favorable image and widespread support within the body politic and that acquiescing to or anticipating student sentiments and demands is politically expedient or at least acceptable.

France, during the Fourth Republic, provides us with a case of students exerting considerable political influence because of indulgent attitudes among both the general public and government decision-makers. In both sectors there existed a veritable cult of youth. Youth was viewed as something important because the future of French culture and civilization was in its hands.

In more concrete terms, the subsidy which had first been granted to the national student union (UNEF) as an organization of public service during the Third Republic was continued throughout the Fourth Republic. UNEF enjoyed very good relations with the Education Committee of the Chamber of Deputies and generally enjoyed good relations with the Ministry of

---

[2] Even if the constitutional amendment should pass, the question of where students will be permitted to vote is a crucial one. Local registrars in my community are in the habit of refusing students the right to register even if they are twenty-one on the grounds that they should register where their parents vote—even if they never reside with their parents! They do not want "outsiders" upsetting the local conservative political apple cart. And an Illinois state legislator has introduced a one-sentence bill that would deny students the right to vote in a university area unless they resided there before attending the university.

Education. The students obtained a student insurance program which was administered by students themselves and very important representation on the body which controlled student services. That students should have these services and should bear responsibility for decision-making and administration was viewed as perfectly appropriate by both political leaders and the general population.[3]

The situation changed with the fall of the Fourth Republic and the coming to power of the Gaullists. Even before UNEF took a stand against the Algerian War, there was conflict with the Gaullist regime. But once the organization did decide to take a position on the war in 1960, UNEF felt the full fury of the government. The subsidy was suspended and punitive measures were attempted against at least one of the national leaders. Nevertheless, the organization continued to demonstrate against the war and to spur other labor and teachers' unions to come together in syndical solidarity against it. The students were both the catalysts and the vanguard of the antiwar movement. And while other factors undoubtedly came into play—i.e., de Gaulle's conviction that the French could not win, his conviction that a settlement which would permit good relations in the future was the optimal policy, and problems with army discipline and the OAS (particularly after the 1961 attempted coup) —there is little doubt that the tension which the students were creating in metropolitan France and the clashes between demonstrators and police and the right and left played an important role in the government's decision to give up the ghost and stop the war in 1962.

Until 1968, however, this was the one positive victory to which the students could at least make partial claim during the Fifth Republic. While the general image of the students among the population at large remained favorable, the Gaullists continued a hard line after the war. This experience revealed how important a resource the positive attitude of decision-makers during the Fourth Republic had been. The students were thrown completely on the defensive. UNEF's subsidy was restored for a brief period and then canceled again; its access to decision-makers was terminated; student representation on the body determining policy regarding student benefits was drastically reduced; and students were physically beaten off the streets when they attempted to publicly demonstrate their grievances. The government simply continued to make and enforce policies, like the Fouchet university reforms, which were generally repugnant to the students.

As an observer of all this it was very difficult to see what UNEF or any other student organization could do to reassert its influence on the policy process. At the same time one had the feeling that the government was taking prerogatives which certainly reflected its ability to make decisions and have them stick in the short term but which also might involve serious costs for the regime sometime in the future. Bitterness and alienation from the regime ran deep and wide within the student milieu. And this was more important than the more visible indices of the proliferation of anti-regimist organizations and the ideological fragmentation.

Even so, what could the students do? We had hypothesized before the 1968 revolt that when faced with a resistant set of governmental decision-makers there are three conditions which must be met before students can emerge victorious: (1) they must be prepared to engage in revolutionary activity or convince the decision-makers that they are; (2) there must be a high degree of political instability; and (3) they must

---

[3] See my book, *Student Politics in France: A Study of the Union Nationale des Etudiants de France* (New York: Basic Books, 1970), especially Chapter III.

enjoy the support of powerful nonstudent forces.[4]

These conditions were particularly inspired by the cases of the overthrow of the Rhee regime in South Korea and the Sukarno regime in Indonesia. But the 1968 revolt in France taught us how slight a hold we have on problems of stability and instability in industrialized countries.

Some have contended that the student revolt was worse than a failure for the students, that it backfired. Professor Lipset has written: "In France, the student revolt has had one obvious political consequence; it has given France its first majority party government in history, one which is right wing."[5] This argument, I maintain, is misleading. First, while it is of statistical interest that the Gaullists won a majority in the National Assembly, power relationships were not really changed. The Gaullists were perfectly capable of accomplishing everything in the previous Assembly that they were with their absolute majority.

Second, the revolt did indeed result in important victories for the students, victories which they were unsuccessful in obtaining before the particular set of events that occurred in 1968. The Fouchet reforms were scrapped and reforms that were more acceptable to the students were substituted. These involved decentralization of the university system and the provision for considerable student representation on university governing bodies. This was indeed a very radical shift in policy. There was also the immediate removal of those cabinet members who had been primarily responsible for the Gaullist hard-line policy: Peyrefitte, Fouchet, and Joxe. Another key hard-liner, Debré, was removed from responsibility in domestic policy by being transferred to the Ministry of Foreign Affairs. Amnesty was granted to students who

had been involved in clashes with the police in May. And, almost one year after the revolt itself, the man whom many claimed that the student revolt had ensured unlimited tenure as President of France, General de Gaulle himself, fell from power. And, as we have previously indicated, while some maintain that de Gaulle needlessly put himself in a precarious position over the referendum, the facts are that he did do it and that his decision to do it and the French electorate's loss of faith in him were determined by the revolt.

The first important characteristic of the revolt was, thus, that it brought about important successes in terms of system outputs and personnel. There are two other characteristics of extreme significance. First, the students did indeed pose a threat to the very existence of a political regime in an industrialized country. They themselves created a condition of political instability by their own activity which touched off an imitative response on the part of the workers. They injected a stimulus which rendered the government incapable of performing almost all of its functions. The productive and distributive processes of the country were simply brought to a halt. By posing a credible threat to the existence of the political system, they rendered the costs of a continuation of alienating policies excessive to decision-makers.

Second, the revolt was spontaneous. The dynamism unleashed in 1968 was severe alienation transformed into human energy and activity by action on the part of decision-makers which pushed people beyond the brink. It could not have been channeled through organizations. Indeed, the revolt was the result of the failure of organizational activity to achieve anything at all. This was a "movement" of alienated, frustrated, and angry people.

[4] *Ibid.*
[5] Seymour Martin Lipset, "The Possible Effects of Student Activism on International Politics" in Seymour Martin Lipset and Philip G. Altbach (eds.), *Students in Revolt* (Boston: Houghton Mifflin, 1969), p. 515.

This is not to imply that the revolt was entirely negative. While there was no single highly structured ideology that united the participants, they were united around several themes. First, there was the libertarian theme. The revolt was seen as opening up the possibility of a permanent and effective challenge to social institutions which were viewed as being extremely hierarchical and authoritarian. In place of the ubiquitous "forbidden" signs was scribbled, "it is forbidden to forbid." There was the theme of equalitarianism and the hope that the revolt might lead to a system based upon humanitarian and cooperative norms rather than one dominated by egoistic and exploitative social relationships as the present system was viewed. And there was the theme of decentralization and participation which accompanied the widespread disenchantment with representative democracy à la de Gaulle. During the revolt new structures, "action committees" and "occupation committees" were created, first in the universities and then in factories, and even professional institutions. They represented a search for new modes of participation which would maximize the above values. They were admittedly experimental, they were in many cases cumbersome, they were often ill coordinated, and those that exercized effective power did so for a relatively short period. But for many they represented a real advance, a real political education, in what cannot be expected to be a one-shot process of the transformation of institutions.

What can we say about the ability of students to affect system outputs and changes of personnel in the United States? As opposed to pre-1968 France, American students have had to deal with a plurality of decision-makers. American universities themselves are "political" systems within which is wielded a good deal of power. Faculty bodies, administrators, and boards of trustees must be contended with if students are to attain certain goals. State politi-

cal systems exert control over state university budgets, to a greater or lesser extent they may intrude into internal university governance, and they make laws that regulate the behavior of students. And then there is the national government which must be contended with if students want to affect the broader questions of resource allocation, racial injustice, poverty, and Vietnam. In this sense, one would expect a lesser degree of national cohesion and organizational facility than in France where all students had to confront only one set of decision-makers.

We are sorely lacking in systematic studies of the comparative politics of student activism within American universities which focus on the incidence and conditions of success or failure that students have had in extracting concessions from university decision-makers. Until we have such studies, which ought to be treated just as seriously and rigorously as any other work of comparative politics (it is amazing how lightly and carelessly some scholars tread when it comes to the subject of students—something they would not dare to do if dealing with labor, the business community, or other more powerful sectors) , we are all going to be tempted to generalize from our own most immediate experience or from those situations that receive the most publicity. Largely from my own experience at the University of Illinois and from what I have read and heard about several other campuses, I would offer the following tentative generalizations.

First, while there is a greater tendency than in the past to include students on committees, there is very little commitment on the part of most administrators and faculty members to the proposition that students should wield real power and responsibility as existed in France during the Fourth Republic. Indeed, in France public opinion and political figures were far more convinced of the proposition than those immediately involved in the academic community and the students were able to make no headway in strictly academic areas of governance (as opposed to student services and benefits) even during the Fourth Republic. Where students are gaining access to such committees there is generally great care taken to structure the situation so that their power will be minimized. This is done either by making sure that students are a minority on committees or by posing external checks upon the powers of the committees on which they sit. The student perceptions of attempts at "cooptation" tend thus to be quite correct.

Second, there are two mutually reinforcing sources of the fear of student power within the university community. These are traditional prerogative and fear of political radicalism. In terms of traditional prerogative, administrators and faculty members tend to be most sensitive to different challenges. For the administrators, control over expenditures, facilities, and programs is crucial. For the faculty, the most serious challenges are in hiring and retention of faculty members and course content and pedagogy. While students generally have not been permitted to participate formally in the latter matters, they do exercise some power by refusing to take certain professors or courses and by publishing course critiques. In terms of their fear of political radicalism, administrators and faculty members run neck and neck. SDS is the *bête-noire* which is responsible for all their difficulties

with the students. Indeed, some of our most well-known social scientists on university faculties have engaged in the most simplistic of analyses. The comparison of the new left or SDS with the Nazis or Fascists or somehow implicitly making distinctions that permit repressive behavior toward the "hard-core" or "leaders" but not others is too frequent a theme of these presentations.[6]

Third, student governments or their equivalents at most major universities have indeed turned their attention toward general political and social issues as well as the more constricted issues of student participation. This is entirely normal behavior, as we have seen in France, when the general society is being torn asunder by divisive issues. Moreover, it is not a question of choice. It is based on a realistic assessment of the university operating as a control mechanism in conjunction with external political institutions.

Fourth, in some cases outputs and personnel have been affected through the use of disruptive tactics. At Berkeley, the 1964 revolt did indeed result in loosening up restrictions on speech and the ouster of President Kerr. At Columbia, it took a major conflict with the police in 1968 to bring about a division between faculty and administration, the appointment of the Cox Commission, and an open admission that the internal governance of the university was indeed repressive and that that fact

[6] I would include here Professor Edward Shils' article, "Dreams of Plenitude, Nightmares of Scarcity," in Lipset and Altbach's *Students in Revolt, op. cit.*, in which he accuses activists bent on confrontation of contriving all issues other than Vietnam (p. 26) and contends that "the Nazi abuse of the Weimar 'system' " and "the frequent denunciations of the 'system' " by student radicals in France, Germany, and the United States "bespeaks an affirmity of outlook" (note 7, p. 30). I would also include Professor Daniel Bell's article "Columbia and the New Left" in *The Public Interest*, No. 13 (Fall 1968), which is basically a tirade against the SDS. A sample: "The administration above all failed to understand the *dynamics* of the student protest: That whatever reason there may have been for early police action, when the buildings were seized by hard-core SDS members, the subsequent surge of political support on the part of 500 other students—most of them liberal, moderate, pacifist, and not members of SDS—effectively changed the *political* character of the situation. The failure to make the necessary distinctions between these students and SDS, and then to understand that these students were not wreckers but were now trying to express their inchoate grievances against the university, permitted SDS to call the tune..." (p. 95).

might just have had something to do with the university being torn apart. There too, the president of the university, who had been resistant to change, was displaced. But where the French revolt resulted in victories for French students generally, victories won through disruption on American campuses have been restricted to the particular university where the battle was fought. Students at other universities must contend within their own little political systems. And faculties and administrators on other campuses seem all too often to have drawn the conclusion that there wasn't enough control exerted at Berkeley and Columbia.

Fifth, these confrontations can involve costs. To some extent the events at the University of California undoubtedly aided reactionary forces in gaining control of the executive branch of the state. And most, if not all, of the student activists are not Reagan or Rafferty fans. It is all too fashionable, however, to blame the students exclusively for these costs. Administrators and faculty members who resist all efforts at change and who engage in what students feel to be repressive practices, but who also disapprove of what they feel to be the repressiveness of outside political forces, must bear heavy responsibility for bringing this cost upon themselves. Because one's own interests and prerogatives always seem so reasonable and one is always convinced that one is doing good for other people, it is difficult for these administrators and faculty members to see the parallel between repressive external political forces and repressive university governance which is evident to many students.

Sixth, the decline of *in loco parentis* on most large campuses in the United States is due less to the exercise of student power than to the impossibility of enforcement within the huge university environment. However, while surveillance and control over student life in this regard is diminishing, it is frighteningly increasing in the areas of drug usage and political expression and behavior. In these areas, as opposed to the case of *in loco parentis,* university security offices (often staffed by former local law-enforcement officers or by ex-FBI men who belong to the FBI Association) and ever-expanding university police forces (on the campus at which I work we now have a force of seventy officers) work in conjunction with federal and state authorities.

On the general political level, students appear to have had very little positive impact upon policy-making or makers within the state legislatures. Indeed, at the present time we are witnessing an unprecedented vindictiveness directed toward students from state legislatures because of what their members feel is unwarranted disruptive and destructive tactics. At least in Illinois, the legislature has narrowed the prerogatives of administrators in dealing with people who are defined as disruptive or destructive.

At the national level the major issues have been civil rights and racial equality and foreign policy, especially Vietnam. Let us take these issue areas and assess the impact which students have had and might have in the future.

It is often forgotten that accompanying the movement for civil rights for the black population of the South were two other causes of students in the early 1960s, the Fair Play for Cuba movement and the movement against the tactics of the House Un-American Activities Committee (HUAC). That committee was determined to seek out Communists and/or "subversives" and expose them to the public. And it decided that the pickings were especially good within the academic community in the Bay area of California. HUAC's visit to California resulted in demonstrations and confrontations which the committee claimed impeded it from effectively performing its function. And, in order to counterattack, it made the very serious error of making and distributing what was one of the most patently stupid and radicalizing films of all time, "Operation Abolition." Due to the confrontation of the students, and some courageous faculty members it must be acknowledged, what was once an effective group of political witch hunters and intimidators was forced into the open. Through the distribution of the film, particularly on campuses, HUAC made itself look ridiculous. This marked the end of its reign of political terror.

The other major civil-rights battle was fought in the South. This was the combined struggle of the Student Non-Violent Coordinating Committee and white civil-rights workers (the Freedom Riders) from northern campuses for equal political rights for black people in the South. While the Brown versus Board of Education decision had marked the interest of the federal government in equal education in the South, the government did not interject itself seriously into the problem of political rights before the agitation began in 1960. Again, using confrontation tactics of a nonviolent variety, SNCC and the Freedom Riders, along with the Southern Christian Leadership Conference, focused national and worldwide attention on the oppression of the black in the American South. At a cost of life and physical injury to the activists, some gains were made in the form of national legislation covering voting rights and equal accommodations. However, very little was accomplished in terms of a shift in power relationships or resource distribution. And it soon became very clear to the activists that when one thinks in these terms, the problem of racism is not a regional but a national one. The legislative gains thus turned out to be largely symbolic. And despite the continued interest of black and white student activists in racism throughout the American institutional structure, about the only real gain has been in opening up some of the larger universities and colleges more to minority groups than they have

been in the past. Moreover, alliances between black and white student groups have been made very difficult by a shift toward a separatist position on the part of the blacks. The Panthers are an exception but even among the Panthers there is a suspicion that most of the white activists would not be prepared to take up guns when the chips were down as the Panthers are prepared to do. Thus while the theme of racism is still raised in white-student activists circles, action has recently been centered around other issues.

Student interest in the cold war and foreign policy has a postwar history that antedates the Vietnam war. Immediately after the Second World War, in 1947, the United States National Student Association was formed. Up to 80 percent of the yearly budget of this organization was supplied covertly by the Central Intelligence Agency. And a small group of national leaders which changed each year were aware of the source of funds and performed intelligence functions for the Agency at international meetings. In 1950, they cooperated with the Agency in forming the International Student Conference which was to be the American cold-war rival to the communist-dominated International Union of Students. Until the 1960s the student role in international politics was a small group of leaders of NSA serving the CIA and its cold-war efforts either because they were in tune with the efforts or, a little later, because they were under the threat of prosecution under the National Security Act. At the mass level students either were genuinely not interested in international politics or feared the repercussions if they should speak out in a critical manner during the McCarthy period. Such interest as did exist could be channeled through safe enterprises like international relations clubs and mock United Nations meetings. These were characterized by a low intensity of commitment to most issues. The Arab-Israeli conflict was the notable exception.

In 1959 and 1960, the first really critical approach to American foreign policy which involved a commitment to political action was taken by the Fair Play for Cuba groups. They were immediately branded as communists or dupes of the communists. But students were now less intimidated by this kind of attack as would be soon indicated by the confrontation with HUAC. The issue of Cuba was crucial. For some, Kennedy's attacks on the Republicans for permitting communism to exist ninety miles off of our shores in the television debates with Nixon and his Bay of Pigs and missile decisions were convincing proof that the United States was suffering from a cold-war anti-communist mania which transcended parties and personalities. While Kennedy was successful in appealing to many young people who were attracted by his sophisticated and intellectual style, his peace-corps program, and his obvious concern for the race and poverty issues, the Cuban and Vietnamese policies and the development of the general counterinsurgency strategy were crucial steps in the process which was to alienate so many American students from the political system.

The next fateful steps were taken by President Johnson in 1965: the large-scale expansion of the war in Vietnam and the intervention in the Dominican Republic. In the election campaign of 1964 Johnson had differentiated himself from the more aggressive Goldwater and promised that he would not commit American boys to a land war in Asia. And we students (I was a student then) were impressed and if of voting age voted for him. Not only did Johnson expand the war but he did so on the most implausible of pretexts: the so-called Pleiku incident; the so-called Gulf of Tonkin incident; and that lovely pamphlet distributed by the State Department entitled "Aggression from the North." The collective behavioral response to this was the first mass march on Washington to protest the war in April 1965.

Following on the heels of the national antiwar march was the intervention in the Dominican Republic and an attempted justification of this which informed us whose uncles were communists down there by the same publishing house which had brought us "Aggression from the North." It was as if the government was trying to clear things up for those who might have missed the point and viewed Vietnam as an aberration or a mistake. Cuba, Vietnam, and the Dominican Republic were part of a systematic response process of this nation which was to stifle any attempt at social change in a more equalitarian direction wherever it thought it could get away with it.

From 1965 to the present, Vietnam has been the major area of concern for student activists. And a number of tactics have been attempted. There was the "teach-in," the effect of which was confined within academic communities. National and local demonstrations were continued and the largest demonstrations in the history of the nation assembled. The electoral process was attempted in the form of the McCarthy primary races and the electoral races of other peace candidates. The rates of draft resistance and desertion from the armed forces swelled. ROTC, military and industrial recruiters with defense contracts, and university relations with the Defense Department were challenged. And lately industrial, commercial, financial, and military establishments which are being blamed for American policies have been the subject of bombing attacks numbering in the thousands per year.[7]

In 1968 the antiwar movement was having an important effect upon public opinion. Immediately after the polls reported a new low in confidence in Johnson's han-

[7] On the rate of bombing in New York City (368 from January 1969 through May 1970), see the *New York Times* (July 17, 1970), p. 1.

dling of the war, the President announced that he would not serve another term. He admitted that it would take someone else to bring any unity to the people. Of the four major contenders for the Democratic nomination—McCarthy, Kennedy, Humphrey, and McGovern—three were peace candidates. And before the assassination of Kennedy it looked as though the nomination might be decided in negotiations or combat between the Kennedy and McCarthy forces. But Kennedy was assassinated and the Democratic Party decided to commit suicide both inside and outside its convention hall.

Both Nixon and Humphrey felt the necessity to run on a program that called for withdrawal from Vietnam. Nixon claimed to have a plan which he could not reveal and, in retrospect, he could not have revealed it. The Nixon strategy has been twofold. Attempt to defuse the peace movement by announcing a policy of phased withdrawal, by introducing a draft lottery and the intention to go to a completely voluntary army, by announcing that there will be no more Vietnams, and by getting people interested in other issues like pollution. The other aspect to the strategy has been the attempt to suppress and intimidate those who persist in the peace movement through activities of the FBI, military intelligence, and prosecution in the courts. The performance of the intimidation function (we should add that to Almond's list) has been shifted from the legislature and HUAC to the executive.

Despite the downfall of President Johnson and the Democratic Party and the promises of Nixon to end the war and the draft and not to engage in more Vietnams, the war did in fact continue. The aim of the peace movement became total and immediate withdrawal without gimmicks like "Vietnamization." There was an attempt to exert further pressure by reviving the technique of the national demonstration and combining it with a cessation of normal activity. This took the form of the several

"Moratoria" held during the academic year 1969–1970. By the spring of 1970, the National Mobilization Committee found that it was impossible to maintain the momentum of the October moratorium in the face of no visible impact on policy and went out of business, ostensibly to work at the grass roots. With the exception of a minority of the most alienated who were willing to take large personal risks and a minority of the most tenacious who were willing to continue antiwar publicity campaigns and work within the system, the antiwar movement was demoralized. There was a brief mass transfer of energy and activity over to the pollution issue. After all, the government seemed to be on the side of the angels here and one could even get in a few licks at big business. And maybe one could forget the war.

In reality few were kidding themselves. The frustration over the war issue had been accumulated to a point where the transfer would not work. The attitude toward the war and the government within the student milieu was similar to the hostility which the Gaullists had managed to generate against themselves in France. And having observed the ravaged state in which the Algerian War had left France and the Gaullists continued to push people to the brink, it was incredible to watch the Nixon Administration, which talked withdrawal, the end of the draft, and deescalation of the conflict at home out of one side of its mouth, feed the alienation by taking the offensive against the dissidents. In many instances even the language used by the Vice-President, the Attorney General, and the President himself was the very same as that used by French hard-liners. While I had been convinced for some time that the Vice-President's speech writers had been going over old French texts, the expressions "carnival in the streets," an echo of President de Gaulle's characterization of the French student revolt two years previously, and "effete intellectual snobs," reminiscent of Minister of Algerian Affairs Lacoste's "exhibitionists of the heart and mind" remark made during the Algerian War in a speech to a group of war veterans, did at least raise the possibility of an international conspiracy.

In good Gaullist tradition, the Nixon Administration not only fed the alienation by pursuing the obnoxious policies and by taking the offensive against the antiwar movement but, in ordering the Cambodian invasion, also provided a catalyst which set off an explosion of spontaneous responsive activity.

The Gaullists and the French students have provided us with an example of political behavior and outcomes when decision-makers pursue policies which highly alienate the student population. Up to this point in time, the behavior of the decision-makers and the behavior of the students in the United States bear such a similarity to France between the end of the Algerian War and the 1968 revolt that we may well have a model which can be generalized to such conflict when it arises in industrialized societies. We may also be able to extend the model to cover other groups deprived of resource bases within these societies.

The model takes the form of a scenario in which time and memory play key roles. The starting point is policies which violate the formal values of the society. Students view them as immoral and refuse to rationalize them. Although UNEF had been politically active since its inception and had shifted its concern after World War II from exclusive attention to educational issues (1945–46) to both educational and general issues (1946–50) and back again to exclusive concern with educational issues (1950–56), in both France and the United States the policies which began the process of alienation did not have to do with education. They were "environmental," the Algerian War in France and civil rights and the Vietnam War in the United States. In both cases, however, the initial response of the students was to work through organizations to influence these specific policies and to conduct political education both within and without the student milieu. There is great similarity in the relative moderation of UNEF throughout the Algerian War (the war ended two years after UNEF took a position) and in the early positions of SNCC, SDS, and the *ad hoc* committees on Vietnam. This is what I refer to as the "apple pie" stage.

The government resists the demands for change. The students do not possess the resources to compel change or even to open up direct channels of access to decision-makers. In the absence of such resources students turn to direct-action techniques, such as peaceful demonstrations, in order to demonstrate the intensity of their feeling to the government and to public opinion. They attempt to include nonstudent allies in these demonstrations of sentiment.

The government has a low degree of tolerance for such public demonstrations. It uses bans, unacceptable restrictions, violence, threats, and actual prosecutions to discourage such behavior. The students persist. Some might even attempt to fight back in the streets but, because of the disparity of resources, the students lose there also. And the government attempts to place the blame upon the students for whatever violence occurs.

Disaffection from the government transcends the original issue or issues. There develops a general antiregimist sentiment which spreads to a much larger group than the activists. In fact, as the antiregimism spreads it is accompanied by a sentiment of powerlessness and frustration. Activist groups diminish in size and fragment according to narrow ideological interpretations. This is a stage of sectarianism.

A small minority forms activist guerrilla groups. While the groups might engage in open confrontation initially, as in The Weathermen's 1968 Days of Rage, in short order they are forced underground.[8] Some participants see this activity as literally the vanguard of a coming revolution. Others view it as the only possible hope for effective disruption. Some see it as the only way to take a stand on the moral issue regardless of the probable effect on the system. Most of those involved in activism at an earlier stage, however, doubt the feasibility of such activity and are unwilling to engage in activities for which serious criminal penalties might be incurred.

At some point, however, the government overestimates its power and pushes too far. It supplies a catalyst which the student population regards as so outrageous that the normal incentive system upon which the government relies for control is rendered ineffective. The underlying discontent and alienation blow up in spontaneous action.

The spontaneous action may or may not pose a real and immediate threat to the existence of the regime. The key variables will be how far the students are willing to go in terms of running risks (a function of the spread and depth of the alienation and the degree to which the catalyst is viewed as "outrageous") and how the explosion is responded to by decision-makers, other groups in the society, and public opinion.

In France, the attitude of the hard-liners during the early stages of the revolt was rejection of all demands and the ordering of police charges. On the night of May 10–11, the "Night of the Barricades," the students broke with the normal incentive system. They did not flee from the barricades. They stood their ground and fought a night-long pitched battle with the police and paramilitary CRS.[9]

Public opinion, which had been favorable to the demands of the students in the area of education before the revolt, reacted with indignation against the behavior of the government and police. The students had the continuing support of the largest teachers' union and the small *Parti Socialiste Unifié*. On May 13, all of the major labor unions protested the action of the government by calling a twenty-four-hour strike and by participating in a march and demonstration in which between one-half and one million people took to the streets of Paris. The most threatening action for the government, however, was the long wild-cat strike of between nine and ten million workers.

The situation is obviously different in the United States. The response to the Cambodian invasion provided some very interesting data. Even though lines of communication among American campuses are much weaker than in France, American students can act in unison. The mind-sets at major American universities and colleges are sufficiently in tune that a political stimulus can set off similar spontaneous responses.

The President was obviously surprised and frightened although it was reported that he had been warned of the possible repercussions on the campuses by his advisors. Unable to sleep in the predawn hours, he aroused his valet who drove him to the Lincoln Memorial where he subjected young protestors who were trying to sleep to what they described as disjointed and incoherent rambling.

Although the American students were generally not prepared to fight the kind of pitched battle that the French students had fought, the reaction of locally controlled police and National Guard units was more brutal than that of the French police. Four students lay dead at Kent State and two at Jackson State. This was

---

[8] The government has not been as effective in tracking down members of these groups as many, including myself, had thought they would be. At any point in time there is a tremendous base of support for these people among those who are alienated but who are not willing to engage in guerrilla activities themselves.

[9] See my "The Revolution Betrayed: The French Student Revolt of May–June 1968" in Lipset and Altbach, *op. cit.*, pp. 127–166.

consistent with the previous pattern of a much greater propensity among American police to use bullets on demonstrators or dissidents (e.g., the Alameda County Sheriff's office in 1969, the murders of Fred Hampton and Mark Clark, and numerous killings of black Panthers and students in the South) than is the case in France. During the entire revolt in France, I could not document one shooting by law-enforcement officers.

In the United States, the Administration has invested a great deal of energy in attempting to polarize opinion against the dissidents and public opinion has tended to be negative. While a couple of liberal labor leaders were stirred to expressions of open opposition to the war, the Executive Council of the AFL-CIO approved of the President's Cambodian action. In several cities, construction workers formed violent vigilante groups and/or launched counter demonstrations.

There were, however, more favorable responses from the students' point of view. Bureaucrats charged with the execution of policy in both HEW and the State Department openly expressed their strong opposition to the President's policies. The Commissioner of Education attacked the Cambodian adventure. He was fired. The Secretary of the Interior accused the President and his political associates of being insensitive to the concerns of youth and he too was subsequently dismissed. It appeared that the President and his most right-wing associates, Mr. Mitchell and Mr. Agnew, were being isolated within their own executive branch.

The Senate was clearly impressed. This was indicated by the passage of the Cooper-Church Amendment. Thus both within the executive and legislative branches the student action of May stimulated some very bold antiwar behavior. But the behavior of the bureaucrats, upon whom the execution of policy depends, was the more interesting. And that the President seems to have perceived the danger to his position is reflected in the shift of some responsibilities from State to Defense and in both the threat of dismissal and actual dismissal of dissidents.

From the point of view of the students, the reaction of investors was also favorable. Economists admit that the most important determinant of the direction of the stock market is psychological. The student revolt in France cost that country a fortune and necessitated a devaluation in the franc. The comparatively mild action of the American students wreaked havoc with the market. After all is said and done, it may well be that the most potent support which the student movement will generate on the war issue will not come from other powerless anti-establishment forces like ghetto blacks but from within the establishment itself, particularly from government bureaucrats and market investors.

Less important in terms of potential effect but important in symbolic terms was the support generated within the academic community. More faculty members than ever before became active participants in the events of May. In general, the faculty became much more honest with themselves and their students over what was happening. A permanent antiwar lobby of academics in Washington was formed. And even some administrators who had opposed any political commitment on the part of the university broke their silence under pressure.

The French case demonstrates that there is always a danger of instability in any political system when the government insensitively attempts to push beyond the effectiveness of the incentive system. I know of no one who considered the French political system before May 1968 to be unstable. All of the usual indices which have been used by social scientists to measure stability were there—it was an industrialized country, there was inflation but the economy was not in trouble from the point of view of investors and financiers, de Gaulle had been in power for a full decade, the extreme right was virtually nonexistent, the Communist Party was playing within the system, and the dissident student organizations had been immobilized by the government at every turn. In very short order the students changed all that.

The major lesson of both the French and American cases is the futility of traditional organizational efforts to bring about specific policy changes when students are faced with a government in a relatively "efficiently" operating industrialized society which is determined to resist their demands. Such organizational efforts are inherently conservative and are viable mechanisms only for those categories that already possess greater resource bases. In order for the students to emerge victorious they must clearly indicate to the government that they are prepared to incur the serious risks involved in breaking through the system's incentive structure. In other words, they must show that they are prepared to engage in disruptive behavior despite costs to themselves which will involve costs to the system which decision-makers do not want to incur. The ultimate cost would be, of course, the termination of the regime. But there are also intermediate costs—both political and economic—which the government will not wish to incur. All political decision-makers are eager to foster the impression that they can keep things under control in the streets, provide efficient policy execution and services, and maintain a favorable climate for economic growth.

The 1968 uprising in France and the reaction to the Cambodian invasion in the United States may well indicate that the only way that such disruptive behavior which is not easily "managed" can come about under the above conditions is through spontaneous action. There is some room for strategic maneuvering on the part of students—i.e., the maintenance of a certain level of political consciousness within their own ranks and in the ranks of potential allies and of a certain level of tension or threat. But the structuring of the situation must be done by the government itself. But the government must act according to the scenario. It must develop alienation through resistance to demands and repressive responses and it must provide the catalyst that makes possible the mass transcendance of the incentive structure upon which it relies for effective control. Once this has been accomplished, once spontaneity has been experienced on a mass scale, a new state of mind or consciousness and a new political context has been created. The Gaullists learned this the hard way. All at once, concessions to the students on specific issues and personnel seemed a reasonable price to preserve power. But by this point most of the activists are no longer just thinking in terms of changing specific policies or office holders. They are thinking in terms of basic systemic change.

BASIC SYSTEMIC CHANGE

On numerous occasions the question is raised as to whether or not we are experiencing a phenomenon which is significantly different from left-wing student activism in American universities in the 1930s. There is usually an implicit assumption and question behind this. The assumption is that the activism of the 1930s either faded away as the participants aged or was absorbed by the war and the New Deal without having significant impact upon the political system. The question is: will the same fate not befall contemporary student activism?

I am cognizant of Professor Lipset's criticism of Professor Andrew Hacker and Mr.

William Braden for "their ahistoricism, their exaggeration of the uniqueness of the contemporary."[10] Nevertheless, I will argue that student activism today is different from student activism in the 1930s in that it is occurring within the context of a "counterculture."

Of course, I am not the first one to put forward the idea of a counterculture. It runs through the writings of Herbert Marcuse. Theodore Roszak, in his *The Making of a Counter Culture,* discusses the counterculture but actually devotes almost all of his attention to the technocracy which he sees as responsible for its growth.[11] In his very recent book, Philip E. Slater speaks of

two separate cultures in America ... the opposition between the old scarcity-oriented technological culture that still predominates and the somewhat amorphous counterculture that is growing up to challenge it. At times this distinction may seem synonymous with old-versus-young, or radical-versus-conservative, but the overlap is only approximate. There are many young people who are dedicated to the old culture and a few old people dedicated to the new.[12]

Margaret Mead argues that the generation gap is worldwide and that we are now entering a new and universal anthropological stage which she calls "prefigurative culture.[13] In prefigurative culture young people learn from their peers rather than from their elders. Thus cumulative patterns of political socialization are broken by peer-group interaction. In 1967, Kenneth Keniston argued that there were really two

kinds of youth dissent in the United States, the "romantic-alienated" (the culturally oriented) and that "universalistic-activist" (the politically oriented), that these were going in different directions, and that the tension between them would probably increase.[14] I argue, and Keniston now agrees, that these are aspects of the same phenomenon and that they are mutually reinforcing.

Let me be more explicit in regard to the differences with the 1930s. While I shall deal elsewhere in more detail and in a more rigorous comparative fashion with these characteristics, here space permits little more than a brief enumeration.

First, we now have a differentiation running along generational lines in regard to language, dress, art, drugs, and sex. Attitudes and behavior in regard to these phenomena are very different in the new youth culture from what they are in the dominant culture.

Second, the youth culture exhibits far greater spread than it did in the 1930s. It is widely spread within the university student milieu wherein we find the children of those especially rewarded during the postwar period of economic abundance,[15] it is affecting people who come into constant contact with students like faculty members (some of whom were students themselves only a short time ago), it is being carried by graduating students in the various professional areas of life, and, most importantly, it is spreading downward into high schools, junior high schools, and even gram-

[10] Seymour Martin Lipset, "The Banality of Revolt," *Saturday Review* (July 18, 1970), p. 34.

[11] Theodore Roszak, *The Making of a Counter Culture* (Garden City, N.Y.: Anchor, 1969).

[12] Philip E. Slater, "America's Changing Culture," *Current* (June 1970), p. 15.

[13] Margaret Mead, *Culture and Commitment: A Study of the Generation Gap* (Garden City, N.Y.: Natural History Press/Doubleday, 1970).

[14] Kenneth Keniston, "The Sources of Student Dissent," *Journal of Social Issues,* 23 (1967), pp. 108–137 reprinted in his *Young Radicals: Notes on Committed Youth* (New York: Harcourt, Brace, and World, 1968).

[15] However, students are now rapidly finding themselves economically deprived by the spiraling unemployment. This will act as a further radicalizing factor as it has in France since 1963.

mar schools at a rapid rate. Over the past five years each freshman class has been more deeply touched than the previous one. It is through this downward spread that the counterculture is affecting young people who will not go into universities or the professions but into the blue-collar labor force.

Third, there is a high degree of political separatism or the shunning of traditional political structures. The student activism of the 1930s tended to be centered around either establishment parties or adult-controlled anti-establishment parties like the Communist or Socialist parties. Neither the establishment parties nor these anti-establishment parties have much attraction for today's students.

Fourth, we have the rise and fragmentation of ideological organizations and movements which goes well beyond the fragmentation of the left-wing parties of the 1930s. Moreover, the fragmentation stems from the base as opposed to the 1930s in which the lines of fragmentation followed disaffection at the leadership level. I would argue that the present fragmentation indicates a higher degree of alienation and frustration than existed in the 1930s.

And, *fifth,* we have the progressive escalation in the use of direct-action techniques which was more characteristic of the labor movement than of student activism in the 1930s.

It is generally argued that the counterculture is a result of technological growth and the attendant increase in impersonality and hierarchical control. Margaret Mead sees prefigurative culture as a universal phenomenon. While I would agree that the revolt against impersonality and hierarchical control transcends national boundaries and is probably found in all industrialized societies in greater or lesser intensity, I would argue that there are differences in the nature of the challenges. The second through fifth characteristics

which we have attributed to the American counterculture would apply in France as well. While formulated in more rigorous Marxian theoretical terms in France, the two youth milieux also share in a negative attitude toward capitalism. But in France, the expression of political differentiation and alienation is not reinforced by differentiations in language, dress, art, sex, and drugs as it is in the United States.

At this point I would advance two propositions. First, despite the difference in manifestation of the challenges to the dominant system, I would contend that basic systemic change is inevitable in France and the United States as in all of the industrialized countries. For within the youth milieux there is a new "mind-set." Culture is composed of mind-sets. They are both cognitive and normative, both prescriptive ideas and ways of perceiving the world. They are based upon felt human needs and, in the long run, are the crucial variables in political change. And, some of the work on American political socialization notwithstanding, at critical points in history they are not simply the result of cumulative political socialization extending in a linear direction from the family through the work experience.

We are now in a period in which the requisites of Weber's impersonal hierarchical organizations no longer conform to the felt needs of the individuals who are subjected to them. Hierarchy and impersonal authority have simply gone beyond the point of diminishing returns. Just as Marx, at least in his later writings, went too far when he attempted to demystify Hegel by substituting materialism and economic determinism for idealism, so Weber and the sociologists influenced by him fall into a similar error by asserting the absolute primacy of the requirements of systems of production, distribution, and control over all other determinants. Thus I would expect that the more dehumanizing and authoritarian aspects of industrialized societies will be minimized as the new mindsets replace the old ones presently dominant.[16]

The second proposition is that because of the mutually fortifying impact of the political and more broadly cultural aspects of the youth and student counterculture in the United States, change will be even more basic and more rapid in this country than in France.

The question remains, however—what about the short term? If our analysis is correct, if the only way that students can hope to change policy in the face of a resistant government is by disruption, does this not threaten a change in the system toward more repression and a drastic reduction in civil liberties?

I do not think that anyone, even within the youth culture, takes this prospect lightly. The older generation too has a mind-set and is in control of tremendous resources. Philip E. Slater has written:

If the issue is left to generational confrontation, with new culture adherents attempting simply to push their elders out of the way and into the grave, the results will probably be catastrophic. The old culture will not simply fall of its own weight. It is not rotten but wildly malfunctioning, not weak and failing but strong and demented, not a sick old horse but a healty runaway. It no longer performs its fundamental task of satisfying the needs of its adherents, but it still performs the task of feeding and perpetuating itself. Nor do the young have the knowledge and skill successfully to dismantle it. If the matter is left to the collision of generational change it seems to me inevitable that a radical-right revolution will occur as a last-ditch effort to stave off change.[17]

If we are correct, then the choice obviously comes down to dropping one's goals or running the risk of the shift to the right which Slater talks about. Several points need to be made. *First,* since the goals relate to deeply felt needs and commitments, the goals will not be dropped. Students will continue to oppose the unconscionable Vietnam War in which they or their friends or husbands must participate or opt for prison or exile. And once we are out, if indeed we will ever be out, they will continue to oppose racism, poverty, the cold-war mentality, and the impersonalization and authoritarianism of social institutions.

Second, it is widely believed in the counterculture that we are either already in a state of fascism or inevitably and rapidly moving toward it. Therefore, while action might indeed hasten the process, it is also seen as the only possibility for resistance. And if enough people act, it might, *just might,* be possible to reverse the trend.

Third, it is the establishment, not the counterculture, that has structured the situation. While there is romanticism in the counterculture, there is also anguish and fear. Indeed, it is the government that is attempting to play on the danger of backlash and to use it as a resource. The rhetoric of the Administration, and particularly that of Mr. Agnew, seems to be consciously designed to this end.

Our governmental decision-makers thus bear the responsibility for the situation they have structured. But if men like Nixon, Agnew, and Mitchell are not terribly concerned about a shift to the right

---

[16] Here, of course, I am in agreement with Professor Flacks in his critique of Professor Bell's contention that the increasingly militant tactics of students are simply the "guttering last gasps of a romanticism soured by rancor and impotence." This interpretation might save the end-of-ideology thesis but I do not think that it conforms to the reality "out there" either in France or the United States. See Daniel Bell, *op. cit.,* p. 100; and Richard Flacks, "Social and Cultural Meanings of Student Revolt: Some Informal Comparative Observations," *Social Problems,* **17**:3 (Winter 1970), pp. 354–357.

[17] Slater, *op. cit.,* p. 16.

and are willing to play on it, those of us who share or pretend to share many of the aspirations of the students—e.g., an end to the war, to racism, to poverty—ought to be concerned. Yet too often university administrators and academics have served the cause of the reaction. Too often serious analysis of the causes and nature of student activism has been replaced by denunciations that conjure up images of a totally destructive fascist-like radical student movement, denunciations that can only contribute to public panic rather than understanding. Too often have men who claim to agree with the goals of the students criticized them for their tactics without offering viable alternatives and without active engagement themselves on the vital issues. And too often have those "liberal" administrators who advance the concept of institutional "neutrality" justified and participated with federal and state authorities in turning universities into virtual totalitarian police states replete with spies, informers, and files. They seem to have forgotten the lesson of McCarthyism, when there were no activist students to blame, that no social institution escapes general repression unless it resists it.

Up to this point the French example has provided a model offering a high degree of predictability for the behavior of both the political system and its youthful dissidents. Like the French, the American system seems determined to force the younger generation to choose between their most deeply felt needs and humanitarian instincts and attachment to the system itself. And, like the French system, it thereby loses the most potent binding force and its very *raison d'être*. There is no greater sign of social degeneration than a general policy of infanticide. Both at home and in Vietnam that seems to be our choice.

LET US SHAPE THE FUTURE

Carl Oglesby

Seven months ago at the April march on Washington, Paul Potter, then president of Students for a Democratic Society, stood in approximately this spot and said that we must name the system that creates and sustains the war in Vietnam—name it, describe it, analyze it, understand it, and change it.

Today I will try to name it—to suggest an analysis which, to be quite frank, may disturb some of you—and to suggest what changing it may require of us.

We are here again to protest again a growing war. Since it is a very bad war, we acquire the habit of thinking that it must be caused by very bad men. But we only conceal reality, I think, to denounce on such grounds the menacing coalition of industrial and military power, or the brutality of the blitzkrieg we are waging against Vietnam, or the ominous signs around us that heresy may soon no longer be permitted. We must simply observe, and quite plainly say, that this coalition, this blitzkrieg, and this demand for acquiescence are creatures, all of them, of a government that since 1932 has considered itself to be fundamentally liberal.

The original commitment in Vietnam was made by President Truman, a main-

Reprinted by permission from Liberation *(January 1966).*

stream liberal. It was seconded by President Eisenhower, a moderate liberal. It was intensified by the late President Kennedy, a flaming liberal. Think of the men who now engineer that war—those who study the maps, give the commands, push the buttons, and tally the dead: Bundy, McNamara, Rusk, Lodge, Goldberg, the President himself.

They are not moral monsters.

They are all honorable men.

They are all liberals.

But so, I'm sure, are many of us who are here today in protest. To understand the war, then, it seems necessary to take a closer look at this American liberalism. Maybe we are in for some surprises. Maybe we have here two quite different liberalisms: one authentically humanist; the other not so human at all.

Not long ago, I considered myself a liberal. And if someone had asked me what I meant by that, I'd perhaps have quoted Thomas Jefferson or Thomas Paine, who first made plain our nation's unprovisional commitment to human rights. But what do you think would happen if these two heroes could sit down now for a chat with President Johnson and McGeorge Bundy?

They would surely talk of the Vietnam war. Our dead revolutionaries would soon wonder why their country was fighting against what appeared to be a revolution. The living liberals would hotly deny that it is one: there are troops coming in from outside, the rebels get arms from other countries, most of the people are not on their side, and they practice terror against their own. Therefore, not a revolution.

What would our dead revolutionaries answer? They might say: "What fools and bandits, sir, you make then of us. Outside help? Do you remember Lafayette? Or the 2000 British freighters the French navy sunk for our side? Or the arms and men we got from France and Spain? And what's this about terror? Did you never hear what

we did to our own loyalists? Or about the thousands of rich American Tories who fled for their lives to Canada? And as for popular support, do you not know that we had less than one-third of our people with us? That, in fact, the colony of New York recruited more troops for the British than for the revolution? Should we give it all back?"

Revolutions do not take place in velvet boxes. They never have. It is only the poets who make them lovely. What the National Liberation Front is fighting in Vietnam is a complex and vicious war. This war is also a revolution, as honest a revolution as you can find anywhere in history. And this is a fact which all our intricate denials will never change.

But it doesn't make any difference to our leaders anyway. Their aim in Vietnam is really much simpler than this implies. It is to safeguard what they take to be American interests around the world against revolution or revolutionary change, which they always call communism—as if it were that. In the case of Vietnam, this interest is, first, the principle that revolution shall not be tolerated anywhere, and second, that South Vietnam shall never sell its rice to China—or even to North Vietnam.

There is simply no such thing now, for us, as a just revolution—never mind that for two-thirds of the world's people the twentieth century might as well be the Stone Age; never mind the melting poverty and hopelessness that are the basic facts of life for most of modern men; and never mind that for those millions there is now an increasingly perceptible relationship between their sorrow and our contentment.

Can we understand why the Negroes of Watts rebelled? Then why do we need a devil theory to explain the rebellion of the South Vietnamese? Can we understand the oppression in Mississippi, or the anguish that our Northern ghettos makes epidemic?

Then why can't we see that our proper human struggle is not with communism or revolutionaries, but with the social desperation that drives good men to violence, both here and abroad?

To be sure, we have been most generous with our aid, and in Western Europe, a mature industrial society, that aid worked. But there are always political and financial strings. And we have never shown ourselves capable of allowing others to make those traumatic institutional changes that are often the prerequisites of progress in colonial societies. For all our official feeling for the millions who are enslaved to what we so self-righteously call the yoke of communist tyranny, we make no real effort at all to crack through the much more vicious right-wing tyrannies that our businessmen traffic with and our nation profits from everyday. And for all our cries about the international Red conspiracy to take over the world, we take only pride in the fact of our 6000 military bases on foreign soil.

We gave Rhodesia a grave look just now —but we keep on buying her chromium which is cheap because black slave labor mines it.

We deplore the racism of Verwoert's fascist South Africa—but our banks make big loans to that country and our private technology makes it a nuclear power.

We are saddened and puzzled by random back-page stories of revolt in this or that Latin American state—but are convinced by a few pretty photos in the Sunday supplement that things are getting better, that the world is coming our way, that change from disorder can be orderly, that our benevolence will pacify the distressed, that our might will intimidate the angry.

Optimists, may I suggest that these are quite unlikely fantasies. They are fantasies because we have lost that mysterious social desire for human equity that from time to time has given us genuine moral drive. We have become a nation of young bright-eyed, hard-hearted, slim-waisted, bullet-headed, make-out artists. A nation—may I say it?—of beardless liberals.

You say I am being hard? Only think.

This country, with its thirty-some years of liberalism, can send 200,000 young men to Vietnam to kill and die in the most dubious of wars, but it cannot get 100 voter registrars to go into Mississippi.

What do you make of it?

The financial burden of the war obliges us to cut millions from an already pathetic War on Poverty budget. But in almost the same breath, Congress appropriates $140 million for the Lockheed and Boeing companies to compete with each other on the supersonic-transport project—that Disneyland creation will cost us all about $2 billion before it's done.

What do you make of it?

Many of us have been earnestly resisting for some years now the idea of putting atomic weapons into West German hands, an action that would perpetuate the division of Europe and thus the cold war. Now just this week we find out that, with the meagerest of security systems, West Germany has had nuclear weapons in her hands for the past six years.

What do you make of it?

Some will make of it that I overdraw the matter. Many will ask: What about the other side? To be sure, there is the bitter ugliness of Czechoslovakia, Poland, those infamous Russian tanks in the streets of Budapest. But my anger only rises to hear some say that sorrow cancels sorrow, or that *this* one's shame deposits in *that* one's account the right to shamefulness.

And others will make of it that I sound mighty anti-American. To these, I say: Don't blame *me* for *that!* Blame those who mouthed my liberal values and broke my American heart.

Just who might they be, by the way? Let's take a brief factual inventory of the latter-day cold war.

In 1953 our Central Intelligence Agency managed to overthrow Mossadegh in Iran; the complaint being his neutralism in the cold war and his plans to nationalize the country's oil resources to improve his people's lives. Most evil aims, most evil man. In his place we put in General Zahedi, a World War II Nazi collaborator. New arrangements on Iran's oil gave 25-year leases on 40 percent of it to three U.S. firms, one of which was Gulf Oil. The CIA's leader for this coup was Kermit Roosevelt. In 1960 Kermit Roosevelt became a vice president of Gulf Oil.

In 1954, the democratically elected Arbenz of Guatemala wanted to nationalize a portion of United Fruit Company's plantations in his country, land he badly needed for a modest program of agrarian reform. His government was overthrown by a CIA-supported right-wing coup. The following year, Gen. Walter Bedell Smith, director of the CIA when the Guatemala venture was being planned, joined the board of directors of the United Fruit Company.

Comes 1960 and Castro cries we are about to invade Cuba. The Administration sneers, "poppycock," and we Americans believe it. Comes 1961 and the invasion. Comes with it the awful realization that the United States Government had lied.

Comes 1962 and the missile crisis, and our Administration stands prepared to fight global atomic war on the curious principle that another state does not have the right to its own foreign policy.

Comes 1963 and British Guiana, where Cheddi Jagan wants independence from England and a labor law modeled on the Wagner Act. And Jay Lovestone, the AFL-CIO foreign policy chief, acting, as always, quite independently of labor's rank and file, arranges with our government to finance an eleven-week dock strike that brings Jagan down, ensuring that the state will remain *British* Guiana, and that any workingman who wants a wage better than 50 cents a day is a dupe of communism.

Comes 1964. Two weeks after Undersecretary Thomas Mann announces that we have abandoned the *Alianza's* principle of no aid to tyrants, Brazil's Goulart is overthrown by the vicious right-winger, Ademar Barros, supported by a show of American gunboats at Rio de Janeiro. Within 24 hours, the new head of state, Mazzilli, receives a congratulatory wire from our President.

Comes 1965. The Dominican Republic. Rebellion in the streets. We scurry to the spot with 20,000 neutral Marines and our neutral peacemakers—like Ellsworth Bunkers, Jr., ambassador to the Organization of American States. Most of us know that our neutral Marines fought openly on the side of the junta, a fact that the Administration still denies. But how many also know that what was at stake was our new Caribbean Sugar Bowl? That this same neutral peacemaking Bunker is a board member and stock owner of the National Sugar Refining Company, a firm his father founded in the good old days, and one which has a major interest in maintaining the status quo in the Dominican Republic? Or that the President's close personal friend and advisor, our new Supreme Court Justice Abe Fortas, has sat for the past nineteen years on the board of the Sucrest Company, which imports black-strap molasses from the Dominican Republic? Or that the rhetorician of corporate liberalism, and the late President Kennedy's close friend, Adolf Berle, was chairman of that same board? Or that our roving ambassador Averill Harriman's brother Roland is on the board of National Sugar? Or that our former ambassador to the Dominican Republic, Joseph Farland, is a board member of the South Puerto Rico Sugar Co., which owns 275,000 acres of rich land in the Dominican Republic and is the largest employer on the island—at about one dollar a day?

Neutralists! God save the hungry people of the world from such neutralists!

We do not say these men are evil. We say, rather, that good men can be divided from their compassion by the institutional system that inherits us all. Generation in and out, we are put to use. People become instruments. Generals do not hear the screams of the bombed; sugar executives do not see the misery of the cane cutters: for to do so is to be that much *less* the general, that much *less* the executive.

The foregoing facts of recent history describe one main aspect of the estate of Western liberalism. Where is our American humanism hero? What went wrong? Let's stare our situation coldly in the face. All of us are born to the colossus of history, our American corporate system—in many ways, an awesome organism. There is one fact that describes it: with about 5 percent of the world's people, we consume about half the world's goods. We take a richness that is in good part not our own, and we put it in our pockets, our garages, our split-levels, our bellies, and our futures.

On the *face* of it, it is a crime that so few should have so much at the expense of so many. Where is the moral imagination so abused as to call this just? Perhaps many of us feel a bit uneasy in our sleep. We are not, after all, a cruel people. And perhaps we don't really need this superdominance that deforms others. But what can we do? The investments are made. The financial ties are established. The plants abroad are built. Our system *exists*. One is swept up into it. How intolerable—to be born moral, but addicted to a stolen and maybe surplus luxury. Our goodness threatens to become counterfeit before our eyes—unless we change. But change threatens us with uncertainty—at least.

Our problem, then, is to justify this system and give its theft another name—to make kind and moral what is neither, to perform some alchemy with language that will make this injustice seem to be a most magnanimous gift.

A hard problem. But the Western democracies, in the heyday of their colonial expansionism, produced a hero worthy of the task.

Its name was free enterprise, and its partner was an *illiberal liberalism* that said to the poor and the dispossessed: What we acquire of your resources we repay in civilization. The white man's burden. But this was too poetic. So a much more hardheaded theory was produced. This theory said that colonial status is in fact a *boon* to the colonized. We give them technology and bring them into modern times.

But this deceived no one but ourselves. We were delighted with this new theory. The poor saw in it merely an admission that their claims were irrefutable. They stood up to us, without gratitude. We were shocked—but also confused, for the poor seemed again to be right. How long is it going to be the case, we wondered, that the poor will be right and the rich will be wrong?

Liberalism faced a crisis. In the face of the collapse of the European empires, how could it continue to hold together our twin need for richness and righteousness? How can we continue to sack the ports of Asia and still dream of Jesus?

The challenge was met with a most ingenious solution: the ideology of anti-communism. This was the bind: we cannot call revolution bad, because we started that way ourselves, and because it is all too easy to see why the dispossessed should rebel. So we will call revolution *communism*. And we will reserve the right to say what communism means. We take note of revolution's enormities, wrenching them where necessary from their historical context and often exaggerating them, and say: Behold, communism is a bloodbath. We take note of those reactionaries who stole the revolution's need to consolidate itself, and say: Behold, communism is a tyranny.

It has been all these things, and it will be these things again, and we will never be at a loss for those tales of atrocity that comfort us so in our self-righteousness. Nuns will be raped and bureaucrats will be disemboweled. Indeed, revolution is a *fury*. For it is a letting loose of outrages pent up sometimes over centuries. But the more brutal and longer lasting the suppression of this energy, all the more ferocious will be its explosive release.

Far from helping Americans to deal with this truth, the anti-communist ideology merely tries to disguise it so that things may stay the way they are. Thus, it depicts our presence in other lands not as a coercion, but a protection. It allows us even to say that napalm in Vietnam is only another aspect of our humanitarian love—like those exorcisms in the Middle Ages that so often killed the patient. So we say to the Vietnamese peasant, the Cuban intellectual, the Peruvian worker: You are better dead than Red. If it hurts or if you don't understand why—sorry about that.

This is the action of *corporate liberalism*. It performs for the corporate state a function quite like what the Church once performed for the feudal state. It seeks to justify its burdens and protect it from change. As the Church exaggerated this office in the Inquisition, so with liberalism in the McCarthy time—which, if it was a reactionary phenomenon, was still made possible by our anti-communist corporate liberalism.

Let me then speak directly to humanist liberals. If my facts are wrong, I will soon be corrected. But if they are right, then you may face a crisis of conscience.

Corporatism or humanism: which? For it has come to that. Will you let your dreams be used? Will you be grudging apologists for the corporate state? Or will you help try to change it—not in the name of this or that blueprint *ism*, but in the name of simple human decency and democracy and the vision that wise and brave men saw in the time of our own revolution?

And if your commitment to human value is unconditional, then disabuse yourselves of the notion that statements will bring change, if only the right statement can be written, or that interviews with the mighty will bring change if only the mighty can be reached, or that marches will bring change if only we can make them reasonable enough.

We are dealing now with a colossus that does not want to be changed. It will not change itself. It will not cooperate with those who want to change it. Those allies of ours in the government—are they really our allies? If they are, then they don't need advice, they need constituencies; they don't need study groups, they need a movement. And if they are not, then all the more reason for building that movement with a most relentless conviction.

There are people in this country who are trying to build that movement, who aim at nothing less than a humanist reformation. And the humanist liberals must understand that it is this movement with which their own best hopes are most in tune. We radicals know the same history that you liberals know, and we can understand your occasional cynicism, exasperation, and even distrust. But we ask you to put these aside and help us risk a leap. Help us find enough time for the enormous work that needs doing here. Help us build. Help us shape the future in the name of plain human hope.

DOMESTIC LAW AND INTERNATIONAL ORDER

Eldridge Cleaver

The police department and the armed forces are the two arms of the power structure, the muscles of control and enforcement. They have deadly weapons with which to inflict pain on the human body. They know how to bring about horrible deaths. They have clubs with which to beat the body and the head. They have bullets and guns with which to tear holes in the flesh, to smash bones, to disable, and kill. They use force, to make you do what the deciders have decided you must do.

Every country on earth has these agencies of force. The people everywhere fear this terror and force. To them it is like a snarling wild beast which can put an end to one's dreams. They punish. They have cells and prisons to lock you up in. They pass out sentences. They won't let you go when you want to. You have to stay put until they give the word. If your mother is dying, you can't go to her bedside to say goodbye or to her graveside to see her lowered into the earth, to see her, for the last time, swallowed up by that black hole.

The techniques of the enforcers are many: firing squads, gas chambers, electric chairs, torture chambers, the garrote, the guillotine, the tightening rope around your throat. It has been found that the death penalty is necessary to back up the law, to make it easier to enforce, to deter transgressions against the penal code. That everybody doesn't believe in the same laws is beside the point.

Which laws get enforced depends on who is in power. If the capitalists are in power, they enforce laws designed to protect their system, their way of life. They have a particular abhorrence for crimes against property, but are prepared to be liberal and show a modicum of compassion for crimes against the person—unless, of course, an instance of the latter is combined with an instance of the former. In such cases, nothing can stop them from throwing the whole book at the offender. For instance, armed robbery with violence, to a capitalist, is the very epitome of evil. Ask any banker what he thinks of it.

If communists are in power, they enforce laws designed to protect their system, their way of life. To them, the horror of horrors is the speculator, that man of magic who has mastered the art of getting something with nothing and who in America would be a member in good standing of his local Chamber of Commerce.

"The people," however, are nowhere consulted, although everywhere everything is done always in their name and ostensibly for their betterment, while their real-life problems go unsolved. "The people" are a rubber stamp for the crafty and sly. And no problem can be solved without taking the police department and the armed forces into account. Both kings and bookies understand this, as do first ladies and common prostitutes.

The police do on the domestic level what the armed forces do on the international level: protect the way of life of those in power. The police patrol the city, cordon off communities, blockade neighborhoods, invade homes, search for that which is hidden. The armed forces patrol the world, invade countries and continents, cordon off nations, blockade islands and whole peoples; they will also overrun villages, neighborhoods, enter homes, huts, caves, searching for that which is hidden. The policeman and the soldier will violate your person, smoke you out with various gases. Each will shoot you, beat your head and body with sticks and clubs, with rifle butts, run you through with bayonets, shoot holes in your flesh, kill you. They each have unlimited firepower. They will use all that is necessary to bring you to your knees. They won't take no for an answer. If you resist their sticks, they draw their guns. If you resist their guns, they call for reinforcements with bigger guns. Eventually they will come in tanks, in jets, in ships. They will not rest until you surrender or are killed. The policeman and the soldier will have the last word.

Both police and the armed forces follow orders. Orders. Orders flow from the top down. Up there, behind closed doors, in antechambers, in conference rooms, gavels bang on the tables, the tinkling of silver decanters can be heard as icewater is poured by well-fed, conservatively dressed men in horn-rimmed glasses, fashionably dressed American widows with rejuvenated faces and tinted hair, the air permeated with the square humor of Bob Hope jokes. Here all the talking in done, all the thinking, all the deciding. Gray rabbits of men scurry forth from the conference room to spread the decisions throughout the city, as News. Carrying out orders is a job, a way

of meeting the payments on the house, a way of providing for one's kiddies. In the armed forces it is also a duty, patriotism. Not to do so is treason.

Every city has its police department. No city would be complete without one. It would be sheer madness to try operating an American city without the heat, the fuzz, the man. Americans are too far gone, or else they haven't arrived yet; the center does not exist, only the extremes. Take away the cops and Americans would have a coast-to-coast free-for-all. There are, of course, a few citizens who carry their own private cops around with them, built into their souls. But there is robbery in the land, and larceny, murder, rape, burglary, theft, swindles, all brands of crime, profit, rent, interest—and these blasé descendants of Pilgrims are at each other throats. To complicate matters, there are also rich people and poor people in America. There are Negroes and whites, Indians, Puerto Ricans, Mexicans, Jews, Chinese, Arabs, Japanese—all with equal rights but unequal possessions. Some are haves and some are have-nots. All have been taught to worship at the shrine of General Motors. The whites are on top in America and they want to stay there, up there. They are also on top in the world, on the international level, and they want to stay up there, too. Everywhere there are those who want to smash this precious toy clock of a system, they want ever so much to change it, to rearrange things, to pull the whites down off their high horse and make them equal. Everywhere the whites are fighting to prolong their status, to retard the erosion of their position. In America, when everything else fails, they call out the police. On the international level, when everything else fails, they call out the armed forces.

A strange thing happened in Watts, in 1965, August. The blacks, who in this land of private property have all private and no property, got excited into an uproar because they noticed a cop before he had a chance to wash the blood off his hands. Usually the police department can handle such flare-ups. But this time it was different. Things got out of hand. The blacks were running amok, burning, shooting, breaking. The police department was powerless to control them; the chief called for reinforcements. Out came the National Guard, that ambiguous hybrid from the twilight zone where the domestic army merges with the international; that hypocritical force poised within America and capable of action on either level, capable of backing up either the police or the armed forces. Unleashing their formidable firepower, they crushed the blacks. But things will never be the same again. Too many people saw that those who turned the other cheek in Watts got their whole heads blown off. At the same time, heads were being blown off in Vietnam. America was embarrassed, not by the quality of her deeds but by the surplus of publicity focused upon her negative selling points, and a little frightened because of what all those dead bodies, on two fronts, implied. Those corpses spoke eloquently of potential allies and alliances. A community of interest began to emerge, dripping with blood, out of the ashes of Watts. The blacks in Watts and all over America could now see the Viet Cong's point: both were on the receiving end of what the armed forces were dishing out.

So now the blacks, stung by the new knowledge they have unearthed, cry out: *"POLICE BRUTALITY!"* From one end of the country to the other, the new war cry is raised. The youth, those nodes of compulsive energy who are all fuel and muscle, race their motors, itch to do something. The Uncle Toms, no longer willing to get down on their knees to lick boots, do so from a squatting position. The black bourgeoisie call for Citizens' Review Boards, to assert civilian control over the activity of the police. In back rooms, in dark stinking corners of the ghettos, self-conscious black men curse their own cowardice and stare at their rifles and pistols and shotguns laid out on tables before them, trembling as they wish for a manly impulse to course through their bodies and send them screaming mad into the streets shooting from the hip. Black women look at their men as if they are bugs, curious growths of flesh playing an inscrutable waiting game. Violence becomes a homing pigeon floating through the ghettos seeking a black brain in which to roost for a season.

In their rage against the police, against police brutality, the blacks lose sight of the fundamental reality: that the police are only an instrument for the implementation of the policies of those who make the decisions. Police brutality is only one facet of the crystal of terror and oppression. Behind police brutality there is social brutality, economic brutality, and political brutality. From the perspective of the ghetto, this is not easy to discern: the TV newscaster and the radio announcer and the editorialists of the newspapers are wizards of the smoke screen and the snow job.

What is true on the international level is true also at home; except that the ace up the sleeve is easier to detect in the international arena. Who would maintain that American soldiers are in Vietnam on their own motion? They were conscripted into the armed forces and taught the wisdom of obeying orders. They were sent to Vietnam by orders of the generals in the Pentagon, who receive them from the Secretary of Defense, who receives them from the President, who is shrouded in mystery. The soldier in the field in Vietnam, the man who lies in the grass and squeezes the trigger when a little half-starved, trembling Vietnamese peasant crosses his sights, is only following orders, carrying out a policy and a plan. He hardly knows what it is all about. They have him wired-up tight with the slogans of TV and the World Series.

All he knows is that he has been assigned to carry out a certain ritual of duties. He is well trained and does the best he can. He does a good job. He may want to please those above him with the quality of his performance. He may want to make sergeant, or better. This man is from some hicky farm in Shit Creek, Georgia. He only knew whom to kill after passing through boot camp. He could just as well come out ready to kill Swedes. He will kill a Swede dead, if he is ordered to do so.

Same for the policeman in Watts. He is not there on his own. They have all been assigned. They have been told what to do and what not to do. They have also been told what they better not do. So when they continually do something, in every filthy ghetto in this shitty land, it means only that they are following orders.

It's no secret that in America the blacks are in total rebellion against the System. They want to get their nuts out of the sand. They don't like the way America is run, from top to bottom. In America, everything is owned. Everything is held as private property. Someone has a brand on everything. There is nothing left over. Until recently, the blacks themselves were counted as part of somebody's private property, along with the chickens and goats. The blacks have not forgotten this, principally because they are still treated as if they are part of someone's inventory of assets—or perhaps, in this day of rage against the costs of welfare, blacks are listed among the nation's liabilities. On any account, however, blacks are in no position to respect or help maintain the institution of private property. What they want is to figure out a way to get some of that property for themselves, to divert it to their own needs. This is what it is all about, and this is the real brutality involved. This is the source of all brutality.

The police are the armed guardians of the social order. The blacks are the chief domestic victims of the American social order. A conflict of interest exists, therefore, between the blacks and the police. It is not solely a matter of trigger-happy cops, of brutal cops who love to crack black heads. Mostly it's a job to them. It pays good. And there are numerous fringe benefits. The real problem is a trigger-happy social order.

The Utopians speak of a day when there will be no police. There will be nothing for them to do. Every man will do his duty, will respect the rights of his neighbor, will not disturb the peace. The needs of all will be taken care of. Everyone will have sympathy for his fellow man. There will be no such thing as crime. There will be, of course, no prisons. No electric chairs, no gas chambers. The hangman's rope will be the thing of the past. The entire earth will be a land of plenty. There will be no crimes against property, no speculation.

It is easy to see that we are not on the verge of entering Utopia: there are cops everywhere. North and South, the Negroes are the have-nots. They see property all around them, property that is owned by whites. In this regard, the black bourgeoisie has become nothing but a ridiculous-nuisance. Having waged a battle for entrance into the American mainstream continually for fifty years, all of the black bourgeoisie's defenses are directed outward, against the whites. They have no defenses against the blacks and no time to erect any. The black masses can handle them any time they choose, with one mighty blow. But the white bourgeoisie presents a bigger problem, those whites who own everything. With many shackled by unemployment, hatred in black hearts for this system of private property increases daily. The sanctity surrounding property is being called into question. The mystique of the deed of ownership is melting away. In other parts of the world, peasants rise up and expropriate the land from the former owners. Blacks in America see that the deed is not eternal, that it is not signed by God; and that new deeds, making blacks the owners, can be drawn up.

The Black Muslims raised the cry, *"WE MUST HAVE SOME LAND!" "SOME LAND OF OUR OWN OR ELSE!"* Blacks in America shrink from the colossus of General Motors. They can't see how to wade through that thicket of common stocks, preferred stocks, bonds and debentures. They only know that General Motors is huge, that it has billions of dollars under its control, that it owns land, that its subsidiaries are legion, that it is a repository of vast powers. The blacks went to crack the nut of General Motors. They are meditating on it. Meanwhile, they must learn that the police take orders from General Motors. And that the Bank of America has something to do with them even though they don't have a righteous penny in the bank. They have no bank accounts, only bills to pay. The only way they know of making withdrawals from the bank is at the point of a gun. The shiny fronts of skyscrapers intimidate them. They do not own them. They feel alienated from the very sidewalks on which they walk. This white man's country, this white man's world. Overflowing with men of color. An economy consecrated to the succor of the whites. Blacks are incidental. The war on poverty, that monstrous insult to the rippling muscles in a black man's arms, is an index of how men actually sit down and plot each other's deaths, actually sit down with slide rules and calculate how to hide bread from the hungry. And the black bourgeoisie greedily sopping up what crumbs are tossed into their dark corner.

There are 20,000,000 of these blacks in America, probably more. Today they repeat, in awe, this magic number to themselves: there are 20,000,000 of us! They shout this to each other in humiliated astonishment. No one need tell them that there is vast power latent in their mass. They know that 20,000,000 of anything is enough to get some recognition and consideration. They know also that they must harness their number and hone it into a sword with a sharp cutting edge. White General Motors also knows that the unity of these 20,000,000 ragamuffins will spell the death of the system of its being. At all costs, then, they will seek to keep these blacks from uniting, from becoming bold and revolutionary. These white property owners know that they must keep the blacks cowardly and intimidated. By a complex communications system of hints and signals, certain orders are given to the chief of police and the sheriff, who pass them on to their men, the foot soldiers in the trenches of the ghetto.

We experience this system of control as madness. So that Leonard Deadwyler, one of these 20,000,000 blacks, is rushing his pregnant wife to the hospital and is shot dead by a policeman. An accident. That the sun rises in the east and sets in the west is also an accident, by design. The blacks are up in arms. From one end of America to the other, blacks are outraged at this accident, this latest evidence of what an accident-prone people they are, of the cruelty and pain of their lives, these blacks at the mercy of trigger-happy Yankees and Rebs in coalition against their skin. They want the policeman's blood as a sign that the Viet Cong is not the only answer. A sign to save them from the deaths they must die, and inflict. The power structure, without so much as blinking an eye, wouldn't mind tossing Bova to the mob, to restore law and order, but it knows in the vaults of its strength that at all cost the blacks must be kept at bay, that it must uphold the police department, its Guardian. Nothing must be allowed to threaten the set-up. Justice is secondary. Security is the byword.

Meanwhile, blacks are looking on and asking tactical questions. They are asked to die for the System in Vietnam. In Watts they are killed by it. Now—*NOW!*—they are asking each other, in dead earnest: Why not die right here in Babylon fighting for a better life, like the Viet Cong? If those little cats can do it, what's wrong with big studs like us?

A mood sets in, spreads across America, across the face of Babylon, jells in black hearts everywhere.

SEXUAL POLITICS

Kate Millett

Is it possible to regard the relation of the sexes in a political light at all?

It depends on how one defines "politics." I do not define the political area here as that narrow and exclusive sector known as institutional politics of the Democrat or Republican—we all have reason to be tired and suspicious of them. By politics I mean power-structured relationships, the entire arrangement whereby one group of people is governed by another, one group is dominant and the other subordinate.

It is time we developed a more cogent and relevant psychology and philosophy of power relationships not yet considered in our institutional politics. It is time we gave attention to defining a theory of politics which treats of power relationships on the less formal than establishmentarian grounds of personal intercourse between members of well-defined and coherent groups—races, castes, classes, and sexes. It is precisely because such groups have no representation in formal political structures that their oppression is so entire and so continuous.

In the recent past, we have been forced to acknowledge that the relationship between the races in the United States is indeed a political one—and one of the control of a collectivity defined as birth, by another collectivity also defined by birth. Groups who rule by birth are fast disappearing in the West and white supremacists are fated to go the way of aristocrats and other extinct upper castes. We have yet one ancient and universal arrangement for the political exploitation of one birth group by another—in the area of sex.

Just as the study of racism has convinced us that there exists a truly political relationship between races, and an oppressive situation from which the subordinated group had no redress through formal political structures whereby they might organize into conventional political struggle and opposition—just so any intelligent and objective examination of our system of sexual politics or sex-role structure will prove that the relationship between the sexes now, and throughout history, is one of what Max Weber once termed *Herrschaft*, or dominance and subordination—the birthright control of one group by another, the male to rule and the female to be ruled. Women have been placed in the position of minority status throughout history and even after the grudging extension of certain minimal rights of citizenship and suffrage at the beginning of this century. It is fatuous to suppose that women—white or black—have any greater representation now that they vote than they ever did. Previous history has made it clear that the possession of the vote for 100 years has done the black man precious little good at all.

Why, when this arrangement of male rule and control of our society is so obvious, is it never acknowledged or discussed? Partly, I suspect, because such discussion is regarded as dangerous in the extreme—and because a culture does not discuss its most basic assumptions and most cherished bigotries. Why does no one ever remark that the military, industry, the universities, the sciences, political offices, and finance (despite absurd declarations to the contrary on the evidence that some little old lady owns stock over which she has no control) —in short, every avenue of power in our culture, including the repressive forces of the police—is entirely in male hands? Money, guns, authority itself, are male provinces. Even God is male—and a white male at that.

The reasons for this gigantic evasion of the very facts of our situation are many and obvious. They are also rather amusing. Let's look at a few of the thousand defenses the masculine culture has built against any infringement or even exposure of its control. One is to react with ridicule and the primitive mechanism of laughter and denial. Sex is funny—it's dirty—and it is something women have. Men are not sexual beings—they are people—they are humanity. Therefore, any rational discussion of the realities of sexual life degenerates as quickly as men can make them into sniggering sessions, where through cliches so ancient as to have almost ritual value, women who might be anxious to carry on an adult dialogue are bullied back into "their place."

At the level of common attitudes, sex—and particularly that very explosive subject of the relationship of the sexes—is a subject closed to intelligent investigation and accessible only to persiflage and levity.

The second evasion our culture has evolved is via folk myth. From Dagwood to the college professor, sex is folklore and the official version of both is that the male is the "victim" of a widespread conspiracy. From the folk figure of Jiggs or Punch to the very latest study of the damage which mothers wreak on their sons, we are assailed by the bogey of the overbearing woman—woman as some terrible and primitive natural evil, our twentieth-century remnant of the primitive fear of the unknown, unknown at least to the male, and remember that it is the male in our culture who defines reality. Man is innocent, he is put upon, everywhere he is in danger of being dethroned. Dagwood—the archetypical henpecked husband—is a figure of folk fun only because the culture assumes that a man will rule his wife or cease to be very much of a man. Like a dim-witted plantation owner who is virtually controlled by his far cleverer black steward or valet, Dagwood is a member of the ruling class held up both to scorn and to sympathy—scorn for being too human or too incompetent to rule, yet sympathetic because every other member of the privileged group knows in his heart how burdensome it is to maintain the illusory façade of superiority over those who are your natural equals.

The fantasy of the male victim is not only myth, it is politically expedient myth, myth either invented or disseminated to serve the political end of a rationalization or a softening and partial denial of power. The actual relation of the sexes in our culture from the dawn of history has been diametrically opposite to the official cult of the downtrodden male—yet our culture seeks on every level of discussion to deny this. To the logical charge of oppression which any objective view of the sex structure would bring up, masculine society has a fascinating tactic of appropriating all sympathy for itself. It has lately taken up the practice of screaming out that it is the victim of unnatural surgery . . . it has been "castrated." Even Albert Shanker has discovered of late that black community control, the Mayor, and the Board of Education have performed this abomination upon his person. To those in fear of castration, one word of comfort. The last instance of its practice on a white man in Western culture was the late eighteenth century when the last castrati lost a vital section of his anatomy in the cause of the art of music —at the hands of another male, I must add. For castration is an ancient cruelty which males practice on each other. In the American South it was as a way to humiliate black victims of the Klan. In the Ancient East it was as a barbarous form of punishment for crime. In the courts of the Italian Renaissance castration was a perverse method of providing soprano voices for the Papal Choir. It was felt that women were too profane to sing the holy offices, so to supply the demand for the higher musical register, eunuchs were created through putting young men to the knife.

As the practice of physical castration has been abolished, it is clear that the word in current usage must be accepted in a metaphoric rather than a literal connotation, if we are to make any sense of the fantastic anxiety which assails contemporary male egos; for on every hand, in the media and in the culture both high and low, men today have come to see the terrible specter of the "castrating female" all about them, and their paranoic delusions are taken for social fact. Having, in a confused way, associated his genitalia with his power, the male now bellows in physical pain and true

hysteria every time his social and political prerogatives are threatened. If by castration is meant a loss through being forced to share power with oppressed groups deprived of power or even of human status, then there are many white men in America who will suffer this psychic operation, but it will be the removal of a cancer in the brain and heart, not of any pleasurable or creative organ. To argue that any woman who insists on full human status is a "castrating bitch" or guilty of the obscure evil of "penis envy" (only the most consummate male chauvinist could have imagined this term) is as patently silly as to argue that dispossessed blacks want to become white men—the issue is not to be Whitey but to have a fair share of what Whitey has: the whole world of human possibility.

While I am fully aware that equal rights entails equal responsibility, there are some things Whitey has which I am very sure I don't want, for example a Green Beret, a Zippo for burning down villages, the ear of a dead peasant, or the burden of the charred flesh of a Vietnamese child. Nor do I have any interest in acquiring the habits of violence, warfare (unless in the just cause of self-defense, a cause I cannot foresee ever happening in American foreign policy), or the white man's imperialist racism, or rape, or the capitalist exploitation of poverty and ignorance.

Because of the smokescreen of masculine propaganda one hears endless cant about "castration," whereas real and actual crimes men commit against women are never mentioned. It is considered bad taste—or unsportsmanlike—to refer to the fact that there are ten thousand rapes—or crimes against female personality—in New York City each year—and of course I speak only of those instances which are reported, probably one-tenth of those which occur. It is also generally accepted that to regard Richard Speck and so many others like him in anything but the light of exceptional and irrelevant instances of individual pathology, is another instance of not playing fair. But I submit that Speck merely enacted the presuppositions of the majority of male supremacists of the sterner sort—and they are legion. That his murders echo in the surrealist chambers of masculine fantasy and wish fulfillment is testified to by every sleazy essay into sadism and white slave traffic on the dirty movie belt of 42nd Street in Manhattan, and in the antisocial character of hard-core pornography. *The Story of O* tells it like it is about masculine fantasy better than does *Romeo and Juliet*. So does the Playboy, chortling over the con game he has played on that Rabbit he dreams of screwing—the Bunny, or woman reduced to a meek and docile animal toy.

For the extent and depth of the male's hatred and hostility toward his subject colony of women is a source of continual astonishment. Just as behind the glowing mirage of "darkeys crooning in the twilight" is the reality of the block, the whip, and the manacle, the history of women is full of colorful artifact: the bound feet of all old China's women, deliberately deformed that they might be better controlled (you can work with those useless feet, but you cannot run away); the veil of Islam (or an attenuated existence as a human soul condemned to wear a cloth sack over her head all the days of her half-life); the lash, the rod, the rope; domestic imprisonment through most of the world's history; rape concubinage, prostitution . . . yes, we have our own impressive catalogue of open tyrannies. Women are still sold in Saudi Arabia and elsewhere. In Switzerland, they are even today disenfranchised. And in nearly every rod of ground on this earth they live only via the barter system of sex in return for food and security—and often very little of the latter. Like every system of oppression, male supremacy rests finally on force, physical power, rape, assault and the threat of assault. As a final resource

when all else has failed, the male resorts to attack. But the fear of force is there before every woman always as a deterrent—dismissal, divorce, violence—personal, sexual, or economic.

As in any society in a state of war, the enforcement of male rule which euphemism calls "the battle of the sexes," is possible to maintain only through the usual lies convenient to countries at war—the Enemy is Evil—the Enemy is not Human. And men have always been able to believe in the innate evil of woman. Studies of primitive societies—just as studies of our own religious texts—illustrate over and over the innumerable instances of taboos practiced against women. A group of aborigines agree with Judaism in the faith that a menstruating woman is "unclean," taboo, untouchable. Should she have access to weapons or other sacred and ritual articles of the male, she will place a hex or a spell upon them that their masculine owners will not survive. Everything that pertains to her physical makeup or function is despicable or subversive. Let her go outside the village and inhabit a hut alone and without food during her period—let her be forbidden the temple, even those outer precincts assigned to her, for a specified number of days after, as the Gospels coolly inform us, she has given birth to the very saviour of the world —for she is still dirty. Dirty and mysterious. Have you ever thought it curious that nocturnal emissions were not regarded as either dirty or mysterious, that the penis was (until industrialism decided to veil it again for greater effect) never considered as dirty, but so regal and imperious that its shape is the one assigned to sceptres, bombs, guns, and airplanes? In history, vast numbers of peoples have worshipped the phallus openly.

It may also be true that even larger numbers of peoples once worshipped the womb or the fertility powers of the earth. It may also be true that one of the many causes for the commencement of that now-universal oppression and contempt for women lay in the male's very fear of the female's powers of giving life and perhaps inspired that enormous change in world affairs we call the patriarchal takeover. Living so close to the earth, without having yet developed toys of his own in warfare and the rise of princely city-states full of toiling slaves building him empty monuments, and unaware of his own vital role in conception, the male may well have cast glances of fearful envy on the woman and what was, in those conditions, her rather miraculous capacity to bring another human life out of her very belly—and seen in it a connection with the phases of the moon and the seasons of the earth's vegetation—and stood both in awe and in terror, and finally in hatred, and decided to cast this function down from what he rather naturally assumed was its collusion with the supernatural, the terrible, and the uncontrollable forces of nature—and denigrate it to the level of the bestial, the filthy, the pernicious, and the obscene. And thus totem was appropriated by the male and taboo assigned in a thousand ways to operate against the female.

Having vitiated all effects of the female power, the male set about aggrandizing his own. Having finally appropriated all access to the supernatural for himself, he established an alliance with the new male god (both his brother and his father, depending on auspicious or inauspicious circumstance), he then proceeded to announce his kinship with the divine through a long and impressive list of patriarchs and prophets, high priests and emperors. Now that he had gone into partnership with God, the male set himself up as God to the female. Milton puts it this way: "He for God only, she for God in him."

In some cultures females were allowed to participate on an inferior level as figures of identification for human females—useful in encouraging them to an enforced co-operation in their own control. So they can see themselves as honored through the rapes of Jove on Europa and Leda, favored in divine seduction scenarios as in endless scenes of wood nymphs, possibly debased versions of other tribal goddesses at loose ends now their matriarchal reign had ended—or incarnate in that first troublesome woman, Juno, the insubordinate wife.

But in sterner patriarchal societies such as the Judaic and Christian there was never any kidding around about goddesses. Christianity did not elevate the Virgin to goddess status until the twelfth century, and the Protestants dethroned her a mere four hundred years later. The device of making her both virgin and mother not only excites admiration for its ingenuity but astonishment as its perfection of effect—here is divine or nearly divine woman completely relieved of that insidious sexuality by which woman herself has always been defined.

Mere mortal women in the Christian ages were continuously assured of their inherent evil and inferiority by a whole procession of fanatic male supremists—from Paul, who found even the exhibition of their hair in church a powerful provocation and an indelicate enticement to hellish practices more apparent in his mind than in others (such it is to represent the sexuality of the whole race in only one half of it), to Jerome, Augustine, Aquinas, and a whole parade of ascetics, hermits, and other nonparticipating types who have projected their own teeming sexuality onto the female. For so strong is the hold of the Christian assumption through Eve and other notable exempla that the "evil" of sex was introduced via the female alone, that today even *women* think of *women* when they think of sex, sexiness, sex objects, sexuality, and sex symbols—a state of rather surprising paradox in a society which rigidly enforces heterosexuality for women.

Judaism is even more punctilious than Christianity in the matter of male supremacy. First thing in the morning every male Jew is enjoined to thank God for creating him a male and therefore a superior order of being. I have never been informed as to what Jewish women are instructed to say on such occasions of coming to consciousness—perhaps it is some little bit of advice to themselves not to fall into the much-satirized posture of the overbearing Jewish mother.

Of course it is not surprising that religion as we know it takes the enforcement of male supremacy by divine fiat as part of its function in a patriarchy. So too does literature, all traditional and contemporary notions of government, those platitudes which currently pass for social science—and even, despite the influence of the Enlightenment, science itself cooperates in a number of transparently expedient rationalizations in maintaining the traditional sexual politics on grounds so specious as to have a certain comic charm.

A further way in which contemporary masculine culture refuses to face the issue of sexual politics is through the reduction of the two sexual collectivities of male and female into an endless variety of purely individual situations, whereby all cases are unique—each a delicate matter of adjustment of one diverse character to another, all of them merely the very private matter of one-to-one relationships. That this is so largely our favorite method of portraying sexual relationships today—since Freud and the development of the very private science of psychoanalysis—is probably due in good part to the convenience it offers in shielding us from the unpleasant reality of sexual relations should we begin to view them on general or class/caste terms as we have

learned to see race. For we know very well now that race is not a matter between one employer and his "boy" or one family and its "maid," but it is to be perceived in the far more pertinent light of one race's control over the other.

The Individual Case translates our older myth of the dangerous female into a newer but by now rather shop-worn cliche of the bitch stereotype—the most stock figure of the contemporary media. It is interesting to note how this bitch leads one to fancy— without ever coming right out and saying it —that all women are bitches. It is puzzling, too, how, as woman—with woman's minority status and therefore a creature completely out of the male power structure— she is arbitrarily and unjustly blamed for nearly every fault in American life today, and turned into a veritable symbol of the hateful establishment. As beauty queen, the male establishment is willing to allow woman a place as mascot or cheerleader— but it is a long way from admitting her to any personal stake in the establishment's show. As a girlfriend or a wife, she may participate vicariously for a time, but she is easy to replace and the trade-ins on old models of wife and mistress is pretty brisk. She may sleep with so many thousands a year or such and such an office, but she is dreaming if she ever fancies such glory is her own.

For the purpose of male propaganda, one of the most felicitous effects of the Individual Case myth is that it immediately translates any resistance to the present political situation in sex relations into a damning conviction of the sin of neurosis. As psychology has replaced religion as the conformist force in social behavior, it has branded any activity at odds with the status quo (which, by the way, it has taken to be "normality") as deranged, pitiable, or dangerous behavior. By this criterion, current "normality" in the United States is racism, police brutality, and ruthless economic exploitation. This is what happens, if, like the shrinks, you take nineteenth-century social life as both the state of nature and the state of a healthy society. Any woman who fails to conform to the sterile stereotype of wife and motherhood as all and only, or who fails to bow in elaborate deference to male authority and opinion on any and all questions, is clearly off her nut. Men have said it.

One other device to maintain the current and traditional sexual politics is to claim that the whole thing has already been settled a long time ago—"we gave you the vote," as the male authoritarian puts it with such stunning arrogance; "we went to the polls and elected you into the human race because one day you mentioned the oversight of your exclusion and, obliging fellows that we are, we immediately rectified this very trivial detail."

The foregoing is both a distortion of history and a denial of reality. Women fought hard and almost without hope, driven to massive and forceful protest which has served as a model both for the labor movement and the black movement. They struggled on against overwhelming odds of power and repression for over one hundred and fifty years to get this worthless rag known as the ballot. We got it last of all —women, black and white, are the last citizens of the United States—and we had to work hardest of all to get it.

And now we have it we realize how badly we were cheated—we had fought so long, worked so hard, pushed back despair so many times that we were exhausted, that we just said: "Give us that and we will do the rest ourselves." But then we didn't realize, as perhaps blacks never realized until the civil-rights movement, that the ballot is no real admission to civil life in America; it means nothing at all if you are not represented in a representative democracy. And we are not represented

now any more than black people; both groups have only one senator—one Tom apiece. The United States has fewer women in public office than almost any nation in the world—we are more effectively ostracized from political life in this country than any other constituency in America, and we are 53 percent of its population. Political nominees announced their intention of helping asthmatic children and the mentally retarded of every age, if elected—but not a word about women—half the population—but not a word—the largest minority status group in history. But not one word.

It is time the official fallacy of the West and of the United States particularly—that the sexes are now equal socially and politically—be exploded for the hoax it really is. For at present any gainsaying of this piety is countered with the threat that "women have got too much power," "they're running the world," and other tidbits of frivolity which the speaker, strange as it may seem, might often enough believe. For the more petty male ego, like that of the cracker or the union man in the North who voted for Wallace, in his paranoia is likely to believe that because one woman or one black man in millions can earn nearly as much or even a bit more than he does, the whole bunch are taking over that sordid little corner of the world he regarded as his birthright because he was white and a male, and on which he had staked his very identity—just because it prevented him from seeing himself as exploited by the very caste he had imagined he was part of and with whom, despite all evidence to the contrary, he fancied he shared the gifts of the earth and the American dream—nightmare that it is.

The actual facts of the situation of women in America today are sufficient evidence that, white or black, women are at the bottom unless they sleep with the top. On their own they are Nobody and taught every day they are Nobody and taught so well they have come to internalize that destructive notion and even believe it. The Department of Labor statistics can't hide the fact that this is a man's world—a white man's world: the average year-round income of the white male is $6,704; of a black male $4,277; of a white female $3,991; and of the black woman $2,816. As students you live in a Utopia—enjoy it, for it is the only moment in your lives when you will be treated nearly as equals. When you get married or get a job you will be made to see where power is, but then it will be too late. That is why you should organize now: look at your curriculum and look at your housing rules—that's a start at realizing how you are treated unfairly.

But the oppression of women is not only economic; that's just part of it. The oppression of women is Total, and therefore it exists in the mind—it is psychological oppression. Let's have a look at how it works, for it works like a charm. From earliest childhood every female child is carefully taught that she is to be a lifelong incompetent at every sphere of significant human activity; therefore, she must convert herself into a sex object—a Thing. She must be pretty and assessed by the world: weighed, judged, and measured by her looks alone. If she's pretty she can marry; then she can concentrate her energies on pregnancy and diapers. That's life—that's female life. That's what it is to reduce and limit the expectations and potentialities of one-half of the human race to the level of animal behavior.

It is time we realized that the whole structure of male and female personality is arbitrarily imposed by social conditioning —a social conditioning which has taken all the possible traits of human personality, which Margaret Mead once, by way of analogy, compared to the many colors of the rainbow's spectrum, and arbitrarily assigned traits into two categories; thus aggression is masculine, passivity feminine,

violence masculine, tenderness feminine, intelligence masculine, and emotion feminine, etc., etc. . . . arbitrarily departmentalizing human qualities into two neat little piles which are drilled into children by toys, games, the social propaganda of television, and the board of education's deranged whim as to what is proper male-female "role building." What we must now set about doing is to reexamine this whole foolish and segregated house of cards, and pick from it what we can use: Dante, Shakespeare, Lady Murasaki and Mozart, Einstein and the care for life which we have bred into women—and accept these as human traits. Then we must get busy to eliminate what are not properly humane or even human ideas—the warrior, the killer, the hero as homicide, the passive dumb cow victim.

We must now begin to realize and to retrain ourselves to see that both intelligence and a reverence for life are HUMAN qualities. It is high time we began to be reasonable about the relationship of sexuality to personality and admit the facts—the present assignment of temperamental traits to sex is moronic, limiting, and hazardous. Virility—the murderer's complex or self-definition in terms of how many or how often or how efficiently he can oppress his fellow—this has got to go.

There is a whole generation coming of age in America who have already thoroughly sickened of the military male ideal, who know they were born men and don't have to prove it by killing someone . . . or wearing crew cuts. There is also a vast number of women who are beginning to wake out of the long sleep known as cooperating in one's own oppression and self-denigration, and they are banding together, in nationwide chapters of the National Organization for Women, in the myriad groups of radical women springing up in cities all other the country and the world, in the women's liberation groups of

SDS and in other groups on campus, and they are joining together to make the beginnings of a new and massive women's movement in America and in the world— to establish true equality between the sexes, to break the old machine of sexual politics and replace it with a more human and civilized world for both sexes, and to end the present system's oppression of men as well as women.

There are other forces at work to change the whole face of American society: the black movement to end racism, the student movement with its numbers and powers for spreading the idea of a new society founded on democratic principles, free of the war reflex, free of the economic and racial exploitation reflex. Black people, students, and women—that's a lot of people; with our combined numbers it is probably 70 percent of the population or more. It is more than enough to change the course and character of our society, surely enough to cause a radical social revolution. And maybe it will also be the first real revolution . . . the first to avoid the pitfall of bloodshed, a mere change of dictators and the inevitable counterrevolution which follows upon such betrayal and loss of purpose.

We are numbers sufficient to alter the course of human history by changing fundamental values, by effecting an entire change of consciousness. We cannot have such a change of consciousness unless we rebuild values—we cannot rebuild values unless we restructure personality. But we cannot do this or solve racial and economic crimes unless we end the oppression of all people —unless we end the idea of violence, of dominance, of power—unless we end the idea of oppression itself—unless we realize that a revolution in sexual policy is not only part of but basic to any real change in the quality of life.

Social and cultural revolution in America and the world depends on this change of consciousness of which a new relationship between the sexes and a new definition of humanity and human personality are an integral part.

As we awake and begin to take action there will be enough of us and we will have both a purpose and a goal—the first truly human condition, the first really human society. Let us begin the revolution and let us begin it with love: all of us, black, white, and gold, male and female, have it within our power to create a world we could bear out of the desert we inhabit, for we hold our very fate in our hands.

ALL FOR VIETNAM

Tom Hayden

The Cambodian invasion, the killings at Kent State, and Nixon's cold-war rhetoric all caused a sudden panic among millions of Americans who yearned to believe in "Vietnamization" and other promises of peace in Southeast Asia. The national reaction was great enough to send Nixon before the TV cameras, and ultimately to the Washington Monument, to cool the threat of disruption in his own capital. Nixon's promise to withdraw from Cambodia did have a temporary cooling effect, but it also blew away many lingering illusions about peace in Asia. The government had served notice to all but the most blind that its intention was to win the war through escalation—even with nuclear weapons, if necessary.

Why did anyone ever doubt it?

The U.S. government already had demonstrated its willingness to attempt subtle genocide in Vietnam under the pretense of waging a "war of attrition." The military ruthlessly bombed the social structure —schools, hospitals; used chemicals to poison the dams of Vietnam, the rivers and farmlands; drove the rural population in the South into concentration camps; and spoke of "destroying cities to save them," "fighting against the Vietnamese birth rate," and "threatening their existence as a nation." The toll of suffering in Vietnam long ago surpassed that which would have resulted from a Hiroshima-type attack. Genocide by any other name is still genocide. Regardless of the intent of particular

officials during the last twenty-one years of American intervention, the dynamic is unmistakable: relentless American military action has attempted to crush the Vietnamese revolution by any means necessary, by any escalation required.

THE PATTERN OF LIBERAL PROTEST

But there is a very human desire to recover from shock, to return to normalcy, to disbelieve that nightmare can become reality. All these feelings operate among Americans who want peace, and it is precisely these feelings that Nixon has sought to manipulate. Feelings such as these quite likely moved people involved in national protests against the Cambodian invasion to feel satisfaction with Nixon's agreement to "withdraw" in two months.

If the New Haven weekend offered a glimpse of the Apocalypse, the calm protest in Washington, D.C., just one week later returned most people to the conventional world of antiwar protest.

It was not the Nixon Administration which implemented this pacifying strategy but, paradoxically, the liberal establishment that Nixon and Agnew despise. Much of the effort to keep young people from believing that the nightmare had come was made by liberal politicians and college administrators.

On Yale's signal, college administrators

Reprinted by permission from Ramparts *(September 1970), pp. 26–27, 46–49; this article is an abridged chapter from Tom Hayden's* The Trial, *published by Holt, Rinehart, and Winston; copyright © 1970, Tom Hayden.*

adopted a sudden new tolerance, even co-operation, towards dissent on the campuses. Just as Yale was "reconstituted" for a weekend to accommodate the Panther protests, so did schools everywhere allow students and faculty to work against the war. On the political front, a score of senators came forward with antiwar amendments and proposals for channeling student energies into fall electoral campaigns.

The underlying motive of the administrators and politicians in all this was certainly not withdrawal of troops from Vietnam or radical transformation of the war-oriented university. Their immediate concern was peace in the schools and peace between the generations.

A perfect embodiment of this concern could be found in the figure of Cyrus Vance, a Yale trustee who was intimately involved in keeping his alma mater from being destroyed during the May Day protests. Vance, of course, previously represented the U.S. government in the Paris peace talks. Like Yale President Brewster and Yale trustee John Lindsay, Vance by now preferred a retreat in Vietnam to save America's interests elsewhere, particularly at home.

These men knew quite well the level of discontent on the campuses. They knew that the school year's two peaceful and legitimate moratoriums had only widened the generation gap. They knew that the Chicago conspiracy trial had added greatly to the despair the young felt toward established institutions. Above all they knew that since the beginning of the year the level of revolutionary violence in America had taken a quantum jump forward. Demonstrators in large numbers were breaking windows and trashing buildings. Young guerrillas were burning and bombing hundreds of institutions, such as ROTC and draft boards. They knew, finally, that Yale would be leveled in any confrontation during May Day weekend, setting off perhaps hundreds of violent rebellions on less guarded campuses. In their calculation it was time for a new policy: to allow for peaceful dissent within their institutions even at the risk of ruffling Establishment feathers and exciting Spiro T. Agnew.

This is not to say that all the protest energy generated by the spontaneous national student strike was wasted or coopted. Overnight, thousands of new activists were made; Nixon was forced to limit the timetable of his invasion; and shock over the blood spilled at Kent State, Augusta, Jackson, and Cambodia probably increased the conviction of millions of Americans that the war was wrong.

Now that the strike is over, however, we can see its limits clearly. No colleges were really "reconstituted"; no fundamental pressures were built against the war machine; most of the activity dissipated into summer vacation; most college administrations were able finally to preserve their buildings from violence. In contrast to this, there was a bloodbath in Cambodia; 40,000 South Vietnamese troops remain there; and the U.S. is planning to bomb Cambodia as mercilessly as it does Laos.

The sense of *déja vu* this syndrome creates is overpowering. We went through a precisely analogous experience in 1967–68 leading up to the Chicago confrontation. Then members of the "lunatic fringe" of the American left were not guerrilla bombers; they were burning draft cards, obstructing Dow recruiters and storming Pentagon walls. Then, too, the Establishment's crisis managers (McGeorge Bundy comes to mind) were urging a cutback in Vietnam to prevent a breakdown at home. Then as now the message to young America was: don't believe the radicals, work within the system, create a constructive alternative to nihilism—and remember, you'll be crushed if you try to rebel. Then also the young people went to the Silent Majority, worked in the very guts of the electoral system, became Clean for Gene. Then came the bloody finish in Chicago. Senator Mc-

Carthy went off to cover the World Series for *Life* magazine. The moderates won their demands—negotiations with the other side, an end to the bombing of North Vietnam —only to realize they were meaningless. The government had ended the antiwar movement under the pretext of ending the war.

It is amazing that within a year optimism could bloom again among the same liberal forces that were shattered in Chicago. A group of former McCarthy and Kennedy workers (and politicians, even including Averill Harriman) formed a movement curiously called The Moratorium. Everyone hailed it as a respectable alternative to the kind of politics the Chicago conspiracy represented (we had to fight their bureaucracy even to appear on stage in the Chicago moratorium in October). Indeed, a million people were mobilized around rather humble slogans like "Give peace a chance." The response to this upstanding, respectable protest? Nixon declared he would be unaffected by their numbers, and Agnew branded the organizers "effete snobs."

Evidently the Agnew criticism contained some truth, since the Moratorium organizers swiftly gave up their plans for an escalating, month-by-month boycott and work stoppage and closed the Moratorium to return to the more familiar environment of electoral politics. The Cambodian invasion came three weeks later.

The pattern of liberal failure is by now obvious. From the McCarthy campaign to the Moratorium to the present campus "reconstitution" movement, we have seen a moderate, Democratic Party-oriented program tried and frustrated again and again. The problem in this political strategy seems to be an overreliance on politicians and an underreliance on popular pressure. This is not the way liberal strategists would argue their cause, of course. They would say that the war can only be ended by respectable efforts within the mainstream of politics,

and that disruptive protest only alienates the public and strengthens the hawks. But they cannot be blind to the fact that if they have any leverage at all, it is precisely because they are a safe alternative to radicalism. For a better explanation of their politics we would have to conclude that they want to end the war but also save the system. They do not themselves follow the natural path of radicalization which many of their followers do. They remain instead a loyal opposition working within the electoral arena for changes—changes, not in the system, but in its priorities.

The tragedy is that many young people who accept the liberal theory of change are simply not aware of their own power. It is not that they want above all to stay within the system, but only that they are conditioned to believe that working outside the system is impossible. They are still blind to the source of their tremendous power, the power to make Nixon rush to the Washington Monument. That power does not reside in their electoral potential but only in their potential to disrupt the vital institutions containing them—the universities— and to threaten the stability of the country's future. It was this threat which caused Brewster to "open" Yale, and Nixon to pledge "withdrawal" from Cambodia. There is a constant tendency among students and young people in general to disbelieve the reality of their own power, to continue believing that power is with their parents or the politicians. But they should instead consider the formula the Vietnamese have for American politics: *if we are strong, even a Goldwater will withdraw; if we are weak, even a McCarthy will attack.*

RADICALISM AND ITS IMPASSE

The radicals have always been more correct about Vietnam than have the architects of liberal protest. The former goals of the radicals, once condemned by liberals as utopian, now are quite acceptable—for example, the demand for immediate withdrawal instead of negotiations. The radical strategy of relying on people in the streets instead of in the ballot box has also been productive, at least up through 1968, when the radical strategy reached a peak of success which has been followed by a prolonged impasse.

In 1968 we administered the first clear setback to America's strategy of escalation. It was the year of military defeat (the Tet offensive) and of political catastrophe, with Westmoreland, McNamara, and Johnson bowing out unceremoniously. Those who came to Chicago to protest were prophets without honor holding to two convictions: that despite Johnson's retirement, despite the Paris talks, the U.S. aggression would continue; and that the antiwar movement should remain independent in the streets instead of placing itself at the disposal of "peace candidates." The Chicago confrontation was the peak in a year of demonstrations showing that any political leadership committed to staying in Vietnam would face domestic chaos and, ultimately, electoral defeat.

But at the same time we learned that in the face of chaos, "law and order" would be implemented long before withdrawal from Vietnam. Moreover, from Johnson's abdication we realized that America's stake in Vietnam took precedence over the personal fortunes of whoever happened to be President. The costs we were imposing on the American Establishment were real but (at least for a while) acceptable.

And with that discovery, radicalism came to an impasse.

Up to that point, and even today, most peace activists and radicals believe that Vietnam is a flaw—a terrible flaw—in the working of the American Empire, which could be repaired by a loud enough outcry

of disagreement. Who would have believed that a supreme egomaniac like Lyndon Johnson would make winning the war more important than winning reelection? Who would have thought that with half the Senate and most of the press and public believing the war a "mistake," it would nevertheless continue to expand?

There has been a widespread failure to recognize in Vietnam the most serious international showdown of our time.

Radical intellectual theories about Vietnam, for example, have assumed that U.S. involvement is irrational—not in the sense liberals assert when they blame faulty Presidential advisers for our Vietnam commitment, but "irrational" in the sense that Vietnam is not in the "true interests" of corporate capitalism. In the radical view, America is ruled by a flexible corporate elite with many interests throughout the world. In this empire, Vietnam is a rather unimportant economic and political area (compared to India, Indonesia, Japan, or Brazil). Since the corporate elite is concerned with the smooth overall maintenance of empire, and not with the occasional loss of a small domino (the radical reasoning goes), our powerful gentry will cut their losses in Vietnam and dig in better elsewhere. In this view, the U.S. can withdraw to Thailand and India-Indonesia, keeping a forward base against China while consolidating its grip on richer possessions.

This world view provided most of the operating assumptions of the major antiwar groups in the late Sixties—the Mobilization and the SDS—even though the two organizations were constantly at odds over strategy.

The Mobe did just what its name implied: it mobilized people to demand withdrawal from Vietnam. In most cases its demonstrations were large, legal, and peaceful, designed to allow a variety of people to surface their opposition to Vietnam. Between mass mobilizations there were numerous attempts to do educational work among new constituencies, but local branches of the Mobe existed primarily to pull out people to rallies. The presence of ever larger numbers in the streets was effective in several ways: first, it helped individuals feel they were not alone in opposing the war; second, it gave politicians and influential figures confidence that they could oppose the war without being crucified, which in turn legitimized dissent among larger numbers of people; and third, it gave encouragement to the Vietnamese revolutionaries while demoralizing the American military and the puppets they supported.

But eventually the underlying assumption—that decision-makers would end the war if enough widespread pressure was created—was proven inadequate by the government's repeated escalation. While its structure remains, the Mobe direction has blurred and support has waned since 1968.

The SDS radicals actually created the first national mobilization in the spring of 1965, but then very quickly shunned a leadership role in the antiwar protests because they did not believe in the "pressure" strategy. Their radicalism, however, often led in perverse and sectarian directions. They assumed the antiwar mobilizations would be deceptively "successful" because the American Establishment, sensing a bad investment in Vietnam, would use the antiwar sentiment as a popular basis for pulling out. The peace movement would be coopted in the process, used by a new set of politicians (Robert Kennedy) for their rise to power. The real issue, for SDS, was not Vietnam but the imperialist system which would continue beyond the withdrawal, a system which would strangle and threaten Vietnam (as the American blockade does Cuba) and other nations, until overthrown. In SDS language, there had to be an anti-imperialist movement able to muster resistance "seven wars from now."

In various local actions, SDS chapters made important antiwar contributions by their confrontations with recruiters and official spokesmen. But in the two major national confrontations against the war—at the Pentagon and Chicago—SDS stayed aloof and hostile until the sheer heat of the conflict persuaded them to participate.

The SDS outlook was clearer than the liberal and humanitarian politics of most of the movement, but it was a terribly elitist view. Instead of regarding Vietnam as the crisis which would tear America apart and create conditions for domestic radicalism, a crisis which SDS would be deeply involved in resolving, they saw it more as an important issue for liberals.

There were other strands of radicalism—the life-style, or cultural, rebellions—which were even further removed from the issue of the war. Taking Vietnam only as a symptom of what was wrong with the country, many chose to fight primarily against their own oppression as longhairs. They opted totally out of the antiwar movement into what would become the Woodstock Nation. To the early Merry Pranksters as well as to the later Yippies, the antiwar activists were "straight" or "too political" or "on a death trip," not in touch with their own oppression and therefore building no alternative to America. And so there developed a genuine alternative culture, but its outlook, until quite recently, has been that of revolution-for-the-hell-of-it, revolution-for-ourselves, "Dope, Rock 'n' Roll and Fucking in the Street," etc. Whatever impulse there has been in this culture against the war has had no outlet (except during Chicago) or has been channeled into a diffuse rage against America.

The women's liberation movement, too, has been through a long alienation from the issues of Vietnam and the Third World. Rebelling against male-dominated structures in the antiwar movement, and focusing primarily on their particular oppression, they have assumed that the problem of Vietnam would be solved by others.

Even during our Chicago trial, though it was aimed at the antiwar movement, we could not generate a new level of interest in Vietnam. In our speeches we emphasized the government's attack on antiwar militants. We observed the Moratorium in court. We sent Bill Kunstler to Paris to obtain news of American prisoners held in North Vietnam. We supported the idea of a release of U.S. prisoners in exchange for Bobby Seale and Huey Newton . . . yet Yippie theatrics and Judge Hoffman's personal quirks dominated popular consciousness of the trial. The same people whose nerves were deadened to the massive atrocity of Vietnam could be aroused by the relatively minor oppressiveness of our Chicago courtroom.

Paradoxically, the Vietnamese knew best that the trial was about the future of the antiwar struggle. Throughout Vietnam, people were concerned about our fate and, when we were jailed after the trial, our immediate release was demanded at the Paris peace talks.

Given the vacuum of militant antiwar leadership, it was predictable that a group like Weatherman would reassert a revolutionary interest in third-world struggles. And the vacuum may also explain the extreme one-sidedness with which they would assert their politics.

Against the view that emphasized the stability and flexibility of imperialism, the Weathermen began with the view that the Vietnamese and other third-world peoples are winning; that imperialism is in its death throes. They advanced a fifth-column strategy, although cloaked in a hippie life style and invoking Dylan and the Stones as well as Regis Debray and Lin Piao.

Their view: "The pump don't work 'cause the vandals stole the handle." The exclusive task of white radicals, in their view, is irregular warfare behind enemy lines inside American imperialism's fragile structure. Irregular, rather than conventional, guerrilla warfare, because the Weathermen are doubtful of ever achieving broad popular support inside the United States. They are essentially agents, John Browns, for the Third World revolution, with the goal of materially weakening imperialism by overextending its resources.

The immense contribution of the Weathermen has been in their assertion of internationalism and in their commitment to give their lives, rather than lip service, in solidarity with third-world people. But the problem in their vandalism or fifth-column strategy is that it fails to embrace the legitimacy of other struggles against oppression: women's liberation, the cultural revolution, and so forth. Thus the Weathermen create a basic rupture between themselves and their natural base for revolution. The intertwined problem is that the Weathermen are underground by choice and necessity, thus cutting themselves off from any open leadership role in mass struggles against the war. They do not carry out the basic Vietnamese teaching that legal demonstrations, even activity by the liberal wing of the Establishment, can be more important on certain occasions than guerrilla attack.

So the liberal antiwar movement is trapped in electoral politics, the radical strategy is at an impasse, other revolutionaries have abandoned Vietnam for the issue of their own oppression, and a few people have gone underground. Clearly, we have come to the crossroads; either the Vietnamese people will win, or they will be maimed horribly in a larger war. Either we will stop this war, or we will live under an intolerable barbarism. *Our task: an all-out siege against the war machine. Our watchword: All for Vietnam.*

WHAT IS TO BE DONE

First and foremost, we need an Emergency Consciousness about the real danger of further escalation. The only way the Vietnamese, the Cambodians, and the Laotians can secure their national rights is if the U.S. government is prevented from enlarging the war to include China and the use of advanced chemical or nuclear weapons. We cannot rely on liberal politicians to initiate this alert. At most we can include them in a united front, but the strongest Emergency must be sounded by students on campuses like the University of California, where the bombs are being processed, by the scientists who know what is going on, by the local antiwar groups outside military institutions, and by all groups who are supposedly defending the Vietnamese Revolution. By forcing the government to answer in advance whether it is planning an ultimate genocidal blow, we can develop an international alarm which will make such an escalation far more difficult. We will also be laying the foundation for renewed militancy at home, since no tactics are too extreme in the face of this threat.

Second, Vietnam has become once more a leading priority for all groups struggling to change the country. It cannot be assigned to an antiwar movement that is no more than a bureaucratic skeleton which goes into motion several times annually. The practice of organizing *only* around one's particular oppression must be seen as self-indulgence in the face of what threatens Vietnam. It is also illogical because there are no Vietnamese inside this country, and therefore we have to speak for them.

Third, the Vietnam war should be linked always with the issues of racism and repression at home. There still are many who prefer to keep the issue of Vietnam "separate" for the purpose of drawing the greatest popular support. This political line is self-defeating for at least two reasons: it depresses and holds back the swiftly growing consciousness of hundreds of thousands of people who long ago were awakened to the war issue; and it neglects the obvious repression of the antiwar radicals and blacks who are being crushed precisely because they are causing difficulties for imperialism. If the Administration can gun down and silence Panthers, one might ask, why would that Administration have to worry about an unarmed and less disciplined peace movement?

Fourth, it is time for the core of the anti-war movement to intensify the struggle with the goal of "cutting the supply lines" that feed the war machine. It is all well and good to make "reaching larger numbers of people" the goal of organizing, but there comes a moment when time is running out, when there can be no more waiting for the Silent Majority or the Working Class to be taking the stand we have to take. It is time to ask what has become of the hundreds of thousands who have been mobilized in the past for orthodox demonstrations, but who are never called upon to do more than repeat those performances. Is our "lack of numbers" and "isolation" the problem, or is it the cynicism and defeatism of those who have given up on stopping the war machine?

The image of "cutting the supply lines" is meant to deflect focus away from politicians and toward the precious institutions that must run smoothly if this war is to go forward. Now is the time to cripple this machinery of war by extending the "siege of the Pentagon" from one end of the country to another. The revolt of black GIs—and many whites as well—is a prime example of the way to do it. Delegitimizing and shutting down ROTC, which supplies the junior officers, is another example. Preventing nuclear and chemical warfare research is another. We need to be assailing corporations doing Vietnam business, striking at the authority of every important individual and agency involved in Vietnam, exposing and identifying the Vietnam lobby as a group of war criminals, isolating, weakening, and stopping their murderous program.

This siege strategy embraces both "mobilization" and "guerrilla" tactics. The immediate problem is not whether the tactics are too moderate or too militant. The problem is to recommit the energies of every sincere person for a last stand on Vietnam. The problem is to make people see that Vietnam is not a permanent part of the American Way of Life; it is a war with a dynamic leading to a showdown.

The only way to brush off our cynicism is to realize that we are not alone and isolated inside the United States. We should follow the war not as a "tragedy" but as a struggle in which the side of humanity is making a stand so heroic that it should shatter the hardest cynicism.

One of the best ways to gain strength for the struggle is to explore and measure the contribution of the Vietnamese people to ourselves and to the rest of the world. Developing this sense of internationalism means going beyond the conceptions of Vietnam offered by dove professors in the teach-ins. Their view, accepted widely in the antiwar movement, is that Vietnam is a case of "civil war" in which the U.S. should not have intervened. The notion of "civil war" suggests that there are several Vietnamese sides with different ethnic, religious, and political backgrounds, all quarreling among themselves. The implication is that Vietnam always has had internal problems which should not be important to the U.S. government. There is no basis for solidarity with Vietnam in this view, only a basis for paternalistic regret.

This kind of thinking hides from people a history which is both informative and stirring. What has happened in Vietnam is no more a "civil war" than the American Revolution was a "civil war." The fact that some Vietnamese have identified first with the French and now with the Americans is no more significant than the fact that some American colonists were linked to the British.

The real history of Vietnam is a history of successful revolution which the Western powers have been trying to erase for twenty-five years. The important fact about Ho Chi Minh's 1945 Proclamation of Independence is not that he quoted the American Declaration (which the doves constantly use to show how cooperation would have been possible with him) but that he declared the independence of his country. The basic conflict since that time has not been among the Vietnamese. The Diem government and the Thieu-Ky government were established by the U.S. and would fall without the U.S.: they have no significant roots among the Vietnamese people. The basic conflict is between the Vietnamese Nation and American Imperialism.

This Vietnamese Nation is a threat not only to American generals but to American professors and liberals, because of the revolutionary example it is establishing. The Vietnamese defy the military assumption that weapons can preserve America's power, and in their defiance revive a romantic revolutionary spirit that is supposed to be out of style.

In Vietnam the word "individualism" does not exist. The Vietnamese word that comes closest to individualism is "cannibalism." Their culture and their oppression have helped them approach the communist ideal of suffering, sharing, and struggling together. In order to survive they have had to become brothers and sisters in everything *before* achieving the technology and abundance that is supposed to make such a socialist life style possible.

Their age-old fight against foreign aggression makes struggle seem to be in their blood. Their existence, like that of Cuba and Korea, demonstrates not only that socialist and national liberation struggles can be joined; it demonstrates that the Modern Imperial Colossus can be fought and beaten by a small country with primitive technology.

The Vietnamese people have fired the modern "shots heard round the world." They are defeating the United States in war, destroying the myth of American superiority.

In this triumph they have raised the spirit of millions of third-world people.

They have provided the triggering issue for the new student movements in Western Europe.

They have inspired black and brown people, and young white people, inside the United States itself.

More than any other people, they have come to represent the conscience of humanity. When Ho Chi Minh died he was the most revered statesman in the world.

And they have done all this alone. The initiative has been theirs. They began fighting and dying long before there was a peace movement in America. They fought despite the fact that their communist allies were impossibly divided.

If it seems embarrassing or fuzzy-headed to mention these truths in America, it is only because our country is an emotional wasteland too decadent to believe in being born again.

But if these truths continue to inspire greater numbers of Americans, the Vietnamese people will have to be thanked for a final gift: opening our eyes to our own history as a genocidal nation, and starting us on the road to our own revolution.